The Spanish conquest of America generated a profusion of chronicles, tracts and poetry, among which figured several classics of the Renaissance. It also provoked a fierce debate between Bartolomé de las Casas, who defended the Indians, and the humanist historians who glorified the conquerors. Thereafter, imperial jurists and churchmen acclaimed the Spanish monarchy as chosen by Divine Providence to establish a Catholic empire in the New World. Within the bounds of this universal monarchy, American Spaniards sought to define their social identity by installing Aztec and Inca civilisation as the historical foundations of their countries and by accepting Our Lady of Guadalupe and St Rosa of Lima as their patrons. When the Enlightenment re-stated the imperial critique of the New World's inhabitants, creole patriots vigorously responded; and if in South America Simón Bolívar cited classical republicanism to justify independence, in Mexico creole patriotism was transmuted into an insurgent nationalism that did not succumb to liberal ideas until the victory of the reform movement led by Benito Juárez.

This book is about the quest of Spaniards born in the New World to define their American identity. It demonstrates that across the three centuries of colonial rule creole patriots succeeded in creating an intellectual and political tradition that by reason of its engagement with native history and American reality was idiosyncratic, regionally diverse, and distinct from any European model.

THE FIRST AMERICA

The arrival of the Spaniards in Mexico

THE
FIRST AMERICA

The Spanish monarchy, Creole patriots, and
the Liberal state 1492–1867

D. A. BRADING

Lecturer in Latin American History,
University of Cambridge

The right of the
University of Cambridge
to print and sell
all manner of books
was granted by
Henry VIII in 1534.
The University has printed
and published continuously
since 1584

CAMBRIDGE UNIVERSITY PRESS

CAMBRIDGE

NEW YORK   PORT CHESTER   MELBOURNE   SYDNEY

Published by the Press Syndicate of the University of Cambridge
The Pitt Building, Trumpington Street, Cambridge CB2 1RP
40 West 20th Street, New York, NY 10011, USA
10 Stamford Road, Oakleigh, Melbourne 3166, Australia

First published 1991

Printed in Great Britain by the Bath Press, Avon

British Library cataloguing in publication data

Brading, D. A. (David Anthony,) *1936–*
The First America: the Spanish monarchy, Creole patriots
and the Liberal state, 1492–1867.
1. Spanish America, history
I. Title
980

Library of Congress cataloguing in publication data

Brading, D. A.
The first America / by D. A. Brading.
p.   cm.
Includes bibliographical references.
ISBN 0 521 39130 X
1. Latin America – History – To 1830.   2. Nationalism – Latin
America – History.   3. Church and state – Latin America – History.
I. Title.
F1412.B79   1991
908'.013 – DC20   89-77364   CIP

ISBN 0 521 39130 X hardback

For Celia Wu

To seek new worlds, for golde,
for prayse, for glory.

SIR WALTER RALEIGH

By the rivers of Babylon, there
we sat down, yea, we wept, when
we remembered Zion.

PSALM CXXXVii.1

CONTENTS

ILLUSTRATIONS

PREFACE

ALTHOUGH THE idea of this book came to me in 1971 when I was teaching at Yale, its intellectual origin can be traced back still further to the bafflement and fascination I felt on first reading Fray Servando Teresa de Mier's *Historia de la revolución de Nueva España, antiguamente Anáhuac* (1813) in the British Library reading room in 1963. It was a book, I was later amused to learn, which had so puzzled a contemporary Englishman that Simón Bolívar wrote his famous Jamaica Letter to reassure him that the Mexican insurgents had no intention of reviving the worship of the Aztec god Quetzalcoatl, whom Mier had identified as St Thomas the Apostle. To resolve my own confusion, I wrote *The Origins of Mexican Nationalism*, published in Mexico in 1973; and without the welcome accorded it, I doubt whether I would have persevered with this present work. At the outset, what I had in mind was a series of essays designed to exhibit the historical interest of a set of Spanish American authors. Over the years the plan and scale changed considerably and towards the end I often had the sensation that the book already existed and that my task was simply to discover its true form and content. But the original purpose of exhibition or representation, what Greek historians called mimesis, remained constant. Some caveats should be taken into account. If the secondary bibliography and notes are not more extensive, it is because I have concentrated on reading primary sources, only citing those studies which have positively assisted my understanding. At the same time, I am conscious that the book is far too short to deal adequately with all the texts that are discussed and that I offer but one reading of often complex works. If Mexico figures more prominently than Peru in the chapters dealing with independence and its aftermath, it is simply because the terms of its political debate were more systematically defined than was the case elsewhere.

At the start of what has proved to be an intellectual route-march, I was guided by the writings of Edmundo O'Gorman, John Leddy Phelan, Antonello Gerbi, Luis Villoro and Francisco de la Maza. Thereafter, the works of J. H. Hexter, J. G. A. Pocock and R. J. W. Evans illuminated key moments of my journey. An understanding of the way an intellectual tradition exercises its influence came from reading Harold Bloom, George Kubler, Clifford Geertz, David Douglas, Edmund Wilson, and Gerhard von Rad. Conversation with Quentin Skinner and T. C. Blanning in Cambridge clarified my ideas on certain points of cultural terminology. Beyond that, I wish to acknowledge the encouragement given to me in Mexico by Edmundo O'Gorman, Enrique Florescano, Arnaldo Córdova and Enrique Krauze; and in Peru by Félix Denegri Luna and José Durand. In Cambridge I am indebted to the Centre of Latin American Studies where I delivered preliminary lectures on Las Casas, Simón Bolívar and Garcilaso de la Vega. Without the grant of a year's sabbatical leave in 1984–5 by Cambridge University the book could not have been written; I have received no other financial assistance. All the final typing was done by Margaret Rankine who has patiently disentangled my text and often corrected my errors. As regards the illustrations, I thank Félix Denegri Luna, Enrique Florescano, Martin Murphy and Clara García Ayluardo for their assistance. Permission to reproduce from books and paintings in their possession was kindly given by Lord Methuen, the British Library, Cambridge University Library, Manchester College, the Museo Nacional de Historia in Mexico City, the Palacio de Gobierno in Caracas, the Museo Nacional de Historia in Lima, and the Museo del Prado. Finally, I wish to thank Christopher Brading for his patience, and Celia Wu for her unfailing support across the nine years that went into this book.

PROLOGUE

IN HIS review about Clive of India, Lord Macaulay remarked that, whereas few Englishmen knew anything about British exploits in the East, 'every schoolboy knows who imprisoned Montezuma and who strangled Atahualpa'.[1] But what is there in English literature that can compare to the letters of Hernán Cortés or the 'true history' of Bernal Díaz? If the Italian humanists created the image of America as a New World populated by primitive men who lived close to nature, by contrast, the Spanish conquerors told the tale of how small bands of warriors invaded realms with populous cities and a settled peasantry, defeating their foes in fierce warfare. Nor did the conquerors rest content with simple accounts of their battles, since Cortés had his chaplain, Francisco López de Gómara, celebrate his deeds in elegant, Tacitean prose. Spanish humanists had no hesitation in praising the exploits of their compatriots and trumpeted an exuberant eulogy of their nation's overseas conquests. In Chile, Alonso de Ercilla composed the first drafts of *La Araucana* while serving in the frontier wars that haunted that country. Although inspired by writers of the Italian Renaissance, his epic poem harked back to *El Cid* and to the countless romances that recounted battles between Moors and Christians. The conquest of America thus generated a small library of chronicles, narratives and verse, among which figure several classics of Spanish prose and poetry.

But the deeds of the conquerors were sharply questioned by Bartolomé de las Casas, the great Dominican defender of the Indians. Where, in all the long centuries of European imperialism, was there a scene to equal the public debate staged at Valladolid between Juan Ginés de Sepúlveda and Las Casas? Had the dispute dealt simply with the crimes of the Spaniards in the New World it could be compared to the trial of Warren Hastings for his alleged tyranny in India. But the central issue at Valladolid was Sepúlveda's Aristotelian thesis that the natives of America were slaves by nature and hence unfit to govern themselves. In reply, Las Casas prepared a massive treatise in which he drew on missionary research into Indian religion, history and government to demonstrate that the Incas and Aztecs were as civilised as the ancient Romans and Greeks. If Las Casas denounced the cruelties of the conquerors so violently, it was because he attributed the discovery of America to a providential decision to provide the American Indians with the means of salvation. It was for this reason that he accepted the papal donation of 1493 as the charter of Spain's dominion, since the Holy See had granted to the kings of Castile sovereignty over the New World on condition that they ensured the conversion of its inhabitants.

If the grand debate over the justice of the Spanish conquest has been often discussed, it has been much less commonly remarked that the imperial tradition was re-stated and indeed much strengthened during the long reign of Philip II. In Peru, Viceroy Francisco de Toledo assembled a circle of jurists and theologians who accepted Sepúlveda's thesis and agreed that before the Indian could become a true Christian he had to be taught how to be a man. An indispensable part of his education consisted in working for low wages in the mines at Potosí and Huancavelica. What distinguished the new imperial school was that instead of praising the conquerors they now celebrated the benign authority of the Catholic Kings of Spain. The Jesuit theologian, José de Acosta, asserted that Divine Providence had planted mineral wealth in the New World so as to attract settlement and hence endow the Spanish monarchy with the financial means to defend the Catholic Church in Europe from both Turkish infidel and Protestant heretic. When Antonio de Herrera at last published the official history of the 'the deeds of the Castilians' in America, he cited Charles V's support of Las Casas' campaign on behalf of the Indians as proof of the Catholic Kings' concern for the welfare of their new subjects. In the seventeenth century, Juan de Solórzano, a learned jurist who wrote the standard commentary on the Laws of the Indies, reaffirmed the providential election of the Catholic monarchy and defined its authority as absolute. By then, theologians of neo-Platonic bent saluted their king as God's image on earth, not merely the head, but even the soul of the commonwealth.

It was in the early seventeenth century that creole patriotism – which is the primary theme of this book – first emerged. At this time the descendants of the conquerors and early settlers were haunted by an all-pervasive fear of dispossession, a sense that they had lost their birthright, the governance of the countries which their ancestors had won for the Catholic Kings. In this epoch the Spaniards born in America besieged the Crown with pleas for appointments to high office in Church and State and crowded into the priesthood, filling the colleges, cathedral chapters and priories in all the leading cities of the New World. The effect of their religious fervour was to endow Lima and Mexico City with a formidable ecclesiastical establishment, their numerous churches built and decorated in the most ornate style of the Baroque era. But the creoles found formidable rivals in new waves of immigrants from the Peninsula whose seizure of control of trade and rapid acquisition of riches and honours they bitterly resented. It was at this time also that creole nostalgia for both the heroic epoch of the conquest and the exotic grandeur of the native empires was deepened by the publication of Juan de Torquemada's *Monarquía indiana* and the Inca Garcilaso de la Vega's *Comentarios reales de los Incas*. For in these remarkable works they encountered a persuasive account of the origin and development of Indian civilisation in Mexico and Peru, combined with an exuberant celebration of the conquest, be it military or spiritual. That both these chronicles drew on Las Casas and on the native elite who had assisted missionaries and magistrates in their inquiries into Aztec and Inca culture meant that they bequeathed to posterity a perspective on Indian history that differed substantially from the scornful views of the imperial school. These works were destined to figure as the prime texts of the patriotic tradition in Mexico and Peru. That one was written by the mestizo son of an Inca princess and the other by a Franciscan educated in Mexico was all-important.

In his portrait of Victorian England, G. M. Young argued that 'the real central theme of History is not what happened, but what people felt about it when it was happening'.[2] If this maxim be enlarged to include what people felt about what had happened in the past, then it affords the best approach to the majestic sequence of seventeenth-century chronicles which articulated the nascent consciousness of creole identity. To read Antonio de la Calancha's history of the Augustinian order is to enter the introverted culture of the provincial Baroque, where devils and saints competed for souls, acting through dreams and apparitions. That Calancha should have attributed the wise laws of the Incas to the preaching of the Christian gospel by St Thomas the Apostle demonstrated his ambition to subjugate the native past, thereby uniting the Inca and Catholic phases of his country's history within a common, Christian frame. In practice, however, the creoles found it difficult to install the Inca empire as the foundation of their *patria*, since in Cuzco the native elite continued to parade in their traditional finery in public testimony of their historic claims. In effect, Peruvian patriots failed to advance any concept or symbol that might have served to express the common identity of the Andean empire; instead, their loyalty centred on each provincial capital, with Lima no more regarded than Potosí, Chuquisaca, Cuzco or Quito. By contrast, in New Spain, creole patriots insisted on the continuity between Tenochtitlan and the viceregal capital that was built on its ruins. There existed a corpus of Indian codices and annals in Nahuatl which offered the possibility of a reconstruction of native history on more imaginative lines than the version offered by Torquemada. More important, in 1648, Miguel Sánchez published his account of the apparition of the Virgin Mary to a poor Indian shortly after the conquest and of the miraculous imprinting of her image on his cape. The cult of Our Lady of Guadalupe at Tepeyac, a hillside sanctuary outside Mexico City, attracted the devotion of both creoles and Indians, nobles and commoners, and soon extended across all the dioceses of New Spain. The significance of this cult was that it affirmed that the Mother of God had chosen the Mexican people, no matter what their race, for her especial protection. In an epoch when the Catholic monarchy exercised a rigorous censorship and attracted a quasi-religious veneration, patriotic sentiment could only find expression in historical or religious myths and symbols.

Whatever hopes the creoles entertained of obtaining some measure of home rule within the framework of the Catholic monarchy were shattered by the accession of the Bourbon dynasty which, in the second half of the eighteenth century, sought to reduce its American kingdoms to the condition of mere possessions. In this context we should recall that, when George Kubler reflected on the sequence of art forms which dominated Spanish–American painting, sculpture and architecture, he defined the empire as a cultural colony, which is to say, as 'a society in which no major discoveries or inventions occur, where the principal initiative comes from outside rather than from within the society . . .'[3] Prime images brought in from Europe were endlessly replicated but frequently suffered deterioration owing to poor technique. In effect, the grand transitions in style from late Gothic and early Renaissance to Mannerism and the Baroque, from Churrigueresque to neo-classic, were all re-enacted in Spanish America. At no point, however, was European primacy more brutally evident than when the enlightened ministers of Charles III cut short the final flowering of the Mexican Churrigueresque in favour of an arid neo-classicism. By then, Spain itself was a cultural colony, desperately attempting to regain lost ground, importing ideas and experts from France. During the Bourbon drive to revitalise the colonial economy and exploit American resources to finance the Spanish monarchy's revival, creoles found themselves once more excluded from high office. The Jesuits were expelled and the Church subjected to a determined campaign to reduce its authority and wealth. At the same time, leading European historians now intervened, invoking the theory of climatic determinism to depreciate the cultural achievements of the Incas and Aztecs and to scorn the creoles. It was left to the American Jesuits, exiled in Italy, to defend the possibility of obtaining accurate historical knowledge about ancient civilisation in the New World. Once more the patriotic tradition opposed the imperial school, the latter oddly revived by the 'philosophers' of the Enlightenment. It comes as no surprise to find that when the Peruvian Jesuit, Juan Viscardo y Guzmán, called upon the American Spaniards to liberate their countries, he should have cited Las Casas and Garcilaso rather than Voltaire and Rousseau in support of his indictment of Spanish tyranny.

When the Napoleonic invasion of Spain finally broke the power of the absolute monarchy, the creoles at once demanded autonomy and established juntas in most provincial capitals. In South America liberal ideas were warmly welcomed and the new republics copied the constitutions of the United States and France. Simón Bolívar invoked the fashionable creed of classical republicanism, boldly presenting himself as a patriot hero dedicated to the pursuit of glory. Only Peru remained loyal to the Crown, still haunted by the Tupac Amaru rebellion, in which a descendant of the Incas had led a popular movement to restore their empire, in part inspired by his reading of Garcilaso's *Comentarios reales*. It was in New Spain that creole patriotism at last became a political ideology. For when the creole clergy incited the masses to rebel against the colonial authorities, they offered them the image of Our Lady of Guadalupe as their flag and patron. Moreover, the first congress to proclaim independence boldly advanced the concept of a Mexican nation, already in existence prior to the advent of the Spaniards and now about to recover its freedom, thus reversing the injustice of the conquest. The atrocities of royalist generals were freely compared to the crimes of the conquerors and Las Casas saluted as the apostle of America. All this was tied to a demand for the establishment of a Mexican republic and the abolition of the laws which had hitherto differentiated the ethnic groups into which the population was divided. In effect, creole patriotism here flowered into an ideology that advocated a Catholic republicanism and an insurgent nationalism.

As the bitter experience of both Simón Bolívar and the Mexican insurgents proved, the destruction of the Catholic monarchy's traditional authority soon allowed countless petty chieftains to emerge, *caudillos* and *caciques*, who came to exercise despotic power in their districts. It was Domingo Faustino Sarmiento who denounced these men as the chief obstacle to progress in Argentina, characterising them as the exponents of rural barbarism. In Mexico the survival of the royalist army prevented such leaders from seizing power, but in itself became an agent of disorder. It was after independence that creole patriotism in Mexico fell victim to the growing conflict between Catholic conservatives and anti-clerical radicals. During the Liberal Reform the radicals completed the Bourbon assault on Church wealth and privilege, expelling the clergy from public life. Challenged by military revolt and French invasion, the radicals imported the ideals of classical republicanism and invited their fellow citizens to defend their liberal *patria*, which now embodied the principles of the French Revolution.

It is thus the purpose of this book to demonstrate that, no matter how much Spanish America depended on Europe for its art forms, literature and general culture, its chroniclers and patriots succeeded in creating an intellectual tradition that, by reason of its engagement with the historical experience and contemporary reality of America, was original, idiosyncratic, complex, and quite distinct from any European model. The sheer intensity of the wars of conquest and independence, the fascination exerted by the spectacle of native civilisation, the virulence of the polemic against the tyranny of the conquerors and caudillos, the remarkable fervour of the first missionaries and the colonial Church – all these elements found expression in the chronicles and memorials which slowly articulated the creole quest for an American identity. At all moments there was a subtle counterpoint between the patriotic and imperial traditions and between the prime texts of Mexico and Peru. That many of the Spanish imperial school's cherished maxims were later revived by the philosophic historians of the Enlightenment and thereafter retailed by Mexican and Argentine liberals, only adds to the complexity of the case. What is readily apparent, however, is that the historical arguments and religious myths which figured so largely in the patriotic tradition were always liable to acquire a political resonance, even if their influence was more exerted across the centuries than by decades.

PART 1

CONQUEST AND EMPIRE

Remove justice, and what are kingdoms but bands of criminals on a large scale?

ST AUGUSTINE

1

A NEW WORLD

I

IN *The Divine Comedy* Dante portrayed Ulysses setting forth on his last voyage, animated by a desire for 'experience of all lands that be and of man's nature whether good or bad'. Accompanied by a small band of faithful followers, the Greek hero sailed past Seville and Ceuta, out through the Pillars of Hercules into the open waters of the western ocean, only there, after several days journey, to encounter a great island mountain, later identified by Dante as Mount Purgatory, before which a raging whirlpool hurled his ship and crew to an untimely grave beneath the sea. Already in his *Medea* Seneca had prophesied that 'after many years an age will come when the ocean will loose the chains of things and a huge land lie revealed, when Tethys will disclose new worlds and Thule no more be ultimate'. So also, the prophet Isaiah foretold that the nations of 'isles afar off', as yet unknown, would foregather in Jerusalem at the last day. Thus, when Christopher Columbus (1451–1506) ventured across the Atlantic, sailing for thirty-two days through uncharted seas before first sight of land, with no more than the stars in the heavens, the winds and currents of the ocean, and a simple compass and astrolabe to guide him, in effect the Genoese mariner assumed the mantle of Ulysses and boldly sought to fulfil the predictions of Seneca and Isaiah. But whereas Dante described the Greeks as impelled by a quest for 'virtue and knowledge', neither contemporaries nor posterity ever succeeded in deciphering the complex, idiosyncratic amalgam of nautical assurance, material ambition and spiritual presumption which drove Columbus to conceive and undertake such an apparently foolhardy enterprise. To this day the man remains something of an enigma.[1]

Few great events in the history of the world bear so personal an impress as the discovery of America. It took the Portuguese close to a hundred years to effect the passage to India, starting with a cautious exploration of the coasts of Africa, pausing for the settlement of Madeira and the Azores, and allowing a full decade to elapse between Bartholomew Díaz's traversing of the Cape of Good Hope in 1486 and Vasco da Gama's final voyage to Calicut in 1498. So too, although the English, led by John Cabot, first sighted Newfoundland in 1497, that tardy nation required more than a century of exploration and projects before finally establishing permanent settlements along the coasts of North America. In both cases, an entire series of voyages, backed by the court, merchants and the nobility, preceded the final, successful outcome. By contrast, Columbus appears to have become possessed of the idea of sailing westwards to Asia in the silence of his own heart, unprompted and largely unassisted. So strong was his conviction of its practicality that he survived seven years of rebuff in the courts of Portugal and Castile without relinquishing his enterprise. Although there can be little doubt that the Portuguese and English were bound eventually to sight Brazil and Newfoundland, the discovery of a direct route across the Atlantic from the Azores or Canaries to the Antilles was entirely the achievement of Columbus. That he found backing in Spain rather than in Portugal or England changed the course of history. Without his personal intervention, Spanish America might well never have been summoned forth into existence.

At the same time, there was nothing fortuitous about the discovery of America. In his biography of his father, Hernando Colón drew attention to Colombus' unrivalled experience of the Atlantic seaboard, based on voyages ranging from the Gulf of Guinea to Iceland, which enabled him to acquire an intimate knowledge of the varied currents and winds of the ocean. It was during these journeys that he heard stories of the bodies of a strange race of men washed ashore, of wooden carvings of unknown source found on the coasts of Galway and the Azores. As an expert navigator, he had acquired all the elements of astronomy, geometry and algebra that were necessary for nautical calculation. He was a skilled cartographer. Equally important, Columbus complemented his practical skills by a study of geography, reading Ptolemy's *Geography*, only recently printed, and Pierre d'Ailly's *Imago mundi*. He also delved into travel literature, with Marco Polo's description of Cathay and the Great Khan strengthening his resolve to reach Asia. In short, Columbus took full advantage both of the contemporary revival of geographical knowledge and the growing expertise in navigation, a union of theory and practice already given an institutional base in the early decades of the fifteenth century by the Portuguese Prince, Henry the Navigator.[2] Without this deepening interest in exploration and overseas trade, systematically pursued, the transatlantic voyages would have been unimaginable.

Contemporary interest in maritime expansion was closely linked to commercial interest. In the wake of Portuguese sailors, Genoese merchants moved to exploit the trading possibilities of the tropics, importing slaves from Africa and introducing sugar planting into Madeira. Here also, Columbus applied in America the perceptions and practices already in operation across the Atlantic. Although his first accounts of the Antilles expressed his delight in the beauty and natural fertility of the island scenery, his careful appreciation of their human population had the ominous ring of a predator holding his men in restraint so as all the better to calculate the best mode of striking a profit. For he assessed the natives of Hispaniola in these terms: 'They do not have arms and are all naked and with no ability for war and are very cowardly, so that a thousand could not resist three (Spaniards) and thus they are fit to be commanded and made to work and to sow and to do anything that is necessary to make towns and be brought to clothe themselves and be taught our religion.' Without hesitation he took possession of the islands in the name of the Catholic Kings of Spain and installed a small garrison to hold them.[3] Moreover, if as governor he subsequently sought to restrain the worst excesses of the settlers, which is to say, he strove to halt the seizure of women, the murder of any native who resisted, and the outright enslavement of entire villages, nevertheless, he himself initiated the slave trade, carrying off for exhibition several Indians on his first voyage, and thereafter despatching an entire cargo of slaves to Seville for sale. At the same time, he became obsessed with the need to find sufficient gold to finance further ventures and sustain the existing colony in Hispaniola. From the start the Genoese merchants resident in Seville invested in the trade with the Indies and were responsible eventually for the introduction of both sugar planting and African slavery in the Caribbean. In short, Columbus placed his nautical skills in the service of European capitalism, then still caught in its commercial phase, but already well equipped to develop and profit from the discovery of America.

   To emphasise the practical, hard headed character of the great admiral is perfectly appropriate. After all, it was a remarkable achievement for a Genoese mariner of humble extraction to raise himself and his family into the ranks of the Castilian nobility, obtaining in perpetuity the title of admiral and viceroy of the isles and mainland of the ocean sea. In the event, he proved unable to command the unruly Spanish hidalgos who swarmed into Hispaniola in the wake of his second voyage, an ineptitude that was to yield a tragic consequence, when he was seized and sent back to Spain loaded with chains. That Columbus refused to rest content with his discoveries, and chose to return again to the Antilles, there once more to seek a passage to Asia, surely demonstrates that considerations of material profit and social advancement by no means offer a persuasive or complete explanation of his motivation. In a letter of protest to the Catholic Kings against his imprisonment, he wrote: 'I should be judged as a captain sent from Spain to the Indies to conquer a large and warlike people . . . Here, by God's will I have brought under the dominion of our sovereigns a new world, whereby Spain, which was called poor, has become rich.' If he sought gold, slaves and other tropical commodities, it was because he realised that trade was necessary to sustain colonisation.[4] For himself, however, he remained more concerned to raise the resources which would finance his voyages of exploration and thus enable him to discover the route to Cathay.

But if practical considerations formed, so to say, the means to an end, what was the great prize that animated Columbus' quest? What was the source of his remarkable tenacity of purpose in the years before and after his discovery of the route across the Atlantic? There is a mystery here which puzzled contemporaries and continues to puzzle all students of the man. For he wantonly opposed expert opinion of the day and raked across a disparate body of texts, some geographical, others scriptural, to argue that the world was much smaller than the calculations of Ptolemy allowed, with the consequence that Spain was much closer to Asia than was commonly imagined. Basing himself on Pierre d'Ailly and on the Florentine geographer, Paolo Toscanelli, he estimated the distance between the Canary Islands and Cipango (modern Japan) at no more than 2,400 nautical miles, a figure wildly distant from reality, since the modern calculation is 10,600 miles. In any case, so he observed, had not the prophet Esdras declared that six out of the seven parts of the earth's surface were covered by land? It was precisely because his assertions were regarded as nonsensical that the geographers and maritime experts of Portugal advised their monarch to refuse all assistance to Columbus, whom they dismissed as a foolhardy visionary rather than as a great mariner.[5] What purpose would be served in despatching an expedition to sail across thousands of miles of open ocean, with only the barest chance of encountering an island to break the journey?

If the balance of rational, expert argument weighed so heavily against Columbus, why did he persist in his project and indeed, how was it possible for him to persuade the Catholic Kings to back the venture? Alas, the available sources do not yield any clear explanation. So obvious was the discrepancy between the weakness in argument and the tenacity of purpose that contemporaries resolved the problem by suggesting outright deception. The first general chronicler of the Indies, Gonzalo Fernández de Oviedo y Valdés, raised the possibility that Columbus had met an unnamed pilot, of Portuguese or Andalucian extraction who, blown off course by a storm, had reached America and then returned home, where on his deathbed he had informed the Genoese of his discovery. It was thus prior knowledge of the existence and general whereabouts of the West Indies that accounted for Columbus' confidence in venturing across the Atlantic, a knowledge which sustained him in the years of neglect at court. This theory, mentioned by Oviedo only as a possibility, was presented as an acknowledged fact by Francisco López de Gómara, the second great chronicler of the Indies, and thereafter was accepted by many Spanish historians of the sixteenth and seventeenth centuries.[6] Although Hernando Colón wrote a biography of his father largely to combat this opinion, his work was published in the 1560s in Italian and did not receive the attention it

warranted. In any case, by then most Spanish chroniclers were more concerned
to celebrate the heroic deeds of Cortés and Pizarro than the maritime exploits
of a Genoese sailor.

The problem with this 'explanation' is that it runs contrary to the testimony
of Columbus himself, who began his journal of the first voyage by stating that
his purpose was to reach Cathay and the Great Khan. Moreover, he apparently
went to his grave persuaded that he had indeed discovered the shores of Asia,
with Hispaniola still identified as Marco Polo's Cipango or Japan. The goal
here was neither the extension of geographical knowledge nor the opening of
new trade routes. Instead, it was the conversion of the Great Khan to
Christianity, followed by an alliance against Islam, the prelude, so it was
hoped, to the reconquest of Jerusalem by the Catholic Kings. In short,
Columbus thus viewed himself as the instrument of Divine Providence chosen
to set in motion the events which would initiate the last age of the world's
history, an epoch scheduled to be enacted before the Second Coming of Christ
and the Last Judgement. With St Augustine and Pierre d'Ailly as his guides, he
calculated that of the 6,000 years allowed for the world's duration, a mere 155
years remained, a period barely sufficient to achieve the preaching of the gospel
to all nations, the conversion of mankind to the Christian faith, and the
liberation of the Holy Places. Illumined by such convictions, what need had
Columbus with mere facts or material gain? If he had paused to calculate, he
would never have embarked on his perilous venture. As he himself wrote: 'For
the prosecution of the enterprise of the Indies, I did not profit from reason, nor
mathematics, nor maps of the world: in all things what Isaiah foretold has been
fulfilled.' That an ignorant layman rather than a great divine had been chosen
for this purpose was all the more proof of the hidden design of Providence.[7]

There was little that was exceptional or personal in these cosmic hopes of
Columbus. Since the twelfth century Christendom had been haunted by waves
of millennial expectation, with the passing events of political history at times
invested with prophetic significance. The reconquest of Jerusalem was associated with the imminent rise to power of a world emperor, a new Charlemagne, chosen to unite Europe and overthrow Islam. In Spain, the excitement
generated by the final reconquest of Granada in 1492, followed by the
expulsion of the Moors and Jews, found expression in patriotic and religious
eulogy of the Catholic Kings as the favoured instruments of Providence,
sentiments entertained as much at court as in Church circles. Is it too much to
suggest that if the Spanish monarchs chose to disregard expert opinion and
provide financial support for Columbus' first voyage, it was in large measure
because they shared the religious euphoria occasioned by the victory over the
Moors? Here, it is pertinent to recall that the vital nexus between Columbus
and the court was the Franciscan friar, Juan Pérez, a member of the observant
branch of the order which in Spain was strongly influenced by the millennial

ideas of Joachim de Fiore, a Calabrian abbot of the twelfth century. Moreover, Columbus paid tribute to two Franciscans, Juan Marchena and Juan Pérez, as the only men who had supported him during the fruitless years prior to 1492. Clearly, if he had been simply preoccupied with commercial interests or private gain, he would not have obtained their backing: it was precisely the prospect of reopening the mission to China – the Franciscans had already despatched a mission to Peking in the thirteenth century – together with the intimation that the last age of humanity was possibly imminent, that drove Pérez to enlist royal approval for the exploratory voyage.[8]

Ironically, it was precisely this sense of providential design and election that prevented Columbus from recognising that he had discovered a new world. Instead, on his third voyage, undertaken in 1497, he identified the great Orinoco as one of the four rivers that watered the Garden of Eden, an observation that led him to conclude that he had discovered the original site of the earthly paradise. Added weight to the identification was provided by the medieval siting of Paradise at the furthest extremity of Asia. Furthermore, when on his fourth voyage along the coasts of Central America, he found evidence of abundant gold in Veragua, he argued that the province was biblical Ophir, the mines from which Solomon had taken the gold to build the temple at Jerusalem. What could be more appropriate than that the same mines, now rediscovered, would enable the Catholic Kings to liberate the Holy City from Islam? In this context Columbus wrote: 'Gold is most excellent, Gold constitutes treasure and anyone who has it can do whatever he likes in this world. With it he can succeed in bringing souls to Paradise.'[9] It was in his account of the disastrous fourth and last voyage, of 1504, when his ships were buffeted by storms, his landing parties ambushed by hostile Indians, and his ill-disciplined crew mutinous, that Columbus confessed that he feared for the very lives of his young son and brother who accompanied him. In a moment of exhaustion and despair he fell into a deep slumber, only then to hear a voice which reminded him that it was God the All Mighty who 'gave you the Indies ... against the barriers of the ocean-sea, which were closed with such mighty chains, he gave you the keys'. Did not the Admiral now enjoy fame throughout Christendom? What more had God done for Moses or for David, 'whom from being a shepherd he made a king of Judah'.[10] Prior to embarking on this last expedition, Columbus had commissioned a Carthusian monk to compile an anthology of prophecies culled from Scripture and the Church Fathers, all chosen to illumine the spiritual significance of the discoveries. Obviously, the success of his first voyages magnified Columbus' conviction of Divine election; but we do well to remember that he was already some forty years old when he sallied forth across the Atlantic, so that the fulfilment of his hopes and plans more probably confirmed rather than initiated that conviction. But as to just when the idea took possession of his mind and spirit the sources are silent.

II

Although Columbus' brief account of his first voyage was published in Barcelona almost immediately after his return to Spain and attracted considerable attention throughout Europe, it was Amerigo Vespucci's *Novus mundus* (1503) which caught the imagination of the educated classes, its elegant Latin prose soon translated into all the principal European languages. So great was its circulation that in 1507 when Martin Waldeseemuller, a German cartographer, was commissioned to illustrate an edition of Vespucci's letters with a world map, he boldly named the newly discovered continent as America, albeit applying the term to the land-mass situated below the equator. Yet Vespucci was little more than a Florentine adventurer, a subordinate pilot in Portuguese expeditions, who in his letters to Lorenzo di Pier de' Medici and other luminaries, sought to create the impression that he was the first discoverer of the New World.[11] His real achievement was essentially literary. For *Novus mundus* is a Renaissance fable, a relatively short, simply written tale of a journey to unknown shores. Devoid of all circumstantial detail or personal pleading, its focus was directed entirely on the New World and its inhabitants with little mention of the European intruders or their nefarious slave-raiding. It was all as if the poetic accounts of classical authors such as Lucian and Virgil concerning the golden age of the first men living in the woods was now found to exist in reality across the Atlantic.

The sense of excitement in Vespucci's description was unmistakable. Here was an entire continent, rather than a new chain of islands, filled with immense trees and dense forests, populated with countless species of birds and beasts unknown to Europe, all uncatalogued by any ancient naturalist; the very heavens displayed a different system of stars. This new world, so Vespucci declared, offered so propitious a terrain for human habitation that 'if the terrestrial paradise is to be found in any part of the world, it will not be far distant from these countries'. All in all, it was 'a continent inhabited by a greater number of people and animals than found in our Europe or Asia or even Africa'. This image of an earthly paradise was sustained by the observation that the natives of these lands went stark naked, dwelt freely together, without the constraints of individual property, law or religion, and were untroubled by much illness or ravages of the plague. 'Neither do they have their own goods, but hold everything in common. They live together without a king, without authority, so that each man is lord of himself.' This tropical idyll was further spiced by Vespucci's insistence that sexual relations were governed by absolute freedom, with promiscuity the rule and marriage unknown. Moreover, the women were both beautiful and amorous, eagerly seeking the embraces of any passing European. In sum, the inhabitants of this other Eden 'live according to nature and can be more justly called epicureans than stoics'.[12]

In his subsequently published *Letters*, Vespucci heightened what was the only dissonant note in this image of natural man, when he confessed that the inhabitants of the New World greatly enjoyed fighting each other, albeit without much skill or order, with the flesh of their captives eaten with considerable gusto. Indeed, the quarrelsome nature and cruelty of the men and the very promiscuity of the women now led Vespucci to conclude that 'their way of life is barbarous'. He also admitted that the Indians made frequent attacks on visiting Europeans. However, he still maintained that their wars derived more from a desire for vengeance than from any ambition for power or wealth, since they had no use of gold other than for adornment, did not exchange goods in trade, and lived content with whatever nature provided them. In all this, Vespucci offered a remarkably faithful image of the ideal savage, setting off ideological hares that were to be chased with remarkable energy across the centuries.[13]

The degree to which the preoccupations of the Italian Renaissance determined the manner in which the New World was viewed is best shown by *De orbe novo* (1514), a collection of letters written in stylish Latin to Cardinal Ascanio Sforza and Pope Leo X by Peter Martyr d'Anghera (1457–1526), a Milanese humanist resident at the Spanish court. Weary of his task of teaching Latin and letters to the recalcitrant offspring of the Castilian nobility, Martyr made it his concern to keep abreast of all the most recent news of the new discoveries, conversing with Columbus and other explorers, with the aim of despatching the gist of his enquiries to Italy. Like Vespucci, he boldly characterised the inhabitants of the Indies in terms taken from classical literature, observing that 'they go naked and know neither weights nor measures, nor that source of all misfortune, money: living in a golden age, without laws, without lying judges, without books . . .'[14] Not merely did the Indians lack all knowledge of writings, they also practised primitive communism, since 'among them the land belongs to everybody, just as the sun and the water. They know no difference between *meum* and *tuum*, the source of all evil . . .' Here, then, was the image of a society still living in some pre-lapsarian stage of human existence, a stage familiar to any reader of Ovid's *Metamorphoses*, skilfully deployed so as to offer an implicit critique of contemporary Europe. At the same time, Martyr freely admitted the prevalence of warfare between villages and expressed his repugnance at reports of cannibalism practised by Caribs in their raids on other islands. As a priest writing for the benefit of ecclesiastical dignitaries, he refrained from any comment on the alleged promiscuity of the womenfolk.

Quick to appreciate the value of travellers' reports, Martyr declared that he found accounts of native religion far more interesting than all the stories of Lucian, since in place of poetic fictions they dealt in the realities of human belief. So too, on learning that some tribes inserted a piece of gold in their lips, so as to beautify themselves, he marvelled at the relativity of human taste and standards of beauty. 'What they think elegant, we think hideous. This example proves the blindness and the foolishness of the human race; it likewise proves how much we deceive ourselves. The Ethiopian thinks that black is a more beautiful colour than white, while the white man thinks the reverse ... each country following its own fancy.' It was this readiness to appreciate novelty and accept divergence from European norms that led him to admire the gold discs and elaborate Aztec plumage that Cortés sent back from Mexico, exclaiming 'I have never seen anything, which for beauty could more delight the human eye.'[15]

If in his first letters Martyr celebrated the discoveries in terms taken from classical fables, subsequently he chronicled Spanish exploits with mounting disapproval. Already, he had noted that the men who accompanied Columbus on his second voyage were 'for the most part undisciplined, unscrupulous vagabonds who carried off women'. Thereafter, on hearing of the quarrels and murders that marred the conquest of Darien in central America, he lamented: 'these discoverers of new countries ruined and exhausted themselves by their own folly and civil strife, failing absolutely to rise to the greatness expected of men who accomplish such wonderful things'. True, he never ceased to marvel at the indomitable courage of the Spaniards, the more especially as news arrived of the conquest of Mexico by small bands of adventurers, but he grew weary of the persistent reports of civil conflict among the conquerers and of their ill-treatment of the native population, commenting once more on events in Darien that it was 'nothing but killing and being killed, massacring and being massacred'.[16]

In the last letters of De orbe novo, published in 1530 after his death, Peter Martyr informed Europe of the enslavement and subsequent destruction of the native population of the Antilles. Conquest, famine and disease, especially smallpox, were responsible for thousands of deaths, but ultimately, so Martyr judged, it was the enforced demands for Indian labour, together with the ill-treatment meted out to these workers, which were the chief causes of this unparalleled demographic catastrophe. 'These simple, naked natives were little accustomed to labour and the immense fatigue they now suffer, labouring in mines, is killing them in great numbers.' He condemned the enslavement of the Lucayos islanders who were seized and shipped to Hispaniola, only there to die, 'exhausted by disease and famine, as well as by excessive labour'. Although he was careful to observe that the King's Council had dictated several laws designed to protect the unfortunate natives of the New World, he concluded that the Spaniards 'carried away by love of gold, became ravenous wolves'.[17] Yet the conquests and empire had been justified by the promise to preach the gospel to the Indians: was there not the danger, Martyr questioned, that Providence would punish Spain for this blasphemy?

The combined effect of Vespucci and Martyr was to bequeath an image of the New World and its inhabitants that was to haunt the mind of Europe for centuries to come. It was as if the classics had come to life, with the accounts of modern travellers confirming the picture of the first men already drawn by ancient poets and satirists. In tropical forests mankind still dwelt as in the infancy of the race, following the dictates of nature, unconstrained by the conventions and laws of civilisation. Here was a line of thought which was to fascinate both Renaissance humanists and Enlightenment philosophers. It was the French humanist, Michel de Montaigne (1533–92) who in his influential essay 'On Cannibals' developed the implications of Martyr's reflections into a sceptical critique of all absolute canons of taste, morals and manners. In what way, he asked, was Christian Europe superior to the pagan New World? The Indian savages who visited France were shocked by the serfdom and poverty of the French peasantry, accustomed as they were to the freedom of their Brazilian forests. Why should European extravagance and finery be preferred to the simple plumage of the natives? Moreover, if the Indians were guilty of cruelty in their wars, had not the Spaniards displayed even greater barbarism in their enslavement and massacre of entire peoples? What was worse: to eat a man once killed or to have him eaten alive by one's dogs? Thus Montaigne both defended the natives of the New World from dismissal as mere savages, more close to beasts than to men, and depicted their manners and society as a standard of natural behaviour by which to measure and condemn contemporary Europe, and in particular, to excoriate Spain, the oppressor of Italy and the enemy of France.[18] In all this cycle of discussion, it was always the inhabitants of the Antilles and Brazil who were cited as examples, with comparatively little reference made to the peoples of Mexico and Peru: natural savagery rather than alien civilisation was the preferred humanist image of the New World.

III

1492 was a Janus year for Spain, a year of warfare and exploration, filled with patriotic euphoria. If the discovery of a route across the Atlantic opened the way for overseas settlement, the fall of Granada marked the culmination of a centuries-long struggle to reconquer the Peninsula from Muslim domination. Both momentous events sprang from the union of the Crowns of Castile and Aragon in 1474, since it was the increased resources and political strength of the Catholic Kings, Isabella and Ferdinand, that enabled the Spaniards to sustain a ten-year campaign against the Moorish kingdom and then finance the despatch of Columbus' expeditions to the Caribbean. Needless to say, in contemporary estimation, it was the victory over Islam which caused most exultation, the more especially since the departure of the Moorish king and nobility was accompanied by the expulsion of all professed Jews from Spain.

Where once the adherents of all three faiths had lived in relative harmony, henceforth only the most orthodox Christianity was to be tolerated. Already at the Council of Basle in 1434–6, the delegates for Castile had claimed precedence over the English, citing their monarch's services in defence of Christendom from the Muslims. By the middle years of the fifteenth century, patriotic chroniclers both celebrated the warlike Gothic ancestry of the Castilians and hailed their kings as chosen by Providence to take the lead in the perennial war against Islam.[19] Small wonder, then, that the Fall of Granada fired yet further the mood of messianic expectation that infected Spain as much as other countries of Western Europe at the close of the Middle Ages. It was such considerations that prompted the despatch of an expedition in 1509 to North Africa, which succeeded in capturing the port of Oran. More important in the context of European politics was the campaign of Gonzalo Fernández de Córdoba, 'the Great Captain', who in 1503 defeated French forces in Southern Italy and thus vindicated King Ferdinand's dynastic claim to the kingdom of Naples and Sicily. The circle of territorial aggrandisement was completed by the acquisition of Navarre, by which all the states of the Peninsula, save only Portugal, were at last united under a common king. Within a generation the Catholic Kings had transformed Spain from a congeries of frontier states into a powerful monarchy occupying the very centre of European politics and warfare. Small wonder that Italian humanists praised Ferdinand of Aragon as the very epitome of statecraft.

In Spain itself both chroniclers and humanists vied to celebrate the great events of these decades. In his *Gramática de la lengua castellana* (1492) Antonio de Nebrija (1444–1522), a leading Spanish humanist educated at Salamanca and Bologna, declared that the example of the ancient Greeks, Jews and Romans all proved beyond doubt that 'language was always the companion of empire', with literature and conquest flowering together. In consequence, so he informed Queen Isabella, he had framed his grammar with the aim of making Castilian a fit medium for the composition of historical narratives, soon to be written, designed to ensure that 'the memory of your deeds will not perish'. Indeed, with perceptible excitement, Nebrija proclaimed that 'this great company which we call the kingdom and commonwealth of Castile' was on the move, its religion now purified, its people united, its arms everywhere victorious. Events certainly justified his rhetoric. In a subsequent history of the Catholic Kings, Nebrija observed that the course of empire had flowed ever westward, from Persia to Rome, adding:

> And who now cannot see that although the title of empire is in Germany its reality lies in the power of the Spanish monarchs, who, masters of the large part of Italy and the isles of the Mediterranean sea, carry the war to Africa and send out the fleet, following the course of the stars, to the isles of the Indies and the New World, linking the Orient to the western boundary of Spain and Africa.[20]

The success of Spanish arms was accompanied by a powerful upsurge of activity in virtually all aspects of Christian life in the Peninsula. The decision of the Catholic Kings to appoint Francisco Jiménez de Cisneros, an ascetic Franciscan friar, as Archbishop of Toledo and Primate of all Spain, expressed their determination to purge Church government of its worst abuses. It was largely thanks to his intervention that the movement of reform and renewal within the mendicant orders proved so successful, with the Franciscans, the most numerous community, transformed by the victory of the observant wing over the lax 'conventuals'. Similarly, the Dominicans received inspiration from the austere preaching of their Florentine confrere, Giralomo Savonarola. It was this strong movement of religious renewal, already under way before the explosion of the Reformation in Germany, which laid the foundation for the heroic age of the Spanish Church when a veritable Pleiad of saints stamped an impress on the Catholic Reformation in Europe which was not to be erased until the Enlightenment. Ignatius Loyola, Francis Xavier, Teresa of Avila and John of the Cross were but the most prominent of an entire generation of saints and ascetics who sought to scale the ramparts of heaven, displaying the same heroic energy and tenacity of purpose as their secular counterparts expended before the walls of Granada and the causeways of Mexico.

At the same time, the intellectual life of Spain experienced a manifest quickening. In this sphere also Cardinal Cisneros intervened, founding a new university at Alcalá with special chairs in Greek and scholastic theology, and funding the publication of the first polyglot Bible with parallel texts in Hebrew, Greek and Latin. In Spain as elsewhere in Europe the early sixteenth century witnessed a pronounced increase in the number of students attending universities. Degrees in civil and canon law offered the prospect of high office in Church and State, the more especially since the Catholic Kings relied upon the trained minds of university lawyers to assist them both as councillors of state and as local magistrates. Such *letrados* were to prove indispensable in the governance of Spain's burgeoning overseas empire. But if the traditional expertise of Spanish academics had been the study of law, leaving theology and philosophy to the religious orders, during the sixteenth century virtually all universities in the Peninsula created new faculties and chairs for the teaching of scholastic theology. In part this expansion catered for the demand created by the prestige of a succession of theologians and philosophers – men such as Francisco de Vitoria, Domingo de Soto, Melchor Cano and Francisco Suárez – who dominated the European revival of the Thomist school of scholastic theology, confidently applying the principles of natural law to contemporary problems.[21]

The very exuberance of the Christian triumph in Spain bred an intolerance that eventually came to border on paranoia and descend into the most obtuse orthodoxy. For although the Moorish nobility and all professed Jews departed the country in 1492, there still remained a large community of poor Muslims,

Moriscos as they were called, and an indeterminate number of *conversos*, Jewish families who had converted to Christianity. Within a decade the Moriscos were forced to become Christian and henceforth throughout the sixteenth century remained a resentful, unreconciled, and occasionally rebellious minority, until the Crown ordered their final expulsion in 1605. If the Moriscos formed a community apart, by contrast the new Christians, or converted Jews, infiltrated Spanish society at all levels and as such were the object of paranoic fear. In 1482 the Inquisition had been established in large measure to deal with Judaisers, as backsliding Jews were called, and thereafter a central feature of its activities was the persecution of new Christians. So intense was the prejudice against the *conversos* that in 1541 the cathedral chapter of Toledo issued an edict demanding that all future canons should present testimonials of *limpieza de sangre*, proof that they derived from old Christian stock without any infection of the 'bad blood' of Jews or Moors.[22] Such documentary proofs soon became necessary for appointment to any high office in Church and State. Yet independent evidence suggests that many noble families, not to mention several leading literary men, and many eminent religious, including St Teresa herself, all possessed Jewish ancestry. In the long run, the all-pervasive presence of the Inquisition in Spanish life was to quell the diversity of cultural influences at work in the early sixteenth century.

Emphasis on the cultural vitality of Spain in this epoch should not be defined as a simple consequence of the Italian Renaissance. It should be recalled that New Castile and Andalucía had not been reconquered and settled until the middle years of the thirteenth century, a frontier expansion which meant that much of Spain trailed far behind the cultural efflorescence of northern Europe in that century. In Seville, for example, it was only in the fifteenth century that the great Gothic cathedral was constructed, a massive stone edifice towering above a city still largely served by churches built in simple *mudéjar* brick. As for Salamanca, it was only in 1512 that the city finally decided to replace its sombre, Romanesque cathedral with the grandiose Gothic monument that still dominates its skyline. As much as in England, the early sixteenth century witnessed the final and most exuberant flowering of the Gothic style. In painting, Flemish art reigned supreme, with Spanish artists as yet untutored in the new developments of Italy. So also, literature was still dominated by the cult of chivalry and the celebration of great deeds of war and love, with only Juan de Mena (1411–56) valiantly attempting to assimilate the lessons of Dante. In short, the presence of a few humanists recently returned from Italy no more affected the medieval character of Spanish culture than the introduction of a few classical motifs into the façades of churches signified the demise of the Gothic. During the epoch of the Catholic Kings, Flanders and Burgundy rather than Florence and Rome were the masters of Spain in the visual arts, in literature, and in religion. It was the Christian Renaissance of northern Europe led by Erasmus rather than its Italian counterpart, that exercised the most immediate influence, since its emphasis on Church Fathers rather than on pagan classics found a warm welcome in clerical circles. The first Castilian poet to master the Petrarchan sonnet was Garcilaso de la Vega (1501–36), a nobleman whose Renaissance cultivation of both 'arms and letters' set a pattern that was to command widespread assent among the Spanish gentry who subsequently enrolled in the service of the Catholic monarchy.[23]

It was in the reign of Charles V (1517–54) that the remarkable range of influences at work in Spain became manifest. For Castile now emerged as the political centre of a Habsburg patrimony that encompassed the Low Countries, Austria, Bohemia, Milan and Naples, a dynastic aggregation of provinces and kingdoms on a scale not witnessed in Europe since the days of Charlemagne. In the first instance, the new king's reliance on Flemish counsellors and the extravagance of his Burgundian court circle, awoke fears of foreign exploitation that found expression in the *comunero* rebellion of 1519 when the towns of Castile and Valencia burst into revolt. But the swift defeat of that movement reinforced the doctrine, already widely accepted in fifteenth-century Castile, that the king's authority was absolute since it derived directly from heaven rather than from any contract with the people.[24] Thereafter, the nobility and impoverished gentry of the Peninsula gladly enlisted in their royal master's armies and followed the emperor in a series of campaigns that took them into Italy, France, North Africa and Germany. The veterans of these wars were never to forget the glorious decade of the 1520s when Charles V defeated the King of France in the struggle for mastery in Italy, allowed his forces to sack Rome, and then led the successful defence of Vienna against the Turkish onslaught of Suleiman the Great. If his subsequent campaigns in North Africa and Germany did not meet with such manifest success, nevertheless, their religious character confirmed the emperor as the chief defender of the Catholic faith, at a time when it was threatened by both Muslim infidels and Protestant heretics. The Habsburgs thus inherited the Christian mission of the Catholic Kings. In Spain the vein of humanist eulogy initiated by Nebrija joined with a widely diffused millennial expectation of a new age, so that Charles was hailed both as another Caesar and a second Charlemagne, chosen by Providence to reunite Christendom, defeat the Turks and reconquer Jerusalem, thereby establishing the long-awaited world monarchy. All these fervid hopes, more medieval than modern, were given eloquent expression by Hernando de Acuña in a poem addressed to the emperor on the eve of his expedition to Tunis.[25]

> Sire, now approaches, or already has arrived
> The glorious age when heaven will proclaim
> One pastor, and a single flock
> By fortune for your times reserved ...
> And now, for its solace, announces to the world

One monarch, one empire and one sword.
Already the orb of earth in part now experiences
And everywhere awaits your empire
Conquered by you in just war.

When bands of Spanish adventurers fought their way into the mountainous
interior of the New World, subjugating entire provinces and great states, they
annexed their conquests in the name of his Caesarian Majesty, Charles V, Holy
Roman Emperor, King of Castile and León, and thus gave yet more substance
to the expectations that he would create a world-monarchy.

IV

In *The Civilization of the Renaissance in Italy* (1860) Jacob Burckhardt
included the discovery of America as an expression of the cultural renovation
of the city-states of Italy in the fourteenth and fifteenth centuries. It is a view
which still enjoys considerable currency among historians. According to this
approach, the Renaissance is to be defined as the grand opening act of the
modern epoch, a period when the human spirit threw off the shackles of the
Middle Ages, exploring both nature and man from a new, more realistic
perspective, in which the ever-widening horizons revealed by maritime expansion played a notable part.[26] Not all the evidence, however, supports this facile
assimilation of the discovery of the New World to the advent of a new age. As
we have seen, Columbus himself was driven forward by religious convictions
that derived from a cycle of prophecy that was initiated in the twelfth century.
That the first cathedral to be built in the New World was constructed in Gothic
style serves to emphasise the essentially medieval ethos of the adventurers and
friars who swarmed across the Atlantic in the first years of conquest. Were it
not for the frontier status of Spain, one might well take Johannes Huizinga's
The Waning of the Middle Ages (1924) as a better guide than Burckhardt to
portray their spirit and aspirations. As it was, the conquerors of America
modelled themselves on the bold, realistic verve of El Cid, seeking to win for
themselves lordships and noble status in the lands they seized with such
incomparable energy. Where the Italian Renaissance exerted a decisive
influence was in the sphere of literary description, in the image created by
Vespucci and Martyr of the discoveries as a New World, its inhabitants still
dwelling in natural bliss, uncontaminated by the vices of civilisation. A
distinction thus has to be drawn between the conquerors and explorers of the
Indies, men more conversant with medieval romances than with the classics,
and the humanists who penned the accounts which caught the imagination of
the educated classes in Europe. Within little more than a decade of the first
sighting of the Caribbean islands, there thus had opened a fissure between the
image of the New World entertained in Europe and the reality of America

experienced by the first settlers, a fissure which, if derived from the Renaissance, was equally destined to become apparent in the Enlightenment.

In the last resort, however, any sharp contrast between the Middle Ages and the Renaissance is best avoided. For many historians the great divide which separates the modern epoch from earlier ages should be located in the seventeenth century, when the scientific revolution succeeded in reducing the physical phenomena of nature to mathematical regularities and thus decisively undermined the authority of ancient science and philosophy, an intellectual revolution which rendered obsolete the entire edifice of scholastic philosophy built upon the union of Aristotle and Christian theology. The same commentators insist on the impressive continuity of scientific endeavour in the long preparatory epoch which stretched from the thirteenth to the seventeenth century, with the Renaissance but one chapter in a complex story. It is an interpretation which enables us to make some sense of Columbus and indeed was first advanced by Alexander von Humboldt, himself a noted naturalist and traveller, who seized upon the paradox that such an apparently hard-headed, skilled mariner as Columbus should have been fired to action by esoteric religious speculations. But Humboldt then observed that many of the great scientists of the sixteenth and seventeenth centuries had possessed a similar, complex amalgam of mystical motivation and material analysis. Isaac Newton's discovery of the laws of gravity was in part prompted by his fascination with alchemical lore, and his mathematical speculations spilled over into an obsession with biblical chronology. More to the point, Humboldt compared Columbus to James Watt, the inventor of the steam engine, saluting both men as responsible for 'the enlargement of the empire of man over the material world, over the forces of nature'. At the same time, he pointed to the continuity in the development of scientific knowledge in the centuries that separated Roger Bacon and Albert the Great from Kepler and Galileo. It was the preceding advances in astronomy, mathematics and cartography which provided the necessary theoretical foundation for Columbus' nautical skills. In sum, the combination of technical expertise and mystical conviction, with both forces harnessed to serve commercial expansion and political power, was a characteristic which united Columbus with several of the greatest figures in Western science and technology.[27] There was nothing accidental or fortuitous in the invention of the New World.

2

CONQUERORS AND CHRONICLERS

I

THE CONQUEST of Mexico abruptly and dramatically transformed the image of the New World. The dismal story narrated by Peter Martyr of a tropical paradise invaded by ruthless bands of marauders intent on enslaving its witless inhabitants was replaced by the epic tale of Christian warriors fighting against great odds to overthrow a glittering, pagan empire. The intrinsic drama of this venture into an unknown interior distinguished the expedition from all other wars fought in the Indies. For the first encounter of Hernán Cortés with Moctezuma's ambassadors on the coast of Tabasco was followed by the establishment of a town at Veracruz, the disavowal of the governor of Cuba's authority, and the decision to march inland. With little more than five hundred men, Cortés first fought and then formed an alliance with the Tlaxcalans, the hereditary enemy of the Aztecs, an alliance which in part led him to massacre the unfortunate inhabitants of Cholula. The first sight of the island city of Tenochtitlan, its pyramid-temples rising high above the surrounding water, remained stamped on the minds of the Spaniards. As in a dream, they descended the mountains to be greeted by Moctezuma, a welcome they repaid by seizing that monarch in his own palace. The peace was broken by Cortés' departure to suborn a newly arrived expedition of Spaniards, and, still more by Pedro de Alvarado's wanton massacre of the Mexican nobility during the feast of Huitzilopochtli, their patron deity. There ensued the ignominious flight of the Spaniards from the city and the final three-month siege of Tenochtitlan by Cortés and his Indian allies. Here, indeed, were feats of arms that had a Homeric quality. Small wonder that Peter Martyr was led to exclaim: 'of all our contemporaries only the Spaniards are capable of withstanding such trials'. In the same way that El Cid, Spain's medieval hero, had conquered Valencia from the Moors, so now Cortés and his heroic band captured Tenochtitlan, the desperate resistance of its defenders magnifying the epic quality of a siege reminiscent, so Cortés averred, of the fall of Jerusalem.[1]

Until the stirring events of 1519–21 the Spaniards had proved remarkably silent about their invasion of the New World, leaving the task of description to Italian adventurers and humanists. But news of the conquest of Mexico reached Europe through the publication of the letters written by Cortés to the emperor informing him of the newly acquired territories. At last, here was a Spaniard telling a very Spanish story, his unvarnished prose rising to the greatness of the occasion, affording the spectacle of a great captain turning from the heat of battle to compose despatches for his royal master. Not content with an arid account of combat, Cortés was at pains to emphasise the alien grandeur of the society he encountered in Anáhuac. For its inhabitants not merely wore clothes, occupied houses often covered with stucco, and practised intensive agriculture, they also dwelt in large cities which were dominated by high temples and great palaces, the dense population offering tribute both to a warrior nobility and a numerous priesthood. The temples, which surmounted soaring stepped pyramids, housed horrific idols and bore abundant evidence of regular human sacrifice. Cortés marvelled at Moctezuma's palace, with its extensive gardens and well-stocked aviary and zoo, all attended by five hundred servants. The image of Asiatic splendour was strengthened by description of native temples as mosques. Cortés compared Cholula to Granada, and estimated that Tenochtitlan was equal in size to contemporary Seville, its great market at times frequented by some fifty thousand people. Indeed, such was the scale of the conquered territories that Cortés sought permission to call the land New Spain, and boldly informed Charles V: 'Your highness ... may call himself once more emperor, with a title and with no less merit than that of Germany, which through the grace of God your sacred Majesty possesses.'[2]

Viewed from the perspective of Europe and of the imperial court, the ability of Cortés to frame persuasive accounts of his deeds was almost as important an achievement as the actual events. For we must recall that his expedition had been largely financed and despatched by Diego de Velásquez, royal governor of Cuba, and despatched with strict instructions simply to reconnoitre the coasts without any attempt to press inland. The establishment of a town council at Veracruz so as to provide a legal basis for the appointment of Cortés as chief justice and captain was a patent act of defiance of the governor. Moreover, since it coincided with the *comunero* rebellion in Spain, it smacked of popular, elective government.[3] To justify his actions, Cortés mounted a bold, literary offensive, denouncing Velásquez' project as 'tyrannical', arguing that all the governor had in mind was a coastal raid in search of gold, one more murderous *razzia* of the kind that had already devastated the Antilles. By contrast, Cortés sought to conquer, to pacify and to settle, thus winning new kingdoms both for the emperor and the Christian faith. Throughout his narrative he exclaimed against the horrors of idolatry and human sacrifice, at times risking the safety of his expedition by entering the temples of his Indian allies to cast down idols and install Christian images in their place. The buoyant tone in which Cortés informed the emperor of his loyalty and Catholic devotion is best displayed in the eloquent speech that he delivered on the eve of battle with the Tlaxcalans, in which he reminded his men that they were subjects of the king and 'in a position to win for Your Majesty the greatest kingdoms and lordships in the world'. Moreover, Spaniards had never been found wanting and 'as Christians were obliged to fight against the enemies of our faith and were gaining glory in the next world for so doing, winning the greatest honour and glory any man had won up to our times'.[4] The ability of Cortés to find the words to describe and justify his actions is all the more impressive if we recall that he had arrived in the New World in 1504 at the age of nineteen, having spent only two years at the university of Salamanca. His smattering of law and letters, however, proved sufficient to secure for him appointment as secretary to the governor of Cuba and a leading place among the rulers of that island. In the event, his literary eloquence, when combined with the remission of bullion, won him royal recognition and appointment as governor and captain-general of New Spain. The pursuit of 'arms and letters', thus raised Cortés from the status of a petty hidalgo to the condition of a great noble, his house and family henceforth figuring among the titled aristocracy of Castile.

Ever fertile in legal resource, Cortés sought to justify his exploits on grounds far removed from mere force of arms and conquest. He seized upon Moctezuma's speech of welcome as evidence that the Indian monarch had freely accepted the sovereignty of Charles V. For in that speech, as Cortés reported it, the master of Anáhuac declared that the Mexica were newcomers to the land. They had been led by a lord who subsequently left them. When he returned he had found that they had married with the existing inhabitants and would no longer recognise his authority. Once more, he departed but warned them that his heirs would one day return to take up their patrimony. The lords of Tenochtitlan were thus mere regents, holding the throne until the return of their first leader, or his sons. Moreover, Cortés already had evidence that Moctezuma identified him as the heir or agent of that lord, since in Tabasco the Aztec ambassadors had brought elaborate gifts and regalia, and had offered him human blood to drink in recognition of his divine status. Taking advantage of this misconception, Cortés invited Moctezuma to pay homage to Charles V as the descendant of this 'great lord or king'. He arranged for the pliable monarch to summon the Aztec nobility so as to adjure them to accept the emperor across the ocean as their rightful lord and sovereign.[5] As a result of these proceedings, Cortés declared that Anáhuac had been won for the emperor, not through force of arms, but rather by peaceful cession of sovereignty. When the Mexica rose in fury to kill Moctezuma and expel the Spaniards form Tenochtitlan, in effect they were guilty of rebellion, since the solemn act of *translatio imperii* had already been staged.

More persuasive than this dubious argument was the emphasis Cortés placed on the preaching of the Christian gospel to the natives of Mexico. From the start, he sought to instruct his Tlaxcalan allies in the elements of his religion and to cast down Indian idols. Upon his return from the fruitless expedition to Honduras, he seized the opportunity of welcoming the first Franciscan mission to New Spain, kneeling in the dust before the assembled nobility to kiss the hand of Martín de Valencia, leader of the twelve travel-stained friars who had walked barefoot from Veracruz to Mexico City. In his last letter to the Emperor, Cortés attested to the remarkable success which had greeted the efforts of this mission, with natives flocking to receive their message. He exclaimed: 'in a very short time we can take it for certain that a new Church will arise, where more than in any other part of the world Our Lord God will be honoured and served'.[6] If the spiritual fruits of conquest were so manifest, how could that passage of arms be condemned?

The skill with which Cortés sought to sever the Mexican venture from its Caribbean matrix should not obscure the identity of purpose and institutions. Apart from the initial Crown financed expeditions to Hispaniola and Darien, all other conquests and voyages were organised privately, the offspring of a dynamic frontier society, supported by merchant capital from Europe, which employed the profits of one venture to finance the next excursion. Conquest and settlement thus acquired a momentum which was sustained by ever-growing numbers of adventurers who swarmed into the New World, with the survivors forming a hardy breed of frontiersmen, able to endure rigours and risks unimaginable in Europe. When enlisted on a venture – an *entrada* – these men constituted a *compaña*, a company united in search of plunder, albeit subject to their captain or *caudillo* who maintained a loose but summary military discipline. The conquerors thus usually referred to themselves not as soldiers but rather as 'companions'. In short, the same type of organisation which had characterised the English conquests in France during the Hundred Years War – the free company – thrived anew in the Indies.[7] However, the eventual aim of these company ventures was not simple booty, but conquest and 'pacification' of the natives, so that Indian labour could then be employed to procure gold, wood and other export commodities. The great prize in this scramble for riches was an *encomienda*, the grant of a number of Indians who were henceforth obliged to offer free labour service and tribute to their Spanish master. This institution had been introduced by Nicolas de Ovando, governor of Hispaniola 1504–9, and thereafter formed the economic basis of conquest society throughout Spanish America. As each new terrritory fell to the conquerors, its native inhabitants were distributed among the captains and leading men of the triumphant expedition, so that the *encomenderos* quickly emerged as a colonial nobility, the labour service of their Indians employed to mine for gold and silver or open up land for agriculture.[8] Once established, the encomenderos generally founded a Spanish town as the capital of their district, where they constructed their chief residences. They dominated the town councils and controlled the annual appointments of *alcaldes ordinarios*, the urban magistrates, whose authority in these early years extended to encompass the surrounding province. Thus, although the encomienda did not carry any rights of jurisdiction over Indians, the encomenderos' control of the urban magistracies conferred extensive powers over the native population.

The conquest and settlement of Mexico drew its leadership, manpower and financial backing from the Antilles and proceeded in much the same fashion as its Caribbean predecessors. Once Tenochtitlan had fallen, Cortés gathered together the treasure seized from the Aztecs, set aside one fifth for the Crown, another fifth for himself, and divided the remainder among his company according to status, a horseman receiving eighty pesos and a footman fifty or sixty pesos, a reward which proved a severe disappointment to most of the conquerors. Thereafter, Cortés moved quickly to distribute encomiendas to his principal lieutenants and followers, carving up central Mexico into a series of these grants. What requires emphasis is that most encomiendas coincided with the boundaries of Indian lordships, which is to say, they comprised entire communities rather than simple levies of labourers. Moreover, Cortés issued a set of regulations designed to safeguard the natives from undue exploitation, much in the same way as he sought to prevent his followers from raiding or looting Indian villages.[9] Although the Indians of New Spain were destined to endure much ill-treatment and to suffer from the inroads of epidemic disease, in general they were not subjected to the violent abuse meted out to the unfortunate inhabitants of the Antilles. The very density of population, the advanced nature of its society and political organisation, and the vision of Cortés, all combined to mitigate the worst excesses of the conquerors.

The very success of Cortés in battle and in government aroused jealousy both in Mexico and at court, where it was rumoured that the conqueror wished to make himself king of the great empire he had won. The publication of his letters to the emperor in several European languages brought him a reputation as a warrior which awoke fears and envy. The result was that although, on his return to Spain, Cortés was welcomed by Charles V, awarded the title of Marquis of the Valley of Oaxaca and given an impressive series of encomiendas encompassing no fewer than 23,000 tributaries, he was denied any further appointment as governor. Henceforth, New Spain was to be ruled, first by a high court of justice – the *audiencia* – and then from 1535 onwards, by a viceroy invariably selected from the ranks of the Castilian nobility. For his part, Cortés had to be content with employing the labour and tribute of his Indian tributaries to initiate a series of economic enterprises, planting sugar on the coast, growing wheat on the central plateau, mining for silver at Taxco, washing for gold in Oaxaca, building ships at Tehuantepec, and exploring the coasts of Lower California for pearls.[10] In 1539, frustrated by the treatment accorded to him by Viceroy Antonio de Mendoza, he returned to Spain, there to frequent court circles and to accompany Charles V on his ill-fated expedition to Algiers.

If public opinion in Spain in the 1540s turned so decisively against the conquerors, in part it was because of the shock of the news from Peru, where the adventurers who had seized possession of the Inca empire not merely executed Atahualpa on trumped-up charges but thereafter set about each other in an entire cycle of fratricidal conflict. The worst excesses of the civil wars that had haunted most European countries in the fifteenth century were once more enacted amidst the ruins of the Inca empire. It was a story which lacked both the drama and the nobility of events in Mexico. For both Francisco Pizarro and Diego Almagro were grimy, illiterate veterans of Darien, notable only for their tenacity of purpose and endurance of hardship. Both men fell victims in the wars caused by their failure to reach an amicable agreement over a just division of the vast territories they had won, Pizarro assassinated and Almagro executed. Moreover, when the Crown sought to pacify the unruly settlers by installing a viceroy, Blasco Núñez de Vela, his high-handed measures soon provoked open rebellion led by Gonzalo Pizarro against the authority of the Crown. In all, the sequence of conquest, civil war, and rebellion lasted a quarter of a century, 1530–55, during which the native population inevitably suffered at the hands of this murderous breed of conqueror. The spirit which animated many of these men was expressed with startling frankness by a licentiate in law, who observed that in Peru he had lost all scruples of conscience and sought no other glory than to kill his enemies, reproaching a companion for his leniency in blasphemous terms: 'it was no time to be a Christian, but rather time to put the soul, and if it were necessary, the body, into hell . . .'.[11]

The task of writing 'a true account' of the conquest of Peru was assumed by Francisco de Jerez, the secretary of the first expedition to Cajamarca, whose report was published in 1534. In the prologue addressed to Charles V, Jerez sounded a triumphal note: 'Who can equal the deeds of Spain . . . when have either the ancients or the moderns witnessed such great deeds with so few people against so many climes of heaven and gulfs of sea and distance of land, to conquer what has not been seen or known?' But his succinct narrative entirely lacked the skill or interest of Cortés' letters. Although he drew attention to the Inca roads, their strong fortresses and warehouses, noted the wealth of Cuzco and the temple of Pachacamac, and admitted that 'the cloth is best that has been seen in the Indies', Jerez betrayed little interest or sympathy for native society. He defended the seizure of Atahualpa at Cajamarca and the subsequent massacre of his entourage on the grounds that the Inca emperor had failed to listen to the exhortations of the Dominican friar, Vicente de Valverde, that he should at once accept the Christian faith and recognise Charles V as his sovereign. Moreover, although he noted that the Spaniards 'were astonished to see so much prudence in a barbarian', he justified Atahualpa's execution by Pizarro, notwithstanding the payment of the ransom, by the observation that 'he was the greatest and cruellest butcher men had seen'.[12]

Apart from the calculated murder of Atahualpa, what most impressed contemporaries in this account was the extraordinary plunder that the conquerors of Peru won for themselves. For the 169 Spaniards who marched across the highlands to Cajamarca secured over a million pesos for division, with a horseman receiving some 8,800 gold pesos and 362 marks of silver, and footmen about half that amount. The Pizarro brothers despatched to the emperor 153,000 gold pesos and another 5,058 marks of silver. Thus whereas Tenochtitlan had yielded comparatively little reward to its conquerors, by contrast Peru satisfied the wildest dreams of every 'companion' who had joined Pizarro in his foolhardy venture into the Inca empire.[13] Henceforth Peru was to be synonymous with great riches and became a magnet attracting every footloose adventurer and impoverished hidalgo in the Indies. Small wonder that for a generation the country equally became renowned for its civil wars and public disorders. The remarkable difference between the sequence of events in Mexico and Peru in the years immediately following their conquest meant that when their respective histories came to be written the focus and interest proved equally distinctive, with the heroic quality of Cortés set against the murderous character of the Pizarros and the Almagros, a contrast in large measure derived from the impression created by Cortés' own letters. But what care had these frontiersmen for the opinion of posterity when the prizes were so high and the temptations so great?

II

The only chronicler who captured the character and spirit of the entire tumultuous sequence of exploration and conquest that stretched from the first voyages of Columbus to the civil wars of Peru was Gonzalo Fernández de Oviedo y Valdés (1478–1557), a former courtier and treasury official. Whereas Cortés and other captains despatched accounts of their deeds to Spain, so as to obtain royal reward, Oviedo took upon himself the task first of describing the flora and fauna of the hemisphere, and then, more importantly, of narrating the complete history of its occupation by the Spaniards. The result of his life-long endeavour was the *Historia general y natural de las Indias*, a vast, sprawling chronicle, divided into fifty 'books', which in a densely printed modern edition fills five volumes of text. Resident for many years in Santo Domingo, still the chief port of entrance and departure for all travellers in the Indies, Oviedo kept an open file on each province of the empire, often inserting without much change the accounts he copied from conquerors on journey to Spain.[14] At times, his chronicle possesses all the immediacy of a work in progress, with his own often acerbic interjections adding a diary-like quality to the text. With the indomitable assurance that such an enterprise required, Oviedo declared that future generations would marvel 'that a single man could have written such a multitude of histories and secrets of nature' and boldly defined his chronicle as 'not one of the least but rather one of the most high and copious that has been written by any man since Adam'.[15] In effect, Oviedo was an intellectual conquistador, who sought to achieve lasting fame as both the Pliny and the Herodotus of the New World.

The dictum that no man of any quality has ever gone to America save because of the disappointment of his hopes in Europe, was abundantly proved in the case of Oviedo. Reared at court as a *mozo*, an inferior page in the household of Prince Juan, the heir to the Catholic Kings, the sudden death of his master in 1497 drove Oviedo 'to wander through the world' in search of a livelihood, a search rendered all the more desperate in later years by his acquisition of a beautiful young wife. As a young man, he travelled in Italy, acquiring an extensive knowledge of its literature and leading men. To the end of his days he was to cite the satires of Aretino with delight, a taste in part derived from the scandal of the excesses of Pope Alexander VI and his son, Cesare Borgia. Thereafter, he served briefly as secretary to the Great Captain, Gonzalo Fernández de Cordoba. Very much the Spanish gentleman abroad, he failed to gain any mastery over Latin, so that his knowledge of classical literature was based on Italian and Spanish translations. Moreover, although his experiences in Italy left an indelible mark on his mind, when at the end of his life in Santo Domingo he came to write his *Quinquagenas de la nobleza de España*, a poetic gallimaufry of reminiscence and reflection, he dwelt more upon the heroic feats of arms of the Spaniards in Italy than on the splendours of Renaissance art and literature. For Oviedo the purpose of both poetry and history was to celebrate great warriors and their valour.

It was in 1514 at the age of 37 that Oviedo first entered the New World, serving as notary and treasury official in the expedition to Darien led by Pedrarias Dávila, an appointment which entailed supervising the branding of all Indian slaves. Two years later he returned to Spain and subsequently alternated between America and Europe, vainly seeking preferment at court, advancing ill-conceived projects of colonisation and, in 1525, at last winning some measure of reputation by the publication of his *Sumario de la natural historia de las Indias*, the first description of the fauna and flora of the New World. In this project, he was encouraged by Hernán Núñez, a leading Spanish humanist who taught Pliny at the university of Salamanca. Disappointed in his hopes of material enrichment and official preferment, in 1532 Oviedo accepted a life-long appointment as constable of the royal fortress at Santo Domingo

1 Title page of Gonzalo Fernández de Oviedo y Valdés, *Historia general y natural de las Indias*

and, more importantly, was recognised as royal chronicler of the Indies. His ambition to achieve fame as the Pliny of the New World was in part realised in 1535 by the publication of the first fifteen books of his *Historia general y natural de las Indias* which dealt with events up to 1520. However, when in 1548 he returned to Spain to obtain permission to publish the remainder of his chronicle, which covered the conquest of Mexico and the civil wars in Peru, he was denied a licence. It was not until the nineteenth century that the complete text of his great work was published by the Royal Academy of History in Madrid.

Impressed as were all his contemporaries by the sheer magnitude of the events he had witnessed, Oviedo followed Nebrija in adopting a triumphal, providential view of Spain's role in the world, observing of Charles V that

> God has chosen for him the supreme dignity both in the world and in the Christian commonwealth, acting as second sword, with the Vicar of Christ the first ... the climax of the universal monarchy of our Caesar is about to occur ... so that the rest of the world is to be conquered, God placing all infidels under the banner of Jesus Christ, in obedience and service of so Christian a monarch.

As late as the 1550s, when the emperor was about to abdicate, Oviedo expressed the hope that he would lead a crusade to defeat the Turks and reconquer Jerusalem.[16] Within this grand, providential scheme, the Indies were to play a central role, their riches supplying the emperor with the sinews of war, shipping sufficient gold and silver to finance the wars against the Protestants and Turks. Oviedo wrote: 'the continent of these Indies is the other half of the world, as great and indeed possibly greater than Asia, Europe and Africa, so that all the land of the universe is divided but into two parts'. Its discovery was providential: Columbus was not merely praised as 'the first inventor, discoverer and admiral of these Indies', he was also saluted as 'the minister and instrument' of the Holy Spirit who guided his path across the ocean. Nowhere was Oviedo's celebration of the epoch in which he lived better expressed than in his pronouncement on Magellan's voyage around the world: 'the journey that this galleon made was the greatest and most original event since God created the first man and made the world'.[17]

Needless to say, Oviedo reserved his fondest praise for the Spaniards, whose epic deeds and conquests in the New World equalled where they did not surpass the exploits of Alexander and Cyrus. Among the nations of contemporary Europe, the Spaniards were distinguished by their singular ability in war, a quality which derived both from their Gothic ancestry and from their long experience of combat against Islam. Whereas in France and Italy only gentlemen were trained in the practice of arms, by contrast 'in our Spanish nation ... all men are born principally and especially for their devotion to exercise of arms'. Oviedo marvelled how commoners in the Indies fought as bravely as hidalgos, on occasion rising to positions of command. Commenting on the inevitable hardships and often brutal discipline that characterised the expeditions to the New World, he hailed the conquerors as 'men of quality, who are born poor, obliged to observe the military rule, a rule that is more strict than that of the Carthusians and more dangerous'. In a revealing shift in social values, Oviedo here transferred to the adventurers who enlisted in the free companies that invaded the Indies the prestige and dedication once reserved to the Christian knight.[18] The figure who most attracted his praise, perhaps inevitably, was Hernán Cortés, who possessed, so he declared, all the qualities of a great captain as set out in the military treatises of Xenophon and Vegetius, and he boldly compared him to 'that mirror of knighthood, Julius Caesar'. Indeed, it was only in Anáhuac that Oviedo encountered battles and sieges on a scale sufficient to dignify his narrative, so that within the *Historia general* the conquest of Mexico stands apart by reason of the intrinsic drama and grandeur of its action. At the same time, although he described Moctezuma as 'a great king', he criticised him as 'very lacking in spirit or else pusillanimous'. Moreover, he doubted the veracity of Moctezuma's speech of welcome to the Spaniards, as reported by Cortés, characterising it 'as more of a story, a means of inventing a fable to serve his purpose, by an astute, wise and artful captain'.[19]

Not only did Oviedo proclaim the superiority of modern conquests over ancient exploits, he also declared that contemporary voyages and discoveries had rendered classical geography and learning obsolete. 'The ancient writers were ignorant of the greater part of the world and what they did not know was much more than that which they wrote about.' To this joyous dismissal of the ancients, there was conjoined an insistence on the advantage of practical experience over mere book-knowledge as the best guide to action. In warfare, for example, everything depended on the experience of a captain and his followers: mere greenhorns from Europe (*chapetones*) soon died in the New World, failing to adapt to its 'particular constellation'. It was precisely Columbus' practical mastery of the art of navigation, a mastery derived from prolonged observation and experience of the currents, winds and stars of each particular region, which had assured him success in his venture across the ocean. In short, here was a kind of empirical knowledge, far removed from theoretical study based on books and the ancients, 'which cannot be learnt in Salamanca, Bologna and Paris, but only in the chair of the compass'. In these utterances, Oviedo testified to the impact of the new discoveries with unparalleled freshness and perception, broadening the discussion from mere comparison with the classics to an insistence on experience and observation as the basis of all true knowledge.[20]

So to describe Fernández de Oviedo: to extract from his voluminous writings the notes of patriotic exaltation; to point to his acute observation of nature;

and to emphasise his Italian experience – all this is to present Oviedo as a man of the Renaissance, similar to his humanist mentors, Nebrija and Hernán Núñez. Such a portrait, however, is manifestly tendentious or, at best, one-sided.[21] To start with, when in 1515 Oviedo first returned from Darien, he sat down in Spain to compose a chivalrous romance, *Claribalte*, which described how its Arthurian hero defeated France, conquered Constantinople and Jerusalem, united the Greek and Latin Churches and was then acclaimed both Pope and emperor. Admittedly, this summary appears more like a political prospectus for Charles V than a story of knightly deeds, but it serves to remind us of Oviedo's late medieval fascination with such matters.[22] Indeed, in his last book, the *Quinquagenas*, he described the exploits of the Great Captain in Italy in terms of medieval combat, citing the individual acts of valour performed by 'brave knights'. Content to compare his hero with El Cid, Oviedo neglected the political dimension of the struggle for mastery in Italy waged between Spain and France in favour of detailed descriptions of chivalrous feats of arms, employing a vocabulary at times oddly at variance with the realities of contemporary warfare, on one occasion referring to 'three knights, colonels of infantry'.[23]

Despite his praise of Columbus, Oviedo was also the first chronicler to raise the possibility that the New World had been discovered by an unknown Basque or Andalusian pilot, who, blown off course by a storm, had reached America and returned, only soon after to die, albeit not before informing Columbus of the secret of his journey. If Oviedo presented the story as a mere possibility, subsequent Spanish chroniclers were to accept the myth as an article of faith. Moreover, Oviedo also sought to undercut the significance of the papal donation of 1493 by arguing that discovery and conquest created sufficient rights of dominion as to render it unnecessary.[24] Not content with bare assertion, he also had recourse to the history of the false Berosus, a text recently 'discovered', which is to say, invented, by Fr Jacobo Annius in 1497, where it was recorded that the twelfth king of Spain, Hespero, had discovered the Isles of Hesperides, a group of islands situated in the Atlantic, an archipelago identifiable with the Antilles. Similarly, at a later period the Carthaginians had sailed across the Atlantic and encountered the same islands.[25] In short, the Spanish occupation of the New World should be regarded as the reconquest of ancient Iberian domains rather than an entirely new venture headed by an Italian and justified by papal donation. In any case, since Christ had enjoined his Apostles to preach the gospel to all nations, then it followed that at some point missionaries had reached the Indies so as to convert its native inhabitants, a mission which in all probability had been despatched from Spain. In short, Oviedo here delved into myth and legend so as to undercut the providential significance of the discovery of the New World and to assert prior Spanish claims to sovereignty.

Contrary to any triumphant vision of the New World as marking a new start in human affairs, Oviedo frankly admitted that its conquest was accompanied by scenes of unparalleled horror and cruelty. A participant in the expedition to Darien, he calculated that so prevalent and remorseless was the campaign waged against the natives of the region that within a few years its population of 2 million Indians had been virtually destroyed. If Núñez de Balboa, the first captain to enter the province had sought the alliance of native chiefs, by contrast the grim veterans of the Italian wars unleashed by Pedrarias Dávila installed a reign of terror. Of the treatment of Indians meted out by one band of conquerors, Oviedo wrote: 'they tortured them, demanding gold, and some they burnt, and others they gave to be eaten alive by dogs, and others they hanged and on others they practised new forms of torture'. From Darien there sprang an entire breed of frontier captains, who extended their raids northwards into Nicaragua and southwards to Peru, carrying off thousands of slaves, and destroying entire peoples. It was not merely Spaniards who were guilty of these crimes since the cruelties perpetrated by the German Welser in Venezuela were so gross that Oviedo described them as human wolves, adding 'I can only believe that among these sinners the Devil was afoot or that one of these men was none other than Satan himself.'[26]

Nothing scandalised Oviedo more than the boundless greed of self-appointed captains or *caudillos* who led their men to destruction, setting out on foolhardy expeditions without any prospect of success. He singled out the case of Diego Díaz Ordaz, a lieutenant of Cortés in Mexico, who abandoned the comfort and prestige of his encomienda to lead a foray along the coasts of Guiana in which most of his followers lost their lives. Equally memorable was the aimless venture into the interior of Florida mounted by Hernando de Soto, a leading conqueror of Peru, who led 1,000 men in a three-year trek across the southern states, ranging from Florida to Louisiana. The trail of destruction left by the expedition aroused the universal hostility of the warlike Indians of the region so that barely a third of the Spaniards eventually escaped, with little more than scars to show for all their toil and sufferings. Soto, so Oviedo pronounced, had been trained in the school of Pedrarias and Pizarro and was much given 'to the sport of killing Indians', which was 'neither to settle nor to conquer, but rather to disturb and devastate the land and to quit the natives of their liberty'.[27]

Even Cortés did not escape Oviedo's criticism. Despite his eulogy of the captain as another Julius Caesar, he inserted into the *Historia general* a dialogue between himself and Juan Cano, a conqueror in Mexico, who had married Isabel Cortés, a daughter of Moctezuma and the widow of Cuauhté-moc, the last ruler of Tenochtitlan. For Cano, who visited Santo Domingo in 1544, presented a decidedly critical view of his former leader, asserting that Cortés had slaughtered over three thousand Indians at Cholula, in a surprise attack, undertaken, not as was later alleged to forestall native ambush, but simply so as to inspire Moctezuma with terror. Similarly, in Tenochtitlan, Pedro de Alvarado had massacred some six hundred young nobles as they celebrated a religious festival simply to seize their gold ornaments. After the fall of that city, Cortés first had Cuauhtémoc tortured and then killed without reason or remorse.[28] That Oviedo should have wished to have included this devastating critique bears witness to his growing disillusion with the entire process of conquest, a disillusion which became more obvious as his *Historia general* ran its course.

It was the news coming in from Peru that most shocked Oviedo, a shock compounded by the report of the death of his only son in that country. For he had known both Francisco Pizarro and Diego de Almagro when they were mere captains hunting for gold in Darien. Neither man knew how to read or write. Veteran frontiersmen by the time they reached Peru, neither man had the capacity to rule a great empire. Indeed, Oviedo dismissed Pizarro as 'the bastard son of a gentleman squire, a man without letters or skill in governing'. Condemning the execution of Atahualpa as simple murder, he attributed the injustices committed by the Spaniards in Peru to their initiation in the infernal school of Pedrarias in Darien where they had become accustomed to kill and torture Indians without remorse or pity. For all that, Oviedo confessed his astonishment at the savage cycle of civil wars that decimated the conquerors of Peru, with first Pizarro and then Almagro losing their lives. But it was the rebellion led by Gonzalo Pizarro in the 1540s which evoked his strongest condemnation, the more especially when he learnt of the death of Viceroy Nunez de Vela. For here was a threat to the very unity of the Spanish nation, a reversion to the anarchy of the previous century. Significantly, he defined Pizarro as a 'tyrant', applying that term as it was used in the *Siete Partidas*, the Castilian medieval code of law, as a man who seized power in defiance of the rightful authority of the king. It was a term he also employed to describe Cesare Borgia and the *comunero* rebels of 1519.[29]

Confounded by the excesses of the conquerors in the New World, their fortunes and careers so often destroyed by folly or mutual malevolence, Oviedo could find no better explanation to account for these extraordinary vicissitudes than the image of Fortune, which, with blindly spinning wheel, raised obscure men to govern great empires and cast down well-born heroes to early graves. True, he was careful to deny that the stars had any real influence over human affairs and asserted that Fortune was but another name for God's providence. But, in general, Oviedo invoked the concept in a secular fashion as a blind, inexplicable force, operating in the world with arbitrary and unpredictable results.[30] The only other principle he advanced to explain the turbulent course of events in the New World was *codicia*, the virulent cupidity or greed that drove the conquerors ever forward into new, often reckless ventures. Indeed, so often did he appeal to this concept to account for the cruelty and irrational excesses of the Spaniards that at times it appears to operate as an independent force, a demonic possession that destroyed the men it infected. Whereas Italian historians such as Guicciardini depicted men as caught between the influence of Fortune and the exercise of their own *virtu*, their individual moral power deployed in war and politics, by contrast Oviedo described the conquerors as governed by the blind forces of cupidity and Fortune, powerless to resist their ruin.[31]

By the 1540s a veteran settler, Oviedo lamented the failure of the first conquerors to establish themselves in the New World, asserting that their lives and earnings had been squandered without consequence. Out of the two thousand adventurers who had entered Darien only some forty men survived until 1535. All these lands, he complained, were gained 'at the cost of our lives for the profit of the merchants and the settlers who, with their hands clean, now enjoy the fruits of other men's sweat and toil'. Such was the constant turn-over in residence that few men formed fixed attachments to any particular place. Certainly this was the case with Santo Domingo whence the first settlers had migrated to Mexico and Peru in search of riches, so that the city was treated as a stepmother, a *madrasta*, rather than as a *patria*, a homeland in whose service a man might care to die.[32] It was not only the merchants, many of them Genoese, who swarmed into the Indies, scouring the land for profit, but in addition, so Oviedo observed, lawyers, notaries and judges equally flocked to the New World, descending upon the conquerors like carrion crow, seeking to stir litigation so as to enrich themselves. In a splendid phrase, he referred to notaries as 'alchemists of ink, who became rich overnight'. Nor were the crown judges exempt from such charges, since of one such individual in Nicaragua, he commented that he had come 'to enjoy other men's sweat, as is the rule here with judges with degrees ... who have known how to employ their studies in theft and letters rather than in justice'. In one all-encompassing sentence, Oviedo summed up his complaints against the university men who came to the Indies: 'the lawyers take our property and the doctors our lives'.[33]

In the light of these sentiments, it should come as no surprise to learn that Oviedo equally entertained a strong aversion to the clergy, and in particular, to the friars who devoted their lives to the conversion of the Indians to the Christian faith. As late as the 1540s, Oviedo cited the satires of Aretino and Erasmus concerning the vices and hypocrisy of the Catholic clergy, his own experience of the Rome of Alexander VI still a potent influence on his attitude. At the outset, so he wrote, he had imagined that friars came to the Indies in search of souls, but experience had taught him that 'under the shadow of their habit, these fathers are accustomed to contrive much other business'. After his visit to Nicaragua, he commented sarcastically on the numbers of Indians who were baptised there after simply learning one or two prayers by rote, the friars keeping careful count of their converts so as to impress the king and obtain appointment as bishops. In their dealings with Spanish settlers, the friars often abused their role as priests, obtaining handsome legacies for their communities from deathbed repentance. In Santo Domingo the canons of the cathedral speculated in property to the detriment of the city. In any case, the religious were a dangerous breed of men from whose ranks had emerged men like Luther who had led Germany into heresy and broken the unity of Christendom. So also in the Indies, the clergy threatened Spanish dominion by their intrigues and jealousy of the conquerors, the source of their envy often springing from their social origin as foreigners or men of low birth. 'The religious habit and the sack-cloth languages, together with their titles and degrees, serve to hide the base stock and meanness of those not endowed with good blood'.[34]

In certain measure, Oviedo's aversion to priests, lawyers, doctors and merchants derived from the conventional contempt exhibited by knights and gentry for the learned and money-grabbing professions. But it equally sprang from a suspicion, widespread in Spain, that these occupations were infiltrated by Jews and heretics. Recalling that in his youth he had frequently heard Spaniards mocked in Italy and France as Moors or Jews, he praised the Catholic Kings for 'cleansing' Spain in 1492 by their expulsion of all professed Jews. But there still remained the menace of the Jews who had converted to Christianity, since the quality of their Catholic faith was inevitably suspect. So strong were Oviedo's fears on this score that he called for the establishment of the Inquisition in the New World so as to protect the Church from the insidious corruption of the *conversos*. Towards the end of his life, he pronounced emphatic approval of the notorious decree of *limpieza de sangre* promulgated by the Archbishop of Toledo, Francisco Martínez Siliceo, a decree which insisted that henceforth all candidates for canonries in the cathedral chapter should present certificates that they were hidalgos or of old Christian stock, uncontaminated by any admixture of the 'bad blood' of Moors and Jews. Oviedo's enthusiasm for a regulation which soon became a standard requirement for all appointments in Church and State, once again illustrates the degree to which he expressed the common mentality of the sixteenth-century Spanish petty gentry.[35]

Nothing is more shocking in Oviedo to the modern reader than his open denigration of the native inhabitants of the New World. In his first published work, *Sumario de la natural historia*, he described the Indians as guilty of cannibalism, and sodomy, endowed by Nature with skulls that were four times as thick as the European cranium. So also in his *Historia general* he informed the world that: 'This people is by nature lazy and vicious, of little faith, melancholic, cowardly, of low and evil inclinations, liars, and of little memory or constancy ... In the same way that their skulls are thick, so is their understanding beastly and ill-inclined.' Himself the owner of slaves and possessor of an encomienda in Darien, whose Indians he employed mining for gold, Oviedo clearly sought to justify his exploitation of these wretched victims of conquest by depicting them as barely human, little higher than the beasts. Moreover, he did not hesitate, when in Spain, so to advise the Council of the Indies when that body sought his opinion in its review of colonial government. Such was the brutish incapacity and malevolence of the Indians that it was well-nigh impossible for them to understand or accept the Christian faith. Indeed, Oviedo later wrote that after thirty years in the Indies he had yet to meet a native who was a true Christian. The 'spiritual conquest', the mass conversion of the Indian population was thus little more than a charade, a vast fraud perpetrated by mendacious friars on uncomprehending natives.[36]

In all fairness to the memory of Oviedo, it should be noted that in the later, unpublished sections of his chronicle, he inserted more favourable comments on Indian character and quality, writing 'the truth is that I have seen many a naked Indian woman more truly modest than a fully-dressed Christian woman'. When his good friend, Jiménez de Quesada, the conqueror of New Granada, praised the inhabitants of that province for their rationality and civility, Oviedo was content to copy the opinion without qualification. So too, he allowed that the natives of Peru were 'a clean people and of good reason, with virtuous women', all well-dressed and firmly governed. In Nicaragua he was impressed by the intelligent discourse of a chief and confessed that the natives there were more than justified in seeking to defend themselves from the slave-raids of the Spaniards. In one revealing passage, he maintained that the human sacrifice and cannibalism of the Indians were more than matched by the Spanish practice of unleashing their mastiff hounds to tear unfortunate captives to pieces. He admired the jewellery of Mexico and recognised that it was equal in craftsmanship to anything he had seen in Italy.[37] In short, as the tide of conquest swept across the mainland, encompassing the advanced societies of Mesoamerica and the Andes, so Oviedo was forced in part to modify his impression of Indian character and capacity.

Despite these qualifications, Oviedo's views on the Indians remained distinctly hostile. He frankly admitted that it was the virtual enslavement of the inhabitants of the Antilles effected by the encomienda system that had caused the depopulation of the islands, with the entrance of smallpox completing a process already well under way. Elsewhere, slave-raiding and simple massacre were the cause. Despite these admissions, however, Oviedo blamed the destruction of the native population of the New World on the Indians themselves: their sufferings were God's punishment for their abominable sins, the Spaniards thus serving as mere instruments of Divine wrath. 'This blame and punishment principally derives from the crimes, abominable customs and rites of this people.' Moreover, their unnatural vices had brought them under the dominion of the Devil, whose influence clearly lingered in their minds long

after their ostensible conversion to Christianity. One great advantage that
derived from the disappearance of the Indians was the extirpation of all forms
of idolatry: 'Now the Devil is banished from the islands; all that came to an
end, now that most of the Indians' lives have ended.'[38] Not that Oviedo was
much impressed by the African slaves brought in to replace the natives since,
although he admitted that they were so badly treated that they were often
driven into revolt and flight, he condemned them for their essentially vicious
nature, concluding that their souls were as dark as their skins.[39]

With such a swarm of phobias buzzing in his head, it was no doubt inevitable
that Oviedo should have quarrelled with Bartolomé de las Casas, the great
defender of the Indians. In many respects their careers ran parallel, since in the
years 1515–19 both men returned to Europe to canvass their respective projects
for the New World. It was at Barcelona in 1519 when Las Casas won royal
approval for his scheme for the peaceful settlement at Cumaná, that Oviedo
presented his proposals for the establishment in Santo Domingo of a priory-
fortress of the chivalrous order of Santiago, garrisoned with 100 knights to
patrol the confines of empire, subjecting the disorderly tide of conquest to their
rule. The rejection of this fantastical scheme in favour of Las Casas' project
soured relations between the two men, whose cast of mind and natural
sympathies were at opposite poles. Oviedo paid off his score by devoting the
last pages of the published first part of his *Historia general* to a sarcastic
account of the Cumaná fiasco, accusing Las Casas of being responsible for the
deaths of the colonists killed by hostile Indians.[40] He insisted that the failure of
the enterprise signified that all attempts to preach the gospel in the New World
had to be preceded by armed conquest. Unfortunately for Oviedo, the influence
of Las Casas at court and in ministerial circles became paramount in the 1540s,
so that when the chronicler returned to Spain he was refused a licence to print
the second part of his *Historia general*. In his *Quinquagenas*, Oviedo admits
that Las Casas had been greatly mortified by his description of the Cumaná
incident. He also recalled that he had witnessed the Dominican's disembarca-
tion in Santo Domingo, accompanied by a mission of thirty young mendicants,
many of them barely more than boys, adding characteristically: 'in the Indies it
rains friars'. In a bitter complaint of Las Casas' virulent denigration of the
conquerors, he compared him ineptly to Aristophanes, the Greek satirist, and
then denounced 'his demerits and his three faces, first as a layman without
authority, then as a secular priest engaged in business, and finally as a
troublesome and lying friar'. Ironically, while Oviedo in Santo Domingo
penned these remarks, in Spain Las Casas was revising his own *Historia de las
Indias* where he blackened the chronicler's reputation, denouncing him as a
slave-driver, whose slanderous attacks on the Indians sprang from an uneasy
conscience. In both cases, these two old men, both by then in their seventies,

employed their chronicles to pay off old scores and to promote the political causes for which they had campaigned throughout their lives.[41]

From the ruin and vicissitudes of his life in the New World, Fernández de Oviedo sought to erect a lasting monument in the form of his *Historia general y natural* which was designed to serve both as an encyclopaedia and a universal history of the Indies. His ambition, however, outran his literary capacity, so that it is only the professional historian who now cares to plough through his heavy volumes. For in Oviedo we encounter that combination of minute realism, prolixity of language, and absence of literary form that Huizinga defined as the chief characteristics of late medieval prose and poetry. There was a positive obsession with the recording of facts and events, marred by the lack of any corresponding power to organise the material into logical or literary form. In the case of Oviedo, the intention which animated his ambition was admirable: to compile an inventory of 'the secrets of Nature' in the Indies and 'to relate the merits of the conquerors'. But in both branches of his endeavour he employed the same basic method, the description of individual facts and the narration of specific events – in short, the accumulation of what he called *particularidades*, with little more organisation or interpretation than a rough and ready geographical and chronological distribution of material.[42]

If Oviedo won fame in Europe for his description of the flora and fauna of the New World – the first ever penned – his contribution to the development of natural history lay simply in the enumeration of phenomena, with all the emphasis on external description and virtually no attempt at classification, still less at explanation. He admitted: 'as to these things and secrets of Nature, the causes are hidden, given that only the effects are visible'. He lamented that a Leonardo or a Berruguete had not visited the Indies so as to observe and depict the grandeur of its Nature, since 'all this is to be seen rather than written about'. Thus, although he constantly referred to the secrets of nature, he used the term as a synonym for effects or observable facts, secret only in the sense that hitherto they had been hidden from the European eye.[43] At the same time, Oviedo approached his task in realistic vein, eschewing travellers' tales and the fanciful bestiaries of an earlier age, so that he enlarged contemporary knowledge by his provision of relatively accurate data. In the last resort, the emphasis on an inventory of phenomena rather that on their explanation or interpretation, no matter how necessary a prerequisite, was essentially pre-scientific in its approach to the natural world.

As a chronicler, Oviedo was governed by the same obsession with recorded facts, stating: 'I do not write following the authority of some historian or poet, but as an eye-witness', or using 'authentic testimonies signed with names and confirmed by public notary, as in any legal certificate'. The primary material out of which he composed his work was the 'accounts of merits' despatched by purpose of his chronicle was to transmit to posterity a faithful record of the great deeds accomplished in the Indies, which otherwise would soon be lost in the passage of time. He also wrote to instruct and improve, citing the Greek historian Diodorus Siculus that: 'History alone, with words equal to the deeds, is marked by true utility, since it exalts the honourable and spurns the vicious ... by the experience of times past which history gives, we come to live perfectly.' Whereas the law existed but to punish and poetry merely to give delight, History, the testimony of virtue and vice, served as both moral guide and recording angel. In this approach to the profession of historian, Oviedo was closer to medieval chroniclers such as Froissart and Commynes than to Florentine humanists like Bruni and Guicciardini. At the same time, the very emphasis on eye-witness accounts of contemporary affairs is reminiscent of Herodotus.[44]

As much as Columbus, Oviedo thus makes nonsense of any attempt to draw a sharp distinction between the Middle Ages and the Renaissance, or, to put the matter more accurately, reminds us of the empirical, realist bias of large areas of late medieval culture. The celebrated inability of the scholastic mind to ground its syllogisms and universal truths in the empirical particularities of the natural and social world should not blind us to the late medieval talent for sharp, often dramatic, observation and portrayal of that world. At times, of course, observation proved at odds with theory, with the hapless reader left perplexed by apparent contradictions. Thus Oviedo celebrated the grandeur of nature in the New World, but disdained the squalid character of its human inhabitants. More important, he praised the epic quality of the Spanish conquest, yet deplored the cupidity and cruelty of the conquerors with monotonous insistence. So too, although he prophesied the advent of the universal monarchy of Charles V as providentially inspired, he took a secular view of the discovery of the New World, displaying a remarkable hostility to the clergy and their missionary enterprise. Any interpretation of the conquest as the last crusade will not easily survive a close reading of Oviedo. In the last resort, the *Historia general y natural* survives as a copious repository of information, all the more valuable precisely because its author pursued facts rather than theories, content to incorporate personal testimonies virtually untouched rather than subjecting his material to the constraints of historical composition and interpretation.

III

Although Hernán Cortés, upon his return to Spain, attended court and accompanied Charles V on his ill-fated expedition to Algiers, he failed to gain entrance into royal councils or win the recognition he craved, his military experience in the Indies at a discount in the war against the Turks. As much as experience in the Indies at a discount in the war against the Turks. As much as Clive of India after him, his colonial wealth only conferred minor political influence at home. Moreover, such was the ascendancy of Bartolomé de las Casas in ministerial circles that his very reputation as a great captain and magnanimous conqueror was at risk. The rebellion of Gonzalo Pizarro against the New Laws of 1542 brought into question the very loyalty of the conquerors to the emperor. There was a danger here that steps might be taken to confiscate or reduce the vast patrimony that Cortés had secured for himself and his descendants, the basis of his entrance into the ranks of the Castilian nobility. Ever resourceful and perceptive, Cortés now cultivated the company of such literary men and the clergy as cared to frequent his house, at times discussing with them the grand debate then in progress over the justice of the conquest of America. In 1546 he moved to Seville, still the literary capital of Spain, only there to die before he could fulfil his cherished hope of returning to the New World, albeit providing in his will that his bones should be shipped for entombment in the Hospital de Jesús in Mexico City.[45]

Before his death, Cortés evidently chose Francisco López de Gómara, his chaplain, to justify and exalt his achievements, thus assuring his reputation and patrimony for posterity. A humanist trained in Alcalá, who had spent some years in Italy, Gómara (1511–c. 1566) accompanied Cortés to Algiers and had already composed a brief life of Barbarossa, the ruler of that city. He was to spend his last years compiling the *Anales del Emperador Carlos V*, an ambitious, incomplete work, in which he sought to integrate the conquest of the New World with contemporary events in Europe with the aim of offering a universal history of his times. What is remarkable about this last work is the light it throws on Gómara's approach to the historian's task. For he exhibited a deep fascination with the life and character of Cesare Borgia and still more with the warlike feats of the Spaniards in their conquest of Italy under the Great Captain and Charles V. The influence of the Florentine Renaissance is illustrated by his observation on a Spanish captain, whose courage was more than matched by his avarice and cruelty: 'the rose comes forth from the thorns, and only by miracle is great virtue found without vice'. For here we encounter a definition of virtue clearly akin to the Machiavellian *virtu*, which is to say, that moral power and ambition that found expression in war and politics, a concept quite distinct from Christian morality, and which in effect condoned the use of violence for the achievement of glory.[46]

To identify López de Gómara as a humanist, influenced by the Italian Renaissance, offers but a first step in his interpretation. As loyal subjects of Charles V, the Spaniards had little understanding or sympathy for the republican tradition of civic humanism in which Leonardo Bruni grounded his history of Florence. Despite the sentiments which bound Castilians to their cities, which by this time had come to be described as their *patria*, their political loyalties were to the king–emperor who had led them to such high place in the concert of Europe. The preferred model for Gómara was Paolo Giovio, an Italian bishop who wrote, among other things, a *Life of the Great Captain* and a *History of his Own Times*. For Giovio professed to write universal, contemporary history, based on public documents, private letters and information procured by interview. An admirer of Machiavelli and Guicciardini, he took a disenchanted view of human affairs, displaying an innate scepticism concerning the religious professions that infused contemporary political conflict. At the same time, he was profoundly engaged in the exaltation of great men, following the tradition of Plutarch and Seutonius, a celebration that at times afforded contradiction between the demands of truth and the commitments of eulogy.[47] But whereas Italian historians generally followed Bruni in drawing a sharp distinction between the modern and medieval epoch, fixing upon the revival of letters as the great divide, by contrast their Spanish counterparts were more impressed by imperial continuity. In 1545 Pedro Mexía, 'the illustrious knight' of Seville published his *Historia imperial y cesárea* in which he described the lives of all the Caesars, from the conqueror of Gaul until Charles V, depicting the Habsburg dynasty as the heirs of Charlemagne and Augustus, and thus offering an implicit denial of any radical break in historical continuity.[48] Despite differences in style and vocabulary, both Mexia and Gómara still deployed their prose to magnify the valorous deeds of great kings and their knights.

It was in 1552 that Gómara published his *Historia general de las Indias* and *Historia de la conquista de México*, two separate works, almost immediately republished together under the title of *Hispania victrix*. Writing in a style of incomparable concision, Gómara sounded a brazen paean of triumph, which celebrated the Spanish discovery of the New World rather than the revival of letters in Italy as the advent of a new epoch in the history of humanity. In both the introduction and conclusion of his *Historia general*, he expressed the exhilaration experienced by his generation at the sudden explosion of Spanish arms and dominions, boldly affirming that 'the greatest event since the creation of the world, apart from the incarnation of He who created it, is the discovery of the Indies which is thus called the New World'. But if these lands were called a New World, he added, it was not because of their recent discovery, but rather because they comprised as much territory as Europe, Africa and Asia put together. In his dedication to Charles V, Gómara declared that 'God wished the Indies to be discovered in your time and by your vassals, that they would be converted to his holy law', choosing the Spaniards for this task because they had always fought against the infidels. In a formal eulogy of his nation, now renowned throughout the world, he exclaimed that 'Never at any time did a king or people move or subject so much in so short a time as we did . . . as much in warfare and exploration as in preaching the gospel and the conversion of 'it is therefore just that Your Majesty should favour the conquest and the conquerors'.[49]

In line with this jingo exuberance, Gómara took as fact the hint of Oviedo, and boldly announced that the Indies had been discovered by an unknown pilot of Andalusian, Basque or Portuguese extraction, who had died in the house of Columbus. The exploits of the admiral were described in but summary terms, none too favourable. Unlike Oviedo, however, Gómara printed the Latin text of the papal donation of 1493, thus ascribing it capital significance in establishing the legitimacy of Spanish conquest. Needless to say, he followed his predecessor in offering a biting description of the failure of Las Casas' project of peaceful colonisation in Cumaná, accusing him of being responsible for the deaths of the Spanish farmers he had brought out to the Indies. Equally daring, Gómara questioned the wisdom of the New Laws which threatened to deprive many conquerors of their encomiendas, attributing the measure to the intrigue and jealousy of religious like Las Casas. Indeed, the rebellion led by Gonzalo Pizarro was presented as an almost justifiable defence of property and rights gained through conquest.[50] At the same time, Gómara did not exculpate the Spaniards entirely, clearly stating that it was through their oppression and slave-raiding that the population of the Antilles and Central America had been destroyed. So also, he condemned the execution of Atahualpa as an act of cruelty and described Pizarro as a good soldier but unfit to govern a great empire. In exculpation, he noted that God's judgement was already to be discerned in the violent deaths that most of the conquerors of Peru had suffered during the civil wars. If any reader doubted the justice of the conquests, he was advised to read the works of Juan Ginés de Sepúlveda in order to find a satisfactory resolution of the question.[51]

Where Gómara betrayed most clearly his reliance on Oviedo, and indeed, their common perspective, was in his assessment of the Indians. In the introduction to the *Historia general*, he declared them to be the children of Adam, since otherwise they might be thought to be mere beasts, adding: 'they do not have letters, nor money, nor beasts of burden: essential things for society and the welfare of man'. This lack of civility was compounded by their many offences against natural law, arising from their practice of idolatry, human sacrifice, sodomy and cannibalism. In the text Gómara offered some rudimentary account of the native population, seeking to distinguish between provinces, but failed to offer any considered view of the differences that separated the inhabitants of the Antilles from the subjects of the Incas. After noting the drunkenness and promiscuity of the inhabitants of Hispaniola, he echoed Oviedo in his charge that they were 'sodomites, indolent, liars, ungrateful, changeable and base'. Much the same list of qualities were applied indiscriminately to other groups of Indians. With little as yet published on Peru, Gómara was content to admit some of the achievements of the Incas as regards warfare was content to admit some of the achievements of the Incas as regards warfare and the construction of great fortresses. But for the rest, he dismissed their religion as idolatry and criticised their practice of human sacrifice, their drunkenness and the tyranny of their rulers. 'The vulgar do not have, nor want, nor are allowed property. They are liars, thieves, phlegmatic, ungrateful, without honour or shame, charity nor virtue.' In a few brief paragraphs Gómara thus described and condemned one of the greatest empires known to human history.[52] If we compare the almost intuitive sympathy with which Peter Martyr greeted all news about the inhabitants of the Antilles with the scornful dismissal of the Incas and their subjects exhibited by Gómara, then some measure of the difference between Italian and Spanish humanism can be discerned.

It was in his *Conquista de México* that Gómara found a theme worthy of his pen and consonant with his conception of history. Essentially, he wrote a life of Cortés, largely based on the conqueror's original letters and reminiscences, interlarded with accounts of Indian culture and history. If at one stage, Gómara had thought to write parallel lives of Barbarossa and Cortés, in effect the comparison was now with Pizarro, the relatively peaceful settlement of New Spain contrasted with the disorders and rebellion of Peru. From the start, he denied the charges levelled both by Peter Martyr and Oviedo that Cortés had been guilty of virtual treason in his disavowal of the authority of Diego Velásquez, the governor of Cuba, arguing that in large measure the expedition had been financed independently of the governor. At several points in the text, he drew attention to Cortés' concern to set aside the royal fifth, listing the treasures that the conqueror had despatched to Spain. More important, he employed the humanist device, copied by Bruni from classical historians, of providing the complete text of the orations that Cortés was alleged to have delivered, both to his own men and to the Indians. These speeches present Cortés as the loyal Christian warrior, seeking as much to convert as to conquer, emphasising at all points his loyalty to the emperor, his appeal to his fellow Spaniards, and his concern for the salvation of the Indians. The speeches thus contain the ideological nub, the message, so to say, of the book. Yet, more important, Gómara reported the two speeches of Moctezuma in which that unfortunate monarch welcomed the Spaniards into Tenochtitlan, recognising them as the messengers of the Aztecs' previous lord, and thereafter exhorting the Indian nobles to recognise the authority of Charles V as their lawful sovereign. In short, Gómara here developed the theory, already enunciated by Cortés, albeit mistrusted by Oviedo as a stratagem, of a *translatio imperii*, a voluntary cession of sovereignty with the corollary that the Indian attack on the Spaniards, following Alvarado's massacre (justified by Gómara as a preemptive measure of defence) was an act of rebellion against the emperor, the rightful monarch of Mexico. Once more, the essence of the case was advanced in the course of a formal oration. Finally, Gómara took advantage of hindsight to praise Cortés for distributing the conquered Indians among encomiendas awarded to all his lieutenants and leading followers, thus ensuring a true settlement of New Spain.

In his portrait of Indian society in Mexico, Gómara drew upon the information gathered by Fr Toribio de Benevente, better known as Motolinia, a leading Franciscan missionary in New Spain and an ardent supporter of Cortés. Much of this data was published for the first time by Gómara and was far superior in depth and scope to the scatter of dispersed facts he presented for Peru. For here the reader encountered some discussion of native mythology and ritual, of moral instruction and calendrical computation, of history and society, all pointing to the relatively advanced character of Mexican civilisation. Once more, the gardens and palace of Moctezuma figured large, together with accounts of the orders of knights and the fasting and penitence of the priesthood. That the Mexicans were relative newcomers to the land was made clear. However, no matter how favourable these features might appear, Gómara coloured his portrait with the dark background of a society which worshipped the Devil and engaged in massive daily human sacrifice and ritual cannibalism, an emphasis that led to the grand conclusion: 'There was never, so it would appear, a people more or so idolatrous as this: so given over to the killing and eating of men . . .'[53]

Towards the close of his history, Gómara offered a justification of the conquest in terms of the advantages it offered the Indians of New Spain. Once subject to the arbitrary tyranny of an absolute despot, they were now the free subjects of a Christian king, governed by just laws, their property assured and their labour remunerated by wages. The conquest had liberated them from civil slavery and had freed them from the awful necessity of human sacrifice. Moreover, the Spaniards had introduced the Indians to the use of iron, given them domestic animals, and circulated silver money in place of the cacao beans hitherto in use. The nobility had been taught how to read and write and some had even learnt Latin, an all-important acquisition, since 'with letters they are truly men', a dictum that expressed Gómara's humanist bias.[54]

Despite the thoroughly secular temper of Gómara's narrative, at all points he was anxious to justify the conquest by appeal to its religious sanction and benefit, an insistence which distinguished his history from Oviedo's chronicle. Not merely did he print the papal donation in full and depict Cortés as recklessly quick to destroy pagan idols, he also assured his readers that during one desperate battle the Spaniards had been assisted by no less a figure than Santiago himself, an intervention mentioned by Oviedo as hearsay but retailed by Gómara as acknowledged fact. More important, he emphasised the great enthusiasm with which the natives of New Spain welcomed the preaching of the Christian gospel by the Franciscans and other religious. Drawing upon the

memorials of Motolinia, he described scenes of mass penitence and processions, with Indians baptised by the thousand, the destruction of their former
temples and idols leaving them no alternative but to seek heavenly assistance in
the newly erected Christian churches. In this harvest of souls, encouraged by
Cortés, the chief patron of the friars, lay the chief benefit and justification of the
conquest. Once again, the implicit contrast between Peru and Mexico worked
in favour of the northern kingdom, since Gómara confessed that by reason of
the civil wars and rebellion, the preaching of the gospel had made little
advance, the Indians of Peru more noted for their recalcitrant indifference than
for the devotion that characterised the natives of New Spain.[55]

Published at a time when the status of encomiendas and the justice of the
conquest was the subject of public debate and furious agitation within the
councils of the king, Gómara's *Historia general* displayed an audacious
freedom of comment which quickly elicited an official decree ordering its
withdrawal from circulation. Already, however, by 1554 its instant popularity
had attracted no less than three separate editions. Here at last the Spanish
public found a history of the conquest of the Indies which was stylish, succinct,
and triumphant. What impresses anyone familiar with contemporary chronicles is the insouciant brio with which Gómara reduced the sprawling accounts
of Oviedo and other chroniclers into a laconic summary, characterised by acute
judgement and strenuous command of the narrative. Yet despite the sharp
contrast between Oviedo and Gómara as regards their style and formation,
their sentiments and perspective on events prove to be remarkably similar. The
aim and bias are identical. Both Oviedo and Gómara glorified the conquerors
and denigrated the Indians. But whereas the first chronicler inserted first-hand
materials which often offered testimony that ran contrary to his main
argument, by contrast Gómara so ordered his evidence as to frame a coherent
case. The very crimes of a Pizarro or the human failings of Cortés as regards
women were deliberately included so as to emphasise the heroic quality of the
conqueror of Mexico. The two volumes of his work are of a piece, with the
thesis of the *Historia general* exemplified in the life of Cortés.

The impact of Gómara's history was instant, universal and far-reaching. Its
brazen triumphalism provoked the anger of Las Casas and aroused deep
suspicion in official circles. Conversely, fellow humanists such as Cervantes de
Salazar moved quickly to incorporate its text in their projected histories. At the
close of the century, the royal chronicler of the Indies, Antonio de Herrera,
equally plagiarised his narrative and arguments. In short, Gómara played a
decisive role in transmuting the often incoherent materials assembled by
Oviedo into a form which rendered them both accessible and attractive, his
work a constitutive moment in the emergence of the imperial school of New
World history, the rationale of which was the celebration of Spanish conquest
and empire.

IV

Gómara's eulogy of Cortés not merely offended religious and official sensibilities, it also profoundly irritated the conqueror's own companions, many of
whom cherished bitter resentments concerning the apportionment of the spoils
of conquest. By the 1550s such conquerors as still survived were engaged in a
campaign to protect their encomiendas and, in particular, urge on the Crown
the necessity of bequeathing these grants to their sons and grandsons. Had they
not fought battle upon battle to win these lands for the Crown and the
Christian faith? They compiled 'accounts of merit', to record their deeds, so as
to justify their clamour for reward, both for themselves and, more importantly
as their lives drew to a close, for their families and heirs. Indignant at the
denigration of their reputation launched by Las Casas, they found Gómara's
errors and curt narrative equally offensive. Not merely had Cortés obtained the
lion's share of encomienda Indians and wealth, he now enjoyed lasting fame as
the conqueror of Mexico, portrayed as a leader who achieved his victories
virtually unassisted by the counsel or skill of any lieutenant or companion. The
collective experience of an entire band of conquerors had been converted into
the biography of a great captain. If Las Casas denounced them as criminals,
Gómara simply ignored their existence. That a man who had never set foot in
the New World should thus seek to deprive them of their share of glory and
virtually excise their deeds from the annals of the past was indeed a bitter blow.

It was to combat the errors and omissions of Gómara that Bernal Díaz del
Castillo (1495–?1583), a young follower of Cortés, sat down in the 1550s to
write the *Historia verdadera de la conquista de la Nueva España*, a work which
engaged him intermittently until at least 1575. The result was not so much a
polemic as a sustained memoir of the events of the conquest which possessed an
immediacy and life rarely found in other accounts of this period. Taking
Gómara's narrative as a framework, Bernal Díaz recorded his memories of the
events described in that text, enlivening and transforming every scene by a
plethora of circumstantial detail, all related from the perspective of an eye-
witness and a participant. Writing in a vigorous, colloquial style, he thus
relived in old age the great deeds of his youth, setting out on paper his still lively
recollection of what it meant to be a conqueror.[56]

Although the *Historia verdadera* was to be plundered by generations of
romantic historians and popular novelists in quest of racy material, it presented
a sustained argument. Time and again, Bernal Díaz insisted that on all
occasions Cortés took counsel with his chief captains and followers, and that
the most important decisions were subject to collective agreement of the entire
company of conquerors. In particular, it had been the company, not Cortés,
which had decided to break with Velásquez and march into the interior in
search of glory and riches. On occasion, Bernal Díaz' irritation boiled over, as

when he wrote: 'the chronicler Gómara says that Cortés did this, went there, came here, and says so many other things which do not lead anywhere, that even if Cortés had been made of iron . . . he could not have gone everywhere'. Yet more annoying was the impression Gómara gave of effortless victories: 'he makes no mention as to whether they were killing us or whether we were being wounded, nor what work we had nor what sufferings, but instead he writes it all as if we had been going to a wedding'.[57] At the same time, Díaz scornfully dismissed Gómara's story that the conquerors had been assisted during battle by the appearance of Santiago and the Virgin Mary, observing: 'I as a sinner was not worthy to see it.' To the best of his knowledge, no other conqueror had seen an apparition, since otherwise they would certainly have built a chapel to commemorate such a momentous event. Indeed, the first news he had of the apparition was on reading Gómara. Needless to say, he added, the conquerors had always fought for the Catholic faith and were only too conscious of the assistance given them by the Almighty in their battles against the infidels. It was in this context that he defined the motives of the conquerors with lapidary precision: 'To serve God and His Majesty, to bring light to those in darkness, and also to get rich.'[58]

What remains in the minds of all readers of Bernal Díaz is not his complaints against Gómara, but rather the epic quality of his narrative when he relived the great moments of the conquest. On recalling the Spaniards' first sight of the island city of Tenochtitlan, seen from a mountain pass, he exclaimed: 'when we saw all those cities and villages built in the water, and other great towns on dry land . . . and that straight and level causeway leading to Mexico, we were astounded'. Indeed, some of the soldiers asked themselves whether it was not all a dream, since 'those great towns and temples and buildings rising from the water, all made of stone, seemed like an enchanted vision from the tale of Amadis'.[59] So too, Díaz offered a memorable description of the *noche triste*, when the Spaniards, laden down with plunder, fought their way out of Mexico, only to find in many cases that their spoils impeded their escape or caused them to drown. His narrative reaches a climax with the final siege of Tenochtitlan, when the Spaniards, now assisted by thousands of native allies, engaged in fierce hand-to-hand fighting along the causeways leading into the city. Few scenes in history have been preserved with such dramatic intensity as when Díaz recalled the moment when 'the dismal drum of Huichilobos sounded again, accompanied by conches, horns and trumpet-like instruments. It was a terrifying sound, and when we looked at the tall pyramid-temple from which it came, we saw our comrades who had been captured in Cortés' defeat being dragged up the steps to be sacrificed.' Watching from the causeways, powerless to assist, the horror-striken conquerors saw the Indian priests lay their comrades on the altar stone and then cut open their chests, offering the palpitating hearts to their gods.[60] Here, indeed, was material on which William

Prescott was to draw, when he wrote his classic history of the conquest of Mexico.

Whereas both Oviedo and Gómara sought to glorify the conquerors by denigrating the Indians, by contrast Bernal Díaz always referred to his native opponents with respect, emphasising just how hard-fought were the battles of the conquest. He painted an attractive portrait of Moctezuma, and emphasised the services and courage of Marina, the mistress and interpreter of Cortés, without whose assistance communication between the Spaniards and Indians would have proved difficult. Towards the end of his chronicle, he marvelled at the skill and intelligence with which the Indians after the conquest had acquired and applied European arts and crafts, and noted that many of the nobility had already learnt how to read and write. In his recollections of Tenochtitlan, there already entered a note of nostalgia for a glory on earth that had been destroyed, with now only a handful of survivors aware of its grandeur.

Writing in the 1560s, Bernal Díaz was a voice from the past, the voice of a Spain still more medieval than modern, the purpose of his chronicle the commemoration of great deeds and great warriors, comrades and companions in battle. 'Fame, illustrious, praiseworthy Fame' was his inspiration, a fame which had been obscured by Gómara and other chroniclers. On reading Julius Caesar, he found that the Roman general had been in some fifty battles – exactly the same number of engagements in which he himself had joined. Moreover, so he expostulated, had not the achievement of fame through heroic deeds in years past brought royal reward? Certainly, that had been the practice in Spain where the kings of Castile and Aragon had divided the lands seized from the Moors among the knights and nobles who had conquered them. But in New Spain Cortés had appropriated the best encomiendas and richest provinces for himself and his friends, so that many of the original band of conquerors had been forced to seek new lands in the South. Whereas by reason of his letters and remittance of treasure, Cortés had won a title of nobility and great wealth, sufficient to allow his retirement to Spain, by contrast many of his followers and early companions died in remote provinces or lingered without adequate recompense for their toil and struggle. Indeed, by 1568 only five out of the 560 men who had joined Cortés on the first voyage from Cuba still survived, all now 'very poor and burdened with sons and daughters to marry, and grandchildren, and with little income, so that we pass our lives in toil and misery'.[61] Here, in these complaints of neglect and poverty, we encounter the birth of what can only be called a colonial consciousness, a strong current of sentiment, articulated by the lesser conquerors and transmitted to their sons and descendants, which held that the rewards of conquest had been misappropriated and denied to the men who had fought and toiled on the battle-field. Present in Oviedo, it emerged strongly in Bernal Díaz, and was to become a cardinal tenet of the emergent creole patriotism of the seventeenth century. Since Bernal Díaz' *Historia verdadera* was not published until 1634, and only then in an obscure, truncated edition, his work exercised little influence and indeed was little used until seized upon by Prescott. Its importance thus lies more in its immediate testimony than in any influence on subsequent colonial chroniclers.

At issue between Gómara and Bernal Díaz, however, was not just a dispute over the rightful apportionment of the spoils of conquest, but also a clear contrast, albeit not fully articulated by Díaz, as to the way in which history should be written and conceived. The character of this contrast is best observed in *El Antijovio*, a slashing tract dashed off in 1567 by Gonzalo Jiménez de Quesada (1499–1579) after he had read a Spanish translation of Paolo Giovio's *History of his Own Times*. A friend of Fernández de Oviedo, who described him as 'an honourable man with a fine wit and great intelligence', Quesada had spent the years 1527–30 fighting in Italy before organising the expedition that succeeded in conquering and pacifying New Granada.[62] Giovio aroused his ire by criticising the Spaniards for their cruelty, rapacity and lust for dominion in Italy, charges that Quesada was at pains to deny. All nations, even the Portuguese, so he asserted, now envied the Spaniards for their great conquests and possessions, accusing them of great crimes. Yet it had been the German not Spanish troops, who had been most guilty of torturing the inhabitants of Rome during the disastrous sack of that city in 1527. The wars which had devastated Italy had been started by the ambition of the Kings of France, with the Spaniards entering merely to defend the inherited rights of their king and emperor. Indeed, the Italians should be grateful to Charles V for putting down all 'the bands and tyrannies' which had haunted the city-states. Oddly enough, Quesada reproached Giovio for criticising the Florentines for defending their republican liberty, arguing that all ancient and moral philosophy taught that liberty is man's precious gift, superior to all riches, provided it was combined with recognition of the emperor as supreme head of the Christian common-wealth, and in this case ultimate feudal lord of Tuscany with the right to determine by which form of government they should be ruled. As for the territories directly appropriated by Charles V, he observed that the emperor was not a Turkish tyrant, but rather a Christian king who respected 'the laws and rights of each kingdom and province'.[63]

What aroused Quesada's ire was Giovio's secular interpretation of events, an approach derived in good measure from his admiration for the writings of Machiavelli and Guicciardini. Any suggestion that the German princes might have had dynastic reasons for adopting Lutheranism or that Charles V himself had political reasons for combating the Protestants and France was rejected out of hand. The emperor, 'God's lieutenant', had consumed his life in defence of the Catholic faith, waging war on the Turks in Tunis and Austria and seeking at all points to repress the Lutheran heresy. Equally important, Quesada attacked Giovio's essentially political view of warfare, arguing not merely that 'the rules of war cannot be properly put down in writing', but also that the purpose of war was the achievement of glory. Whereas Giovio had praised the emperor's brother, Ferdinand of Austria, for his wise decision not to lead his forces against the Turks in Hungary, Quesada exclaimed that all great princes known to history, from Julius Caesar and Alexander the Great to Charlemagne and Charles V himself, had fought at the head of their armies, a role rendered all the more honourable once it was recalled that in all battles fought against the infidel the fallen Christian warrior was immediately rewarded by a place in heaven. The aim of the chronicler was to offer an unvarnished record of great deeds, without any insertion of invented orations, the literary device so favoured by humanist historians. 'Now the chronicles of Charles ought to be written that ... the Spaniards fought in such a way that their names and immortal deeds should be perpetuated in those writings.' Nor could the great feats of arms wrought by the emperor and the Spaniards be separated since 'we count with our prince ... all as one body, joined as members under that head'.[64] Once again, the patently medieval assumptions of the Spanish conquerors of America stand revealed, all the more clear when contrasted with Giovio's sceptical view of contemporary statecraft.

The contrast between the blunt 'true accounts' of the conquerors and the stylish chronicles of the humanists was finally resolved by recourse to poetry. In *La Araucana* (1569, 1578, 1589) a heroic epic composed and published in three parts, Alonso de Ercilla (1533–94) drew in equal measure upon his own experiences in battle and on the literary techniques of the Italian Renaissance to frame a stirring narrative of frontier warfare in Chile. Educated at court where he served as page to Prince Philip, the future king, Ercilla accompanied the marquis of Cañete, viceroy of Peru, to Lima and thereafter joined Cañete's son Don García Hurtado de Mendoza, in his campaign to suppress the great Araucanian rebellion which threatened the very survival of Spanish settlement in Chile. In the years 1557–9 the young courtier thus enacted the ideal role of the Spanish Renaissance, wielding both pen and sword, writing verse in military encampments in moments of rest between hand-to-hand engagements with native warriors. Unlike other conquerors, however, Ercilla spent but eight years in the New World before returning to Madrid, where, supported by funds derived from inheritance and marriage, he frequented aristocratic society and served Philip II on several diplomatic missions.[65] The contrast with Fernández de Oviedo, whom in some respects he resembled, could not be more clear.

In *La Araucana* Ercilla drew upon the tradition of the heroic epic revived in Italy by Ariosto and Boiardo, and indeed reached back to its classical source in Virgil and Lucan. But whereas the Italian poets portrayed imaginary battles and adventures, by contrast Ercilla followed the example of Camoens' *Lusiads* and took as his theme contemporary events, including scenes which he himself had witnessed. To assist him in the descriptions of armed combat – the entire poem resounds with the clamour of arms – Ercilla drew upon the romances of medieval Castile with their endless recounting of frontier skirmishes between Moors and Christians, a tradition which rested on *El Cid*. Such was the realism with which the poet approached his task that *La Araucana* later served as the primordial text of Chilean history to which subsequent chroniclers paid tribute. At the same time, Ercilla sought to dignify his epic by frequent allusion to classical heroes and scenes, including Virgil's Dido and, equally important, included a lengthy narration of the Christian victory over the Turks at the battle of Lepanto. The desired effect here was to place the Araucanian wars within the universal context of the Catholic monarchy's defence of Christendom, thus integrating an obscure frontier rebellion into the frame of European history.[66]

The most striking feature of *La Araucana* was Ercilla's decision to relate the wars of Chile largely from the perspective of the natives, celebrating Lautaro and Caupolicán, their leading chieftains, as the heroes of his work. Moreover, he depicted the Araucanians as a hardy, freedom-loving nation of barbarian warriors whose 'state' was governed by a confederacy of war-chiefs who met in 'senate' to prepare the defence of their 'patria' from foreign dominion, be it of the Incas or the Spaniards. Without any law or gods to govern them, other than Satan and his soothsayers, the Indians lived for battle, their young men striving to distinguish themselves by daring acts of valour, the only means by which they could win fame, honour and power. In short, the Araucanians were portrayed as primitive heroes, almost Homeric in their passionate courage, possessing a combination of qualities highly reminiscent of the barbaric virtues of the ancient Germans as described by Tacitus. Nor did Ercilla hesitate to compare their chiefs' defence of their country and liberty to ancient Roman heroes and to endow them with a sense of honour as keen as any Spanish hidalgo's. Thus one chief was said to have demanded satisfaction for injuries done to 'my honour, patria and company'.[67] So too, Ercilla commented on the chastity and devotion to their spouses displayed by the daughters of these chiefs. At the same time, he fully acknowledged the justice of the Indian struggle to preserve their freedom, admitting that the first Spanish governor, Pedro de Valdivia, had not restrained the encomenderos from oppressing their native subjects. He deplored the cruelty with which captured Indians were treated and exclaimed in horror at the brutal execution of Caupolicán. Had it not been for their ill-treatment by the Spaniards, the Araucanians might well have welcomed the preaching of the Christian gospel.

Viewed within the context of either the imperial perspective of Oviedo and Gómara or the combatants' view of Cortés and Bernal Díaz, the enlargement of human sympathy achieved by Ercilla was remarkable. Whereas most chroniclers depicted the natives of the New World as bereft of all sense of shame or honour, disfigured by their addiction to unnatural vices, by contrast the Araucanians were portrayed as endowed with the virtues of classical republicanism, impelled by their love of liberty and country to wage unremitting war against the Spanish invaders. Unlike the mendicants whose protests against the conquerors' cruelties often derived from a detestation of all armed aggression, Ercilla exalted the warrior's calling and defended the necessity of war, arguing that it was the means by which God 'afflicts the world, punishes it, amends and corrects it'.[68] Moreover, his approving description of the often ruthless measures adopted by Cañete to pacify the rebellious settlers of Peru testified to his courtier's devotion to the king's authority, a devotion equally revealed in his criticism of the French attack on Spanish forces at Saint Quentin, and his closing defence of the expedition launched by Philip II to assert his claim to the Crown of Portugal left vacant by the death of King Sebastian. Without warfare, how could justice prevail or the rights of the Catholic Kings be defended? What was remarkable in Ercilla was his capacity to recognise the justice of the Araucanian cause and the courage with which they defended their freedom, without in any way conceding the claims of the Spanish monarchy to govern the New World. In the last resort, he bequeathed to Chile a tradition of sympathetic portrayal of native virtue which was rare, not to say, unknown, in other provinces of the Spanish empire, where, as we shall see, quite different lines of defence of Indian culture were advanced.

3

THE UNARMED PROPHET

I

IN 1531 a Dominican friar, resident in Hispaniola, addressed a memorial to the Council of the Indies in which with prophetic authority he warned the ministers that they all risked eternal damnation in allowing the destruction of the New World to continue unchecked. Divine Providence, acting through the Vicar of Christ, the Pope, had enthroned the emperor Charles V as another Joseph to rule over a new Israel, entrusting him with the mission of bringing salvation to the natives of the Indies.[1] As yet, however, only thieves and tyrants had entered the New World, robbing, killing and oppressing, with the result that over 2 million people had already died. Thousands of souls, 'called by Christ at the eleventh hour of the evening' had lost their chance of eternal salvation. Moreover, once the wars of conquest, initiated in contravention of all natural and divine law, were completed, there then had followed 'the second and unmerciful sorrow of tyrannical government'. Apportioned among the conquerors in encomiendas, the Indians were driven to death by gross exploitation. Just why God allowed such terrible punishments was a divine secret, but woe to the instruments of his wrath! 'What are great kingdoms without justice but great *latrocinios*, which is to say, according to St Augustine, the dwellings of thieves?' Yet time still remained for the councillors to save their souls, act as 'the redeemers of this great world', and achieve a great 'increase in the temporal riches of the state of the king' through the abolition of the encomienda.[2] Once the present tyrants were quit from their place of command, the Council could appoint prudent, just royal governors, each assisted by a bishop and up to twenty religious recruited from the Dominicans and Franciscans. Military protection could be left to coastal fortresses each with a garrison of 100 men. All Indians should pay tribute direct to the Crown, with collection entrusted to the religious. As matters stood, Spanish government in the Indies was a gross tyranny and the Indians had just cause to defend their liberty by armed resistance.

The friar who addressed the Council of the Indies in such peremptory and passionate terms, Bartolomé de las Casas, was no stranger to the councils of the king. In his *Historia de las Indias* Las Casas recounted that the refusal of his Dominican confessor to grant him absolution had stirred his conscience which was then, so to say, pierced by the scriptural text assigned for his Easter sermon, which bluntly declared:

> If one sacrifices from what has been wrongfully obtained, the offering is blemished; the gifts of the lawless are not acceptable . . . Like one who kills a son before his father's eyes is the man who offers a sacrifice from the property of the poor. The bread of the needy is the life of the poor; whoever deprives them of it is a man of blood . . .
>
> (Eccl. xxxiv, 18–22)

If these words moved Las Casas so powerfully, it was because since his arrival in Hispaniola at the age of eighteen in 1502, he had supported himself from the unpaid labour of the Indians.[3] Indeed, thanks to his participation in the conquest of Cuba, he had obtained an encomienda and was a partner in a small trading enterprise. At the same time, he had achieved the rare distinction of being the first priest to be ordained in the New World. Moreover, his connection with the Indies had started earlier, since his father and uncle both accompanied Columbus on his second voyage and had brought him an Indian boy for a slave. A native of Seville, of possible *converso* extraction, Las Casas had attended the cathedral school then managed by Spain's leading humanists, an education which left him with fluent Latin and some introduction to classical literature. Living in the Caribbean from 1502 until 1515, he had little opportunity to acquire more than an elementary grasp of theology, especially since at that time secular priests in Spain were not renowned either for their learning or their devotion.[4]

It was the arrival of the Dominicans in Hispaniola in 1510 which started the public debate over the treatment of the Indians. If we accept Las Casas' subsequent account, the friars soon won fame for their austere life and missionary zeal. He recounted that he heard a sermon delivered by Fr Pedro de Córdoba on the theme of Paradise: 'I heard it and on hearing it counted myself happy.' It was two years later, in 1512 that Fr Antonio de Montesinos preached an advent sermon on the text of St John the Baptist 'I am the voice of one crying in the wilderness', in which he denounced the colonists for their exploitation and abuse of the Indians, questioning their right to exact labour from their unfortunate serfs, and concluding with the passionate cry: 'Are they not men? Do they not have rational souls? Are you not obliged to love them as yourselves?' He warned the congregation that they faced the prospect of eternal damnation for their crimes.[5] It was a sermon which evoked the official wrath of both the governor and the authorities in Spain. But it had little effect in restraining the destruction wrought by the invasion of Cuba, where on the pretext of resistance the Spaniards deliberately inflicted atrocities so as to terrorise the natives into submission. Las Casas joined the expedition and witnessed scenes of such horror that in later life he wrote: 'All these deeds and others, foreign to all human nature, mine own eyes saw, and now I fear to relate them, not believing myself, since perhaps I might have dreamt them.'[6] Nevertheless, he obtained an encomienda and set his Indians to work in the mines and on the land, ensuring only that they were adequately fed. His partner in business, Pedro de Rentería, who had an encomienda in Jamaica, raising pigs and growing manioc, tried to set up a school for the Indian children under his care. For all that, it was not until his conscience was pricked both by the Dominicans and by his own Easter sermon text, that in 1514 Las Casas decided to free his Indians and seek reform of the entire system.

With the support of the Dominicans, both in Hispaniola and in Spain, Las Casas returned to the Peninsula in 1515, there to campaign at court on behalf of the American Indians for a period of six years. During this time, he obtained an audience with King Ferdinand, secured the confidence of the regent, Cardinal Francisco Jiménez de Cisneros, and attracted the favour of the Flemish ministers of Charles V. Throughout this period he proved indefatigable in framing proposals for reform of the government of the Indies, drawing upon his first-hand knowledge at a time when reports from the New World increasingly gave notice of the disappearance of the native population of the Caribbean Islands. In 1512, prior to his arrival, the Crown had promulgated the Laws of Burgos, which sought to regulate the operation of the encomienda, ensuring that every Indian had an adequate diet of meat and regular Christian instruction. Nevertheless, although successive monarchs and their chief ministers expressed a concern for the welfare of their new vassals, effective administration of the Indies was left to the Bishop of Burgos, Juan Rodríguez de Fonseca and the secretary of state, Lope Conchillos, both of whom had a vested interest in preserving the current system. In consequence, Las Casas was obliged to word his reform project so as to demonstrate that the changes he advocated would prove of benefit to the Crown as well as assist the Indians. In any case, Las Casas himself still sought to promote rather than deter Spanish settlement of the New World and equally expected some personal profit to accrue from his schemes.

What is startling about Las Casas' early proposals is the degree to which they anticipated the future structure of colonial government. In his 1516 *Memorial de remedios*, he reported that Hispaniola was by then depopulated, with a mere 15,000 Indians left out of an estimated 2 million inhabiting the island in 1492. As for Cuba, some 100,000 natives were obliged to toil for the Spaniards to the point where they were left no time to cultivate their own crops. The first and chief remedy was the outright abolition of the encomienda.[7] Henceforth, Indians should work for the Spaniards only when they were paid a wage for their labour. At the same time there should be a clear separation between the *comunidades* of the Spaniards and the *pueblos* of the Indians. In effect, Indians should be gathered together into villages, each with a church and hospital, governed by a priest, recruited either from the religious or from qualified secular clergy. Spanish settlement was to be encouraged, with farmers rather than mere adventurers sent out as colonists, in the hope that each farmer would take under his wing a number of Indians, teaching them the practice of agriculture and possibly intermarrying with them. In general, relations between settlers and natives were to be strictly regulated so that at any one time no more than one-third of all Indian men between the ages of 25 and 45 were to be summoned to work for the Spaniards for a period of no more than two months and at no more than twenty leagues from their home village. All such labour was to be remunerated. Finally, Las Casas recommended bringing in slave labour from Africa further to assist the colonists. Here, then, was a remarkable forecast of how the colonial system was to operate in the last decades of the sixteenth century.

These plans only applied to the islands of the Caribbean, since for the mainland, still largely uncharted, Las Casas suggested that settlement should be limited to a series of some ten fortresses, situated at intervals of a hundred leagues, each governed by a captain and garrisoned with a hundred men, whose chief occupation would be peaceful trade with the surrounding Indians. All further armed incursions into Indian territory were to be prohibited, so as to attract the natives to Spanish rule by trade and through peaceful conversion. Each fort was to have a bishop, assisted by a band of Dominicans or Franciscans, who was to serve like 'those of the primitive church, walking barefoot, wherever required'. If martyrdom rewarded missionary endeavour, it was a price worth paying for the peaceful foundation of the Church in the New World.[8] As for the interests of the Crown, Las Casas asserted that its income could be assured from the profits of trade and from the tribute that the Indians would willingly pay after their conversion.

Not content simply to circulate memoranda, Las Casas himself eventually obtained the support of the Flemish ministers of Charles V to establish a small colony at Cumaná on the northern coast of Venezuela. Ironic attention has been directed at his archaic suggestion that the settlers under his command should be known as 'knights of the golden spur' and be attired in crusaders' tunics. More important is the scope and nature of the scheme. Originally, Las Casas had applied for a grant of no less than a thousand leagues of coastline, an area which was eventually reduced to a tenth of that figure, which is to say, some three hundred miles, still an appreciable area to control. The economic basis of this venture was to be trade with the Indians, combined with agriculture in the immediate vicinity of the settlement, with profits accruing to the chief colonists, including Las Casas, and to the Crown in the form of taxes.

In short, this was a scheme for peaceful Spanish colonisation, justified by the prospect of some profit, but animated by the long-term expectation of the conversion and pacification of the mainland Indians. What the project lacked was practicability. For Cumaná was situated close to the pearl fishery at Cubagua, an island base for adventurers who had already raided the coast in search of Indian slaves. Indeed, the natives had already murdered two Dominican missionaries in an adjoining district and were determined to resist all further encroachment on their territory. Moreover, Las Casas failed to recruit a sufficient number of farmers to accompany him, relying instead on the usual heterogeneous assortment of Spaniards, to man a settlement which lacked adequate provision for defence. In the event, Indian attacks drove the friars and colonists to abandon the venture, not, however, without loss of life. All the resources poured into the settlement by the Crown were forfeited by its failure. Crushed by this disaster, Las Casas took refuge in Hispaniola, and there in 1524 entered the Dominican order.[9] His failure did not go unnoticed either at court or in the New World, since, as we have seen, it was described in sarcastic terms by Fernández de Oviedo in his *Historia general de las Indias* (1535), as demonstrating the folly of all attempts to convert the Indians before their military conquest by the Spaniards. By contrast, Las Casas himself concluded that the failure of the project sprang from the desire to serve God and Mammon at the same time, to yoke the Christian mission to secular colonisation.

II

The entrance of Las Casas into the Dominican Order meant that henceforth he was to devote himself entirely to the defence of the natives of the New World. Nevertheless, it was not until 1534, which is to say, some fourteen years after the Cumaná disaster, at the age of fifty, that he plunged anew into his mission. By then, of course, the entire pattern of Spanish colonisation had been progressively transformed by the conquest first of Mexico and then of Peru. The slave-raids and marauding incursions across the Caribbean had been replaced by the seizure and settlement of great empires. Frustrated by the civil wars from reaching Peru, his first objective, in 1534 Las Casas entered Nicaragua and both there and in Guatemala soon won the respect of the governor and bishop for his zealous care for the instruction of the Indians. In the light of future accusations against him, it must be emphasised that at this stage of his life he obtained the strong recommendation of his ecclesiastical superiors, who testified that he was a dedicated friar and an ardent missionary. But he did not hesitate to express his shock at the devastation he encountered, writing that although 'Nicaragua is a paradise of the Lord', with fields as green and fertile as any garden in Spain, its population of over 600,000 had been reduced to a mere 15,000 through mass deportation as slaves to the Caribbean and Peru. In a letter to an unnamed personage at court, he defended his own record, asserting that he had laboured for over twenty years 'to serve my God and to assist in the salvation of those whom he bought with his blood and that the state of my king might grow immensely'. He had been the first to draw the court's attention to the destruction of the Indies and to encourage the Dominicans and Franciscans to go to the New World. It was largely thanks to 'those great friars of St Francis of New Spain' that Mexico had escaped the worst ravages of the conquerors. Indeed, 'the only true servants that his Majesty has here are the religious, provided they are good religious'. All the rest was a story of murder and theft, with the German Welser in Venezuela acting like wolves in the sheepfold.[10] Not that the Spaniards lagged far behind since, by his murder of Atahualpa, Pizarro had usurped a kingdom that the Pope had given to the King of Castile.

This passionate letter was followed in 1537 by an agreement with the new governor of Guatemala that the still unpacified zone known as Tuzulutlán, situated in the area bordering modern Chiapas, should be reserved for an experiment in peaceful conversion by the Dominicans, with all other Spaniards forbidden access to the Indians. Although his biographer, Fr Antonio de Remesal, later composed a lively narrative of how a Dominican mission led by Las Casas triumphantly succeeded in pacifying and converting the hostile peoples of this region almost overnight, modern research has shown that there is little basis in fact for this story.[11] The essential achievement of Las Casas here was to reach a secret agreement with the Indian chiefs, to whom protection and honours were promised in return for allowing the religious to preach the gospel. It was in the 1540s that the mission proved successful, so that Las Casas only entered the zone after its pacification in his role as Bishop of Chiapa. Nevertheless, his tactics here, if less dramatic than those suggested by his biographer, derived from the principle, fully elaborated in his later tracts, that the authority of Indian lords should be maintained and that conversion was best assured with their support and protection. His success in obtaining the exclusion of other Spaniards from mission territory set an example which other religious orders, notably the Jesuits, were to imitate.

In 1538 Las Casas travelled to Mexico City, where, far from impressed by the 'spiritual conquest' then in full swing, he protested strongly against the practice of baptism of adults *en masse* without provision of adequate, individual catechesis, and indeed secured an episcopal condemnation of the policy. For Franciscans such as Fr Toribio de Motolinia, who boasted of baptising 14,000 Indians in two days, it was intolerable that Las Casas should seek to prevent their reaping the spiritual harvest of missionary endeavours. The disagreement was of fundamental significance, since it derived from two distinct views of the Church and of the nature of conversion. For whereas Motolinia followed a triumphalist tack, seeking to re-create the primitive church in New Spain, a church which would include all Indians, by contrast Las Casas took the Augustinian line that the City of God was a pilgrim church composed of the predestined elect.[12]

The clearest statement of Las Casas' views on conversion is to be found in the Latin tract *Del único modo de atraer a todos los pueblos a la verdadera religión*, written in Mexico in 1538–40, and found only in an incomplete or unfinished text. By far the most theological of his writings, with much of the argument taken from such Church Fathers as St John Chrysostom and St Augustine, its chief premise was that all peoples in the world possess much the same range of human qualities and that in all nations God has predestined a certain, albeit unknown, number of souls for eternal salvation. In consequence, it was a spiritual necessity that the gospel should be universally preached in the same way to all men. Moreover, all human beings had implanted within them a natural light which impelled them to seek the one true God. Similarly, all men naturally sought to know the truth and, where not hindered by sin, to follow the path of natural virtue. God was wisdom and Christ a liberator-God, who brought freedom from the burden of sin. It thus followed that the kingdom of heaven, which was what the gospel announced, had to be preached with love and by means of rational persuasion. The road to faith was similar to that leading to knowledge, since in both operations of the intellect conviction or a conclusion was attained by examination of a sequence of reasoning, albeit in the case of faith with will rather than reason dictating the final affirmation. Preaching the gospel was thus a work of persuasion, of moving affections and providing reasons. In this context, the figure of the apostle was all-important: offering an example in his own life of the truths he preached, the preacher had to show that he stood to gain no financial profit or political power from the conversion of his audience. In advancing these arguments, Las Casas cited the gospels, presented St Paul as the very image of the true apostle, and alluded to St Augustine of Canterbury's mission as an historical example of peaceful conversion.[13]

With his case established by a multiplicity of citations and arguments, Las Casas then turned to condemn the men who had conquered the New World and to controvert the religious who argued that conquest was necessary if the gospel was to be preached with any success. In dramatic terms, he described the horrors of conquest – the massacre of innocents, the seizure of women, the enslavement of captives, the loss of political freedom, and the murder of kings – all scenes which he had witnessed or which were all too fresh in common memory. What could fill the hearts of the subjugated except terror and hatred? How could the gospel be preached under such circumstances? Where were the occasions of reflection, the opportunities for quiet persuasion, when fear dominated men's minds? How could the gospel be preceded by war? After all, 'war was but murder, a common act of banditry committed among many'. As for the conquerors who paraded their Catholic faith as a rallying cry in battle, they were no servants of Christ but rather so many devils, the children of Satan. Indeed, to attempt to spread the gospel at sword-point was to fall into the heresy of Mahomet, the vilest of the enemies of the one true faith. 'These men [are] the precursors of Anti-Christ and imitators of Mahomet, being thus Christian only in name.' Moreover, citing Aristotle's *Politics*, he further argued that 'the government which is acquired through force of arms or which in any way has been acquired against the will of the subjects is tyrannical and violent'.[14] The true purpose of government was the well-being of the subjects, not the profit or glory of the governor. Furthermore, since the Indians possessed their own forms of political authority, it was against all divine and natural law to deprive them of their government and liberty. In short, the conquerors were thieves and murderers who could only expect salvation if they made an act of restitution of all the goods they had stolen from the Indians. For the present, however, their crimes had thrust them beyond the pale of Christian charity.

In 1540 Las Casas returned to Spain, ostensibly as the agent of the bishop of Guatemala, commissioned to recruit religious as missionaries in that diocese. But he arrived in company of the French Franciscan, Jacobo de Tastera, and supported by letters of recommendation from Francisco de Zumárraga, the Franciscan archbishop of Mexico, and Domingo de Betanzos, the Dominican provincial of New Spain. In no sense was Las Casas alone in his efforts to reform the colonial system. Tastera had already attempted to preach the gospel peacefully to the natives of Yucatán and had access to court circles. Already, in 1537, Pope Paul III had issued a bull at the instigation of the Dominican bishop of Tlaxcala, Julián Garcés, in which he pronounced not only that the Indians were true men with souls to be saved, but also that conversion to Christianity should not be accompanied by any loss of liberty or property. This papal intervention gave an international dimension to royal concern over the Indies which was further heightened by the refusal of the King of France to admit the validity of the original papal donation of 1493. In short, there was a groundswell of pressure, largely emanating from the mendicants and their bishops, for a reform of the colonial system of government. News of civil war in Peru further heightened alarm at the continuing excesses of the conquerors. It was at this juncture, with Charles V at last in residence in Spain, that Las Casas thrust himself into the centre of ministerial debate, circulating papers of such unparalleled virulence that the monarch was left horrified and committed to reform.[15]

It was to persuade the emperor to act that in 1542 Las Casas composed his most notorious tract, *Brevísima relación de la destrucción de las Indias*. First defining the Indians as the most gentle, humble, and kind people in the world, the most ready and fit for conversion to the true faith, Las Casas then described how bands of Spaniards, invariably characterised as tyrants and thieves, had burnt, tortured and murdered their way across an entire world inhabited by

2a Cruelties of the conquerors

innumerable villages of docile, largely defenceless natives. Conquest was then
followed by the exploitation of encomiendas or outright enslavement, leaving a
train of destruction so wanton that after half a century of European settlement
15 million Indians had disappeared from the face of the earth. The absence of
any names in the text invested the cycle of conquest with the impersonal
character of some infernal process, as if, island by island, province by province,
packs of wolves had been unleashed to ravage great flocks of sheep peacefully
grazing in green pastures. It was a bitter, inflammatory diatribe, monotonous
and repetitive in style, but enlivened by vivid incidents of atrocity, some
personally witnessed, all presented without palliation or qualification, leaving
the reader stunned by the appalling scenes it described.[16]

If Las Casas wisely omitted naming any of the conquerors in the published
text of *Brevísima relación*, he apparently gave full references in the version read
by the emperor. If we consider that Hernán Cortés attended the advisory
sessions of the juntas summoned by the emperor to consider the case for
reform, then the impact of Las Casas' denunciation should be clear. Later in
life, the Dominican recalled that he had reproached Cortés to his face for his
crimes in Mexico.[17] Moreover, Las Casas' proposals for changing colonial
government were radical. At the outset, he advocated the immediate emancipa-

2*b* Cruelties of the conquerors

tion of all Indian slaves, no matter how obtained. Then, he called for the outright abolition of the encomienda, defining the Indians as the free vassals of the Crown, liable simply for payment of royal tribute. Only with such radical measures could the unfortunate natives be rescued from a tyranny that had destroyed the majority of the population and reduced the survivors to a condition of such terror that they had become like rabbits awaiting their death-blow. Divine Providence had chosen Spain for the grand mission of making the New World Christian, but in the event it had been Lucifer who had won the victory. As for the encomenderos, the best remedy would be to seize half their property and use the proceeds to attract other settlers. Indeed, in New Spain it was advisable to imprison about twenty of the richest encomenderos, confiscate their property and despatch them home to Seville. As it was, rumour on the streets of Spain had it that the riches of the Indies all derived from murder and theft. If reform of abuse was not forthcoming, surely God would punish Spain for all the evils wrought in the New World.[18]

These powerful memorials, when taken with other reports from the Indies, bore fruit in the code of New Laws promulgated in 1542, which both at the time and subsequently was attributed to the influence of Las Casas. Certainly, the main provisions were in accord with his proposals. All Indian slaves were to be emancipated forthwith. All rebels and royal officials were to be stripped of their encomiendas and all other encomiendas were to revert to the Crown on the death of their present incumbent. Equally important, the obligation of Indians to provide free labour was brought to an end, so that henceforth the encomienda was to consist of the payment of tribute, either in kind or in cash. All labour performed by Indians for Spaniards was to be remunerated with a daily wage. *Audiencias* – crown courts – were established in Guatemala and Lima so as to ensure that these remote provinces would have access to justice. At one stroke, the Crown thus sought to terminate the institution which had been the foundation of the society established by the conquerors.

The uproar which greeted the New Laws revealed their radical nature. In New Spain, the viceroy Antonio de Mendoza invoked the power inherent in his office to suspend their implementation until the Crown had listened to the protests of the encomenderos' agents despatched from Mexico to Spain. He also compiled a series of reports from leading institutions, including the provincials of the three mendicant orders, all of which urged caution. In Peru the reaction was instant. For in that kingdom virtually all encomenderos had participated in the civil wars between the Pizarros and the Almagros and thus stood to lose their grants.

But the newly arrived viceroy, Blasco Núñez de Vela, sought to implement the laws, in part so as to allocate encomiendas for his own entourage. The result was an open rebellion led by Gonzalo Pizarro which culminated in the viceroy's death, a rebellion justified by the assertion that the conquerors had entered into a contract with the Crown and hence could not be dispossessed without due reason. Any laws which prejudiced property and rights within a kingdom required the ratification and consent of the leading citizens of that country. In the event, the Council of the Indies renegued upon the project to abolish the encomienda and in 1545 allowed these grants to continue for at least another life after the death of the original possessor. In Peru, the rebellion was defeated largely by assuring the encomenderos that their grants would be confirmed if they deserted Pizarro and renewed their allegiance to the Crown. Moreover, if the provision of free Indian labour to encomenderos was brought to an end, the colonial authorities soon found it necessary to organise *repartimientos de labor*, which is to say, obligatory drafts of native labourers from each village for work either in agriculture or the mines, albeit now in return for a modest daily wage. As far as the Indians were concerned, the chief benefit brought by the New Laws was the emancipation of slaves and the freedom from any personal dependence on particular settlers. For the conquerors, it signified that the Crown was determined to assert its authority, defining the encomienda as a pension charged on royal tribute rather than as a seigneurial benefice.[19]

In 1543, to assist in the implementation of the New Laws, Las Casas reluctantly accepted appointment as bishop of Chiapa, a poor, remote diocese in the south of New Spain, which had the single advantage of bordering the district of Tuzulutlán, the scene of his experiment in peaceful conversion of Indians who had yet to be conquered by the Spaniards. Accompanied by a numerous mission of young Dominicans, Las Casas soon fell into conflict with his former patron, Francisco Marroquín, the bishop of Guatemala, who resented any challenge to the territorial limits of his diocese. Nor did Marroquín fully concur with Las Casas' determination to employ ecclesiastical, and in particular, episcopal jurisdiction and sanctions as the chief means of protecting Indians from the settlers' exploitation. For Las Casas advised the newly established audiencia of Guatemala that he proposed to take cognizance of all cases of ill-treatment of Indians, calling upon the secular authorities to assist him in the enforcement of the New Laws. Nor did he hesitate to threaten the president and judges of the court with excommunication if they failed to comply with his demands. All native slaves had to be freed forthwith.[20] Equally important, he composed and circulated a *confesionario*, a set of instructions to all priests licensed to hear confessions, in which he insisted that absolution should be forbidden to all conquerors, encomenderos and merchants, even on their deathbeds, until they signed a formal act of restitution, returning to the Indians all the goods and property they had unjustly acquired since their arrival in the New World. Any priest who refused to enforce this edict was to have his licence withdrawn.[21] At the same time, Las Casas insisted on the necessity of maintaining the legal immunity of all ecclesiastics from royal justice as the only way of allowing the clergy to pursue their protection of their flock. In effect, the sacramental powers of the clergy were thus converted into a source of juridical and social authority, the confessor now acting as virtual judge of the penitent.

The enforcement of this policy caused uproar as the leading citizens of Chiapa found themselves unable to comply with their Easter obligations or indeed celebrate Holy Week in the customary fashion, their property and livelihood challenged with threats of eventual hell-fire. If this head-long onslaught against the vested and often corrupt interests of both settlers and royal officials did not actually, as later biographers averred, lead to Las Casas fleeing from Chiapa in danger of his life, certainly he aroused such opposition as to render his position as bishop untenable. Within little more than a year, he chose to abandon his diocese and return to Spain, tarrying in Mexico only for an attempt to rally his fellow bishops and religious to insist on the immediate emancipation of all Indian slaves. By then, of course, news had reached New Spain of the emperor's edict allowing all existing encomiendas to be inherited and maintained for a further life. In short, the attempt by Las Casas to invoke episcopal and sacramental sanctions to challenge and reform the structure of colonial power and property, a campaign in many ways reminiscent of the early medieval hierarchy's conflict with the feudal nobility, had failed to achieve its main objectives.

Despite his setbacks in Chiapa, Las Casas moved swiftly to recoup his influence at court and in the Council of the Indies. In the years 1547–66, which is to say, between the age of 63 and 82, he devoted his still abundant energies to an extraordinary round of activity, attacking the conquerors and their humanist apologists at both the intellectual and political level. By this time the acknowledged advocate of the Indians, he received a stream of letters, petitions and memorials from the New World, a mass of material that he put to good use in both his theoretical writings and in his campaign at court. Although the accession of Philip II to the Spanish throne in 1554 was eventually to lead to a radically distinct approach to the Indies, in the short term Las Casas still succeeded in influencing royal policy. Once again, it was the controversial question of the continued survival of the encomienda which provoked his intervention. For in 1554 the encomenderos of Peru offered the Spanish Crown 4 million ducats for the concession of perpetuity of inheritance of their grants, accompanied by rights of jurisdiction, both criminal and civil, over their Indians. They sought to convert the encomienda into a full-blown feudal benefice or fief, their families henceforth sustained as a hereditary nobility by the tribute of their native subjects, their jurisdiction interposed between the Crown and the Indians. With the new king, Philip II (1554–98), almost bankrupt following his accession to the throne, these proposals met with an initial welcome among his advisers, anxious to raise funds. There then ensued several years of discussion and intense lobbying, with memorials solicited from Lima and Mexico City. Throughout this period, Las Casas played an active role in mobilising official opinion against the encomenderos, at one point promoting a counter-offer from the Indian nobility of Peru who were fearful of any further subjection to the settlers.[22] In the opening stages of the controversy, he had the advantage of support from his good friend and fellow Dominican, Bartolomé Carranza de Miranda, a counsellor of Philip II, who had accompanied that prince on his visit to England and who was rewarded by appointment as archbishop of Toledo. Carranza had been once offered the bishopric of Cuzco and took the view that once the Indians had been fully converted to Christianity Spain should withdraw from America. In a strongly worded letter to Carranza, then resident in London, Las Casas urged that the Peruvian petition should be rejected out of hand, since it would threaten the maintenance of royal dominion in the Indies. The conquerors and encomenderos were tyrants, responsible for the destruction of the native population of the New World, who now sought to perpetuate their misrule, alienating royal jurisdiction. He derided their claims to constitute the bulwark of Spanish possession of the Indies: defence and internal peace could be easily entrusted to garrisons of soldiers paid from the revenue that would accrue to the Crown following the escheatment of encomiendas. All that was needed was strong viceroys and five hundred men in Peru and another three hundred in New Spain.

In a remarkably outspoken letter to Philip II, written in 1556, Las Casas reminded the king that he had first advised his great-grandfather, Ferdinand of Aragon, on the situation in the Indies over forty years before. Now, he protested against 'the tyrants and traitors' of Peru who had virtually destroyed that kingdom and who now wished to alienate what remained from royal jurisdiction. The Indies had been given to the kings of Castile for the conversion of their inhabitants to the Christian faith. The Indians were free subjects of the Crown. With what right did the king and his advisers now seek to deprive them of their freedom and endanger their conversion? In any case, the matter should be discussed in the Cortes since it presented the manifest danger that Castile would lose its dominion in the New World. After all, if the New Laws had been greeted with rebellion and the death of a viceroy, what was there to prevent the sons and heirs of the Peruvian rebels from challenging the Crown in future or indeed from breaking with Spain? In audacious vein, Las Casas argued that the king had no right to alienate free men from his jurisdiction or diminish the royal patrimony which he had inherited and was bound to transmit to his successors.[23]

If these arguments failed to persuade the king, they certainly prompted debate and enquiry into the whole issue, with a further round of memorials and petitions elicited from Peru. But although the current viceroy and key jurists advised in favour of the encomenderos, the royal commissioners appointed to consider the matter warned the king that the American-born sons and descendants of the conquerors lacked any natural loyalty or affection for either Spain or its king, so that to create a feudal nobility in Peru would endanger Spanish possession. In 1562 the Council of the Indies finally persuaded Philip II to refuse both perpetuity and jurisdiction, emphasising the Crown's duty to the Indians, the source of its sovereignty in the papal donation of 1493, and the danger of further rebellion by the settlers. In a subsequent letter, Las Casas attributed the defeat of the petition to the initial intervention of Carranza and to the support of such Dominican theologians as Melchor Cano and Domingo de Soto for his own campaign before the Council of the Indies.[24] By then, the hapless Carranza had himself fallen prey to the persecution of the Inquisition, imprisoned under charge of heresy. Ever outspoken, Las Casas rallied to the support of his old friend, offering passionate testimony as to his orthodoxy.[25]

In his last memorial to the Council of the Indies, written in 1565, Las Casas quietened his conscience by once more presenting a vehement denunciation of the double tyranny of conquest and encomienda. The Indians lived like the Israelites in Egypt, labouring under the oppression of their Spanish Pharaohs. The entire period since the discovery of the New World until the present had been a story of unmitigated exploitation, theft and murder, with kingdoms usurped and their population devastated. Unless complete restitution was made to the Indians, there could be no hope of establishing a just or legitimate government. The natives had full right to defend themselves and engage in just war against their Spanish oppressors. Much the same message was sent to Pope Pius V, whom in the same year Las Casas petitioned for a decree enjoining the bishops in the New World to protect their native flocks from the Spaniards, seeking not to enrich themselves but rather to learn the language of their miserable subjects, so as best to ensure their instruction.[26] Consistent to the last, Las Casas took the occasion of his last will and testament to declare that God Almighty would punish Spain for all the crimes wrought in the New World.

The importance of Las Casas' intervention in the councils of the king in these years cannot be underestimated. What was at stake was the political constitution of the Spanish empire in America. Had the encomenderos succeeded in obtaining their long-cherished aim of converting their grants into feudal fiefs, then the structure of authority in the Indies would have been transformed. The heirs of the conquerors would have emerged as a true feudal nobility, a colonial governing class, endowed with sufficient authority over the Indian peasantry as to protect their subjects from the exactions and levies of the royal magistrates sent over from Spain. The initial pact between Crown and conquerors would thus have issued into a contractual constitution, with royal absolutism tempered and limited by the existence of a powerful colonial aristocracy. If the often intemperate memorials of Las Casas received a hearing at court, it was in part because at all stages of the dispute he looked to the Crown for redress and in so invoking royal authority enlarged its scope and power. His defence of the Indian thus served to strengthen royal authority, and indeed his preference for a military garrison over the feudal levy of the encomenderos betrayed an absolutist bias common among political thinkers of the day.

III

In much the same years, 1552–61, that he fought his last battle at court, Las Casas also revised and amplified his *Historia de las Indias*, a detailed narrative of events and policies of the period 1492 to 1521. Based primarily on materials collected after he had entered the Dominican order in Hispaniola, and started in 1527, the chronicle incorporated a great deal of subsequent reflection and autobiographical reminiscence. It was written, so Las Casas averred, to celebrate the glory of God and his Church, to honour Spain and its kings, to defend the good name of the Indians, and, above all else, to provide an accurate record of the injustices of the conquerors.[27] It was also written to correct, refute and replace the general histories of Oviedo and of Gómara, albeit more with an eye to posterity than to the present, since Las Casas bequeathed the manuscript to his Dominican brethren with strict instructions that it should not be published until at least forty years had elapsed. In these broad aims he was not entirely successful, since his narrative ends with his own failure at Cumaná and does not cover the conquest of Mexico other than by allusion. However, despite the re-occurring monotone of denunciation and its often limp style, the work offers an incomparable portrait of the Caribbean phase of Spanish expansion, the devastation wrought by the conquerors rendered all the more tragic by the paradisical image of the Antilles encountered by Columbus.

Historia de las Indias begins with the solemn affirmation that in all generations in every nation God has predestined a remnant for salvation. The discovery of America was an act of Divine Providence, pre-ordained so as to open the gates of the City of God to the chosen elect among the natives of the New World. This doctrine, which Las Casas derived from St Augustine's *On Predestination and the Gift of Perseverance*, a tract which he praised for its 'beautiful and profound statement', was qualified by an equally strong insistence on the inscrutability of God's will.[28] Although Las Casas argued that Columbus and Spain were the chosen instruments of Providence, he refrained from any apocalyptic interpretation of the great discoveries, asserting that the time and number of souls saved was unknowable. Of the greatness of the achievement of Columbus, however, he had no doubt. For he enjoyed access to the Discoverer's papers as well as to the life written by Hernando Colón, so that he could attest to the difficulties and trials that beset Columbus at all stages of his career. Indeed, the intensity of these trials, raised by the Devil, so he argued, was proof of the Divine origin of the venture. Yet despite his largely sympathetic portrait of Columbus, Las Casas signalised his unprovoked seizure and enslavement of the helpless Indians of the Antilles as a radical error, a crime springing from his ignorance of 'natural and divine law', from which flowed the slave-raiding expeditions that were to devastate the Antilles. Thus, the chosen 'leader and guide of this Divine venture' was himself responsible for its corruption.[29] The torments and disappointments which afflicted the admiral in his last years were both retribution for his sins and possibly – so Las Casas suspected – sufficient punishment as to allow his eventual salvation, since although his acts were wicked, his intentions were good, and his crimes overshadowed by the greatness of his achievement in unlocking the doors of the ocean-sea.

With the death of the Discoverer, the narrative shifted to the devastation wrought by the Spaniards in the islands and coast-lands of the Caribbean. Here is no place once more to recount this story other than to note the immediacy of the horror felt by Las Casas as he recalled scenes of deliberate massacre that he himself had witnessed. What is clear is that he attributed major responsibility of the events he described to Juan Rodríguez de Fonseca, bishop of Burgos, and to the secretary of state, Lope Conchillos, who profited from the system and blocked any proposals for reform. So too, the three royal governors of the period, Nicolás de Ovando of Hispaniola, Diego Velásquez of Cuba and Pedrarias Dávila of Darien formed a sinister triumvirate which presided over the destruction of the Indian population.[30] At the same time, Las Casas commented on great loss of life also suffered by the Spaniards, with over 1,000 of the 2,500 men who accompanied Ovando soon succumbing to disease and the effect of climate. Many expeditions lost most of their members. In a dramatic passage, Las Casas related the shock of Pedrarias and his chief followers, newly arrived, still dressed in European finery, at the sight of Núñez de Balboa, the discoverer of the Pacific, who came to meet them, dressed in a cotton shirt and sandals, content to pass his nights in a straw hut. Very soon after, with their rations consumed, many of the nobles who had accompanied Pedrarias died of hunger, unable to adapt to the tropical environment.

The horror of the European invasion was magnified by Las Casas' idyllic portrait of the fertility of the New World and the beauty and innocence of its inhabitants. Indeed, taking up a suggestion of Columbus, he devoted no less than twenty pages to a discussion as to whether the Antilles were the site of the Garden of Eden, a question he left undecided, but with evident sympathy for such a location. Moreover, he depicted the natives of the Caribbean as still dwelling in some pre-lapsarian paradise, since on recalling his sight of one aged Indian he exclaimed: 'it seemed to me that I saw in him our father Adam when he enjoyed the state of innocence'. Inspired in part by Peter Martyr, he asserted that the inhabitants of the Lucayos Islands, destroyed by slave-raids, 'above all others in the Indies, and I believe in all the world, were distinguished by their gentleness, simplicity, humility, quiet and other natural virtues, to the point where it seemed that Adam had not sinned in them . . . they had that life which people lived in the golden age, so praised by poets and historians'. Who could doubt, he added, that such a people were eminently fitted for the preaching and reception of the Christian gospel. Indeed, the very vices of which they were accused – indolence and lack of the acquisitive spirit – were signs that they were content with nature's gifts. Whereas the Spaniards were consumed with greed and cupidity, the Indians lived close to the dictates of evangelical poverty that were the prized virtue of the Franciscans and Dominicans. After all, if they despised gold, so also 'evangelical perfection and even the true and natural philosophy esteems it as dung'. In short, the inhabitants of the islands of the Caribbean lived 'according to natural law'.[31]

In the event, Divine Providence willed that this earthly paradise should be destroyed by the kingdom of darkness, the conquerors without doubt 'governed and guided by the Devil'.[32] Although the Pope had entrusted the New World to the kings of Spain so as to ensure the conversion of its inhabitants, little effort was made in the first years to preach the gospel to the Indians. The Franciscans in Santo Domingo ignored them and lived quietly in their priory, ministering to the Spanish settlers. Only with the arrival of the Dominicans led by Pedro de Córdoba and Antonio de Montesinos was there a concerted attempt not merely to preach the gospel but also to denounce the exploitation of the Indians. If in this section of his chronicle, Las Casas expatiated on the austerity and virtue of his brother Dominicans, he equally emphasised their prophetic role as defenders of the poor and down-trodden. It was, of course, their sermons and promptings which drove him to embark on his own career as advocate of the Indian. The *Historia de las Indias* concludes with an extended account of Las Casas' mission in Spain in the years 1515–19, ranging from his lobbying of Cardinal Jiménez de Cisneros to his encounter with the Flemish ministers of Charles V, a role which pitted him against the bishop of Burgos and his advisers. Official papers and juntas are cited in some detail and the springs of decision closely examined. The narrative concludes with the bitter anti-climax of the experiment in peaceful colonisation at Cumaná, a venture which caused 'the priest to drink great bitterness'. The failure was God's punishment for his mixing of Divine and material interests in the same venture, seeking both to win souls and produce a profit for the king and the colonists. As much as Columbus, the advocate of the Indians thus suffered defeat and disappointment because of his misconception of the providential significance of the discovery of the New World, failing to understand that the ocean-sea had been opened solely to permit the salvation of the Indians.[33]

One notable revision in his thinking which Las Casas signalised in his chronicle was a newfound condemnation of the African slave-trade. In his first memorials to the Crown, he had favoured the importation of black slaves into the New World as a means of assisting Spanish colonists, with a view to freeing the Indians from this obligation. Even as late as the 1540s he still accepted that slaves brought from Africa were prisoners captured in war or mere criminals. However, in the *Historia de las Indias* he attacked the Portuguese for their slave-raids on African coasts and condemned their historian, Juan de Barros, for his fond description of this trade. Later, he criticised the ill-treatment to which black slaves were subjected on the sugar plantations in Hispaniola and elsewhere in the New World. He thus openly recanted his previous support of African slavery, a sure sign of the growing radicalism of his social thinking in these years.[34]

In the last chapters of his work, Las Casas took the opportunity to settle accounts with his critics and predecessors. Already, he had praised Peter Martyr as the only reliable authority on the Indies, dismissing Vespucci as an ignorant, lying adventurer. But it was Fernández de Oviedo, the great chronicler of the Indies, his rival for royal favour in 1519, who attracted his most devastating attack. For Oviedo was a conqueror, an encomendero and slave-owner, who had participated in the cruelties meted out to the Indians by the followers of Pedrarias. Despite all this, Oviedo attempted to depict as knights-errant men who had set their dogs on luckless natives. Moreover, he was a declared enemy of the Indians, his ignorance and bad conscience driving him to slander them, endowing them with imaginary vices and defects. Worse still, he had advised the bishop of Burgos to the same effect, thus impeding projects of reform. Oviedo's criticism of the Cumaná enterprise thus derived from an evil disposition. Needless to say, López de Gómara incurred much the same derision: his polished prose hid a series of errors and open lies, in large measure the result of his believing everything his master had told him, including the extent of human sacrifice practised by the Indians.[35]

It was, however, the former friend and associate of Las Casas, Hernán Cortés, who attracted the most powerful denunciation, since he was described as 'a pure tyrant and usurper of foreign kingdoms'. A poor squire without means or connexions, he had betrayed the trust vested in him by Velásquez, bribing, threatening and even hanging his companions so as to persuade his company to enter Mexico. In his dealings with the Indians, he had relied on terror to inspire fear, massacring thousands of natives at Cholula without provocation merely to terrify Moctezuma. As much as any tyrant in history, he had sown discord among peoples so as to seize power for his own profit, acting always to the detriment of the conquered peoples. Once rewarded with power and wealth, he had paid literary men like Gómara to magnify his reputation, celebrating him as another Alexander or Caesar. Not merely had Las Casas reproached him to his face for his crimes, but in another memorial of this period he asserted that men like Cortés and Pizarro should have been beheaded rather than receiving titles of nobility and great estates.[36]

At first sight, the *Historia de las Indias* is a simple chronicle with two chief protagonists, Christopher Columbus and Bartolomé de las Casas, both depicted as chosen by Providence to open the New World to the preaching of the Christian gospel. That both men derived from relatively humble circumstances, won a hearing in the highest councils of State, and ended their ventures in disappointment, their set-backs in large measure just retribution for the failure to comprehend the spiritual significance of their earthly mission, only served to confirm the similarity of their vocation. Despite the impersonal fashion in which he referred to his public career, in effect Las Casas wrote an *apologia pro vita sua*, installing his campaign on behalf of the Indians at the very centre of all future accounts of the foundation of the Spanish empire in the New World. Viewed more carefully, the *Historia de las Indias* can be seen as an extended essay in prophetic history, an exploration of the slow, tragic unfolding of God's providence. In this approach Las Casas was deeply influenced by St Augustine's vision of the enduring conflict between the Earthly City and the City of God, a conflict derived from the opposing principles of self-love and love of God, between lust for dominion and Christian obedience. That the Spanish conquerors should have acted as if they were led by the Devil, intent on destroying an earthly paradise, only served to confirm the distinction,

3 Bartolomé de las Casas

already admitted by the African saint, between the visible, institutional
Church – which included both the saved and the damned – and the chosen elect
of the City of God. Whereas it had become common in the Middle Ages to
misconceive the character of the spiritual combat between the two cities, at
times reducing it to public battle between Muslim and Christians, by contrast
Las Casas displayed remarkable fidelity to the delicate, often subtle balance of
the *City of God*. That Las Casas should have insisted on the intrinsic
superiority of spiritual over temporal concerns in the discovery of the New
World; that he avoided all forms of triumphalism, Christian or Spanish; and

that he rejected any kind of apocalyptic interpretation of contemporary events – all this amply confirmed the Augustinian bias of his thought.

IV

In the prologue to his *Apologia*, Las Casas declared that as a bishop he had set himself up as a wall against the evil men who threatened the new Israel, his native flock. So also, in his last will and testament, he affirmed that God had chosen him to defend the Indians from the injustices of 'we Spaniards' and prophesied that God would punish Spain for its crimes in the New World.[37] As this emphasis on judgement reveals, Las Casas did not conceive of himself as an Apostle. Despite his years in Central America, there is little evidence to suggest that he ever learnt a native language or devoted any great portion of his life to the catechesis of Indians. Although he praised the apostolic labours of the Franciscans in New Spain, he never shared their dreams of a millennium about to dawn and indeed questioned the means by which they gathered in their great harvest of souls. His conviction that the City of God was a band of pilgrims, composed of the predestined elect forbade any illusions of universal salvation in history. Instead, he is best defined as a prophet, albeit a court rather than a country prophet, more at home in the council-chamber than in the wilderness. His message was none the less harsh. If his Dominican exemplar, Savonarola, had denounced the worldly corruption of Renaissance Florence as a betrayal of that city's spiritual destiny, so equally at the historical moment when patriotic, imperial euphoria reached its climax under Charles V, Las Casas condemned the conquest of the New World as a betrayal of Spain's providential mission to promote the overseas expansion of the Catholic Church. It has been argued that both Machiavelli and St Thomas More glimpsed, as in a blinding vision, the inner nature of contemporary political power, a vision which led the English thinker to formulate a commonwealth based on contrary principles.[38] Bartolomé de las Casas was possessed by much the same kind of vision, haunted by the remembrance of a living Utopia wantonly destroyed by the advent of the Prince, with leaders like Cortés and Pizarro winning great riches and enduring fame through the destruction of Indian society. It was a vision which did not allow him to palliate, qualify or accommodate so that, from the start of his public career until his death, Las Casas reiterated the same basic message. So powerful and persuasive was his life-long campaign, waged across half a century in learned compositions and in biting state-papers, that he succeeded in bringing into question the entire legitimacy of the Spanish empire, so that subsequent generations of creole chroniclers were at times to attribute current tribulations to the injustices of the original conquest. In the last resort, the career of Las Casas afforded an enduring testimony of the vitality of Christian principles in sixteenth-century Spain.

4

THE GREAT DEBATE

I

FOR MOST Spaniards the title-deed of possession of the New World was the papal donation of 1493 when Alexander VI granted the Catholic Kings dominion over the isles and mainland of the ocean-sea, charging them with the conversion of the inhabitants of these newly discovered lands. That this donation cited the recent conquest of Granada as testimony of their sovereigns' eminent services to the Church, only strengthened popular conviction as to the Christian sanction and purpose of the overseas empire. In the universities, however, that assumption was soon challenged and the justice of Spanish conquest and empire in the Indies called into question. With what right did the Papacy grant possession to the kings of Castile over countries already inhabited and governed by their own rulers? Were the natives of the New World so deficient in common humanity as to justify armed conquest before the despatch of Christian missions? Needless to say, these questions soon became entangled with the thorny problem of the often criminal behaviour of the conquerors. The effect of Las Casas' denunciations was to query the very legitimacy of Spanish dominion in America. Moreover, the promulgation of the New Laws of 1542 failed to quieten Christian consciences or still the conquerors' ambition, so that the councils of the emperor continued to be agitated by memorials and petitions from both sides to the dispute.

It was at this point that Charles V convoked a junta composed of jurists and theologians to consider the justice of further conquests in the New World. In pursuance of this enquiry, the famous debates at Valladolid between Juan Ginés de Sepúlveda and Bartolomé de las Casas were staged in 1550–1 before a jury chiefly composed of Dominican theologians. The polemic between the humanist and the friar, already in train before these sessions, marked a watershed not merely in both men's lives, but also in the entire controversy about the Spanish conquest of America. For Sepúlveda failed to obtain permission to print his notorious defence of the conquerors and thereafter smarted from the concerted criticism of the Dominicans. Equally, Las Casas found himself driven by his opponent's skilful arguments to re-cast his abundant materials on the Indians and to qualify his defence of the Catholic monarchy in the New World. Moreover, in 1552 Las Casas published without licence eight tracts, among which figured both the *Brevísima relación* and Fr Domingo de Soto's summary of the Valladolid debates, which thus entered the public domain, albeit without great circulation. Since neither party in this dispute advanced arguments which were notably original, it is necessary first to trace their intellectual antecedents before examining the terms of their controversy.

II

The first comprehensive juridical defence of Spain's empire in America had been advanced by Juan López de Palacios Rubios (1450–1524), a judge and university professor, who was summoned by King Ferdinand to present an 'expert' opinion at a meeting of jurists and theologians convoked at Burgos in 1512 to consider the charges of injustice and exploitation raised by Fr Antonio de Montesinos. With a doctorate in canon rather than civil law, Palacios Rubios chose to base his claim on principles derived from scholastic theologians and the medieval canonists. To start with, he cited the theory already framed by John Major (Mair), a leading scholastic philosopher teaching at the Sorbonne, who had argued that the natives of the New World were so barbarous as to be classified as 'slaves by nature', and hence in need of correction and government by men fitted to rule. The source of this argument was Aristotle's *Politics*, where the Greek philosopher stated that some men by reason of their lack of judgement and education were incapable of prudent government, either of themselves or of their neighbours. It was a case of the passions overwhelming reason, of the body governing the mind. Obviously, children and women fell into this category, but so also did much of the peasantry and other men whose intellect was clouded by daily manual toil. But Aristotle broadened the concept still further when he declared that most barbarians were equally slavish since their governments were usually based on fear and force rather than on the wisdom and freedom that characterised the Greek city, the contemporary Persian empire offering a striking example of oriental despotism. These doctrines were revived in the Middle Ages and invoked in the influential tract *De regimine principum*, a text ascribed to St Thomas Aquinas, although in fact written by Ptolemy of Lucca. So also, the humanists of the sixteenth century found such ideas attractive, especially the emphasis on the supremacy of mind over body, citing them to contrast European freedom with Turkish tyranny. In all fairness to the proponents of Aristotle, it should be noted that these arguments were employed to defend social hierarchy rather than outright enslavement. Palacios Rubios insisted that the Indians were free men so that if they accepted Spanish rule they should not be seized or enslaved.[1] He cited Major and Aristotle to define the natives of the New World as men incapable of forming a government ordered according to the dictates of natural reason and Christian freedom, since their minds were clouded or, best to say, ruled by their physical passions.

Not content to rest his case on the Indian's natural incapacity, Palacios Rubios also defended the Alexandrine donation as the prime charter of Spain's empire in America. To this end, he adopted the canonist doctrines of Henry of Susa, better known as Ostiensis, and of Augustine of Ancona, who argued that with the passing of the four monarchies of the Assyrians, Medes, Greeks and Romans, Christ had inaugurated the fifth and last monarchy of the world, ruling as both emperor and high-priest of the universe. It followed that the Pope, the vicar of Christ, exercised both spiritual and temporal authority over the entire world. Moreover, Christ's advent had abrogated the political dominion of infidel sovereigns, who thus could be dispossessed of their kingdoms in order to secure their subjects for the Christian Church. Indeed, by reason of his 'supreme dominion, power and jurisdiction', the Pope conferred spiritual authority on bishops and temporal authority on the emperor and other kings. As vicars of Christ, one pope had acclaimed Charlemagne as king of Jerusalem and another pope now granted the Catholic Kings possession of the Indies.[2] If the Indians refused to recognise this donation, the king of Spain had the right to wage war to enforce their subjection. So also, once they were pacified, he was entitled to demand that they should pay tribute. Such had been the practice of the Romans in their empire and such was the invariable burden placed on all conquered peoples.

It was Palacios Rubios who also provided the text of the *requerimiento*, a formal exhortation to the natives of the New World to submit to the king of Spain and embrace the Christian faith. First employed in the Pedrarias expedition to Darien, where Oviedo had the dubious privilege of reading it in public to uncomprehending Indians, this document was a cynical piece of legal gibberish, which proved a source of much merriment both to its author and the conquerors. In effect, it announced that God, the creator of the first men, had chosen St Peter and his successors in Rome as monarchs of the world, superior in authority to all earthly princes. A latter-day pope had conferred possession of the Indies on the king of Spain. In consequence the Indians were commanded to recognise his authority and become his free, Christian subjects. Any denial or delay in accepting these demands would entail instant war, rendering them liable to death or enslavement as rebels. Perhaps the most remarkable feature of the *requerimiento* was the absence of any reference to Christ, his place in the theological scheme allocated to St Peter and the Papacy.[3] That such a text could have been despatched to the New World is commentary enough on the implicit contempt both of the Indians and of the Christian gospel that animated its author.

In the short run, it was not so much the aberrations of canonist doctrine as the crimes of the conquerors which attracted the condemnation of religious and scholars in Spain. In these years the influence of Erasmus was at its height in the Peninsula and his Spanish disciples were impressed by his criticism of the cycle of dynastic wars which haunted contemporary Europe. Both Erasmus and St Thomas More questioned the very ethos of medieval chivalry, and the popular literature that celebrated feats of arms as the source of man's chief glory, describing the warrior class as an idle burden on society. In this critique of the dynastic state and the class that supported it, they drew upon the writings of St Augustine.[4] The extent of their debt to the African saint is best revealed in the works of Juan Luis Vives, a Spanish humanist of Jewish extraction who was their friend and protégé. For in 1519–21 Vives edited for publication the *City of God*, adding an influential commentary that continued to be reprinted until the seventeenth century. In his notes to that work, he declared: 'the world is . . . bathed in floods of mutual blood. When one kills a man, it is called a crime, but when many together do likewise, it is called a virtue. Thus, the greatness of the fact, not respect for innocence, sets it free from penalty.'[5]

Any doubt about the Augustinian inspiration for the northern humanists' condemnation of warfare and the military ethos is allayed by examination of *Concordia et discordia*, a tract Vives wrote in 1529, addressed to the emperor Charles V, at the summit of that monarch's prestige, when it appeared that he had been chosen by God, so Vives averred, for 'some grand and marvellous design'. The overriding concern of the tract lies in its forthright criticism of the wars that then afflicted Europe, wars which derived from 'the infinite desire for power, for domination of the world', and yet which were 'more characteristic of beasts than of men'. Citing Augustine repeatedly, he attributed the prevalence of war to pride or self-love, which prompted the pursuit of military glory. Alexander and Caesar here figured with the recent dukes of Burgundy as arch-villains, whose ambition had caused the death of thousands. Behind the concentration on warfare lay the entire system of honour and nobility, with pride of lineage based on ancestors who never had a useful profession and were mere brigands. Before the rise of the arts and sciences 'men concentrated on honour, glory and fame, on the crimes of war'. Moreover, Vives extended his critique to cover all 'enactments of conflict', which, if in the ancient world had consisted of gladiatorial combat, in his time were manifest in 'military practices, competitions of poetry and oratory, and scholastic disputes . . .' Clerical and intellectual life was as much characterised by the spirit of conflict and domination as any battle-field or political arena.[6]

Despite his parade of Augustine as his chief authority and the striking similarity in his critical approach to the earthly city, Vives offered a quite distinct ideal of positive virtue. Above all else a humanist, he praised the republican heroes of Rome who had sacrificed their lives in service of their country, and drew a sharp distinction between republican virtue and that of the succeeding empire which was based on territorial conquests, discord and corruption. In contradiction to Augustine, he asserted that 'justice is the chief bond of human societies'. The influence of Cicero and Seneca was also manifest in his eulogy of the sage as characterised by his command over the passions, a serene and calm intellect, referring to 'the intelligence of the sage or philosopher, like a terrestrial divinity'. So also, he concluded with an invocation of the union of all nations in their common humanity, living 'as if citizens of the same country'. In short, what the case of Vives reveals is that it was possible to invoke and cite Augustine's arguments despite embracing a governing philosophy that was antithetical to the mainspring of the saint's theological system.[7] Christian Stoicism often echoed the Augustinian critique of empire and warfare, but its moral ideal was quite distinct.

Obviously, one did not have to read St Augustine to find either words or reasons to condemn the excesses of the conquerors. In a private letter, written in 1534, the Dominican, Francisco de Vitoria, leader of the revival of Thomist theology and philosophy at the university of Salamanca, expressed his horror at the recent news from Peru of the execution of Atahualpa, exclaiming that it 'freezes the blood in my veins to think about it'. No doubt it was the flurry of reports from the Indies, especially those derived from the mendicants, that prompted Vitoria in 1539 to deliver his famous Relectio de Indis, a lecture in which he sought to apply his philosophical doctrines to the problems of the New World. His starting point was the celebrated dictum of Aquinas that 'grace does not destroy nature but completes it'. This proposition effectively undermined any simple dualism or contrast between pagan evil and Christian grace by the assertion that the Christian gospel fulfilled and perfected the natural virtue of pagan philosophy and politics. Despite the radical damage wrought by Adam's Fall and subsequent sin, human nature still preserved its own autonomous ends, guided by natural law. After all, man had been created in the image of God and despite the effect of sin still retained all the marks of his creator's hand. Moreover, in regard to political authority Aquinas had followed and developed Aristotle in identifying man as 'a social and political animal', thus defining political associations as both necessary and good. Justice and the rule of law, both natural and positive, were the chief characteristics of the commonwealth, which existed to promote the mutual welfare of its members. By contrast, tyranny was taken to signify a government where the profit of the ruler, usually achieved by exploitation of the subjects, took first place, a regime usually associated with arbitrary exercise of power without restraint of law. In short, Aquinas bequeathed to Vitoria a set of concepts which could be easily adapted to deal with contemporary problems.[8]

To start with, Vitoria attacked the theory that the Indians were slaves by nature by observing that empirical reports despatched from Peru and Mexico testified that the natives of those countries were rational, possessed property and laws, and were governed by duly constituted monarchs. The fact that the kings were idolaters did not offer any grounds for depriving them of their authority. It had been an error of John Wycliffe to argue that sin deprived a prince of his right to govern or be recognised by Christians as their lord. Thus Indian monarchs possessed a natural right to property and dominion which could not be justly abrogated on charges of paganism. In any case, all that Aristotle had meant by defining some men as slaves by nature was that they needed to be governed by others; his doctrine offered no justification for outright enslavement.

In the second place, Vitoria curtly dismissed the canonist doctrine of the universal monarchy of the Papacy as ill-founded. Following the Dominican theologian, Cardinal Torquemada, he declared that Christ had never claimed temporal dominion, since his kingdom was not of this world. On what grounds could his vicar, the Pope, lay claim to jurisdiction over the kings of this world? In fact, there was no universal political authority in the world, only a series of autonomous states, each governed by their own lawful monarchs. It followed that the Pope had no right to dispose of any earthly realms, still less grant dominion to the king of Castile over peoples who already had their own rulers and who had never heard of the Christian gospel. As for the so-called right of discovery, that could only apply to lands that were uninhabited. In short, the papal donation offered no grounds for armed conquest of the New World or indeed of legitimate empire.

In a few succinct lines, Vitoria thus refuted the two most commonly held reasons for defending Spanish rights to empire in America. However, he then sought to devise arguments to justify some form of Spanish presence in the Indies. Drawing upon Roman jurisprudence, he observed that there existed laws governing intercourse between nations, derived eventually from the principles of natural law, which implied universal rights of communication and trade between all peoples. At the same time, there existed the specifically Christian right to preach the gospel to all nations and to protect fellow Christians from persecution. Finally, there was the right to suppress nefarious practices that grossly offended natural law so as to protect the innocent, who might fall victim to these offences. Obviously, when a prince freely invited the Spaniards to intervene, this welcome created a right to govern. Taken together, these principles marked the beginning of the modern theory of international law based as they were on the presumption of a definable nature common to all mankind. At the same time, it followed that the existence of specific rights of communication, trade and Christian mission entailed corresponding duties to preserve or defend these rights by the use of armed force. A Christian prince might well install a fortress or indeed mount a punitive expedition to open another country to trade or to protect fellow Christians from persecution. What they did not justify was the armed conquest and outright enslavement of another people. Vitoria openly doubted the desirability of any violent intervention to suppress such nefarious practices as cannibalism or human sacrifice, since the ensuing war might well provoke greater evils than those already existing. In any case, for a theologian the so-called crimes against nature, such as sodomy or cannibalism, were not more grave than common murder. Similarly, he deplored any conquest designed to effect conversion since such expeditions could only breed hatred of the gospel. On the other hand, if any pagan prince decided to embrace Christianity, then he had the right to command his people to follow his example or to summon a Christian prince to compel them.

At the close of his lecture, Vitoria cautiously re-opened the door he had appeared to close, when he admitted that there were grounds for suggesting that the Indians did not in fact possess such laws, political institutions or a level of knowledge sufficient to maintain a true commonwealth. By reason of their barbarous customs and defective education, they resembled the European peasantry, since they appeared to be more governed by their passions than by reason, unable fully to discern the dictates of natural law. It was doubtful whether they could defend themselves from an attack by a European power. In short, a case could be made for the Spanish king appointing governors to act as their protectors and tutors, teaching them both the Christian faith and the arts of civilisation. It will be observed that in this line of reasoning Vitoria shifted the argument away from assertions about inherent Indian nature towards a debate over the quality of their culture and society.[9] Moreover, as rational men the Indians were presumed to have the innate capacity to receive the gospel and eventually constitute their own commonwealth, a corollary which implied that the justification of Spanish rule applied only for a limited number of years.

The challenge offered by Vitoria to the standard 'case' for Spain's empire in the New World rapidly took Spanish universities by storm, where the theological faculties were dominated by his Dominican disciples. Indeed, the emperor Charles V summarily commanded Vitoria not to engage in any further unauthorised public pronouncements on matters of royal policy. But controversy soon mounted following the arrival of Bartolomé de las Casas from the Indies, the more especially when he presented the emperor with a copy of the *Brevísima relación*, written to obtain a thorough-going reform of imperial government. It was at this juncture, in 1544, two years after the promulgation of the New Laws, that Juan Ginés de Sepúlveda, a distinguished humanist and

Greek scholar, chose to enter the debate. His credentials were impeccable. Educated at Bologna, for many years resident in Rome, where Paolo Giovio figured among his friends, he had already translated several works of Aristotle into elegant Renaissance Latin. In 1536 he had been rewarded with appointment as imperial chronicler and later acted as tutor to Prince Philip. Nor was he a stranger to controversy, since he had published a tract in support of his patron Cardinal Alberto Pio, attacking the Christian pacifism of Erasmus. In a dialogue entitled *Democrates primus* he sought to defend the essential compatibility of Christian morality and the warrior code, thus rejecting the newly revived Augustinian critique of the Caesars of this world. Instead, he argued that provided the cause was just, the profession of arms and the pursuit of military glory were both honourable and Christian. It was in accordance with this view that elsewhere he strongly urged the emperor to lead his army against the Turks and so win the greatest empire known to history.[10] In short, whereas the Northern Renaissance led by Erasmus, More and Vives could discern little profit and less honour in contemporary warfare, by contrast Spanish humanists such as Sepúlveda and Gómara returned from Italy ready and eager to sing the praise of great warriors and kings, their elegant rhetoric thus serving the cause of imperial expansion. What is difficult to appraise is the influence of Machiavelli and Italian humanism as against the continuing appeal of the chivalrous code of fifteenth-century Spain.

Whatever the source of Sepúlveda's sentiments, their drift was unmistakable and decidedly unpalatable to many readers. In the dialogue entitled *Democrates secundus*, written in 1544, possibly at the instigation of Fernando de Valdés, archbishop of Seville, inquisitor-general, and a bitter enemy of Erasmus and his Spanish disciples, Sepúlveda defended the justice of Spanish conquests and empire in the New World. Basing himself primarily on the works of Oviedo, but also encouraged by conversation with Hernán Cortés at court, he sought to revive the arguments of John Mair and Palacios Rubios by demonstrating that the Indians were slaves by nature. Apparently unaware of Vitoria's contribution to the debate, he stated the case in contrasting terms that were peculiarly offensive asserting that

> these barbarians of the New World . . . in prudence, intelligence, virtue and humanity are as inferior to the Spaniards as are children to adults and women to men. The difference between them is as great as between a wild, cruel people and the most merciful, between the grossly intemperate and, the most continent and temperate, and, I am tempted to say, between men and monkeys.

Later, Sepúlveda described the Indians as *homunculi*, little creatures more close to the beasts than to rational men, who only possessed 'the vestige of humanity'.[11]

Where Sepúlveda scored over both Mair and Vitoria was in his analysis of

Indian society. For his contemptuous dismissal of native culture did not simply rest on the application of Aristotle's dictum and indeed in his *Apologia*, published in Rome, he did not employ the term. Instead, Sepúlveda applied humanist criteria to appraise the Indians. To start with, 'They do not know of letters; they do not preserve records of their history . . . and lack written laws.' As for descriptions of the cities and states of New Spain and Peru, all these proved was that the natives were indeed men and not monkeys or bears. After all, ants built towns and spiders wove thread. But the Indians lacked all notion of private property and lived subject to the arbitrary authority of their rulers, who were free to dispose of their lives and lands at whim. Thus, whereas Peter Martyr had fixed upon communality of property as a positive good, reminiscent of the golden age, by contrast Sepúlveda defined individual possession of land as a necessary condition of a free citizenry. Like all humanists, he defined political despotism as characteristic of barbarians, be they Turks or Indians, a definition which derived from Aristotle's description of the Persian empire.

If the Indians' radical incapacity for constituting a society governed by rational, just laws was a sufficient justification for conquest, it was their addiction to unnatural vice which rendered subjugation an imperative. Here the familiar catalogue compiled by Oviedo appeared in all its sorry force, with incest, sodomy, cannibalism and human sacrifice well to the fore. All these offences against the natural law were an insult to humanity and demanded the severest punishment. Instead of the pursuit of glory in just wars, the Indians waged endless warfare to satisfy their relentless appetite for human flesh, sacrificing innocent victims to their gods. So ferocious and savage was their society that only armed intervention could suppress its vices. If the Christian gospel was to be preached, and some degree of civility introduced, then the inevitable first step had to be armed conquest and pacification; any other course would merely lead to unwarranted martyrdoms. Once more, the hand of Oviedo can be discerned in these pronouncements.

If Mair and Palacios Rubios had justified conquest on the twin grounds of Indian nature and the papal donation, Sepúlveda relegated the Alexandrine bull to the status of a confirmatory act, subsequent and subordinate to the rights gained by discovery and conquest. As much as Nebrija and Oviedo, Sepúlveda sang the praise of his own nation, declaring that the campaigns of the Great Captain and Charles V had won for the Spaniards a reputation for constancy, temperance and courage that set them above their European neighbours. He marvelled at the heroic audacity of Cortés and his men venturing into battle against such multitudes of Indians. Indeed, the very ease with which they had conquered the Mexicans demonstrated how 'some men enjoyed a superiority to others in wit, fortitude and courage and how those others were slaves by nature'. In this eulogy of the conquerors, Sepúlveda laid out the foundation upon which Gómara raised his history of the conquest of Mexico. Needless to say, the Spaniards brought with them the Christian gospel and the arts of civilisation, thus liberating the Indians from the savagery in which they had dwelt. However, unlike Vitoria and his Dominican disciples, Sepúlveda did not entertain any hope that Indian nature would be transformed by Spanish rule. For he drew a distinction between the forms of government respectively appropriate to freemen and to serfs and compared the colonial body politic to a household where the Spaniards figured as the king's sons and the Indians as his servants, the latter now much improved by domestication but still needing to be ruled by command rather than by free observance of law.[12]

Perhaps the most striking feature of Sepúlveda's dialogue was its thoroughly secular character. For although he sought to buttress his case by quotations from scripture and the Church Fathers, citing Israel's massacre of the Amalekites and St Augustine's advocacy of force to obtain the submission of the Donatists, nevertheless the kernel of his argument consisted of the stark contrast drawn between Indian servitude and Spanish virtue. In all fairness, it should be noted that Sepúlveda did not advocate outright enslavement of the Indians; nor did he express any approval of the crimes of the conquerors. But his humanist bias in favour of great men and great deeds, both in literature and in arms, led him to magnify Spanish achievements in the New World through a systematic denigration of the Indians. Needless to say, the Dominican disciples of Vitoria, Melchor Cano and Bartolomé Miranda de Carranza, who had to judge whether his dialogue should be licensed for publication unanimously recommended its suppression.[13] Sepúlveda had paid no attention to the teachings of Vitoria and in any case his work was a piece of literature that obtruded into areas of debate which they deemed best reserved for trained theologians. But although *Democrates secundus* mouldered in manuscript until the nineteenth century, its arguments continued to figure in all debates about the character of Spanish rule and Indian nature. Indeed, whereas Vitoria's formulation of the natural rights of international trade and communication failed to attract much attention in future polemics over Spain's overseas empire, by contrast the congenital incapacity of the Indians and the heroic quality of the conquerors were to occupy a central place in subsequent controversy and chronicle. In the short term, however, the prime importance of Sepúlveda's dialogue was that it challenged Las Casas to re-order and re-think the mass of materials he had already collected concerning the culture and beliefs of the American Indians.

III

In the years which followed the debate with Sepúlveda at Valladolid, Las Casas not merely revised his *Historia de las Indias*, he also revised and completed his *Apologética historia sumaria*, a vast systematic treatise in which he sought to demonstrate that the natives of the New World were both as savage and as civilised as the peoples of Europe and the Near East during the classical period. His work has been rightly described as the first known exercise in comparative ethnography.[14] Certainly, both the manner of argument and the materials on which it was based were markedly original. For Las Casas assembled a vast amount of data about most aspects of Indian morality, government, and religion, material mainly dealing with the Incas and Aztecs, but including sections on the Caribbean, and then proceeded to a systematic comparison and contrast, topic by topic, with an equally formidable, but less original corpus of knowledge on the Ancient World culled from classical authors. He drew upon his own observations in Hispaniola and central America, the researches of the Franciscans in Mexico and reports from Dominicans in Peru, supplemented by the usual printed sources such as Cortés' letters, Estete on Peru and the travels of Cabeza de Vaca in North America. At all points, Las Casas was concerned to define, compare and collate so as to establish a framework of analysis which could be invoked to interpret any non-Christian society. In regard to the development of human culture, it must number among the most important essays before Vico transformed the subject.

Quick to sense the threat from climatic determinism, Las Casas devoted a long introduction to a description of the climate and terrain of Hispaniola, which he pronounced as more fertile and propitious for human settlement than any European counterpart. Drawing upon Aristotle's thesis that both intellect and spirit thrived best in warm rather than in cold climes and noting Hippocrates' assertion of the superiority of Asia over Europe for the cultivation of crops, he defined the Americas as essentially an extension of Asia. It was for this reason that he insisted on using the term 'the Indies' and rarely described the hemisphere as a 'New World'. Like most of his contemporaries, Las Casas thus accepted environmental determinism, with the heavens and their constellations deemed to influence mankind through the interplay of the vital elements of water, fire, earth and air which in turn determined human character. It was in part the Asiatic softness of climate in the Indies which rendered its inhabitants such easy prey for European warriors reared in more hardy climes. It also allowed for an unparalleled increase of population since 'they did not have wars among themselves, nor suffered hunger, nor epidemics, they bred and multiplied each day infinite numbers of people, with every married woman having usually three, or four or five children'.[15]

On the question of cultural evolution, Las Casas turned to Cicero and other classical authors for a sketch of the natural history of humanity, texts in which he found a description of the first men living scattered in caves and forests without cultivation, fixed abode or indeed society, each man's hand raised against his neighbour.[16] It was a stage which was brought to an end in part by the pressure of necessity and experience of the advantage of co-operation,

pointing to the truth of Aristotle's dictum that man was a social animal. But it
was a stage which also led to the intervention of a wise lawgiver, such as King
Saturn in Italy, who introduced the golden age by teaching men such arts of
peace as agriculture and stock-raising. Las Casas then took from Cicero the
assertion that men in all nations are essentially the same in nature and hence
argued that the natives of the Indies had passed through much the same
sequence of cultural development as that observed in the Ancient World. 'All
the lineages of man are one', he wrote, which signified that all men were
capable of much the same range of knowledge, skills and religion. Indeed, after
the conquest the Mexican Indians soon acquired most Spanish crafts and a
handful had even learnt Latin. More important, Las Casas directly applied the
sequence of cultural development he found in Cicero, asserting that if the
Aztecs and Incas resembled the Romans and Greeks, the tribes of North
America were best compared to the ancient Scythians since they still roamed 'in
that first rude state'. It was this distinction drawn between the peoples of the
Caribbean and 'Florida' and the advanced societies of Peru and Mexico which
gave the *Apologética* its analytic force.[17]

If the first sections of the work dealt mainly with Hispaniola and its
inhabitants, when Las Casas invoked the Aristotelian definition of the city he
concentrated mainly on the Incas and Aztecs, with the aim of demonstrating
that their societies possessed the six requisites for a city, viz., agriculture,
artisans, warriors, rich men, organised religion and lawful government. In this
regard, Las Casas expatiated on the grandeur of Tenochtitlan and Moctezuma's palace, the density of its population, the activity of its great market, the
skill of its artisans, the enterprise of its merchants and the towering height of
the great pyramid temple for which only Egypt offered a rival. So also, the
irrigated terraces of Peru, the two great highways spanning the Inca empire, the
stone fortresses and storehouses, and the social organisation of Cuzco were
described in some detail. The emphasis on military valour, with the Mexican
orders of warriors similar to Christian knights, was faithfully recorded. In
short, Las Casas had little difficulty in demonstrating that the Incas and Aztecs
fulfilled the first four requisites of the true city or civil community.

Inevitably, the main focus was on religion, the discussion of which comprised almost half the text. Here, Las Casas started by reaffirming the thesis
taken from Augustine and Aquinas that all men by virtue of the natural light
implanted within them by their Creator naturally seek to know and serve God.
All men thus possess a dim sense of the one true God. However, the corruption
of human nature occasioned by original sin and sheer ignorance drove them
into idolatry. Aware of the necessity of worship and sacrifice, they fixed upon
natural phenomena, such as the sun or the stars as the cause of their being.
Later, kings and lawgivers were transformed into deities. In essence, the
descent into idolatry was a natural process derived from the original disorder-

ing of the human soul. However, man's ignorance and depravity were seized upon by the Devil and his cohorts as the opportunity for actively perverting man's natural desire to propitiate the heavens and honour wise men. The worst excesses of paganism, therefore, sprang from demonic intervention. As to the power of evil spirits to influence the material and moral world, Las Casas cited *Malleus maleficarum*, the bible of the witch-hunts which were then gathering momentum in Europe.[18]

Thereafter, Las Casas presented a detailed comparison and analysis of the pantheon of gods, both classical and Indian, and the organisation of religious cults in both systems, all with the purpose of demonstrating that the Aztecs and Incas possessed as complex a system of belief and worship as anything known in the Ancient World. With our knowledge of Las Casas, it comes as no surprise to find that the comparison favoured the peoples of Mexico and Peru. This conclusion in part derived from the bias of the sources. For Las Casas relied heavily on St Augustine's *City of God*, which he described as 'that famous work, so celebrated among books', to guide him through the discussion of classical paganism.[19] By contrast he drew upon contemporary Franciscan and Dominican reports on Indian religion, written at a time when missionary optimism still waxed strong. The result was an emphasis on the puerility of classical mythology and the obscenity of its cult compared to the rigorous fasting and prayer of the Indian priesthood. Idolatry in the New World was more honest and pure, less stained with corruption than its ancient counterpart, and it was for this reason that the conversion of the Indians had proved so successful. Indeed, since the Indians of the Caribbean offered a virtual *tabula rasa* in matters of religion and the Incas with their sun-worship were close to monotheism, then their conversion should prove relatively easy. At the same time, however, Las Casas declared that precisely because the Mexican Indians surpassed all other nations in their commitment to idolatry and the cult of their deities, then once converted they would become the best Christians in the world.[20]

The boldness of Las Casas' approach to Indian religion can be observed at its most audacious in his discussion of the thorny question of human sacrifice and attendant cannibalism, a practice found in many American societies but especially prevalent in Mexico. Once more, comparison with the Ancient World was invoked, since most peoples of that epoch, not least the Jews and Spaniards, at times had been guilty of this offence. Demonic intervention figured as a possible cause of human error and sin. Not content, however, with mere exoneration by comparison, Las Casas returned to his central affirmation that all men naturally seek to know and serve the one true God and that they expressed their worship and service in offering sacrifice. It followed that all sacrifice, no matter which deity it sought to propitiate, embodied man's desire to serve the Almighty. Moreover, the more dedicated men were to the cause of religion, the more valuable would be their offerings. And what more valuable thing did man possess than life itself? Human sacrifice was thus the highest expression of man's desire to serve God. In the absence of any knowledge of positive law, be it Divine or civil, human sacrifice was both a natural and a rational practice. Here, indeed, was an argument to shock the unlearned and confound Sepúlveda! It was an argument which Las Casas had presented in summarised form in his Latin *Apologia* and one in which he took great pride, since in a letter written to the Dominicans of Guatemala in 1563 he declared: 'before me no man dared to touch or write' on such a question.[21]

The treatise continued with a path-breaking discussion of Indian government and social morality. Once more, we are treated to a contrast between the laxity and frequent obscenity of the ancients in regard to marriage and the austere code enforced by the Aztecs and Incas. Las Casas praised the wisdom of the kings of Texcoco and the severe punishments, including the death penalty, meted out for all infractions, including sins such as adultery and crimes like theft and murder. Citing materials supplied by Fr Andrés de Olmos, a Franciscan missionary, he provided specimens of the admirable moral homilies delivered by Indian parents and governors to their children, the strictness of their education surpassing anything known in the ancient world. In short, the Mexican realms were governed according to the dictates of natural law, their kings administering demonstrable justice, without which, Las Casas declared, a true commonwealth could not exist. Even more impressive were the achievements of the Incas. Here the emperor Pachakuti figured as a monarch whose concern for the welfare of his subjects not merely contrasted to the depredations which accompanied Roman conquests, but even offered a lesson to the Catholic Kings. Agriculture was improved by irrigation and the produce stored in regional warehouses was periodically distributed among the population. So anxious was this monarch to make provision for the care of the aged, sick and poor, that communal meals in the main square of each village were introduced, a measure of social charity far exceeding anything known in Christian Europe. Thus, neither the errors of the Indians in matters of religion nor demonic intervention in their cult apparently affected their ability to discern and obey the dictates of natural law, in the application of which they at times scored over nations blessed by Christian revelation. In conclusion, Las Casas declared that the Incas and Aztecs were not merely the equals of the Romans and Greeks, but also 'in many good and better customs they surpassed them, as indeed they did the English and French and some of the people of our Spain'.[22]

All that remained was for Las Casas to elucidate the meaning of the term barbarian, when it was applied to such peoples as the Aztecs and Incas. He distinguished four classes of men commonly reckoned as barbarians: those whose behaviour was ferocious and cruel; those who lacked letters; those who had no government or law; and those who lacked the Christian faith. Obviously, all societies, even Christian countries, possessed members who belonged to the first two classes of barbarians, since they comprised all men grossly defective in morality or knowledge. Among the Indians only the Mexicans appeared to have had anything approaching a book or a script, an obvious defect since the absence of written records prevented any certain account and transmission of history and laws. However, he had already illustrated the quality of their justice and morality. It followed that the only true reason for calling the Indians barbarians was their ignorance of Christianity, a condition which they shared with the Moors and Turks, whose states were highly organised. But whereas the Muslims waged bitter war against Christendom, the Indians had welcomed the preaching of the gospel. As for Sepúlveda's concept of Indians as slaves by nature, that was not worthy of discussion other than as a description of those individuals in any society whose character best fitted them to serve rather than to command.[23]

In the early seventeenth century, Fr Antonio de Remesal exclaimed that the *Apologética historia sumaria* 'shows the bishop to have been one of the greatest humanists in the world'.[24] This is not a characterisation that comes readily to mind in regard to Las Casas. The style and form of his work has little of the controlled perspective or elegance of style that we associate with the humanism of the Renaissance. His sources are as much patristic or medieval as classical, with Augustine as potent an influence as Aquinas or Aristotle. Yet, in essence, there was little that was scholastic in his method or purpose. For what we encounter in the *Apologética* is an obsession with facts, with the collection of data about religion, morality, politics and law, all subjected to 'collation and comparison'.[25] Moreover, despite the interest in demons and their works, the sinew of the argument is naturalistic, starting with the influence of climate and terrain on humanity, proceeding to a description of Indian civilisation interpreted from the viewpoint of natural law, and culminating with a discussion of religious cult defined in equally naturalistic fashion. At the same time, the entire work exhibits a peculiar fissure, not to say contradiction in Las Casas' thought. For whereas the *City of God* is deployed to damn classical paganism as obscene and dominated by the Devil, by contrast Indian religion is defended on the grounds of natural law and man's innate quest for the Godhead. The underlying premise, on which the entire work rests, derived both from Cicero's insistence on the common nature and evolution of all humanity, and on the Christian dogma that all men are the children of Adam, created in the image of God.

In the course of his intellectual battle against the imperial school of Oviedo, Sepúlveda and Gómara, Las Casas wrote the *Historia de las Indias* to define and defend the quality of Indian culture. But he still had to devise reasons to justify the Spanish empire in the New World, the more especially since he had always looked to the Crown for assistance in his campaign on behalf of the Indians. If he enjoyed influence at court, it was in part because he was an advocate of royal authority. To encounter these arguments it is necessary to examine his Latin *Apologia*, the text he read before the jury at Valladolid, and the tracts he published in 1552, notably, *Treinta proposiciones muy jurídicas* and the *Tratado comprobatorio del imperio soberano*. At the same time, the impact of the polemic with Sepúlveda, when taken with the subsequent controversy over the Peruvian encomenderos' plea for jurisdiction and perpetuity of tenure, effectively radicalised his thinking about the legitimacy of imperial rule in the Indies. Equally important, although Las Casas professed great respect for Francisco de Vitoria, he pursued a distinctive line of reasoning which combined natural law theory with doctrines taken from the canonists.

To start with, Las Casas was at pains to deny the accuracy of Sepúlveda's citation of St Augustine and Scripture to support the justice of armed conquest of idolaters. Israel's invasion of the Holy Land belonged to the Old Testament, which had been superseded by the more merciful doctrines of Christ and hence offered no grounds for modern conquests. As for Augustine's approval of use of force to suppress Donatism in North Africa, the saint had always advocated the peaceful conversion of pagans, maintaining that it was first necessary to uproot idolatry from men's hearts before levelling their temples. It was against heretics who had abandoned orthodox, Catholic teachings, not against pagans, that Augustine invoked political coercion. Here was a distinction that Las Casas found attractive. Far removed from the liberalism of his modern admirers, he declared that baptism was the equivalent of a feudal oath of loyalty, so that heretics were guilty of treachery and hence liable for stringent punishment, since they were 'the worst of men and most harmful to the entire universal church'.[26] Indeed, like Oviedo he suggested that the Inquisition should be established in the Indies so as to extirpate any heretical infection.

With this distinction made, Las Casas then developed the standard argument, already expounded by Vitoria, that idolatry and other sins in no way vitiated the natural rights of pagan princes to govern their kingdoms. All men, no matter how barbarous, possessed the same rights to self-government, property and liberty. In the case of the Indians, it was abundantly clear that they had perfectly adequate forms of government. The description offered by Sepúlveda was a tissue of slander taken from Oviedo. It was a positive insult to the Almighty, bordering on blasphemy, to suggest that He would have peopled an entire hemisphere with men so brutish and incapable as Sepúlveda claimed. Even if the crimes reported by Oviedo were in part true – which Las Casas denied – any armed intervention to suppress them would provoke more sin and destruction than the offences it sought to eliminate. So also, to preach the gospel at sword-point was a heresy worthy of Mahomet; as it was, the Indians viewed the conquerors more as agents of the Devil than of Christ. Careful to avoid any confusion between the case of the Indians and that of Islam, Las Casas expressly excepted the Moors and Arabs from the general rule of infidel right to self-government, since from the start they had invaded lands once occupied by Christians. As declared enemies of the faith, all war against them was justified and at all times they could be rightfully deprived of their lands. The principle of the crusade was thus enthusiastically endorsed. So also, Las Casas asserted that a prince had the right to determine the religion of his subjects, so that any Indian ruler could demand that his people embrace Christianity. In line with this principle, he cited with approval the examples of the Roman emperors Constantine and Theodosius, who first proclaimed Christianity the religion of the empire and then decreed the closure of all pagan temples.[27]

If Las Casas thus dismissed all wars of conquest directed against the American Indians as unjust and the subsequent government as tyrannical, on what grounds did he justify Spain's empire in the New World? The only possible source of political legitimacy, so he argued, was the papal donation of 1493. Careful to reject the extreme canonist doctrine of Ostiensis and Palacios Rubios, which he described as almost heretical, that the Pope as vicar of Christ possessed temporal dominion over all kingdoms in the world, Christian and infidel alike, Las Casas followed Vitoria in defining papal authority as spiritual and hence powerless to quit infidel princes of their kingdoms. However, he argued that as vicar of Christ, the Pope had the whole world as his parish, and was responsible for preaching the gospel to all nations. The Pope thus possessed a 'voluntary', spiritual authority over all men. It was in pursuance of this great end, the conversion of all nations to the Christian faith, that the Pope could suspend any temporal authority that presented an obstacle to the Christian mission and by extension empower Christian kings to protect and further that mission. But this suspension of the authority of infidel monarchs was limited to the degree necessary to ensure the peaceful conversion of their subjects.[28] In short, by introducing the Papacy as a world-wide mediator and judge, Las Casas sought to maintain the balance between the positive rights of the universal Christian mission and the natural right of all kingdoms to preserve their independence.

If Las Casas thus re-inserted the papal donation as the title-deed of Spanish sovereignty in the New World, he was at pains to circumscribe the nature of that authority. It was, so he declared, essentially *modal*, which is to say, conditional rather than absolute, its validity dependent on compliance with the terms of the donation. The spiritual purpose and secular *raison d'être* of the empire was the conversion of the native inhabitants, a purpose to which all temporal concerns were subordinate. Moreover, as he argued elsewhere, the Alexandrine bull offered no warrant for armed incursions: the gospel had to be preached in a peaceful manner, preferably in the way he had pioneered in Verapaz. Equally important, the political authority of Indian lords had to be respected and maintained, the gospel preached with their co-operation and agreement. Only when they actively opposed the entrance of missionaries could a moderate use of coercion be invoked. In all this, Las Casas was careful not to offer any comfort to the conquerors, upon whom he continued to pronounce a universal malediction.

But how was it possible for Las Casas both to defend the papal donation and the political authority of Indian lords? Once again, he displayed considerable theoretical ingenuity. Essentially, he re-defined the papal donation as the concession of imperial sovereignty over an entire hemisphere, which hence constituted a new Christian empire, arguing that:

> The Kings of Castile and Leon are true sovereign princes and universal lords and emperors over many kings, to whom by law belongs all the high dominion and universal jurisdiction over the Indies, by the authority, concession and donation of the Holy Apostolic See, and thus by Divine authority ... The Spanish Kings are almost delegates and co-adjutors of the Apostolic See.

In the same way that in the eighth century the Pope had crowned Charlemagne King of Jerusalem and Holy Roman Emperor, so equally Alexander VI had in effect created a Holy Empire of the Indies, conferring on the Catholic kings an imperial jurisdiction.[29] Moreover, if the discovery of the New World was clearly an act of Providence, then it followed that Spain's empire was equally providential, created and maintained to ensure the conversion of the Indians. At the same time, the imperial character of royal government did not entail any abrogation of the local or provincial jurisdiction of Indian lords. Needless to say, this resounding doctrine won for Las Casas a hearing at court that otherwise might have been denied him. Nor did it involve any lessening of his attack on the conquerors, since he continued to argue that the encomienda, an institution that perpetuated the injustice of the conquest, embodied the usurpation of the political authority of both the king–emperor and the Indian lords, intervening between the Crown and its free subjects.

If the debate with Sepúlveda had driven Las Casas to revise his defence of Spain's imperial presence, the petition of the Peruvian encomenderos for perpetuity of tenure and concession of jurisdiction over their native tributaries led him to construe a contractual theory of political obligation. In a short Latin tract, entitled *De regia potestate*, a work later published in Germany but not until recently attributed to Las Casas, he stated that all kings derive their authority from the free consent of the people, which, as the source of sovereignty, preceded the monarch both in essence and in time. The chief purpose of government was the welfare of the subjects. It followed that the concession of sovereign jurisdiction to the king did not diminish the rights of the subjects, whose free consent was required for any measure that might prejudice their liberty and property. For his part, the monarch was the guardian of his inherited jurisdiction and the 'fiscal goods' attached to his office, without any personal right to dispose or diminish them. Any sale of judicial office was inherently vicious, a form of simony. Similarly, although he could bestow honorific titles of nobility, any accompanying concession of jurisdiction was beyond his authority. For the kingdom, essentially a union of cities, formed a 'mystical body', which could not be dismembered without lasting hurt. Citizens owed their chief loyalty to their *patria*, which is to say, to their native city, so that the king as presiding monarch over this federation had no right to alienate any cities or provinces from the common jurisdiction.[30] As it will be observed, the thrust of this line of argument was to limit the monarch's power by insistence on the free consent of the subjects, yet equally to strengthen and magnify his jurisdiction by repudiating both sale of office and concession of feudal benefices as a derogation of his indivisible sovereign power.

Needless to say, Las Casas did not undertake this exercise in political theory without the problems of the New World in mind. Already, in the course of the debate with Sepúlveda, he had come to realise the importance of free consent in the formation of any true polity. In his last major work, the Latin scholastic treatise entitled *Los tesoros del Perú*, written in 1561, he fixed upon the principle of popular or common consent as the final criterion by which to judge the legitimacy of Spain's American empire. Reiterating the Thomist principle that the realm of Christian grace did not supersede or abrogate the 'order of justice' and that the Pope had not power to disregard the dictates of natural law, he declared that 'defence of the patria and of its liberty is a natural right'. The lawful sovereigns of Peru were the Incas and other native lords. Any usurpation of their rightful jurisdiction was the act of a tyrant. All this Las Casas had said many times before, but he now introduced a more radical consideration, observing that even if the Indian kings and lords accepted Spanish rule their subjects still had to offer their free consent to this transfer of sovereignty.[31] If Moctezuma had indeed recognised the authority of Charles V – Las Casas accused Cortés of inventing the story – his decision still had to be ratified by the Mexican people; no king could alienate his realm without consultation. Indeed, in former times the accession of kings and the election of bishops both required popular consent. Moreover, whereas in earlier treatises Las Casas had argued that once Indians were baptised they became the subjects of the Spanish King and hence guilty of rebellion if they combated his decrees, now at the close of his life he declared that the Indians, even if Christians, could still rightfully resist any seizure of property or loss of liberty. It followed that the papal donation of imperial sovereignty over the New World to the Catholic Kings was itself dependent on the free consent and agreement of the native peoples of America. Yet in fact the Indies had been conquered by violence and continued to be governed with violence. At no point had the native kings or their subjects been given the opportunity to offer their free consent. The conquerors were tyrants and the empire they created an unmitigated despotism: the entire cycle of conquest and government, from 1492 until 1561, so Las Casas now averred, was little more than a story of theft, murder and oppression.[32] The Indians had the clearest right to resist and rebel in just war to regain their liberty. As for the Catholic Kings, they had no right to appoint governors or viceroys, still less reward with titles of nobility men like Cortés and Pizarro who should have been hung as common criminals. The only just course of action was to restore to the Indians all the property and land seized from them and reinstate the Incas as lawful monarchs of Peru. Without justice and consent, no true commonwealth could exist: the terms of the papal donation had never been fulfilled and so the Catholic Kings did not enjoy true 'juridical possession' of the Indies. In this last despairing conclusion, Las Casas abandoned his former reliance on the Crown to correct the excesses of the conquerors and finally brought into question the very legitimacy of imperial rule, which until then he had so consistently defended.

To trace the sources of Las Casas' thinking in these last years is no easy matter, the more especially since on occasion he was guilty of citing any number of authorities lifted from the few treatises that he had actually read. Obviously, in defining the conquerors as tyrants, he continued to rely on the *Politics* and *Ethics* of Aristotle and *De regimine principum*. But he also turned to the treatise on tyranny written by Bartolus of Sassaferrato and to a study of feudal benefices published by Baldus of Ubaldis.[33] These Italian jurists had sought to justify the independence of the northern city–states from the authority of the German emperors and to condemn the seizure of power by tyrants. They taught that no king had the right to alienate any part of his realm or jurisdiction, and that to be legitimate all government required the free consent of its subjects. In short, the Italian reaction to the excesses of the *condottieri* offered doctrinal support for Las Casas' condemnation of the conquerors, since in both cases political power derived from armed force and was exercised for the ruler's benefit without reference to the consent or welfare of the subjugated peoples. As much as in his defence of the just rule of the Incas and Aztecs, so equally in his characterisation of the Spanish empire, Las Casas drew upon European jurisprudence and Thomist philosophy to establish the rights of the natives of the New World. At the same time, it should be noted that in contemporary Spanish usage the term *tirano* was loosely employed to describe the leaders of rebellions against the Crown. When Oviedo referred to Gonzalo Pizarro as a tyrant, he mentioned his usurpation of royal authority rather than any act of ill-government. Clearly, Las Casas had this meaning in mind, when he styled the conquerors as tyrants and usurpers, since they had robbed the Indian lords of their rightful authority and interposed their illegitimate power between the Spanish Crown and its native subjects.

The prophetic violence with which Las Casas assailed the conquerors derived from other sources than his readings in Italian jurisprudence. Whereas Sepúlveda and Gómara united to laud Cortés as another Caesar, the Dominican roundly condemned all pursuit of military glory as an expression of man's lust for dominion, the animating principle of the Earthly City. With evident relish he cited St Augustine's anecdote concerning the exchange between Alexander the Great and a captured pirate, in which the robber asserted that the only difference between himself and the king was the scale of their depredations. Moreover, he accepted the African saint's condemnation of the Roman empire, rejecting Sepúlveda's eulogy of the civilising mission of that state with the assertion that 'the Roman empire did not arise through justice but was acquired by tyranny and violence'. If God had allowed it to thrive and continue, it was because He often used tyrants such as Cyrus and Sennacherib to fulfil his providential designs.[34] At the very outset of his public career as a Dominican, in 1531, Las Casas had repeatedly cited the *City of God* to support his attack on the conquerors. The significance of that source should become clear if we read the most telling lines in full.

> Remove justice, and what are kingdoms but bands of criminals on a large scale? What are criminal bands but petty kingdoms? A band is a group of men under the command of a leader, bound together by a compact of association, in which plunder is divided according to an agreed convention. If this villainy wins so many recruits from the ranks of the demoralised that it acquires territory, establishes a base, captures cities and subdues peoples, it then openly arrogates to itself the title of kingdom.

Here in a passage written a thousand years before the discovery of America, we encounter a pretty accurate definition of the free companies who invaded the New World.[35] Indeed, if we turn to a Spanish translation of the *City of God*, we find very much the same words, since the term leader becomes *caudillo* and the compact of association, *compañia*. Moreover, since Las Casas probably used the edition that carried the comments of Luis Vives, he would have read the note appended to this passage, which declared that 'fighting belongs neither to good men nor thieves, nor to any that are men at all, but is a right bestial fury'. If one man kills another man, it is called murder; but when many unite to kill in war, it becomes a virtue. It was through these notes of Vives that Las Casas became familiar with the deployment of arguments taken from Augustine by

Erasmian humanists to bring into question the entire military ethos of contemporary Europe and its governing class.[36]

To assert the underlying Augustinian bias in Las Casas' thought is not to deny his enduring indebtedness to Aquinas, Aristotle and the natural law tradition. In this context, it is significant that he accepted Cicero's dictum that justice was the foundation of any commonwealth, a dictum that had been rejected by Augustine who preferred to emphasise the union of wills in pursuit of an agreed end.[37] It was the natural law tradition, re-stated by Vitoria, which enabled Las Casas to defend the rights of Indian realms to self-government and resistance to unjust conquest. The glaring absence in the *City of God* of any mention of Roman law meant that Augustine's voluntaristic theories of political association could provide little assistance for Las Casas' arguments in favour of native rights. Instead, what he took from the African saint was a condemnation of armed conquest so radical as to bring into question the legitimacy of all government which rested on such foundations. His very insistence on the supremacy of spiritual over temporal interests in the discovery of the New World led him to define the Papal donation as the title-deed of empire and then to invoke sacramental sanctions to reform secular abuses. In practice, his radical rejection of some sixty years of overseas settlement and government derived from Christian principles far removed from the essentially accommodating temper of Thomist political theory, leading him in the last resort to favour either the pipe-dream of restitution of native authority or, in reality, a strengthening of the power of absolute monarchy over the conquerors and their descendants.

V

The influence of Las Casas on the emergence of a political tradition in Spanish America was all-important. At the close of the colonial period, the Mexican insurgent ideologue, Fray Servando Teresa de Mier, hailed him as 'the tutelary genius of the Americas, the father of the Indians', and claimed that the Laws of the Indies were little more than 'conclusions taken from the writings of Las Casas'.[38] Although his major works were not published until the nineteenth century, substantial extracts were quietly incorporated into subsequent chronicles and through this medium enjoyed wide circulation. As we shall see, the works of Antonio de Herrera, the Inca Garcilaso de la Vega and Juan de Torquemada, the three principal historians of the Indies at the beginning of the seventeenth century, were all indebted to the writings of Las Casas. At the same time, the circle assembled by Francisco de Toledo in Peru sharply attacked the campaign of the great Dominican as essentially misguided. The subsequent translation of the *Brevísima relación* into all the leading European languages rendered this tract one of the most widely read political pamphlets in early modern Europe, serving as a basic text for all enemies of Spain and its American empire. But the tract also enjoyed a surreptitious circulation in the New World and influenced creole patriots in the view they adopted about the conquest. That the encomenderos of Peru and Mexico failed to convert their grants into feudal fiefdoms affected the entire course of history in these countries. The legacy of Las Casas both in the actual establishment of imperial government in the New World and in the subsequent interpretation of the history of the conquest was thus all-pervasive and recurrent. In one form or another, each generation of Spanish Americans has had to wrestle with the implications of his prophetic mission.

5

FRANCISCAN MILLENNIUM

I

IN 1524 a Franciscan mission of twelve friars walked barefoot from Veracruz to Mexico City, there to be welcomed by Hernán Cortés, who knelt in the dust before the assembled nobility, both Spanish and Indians, to kiss the hand of their leader, Martín de Valencia. This dramatic moment, so rich in symbolic promise, was cherished and for long remembered by conquerors and friars alike, since it was taken to signify that the preaching of the gospel in New Spain would command the active support of the secular authorities. Nor was this expectation disappointed, since the first two viceroys, Antonio de Mendoza (1535–50) and Luis de Velasco (1550–64) relied on the mendicants to act as both spiritual mentors and political guardians of the native community. In the early decades of conquest society, the three religious orders, Franciscans, Dominicans and Augustinians, competed with the encomenderos for the effective governance of the Indian population, seeking to protect their charges from the worst abuses of the settlers. Indeed, it was the friars who administered the massive resettlement and concentration of the native population, a programme initiated in the late 1540s and at its height in the following decades.[1] The scattered hill-side hamlets in which so many Indians had dwelt were vacated and replaced by new towns, usually situated on the plains, their streets laid out in a formal grid centred on the main square, which was invariably dominated by the parish church. Not merely did the religious preach the gospel, they also re-shaped the pattern of native life and culture, introducing Spanish arts and crafts, and teaching the elite Spanish forms of government.

It was the political authority exercised by the friars which enabled them to set about the extirpation of idolatry with such exemplary vigour. Convinced that pagan religion was the work of the Devil, they quickly moved to level native temples to the ground, smash idols, burn codices as signs of necromancy, and to ban any further celebration of pagan rites. If they did not oblige anyone to accept baptism, they summarily punished any lord or priest who sought to preserve the old religion, not hesitating to whip, imprison, exile, or, on occasion, burn offenders who offered active resistance to their teachings. In 1539 the lord of Texcoco, Don Carlos Ometochtzin, a former pupil of the Franciscans, was burnt at the stake for exhorting his subjects to return to their ancient rites.[2] In Yucatán, in 1562, little more than fifteen years after the conquest of that province, the Franciscans discovered that many of their most trusted assistants had organised surreptitious pagan ceremonies, at times even employing Christian churches for that purpose. In horrified reaction, the mendicants launched a brief reign of terror, imprisoning thousands of unfortunate natives and subjecting the ringleaders to such torture that some died of their pains and others remained permanently crippled. Although the incoming bishop, himself a Franciscan, described the missionaries as 'men of little learning and less charity', and quickly put an end to the affair, the provincial responsible for its instigation was eventually exonerated.[3]

To insist on the peremptory, even violent character of the 'spiritual conquest' is to recall but one side of the story. Martín de Valencia was an ascetic more liable to scourge his own mortified flesh than to whip dissident Indians. Moreover, all the chroniclers testify that after a period of 'coldness', attributable, no doubt, to the shock of seeing their idols cast down and destroyed, the Indians flocked in thousands to hear the gospel and learn the rudiments of Christian doctrine. For his part, Cortés summoned over a thousand children of the Indian nobility, entrusting them to the Franciscans for education.[4] Thereafter, it was the native elite, lords and nobles, who acted as their lieutenants, helping to organise services and to summon the labour drafts necessary for the construction of churches. This intimate collaboration testified to the rapidity with which the Indians assimilated Spanish culture and language. It was also responsible for the scenes of mass enthusiasm which at times greeted the mendicants, the natives clamouring for permission to build churches and chapels to serve the religious needs of their particular communities. The friars marvelled at the zeal with which their neophytes participated in the celebration of the Catholic liturgy. Any scepticism about these reports can be allayed if we consider that in Peru chroniclers constantly complained of the recalcitrant indifference of the natives to their preaching, and drew an explicit contrast between religious behaviour in the two countries.[5] In short, there is a sunlit, euphoric quality about the spiritual conquest in central Mexico, endowing it with a numinous character that still haunts the precincts of such churches as Huejotzingo, Acolman and Tzintzuntzan.

Indian zeal was more than matched by mendicant dedication. During the reign of the Catholic Kings, the Spanish Church had witnessed a profound renewal in the spiritual and intellectual life of the mendicant orders. The Dominicans of Castile were as much influenced by the ascetic teachings of Savaronola as by the revival of Thomist theology. Among the Franciscan provinces the observant wing of the order replaced the lax conventuals. Before heading the mission to Mexico, Martín de Valencia had served as the first provincial of San Gabriel de Extremadura, a new province created from a group of priories already renowned for their austerity and for their commitment to preaching the gospel to the moriscos of Granada. The first archbishop of Mexico, Juan de Zumárraga, a Franciscan well-versed in the writings of Erasmus, composed a catechism which set out Christian doctrine in simple, biblical language. So too, in Michoacán Bishop Vasco de Quiroga established hospitals in all Indian villages and founded two communities along lines suggested by More's *Utopia*.[6] The millennial expectation then current among many Franciscans here fused with the hopes of the Northern Renaissance for a rebirth of the primitive Church, hopes as much alive in these years amidst Catholic circles as among Protestant reformers. In architecture these expectations led the mendicants to construct churches built in late Gothic style, which were distinguished by their high, single-naved simplicity, with only a Renaissance or plateresque façade to indicate the advent of new aesthetic fashions in Europe. For the most part built in the middle years of the century, these churches testify to the essentially medieval quality of the spiritual conquest.[7] In Spain the renewal of religious enthusiasm preceded the Protestant Reformation and the conversion of the natives of New Spain must be counted among the chief works of that renewal. In any discussion of the Catholic Church in the sixteenth century the establishment of the Mexican Church must thus occupy an important place.

II

The chronicler who best expressed the euphoria of the early years of missionary endeavour was Toribio de Benavente (1500?–1569), better known by his Nahuatl name of Motolinia, 'the poor one'. In exultant terms, he celebrated the flight of the new Israel from the Egypt of idolatry into the Promised Land of the Christian Church. The spiritual conquest was thus a liberation and, above all else, an exodus. As one of the first twelve friars to arrive, Motolinia marvelled at the docility and devotion of the Indians, praising their willing attendance at sermons and mass, and their acceptance of penitence and fasting as necessary means of salvation. Terrified by the doctrines of hell-fire and eternal damnation, many natives made heart-felt confessions of their sins. Above all, Motolinia concentrated on the great collective acts of the Catholic liturgy, describing a torch-lit procession, held at night on the eve of Good Friday, where each penitent lashed the back of the man who preceded him. An entire chapter of his work was devoted to a description of the public enactments of the story of Adam and Eve, and of the reconquest of Jerusalem by the emperor and Pope assisted by a joint army of Indians and Spaniards, all the dialogue of these pieces spoken in Nahuatl. By 1540, so he calculated, over 4 million natives

4 The first twelve Franciscans in Mexico

had been baptised, numbers rendered credible by the admission that he himself, assisted by only one other friar, had administered the sacrament to no less than 14,200 Indians in the space of five days.[8]

Not content with this exuberant celebration of the birth of the Mexican Church, Motolinia was also at pains to commend the intelligence and talents of the Mexican Indian. Assisted by instruction from Pedro de Gante, a Flemish Franciscan, the natives of the capital had acquired a knowledge of Spanish arts and crafts with remarkable ease and rapidity. Within a few years, Indians acted as masons, carpenters and sculptors, helping to build churches and convents under the direction of the mendicants. Indeed, within a generation several notable Indian artists emerged, men who produced serviceable copies of the paintings and prints brought over from Flanders and Spain. As for the children of the nobility, not merely did they master Spanish and learn how to read and write, some of the most talented even studied Latin and theology. So impressed were the Franciscans at their progress that three or four young pupils were admitted into the Order, although experience soon proved that the Indians were not ready for the priesthood, since they were better fitted for marriage than celibacy.

If Christian baptism was thus interpreted as an exodus from the land of idolatry, it soon became obvious that the new Israel still hankered after the forbidden rites of Egypt. It was thus necessary for the friars to make a study of pagan religion. In any case, preaching the gospel required an intimate knowledge of native languages and in particular a familiarity with the concepts and vocabulary of religious belief and morality. How else could the words be found for an accurate and persuasive expression of Christian doctrine and worship? At the same time, in his *Historia de los indios de la Nueva España* (1541) Motolinia emphasised the cruelties of Aztec rites, with the unparalleled practice of human sacrifice and ritual cannibalism offering clear evidence that Mexico had formed a veritable kingdom of darkness prior to the Spanish conquest. In the pantheon of deities and the cycle of feasts, he perceived the unmistakable hand of the Devil, who through false oracles had actively intervened to pervert Indian religion. In this emphasis on demonic possession, Motolinia was indebted to Andrés de Olmos, the first Franciscan to make a study of native religion, who before his arrival in New Spain was already an acknowledged expert on magic, superstition and witchcraft, having once assisted Zumárraga in a witch-hunt in the Basque provinces.[9] From the outset the Franciscans in New Spain differed from Las Casas in giving greater weight to the active intervention of the Devil in Indian religion.

At the same time, Motolinia praised the Indians' strict morality both as regards the education of their children and in the severe punishments meted out to anyone found guilty of such offences as adultery and drunkenness. He acknowledged that they possessed *ius gentium et civile*, which is to say, the law of nations and their own positive law.[10] Equally important, he provided the first detailed account of the Mexican calendar, thus initiating a line of analysis that was destined to occupy a central role in any assessment of Indian culture. For the calendar demonstrated that the peoples of Anáhuac possessed a remarkable knowledge of the movements of the heavens. Moreover, properly understood, the calendar offered a key to unlock the mysteries of Indian chronology and of the annual cycle of feasts. It was in this connexion that Motolinia reported that the Aztecs kept a set of illustrated books, now known as codices, which dealt with the chief rites and feasts of their religion, with omens and soothsayings, and 'the count of the years', a book which recorded the chief events and reigns of kings.[11] Although most of the codices were destroyed either during the conquest or by the first missionaries who indiscriminately burnt them as tools of necromancy, they had always required interpretation and commentary by priests and scribes, trained in oral exposition. From these men Motolinia obtained information on native history, learning that the Mexica were relative newcomers to Anáhuac, immigrants from the North whose culture was far inferior to the Culhua Toltecs who preceded them. He calculated that the Mexica had arrived in the central valley in 1092 and that they had founded Tenochtitlan in 1300, the precision of these dates derived from his interpretation of the calendar.[12] For the rest, Motolinia praised the wisdom of the two lords of Texcoco in the fifteenth century, Nezahualcoyotl and Nezahualpilli, rulers famous for their heroic life, poetry and justice. He followed Cortés in marvelling at the grandeur of Tenochtitlan when encountered by the Spanards, offering some measure of the great temple and the wealth of the palace of Moctezuma. In all this, what was entirely lacking was the systematic analysis offered by Las Casas in his *Apologética historia sumaria*, where the concept of natural law and comparison with the Ancient World provided a criterion by which to appraise the quality of the Mexica. By contrast, Motolinia appeared fascinated by the grandeur of Indian civilisation yet repelled by its religion so that in the last resort he depicted an advanced culture radically corrupted by demonic intervention, an approach, it should be noted, remarkably similar to that adopted by St Augustine in his treatment of the Roman Empire and its religious cult.

If the contrast between the terrors of Egypt and the joys of the Promised Land was skilfully drawn, Motolinia made no bones about admitting that the Exodus across the desert offered a bitter passage for the Indians as they were assaulted by ten symbolic plagues. These afflictions consisted of the loss of life in the actual conquest and subsequent civil wars, the enslavement and ill-treatment meted out by the encomenderos, the forced drafts of labour for construction work in the capital, the much abused contingents of labourers required for the mines and agriculture, the effects of famine, and finally, the incursions of smallpox, the plague and other lethal diseases. By 1540 the classic

afflictions of 'war, plague and famine' compounded by pervasive exploitation
of labour for the benefit of the Spanish settlers, had already, so Motolinia
estimated, carried off a third of the native population. The new Israel thus paid
a bitter price for its redemption. At the same time, Motolinia drew comfort
from the comparison of Mexico with Peru and the Caribbean. If the blind
avarice of the Spaniards had left the Islands devastated and Peru dominated by
civil war, by contrast in New Spain the Franciscans had succeeded in protecting
the Indians from the worst excesses of the conquerors. It was largely thanks to
their inspiration that the city of Puebla had been established, a city for Spanish
farmers and artisans rather than of conquerors or encomenderos, where, with
peaceful colonisation under way, many settlers had taken Indian women for
wives, thus rearing a new Christian mestizo population.[13]

If Motolinia proved so ready to justify the sufferings which accompanied the
Exodus, it was in part because he expected the millennium soon to dawn. As we
have seen, the observant wing of the Spanish Franciscans was strongly
influenced by the prophecies of the twelfth-century Cistercian abbot, Joachim
de Fiore, who had divided all history into three great trinitarian stages
governed respectively by God the Father, the Son and the Holy Spirit.
Historical developments thus acquired a providential significance. For if the
present epoch opened with the Incarnation of Jesus Christ, the third age,
animated by the Holy Spirit, was soon to begin, its advent announced by the
emergence of two orders of 'spiritual men', a prophecy which was fulfilled, so it
was claimed, in the foundation of the Franciscans and Dominicans. Moreover,
St Bonaventure, the Seraphic Doctor, later identified St Francis as the angel of
the Apocalpyse who was to unlock the seal of the sixth and penultimate age, an
epoch to be characterised by an unprecedented preaching of the gospel
throughout the world, albeit marred by the simultaneous appearance of Anti-
Christ. The traditional sequence of seven ages was thus conflated with the three
great stages of the Joachite prophecy, the sixth age inaugurating the dominion
of the Spirit, which was to be consummated in the millennium, the seventh and
last age before the Second Coming of Christ and the Last Judgement.[14] All these
dramatic events, it must be noted, were scheduled to occur in history, before
the end of the world, and thus might well be accompanied by the reign of a
world emperor or an angelic pope, prophecies of which easily entered into this
scheme of expectation.

A Mexican dimension to the Joachite prophecies emerged when Motolinia
interpreted the joyous conversion of the Indians of New Spain as a presage of
the approaching reign of the Spirit. Like Columbus before him, he calculated
that with a possible 5,200 years before Christ and 1,542 after his birth, there
remained little time before the last days. Elsewhere, recalling the four empires
of Babylon, the Medes and Persians, the Greeks and the Romans, he saluted
Charles V as 'the leader and captain' of the fifth monarchy of Jesus Christ, a

realm destined to encompass the world. Thus the sixth age inaugurated by St Francis was well advanced, so that little time remained for the conversion of the Indians. In a striking passage he wrote: 'Since at the beginning the Church flourished in the East, which is at the start of the world, now at the end of the centuries, it has to flower in the West, which is at the end of the world.' New Spain resembled Egypt, both in the strength of its paganism and in its Christian fervour, and like its counterpart was 'a most fit land for hermits and contemplatives'. So central a role in Church history was Mexico destined to play that Motolinia speculated that when on Mount Alverna St Francis had conversed with God, there receiving his stigmata, possibly he had been informed of the conversion of these western peoples of the Indies.[15] In accordance with these high expectations, he emphasised the evident sanctity of Martín de Valencia, the Franciscan leader, who, unable to learn an Indian language, had retired to a cave near Amecameca in the district of Puebla, where his long sessions of prayer and penitence won him the veneration of neighbouring Indians. Returning to the theme of conversion, Motolinia apostrophised the city of Mexico in these striking terms: 'You were once Babylon, full of confusion and evil; now you are another Jerusalem, the mother of provinces and kingdoms.' The barbaric decrees of a heathen tyrant had been replaced by the wise laws of the Catholic King. In the temporal sphere, all that remained was for the emperor to send an *infante*, a younger son or a nephew, to govern New Spain; after all, the conquests of Alexander had been divided into several kingdoms.[16]

It was the very strength of Motolinia's millennial expectations that drove him into controversy with Las Casas. Already, in 1538, the Dominican had offended him by obtaining episcopal condemnation for the practice of mass baptism of which he was a proponent. But it was his reading of the *Brevísima relación*, together with the accompanying *Confesionario* that demanded denial of absolution until penitents made instant restitution of their property to Indians, which angered Motolinia and led him to write a letter to Charles V in 1555 roundly attacking the Dominican. For certain, he admitted that the Indian population of New Spain had greatly declined in number, in some parts by two-thirds, in other parts by four-fifths or even seven-eighths. But he denied that the Spaniards were primarily responsible for this dramatic and progressive decline. Once the initial effects of conquest and enslavement were past, it had been the successive plagues – smallpox and typhus – which had despatched most Indians into the next world.[17] The reasons why the Indians proved so susceptible to these epidemics remained a mystery to Motolinia. Possibly, it was a divine punishment for their previous idolatry. Possibly, it was because their 'nature' was weak, with drunkenness an ever-present menace and the plague their chief enemy. Whatever the case, it was wrong to blame all Spaniards. Not all encomenderos were villains; indeed, some had encouraged the religious in their ministry and others were good Christians. As for the charge of seizing land, there was now, with the disappearance of so many Indians, land enough for both Indians and Spaniards.

It was Las Casas' unqualified condemnation of the conquest which most offended Motolinia. After all, the Mexicans themselves were comparative newcomers to Anáhuac who had conquered most of their empire barely a hundred years before the arrival of the Spaniards; they were cruel tyrants guilty of the worst crimes against God and nature. Any attempt at peaceful conversion along the lines prescribed by Las Casas would have provoked instant and unnecessary martyrdom. In any case, once the inevitable bloodshed of the conquest was over, the Indians had been relatively well-treated, their tribute and labour drafts carefully regulated, the law-courts welcoming appeals for protection. Not content with this defence, Motolinia then called into question the very mission of Las Casas, describing him as a false prophet, a man 'so assertive, unquiet, demanding, quarrelsome and litigious', who only knew 'a little canon law' and was not above breaking his own precepts, using unpaid Indians to carry his baggage. He was the enemy of the Spanish nation, whose attacks would be read by both foreigners and Indians, anxious to condemn the conquest.[18] By contrast, Motolinia now drew out the full implications of his exodus theology by arguing that Providence had chosen Cortés to open the door in New Spain for the preaching of the gospel, an affirmation which led him to salute the conqueror as 'the captain of this western land' and as 'a child of salvation', who had always sought to protect the Indians and ensure their conversion.

III

Where Motolinia exalted in triumphalist vein over the new Israel's exodus from its Egyptian idolatry, his chief disciple, Jerónimo de Mendieta (1525–1604), assumed the mantle of the prophet Jeremiah and lamented the fall of the new Jerusalem, with Mexico City now become another Babylon, its native inhabitants thrust into captivity. By 1596, when he completed his *Historia eclesiástica indiana*, mulattos and mestizos, ever growing in numbers, vied with Spaniards to abuse the Indians, actively corrupting where they did not exploit. By then, the Indian population of New Spain, so he concluded, barely reached an eighth of its number prior to the conquest. In the periodic incursion of epidemic disease, the chief cause of this radical decline, Mendieta now discerned the operation of Divine mercy, liberating the luckless natives from further abuse.[19] What for Motolinia had been the incidental sufferings of a desert journey, had become for Mendieta permanent features of Indian life under Spanish rule. Small wonder that he echoed Las Casas in so much of what he had to say.

If he wrote with such evident bitterness, it was because Mendieta had arrived in New Spain in 1554, which is to say, at a time when, although the mendicants were by then caught up in the multifarious business of re-settlement of villages and church building, several figures of the first generation of missionaries still remained active, offering living testimony of the ideals and expectations that had animated their enterprise. In his portrait of Andrés de Olmos, drawn from memory, he noted how the old man, gaunt from continual fasting, had practically lost all taste or appetite for food. What emerged from his nostalgic recollection was the perception of a striking congruence between the nature of the Indians and the social vision of the mendicants. If the Franciscans exalted 'Our Lady Poverty' as their spiritual ideal, then in the Indians of New Spain they encountered a race of men not merely blessed with remarkably few material possessions but who equally appeared to lack an acquisitive spirit. To cap the similarity, the Indians had the simplicity of children and were as obedient to their superiors as any religious bound by oath. It was these characteristics that led Mendieta to exclaim: 'In all the world there has never been discovered a people more ready or fitted to save their souls than the Indians of New Spain.'

To win the devotion of such a people required exemplary dedication from the friars who found themselves driven back to the austere precepts of St Francis. They had 'to walk unshod and barefoot, with habits of thick serge, spare and torn, to sleep on a single mat with a staff or a bundle of dry grass for a pillow, with a *tortilla* of maize and chile, cherries and cactus fruit'. Moreover, this strenuous physical regime was matched by the necessity of adapting themselves to the character of their flock. 'They had to put aside the anger of the Spaniards, their pride and presumption, and make themselves Indians with the Indians, phlegmatic and patient as they are, poor and half-naked, gentle and humble as they are.' In these images conjured by Mendieta, we enter a world reminiscent of the *Fioretti* of St Francis, in which holy men, their bodies torn by fasting and self-flagellation, their nights consumed in prayer, engaged in spiritual combat against Satan to liberate Anáhuac from the kingdom of darkness. Never since the days of the Apostles, wrote a Franciscan provincial, had the Church witnessed such enthusiasm for hearing the gospel or such zeal for winning souls.[20]

It must be confessed that in the last resort Mendieta was more concerned to commemorate the exemplary lives of his fellow Franciscans – he saluted his own province of the Holy Gospel as 'the head and leader of this Church' – than to celebrate the Christian devotion of the Indians as the new Israel. True, he certainly depicted the scenes of initial enthusiasm. Moreover, he explained that the Franciscans had made it 'their first and principal action to congregate and erect colleges for children'. It was from the progeny of the nobility that they learnt native tongues and it was these youngsters who assisted them in acting as

5 Franciscan evangelisation

interpreters. 'Children were the masters of the evangelists, children were also the preachers, and children the agents of the destruction of idolatry.' So loyal were these young disciples that on occasion they even denounced their own parents for persistence in pagan worship, actions which at times led them to being beaten by irate relatives and on occasion suffering martyrdom.[21] But Mendieta had to admit that these initial scenes of ritual euphoria and individual enthusiasm slowly disappeared as the century drew to its close, with the Indians becoming increasingly demoralised. Whereas prior to the conquest drunkenness had been severely punished or restricted to ceremonial occasions, after the arrival of the Spaniards the Indians became addicted to the consumption of pulque, the fermented juice of the maguey cactus, suffering all the attendant vices of promiscuity and violent quarrels. Indeed, they slowly lost their former zeal for religious practice, no longer flocking to the churches as they had done in the first years after their conversion. Part of the problem sprang from the decay of the Indian elite, since with the loss of land and the right to tributary draft labour the nobility were reduced to the condition of commoners, obliged to till the fields to eke out a subsistence. Then again, many Indians had become infected with a mania for litigation and consumed their patrimony in petty disputes over land.

Although Mendieta thus painted a bleak picture of a demoralised society, its morality in decay, he did not doubt that the Indians were still true, devout Christians, whose salvation could be assured, provided they could be separated from the Spaniards and subjected to firm paternal rule. If only, he once exclaimed, the Indians could be all transported to the mythical islands of the Antilles, 'then they would lead quiet and peaceful lives in the service of God, as in an earthly paradise, and at the end of their lives go straight to heaven'.[22] Such a separation, however, entailed perpetual tutelage rather than independence. In a letter, Mendieta defined the average Indian as a grown child, the equivalent of a Spanish boy of twelve, more in need of the protection of a father than of the authority of a governor. Nor did he hesitate to draw the appropriate moral: like most children the Indians were at times all the better for a good beating; they had few sins which could not be cured by twelve strokes of the lash.[23] It logically followed from this definition that the Indians should not be admitted into the priesthood. The experience of the Franciscans at the college of Santa Cruz Tlatelolco, where talented young noblemen studied theology and Latin, had demonstrated that 'for the most part . . . the Indians are not fit to command or govern, but rather to be commanded and governed'. The new Israel led so triumphantly by Motolinia from its Egyptian darkness was thus condemned by Mendieta to a condition of permanent tutelage in its Promised Land.[24]

In any case, the material conditions of the Indians, and, more particularly, of the Indian elite, suffered an obvious decline in the 1560s. For Philip II despatched Juan de Valderrama as general visitor to New Spain, charged with a review of the fiscal system. The result was that tribute payments, hitherto assessed on entire communities, were converted into a strict capitation tax, with the nobility as much as commoners included. The Indian lords, known as caciques, no longer received the free labour service from the peasantry to which they were accustomed. Moreover, during the administration of Viceroy Martín Enríquez (1569–81) Indian labour drafts, known as *repartimientos de labor*, were organised in a more systematic and exploitative fashion than hitherto had been the case. Each community had to make available up to a tenth of its adult males, for work on Spanish haciendas, in silver mines or on urban construction, their labour remunerated by a daily wage barely sufficient to cover their subsistence.[25] Thus although the encomienda, the object of Las Casas' detestation, had been reduced to a mere pension on tribute returns, its successor, the compulsory labour levy, proved equally onerous, the more especially since Indians were often subjected to considerable abuse by their employers.

To his credit, Mendieta protested sharply to the viceroy and to the Council of the Indies about the injustice of the system and its harmful effect on the Indian population, which still continued to decline in number throughout these years. In the 1580s he supported the memorials of Carpio de Ricarte, a French Franciscan, who compared the Mexican Indians to the children of Israel labouring for Pharaoh in Egypt. Citing Las Casas, Ricarte insisted that since the Indians possessed their own rulers and social hierarchy, they had no general obligation to work for the Spaniards. The implications of this argument were elucidated by the provincials of the three mendicant orders who in a memorial presented to the Crown in the 1590s declared that the commonwealth (*república*) of New Spain comprised two distinct nations: they failed to discern any reason or moral obligation which justified Indian labour levies supplied to the Spaniards, the more especially as by then free wage-labour was available to landowners willing to pay the market rate. If the colonial authorities proved deaf to these protests, it was because with the arrival of Martín Enríquez all the emphasis was on the despatch of bullion to Castile to finance Philip II's European wars. For his part, Mendieta pleaded that at least half the revenue collected in Mexico should remain in the country so as to ensure the protection of the northern frontier and to guard coastal towns from the assaults of English privateers like Drake.[26] The reduction of New Spain to the status of a mere overseas colony of Castile did not fit easily with the Franciscan vision of the new Jerusalem.

In the same years the prestige and status of the mendicants came under attack. Valderrama was horrified at the degree of political authority exercised by the religious over their flock, a power, so he charged, which enabled them to employ Indian labour to construct grandiose churches and priories built on a scale far beyond the necessities of the communities they served. Moreover, they had used their influence to exempt many Indians from royal tribute and the draft levies of the *repartimientos de labor*. So too, Viceroy Martín Enríquez broke with the policies of his predecessors and roundly criticised the mendicants for their ambition 'to govern in the spiritual and temporal spheres in these countries'. At the same time, the bishops now challenged the autonomy of the religious, seeking to subject their missions to episcopal visitation, and where possible, replace the friars by secular clergy. Finally, the audiencia, the high court of justice, questioned the right of the religious to impose any punishments on their native charges or indeed exercise any kind of secular jurisdiction, the preserve, so it was contended, of the corregidores, the district magistrates, appointed throughout New Spain during the course of the 1560s.[27] In short, the opening decades of the reign of Philip II witnessed a sustained assault on the privileges and authority of the missionary church created by the three mendicant orders.

It was this weather change in the attitude of the colonial authorities which led Mendieta to contrast 'the golden age and flower of New Spain' under the benign rule of Cortés, Mendoza and Velasco, with the wintry, silver epoch of Philip II. As early as 1562 he argued that the country required a strong viceroy, endowed with 'absolute power', untrammelled by the audiencia's intrusion, who would govern the Indians as a father. Apart from the viceroy, no other Spanish magistrates or courts should be allowed to meddle in Indian affairs other than in the case of grave crime. Instead, government of the native community should be entrusted to the religious acting in conjunction with Indian lords and nobles. For grown children such as the Indians all that was needed in the way of political authority was the friars as schoolmasters and the viceroy as universal father. As it was, Mendieta lamented that the mendicants had lost 'their authority to punish and correct the Indians, who in consequence now consume their possessions in litigation'. In 1571 Mendieta wrote to the president of the Council of the Indies, Juan de Ovando, to propose that in New Spain two distinct sets of bishops should be appointed to govern Indians and Spaniards respectively. The bishops for the Indians were to be chosen exclusively from the three mendicant orders then active in the mission field, with the rider that their 'dioceses' should be restricted to the parishes administered by their own order, a Franciscan bishop governing Franciscan parishes. After all, he added, until the reign of Constantine the Great bishops had lived in modest style, without all the pomp of great cathedrals, chapters of canons and the high income produced by the tithes.[28] Here, then, was a blueprint for the maintenance of the missionary church, designed to preserve the jurisdiction of the mendicants and to protect the Indians, both now under threat from the secular authorities and the ecclesiastical hierarchy.

The nostalgic bitterness which pervaded the *Historia eclesiástica* was all the more intense because Mendieta retained so much of Motolinia's millennial interpretation of the spiritual conquest. The discovery of America was depicted as an act of Providence rendered all the more striking since it coincided with the capture of Granada and the expulsion of the Jews from Spain, thus enabling the Catholic Kings to prove victorious over the 'three demonic squadrons' of Moors, Jews and idolaters. The Caribbean phase, however, was described as a train of destruction wrought by the Spaniards, with the efforts of Las Casas at Cumaná the only redeeming feature. By contrast, Mendieta followed his master in hailing Hernán Cortés as another Moses leading forth the new Israel into their promised land. His greatest deed was not any feat of arms but rather his kneeling in the dust before Martín de Valencia. Moreover, the foundation of the Mexican Church possessed a dramatic significance within the divine economy of the Catholic Church. For Martin Luther and Hernán Cortés were both born in 1484, so Mendieta averred, albeit wrongly, the very same year when the great temple of Huitzilopochtli at Tenochtitlan had been dedicated amidst scenes of unparalleled sacrificial carnage. So also, in 1519 when Luther led the rich, proud nations of northern Europe into heresy and damnation, Cortés overthrew Satan's kingdom in Mexico and led its poor, humble peoples into the fold of the Catholic Church.[29] For the first, if not for the last time, the New World was called in to redress the balance of the Old. With his gaze fixed upon millennial meaning, Mendieta failed to perceive the irony of describing armed conquest as a spiritual exodus, or of dubbing an alien conqueror as a liberator.

At the close of his long chronicle, Mendieta adverted to the contrast between Motolinia's joyous celebration and his own Jeremiah-like laments. The new Israel had entered its Babylonian captivity. Indeed, its condition was much the same as that encountered by Judas Maccabaeus on Mount Zion under the degrading rule of the Seleucids. In despair, Mendieta turned to Psalm 79 of the Vulgate where the Lord is beseeched to rescue from destruction the vine he has brought out of Egypt. 'Lord God of Hosts, how long wilt thou be angry against the prayer of this people?' Implicit within these biblical allusions was the expectancy of an earthly liberator, of a Messiah who would rescue Israel from its oppressors. But Mendieta chose not to pursue this dangerous line of speculation, but rather prayed that the king of Castile, God's elected agent on earth, would free the Indians from the bonds of avarice.[30] Written at the close of the sixteenth century, *Historia eclesiástica* thus offered little hope for the future; its spiritual message was essentially nostalgic; its view of events more close to the bleak realism of Las Casas than to the apocalyptic hopes of Motolinia.

IV

In addition to offering oral instruction to the Indians, the mendicants wrote and printed a series of works in native tongues, ranging from catechisms and prayers to sermons and *autos*, dramatised scenes designed to illustrate stories from Scripture or central doctrines of the Christian faith. Once again, the Franciscans took the lead, accounting for no less than eighty of the 109 titles known to have been published in the years 1524–72. Of these works some sixty-six were in Nahuatl, the chief language of central Mexico. Needless to say, in this conversion of native tongues into a medium of literary discourse, the role of Indian disciples and interpreters was all-important, since no matter what their mastery of these languages few religious could ever hope to rival the fluency or accuracy of a native speaker. In short, the emergence of Nahuatl as a literary medium derived from the intimate collaboration of friars and their native disciples. At the humdrum level of everyday existence, the Indian elite were quick to apply their new-found skill to frame last wills and testaments, to record acts of their town councils, to notarise sales and purchases of property, and to engage in correspondence, all set down in Nahuatl.[31] Municipal archives still preserve the documents that testify to the rapidity with which the nobility acquired and applied the art of reading and writing in their own language. Equally important, at a more elevated level, there was some attempt to preserve or compose pieces of poetry, to translate passages from Christian scriptures, and to compose works of history. In short, the sixteenth century witnessed the emergence of an entire literature in Nahuatl, signalising the conversion of an oral tradition into written form, through which the native elite sought to maintain, if not extend, their cultural and social identity.

Nowhere was the defence of cultural identity more obvious and successful than in the attempt to retrieve the historical record. In central Mexico the Aztecs and other peoples had possessed codices, which recorded 'the deeds and story of conquests and wars, of the succession of the chief lords and in what year and under what lord there had occurred droughts, signs from heaven and general plagues; and all the lords who governed New Spain until the arrival of the Spaniards'. During the conquest the records of Texcoco and Tenochtitlan were burned and what remained were often destroyed by the mendicants. Thereafter, the native authorities in most towns embarked on a sustained effort to compile new records, at first using traditional glyphs, the native pictographs, which, however, were soon annotated by Nahuatl commentaries, and subsequently converted into written annals, and then, if necessary, translated into Spanish to form a coherent narrative. In the remote town of Quauhtinchan, situated in the modern state of Puebla, a complex codex was initiated during the 1550s, now known as the *Historia Tolteca–Chichimeca*, which offered fascinating illustrations, pictographs, and a seemingly impenetrable thicket of place names, genealogies, lists of rulers, enigmatic dialogues and scenes, and bare annals – in short, the bare bones of history, all presented without narrative, and still dependent on extensive commentary for any degree of intelligibility.[32] The recuperation of the historical record did not spring from

6 Title page of Alonso de Molina, *Vocabulario en lengua mexicana y castellana*

any disinterested quest for knowledge, but derived from the practical necessity of authenticating traditional claims to noble status and territorial rights.

At the head of the native elite's quest to reaffirm their cultural identity stood the masters and former students of the College of Santa Cruz Tlatelolco. In the first years after its foundation in 1536 the Franciscans taught their pupils Latin and the elements of theology and philosophy with the aim of preparing them for the priesthood. And although, as Mendieta confessed, they entrusted the college to native masters when they found the students more inclined to marriage than celibacy, nevertheless, they relied upon these one-time disciples to assist them in their translations of sermons, scripture and plays into Nahuatl. It was these same men who often rose to become governors of their districts, acting as political intermediaries between the Indian community and the Spanish authorities. In his *Sermonario en lengua mexicana* (1606) Fr Juan Bautista, a Franciscan born in New Spain, paid tribute to a select number of these first 'sons' of the college of Santa Cruz, praising both their knowledge of Latin and the Christian devotion manifest in their concern to assist the Franciscans prepare works in Nahuatl. In particular, he singled out Antonio Valeriano, governor of the Indian suburb of the capital, San Juan Tenochtitlan, for over thirty years, who spoke and wrote in Latin with remarkable elegance. At the same time, he lamented that with the passing of that generation – Valeriano died in 1605 – there were few Indians who still spoke correct or elegant Nahuatl. Although the Franciscans attempted to revitalise the college at Tlatelolco in the 1570s, with the result that as late as 1584 its pupils were described performing a brief play for the visitor, by the end of the century its buildings had crumbled and it survived merely as a school for young children.[33]

The melancholy decline of Santa Cruz Tlatelolco should not obscure the central role it played in the preservation of knowledge of Indian culture and in the creation of a distinctive Mexican historical tradition. For it was in the college that Bernardino de Sahagún (1499?–1590), the greatest scholar among the Franciscans who mastered Nahuatl, taught in the 1530s and again from the 1570s onwards, and there encountered the native disciples who assisted him in his life-long research into Indian culture. A student at Salamanca before his arrival in New Spain in 1529, Sahagún conceived the project of composing a *Calepino*, which is to say, a demonstrative vocabulary, an illustrated dictionary of literary and spoken Nahuatl. When his pastoral ministry took him to priories at Texcoco, Tepopulco and Mexico, he extended the scope of his inquiries. First in Tepopulco during the 1540s and later at Tlatelolco, Sahagún systematically questioned the Indian lords and nobility and then recorded their depositions in Nahuatl. Here is no place to discuss the complex question of the dates and sources of his great work: sufficient to note that if the first draft dates from 1549, the version in Nahuatl was only completed in 1569. The massive bilingual recension, now known as the *Códice Florentino*, set out in parallel columns of Spanish and Nahuatl, accompanied by lavish illustrations drawn by native artists, was completed in 1575–6 and was followed by another version in Spanish probably copied in 1579. It should be noted that the *Historia general de las cosas de Nueva España* was first composed in Nahuatl and that the Spanish version, some introductory matter apart, is a translation. It was this feature that distinguished the work from all other contemporary chronicles and which raises the question of the degree to which Sahagún's native collaborators should be regarded more as co-authors than as mere assistants. This was especially the case with book twelve which dealt with the Indian account of the conquest. For whereas Sahagún wrote a plain, unadorned Spanish prose, recent analysis and translation has shown that the Nahuatl version of these events often rises to genuine literary eloquence and poetic beauty, its prose distinguished by rhythmic force and assonance.[34]

Divided into twelve books, the *Historia general* described the origin and attributes of the Mexican gods, omens, soothsayers; the heavenly constellations and nature; kings, lords, merchants and commoners; and concluded with specimen orations and prayers and the native account of the conquest. Far from being a history – it was relatively weak on past events – it constituted an encyclopaedia covering virtually all aspects of Mexican religion, society and natural philosophy. Book seven, which dealt with rhetoric and moral philosophy, consisted of a collection of formal orations, prayers and moral exhortations. Much of the text thus formed a vast source-book, an anthology of myths and rhetoric, a guide to literary and linguistic usage. Indeed, at times the linguistic purpose appears to have predominated since the material was deployed more to illustrate usage than to describe the philosophic or social realities it purports to describe. To a marked degree, the *Historia general* is a work of literature: Sahagún effectively presided over the birth – alas, stillborn – of Nahuatl literature, at a time when only the older generation of Indian nobles still preserved the memory and practice of the classic language.

In the event, Sahagún's life-work failed to yield its expected fruit. For many years impeded by lack of funds and encouragement from his immediate superiors, he was heartened in 1575 by a royal decree ordering him to prepare a Spanish version of his text and despatch it to Spain. At that time, Juan de Ovando, president of the Council of the Indies, circularised all colonial authorities, requesting that extant chronicles and manuscripts dealing with the conquest should be sent to Madrid to assist the newly appointed cosmographer royal to compose an authoritative history of the Indies. However, in 1577, after Ovando's death, Philip II issued a notorious decree prohibiting all further inquiry into native history and religion. All material on these subjects was to be confiscated and despatched to Madrid. In Mexico Viceroy Martín Enríquez sought to impound Sahagún's surviving manuscripts and thus deprive the old man of any hope of seeing his life-work in print.[35] Some years before, the scriptural translation of Gilberto Maturini, a fellow Franciscan, had been seized and its author imprisoned by the Inquisition. At much the same time, in Peru, Viceroy Toledo commissioned an official history of the Incas and equally strove to suppress any further inquiry into the native past. It should be recalled that in Spain itself during this decade Fr Luis de León was imprisoned by the

Inquisition on the charge of preferring the Hebrew and Greek texts of the Bible to the Latin Vulgate.[36] With the Counter-Reformation in full tide in the Hispanic world the patient, disinterested scholarship of Sahagún was at a discount. Whatever the cause, all the complete texts of his great work ended up abroad, and it was not until the nineteenth century that it saw the light of day, albeit even then in often corrupt form.

In the Spanish version of the *Historia general*, Sahagún inserted a considerable range of reflections on the progress of the spiritual conquest in New Spain. In a revealing argument, he justified his great enterprise of research by declaring that in the same way that a doctor had to study all types of disease so as to know best how to cure his patients, so equally the Christian missionary had to acquire a profound knowledge of the manifold forms of idolatry so as to enable him both to detect its presence, often hidden, and devise adequate means to destroy it root and branch. Without such specialised knowledge, there was the danger that priests would mistake superficial conformity for true assent to Christian truth, failing to discern the survival of pagan beliefs and practices. Equally important, it was through a thorough mastery over native language and modes of thought that the religious could find the words and the ways in which to express Christian doctrine and worship in an accurate and persuasive fashion. Indeed, without precision in the use of language, heresy or blasphemy could easily infect or mar the best-intentioned translation. In final defence of his endeavours, Sahagún appealed to the precedent of the *City of God*, where St Augustine had conducted a detailed discussion of Roman religion.[37]

What does emerge from the Spanish version of 1579 is Sahagún's deep-seated pessimism about the entire missionary enterprise, a pessimism which amounted to outright scepticism as to its final value. It was not that he was tempted to deny the quality or talent of the Mexican Indians: 'there is no art which they do not have the intelligence to learn or use'. They were quite capable of learning grammar, rhetoric and theology. It was only ill-informed prejudice which led Spaniards to criticise the Santa Cruz College on the grounds that it was impossible for Indians to learn Latin and positively dangerous for them to study theology. Yet some students had acquired an excellent knowledge of Latin and none had been tempted into heresy. However, Sahagún admitted that no Indian had been admitted into the priesthood, largely because it was thought they could not sustain the requirement of celibacy. The problem here was that 'the temperature and abundant character of this land and the constellations which govern it greatly assist human nature to be vicious, indolent and given over to sensual vices'. Before the conquest the Indians had certainly obeyed a strict morality, but at that time the determining bias of the constellations had been countered by a rigorous education, the practice of warfare, and severe punishment for all offences. By the 1570s the old forms of government had disappeared: the conquest had destroyed morality as much as idolatry, so that the Indians were now submerged in drunkenness, a vice which in turn led to violent quarrels and sexual promiscuity. Sahagún confessed that the Franciscans had expected too much of their young disciples, subjecting mere boys to fasting, night-prayers and penitence, without allowing them any exercise. Even so, in the first years the Santa Cruz College had worked reasonably well, its pupils helping the friars to compose sermons and catechisms. But now, some forty years on, the situation was beyond remedy. The Indians were no longer docile but more often drunk and deceitful, and were 'burdensome to govern and little inclined to learn'.[38] They were certainly no longer fit to become priests.

So severe was the onslaught of the great plague of 1575–7, when 2 million Indians were thought to have died, that Sahagún openly wondered whether the native population of New Spain would survive. Sufficiently Franciscan to praise Cortés as another Joshua, a servant of God chosen by Providence to overthrow paganism, Sahagún concluded that the Indians of New Spain had suffered the fate that the prophet Jeremiah had foretold of the Jews: that Israel would be conquered by an ancient, mighty nation 'who would consume the harvest, the vines, the flocks and overthrow their cities'. At the same time, his experience of listening to confessions during the great plague of those years had caused him to doubt the reality of the Christian faith of his native penitents. New Spain, he concluded despondently, had turned out to be 'a sterile land, needing much toil to work it'. Were the Spaniards now to abandon it, then within fifty years no trace of Christianity would linger in the minds of the Mexican Indians.[39] It was this despairing view of native religion that led Sahagún to condemn the pilgrimages to the chapel of Our Lady of Guadalupe at Tepeyac, a small hillside sanctuary situated outside Mexico City. Prior to the conquest there had stood a temple on the same site dedicated to Tonanztin, the Mother of the Gods, which had equally attracted pilgrims. Clearly, the veneration for the Virgin Mary expressed by Indians was but a subterfuge, so Sahagún averred, for continued idolatry. In conclusion, the true significance of the conquest of Mexico, he surmised, might well have been to provide a road, a stepping-stone to China, 'where there are a very clever people, of great knowledge and good government'.[40] Unlike the case of Mexico, if the Christian faith was planted in China, it would endure and thrive.

It would be wrong to conclude our discussion of Sahagún on a note of despair prompted in part by the terrible years of the 1570s when, as epidemic disease carried off thousands, the vice-regal administration increased its demands for Indian labour and enforced the collection of tribute in a rigorous fashion. In any case, Sahagún was by then a man close to eighty whose memories stretched back to the great moments of the spiritual conquest, so exuberantly celebrated by Motolinia. Moreover, he had suffered the bitter disappointment of having the finished manuscripts of his great work despatched to Spain, there to moulder in archives without any hope of publication. In the last decade of his life – he died in 1590 – Sahagún returned to work on his materials dealing with the Mexican Calendar and the allied subjects of native astrology and divination. In 1582 he published a Nahuatl psalmody, a collection of prayers, sermons and scriptural translations, designed to assist the mendicants in their pastoral ministry. Equally important, he composed yet another Nahuatl version of book 12 of his *Historia general* devoted to the native view of the conquest. In this work, above all others, we sense the intervention of that select circle of *colegiales*, college men such as Valeriano and Jacobitin, who had assisted him throughout his enquiries. For we here encounter a narrative of tragic, sombre power, written in a classic Nahuatl which exploits all the poetic resources of the language.[41] At the same time, it offered an interpretation of the conquest which was obviously at odds with the accounts of Gómara and Córtes, soon to be revived and perpetuated by Antonio de Herrera.

To start with, Book 12 provided a striking description of Moctezuma, haunted by omens of ill promise, torn by anguish at the news of the arrival on the coast, and fearful that the Spaniards were the emissaries of Quetzalcoatl, the ancient god of Tula and Cholula, who according to myth had departed across the western seas promising one day to return to Anáhuac. Although the Mexica worshipped Quetzalcoatl, they had assigned the god a place in their pantheon inferior to Huitzilopochtli, their tribal deity, whom they had elevated into the lordship of the universe. Moctezuma sent ambassadors to Córtes bearing gifts appropriate to the god, with instructions to clothe him in the regalia of Quetzalcoatl and offer him human blood to drink.[42] Needless to say, the ambassador's dramatic report of the Spaniards' ships, cannons, horses and mastiffs all filled the Indian monarch with even greater anguish. At the same time, the nobles noted that the Spaniards had fingered gold objects in the presents as if they were monkeys. The text insists that Moctezuma welcomed Cortés into Tenochtitlan, inviting him as Quetzalcoatl to take up his throne, confessing that he felt as if in a dream witnessing ancient prophecies now realised. There is remarkable power in the description of the conquerors entering the city, the hounds panting and sniffing, the standard-bearer tossing his banner, the horses neighing, their bells jingling, their mouths afoam, the arquebusiers firing their weapons, the air filled with the smoke and smell of gunpowder – all this has the poetic force of an eye-witness account, conveying the sheer terror of the Indians at the fierce apparitions from another world. So also, the full horror of Alvarado's massacre of the young Mexica noblemen is conveyed through an almost bemused description of the impact of steel swords on human flesh, with bodies ripped asunder, their intestines spilling to the ground. Finally, the text achieved epic intensity in its portrayal of the siege of Tenochtitlan, the population suffering from hunger and smallpox, the warriors sallying forth in daily battle against both Spaniards and their erstwhile Indian allies and subjects. The courage of the young Cuauhtémoc was contrasted to the fate of Moctezuma, casually murdered by the Spaniards before they fled the city. With the city taken, the Mexica found themselves at the mercy of a ruthless enemy, their young women taken for concubines, their young men branded on their faces as slaves, their leaders tortured for news of treasure.[43] Such is the intensity of the narrative, its text an amplification of post-conquest annals, that we must surely assume native authorship, or, alternatively, endow Sahagún with a literary power in Nahuatl that was quite unavailable to him in writing Spanish. Whatever the case, it should be emphasised that this native account clearly asserted that Cortés was welcomed peacefully into Tenochtitlan as Quetzalcoatl, so that the Mexica thus accepted a *translatio imperii*; armed conflict only started after Alvarado's treacherous attack. Here were themes that were to echo across much of subsequent interpretation of the conquest.

V

The singular quality of the Franciscan enterprise in New Spain is confirmed by the contrast offered by the Mexican Dominicans. From the start, the first provincial, Domingo de Betanzos, had been notorious for his scornful opinion of the abilities and talents of the Indians, uttering a deathbed repentence of his views only after being subjected to forceful remonstrance from Las Casas. Of course the Dominicans soon learnt native tongues and assumed direction of the conversion of many communities, especially in the southern provinces of New Spain. At least one friar of their province, Diego Durán, displayed a keen interest in the Indian past and indeed composed an extensive chronicle about the Mexica which numbers among the most important sources on their history. But his interest was apparently peculiar to himself, his chronicle soon lost, and his Dominican brethren unconcerned by its suppression. When in 1596 Agustín Dávila Padilla, a Mexican-born Dominican, used his prerogative and income as archbishop of Santo Domingo, to publish a history of his Order's apostolic labours in New Spain, he abruptly began his narrative with the arrival of the first friars in 1526, thus omitting any description of the Indian past or any discussion of the conquest. In appearance, his chronicle was a simple, staid account of the lives of holy friars, all praised for their asceticism or their labours as evangelists. In particular, Betanzos was extolled in terms remarkably similar to the portrait of Martín de Valencia penned by Motolinia. Both men were depicted as great ascetics; neither managed to learn an Indian language; and together once projected a journey across the ocean to China, anxious to encounter a more propitious soil for the gospel seed than New Spain. Indeed, Dávila remarked that Betanzos had predicted that the Mexican Indians were destined to disappear from the face of the earth, a prophecy which the subsequent ravages of the plague seemed likely to confirm.[44]

Unlike Sahagún, Dávila displayed great confidence in the results of the spiritual conquest. Marvelling at the devotion of the Mexican Indians, he commented on the long hours many of them spent in church, their devotion to the celebration of the Catholic liturgy, and the reverence they displayed to the religious. Himself born in Mexico, he thus rejected the reservations entertained by Spanish mendicants. At the same time, he roundly criticised the viceregal policy, revived in the 1590s, of resettling and concentrating in new towns the remnants of the native population. He provided a list of all the plagues they had suffered with estimates of the millions who had perished. More important, he argued that if the Indians were left in their scattered hill-side hamlets, they were far more likely to escape the worst effects of the plague than if they were exposed to urban contamination. In short, the entire policy of resettlement was here called into question and in part held responsible for the horrendous decline in Indian numbers.[45]

There are other surprises in the staid pages of Dávila. For he strongly endorsed the Dominican campaign on behalf of the American Indians, noting that it was the Dominican bishop of Tlaxcala, Julián Garcés, who had obtained from Pope Paul III the declaration that the natives of the New World were fully human and as such entitled to live as free subjects of the king of Spain. Nor did he hesitate to deplore the devastation of the Caribbean or to condemn Alvarado's massacre as wanton murder, accepting the estimate that by 1542 some 15 million Indians had lost their lives as a direct result of the Spanish conquest. He castigated the attempt to preach the gospel at sword-point as a heresy worthy of Mahomet. In short, Dávila adopted almost in their entirety the denunciations of Las Casas. More important, he provided the first public account of the life of the great Dominican, listing all his principal writings with a brief description of their content. Needless to say, he was careful to insist that at all points in his career Las Casas had enjoyed the support of both Charles V and Philip II, observing that after his term as bishop of Chiapa he was summoned to Spain to advise the court and Council of the Indies on all matters affecting the New World. He declared that Las Casas was a perfect religious, a holy bishop and, above all else, an apostle of the Indians, concluding: 'he spoke like a saint; argued like a jurist; pronounced like a theologian; testified as an eye-witness; and preached with the liberty of a true friar, unconcerned with temporal matters . . .'. Coming as it did from an archbishop and the son of a conqueror, a more authoritative endorsement of Las Casas would be hard to imagine.[46] The implications of this eulogy of the great Dominican were made clear when Dávila adverted to the growing incidence of pirate raids on colonial settlements. He inserted a long description of Sir Francis Drake's sack of Santo Domingo in 1585, lamenting the desecration of churches, the looting of private homes, and the ransom demanded of leading citizens. How was it possible for a mere pirate to challenge the power and might of the Catholic King, a monarch who had defeated the Great Turk, and imposed his will on Italy, Flanders and France? Las Casas had prophesied that God would punish Spain for the crimes wrought by the conquerors in the New World. Was it not possible to discern in these piratical assaults divine retribution at work?[47]

It would be a mistake to dismiss the initial jealousy between Motolinia and Las Casas as the expression of rivalry between the two great orders of friars. From the outset there were at issue two distinct views of the Church and the nature of conversion. For the early Franciscans conceived the foundation of the Mexican Church as making the advent of the sixth age, with collective salvation in history an imminent prospect. By contrast, for Las Casas the Augustinian doctrine of the predestined salvation of the elect ruled out any hope of mass conversion. Whereas Motolinia devoted his life to creating a Church, initiating entire Indian communities into the practice and devotions of medieval Catholicism, a religion which in certain measures endures to this day, Las Casas devoted his formidable energies to promoting reform in the very structure of colonial society, campaigning to secure for the Indians a just recompense for their labour and some degree of civil liberty. If the Franciscan laboured as an apostle, seeking to bring sacramental grace to those in darkness, the Dominican acted as a prophet, denouncing the crimes of men in power and proclaiming the necessity of justice for the poor and oppressed. The irony here was that the spiritual interpretation of historical events, derived from the Joachite prophecies, should have led the Franciscans to defend military conquest as a necessary prelude to the expansion of the Kingdom of God. In the same way as in ancient Judaism the apocalyptic tradition vested its hopes in the advent of an earthly, triumphant Messiah, so equally the millennial movement of the late Middle Ages awaited the appearance of a world emperor, and, in the case of New Spain, did not hesitate to proclaim Cortés as another Moses.

If the spiritual euphoria which possessed the first Franciscans in Mexico drove them into administering baptisms *en masse*, they were also distinguished for their corporate endeavour to penetrate the alien obscurity of native religion and culture. It was an endeavour which drove them to form a close alliance with the Indian elite, and, indeed, through education and conversion create a new elite, better able to transmit their message to the population at large. Moreover, whereas the chronicles of other orders celebrated the heroic zeal of the missionaries, by contrast, in the pages of Motolinia, Sahagún and much of Mendieta, it is the natives of New Spain who occupy the centre of the stage. Indeed, in the great work of Sahagún, the voice of the chronicler is present only in the introductory sections written for the Spanish version; all else derives from native sources. It was precisely this reliance on Indian disciples, which enabled a select elite of native intellectuals to preserve for posterity the memory of their ancestral culture and, equally important, to help the mendicants devise forms of religious devotion appropriate for the Indian peasantry. If the experiment appears to have ended in disillusionment, with Mendieta adopting the prophetic despondency of Las Casas, nevertheless, the writings of the first two generations of Franciscans in Mexico form impressive testimony to a shared religious experience, a euphoric moment when mendicants and Indians joined to celebrate the Christian gospel, the memory of which still illumines the pages of their chronicles.

6

THE PROCONSUL

I

IN 1572 the viceroy of Peru, Francisco de Toledo, despatched an armed
expedition to the jungle fastness of Vilcabamba to capture Tupac Amaru, the
last claimant to the Inca throne. Once in Cuzco the unfortunate young prince
was summarily condemned to death on the charge that he had connived at the
murder of an Augustinian friar; in more general terms the survival of an
independent Inca state, no matter how small, was viewed as a menace to the
peace and stability of Spanish dominion in Peru. Despite pleas for mercy from
all the heads of the religious communities in Cuzco, Toledo invoked his
authority as captain-general, entrusted with the security and defence of the
realm, and ordered Tupac Amaru to be beheaded in the main square, where the
execution was witnessed by thousands of grieving Indians. Subsequent despatches by the archbishop and the audiencia of Lima deplored the unnecessary
scale and expense of the expedition and the undue severity of the sentence. The
execution of the last Inca monarch, performed with such symbolic solemnity,
created a profound impression on both Spaniards and Indians, since it marked
the end of the post-conquest epoch in which Peru had been governed by an
incoherent alliance of encomenderos and native lords. In the seventeenth
century the Augustinian chronicler, Antonio de la Calancha, described the
proceedings as an act of *raison d'état* and characterised Toledo as a disciple of
Machiavelli, since he elevated political expediency above the dictates of
justice.[1]

For his part, the viceroy justified the execution by arguing that the existence
of Vilcabamba prevented Peru from obtaining *asiento*, which is to say, a firm
and enduring settlement of its political order. After Pizarro's judicial murder of
Atahualpa, the Spaniards had recognised his half-brother, Manco Inca, as
emperor, only then so to ill-treat and humiliate the unfortunate prince as to
drive him into leading a general uprising against the conquerors. In 1539,
following the failure of this movement, Manco Inca established himself at
Vilcabamba, carrying with him the gold disc, its centre filled with the ashes of

the hearts of previous emperors, which had been worshipped in the great temple of Coricancha at Cuzco. Thereafter, his sons, Sayri Tupac and Titu Cusi Yupanqui, preserved the independence of their small principality, on occasion sallying forth to treat with the Spanish authorities. During the 1560s, however, a group of kurakas – the Indian lords of the central Highlands – projected a general uprising to restore the Incas to their throne, their conspiracy offering clear evidence of the political role still played by the Inca prince at Vilcabamba. At the same time, it should be noted that another half-brother of Atahualpa, Paullu Inca, had welcomed Spanish rule, remaining in Cuzco, and as reward for his loyalty during the civil wars and rebellion was awarded an extensive encomienda. Despite the services of this branch of the Inca royal family, Toledo arrested the sons of Paullu Inca, confiscated their impressive palace, and sentenced them to exile on trumped-up charges. In this case, the audiencia in Lima succeeded in quashing the sentence, pronouncing the viceroy's assumption of jurisdiction quite unwarranted, a view which was shared by Philip II, who ordered the Indian princes to be restored to their homes and dignity.[2]

That the author of these calculated acts of political terror was a distant relative of the Duke of Alba, whose harsh rule of the Low Countries provoked the Dutch revolt of 1572 tells its own story. Francisco de Toledo (1515–82), the son of the Count of Oropesa, was a life-long courtier, who had accompanied Charles V on his campaigns in Tunis, Germany and Italy, and followed his royal master into retirement at the monastery of Yuste. A *mayordomo* of the king – a title he shared with Viceroy Martín Enríquez – and a knight of the Order of Alcántara, in which he had sworn vows of obedience and celibacy, Toledo displayed all the imperious confidence of a man born to govern. Whereas other viceroys were content to limit their activities to Lima, he travelled extensively across the highlands, personally leading an armed expedition against unpacified Indians of the jungle lowlands. His ambition and ruthless energy were best expressed in a letter to Philip II where he declared: 'I have sought to see everything and have attempted to conquer this kingdom anew for Your Majesty.'[3] The moment was propitious. During the 1560s a general visitation had been conducted by Lope García de Castro, so that much information on Indian communities was already available. At the same time, the debate over the future and status of the encomiendas had been resolved. In particular, Toledo could draw upon the *Gobierno del Perú* (1567) an invaluable treatise composed by Juan de Matienzo (1520–79) a judge of the high court in Charcas, which both analysed the problems of the country and proposed a series of reforms. To implement his policies, Toledo recruited a circle of trusted lieutenants, among whom figured both his Dominican cousin, Fr García de Toledo and the talented adventurer, Pedro Sarmiento de Gamboa. At all points, he took counsel with those settlers and officials who had acquired an

7 Francisco de Toledo

expert knowledge of native language and culture, with men such as Polo de Ondegardo and Juan de Betanzos. What distinguished the twelve years, 1569–81, in which Toledo governed Peru, was the ruthless application of fundamental measures designed to transform and reconstruct on enduring foundations the entire political and social order of the country. Equally remarkable was his insistence on delving into the Inca past to procure evidence to justify his policies and to bequeath to posterity a code of laws, by which Peru was to be governed for many years. It was in recognition of these achievements that Juan de Solórzano, the chief jurist of the empire, later hailed him as 'the Solon of Peru' and a viceroy described him simply as 'our master'.[4] Certainly, dynastic absolutism had few more faithful exponents than Francisco de Toledo.

II

By 1569, when Toledo arrived in Peru the threat to stability emanating from Spanish settlers was largely a matter of the past. The cycle of civil war and rebellion had ended in 1554 and the viceroys who governed the country in subsequent years, the marquis of Cañete and the count of Nieva, took strong measures against the turbulent breed of footloose adventurers who had enlisted in the disturbances of the first thirty years of Spanish rule. Yet as late as 1559–61, Lope de Aguirre recruited his infamous Marañones from these men and led them on a trail of devastation across the backlands of Venezuela. Moreover, only in 1564, after almost a decade of deliberation and inquiry, did the Crown accept the advice of the Council of the Indies and deny the encomenderos their plea for grants in perpetuity, accompanied by jurisdiction, both criminal and civil, over the Indians. It was in these same years that Bartolomé de las Casas denounced Spanish rule in Peru as an unmitigated tyranny, arguing that the kurakas, the Indian lords, were the only legitimate rulers of the country and that the Incas should be restored to some measure of authority.

When Toledo came to consider the matter, he found that Juan de Matienzo strongly recommended that the encomiendas should be given outright as inheritable entails to their present incumbents. 'It is clear that the encomenderos sustain the country and that without them there would be no commonwealth.' In each Spanish town the encomenderos formed a local nobility, their residence an open house for a small entourage of Spaniards. They dominated the town councils and acted as municipal magistrates. Yet they were haunted by the fear that the Crown might decide not to renew their grants for another life and thus deprive their children of their status and source of income. It was for this reason that the Dominican, García de Toledo, argued that the encomiendas should be converted into entails, to allow the Spaniards to take root in Peru, so as 'now to make it into another Spain'. As it was, the Indians lacked any protection from marauding Spaniards and men came to Peru to make their fortunes and then return home. At the same time, Matienzo strongly urged that all exercise of jurisdiction should be reserved to the corregidores, the crown magistrates, who were usually appointed for terms of five years, so that the encomienda should survive as a simple charge on the tribute list rather than become a full-blown feudal institution. However, he then qualified this recommendation by further suggesting that titles of nobility such as duke or marquis should be awarded to 'two or three men in each city, to those who have the largest encomiendas, accompanied with civil and criminal jurisdiction'. In short, he advocated a mixed system of royal and seigneurial government for the Indians.[5]

On this great question, Toledo adopted a compromise solution. His predecessor, the Count of Nieva, had suggested dividing the encomiendas into three distinct classes, the first issued in perpetuity, the second for but one life, and the third reserved to the Crown. So also, Toledo now recommended that a few should be granted in perpetuity in each city and that the rest should revert to the Crown on the death of their present possessor or be merely extended for one further life. By this time, of the 368 encomiendas in central and southern Peru no less than 81 were vacant, so that there was ample room for manoeuvre. In this instance, Toledo's intervention proved less than decisive, since the Council of the Indies decided to confirm succession for a second or a third life, depending on the case, without any promise of perpetuity. In any case, Toledo resolutely opposed any concession of jurisdiction and indeed insisted that encomenderos should fix their residence in Spanish towns. Furthermore, he affirmed that they should not possess any land within the territory of their encomiendas and that they had no right to free labour from the Indians of their grant. At the same time, he challenged the hegemony hitherto exercised by encomenderos within Spanish towns by demanding that at least one of the two annually elected municipal magistrates, *alcaldes ordinarios*, should be chosen from citizens who did not hold an encomienda. When the city council of Cuzco refused to obey this injunction, he imposed his authority by threatening to imprison the councillors who opposed him. One last point requires emphasis. When Toledo recommended the concession of some encomiendas in perpetuity, he justified this measure by observing that, in contrast to tyrants and barbarians such as the Turks, the Christian kings of Europe had always governed their realms with the assistance of a nobility which either possessed landed entails or feudal jurisdiction. It was a revealing observation, the full significance of which should later become apparent.[6]

It was primarily in his dealings with the Indian population, however, that Toledo set his mark on Peru. Adopting the counsel of Matienzo, he set in motion and drove forward a thoroughgoing general visitation, despatching sixty visitors, men chosen for their knowledge of the country and its people, to compile a detailed census of the native population. In addition, they took notice of the distribution of land and the incidence of tribute and labour services. They were also required to question local rulers on the character of Inca government and to assess the nature and scope of Inca exactions. Once assembled, the visitors' reports provided Toledo with the Peruvian equivalent of the Domesday Book, a document compiled with the same ends in view. With its information to hand, Toledo could calculate both the supply of available Indian manpower and the range of customary tribute and services to the State.

To effect his transformation of Peru, Toledo abandoned Lima and ensconced himself in the highlands, travelling extensively for some five years, 1570–5, with the aim of examining at first-hand the problems and possibilities of the viceroyalty. It was his personal intervention that was responsible for the exemplary thoroughness and rapidity with which the next great stage of the visitation was implemented. For once the results of the general survey were known, Toledo imposed a 'reduction' or general re-settlement of the Indian population, concentrating the inhabitants of scattered hill-side hamlets into small towns, each possessed of at least five hundred families. Laid out on a familiar grid system, these towns were all endowed with a church, council chambers and a prison, with the Indians enjoined to establish councils and elect annual magistrates on the Spanish model. Although in subsequent years considerable seepage of population occurred, with many Indians pitching their residence in more convenient sites, all the evidence suggests that a major and permanent relocation of the native community occurred. To this day, the towns established by Toledo still survive as important centres of native life. Recent research for Huarochirí has found that some 121 hamlets were concentrated to form eleven towns.[7]

Unlike similar projects in Mexico, the re-settlement programme did not apparently result in any loss of Indian land; indeed, Toledo sought to halt Spanish encroachment and where necessary even ordered the return of land to the native communities. So also, he demanded strict compliance with the New Laws, urging that all work performed by Indians for the hispanic sector should be remunerated by payment of a wage, preferably in cash: no Spaniard had any right to free labour service. In all this, Toledo's aim was to provide the peasantry with a firm basis in the land while at the same time carefully regulating their economic relations with the settler community. The reason for this concern, however, was not particularly altruistic, since he commanded the district magistrates to maintain detailed lists of all Indian tributaries, which is to say, of all married males between the ages of 18 and 55, and raised the rate to $5\frac{1}{2}$ pesos a head.[8] Since this poll-tax was almost triple the 2 pesos demanded of the Mexican Indians, the presumption here must have been that the natives of Peru were better placed to pay such a sum or, alternatively, that there was simply more money available in the southern viceroyalty. In mitigation, it should be observed that in Peru the clergy were supported by a deduction from the tribute, whereas in New Spain they charged separate fees for the administration of the sacraments. At the same time, Toledo decreed that the class of Indian peasants known as *yanaconas*, who resided on Spanish estates rather than in native communities should henceforth be defined as permanently ascribed to those estates; they were denied freedom of movement, but were guaranteed a plot of ground. Since an estimated 40,000 tributaries were included within the terms of this decree, Toledo clearly sought to endow the colonial landlords with a supply of labour which would not conflict with the demands of the mining sector.[9]

Although he initially adopted a critical attitude to the kurakas, the native lords, accusing them of exercising a tyrannical authority over their subjects, Toledo eventually concluded that 'to govern the Indians, it is necessary to use the caciques'. If tributes were to be collected or labour levies summoned, the experience and authority of the nobility was indispensable. But Toledo was at pains to deny that the kurakas possessed any hereditary right to their titles, insisting that they constituted a class of state officers, appointed by the Crown and paid a small salary deducted from the tributes for their work. All appointments required the viceroy's approval and commoners as much as noblemen could be promoted. To ensure the emergence of a class of men qualified to act as intermediaries between the colonial authorities and the Indian communities, Toledo proposed to establish two colleges, situated respectively at Lima and Cuzco, for the education of the children of the existing nobility. In effect, the kurakas did constitute a hereditary nobility and displayed considerable skill in navigating the stormy waters of post-conquest society.[10] Indeed, in contrast to central Mexico, where the reign of Philip II witnessed a fundamental decline in the fortunes of Indian rulers, in Peru the native nobility emerged strengthened by the effects of Toledo's legislation.

The reform of provincial government was completed by the appointment of corregidores, royal magistrates charged with the collection of tributes, and the administration of all first-instance justice. Although many such officials had been appointed in the 1560s, it was left to Toledo to organise the system on a permanent footing, dividing the viceroyalty into about seventy large districts. Since these officers also presided over the council of any Spanish town or city that fell within their jurisdiction, they effectively replaced the encomenderos and municipal magistrates as the central figure in local administration. Like the local clergy and kurakas, they received a salary deducted from the tributes, an income supplemented by the fruits of justice and other more irregular sources. Although the most lucrative of these posts went to candidates appointed in Madrid, the majority of magistrates were chosen by the viceroy, who used these offices both to reward and enrich members of his own official family and to conciliate the bureaucratic and settler elite. Since tributes were still often paid in kind rather than in cash, corregidores rapidly became involved in commercial activity, selling the produce they collected for the Crown and using tribute monies to fund their own trading ventures. In clear abuse of their position, they levied labour for the manufacture of woollens and employed their native subjects to transport goods for sale in the mining camps, in both cases justifying their exploitation by the necessity of providing the means for the Indians to raise cash to meet their tribute payments. Appointed for limited terms – generally for no more than five years in any one district – the corregidores soon became notorious for their remorseless search for profit, usually obtained at the expense of their subjects.[11] Their replacement of the encomenderos as the chief agent of local government certainly strengthened royal authority, but did little to improve the condition or treatment of the Indians. Indeed, in the long term, the union of trading and judicial functions in the same class of official was to constitute a major source of oppression of the native population.

An essential feature of the Toledan reforms was the destruction of idolatry and the provision of Christian instruction for the native population, each town assigned a priest supported from the tributes. Well aware of the contrast between Mexico and Peru as regards Christian devotion – the recalcitrance of the Andean Indians had been the subject of public comment since the chronicle of Gómara – Toledo complained about the poor quality of the clergy who entered the southern viceroyalty: 'as the first born, New Spain took the cream from the start, and succeeded both in the choice of Church prelates and of religious, so that all were holy, humble men devoted to implanting the gospel among the natives'. By contrast, the civil wars in Peru had deterred the mendicants from entering the country, with the result that secular priests took the lead, men of low morals, more interested in personal profit than in preaching the gospel, who took advantage of their position to abuse the Indians. Whatever the cause, all observers agreed that despite baptism, the natives of Peru remained essentially pagan. Indeed, during the 1560s the central highlands had been swept by a movement known as *taki onkoy* in which native prophets foretold the end of Spanish rule and in frenzied meetings called for the return of the old gods. For their part, the clergy mistrusted their flock to such an extent that the Church Councils held in Lima in 1567 and 1582 not merely denied Indians admission to Holy Orders but also forbade them to receive the Eucharist.[12]

In accordance with his usual defence of royal prerogative, Toledo reproved the clergy, especially the religious, for seeking to exercise political authority over the Indians and commanded them to refrain from either whipping or imprisoning their native flock. The administration of all such punishment was reserved to civil magistrates. He also insisted on the rights of the Crown as universal Patron of the Church, demanding that all ecclesiastical appointments be forwarded to the viceroy for confirmation. To ensure that the clergy should be able to preach the gospel in Quechua, the general tongue of Peru, he founded a chair in that language at the university of San Marcos and decreed that all candidates for parishes should be examined in their knowledge of Quechua. In general, he favoured the religious over the secular clergy as better fitted for the task of converting the natives and in particular sought to enrol the newly arrived Jesuits to enter this field. By this time, however, considerable tension existed between the bishops and the religious over the question of episcopal visitation of all parishes in their dioceses and in consequence the Jesuits refused to become embroiled in this controversy, reserving their efforts for periodic missions rather than accepting the regular administration of parishes. If Toledo proved successful in ensuring the appointment of priests in the towns in which the native population had been re-settled, thus ensuring the presence of active agents of acculturation and conversion, nevertheless, he failed to effect any substantial change in the way the Indians of Peru viewed their new religion. At the beginning of the seventeenth century, the ecclesiastical authorities were shocked to learn of widespread idolatry and in consequence launched a concerted campaign for its extirpation, which was destined to continue for several decades, albeit with only indifferent success.[13]

The central achievement of Toledo's government lay in the revival of the mining industry. Since its discovery in 1545 the *cerro rico* at Potosí had been the scene of unparalleled production of silver, its rich ores easily smelted in clay furnaces built and operated by Indians. However, in the 1560s output suffered a radical decline owing to the exhaustion of the surface veins within the peak, with the result that the despatch of royal treasure across the Atlantic equally faltered. Yet there had been already discovered in New Spain a new technique whereby low grade ores could be refined by a process of amalgamation with mercury, assisted by admixtures of salt, lime and copper compounds. But it was not until Toledo himself went to Potosí and personally presided over experiments that the technique was successfully applied to the ores of the *cerro rico*. Overnight the entire structure and pace of production of the industry was transformed. Spanish entrepreneurs now took command of the refining sector, hitherto operated by Indians, building water-driven crush-mills, elaborate patios and vats to house their operations. Behind the town a series of dams were constructed so as to create artificial lakes sufficient to ensure a regulated supply of water to power the mills. Equally important, whereas in New Spain the industry had to rely on imports of mercury from Almadén in Spain, by contrast, explorations in Peru revealed plentiful deposits of mercury at Huancavelica in the central highlands. Once again, it was Toledo who took the lead in initiating production at this mine, leasing it on contract to independent entrepreneurs. The result of these measures was that by the late 1570s silver output in Peru rose dramatically, with royal revenues, the fifth levied on all production, rising from less than 200,000 pesos a year to well over 1 million in the next decade.[14]

The dramatic increase in silver production did not derive simply from technological innovation and capital investment in new plant; it also depended on the massive, enforced mobilisation of the Andean peasantry. The principle of labour levies was not new. In Peru as much as in New Spain the abrogation of the encomenderos' right to free labour service led to the introduction of *repartimientos de labor*, known locally by the Quechua term *mita*, by which a fixed proportion of Indian tributaries were required to present themselves for work in the hispanic sector, albeit now in return for a wage. The municipal magistrates and the corregidores distributed these workers for a variety of tasks, in mines and agriculture, in towns and for wayside inns, with the kurakas generally held responsible for the supply of a sufficient number of men. As regards the mining industry at Potosí, Indian rulers in the surrounding provinces had despatched contingents of labourers to offer themselves for work, their earnings set aside for the payment of tribute of the home district. Moreover, the inquiries of the 1560s and the subsequent general visitation revealed that the Incas had demanded labour service rather than tribute as the chief obligation of the subject population. Already, in his *Gobierno del Perú* Matienzo had advocated the introduction of a system of compulsory labour, arguing that the wages the Indians earned in this fashion would allow them to pay the tribute which they owed the Crown.[15]

Despite ample Inca precedent and recent practice, the scale on which Toledo made provision for the manpower necessities of the mining industry was startling. Basing his calculations on the census, he summoned 13,500 men, or no less than a seventh of all adult males from a vast area stretching from Potosí to Cuzco, embracing some fourteen provinces, to work each year in the *cerro rico*. A similar arrangement supplied Huancavelica with 3,280 Indians recruited from the surrounding districts. Some lesser minefields were also consigned small levies. Since Potosí already possessed a certain number of free workers, attracted by high wages, the *mita* embodied a massive input of cheap labour, since the *mitayos* were paid less than half the rate offered to other workers. The social effects of this mobilisation of the Andean peasantry were all-pervasive. In the case of Potosí, the *mita* came to resemble a great annual migration, with contingents from the region adjoining Lake Titicaca taking up to two months to cover the 600 miles journey across the *altiplano*, often travelling in company of their wives and families, sustained by flocks of llamas bearing provisions. For the Crown the results were equally impressive, since the combination of technological improvement with a massive supply of labour prompted a dramatic increase in silver production. Thanks to the Toledan reforms, Potosí came to account for at least 70 per cent of Peruvian silver and more than half of all silver produced in America. For a brief moment the *cerro rico* acted as a magnet for the entire Atlantic economy.[16]

The logical conclusion of the Toledan settlement would have been the transfer of the Peruvian capital from Lima to Cuzco, combined with the opening of the sea routes to the River Plate. This was indeed the proposal of Matienzo and Toledo appears to have agreed on its feasibility. The wealth and population of the country lay in the highlands. Cuzco had all the prestige of its Incaic past. Moreover, such a shift in the geo-political centre of the colonial system would have completed the Spanish assumption of the power and authority of the Incas. As it was, Lima remained the capital, drawing its wealth and sustenance from a vast hinterland which its governors rarely, if ever, visited, a permanent testimony and partial cause of the deep fissure in Peruvian history which separated the Habsburg realm from its native predecessor.[17]

III

Although the central achievements of the Toledan settlement clearly derived from the financial exigencies of the Crown and the political incoherence of post-conquest Peru, the inspiration and justification of the project rested on a remarkably harsh interpretation of Andean history and society. To anticipate our argument, the circle of lawyers, priests and soldiers who surrounded the viceroy subscribed to the imperial, humanist ideology of Sepúlveda and Gómara. But whereas in the 1540s controversy had centred on the justice of the conquest, for the Toledan circle the main question at issue was the form of government that Peru and its native inhabitants required if the necessities of the Crown were to be satisfied. Whereas Sepúlveda had based his case on the often naïve chronicles of Oviedo, his disciples in Peru could boast practical experience of colonial administration, several having participated in the inquiries and debates of the 1560s. The most distinctive feature of their approach was the perusal of the Inca past for precedent and arguments on which to base and justify their measures of reform. Indeed, without that precedent and the experience it generated, they may well have been obliged to adopt alternative expedients. In the case of the *mita* – to take the most obvious example – if the Incas had not already summoned thousands of peasants to travel long distances for work on imperial projects, would Toledo and his advisers have dared to organise the labour levies for Potosí on such a scale? In New Spain no Indian was called upon to travel more than thirty miles when summoned to work by the *repartimiento de labor* levy. In many ways, the Toledan project for Peru created what can only be called a successor-state to the Incas, with key institutions modelled on native practice.

To ascertain the central features of the Toledan vision of Peru and its inhabitants, it is necessary to consult the viceroy's voluminous correspondence with Philip II together with the final report he presented to his successor. As we have seen, Matienzo's *Gobierno del Perú* offered a blueprint of much that was to be implemented during the 1570s. To obtain further access to the viceroy's thinking, the long memorial written at Yucay by his Dominican cousin, García de Toledo, is invaluable. Finally, the *Historia indica* (1572) written by Pedro Sarmiento de Gamboa (1530?–92) summarised the depositions of the native nobility about the history of the Incas. Through an analysis of these texts we can obtain a relatively coherent impression of the intellectual foundations of the Toledan school.

At the outset of their inquiries the Toledan circle found it necessary to confront the arguments of Las Casas, set out in his *Los tesoros del Perú* (1564), where he had denounced Spanish rule as mere tyranny, identified the kurakas as the native, rightful lords of Peru, and called for a restitution of the Incas, all the while defending the Indian's right to rebel and resist Spanish exactions. The task of undermining Las Casas' authority was assumed by García de Toledo, who roundly declared that all doubts about the legitimacy of colonial rule derived from the life-long campaign of one man – Bartolomé de las Casas – 'whose qualities were to be a very good religious, but in matters of the Indies very passionate and in the most substantial matters very deceived . . .' Indeed, he was so overcome by his passion that 'it sprang forth from his eyes . . .' It was his denunciations of the conquerors that had unsettled the Emperor Charles V, allowing the friar to dominate the Council of the Indies. All the world was upset by his assertion that the Incas and kurakas were 'the legitimate native lords' of Peru, an assertion which had misled jurists and theologians such as Francisco de Vitoria to approve his arguments. The problem here was that Las Casas had been treated 'as if he were an apostle' and by reason of 'his good life and authority as bishop' had been trusted by the emperor and the Council of the Indies. Yet his fundamental premise was mistaken: the fact of the matter was that the Incas were tyrants, themselves but recent conquerors, their empire in existence for little more than eighty years, who had deprived their subjects of both land and liberty, exacting tribute and services from them as if they were slaves. Moreover, it followed that the kurakas were an equally transient phenomenon, the mere henchmen of the Incas, appointed recently, without any right of hereditary succession, whose retention of power at the local level threatened to impede the work of conversion. To cap his argument, García de Toledo claimed to perceive 'the most subtle work of the Devil' in deceiving Las Casas and using the good intentions of the Dominican to unsettle the Indies, undermine the work of conversion and defame the good name of Spain.[18]

Needless to say, Toledo largely agreed with the analysis offered by his cousin. For he informed Philip II that he had given orders to ensure that 'the books of the Bishop of Chiapa and other publications without licence of the

Royal Council are being collected as Your Majesty commanded: those of Chiapa were the heart of most friars of this kingdom and have done most harm in it . . .' Similarly, he fixed upon errors in 'matters of fact' as the chief cause of complaint against Las Casas and firmly denied that the Incas ever exercised any legitimate authority in Peru. It was for this reason that he called for the withdrawal of Diego Fernández' *Historia del Perú*, a chronicle of recent rebellions, since it described the Incas as the 'native lords' of the country.[19]

It should not be imagined that this censure of Las Casas entailed any approval for the conquerors. Toledo himself denounced the Pizarros for their 'vicious liberty which caused their tyrannical disobedience', and in general condemned the 'liberty' which had characterised post-conquest society. For his part, Matienzo followed Gómara in observing that if the apparitions of Santiago and the Virgin Mary at the siege of Cuzco indicated that divine providence favoured the Spaniards, nevertheless, divine justice had equally intervened to ensure that most of the conquerors responsible for the ill-treatment of Indians had lost their lives in the subsequent civil wars. So too, García de Toledo admitted that the conquerors had committed many crimes and atrocities, albeit he then observed that they were simple warriors, who had subsequently testified that: 'they had it by faith that it was a great virtue to kill these Indians and lance them, since they perceived them as idolaters, adoring stones, sacrificing men and eating human flesh; and since they were not theologians, they thought they were serving God in killing his enemies'. Even so, when they learnt of Las Casas' condemnation of their crimes, some conquerors became so conscience-stricken and preoccupied that they married Inca heiresses, so as to obtain property through marriage and inheritance rather than sustain any claim by right of conquest.[20]

But what were the grounds for pronouncing the Incas to have been tyrants? Obviously, the issue could only be resolved by an appeal to history. Unfortunately, there was precious little written evidence on which to base any judgement. Unlike the natives of New Spain, the Indians of Peru had not devised any form of script, so that the only historical record available was a set of paintings of the monarchs of the Inca dynasty that had been commissioned by the emperor Pachakuti some eighty or more years before the arrival of the Spaniards. Andean culture entirely lacked the obsessive concern with the passage of time that characterised Mesoamerica. All that oral tradition had to offer was the testimony of the Cuzco elite as to the grandeur, benevolence and duration of their empire as against the contrasting plaints of the provincial nobility about the cruelty and recent date of Inca conquests. The materials collected by Fr Domingo de Santo Tomás, author of the first Quechua dictionary, had been sent to Las Casas for incorporation in the *Apologética historia sumaria*. On the Spanish side, therefore, all that was known about the Incas was to be found either in Gómara, who in his *Historia general* had fixed upon the absence of private property, money and the demand for labour service as clear evidence of tyranny, or alternatively, in the summary exclamations about the greatness of the fortresses, roads and sheer extent of the empire that were in the introductory sections of Agustín de Zárate and Diego Fernández, the two leading chroniclers of the conquest and civil wars.

The picture would have been substantially altered had Pedro de Cieza de León (1518–53) lived to publish the second part of his *La crónica del Perú* which dealt with the Inca state. For there he offered an account of the bestial savagery in which the natives of Peru had dwelt before the Incas succeeded in establishing both dominion and civilization. Although Cieza de León certainly drew attention to the cruelty and massacres which at times accompanied Inca expansion and clearly depicted the Devil as the chief source of their religion, nevertheless, he offered a remarkably favourable assessment of their laws and institutions, emphasising the degree to which they attracted veneration of their subjects. Indeed, he presented the Inca empire as a model of statecraft worthy of Spanish emulation. He openly admitted: 'it is no small sorrow that, being the Incas gentiles and idolaters, they should have had such good order so as to know how to govern and conserve such extensive lands, and we, being Christians, should have destroyed so many kingdoms ...' Resident in the last years of his life at Seville, after spending nearly twenty years in Peru, Cieza de León bequeathed his manuscripts to Las Casas, whom he may well have met in Spain.[21] Moreover, he succeeded in publishing the introductory part of the *La crónica del Perú* (1552) which reported his travels from Panama to Potosí, thus offering a description of monuments and scenes on his route. Sure enough, he described the natives of New Granada as guilty of human sacrifice, cannibalism and sodomy, asserting that in Peru also the Indians had practised similar vices prior to the advent of the Incas. So too, he lamented the massacre that had accompanied Huayna Capac's capture of Quito. The temples of the Incas were sanctuaries of the Devil. But across his narrative, there emerged a persistent note of nostalgia and regret that the Indians of Peru, once so numerous and prosperous, had suffered depopulation and destruction at the hands of the Spaniards. Not merely did he exclaim over the grandeur of Inca fortresses and roads, he also praised their laws and care for the well-being of their subjects, exclaiming 'how the Inca kings who governed this empire were so wise and of such good government and so well provided'. Such remarks, uttered, so to say, in passing, were to be seized upon by later historians and certainly ran counter to theses advanced by the Toledan school.[22]

The contrast presented by the *Historia indica* (1572) could not have been greater. For the aim of Pedro Sarmiento de Gamboa was to demonstrate by exposition of the historical record that the Incas were tyrants in origin and tyrants in practice, their government thus defined as radically illegitimate. After a fanciful prologue, in which, inspired by Zárate, he speculated that the natives

of Peru descended from the inhabitants of Atlantis, with the Greeks subsequently colonising Yucatán, Gamboa then described the mysterious mission of
Viracocha, a powerful, almost apostolic figure who had dwelt in Peru at the
beginning of its history. Thereafter, the country fell into anarchy, its inhabitants dominated by vice and civil war, a condition from which they were
rescued by the Incas. Although Gamboa provided a list of twelve Incas, with
the fanciful appearance of Manco Capac dated as far back as 665, he insisted
that it was only during the reign of Pachakuti, the ninth monarch, that the Incas
extended their dominion beyond the immediate vicinity of Cuzco. It was this
ruler who was responsible for the construction of so many fortresses, the
rebuilding of the capital and the re-settlement of the population. It was under
the same monarch that the great temple of the Sun at Cuzco came to house the
mummified remains of previous sovereigns. At the same time, Gamboa
condemned Pachakuti as a tyrant who suppressed all rebellion with great
cruelty, re-settled much of the population, and appointed new kurakas to
govern the conquered peoples. His successors, Tupa Inca and Huayna Capac,
each had to reconquer much of the same territory already held by Pachakuti,
crushing the revolts which greeted their accession, and thereafter extending the
frontiers of their empire still further. Their conquests were accompanied by the
construction of roads and the introduction of irrigation channels and terracing
to extend the lands available for cultivation.[23]

Although Gamboa's chronology was sadly amiss – he attributed the reign of
Pachakuti, the grandfather of Huayna Capac who died in 1525, to the
thirteenth century – his central aim was to demonstrate that the Inca empire
was a recent creation, which had grown through a process of warfare, in which
each ruler's accession had been greeted by rebellion and civil war. At all points,
he insisted on the despotism of their government, with their subjects deprived
of property and liberty, and compelled to labour for their masters without
recompense. Human sacrifice was a regular part of religious ritual. Since each
succession to the throne was contested by other claimants, no Inca could be
described as enjoying the legitimate authority which derived from rightful
inheritance, an observation which applied with especial force to Atahualpa and
Huascar, the rival contenders at the moment when the Spaniards arrived in
Peru. In short, Gamboa extracted from native depositions, compiled during the
general visitation, a remarkably bleak interpretation of Inca history and
government. In part, it reflected the long-cherished hostility of the provincial
nobility to their Inca masters. More important, it both exculpated the Spanish
conquest by describing it as effecting a liberation from tyranny, and, by
implication, justified the Toledan settlement as a replication, albeit undertaken
for other, more Christian ends, of Pachakuti's great achievement.[24] History was
thus rewritten with an eye to contemporary exigencies.

The importance that Toledo attributed to these historical arguments was demonstrated by the sinister farce he staged at Cuzco in 1572, when representatives of the twelve Inca *ayllus* or lineages, all ostensibly descended from former rulers, were summoned to listen to a public reading of the *Historia indica*. Once the session was completed, they were called upon to sign a notarised declaration testifying their assent to its accuracy. In such fashion Toledo sought to rewrite history, or, best to say, extend his command over the Peruvian past. After all, had not Pachakuti done likewise when he had painted the succession of the Incas? In this context, it should be noted that it was in part thanks to Toledo's counsel that in 1577 Philip II circulated the notorious decree, which prohibited all further inquiry into native religion and history and ordered the colonial authorities to confiscate all manuscripts dealing with such topics. The past constituted too dangerous an arsenal to be left open for random or ill-intentioned inspection.[25]

Not content with the appeal to history, Toledo also invoked the servile nature of the Indians as further justification of his settlement. To ascertain the immediate origin of this view, we have only to turn to Matienzo's *Gobierno del Perú*. For there it was argued that fear was the basis of the devilish tyranny of the Incas, with the Spanish conquest an act of Christian liberation. Authority had been restored to the kurakas and the peasantry had been given the opportunity to improve their lot by earning wages in the mines and agriculture. Unfortunately, so Matienzo argued, the Indians were neither fit nor ready to take advantage of the freedom offered by Spanish rule. Instead of freely entering the market economy, selling produce and offering themselves for wage-labour, they simply retreated into a regime of mere subsistence, passing their days in idleness. The reasons for this failure were to be found in the absence of individual property within the Indian community and in their collective subjection to the despotic authority of the kurakas, which meant that the peasantry had little incentive to seek any improvement in their condition, since the wages they earned were often appropriated for communal purposes.[26] Moreover, Matienzo advanced a second, more general reason: by nature the Indians were low-spirited, timid, melancholic, credulous, prone to drunkenness, and rarely endowed with any thought or concern for the future. 'They are the enemies of work, and, if not compelled to work, friends of idleness.' All these observations led to the familiar, inevitable conclusion: 'they are naturally born and bred to serve and it is more profitable for them to serve than to command, because, as Aristotle says, for men such as these Nature created stronger bodies and gave less understanding and to those born free less strength of body and better understanding'. Matienzo's debt to Sepúlveda and Gómara here stands revealed: there was the same humanist insistence on the cash economy and individual property as the basis of civil liberty, combined with the same contempt for the servile condition of the native peasantry. The conclusions that Matienzo drew from his analysis were equally uncompromis-

ing and harsh. If by reason of their history and nature the Indians were unable
to enjoy the fruits of Christian liberty, then they should be compelled to work
for the Spaniards. So enamoured was Matienzo with this idea, that he compiled
an elaborate schedule, proposing that every Indian should be required to work
for 140 days every year, his services as a wage-earner supplied to a variety of
authorities. At the time he wrote, the mines of Potosí lacked sufficient labour.
In a revealing comment, Matienzo justified these obligations as an equitable
exchange between Spaniards and Indians: 'we give them doctrine, teaching
them how to live as men, and they give us silver, gold or things of value'.[27]
Gómara himself could not have put the matter more concisely.

It was Toledo who pulled together the conclusions of Gamboa and Matienzo
in a summarised account of native depositions that he sent to Philip II in 1572,
citing both Inca precedent and Indian nature as the chief justification for the
peremptory rigour of his general settlement of Peru. For a start, he declared
that until the recent conquests of Pachakuti Inca Yupanqui the Andean
Indians 'were masterless, without any kind of government among them, so that
everyone enjoyed what he had and lived as he wished'. It was a period of
endemic warfare in which 'everyone was lord in his own house'. It was Tupa
Inca who created the empire, by cruel armed conquest, thereafter appointing
such kurakas as he saw fit, and transplanting entire communities. The essential
argument here was that the Incas knew that 'the inclination and nature of the
Indians was to be idle and indolent'. To correct this unfortunate character, they
despatched their subjects on an entire series of public works, always keeping
them occupied, their government always sustained by appropriate rigour.
Indeed, without leadership and firm control, the natives were lost, unable to
conserve either their own souls or their property. All this led to the general
conclusion that since the Incas and the kurakas were tyrants, then Philip II was
undoubtedly the legitimate sovereign of Peru. Moreover, the king was free to
appoint such kurakas as he saw fit, distribute land to the Spaniards, and
appropriate local treasure. Equally important, 'the weakness of reason and
little understanding' of the Indians meant that the king had the duty to dictate
laws for their preservation and enforce them 'with some rigour', with the aim
of preventing them from ruining their lands through idleness and undue
liberty.[28] Thus Toledo first defined the Inca empire as a tyranny based on fear;
argued that state direction of labour was a necessary remedy for native sloth;
and then cited this precedent to justify the colonial despotism he proposed to
establish. In this context, the observation he made when discussing encomiendas that Christian kings in contrast to tyrants and barbarian lords had always
governed through an hereditary nobility assumes a new-found significance. For
his insistence that the kurakas were no more than appointed officers of the
Crown, without any rights of inheritance, clearly indicated the tyrannical
nature of the regime he consciously sought to establish in Peru.

Despite his protestations of Christian concern for Indian salvation, Toledo had essentially secular ends in view. In his final report to Philip II, he wrote, 'the government which the Indians had before I personally visited them was the same and little more politic than that which they had had during the time of the tyranny of the Incas'. Thanks to the resettlement in towns and the close supervision exercised by the district magistrates and the parish priests, they were now on the road to improvement, albeit rarely as yet ready for Christianity. He defended his measures in uncompromising terms: 'to learn to be Christians, they first have to be men and be introduced to a politic and rational mode of government and life'. In short, civilisation, which is to say, acculturation to Spanish forms, was necessary before any start could be made on the task of conversion.[29] At all stages in this long journey, however, compulsion and control were inevitable, since without some measure of fear the Indians, by reason of their lack of ambition for honours or covetousness for material possessions, would sink back into mere subsistent idleness. If Toledo restored a command economy in the Andes, it was because he feared that the inducements of the market-place, of wages and property, were insufficient to attract the Indians into working for the Spaniards. Mercantile capitalism in Peru, based on the diffusion of money as the measure of value, thus depended on state intervention to mobilise the peasantry to service the mining industry and commercial agriculture.

In retrospect, what is striking about the Toledan system is both its similarity and contrast to the Franciscan settlement in New Spain. For in both Mexico and Peru the native population was uprooted from its scattered hamlets and concentrated in towns or large villages, designed to promote both acculturation and conversion. Moreover, both the Franciscans and the Toledan circle probed deeply into native history and culture so as to devise the most effective means of transforming the Indians into a Catholic peasantry. As we have seen, Mendieta as much as Matienzo defined the Indian as more fitted to serve than to command, with corporal punishment or compulsion necessary for his government. But whereas the Franciscans sought to capture the essence of native thought on religion, mastering Nahuatl to create a new literature and history, by contrast the Toledan circle were obsessed with the material achievements of the Inca empire, more concerned to encounter the means of mobilising native labour, with acculturation rather than conversion their priority. In the last resort, if the Franciscans interpreted their mission as a central event within the history of the universal Church, Toledo strove to transform Peru into the Spanish Crown's most profitable possession.

IV

In his final report to Philip II, Toledo complained that his devotion to the king's service had caused him to be accused of being 'a tyrant, a bad Christian and a thief'. Despite his achievements, the king had failed to answer his letters in the last years of his administration; nor had he been rewarded by any token of royal favour. With his health already broken by his long period in office – he was sixty-six years of age when he retired – Toledo did not survive the journey across the Atlantic to Spain by more than a few weeks. Rumour had it that in his audience with the king, Philip II coldly reproved him for his harsh measures and, in particular, condemned the public execution of Tupac Amaru. Whatever the truth of the matter – there is no documentary evidence to sustain the charge – the king certainly encouraged the Council of the Indies to pursue Toledo's executors with demands for the repayment of the 50,000 ducats that the viceroy had appropriated from Indian community funds to cover the expense of his five-year visitation of the highlands. Since the issue was not resolved until 1597, there is some reason to suspect royal displeasure. More-over, Toledo's successor as viceroy, Martín Enríquez, informed Madrid that he was appalled to learn that Toledo had not kept any clear accounts of expenditure so that it was difficult to trace the flow of royal revenue. Then again, Toledo had frequently taken decisions on important matters without consultation with the audiencia or approval from the Council of the Indies, hastening to promulgate such a body of law and ordinances on so many aspects of colonial life that future viceroys were destined to remain mere executors of his legislation.[30] To cap it all, Toledo had affixed his coat of arms to the viceregal palace, sure sign of his imperious ostentation.

If Philip II did not relish the style of Toledo's regime, he certainly drew great benefit from its results. The revival of Potosí yielded the Crown an extraordi-nary increase in revenue, with the fifth levied on silver production rising from under 200,000 to over 1 million pesos a year during the 1570s. It was this dramatic and massive influx of bullion which rescued the Crown from virtual bankruptcy and enabled Philip II to finance his wars in Europe. Without the annual arrival of the treasure fleets from the Indies, it would have been impossible for the Catholic monarchy to maintain its army in Flanders and intervene in France and Germany.[31] If the Spanish Crown emerged as the bulwark of the Counter-Reformation and the leading power in Europe during the last decades of the sixteenth century, it was in large measure thanks to the harsh measures of Toledo, or, to put the matter more fairly, thanks to the toil and suffering of the Andean peasantry who laboured in the mines of Potosí and Huancavelica. Whatever the verdict of posterity, there can be little doubt that Francisco de Toledo succeeded in stamping an impress on Peru that was in varying degree to endure until the close of the colonial period.

7

ANDEAN PILGRIM

I

IN 1614 or thereabouts an elderly Indian, aged, so he claimed, about eighty, returned to his home village in the province of Lucanas, a district in the central highlands of Peru. The grandson of a king, he had once dressed in fine cloth but now after thirty years in the world serving God, the king and the poor, he had only rags to cover him. On arrival he found that his lands had been taken from him and his house occupied. Observing that the local peasantry was ill-treated by the Spanish district magistrate, subjected to forced labour levies, he at once complained to the authorities, only to find himself expelled from the province by the corregidor acting in union with the parish priest. Angered by the blatant disregard for the royal laws and viceregal ordinances that sought to protect the Indians from abuse, he decided to set out for Lima, there to present his case to the viceroy and urge remedies to be undertaken. To accompany him on the journey, he took a horse, a dog and his young son, all of which he was destined to lose as he made his way down across the mountain trails.[1]

The scenes he encountered on his journey could not have been more dramatic. For on entering the town of Huancavelica, the site of the great mercury mine, he found Spanish overseers beating Indian headsmen, calling them dogs and dumb brutes, adding 'it appeared as if all the devils had sallied forth from hell to disturb the poor of Jesus Christ'. The cause of all the disturbance and abuse was that the labour draft for the mine, the *mita*, was incomplete because the district magistrates had summoned Indians for their own purposes, using them to transport wine to distant markets. Elsewhere, he met three old women who had fled their homes in Huarochirí, because the former parish priest, Dr Francisco de Avila, had initiated a general campaign to extirpate idolatry, using his powers as visitor-general to seize native property.[2] Noting that a Spaniard had demanded free Indian labour for the purpose of weaving cloth destined for sale in Potosí, the traveller reproached him, observing that the ordinances of Viceroy Toledo prescribed that all native labour should be remunerated with a wage. To which admonition the Spaniard

8 Guaman Poma de Ayala on his last journey to Lima

replied that the viceroy's legislation only covered Indians and that as a Spaniard he was a free man who could do as he pleased. If the local cacique did not comply with his demands for labour, he would be dismissed from office and imprisoned. As for his interlocutor, he was just a *pleitista*, a barrack-room lawyer, or, as one priest put it, *un santito ladinejo*, which is to say, a sanctimonious hispanified native. At this point Guaman Poma de Ayala informed the Spaniard that he descended from great lords and Incas, that his mother was a queen and that Don Melchor Inca, who had recently taken up residence in Spain, was a close relative. His father had served God and His Majesty the King all his life. These claims were then followed by an extraordinary declaration: 'I as Guaman, the condor, king of birds, fly more and are worth more.' He was also Poma, the lion, the king of beasts, and Ayala, faithful knight of Biscay, and Chava, a sword, cruel against tyrants. Obviously mystified, but suitably impressed by this resounding declamation, the Spaniard advised him to go to Castile so as to obtain a reward from the king for all his service.[3]

On his arrival in Lima, by this time penniless and hungry, Guaman Poma failed to find any immediate shelter and was obliged to seek refuge in a church. Although he encountered some means of support, he found access to the viceroy much more difficult than he had imagined, the more especially since he lacked any means of bribing the guards and lesser officials. The result was that he wearily concluded his narrative with the bitter reflection that the world was turned upside down and that in Peru 'there is no God or king: they are in Rome and Castile'. If by justice was meant the punishment of the poor, then it could be found in abundance across the country. But for the rich, there was no justice, since no punishment was meted out on their crimes.[4]

What became of Guaman Poma de Ayala after his fruitless journey to Lima is not known. Even if he was ten or fifteen years younger than he claimed, his life was still obviously approaching its close. Viewed from the perspective of posterity, however, his journey to Lima was not without consequence. For he was apparently allowed to present either to the viceroy or to his secretary a massive manuscript of 1190 folio pages and 496 illustrations entitled *El primer nueva corónica y buen gobierno*, which then was sent to Spain, albeit more as a curiosity than as a political tract. Thereafter, it was probably purchased by the Danish ambassador, since it was later deposited in the royal library at Copenhagen, where it still remains, unknown to the world at large until its 'discovery' in 1895. Subsequently published in facsimile, the scholarly world had to wait until 1973 before obtaining an edition which applied modern rules of punctuation to Guaman Poma's garrulous, straggling prose, and, more important, offered translation of its frequent interjections of Quechua and the occasional phrases of Aymara. It is thus only in the last few years that the true stature of Guaman Poma has come to be recognised. For what he offered the king of Spain was a history of Peru since creation, a passionate denunciation of the country's misgovernment after the Spanish conquest, and proposals for reform. Above all, the *Nueva corónica* provides the modern reader with an unparalleled opportunity to listen to the testimony of a half-educated, acculturated Indian, writing in all confidence, without censorship, about Peru and its people. For many years an interpreter and assistant to Spanish visitors, magistrates and priests, Guaman Poma participated in the grand inquiry into Inca history and government launched by Toledo in the 1570s, a decisive experience in his cultural formation, since it taught him how to compile and present information drawn from native sources.[5] At the same time, he demonstrated a sound grasp of Christian doctrine and the Toledan ordinances, no doubt acquired both through sermons and court sessions. A member of the provincial nobility rather than of the Cuzqueño elite, Guaman Poma was obviously self-educated, obtaining only an imperfect command over the Spanish language. Yet whatever its faults of grammar, almost every page of the *Nueva corónica* attests to a powerful and often mordant intelligence, its inadequacies of style more than compensated by the originality of its substance, with the journey of the author to Lima figuring among the most vivid narratives in Spanish American literature.

II

No aspect of the *Nueva corónica* was more original or surprising than its account of the early history of Peru. For whereas most Spanish chronicles adopted the perspective of the Cuzqueño elite, assuming that the natives of Peru dwelt in a state of savagery prior to the advent of the Incas, by contrast Guaman Poma boldly sketched a sequence of no less than four ages of cultural and social development prior to the appearance of Manco Capac. Drawing upon standard Biblical chronology, albeit with some deviations, he postulated a million years after the creation of Adam, but fixed the effective beginning of New World history with the arrival of a descendant of Noah some time after the great Flood. There then followed four ages covering some 5,300 years, the equivalent of the three Biblical epochs initiated respectively by Noah, Abraham and David. These ages were described in terms of ascending social complexity, so that if at the start men lived in the jungle and in caves, hunted for food and went naked, in the second stage, although still comparatively barbarous, they developed agriculture and established fixed settlements. In the third age, kings appeared who issued laws and the Andean population began to wear clothes. Finally, in the last stage within this scheme, corresponding to the bibilical epoch inaugurated by King David, these petty kings built fortresses and engaged in warfare. Here, then, was a scheme of evolutionary development, reminiscent of that advanced by Cicero and applied by Las Casas to the New

World. The contemporary existence of savages in the Amazonian jungles bordering the Andes obviously offered any observer the basis of such a contrast; what is striking is that Guaman Poma ascribed to each stage particular social and political characteristics. Moreover, the entire historical sequence, which lasted from the great Flood until the incarnation of Christ, was defined by Guaman Poma as a period when the natives of Peru refrained from idolatry and worshipped the one true God, albeit dimly conceived. Equally important, they practised a strict morality, obeying the ten command-ments and punishing all sins with great severity. Then again, since communal meals were the rule, no-one went hungry, the more especially since at birth everyone, male and female alike, was assigned a tract of land for their subsistence, with the community assuming the responsibility for feeding the elderly, infirm and orphans.[6] In short, by implication, Guaman Poma depicted human society in early Peru as governed by the dictates of natural law, the practice of virtue unimpeded either by the effects of original sin or the intervention of the Devil.

Needless to say, corruption entered the Andean paradise long before the advent of the Spaniards. Essentially, Guaman Poma asserted that it was the first Inca, Manco Capac, and still more his mother and wife, Mama Occlo, a woman notorious for her immorality, who introduced idolatry into Peru, thus effectively entrusting the country to the dominion of the Devil. The empire they created was established through force of arms and imposed heavy burdens on their subjects. The evil rule of the *amarus*, the serpent-demons, was thus a tyranny. However, these dark events, which occurred in the years just prior to the birth of Christ, were mitigated in their effect by the apostolic mission of St Bartholomew, who arrived in Peru during the reign of the second Inca, preaching the gospel, working miracles and bequeathing to posterity as testimony of his mission the famous cross at Carabuco, still in existence at the time of the Spanish conquest. Such was the enduring influence of his teaching that Viracocha Inca sought to abolish idolatry in Peru. Not all rulers were so benevolent, and Guaman Poma singled out Pachakuti, usually described as a wise legislator, as a harsh tyrant, his reign stained by cruel conquests, pestilence and great mortality – inflictions sent from heaven – to punish the land for his sins.[7] Whether it was his status as a provincial noble or alternatively his employment as interpreter in the Toledan visitation that drove Guaman Poma to adopt such a hostile view of the Incas is difficult to know. Whatever the case, it is an interpretation of native history, advanced by an Indian which at first sight appears to be totally at variance with the idealised version purveyed by the Cuzqueño elite.

Although Guaman Poma condemned the Incas for their idolatry and tyranny, describing in some detail their annual sacrifices of women and children to the gods, he also was at pains to emphasise that they continued to observe much of the morality and admirable practices of the first ages of native society. In particular, he drew attention to the Incas' laws which provided for severe chastisement for breaches of morality, with offences such as adultery punished by death and drunkenness treated as a crime. Similarly, he insisted that the community still continued to take care of the elderly, the infirm and the poor in a fashion unknown in Christendom. In short, Guaman Poma depicted the Inca state as a tyrannical super-imposition on a native society which in many important aspects maintained its original integrity and cohesion. Moreover, if we consider that Guaman Poma chose to conclude his vast manuscript, not with the account of his journey to Lima, the section he wrote last, but with an extended description of the agricultural year, with its cycle of monthly and seasonal tasks offering an image of the good life, of man working in harmony with both nature and his fellows, his toil for the common good blessed by heaven, then we must conclude that his essential purpose was to defend the natural virtue and value of Indian life and society. This view was best resumed in his exclamation: 'How the Indians of old were Christian: although they were pagans, they observed God's commandments and the good works of compassion.' In effect, Guaman Poma here identified Christianity as a form of natural religion, with observance of the natural law and the worship of the one true God, its defining characteristics.[8]

In contrast to this ideal Andean past, the present age was described as an epoch in which everything was al revés, back to front, or, to use the old English expression, when the world had been turned upside down. The causes of this unhappy state of affairs lay deep within the Spanish conquest and the form of government thereafter established. To illustrate the avarice of the conquerors, Guaman Poma drew a satirical picture of Pedro de Candia avidly trying to eat gold. So also, he drew various scenes of conquistador cruelty and violence, depicting the tortures of captives, the seizure of women, and the general assault on the subject population. At the same time, he was at pains to emphasise the illiteracy of Francisco Pizarro, a sign of his unfitness to rule. Many of the conquerors were mere commoners, often Jews or Greeks, prone to rebel against the Crown, men damned by the Almighty for their crimes, who by reason of their failure to make any restitution of the goods they had stolen from the Indians would roast in hell-fire for all eternity. Once again, it is difficult to ascertain the precise sources of these fulminations. In his garbled account of the conquest, Guaman Poma apparently drew upon the chronicle of Agustín de Zárate. But his narrative is full of errors, some the result, no doubt, of ignorance, others, one suspects, the effect of malice, irony or prejudice. Why does Pedro de Candia, the Greek artillery man, figure so large in his version? That he should have described Vicente de Valverde, the friar who accompanied Pizarro's first expedition as a Franciscan rather than as a Dominican may have derived from the conviction that the first preacher of the Christian gospel in

Peru should have been a disciple of St Francis. Was it irony or inadvertence that led him to dub the general chronicler of the Indies, a man noted for his contempt for the natives of the New World, as Gonzalo *Pizarro* de Oviedo? For the rest, it is clear that Guaman Poma drew upon the doctrines of Las Casas, retailed to him, no doubt, in sermons or in conversation with the friars with whom he dealt.[9] Life in the highland parishes was often lonely and the company of an intelligent, inquisitive Indian interpreter was not always to be despised; a great deal of Spanish culture was transmitted in casual conversation and social intercourse.

Condemnation of the conquest did not entail any rejection of Spanish rule. As much as the *colegiales* of Santa Cruz Tlatelolco, who assisted Sahagún frame the Mexican Indian version of the conquest, so also Guaman Poma sought to depict that event as a freely accepted *translatio imperii*, claiming that it was his own grandfather, identified as the 'second person' of the emperor Huascar, who led an embassy to Tumbes to inform Pizarro that his master peacefully recognised Charles V as sovereign lord of Peru. He gladly purveyed the story that at the siege of Cuzco, where the forces of Manco Inca greatly outnumbered the Spaniards, the Virgin Mary and Santiago appeared, assisting the conquerors to repel the Indian army. Indeed, he averred that it was owing to this clear expression of the will of heaven that the Indians remained loyal to the Crown throughout the subsequent cycle of civil war and rebellion.[10] Guaman Poma's father fought with Almagro against the Pizarros and later assisted in the repression of several revolts, especially that led by Hernández Girón. In short, the mandate of heaven had passed from Cuzco to Rome and Castile, a conviction that led him to hail the Catholic King as universal Inca, the 'second person' of the Pope, the Vicar of Christ on earth. Already, in anticipation of this unified world monarchy, the three kings had worshipped Christ in the stable at Bethlehem, kings identified by Guaman Poma as Baltazar the Spaniard, Gaspar the black, and Melchor the Indian. In a crude map drawn to illustrate this idea, he divided the world into four quarters, after the model of Inca Tawantinsuyo, with Castile, the equivalent of Cuzco, at the centre, surrounded by the four kingdoms of Rome, Guinea, Turkey and the Indies. In another map, however, illustrating the relation of Peru to Castile, he placed the Indies above Spain as the superior moiety, thus dividing the Catholic monarchy into two halves or moieties following the basic social division of all Peruvian communities. In this context, it should be noted that he interpreted the meaning of *Indias*, the Indies, as a shortened form of *tierra en el día*, which is to say, the 'land in the day', or, by extension, the land of the sun, the ancient Inca deity.[11]

If the Catholic King was thus acknowledged as the universal Inca, it was only to be expected that his representatives in Peru, the succession of viceroys, should be described as wise, just rulers, zealous for the welfare of their subjects.

In point of fact, only the government and person of Francisco de Toledo appears to have left any lasting impression on Guaman Poma. Throughout the *Nueva corónica y buen gobierno*, there are repeated references to this viceroy, who was praised for his decision to reside in Cuzco, and yet more for his ordinances that safeguarded Indian possession of land, prohibited Spaniards from living in Indian villages, and insisted that all work undertaken by Indians for the Spanish sector should be rewarded with a wage. In particular, Guaman Poma praised Toledo for his attempts to ascertain the laws of Incas and indeed argued that the most beneficial elements within the Toledan ordinances all derived from Inca precedent.[12] What is remarkable here is the degree of familiarity with the viceroy's legislation he displayed and his readiness to appeal to those laws when criticising the exploitation of Indian man-power by district magistrates.

This relatively favourable assessment of Toledo's measures, however, has to be balanced against a withering attack on the viceroy's enforced re-settlement of the population. The former sites of native dwellings and hamlets had not been fixed at random, so Guaman Poma asserted, but rather derived from the careful inspection of judges and astrologers, who by reason of prolonged experience and study were acquainted with the particular qualities of the terrain and climate of each district of the highly variegated landscape of the Andes. In general, for permanent residence they chose places situated at some height which were likely to prove healthy. By contrast, Toledo's visitors lacked all comprehension of Indian needs and built towns in low-lying, unhealthy zones, often pitching the sites at considerable distances from the fields under cultivation. The inevitable result was that the Indians gathered into these towns fell victim to the plague and to famine, their very concentration rendering them more vulnerable to these afflictions. Moreover, the decline in population, combined with the introduction of European livestock, meant that it was no longer possible to maintain the long-range water channels which had allowed the hill-side terraces to be irrigated. In short, Guaman Poma offered a persuasive critique of the Toledan programme which modern research has in essentials confirmed.[13] Equally important, he strongly condemned the execution of Tupac Amaru as an act of injustice, arguing that Toledo had refused the Inca a trial and in sentencing him to death had far exceeded the limits of his authority, since only a king had the right to judge another king. Indeed, so biting was the reproof administered by Philip II to Toledo on his return to Spain that the erring viceroy died almost at once, overcome by shame and grief.[14] The account provided by Guaman Poma of this dramatic scene points to the existence of a widely diffused tradition, in part no doubt inspired by a revulsion against the execution of Tupac Amaru, and strengthened by an unwillingness to accept that the Catholic King, the fount of earthly justice, could have condoned the actions of his viceroy.

III

In the second part of his work, entitled *Buen gobierno*, Guaman Poma conducted, so to say, a general visitation of Peru, and then, envisaging the presentation of its written text to Philip III, offered remedial proposals. The picture he presented could not have been drawn in darker colours. Two generations after its conquest, Peru constituted a world turned upside down, with everything *al revés*, a country ravaged and tormented by alien rulers, where the constituted authorities actively conspired to exploit, corrupt and destroy their unfortunate subjects. Despite ordinances to the contrary, the encomenderos still demanded that Indians should be sent to them for personal labour service in the city and expected to be treated as if they were Incas when they visited the district of their tributaries. By this time, however, the chief oppressors of the native population were the corregidores, the provincial magistrates, who although paid only an annual salary of 1,000 or 2,000 pesos expected to accumulate a profit of some 50,000 pesos from their five-year term of office. Charged with the collection of tributes, they employed the Indians of their jurisdiction on a variety of tasks ranging from weaving cloth and growing coca, to transporting goods to the mining camps, all under the pretext of satisfying the tax assessments of the subject communities. It was also the corregidores who were responsible for the despatch of the *mita* levies to Potosí and Huancavelica, where with neither adequate rest nor medical treatment available, many Indians died of accidents or mercury poisoning. Any resistance to the incessant demands for labour was quelled by whipping and imprisonment, and any resort to violent protest repressed by instant execution. So also, the attempts by Indian caciques to protect the natives were answered by coercion or seizure of their goods. When Guaman Poma's chief disciple, a cacique called Cristóbal de León, refused to collaborate with the exactions of the magistrates, he found himself imprisoned and his house burnt down. Nor did the Church offer the natives of Peru any assistance, since, if we are to believe Guaman Poma's account, the parochial clergy, both secular and religious, collaborated closely with the provincial magistrates and equally sought to employ Indian labour for their own profit.[15] Once again, any protest was brutally suppressed, with the bishops' visitors simply bought off.

Running through the entire text is an almost obsessive concern with the sexual exploitation of Indian women by the Spaniards. The proclivities of the conquerors in this respect are well documented from other sources which attest that the very wives and daughters of leading Incas were not safe from violation. But Guaman Poma claimed that the Indian women who were sent to the houses of the corregidores and encomenderos to act as servants or to weave cloth were equally subject to abuse. Much the same problem occurred in the tambos, the wayside inns, where Spanish travellers often beat the Indians charged with their maintenance and attacked their womenfolk. As for the clergy, Guaman Poma depicted them as veritable satyrs, at times setting up entire harems of native women, off whom they bred broods of illegitimate children. Under the pretext of doctrinal instruction or of weaving cloth, parish priests summoned local women to their residences, only then to corrupt them.[16] Finally, even the black slaves at times joined with their Spanish masters in ill-treating and abusing the Indians.

The inevitable result of this all-pervasive oppression was the profound demoralisation of the Peruvian Indian, a demoralisation which found expression in a new-found addiction to alcohol. Guaman Poma was well aware that in the Andes the rites of popular religion had always been accompanied by a generous consumption of *chicha* and indeed he asserted that drunkenness was usually the occasion of idolatry, so close was its association with native religion. But whereas the Incas had severely punished casual drunkenness, now it had become the rule both for caciques and commoners. The effects of this demoralisation were all too obvious. To escape from the burdens of labour levies and tribute, many Indians deserted their families and villages, seeking refuge and employment in the mining camps in Spanish cities, or in distant provinces. The *mitayos* sent to Potosí often did not return home. Many natives chose to become *yanaconas*, a term Guaman Poma used to describe those Indians who became the servants of the Spaniards, often adopting European dress, or who settled on Spanish estates as labourers enjoying the landlords' protection from the provincial magistrates. Then again, the numerous women who had been corrupted by the Spaniards often turned to drink, with some becoming common whores and others choosing to consort with mestizos, blacks and poor Spaniards, producing an equally numerous breed of mestizos who in turn sought out native women. Small wonder, therefore, that the native population of Peru was fast disappearing. In districts where under the Incas a thousand tributaries had flourished and multiplied, often only a hundred survived, languishing in poverty and despair.[17]

In a graphic image, Guaman Poma depicted a terror-stricken Indian surrounded by a dragon-serpent, a lion, a fox, a tiger and a rat, all seeking to rend him apart, these animals the rapacious symbols respectively of the provincial magistrates, the encomenderos, the parish priests, Spanish travellers and the Indian nobility. Elsewhere, he compared Peru to the land of Sodom and Gomorrah, awaiting fire from heaven to consume its iniquities. The more he described the sufferings of the Indians, the more he was moved to invoke the prophet Habakkuk, exclaiming: 'O Lord, how long shall I cry, and thou wilt not hear, even cry out to thee of violence, and thou wilt not save.' He invited the Indians of Peru to join with the prophets of Israel and plead with God for mercy and deliverance. In this context, one cannot but wonder whether Guaman Poma had read further in the same chapter of Habakkuk, since in the same first chapter from which he quoted the Lord answered the prophet declaring that to punish Israel he would raise up the Chaldeans, 'that bitter and hasty nation', with horses 'swifter than leopards, more fierce than the evening wolves', who like eagles shall sally forth to enslave the Chosen People. In this image, the Peruvian Indians could thus be identified as a new Israel oppressed by the agents of darkness. Certainly, in later centuries, Indian leaders were to clamour for a Moses to lead them out of the house of bondage. In the short term, however, Guaman Poma was more animated by a stoic resignation than by any prophetic expectancy of deliverance, repeatedly concluding his account of oppression with the refrain *y no hay remedio* – and there is no remedy – a refrain in turn justified by the grim dictum: 'To every man and every house God sends his punishment.'[18]

To emphasise the prophetic quality in Guaman Poma and extract from his massive text a bleak, all-compassing denunciation of Spanish rule reminiscent of Las Casas is to present but one aspect of his achievement. For an entire world parades through his chronicle, described at times with consummate irony. He maliciously reports the quality of Quechua employed by preachers elsewhere renowned for their mastery of the native tongue and records the domestic conversation of Spanish magistrates with inimitable sarcasm. At the same time, he inserts Quechua love-songs and prayers, often of rare beauty, even in translation. Moreover, no matter how damning his general indictment of the colonial authorities, when he came to pronounce on individuals, he readily mentioned several examples of both corregidores and other Spaniards who were both upright and generous in their dealings with the Indians. So also, he cited several cases of devout, austere priests who devoted their lives to the service of their native flocks without any cause for complaint. Indeed, his own half-brother, the mestizo Martín de Ayala, was a priest who passed his time in prayer and penitence, serving the poor and the afflicted in the hospital at Huamanga. When assessing the religious, he drew a clear distinction between the members of the different orders, in general condemning the Dominicans, the Augustinians and Mercedarians for their pride, anger and harsh treatment of the Indians, while praising the Jesuits and the Franciscans, writing of the latter 'the reverend priests are all holy and very Christian, of great obedience, humility and charity, with love of their neighbours and great love for the poor of Jesus Christ'.[19]

As the terms in which Guaman Poma framed his indictment of the colonial authorities make clear, his denunciations did not entail any rejection of Spanish rule and still less of Christianity. As a young man he had served as interpreter or assistant to Cristóbal de Albornoz, the ecclesiastical visitor responsible for the suppression of the *taki onquoy* movement in Huamanga, a nativistic movement which had preached the return of the old gods. In his text, Guaman Poma always took care to condemn the worship of *huacas* as idolatry. More important, he was obviously influenced by Franciscan preaching and conceived of the Christian gospel in Franciscan terms as bringing relief to the poor and afflicted of this world, observing 'Our Lord Jesus Christ became poor and humble in order to gather and attract poor sinners.' If he criticised the clergy in Peru so harshly, it was because they had betrayed the gospel, acting as the servants of Mammon. Since Christ had quit himself of his Divine Majesty to bring light to the poor, how much more should his apostles rid themselves of worldly encumbrances so as best to preach the gospel. In this context, Guaman Poma adverted that he himself, although by birth and calling a nobleman, had chosen to dress as a commoner, living among the poor so as to observe their sufferings and the injustice with which they were treated.

> To give testimony of all this, it is convenient to write as if giving sentence as an eye-witness, relating what has happened to me and how they persecuted me. It was for this that I made myself poor, placing myself among them . . . to learn how the rich and proud scorned the poor, so that it appeared that where were the poor, there was no God or justice. Yet it is clearly known from faith that where the poor are, there Jesus Christ himself is, and where God is, there is justice.[20]

Guaman Poma so far adopted the prophetic office that not merely did he denounce oppression and corruption, but presented himself as a suffering servant, the prophet persecuted for his witness as another Christ.

His acceptance of Christianity and his loyalty to the Crown, however, did not prevent Guaman Poma from a defence of the interests of his class and lineage, the Indian provincial nobility whom, in terms already set out by Las Casas, he defined as the only 'natural rulers' of Peru. The case was simple enough: 'only the Indians are the legitimate proprietors that God planted in this kingdom'. It followed that the encomenderos were mere *mitimac*, which is to say, alien colonists, who lacked the ancestral rights of the native-born. In any case, many of the conquerors had been mere commoners, often Jews, Moors and other foreigners, their claim to rights and tribute and labour as the rewards of conquest quite groundless, since the last Incas had peacefully accepted the sovereignty of Charles V. It was this vision of Peru as essentially Indian that led Guaman Poma to contrast the relative virtues of Europeans and Africans with the absolute vices of the Spaniards and blacks born in Peru, describing the Creoles as 'fierce, proud, lazy, liars, gamblers, avaricious, of little charity, miserable tricksters, enemies of the poor Indians and of the Spaniards, thus are the Creoles, just like the mestizos, only worse than the mestizos'.[21] Since all Spaniards were defined as intruders, as mere aliens, it followed that the provincial magistrates and parochial clergy only enjoyed interim authority and in no sense could be regarded as endowed with lasting or legitimate rights to their offices.

Despite his concern for the poor and downtrodden, Guaman Poma adopted an aristocratic stance, declaring 'caste makes a man ... without good blood and without letters, one cannot rule or govern according to the letter of God, nor will the laws of these kingdoms be obeyed or respected'. Only the class he described as the *caciques principales* were the rightful rulers of Peru, their authority derived from God and confirmed by the Catholic King, the universal Inca. In this context, he observed that although Christ 'wished to be poor, he did not desire to come forth from the common people, but from the caste of kings', the royal house of Judah. Once again, the general argument coincided with his personal case. For Guaman Poma claimed to be descended from the Yarovilcas of Huánuco, the ancient kings of Chinchasuyo, who after their conquest by the Incas were rewarded with high office. His own grandfather or great-grandfather, Guaman Chava-Yarovilca, had served as 'second person' to the Inca Tupac Yupanqui. His mother, Juana Curi Occllo, was the daughter of that emperor. Admittedly, none of these claims can be substantiated and may well have been unfounded. His father, Martín Guaman Mallqui de Ayala, apparently participated in the civil wars; his mother had a mestizo child by the conqueror, Luis Avalos de Ayala. Just what the family status was is unclear, since although documentary evidence has been discovered which shows that Guaman Poma acted as general lieutenant of the corregidor in his native province of Lucanas, it also reveals that on one occasion he was denounced as a mere commoner falsely passing himself off as a cacique.[22] Whatever the case, he certainly viewed himself as a spokesman for the hereditary nobility of Peru, denouncing Spanish attempts to appoint commoners as caciques, accusing the latter of drunkenness and oppression.

At the close of *Buen gobierno*, Guaman Poma described an imagined audience in which he conversed with King Philip III, 'the monarch of the world', presenting his chronicle and offering counsel as to the ways in which Peru could be restored to prosperity and order. The king first enquired the reason why the population had thrived and multiplied under the Incas but was now dwindling and afflicted with poverty. In reply, Guaman Poma advised the exclusion of all Spanish magistrates from any dealings with the native population, leaving its governance entirely in the hands of the caciques. The next step would be to restrict Spaniards to the cities, restore the land to Indian communities and procure the return of all natives to their home-villages. Henceforth, no Indian should ever be required to offer personal service to any Spaniard. Obviously, such a drastic reorganisation would require a general visitation, the guiding text and inspiration of which should be the *Nueva corónica y buen gobierno*. To render this plan practicable, it was necessary for the Indian nobility to take the lead, adopting Spanish clothes, and learning how to read and write, so as to administer the laws of the Indies and to impart a Christian example to their people. Equally important, Indians should be ordained for the priesthood. Although Spanish magistrates and clergy jeered at

9 Guaman Poma de Ayala presents his chronicle to Philip III

the quality of native intelligence, their mockery sprang from self-interest and
prejudice, since experience had shown that the natives of Peru were capable of
practising all the arts, crafts and professions of the Spaniards. Indeed, there was
no man whom the authorities feared more than an educated Indian, against
whom they invariably conspired, denouncing him as a *pleitista*, simply because
he was conversant with his rights at law. With the restoration of the authority

of the Indian nobility, steps could then be taken to recover the native social virtues, well-nigh lost, of obedience, co-operation and compassion. After all, under the Incas 'neither the Indians of great China [sic] nor of Mexico nor of any other people in the world, but only the Indians of Peru had such great obedience'. The undue liberty introduced by the Spaniards had led to a breakdown in social co-operation and in a failure to care for the sick and the elderly. But with the native nobility once more in command, no doubt free to enforce their authority with customary punishments, then the old order could be restored.[23] The fact, as we have noted, that Guaman Poma chose to end his chronicle with a description of the agricultural calendar of monthly tasks confirms his nostalgia for a golden age that lay remote in Peruvian history. The ideal future could only be attained by a return to the past; the Promised Land was more of a memory than a prospect.

IV

Challenged by the shock of conquest and the obvious contempt with which the conquerors viewed their knowledge and talents, the Indian elite desperately sought both to assimilate the Spanish language and religion and also to maintain certain strands of their own culture. In particular, they sought to retrieve the historical record from oblivion and to assert the value of native morality. As the case of Guaman Poma demonstrates, it was through a positive avowal of Christianity that they encountered the concepts which enabled them to frame an acceptable defence of their social identity. Whereas the peasantry could evade the challenge of acculturation by a mixture of stoic resignation and dissimulation, by contrast, the Indian nobility found themselves in constant contact with the colonial authorities and other Spaniards, since they were obliged to act as both intermediaries and assistants. The same men who organised Catholic liturgy for the clergy also had to countenance the maintenance of pagan rites by their communities. At times, the strain proved intolerable, but for the more intellectually adept the result was a fruitful adaptation of certain Christian themes to native concepts.

The scale of the challenge to the native elite can be gauged from a Quechua text now known as *Dioses y hombres de Huarochirí* (1598) a collection of depositions compiled by Francisco de Avila, a mestizo priest concerned at the survival of idolatry in his parish. His informants freely admitted that many of the villagers continued to worship their ancient gods, especially Pariacaca, the chief mountain of the district. Many of the Christian feasts they chose to celebrate coincided with the former calendar of rites held in honour of their deities. Some informants thought that those Indians who held fast to the old ways were more blessed with progeny than the natives who accepted the priest's admonitions. But the document also attests to the mental conflict that the rival claims of Christianity and paganism could generate in Indian minds, especially in the case of the native elite. For the text informs us that a cacique of Huarochirí, don Cristóbal Choquecaca, 'had left off believing in the *huaca* and did not even remember that it had existed'. However, his unconscious mind betrayed him, since his dreams were invaded by angry gods, whom he now identified as devils. So powerful was his experience, that he boastfully recounted to the villagers the victories he had won in these frequent night battles. 'The huaca Llocllayhuanca, of which we make so much, is only a demon owl. Last night, with the help of our mother, the Virgin Mary, I conquered him. From today onwards you should not enter his house, none of you. If I see anyone enter the house, I may well accuse him before the Father.'[24] Some years after, Choquecaca made good his threat and denounced the secret worship of the Indians to Francisco de Avila, who in turn informed the archbishop of Lima, the accusation thus sparking off a widespread campaign to extirpate idolatry in Peru.

Written affirmations of Indian beliefs, independent of mendicant inquiry, were of necessity rare, since any overt doubts about Christian doctrine or sympathy for pagan myths could well entail imprisonment. By far the most impressive maintenance of native tradition was to be found in Yucatán, where the Maya jaguar priests, historically charged with elaborate calendrical computations stretching back across millennia, continued their calculations and prophecies across the colonial period. There still survives a small library of their writings known generically as Chilam Balam, books of counsel, written in Maya, using the Spanish alphabet. The common feature of these anthologies is their obsession with the measure of time, its passage divided into twenty-year periods called *k'atun*. So accurate were their calculations that the sequence of Maya history for over 500 years before the arrival of the Spaniards can be traced from them. Possibly the most startling feature of their approach to events is the interpretation of the Spanish conquest as one further invasion of the peninsula, comparable to the arrival of the Itza some 800 years before. Indeed, one anthology records a conference of Indian governors, called in 1577 to determine the territorial boundaries of each community without mention or intervention of the colonial authorities.[25] More important, the study of the past was undertaken to uncover the secret of the future, since the sequence of *k'atuns* was held to be cyclical, at times bringing inevitable catastrophe, at times yielding some measure of relief. Cast in language that was highly poetic, elliptical and allusive in the extreme, nevertheless, in places these books offer remarkably forthright appraisals of the situation of the colonial Maya.

For example, the *Chilam Balam* of Chumayel offers a dramatic if stoically resigned account of the calamities associated with Spanish rule. 'It was only because these priests of ours were to come to an end when misery was introduced, when Christianity was introduced by real Christians. Then with the true God, the true *dios*, came the beginning of our misery.' For the author makes it clear that the conquest entailed enforced tribute, excessive labour service, outright theft of land, seizure of women and general ill-treatment. The passage concludes: 'it is by Anti-Christ on earth . . . by the foxes of the towns, by the blood-sucking insects of the towns, which drained the poverty of the working people'. In another anthology, we encounter the statement that 'time had gone mad'. Yet despite the lamentations, there also occurs an all-pervasive note of resignation. Indeed, so great was the expectation of cyclical catastrophe that in 1696 the priests of the small community of Itza who retained their independence of Spanish rule deep within the jungles of Peten, advised their people to accept Christianity and Spanish rule precisely because their reading of the *k'atun* sequence indicated the inevitability of this infliction.[26]

At the same time, as the reference to Anti-Christ suggests, their emphasis on prophecy led them to accept a strain of Christian millenarian doctrine that derived from the Books of Revelation and Daniel. It must be remembered that in all likelihood the authors of these anthologies also officiated as masters of ceremonies in the parish church and thus had considerable knowledge of Catholic doctrine. In one collection we find an attempt at an exact correlation of the Maya count of years with Christian chronology. It should come as no surprise, therefore, to encounter a prophecy of the second coming of Christ in which the Mayas were to be liberated from their sufferings. A great deluge would flood the world and the Lord Jesus would return to the valley of Jehosophat near Jerusalem. 'But it shall come to pass that tears shall come to the eyes of our Lord God. The justice of our Lord God shall descend on every part of the world.' Here, in a text written in a remote village on the Yucatán peninsula, apocalyptic expectation provided, once more, the hope of earthly deliverance.[27] Whether that reassurance derived from the Mayas' Franciscan mentors – the order had numbered many exponents of millennial doctrines in its strife-torn history – or whether it was taken directly from the Book of Revelation and other biblical texts is still a matter for research.

Comparison of the prophetic books of the Mayas with the *Nueva corónica y buen gobierno* at once reveals both the originality of Guaman Poma and the underlying similarity of these cultural projects. In both cases, there was an insistence on the basic continuity of Indian history, with the conquest viewed as a traumatic but essentially surface phenomenon, and the integrity of native society threatened but as yet maintained. So also there was a common appeal to the prophetic strand in the Christian tradition, a combination of the Franciscan emphasis on the poor as Christ's chosen flock and millennial hopes of salvation in history, all counter-balanced by a stoic resignation at the sufferings meted out by the inevitable unfolding of human fate. But whereas the books of Chilam Balam were anonymous and preserved an oral tradition, by contrast Guaman Poma, although undoubtedly familiar with a similar kind of orally transmitted knowledge, chose to bequeath to posterity a literary text of surprising complexity. Unlike his Maya counterparts, he made no claim to personal revelation; his role as prophet was limited to the witness and denunciation of Indian sufferings; his pretensions extended only to the claim of royal descent. In essence his ambition and presumed role were best defined in the illustrations in which he presented himself as *el autor*, 'the author', depicted first as dressed as a Spaniard, listening to the account of Inca history and laws given by Indian sages and record-keepers; then on journey as a poor pilgrim to Lima; and finally, in audience with Philip III, offering counsel on how best to restore justice and prosperity to Peru.[28] To leap thus across centuries of human history, to move within a single generation from a pre-literate culture to a full-blown consciousness of the individual writer as an author, with his life-work identified as the composition of an extended chronicle which took the form both of a history and a visitation of his country and people, was clearly the achievement of no ordinary man. Certainly, he had no rivals in this field either in Peru or in Mexico.

Obviously, such a work did not emerge from a cultural vacuum. Indeed, Guaman Poma made boast that he was familiar with the works of Zárate, Fernández, Oviedo and others. He had read something of Luis de Granada and the work of the Peruvian Franciscan, Jerónimo de Oré. He apparently knew Martín de Morúa, a Mercedarian friar, whose chronicle of Inca religion and history at times resembles his own work. That he accused Morúa of carrying off his wife points to a close, albeit unhappy relation.[29] However, it was undeniably the precedent and example of the Toledan visitation, in which he participated as an interpreter, which offered the most likely model for his enterprise. But it should be noted that the series of illustrations which accompanied the text are original and at times convey their message in images which were more powerful than anything in the accompanying prose, which in places consists of little more than an extended commentary on individual scenes. That Guaman Poma was conscious of the extraordinary originality of his life-work is demonstrated by a remarkable passage in which he offers a statement of his purpose:

> The Christian reader will be filled with amazement and fear on reading this book and chronicle and chapters and will ask who taught me and how can I know so much. Well, I say to you that it has cost me thirty years of work, if I am correct, or certainly twenty years of work and poverty, leaving my house, children and property, and working and entering among the poor and serving God, and his Majesty, learning languages, serving the learned, and those who do not know and those who do know. And I was raised in the palace, in the house of good government and in the high court, and I have served viceroys, judges, presidents of court, and lesser judges and most illustrious bishops and commissioners. And I have dealt with priests, corregidores, encomenderos, visitors, serving and asking

the poor Spaniards and the poor Indians and blacks. I have seen the visitor of the holy Church and the general visitor of Indian tributaries and the review and settlement of lands. And as a poor man among them, they revealed to me their poverty and the others their pride, of which were I to write of all that has occurred before me in all the work of the pride of the priests, corregidores, encomenderos and chief caciques, those who persecute the poor of Jesus Christ, at times it is a matter for tears and at times for laughter and at times for pity.[30]

Although Guaman Poma has been described as a sarcastic, resentful spectre glowering at the feast of culture currently enacted in the colleges, cathedrals and convents of Lima and Cuzco, his chronicle an expression of 'the inert world of the Stone Age and of pre-history which uselessly rebels against the world of the Renaissance and adventure', it is not so easy for a modern audience to exorcise Banquo's ghost in such cavalier fashion.[31] For Guaman Poma must surely figure as the chief native disciple of Bartolomé de las Casas, his hopes for Peru a faithful application of the doctrines of the great Dominican. Where else in colonial literature can we encounter so powerful an affirmation of the Franciscan exaltation of the poor and downtrodden as Christ's chosen flock? For an English reader, the chronicle at times evokes the social radicalism and medieval piety of William Langland's *Piers Plowman*. If modern anthropologists have hailed the *Nueva coronica*'s testimony regarding native social practice, there has been remarkably little theological assessment of Guaman Poma's fundamental premise that Christian revelation should be regarded as the fulfilment rather than as the negation of the social morality and cosmic reverence of Andean society. It was an argument already advanced by Las Casas, and yet more forcefully developed by the Inca Garcilaso de la Vega.

8

JESUIT TRIUMPHS

I

ON HIS way to the Jesuit mission in Peru in 1571, José de Acosta stopped at Santo Domingo where he was sharply questioned by the archbishop, himself a Franciscan, about the Company of Jesus. Why did its members not sing the daily office in choir like other religious orders? Why did they not practise systematic bodily mortification? He complained that: 'They eat very well, they dress very well in fine cloth . . . they do not profess penitence . . .'. Then again, why did the new institute presume to take the name of Jesus, when all other orders chose to be called after their founders? Their name was all the more offensive since whereas Jesus Christ had come to serve the poor and downtrodden of this world, the Jesuits catered for the needs of the rich and the learned, their abundantly endowed colleges primarily devoted to the education of the social elite. Moreover, they admitted only the most intelligent of their students into the ranks of the Company, directing the remainder to enter other religious orders. Confronted with such an all-encompassing broadside, Acosta vigorously defended the Company, arguing that the alternative to endowments was a wearisome hunt for alms. In any case, the wealth of the Jesuits had been greatly exaggerated; it was the lack of adequate means which had obliged rectors to discourage poor students from entering their colleges. As for mortification of the flesh, Acosta declared that the external forms of asceticism were more characteristic of St John the Baptist than of Christ. What the Jesuits pursued was mortification of the will, seeking to subject themselves in all things to the command of their superiors. He also defended the Company's policy of expelling unsatisfactory members as the only means of maintaining strict observance of the rule.[1]

This little dialogue, reported by Acosta to the Father General in Rome, illustrates the shock experienced by the mendicant orders at the appearance of the Jesuits in America. The image of St Francis as another Christ, the sixth angel of the Apocalypse, summoned to inaugurate a new epoch in the history of the Church, an epoch guided by the ideals of material poverty and bodily penitence, was now challenged by an association of priests, university men endowed with a keen instinct for political influence, quite unabashed by the problems of dealing with property, who quickly moved to establish colleges in all the leading cities of the Catholic world, thereafter constructing churches which in grandeur were only surpassed by the cathedrals.[2] Within little more than a generation after their foundation, Jesuits were to be encountered in assiduous attendance at courts as distant as Vienna and Peking, Madrid and Delhi, their world-wide missions yielding a rich harvest in conversions and reports. From the start, the new order operated on an international scale, the monarchical authority of the Father General overriding any mere provincial or national sentiments. Distinguished by their intellectual talents, by their practical gifts, and by their moral discipline, the Jesuits soon figured as the shock troops of the Counter-Reformation. At the same time, their success attracted the envy of the mendicants, whose prestige and ideals were undermined and diminished, and on occasion provoked the outright hostility of the bishops whose authority they sedulously avoided. It was to counter the mounting wave of criticism that they dealt only with the rich and powerful, that in the early seventeenth century the Jesuits authorised the publication of several chronicles, all designed to prove that in the New World their apostolic mission encompassed the most miserable and barbaric subjects of the Spanish Crown. By then the Jesuits had outstripped the mendicants, both in preaching the gospel beyond the frontiers of empire and in ministering to the African slaves who constituted much of the urban work-force.

II

In *De instauranda Aethiopum salute* (1627), a work first published in Spanish, Alonso de Sandoval described how he and his faithful assistant, Pedro Claver, made it their duty to meet the slave ships arriving at the port of Cartagena. By the early seventeenth century some twelve or fourteen ships a year disembarked their grim cargo of three to six hundred African slaves, destined for auction, sale and distribution across the empire. The two Jesuits, accompanied by interpreters whom they kept especially for the purpose, entered the ships to minister to the sick and dying. The scenes they encountered were appalling. For throughout their long voyage across the Atlantic the slaves were kept chained underdeck and only fed a meagre diet of maize. In these conditions, typhus, fevers and other infectious diseases could easily rage through the entire contingent so that it was not uncommon for ships to lose a third of their slaves, either from hunger or disease, before reaching Cartagena. On entering the ship, so Sandoval reported, the fetid stench was sufficient to deter all but the most determined or dedicated. Often, he found corpses still chained in place, the flies swarming in their open mouths. Other slaves died shortly after disembarkation, their bodies cast to one side in the port compound without anyone attempting to cover them, or paying them more attention than if they had been dogs. 'All this', wrote Sandoval, 'mine own eyes saw and wept.'[3]

The purpose of the Jesuits was to convert and baptise the newly arrived Africans so as to ensure their eternal salvation. To this end, they ministered to the slaves underdeck, offering them water to drink, handing out clothes to cover their nakedness, and ensuring that the dead were given prompt burial. Thereafter, as the slaves recovered their strength in the compound on shore, Sandoval and Claver continued to visit them so as to begin their catechesis in Christian doctrine. The great problem here was to ascertain the language of any individual, so that in addition to the handful of interpreters, themselves slaves, maintained by the Jesuits, it was at times necessary to fetch other blacks resident in Cartagena who might be familiar with the language in question. To assist him in this respect, Sandoval kept a directory of all local slaves, noting down their 'nation' and whether their owners would allow them to be used for this purpose. From the start, Sandoval expounded the chief doctrines of the Christian faith to the unhappy Africans, declaring that there was but one, triune God, that his Son had become man; that all men were faced after death with the last judgement, at which they were sentenced for all eternity either to life in hell or in heaven; and that Christ had come to save all those who kept the ten commandments and who displayed contrition for their sins. The slaves were then asked whether they understood these doctrines and whether they freely accepted them, with the choice between heavenly bliss and the torments of hell-fire rendered explicit, a contrast at times assisted by the presentation of simple but suitably dramatic drawings. Upon assent, a formal ceremony of baptism was enacted and each newly converted slave was given a small holy medal to wear about his neck. In this context, Sandoval condemned the practice of priests in Africa administering baptism *en masse* to entire shipments of slaves, arguing that without individual catechesis and consent the sacrament was null and void and the ceremony sacrilegious. Similarly, it should be noted that the Jesuits possessed the right granted by the Papacy to baptise and confess in their missions without the authorisation of either bishops or parish priests. If the local clergy were tempted to question this right, Sandoval simply invited them to accompany him when boarding a ship, only to find them beating a quick retreat, horrified by the stench and the sights that awaited them.[4]

Under no illusion that the preliminary exposition of doctrine in any way sufficed, Sandoval declared that baptism merely opened the gate, so to say, marking the start of instruction and an initiation into Christian life that would continue for years to come. At the same time, he maintained that the Africans drew immediate comfort from the gospel message that God was their father and that heaven awaited those who believed in Him. Certainly, the need for any scrap of consolation was urgent, since Sandoval admitted that the prospect facing them was decidedly bleak. Some slaves were mercilessly beaten by their owners, their wounds left to fester untended; a few were even beaten to death or left in chains; others barely had enough to eat and went about half-naked; many were driven to the point of exhaustion, working in mines or in the fields, often treated worse than oxen or mules. To justify this treatment, their owners argued that the blacks were little better than beasts, far too rustic and barbarous to understand Christian doctrine, let alone receive the Eucharist. As a result, it required constant reproof and urging from the clergy to ensure that baptised slaves were allowed to attend church so as to receive further instruction. As for marriage, some owners preferred to prostitute their female slaves rather than allow them to establish any legitimate relations.

In passages as impressive as any written by Las Casas, Sandoval protested both at the treatment of the slaves and against the view that they were mere brutes. All men had been created equal, he declared, endowed by God with a common nature, destined for the same end, with no distinction of lineage or estate. True nobility was of the spirit, not of the body, or based on ancestry. In any case, practical experience showed that the blacks were true men, not children or beasts, since they were animated by a free will and reason, and were capable of much the same actions as a Spaniard. In Africa, 'they have war and make peace, they marry, they buy and sell, barter and exchange like ourselves'. They certainly had the capacity to understand the mysteries of the Christian faith and indeed, once converted, many became remarkably devout. As slaves they had the obligation of obeying their masters, but conversely their owners had the duty to care for their welfare and ensure their practice of the religion. 'Lords and servants are brothers, both in nature and in faith and grace, and have the same Father and Creator.' Had not St Paul gloried in becoming a slave of Christ? In conclusion to this resounding declaration of the common nature and condition of all men, Sandoval warned slave-owners of the four sins that cried out to heaven for vengeance – murder, sodomy, oppression of the innocent, and defrauding workers of their just wage.[5] As it was, he had been informed by a fellow Spaniard that the Moors in Algiers treated their Christian slaves better than the Spaniards treated the blacks in their power.

The primary purpose of *De instauranda Aethiopum salute*, however, was not to denounce either the institution of slavery or the ill-treatment of slaves, but rather to describe and defend Sandoval's methods of catechesis and to attract other Jesuits to embrace this ministry. It was to this end that he prefaced his work with a detailed enumeration of the diverse peoples of Africa, clearly distinguishing the natives of the Gulf of Guinea, whom he described as the most willing, intelligent and attractive of slaves, from the peoples of the Congo and Angola who were less fit for work, soon dying in captivity. Drawing upon the fruits of his own inquiries and from the reports he had obtained from traders and Jesuits stationed in Luanda, he compiled a catalogue of African tribes and nations, ranging from peoples who were mere 'savages of the jungle', without agriculture, laws or trade, to the great kingdoms of the Congo, Monomotompa and Ethiopia. The purpose of this description was to provide practical guidance for priests who had to deal with slaves, helping them to distinguish the languages and peoples of the different regions. However, unlike Las Casas, Sandoval did not entertain a particularly high view of the race to whom he devoted his life. Accepting the view that a black skin derived from ancestry rather than from effect of climate, he adopted the interpretation that it originated in Noah's curse on his son Ham, which condemned his descendants to be 'servants of servants', their blackness thus the outward expression of the Africans' inferior lineage and servile destiny.[6]

Whereas Las Casas in his *Historia de las Indias* had condemned the Portuguese for their engagement in the slave trade, by contrast, Sandoval, although clearly tormented by the glaring inhumanity of the trade, failed to encounter any reasons for its abolition. His efforts in this direction went as far as to query the Portuguese Jesuits at Luanda for their opinion about the justice of this commerce in human flesh. But their answer was peremptory. Neither in Africa nor in Brazil had any priest or theologian ever urged any doubts as to the right of Christians to purchase and possess African slaves. Indeed, the Jesuits themselves owned many slaves in Brazil, employing them both as domestic servants and as field-hands on their plantations. The case here was simple. Most of the Africans sent across the Atlantic had been first enslaved by native kings and lords of the interior, either in punishment for crimes or as captives taken in warfare. Thereafter, they were sold at inland fairs to coastal traders who in turn sold them to Portuguese shippers. What guilt could be attached to the purchase of slaves who had already changed hands several times before their oceanic passage? The Luanda Jesuits admitted that some coastal traders occasionally raided the interior, carrying off innocent villagers, an act of obvious injustice, but the victims of these raids formed but a small minority within the great mass of exported slaves and there was no easy way of distinguishing them from war-captives and criminals. In any case, it had to be borne in mind that shipment to the Indies afforded the opportunity of offering the means of salvation to countless Africans who otherwise would have been condemned to eternal damnation. Was it desirable to endanger the salvation of so many by questioning the justice of the enslavement of so few? To these powerful arguments of the Luanda Jesuits, Sandoval could offer no reply, the more especially since, like Motolinia before him, he was more concerned to win souls for heaven than to campaign for earthly justice.[7]

A native of Seville, albeit raised and educated in Lima, Alonso de Sandoval (1576–1651) became a Jesuit at the age of sixteen and after completing his studies spent the remainder of life, from 1605 onwards, at Cartagena devoting his life to the catechesis of the blacks. It was not given to him to foresee that his humble, Catalan assistant, Pedro Claver, a priest who ministered to the blacks by day and passed his nights in prayer and self-scourging, was destined to be canonised as a saint.[8] Instead, he was inspired by the heroic mission of St Francis Xavier, whose life, written by Juan de Lucena, he translated from Portuguese into Castilian. Sandoval praised the great missionary not so much for his oft celebrated entrance into Japan, but rather for his preaching the gospel in Africa and southern India, arguing that he should be acclaimed as the chief apostle of the black nations of the world. Moreover, the path he had blazed had then been followed by many Jesuits, who had entered the kingdoms of Ethiopia, the Congo and Monomotompa, with several priests winning the glorious prize of martyrdom in their eagerness to evangelise the Africans. In southern India their converts already numbered thousands. In the Philippines they had laboured among the *negritos*, the most primitive peoples of the archipelago. In short, so Sandoval argued, the Jesuit mission was primarily directed to the poorest and most humble peoples of the earth, thus fulfilling the injunction of St Ignatius when he sent his first disciples to work in hospitals and among the poor. Anxious to dismiss the canard that Jesuits resided at oriental courts dressed in silks, he insisted that their primary mission was to the black nations of the world, including in a common rubric, the peoples of Africa, southern India, the Philippines and slaves in America.[9]

In his eagerness to attract his brethren into the mission field, Sandoval insisted that the Company of Jesus was 'a religion of apostles', and interpreted the famous fourth vow as entailing a fundamental commitment to preach the gospel throughout the world. Indeed, it was this vocation which distinguished the Jesuits from other religious orders in the Catholic Church, since whereas, for example, Franciscans were characterised by their love of poverty and Dominicans by their pursuit of truth, the Jesuits sacrificed everything to the task of winning souls. As for those priests who figured as professors or preachers in city churches, their lives spent in study or mediation, he exhorted them to seek eternal glory in an active ministry among the blacks and the poor; it was in this field of apostolic labour that heavenly crowns were to be won. To clinch his case, Sandoval cited a story taken from the Desert Fathers of Egypt, where a monk, after spending fifteen days working among the poor then passed fifteen years in prayer and penitence, suffering countless temptations in the desert, only to learn that he had gained more merit in heaven for his two weeks of selfless action helping others than in all the long years of solitary retreat. In devoting himself to the salvation of his neighbours, a man of God would always receive sufficient grace to overcome the temptations encountered in his ministry.[10]

Whereas Motolinia had interpreted the conversion of the Mexican Indians as an evident sign of the approach of the millennium, in part already announced by the advent of St Francis, so equally, Sandoval fixed upon the emergence of the Jesuits as signalising the renewal of apostolic life within the Church. In terms reminiscent of the paintings undertaken by Rubens at much the same time in Antwerp, he hailed St Ignatius Loyola as 'the sun of the Catholic Church', illuminating the universe with his radiance. Not content with this extravaganza, he proceeded to salute St Ignatius and St Francis Xavier as sun and moon, as Elias and Moses, and as Peter and Paul. Written only a few years after the spectacular celebrations that had greeted the canonization of the two men in 1622, their apotheosis was taken to signify the rebirth of the apostolic Church, the journeys and achievements of St Paul now re-enacted by the Jesuits on a world stage. It was this conviction of renascence that accounted for Sandoval's emphasis on the legendary travels of St Thomas the Apostle, who before his final martyrdom in southern India, where his tomb was conventionally located, had preached the gospel in Africa, India, China and even Brazil. St Francis Xavier had thus followed closely in the footsteps of St Thomas, the initial promise of whose mission was now finally realised. In a closing image, Sandoval observed that the Indies was a land of merchants and that Christ was 'the sovereign merchant of the gospel', who 'made and instituted a Company, with men whose purpose is to search for souls', priests who were thus 'merchants by profession, partners of the high merchant', engaged in the pursuit of spiritual riches.[11]

III

By far the most renowned Jesuit enterprise in Spanish America unfolded in a remote but vast corner of empire in the jungle zones that lay between Brazil and Paraguay, mainly inhabited by unsubdued villages of Guaraní Indians. In the *Conquista espiritual ... en las provincias del Paraguay, Paraná, Uruguay y Tape* (1639), Antonio Ruiz de Montoya, a native of Lima, who had participated in the mission almost from its start in 1603, described how it was the practice for two or three Jesuits to enter a given territory, usually far removed from the zone of Spanish settlement, accompanied by only a few Indian disciples. Opposition to their arrival was often intense, with martyrdom a constant threat and flight at times offering the only escape from danger. All the first efforts were directed to winning the friendship of the caciques, whose protection was often purchased by gifts of iron axes and other useful or attractive objects. What distinguished the venture in Paraguay from most frontier missions was the absence of other Spaniards. For whereas elsewhere it was the rule for armed expeditions either to precede or to accompany the missionaries, by contrast, in Paraguay the local settlers had failed miserably in their attempts to subdue the natives of the jungle zone. The result was that when the Jesuits, relying on the gospel, alone and unaided 'conquered the unconquerable', they were granted exclusive rights over the pacified territory, the Crown allowing them to exclude all Spaniards from their stations. In a charming description of how he went about 'capturing' a village, Montoya recalled that he had entered its district with a procession, headed by a cross and carrying a large board on which were painted the seven archangels, 'princes of the divine militia', to whom he prayed for protection.[12] In short, in their Paraguay missions, the Jesuits fulfilled almost to the letter the principles and methods of peaceful conversion enunciated by Las Casas in his Verapaz experiment.

Once pacified, the Indians were concentrated into a series of villages, each dominated by its church, the streets laid out on a grid system, the life of the community dominated by the liturgical calendar, with choirs and orchestras employed to celebrate solemnities in a manner best calculated to impress the neophytes. In addition, the Jesuits taught the children of the caciques how to read and write and provided instruction in an entire range of artisan crafts. Drunkenness was punished and any persistent illicit sexual relations rewarded by expulsion from the settlements. The Jesuits lived among their flock, dressed simply and ate much the same diet as the Indians. The scale of their mission can be gauged by the estimate provided by Montoya that in the years 1612–26 no less than 95,000 natives were baptised. Unlike other missionary chroniclers, Montoya declared that he would refrain from singing the praises of his brethren who had relinquished the honours of university chairs and the pulpit to live a penurious life among the Indians. In Paraguay, there were no silks or palaces as in Japan, but merely jungle clearings and the simple food and clothing of the natives.[13] Nor did he dwell on the three Jesuits who were martyred in the course of the spiritual conquest. In short, Montoya was content to let the facts speak for themselves, the pace and drama of his lively narrative telling its own story, without any of the evangelical exuberance or millennial expectation of a Motolinia.

One myth, however, certainly haunted the Jesuit enterprise, and that myth, appropriately enough, concerned the apostolic mission of St Thomas. Basing himself on the accounts of an Augustinian chronicler in Peru, Alonso Ramos, and the Portuguese Jesuit historian, Manuel Nóbrega in Brazil, Montoya declared that if the natives of Paraguay had proved so receptive to the preaching of the gospel, it was because they already possessed a dim, uncertain knowledge of the one true God, a doctrine imparted to their ancestors by no less a master than St Thomas the Apostle, who had conducted a mission across a wide belt of territory in South America, extending from Brazil through Paraguay into Peru. Numerous relics of his mission survived, including of course the famous cross of Carabuco in Peru. Equally important, the apostle had prophesied that one day his disciples would return to continue his work, an event that the Indians identified with the arrival of the Jesuits. Viewing this mission in the context of his journeys in Africa and India, Montoya declared that St Thomas had been chosen as the 'apostle of the most humble people in the whole world, the blacks and the Indians', a clear echo of the arguments already advanced by Alonso de Sandoval.[14]

Although the Jesuits succeeded in obtaining royal permission to exclude Spaniards from their mission territory, they soon attracted the envy and hostility of the settlers at Asunción, a small town of no more than 300 citizens. Montoya did not hesitate to present a strong criticism of the Paraguayan encomenderos who despite the New Laws still continued to exact personal service from their Indians, at times for periods of up to six months, so as to procure a work-force for the cultivation of yerba mate, the region's only cash-crop. The ill-treatment meted out to the natives had greatly reduced the population driving some villages into flight and others into rebellion. Observing that the local Spaniards sought to carve out new encomiendas from among the Indians converted by the Jesuits, he declared that to allow this to happen would be like leading lambs to the slaughterhouse. If at times the Jesuits gave shelter to natives who had fled from the zones of Spanish settlement, it was because they respected the dictates of natural law which gave the Indians the right to preserve their liberty by flight from their oppressors. As it was, the citizens of Asunción were more famous for their worship of Venus than of Christ, a reference to their notorious fondness for native women. The rivalry between the Jesuits and the settlers was to turn into outright hostility when the missions started to cultivate yerba mate, its sale organised through the network of Jesuit colleges.[15]

The purpose of Montoya's chronicle was not merely to celebrate the apostolic achievements of the Company of Jesus, but also to seek royal approval for measures undertaken to secure their work from total destruction. In 1628 the missions were attacked by an armed band of slave-raiders recruited in the Brazilian city of São Paulo. Thereafter, in the years which followed, successive bands invaded the mission territory, carrying off their defenceless inhabitants and murdering anyone who tried to resist, quite deaf to the protests of the Jesuits. Since at this time Portugal and Castile were subject to a common monarch, two priests journeyed to São Paulo to remonstrate with the governor, only to find that the riotous populace threatened their lives. The reasons here were simple. Over the years São Paulo had become the base of a murderous breed of frontiersmen known as *bandeirantes*, who wandered for years at a time across the interior of southern Brazil in search of slaves and gold. With Indian women for companions, they bred an offspring that followed the same career, men not easily subject to the control of the colonial authorities either in Brazil or Paraguay. In any case, Montoya alleged that the governors at Asunción proved either impotent or indifferent to the plight of the missions, with one incumbent actively conspiring with the invaders so as to participate in the profits of the raids. Confronted with the prospect of the total destruction of their enterprise – one source claimed that the Paulistas had carried off some 60,000 natives – the Jesuits decided to evacuate their flock to more distant zones, far removed from the slaver's orbit. In dramatic tones, Montoya described the migration of over 12,000 Indians, travelling by canoe up the Paraná river, their numbers soon depleted by hunger, illness and drowning.

Flight brought but temporary relief, since in 1637 a band of a hundred Paulistas, accompanied by a contingent of Tupi Indians, surprised a mission village at mass on Sunday. Murdering anyone who resisted their attack, they raped and abducted the women and, as a parting gesture, burnt to death all those Indians who were unfit for the long journey through the jungle. Montoya visited the village soon after the assault and was thus able to describe in vivid detail the carnage he encountered.[16] By this time, however, the Jesuits had decided to arm their flock, training them in the arts of defence, so that the next Paulista band to enter their territory was ambushed and forced to retreat after suffering considerable losses. It was precisely this enduring threat to the mission presented both by the *bandeirantes* and the indifference of the authorities in Asunción, that drove Montoya to journey to Madrid, there both to publish his chronicle and to negotiate with the Crown. In the event, his diplomatic mission proved as successful as his incursion into literary composition, since the Jesuits obtained royal blessing for the continued exclusion of Spaniards from their missions and, more important, royal permission to arm their native subjects so as to protect them from further Paulista attacks.

In effect, the missions in Paraguay constituted the fulfilment of the dreams and projects of Las Casas and Mendieta. Here, indeed, the Indians lived as in an earthly paradise, segregated from European contamination, their lives peacefully expended in agriculture, the crafts, and in the celebration of Catholic rites. Although the Jesuits were to be accused of creating an independent state, which in later years was to be both praised as a Platonic utopia and condemned as a Socialist prison, in fact their methods and purpose did not differ greatly from their Franciscan predecessors in New Spain. Indeed, the missions remained subject to the authority of the Spanish governor in Asunción, their inhabitants paying tribute to the Crown at the usual rate. Similarly, the bishop of Paraguay was entitled to conduct a visitation and was sent at least a token tithe. Where these missions differed from their counterparts in New Spain was in the total exclusion of other Spaniards from a wide stretch of territory and in the organisation of an armed militia directly subject to the Jesuits. In subsequent decades when Asunción became the scene of convulsive faction and incessant riot, the ability of the Jesuits to put into the field a disciplined, well armed militia both constituted a point of stability in the province, and rendered the missions virtually immune from any challenge from the settler elite. By the early eighteenth century, when the missions encompassed close to 100,000 inhabitants, the existence of this autonomous political entity, close to the frontiers with Brazil, came increasingly to be viewed as a threat to royal authority in South America.[17] But that is another story. What is clear is that the exceptional character of the Jesuit missions in Paraguay derived more from the exigencies of the frontier and the sheer remoteness of the province than from any sustained ambition of the Jesuits to render themselves independent of the Crown. Which is not to deny, however, that the structure of their little state was the fulfilment of every missionary's dream.

IV

The note of defiant magnification of the achievements of the Jesuits already apparent in the works of Sandoval and Ruiz de Montoya was rendered explicit in a prolix chronicle, written by Andrés Pérez de Ribas, in 1645, the Spanish provincial of the Mexican Province, which provided a detailed account of the foundation and growth of the Jesuit mission in Sinaloa, Sonora and among the Tepehuanas of Chihuahua, together with some discussion of the work undertaken by the Company among the Indians of the capital. It was entitled 'The history of the triumphs of Our Holy Faith among the most barbarous peoples of our globe, obtained by the soldiers of the militia of the Company of Jesus'. The purpose behind the chronicle emerged in the author's observation that an unnamed heretic had accused the Jesuits of choosing to work in 'countries of renown, wealthy and powerful' such as China and Japan, to the neglect of the poor and humble. In fact, as we have seen, it was not just heretics but equally the mendicants – Dominicans, Franciscans and Augustinians – who reproached the Company of Jesus for dealing so exclusively with the social elite, wearing silks in the Orient and cultivating the nobility in Europe. The evidence for such charges was not always forthcoming. Pérez de Ribas argued that the Jesuits had always addressed their ministry towards the poor and humble and had preached the gospel to many barbaric peoples. Of the four hundred members of the Mexican province, no less than sixty-five were to be found outside the colleges established in the cities, working on the mission stations. Indeed, over twenty priests had already suffered martyrdom at the hands of the northern Indians. Concurring with Sandoval, he interpreted the famous fourth vow taken by tried and trusted members of the Company – to go where the Pope directed – as a commitment to undertake a universal aposto-late, with St Paul's famous injunction, 'to be all things to all men', their guiding light. In triumphal spirit, he pointed to 'the militia and Company of Jesus, squadrons of the Divine captain, that are spread across the world', an apostolate which as much as in the first centuries had yielded a rich harvest 'full of triumphs and martyrs and confessors of the Church'.[18]

The story Pérez de Ribas had to tell was as impressive as any told by Montoya. For not merely had the Jesuits won numerous converts in Sinaloa,

they also succeeded in pacifying the Yaquis of Sonora, renowned 'to be a nation
so populous, warlike and arrogant that never had commerce nor friendship
with the Spaniards . . .' In all, some 30,000 natives of this tribe, dwelling in over
eighty separate settlements, were persuaded to accept the ministrations of the
Jesuits. Despite their ferocity, so he averred, there were 'many of very good
character, grateful and loyal'. If in general the Indians of the north-east did not
require much persuasion to become Christians, it was in part because they did
not possess any traditional pantheon of deities to hold their devotion, since
their religion was more a question of superstition, their lives dominated by
shamans, agents of the Devil, who wielded influence through preying on their
fears. Once converted, the Indians lost their taste for warfare and unlike the
Mexicans proved remarkably open to Jesuit exhortations to abandon their
excessive consumption of alcohol. Indeed, Pérez de Ribas described the Indians
of the region as good Christians, docile and faithful, without any of the malice
and hypocrisy of 'civilized nations'. Here, as elsewhere, the Jesuits established a
series of mission stations, laying out the surrounding towns in the usual
fashion, instructing their flock in artisan crafts, and supplying them with horses
and sheep as well as iron implements.[19] If we pause to consider that after
Independence the Yaquis were to engage in almost perpetual warfare with the
Mexican authorities in Sonora, then the achievement of the Jesuits in both
pacifying and governing such a nation appears all the more remarkable.

Although the conversion of the Yaquis was apparently obtained by an
expedition of two priests entering their territory accompanied only by four
Indian disciples, in the previous venture into Sinaloa the Jesuits had requested
the authorities to establish a small fort, which in 1596 was garrisoned by a
platoon of twenty-four soldiers. In this instance, Pérez de Ribas had no
hesitation in invoking such protection, arguing that in areas where the Devil
inspired the natives to resist the preaching of the gospel, with the lives of
missionaries placed at risk, the Catholic Kings, by reason of their universal
patronato in the New World, had the positive duty to intervene with force of
arms. After all, the emperors Constantine and Theodosius had wielded their
authority to encourage the advance of the faith and to suppress paganism.
Certainly baptism had to be freely accepted, but it often happened that those
natives who wished to be baptised were deterred by fear of attack from their
neighbours. In general, the existence of frontier garrisons, no matter how
small, had proved of great assistance to the progress of the Jesuit missions and
certainly prevented undue martyrdoms. In this line of reasoning, Pérez de Ribas
wrote with the experience of sixteen years spent in the northern missions. It
was in this context that he provided an admirable definition of what was then
meant by the term 'spiritual conquest', when he praised the virtues of 'those
labourers of the gospel and soldiers of the militia of Christ who were employed
in the apostolic ministry of these spiritual conquests and enterprises, waged so

as to liberate the souls God had ransomed with his blood, and to overthrow the fortresses where the Devil held them captive'. The enemy here was thus the Devil, with the hapless Indians the mere battleground and prize of this spiritual combat between the forces of heaven and hell.[20]

In addition to his account of the northern missions, Pérez de Ribas also described the urban ministry of the Jesuits, observing that in Mexico City they had several priests who were expert in native languages. As much as in Peru, however, they were careful not to enter into competition with the mendicants or incur the danger of episcopal visitation by accepting the charge of any native parishes, the only exception to this rule being the small Otomí *doctrina* of Tepozotlán, where they also maintained a house of studies. Here and at the college of San Gregorio in the capital, the Jesuits educated the sons of the Indian nobility, each school taking up to fifty students. Some of their pupils went on to attend the university and at least one student had not merely obtained his bachelor's degree but was also ordained a priest and appointed as a beneficed *cura* of a parish. Here, in an unexpected place, we encounter valuable testimony of the growing hispanisation of the Indian elite of New Spain which now allowed the children of the nobility to master the rudiments of higher education and enter the priesthood, albeit still in small numbers.[21]

In his account of the college of San Gregorio, Pérez de Ribas noted that two Indian confraternities were based in its church and that the Indians of the capital celebrated certain feasts with special dances and costumes. The native sacristan was well known for his penitence and holiness. It was, however, the life and works of Juan de Ledesma, a Mexican-born Jesuit, which dominated this account, since he devoted his life to the college and indeed was responsible for the construction of its church. In open contradiction to the calumny that Jesuits only dealt with 'people of wealth and renown', Ledesma refused to meet rich Spanish women, preferring to spend days hearing the confessions of Indians and preaching to his congregation in Nahuatl. During the great plague of 1629–30, he had proved tireless in his ministrations to the natives who were generally the most afflicted by the epidemics that still ravaged New Spain. The most striking feature of this description of a holy priest was the emphasis that Pérez de Ribas placed on Ledesma's asceticism, claiming that so rigorously did he scourge his flesh during nightly sessions of self-discipline that the walls of his cell were often found flecked with blood. During Holy Week he passed the entire day in the confessional and only slept in a chair.[22] In short, here was an image of the Christian saint defined by the practice of asceticism and service of the poor, a reminder of the degree to which the Jesuits still subscribed – at least for the purpose of propaganda – to the Franciscan ideals of sanctity.

What was entirely absent from the chronicle of Pérez de Ribas was any discussion of the main activity of the Jesuits in New Spain, the education of the creole elite in the circuit of colleges established in all the leading cities of the kingdom. Still less did he mention the impressive chain of haciendas which the eight colleges of New Spain had acquired so as to support their operations. Yet the first priority of the Jesuits upon their arrival in 1572 had been to establish a college in Mexico City, a venture which soon attracted the charitable munificence of Alonso de Villaseca, one of the wealthiest individuals in the colony. An indignant grandson of the benefactor, whose own brother entered the Company, estimated that Villaseca and his son-in-law, Agustín Guerrero, gave some 229,000 pesos to the Company of Jesus.[23] It was with the assistance of such donations that the Jesuits in Mexico moved so rapidly to establish colleges which offered a respectable education for the children of the elite and, equally important, prepared an entire generation of young creoles for the priesthood, their pupils soon ascending to the highest ranks in the ecclesiastical hierarchy. The rise of the creole clergy, a major feature of the seventeenth-century Church throughout Spanish America, was intimately connected to the preceding arrival of the Jesuits and the education they provided.

The degree to which the Jesuits in New Spain moved to acquire landed estates has only recently become clear. In 1643, only two years before Pérez de Ribas published his chronicle, the Mexican Province reached a settlement with the Crown whereby the colleges agreed to pay 7,000 pesos to obtain legal recognition of their claim to the lands occupied without due title, sections that in all encompassed no less than 1,004 square kilometres of pasture and 6,880 hectares of farmland. In 1650 the provincial compiled a report for the Father General of the Company in which he stated that his province had 336 members, of whom 60 were engaged in the northern missions, leaving 276 priests and brothers resident in some 21 colleges and houses. This impressive array of institutions was supported by a collective income of 156,500 pesos, a sum from which 37,000 pesos had to be subtracted in order to cover interest payments on debts and mortgages that amounted to 740,170 pesos, monies borrowed either to acquire more land or to finance the construction of churches and other buildings. If we apply the rate of 5 per cent return on capital, the conventional return on all loans in colonial Mexico, then we obtain a figure of over 3 million pesos as the capital value of all Jesuit properties in New Spain.[24] A modern study of the hacienda of Santa Lucía in the central valley owned by the college of St Peter and Paul found that in these years this vast estate possessed flocks of sheep which numbered over 100,000 head, from which the college obtained an annual income of close to 20,000 pesos. Moreover, it is clear that Jesuit landholdings grew almost continuously, decade by decade, across the two centuries that elapsed between their arrival in 1572 and their expulsion in 1767.[25] As we shall observe, it was the increasing wealth of the Company that provoked the condemnation of the bishop of Puebla, Juan de Palafox, and led to a bitter dispute in which the Jesuits obtained an ultimately pyrrhic victory. It should be noted that this dispute was already in train when Pérez de Ribas chose to publish his chronicle, its very title and content a defence of the Company's reputation.

In many ways, the most attractive of these early Jesuit chronicles was the *Histórica relación del reyno de Chile* (1646) written and published in Rome by Alonso de Ovalle, who, as his title suggests, wrote as much to laud his *patria* as to celebrate the achievements of his Order, the more especially since he found that even the name of his country was barely known in Europe. Yet when he came to consider the climate, flora and fauna of his native land, he declared that 'in all that has been discovered in America there is no region or part which is so similar to everything in Europe'. But that was as far as the similarity went, since he proceeded to depict a country that was still dominated by incessant frontier warfare, its destiny and identity, so to say, defined by Ercilla's *La Araucana*, written at the very start of its history as a Spanish colony. In large measure, so he declared, it was the climate or the constellation which determined the course of events, since their influence in Chile made the natives so brave as to render their conquest impossible. Citing Ercilla, whom he saluted as an author 'worthy of mortal memory', Ovalle maintained that the Araucanians were 'the brave Cantabrians of America, who like those of Europe merit the title of nobles through the valour with which they have defended themselves from their enemies'. Their leaders exhorted the young warriors to seek 'a glorious death for the esteemed liberty of their country', encountering in warfare the path of honour. Needless to say, Ovalle's fellow countrymen, the creoles or Spaniards born in Chile, equally benefited from the same benign climate and constellation since he praised them for their 'good wits and talents', averring that 'they are the best youth in the Indies ... as much in the docility and nobility of their character as in the acuity of their mind'. At the same time, the demands of frontier warfare inevitably entailed that 'they, more than others, are inclined to warfare and thus very few apply themselves to trade', and still fewer, he added, to any kind of studies.[26] In effect, the entire seventeenth century in Chile was to be dominated by armed struggle between Indians and settlers, with constant inroads and raids, the forces maintained by the Crown barely sufficient to maintain the frontier forts.

It was the first Jesuit provincial in Chile, Luis de Valdivia, who sought to end the deadlock by advocating a general peace treaty, in which the rights of the Indians to local autonomy and possession of their land would be safeguarded. In particular, the general licence issued by the governor for the enslavement of any 'rebel' natives who were captured was to be suspended. In the event, although his efforts led to the signing of a peace treaty in 1612, agreed between the leading Araucanian chiefs and the governor, tragedy intervened when he despatched a mission of three Jesuits across the frontier to initiate the work of conversion. For one cacique, infuriated by the flight of his wives to the Spanish fort, murdered the priests and at one stroke brought a renewal of the cycle of raids and counter-raids, with each side taking captives. In the years which followed, the Jesuits were obliged to restrict their efforts to pacified or friendly Indians who worked as labourers on Spanish estates or who clustered close to the frontier forts.[27] With so many captives taken, however, there also emerged a population of Christian women and children living among the free Indians. Moreover, some caciques proved sufficiently impressed by the priests as to afford them a certain measure of protection if they ventured beyond the limits of Spanish authority.

In addition to his review of the frontier wars, Ovalle provided an invaluable account of the Jesuit ministry in Santiago and other towns in Chile. For their priests did not restrict themselves to the colleges, but also engaged in regular visits to gaols and hospitals, and preached the gospel in public squares and in churches. Great emphasis was placed on hearing confessions, especially during Lent and Holy Week, with some priests available until late at night. Their church offered a warm welcome to the confraternities organised by Spaniards, Indians and blacks. Ovalle offered a lively description of penitential sessions during Lent when members of these bodies entered the church at night carrying crosses and scourging themselves in 'the discipline of blood'. On Easter Sunday all the Indian confraternities sallied forth in procession through the streets, carrying banners, candles and images, their march accompanied by 'much music and dances'. So also, at the feast of the Three Kings at Christmas, the black confraternities elected their own king dressed as a Spaniard and danced in his honour. In a charming passage, Ovalle described how one Jesuit provincial led such a procession, singing *coplas* in praise of the Virgin Mary.[28] The priests of the Company also toured the countryside, visiting haciendas, and ministering both to Indian labourers and African slaves. Commending the labours of Sandoval, whom he had met when passing through Cartagena, Ovalle admitted that the aspect of the Jesuit ministry which caused most work was the catechesis of slaves newly arrived from Africa, since 'these are so incapable (I do not speak of the blacks born here nor of those who have learnt Spanish, since these have as much capacity as the Spaniards, but of the newcomers) that they appear more like beasts than men . . .' Even so, he related a story to show that even the most obdurate and apparently insensible blacks could be won over to the faith provided they were treated with kindness and persistent effort.[29]

In sum, Ovalle painted a remarkably attractive picture of the variegated gamut of Jesuit activities in Chile, tasks which ranged from the education of the creole elite to extensive frontier missions and urban ministry among Indians and blacks. His chronicle thus afforded an effective rebuttal of current slanders of the Company. In its praise of both the Araucanians and the creoles, it amply illustrated the demands of local patriotism. At the same time, Ovalle lamented that the unsettled state of the country meant that the Jesuits were not able to obtain sufficient recruits, so that the fifty priests of the Chilean province were quite unable to deal with all the demands on their time and attention. His chronicle thus ended with an appeal that more Jesuits be sent from Europe to Chile. After all, thanks to the authority of the Catholic monarchy, more souls were to be harvested in America than in Asia.

IV

For two hundred years the Jesuits in Spanish America grew steadily in numbers, wealth and influence. Their heroic labour in the frontier missions was matched by their unceasing toil in colleges, the pulpit and the confessional. Whereas the mendicant orders came to be plagued by disorders arising from partisan conflict and failure to observe their rule, the Company of Jesus maintained its cohesion and moral discipline, expelling dissidents and back-sliders without compunction. To account for this success we should remember that all Jesuits were formed by *The Spiritual Exercises*, a set of meditations devised by St Ignatius Loyola and always taken under the guidance of a skilled spiritual director. In good Spanish fashion the initiate was called to enlist in the service of Christ, the Lord of the Universe, in much the same spirit as a loyal subject might follow his king into battle against the infidel. But he was then enjoined to reflect on the long, obscure life of Christ at Nazareth before picturing in his mind's eye 'a vast plain embracing the whole region of Jerusalem, where the supreme Captain-General of the good is Christ our Lord: and another plain, in the region of Babylon, where the chief of the enemy is Lucifer'. In this war between 'the two standards' Satan despatched an innumerable army of demons to deprave and subvert every nation on earth, whereas Christ relied on his apostles and disciples to preach the gospel to all men. At issue were the opposing values of riches, honour and pride as against poverty, shame and humility.[30]

If St Ignatius thus invoked the grand Augustinian image of the Two Cities, Jerusalem and Babylon, engaged in cosmic conflict across the ages, in his 'Rules for thinking with the Church', he exhorted the Jesuits to sustain the devotional practices of medieval Catholicism, encouraging veneration of saints' relics, candles and holy images, the frequent hearing of mass and reception of communion, and the practice of pilgrimage. Although he recognised that positive theologians such as St Augustine, St Jerome and St Gregory had the power 'to move the affections to love and serve God our Lord in all things', he especially commended the great scholastics, St Thomas, St Bonaventure, and Peter Lombard, whose merit was 'to define and explain for our times the things necessary to eternal salvation and to take the lead in impugning and exposing all errors and fallacies'. Since they drew on Church councils and canon law to supplement their reading of scripture and the early Fathers, they were 'more modern' and reliable than their predecessors.[31]

Although the Jesuits never renegued on their founder's injunction to defend the intellectual and devotional culture of medieval Catholicism, they also moved quickly to master the literary and philosophic advances of the Renaissance. Moreover, their missions in China, Japan and India soon confronted them with the task of reconciling the Christian gospel with oriental philosophy and religion. To assist them they first invoked the distinction between nature and grace, between human wisdom and Christian truth, so clearly set out by St Thomas Aquinas. For further inspiration they turned to the Florentine revival of Alexandrian neo-Platonism, a school which had attempted to reconcile Plato and Moses, Christian revelation and Greek philosophy. By the seventeenth century there emerged Jesuit theologians who framed a vast, historico-cosmological synthesis in which the Catholicism of the Baroque era was presented as the triumphant fulfilment of mankind's universal quest for natural wisdom and spiritual knowledge of the Deity. The very organisation of the Company of Jesus was interpreted as a practical application of the principles of human government set out in Plato's *Republic*.[32]

If modern scholars have baulked at any facile equation of Jesuit and military discipline, it is clear that St Ignatius shaped his institute in accordance with the nascent ideals of absolute monarchy. Whereas the mendicant orders formed confederations of relatively autonomous provinces in which superiors were chosen by periodic election, the Company of Jesus was governed by a Father General elected for life and resident in Rome, who had the power to appoint all provincials and college rectors. From their inception the Jesuits eschewed any narrow European ambit and despatched missions across the globe. In this respect they acted as the ideal instruments of a revived Papacy which equally took the whole world for its parish. At the Council of Trent, Diego Lainez, St Ignatius' first successor as Father General, boldly queried the universal necessity of episcopal jurisdiction, attacking the immobile hierarchy of dioceses and parishes as an obstacle to the expansion of the missionary church. Although his arguments were rejected by the Council, which magnified the authority of the bishops, albeit often as delegates of the Pope, the Jesuits thereafter sedulously evaded all episcopal intrusion into their affairs.[33] In Spanish America they refused to accept the administration of parishes so as to avoid potential conflict with the hierarchy, confining their governance of souls to the frontier missions. Nevertheless, their international character, the sheer *élan* of their expansion, their growing wealth and influence, and their resolute independence, all combined to arouse the suspicion and resentment of both the mendicant orders and of many bishops.

9

HISTORY AND MYTH

I

THE APPEARANCE of José de Acosta's *Historia natural y moral de las Indias* (1590) marked an epoch in the European comprehension of the New World. The book was immediately republished in several editions and within a few years had been translated into all the principal languages of Europe. It soon attained the rank of a classic and as late as the eighteenth century the Scots historian, William Robertson, pronounced it to be 'one of the most accurate and best informed writings concerning the West Indies', and saluted its author as 'a philosopher'.[1] The reasons for its popularity and enduring influence are not hard to seek. In relatively modest compass, the reader was provided with a description of nature in the New World, a disquisition on the origin of its native inhabitants, and a brief history of the Inca and Aztec empires. The work was distinguished by an easy, fluent style, by a confident lucid exposition of often complicated matters, and above all, by the critical acumen of its arguments. Where his predecessors had been content to describe, Acosta always sought to explain, weighing both cause and effect with masterly precision. Not since the days of Vespucci had any author combined first-hand experience of the Indies with such evident literary talent. But if the Florentine had composed a classical fable, the Jesuit demonstrated that he had assimilated the lessons of the Renaissance both as regards style and perspective, at all points rejecting myth and authority in favour of observation and reason. That he also wrote to glorify God's providential election of the Catholic monarchy as ruler of the Indies did not in any way obscure the quality of his reasoning.

A heavy man, of uncertain, melancholic temper, a Jew by descent, José de Acosta (1540–1600) was educated at the universities of Alcalá and Salamanca, where the Jesuits were then challenging the Dominican mastery of the faculties of theology and philosophy. Once qualified, he was considered for a theological lectureship at Rome, but, if we are to believe his testimony, 'I pleaded to be sent to the Indies to work among barbarous peoples without esteem or honour.' In the event, he spent the years 1571–86 in Peru, where, far from ministering to the

Indians, he won recognition in Lima for his eloquent and learned sermons. He lectured in the university of San Marcos, acted as chief theologian of the third Provincial Church Council held in Lima in 1581, and served as provincial of his Order. Such was his distinction that Francisco de Toledo sought his company and indeed attempted to enroll him within the circle of his advisers. The two men quarrelled, however, on the vital question of the Jesuit mission, the viceroy seeking to entrust the Company with the administration of Indian parishes, only to find that Acosta rejected the proposal on the grounds that such responsibility would bring his Order into inevitable conflict with the bishops over the question of jurisdiction and visitation. Instead, the Jesuits in Peru chose to concentrate their efforts in establishing colleges in the leading cities for the purpose of educating the children of the chief settlers, the chief exception to this rule being their college at Juli, situated in Chucuito, where they catered for the needs of the local Aymara.[2]

In 1587 Acosta returned to Spain, breaking his journey to spend a few, but instructive, months in Mexico. It is testimony to his remarkable abilities that soon after his arrival in the Peninsula he attracted royal favour and was subsequently chosen to serve as the king's emissary to Rome, where he conducted delicate and eventually unsuccessful negotiations with both the Pope and the Jesuit General concerning Philip II's desire to subject the Company in Spain to the jurisdiction of the Inquisition and to assert a greater degree of royal authority over the Iberian provinces of the Order. This involvement with the Crown discredited Acosta in the eyes of fellow Jesuits, although it did not prevent him from becoming rector of the college at Salamanca. In 1588 he succeeded in obtaining royal licence to publish two Latin tracts dealing with Nature in the New World and missionary methods and theory, the latter entitled De procuranda Indorum salute.[3] Two years later he won enduring fame with the publication of the Historia natural y moral de las Indias, which consisted of a translation of the first Latin tract, written in Peru, together with materials on native history in part gathered during his visit to Mexico. A man of great learning, Acosta displayed a greater familiarity with the writings of the Church Fathers and the classics than with the works of Aquinas and other scholastic theologians. A denizen of the sombre world of Philip II, he displayed a peculiar combination of acute intelligence and brazen triumphalism, salted in places with a political cynicism more reminiscent of Gómara than of Las Casas, whose name, significantly enough, never once appears in his books or letters.

The most original part of Acosta's work lay in his discussion of nature in the New World. In the opening pages of his Historia natural, he deliberately chose to emphasise the geographical errors of Aristotle and St Augustine, albeit carefully adverting that it was not the responsibility of a Church Father to be an expert in such matters. The natural philosopher in his examination of the causes and effects of phenomena had to be guided 'not so much by the doctrine of ancient philosophers, as by true reason and certain experience'. The same point, of course, had been made by Oviedo over half a century earlier, but with far less wit and force. Not content to exclaim over the absurdity of Aristotle's contention that the torrid zones of the world were uninhabitable, Acosta sought to encounter reasons to explain why the heat of these regions was not so great as had been imagined by the ancients. The chief cause, he argued, was the sheer humidity of the tropics, adding 'nowhere in the universe are there more or greater rivers or more swamps. The greater part of America is uninhabitable because of the superabundance of water ...' The sheer depth of the oceans, when combined with a burning sun and the high frequency of strong winds produced an abundant rainfall which kept the soil fertile and humid and the air fresh and benign. With equal care, Acosta analysed the effect of altitude on climate, observing that the highlands of Peru offered a favourable environment for human settlement in the tropics. Although he provided a considerable range of information on the metals, crops and livestock of the New World, Acosta's main achievement was to advance a rational explanation of the causes and effects of tropical climate, virtually identifying the Americas with this zone. Whereas Oviedo had offered little more than an inventory or catalogue of flora and fauna, mere *particularidades*, by contrast, Acosta at all points sought to ascertain the causes of phenomena, generalising from observation. It was precisely in this pursuit of causality and generality rather than in any mere observation of effects that Acosta most closely approached the purpose and method of the modern scientist, and most obviously merited Robertson's description of him as a philosopher.[4]

In his discussion of the much controverted question of the origin of mankind in the New World, Acosta displayed great judgement, cutting through the fog of speculation that surrounded the subject with incisive logic. The theory advanced by Zárate and Sarmiento de Gamboa, that the Indians descended from the peoples of the lost continent of Atlantis, was dismissed out of hand, the account found in Plato's dialogue, *Timaeus*, discounted as mere fable. As for the commonly canvassed notion that Peru was the biblical Ophir, the site of King Solomon's mines, he argued that Africa or the East Indies were a far more likely location. After all, until the modern discovery of the magnetic compass, no mariner had ever dared to venture into the open ocean, but rather had always sought to remain close to land, hugging the shore-line. How then was it possible for Solomon's ships to sail across the Pacific to Peru? Then again, Acosta rejected the popular opinion that the Indians descended from the Ten Lost Tribes of Israel, arguing that whereas the natives of the New World retained no recollection of any script or much idea of God, of all peoples on earth the Jews were the most renowned for the tenacity with which they clung to their traditions and lineage. What lent interest to this argument was that Acosta himself came from *converso* stock, his family of Jewish descent.[5] It should be noted that underlying the identification of the Indians with the Israelites was the millennial premise that the conversion of the Jews would mark the advent of the last age before the Second Coming of Christ. With all such myths dismissed with contempt, Acosta then argued for the probability that the first men to arrive in the New World came by land rather than by sea, crossing from Asia in the north-eastern corner of the hemisphere in the direction of modern Alaska, at that time still unmapped. He surmised that on arrival these men were mere savages, travelling in small bands, slowly spreading across the entire landmass during a lengthy period of time, a hypothesis supported by the multiplicity of unrelated languages spoken by contemporary Indians. That they came from a common source in East Asia was demonstrated by the similarity of their physique and appearance to the natives of that region. The conclusion that Acosta derived from these arguments was that all social and political development in the New World derived from autochthonous forces, with leaders of great courage and intelligence emerging to form states and eventually empires, leading their subjects out of their hitherto savage condition.[6]

It was in his tract on missionary tactics, entitled *De procuranda Indorum salute*, that Acosta continued the discussion of Indian social development, advancing his celebrated division of all 'barbarians' into three broad categories, arranged in evolutionary sequence. The first class, to which the Chinese, Japanese and some East Indians belonged, was defined by the possession of cities, laws, stable government, and, above all else, by the possession of a script which allowed for written laws, books and records of the past. The second class, which comprised the Aztecs and Incas, had fixed settlements, a religious cult, strong rulers and some memory of the past, but lacked books or a script. The third stratum comprised mere savages, such as the natives of Amazonia, 'without laws, without kings, without priests, without magistrates and without government'. Elsewhere, Acosta interpolated another stratum or stage, inserted between the Incas and savages, so as to cover the societies of New Granada and Chile which possessed the rudiments of government and religion. In general terms, there was little that was new in this scheme. Already, as we have seen, Las Casas had drawn a sharp distinction between the advanced states of the Incas and Aztecs, the equal in all but Christianity and the possession of a script to the ancient Romans and Greeks, and the simple islanders of the Caribbean or the nomads of Florida, still dwelling in the first age of humanity. It was a contrast found in Cicero and in classical poets. The originality of Acosta's approach lay in his replacement of the simple contrast of civilization and savagery by a sharply delineated, ascending scale of societies, defining each stage with carefully listed characteristics. The inclusion of the Chinese and Japanese, based on data provided by Jesuit missionaries, offered a more ample perspective than that afforded by the comparison with the ancient world. At the same time, the emphasis on a written script as the defining mark of true humanity and political culture, betrayed Acosta's humanist bias, and obviously echoed the arguments of Sepúlveda and Gómara.[7] Moreover, Acosta was insistent that societies in all three stages were essentially barbaric owing to their ignorance of Christian doctrine and morals.

The purpose of this division of all humanity outside Christendom into three classes lay not in its utility for anthropological research but rather in affording a yardstick by which to measure what reliance should be placed on force of arms in the preaching of the Christian gospel. In dealing with nations such as the Chinese and Japanese, so Acosta argued, there existed no justification for conquest by a Christian prince. In Mexico, he composed a memorandum opposing the mad schemes of his fellow Jesuit, Alonso de Sánchez, who had urged the Spanish Crown to launch an attack on China, so as to bring that empire into the fold of the Catholic Church. On both practical and theological grounds, Acosta denounced the plan, declaring that it was unjust, impracticable, and would cause grave scandal. If the Chinese were reluctant to admit Spanish merchants and missionaries, it was in large measure because of their fear of aggression. Granted that the emperor and his mandarins maintained internal peace and government, the gospel should be preached peacefully, as had been the case in the Roman Empire. In this connexion, it should be noted that Acosta remained resolutely unimpressed by contemporary Jesuit praise of Chinese culture, arguing that their reliance on characters rather than on an alphabet meant that the *literati* had to devote all their energies to learning how to read and write rather than in acquiring knowledge of the sciences and philosophy.[8] Any American Indian who learnt the alphabet would soon come to know more than the wisest Chinese savant.

In the approach to mere savages, such as the peoples of Amazonia, Acosta defended the right of the Christian prince to intervene with force of arms for the purpose of establishing a protectorate, obliging the natives to form settlements, so that they could learn the crafts of Europe and eventually come to accept the gospel. If land lay idle, it could be legitimately granted to Spanish settlers who could then assist in the pacification of the region. Where the savages resisted this encroachment on their territory, it was permissible for the authorities to repress their rebellion, albeit more with paternal admonition and punishment than by fire and the sword. In short, Acosta fully endorsed the steady expansion of the Spanish frontier in the Americas, and thus provided a justification of contemporary practice.[9]

But what of the Incas and Aztecs, the second class of barbarians: was their conquest an act of justice? Had warfare offered the best means of preaching the gospel to these peoples? Needless to say, in raising this question Acosta entered a political and ideological mine-field. A fellow Jesuit in Peru already had been severely reprimanded for questioning the justice of Spanish conquest and dominion. As we have seen, Viceroy Toledo had endeavoured to close the question, sharply condemning Las Casas as a pernicious influence, whose tracts upset Christian consciences to no good purpose. So too, in much the same vein Acosta now argued that by the 1580s the time was long since past for any restitution of goods or restoration of the old order: Spanish conquest and empire was a political fact and had to be accepted as such. To continue to question the justice of the venture would imperil the task of evangelising the Indian. Far from obeying his own dictum, however, Acosta then cited the propositions enunciated by Francisco de Vitoria, theories still dominant in Spanish universities, so as to challenge the conventional justification of Spanish expansion. He denied that the Pope possessed any right to confer jurisdiction over infidel kingdoms. Similarly, Christian kings had no God-given mandate to invade other states in order to punish crimes against nature. Each common-wealth was endowed with its own sovereignty and territorial integrity: to admit otherwise would open the door for English or French intervention in Spain itself on some trumped-up pretext of injustice.[10] With these observations in hand, Acosta then denounced as 'a vulgar error' the widely held belief that the Catholic King had been authorised by the Pope to conquer the Indians in order to repress their idolatry and prevent their crimes against nature. The arguments of 'a certain author', which is to say, Sepúlveda, could not be countenanced. Conversely, Acosta judiciously framed a case for European maritime expansion by developing Vitoria's doctrines that all nations have the natural right to communicate and to trade, and, if Christian, to preach the gospel, principles he deployed to justify the establishment of armed ports and fortresses on foreign coasts to defend merchants and protect missionaries, a formula reminiscent of the first proposals of Las Casas for settlement on the mainland of America.[11]

Granted this reliance on Vitoria and the school of Salamanca, it should come as no surprise to observe that Acosta contemptuously dismissed the favourite argument of the Toledan circle, that the tyranny of the Incas justified Spanish conquest and dominion. If crimes against nature did not offer a pretext for military intervention, how could the character of a political regime affect the issue? In any case, were not all empires founded by violence and war? Had not St Augustine in his *City of God* declared that the Roman Empire had been tyrannically established, its great men seeking glory through the death of thousands? Yet the Apostles had never sought to encompass its destruction nor questioned its rule. If this be allowed, then what cause was there to query the right of the Spanish Crown to govern the New World? In this extraordinary application of Augustine's doctrines, Acosta argued in effect that both the Inca and the Spanish empires were founded on unjust conquest and violence and hence, by implication, were both tyrannies.[12] But neither their origin nor their eventual constitution offered any justification for outside intervention, still less any cause to question their legitimacy.[13]

With tender consciences, no doubt comforted by this Machiavellian defence of *raison d'état*, so typical of the servants of absolute monarchy, Acosta then urged the clergy to draw practical encouragement from the papal commission to the Catholic Kings to ensure the conversion of the native inhabitants of the New World. Contemporary Jesuit experience in Africa had demonstrated that in countries where the gospel had been preached in peaceful fashion without European intervention, the unstable nature of barbarian monarchs easily led to a loss of faith and relapse into idolatry. Where the subjects of a given state were accustomed to be governed tyrannically, it was necessary to procure and maintain conversion by a certain measure of compulsion. In short, priests should not seek to debate grand questions of political justice, but rather should concentrate their energies on the task of preaching the gospel, taking advantage of the authority and assistance offered by the Catholic Kings.[13]

Despite his evident reservations about Toledo's powers of ratiocination, Acosta entirely agreed with the viceroy in defining the natives of Peru as barbarians, which is to say, as persons deficient in rational judgement and hence unfit for political liberty. In a clear echo of Sepúlveda and Matienzo, he bluntly declared that 'the character of the Indian is servile'. True, he defended the natives' rationality, condemning those Spaniards who treated them as mere brutes. Like all the sons of Adam, they had souls in need of salvation and the Church had the obligation to protect them and ensure their conversion. But he also cited St John Chrysostom to the effect that the nature of slaves was shameless, lascivious, stupid, and difficult to change by instruction, concluding that this description applied to both Africans and Indians with equal force. To remedy the defects of such a character, strict discipline was required: 'with the healthy burden of assiduous toil, they are separated from idleness and license, and, braked by fear, are kept within their duty'.[14] But their character was not innate, merely the result of their upbringing, so that across the passage of generations it would be possible to effect change by means of strict education and continuous instruction. As Aristotle had said, custom was second nature. Not that such a transformation could be wrought through the education of individuals: the entire society had to be re-founded. It was for this reason, so Acosta declared, that it was necessary to concentrate the Indians into towns, provide them with clothing, introduce the use of money, and install a priest and magistrates to supervise them, with schools for commoners and colleges for the nobility an essential part of the programme. In effect, Acosta entirely supported the Toledan policy of enforced resettlement and cited with approval the viceregal dictum that 'it was first necessary for the Indians to learn how to be men and afterwards to be Christians'. As much as Mendieta in New Spain, he defended the sanction of physical punishment, so as to allow priests and magistrates to correct bad habits or offences, advocating 'some light monetary fine, putting them in the stocks for a day, sometimes a few strokes of the lash, and the most grave of all, shaving their heads, which is deemed a major affront among Indians'. Clearly, whether one saw the Indians as mere children or as virtual slaves made little difference when it came to the sort of punishment envisaged.[15]

As befitted a tract addressed to future missionaries, *De procuranda* was filled with exhortations as to the need for sacerdotal humility and patience, without any mitigation of the difficulties and tedium of the task: 'We suffer the inconstancy and the natural imbecility of the Indians, obliged to scatter the divine seed on ground that is sandy and shifting.' At the same time, he noted that 'for a bad teacher all the pupils are stupid', admitting that the method of catechesis in Peru had been sorely deficient, since it had largely consisted in training the Indian to recite by rote a few prayers and enforcing attendance at mass without much exlication of the gospel. Indeed, the Indians had been often positively deterred by the avarice, lust and tyranny of the priests put in charge of their parishes. Yet it was precisely these 'mercenary ministers' who were loudest in proclaiming the irrationality of the Indians so as the more easily to defend their brutal exploitation. On two key issues, Acosta agreed with the Franciscans in Mexico, when he advocated that Indians should be allowed to receive the Eucharist (which some priests wished to deny them) but counselled that they should not be admitted to the priesthood. As provincial of the Jesuits he had insisted on the necessity of mastery of Indian languages if the gospel was to be preached to all natives. To deal with this problem, he had initially favoured the acceptance of mestizos as Jesuits, but confessed that experience had demonstrated that although some became dedicated priests many had clearly imbibed Indian vices along with the milk of their native mothers.[16]

Broadening his discussion to review recent legislation, Acosta expressed approval of virtually all the central features of the Toledan settlement, seeking only to temper the wind to the shorn lamb. He defended the right of the Crown to demand tribute from its native subjects and did not quarrel with the principle of forced labour recruitment for work in the mines and agriculture. He agreed with Matienzo that it would be better for the Indians if the encomenderos be given their grants in perpetuity, since they should be regarded as a nobility which was essential for the defence and stability of the kingdom. This defence both of encomiendas and the *mita* demonstrates the gulf separating Acosta from Las Casas and Mendieta and the degree to which he shared the ideas of the Toledan circle. At best, he protested against abuses in the system demanding more effective regulation of tributes and labour levies. For the rest, he simply questioned the principle set forth by Matienzo and implemented by Toledo, that the Indians should be taxed according to their capacity to pay, which is to say, exploited to the degree consonant with their physical survival.[17]

In the second part of his *Historia natural y moral*, composed in Europe,

Acosta drew upon the researches of Polo de Ondegardo in Peru and of Juan de
Tovar, a fellow Jesuit, in Mexico, to offer a summary description of the Aztec
and Inca empires. Whether he enjoyed the opportunity to consult the manuscript copy of Las Casas' *Apologética historia sumaria* that was kept in the
Dominican priory in Mexico is not known, but undoubtedly his few months in
New Spain appear to have persuaded him to take a more favourable view of
Indian achievements than had been evident in *De procuranda*, a tract written
when still in Peru. Whatever the case, he prefaced his account with the
observation that his purpose was to counter the false but common opinion that
the Indians were 'a brutish and bestial people, without intelligence or so little as
barely to warrant the name'. In fact, their laws and institutions had many
features worthy of respect in any nation of the world. If they were guilty of
vices and idolatry, so equally had been the ancient Romans and Greeks, an
admission which in no way detracted from their obvious virtues. Acosta then
qualified the force of this comparison with the classical world, so favoured by
Las Casas, by adding: 'Although the ancient gentiles have far surpassed in
valour and natural knowledge the peoples of the New World, yet we may
observe many things in them worthy of respect. But, to conclude, they show
them to be barbarous, a people who being deprived of supernatural light, also
lack philosophy and natural knowledge.'[18]

The radical contrast to Las Casas, implicit in these words, was reflected in
the way in which Acosta presented his material and arguments. For whereas
the Dominican invoked Aristotle's criteria for a true city, and only moved to
discuss the question of religion once he had demonstrated the secular foundations of native society, the Jesuit initiated his discussion of Inca and Aztec
culture by a rabid denunciation of the Devil who as author and fount of all
idolatry governed the New World in a monstrous empire of darkness. Although
Acosta admitted that many natives entertained a vague idea of a creator of the
universe, a divine being similar to the unknown god whose altar St Paul
encountered in Athens, nevertheless, he attributed the prevalence of idolatry to
the direct intervention of Satan, who so influenced Indian religion as to create a
blasphemous parody of Christianity, imitating both its rites and beliefs, all with
the purpose of leading the natives further astray into crime and immorality.
Thus, whereas Las Casas had elaborated an essentially naturalistic argument,
tracing the origin of idolatry to human fears and ambitions, the effect of man's
fallen nature, with the Devil merely intervening to take advantage of this
weakness, by contrast, Acosta defined Satan as the fountain-head and source of
pagan religion, his dominion imposed to prevent or pervert the observance of
the dictates of natural law. If Las Casas had invoked Aquinas to defend the
autonomy of human nature, Acosta cited Augustine's *City of God* to confirm
his identification of all manifestations of native religion as the work of the Lord
of Darkness. Once more, the vision of the Two Cities, Jerusalem and Babylon,

locked in spiritual combat across the ages, was deployed so as to prevent any accommodation with non-Christian religion.[19]

The discussion of Indian government and law was governed by much the same unsympathetic approach. At the outset, Acosta observed that all barbarians exhibit the quality of their nature in the form of government they adopt, which was to say, that they were invariably ruled by tyrants, with kings treated as gods and subjects as slaves. This was a rule that was as much applicable to the Chinese and Turks as to the Incas and Aztecs. Despite this unpromising start, Acosta then skilfully compressed a great deal of information into short, incisive chapters in which he described the most striking achievements of the two empires. For Peru the emphasis was obviously on the impressive roads, the great fortresses and temples constructed by the Incas, followed by an approving discussion of the equitable forms of land distribution, the austere diet and the benevolent forms of social co-operation and welfare, worthy, so he averred, of a religious community. By contrast in New Spain it was the complexity of the Mexican calendar and the approximation to a written script which occupied the centre of the stage, topics based on papers supplied by Juan de Tovar. On the question of historical sequence, Acosta found that whereas for Peru little trustworthy data could be found on the Incas prior to the reign of the emperor Pachakuti in the early fifteenth century, in New Spain it was possible to encounter a detailed chronology stretching back several centuries, starting with the migration of the Aztecs southwards and continuing with the succession of monarchs who ruled in Tenochtitlan since its foundation. The emphasis on the role of the Devil in the guise of Huitzilopochtli, the tutelary deity of the Mexica, was counter-balanced by a eulogy of the wisdom of the lords of Texcoco. Throughout Acosta's discussion of the Aztecs and Incas there can be discerned a latent contradiction which he fails to resolve in any satisfactory manner.[20]

In his concluding account of the conquest of Mexico, Acosta provided an answer to the questions that he had preferred to leave unresolved in De procuranda. Invoking the authority of Eusebius of Caesarea, the Church historian and biographer of Constantine the Great, he now chose to present the conquest of the New World as a manifest act of Divine Providence. In the same way that the Roman unification of the ancient world had prepared the way for the preaching of the gospel, so equally the rise of the Inca and Aztec empires had smoothed the path for the entrance of Christianity, their reliance on a single tongue easing the task of the mendicants. As for the massacres perpetrated by Cortés at Cholula and by Alvarado in Tenochtitlan, they were best seen as God's punishment on the Indians for their idolatry and cruelties. Equally important, Acosta did not hesitate to accept the intimations of Gómara and Cieza de León that in both Peru and Mexico the conquerors had been assisted in their battles against the Indians by the appearance of Santiago and the Virgin Mary. The conquest was thus defined as a providential act of liberation through which the natives of the New World were freed from the dominion of both Satan and human tyrants and offered the means of salvation. Thus, whereas in *De procuranda* Acosta had counselled against any further discussion of the justice of the conquest as politically inexpedient, albeit ready to condemn the murder of Atahualpa, in his *Historia natural y moral* he assumed the mantle of Gómara and sounded a triumphalist note far removed in spirit from the diatribes of Las Casas.[21]

His subordination of religious and humanitarian interests to political expediency is nowhere better illustrated than in Acosta's description of Potosí. For he provided a careful survey of the mining industry and of the techniques on which it depended, fixing upon Toledo's introduction of the process of amalgamation with mercury as the salvation of the *cerro rico*. At the same time, he offered a lively portrait of the town prior to recent changes, recalling the spectacle of the surrounding hills illumined by the flickering light of over 6,000 Indian clay furnaces used for smelting the ore. Once again, Acosta scored by his keen attention to matters of contemporary interest and by his mastery of mineralogical and technical subjects. Equally significant, however, he made no mention of the other, indispensable feature of Toledo's revival of Potosí, the organisation of the *mita*, the enforced draft of over 13,500 Indian peasants, summoned from a vast area to labour in the mines and mills of the great peak. Moreover, echoing Toledo's Dominican cousin, Acosta boldly declared that Divine Providence had carefully sowed the New World with plentiful deposits of precious metals so as to attract Christian settlement and thus ensure the conversion of the Indians. The discovery and renovation of Potosí had provided Philip II with the means of uniting the Crowns of Portugal and Castile, and thus bringing the West and East Indies under one Catholic monarch charged by Providence with the defence of Christendom from the onslaught of both infidel and heretic.[22] Eusebius of Caesarea himself could not have claimed better acquaintance with the design of the Triune Godhead than Acosta did in these presumptuous asseverations.

The selective reliance of Acosta on certain doctrines of St Augustine was also manifest in his approach to the all-important question of the possible salvation of the virtuous pagan. For he resolutely denied the possibility of eternal salvation outside the Christian Church and strongly criticised those Jesuits who argued that non-Christians who observed the dictates of natural law might well enter heaven by means of what in theological terms was called baptism of desire. Indeed, in Peru, Acosta had been active in condemning the Dominican, Francisco de la Cruz, for teaching (among other things) that Indians could win salvation through implicit faith without any formal knowledge of Christian dogma. So too, the third Church Council held in Lima, which Acosta attended as theological adviser, pronounced that by reason of their idolatry all Indians

who had dwelt in Peru prior to the advent of the Spaniards were the children of
Satan, irrevocably sentenced to eternal damnation.[23] To appreciate the implications and context of this judgement, it should be noted that at much the same
time, Matteo Ricci, the founder of the Jesuit mission in Peking, declared that
Confucius had taught the worship of the one, true God and had imparted an
admirable code of ethics, perfectly consonant with Christian morality. Further,
he wrote: 'One can confidently hope that in the mercy of God, many of the
ancient Chinese found salvation in the natural law, assisted as they must have
been by the special help which, as the theologians teach, is denied to no-one
who does what he can towards salvation, according to the light of his
conscience.' In this pronouncement Ricci established the theological foundation of the Jesuit mission in China, and by extension, in any country where the
observance of natural law appeared to be uncontaminated by the prevalence of
idolatry. The contrast with Acosta could not have been greater.[24] At dispute
was the calculated eclecticism which allowed Acosta to invoke St Augustine to
depict Indian society as corrupted to its very core by the dominance of the Devil
while at the same time celebrating in Eusebian strain the triumph of Spanish
arms in the New World as the fulfilment of Providential design.

III

The summary confidence with which Acosta dismissed several much-cherished
theories about the origin of the American Indians affronted minds unsympathetic to the critical lessons of the Renaissance. In Europe itself great tracts of the
past remained uncharted terrain inhabited only by the fanciful projections of
pious mythographers and patriotic speculators. Moreover, if some humanists
sharpened their linguistic analysis of texts, others were attracted to delve
deeply into the arcane lore of Egyptian hieroglyphs and the Kabala. Since the
discovery of America had been in part prompted and was certainly accompanied by an outburst of millennial expectations, it should come as no surprise to
learn that the origin of its native inhabitants provoked almost as much
speculation and controversy as the often-studied polemic concerning their
nature and talents. It will be recalled that Oviedo had identified the Antilles as
the Hesperides, the ancient Islands of the Fortunate, and had advanced the
hypothesis of a pre-historic Spanish colonisation. So too, both Zárate and
Sarmiento de Gamboa had cited Plato's *Timaeus* as evidence of the existence of
Atlantis, suggesting that the Indians were the descendants of its inhabitants.
Similarly, superficial resemblances between native cults and myths and the rites
and doctrines of Christianity or of the Jews, were interpreted as proof either of
early apostolic evangelisation of the New World, or, alternatively, of actual
settlement by the Israelites. What all these theories had in common was an
unstated purpose of subjecting the Indians to the universal scheme of biblical

history, an endeavour inspired by the presumption that the Indians lacked the capacity either to discover the dictates of natural law or approach any knowledge of the one true God without the assistance of teachers or settlers from abroad.

The fountain-head and enduring repository of all such myths was the *Origen de los Indios del Nuevo Mundo* (1607), a stout little volume published in Valencia by Gregorio García, a Dominican who had spent nine years in Peru. Its chief inspiration was the Latin commentary on ancient historians written by a fellow Dominican, Fr Jacobo Annius de Viterbo, who in 1498 published a range of texts hitherto deemed lost, chief among which was the history of Babylon from the days of Noah and the Ark composed by Berosus. Although some scholars almost immediately denounced Annius' discoveries as mere forgery, the information he provided about the first epoch of humanity on earth attracted a wide audience and continued to enjoy a certain vogue until the early eighteenth century.[25] Orthodox interpretation of biblical chronology at this time only made provision for six thousand years of history, so that the vista of a relatively civilised primitive age offered by the false Berosus was not inherently implausible. In particular, Noah was depicted as a philosopher conversant with many sciences, who instructed his children in the arts of astronomy and ship-building, thus allowing them to explore the globe without hurt. The diaspora of the descendants of his three sons, Shem, Japhet and Ham, was taken to explain the origin of the different races of mankind. Thus Misraim, the son of Shem, was identified as both a philosopher and a devilish mage, the founder of Egypt and its religion. Information was also forthcoming on the first settlement of Spain and its succession of twelve kings, including such eponymous monarchs as Ibero, Hispalo and Hesper. Although the great Jesuit historian, Juan de Mariana, poured scorn on these genealogies, several distinguished Spanish biblical scholars, including Benito Arias Montano and Juan de Pineda, accepted the data provided by Annius as throwing light on the early days of mankind.

It was in this heady context of biblical commentary and mythical history that García set about tracing the origin of the American Indians. Granted the contemporary obsession with the dimensions of Noah's ark and the duration of its voyages, it was only to be expected that García should assert that the ancients had little problem in navigating a course across the oceans of the world. The argument put forward by Acosta that before the discovery of the magnetic compass no mariner had ever dared to abandon the coast-line, was dismissed by simple appeal to the authority of the Bible. Whether one of Noah's grandsons had sailed to the New World was a question, however, on which he did not pronounce. Indeed, García found it difficult to explain just how the hemisphere was re-stocked with animals after the great Flood. Possibly, so he opined, the Almighty had employed angels to transport them across the oceans. On the other hand, the difference between the animals of the New World and the Old was easily explained by the effect of climate and in particular by the exceptional humidity of the Americas caused by its great lakes, rivers and super-abundant rainfall. After all, if Indians and blacks differed from Europeans, it was owing to the effect of climate. In time, García added, the Spaniards born in America would come to resemble the Indians.[26]

With his general principles established, García then presented his case, purporting to demonstrate that the Indians took their origin in successive waves of settlement emanating from Asia, Europe and North Africa. The theory to which he obviously attached the greatest weight was that the Indians descended from the Ten Lost Tribes of Israel. His authority here was the apocryphal Book IV of Esdras, a text much cited by Columbus, where in chapter 13 it is stated that the tribes taken captive by the king of Assyria fled across the Euphrates to the distant land of Arzareth where they would dwell until the last days. Since it took them a year and a half to reach this haven, it clearly lay in Central Asia, from which it was perfectly plausible to suppose a further migration by land into the New World. For García the proof of this identification rested on the similarity of character that he discerned in Jews and Indians, writing of the latter: 'How timid and full of fear they are: how given over to ceremonies, sharp-witted, lying and inclined to idolatry, all of which the Jews had.' Drawing on his experience as a missionary in Peru, he declared that the natives had to be forced to attend to Church and obliged to follow the path of virtue. In general, the Indians were incredulous, ungrateful, idolatrous and displayed little compassion for their neighbours. Yet they were so timid that on one occasion he himself had broken up a drunken party of over three hundred natives. Further proof of their Jewish origin was to be found in their ceremonies and customs, since both their burial rites and sacrifice of children were cited in the Bible among the many failings of the children of Israel. About the only objection to all this reasoning that occurred to García was that the Jews were generally taken to be an intelligent and good-looking race, whereas the Indians were 'of rude and clumsy understanding, ugly in body and face, and the nation least esteemed in all the world'. Although the black slaves imported from Africa were slaves by law and serfs by nature, even they were counted as a better caste and more endowed with high spirits than the Indians. To explain the conundrum, he cited Hippocrates concerning the determining effect of climate on human character and concluded that the New World had trans-formed the children of Israel, who in any case had been more addicted to idolatry than their cousins of Judah. If they had lost all recollection of their religion, well, so had that 'accursed rabble', the English, who had sunk so deep into heresy as to relinquish their Christianity. Moreover, there were traces of certain traditional practices and beliefs, since the Indians of Peru observed the laws set out in the Book of Leviticus and worshipped a Creator-God. So too, there was evidence of Hebrew words in native languages, of which by far the most notable was Mexico, which García interpreted as derived from the Hebrew word 'Mexi', meaning leader or head.[27]

Not content simply to trace the migration of the Ten Lost Tribes from Asia, García also found evidence of extensive settlement from across the Atlantic. The proof was essentially inferential and comparative. He argued that the impressive ruins of Tiahuanaco and the great stone fortress of Saccashuaman outside Cuzco both pre-dated the Incas and possessed a grandeur which far exceeded the architectural skills of any Indian. He also cited the ruined pyramids, towers and sculptures of Yucatán, which equally soared far above the vision of the Maya peasantry who dwelt in mere huts pitched close to these sites. The people responsible for such monuments were obviously those great seafarers, the Carthaginians, whose religion and temples resembled those of the Indians. Like the Mexica they used pictographs rather than the alphabet. After thus depriving the natives of the New World of any credit for their most notable cultural achievements, García then proceeded to enter the celebrated controversy as to the meaning and origin of the word Peru. Once again, he preferred the authority of such biblical commentators as Benito Arias Montano and Tomás Malvenda to the arguments of Acosta and identified Peru as the biblical Ophir, which is to say, the site of King Solomon's mines. Since the Hebrew original, Puraim, was plural, it was probable that Solomon's ships had traded with Mexico as much as with Peru, their passage across the Pacific offering no problem.[28]

A born eclectic, García now broadened his terms of reference and accepted Plato's account of Atlantis as veridical. Indeed, he sharply reproved Acosta for his dismissal of the fable, 'who mocks this with much wit', arguing that a recent translation of the *Timaeus* had made it clear that the dialogue was not dealing in allegory but in literal truth. Had not Melchor Cano, the celebrated Dominican theologian, affirmed that it was necessary to accept the authority of such authors as Plato? Acosta relied too much on his native wit, failing to pay due respect to time-honoured sources. In any case, many of the features of Atlantis described by Plato, such as the maintenance of warehouses for provisions and the division of society into separate classes, were to be encountered among the Indians. From the lost continent to the Spanish Peninsula was but a short step for García, who relying once more on the false Berosus printed by Annius, gladly accepted the hypothesis first advanced by Oviedo that the Spaniards themselves, led by King Hesper, had conquered the Antilles, naming the archipelago the Isles of Hesperides.[29] After all, the early Spaniards were generally described as a primitive race of men, warlike and with little acquaintance with any science, addicted to idolatry and feasting – in short, the mirror image of the contemporary Indian. The memory of these Spanish expeditions, launched some 1658 years before the birth of Christ had never been entirely lost, since in due course the Phoenicians, Romans and Greeks all crossed the Atlantic at some stage, leaving behind evidence of their presence in the New World in the form of roads and in the pantheon of pagan deities worshipped by the Indians. Finally, in deference to Acosta's arguments, García also pronounced that the Chinese and Tartars had entered the New World, their migration demonstrated by the Indian employment of both the solar and lunar calendars, and their use of such devices as the *quipus*, or knotted strings, to assist in computation. All this led to the resounding conclusion that the New World, far from existing in virginal isolation from the rest of humanity, had been persistently and periodically invaded by migrants from Asia, Europe and North Africa and hence that the American Indians were the descendants of all these successive waves of settlement.

Between García and Acosta there was an unbridgeable divide, both as regards their view of human history and in their method of reasoning. Whereas Acosta adopted an essentially evolutionary scheme of cultural development, with a progressive ascent from mere savagery to civilisation, by contrast, García depicted the natives of the New World as the degenerate descendants of once civilised settlers from the Old World. All the cultural achievements and moral behaviour that Las Casas had enumerated as evidence of Indian quality were attributed to the arrival of the Jews, the Carthaginians, the Atlanteans and others. There had occurred little or no autochthonous development in the New World. If its native inhabitants had observed the natural law or dimly approached the one true God, it was not thanks to any innate light or quality, but rather owing to half-forgotten beliefs and practices bequeathed them by their more advanced ancestors. To sustain his case, García cited the authority of the Bible, Plato and other venerable texts, rejecting Acosta's reliance on observation and argument. The evidence he deployed comprised a series of cultural comparisons, with similarity the proof of origin. If both Indians and Carthaginians built pyramids, it followed not merely that these monuments had a common source and identity but also that they originated outside the New World. At all points, García displayed a profound contempt for native capacity and character, attributing all that was positive in their history to external impact.

One last point requires emphasis. Although García might appear to be entirely fanciful in his historical speculations, there was a naturalistic argument imbedded in his scheme of human history. What had caused the Ten Lost Tribes to descend to the condition of the contemporary Indian? Why had the Carthaginians and other European settlers failed to establish a thriving civilisation in the New World? In short, what was the cause of the progressive cultural and moral degeneration of all the successive waves of human settlement in the New World which rendered their ignoble descendants so inferior to the peoples of Europe and Asia? The only answer that García offered to solve this conundrum was to cite Galen and Hippocrates and attribute degeneration to the effect of climate. There was something in the humid landscape and weather of the New World which had a gradual yet dramatic effect on all the variegated peoples that had migrated to the hemisphere.[30] It was an argument, ironically enough, that was to surface again with renewed vigour in the eighteenth-century Enlightenment.

The influence of García's enthusiasm for pseudo-biblical myth and astrological determinism was manifest on both sides of the Atlantic. In his *Conveniencia de las dos monarquías Catolicas, la de la Iglesia Romana y la del Imperio Español* (1612) – a work whose content belied its resounding title – Juan de la Puente, a Dominican theologian resident in Madrid, not merely traced the travels of Noah's sons but also sketched out an itinerary of the preaching tours of the twelve Apostles. The object here was to demonstrate that the Church in Spain owed its foundation as much to the intervention of St Peter and St Paul as to the more generally acknowledged arrival of St James. That de la Puente did not rule out the possibility that St Thomas may well have preached the gospel in both Brazil and Mexico indicates the attraction of that myth, even if he openly admitted that there was little evidence of any survival of Christian beliefs among the natives of those countries. He followed García in canvassing the theory that the American Indians descended from the Ten Lost Tribes of Israel, noting that in the world-map compiled by Abraham Ortelius their eventual destination of Arzareth was located on the north-eastern extremity of Asia, close to both the Tartars and America. In an intriguing observation on the Jews, he pronounced them to be perpetual wanderers, fated never to encounter a fixed patria, chosen by the Almighty to diffuse universal knowledge of the one, true God.[31] In this context he declared that 'the natural love which a man has for his country is born in the stars which engender us and preserve us in our first years'. It was this emphasis on the power of the stars which led him to' insert the notorious oft-cited note: 'the heavens of America induce inconstancy, lasciviousness and lies: vices characteristic of the Indians and which the constellations make characteristic of the Spaniards who are born and bred there'.[32] Here was an affirmation against which creole patriots were to rage for more than a century but which was destined to enjoy wide circulation.

Not all imperial mythographers were credulous friars. In 1650 Antonio de León Pinelo (1590–1660), soon to serve briefly as Historiographer and General Chronicler of the Indies, completed his *El paraíso en el Nuevo Mundo*, a sprawling mass of Baroque erudition, not published until the present century, in which he revived the thesis that had so attracted Columbus, that America had been the site of the Garden of Eden. The author óf the *Epítome de la biblioteca oriental i occidental* (1629), the first comprehensive bibliography of all known works both printed and in manuscript which dealt with the Indies, Pinelo was also responsible for framing the first drafts of the consolidated collection of the Laws of the Indies. Drawing inspiration from the great corpus of biblical commentary that had emerged during the early seventeenth century, he now fixed upon the recently translated writings of St Ephrem, as transmitted by the Syriac bishop Moses Bar Cefas, where it was argued that Paradise had been situated in another world, which the descendants of Adam had abandoned with the Great Flood. This other world, so Pinelo argued was not a different planet, but was in fact America, a hemisphere, however, which he preferred to call Iberica. It was especially in Amazonia that traces of Eden were to be found. Even now, in this region Nature was at its most abundant and fertile, supporting a huge variety of plants, trees and animals. Above all, the existence of the four great rivers of the Amazon, Orinoco, Cauca or Magdalena, and the Plate, all watering the heart of the continent, demonstrated the truth of this thesis. It was a zone which enjoyed 'an eternal summer and a perpetual spring'. If there were also to be encountered a great number of cacti, thorns, and serpents breeding from swamp mud, all this served as but a reminder of Adam's expulsion, an argument confirmed by the presence of a chain of volcanoes surrounding the region like the biblical swords of fire which banned the first man from Paradise.[33]

Just why Pinelo was so enamoured with this bizarre theory is hard to say. Although born in Spain, he had been taken as a boy to South America and there passed eighteen years, studying with the Jesuits and qualifying in the university of San Marcos in Lima. The reasons for this migration could not have been more urgent: both his grandfathers had been burnt at the stake as judaisers by the Inquisition in Lisbon. Yet despite subsequent accusations of *converso* malpractice, his father, once widowed, entered the priesthood and became the trusted chaplain of the creole archbishop of Lima, Fernando Arias de Ugarte. Moreover, his two brothers studied for doctorates at Salamanca, one obtaining appointment as canon in the cathedral at Puebla and the other practising as professor of law and rector of the university of San Marcos. As for Pinelo himself, he returned to Spain in 1622 and thereafter served for many years as a *relator* for the Council of the Indies. It is tempting to connect his theories to his parentage, but in reality difficult to trace any specifically Jewish line of reasoning other than his insistence that the first language of humanity was Hebrew, a theory, however, widely canvassed at that time.[34] Perhaps his obsession may have derived from pride in his adopted patria. Whatever the case, he was more concerned to describe the natural glories of South America than to speculate on the long history of mankind in that hemisphere. Only on the much controverted question of Noah and his ark did his interest quicken, since here was a subject which had aroused considerable erudite speculation. Pinelo argued that the purpose of the Flood was to transport Noah and his progeny to Mount Ararat in the Middle East, a journey which lasted 150 days and required a ship with the carrying capacity of fourteen contemporary galleons. That the direction of the journey was westwards to Asia was taken as self-evident, since the ark had always figured as a type and symbol of the Church, whose mystical passage from Jerusalem to Rome was equally ever westward.[35]

The imperial bias in Pinelo's approach to the American past emerged clearly in his discussion of the Indians. For he argued that the cultural achievements of these 'two great monarchies' of Peru and Mexico were very recent and decidedly untypical, since outside their realms and before their establishment, the natives of the New World had dwelt in bestial savagery, their natural increase limited by a universal addiction to warfare, human sacrifice and cannibalism. A simple, even honest people, the Indians lacked both avarice and art, the twin motives that impelled mankind to achievement and, although in appearance they resembled the inhabitants of Asia, in character they displayed the same qualities as the Africans, a sure sign that they descended from Noah's accursed son, Ham. Their understanding was feeble and their bodies, although strong, easily fell prey to illness. All this led to the familiar refrain: 'the Spaniards entered as lords over the Indians, serfs by nature, as the philosopher says'.[36]

Not content with this time-honoured disparagement of the natives of the New World, Pinelo sought to deprive them of credit for their most impressive visible achievements. For he asserted that the greatest monuments of Peru and New Spain – the ruins at Tiahuanaco, the fortress of Sacsayhuaman outside Cuzco, and the pyramids and carved pillars of Copan in Honduras – had been constructed prior to the great Flood by early descendants of Adam. After all, so he argued, post-lapsarian men were conversant with all the arts and sciences known to the modern age. Nor did he discount the possibility that parts of 'Iberica' may have been inhabited by a race of giants. In short, the Indians were but barbarous late-comers to the New World. All their most advanced societies had achieved was to copy or to restore the buildings bequeathed by the pre-deluge epoch, erecting mere superstructures so to say, on the grand foundations laid by the first men. Moreover, Pinelo rejected García's theory that the Indians were descendants of the Lost Tribes of Israel and discounted the notion of any apostolic mission to the New World. Indeed, he argued that 'Iberica' had laboured under God's curse from the epoch of the Flood to the incarnation of Christ, with the result that the Indians had only appeared in the first centuries of the Christian era. In this bizarre strain of reasoning, the imperial tradition reached a logical conclusion: if the American Indians were as barbarous and low-spirited as their critics averred, then the obvious inference was that they were incapable of creating monuments which in scale and quality rivalled Old World equivalents.[37]

If all was darkness in America from the Deluge to Columbus, with the advent of the Spaniards the hemisphere poured forth its natural riches for the benefit of the Catholic monarchy. After a description of the great drainage trench at Huehuetoca, cut to free Mexico City from endemic flooding and which had already cost the Crown some 3 million pesos, Pinelo offered a detailed account of the silver mines of Peru. Like all his generation in Lima, he was obsessed by the *cerro rico* at Potosí, a magic mountain, which for a few dramatic decades dominated the entire Atlantic economy. He subscribed to the comforting alchemical theory that the precious metals took the form of great trees set deep in the earth, the lodes encountered by miners but the uppermost branches that were slowly, if constantly, renewed by the upward flow of natural ore. After an account of the refining process and the enforced levy of Indians summoned to labour in the mines, he set out a series of calculations about the total production of precious metals in the New World since the first gold was found on Hispaniola. By 1640, so he estimated, the total output of gold and silver amounted to no less than 3,249 million pesos, with Peru by then producing at least twice as much as New Spain. All this led to the conclusion that 'the greatest riches of the universe in silver ore have been placed by the Creator in the provinces of Peru'. That such vast shipments of bullion had left Spain more poverty-stricken than it was prior to the discovery of America was a paradox that Pinelo mentioned, only to leave unanswered, more anxious to find the mystical comfort that 'the Catholic monarchs of Spain are the legitimate kings of the earthly paradise'.[38]

As a young man aspiring to high office, Pinelo had boldly stated that to master the history of the New World the chronicler had to be familiar with at least one province of the empire; to have resided at court, 'the common patria'; to be acquainted with the geography of the Indies; and to display a 'knowledge of letters'. Despite such ambition, Pinelo completed remarkably few of the historical projects he listed so carefully in his *Epitome*.[39] His one substantial work, *El paraíso en el Nuevo Mundo* was not printed until the present century. For the appointment to which he aspired, of Chief Chronicler of the Indies, came but two years before his death, so that he eked out the best part of his life as *relator* for the Council of the Indies. But it was in this relatively modest position that he undertook the all-important task of framing a general compilation of the innumerable rescripts issued by the Council since the discovery and conquest of America. Even here, Pinelo failed to see his work yield fruit, since publication was delayed until long after his death and then made but passing reference to his name.

IV

The decision of the Council of the Indies, taken on the advice of Las Casas, to withdraw Gómara's *Historia general* from circulation and to refuse Oviedo permission to publish the remainder of his great chronicle meant that there was no text dealing with the discovery and conquest of America which presented the Spanish version of events. It was this vacuum which allowed Girolamo Benzoni, an Italian traveller, to capture the market, so to say, by publishing in Venice a short *Historia del Mondo Nuovo* (1565) in which he presented a severe indictment of Spanish conquests. Scornfully dismissing Gómara's theory of the unknown pilot's prior discovery of America as a pitiful example of Spanish envy of Italian glory, he offered what purported to be an eye-witness description of the destruction of the native population in the Caribbean and Central America, the result, so he averred, of slave-raiding and outright massacre. Benzoni condemned the cruelty of the conquerors who instead of preaching the Christian gospel in peace had acted as the children of Satan. Not that he was particularly enamoured of the Indians, since he described them as 'this race of irrational beings', more close to the beasts than to men, guilty of the worst vices. At the same time, he praised the Dominicans for their defence of the natives and admitted the beneficial results of the New Laws and the accompanying emancipation of Indian slaves. However, he openly queried whether any natives had ever become true Christians, since their minds were so filled with terror and hatred of the Spaniards. Finally, he mocked the pretensions of adventurers such as Núñez de Balboa to be acclaimed as great conquerors when all they had done was to subdue a few half-naked savages. In short, Benzoni offered the European public a remarkably bleak assessment of the Spanish record in the New World, clearly drawing on the latter *Decades* of Peter Martyr and possibly the tracts of Las Casas. His work was translated into most European tongues and was used by Montaigne when he came to write his famous essay on Cannibals.[40]

It was in part to counter the rising tide of foreign criticism that in 1571 Philip II appointed Juan López de Velasco as 'chief cosmographer-chronicler of the Indies', charged with the dual task of compiling an accurate description of Spanish possessions and of composing an official history of their conquest. To facilitate his task circulars were despatched to the viceroys of Mexico and Peru, demanding remission of all manuscripts which dealt with the history of the New World. In the event, little progress was made and nothing published. Meanwhile, in 1578 there appeared the first Dutch translation of Las Casas' inflammatory tract, the *Brevísima relación*. It was soon followed by editions in French and English and by the Latin and German versions of 1598–9 published by the De Bry brothers, which were lavishly illustrated by engravings of Spanish atrocities. The legitimacy of the Spanish Crown's vast empire in the New World was thus called into question, with European opinion, both Catholic and Protestant, united in condemning the conquerors for their massacres of the native inhabitants of America.[41] It was thus left to Antonio de Herrera y Tordesillas (1549–1625), appointed 'chief historiographical chronicler of the Indies' in 1596, to provide the Spanish version of the conquest. His task, however, was not to emulate Gómara and glorify Cortés, but rather to demonstrate the ever-vigilant concern of the Catholic Kings for the welfare of their Indian subjects, albeit quietly restoring such reputation for the conquerors as could be secured without undue distortion of the narrative facts.

The result of his labours was the *Historia general de los hechos de los castellanos en las islas i tierra firme del mar océano* (1601), a massive work divided into four *Decades* which covered the years 1492–1531, and prefaced by a 'description of the West Indies'. In 1615 another three *Decades* were published, taking the story up to 1546. Granted access both to official papers and to the manuscript chronicles confiscated during the 1570s, Herrera succeeded in at last providing the world with an authoritative history of the conquest, which by reason of its wealth of data and succinct, flowing prose at once obtained recognition as the chief source and record of Spanish settlement of the New World. If Herrera succeeded where others failed or dared not venture, it was in large measure because he was a professional man of letters, educated in Italy, a secretary of viceroys who, before his appointment as royal chronicler, already had to his credit an impressive range of works, including a translation of Giovanni of Botero's *The Reason of State*. Heir to the Italian humanist tradition of universal history, of which the chief exponent was Paolo Giovio, Herrera also wrote a history of the world, which, despite its pretentious title, chronicled the events of the reign of Philip II, 'the Prudent'. Whereas Gómara had placed his literary skills at the service of Cortés and the conquerors, Herrera took advantage of his own impressive talents to advance the cause of the Spanish Crown.[42]

The purpose of the *Historia general* was set out in its dedication, where Herrera declared that he wrote to preserve 'the memory of the glorious deeds of the Catholic Kings and the Castilian nation', which foreign envy, in particular Italian envy, had sought to blacken or ridicule, much in the same way as the Greeks had mocked the triumphs of the Romans. The purpose of a chronicle was to honour virtue, condemn evil and by example teach posterity. If an authorised, official chronicle had become a necessity, it was because in regard to the Indies 'one cannot give faith to almost anything that has been written until now, since it has been done with too great a freedom'. What Herrera had in mind was made explicit during the course of a lawsuit brought by the Count of Puñonrostro, the grandson of Pedrarias Dávila, the infamous governor of Darien, who accused him of blackening his ancestor's reputation. For he observed that Philip II had called upon him to write an authorised account of the conquest so that foreign criticism of the undoubted cruelties and cupidity of some conquerors should not be seen to detract from the great deeds and glories of many other conquerors. Papers in his possession made it quite clear that Pedrarias was responsible for the death of thousands of Indians, with Benzoni's charges fully substantiated by contemporary Spanish sources. He referred to

10 Title page of Antonio de Herrera y Tordesillas, *Historia general de los hechos de los castellanos en las islas i tierra firme del mar océano*

the estimates of Las Casas and his Dominican biographer, Fr Agustín Dávila Padilla, archbishop of Santo Domingo, concluding that in the period from 1492 to 1560 'there died at the hands of our Castilians, with fire and the sword, through hunger and other ill-treatment, forty million souls'. Needless to say, Herrera did not propose to publish such damaging admissions in his *Historia general*, where he sought to demonstrate that the Catholic Kings had faithfully observed the terms of the Papal Bull of 1493, taking all possible measures both to ensure the welfare of their new subjects and to provide for their conversion to the Catholic faith. In short, the aim here was more to justify the empire and its government than to defend or exalt the conquerors.[43]

As befitted an imperial chronicler, Herrera began, not with any account of the formation of the Inca and Aztec states, but rather with a description of the Spanish empire that had been superimposed on the ruins of these kingdoms. A perfunctory account, based largely on data compiled by his predecessor, Juan López de Velasco, the 'Description of the West Indies' nevertheless served to remind contemporary readers of the greatness of Spain's empire, which by then stretched from Florida and New Mexico to Chile and the River Plate, with outriders in the island archipelagos of the Caribbean and the Philippines. The mere description, province by province, city by city, in itself set out an entire world created by the Spaniards, with the two viceregal capitals, Lima and Mexico City, housing an impressive range of institutions, both civil and religious. It was a world which supported no less than five archbishops, twenty-seven bishops, two universities, over four hundred priories and colleges of the religious orders, and an innumerable quantity of parishes and confraternities. In the civil sphere, the two viceroys of Peru and New Spain were assisted by a number of provincial governors, corregidores and by nine audiencias or royal chanceries resident in Santo Domingo, Mexico City, Guadalajara, Guatemala, Panama, Bogotá, Quito, Lima and Charcas. Above all, Herrera stressed that the Catholic Kings were the universal patrons of the Church in their overseas empire, with effective rights of appointment to all positions, and in possession of all ecclesiastical tithes. At the same time, the Crown graciously allocated the tithes to support the secular clergy, setting aside funds for the construction of churches and cathedrals. The description concluded with a list of viceroys and members of the Council of the Indies, the supreme governing body of this vast empire.[44]

In accordance with the European perspective of the work, Herrera commenced his history proper with a narrative of Columbus and the first voyages. Unlike Gómara and Oviedo, there was no attempt to rob the great discoverer of his glory by suggesting that the New World had been first encountered by some unknown pilot. Moreover, the ravages of the Spaniards that led to the destruction of the Indian population of the Caribbean region were admitted, albeit without any emphasis or condemnation, offset by the clear suggestion that often they were provoked by native hostilities. But the extraordinary feature of Herrera's account of the Caribbean phase of exploration is the degree to which he relied on Las Casas' *Historia de las Indias*, the manuscript of which had been transferred from the Dominican priory of San Gregorio into royal possession. Not merely did he follow the great Dominican in his account of Columbus and the conquest of Cuba, he also outlined the stages of Las Casas' campaign on behalf of the American Indian. He defended the experiment in peaceful colonisation at Cumaná, reproaching Gómara and Oviedo for their mockery of the future bishop of Chiapa. So too, he described the role of Las Casas in framing the New Laws of 1542. The object here was quite simple. Throughout the narrative of these events, attention was repeatedly drawn to the welcome accorded to Las Casas at court and the continued support he received from Charles V throughout his campaign. At the same time, the moral violence with which the Dominican attacked the conquerors was quietly suppressed.[45] Ironically, Las Casas was thus incorporated into the authorised history of the Indies, his crusade invoked in such a way as to serve to legitimise the dominion of the Spanish Crown, since at all points it demonstrated that the Catholic Kings had sought to procure the welfare of their native subjects. This reliance on Las Casas was further strengthened by Herrera's acceptance of the Alexandrine Donation as the title-deed of empire. Either ignorant of, or hostile to, the arguments of Vitoria and his school, the chronicler simply asserted that the Pope, acting as 'universal pastor of the world', possessed the right to dispose of lands belonging to infidels. In an echo of Las Casas' earlier arguments, he declared that if the Papacy had once anointed Charlemagne king of Jerusalem, then Alexander VI equally possessed the power to confer 'the sovereign empire and principality of the Indies' on the Catholic Kings. Between the worlds of scholastic theologians and humanists there apparently stretched an unbridgeable abyss.[46]

Granted the purpose of his work, it should come as no surprise to observe that Herrera did not expatiate on the glories of the conquests of Mexico and Peru, content rather to allow the scale of events to speak for themselves. The very pace of his fast-moving narrative allowed him to avoid any judgement or comment on the action he described. At the same time, he quietly exculpated most of the conquerors of the worst charges levelled against them, excusing Cortés' massacre at Cholula as a response to Indian plot and Alvarado's attack on the young nobles in Tenochtitlan as pre-emptive strikes against under-cover attack. What recent study of the text has revealed is the sheer scale of Herrera's debt to previous chroniclers, with the conquest of Mexico mainly copied from a manuscript of Dr Cervantes de Salazar, a humanist resident in Mexico who in turn had borrowed heavily from Gómara. For Peru the chief source was the great chronicle of Pedro Cieza de León, a plagiarism so entire that a later Spanish historian indignantly denounced Herrera for having 'dared to bury within his Decades an entire chronicle, a model of its class'.[47] The most significant feature here was the quiet defence of Pizarro's decision to execute Atahualpa 'for convenience of the public good', describing the act as a political necessity if the dominion of the Crown of Castile was to be firmly established. Noting that many Spaniards were horrified by the judicial murder of the emperor, Herrera loftily commented: 'the vulgar always are moved by the news of events, without other considerations', contrasting this reaction to Pizarro's steely determination, long guarded in the secret of his heart, adding in courtier fashion: 'the fruits of secrecy are great and especially in those who govern'. In this application of the lessons of contemporary European statecraft, there was obviously no room for the triumphalism of Gómara, and still less for the insistent invocation of Divine Providence proffered by Acosta; instead we encounter the Machiavellian doctrine of *raison d'état*, by which judicial murder was defended in the name of political necessity.[48]

If Herrera thus adopted a decidedly muted approach to so many controversial questions, skirting treacherous ground by the speed of his narrative, nevertheless, when he came to describe the natives of the New World he stood four square in the tradition of Oviedo, Gómara and Sepúlveda. In particular, he followed the example set by Gómara of including materials on the pre-hispanic cultures as picturesque inserts, introduced as a background to a narrative centred on the exploits of the Spaniards. Once more, the favourable image of relatively complex societies with great temples and cities in Mexico and impressive roads and fortresses in Peru was darkened by an emphasis on human sacrifice, idolatry and tyranny. So also, pell-mell lists of native customs and qualities were bundled together in a manner copied directly from Gómara. Moreover, at the very outset of his work, Herrera boldly pronounced that as regards climate, crops and genius of its inhabitants Europe was superior to the New World. That the Indians lacked any knowledge of iron, gunpowder and letters and did not practise trade or possess true cities, all demonstrated that 'their culture and government was barbarous'. In assessing the natives of Mexico, he observed: 'the greater part of this people is of low talent and weak both in their spirits and in physical energy, being pusillanimous, of low thoughts, incapable of anything serious. They have to be corrected and treated with love.' Although he admitted that Incas and Aztecs had displayed signs of intellect and political ability, which raised them far above the beasts, he also asserted that their natural constitution was so weak that after the conquest they had fallen victim to smallpox and the plague and had been quite unable to resist the inroads of wine and toil. Lamenting the widespread depopulation which had occurred, together with the accompanying exploitation, he exclaimed that the Indians 'were so spineless and idle and so given over to drunkenness' that they had failed to profit from the economic activity and opportunities offered by Spanish settlement. In any case, throughout the New World, the Indians had proved themselves to be 'great liars, drunkards, thieves, and in some cases, sodomites', being often dirty both in their clothes and in their manner of eating. In regard to the natives of Peru, he echoed Matienzo with the observation that 'for good government it is necessary to compel them to work both for their own benefit and for the conservation of their community'. Once more, the Toledan settlement found a defence on the firm ground of the servile nature of the Indians.[49]

In sum, Herrera achieved a remarkable *coup de main* since his praise of the humanitarian work of 'the most learned Bishop of Chiapa' allowed him to defuse the trimphalism of Gómara, while quietly presenting Oviedo's view of the American Indian as based on common agreement. He admitted the abuses of the conquerors so as to emphasise the efforts of the Crown to protect its native subjects. It should be recalled that Botero in his *Reason of State*, which Herrera had translated into Spanish, advised all princes to defend and encourage religion as the chief buttress of their authority, a concern always subordinate to the pursuit of self-interest that was the defining characteristic of all sovereign power. The recognition of the Papal donation and the protection accorded to Las Casas could thus be paraded as potent signs of the Spanish Monarchy's international role as bulwark of Catholic orthodoxy.[50] In short, the *Décadas* marked the culminating point in the formation of an imperial tradition in New World history, a tradition initiated by Fernández de Oviedo, re-stated with brazen confidence by Gómara and Sepúlveda, and now consolidated by Herrera in quiet, fluent style that masked the continuity in perspective by skilful concession and omission, all designed to confirm the justice and right of the Spanish Crown's claim to dominion over the isles and main of the Ocean Sea.

V

As foreign criticism of Spain mounted, fuelled by successive editions of Las Casas and Benzoni, so in the course of the seventeenth century Spanish historians and jurists now expressed overt criticism of the bishop of Chiapa. In his *Historia de la conquista de México* (1684), Antonio de Solís y Rivadeneyra (1610–86) deployed his considerable literary talent – he was both a playwright and poet – to celebrate the deeds of Hernán Cortés – deeds, so he exclaimed, of an illustrious captain performed on a scale rarely witnessed in history. Of his predecessors in the field he judged that Gómara had failed to rise to the occasion, leaving a narrative strewn with errors. As for Bernal Díaz del Castillo's *Historia verdadera*, available in print since 1632, he found its outspoken criticism of Cortés and his biographer as intolerable as its vulgar style, offering a clear demonstration of the danger of 'permitting discussion to those who are born to obey'. By contrast, Solís sought to emulate the Roman historian Livy and employ the resources of humanist historiography to celebrate the glorious achievements of his nation.[51] The frigid classicism of his style won him much praise and many readers in the eighteenth century, but modern taste now finds his reliance on sententious orations both tedious and false, all the more since both Cortés and Moctezuma declaim in virtually identical and equally inappropriate fashion.

The apologetical intent which animated Solís can be best observed in his treatment of the two Spanish massacres wrought by Cortés at Cholula and by Alvarado at Tenochtitlan. It was not simply the case that he exculpated the Spaniards on the usual grounds of pre-emptive action to avert ambush. Instead, he rounded on foreign critics who had seized on these incidents to insult his nation, and then lamented that their abuse stemmed from Las Casas, 'whose words they copy and translate, attacking us with the argument of our author and qualified witness', a man who thus 'obtained by this means the miserable applause of seeing himself cited against his own nation'. To fix upon the inevitable cruelties of conquest was to mistake appearances for substance, and to question the means chosen by Providence to effect its Divine purpose, the salvation of the New World and its inhabitants. Not that Solís sought to invoke any supernatural effects to justify this thesis, since he accepted Bernal Díaz' denial of any apparition by Santiago to assist the conquerors in battle. So too, although he cited Acosta's account of the Devil appearing to Moctezuma, his endorsement was less than enthusiastic, since he preferred to trace 'natural causes' rather than rely on supernatural agencies to explain the course of events.[52]

Impressed by Acosta's account of Mexican culture, he defined the Indians as rational, courageous barbarians, the more especially since he noted that: 'Some writers who show little affection for the Spanish nation treat the Indians as beasts incapable of reason, in order to give less esteem to their conquest.' Far from innocent or defenceless, the natives proved themselves worthy foes, their performance in battle reminiscent of the German war tactics described by Tacitus. This said, Solís chose not to let his pen dwell for long on the subject of Indian culture or society, matters he observed, much canvassed in preceding chronicles of the Indies, but which offered 'a reading that is little necessary, which lacks sweetness and is far from useful'. Like both Gómara and Herrera, he inserted all such material in the middle of his narrative, after Cortés had reached Tenochtitlan, so as to form a picturesque background to a course of action which was initiated in Spain and reached its climax with the siege and capture of Mexico. His account concluded with an emphasis on the bestial horror of human sacrifice and cannibalism, the latter practice so common, he averred, that the flesh of victims was sold in the market-place. It was in his portrait of Moctezuma, however, that Solís best explored the meaning of native barbarism, when he depicted that monarch as a proud, imperious tyrant who descended into a grovelling, pusillanimous abjection once reduced to captivity, a characterisation that William Prescott was to dramatise yet further.[53]

Nowhere did Solís display his apologetical intent more skilfully than in the emphasis he accorded Moctezuma's welcome of Cortés as Quetzalcoatl or as that god's messenger. Of course Cortés himself had first expounded the theory of a voluntary cession of dominion in his letters to Charles V with the aim of condemning Indian resistance as rebellion. But Solís now identified Quetzalcoatl as the founder of the Mexican empire, who had departed before his death, bequeathing his successors a prophecy of eventual return. Once Moctezuma had listened to Cortés, he accepted Charles V as the descendant of Quetzalcoatl, acknowledging him as the rightful lord of the empire founded by his ancestor. Solís concluded that the Habsburg emperor was thus the true ruler of Mexico, 'legitimate and hereditary in the sense of those people and in truth destined by heaven for the better possession of that Crown'. With this ingenious invention, the imperial historian wiped clean the historical record and deployed the time-honoured theory of translatio imperii in a manner which allowed him to adduce further grounds for imperial possession. That he should have ended his narrative with praise for the kind liberality of Cortés' treatment of Cuauhtémoc should come as no surprise; the doctrine of 'reason of state' purveyed by Botero found in Solís an able, historical practitioner.[54]

More of a literary man than an historian, Solís had little to offer other than fine words. Despite his appointment as Historiographer and General Chronicler of the Indies, he failed to consult the vast store of manuscripts available in royal libraries and archives. The contrast with Herrera could not have been greater. Yet in his anxiety to employ a pure, classical prose, Solís applied Spanish nomenclature to native institutions, so that the Tlaxcalans were described as meeting in senate and possessing a nobility and knights. Similarly, the Mexican state was endowed with councils of war, justice and exchequer, all supported by roving high courts and revenues which comprised no less than one-third of all produce.[55] It was in this assimilation of native culture to European models through deployment of a classical vocabulary that Solís was destined to influence the Mexican patriot historian of the eighteenth century, Javier Francisco Clavijero, who sought to defend the Aztecs from the disdain of the Enlightenment.

10

THE CATHOLIC MONARCHY

I

IN A state paper defending the pre-eminence of the Council of the Indies over the newly established Council of Flanders, written in 1629, Juan de Solórzano Pereira declared that the Indies were 'an empire which embraces in itself so many kingdoms and such rich and powerful provinces. Or, better to say, it is the most extensive and far flung empire that the world has known.' With the union of the Crowns of Castile and Portugal in 1580, it was possible for a subject of the Catholic monarchy to encircle the globe without leaving his sovereign's dominions. Since their discovery, the Indies had despatched over 1,600 million pesos of gold and silver to Europe. Whereas in Flanders the king was in theory subject to the jurisdiction of the Holy Roman Emperor, in the New World he was 'free, absolute and sovereign', especially since the kingdoms of Spanish America figured constitutionally as overseas provinces of the Crown of Castile. The possession of the New World, so Solórzano affirmed, had raised Spain far beyond France in power and prestige. It was for this reason that the Catholic monarch styled himself: 'Through the Grace of God, King of the Spains and the Indies.'[1]

In 1624 the Council of the Indies decided to prepare for publication a systematic collection of existing laws dealing with America, an herculean venture, since for more than a century an almost continuous stream of rescripts had flowed across the Atlantic. The lawyer who bore the brunt of the task, Antonio de León Pinelo, later complained that he had been obliged to scan over 600 manuscript volumes in which these rescripts were inscribed. By 1635 he had completed his work and presented a draft to the Council, requesting resolution of some 600 'doubts' that he entertained. In the event, it required seven months of almost daily meetings between Pinelo and Solórzano, at that time Councillor of the Indies, to frame a final draft, only then to find their labours nullified by the financial and political crisis of the monarchy. It was in 1681 that the *Recopilación de leyes de los reynos de las Indias* was finally published, and then without adequate acknowledgement of its true authors.[2]

That the *Recopilacíon* was a systematised collection of extracted rescripts rather than a legal code in the modern or Napoleonic sense of the word meant that the text preserved, usually in the original wording, the Crown's response to the great debates of the sixteenth century over the juridical status of the Indians, the justice of the conquest, and the distribution of encomiendas. The collection opened with the resounding affirmation that the Lord God had given the king possession of the newly discovered lands across the ocean-sea and that in consequence the king was 'more obliged than any other prince in the world' to promote the enlistment of the native peoples of the Indies into the guild of the Holy Roman Catholic Church. In thus basing royal authority on the mandate of Heaven, the Laws of the Indies echoed the medieval Castilian *Siete Partidas* which had pronounced that 'Kings are the vicars of God, each one in his kingdom, placed over the people in order to maintain them in justice and truth in temporal matters.' It was in accordance with this absolutist tradition, derived in large measure from Roman law, that Solórzano asserted that 'in sovereign and absolute emperors, kings and princes, there is and resides the root and source of all jurisdiction in their States'.[3] Even on the all-important question of the Crown's exercise of ecclesiastical patronage, the *Recopilación* attributed those powers as much to rights conferred by discovery and church-building as to any grant from the Papacy. Only in the preamble to Book III of the *Recopilación* do we encounter the more familiar thesis, embodied in a rescript issued by Charles V in 1519, that: 'Through the donation of the Holy Apostolic See and other just legitimate titles, we are Lord of the West Indies, Isles and Main of the Ocean Sea ... incorporated in our royal Crown of Castile.'[4] Equally important, the *Recopilación* set out the fundamental principle that the Indians were the free subjects of the Crown and that they could not be enslaved or compelled to work without remuneration. In effect, Herrera's thesis, that the Catholic Kings had always supported Las Casas' campaign on behalf of the native peoples of America, was here demonstrated in the very text of the governing laws of the Indies, finally rescued from the obscurity of the council chamber, the courts and archives, and given wide public circulation. The object of the *Recopilación* was thus not merely to provide an indispensable instrument of government for magistrates and courts, it also demonstrated the justice and legitimacy of Spanish rule in the New World.

The ideological purpose of the *Recopilación* becomes readily apparent if we examine the subsidiary writings of Antonio de León Pinelo who, in his treatise on encomiendas and other offices, saluted the title of 'conqueror of a New World' as glorious, and pronounced that 'this name of conqueror is that which confers most honour in the Indies both to those who have been so and to their sons and descendants'. Such men should enjoy preference in the allocation of offices and rewards, since their rights derived from a 'contract' with the king. In the light of such sentiments it comes as no surprise to find Pinelo bluntly criticising Las Casas, whom he blamed for all the unrest and rebellion caused by the New Laws of 1542. Not that he denied that Indians had been exploited by the first conquerors and encomenderos; but he asserted that the Crown's command to replace labour services by payment of tribute had eliminated most of the injustice hitherto associated with encomiendas.[5]

As it was, Pinelo noted with dismay that the *Brevísima relación* had been translated into Latin by Theodore de Bry and lavishly illustrated with scenes of Spanish cruelty, so that all foreign critics of imperial rule cited the work, attracted by 'the great liberty and asperity with which this author treats of the Spaniards of the Indies'. All the leading discoverers and conquerors were now accused of 'ambition and avarice', their great deeds and honourable fame overshadowed by charges of cruelty and abuse of the natives. To counter Las Casas' questioning of the legitimacy of Spanish rule Pinelo had recourse to Acosta's *De procuranda*, from which he took the classification of all barbarians into three ascending categories, arguing that both the Incas and Mexicans, as well as the more primitive peoples of the Indies, required a Christian prince as 'sovereign lord' if the imperfect knowledge of the Christian faith they had acquired was to be preserved. In any case, the Indians had been guilty of idolatry and were servile in nature. To clinch this familiar line of argument, Pinelo repeated Acosta's pronouncement that no matter what doubts there were concerning the original justice of the conquest, it was now necessary to maintain Spanish rule so as to preserve the influence of the Church among the newly converted natives.[6] After all, although the Roman empire had originated in warfare and armed conquest, had not Christ himself honoured and obeyed its magistrates? Any lingering doubts as to the imperial bias of Acosta's works are soon dissipated if we observe their citation by Pinelo in his attack on Las Casas.

II

If modern research has fixed upon León Pinelo as the prime author of the *Recopilación*, the role of Juan de Solórzano Pereira (1575–1655) in determining the form of the final draft was clearly all important. Author of *De Indiarum iure*, published in successive volumes in 1629 and 1639, Solórzano was already recognised as the most distinguished jurist ever to devote himself to the study of colonial law. Deeply versed in the classics of Roman law and in the works of their Italian commentators, a school led by Bartolus de Sassaferato, he had qualified as doctor of civil and canon law at the university of Salamanca, where he also lectured. The turning point in his life came in 1609 when he accepted an appointment as judge of the high court at Lima. Practical experience of the harsh realities of colonial life came when he superintended the renovation of the great mercury mine at Hunacavelica. Further insight into Peruvian society, no doubt, was afforded by his marriage to the creole daughter of the governor of Cuzco. Although Solórzano was to regard the eighteen years he spent in the New World as an enforced exile, a time when he was denied the promotion accorded to less talented contemporaries, he obviously took advantage of the oportunity to master the contentious law and history of the Indies. In particular, he was influenced by the views and policies of Viceroy Toledo and by the writings of Acosta and Herrera. In 1627 he returned to Madrid and there served first as attorney and then as Councillor of the Indies. Although age and deafness compelled him to retire in 1644, rewarded with the title of Knight of Santiago, he then prepared for publication the *Política indiana* (1648), a massive commentary on the laws of the Indies, in which he translated, in part abbreviated and in part expanded, his earlier work, *De Indiarum iure*.[7]

Nowhere was the imperial ethos which animated the servants of the Catholic monarchy more clearly stated than in the opening pages of *Política indiana* where Solórzano boldly affirmed that the Spanish empire in the New World did not spring from mere human endeavours or from the accidents of discovery and conquest: instead, it derived from the providential design of God the Almighty, absolute Lord of the universe, who had chosen Spain from amidst the nations of Christendom to bring the gift of the Catholic faith to the natives of the New World. In a remarkable appropriation of Mendieta's millennial pronouncements, he recalled that at the very moment that Luther had led the northern peoples of Europe into heresy, Spanish forces, assisted by apparitions of Santiago and the Virgin Mary, had conquered the new lands for the Church. Nor was there anything arbitrary in this venture, since the Catholic Kings and their Spanish subjects were 'the most firm, pure and clean in the Catholic faith and in obedience to the Holy Roman Church, without the mixture of heresy with which so many other nations have been stained'. It followed from this train of argument, so Solórzano averred, that the best and surest title-deed of empire was the papal donation of 1493, the text of which he printed in full. After all, as Cardinal Ostensius had declared, the Pope as Vicar of Christ was the universal monarch of the world and had full right to quit infidel kings of their lands so as to ensure the preaching of the Christian gospel. In this extraordinary admission, Solórzano accepted the political theorems of canon law and thus repeated the arguments of Palacios Rubios first advanced in 1512. There were, of course, potent reasons for this tactic. By the early seventeenth century the Dutch jurist, Hugo Grotius, had recycled Francisco de Vitoria's theses on universal rights of trade and communication between nations so as to call into question Spain's particular claims to possess the New World. In this context, the universal monarchy of the Papacy offered less threat than the equally universal, but more pressing dictates of natural law.[8]

It was Spain's privilege not merely to preach the Christian gospel but also to teach the Indians the arts of civilisation, introducing them to the practice of

11 Juan de Solórzano Pereira

agriculture, the use of money and iron, and life in formed communities. At the time of the conquest most natives of the New World were 'so barbarous, uncultivated and wild that they hardly merited the name of men'. Had not Aristotle long since declared that some men were slaves by nature? Moreover, although Acosta had differentiated the Incas and Mexica from the naked dwellers of the Caribbean, nevertheless, their states had been stained by idolatry, abominable vices and gross tyranny. No matter what their level of culture, all the natives of the New World required the just, prudent governance of a Christian monarch to reduce them to civilisation and true religion. Here, then, Solórzano retailed the key concepts of the imperial humanism of Sepúlveda, Matienzo, Toledo and Herrera. Moreover, he was at pains to lament the slanders of Las Casas, whose *Brevísima relación*, by now printed in various languages, had offered so much ammunition to foreign onslaughts on Spain's mission in the Indies. It was not so much the cruelties of the conquerors as the Indians' vices and drunkenness and their exposure to epidemic disease which had caused such depopulation, a process which could only be interpreted as God's punishment for their idolatry and tyranny. In this context, it comes as no surprise to observe that Solórzano dismissed out of hand contemporary fantasies about the origin of the Indians and the possibility of an apostolic mission to the New World. Acosta rather than García was his preferred authority and he followed the Jesuit in supposing that the first men in America had entered the hemisphere from the north-west, crossing the sea in short journeys or by land. He rejected the notion that St Thomas the Apostle had preached the gospel to the Indian, since that was a privilege and glory reserved by Providence to Spain.[9]

In regard to the condition of the Indians under Spanish rule, Solórzano displayed an uncompromising but compassionate approach. He insisted that by reason of the New Laws of 1542 Indians had to be defined and treated as free subjects of the Crown and in consequence criticised the viceregal ordinances of Toledo, which decreed that the *yanaconas* resident on Spanish estates could neither be expelled nor yet were free to leave, as contrary to the general principle of Indian liberty. At the same time, he insisted that the Crown had the right to compel all its subjects who were 'of servile condition' to work so as to prevent idleness and to ensure that the labour necessary for the maintenance of the realm was forthcoming. In the case of the Indians, compulsion was required because they were rarely attracted by the prospect of high wages 'since in great measure they are lazy and friends of sloth, giving themselves over to drunkenness, lust and the other vices which their idolatry occasions, so that it is with ill-will that they ever leave their native haunts and climes, especially to engage in such laborious tasks'. Like beasts, the natives were content with a mere subsistence, lacking all spirit of avarice or desire to consume more than their daily needs. In any case, both the Incas and Aztecs had obliged their subjects to work on state projects. Granted the insufficiency of alternative supplies of labour, the Crown had decreed that by means of the system of repartimientos and *mita* Indians could be recruited for work in agriculture, the mines, and *obrajes*, the textile workshops. In Peru, however, it was forbidden to despatch Indians to vineyards, sugar plantations or for the cultivation of coca. Moreover, in Mexico only voluntary native labour was allowed in textile workshops and in Peru the licence granted for this purpose by Toledo had been restricted to *obrajes* owned by Indian communities.[10]

Despite his defence of the necessity of forced labour levies, Solórzano was fully conscious of its deleterious consequences. The power of the Spanish monarchy, the protection of the Catholic Church, and the very union of Spain and the Indies all depended on the continued output of gold and silver. With these grand ends in view, the Crown could employ its 'coercive power over its vassals' to compel them to work in the mines. By this time, there was indeed a supply of free labour both in New Spain and Peru attracted by the prospect of high earnings, but it was insufficient to maintain production, especially at Potosí. Despite the decline in the native population, the Indians of the provinces subject to the *mita* still had to despatch contingents of labourers to both Potosí and Huancavelica. Yet Solórzano testified that mining was an arduous and dangerous occupation, so demanding that in the ancient world the Romans had condemned criminals for this task. From personal observation he testified that at Huancavelica the fumes of mercury were so lethal that men emerged greatly weakened and often died within four years. Here then was the moral conundrum: the aim of a good prince was to promote the welfare of his subjects, yet mine-labour, so necessary for the monarchy's survival, destroyed the native population. Already, the Jesuit Francisco Coello had denounced the morality of the *mita*. Solórzano himself admitted: 'the Indian sees that all the weight of that which sustains the kingdom is placed on their shoulders, without all those who take the profit wishing to raise a finger, let alone assist with the burden'. The conclusion was peremptory. The Indies, so Solórzano opined, was like the fourth empire of the prophet Daniel, its feet and foundations built on clay, and the Indians best compared to the children of Israel labouring for Pharaoh in Egypt.[11]

For the rest, Solórzano invoked Roman precedent and Acosta's arguments to justify the broad outlines of the Toledan settlement. Not merely did he defend the collection of tribute, he also advocated that Indians should pay Church tithes, albeit admitting that with such a great variety of payments to the parochial clergy in existence 'prescription and custom' had to prevail. So too, he approved of the policy of reducing the Indians to living in constituted towns, arguing that it was wrong to allow them to live 'scattered and without political form in the hills and fields'. After all, the Romans had enforced similar measures in Spain. Nor did he refrain from citing the familiar dictum that before the Indians could become true Christians, they had to be taught to live as civilized men – *hombres políticos* – with beds to sleep in, tables to eat off, and a change of clothes for attendance at Church. Contrary to Acosta and other authorities, he deplored the decision of Church Councils to teach Christian doctrine in native languages, asserting that the Indians should be obliged to learn Spanish, clinching the argument once more by appeal to the practice of the Romans in Spain. By way of conclusion, Solórzano emphasised that owing to 'their humble, servile and exhausted condition . . . their imbecility, rusticity, poverty, low spirits, continual work and services', the Indians required the protection of the Crown and its magistrates, since otherwise all other groups and races in colonial society would take advantage and exploit them. The lowest Spaniard counted for more than the highest Indian.[12]

If in his discussion of 'the native problem', Solórzano repeatedly invoked Roman precedent, consciously comparing the Spanish empire to its classical predecessor, when he came to discuss the controverted question of encomiendas, he cited medieval, feudal law and practice. In the same way that the nobles who participated in the reconquest of Spain had been granted landed entails and lordships, so equally the conquerors of the Indies received encomiendas designed to reward a warrior nobility with the means of sustaining the defence of the realm. On receiving their grants, the encomenderos had to swear an oath of 'fidelity, especial services and vassalage for this grace and be ready and fit with arms and horse for war . . .' The task of defending the Indies from internal rebellion or foreign invasion thus lay with the encomenderos, 'not only as ordinary vassals, but as *feudatarios* in the service of the King . . .' Moreover, they were expected 'to have an established house in the head cities of their encomiendas'. As much as Toledo, Solórzano asserted that the preservation of all kingdoms depended on the existence of a class of noble, rich vassals. However, despite his emphasis on the feudal character of encomiendas, Solórzano equally noted the essential differences. In the first place, the grants carried no right of jurisdiction, so that the Indians remained free vassals of the Crown. Equally important, an encomienda was essentially a grant made to a particular person; it carried no inherent right of inheritance, still less of transfer, so that the incumbents possessed no rights of property. Although Charles V had suspended the operation of the New Laws, allowing inheritance for a further life, each successive 'life' thereafter had to be negotiated with the Crown, which maintained a general right of reversion. For the rest, although Solórzano admitted that the replacement of native labour service by tribute payments was a necessary and beneficial reform, he criticised Las Casas for exaggerating the abuses of the initial system, adverting that the Dominican generalised from his experience of the Caribbean and Central America. Had the New Laws been strictly enforced, the result would have been universal unrest and riot.[13]

At the close of his review of the laws governing encomiendas, Solórzano expressed his regrets that the conquerors had not been awarded titles of nobility, and the means to support their families, since by his day some of their descendants lived 'in a total nakedness and misery and in such extreme necessity, that they have to beg from others their very sustenance'. He noted the argument that if encomiendas had been given in perpetuity and accompanied by jurisdiction, then their possessors would have protected the Indians against the abuses of the local magistrates and parish priests, defending their vassals 'like that of their sons, their estates and wealth'. He also pointed to the contradiction between the laws which insisted on the Indians' liberty and any proposal of perpetual vassalage. Moreover, with the growth of the mestizo population and the decline in native numbers, it was difficult to see how any grant of jurisdiction could be put into practice. By way of summary, Solórzano declared that in accordance with the views of Toledo and Matienzo, it would have been prudent and just in the 1560s to have created a select number of perpetual encomiendas in each province. But the time had passed, since by now many encomiendas were allocated to men living in Spain or to persons who were not descendants of the conquerors, and the Indian population had declined in number: for which reasons, he did not advocate any change.[14]

If the grand questions of the rights of Indians and encomenderos enabled Solórzano to display his command of the historical literature, the subject of contemporary government did not arouse his interest. There was little to say about town councils and their annually elected magistrates other than to note the prevailing practice of sale of office of the posts of councillors and notaries. By contrast, he sharply criticised the district magistrates, since although these corregidores should act as 'the guardian angels' of the Indians, in fact they resembled the Roman procurators whom Cicero had denounced for their depredations. Only a small number of these posts were appointed in Madrid, with the rest filled by the viceroys for short terms. As a former judge in the high court of Lima, Solórzano stressed the variegated responsibilities of the eleven audiencias of the Indies, situated in Mexico, Lima, Santo Domingo, Guadalajara, Guatemala, Bogota, Quito, Charcas, Panama, Santiago de Chile and Manila. Contrary to his own experience, he recommended that judges should not be allowed to marry within the districts of their jurisdiction and that judges should not be allowed to serve in courts situated in their own patrias, which is to say, in their home cities. By far the most important offices in the Indies were the two viceroys of Peru and New Spain, who as the *alter ego* of the King 'exercise the same power, hand and jurisdiction as the king who names them ... there is no matter in these provinces which they do not despatch'. It was the viceroys who distributed encomiendas when they fell vacant, appointed most district magistrates, issued land grants to Spanish settlers, confirmed all ecclesiastical appointments made by the bishops, acted as presidents of the high

courts of justice in their capitals, supervised the treasury officials and despatched surplus revenue to Spain; and as captain-generals, were responsible for
ensuring the defence of the realm. Small wonder that Solórzano compared them
to the proconsuls of the Roman empire. But although on all ceremonial
occasions they were treated as if they were kings, they were obliged to observe
the laws of the Indies and Castile, not possessing any power to suspend their
operation or to pardon offenders: 'in nothing can they or ought they to proceed
with absolute power'. Indeed, the high courts of justice could admit appeals
against their decrees and refer disputes of jurisdiction to the Council of the
Indies for resolution. They were not free from the threat of excommunication
by prelates of the Church and could not invade the jurisdiction of Church
courts. However, they possessed the right to suspend the operation of any new
rescript or provision emanating from Madrid on the grounds of inexpediency
or injustice, using the celebrated formula: *obedezco pero no cumplo* – 'I obey,
but I do not implement'.[15]

Anxious in his discussion of civil administration to assimilate Spanish
practice to Roman precedent, Solórzano adopted a decidedly regalist attitude
to the Church. Contrary to the tenets of Machiavelli, 'the sure, certain buttress
and foundation of empires consists in establishing, propagating, conserving
and increasing the faith, religion and cult of our True God and Lord'. It
followed that all heresy threatened 'to pervert or subvert utterly the political
state of the realm', so that 'in no Catholic or well-governed commonwealth
should it be permitted'. It was to prevent such upheaval that the Catholic Kings
had founded the Inquisition, with the happy result that Spain and its provinces
'are today the most Christian in the world'. But although the Inquisition had
been established in Mexico and Lima in 1571, its officers operating in complete
independence of the civil and episcopal courts, it was forbidden to meddle with
Indians by reason of 'their rude character and incapacity'. Although Solórzano
thus emphasised the monarch's care for the orthodoxy of the Spanish American
Church, he also insisted on its virtual independence from papal authority, other
than in matters of faith. By reason of the bull of Julius II in 1508 and through
having constructed so many churches and monasteries, the king exercised the
right of Ecclesiastical Patronage throughout the vast overseas empire, acting as
'Vicars of the Roman Pontificate and as Constable of the army of God and of
the preachers of the Divine word'. In consequence, the king appointed all
bishops and canons in the Indies, with the Pope obliged to confirm all
candidates without question. It was a formidable Church over which the
Catholic King presided, since it comprised no less than six archbishops, thirty-
two bishops and some 960 diocesan dignitaries, canons and prebends, all of
whom were selected in Madrid. The power and wealth of this body was great
since it possessed its own courts and law and collected its own taxes. As a
zealous servant of the Crown, Solórzano counselled prelates to avoid all

conflict with royal magistrates and warned them to exercise their powers of excommunication with extreme caution. He stressed that the Church tithes they collected were a gift from the Crown, and that the residual of episcopal estates reverted to the royal exchequer. More controversially, he pronounced that all ecclesiastical lawsuits had to be settled in the Indies with the archbishops acting as the last source of appeal: there could be no remission of cases to Rome for resolution. Conversely, all papal bulls and provisions had to be approved by the Council of the Indies before despatch to the New World. In all this, Solórzano's intent was not to limit the powers of the Church hierarchy but rather to deploy them in service of the king. In a formula reminiscent of Thomas Hooker, he concluded apropos ecclesiastical and secular jurisdiction that 'of one and the other arm the State of the Commonwealth is composed and in both the care of our kings is manifest . . .'[16]

The ecclesiastical questions that aroused Solórzano's commentary did not derive from any conflict between Church and State – in this context an anachronistic formula – but rather centred on the struggle within the Church between the hierarchy and the religious orders. Most important was the controversy over the *doctrinas* administered by the mendicants, a question which, as we have seen, had already preoccupied both Mendieta and Torquemada. Indeed, Solórzano emphasised that the problem was most pressing in New Spain, since in Peru Francisco de Toledo had succeeded in enforcing a policy whereby the religious were obliged to submit their candidates for parish priest to the viceroy for approval, and then obtain from the relevant bishop his 'canonical institution'. At issue here was whether the Church in the Indies should continue to enjoy missionary status or whether it should comply with the legislation of the Council of Trent, the provisions of which tended at all points to strengthen the authority of the bishops. For Solórzano the Tridentine system was preferable since whereas the Crown appointed bishops, it possessed few powers of intervention in the religious orders who elected their own superiors. In New Spain the mendicants strenuously resisted all attempts of the Mexican hierarchy to conduct inspections and appoint *curas*, preferring to administer their *doctrinas* with small groups of friars. In response, the bishops sought to transfer parishes into the hands of the secular clergy. It was not until 1624 and again in 1634 that the Council of the Indies finally issued rescripts demanding observance of the Tridentine laws. By way of final commentary, Solórzano suggested that the mendicants should only retain parishes which were close to their priories, leaving the remainder to be administered by the secular clergy, by then rapidly increasing in number owing to the influx of young creoles into the priesthood.[17]

In line with his previous support for the hierarchy in their dealings with the religious, Solórzano strongly deplored the prolonged attempt by both friars and Jesuits to escape paying Church tithes on the produce of their landed estates. As early as 1501 the Papacy had conceded all rights to collect tithes to the Crown on the condition that the proceeds went to build and support churches in the New World. In practice, tithe receipts constituted the revenue which maintained the bishops, their chapters and cathedrals, and hence were of vital interest to the hierarchy. Moreover, since Indian villages rarely paid anything other than nominal sums, monies had to be collected from Spanish landowners and farmers. Yet the religious orders and in particular the Jesuits had come to own entire chains of haciendas, all yielding a handsome income, on which they refused to pay tithe. Already, the case had lasted for sixty years and was still no closer to settlement. Once more, Solórzano attacked the pretensions of the religious, arguing that since tithes formed part of the regalian rights of the Spanish Crown in its role as Church Patron, it followed that the religious were calling into question the very authority of the king. Here was an issue which at the very time that Solórzano composed his work created an explosive conflict in New Spain between the Jesuits and the bishop of Puebla, Juan de Palafox, his former associate on the Council of the Indies. Although a rescript was issued in 1655 deciding the case in favour of the hierarchy, it remains doubtful whether the Jesuits ever complied with its provisions other than in the most nominal sense.[18]

It was in his discussion of Church affairs that Solórzano first broached the issue of creole rights to high office, an issue which was thereafter to loom so large in debates on the political constitution of Spain's overseas empire. To start with, he noted that canon law required that Church benefices be occupied by the natives of any given diocese or kingdom, it being contrary to 'natural and canon law' for such posts to go to foreigners. So too, a rescript of 1609 had declared that in appointments of bishops 'the sons of Spanish fathers and mothers, born in those provinces should be preferred . . .', always provided they were 'equally worthy to the other candidates, born in these kingdoms'. As a general rule, the descendants of the first conquerors and settlers thus possessed a preferential right to Church benefices, all the more necessary since so many creole families had declined into poverty. In this context, Solórzano commented that this principle equally applied to Indians and mestizos, who should not be barred from the priesthood, always provided they possessed the necessary qualifications and were of legitimate parentage. At the same time, he noted that since the Indies and Castile belonged to the same Crown, it followed that among peninsular Spaniards only the subjects of the Crown of Aragon counted as foreigners for legal purposes. His preoccupation in favour of the creoles led Solórzano to deplore the practice first introduced in 1622 whereby in all the chief provinces of the mendicant orders elections to high office alternated between creoles and peninsulars. The pretext was that European religious were more observant of the rule than their American brethren. Yet it led to equality of status even in provinces where the peninsulars were 'foreigners, newcomers and very few in number'. It was a system which caused 'great sorrow and upset to the creoles to see themselves excluded from these honours in their own country and that strangers should come to govern and lord it over them'. Solórzano could see no justification for continuing the system, once the creoles formed the great majority of the religious in any given province.[19]

Not content with a merely legal defence of creole rights, Solórzano sought to rebut the opinion that Spaniards born in the Indies 'degenerate so much with the heavens and climate of those provinces'. As we have seen, the Dominican, Juan de la Puente had declared that by reason of 'the constellation of the land', creoles had much the same undesirable character as the Indians. But Solórzano adverted that the chief proponents of such views were religious from the Peninsula who sought to discredit the creoles so as to command the chief offices in the American provinces of their order. He drew attention to the large number of creoles, many of whom he knew personally, who were as distinguished for their learning as for their virtue. As Spaniards, they should enjoy access to honours on an equal basis with the peninsulars. Indeed, in his discussion of the audiencias, Solórzano insisted that although judges should not be appointed to courts situated in their home cities, this rule did not apply to the kingdom where 'both in these offices and in other secular, ecclesiastical and military places the natives of a kingdom are generally to be preferred and, as some say, to the total exclusion of foreigners, strangers, and newcomers'. Nor did Solórzano hesitate to apply this rule to the highest level of state, since on stressing the need of Councillors of the Indies to be acquainted with the history and geography of the vast empire they governed, he concluded that it was advisable that 'ordinarily there should be some councillors who are natives of them (the Indies) or at the least have served some years in their high courts'. After all, the Councils of Aragon, Italy and Portugal were composed of natives of these kingdoms or of men who had served in them.[20] Here were potent arguments which were to be much cited by creole patriots in years to come and indeed were revived during the debates on independence at the beginning of the nineteenth century.

III

In both the *Recopilación* and *Política indiana,* we encounter a triumphant, retrospective proclamation of the providential mission of the Catholic monarchy. Underlying that vision was the old medieval idea of the universal Christian empire. In this context, 'the kingdoms of the Indies' figured alongside the kingdoms of Castile, Aragon, Naples and Portugal as states endowed with the full panoply of institutions, both secular and ecclesiastical, governed by their own Council and possessing their own distinctive laws. That in the technical, constitutional sense they counted as overseas provinces of the Crown of Castile did not affect the reality of their status, all the more since their monarch was most commonly styled 'King of the Spains and the Indies'. In comparison with the ever more evident grandeur of Spanish America, the Habsburg possessions in Italy and Flanders dwindled in importance. Without the riches of the treasure fleets which sailed from Veracruz and Porto Bello to Seville, the Catholic monarchy could not have sustained the haemorrhage of resources caused by its European wars and alliances.

If the absolutist principles and practices of Roman law, themselves elaborated in an imperial context, effectively sustained the authority of the king, the prestige of the monarchy was further buttressed by the neo-Platonic, Hermetic philosophy that flowered in the Baroque culture of post-Tridentine Catholicism. The leading Jesuit theologian of this school, Juan Eusebio Nieremberg (1595–1658), affirmed that 'the will of the Prince is the image of Divine omnipotence', adding that 'the king is defined in the holy book of the Egyptian philosopher as the last of the gods and the first of men'. Whereas medieval jurists had defined a kingdom as a mystical body with the prince at its head, Nieremberg declared that the king was the soul of this mystical body, on whose animating presence all political life depended. As a good Jesuit, he praised obedience as the supreme virtue, as much at court as in war or in religion.[21] In a similar vein, Bishop Juan de Caramuel Lobkowitz (1607–80) saluted Philip IV as 'a vice-God on earth'. In all this there was a strong reminiscence of Eusebius of Caesarea's panegyric of Constantine the Great, whom he described as the only true philosopher, exercising perfect control over his passions, dwelling in communion with his Divine original, and acting as virtual intermediary between heaven and earth. In Spain the succession from Charles V to Philip II had marked the transition from a warrior king to a sedentary monarch, invested with a sacral aura through his residence at the Escorial, a palace that was also a monastery, church and dynastic sepulchre. If God Almighty Himself was the architect of Solomon's Temple, so Caramuel asserted, how great was the vision of Philip II who had constructed an edifice that not merely marked the high point of European architecture since its revival in Italy by Bramante, but which of all modern buildings alone rivalled the Temple in grandeur and conception.[22] If Charles V was acclaimed a new David constantly engaged in battle, Philip II could only figure as another Solomon, an exemplar of wisdom and justice.

It was this quasi-Byzantine perception of kingship that underpinned and corroborated Solórzano's vision of the Catholic monarchy as a universal realm composed of many kingdoms, in which all power flowed downwards from the sovereign, whose state was supported by the two great orders of government, the secular and the ecclesiastical, each endowed with their own laws, courts, officers and revenue, both led by hierarchs appointed by the king. For

Solórzano as for Herrera, the history of the Indies only began with their discovery, conquest and incorporation into the Habsburg state, their native past but a sorry tale of barbarism, superstition and tyranny. The positive results of Las Casas' campaign on behalf of the Indians were quietly appropriated as affording proof of the Spanish king's concern for their native subjects. As for the encomiendas, they were but a vestige of the past, their feudal character a troublesome reminder of the medieval foundations of conquest. So too, the inordinate influence of the mendicants in the native ministry smacked of missionary expectations now deemed irrelevant. Yet no matter how much Solórzano sought to present the Indies as fully formed kingdoms, similar in status to their European counterparts, he foundered in the morass of native debility. Unmoved by the prospect of high earnings in the Spanish economy, the Indians had to be coerced by state decree to offer their labour in the mines of Peru. And there they perished. The entire, triumphant Catholic monarchy had feet of clay and was thus destined to crumble. Toledo had deliberately created a tyrannical regime and the consequences were all too evident. Such, however, was not the most immediate lesson that Spaniards born in America took from his commentary. Instead, they were impressed by his defence of the rights of creoles to high office in Church and State. Here was the positive side of his imperial perspective: if the Indies formed true kingdoms, then creole nobles, jurists and churchmen should govern their respective countries as loyal subjects of the Crown. There was no conflict between the local patriotism and allegiance to the Catholic monarchy. Although Solórzano is best regarded as the heir of Acosta, Herrera and Toledo, nevertheless, he thus came to figure within the tradition of creole patriotism as a leading advocate of the political rights of the American Spaniards.

11

TRIDENTINE PRELATE

I

IN 1647 Philip IV and the Council of the Indies were startled to learn that the bishop of Puebla had abandoned his episcopal palace to take refuge in the mountains that lay close to the city. Writing from 'a miserable hovel', accompanied, so he averred, only by his chaplain, secretary and guide, Juan de Palafox y Mendoza (1600–59) defended his flight as a necessary measure to avoid the danger of popular riot and insurrection. For the viceroy, the Count of Salvatierra, had despatched an armed expedition to imprison him and its arrival in Puebla would have provoked violent protests from his faithful flock. Mindful of the events of 1624 when a dispute between the viceroy and archbishop subjected Mexico City to mob rule, Palafox had chosen to evade the daunting choice between captivity and riot, by flight into Puebla's mountainous surrounds. From his rural retreat, the embattled prelate wrote numerous letters to both the king and the Pope, setting out the elements of his case. Quick to dramatise his situation, Palafox appealed to the examples of St Athanasius of Alexandria and St Thomas of Canterbury, two bishops whose defence of Church jurisdiction and doctrine had equally exposed them to persecution by the secular authorities.[1]

For ministers in Madrid, the news was all the more shocking since only eight years before, in 1639, Palafox had been sent to New Spain to conduct a general visitation in which he had displayed such energy and initiative as to warrant his interim appointment as viceroy. Here was no case of a priest of humble extraction who had stumbled into an unfortunate quarrel with his superiors, for Palafox was the son of the Marquis of Ariaza, a leading figure of the Aragonese nobility, who after his ordination in 1629 had accompanied the Infanta María as chaplain on her bridal journey to Vienna. Moreover, on return from his travels in Germany, Italy and Flanders, he had been appointed a member of the Council of the Indies where his quick intelligence and fluent pen soon won him the favour of the imperious Count-Duke of Olivares, the chief minister of Philip IV, then engaged on the Herculean task of reshaping and

uniting the vast scattered patrimony of the Spanish Habsburgs. The flight of
Palafox was thus the calculated act of an experienced minister and courtier,
playing for high stakes in a bitter conflict which demonstrated the enfeebled
quality of royal authority in the middle years of the seventeenth century. For
although the quarrel originated in a dispute with the Jesuits over episcopal
jurisdiction, it was animated and given impetus by the alarm of the colonial
establishment at the threat offered to their interests by Palafox's policies and
views in both Church and State. His failure was a decisive manifestation of
Spain's decline.[2]

II

The arrival of Palafox in New Spain as visitor-general and Bishop of Puebla
could not have occurred at a more inauspicious moment for the Catholic
monarchy. In 1640 both Portugal and Catalonia rebelled in protest against the
fiscal exactions proposed by Olivares, measures designed to raise resources to
sustain Spain's ever more costly campaign against France, a conflict occasioned
by the mounting engagement of both countries in the Thirty Years War in
Germany. The dissolution of the sixty years' union of the Crowns of Portugal
and Castile entailed the loss of Brazil and brought into question the loyalty of
the numerous class of Portuguese merchants, often of Jewish extraction, active
in most provinces of Spain's overseas empire. For Palafox the situation was all
the more alarming when he considered that the new viceroy of New Spain, the
Duke of Escalona, was not merely the first grandee of Spain ever to have been
appointed to that office, but was also cousin of the Duke of Braganza, the
upstart king of Portugal. In conversation, so it was reported, the Duke had
recounted that on hearing that he had been appointed as viceroy a fellow
grandee at court had exclaimed: 'Why go to the Indies? Either you will be a
great thief or you will set off a revolt.' Just why an aristocrat of his standing
should have wished to accept such an onerous post was a mystery, since in
Spain his possessions amounted to a veritable principality, with no less than
56,000 vassals and 145,000 ducats of revenue. In Mexico the duke was seen to
favour Portuguese merchants, despite doubts as to their loyalty. The result of
these apprehensions was that Palafox assembled a case against the viceroy,
largely based on loose talk, and persuaded the Crown to recall Escalona in
1642, and appoint a more reliable successor. In the interim period, which lasted
five months, Palafox himself acted as viceroy, while still remaining visitor-
general.[3] Offered appointment as archbishop of Mexico, he chose to remain
loyal to Puebla, a decision in part taken so as to avoid any conflict with the
incoming viceroy, the Count of Salvatierra, but in part possibly affected by the
consideration that the diocese yielded its bishop an income double that received
by the archbishop.[4]

As viceroy and visitor, Palafox fixed upon the practice of *repartimientos de comercio* as the chief abuse of colonial government. It was a system whereby the district magistrates – alcaldes mayores and corregidores – distributed both cash and merchandise to their Indian subjects, and then employed their judicial authority to enforce the collection of all payments, imprisoning and beating any unfortunate natives who were unable to meet the often excessive rates charged for the goods they received. Many magistrates used the monies they collected as royal tribute to finance their trading ventures and sought to evade the payment of the *alcabala*, the sales-tax, on their transactions. Since these officials were generally only appointed for five years, the incentive to pursue high profit at the expense of their subjects was great. The abuses inherent in the system were compounded by the powers vested in the viceroy to appoint these magistrates, since the Crown only reserved a relatively small number of the posts for nomination in Madrid. The result was that the viceroy usually sought to reward members of his own official and personal family with appointments. At the same time, since all magistrates were exposed to an official review at the end of their term of office, a *residencia* as it was called, most viceroys curried favour with the high court of justice by conferring magistracies on the sons and relatives of the audiencia judges. The circle of official complicity was completed by the participation of the leading merchants of Mexico City, usually peninsular Spaniards, who supplied the district magistrates with the cash and merchandise necessary to sustain their trading operations.

In his anxiety to denounce the system to the Council of the Indies, Palafox did not hesitate to provide the names of the sons and other relatives of the audiencia judges who had received magistracies, observing: 'It is a constant and moral judgement that all these ministers of justice have dealings and contracts with many merchants of this city, acting through their sons and relatives.' It was, of course, the unfortunate Indians who bore the burden of the system, since they could not obtain any legal redress from the abuses of their rapacious magistrates. Palafox wrote: 'these poor subjects have no-one to whom to appeal, so that many times when they come to see me I have to weep with them'. In effect, Palafox here advocated the dismantling of a peculiarly colonial mode of exploitation, in which the entrenched Mexican establishment, mercantile and bureaucratic in composition, composed for the most part of peninsular Spaniards, dominated both local government and the judiciary for the purposes of personal profit, acting to the detriment of both the Indians and the Crown.[5]

The system of colonial government favoured by Palafox derived from his vision of the Catholic monarchy as a union of relatively autonomous kingdoms and his profound sense of aristocratic rights. The monarchy's natural allies and agents were the territorial nobility. In consequence, as viceroy he appointed several creoles as district magistrates, and generally sought to cultivate the creole elite. In the report he handed his successor, he advised him 'to honour

12 Juan de Palafox y Mendoza

the nobility', reminding him of the existence of several royal rescripts which provided for the appointment of the descendants of the conquerors and first settlers to district magistracies and other official posts.[6] Within the Church, Palafox also favoured the promotion of creole clergymen as canons and parish priests and as regards the religious orders advocated the election of creoles as provincials and priors. It was this policy which won him the support of the Franciscan commissary-general, Fr Buenaventura de Salinas, an ardent creole patriot, who succeeded in procuring the election of the first creole to the descalced wing of his order in Mexico. Although it is difficult to locate in Palafox's writings any open commendation of the American-born Spaniards, his enemies certainly accused him of seeking to place himself at the head of a creole party within the politics of the colonial establishment.[7]

In accordance with his desire to identify with his diocese and his adopted country, Palafox took a decidedly favourable view of the Mexican Indians, composing an attractive and much-cherished treatise on native virtues and qualities. For a start, he lauded their natural bravery, observing that the conquest had been a hard-fought affair and that on the northern frontier they continued to resist Spanish advances with equal valour. Once conquered, however, they had accepted the gospel with great enthusiasm and were now both docile subjects and devout Christians. Assiduous in their attendance at church and in their participation in religious processions and feasts, they provided liberal offerings to the clergy. In their homes they had small altars with crucifixes and images of saints who evoked their veneration. Nor were they deficient in morality since they were generally exempt from such typically Spanish sins as avarice, pride, ambition, anger and envy. If they were notorious for their drunkenness, this was to be explained by their desire to find some relief from the misery in which they lived. In any case, their addiction had been over-emphasised, so Palafox argued, since it was certainly no greater than what he had observed among the Germans. For the rest, the Indians lived in great poverty – far more than that practised by the religious – yet were generally resigned to their lot. By nature, they were intelligent and had proved themselves to be excellent painters, sculptors and the like. Indeed, the son of a cacique had been recently ordained and given a parish to administer. All the world, so he observed, united to condemn the Indians for their sloth, yet everyone in New Spain depended on their labour. Writing as bishop to his parochial clergy, Palafox urged them to be patient with the natives, encouraging them to take communion each year, since despite their drunkenness they were often more virtuous than the Spaniards. As for the survival of idolatry, he claimed that 'for the most part, it is now vanquished and banished from among them'. Only in the mountains did the poisonous influence of the Devil still lurk in hidden corners.[8]

The most striking feature of this commendation of Indian talents, is its abstraction and its lack of historical context. There is no evidence to suggest that Palafox took any interest in native antiquities or history. Instead, he was happy to characterise the Indians as a dutiful Catholic peasantry, subject, no doubt, to much the same range of superstitions and failings as their counterparts in Europe, but not qualitatively different. It was a view which, when taken with his advocacy of the creole nobility, led him as viceroy to decree that all hacienda peons in debt to their employers were obliged to remain on the estates until their debts had been redeemed. Whereas the colonial authorities in New Spain had been hitherto anxious to protect the status of the Indians as free vassals of the Crown, with liberty of movement protected at law, Palafox now re-defined those natives who dwelt on Spanish haciendas as serfs bound to the estates for life.[9] Once more, he interpreted colonial realities from the perspective of seventeenth-century Europe, where rural society and government were sustained by the alliance of nobility and Crown, an alliance generally forged at the expense of the peasantry.

If as visitor and viceroy Palafox could do little to change the prevailing order, by contrast, as bishop of Puebla he possessed both authority and income sufficient to make a strong impact on his diocese. The first and most obvious manifestation of his zeal was the programme of church construction and renewal that he launched. Later, he proudly informed the king that he was responsible for the building of no less than 50 churches in the diocese and the construction of some 140 *retablos*, or decorated altar-pieces. To ensure that the diocese would have an adequate supply of qualified candidates for the priesthood, he established a Tridentine Seminary in Puebla, named after St Peter and Paul, providing it with an endowment sufficient both to maintain its Faculty and also to offer small bursaries for poor scholars. A professor was appointed to teach Nahuatl, the most widely used Indian tongue in the region, who was charged with the task of examining the proficiency in that language of all candidates nominated as parish priests. It was a measure of his affection for the Seminary that prior to his departure from New Spain, Palafox bequeathed it his splendid library of six thousand volumes. Not content with such an important achievement, he established a preparatory college and another establishment for women. He also re-built the episcopal palace. The greatest monument to his driving energy was the completion of the magnificent cathedral in Puebla, an edifice constructed in the Renaissance style of the Escorial, its interior dominated by a resplendent retablo that soared to the vaults above the high altar. Although construction on this building had started in the 1570s, all further work had been halted in 1618, when apart from the foundations all that had been acomplished was to raise the main pillars to about half their eventual height. In little more than eight years, Palafox drove forward its completion so that in 1649 he was able to preach at its formal consecration. Setting aside 12,000 pesos from his own annual income, together with another 3,000 pesos each from the cathedral chapter and Crown, he invested some 370,000 pesos in the cathedral, a sum which left him in debt for some years to come.[10] Surpassed only by the cathedral in Mexico City, completed sixteen years later, the church dominated the city of Puebla, confirming its position as capital of a great province. That such an imposing edifice could have been completed in the 1640s, at a time when Spanish armies in Europe suffered defeat and the power of the monarchy crumbled, serves to remind us of the sheer scale of clerical revenue in the middle years of the seventeenth century. As bishop, Palafox was entitled to a quarter of the agricultural tithe collected in his diocese, a source which yielded him an annual income of close to 50,000 pesos.

At the dedication of the cathedral, Palafox preached a powerful, dramatic sermon, rendered all the more moving by the prospect of his imminent departure for Spain, in which he declared that the image and prototype of all churches on earth was Bethel, where the patriarch Jacob had seen, as in a vision, a ladder to heaven, with angels ascending and descending, the messengers and agents of the Almighty. God, so Palafox averred, was everywhere, but He dwelt with especial majesty in heaven and in churches. 'In the empyrean heaven, He works the things of glory and in the temple He works the things of grace.' He recalled the words of Jacob: 'Surely the Lord is in this place . . . How full of dread is this place.' A church was holy ground which should evoke reverent dread since it was inhabited by armies of angels who, like the seraphim who had once guarded the Ark of the Covenant, now daily assisted at mass. 'The house of God is the gate of heaven', where priests, the soldiers of God, fought their sacramental battle against the Devil and his cohorts, their labour so holy that no-one, not even emperors, dared to invade the sanctuary. Palafox reminded the congregation that the only occasion Christ had displayed anger was at the sight of the money-changers in the Temple at Jerusalem, a potent warning to the secular authorities to desist from any desecration of churches. He concluded his sermon with an image of heaven as a perpetual mass, with Christ the celebrant, surrounded by angels and the faithful.[11]

It was only to be expected that so zealous and imperious a prelate as Palafox should take a high view of his office. As a youth he had studied canon law at the universities of Salamanca and Alcalá and it was as a canonist that he interpreted his rights as bishop, arguing that the three chief obligations of a bishop were 'first, to exercise and defend his jurisdiction; second, to impart spiritual doctrine; and third, to provide material assistance'. Bishops, so he declared, were 'masters of true doctrine, doctors of the people, light and salt of the world . . . high priests and generals of God's army.' It followed that the chief assistants and agents of the episcopate were the secular clergy, who through ordination were vested in 'the sacred habit of St Peter', and constituted 'the main trunk of the universal tree of the Church'. The effect of this pronouncement was to relegate the religious orders to the side-lines or, to retain his metaphor, to define them as 'illustrious branches of this trunk'. Elsewhere, he described them as 'useful workers' and as 'light cavalry', always subordinate in their operation to the main body of the Church constituted by the bishops and the parochial clergy.[12] Whereas both in the Middle Ages and in sixteenth-century Spain, the religious orders had enjoyed a prestige far superior to the uncertain fame of the secular clergy, Palafox now sought to raise both the quality and reputation of the parish priests.

This sacramental, hierarchical view of the Church soon led Palafox into an open attack on the mendicants in his diocese. By the early seventeenth century the rights of the Franciscans, Dominicans and Augustinians to continue to administer their Indian *doctrinas* had been called into question by the Mexican hierarchy. A certain number of parishes, especially in communities close to towns of Spanish foundation had been entrusted to the secular clergy. Moreover, the bishops had sought with ever-mounting urgency to subject the parishes administered by the mendicants to regular episcopal visitation. However, although the friars had agreed to nominate one of their community to act as parish priest, in practice the doctrinas continued to be managed by a group of religious residing in a small priory, the ostensible *curas* often shifting residence according to the dictates of their superiors. For Palafox the retention of parishes by the mendicants was an affront to the divine order of the Church, an infringement of the canons of the Council of Trent. To interpose any body of men or any alien authority between a bishop and his flock was to deform 'that most beautiful and ineffable harmony of the hierarchies which unites the Church Militant and the Church Triumphant', since it divorced 'the path of jurisdiction' from 'the path of grace'. Indeed, the proposal that in New Mexico the Franciscan mission should be exempted from episcopal authority he deemed close to heresy.[13]

The situation in Puebla was exacerbated by a scandalous paradox. Despite their commitment to a life of evangelical poverty, the mendicants occupied many of the wealthiest parishes in the diocese, the handsome income from their ministry the material source of the magnificence of their churches and priories. By contrast, the secular clergy in Puebla now numbered, so Palafox claimed, anywhere between seven hundred and a thousand priests, most of whom lacked a regular benefice, so that they survived either through endowments or by casual mass fees. In some cases, they even obtained an income by hiring their services to the religious in charge of the doctrinas. At the same time, the mendicants persisted in their customary opposition to episcopal visitation and the canonical installation of *curas*. Never a man to brook denial of his authority, in 1640–1 Palafox acted swiftly to eject the religious from their doctrinas, depriving them of no less than thirty-seven areas. Since the doctrinas, administered by the country priories were usually considerably larger than the usual parishes, he was able to multiply the number of benefices, installing no less than 150 secular clergy to act as *curas* and vicars. In contrast to what was to be the pattern of secularisation in the eighteenth century, Palafox allowed the friars to retain both their priories and churches, so that he was obliged to construct a considerable number of churches for the parishes now administered by the secular clergy. That this measure could be applied without any undue excitement among the populace suggests that the friars no longer enjoyed the esteem which they had once attracted. Certainly, his policy was attacked both in pamphlets and in the pulpit, with young friars attempting to incite popular protests, but all to little effect.[14] At the same time, no other bishop decided to follow Palafox's example, so that in all other dioceses in New Spain the mendicants continued to administer a large proportion of parishes – up to two-fifths of the total number in Mexico and Michoacán – until the middle decades of the eighteenth century, when the Crown introduced a far-reaching programme of secularisation and curtailment of the religious orders.[15] In this respect, Palafox anticipated subsequent measures and indeed was to be saluted as a forerunner and patron of the Bourbon reform.

Anxious to justify his advancement of the secular clergy, Palafox directed a series of pastoral letters to the parish priests, exhorting them to the path of perfection, exclaiming: 'To conquer the passions of the flesh, what other arms does the spirit have but prayer and mortification? For prayer gives counsel and mortification executes.' He sponsored the formation of congregations of secular clergy in the leading towns of his diocese, enjoining on them a rigorous devotion, declaring that the office of priest was superior to the status of a hermit or nun. He warned them from frequenting any public festivities or even family celebrations with the aim of avoiding temptations, especially that presented by the company of women. More to the point, he commended them to acquire a knowledge of Indian tongues so that they could preach to their flock in native languages, such knowledge being 'the key to the science of this ministry'. So too, they should keep a small stock of books, including a bible, a breviary, a book of sermons or a 'Nieremberg', a catechism of Fr Juan de Santo Tomás, the ordinances of the Council of Trent, a native vocabulary and grammar, and a manual of liturgical ceremonies and charges. He advised them to be ready to expend their income on the cult and ornament of their church, since these edifices were like the wife of a parish priest, which they should love, since 'it is that which gives him a position, sustenance, reputation and fortune, as the cathedral gives me'.[16]

Finally, we should note that Palafox not merely sought to encourage popular devotions, but also was himself a fervid participant. That he should have dedicated the main retablo of the cathedral to the Immaculate Conception of the Virgin Mary was perhaps only to be expected, since that dogma had become a matter of official commitment in seventeenth-century Spain. But he was also devoted to the cult of the Child Jesus, bringing to Mexico an image that he had acquired in Flanders and which accompanied him on his travels. His most treasured image was a broken crucifix, which he had rescued from a disused chapel in Germany, its arms broken by heretics, an image he kept by him until his death. In Puebla, he greatly encouraged Indian devotion to the famous image of the Virgin Mary at Ocotlán, on the hill above Tlaxcala. Like many men of his time, he had a gift for tears and on one occasion he led a procession from the cathedral to a deserted hermitage, situated about a mile outside the city, walking barefoot and carrying a cross, weeping copiously as he preached a penitential sermon.[17] On the score of public morality, he was a rigorist, seeking to ban popular comedies, or, at the least, dissuade the devout from frequenting them.

III

Towards the end of his life, Palafox composed a spiritual memoir, blessed with the title *Confesiones y confusiones*, in which he admitted that he was 'a child of transgression', which is to say, a bastard, who had been left exposed in a basket on a hillside, saved from death only by a passing shepherd and his wife who nursed him back to health. His mother, the daughter of honourable parents, redeemed her sin by becoming a Carmelite nun, rising to become a prioress and founder of a new convent. After his childhood, Palafox was recognised by his father, the Marquis of Araiza, and eventually sent to university where he made a desultory study of canon law. At some point in his twenties, the young man experienced a spiritual conversion and passed eight months of joy, engaged in prayer, living as if immersed in the light of God, without suffering temptation. It was then that he found lasting inspiration in St Augustine's *Confessions* and in the autobiography of St Teresa of Avila, the great Carmelite mystic and Spain's new patron. Henceforth, so Palafox claimed, it was his practice to rise at three or four in the morning to start the day with prayer. He applied the discipline to his flesh, using a scourge with metal pellets on the thongs, three times a day. At night he slept with cilices, bristle circlets tied tightly around his limbs, and embraced a spiked iron crucifix. When young, he had slept on boards, but in age he used a bolster with a coarse shawl to cover him. He made a point of dressing in plain cloth; he fasted three times a week, abstained from wine, visited hospitals and gave alms to the poor. In short, Palafox sought to mortify his flesh in a manner more commonly observed by mendicants than by prelates. His biographer recounted that after his death his officers found a small arsenal of cilices and other instruments of physical penitence.[18]

The object of these ascetic practices was to so quell the body as to free the soul from earthly desire, opening the way to contemplation and eventual union with God. To guide him on this upward path, Palafox turned to the writings of

St Teresa, whose letters he edited, inserting his own commentary. In his tract, *El varón de deseos*, he described the three-fold paths of the purgative, illuminative and unitive ways to heaven. At the same time, he admitted that after the first raptures of his conversion had passed, he himself experienced all the normal round of temptations, and was battered by the onslaught of incredulity, sensuality and despair, afflictions mounted by the Devil, against which, so he averred, the most efficacious remedies were holy water and verbal prayer. By contrast, the ravages of ambition, the child of pride, admitted no more remedy than constant prayer and love of God. Despite his devotion to St Teresa and his study of the great mystics, there is little reason to suppose that Palafox himself was a mystic in the technical sense of the word, since he wrote: 'I have never been able to keep my thoughts quiet enough for meditation.' His imagination was too wild, and the burden of the day's business too pressing for him to perform the spiritual exercises favoured by directors of conscience in this epoch. Instead, he found refuge and consolation in verbal prayer and in writing, confessing that 'although through his incapacity, distractions, laxity and fantasy, this sinner was incapable of prayer ... he framed treatises of prayer so easily that he never or hardly ever thought about what he wrote ...', his literary labours accompanied by profuse tears, as if inspired by the Holy Spirit. By this period, of course, there existed in Spain an entire literature dealing with the methods and problems of mystical and devotional life.[19] With the words and concepts ready-made, so to say, it was as easy for Palafox to compose yet one more spiritual tract as it was for a Wiseman or a Newman to write a novel.

In a revealing admonition, Palafox once declared that 'we have to be more ambitious to conquer the kingdom of heaven in a short time, than was Alexander the Great to win the kingdom of the world'. Since he suffered the afflictions of dryness and emptiness experienced by most men of devotion, he always sought to rally his sentiments by affective effusions, which is to say, by spoken exclamations of love of God, that emotion 'which governs the dance of this interior harmony'. In his memoir, he required no less than thirty pages to describe his daily devotions. To judge from all this, it appears that in his private chamber he prayed as if he were in some great baroque church, each day moving slowly down the nave, pausing to salute the images of the prophets, apostles, Church fathers and saints, at times entering side-chapels, there to prostrate himself before the Crucifix or to venerate the Virgin Mary.[20] In private as in public, Palafox was always the priest, surrounded by the hierarchies of angels and saints, constantly engaged in formal acts of worship, always conscious of the figure he cut on the universal stage of heaven and earth.

By training a canonist and in aspiration a mystic, Palafox had apparently read little theology and less philosophy, his imagination more fired by the living example of Church history than by the writings of the great scholastics.

Perhaps the most striking feature of his approach to Christianity was his contemptuous dismissal of its Hebraic origin, asserting that prior to Christ's advent the effects of both written and natural law were so feeble that barely a hundred men had qualified for salvation. Moreover, the apostles and subsequent saints far exceeded in virtue and heavenly rank the Jewish prophets and patriarchs, with St Peter soaring far above Moses. After all, it was only with the establishment of the Church that the chief means of human salvation, the divine grace that poured out to humanity through the sacraments, had become available. Thereafter, the history of the Church was distinguished by the glorious line of saints, starting with the early Fathers, achieving a climax with the emergence of St Francis and St Dominic; only then to reach a new apogee in the heroic figures of the Catholic Reformation, with Teresa of Avila, Ignatius Loyola, Francis Xavier, Philip Neri and Charles Borromeo but the vanguard of a formidable army of martyrs, confessors and other holy men and women, whose lives and works constituted the proof that the Catholic Church still enjoyed God's blessing and was still animated by the Holy Spirit.[21]

As much a courtier and a royal minister as a churchman, Palafox drew little distinction between the spiritual and secular modes of power, declaring that all authority derived from Heaven, with monarchy and hierarchy its animating principles. In a political application of neo-Platonism, he argued that since there was but one God in heaven, there should be but one Pope and one king on earth. In consequence, Palafox affirmed that 'all government without a head is perdition and confusion', drawing the conclusion that 'to leave the Church to the rule of the few which is aristocracy, or to the rule of the many which is democracy, would be its perdition, leaving it subject to infinite emulation, jealousy and sedition, since all political and natural government rests solely in monarchy'. This principle led him to salute St Peter as the prince of the apostles and the rock on which the Church was founded, arguing that whereas the vocation of the other apostles was personal, ending with their deaths, by contrast the naming of St Peter as their leader was a perpetual office, transmitted to his successors. Since the Church Militant on earth was formed in the image of the Church Triumphant in heaven, it was obvious that one God in heaven had to be matched by but one lieutenant on earth, St Peter and his successors thus acting as universal vicars of Christ, pastors of the world, heads of the Church, with other bishops their sons or younger brothers.[22] After this typically canonist elevation of the Papacy, it comes as no surprise to observe that Palafox failed to define with any clarity the precise relation of the Papacy and the Catholic monarchy of Spain, other than to invoke the time-honoured image of the two swords, governing the spiritual and the temporal spheres.

Palafox described the kings of Spain as guided by the dictates of justice and religion, ruling their realm through the twin hierarchies of the ecclesiastical and secular arms of government, with ministers and magistrates defined as 'images of their princes'. The essential division here was between the rulers and the ruled, the duties of the subject described curtly and simply as obedience to his superiors, which is to say, to the serried ranks of kings and princes, bishops and prelates, the lesser clergy, ministers and magistrates, generals and nobles.[23] In his history of King David, written primarily to provide a biblical refutation of Machiavelli's divorce of political action and Christian ethics, Palafox discounted the prophet Samuel's warning against the tyranny of kings by arguing that Israel's misfortunes had demonstrated the dangers of popular government, the deliberations of a senate always a source of discord. After tracing the story of David's family quarrels, he observed: 'royal palaces are the heart of this world, where ambition and human power are most at play, where all that is high, great and sovereign in the temporal sphere is to be found'. Lest this description be thought to strike too secular a note, he hastened to add that in Catholic palaces prayer and virtue were equally to be found. Elsewhere, in proof of this maxim, he wrote the life of a sister of the emperor Rudolph who died in an odour of sanctity as a nun in the Franciscan convent at Madrid. In his concluding reflections on King David, he adverted to the great tact required of that monarch in governing twelve distinct tribes, all jealous of their autonomy. It had been a master-stroke of David to bring the Ark of the Covenant to his new capital at Jerusalem, thus contriving to endow his office with the blessing of heaven. So also, Palafox counselled, the diverse kingdoms and provinces of the Catholic monarchy should be bound together by an insistence on the king's religious character and role both in Europe and overseas.[24] In a clear echo of Botero, the Church was thus seen as the chief buttress of the Spanish state: Eusebius of Caesarea's panegyric of Constantine the Great rather than St Augustine's distrust of all earthly dominion was the distant model.

Although Palafox asserted that 'the same virtues govern the hierarchies, since the ecclesiastical and the secular greatly resemble each other', in both spheres he clearly expected the nobility to dominate the upper echelons of each ladder. In an explicit distinction between a free commonwealth and a monarchy, he declared that in a monarchy the obligations of a noble were to God, the king, his father and his country, whereas in the commonwealth the first loyalty of all citizens was always to their patria. 'In monarchies and kingdoms the good vassal is not born in his patria but in the heart of his king.' These distinctions only applied to the nobility, since whereas commoners and mere subjects were governed by reason and appetite, the nobility obeyed the dictates of reason and shame, which is to say, they were inspired by 'honour, which in a man of blood is the essence of nobility'.[25]

All these reflections appeared in distilled, applied form, when Palafox chose to examine the contrasting virtues and policies of two canonised archbishops of the previous century, St Thomas Villanueva of Valencia and St Charles

Borromeo of Milan. For the Spaniard was an Augustinian friar, a man of humble social extraction, who, despite his elevation to the rank of archbishop, continued to live as a friar, still dressing in poor cloth, with no more than six chaplains and companions in his palace. The vast income accruing to his office was primarily expended in the service of the poor, with thousands of unfortunates assisted by alms. By contrast, the Italian was an aristocrat who lived in great style, converting his palace into a veritable seminary, with a hundred young clerics in residence, all recruited from noble families, studying under his direct supervision and encouragement. The resources of the diocese were employed to finance the construction of a Tridentine seminary and other colleges, all dedicated to the education and spiritual formation of the secular clergy. Only God in all his wisdom could decide which was the better path to follow, Palafox concluded, but to merely human eyes the work of Borromeo was 'the most useful to the public'. If we note that the Milanese archbishop won fame through his rigorous enforcement of the decrees of the Council of Trent and in particular for his insistence on the reform of the secular clergy which that Council enjoined, then the reasons for Palafox's approbation become clear. It was in a moment of affliction, when he fled from Puebla, that he wrote: 'The Holy Council of Trent is the treasure of the Church, where the truths of the Faith shine resplendent.'[26] Since that assembly had re-asserted the authority and jurisdiction of bishops, albeit conceiving of them as delegates of the Papacy, then the choice of Borromeo as an exemplary Tridentine prelate served to define the true character of Palafox's conception of the Church.

IV

If Palafox succeeded in ousting the mendicants from the parishes they held in his diocese without undue commotion, by contrast, his quarrel with the Jesuits cost him his See and widened into a dispute which acquired international resonance. Although his career was to end in virtual disgrace, his admirers proved sufficiently powerful to procure permission for the Carmelites to publish a collected edition of his works after his death, accompanied by a laudatory biography written by a Spanish cleric later accused of Jansenist sympathies. By the middle decades of the seventeenth century, the Jesuits had acquired numerous enemies and the virulent attack on their pretensions launched by Palafox at the height of the dispute was translated into French and served as further ammunition in the Jansenist onslaught. However, the issues at stake in Mexico were never theological in character, but rather centred on questions of jurisdiction and property. At the same time, the failure of the Spanish Court to sustain the Bishop of Puebla can be interpreted as further evidence of the growing enfeeblement of the Catholic monarchy: by reason of its *Patronato* the Crown was the effective head of the Spanish American

Church, so that any derogation of episcopal jurisdiction entailed an injury to the royal prerogative. Secular and ecclesiastical politics were intertwined and both hierarchies, as Palafox had observed, derived their authority from a common source, the Catholic Kings, who in the Indies acted as delegates of the Papacy.

The opening shots in the battle against the Jesuits occurred in 1642 when Palafox, supported by his cathedral chapter, protested against the donation of an hacienda to the Jesuit College of Puebla. The reasons were simple. Already, the hierarchy in New Spain had presented a formal plea to the Council of the Indies demanding that all religious orders should pay the regular ecclesiastical tithe on the produce of their agricultural estates. As yet, the matter had not been resolved and the Jesuits already had given sign of being the most intransigent opponents of the hierarchy on this question, in large measure because they were already the wealthiest landowners among the religious communities, easily surpassing the Dominicans and Augustinians. On encountering determined resistance, Palafox proceeded to broaden the dispute by denouncing the extraordinary wealth already accumulated by the Jesuits. In a letter to Pope Innocent XI, he declared that the two colleges alone owned over 300,000 head of sheep, operated six sugar planations worth over 1 million pesos and enjoyed an income of at least 100,000 pesos. Since their circuit of missions was maintained by royal subsidy, he calculated that the revenue of the Mexican province was sufficient to give every professed Jesuit an income of 2,500 pesos. These charges were bitterly resented by the province which asserted that the proceeds of their estates went to maintain their colleges and assist in the construction of their churches. Obviously, they could not deny their wealth, since, as we have seen, by their own reckoning the capital value of their possessions at this time was close to 3 to 4 million pesos, although their net income was decidedly less than the estimates provided by Palafox, in part because of the high debts incurred either in the purchase of estates or through church building.[27]

In later years, Palafox composed a small treatise on the general question of church tithes, arguing in characteristic vein that in the same way that all subjects had an obligation to pay taxes to their king, so equally all Christians had the duty to pay tithes to the ecclesiastical authorities. Contrary to the position adopted by Crown lawyers, he asserted that the payment of tithes was an entirely spiritual act, destined to support the priesthood and bishops, maintain the fabric of the cathedral, and assist the poor and infirm. In all nations there had existed a system of contributions for the support of temples and the religious cult. Failure to pay tithes was tantamount to a denial of God's authority, stealing the very garments of Christ. What was at stake here, of course, was the material interest of the cathedral chapters and prelates. In Puebla, the tithe levied chiefly on the agricultural produce of Spanish estates throughout the diocese was expended almost entirely in the city, where it served to maintain the physical fabric of the cathedral, support the hospital, and pay handsome salaries to the twenty-seven canons and prebendaries of the chapter. In 1652 the Council of the Indies decreed that all religious orders should henceforth pay tithes to the authorities of the dioceses in which their estates were located, a ruling which all communities other than the Jesuits reluctantly accepted as definitive since they had already consumed almost half a century in appeals and counter-appeals. However, to judge from later allegations, it remains doubtful whether the Jesuits ever paid more than a nominal tithe on the vast produce of their estates, bishops fearing to provoke yet another round of controversy and polemic.[28]

The ultimate cause of the bitter hostility between Palafox and the Jesuits has yet to be fully explored. In an intriguing report written as early as 1641, the Jesuit provincial advised Rome that Palafox openly sought to interfere in the internal politics of the Mexican province. Apparently, he criticised the failure of the Jesuits in New Spain to elect creoles of good birth and letters to high office, always choosing peninsular Spaniards of low extraction and modest virtue for positions of responsibility. In seventy years since their arrival, there had never been a creole provincial. The letter concluded: 'The good bishop, as a politician, wishes to place himself at the head of this band.' In short, Palafox clearly favoured the introduction of some form of *alternativa*, the system of alternate election of creoles and peninsulars, which had given rise to so many factional disputes within the mendicant orders. Indeed, he equally criticised the friars for importing men from Spain merely for the purpose of electing European Spaniards to high office. At the same time, he was to report that the Jesuits maintained their firm discipline by a policy of expulsions, so that any attempt to form a creole party within the Province was likely to be quashed by strong reprisals and dismissal.[29] It is an ironic commentary on these allegations that at the height of the quarrel with Palafox, the Jesuits were led by their first creole provincial, Pedro de Velasco, a nephew of the second viceroy of that name. The degree to which the dispute can be interpreted through the perspective of the creole aspirations to office is by no means clear.

The climax of the quarrel with the Jesuits occurred in 1647 when the vicar-general of the Puebla diocese, obviously acting on Palafox's instigation peremptorily ordered all Jesuits to exhibit their licences to preach and hear confession, it being a rule of canon law that all priests had to obtain episcopal licence to undertake a public ministry in any particular diocese. Already, Palafox had complained that Jesuit priests had exercised their sacerdotal functions on the haciendas owned by the colleges without permission from the bishop. In the event, the Jesuits refused to comply with the vicar-general's demand, declaring that the Holy See had granted the Company of Jesus a world-wide privilege to exercise their ministry without necessity of episcopal authorisation. Included within this privilege, so it was averred, was the right to refuse to exhibit any documents to justify its exercise. Confronted with this summary dismissal of the principle of episcopal jurisdiction, the vicar-general equally summarily prohibited the Jesuits from any further activity as priests in Puebla, a city where they possessed a college and a leading church. As Palafox later declared, the general privilege cited by the Jesuits essentially applied to mission territory; it certainly did not cover the case of Puebla where the faith had been established for over a century. To concede the case would be to strip the bishop of his staff of office, to deny him the exercise of the jurisdiction conferred by the Council of Trent, to introduce an alien authority between him and his flock.[30]

Rather than submit to Palafox's demands, the Jesuits then engineered the appointment of two judges, *jueces conservadores*, to resolve the dispute, a measure provided for by canon law so as to settle conflicts between two ecclesiastical institutions. However, in this case both judges were Dominican friars, who immediately pronounced in favour of the Jesuits and demanded restitution of their rights to preach and confess, threatening excommunication of the vicar-general and a fine for Palafox if their decision was not accepted. They also extended their purview to assure the Jesuits continuing exemption from payment of tithe. By this time, the Jesuits had also won the support of both the viceroy and the archbishop, the latter bringing with him the Inquisition. A bitter scurry of pamphlets added to the animosity of the conflict, filling the air with personal attacks and insinuations of corruption and ambition. Undeterred by this formidable coalition, Palafox rallied his cathedral chapter behind him and retaliated by excommunicating the two Dominican judges. But the agents he sent to the capital to negotiate were imprisoned and the viceroy mounted an armed expedition to coerce the bishop into submission.

It was at this juncture of the dispute that Palafox took refuge in the hills, protected by a loyal landowner. There he remained hidden for four months, writing a formidable series of despatches to the King, the Pope and the inquisitor-general. Although his opponents later derided his flight as a piece of theatrical nonsense, Palafox was able to cite letters written at the time by Fr Buenaventura de Salinas, the Franciscan commissary-general, warning that the viceroy and his party were determined to humiliate him. Any supporters he had in the capital had been silenced. In particular, the Jesuits sought to expel him from the country, determined to establish the rule that 'no-one should take the Company to court or if they did that it should cost them dear'. For his part, Palafox defended his decision on the grounds that as former minister of the Crown he had no desire to appeal to mob violence. Had he awaited the arrival of the viceroy's men, there might well have occurred a popular outburst, similar to that of 1624 when the masses took command of the capital after a quarrel between the viceroy and the archbishop. By no means averse to self-dramatisation, he appealed to the example of St Athanasius in the desert and to St Thomas of Canterbury, who had died for the principle of 'ecclesiastical immunity'. At the same time, he did not hesitate to attribute the true cause of the conflict to material interests.[31] The Jesuits remained incensed over his demand that they pay tithes on the produce of their estates, and if the archbishop and viceroy supported them it was because his vigilance as visitor-general had injured the vested interests and profits of the colonial establishment. The fall of Olivares, his former protector, had strengthened their determination to pay off old scores.

In the short term, Palafox's tactics met with success, the more especially as his enemies grossly over-played their hand. The Dominican judges excommunicated the bishop in his absence; the Jesuits paraded through the streets in triumph, displaying a grotesque figure of Palafox and brandishing an image of St Ignatius; and a cowed rump of the cathedral chapter approved the Jesuit licences and then declared the See of Puebla to be vacant, its government thus devolving on their own unworthy shoulders. All these excesses worked to Palafox's advantage, as the authorities in both Madrid and Rome rallied to his support, despatching sharply worded reprimands across the Atlantic. The Dominican judges were soon removed and ordered back to Spain. The canons of the cathedral were accused of usurping the Crown's rights of patronage and were put under house arrest. The Jesuits were instructed to exhibit their licences so as to obtain confirmation from the bishop. Palafox returned to Puebla amidst great rejoicing and remained there until 1649, time enough for him to preside over the consecration of the cathedral. But the vehemence of his denunciations of the Jesuits soon provoked alarm at the highest levels of the Company, the more especially as he broadened the terms of the dispute so as to bring into question its very existence, declaring that since their foundation the Jesuits had filled the Church with dissension. Moreover, although the Mexican Jesuits had been reproved both by their own superiors in Rome and by the Crown, they continued to manoeuvre, press for further review of the case, and in general refuse to admit any fault. Indeed, the new provincial, Martín de Rada, coolly informed Palafox that the entire dispute was of his own making. The result was that in 1649 Palafox was summoned home to Madrid, only to find that the Spanish Jesuits had prepared for him 'a bed of sharpest thorns', with scurrilous pamphlets issued to defame his character and career. When he replied in equally polemical fashion, inserting his previous letters to Pope Innocent XI in his *Defensa canónica*, published in 1652 at Rome, the Crown became alarmed at the ever-widening implications of the quarrel. The result was that Palafox was obliged to resign his see in 1654 and accept appointment as bishop of Osma, an impoverished diocese in Castile, where he remained until his death, desperately endeavouring to pay off the debts he had incurred in Puebla.[32] The disgrace of so influential a prelate, a great nobleman and former minister of the Crown, offered potent warning to all enemies of the Company of Jesus to desist from further recrimination.

The reasons for Palafox's downfall become obvious if we consider the character of his final attacks on the Jesuits. He observed that not merely had they initiated an entire series of disputes within the Church, but that they always fought as soldiers seeking victory, no matter what the cost to their opponents or to the Church. From the start, they had questioned the time-honoured doctrine of Predestination taught by both Augustine and Aquinas. In moral theology, they had espoused the dubious and lax doctrine of Probabilism. As regards the mendicants they had insulted the Carmelites by refusing to accept the biblical origin of that order and had derided the coarse serge worn by the Franciscans, asserting that it filled the laity with horror. So arrogant and aggressive had the Jesuits become, that they declared their own rule to be superior to the way followed by other religious orders, obliging the mendicants to defend their practice of penitence and poverty and the retention of singing the office in choir. In Germany, as lands were recovered from heretic princes, they seized the property and even churches that once had belonged to other religious orders. In China, the Jesuits sought to monopolise the mission, preventing friars from entering the celestial empire. Yet the doctrines they imparted to their Chinese neophytes were barely recognisable as Christian, since they suppressed the display of the crucifix and allowed their converts to continue to worship their ancestors. The Church of the Fathers had been founded on the blood of the martyrs: where were the Christian or Jesuit martyrs in China? This grapeshot broadside led Palafox to query the very existence of the Company of Jesus, arguing that it should either be subjected to drastic reform or be suppressed.[33]

Here is no place to comment on the substance of these charges. It was certainly the case that the Jesuits were embroiled in any number of disputes with the theologians of other orders. Their quarrel with the Jansenists in France was to provoke the irony of Pascal. The degree to which their rejection of Augustinian doctrines was bound up with their quest to define the Christian gospel as the fulfilment of natural religion is a question still as yet unresolved. But it was clearly unwise of Palafox to launch his frail bark on such stormy seas. His formation as a canonist did not provide him with the intellectual resources to handle such questions with either competence or tact. In any case, it was singularly unwise to sneer at the Jesuits for their lack of martyrs in China when elsewhere, in Canada, Japan and England, they had precisely distinguished themselves by their heroic aptitude for this apostolic calling. Had he stuck to the questions of tithes and licences, he might well have survived the tempest. On these grounds the facts of the case favoured him. The Jesuits were indeed a wealthy order and although they devoted their vast income to worthy ends they had no particular justification to seek exemption from the general obligation to pay tithes. Moreover, the tenacity and arrogance with which they fought their battle might well have tempted a prelate less imperious than Palafox to angry response. The stakes involved were deemed to be high and they did not hesitate to employ all their resources to rally official opinion to their side. At the same time, by no means all Jesuits approved the actions of their provincials; the inner history of the Company in Mexico, or indeed, for that matter, in Europe, has yet to be written. Whatever the case, the result of Palafox's disgrace was that the Jesuits in New Spain were destined to grow in numbers, wealth and influence, opening new colleges, buying more estates, extending their northern missions, all without cease until their expulsion in 1767.

V

A keen observer of the contemporary scene, Palafox wrote a series of reflections that expressed official opinion with remarkable fidelity. In both the diary he kept of his journey to Vienna in 1629 and in the report he presented to Olivares, he emphasised that the Thirty Years War was above all else a struggle between the one true faith, upheld by the House of Austria, and 'the Lutheran venom'. He praised the emperor Ferdinand II for cleansing his realm of Calvinists, viewing his reconquest of Bohemia as a great Catholic victory. By contrast, he was to criticise the previous emperor, Rudolph II, who had succeeded in avoiding any entanglement in religious wars, for his 'retirement and futile inquiry into natural causes, mathematics and other exercises'. He warned Olivares of Wallenstein, the great *condottiere*, whose ambition and power threatened Habsburg influence. By contrast, he lauded 'the great Count Tilly', commander of the forces of the Catholic League, who 'never set out to fight or to conquer were it no preceded by a prayer, with rosary in one hand and a pistol in the other'. Needless to say, in later years he was bitterly to lament the intervention of France, whose Most Christian King tolerated heretics at home and assisted Gustavus Adolphus and other Protestant powers abroad, all to the detriment of the Catholic faith.[34] Raising his view to survey all Europe, Palafox depicted a continent torn apart by warfare, with heresy and witchcraft on the increase in all regions. How different was the situation of Spain in the early 1630s! Here was a country that enjoyed the supreme blessing of 'one King, one Faith, one Law', protected by strong, natural frontiers, sustained by a rich thriving agriculture, united in loyalty to the Catholic monarchy. 'Today Spain is the most happy country in the world.' Of course, Palafox was well aware of the threats posed by the almost universal enmity to Spain in Europe, with only Austria a faithful, albeit weak ally. So too, the decline in industry had not escaped his attention. But he argued that it was men and courage, not riches that sustained a kingdom. In any case, he reported to

Olivares on passing through Catalonia that 'this principality is the arm of most blood in the exhausted body of Spain'. However, the city council of Barcelona was dominated by merchants and artisans, and the populace were 'overly free' and unquiet. It was necessary to attract the support of the nobility so as to crush the commons and thus employ the resources of the province to assist Castile.[35]

In his *Juicio político*, written after the disasters of 1640, when both Portugal and Catalonia burst into revolt, Palafox offered a melancholy analysis of the decline of Spain. Reflecting on the cycle of international conflict, he declared that it was only during the reign of Charles V that Spain had assumed the 'monarchy' of Europe. Even after the union of the Crowns of Castile and Aragon, the country still only counted as one kingdom among others in the European concert. But with the conquest of Italy, the discovery of the Indies, the defeat of France and the Turks, and the acquisition of Portugal, then Spain became a true monarchy: 'the world trembled and Spain made itself superior to all the nations of Europe and comparable to all the greatest of Africa and America'. If the foundation had been laid by the prudence and parsimony of Ferdinand the Catholic, the monarchy had been created by the valour of Charles V, and then perfected by the zeal for religion and justice of Philip II. But barely had this universal state reached perfection when signs of decay appeared, as if like Daniel's Fourth Kingdom it rested on feet of clay. Essentially, it was the Dutch revolt and the subsequent endless wars in Flanders which had been the chief cause of Spain's ruin. If only Philip II had personally supervised the suppression of the rebellion at its first appearance, the situation might have been saved. Then again, the opportunities for recovery presented by the years of truce in 1606–20 had been wasted, with the pursuit of luxury all the rage, instead of the king laying in treasure to finance future wars. The conflict with France over Italy was the final blow in this chain of errors. Moreover, in the years which followed, Olivares neglected the advice of the councillors of the various states which composed the monarchy, seeking rather to reduce these kingdoms and provinces to a common rule and law. It had been the neglect of the right of each kingdom to be governed by its natives, preserving their separate constitutions, that had led to the disaster of 1640.[36] The heyday of the Catholic monarchy, so Palafox declared, had lasted barely more than thirty years before its hegemony was threatened on all sides.

In his history of the fall of the Ming Empire in China, which also occurred in 1640, that 'fatal year for many empires', Palafox drew the lessons he thought appropriate, praising the invading Manchus for their hardy character, honesty and military valour. By contrast, the Chinese had become effeminate through lack of practice in war, a weakness compounded by the preference given to letters over arms. Mandarins rather than soldiers commanded the imperial armies, a class of men who were notoriously corrupt and tyrannical, their excesses leaving the country defenceless. All this pointed to the conclusion that riches brought undue luxury and sapped military courage, so that 'since the beginning of the world, the poor nations have conquered the rich'. It was a principle that admitted hope for Spain, since although poverty-stricken her population was still vigorous and her soldiers full of courage. At the same time, courage and poverty were insufficient unless based on Christian morality since a kingdom without virtue was like 'a body without blood'.[37]

Towards the end of his life, in 1656, when Spain's defeat by France was all too apparent, Palafox presented a memorial to the Crown designed to protest against ministers levying taxes on clerical income without prior consultation or consent. If the Cortés had to be summoned to approve any new imposts on the laity, so equally the clergy should be consulted on any additional charges they had to pay. He insisted on the political, not to mention the military, value of their prayers, denying charges of idleness, arguing that: 'More is conquered on the altar than in battle, since all victories in battle are owed to the altar.' Prayer conquered all. How then could the 'secret mystery' of Spain's decline and defeat be explained? There was genuine pathos in his query and yet more pathos in his reply.

> The secular and religious clergy of Spain are resplendent in virtue, spirit and example throughout Christendom. The understanding, valour and constancy of the Spaniards is greater than that of other nations. The forces, nerve and power of the monarchy exceed all the Crowns of Europe. The subsidies from America are innumerable. The efforts of the soldiers of Your Majesty and the military skill of the generals can not be greater. What then, is the 'secret mystery' that we can discern as inspiring the public misfortunes . . .?

In these words, Palafox gave vent to that profound sense of bewilderment and betrayal that was to haunt Spain in years to come.[38] The nation had poured forth its blood and wealth persuaded that Providence had chosen Spain as the chief bulwark and sentinel of the Catholic Church. Its armies had been supported by the holocaust of prayer and penitence that arose from the countless cloisters. Yet, at the end of the reign of Philip IV, Spain lay exhausted and bankrupt, about to enter a decline as much cultural as political, when the lights of its brilliant literature, theatre, art and theology, all slowly dimmed. Unwittingly, Palafox offered some clue as to the explanation of this ebbing tide. For, after posing his question so dramatically, he then proceeded to attribute all the public disasters suffered by his country to the decision of the Crown, first taken in 1591, to levy taxes on the clergy. Since that day things had gone from bad to worse for Spain. Nor was historical precedent lacking, since equally in Byzantium the seizure of clerical property had been followed by defeat. That such an explanation should have occurred to a man with the political experience of Palafox surely illustrates both the inward decay of the Spanish intellect and the pre-eminence by then accorded to corporate interest.

VI

The imperious intervention of Juan de Palafox y Mendoza in the public affairs
of New Spain had all the effect of a comet entering and disturbing the fixed
orbits of a planetary system. The effects were both immediate and enduring.
For the humiliation administered to Palafox signified that the Catholic King
and his ministers no longer possessed the political strength to resist the pressure
exerted by a powerful ecclesiastical corporation intent on defending its
exemption from episcopal authority. That a former councillor of the Indies, a
visitor-general and interim viceroy, should have been driven from his bishopric
attested to the patent incapacity of the court at Madrid to defend its trusted
servants. In his brief years of power, Palafox had challenged the vested interests
of the colonial establishment, both secular and clerical, only then to face their
combined onslaught. To put the case into perspective, it should be recalled that
Solórzano had depicted the Indies as governed by two parallel systems of law,
civil and canon, each with its own courts and officers, the king as the Pope's
delegate acting as the respective fount and patron of these two great spheres of
jurisdiction. On this interpretation, bishops and parish priests were as much
officers of the Crown as any royal governor or district magistrate, so that any
derogation of their authority entailed loss of power for the king's State. So
obvious were these conclusions that for more than a century Madrid refrained
from despatching any further visitors to New Spain, henceforth choosing to
avoid any direct confrontation with the corporate and economic interests of the
country. Not until the epoch of Charles III (1759–88) was any challenge offered
to the existing balance of power within colonial government. The result was
that the judges of the high courts continued to conspire with peninsular
merchants resident in the Indies to afford legal protection for the depredations
of the district magistrates who arrived in America with the aim of exacting a
high profit from their hapless native subjects. So too, the *alternativa* in office
between European and American Spaniards was maintained despite its malign
influence on the discipline of the mendicant orders. Only slowly did the creoles
encroach on the upper echelons of colonial administration and then never on
the scale that satisfied their pretensions.

In the long term, the Jesuit triumph over Palafox proved a pyrrhic victory.
Within a decade of his death, the Carmelite order, to whom he had bequeathed
his literary estate, brought out a collected edition of his works, accompanied by
a laudatory biography which presented him as little less than a saint. His
critique of the Jesuits was translated and much cited by French Jansenists, then
engaged in fierce theological controversy with that order. By the eighteenth
century the regalist lawyers who sought to strengthen the king's authority over
the Church hailed him as both a precursor and an inspiration. Indeed, Charles
III warmly espoused the cause of Palafox's canonisation in Rome and

promoted a lavish new collected edition of his works in fourteen folio volumes. In the official memorials and discussions that preceded the expulsion of the Jesuits in 1767 from all Spanish domains, the persecution suffered by the bishop of Puebla was much cited as an example of the subersive, overweening character of the Company of Jesus.[39] In short, the memory of the tumultuous events of the 1640s, carefully preserved in passionate polemic, served eventually to undermine the prestige and position of the Jesuits, offering a convenient whipping-boy for all their opponents.

Despite his obvious encouragement of creole pretensions and his favourable opinion of Indian character, Palafox appears to have taken little interest in the history of his adopted country, his pen more apt to applaud Manchu virtue or to narrate the adventures of King David than to dwell on the life and thought of Nezahualcoyotl. There is no evidence that he ever studied the great sequence of chronicles that dealt with the Mexican past and the feats of the conquerors. He was untouched by the millennial vision of the Franciscans which had conferred on Mexico a central role in the spiritual economy of the contemporary Church. Nor did the anguished denunciations of Las Casas ever attract his attention. Although Palafox certainly read St Augustine's *Confessions* with eager interest, he consciously rejected the dualism of the *City of God*, and quietly ignored its profound distrust of all forms of earthly dominion. Despite subsequent Jansenist citation of his writings, he was much more close to Pierre Berulle, founder of the French Oratory, who practised a similar devotional asceticism, combined with an emphasis on the elevated role of the secular priesthood and a criticical view of the Jesuits. More important, Palafox reached back to Eusebius of Caesarea and his neo-Platonic panegyric of Constantine the Great and politicised the celestial hierarchies of Dionysius the Areopagite.[40] In his vision of the world, Habsburg Spain figured as another Byzantium, a Christian commonwealth in which the bishops, saints and clergy preached and prayed to Heaven to beseech divine protection and assistance for its rulers, magistrates and armies. As much as chroniclers like Gómara and Acosta, Palafox believed that Providence had chosen the Catholic monarchy to promote the cause of the Church throughout the world, its treasure and manpower poured forth to defend its territories from the assaults of both infidel and heretic. Unlike the Franciscans or Las Casas, however, he did not attribute any spiritual signifi- cance to the discovery of America; still less entertain any idea of the New World possessing a special role in the progress of the City of God. In the last resort, Palafox was an imperial visitor in the New World, anxious to define New Spain as an integral province of the Tridentine Church and as an overseas kingdom of the universal Catholic monarchy.

PART 2

STRANGERS IN THEIR OWN LAND

Non fecit taliter omni nationi

12

INCA HUMANIST

I

IN 1560 a young Peruvian mestizo named Gómez Suárez de Figueroa arrived in Spain to seek his fortune. As he was to announce to the world in his first book, he was the son of Garcilaso de la Vega, a leading conqueror and corregidor of Cuzco, and of the Inca princess, Isabel Chimpu Occllo, a grand-daughter of the emperor Tupac Inca Yupanqui. Born in 1539, he had been reared in his father's house but at the age of ten suffered the mortification of seeing his father take a young Spanish noblewoman for his wife, marrying off his native concubine to a common Spanish foot-soldier, by whom she had two other children. Given a rudimentary education in company with other mestizo sons of the conquerors and scions of the Inca nobility, he had observed at first hand the tumultuous cycle of civil wars which dominated the history of Peru until 1555, conflicts in which his father played a leading role. At the same time, he inquired about the Inca past from his mother's family and relatives.[1] The memory of the stirring events of his boyhood was to haunt the *émigré* in all the long years of his Spanish expatriation.

At some undisclosed point after his arrival in Spain at the age of twenty-one, the young mestizo adopted his father's name, a name already rendered illustrious by the great poet and courtier, Juan Garcilaso de la Vega, a distant relative. However, when he approached the noble house of Figueroa, to which he was also related, 'they refused to acknowledge me, despite the news they had of me, because I was an Antarctic Indian'. At court he also encountered rebuff, in this case largely because in Gómara's *Historia general* and in Diego Fernández' *Historia del Perú* his father was identified as a partisan of Gonzalo Pizarro's rebellion. Although in 1569 he expended his meagre resources in equipping himself as a captain in the campaign to suppress the Morisco revolt in Granada, he failed to win any recognition either for his efforts or expense. Thereafter, befriended by his uncle, Alonso de Vargas, he retired to the small Andalusian town of Montilla, only moving to the nearby city of Córdoba in 1593 when he inherited his uncle's estate. Reflecting on his disappointed hopes,

Garcilaso wrote: 'the ingratitude of a prince and the absence of any reward from the King shut me in a corner', with the result that 'although my profession has been more to breed and train horses than to write books ... I had to hearten myself in the corners of solitude and poverty ... I lived a quiet and peaceful life, as a man disillusioned and in exile from this world.' By the year of his death in 1615, however, he had become an honoured figure in the literary and clerical circles of Córdoba and was buried with a commemoratory plaque in the great cathedral which once had served as an Islamic mosque.[2]

As a young man, so he confessed, Inca Garcilaso de la Vega had been entranced by the chivalrous romances that were at that time all the rage in Spain. It was the influence of Pedro Mexía's *Historia imperial y cesárea* which persuaded him to abandon such reading in favour of works about real events. By then the Renaissance ideal of the joint pursuit of arms and letters, already typified by his glorious namesake, had captivated his spirit. With all hopes of advancement dashed to the ground, he concentrated his energies on literary composition, seeking thus to win a name in the world of letters so as to redeem his failure to obtain recognition at court and on campaign. In his provincial retreat at Montilla, he learnt Italian and explored the literature and philosophy of the Renaissance. In addition to the epic poetry of Ariosto and Boiardo, he familiarised himself with the historical works of Biondo, Guicciardini, Bodin and Botero. The first book he published was a translation from the Italian of an exercise in neo-Platonic philosophy. Whereas Oviedo had dipped into much the same range of sources without much profit, by contrast, Garcilaso thoroughly assimilated both the critical method and the patriotic intent that had animated humanist historiography since the days of Bruni. In his major works, the Inca, to give him the title he assumed, wrote not merely to win personal fame, but also and more importantly, to defend the good name of the Indian race and to laud the achievements of his Inca ancestors. In the introduction to his first book, *La traducción del Indio de los tres diálogos de amor de León Hebreo* (1589), published when he was over fifty, he testified to his own mixed parentage and boldly presented the work as the literary first-fruits of Spain's new kingdom in Peru, writing as a son of his *patria*, Cuzco, which regardless of Lima he defined as the head of that empire. In the same preface, he mentioned that he was preparing a work on the history of the Incas, proof of the long genesis of the *Comentarios reales*.[3] What he obviously did not choose to confess was that his life-work was a carefully meditated, sustained rebuttal of the imperial tradition of conquest history, with Gómara and Acosta subjected to thorough-going revision and criticism. Nor did he reveal that he drew upon the writings and arguments of Las Casas to support his defence of the natives of the New World. However, the chief target of his attack was not the Spanish conquest, of which he was the child, but rather the imperial regime inaugurated by Philip II and his viceroys.

The opening shot in Garcilaso's literary battle to rehabilitate the good name of the American Indian was *La Florida del Inca*, published in Lisbon in 1605 but conceived and largely written many years before. The book narrated the story of the disastrous expedition led by Hernando de Soto, a chief lieutenant of Pizarro in Peru, which from 1539 to 1543 wandered aimlessly and destructively across a vast area from the modern states of Florida and Georgia to Mississippi and Lousiana. Seizing women for companions and men for bearers, often attacking villages without provocation, the Spaniards soon attracted the universal hostility of the Indians they encountered, so that their passage was beset by skirmishes, ambushes and assaults. Barely a third of the thousand men who had sailed from Europe survived the long trek through an unmapped wilderness, eventually to flee ignominiously down the Mississippi river, with scars the only reward for their endeavours. Out of this sad affair, already dismissed by Fernández de Oviedo as an ill-conceived, murderous razzia, Garcilaso wove an attractive tale of adventure, full of lively incidents, heroic courage, admirable dialogue and vivid description of Indian society, with the pace of the narrative sustained by the challenge of exploring the unknown.[4] As a work of literature, *La Florida* can still be read today with pleasure.

To make literature out of the brief accounts left by de Soto's followers was no mean achievement. But Garcilaso had another, more 'political' purpose in mind. In large measure, he followed the route already blazed by Alonso de Ercilla in *La Araucana*, that heroic epic which celebrated Indian resistance to Spanish conquest. It will be recalled that the poet described the Araucanians as a hardy, war-like, freedom-loving nation of barbarians, governed by a confederacy of war-chiefs, who met in senate to defend their country and liberty from the Spaniards. Avid for honour and fame, young warriors sought to distinguish themselves by individual acts of valour. In short, we here encounter an image of the barbarian highly reminiscent of the Germans as described by the Roman historian Tacitus. Then again, although undoubtedly influenced by the heroic epics of Ariosto and Boiardo, Ercilla also looked back to the medieval Spanish epic of *El Cid* and its successors, for his poem described historical events rather than inventions of fantasy, with the frontier war between Spaniards and Indians re-enacting the traditional struggle between Moors and Christians.[5]

If Garcilaso proved more conservative than Ercilla in choosing to narrate the story from the perspective of the Spanish invaders, nevertheless, he also depicted the Indians in a favourable light. For the natives of Florida were presented as remarkably exempt from all the vices usually attributed to them by the Spaniards. They generally took but one wife, punished adultery severely, condemned sodomy and refrained from cannibalism and human sacrifice. Their religion was simple and pure, since 'they adore the sun and the moon, with none of the ceremonies of idols, offering of sacrifices or prayers and superstitions found in other pagans'. Equally important, they were singularly warlike, their young warriors inspired by 'the desire and ambition for honour and fame'. Indeed, so redoubtable did their attacks prove that the Spaniards decided to abandon all hope of conquest since 'it was impossible to tame so warlike a people or to subjugate men so free . . .'. In the same way that Ercilla dignified the Araucanian council by calling it a senate, so equally Garcilaso chose epithets which assimilated Indians to European society, referring on occasion to 'an Indian knight' and describing the leading men of one village as 'gentlemen'.[6]

The underlying purpose of *La Florida* was rendered explicit in a passage where Garcilaso commented that most chronicles of the conquest failed to make any mention of the speeches uttered by Indians, 'because they are generally held to be a simple people, without reason and understanding, and that in war and peace, they are little more than beasts'. To remedy this damaging impression, Garcilaso inserted a number of speeches, all without doubt invented, in which he offered an eloquent denunciation of the conquerors. Thus one chief was reported as denouncing the Spaniards as sons of the Devil, guilty of theft, rape and murder. Another chief proclaimed that he was willing to die in defence of his liberty, the more especially since he knew that the Spaniards 'took as their profession to wander like vagabonds from land to land, living by robbing, plundering and killing'. Both in the method and sentiments uttered, Garcilaso here echoed Tacitus, who in his *Agricola* praised Roman imperial expansion, yet reported the eloquent speech of the British chieftains who defended their freedom against the crimes of the invader, declaring: 'Robbery, butchery and rapine the liars call empire; they create a desolation and call it peace.' In much the same way, Garcilaso took care to balance the outspoken protests of the Indians by lauding the exploits of the Spaniards as being as great as any conquest of the Romans and Greeks, accompanied by acts of courage as noble as any deed recorded in *El Cid*. With an eye to the king, he concluded with the pious hope that a land as extensive as Peru and Mexico should soon be conquered by Spain so that its inhabitants might be blessed with the preaching of the Christian gospel.[7]

To emphasise the influence of Ercilla and Ariosto does not exhaust the sources of Garcilaso's philosophy of history. The technique he adopted of encoding the message of his work in speeches attributed to leading personages was a form much favoured by Italian humanist historians such as Bruni and ultimately derived from their classical mentors, Thucydides, Tacitus and Livy.[8] Equally important, in his later works Garcilaso cited Jean Bodin, the French *politique*, whose *Method of History* (1566) divided the past into three ages, the first marked by primitive anarchy and savagery, the second defined by the Mosaic dispensation of the Old Testament and the third, the current age of the kingdom of Christ. In particular, Bodin was at pains to deny the existence of a golden age at the start of history, insistent on man's fallen status.[9] By far the most potent influence on Garcilaso's thinking, however, was the work he himself translated into Spanish, the *Diálogos de amor*. Here is no place for any extended examination of this neo-Platonic treatise written by an *émigré* Jewish philospher. Suffice to say that Leone Ebreo sought to reconcile the wisdom of the Greeks and the theology of the Jews, to join Plato and Aristotle with Moses and Maimonides, to link the Hermetica with the Kabala. Classical mythology and philosophy were interpreted in the light of biblical theology and history and found to teach much the same truths. More positively, Leo declared that the sun was made in the image and likeness of the Deity and that the entire universe was animated by the descending rays of Divine intelligence, so that all men, in so far as they were rational, participated in the 'clarity of God', inspired by the Divine light within them. At the same time, Leo propounded the Empedoclean thesis that the universe was dominated by the alternating principles of Love and Strife. In this scheme, corruption and evil were necessary elements and indeed natural growth was invariably preceded by decomposition and destruction. Leo cited the myth of the Demigorgon who was created out of primaeval chaos, with discord the necessary stage before the achievement of harmony and love.[10] Part of the strife in the world derived from the struggle between the masculine and feminine elements, identified here as intellect and body, with carnal appetite undermining the divine element in men, so that 'restless and insatiable', they descended to the level of beasts.

All this was grist to Garcilaso's historical mill. For here in this philosophy, he found justification to interpret Inca myths and doctrines as an autonomous source of wisdom, derived from the Divine intelligence, which illumines all secular philosophy, and as such existing in harmony with the truths and precepts of Christian revelation. At the same time, the Empedoclean emphasis on the necessity of strife and destruction enabled Garcilaso to interpret the Conquest as a tragic but inevitable event, to be accepted as the prelude or gateway to a new synthesis based on the union of Spaniard and Indian, guided by the inner harmony of Christian and Inca laws and wisdom. Then again, Leo the Hebrew praised the literary devices of allegory and myth as the means of teaching different classes of readers diverse kinds of truth. 'It appears to me no small art or weak invention to enclose within a narrative account, whether true or a fiction, so many, so diverse and high meanings.' In short, by means of entertaining fables and myths, important doctrines could be preserved, even in ages of barbarism, since where the vulgar delighted in the surface incidents of the story, the learned could discern hidden moral and metaphysical truths.[11] Who can doubt that Garcilaso here found inspiration for his literary enterprise? At a time, when Spain appeared chosen by Providence to defend the Catholic faith against heretic and infidel and thus dominate both Europe and America, it required what in nineteenth-century Russia was called Aesopian language to combat the dominant imperial ideology.

II

Although the *Comentarios reales de los Incas* (Lisbon, 1609) and the *Historia general del Perú* (Córdoba, 1617) were conceived by Garcilaso as successive parts of a single work, the first written in honour of his mother and the second in honour of his father, the different titles accurately suggest the radical disparity both in the structure and spirit of these two books. Whereas the history of the Inca dynasty is interrupted by discussions of religion, laws and agriculture, the conquest and civil wars are handled in strict narrative strain. If the *Comentarios reales* possess the dream-like quality of a Renaissance fable, reminiscent of *Utopia* or *The City of the Sun*, the *Historia general* is filled with all the clamour of arms and human passion of the chronicles of Froissart and Commynes. Composed by an elderly expatriate, his best years wasted in provincial obscurity, the entire work is pervaded by a nostalgia for the heroic, tumultuous years of his boyhood and youth, when Gonzalo Pizarro dined at his father's table, and when he himself conversed with Sayri Tupac, on the occasion when that prince left Vilcabamba to visit Cuzco. It was this privileged, personal access both to Inca ancestral memories and to the events of the civil wars either retailed by his father or seen as an eye-witness, which Garcilaso continually cited so as to gain the confidence of readers in his authority as an historian. Although the books were published at the beginning of the seventeenth century, their language, style and ethos all belonged to the early Spanish Renaissance, an indication of the fixity of this author's vision.

To measure the impact of the *Comentarios reales*, we must recall that until its appearance remarkably little had been published about the Incas. True, the conquest chronicles of Jerez, Zárate and Gómara all attested to the grandeur of the empire encountered by the Spaniards, who marvelled at the fine stone-work of temples and fortresses, the provision of public granaries and the Roman quality of the roads. In *La crónica del Perú* (1554) Pedro de Cieza de León praised the wise and prudent laws introduced by Manco Capac, the founder of the Inca dynasty, before which, so he claimed, the Indians had dwelt in a state of savagery. But these striking assertions were uttered, so to say, in passing, since his main concern was to describe the cities and landscape as he observed them, leaving a historical description of the Incas to the second part of his vast chronicle, a treatise which was not published until the nineteenth century. The same fate awaited the mass of information on native history collected by Viceroy Toledo, including Sarmiento de Gamboa's *Historia índica* which similarly failed to reach the public domain.

In short, there were only two authors on whom Garcilaso could draw for data on the Incas, Jerónimo Román y Zamora, an Augustinian friar, and José de Acosta. To start with the *Repúblicas del mundo* (1575 and 1593), a work covering a number of states, both ancient and modern, we find that in the description of the Incas and Aztecs, Román y Zamora simply extracted and summarised the data on native laws, religion, government and history presented by Las Casas in his *Apologética historia sumaria*, material in the case of Peru probably derived from Fr Domingo de Santo Tomás, author of the first grammar of Quechua, or from Cieza de León. Here, once again, Indian history was divided into two clear stages, with the Incas credited with the introduction of *policía*, which is to say, civilisation. Pachakuti, the fifteenth-century emperor, here figures as a virtual monotheist, worshipping Pachacamac, the Creator of the world, with the sun venerated as God's chief image, a concept Román observed which was equally found in the works of the neo-Platonic theologian, Dionysius the Aeropagite. Pachakuti was also depicted as the founder of the Inca state, issuing just and prudent laws, which ensured against poverty and hunger by the provision of communal meals in the main squares of all villages. Román marvelled at 'things so much in conformity with good government and that a people so far from God should attain to so many virtues through their natural light'. Deriding those authors who depicted the Indian as bestial and witless, he asserted that 'they had a natural order and in all things displayed great *policía*'. What was important in Román's work was the confession, already advanced yet more forcefully by Las Casas, that the practice of what in Christian eyes was simple idolatry, be it inspired directly by the Devil or derived from man's inherent sinfulness, did not radically impair human capacity to frame just laws and observe a moral code which equalled or at times bettered the current practice of Christian Europe.[12]

By far the most important source of contemporary knowledge of the Incas, however, was José de Acosta's *Historia natural y moral de las Indias*. In deference to the Jesuit's reputation, Garcilaso always took care to cite his opinions with the greatest respect, referring to him as 'el maestro Padre Acosta'.[13] After all, here was an author on record as seeking to defend the Indians from the charge that they were a brutish, unintelligent people. His succinct paragraphs on Inca achievements, where Pachakuti once more figured as the legislator and effective founder of the empire, had in certain measure pre-empted Garcilaso's chosen literary domain. Yet in *De procuranda* the Jesuit had contemptuously dismissed the Indians as barbarians, endowed with a servile character, who had to be governed by force and fear. Moreover, his insistence on Satan's all-pervasive dominion of native religion had led him to advise the Third Church Council held in Lima that all Indians in Peru prior to the advent of the Spaniards were of necessity condemned to eternal damnation. Thus, although Garcilaso could cull particular items of data from Acosta favourable to his designs, the overall bias and perspective was as intolerable to him as anything written by Gómara.

Careful to offer no hostages to fortune, Garcilaso neither sought to speculate on the origins of mankind in the New World nor defend the entire race of Indians from European slander. Although he always referred to himself as an Indian, and hence distinct from the Spanish chroniclers who had written about the history of his nation and patria, at this stage in his intellectual campaign he was merely concerned to laud the achievements of the Incas. Indeed, at the outset he openly admitted that the natives of Peru had once dwelt in a state of savagery, scattered across the land in small bands, practising unnatural vices, worshipping an untold number of absurd deities, with each man's hand raised in war against his neighbour. It was a condition still to be found among the peoples of Amazonia and indeed, if the reports of Cieza de León were to be accepted, even in parts of New Granada and the Caribbean. The denial of a primitive golden age by Bodin was thus reinforced by citation from Spanish chroniclers, a reminder that Garcilaso had ends in mind quite distinct from the overall defence of the American Indian conducted by Las Casas.[14]

It was the Incas, so Garcilaso argued, who rescued the natives of Peru from their Hobbesian state of nature, introducing fixed settlements, agriculture and other indispensable elements of civil live. With exquisite tact, he made no attempt to explain their sudden appearance some 400 years or more prior to the advent of the Spaniards, content merely to retail the fables about their origin that his Inca uncle had told to him as a boy. Manco Capac and his sister were the children of the Sun, who were charged with the task of teaching the Indians the arts and manners of civilisation. These fables were prefaced by a strong hint that Providence had chosen to illumine the obscurity of native savagery with some ray of Divine light so as to prepare the way for the future preaching of the Christian gospel. Combining the doctrine of Eusebius of Caeserea with the ideas of Bodin, Garcilaso implicitly identified the age of the Incas with the epoch of Mosaic revelation and directly compared their state to the Roman empire, offering thus in both the spiritual and the political sphere an ideal preparation for the successful establishment of the kingdom of Christ in Peru.[15]

Fundamental to Garcilaso's case was his assertion that the Incas venerated the Sun rather than a multiplicity of deities and that they had come to worship the one true God, known as Pachacamac, a term best translated as the informing spirit and source of the world rather than as its creator. Although they allowed their subjects to worship local gods, the Incas quietly suppressed the worst superstitions and practices, diffusing the cult of the sun as the material image of the supreme deity throughout their dominions. In any case, idolatry was far less pervasive than the Spaniards imagined since the term *huaca*, generally taken to signify a god, in fact denoted little more than a sacred object. Not merely had the Incas 'discovered the one true God and our Lord through the natural light of their reason', they also subscribed to the doctrines that every man had a body and a soul, that souls had a life after death, and that men entered heaven or hell according to their deserts. As for morality, Garcilaso affirmed that the Incas punished sodomy and adultery with the death penalty. Contrary to the assertions of Gómara, human sacrifice was unknown, a point very dear to Garcilaso since he annotated his copy of the *Historia general* to that effect. True, he did not deny that the Devil was at work in Peru as elsewhere, misleading people into idolatry and immorality, but he claimed that the Incas themselves derided such cults and practised a superior ethic. In sum, Garcilaso followed Las Casas, as summarised by Román y Zamora, infused his narrative with a neo-Platonic bias taken from Leo the Hebrew, and portrayed the Incas as philosopher-kings who practised a natural religion, its fundamental truths discovered through the exercise of their human intellect which participated in the Divine Light which illumined the rational universe. In all this account, the *amautas*, the seers and philosophers who advised the rulers, figured more than the priests who administered the temples.[16]

Whereas both Román y Zamora and Acosta had fixed upon Pachakuti, the ninth Inca as the practical founder of the empire, Garcilaso insisted on the role of Manco Capac, the first ruler, as the author of civilisation in Peru, a vital distinction since it extended the period of Inca rule from about 80 to over 400 years. Moreover, although he described the sequence of territorial expansion, undertaken by each ruler, he interpolated chapters on various aspects of Indian religion and government so as to create the impression that Inca culture emerged well-nigh full-grown and perfect from its first appearance in Cuzco. Similarly, if the empire had been established by force of arms, its expansion was accompanied by the construction of irrigation channels and terraces which greatly increased the amount of land available for agriculture. Indeed, so benevolent was their government and so attractive their prestige that distant chiefs at times voluntarily submitted to their rule. Not merely was land regularly distributed to each family according to its needs, but all produce was subsequently stored in communal granaries and deposits, thereafter to be allocated according to needs. Although Garcilaso did not follow Román y Zamora on the question of communal meals in the main squares of each village, he certainly insisted that all families, sick and elderly included, received an adequate sustenance thanks to the beneficent disposition of the Incas. As for the demands of the state, these took the form of labour service rather than of taxation, with the peasantry supplying levies carefully organised according to the capacity of each community. The produce of Inca lands was stored so as to provision the army and the temples, thus allowing soldiers and other emissaries of the state to travel across the empire without detriment to the local population. It was this elaborate organisation of manpower and agricultural resources, all based on the calculations recorded in *quipus*, knotted strings that served as mnemonic devices for censuses and accounts, which permitted the Incas to engage in the construction of the fortresses, temples and roads which so impressed the Spanish conquerors. In the sheer grandeur and extent of their conquests and empire, in the skill with which they built their stone roads and strongholds, in the wisdom and justice of their laws – in short, in all but the possession of a written script – the Incas resembled and rivalled the ancient Romans.[17]

Fundamental to Garcilaso's panegyric of his ancestors was his insistence that the Incas governed their great empire in accordance with the dictates of natural law. It was a thesis that he reiterated at several points in the text, but which was best expressed in a passage where he declared that the natives of Peru would never forget that the Incas 'had rescued them from their wild life and had made them human, leaving them everything that was not contrary to the natural law, which was what the Incas most desired to observe'.[18] Moreover, as applied to Peru, the dictates of natural law often surpassed the practices of Christian charity in Europe. This line of argument demonstrated the diversity of intellectual influences that rendered the *Comentarios reales* so distinctive a work within the spectrum of colonial chronicles. On the all-important question of the nature and relation of pagan worship and morality, Garcilaso found inspiration in both Las Casas, as transmitted by Román y Zamora, and in Leo the Hebrew. The classic dictum of Aquinas that divine grace perfects rather than destroys nature was deployed to signify that it was perfectly possible for men to observe natural law and hence frame wise, just laws, without the assistance of Christian revelation, a principle which Acosta had instinctively rejected. Equally important, the neo-Platonic concept of human reason illumined by its participation in the Divine intelligence enabled Garcilaso to predicate for the Incas a knowledge of the one true God, without any recourse to such myths as descent from the Israelites or a possible apostolic mission, so favoured by García and others. Human reason, alone and unassisted, could thus attain to a dim knowledge of God and of the natural law which informed his creation. Plato and Solon thus found counterparts in Manco Capac and Pachakuti.

In a famous passage the Spanish critic, Marcelino Menéndez Pelayo, delcared: '*The Royal Commentaries* are not a historical text; they are a utopian novel like that of Thomas More or like Campanella's *City of the Sun*.' Almost from the start the similarity of Garcilaso's portrayal of the Incas with Plato's *The Republic* was remarked.[19] In point of fact, Garcilaso presented an impressive mass of historical data, in part culled from his predecessors, in part derived from his own conversations with Polo de Ondegardo and his Inca relatives. There is a general similarity in emphasis and perspective between the *Comentarios reales* and Cieza de León's unpublished treatise on the Incas. In both cases, the angle of historical observation derived from Cuzco and the Inca elite, with the viewpoint of the provincial Indians, the conquered subjects of the empire, quite neglected. Just how different the provincial perspective could be is obvious if we recall the fulminations of Guaman Poma de Ayala against the Incas. Modern historians, distrustful of Garcilaso's idealisation of his ancestors, look more to Bernabé Cobo's *Historia del Nuevo Mundo* (1653) which presented a wealth of information not always available elsewhere. But the Spanish Jesuit belonged to the Toledan–Acostan tradition and denounced the Incas as tyrants and barbarians who as subjects of the Devil mercilessly exploited the peoples they conquered. Once more, the character of the Indians was described as essentially malignant, idle and low-spirited. In Cobo, as in his predecessors, there existed a basic contradiction between the evidence he marshalled concerning the complexity and greatness of the Inca state and his interpretation of Indian nature and culture.[20] Whereas Garcilaso, either consciously or unconsciously, bent the available evidence by judicious citation and omission, Cobo drew conclusions which were often at variance with the data he compiled.

One unexplored question is the degree of Jesuit influence on Garcilaso at Córdoba. There was an unrealised project of literary collaboration with Juan de Pineda, a famous biblical scholar who taught at the Jesuit college in that city. Indeed, it was the Jesuits who were responsible for publishing the second part of *Comentarios reales* immediately after Garcilaso's death. His appreciation of the work of the Company was made clear in a passage where he declared that it was only with the arrival of the Jesuits in Peru, some forty years after the first Spanish expedition, that any serious attempt was made to convert the Indians to Christianity. Moreover, it was the Jesuits who entrusted Garcilaso with the battered Latin manuscript of Blas Valera, a Peruvian mestizo member of the Company of Jesus, renowned for his knowledge of Quechua and Inca antiquities. Examination of *Comentarios reales* reveals that Garcilaso repeatedly cited Valera for confirmation on precisely those aspects of Inca culture which defined it as an advanced civilisation. In his discussion of Pachakuti, Valera was cited as affirming that in regard to their laws 'these Incas of Peru should be preferred, not merely to the Chinese, Japanese and East Indians, but also to the pagan peoples of Asia and Greece'.[21] In this boast is there not some clue which would enable us to explain the haunting similarity between Garcilaso's Inca state and the celestial empire of China? For both these polities were described as governed by philosopher-kings, assisted by literati, monotheistic in religion, with the welfare of the subjects the main concern of the rulers. In short, may not the *Comentarios reales* be in part influenced by the fierce debate then in train within the Jesuit Order concerning the salvation of the virtuous pagan and the relation of natural religion and ethics to Christian revelation and morality? The contrast between the views of Acosta and Ricci require no further emphasis. What was at issue here, both in China and in

Europe, was the growing Jesuit attack on the way in which the doctrines of St Augustine had been employed to ascribe a demonic origin to all idolatry and to erect an unbridgeable barrier between Christan and pagan values.

III

With the *Historia general del Perú* we enter the world of the Spanish conquest and the civil wars between the conquerors. These events had already been described in considerable detail by Jerez, Zárate, Gómara and Diego Fernández. In the very year that it was published, Herrera completed the Decades of his *Historia general* dealing with Peru, which incorporated entire sections of Cieza de León's chronicles. All this meant that Garcilaso's contribution was here seen to be far less original than in the *Comentarios reales* and in places demonstrably incorrect. The Incas virtually disappeared from sight and all the attention was on the deeds of the conquerors which Garcilaso hailed as 'greater and more heroic than those of Alexander of Greece or of Caesar of Rome'. Thus, whereas Román y Zamora echoed Las Casas and bluntly dubbed the Pizarros as 'the worst men who ever set out from any nation and who with their companions most dishonoured the kings of Spain', Garcilaso declared that he was 'proud to be the son of a conqueror' and wrote a formal eulogy of his father. Indeed, he criticised Gómara for dwelling on the illegitimacy of Pizarro, arguing that he derived from a noble family of Extremadura. In any case, so he averred, it was deeds rather than birth which constituted the true source of nobility. Yet he accepted Gómara's theory of the unknown pilot's prior discovery of the Atlantic crossing, and indeed identified him as one Alvaro Sánchez of Huelva. Seeking to dignify the conquest of Peru by classical allusion, he compared Pizarro, Almagro and Luque to the famous Roman triumvirate of Octavius, Antony and Lepidus, who had divided the Mediterranean world between them.[22]

Underlying the vein of eulogy, however, we encounter a stratum of thinly masked criticism. At certain incidents in the narrative, there are remarkable differences between Garcilaso's commentary and the version we find in other, earlier chroniclers. To start with, the dialogue between the Dominican friar, Vicente de Valverde and the emperor Atahualpa is deployed with devastating effect. True, Zárate had already confessed that Valverde threatened the Inca with fire and the sword if he did not at once renounce idolatry and accept Charles V as his sovereign lord, utterances which Garcilaso simply extended. But whereas in Gómara and Zárate Atahualpa simply rejects any cession of his kingdom, defends the worship of the sun, and casts Valverde's breviary or bible to the ground, in Garcilaso the Inca waxes eloquent, asserting that either the Spaniards were 'tyrants who sally forth to destroy the world, seizing foreign kingdoms, killing and robbing those who have done you no harm and do not owe you anything, or else you are ministers of God whom we call Pachacamac, who has chosen you for our destruction and punishment'. Garcilaso then reported the Inca as accepting the Spaniard's claims on the grounds that his father, Emperor Huayna Capac, had prophesied on his deathbed the advent of bearded men from overseas, messengers of the God Viracocha, who would effect the destruction of the Inca state.[23] This same prophecy, Garcilaso added, accounted for the failure of the Peruvian Indians to resist the Spanish invasion.

It was in his narrative of the rebellion of Gonzalo Pizarro against the attempt of Viceroy Blasco Núñez de Vela to impose the New Laws of 1542 that Garcilaso was at his most original. For these events he could draw on personal memories and family anecdote, since his father, a leading encomendero of Cuzco, reluctantly joined Pizarro in his repudiation of the authority of the viceroy, and figured in the chronicles of Gómara and Fernández as a leading participant in the movement, only deserting the cause at the last moment when it was clearly doomed to defeat. As to the imprudence and injustice of the New Laws, Garcilaso had no doubt, agreeing with both Fernández and Gómara that they were inspired by Las Casas' vendetta against the conquerors and which, if implemented, would have stripped them of their encomiendas and wealth. In passing, he noted that he had met Las Casas at court but had failed to catch the old man's interest. In short, Garcilaso firmly arrayed himself in the conquistador camp, unimpressed by the Dominican's campaign on behalf of the American Indian.[24] Indeed, he went further and implicitly endorsed the rebellion, suggesting that the desirable outcome would have been the creation of an independent kingdom of Peru.

To advance such a dangerous proposition, Garcilaso had recourse to the favourite literary device of the Italian humanists in setting his own ideas into the mouth of his historical characters. In this case, he invented the text of a letter sent by Pizarro's trusted lieutenant, Francisco de Carbajal, to his leader, advising him to declare himself king of Peru. True, both Gómara and Fernández mention the existence of this letter which they summarise as arguing that since the Pizarros conquered Peru they had more right to govern the country than the king of Spain. But Garcilaso alone gives us the complete text.[25] In this version, Carbajal counsels Pizarro to make himself king, winning support by conferring all encomiendas in perpetual entail, awarding titles of nobility and founding orders of knighthood. In addition, Pizarro was advised to summon the Inca from his mountain stronghold at Vilcabamba and restore him to the throne, so as to obtain the allegiance of the Indians. By this restoration of the Incas, he would comply with natural law, since they were still the legitimate sovereigns of Peru, while by proclaiming himself king he would assert the rights of conquest. Union between Spaniards and Indians could be assured by Pizarro's marriage to the Inca's daughter or sister, thus effecting a peaceful transmission of authority. With all the riches of Peru's mines at his command, Pizarro could purchase the recognition of the world.

The chief villain of the *Historia general del Perú* was thus not Gonzalo Pizarro, whom other chroniclers unite to execrate, but rather Francisco de Toledo, viceroy of Peru. Needless to say, it was not the resettlement of the Indian peasantry into new villages or the compulsory levy of labour for the mines at Potosí and Huancavelica which attracted Garcilaso's ire. After all, his Inca ancestors had done much the same sort of thing and these measures of Toledo were based on Inca precedent, albeit with different aims in view. Instead, he concentrated his attack on the viceroy's decision to mount an expedition to destroy Vilcabamba, and thereafter stage a public execution of Tupac Amaru in the main square of Cuzco. He strongly criticised Toledo's persecution of the members of the Inca royal family and deprecated the exile of mestizos from Cuzco, many of whom were his boyhood friends. In all this, he expressed the bitterness of the encomendero elite at a viceregal regime which now relied more on lawyers than on conquerors to staff its administration and chose to govern the Indians through corregidores rather than by encomenderos. Moreover, with the arrival of officials, merchants and other settlers from the Peninsula, the group of mestizos, offspring for the most part of irregular unions between conquerors and Inca noblewomen, once cherished by their fathers, now found themselves the object of scorn in a society increasingly divided into a hierarchy of ethnic strata. If Garcilaso's account of Toledo exiling all mestizos *en masse* was clearly overdrawn, nevertheless, his bitter conclusion encoded a strong political message.[26]

> Being sons of the conquerors of that empire and with native mothers, some of whom were of royal blood and others noblewomen ... yet neither through the merits of their fathers nor by the nature and inheritance of their mothers and grandfathers, did they obtain anything ... because royal governors gave to their own relatives and friends what their fathers had won and what had belonged to their maternal grandfathers, leaving them without means of support, obliged to beg for alms so as to eat, or forced to rob on the highways and then die on the gallows.

Anxious to damn Toledo's execution of Tupac Amaru with the mark of royal disapproval, Garcilaso claimed that upon the viceroy's return to Spain, Philip II sternly repreached him, declaring that he had sent him to Peru to govern kings, not to kill them. Although the story is unsubstantiated by other sources, we do know that the Crown certainly pursued Toledo's heirs with demands for repayment of Indian funds which the viceroy had appropriated to cover the expenses of his general visitation.

By now it should be clear that when, in his prologue and conclusion,

13 The marriage of Martín če Loyola and Beatriz Ñusta

Garcilaso announced his intention to celebrate the glorious deeds of both Incas and Spaniards, dedicating his book to 'the Indians, mestizos and Creoles . . . of the great and rich empire of Peru', he was not in the least insincere. Despite his idealisation of the Inca state, he did not regret the passing of Tawantinsuyu. True, he lamented the wanton cruelties of the conquest, observing that although the alleged purpose of Spanish expansion was the preaching of the Christian gospel, in fact the Devil had intervened sowing the seeds of discord between the conquerors, thus prolonging the civil wars for over two decades. Indeed, in his text the Devil appears to have enjoyed a more powerful dominion in Peru after rather than before the conquest. It was only with the arrival of the Jesuits years after the first Spanish expedition reached Peru, that the first serious attempt was made to convert the Indians to Christianity.[27] Yet despite these reservations, Garcilaso accepted the conquest as inevitable and providential. After all, had not Empedocles taught that growth and harmony, as much in human affairs as in nature, were always preceded by corruption and destruction? In his description of the rebellion of Gonzalo Pizarro, the figure of Francisco de Carbajal, an aged veteran of the wars in Italy, looms as the embodiment of all the destructive, demonic forces unleashed by the civil wars, a veritable Demigorgon fomenting chaos and discord with bitter jokes and inhuman energy. Yet it was Carbajal, in Garcilaso's narrative, who also boldly proposed the true remedy for the ills of Peru, the union of Inca and Spaniard in an independent kingdom. Out of destruction wrought by the conquest was to come a new country and a new race of men. It thus comes as no surprise to observe that Garcilaso endorsed Acosta's thesis that in the same way that the Roman unification of the Mediterranean world was assisted by Divine Providence so as to prepare for the preaching of the gospel, so also the expansion of the Inca empire across the Andes served a providential purpose in smoothing the way for the entrance of Christianity. That the Virgin Mary and Santiago materially assisted the Spaniards in their defence of Cuzco against the forces of Manco Inca was as much accepted by Garcilaso as by Acosta and Cieza de León.[28] Moreover, the Inca also drew confirmation from Bodin's *Method of History*, identifying the Inca period as the Andean equivalent of the Mosaic epoch, the prelude to the final age of Christian grace.[29] All his philosophy and reading thus taught Garcilaso to accept rather than to deny the conquest. It was for this reason that his works proved so attractive to subsequent creole patriots, descendants of the conquerors, who nevertheless came to take more pride in their country's ancient civilisation than in its colonial dependence on the Peninsula.

Needless to say, there were powerful reasons why Garcilaso should have welcomed the conquest. Despite his assumed title of Inca, he was a mestizo, the acknowledged son of a leading encomendero, raised and educated in his father's house. During his boyhood there were only about eighty encomenderos in Cuzco, who formed a true conquest nobility, and alone counted as *vecinos*, serving as city councillors and magistrates. Each of these men maintained open board for at least six or more soldiers and companions, a number which might rise to thirty during the perennial conflicts of the period. Little wonder that in his *Historia general* Garcilaso should have referred to these men as 'Lords of vassals', thus catching the medieval quality of this colonial society. Despite his affection for his Inca relatives, it is clear that the young mestizo was shaped and determined by the influence of his father's house and class. At the same time, it was an inheritance that was denied him. Commenting on Viceroy Cañete's policy of persuading encomenderos to marry women brought over from Spain, he observed with regret that few Spaniards chose to marry the Indian women, often taken from the Inca nobility, who had borne them children and whose brothers and relatives had assisted them as allies in the civil wars.[30] Remember that his own father had married a woman twenty years his junior, giving Garcilaso's mother as wife to a common foot-soldier. Here, then, is the cause of the peculiar bitterness that filled the last pages of the *Historia general del Perú*. Historical reality had not conformed with his philosophy. The destruction wrought by the conquest had not yielded the expected growth and union. The creation of a Holy Inca empire, based on the marriage of conquerors and Inca noblewomen, governed by a mestizo encomendero class, Christian in religion, ruling a native peasantry in accordance with the principles of Inca legislation, had failed to emerge.

IV

In his *Portrait of the Artist as a Young Man*, James Joyce depicted his hero as torn between the competing demands of the Catholic Church, Irish nationalism, and his personal vocation as an artist.[31] In a key passage, the young man rejects the claims of both Church and country, declaring: 'I will not serve.' Instead, he opts for a life as an artist, henceforth defending himself with the weapons of 'exile, silence and cunning'. The comparison with Garcilaso is instructive. For the young mestizo, either by choice or necessity, also opted for exile and suffered long years of silence. When at last he entered the public realm, he defended himself from censorship by guile and wit, adopting the persona of an 'Antarctic Indian' and an Inca. True, unlike Joyce's hero, he chose to serve both country and nation, acting as spokesman and representative figure of his people and city. But we should remember that at the time when he wrote, that *patria* and nation were still more a figment of his prophetic imagination than a current reality. Moreover, as we have seen, his fondest dream was of a Holy Inca empire, with a mestizo nobility governing a Christian realm built on native foundations. In a very real sense, Garcilaso also chose not to serve. He chose not to serve the imperial, Catholic monarchy of Philip II, then regarded by most Spaniards as called by Providence to defend the Catholic Church in a world-wide crusade against the infidel, the pagan and the heretic. The values Garcilaso celebrated in his works were far removed from the exigencies of the Counter-Reformation: Inca virtue and feudal valour were the very antithesis of the Toledan project for Peru. Yet although such authors as Bernabé Cobo protested against Garcilaso's idealisation of his ancestors, it was not until the eighteenth century that the political implications of the *Comentarios reales* became explicit when it served as a text for the rebellion led by Tupac Amaru II.[32] In the short term, therefore, Garcilaso extracted from the disappointment and isolation of exile a personal victory, albeit symbolic of his race, by winning the fame and respect he craved through literary achievement. In the long run, however, he created the prime text, the primordial image of Peru, the starting point of all inquiry into the history and reality of his country.

13

THE TWO CITIES

I

IN ASPIRATION and sentiment, the Mexican equivalent of the Inca Garcilaso de la Vega was Fernando de Alva Ixtlilxochitl (1578–1650), a mestizo descendant of the royal house of Texcoco, whose family figured as lords of San Juan Teotihuacan. Once a student at the Franciscan college of Santa Cruz Tlatelolco, where he studied classical Nahuatl with Antonio Valeriano, Sahagún's native collaborator, he later recorded: 'From my boyhood, I always had a great desire to learn about the things which happened in this New World, which were no less important than those of the Romans, Greeks, Medes and other pagan states which enjoy fame in the universe.' To this end, Ixtlilxochitl collected Indian codices and discussed their interpretation with elderly nobles, men often aged over eighty, so he averred, who still preserved an active memory of pre-conquest traditions. In addition, he drew on earlier narratives of Texcoco and benefited from consultation with Fr Juan de Torquemada, the leading Franciscan chronicler of his generation. Unlike his Peruvian counterpart, however, Ixtlilxochitl failed to complete or publish his historical projects and bequeathed posterity a complex series of drafts, dealing respectively with the rise of the Chichimeca empire, the heyday of Texcoco and its kings, and native participation in the Spanish conquest of Tenochtitlan. Instead, he passed his life acting as governor of several native communities in the central valley of Mexico and ended his days as official interpreter in the Indian Court, a tribunal established to deal with native grievances.[1] Bereft of the stimulus of European exile and education, Ixtlilxochitl appears to have lacked both the opportunity and means possessed by Garcilaso; nor did he have any eye-witness testimony to offer, since he was born a half a century after the conquest.

The most striking feature of Ixtlilxochitl's approach to the ancient history of Mexico was his affirmation that the Olmecs, a barbarous people who settled Anáhuac after the legendary epoch of the giants, were taught the rules of morality and arts of civilisation by a bearded, white sage, known as Quetzalcoatl-Huemac, who arrived from afar. Although the mestizo chronicler chose not to identify this wise legislator as a Christian apostle, he firmly placed his mission in the epoch of Christ's incarnation, a clear enough hint that Quetzalcoatl was probably St Thomas the Apostle. Thereafter, in AD 387 the Toltecs arrived in Mexico, having wandered across Asia in the millennia following the collapse of the Tower of Babel. Their empire, based on the great cities of Tula, Teotihuacan and Cholula, survived until 959 when it was overthrown by the invasion of the Chichimecas, barbarous Indians invading Mexico from the north. However, the royal house of Texcoco descended from the Toltecs and succeeded in maintaining the elements of their culture despite Chichimeca hegemony and in 1427 joined with Tenochtitlan and Tlacopan to form the Triple Alliance, the dominant power in Anáhuac until the advent of the Spaniards. As will be observed, at all key points in his narrative, Ixtlilxochitl strove to provide precise dates, at times listing contemporary events from European annals, so as to insert the cycle of native civilisation within the context of world history. The source on which Ixtlilxochitl most relied was the famous Codice Xolotl, a post-conquest document which presented the annals of the Chichimecas and of Texcoco in pictographic form, providing detail sufficient as to allow some semblance of a coherent narrative from the twelfth century until the conquest.[2]

At the centre of Ixtlilxochitl's vision of the Mexican past was the dashing figure of Nezahualcoyotl, king of Texcoco, whose adventures and achievements he described in lively flowing prose. All the emphasis was on the monarch's distinction as law-giver and poet, whose prowess on the battle-field was matched only by his romantic exploits. In essence, data on laws, tribute and religion was interpersed amidst a racy narrative of events. But the work was animated by an ideological insistence on the moral virtues of the Texcocan monarchs, an insistence rendered all the more persuasive by the omission of any reference to the Devil and his malign influence over native religion. In terms remarkably similar to Garcilaso's interpretation of the Incas, Nezahualcoyotl was celebrated as 'one of the great sages of this earth, since he was a great astrologer and philosopher, who brought together all the philosophers and learned men of his time'. So profound was his scrutiny of 'divine secrets', that he eventually declared that 'beyond the nine heavens there was a creator of all things and one true god . . . and that there was a paradise for the just and a hell for the wicked . . . he also affirmed that the idols were demons'.[3] Although Ixtlilxochitl could not deny the reality of human sacrifices in Texcoco, he asserted that Nezahualcoyotl came to deplore such atrocities and only allowed them to continue in order not to offend his subjects, or, more important, his allies at Tenochtitlan, where daily holocausts were offered to the gods.

In his account of the Spanish Conquest, by far the most polished of his drafts, Ixtlilxochitl sought to exalt the services of his namesake, the last king of Texcoco, who had figured, so he averred, as the chief native lieutenant of

Cortés at the siege of Tenochtitlan, and who also raised the Indian levies necessary for the reconstruction of the city. It was the first Ixtlilxochitl's decision to accept baptism from Martín de Valencia which encouraged the native nobility to enter the Catholic fold. Despite these services, however, he was not rewarded by either Cortés or the Crown, and indeed went unmentioned in Spanish chronicles. Moreover, with the refusal of the viceroys to allow Texcoco to figure any more as a capital city, enjoying the rights of tribute from subordinate districts, the royal house slowly declined into obscurity. By the close of the sixteenth century, descendants of Nezahualcoyotl could be observed ploughing the fields, obliged to gather a meagre subsistence by the sweat of their brow, their sparse earnings reduced by demands for tribute from royal officials who refused to recognise their noble status. Although Ixtlilxochitl later praised Cortés in conventional terms as another Caesar or Alexander, in his first draft he sharply condemned the conqueror's cruelty in both torturing and executing Cuauhtémoc. At the same time, he displayed a strong animus against the Tlaxcalans, whom he accused of inspiring the Spanish massacres at both Cholula and Tenochtitlan.[4] The overall effect here was of an 'account of merit', written on behalf of the royal house of Texcoco, so as to procure for them privileges equal at least to those enjoyed by their Tlaxcalan rivals. As this strictly local strain of sentiment attests, Ixtlilxochitl lacked both the philosophic perspective and the literary talent of Garcilaso de la Vega and thus proved unable to compose or complete any text of comparable magnitude to the Inca's history of Peru.

II

That the true Mexican equivalent of *Comentarios reales* was the *Monarquía indiana* (1615) a vast, sprawling chronicle published at Seville in three stout folio volumes, attests to the intellectual fissure that separated New Spain from Peru.[5] For its author was Fr Juan de Torquemada, a Franciscan friar who wove together the multifarious works of his predecessors to provide a prolix account of native civilisation and the spiritual conquest. At first sight, few works could have been more disparate in style, substance and perspective, the one a Renaissance fable, distinguished for its style and control, the other a garrulous monastic chronicle, worthy of the late Middle Ages. Yet both authors sought to rescue the good name of the Indians from the disparagement and contempt of the imperial school of history and also to celebrate the conquerors, be they spiritual or military. The Franciscan echoed the Inca in his attack on Herrera, Acosta, and, to a lesser extent, Gómara, for their errors, omissions and misapprehension of American history. How could men who had never set foot in the New World, he queried, distinguish between fact and fiction, the more especially since in the case of Herrera more faith was given to foreign

14 Title page of Juan de Torquemada's *Monarquía indiana*

than to Spanish sources? So blunt a critique did not pass unnoticed, since in the very same year of 1615, when Herrera published his second set of *Décadas*, dealing with Peru, he inserted a defence of his method, citing the use made of state papers, the manuscripts of Las Casas, Cieza de León and others, as well as the chronicles of Gómara, Acosta and Oviedo. Moving to the offensive, he derided Torquemada's chosen authorities – Olmos, Motolinia, Sahagún and Mendieta – as unknown men without reputation and observed that 'he did not know what more to condemn in this author, his ambition or his failure to observe the rules of history'.[6] Despite this scathing dismissal, the *Monarquía indiana* was soon recognised as the prime text of Mexican history, and was destined to influence all subsequent chronicles until the twentieth century. That it was republished in the 1720s along with *Comentarios reales* demonstrated its canonical status as a national classic, a work which incorporated and concluded an entire cycle of research and composition.

The apparent similarity in the intellectual purpose of the Inca Garcilaso and Torquemada should not mask the radical divergence in their personal circumstances and motivation. Juan de Torquemada (1562?–1624) was a Spaniard, taken to Mexico as a child, who entered the Franciscan order in 1579, at a time when both Sahagún and Mendieta were still active in its affairs. After serving briefly in the northern mission, he spent the remainder of his life in central Mexico, engaged in pastoral ministry at several priories. He became distinguished for his mastery of Nahuatl, studying with Antonio Valeriano, whom he warmly acknowledged as his teacher. In the years 1603–12 he served as guardian of the priory at Tlatelolco, where he took charge of the construction of a new church and the repair of the nearby causeway of Guadalupe which spanned the surrounding marshlands. At this time he also lectured at the College of Santa Cruz, which, however, by then catered more for children than for advanced students. It was during this period, labouring 'in the silence of my solitude', in his cell at night, that he devoted some seven years to the composition of his great work, the harvest of at least another fourteen years of study and research. The project was undertaken at the express orders of the Franciscan commissary-general in New Spain, and, to judge from the prior commendation of his mentor, Fr Juan Bautista, was widely expected to comprise a revised version of Mendieta's *Historia eclesiástica indiana*. After a brief excursus to Seville to obtain a licence to publish, Torquemada served as provincial for three years, at a time when the mendicants were engaged both in fierce internal disputes and in controversy with the Mexican bishops.[7] As much as any other chronicle of this period, *Monarquía indiana* was written to defend the record of its protagonists; it was 'an account of merits' of the Franciscans in New Spain, conjoined to an exploration and defence of native culture.

In his approach to Indian history and religion, Torquemada moved far beyond the delvings of his Franciscan predecessors to gather and interpret several codices dealing with the kings of Tenochtitlan and Texcoco and equally benefited from a number of native annals and accounts written in either Nahuatl or Spanish, including an extended history of Tlaxcala by Diego Muñoz Camargo, a mestizo chronicler. In the interpretation of these pictographs and annals, he collaborated closely with Fernando de Alva Ixtlilxochitl, who later hailed him as 'the first discoverer of the meaning of the codices and songs' of New Spain. It is by no means clear as to which man was the more original in this project; certainly, their accounts of Texcoco proved remarkably similar. But Torquemada scored over his mestizo contemporary by his mastery of diverse materials which allowed him to collate the disparate annals of several native states. Moreover, although the despatch of Sahagún's massive compilation to Spain prevented him from pillaging its contents, he made extensive use of Book 12, which afforded the native view of the conquest. Yet more important, he was given unrestricted access to the copy of Las Casas' *Apologética historia sumaria* preserved in the Dominican priory in Mexico City. The result was that if the first volume of *Monarquía indiana* derived from Torquemada's research into the primary sources of native history, by contrast, the second volume, which dealt with religion and government, essentially consisted of transcripts from Las Casas, supplemented by editorial comments and occasional interpolations of material taken from other authors. The other great influence was José de Acosta, since although Torquemada frequently criticised the Jesuit's work, he drew liberally on his arguments about Indian religion and its origins. The effect of this variegated, often conflicting group of sources was that the Franciscan frequently transcribed views and interpretations of events which contradicted each other, depriving his work of intellectual coherence.[8] All this, however, was but a small price to pay for his achievement in providing the public with such an extraordinary wealth of information about the native civilisation of Anáhuac.

In his opening discussion of the origin of the American Indians, Torquemada dismissed out of hand the theories advanced by Gregorio García that the natives of the New World descended from the Carthaginians, from the inhabitants of Atlantis, or from the Ten Lost Tribes of Israel. Pagan beliefs and ritual, he argued, were so widely diffused across the world that similarities did not afford any proof of common ancestry. In any case, the Jews had adopted idolatry from their gentile neighbours. As for transatlantic migrations, the knowledge and instruments of navigation available to ancient mariners were insufficient for oceanic voyages. It was far more likely that the Indians had come by land, crossing the north-eastern straits which separated America from Asia, and then moving southwards.[9] The pleasing semblance of this rational line of argument, taken without attribution from Acosta, was diminished, however, by Torquemada's affirmation that the Indians descended from Ham, the son of Noah, whose descendants were cursed for his mockery of his father's nakedness and condemned to be servants of servants. The consequence of this attribution was revealed in Torquemada's denial of the common supposition that the colour of the human races derived from the influence of climate, since he observed that it was apparent that whites born in the tropics did not darken with the passage of generations any more than blacks grew pale in temperate zones. Therefore, if the Africans possessed a servile nature, as was generally admitted, it was because they were descended from Ham. Much the same was true of the Indians. For Torquemada cited the familiar dictum taken from Aristotle that some men had characters that best fitted them to serve, and added that other men, by reason of their accursed ancestry, were equally born to be servants. Although elsewhere he praised the handsome physiognomy of the Indians and lauded their capacity to learn and apply all the arts and crafts of Europe, his insistence on their descent from Ham signified that they possessed the same servile character as the Africans. In this context, his reiteration of Mendieta's pronouncement that the natives of Mexico were best fitted to be disciples rather than masters, albeit explaining their incapacity by their recently acquired vice of drunkenness, pointed in the same direction.[10] It was a line of argument also encountered in Acosta's *De procuranda*.

Nowhere was Torquemada more original or more confused than in his account of the first human settlement of Anáhuac, a narrative based on the Codice Xolotl, which he had studied with Ixtlilxochitl, albeit deriving a different sequence of events. After an initial age of giants, who exhausted themselves in pursuit of material sustenance, there appeared the Toltecs, a people already civilised, who possessed a knowledge of agriculture and the crafts, sufficiently advanced as to enable them to build the cities of Tula and Teotihuacan. Their peaceful dominion was rudely overthrown by the invasion of the Chichimecas, a savage, half-naked tribe, mere hunters and warriors, who under the leadership of Xolotl created a new empire in Anáhuac. The surviving Toltecs taught these barbaric marauders agriculture and introduced the cultivation of cotton and maize. Throughout this account there lurked a striking contrast, not to say contradiction, between the description of Xolotl and his sons as emperors who ruled cities and extensive fiefdoms, and the occasional, interpolated reminder that they were little more than savage nomads, poised at the same level of culture as the untamed Indians still dwelling on the northern frontiers of New Spain. Equally important, Torquemada insisted that despite their cultural differences both Toltecs and Chichimecas worshipped forces of nature such as the sun and the moon and did not practise human sacrifice.[11]

The oddity of this image of primordial civilisation and subsequent decline was thrown into high relief by Torquemada's inclusion of a chapter transcribed directly from Las Casas, where it was argued that all peoples of the world first lived in caves and woods, hunting and gathering food, dressing in furs and skins, only then slowly to congregate in small communities, building houses, farming the land and weaving cloth, their advance into civilisation hastened by the appearance of sages and lawgivers who framed wise laws, established political institutions and improved the arts. It was a familiar, evolutionary sequence, taken from Cicero and the classical poets, which Las Casas applied to the Americas, describing the natives of Florida as dwelling in the first age of humanity, and attributing the advanced culture of the Incas to the wise laws of Pachakuti.[12] Yet Torquemada failed to relate the general principles of human development to the particular case of Mexico, and presented the Toltecs as already civilised at their first appearance on the historical stage, quite bereft of savage ancestors or primitive stages of development.

But what of Quetzalcoatl, the bearded white sage, to whom Ixtlilxochitl had attributed the advent of civilisation in Anáhuac? Were not the morality and culture of the Toltecs the result of an early Apostolic mission to the New World? Once again, Torquemada refused to entertain any fanciful speculations about the native past, insisting that similarities in religious practice and myth did not entail direct contact, the more especially since the Devil took delight in parodying the Christian faith. As for Quetzalcoatl, he dismissed this haunting figure as a magician who had tricked the Indians into accepting him as a god. However, Torquemada also drew attention to the story of the arrival in Tula of a band of men from Panuco dressed like priests, who may well have arrived on the coast coming from Ireland or even Rome. Their leader, Quetzalcoatl, was described as the bearded white sage of legend, who soon quarrelled with Huemac, the lord of Tula, and hence had to flee southwards where he founded the city of Cholula. Although these immigrants were described as great craftsmen, they were not identified as Christian missionaries, nor were they held responsible for the introduction of civilisation among the Toltecs. Moreover, Torquemada explicitly dated these dramatic events to about AD 750, an epoch far removed from the travels of the Apostle.[13]

It is startling to observe that the Devil only surfaced in Torquemada's text with the advent of the Mexica. Obviously impressed by the force of Acosta's arguments, the Franciscan identified Huitzilopochtli, the Aztecs' tribal god, as Satan himself, who first guided his chosen people across the northern steppe-lands by means of oracles and then induced them to pitch their permanent settlement in the mud-swamps at Tenochtitlan, a place signalised by the apparition of an eagle with outspread wings, perched on a cactus, a serpent or bird clutched in its talons. Here is no place to recount the sequence of battles and alliances by which the Mexica fought their way to dominion over their neighbours. Torquemada was not a born story-teller and for some reason he dismissed as 'a false account' the sinister figure of Tlacallel, counsellor to four monarchs, the man elsewhere held responsible for the Aztecs' dedication to human sacrifice. On this score, however, he identified the Mexica as the first rulers of Anáhuac to introduce both the worship of idols and the offering of human sacrifice to these gods, asserting that until their arrival the Chichimecas and Toltecs had propitiated the forces of nature without such rites. Small wonder, then, that Torquemada repeatedly compared the Aztecs to the children of Israel, albeit with Satan rather than Jehovah as their lord and master.[14] At the same time, he followed Las Casas in evoking appropriate classical comparisons, describing Moctezuma I, whom he compared to Alexander the Great, as 'this king (who for being an Indian the Spaniards call a barbarian) was not an example of a barbarian, but rather of a man who figures among the sages of this world'. So also, after recounting the prudent policy of Moctezuma II, he asserted that the emperor 'never read this law in Greek codes or annals, but read it in the books of good reason'.[15] In short, Torquemada strove to depict Tenochtitlan and its empire as another Babylon, glittering in earthly glory, but darkened by the Devil's dominion, the prudent justice of its rulers undercut by the bloody rites of its religion.

This sombre, demonic image of Tenochtitlan was contrasted to the sunlit court of Texcoco where two great monarchs, Nezahualcoyotl and Nezahualpilli, pursued poetry and philosophy with equal ardour. Drawing upon accounts of its history, written by Juan Bautista Pomar, Antonio de Pimentel and Fernando de Alva Ixtlilxochitl, the mestizo descendants of its royal house, Torquemada transmitted to posterity an attractive picture of Nezahualcoyotl as a philosopher-king who promulgated a code of laws in which such offences as adultery, sodomy and theft were punished by death. Nor did the king hesitate to enforce justice on erring members of his own household, condemning a son to death for sleeping with a royal concubine. As much a warrior as a poet, Nezahualcoyotl led a life punctuated by incidents of sudden flight, eventual victory, and romance, experiences which led Torquemada to compare him to King David. Moreover, the Franciscan adopted Ixtlilxochitl's thesis that these Texcocan monarchs venerated the one true God, the supreme lord of the universe, a belief that led them to dismiss the worship of other gods as idolatry and to seek to halt or lessen the human sacrifices that stained native religion. On his death-bed, Nezahualpilli prophesied the coming of the Spaniards and the destruction of the Triple Alliance.[16]

It was in his second volume that Torquemada forsook historical narrative in favour of a systematic review of native religion, laws and government, a project which entailed the patient transcription of the chapters and sections of Las Casas' *Apologética historia sumaria* which dealt with Mexico, supplemented by materials taken from Sahagún and his own research. The result was a remarkably dense text, with the Dominican's heavy cargo of classical comparison rendered more wearisome by his editor's garrulous commentary. Once more, the basic thesis was that the Mexica were as civilised and moral as the ancient Romans and Greeks. Here too, was to be found not merely Las Casas' initial premise that all men, guided by 'light of reason' had implanted in them zeal to know and worship God, but also his audacious argument that human sacrifice was not an 'unnatural' act, since it sprang from the desire to offer God the most valuable gift possible, human life itself. After a general statement of the three descending levels of law which governed the universe – divine, natural and positive – Torquemada compared the laws of Nezahualcoyotl to the codes of Solon and Moses, thus implicitly asserting that the peoples of Anáhuac generally lived in accordance with the dictates of natural law. Indeed, after presenting the moral exhortations collected by Andrés de Olmos, he commented that they presented 'admirable moral doctrine', equal to the commandments of the Church. Since education was largely conducted by the native priesthood, it followed that these men also warranted praise, the attendants of Quetzalcoatl commended in particular for their chastity and penitential life.[17] In all this line of reasoning Torquemada faithfully expounded the paradox, first set out by Las Casas, that the demonic cult enacted in the temples did not diminish the natives' ability to frame just laws and observe the rules of universal morality.

Among the most spectacular parts of the work was the description of Tenochtitlan, an island city into which were crowded no less than sixty thousand dwellings, each housing four to six residents, a calculation that yielded a total population of over three hundred thousand inhabitants. Connected to the mainland by three great causeways, the metropolis was also supplied with foodstuffs by hundreds of canoes which crossed the lakes and trafficked along its canals. Drawing upon certain drafts of Sahagún in his possesion, Torquemada expatiated on the grandeur of the great temple which towered above the city, constituting a pyramid 360 feet square at its base, with a platform sixty feet wide at the top, on which were raised two temples dedicated respectively to Huitzilopochtli and Tlaloc, the god of rain. Surrounding the pyramid was a great patio in which were located some forty other temples, including a fearsome sanctuary of Quetzalcoatl, with three hundred towers of all sizes rising to the sky. An horrific feature of this impressive scene was the quantity of skulls and drying heads exposed to view, with five hundred or a thousand fixed in line on racks which adorned many of the temple walls, their grisly presence illumined at night by the flickering light of the perpetual fires maintained on two altars at the base of the great pyramid.[18] Less novel was Torquemada's description of the palace and gardens of Moctezuma, since its zoo, aviary and great number of attendants had already attracted the pen of Cortés. At this point, it is worth noting that whereas the conqueror had referred to the ruler of Tenochtitlan as its 'lord', the Franciscan dubbed him an 'emperor'.

To emphasise the fidelity with which Torquemada transcribed the text of Las Casas is not to deny that he frequently imposed a radical new gloss on the

Dominican's arguments. The divergence sprang either from the superficial Augustinianism purveyed by José de Acosta or derived from the direct influence of the *City of God*. For whereas Las Casas attributed the emergence of idolatry to man's fears and the debility caused by original sin, Torquemada insisted on the direct intervention of Satan and his legion of fallen angels who actively promoted the worship of false gods through visions and oracles, thereafter sowing moral corruption through their control of pagan cults. Moreover, he traced the appearance and propagation of idolatry first to Cain and then to Ham and his descendants in Egypt, where the number of gods worshipped had multiplied beyond count. He implied that the Mexica were Satan's chosen people and Anáhuac his especial kingdom, the very scale of human sacrifice taken as proof of this assertion. The result was that at all points in his discussion of native religion, Torquemada stressed the malign influence of the kingdom of darkness. So also, he concluded that all Indians, no matter how virtuous, were condemned to hell-fire for all eternity. After all, St Augustine had argued that the republican virtues of Roman heroes did not release them from the bonds of Babylon, the earthly City, since their actions were undertaken in pursuit of worldly glory. In similar strain, Torquemada asserted that the often admirable morality of the Indians did not suffice to save them from damnation, commenting that 'as far as good customs are concerned neither the natural law, nor that of grace, nor human welfare could ask for more, leaving to one side the true knowledge of God, without which all things, no matter how good they are in themselves, have no value or price'. Without the assistance of Divine grace and Christian revelation, no man could be saved.[19] In this bleak conclusion Torquemada laid the theological foundation on which to raise his celebration of the spiritual conquest.

If the *Monarquía indiana* constituted an enduring monument to the research and historical endeavours of an earlier generation of Franciscans and their Indian collaborators, its underlying Augustinian bias, once understood, provoked increasing irritation among creole patriots, anxious to relieve the Indian past of the burden of demonic possession. Some indication of the manner in which they sought to elude Torquemada's authority can be found, oddly enough, in a chronicle composed in the 1570s by Diego Durán, a Dominican who had been brought to Mexico as a child but who identified clearly with his adopted patria. For Durán averred that the Indians descended from the Ten Lost Tribes of Israel and that the Toltecs at Tula had been partially evangelised by a Christian apostle, probably St Thomas, whose memory was preserved under the name of Topoltsin-Huemac. The point of these myths was that they explained both the excellence of the native moral code and the similarity of their religious ritual to Christian practice. After a sharp condemnation of those Spaniards who scorned the Indians as more close to beasts than to men, he declared: 'if in their rites and idolatry they displayed blindness and diabolical deceit, at least in the matter of government and politics, in obedience and reverence, in grandeur, they were not surpassed by anyone'. Basing his chronicle on a native source which had been employed also by his cousin, Juan de Tovar (Acosta's Jesuit informant) Durán composed a vivid narrative, replete with orations and debate, interspersed with often gruesome incident. His purpose was 'to resuscitate from the grave and oblivion, the glorious deeds of the Mexican nation' whose heroes, so he averred, could be justly compared to the twelve peers of Charlemagne or to El Cid. With his focus entirely fixed on the Mexica, he traced their history from the initial journey across the northern deserts to the foundation of Tenochtitlan, with their rise to empire dominated by the sinister figure of Tlacallel, counsellor to no less than four kings, and the promoter of human sacrifice. In sheer verve, Durán easily surpassed Torquemada, his account of the holocaust of victims which accompanied the dedication of the great temple in 1484 a masterpiece of literary horror.[20] What is by no means clear or indeed ascertainable is the degree to which Durán depended on native oral tradition and the extent to which his fertile imagination expanded the bare annals of the codices into flowing narrative. That his chronicle remained unpublished, despatched to Spain by Martín Enríquez, signified that the chief alternative to the Franciscan version of the Mexican history remained unknown, its patriotic and mythic emphases unevoked.

III

In his treatment of the Spanish conquest, Torquemada openly confessed his debt to Herrera and Gómara, liberally transcribing the former's fluent prose, on the grounds that warfare was no fit study for a friar. But he also drew upon Book 12 of Sahagún and the native annals on which it was based. At all critical moments in his narrative, Torquemada thus cautiously counterposed the Spanish and Indian version of events. To comprehend the risks involved in such a manoeuvre, turn only to Durán's chronicle, where the Dominican lamented Alvarado's massacre of the Indian nobility at Tenochtitlan and sharply condemned the cruelty and avarice of 'this preacher of the gospel'. Moreover, he also blamed the Spaniards both for the murder of Moctezuma and the torture of Cuauhtémoc. Commenting on the sufferings experienced by the Mexica during the final siege of Tenochtitlan, Durán recalled that as a boy he had seen many former Indian slaves, their faces branded after the conquest as if they were cattle.[21] As we have seen, the circle of colegiales who had assisted Sahagún in his presentation of the native account of the conquest, were equally critical of the conquerors. To frame a text which integrated both a eulogy and a critique of Cortés and his followers was thus no easy task.

To start with, Torquemada insisted that Moctezuma identified Cortés as

Quetzalcoatl, despatching ambassadors to the coast of Tabasco to offer the Spaniard the appropriate regalia and gifts. The Indian monarch freely welcomed the conquerors into Tenochtitlan and in an important speech acknowledged their authority. In a word, the Franciscan confirmed the thesis, already advanced by Gómara, of a peaceful *translatio imperii*. Moreover, he accepted the explanation offered by Cortés that the massacre at Cholula was a pre-emptive action, undertaken to forestall a carefully planned ambush. By contrast, he openly questioned the justification of Alvarado's slaughter of the young Mexica nobility at Tenochtitlan, since, although he first excused it as a necessary measure designed to avert a native assault, he also cited an Indian account, written by a young eye-witness, which affirmed that the Spaniards launched a cruel, unprovoked attack. It was a version accepted by Sahagún. This inclusion of a critical view of the conquerors becomes all the more significant if we note that Herrera silently suppressed any mention of the incident in his chronicle and that Torquemada's account was excised by the censor from the 1615 edition, its insertion in 1723 the single most important difference between these two editions of his work.[22] Much the same counterpoint was employed in the description of Moctezuma's death, since, after relating the Spanish version that the emperor died from the impact of stones hurled by an infuriated populace, Torquemada printed an extract from Sahagún in which the conquerors were portrayed as strangling Moctezuma and other native lords before they fled the palace, throwing their bodies into the mud without more compunction than if they had been dogs. So too, he admitted that the torture and final execution of Cuauhtémoc had been bitterly denounced by native historians as judicial murder. In short, Torquemada transmitted to posterity a decidedly ambiguous image of the conquerors and their deeds, an ambiguity far removed from the brazen trumpetings of Gómara or the exculpatory silences of Herrera.[23]

The siege and fall of Mexico–Tenochtitlan prompted Torquemada to offer some general, if none too acute, reflections about the rise and fall of human empire, the four great monarchies of the Chaldeans, the Persians, the Greeks and the Romans defined as the transient embodiments of Babylon, the earthly city, all destined to give way to the fifth and final monarchy of Christ. The sufferings of the Mexica in the final siege evoked comparison with the fall of Jerusalem. But their destruction was justified as the manifest judgement of the Almighty, inflicting punishment for their many sins. According to the prophet Amos, the three gravest offences which invited divine remedy were idolatry, incest and fornication, all sins of which the Mexica were supremely guilty. Their veritable pantheon of false gods, their many concubines, their human sacrifices and endless wars – all these crimes cried out to heaven for punishment. Here was a judgement in which Torquemada, notwithstanding his sympathy for native afflictions, defended the conquest as the providential means by which Babylon could be overthrown and the way opened for the new Jerusalem to be built.[24]

It should come as no surprise to find that Torquemada drew on both Motolinia and Mendieta to define Cortés as a great Christian captain, a veritable Gideon chosen by God to lead his small band of followers to victory over the native hordes. Indeed, he saluted the conqueror as another Moses who had liberated the peoples of Anáhuac from the Devil's dominion, leading them out of the Egypt of idolatry into the promised land of the Christian Church. So also, he followed Mendieta in contrasting Cortés to Luther, the two men both born allegedly in 1485, the very year when the great temple of Huitzilopochli had been dedicated amidst scenes of unparalleled cultic carnage. Whereas in 1519 the German had betrayed entire nations into heresy and damnation, the Spaniard had opened the door to salvation for the natives of Mexico. The only qualification that Torquemada made to these time-honoured tropes was the admission that some reputable authorities accused the conqueror of being a tyrant, guilty of many excesses against the Indians. By way of response he did not seek to palliate any possible offences, but simply observed that Cortés had led a band of adventurers who were undisciplined and often inclined to disobedience, at all times under great pressure from millions of natives. In any case, Cortés had not greatly prospered after his great victory and thereafter suffered the mortification of seeing other men govern the realm he had won for the Spanish Crown.[25]

IV

In the third volume of the *Monarquía indiana*, Torquemada incorporated entire chapters of Mendieta's *Historia eclesiástica* so as to dramatise the heroic endeavours of the first Franciscans in New Spain. Here is no place once more to recall the scenes of native enthusiasm which greeted the mendicants' preaching of the gospel, still less to describe the deployment of children as disciples and interpreters, the construction of churches, the daily instruction, the great processions, theatrical enactments of Christian doctrine and the overall ritual euphoria which characterised the early years after the conquest. But whereas Mendieta cited these scenes only then to deplore their disappearance, lamenting the decline in Indian fervour, by contrast Torquemada silently excised these exclamations of despair from his text. Instead, he transmitted an image of native devotion and mendicant dedication which was thereafter to dominate all evocations of that epoch. Ever faithful to his brief, he praised the handsome appearance and manifold attainments of the Indians, pronouncing them capable of practising all the arts and crafts of Europe, their painters and sculptors already displaying great skill. As for the quality of their religion, he had no doubt that they had become true Christians and that by reason of their gentleness, obedience, simplicity, poverty and patience they were eminently fitted for salvation. Echoing Mendieta, he lamented only their drunkenness, a vice found at all social levels, both as a barrier to perfection and as a sign that they were better suited to be disciples than masters, more fit to be governed than to lead. As proof of their devotion Torquemada described the Holy Week ceremonies in Mexico City, during which thousands of Indians paraded through the streets carrying crucifixes and other images of Christ and the Virgin Mary, with great numbers of penitents – some three thousand on Maundy Thursday – scourging themselves as they walked. The great seven-naved 'chapel' of St Joseph, the principal Franciscan church in the capital, served as the starting place of these processions, its altars a permanent shrine for many of the images most venerated by the Indians.[26]

It was in an extended memorial to the Crown, written to defend the retention of parishes by the three mendicant orders, that Torquemada best defined the character of Indian Christianity. For he there admitted that although the faith of the natives was both lively and sincere, it still required the pastoral care and constant instruction provided by the friars, who alone among the clergy ministered to the Indians in their own, often diverse, languages. At the same time, he emphasised the necessity of celebrating the Catholic liturgy with all due pomp and ceremony. In order to impress the peasantry with 'the authority and greatness' of the Holy Sacrament, it was advisable to maintain great churches, decorated with rich altarpieces, images and paintings. Since the Indians 'by their very nature are so addicted to the religious cult' (ceremoniaticos), their tastes had to be gratified by architectural and liturgical splendour. That Torquemada himself shared this enthusiasm for elaborate ceremony cannot be doubted, since he affirmed that on officiating at high mass, accompanied by the music of instruments and voices, surrounded by deacons and acolytes in their coloured cassocks and white capes, the air filled with incense, then 'at the moment when the Host and Body of Christ Our Lord is elevated, the entire place with its adornments, persons and sound of bells, seems like heaven encompassed on earth'. Is there any reason to doubt that the liturgical pomp which so affected this friar also moved the hearts and senses of the native peasantry, the more especially if it be recalled that their chief men were often present at the altar, directing the acolytes or leading the choir and its assorted orchestra?[27]

In order to obtain the censor's approval of his work, Torquemada quietly suppressed Mendieta's virulent denunciation of repartimientos de labor as the chief cause of Indian suffering and decline. In any case, by the time he wrote Sahagún's fears that the native peoples of Mexico would disappear from the face of the earth appeared unfounded as the overall number of inhabitants stabilised. Not that Torquemada ignored the scale of population decline, since he admitted that official estimates reckoned that over 2 million Indians had died during the great plague of 1576 as against some 800,000 during the preceding epidemic of 1545. Although he remained silent about the dire effects of forced labour drafts, he concluded his first volume by printing a royal rescript of 1609 in which the Crown sought to regulate and limit such *repartimientos*, openly confessing that the very principle of forced labour was distasteful. The hope was expressed that both landowners and miners would soon encounter a sufficiently numerous work-force through a combination of wage-labourers and African slaves. Moreover, when Torquemada described the effects of *congregaciones*, a measure implemented in the years 1593 to 1604, whereby Indians were uprooted from their villages and concentrated in newly established towns, often far removed from their former dwellings, he framed as passionate an indictment as any composed by Mendieta. For the hapless natives had been expelled from their homes and forced to start their lives anew, usually without assistance, on sites which were often inhospitable and barren, their former lands seized by neighbouring Spanish farmers and estate-owners. Despite the protests of the mendicants, the viceroys then governing Mexico had employed secular commissioners to enforce the policy, men prone more to listen to the demands of landlords than to hear the cries of the peasantry. As a result of these measures, thousands of Indians died and many more fled their communities in search of the bare means of subsistence. It is small wonder that Torquemada should have compared the natives of New Spain to the children of Israel in Egypt, suffering Pharaoh's oppression.[28]

The chief purpose of a monastic chronicle, however, was to edify its readers, especially the order's young members, by describing the holy lives of its founders and leading men. From their very inception, so Torquemada asserted, the Franciscans had preached the gospel to the infidel, St Francis himself travelling to Egypt for that purpose. It was thus only to be expected that they would take the lead in the New World. Indeed, was it not the work of Providence that a Franciscan, Juan Pérez de Marchena, had encouraged Columbus to persevere in his great project, promoting his cause at court when all others doubted him? The fact that the leader of the first mission to Mexico, Martín de Valencia, bore the same name as Luther was yet a further sign of the spiritual significance of the conversion of the natives of New Spain. For the most part, Torquemada was content to copy the short biographies of holy friars written by Mendieta, in which all the emphasis was on prayer, penitence, observance of the rule, and austerity in diet and clothing. Although the Franciscans of the Santo Evangelio province occupied the centre of the stage, some mention was made of the Dominicans, Augustinians, and the handful of secular priests who devoted their lives to the Indian ministry. In light of his authorial debt to Las Casas, it was only fitting that Torquemada should have praised the great Dominican for his efforts to win justice for the Indians and described him as a learned and holy priest, observing that 'the glory he enjoys in heaven is very special'.[29] So also, he lauded Bernardino de Sahagún for both his unsparing observance of the rule and for his unparalleled knowledge of Nahuatl, pronouncing that 'no-one has yet equalled him in uncovering its secrets and no-one has so occupied himself in writing in it'. He described Sahagún's great chronicle as 'a work of marvellous artifice', and lamented its wanton confiscation by Viceroy Martín Enríquez who had despatched the first eleven books to an historian in Spain who could not even understand them, let alone use their data.[30] The most significant addition to these lives of holy friars was the biography of Jerónimo de Mendieta, whom Torquemada hailed as 'the Cicero of the Province', his fine style manifest in both sermons and in letters to viceroys and councillors of the Crown, a reminder here that the simplicity of Mendieta's prose, which nineteenth-century intellectuals dubbed naïve, derived from literary artifice. Noted for his strict observance of the rule, Mendieta served until the day he died as a living testimony of 'that golden age' of the order, when Franciscans in New Spain dwelt in harmony, unmoved by party strife or clamour for office.[31]

Towards the close of his life, Torquemada was active in the campaign, launched by the three mendicant orders, to defend the retention of their missionary *doctrinas*. At issue here was the survival of the missionary Church. For the Mexican hierarchy sought to apply the provisions of the Council of Trent and entrust all parishes to the secular clergy. The fact that in 1567 the mendicants had obtained a papal breve from Pius V which allowed them to continue their native ministry did not prevent the bishops from securing from the Crown in 1583 a rescript ordering the transfer of parishes. Moreover, although vigorous protests from the friars led to the partial suspension of this decree, conflict between the bishops and friars still continued, with the hierarchy pressing for recognition of their right to conduct episcopal visitations of all mendicant parishes. More important, the bishops insisted on the canonical appointment of individual friars as *curas*, the candidates to be subjected to examination and licence. Needless to say, these demands were vigorously resisted, since if a friar was appointed to a parish for life, he would be effectively released from the obedience he owed to his superiors in the order. In practice, the native doctrinas established by the mendicants were administered by teams of religious operating from small country priories, the friars moving about according to the needs of their province. In his memorial to the Crown, Torquemada appealed to the king to protect the mendicants, arguing that if the Pope as Vicar of Christ exercised 'the plenitude of power and spiritual jurisdiction' over the entire Church, then it followed that the Catholic King as the Pope's delegate and patron of the Church in the Indies possessed the right to exempt parishes from the intrusion of the local hierarchy. Already, the secular clergy occupied seventy parishes in the archdiocese of Mexico, often administering the sacraments to natives whose language they never learnt and from whom they exacted heavy charges. By contrast, the friars were especially trained for the native ministry, with instruction in local languages regularly imparted. In any case, as 'the chief conquerors', the mendicants enjoyed historic rights to possession of their *doctrinas*, since their ministry preceded the installation of the hierarchy.[32]

Although Torquemada has been accused of censoring Mendieta's critique of Martín Enríquez, in fact he preserved the essential contrast drawn by his predecessor between the golden summer of Charles V and the silvery winter of Philip II. For he praised the first two viceroys, Mendoza and Velasco, for their manifest concern for Indian welfare and their support of the mendicants. In particular, he signalised Luis de Velasco as another Solomon, pausing only to lament that his authority had been increasingly limited by the intervention of the audiencia. If we recall that Velasco's son also served as viceroy, that his second term coincided with the composition of the *Monarquía indiana* and that he served as president of the Council of the Indies precisely when Torquemada went to Spain to obtain a licence to publish, then the links of patronage binding the Franciscans to this noble family will be appreciated. It was for the years that followed that Torquemada reserved his harshest judgement, since he penned a bitter portrait of the visitor, Alonso de Muñoz, a lawyer sent to Mexico in 1566, who installed a virtual reign of terror. The cause lay in the overly exuberant festivities with which the leading encomenderos, the sons of the conquerors, had greeted the return of Martín Cortés, Marquis of the Valley of Oaxaca. Fears soon became rife in official circles that they sought to acclaim him king of New Spain with the result that the audiencia ordered the summary imprisonment of several nobles. Events turned to tragedy when Muñoz arrived and immediately set in train further arrests, the torture of prisoners, and the execution of several young encomenderos. Even Cortés' half-brother, the conqueror's son by an Indian woman, was seized and tortured. The Marquis himself was subjected to confinement and then despatched to Spain, his departure ending any further involvement of the Cortés dynasty in Mexican affairs. Once news of the affair reached Spain, Muñoz was summoned back to Madrid, there to be coldly reproved by Philip II with the damning words: 'I did not send you to the Indies to destroy the kingdom.' Such was the force of this reproof that Muñoz died that very night from its shock.[33] As with the case of Toledo recounted by Garcilaso de la Vega, there is no means of substantiating this fitting conclusion to an unhappy story. Both the Inca and the Franciscan expressed a common hope that the Crown, as fount of justice, would punish all malefactors, no matter how highly placed.

If the execution of the Mexican encomenderos and of Tupac Amaru both expressed the remorseless character of absolute monarchy which would brook no threats to its authority, so equally the administration of Martín Enríquez

(1569–81) was depicted by Torquemada as marking a watershed in colonial government, similar in character, if not so drastic in policy, to the regime imposed by Toledo on Peru. The increased reliance on *repartimientos de labor*, already denounced by Mendieta, was matched by a campaign of 'fire and blood' on the northern territories where a frontier war was launched to punish the savage Chichimecas for their raids on the trade routes which connected the mining camps to the central valleys. As regards the mendicants, Martín Enríquez adopted a decidedly critical attitude, warning his successor that 'in both the spiritual and temporal spheres their ambition is to govern these countries'. Although Torquemada was careful to describe the viceroy as 'a very prudent man, of great severity', he also observed that Enríquez kept himself aloof from colonial society, so that 'the office of viceroy was thus greatly raised, having been until this time something more simple and open to conversation'. Indeed, Enríquez left the Franciscan commissary-general kicking his heels at the palace, and when that cleric complained of the discourtesy in a sermon, promptly ordered the prelate to leave for Spain.[34] Nor was Torquemada alone in noting the wintry coldness of the new epoch, since a contemporary chronicler complained that whereas the first viceroys had acted as the leaders of colonial society, with Luis de Velasco distinguished for his horsemanship, liberality and love of hunting and bull-fights, by contrast Martín Enríquez preserved a retired mode of life, his chief aim the remittance of increased revenue to Spain.[35]

It would be false to conclude on this note of bitter displacement, since Torquemada wrote as the authorised spokesman of a Franciscan province which still retained possession of much of the domain it had won during the spiritual conquest. The *Monarquía indiana* was the work of a peninsular Spaniard who openly confessed that Mexico was not his patria, albeit asserting 'although it is not mine, at least I take it as my own, through having been raised in it'. Accordingly, he framed an exuberant portrait of Mexico City, observing that such was its wealth that when on Sundays all its Spanish inhabitants paraded through its broad, open streets and great squares it was difficult to distinguish the nobleman from an artisan since everyone wore the same rich attire. By this time the capital possessed a university, some thirteen priories and colleges and an equal number of convents for nuns. An island city, it was surrounded by a lake which resembled the Sea of Galilee, its shores lined with towns and villages. More to the point, Torquemada compared Mexico to Rome, once the capital of a pagan empire, and now the head of a Christian kingdom. Turning to an image expounded by Mendieta, he concluded that if Mexico–Tenochtitlan had once figured as another Babylon, it was now a new Jerusalem. Where once fires had burnt on the altars of Huitzilopochtli, accompanied by daily human sacrifice, now, so he calculated, over 600 masses were celebrated every day in some forty churches and chapels, all offered in praise and remembrance of Jesus Christ.[36] What better testimony could be found of the enduring achievement of the spiritual conquest?

V

To insist on the equivalence in canonical status of the *Comentarios reales* and *Monarquía indiana* as prime texts in the respective historical traditions of Peru and Mexico is not to deny the equally significant divergence in purpose and effect that separates the two classics. It is not a question here of the obvious contrast between the early Renaissance and late Middle Ages. It is rather the striking dissimilarity in the ideological purpose of these chronicles and the reactions they provoked in subsequent generations. The Inca Garcilaso de la Vega wrote as a patriot setting out the historical foundations of an emergent nation. His naturalistic approach to the thorny problem of native religion was to prove eminently attractive to the Enlightenment where the Incas were ranked with the Chinese as exemplars of the possibility of practising natural morality without the benefit of Christian revelation. By contrast, Torquemada wrote as the avowed heir of the spiritual conquerors of Mexico seeking to defend the interests of his order. Both his emphasis on the Devil's dominion in Anáhuac and his evangelical triumphalism were destined to prove offensive to creole patriots. Indeed, at the close of the seventeenth century, the Franciscan chronicler, Agustín de Betancur, published a summary account of Mexican history in which he accused his predecessor of plagiarising Mendieta. More to the point, in the eighteenth century the exiled Jesuit, Francisco Javier Clavijero, rewrote Torquemada's history of ancient Mexico in fluent, neo-classic prose; expunged all mention of the Devil from his account of Aztec religion; and brought his narrative to a close with the Spanish capture of Tenochtitlan. The effect was thus to liberate the native past from any real connexion with the spiritual conquest: neither Babylon or Jerusalem figured in his post-Augustinian approach to national history. That it took Mexican chroniclers almost 200 years to master the philosophic premises of the Inca Garcilaso is both testimony to his achievement and proof enough of the ideological force of the Franciscan tradition in New Spain.

14

CREOLE PATRIOTS

I

DURING THE 1590s the Spanish Crown was besieged by a flurry of petitions from New Spain pleading for the grant of 'a fourth life' on all existing encomiendas, which is to say, that inheritance be extended for another generation. The Council of Mexico City warned that many descendants of the conquerors now dwelt in poverty so that the country lay virtually defenceless, the more especially since recent settlers were more intent on enrichment in trade, mining and stock-raising than on bearing arms. If the men of honour were not provided with some means of subsistence, they might well conspire with the 'mulattoes, blacks and other lost people' in a general insurrection.[1] What is remarkable about these petitions and memorials of the 1590s is the degree to which they attested to the emergence of a creole identity, a collective consciousness that separated Spaniards born in the New World from their European ancestors and cousins. It was an identity, however, that found expression in terms of anguish, nostalgia and resentment. From the start, creoles appear to have conceived of themselves as dispossessed heirs, stripped of their patrimony by an unjust Crown and the usurpations of recent migrants from the Peninsula. In part, their resentment derived from the conquerors, from men such as Bernal Díaz del Castillo, who charged that the Crown had failed to reward their heroic services with adequate recompense. In part, it stemmed from the inability of many creoles to profit from opportunities afforded by the expansion of the export economy based on silver-mining, transatlantic trade and the opening of new frontiers. But it also expressed the grievance of a colonial elite denied their birthright, the governance of their country and the enjoyment of the privileges and profit derived from political dominion. The memorials of this period, addressed to the Crown, both reiterate earlier grievances and introduce themes that were to haunt the creole mind until the attainment of independence.

The continuity between the ambitions and plaints of the conquerors and the creoles is best observed in a memorial of 1599 presented by Gonzalo Gómez de

Cervantes who openly called for 'a general and perpetual distribution of Indians to the sons, grandsons and other descendants of the conquerors and first settlers'. The encomenderos should receive titles of nobility and be made 'perpetual lords with civil and criminal jurisdiction'. In addition, public offices should be sold to creoles on a permanent basis. Only by such measures could the Indians be protected from the ill-treatment they received from Spaniards and mulattos. More positively, these concessions would fortify 'the houses and lineages' of New Spain and ensure the prosperity of the country, since it would be then founded on 'the virtue and nobility of knights and gentlemen with vassals'. With their estates and income protected by entail, these aristocrats could maintain up to thirty or forty dependants at their tables and thus assure the safety of New Spain from attack or rebellion, since 'rich men and entailed estates are the best defence of kingdoms'. In short, here was the conquerors' project of establishing themselves as a feudal aristocracy once more advanced without modification more than a generation later.[2]

If such was the dream, the reality was decidedly different. For New Spain, so Gómez de Cervantes insinuated, was not so much a kingdom as a mere colony, its government and wealth used for the rapid enrichment of migrants and intermediaries rather than catering for the vested interests of the native-born. Each viceroy brought over an extensive entourage of relatives and clients whom he installed in public office, appointing his favourites as district magistrates without regard for the long-standing creole clamour for such posts. So also, royal officials employed their influence to obtain speculative land-grants, from which they took a quick profit so as to return to Spain with their fortunes made. Yet more pernicious was the dominance of merchants in economic life, a dominance exercised to the detriment of both landlords and miners. Indeed, if men chose to return to Spain once they obtained wealth, it was largely because 'there is nothing in which to employ their capital (haciendas) that would be permanent other than in merchandise'. Agriculture was on the decline, since 'those who have haciendas in the country abandon them because they cannot find anyone to whom they can entrust them'. Miners were afflicted by the oppression of the treasury officials and the exploitation of the merchants, so that little of the profits accruing from the industry went to the men responsible for the production of silver. The result was that immigrant Spaniards generally chose to enter trade, preferring more to sell goods on the streets or set up small taverns than to engage in agriculture or mining. By the close of the sixteenth century, so Gómez de Cervantes asserted:

> it is clear that monies are found in the power of the merchants and traders and not in the leading citizens and nobles ... Those men who but yesterday served in stores, taverns and low occupations are today in possession of the best and most honourable positions in the country, whereas the descendants of those who conquered and settled it are poor, humiliated, disfavoured and cast down.[3]

Indeed, the very judges of the high court and other magistrates who arrived from Spain without other means of support than their official salaries competed to win the hand of rich merchants' daughters, whereas by contrast the daughters of the creole gentry found refuge in convents. The ultimate beneficiary of this system was the Church which grew steadily in wealth and new foundations. Gómez de Cervantes adverted to the scale of the estates of the Augustinians and Dominicans, and marvelled at the rapidity with which the Jesuits had moved to acquire entire chains of haciendas. Moreover, all young creoles of good family were now educated at the Jesuit colleges in Mexico City and Puebla, with the result that no-one wished to follow the profession of their parents but rather sought to devote themselves to the study of letters so as best to prepare themselves for entry into the priesthood and the religious orders.

In his proposals for a permanent allocation of encomiendas, Gómez de Cervantes clearly did not envisage any simple return to the post-conquest system, since he admitted that in the course of the century some nine-tenths of the native population had disappeared. The problem was to find the means of protecting the remnant that survived from the depredations of vagabond Spaniards, numbering at least a thousand, who preyed on their villages. At the same time, mulattos and blacks dominated petty commerce and equally sought to exploit the unfortunate natives. Indians were also ill-treated by overseers on the haciendas to which they were consigned by the *repartimiento de labor*. But Gómez de Cervantes defended the necessity of forced labour levies on the grounds that without compulsion the natives would not work for the Spaniards; and without Indian labour the haciendas would not produce and the kingdom would go hungry. In any case, despite the allegations of the friars, ill-treatment had not been a major cause of native depopulation, which had been largely the result of the periodic incursions of epidemic disease.[4] After all, Tlaxcala as the ally of the conquerors had been exempted from both tribute and labour levies, yet had still suffered much the same loss of population.

Whereas Gómez de Cervantes presented his case in concise, unemotional prose, Baltazar Dorantes de Carranza in his *Sumaria relación de las cosas de la Nueva España* (1604) invoked both poetry and rhetoric to advance the creole cause. The purpose of his memorial was to provide a complete list of the conquerors of Mexico, together with a description of their descendants. The facts were dramatic. From the 1,326 original conquerors there had emerged but 196 families, which in 1604 comprised some 934 male members, covering four generations. Obviously, this table did not include men who had moved to other provinces or who had returned to Spain and established families in the Peninsula. What the list made clear was that although some families had acquired great wealth, many survived in but modest circumstances, their position still sustained by the income from their encomiendas. Unlike Gómez de Cervantes, however, Carranza recognised that 'the gate was shut and all hope lost for any general and perpetual distribution of Indians'. All that could be expected was the extension of the encomiendas for a fourth life before their final escheatment to the Crown. The chief hope of the creoles, he declared, lay in public office, especially in appointments as district magistrates.[5] Indeed, one purpose of his table of families was to enable the viceroys to distinguish between legitimate and illegitimate descendants of the conquerors, the latter to be excluded from such positions, the more especially as many were mestizos.

As much as other creoles of this period, Carranza lamented the rapid enrichment of immigrants from Spain, their commercial monopoly yielding both wealth and honours. He noted with scorn that the poorest Spaniard on arrival in the New World adopted the airs of a nobleman and claimed preference over the creoles; and quoted the lines of Mateo Rosa de Oquendo, a Peruvian poet, to the effect that men who once had traded trinkets and pins in the streets were now as wealthy as the Fuggers, the German merchant princes, and honoured by titles of nobility. The bitter sense of displacement, not to say, of disinheritance, that such a spectacle provoked among the descendants of the conquerors was expressed by Carranza with impassioned rhetoric, when he exclaimed: 'O Indies! Mother of strangers, a shelter for thieves and delinquents, a homeland for foreigners, sweet kiss and peace for newcomers. O Indies! Stepmother to your own children and exile for your native sons, a scourge and knife for your own people . . . '[6] In effect, the failure of the conquerors to win from the Crown the practical governance of the countries they had fought to possess left their sons and heirs exposed to the competition of both royal officials and new waves of settlers. Creole grievances were thus directed towards the Crown and to recent immigrants from Spain, sentiments which were given lapidary expression by the Peruvian chronicler, Antonio de la Calancha, who asserted that 'those born here are strangers in their own countries: newcomers are the heirs to its honours'. The creole was an American Jacob, robbed of his birthright by a peninsular Esau.[7]

Not content merely to vent the grievances of his class, Carranza also offered reflections on the native history of his country and cited stretches of verse from an unfinished epic on the conquest written by the creole poet, Francisco de Terrazas. In addition, he quoted sections of Las Casas' *Apologética historia sumaria*, no doubt using the copy deposited in the Dominican priory in Mexico City. What is notable here is the pride with which Carranza described the grandeur of Mexico–Tenochtitlan, a city founded in 1318 and which at the arrival of the Spaniards encompassed over 50,000 houses, or, so Carranza calculated, over 1 million inhabitants. He added: 'these lands were everywhere then so full of people that in all the world it seems that there was never a land so populated or where humanity more multiplied'. It was an increase, so Carranza averred, that largely derived from the sheer beneficence of the climate, a view of the New World that he took from Las Casas.[8]

Although he was the son of a conqueror – his father had accompanied Núñez Cabeza de Vaca in his peregrination of North America – Carranza displayed an ambiguous approach to the conquest, an ambiguity that was to characterise many creole assessments of that event. For sure, he saluted Cortés as a second Caesar and cited a passage from Terrazas where the conqueror is hailed in Franciscan fashion as another Moses. But he also echoed the plaint of Bernal Díaz that although Cortés was quick to enrich himself he neglected the interests of his followers. Moreover, he reproached the conquerors for their cruelty to the Indians, especially for the massacres at Cholula and in Tenochtitlan at the feast of Huitzilopochtli, singling out Pedro de Alvarado as 'cruel, hard and avaricious'. By contrast, he praised Cuauhtémoc as 'a most valorous man'. Although he accepted Gómara's story of Santiago and the Virgin Mary appearing in battle to assist the Spaniards, he lamented the loss of Indian life, reckoning that some 40,000 natives had died during the final siege of Tenochtitlan. He exclaimed: 'to preach the gospel, sword in hand, shedding blood, is a fearful thing'. Indeed, might not the decline in the fortunes of conquest-families be in part explained by Divine retribution for their part in such events? The lands and goods seized from the Indians had not proved of lasting value, since 'goods so acquired all dissolve like smoke or like salt in water'.[9] What we here encounter is evidence of an emotional distancing of the creoles from the conquest, a repudiation which was matched by a growing sympathy for the Indians. The legacy of Las Casas thus led creole chroniclers such as Dávila Padilla and Dorantes de Carranza to question the justice of the conquest and to define colonial society as labouring under Heaven's curse.

If petitions for the renewal of encomiendas prompted a range of general reflections about the state of colonial society, the mounting struggle for dominance in the mendicant orders, then in progress, elicited a series of pointed charges and counter-affirmations that gravely impaired relations between European and American Spaniards. In his life of Mendieta, Torquemada printed a letter in which his aged mentor had proposed the establishment of a brotherhood within the province, all of whose members were to swear to vote in all elections to office without prejudice to the origin of candidates, taking no account of whether they had professed their vows in Spain or in Mexico, or whether they were born in Europe or the New World. What he did not mention was that in 1574 Mendieta had warned that 'when the order of St Francis in the Indies ceases to be nourished by friars from Spain, it will be lost'. What caused concern was that Spaniards who professed in Mexico usually had family connexions and relatives living in the country, so that they were no longer free to defend the Indians, unhampered by the temporal interests of the settler community. As for creoles, as Spaniards born in the Indies were called, a few were fit to become priests, 'but the greater part take the nature and customs of the Indians, since they are born in the same climate and reared among them', so that they were manifestly unsuitable for the religious life and ordination. In this context, it should be noted that the aged Sahagún had despondently blamed the climate and heavenly constellations for creole corruption, observing that 'those who are born here [are] very similar to the character of the Indians, in aspect they appear Spaniards and in their condition they are not . . . ', adding that they were 'intolerable to govern and most difficult to save'.[10] Such harsh frankness was not palatable to Torquemada, the more especially since he himself was a Spaniard who had entered the order in Mexico. Moreover, in his lifetime the Franciscans in New Spain became bitterly divided into no less than three parties, comprising gachupines, which is to say, friars born and professed in the Peninsula; 'sons of the province', men born in Spain but who professed in Mexico; and creoles, some of whom were in reality mestizos, albeit with Spanish status. The formation of these parties derived from the decision, taken in the 1570s by the commissary-general in New Spain, to admit novices recruited locally so as to provide sufficient priests for the parishes under Franciscan control. The result was a striking increase in numbers, from 225 friars in 1569 to about 600 by the turn of the century, of whom only fifty had come to Mexico after taking their vows in Spain. It was only in 1611 that a creole first became provincial and not until 1624 that the party controversy was resolved, albeit in none too satisfactory fashion, by the introduction of the *alternativa*, a system whereby the three parties alternated in control of all leading offices within the province.[11] It should be noted that Torquemada served as provincial in 1614–17 and suffered considerably from the effects of this internal strife.

In 1612 there appeared a note in a widely read work, written by the Dominican, Juan de la Puente, which roundly declared that 'the heavens of America induce inconstancy, lasciviousness and lies: vices characteristic of the Indians and which the constellations make characteristic of the Spaniards who are born and bred there'. Not all Europeans subscribed to these views and in Mexico no less than three works appeared, written respectively by a German engineer and two Spanish physicians, which offered a positive affirmation of creole character and intelligence. Employing the current system of humours and the principle of astrological determinism, set out by Hippocrates and Aristotle, both Enrico Martínez and Diego Cisneros agreed that the creoles differed from Spaniards in that the choleric disposition of their peninsular forebears was rendered more tractable by the benign climate in which they were reared. 'A temperate region makes men who are temperate and docile, of acute wits, and perfectly equipped for the sciences.'[12]

Despite this array of medical and astrological texts, the indignant affirmations of creole chroniclers suggest that denigration of their talents and character continued unabated, fired, as Solórzano averred, by partisan conflict within the cloisters of the mendicants. In his chronicle of the Augustinian friars in New

Spain, published in 1624, Juan de Grijalva, a native of Colima, once more sought to exalt the spiritual conquest, affirming that the Indians were by now notable for their devotion to the Catholic faith. Needless to say, he enlarged on the role of his own order in this conversion and in particular fixed upon Fr Alonso de Veracruz, a disciple of Las Casas and a profound theologian who had figured prominently in the defence of mendicant privileges. At the same time, he lamented, somewhat oddly, the absence of any histories of the conquest, asserting that the memory of Cortés was almost lost. Indeed, he questioned whether some hidden curse afflicted New Spain, some malign star which determined the outcome of events in 'this miserable land'. More to the point, he reproached those Spaniards who came to Mexico to seek their fortune and to enjoy its honours, only then to slander the character and good name of its inhabitants, pining for return to the Peninsula. Of his own 'nation', which is to say, the Spaniards born in Mexico, he wrote: 'generally speaking their wits are so lively that at eleven or twelve the boys read, write, count, know Latin and make verses like the famous men of Italy; at fourteen or fifteen they graduate in arts ... ' The university of Mexico, where both the faculty and students were mainly creole, could figure among the most illustrious of Europe. And yet, so he exclaimed,

> despite so much experience, they still ask us, who are born in this land, whether we speak Castilian or Indian. The Church is filled with creole bishops and prebends, the religious orders with prelates, the high courts with judges, the provinces with governors, all creoles, who govern with great judgement and head, and despite it all, they doubt whether we are capable.[13]

In these indignant affirmations, written by a chronicler who had participated in the struggle within his own order to obtain election of creoles to high office, we can observe the bitter resentments engendered by a colonial system that denied the Mexican elite its political birthright in Church and State.

Although in 1607 the Spanish Crown sanctioned the grant of encomiendas for a fourth life, in general its response to creole aspirations and complaints was perfunctory. The reasons for this caution were made clear by several viceroys. As early as the 1570s, Martín Enríquez reported that although the king had commanded that the sons and descendants of the conquerors should be given preference in all appointments to public office, in practice he had found many of them completely unworthy of trust. So also, in 1605, the Marquis of Montesclaros observed that although 'it is common opinion that all district magistrates and other ministers of justice should necessarily be descendants of the conquerors', such creoles were usually quite unfit for high office. After all, many of the adventurers who had come to Mexico were of artisan or peasant stock; moreover, since few Spanish women had arrived in the early years of settlement, many of these men had children who were mestizos or mulattos and as such disqualified from office. With such sentiments, it comes as no surprise to learn that most viceroys should have used their considerable powers to assist their own official family, or alternatively, appointed magistrates from the relatively small circle of creole aristocrats.[14]

To emphasise the embittered negative character of creole patriotism in the early seventeenth century is to tell but one part of the story. The publication of Torquemada's *Monarquía indiana* immeasurably enlarged the elite's consciousness that the capital was not merely a Spanish city but possessed an extensive native history stretching back to the beginning of the fourteenth century. One did not have to be a student of history to take pride in the grandeurs of Tenochtitlan. Almost from the start, therefore, creoles appear to have accepted the pre-Columbian sequence as an integral part of the history of their patria. At the same time, they exhibited a pervasive pride in the greatness and wealth of contemporary Mexico, fixing upon the numerous convents, colleges and churches that dominated its skyline. The rhetoric which was employed to celebrate such urban splendours owed much to the Spanish humanists of the sixteenth century who had lauded the glories of Seville, at that time the effective metropolis of the Indies. Once a frontier city, as much Moorish and Jewish as Spanish, Seville was depicted as a new Rome, and the universal emporium of world commerce. The inflated hyperbole of this rhetoric found immediate echo in the Indies, where it was employed to celebrate both Lima and Mexico City in a vein of civic patriotism which appeared exempt from the republican associations of its Italian counterpart. In 1623 the creole poet, Arias de Villalobos, marked the entrance of a new viceroy into the capital with an invocation of Mexico as:

> Rome of the New World in a golden century
> Venice in form, a Tyre in wealth,
> In artifice a Corinth, a Cairo in trade,
> Athens in knowledge, in treasure a Thebes.
> In you, new city of Charles V,
> A new Venice, we find a new Athens.

By far the most distinguished example of this dithyrambic genre was composed by an *émigré* cleric, Bernardo de Balbuena, who in his *Grandeza mexicana* (1604) sang in harmonious verse of the beauty of the city's women, of the brio and verve of its horsemen, of the splendour of its churches and convents, of the sanctity of its religious, and of the wisdom and prudence of its magistrates. The island-city, riding high amidst the waters of the lake, surrounded by mountains, all covered by gardens and trees, the landscape illumined by the transparent air of its ever-blue sky, passed the year in 'an eternal spring', its fortunate inhabitants dwelling in what Balbuena dubbed 'this Mexican paradise'.[15] Here, indeed, were images more potent and evocative than any comparisons with the faded glories of Europe, images destined to capture the imagination of future Mexican poets.

II

Not all American Spaniards of talent entered the priesthood, still less passed their lives lamenting the decline of their class. Outside the narrow ambit of the viceregal capitals, the provinces and frontiers of the empire offered opportunities for self-advancement and enterprise and sustained a social life that was at times decidedly hectic. In the open ranges of the northern frontiers of New Spain, the creole sons of the first settlers and conquerors maintained the martial, enterprising spirit of their fathers. Thus the expedition which set forth in 1598 to conquer and 'pacify' New Mexico was led by Juan de Oñate, the American-born son of a leading conqueror and miner at Zacatecas, whose wife descended from a union between Hernán Cortés and a daughter of Moctezuma. In the event, the atrocities which accompanied the subjugation of the Pueblo Indians of New Mexico demonstrated that the creoles of New Spain had much the same vices and virtues as their European ancestors. At the same time, the expedition was celebrated by Gaspar Pérez de Villagra, a native of Puebla, who in tedious verse sought to win fame as a Mexican Ercilla, his military exploits matched by literary achievement, his hands adept at wielding both 'lance and pen'.[16]

Similarly, the chief chronicler of the New Kingdom of Granada, Juan Rodríguez Freyle (1566–1642), a native of Santa Fe de Bogotá, displayed little animus against peninsular immigrants and small concern for the fate of the Indian population. Indeed, he dismissed the latter as barbarians 'without law or knowledge of God', ruled by chiefs who were as drunken as they were cruel, their religion and society governed by the Devil. For the rest, Freyle provided a summary account of the initial Spanish conquest and a perfunctory history of subsequent governors, pausing only to signalise the 1590s as a watershed in his country's development when the Crown's quest for additional revenue brought in new taxes and encouraged successive governors to enlarge the scope of their peculations. But he also noted that by the 1620s most of the cathedral canons were creoles and that several of the high court judges were graduates of San Marcos in Lima. In particular, the remarkable career of Fernando Arias de Ugarte, son of a leading family in Bogotá, who had sailed for Spain to complete his studies at the age of fifteen, was a source of great pride.[17]

A born story-teller, Rodríguez Freyle allowed his pen to divagate far from the dry notations of historical annals in quest of tales of intrigue and passion, of incidents which had enlivened the otherwise stale life of a provincial capital. El Carnero, as his chronicle was entitled, dealt in themes of honour, love and jealouy, themes which dominated Spanish theatre of the period. It was the awful temptations afforded by the beauty of women, the source of all human confusion since the fall of Adam, which obsessed Freyle. In a startling affirmation, he exclaimed that 'women generally govern the world', since by means of their counsel, exhortations and intrigue, wives and mistresses governed the men who held positions of authority. At the same time, their beauty and passions were the source of countless crimes and quarrels. 'It is a dangerous thing to have a beautiful wife', he warned, only then to add, and 'most irksome to have one who is ugly.' Against lies and slander, the staple gossip of provincial society, there was no defence. In proof of these observations, Freyle recounted an entire series of dramatic tales, of how a jealous husband killed his wife and her lover in bed; of how an evil beautiful woman had two successive husbands murdered; of a man who killed his sister for dishonouring their family name; and so on.[18] Here was a new genre of chronicle, in which crimes of passion and honour ousted the usual concerns of creole patriots, a genre familiar to readers of Ricardo Palma, the nineteenth-century Peruvian novelist, and at times to be still encountered in the tales of Gabriel García Márquez. Needless to say, although Freyle illumined a side of colonial society left untouched by most clerical chroniclers, the border between fact and fiction in El Carnero was by no means clearly established.

The most piquant of these early creole chronicles, however, was written by a Chilean soldier, Francisco Núñez de Pineda y Bascuñan (1608–80) who towards the close of a life filled with upset and incident, sat down to recount his memories of 1629 when he had spent seven months as a prisoner of the Araucanians. His chronicle, entitled Cautiverio felíz (1673) was rendered more weighty, if less attractive, by the interpolation of lengthy disquisitions as to the causes of the Indian wars in Chile, spiced by imprecations against bad government and laments about his own ruin and lack of recognition. The son of a distinguished Spanish soldier, who spent forty years in Chile fighting the Indians, Pineda himself eventually became a maestro de campo, or general, and passed most of his career on the frontier, eventually serving as corregidor of Concepción. Such were the vicissitudes of his life that in the great Indian rebellion of 1653 he lost most of his fortune, his estancias and encomienda left devastated. In 1670 he went to Lima in search of reward for over thirty years of service, 'only to find myself at the end of my days in a strange land, looking for some relief and rest for my old age ... in a country and under a government where the door of comfort is shut to whose who are poor and worthy'. In his exordium, Pineda declared that he chose to write in a simple style, his account based on 'true experience', rather than attempt to imitate the 'refined and elevated style to which the language has become accustomed'. Such a declaration should not be interpreted as soldierly naïvety, since Pineda had been educated by the Jesuits, read Latin, and was conversant with a wide range of authors, including learned biblical commentaries and certain doctrines of Aquinas.[19]

Few scenes in colonial literature are more memorable or diverting than the picture Pineda drew of himself thrust by a kindly native host into a chicken coop so as to avoid seizure by a drunken cacique who had vowed to kill him. The young creole, barely of age, spent the entire night in the hen-house listening to the drunken shouts of the Indians, not daring to move for fear of causing a commotion among the chickens, 'here for one part the rain, wind and cold molested me and for the other the droppings of the fowl very often fell on my head'. Generally well treated by his captors, who had cause to be grateful to his father, Pineda recounted a terrifying incident where he witnessed the execution of a Spanish prisoner, the assembled caciques drinking the blood from the man's heart which they had cut from his body. So too, he described a *curandero*, a native shaman and healer, who appeared as a veritable Lucifer, with his long hair and unwashed, grimy countenance, inspiring fear. Moreover, at all times he had to be on guard since several caciques sought his death. At the round of feasts, where drunkenness was the rule, he had to take care to avoid the unattached young women who freely offered their embraces to the young creole, since any entanglements could easily lead to jealousy and quarrels. In any case, as a good Christian, so he averred, he deplored promiscuity and illicit relations. His worst temptations came when he was offered as wife the beautiful mestiza daughter of a friendly cacique, the child of a captured Spanish woman. In all the narrative there is a delightful vivacity and an intimate, affectionate portrayal of Indian life and character which was rare in colonial chronicles, the natives of Chile described as human beings endowed with much the same range of sentiments as the Spaniards rather than dismissed as idolaters and savages.[20]

Nor did Pineda refrain from drawing the appropriate conclusions from his experience as a captive, since he openly commended the Indians for their 'generosity of spirit, noble hearts, illustrious blood and intelligent character, directed and governed by a lively and cultivated understanding'. In many aspects they compared favourably to the Spaniards since, unlike their foes, their word could be trusted and they often treated their prisoners well, or inflicted a swift death rather than imprisoning men in chains. Apart from their drunken feasts, they lived in hardy, abstemious manner, the men training themselves from childhood in the practice of arms. Indeed, on the outbreak of war, the men abstained from any physical contact with their wives, so as all the more to strengthen their spirits. It was through brave exploits in war that warriors earned a reputation, their caciques all leaders who had distinguished themselves on the field of battle. For Pineda this type of barbarian virtue appeared reminiscent of the early Romans or of the children of Israel in the age

of Judges. Moreover, the natives were by no means obdurate pagans, hostile to
the Christian faith, since during his captivity Pineda taught the children of the
cacique with whom he stayed both Christian doctrine and prayers and in fact
baptised one young friend shortly before his death. If the gospel was explained
in native language, peacefully and without recrimination or violence, it often
met with ready acceptance. Pineda concluded that since St Thomas taught that
the faith was God's free gift, it was clear that the Holy Spirit was present
among the Indians, inclining their minds and hearts to accept the Christian
gospel.[21]

The obverse of this praise of native virtue was an acerbic condemnation of
Spanish vice. On several occasions during his captivity he questioned elderly
chiefs as to the cause of their constant war against the European settlers, only
to receive the same reply. It was the Spaniards' cruelty and oppression which
had prompted the first great uprising against Pedro de Valdivia in the 1550s and
which again caused the rebellion of the 1590s. Initially distributed in encomiendas, the Indians had been driven to work like dogs, their chiefs scorned, and
their women raped or employed as domestic servants subject to ill-usage, and
their children at times seized and sold as slaves, with some shipped to Lima.
Accustomed as they had been to freedom, reared from youth as warriors, the
Araucanians had rebelled to rid themselves of their oppressors. Nor had the
Church at this period endeavoured to assist the natives, since priests neglected
to teach them anything more than the most elementary prayers and at times
were guilty of actively corrupting Indian women. In all this familiar sequence
Pineda perceived the determining influence of greed, *codicia*, the same vice
which both Las Casas and Oviedo had united to condemn.[22]

It was not just the crimes of the past century that Pineda chose to excoriate
through the speeches of Araucanian chieftains. In his own time, it was not
unknown for children to be seized from 'pacified' natives and sold into slavery.
Indeed, most of the governors who had ruled Chile in his lifetime had allowed
their lieutenants to conduct raids across the frontier with little more purpose in
mind than slave-raiding. If the initiative of Luis de Valdivia, the Jesuit
provincial, to despatch a mission into Indian territory to seek the peaceful
conversion of the natives had ended in the martyrdom of two priests, it was
because Ancanamon, the chief into whose domain they ventured, was infuriated by the deceit of the Spanish interpreter who ran off with his wives. In a
closely argued passage, Pineda recalled that for St Thomas war was justified
when it was sanctioned by the authority of the prince; when it had a just cause,
which is to say, when it was fought in defence of liberty or to punish crimes;
and when it had a just aim in view. None of these conditions could be invoked
to justify Spanish actions in Chile. If there were grounds for war, justice lay
entirely on the side of the Indians, since they had fought to defend their liberty
and free themselves from Spanish tyranny. 'There is not a nation in the world

which so loves the soil where it was born than this of Chile.' Although Pineda did not cite Las Casas, the influence of the great advocate of the Indians, transmitted through the teachings of the Jesuit Valdivia, was obvious in these radical conclusions.[23]

Not content simply to condemn Spanish policy towards the Indians, Pineda attributed the ruin of Chile to its government by men from Europe who came to enrich themselves at the cost of their subjects. What greater evil was there for 'the sons of the patria' than to be ruled by '*advenedizos* and foreigners ... the known enemies of the country'. In advancing this familiar creole plaint, however, Pineda struck a rare note of qualification, when he declared that he abominated any quarrel between fathers and sons, honoured his own father, and explained that 'by sons of the patria, I mean and as such accept all those who are settled here with wives, children, houses and estates and with sufficient experience of twenty or thirty years' experience in this war ... ' As it was, governors failed to equip or maintain frontier forces at the necessary level. The subsidies sent down from Lima served to enrich the treasury officials or corrupt military men whom governors appointed from their own entourage. Soldiers often seized horses from private estancias on pretext of war, their thefts condoned by governors who invoked the malevolent principle of 'reason of state'. The result of the all-pervasive corruption was that veteran soldiers were neglected and merchants and lawyers favoured. The creole nobility was 'shut in a corner and downtrodden', and, too poor to purchase offices, was mortified to observe mere merchants employ their wealth to become town councillors and magistrates, abusing these honours to further oppress and rob the poor. Beyond this sphere lay the audiencia and its attendant lawyers, who equally conspired to corrupt the country, Pineda concluding that 'this multitude of councils, audiencias and courts is the perdition and total ruin of our kingdoms'. It was this dominance of Castilians in Chile that led to the disastrous expeditions that unleashed the general Indian uprising of 1653 which threatened to drive Spanish settlement back to the suburbs of Santiago and which cost Pineda his encomienda and estancias. At that point the governor was obliged to promote creole soldiers, men with long experience of the frontier, to save the situation.[24]

In addition to this unsparing condemnation of the Crown's reliance on peninsular Spaniards to rule Chile, Pineda also enunciated certain general principles of government. Citing the well-known tract of Baldus on tyranny, he observed that whereas the true prince seeks the welfare of his subject, the rulers of Chile had acted as tyrants, since personal profit was their sole objective. He drew upon the biblical commentaries of Gaspar de Villaroel, the creole archbishop of Charcas and of Francisco de Mendoza, a Portuguese Jesuit, to compare certain governors to King Ahab of Israel. Did not the Bible provide examples of prophets opposing their kings in the name of justice? After all, 'the

Law is the true queen ... reason, justice and established rights, against whose power all the majesty of princes and sovereign kings has neither force nor dominion'. Kings were the shepherds of their people, earthly gods; but if justice was absent and the poor oppressed, then what was a kingdom, but, as St Augustine declared, 'a deposit of thieves'. Was there not, Pineda pleaded, a preacher who would denounce the tyranny of governors in Chile and bring to the king's attention the ruin of the frontiers. 'Is there not a prophet among us who has a voice?'[25]

III

Many descendants of the conquerors were more angered than gratified by Las Casas' denunciation of the men whose courage in battle had won the New World for Spain. The great-great-grandson of Bernal Díaz del Castillo, no less, bitterly dismissed the *Brevísima relación* as a gross slander which had blackened the honour and fame of the conquerors, encouraged Indians to rebel, and had been cited by foreigners to justify their assault on Spanish possessions. Such had been the confusion and resentment over the promulgation of the New Laws that all 'America burnt'. In his prolix chronicle of the kingdom of Guatemala, entitled *Recordación florida* (1695), Francisco Antonio de Fuentes y Guzmán (1642–99) drew on local tradition to assert that Las Casas had always been on the move, 'without fixed residence in any of these parts', and that as bishop of Chiapa he had offended everyone by 'the dry style, full of severity and sharpness, with which he treated everyone who approached him'. He had even quarrelled with Francisco Marroquín, first bishop of Guatemala, a prelate renowned for his pastoral zeal, who had assisted him in his first missionary ventures.[26] If Fuentes waxed so indignant in describing events which had occurred almost a century before his birth, it was because the career of Las Casas had been magnified by Fr Antonio de Remesal (1570–16-?) in his chronicle of the Dominican province of Chiapa and Guatemala, published under the pretentious title of *Historia general de las Indias Occidentales* (1619). The offence was compounded by the absence of any other history of the foundation of Guatemala, since the conquerors of that kingdom had failed to write or publish any account of their battles and settlement. A Dominican from Spain who had studied Las Casas' manuscripts in Valladolid, Remesal boldly contrasted the prophetic virtues of the bishop of Chiapa with the crimes and injustices of Pedro de Alvarado and his followers. It was to provide his patria with an honourable, glorious foundation, and to query the authority of Remesal, that Fuentes composed his chronicle, meticulously combing the city archives for imperial rescripts and early ordinances. To this end he embellished his work with lively descriptions of battles and saluted Alvarado as a Spanish Hercules and, in respect to his prudent and just laws, a veritable Numa. Like so many other chroniclers, he cited the full text of the papal donation, and, more oddly, the *requerimiento*, as proof that 'the only and chief purpose of the discovery, conquest and settlement of these kingdoms was the establishment of our holy and Catholic faith among the peoples who inhabited them'. A city councillor, a former district magistrate of Soconusco, and a wealthy landowner, descended on both sides of his family from conquerors and magistrates, Fuentes here expressed the common belief of the creole elite that their society derived from providential design and hence rested on heaven's mandate to the Catholic monarchy.[27]

The defence of the conquerors did not entail any slighting of the cultural achievements of the Guatemalan Indians. For Fuentes noted the number of stelae that were to be found in Atitlán, impresive pillars crowned with sculptured heads, elaborately inscribed with glyphs which, so he averred, commemorated the great deeds and conquests of native monarchs. Yet more impressive was the city of Copan where the ruins of its pyramids, great plazas, temples, and stelae offered persuasive testimony as to the quality of Mayan civilisation. Indeed, so fine were its sculptured remains that many visitors thought that they had been constructed by Carthaginians or by 'Spaniards of old'. But Fuentes derided all such theories – which both García and Pinelo had found plausible – and emphatically pronounced that the monuments were the 'work of the Indians'. On the controverted question of the origin of the natives of the New World, he recorded that he had discovered a manuscript, written in 1544 by a member of the royal dynasty of Quetzaltenango, which claimed that the Indians had migrated from Babylonia. So also, he cited an account in Quiché found by Fr Francisco Vásquez where the Indians were described as a tribe of Israel which, after escaping from Egypt with Moses, moved to Babylon rather than Palestine, and thereafter slowly wandered across Asia. That the natives of Guatemala had much the same ancestry as the Toltecs and Mexica was not in doubt, albeit Fuentes was resolute in proclaiming the independence of the Quiché kingdom from northern intrusion. Moreover, although he countenanced the possibility of Hebraic ancestry, he was more concerned to insist on the Egyptian or Babylonian antecedents of Indian pyramids and hieroglyphs. In no sense, other than on the score of religion, could the Indians be described as barbarians prior to the advent of the Spaniards.[28]

In his approach to contemporary Indians, Fuentes provided an ambiguous, even contradictory assessment, his comments varying according to the theme of discussion. For a start, he stoutly denied that they were slaves by nature, a theory, he asserted, devised to justify the worst excesses of governors like Pedrarias. Anyone who dealt with the natives could testify that there were men of talent among them, fitted for government, endowed with prudence and piety, who spoke Spanish and managed their affairs competently. At the same time, he testified to their alien, intractable quality, observing that 'their character is indomitable and hard', not affected either by punishment or flattery. Moreover, he conceded that the Spanish conquest had wrought havoc with their society and culture. As much as in Mexico, population had declined precipitately, so that Quetzaltenango, which had once housed 80,000 tributaries, now had but 3,000; and in Totonicapa there were but 2,030 men in place of 52,000. Not that this dramatic loss could be ascribed either to the horrors of conquest or to the despatch of workers to the coastal plantations, since the prime cause was the plague and smallpox, their effects made worse by native addiction to alcohol. Then again, the authority and prosperity of the Indian nobility had dwindled so that mere commoners now dominated town councils, a trend that led Fuentes to lament that the natives had lost their former distinction and were now 'cowardly, rustic, without talent or government, slovenly, without art and filled with malice'. To explain this transformation he invoked the influence of the stars and planets which governed the destiny of monarchies and nations. Nor was the change without precedent or parallel, since the descendants of Alexander's gallant soldiers were now but serfs subject to the Ottoman Turks.[29]

In his comments on native religion, Fuentes proved equally ambiguous, since although he praised the Catholic piety of the Indians, who revered saints' images in their houses and expended their exiguous resources on celebration of the liturgy, he also accused them of being 'superstitious and sorcerers'. Indeed, he reported that as a magistrate he had had a group of Indians whipped, since they had used their church for idolatrous rites and when discovered by a visiting priest had forcibly expelled him. So too, the newly arrived Franciscan missionaries in Soconusco, led by Fr Antonio de Margil, had discovered widespread evidence of idolatry. That Indians often endowed their confraternities with lavish donations of land and livestock demonstrated that they were far from poverty-stricken. In fact, Fuentes complained that the sugar plantations owned by creoles were threatened by competition from native *trapiches* which produced cheap brandy and coarse sugar at low prices. Much the same was true for wheat cultivation and the ranching of cattle and sheep. Moreover, since Indians rarely if ever paid any tithes to the Church on their production, their costs were correspondingly lower.[30] In all this, Fuentes testified to the survival in Guatemala of a prosperous Indian economy and a native religion which resisted clerical intrusion.

The polemical rancour with which Fuentes assailed Las Casas and Remesal spilled over into a critique of contemporary Dominicans, whose continued possession of so many native parishes he denounced as 'prejudicial to the sons of the conquerors'. In many districts the word of the Dominican provincial carried more weight than the commands of the bishop, especially since mendicant authority was enforced by resort to the whipping and imprisonment of any recalcitrant native. In effect, the primacy of the religious entailed the deprivation of the secular clergy, almost entirely creole, who failed to encounter any means of subsistence in the parochial ministry. In this context, Fuentes criticised the friars for preaching and ministering to the Indians in their native tongues. It would have been far preferable to have obliged the Indians to learn Spanish, since the survival of 'such difficult and barbaric languages' meant that the mendicants devoted time and energy to mastering these tongues which would have been better expended in the study of theology. In any case, it was surely regrettable that men of such intelligence and learning should bury their talents in the country, dwelling amidst ignorant villagers whose faith and loyalty were suspect. Had the Indians learnt Spanish, it would have proved possible to replace the friars by secular priests. In part these comments, inspired by creole resentment against peninsular dominion, had been overtaken by events, since Fuentes noted that in 1651 the Dominicans in Guatemala elected Jacinto del Castillo, his uncle, as their first creole provincial, and thereafter observed the alternativa between European and American Spaniards. At much the same time the Franciscans followed suit. But the new system had required much struggle and petitioning and prior to its introduction peninsular friars had mocked their creole brethren as *padre indios*. It was a source of pride for local families, Fuentes declared, to observe their offspring winning appointments as priors, provincials and even bishops, epecially since 'those who come from Spain' so often sought to denigrate their talents, relegating them to rural obscurity.[31]

As much as Carranza, Fuentes waxed eloquent when he came to describe his creole patria, blending land and lament in equal measure. Capital cities, he asserted, were the very foundation of kingdoms, since they encompassed palaces and courts, commerce and religious cult, arms and government. The 8,000 Spanish citizens and the Indian populace of Guatemala were served by a cathedral, three parishes, twenty-four churches, seven religious houses and three convents of nuns. It was not until 1678 that the city finally acquired its own university. For the rest, Fuentes expatiated on the miraculous images housed in diverse chapels and dwelt on the splendour of their cult. But the exuberance of his conventional civic eulogy was interrupted by the lament that it was increasingly difficult to find men to act as councillors. At one time, leading citizens had sought to embellish the city and its institutions through donations, but such was the prevailing decline in fortunes that virtually everyone appeared 'driven by blows to the very precipice and total ruin'. After compiling a list of conquerors, Fuentes exclaimed that only a handful of their descendants still figured on the city council, the majority eking out a penurious subsistence in the country, unable to purchase the clothes they needed to appear in public. The glory of the conquerors thus stood in vivid contrast to 'the universal clamour of their poor and ruined descendants'.[32]

Unlike many creole chroniclers, Fuentes did not fix upon immigrant merchants from the Peninsula as the villains who had effected the decline of his class. Instead, he returned to the initial failure of many conquerors to obtain encomiendas and the subsequent failure of encomenderos to secure perpetuity of tenure, noting that since 1643 Guatemala had been unable to cover the costs of maintaining an agent in Madrid to press their claims. Moreover, there was a marked tendency for each incoming president of the high court to bring over an extensive official 'family', who were usually rewarded by appointments as district magistrates, thus denying creoles access to these often lucrative posts. Then again, rescripts had been issued in 1662 and 1667 prohibiting all further official levies of native labour for work on sugar plantations and mines, a serious blow to the interests of creole landowners. Even drafts of labourers for the cultivation of wheat were hard to come by. In effect, the colonial state thus offered little assistance to the creole elite in its struggle for survival. It was in this context that Fuentes cited Solórzano and the newly published Laws of the Indies as to the preference that creoles should enjoy in all appointments to high office in the Indies. In a striking metaphor, he declared that the commonwealth was animated by law and founded on justice, the diverse estates acting in concert, so as to produce a social harmony reminiscent of the music played by different instruments in an orchestra. In practice, however, he complained of the abuses of royal governors and the difficulty in obtaining redress for creole grievances from Madrid. Such was his impression of decline that he declared that: 'in this world there is nothing fixed or settled', and then added: 'it is a grave affliction, perhaps even an incurable one, in my opinion, for a people to have a king who is far away'.[33]

IV

By the early eighteenth century the rhetoric of creole patriotism had become an established convention which was eagerly deployed by the chroniclers of newly emergent cities and provinces. In his *Historia . . . de Venezuela* (1723), José de Oviedo y Baños (1671–1738), a native of Bogotá but for long resident in Caracas, had no hesitation in condemning the wanton razzias led by Ambrosio de Alfinger, which had devastated the country in a merciless hunt for slaves. Such atrocities were not a German prerogative, since the first Spanish conquerors had also tortured Indian chieftains in their quest for gold, often throwing them to their dogs. Not that Oviedo displayed much concern for the Indians, commenting that 'their gentile customs were barbaric, without polish, government or religion'. By the time he wrote there were few Indians left in the area settled by the Spaniards, since smallpox epidemics had completed the desolation wrought by conquest. The most dramatic section of his work dealt with the infamous Lope de Aguirre who in 1561 invaded the island of Margarita, murdering the governor, and hanging both a friar and a woman. In flowing prose, Oviedo drew on earlier chronicles to recount the extraordinary story of how an expedition, launched from Peru to explore the uncharted territories of Amazonia, was taken over by Aguirre, who first had Fernando de Guzmán elected king of Peru, then quarrelled with his protégé and killed him, and finally led a band of two hundred *Marañones*, all armed with arquebuses, some 1,500 leagues across the jungle to Trinidad. For posterity perhaps the most remarkable feature of the text was Aguirre's open letter to Philip II, in which the conqueror complained that his twenty-four years of service and hardship in the Indies had brought him little reward or recognition, especially since the current viceroy in Peru, the Marquis of Cañete, was more prone to hang former conquerors as trouble-makers than honour them. As much as Fernández de Oviedo, Aguirre denounced the friars who sold the sacraments for money and the judges and lawyers who profited from the sufferings of the conquerors. All the wealth of the Indies now went to Spain, where it was used to help the king reconquer Flanders. He boldly informed Philip that he and his companions had 'denaturalised' themselves and henceforth should be regarded as enemies rather than as subjects. He warned him that few kings went to heaven. That Oviedo should have chosen to print this vehement outburst, no matter how critical its frame, was something of an event, since it reminded creoles of the turbulent early history of their country.[34] Were some patriot pulses quickened by the intensity of this defiant challenge to royal authority?

For the rest, Oviedo lauded the fertility and wealth of Venezuela, especially of the valleys surrounding Caracas, where plantations of cacao and sugar offered abundant promise of future wealth. Many of the coastal towns, however, had been sacked by French and Dutch pirates during the last decades of the seventeenth century. But it was Caracas and its inhabitants which most attracted his praise, since 'its creoles are of acute and rapid wits, courteous, affable and polished, without those vices which disfigure most places in the Indies'. Indeed, such was the benevolence of its climate that the town bred a handsome people 'of brave spirits and lovely hearts, and so inclined to all that is civilised that even the blacks, if they are native born, are contemptuous of anyone who does not know how to read and write'. The women, needless to say, were beautiful, pure and devout. It is salutary, when considering this civic eulogy, to recall that at this period Caracas was but a small town, with a thousand Spanish householders, a bishop whose income did not exceed 10,000 pesos, and less than a hundred resident Dominicans and Franciscans. In the course of the century, however, it was destined to become the thriving capital of a wealthy province.[35]

That the new-found prosperity of the Bourbon era did not allay political disquiet can be clearly observed in the *Llave del Nuevo Mundo* (1761), a history and description of Havana, written by José Martín Félix de Arrate (1701–65), a city councillor and member of its aristocracy. Protected by massive fortifications, its garrison maintained by an annual subsidy from Mexico, Havana had emerged as a powerful naval base, its resident squadron of warships a major deterrent against the pirate raids that had devastated the Caribbean coastlands a generation earlier. In the years 1724–61, the royal arsenal constructed no less than forty-two ships, ranging from modest frigates to imposing ships of the line fitted with eighty cannon. All this development, however, had come quite recently, since although the city had long since possessed a cathedral, mendicant priories, and three nunneries, its Jesuit college only dated from 1724 and its Dominican university had been founded in but 1728. The prosperity of Cuba depended on the cultivation of tobacco and sugar, which were shipped to Spain in ever-increasing quantities.[36]

In his historical survey, Arrate lamented the disappearance of the Cuban Indians, on whom he cited Torquemada as observing that they were 'pacific, docile, modest, respectful of their superiors and of much cleverness and aptitude for instruction in the faith . . . ' So harsh had been their conquest and subsequent exploitation that many had chosen to commit suicide. Their loss had meant that plantation owners now had to rely on imported slaves, a regrettable necessity, since although shipping blacks from Africa certainly liberated them from the Devil, the cost of their labour was high when compared to the wages paid to free peons in New Spain. Moreover, there was a constant drain of capital arising from their purchase, since the slave trade was controlled by foreign shipping. No matter what the lament, however, the immediate development of Cuba depended on an ever growing number of African slaves brought in to cultivate its fertile land.[37]

Where Arrate struck a thoroughly traditional note was in his defence of creole aptitudes, indignantly raking across the literature to fix upon the Dominican, Juan de la Puente, as the prime source of slanders that had been recently revived by the dean of Alicante, Manuel Marti. Had not scions of the first families of Spain settled in Havana? Was not the intelligence, liveliness and handsome air of its creoles recognised as far away as Mexico? More positively, he compiled lists of creoles who had distinguished themselves as bishops and canons, as judges and corregidores, and as military men. Indeed, his own brother had died at an early age fighting for Philip V at the battle of Badajoz in 1708. Yet, despite their evident talents, creoles often found it difficult to obtain high office in Church and State, appointments going to peninsular Spaniards who possessed influence and often relatives in the king's councils. To clinch his argument, he recalled that in 1702 the concurrent deaths of the bishop and governor in Havana had left all the chief positions of command in the city held by creoles, men who at a time of great threat from British forces, had distinguished themselves and kept the island firmly on the side of King Philip.[38] In this strongly expressed plaint, Arrate invoked Solórzano and thus indicated how little the passage of time had assuaged the creole elite's grievance at its exclusion from the governance of their own country. It was a theme which was destined to emerge with renewed force during the last decades of the eighteenth century.

15

ANNALS OF OPHIR

I

THE IDENTITY of Peru as Ophir, the source of Solomon's gold, captivated the great biblical exegetes of late sixteenth-century Spain. What could be more fitting than that the Catholic King who dwelt in a convent-palace modelled on the sober lines of the Temple at Jerusalem should be sustained by a redis-covered Ophir? The names appeared to be so similar, especially if one had recourse to the Hebrew plural, *Puraim*. Although both Acosta and Garcilaso protested at the absurdity of the theory, insisting that the term of Peru derived from a northern river or even from an individual Indian, whose name the Spaniards mistakenly applied to the entire country, nevertheless, the ever-credulous Gregorio García pronounced in its favour, arguing that Peru was a synonym for riches.[1] At the level of patriotic symbolism, there was a logic in García's arguments which attracted some chroniclers. Was not Peru founded on two great cities, Lima and Potosí, Byzantium and Ophir, the sacred metropolis and the gates of hell, their grandeur based on the exploitation of the native peasantry? No creole patriot in Peru appeared able to omit reference to his country's riches, no matter what his theme. In the seventeenth century, Garcilaso's *Comentarios reales* failed to engender a tradition of scholarly enquiry into the Inca past among the clerical elite of Lima. Instead, the text which most inspired creole chroniclers was Salinas' *Memorial*, where they encountered an exemplary celebration of the ecclesiastical glories of the capital and the riches of the mines. If his passionate condemnation of native sufferings failed to elicit much response, it was in part because Lima was a coastal city, more African than Indian in population. In any case, their attention was absorbed by efflorescence of the creole Church, untroubled by any nostalgia for the heroic days of the spiritual conquest, since in Peru the Indians had always proved more recalcitrant to mendicant preaching than their Mexican counter-parts. The grandeur of Lima in the early seventeenth century rested on the prosperity created by the Toledan settlement; there was little sense of continuity binding the city either to the Inca empire or even to the tumultuous society of the conquerors.

II

By far the most powerful, public and eloquent statement of early creole patriotism was penned by a Peruvian Franciscan, Fr Buenaventura de Salinas y Córdova (1592–1653), the grandson of a conqueror, who in his *Memorial de las historias del Nuevo Mundo, Pirú*, a tract published at Lima in 1630, not merely echoed with remarkable fidelity the grievances voiced by Dorantes de Carranza and Gómez de Cervantes, but also drew upon Las Casas and Guaman Poma de Ayala to frame a biting condemnation of Spanish exploitation of the Peruvian Indians. That Salinas equally celebrated the ecclesiastical glories of contemporary Lima and described both Pachakuti and Pizarro with even-handed praise only confirmed the unanimity of sentiment that joined the creoles of Peru and Mexico, with the Inca Garcilaso de la Vega a better guide in this context than Torquemada. Indeed, the *Memorial* circulated in New Spain and subsequent Mexican chroniclers, in particular the Franciscans Baltazar de Medina and Agustín de Betancur, were to find inspiration in its portrayal of creole character and its description of Lima. But few other colonial authors chose to write with such frankness as Salinas, and, if they did, almost invariably failed to publish their works. Just how it was possible for the *Memorial* to be released to the public is not clear. Subsequently, Salinas preached sermons in which he both complained that the descendants of the conquerors had been deprived of their encomiendas and attacked the ill-treatment of the Indians, sermons which caused him to be denounced to the Crown. In 1637 he was sent to Europe to pursue the canonisation of Francisco de Solano, a Franciscan missionary in Peru, and once he was in Spain, strict orders were given forbidding his return to Lima. Instead, he spent time in Italy, in part at Rome where he defended the works of Juan de Solórzano, the leading colonial jurist, from papal condemnation. In 1648 Salinas was sent to New Spain as commissary-general of the Franciscan provinces of that viceroyalty, a post which he used to forward creole pretensions to high office. At the time of his death he was about to return to Peru as bishop of Arequipa. The son of a viceregal secretary, Salinas acted as page to Viceroy Luis de Velasco in Lima and then served in the viceregal secretariat until the age of twenty-four when he entered the Franciscan order.[7] It was this experience of government which possibly accounted for the confidence with which he wrote. It equally provided him with access to the vast text that Guaman Poma de Ayala submitted to the viceroy. That the publication of his *Memorial* should have occurred when the archbishop of Lima, Fernando Arias de Ugarte, was a creole, albeit of New Granada, may well have influenced the matter.

The purpose of the *Memorial*, so Salinas boldly declared, was to awaken the conscience of the king and alert him to the danger of damnation if he failed in his duties to his subjects in the New World. 'To govern is to watch. He who sleeps fails to govern.' Indeed, the just right of the Catholic Kings to govern the New World, a right conferred by the Holy See, could not be sustained in face of the torments and injustices suffered by the natives of Peru, who included the Church and its ministers among their many oppressors. If only the king would come to govern this great world, Salinas lamented, or at least send a member of the royal family to rule, then some measure of justice could be maintained. As it was, Spaniards in Peru, both magistrates and merchants, conspired to wreak destruction. Where once 170 million natives had thrived there now survived only 2 million Indians. Despite the efforts and laws of the king and his viceroys, the terrible prospect opened that 'an entire world is coming to its end, rotting away'. For there was an unholy alliance between the State and economic interests, between district magistrates and merchants and miners, to exploit the native population to the point of death. If Hispaniola had lost its population, so now Peru was facing the same fate, a prospect which led Salinas to cite 'the holy bishop of Chiapa, in those divine and burning apologias that he wrote against Ginés de Sepúlveda in favour of the Indians'. He himself had once met an Indian who had been despatched by the local corregidor to carry a great basket on his shoulders for over thirty leagues. On learning that his name was Don Martín, Salinas exclaimed that he should have been called Don Martyr.[3]

If Las Casas had attacked the conquerors and their encomiendas, Salinas condemned the Toledan settlement and the exploitation it entailed. But he also gloried in the wealth and greatness of Peru and Lima and offered remarkably little in the way of principled reform. Throughout his tract there runs the explicit suggestion that it was because the district magistrates and entrepreneurs were generally European rather than creoles that the oppression of the Indian had proved so merciless. He advocated an ordinance whereby all Spaniards who came to Peru in search of wealth should be compelled 'to buy haciendas and urban property', with the aim of building up the country rather than draining off capital by returning to the Peninsula. As it was, district magistrates were appointed in Madrid or by the viceroy from his entourage; served for periods of two to five years; accumulated profits of up to fifty thousand pesos; and then took their ill-gotten gains home to Spain. Moreover, the same complaint could be levelled at the Crown itself, since so much revenue was despatched to Madrid as to leave Peru defenceless. Taxes levied in Potosí and Lima sustained Spanish armies in Flanders, leaving the viceroy without sufficient means to defend the Pacific coast from Dutch marauders, with the result that Callao was sacked in 1614 and again in 1624. 'Spain never helps', Salinas lamented; Peru was but an overseas possession, a royal milch-cow, a world in decay, its sovereign all too distant and uncaring.[4]

It was the sheer distance of Peru from Madrid that denied the creoles easy access to the royal court, the fount of all favours and office, so that the sons of the conquerors 'through misfortune have lost their rights and privileges of descent'. So mortifying did Salinas view their situation that he was moved to exclaim: 'Are those who are born in Peru made of a different stuff from those of Spain?' In fact, the constellation and climate of the New World 'raises and ennobles spirits', with the result that all creoles 'in general emerge with such high spirits that there are none who are inclined to learn the mechanical arts and crafts that their fathers brought from Spain; thus one does not speak of creole cobblers, barbers, smiths and taverners'. Equal in character and intelligence to the European Spaniards, they failed to obtain high office precisely because of the Crown's neglect. As it was, 'newcomers and foreigners' were appointed as district magistrates. Moreover, the *advenedizos*, immigrants from Spain, dominated commerce and were more to be feared by the creoles than the Dutch or English pirates, since not merely did they exploit the unfortunate Indians, but also sought to monopolise all honours and credit within the country. Referring to such merchants, Salinas declared: 'I know many who, after starting with ten or twelve pesos, dealing in packages carried through the streets on their shoulders, poor, broken and distressed men, within eight or twelve years have accumulated eighty or a hundred thousand pesos.' The source of these riches was usually the ill-treatment of the natives, since the newcomers 'live among us squeezing the land like a sponge, sucking the blood of the Indians like mosquitoes'.[5] In Peru, as much as in Mexico, it was thus the rule that peninsular immigrants dominated commerce, with the creoles more anxious to obtain public office than stain their hands by entering trade.

If Salinas lamented the fate of both Indians and creoles, nevertheless, he gloried in the grandeur of his native city, Lima, saluting it as 'a holy Rome in its temples, ornaments and religious cult, a proud Genoa in the style and brio of those who are born in it, a beautiful Florence for its benign climate ... a wealthy Venice for the riches it produces for Spain and prodigally distributes to all, remaining as wealthy as ever ... a Salamanca for its thriving university and colleges'. Small wonder that after such a eulogy, he should have exclaimed that 'the patria is a second God and a first ancestor'. Not at all reluctant to substantiate his case by appeal to statistics, he claimed that Lima consumed every year no less than 200,000 sheep, 200,00 *botijas* of wine, 30,000 *arrobas* of sugar, and 240,000 *fanegas* of wheat. In addition to this consumption of local produce, the city imported a great range of merchandise from Europe and Asia, despatching by way of payment over 5 million pesos for cloth from Castile and another million for the silks and calicoes of China and Japan, the trade handled by some twenty great import houses. Behind the prosperity of Lima lay the unparalleled riches of Peru, the treasure-house of the world, so great indeed, that Salinas declared Peru to be the wetnurse of the world, a veritable pelican mother, 'maintaining with her blood the milk now converted from gold and silver'.[6]

The commerce of Peru and the wealth of Lima all depended on the prodigious output of silver of the *cerro rico*, the rich peak of Potosí. Basing himself on information supplied by the treasury official, Francisco López de Caravantes, Salinas observed that by 1630 the number of Indians arriving for *mita* service had dwindled to some five thousand men, their labour supplemented by the exertions of a thousand free workers resident in the town. The more difficult and skilled task of mining the ore was assumed by these wage-earners who were paid 9 pesos a week as compared to $2\frac{1}{2}$ pesos obtained by the *mitayos* for their labours as porters. In the seventy refining mills no less than $2\frac{1}{2}$ million hundredweight of ore was processed each year, consuming some 6,000 quintals of mercury. The total wages of both types of workers came close to a million pesos, a sum which enabled them to consume some 50,000 *fanegas* of maize used to brew *chicha* beer and another 91,000 *fanegas* of wheat for flour. The magnet of a trading network that extended across the Andes, Potosí was supplied by 30,000 llamas carrying goods, together with another 50,000 llamas employed by the Indians. In all, the annual value of silver produced by the mines was about 10 million pesos. It was the output of the *cerro rico* which sustained the might of the Spanish monarchy, so that Potosí was hailed by Salinas as 'the insensible Pelican, the column and obelisk of the Faith ... the scourge of the Turk, the envy of the Moor, that which makes Flanders tremble, and is the terror of England'.[7]

No matter how much Salinas burnished his prose to magnify Peru, inevitably he had to admit that it was built upon the toil and suffering of the Indians, its economy animated by greed. At the great mercury mine of Huancavelica he was informed that the summons for *mita* duty was taken by the Indians as a sentence of death, since by 1630 the shafts were some 500 feet deep. Some wretched natives committed suicide, others offered their daughters to Spaniards to escape the levy, and all who arrived were cursed and beaten by mestizo and Spanish overseers. In terms highly reminiscent of Guaman Poma de Ayala's earlier description, Salinas pronounced that Huancavelica was 'a living image of death and a dark shadow of hell'. He reported that the Crown Protector of the Indians had provided him with information about ill-treatment so that he could print the material and thus awaken the king's conscience. For it was not just the miners who were responsible for oppressing the Indian, since the district magistrates numbered among the worst offenders, imprisoning natives in *obrajes* for textiles and forcing their subjects to work without payment on the pretext of fulfilling their tribute liabilities. Moreover, they demanded that Indians use their llamas to transport coca, maize, wine and flour to the mining camps, all for the profit of the magistrate. In conclusion, Salinas cited Juan de Solórzano's *De Indiarum iure*, published in 1629, in which the great colonial jurist openly admitted that the Indians of Peru suffered greater oppression under the Spaniards than under the Incas. He had terminated his work almost 'weeping at the calamities, the serfdom and the wasting of the Indians'. For his part, Salinas concluded that his experience as a priest had taught him that the Indians were as other men, endowed with much the same nature, albeit more quiet and docile, meek and humble, more close to the virtues of the Beatitudes.[8] It was only those Spaniards who lived off the toil of the natives who sought to justify their exploitation by describing them as insensible brutes.

The influence of Guaman Poma de Ayala on Salinas can be most clearly observed in his brief discussion of the Indian past, since in his sketch of the first age of humanity in Peru, he asserted that the natives observed the natural law and worshipped the one true God, a primal idyll, later replaced by a descent into warfare and tyranny. However, he also defined the Indians as descendants of Ham, thus belonging to the same servile race as the blacks of Africa and the 'Indians' of Asia. In contradiction to Garcilaso de la Vega, he declared that Manco Capac, the first Inca, achieved power with the assistance of the Devil and inaugurated 'the tyrannical monarchy of the Incas'. Nevertheless, Salinas praised Viracocha Inca as a philosopher comparable to Aristotle, who both believed in the existence of a hidden First Mover of the universe, a deity superior to the Sun, and who also sought to destroy the worship of idols. Thereafter, he cited various authors as to the greatness and wealth of the Inca empire, pronouncing that Huayna Capac was 'the greatest emperor that historians mention'. The great walls of the fortress at Cuzco and the highways stretching along the Andes numbered among the marvels of the world.[9]

Although Salinas described the conquerors as 'the cruellest tyrants' primarily animated by greed, who replaced the 'soft, suave and attractive' rule of the Incas by hellish oppression, nevertheless, he also praised the Spaniards for their heroic courage. In particular, he hailed 'the valour and grandeur of the incredible spirit of Pizarro', and saluted him as 'an incomparable Alexander', who in the person of Atahualpa overthrew another Darius at the head of an army of no less than a million men. Whereas circumstances had always favoured Cortés, by contrast Pizarro displayed his greatness by overcoming innumerable difficulties. Indeed, the conquest could be justly termed 'miraculous', since without the intervention of the Virgin Mary and Santiago it would have been impossible for the Spaniards to defeat so courageous and numerous an enemy as the Incas. Defending the reputation and right of Spain to empire from the attacks of Benzoni, Salinas lamented that the heroic deeds of the conquerors were fast sinking into oblivion since no poet had written the epic they warranted. In this dual eulogy of both Incas and conquerors, Salinas exhibited an intellectual dichotomy that was to haunt creole patriotism until its demise.[10]

Just as Torquemada sought both to defend the quality of Indian culture and
exalt Franciscan achievements, so equally Salinas wrote not merely to testify to
native exploitation but also to celebrate the spiritual establishment of Lima. In
less than a century of existence, the city had come to house some 40 churches
and chapels where each year, so Salinas calculated, 300,000 masses were
offered to heaven. Obviously, as viceregal capital and commercial emporium of
the Pacific coast, Lima supported extensive communities of merchants and
royal officials. So also, the descendants of the leading encomenderos formed a
small nobility who resided in the city. The needs of the social elite were met by
a numerous class of Spanish artisans and professional men. But all these groups
and classes palled into insignificance when compared to the institutional weight
and sheer concentration of talent and wealth embodied in the Church.
According to the census of 1614 Lima had a population of 25,454 persons,
divided into 9,511 Spaniards, 10,386 blacks, mainly slaves, and an assortment
of mulattos and mestizos. By 1630, so Salinas declared, the city had risen to
about 40,000 inhabitants whose spiritual needs were satisfied by a cathedral, 4
parishes and the priories and colleges of the religious orders. The size and
wealth of this ecclesiastical establishment was remarkable, since the cathedral
drew upon an annual tithe income of 60,000 pesos to support a chapter of
27 canons and prebendaries, assisted in their duties by another 14 chaplains
and by 24 students. In addition, Salinas calculated that there were between
300 and 400 secular priests resident in the city, supported by family inheritance, annuities and mass fees. Yet this regiment of clerics was overshadowed by the massed battalions of the religious orders, which although
administering a series of country parishes and provincial priories, maintained
their novitiates and headquarters in Lima. Thus, if the Dominican province
numbered 700 friars who were collectively responsible for 63 Indian doctrinas
and 27 priories, no less than 250 men resided in the capital. Much the same
was true of the Franciscans, with 260 friars in Lima, the Augustinians with
170 and the Merced with 130. The Jesuits were yet more concentrated, since in
a province numbering 250 members, they maintained 150 clerics in Lima to
administer their two colleges, the novitiate, and their Indian parish in *el
Cercado*.[11]

Just how this army of priests spent their time is difficult to say. The most
elaborate celebration of the Catholic liturgy, with periodic processions through
the streets, the prolonged study of scholastic theology and philosophy, the
inevitable round of sermons and lectures, and, not least, the practice of
personal asceticism and meditation: here was the substance of their lives,
supplemented, and marred no doubt, by factional politics and individual
backsliding. To judge from Salinas, a reputation for sanctity was achieved by
holy works, which is to say, by self-flagellation, fasting and prayer. Of one
saintly Mercedarian, a native of Chuquisaca, he wrote that he had 'armed a

cuirass of iron against his flesh, the body rotting with cords and chains, so that by cutting the flesh the bones were revealed'. At his death, it proved impossible to remove this ascetic device. Such was the prestige of the cloister at this time that there was great competition to enter the novitiate so that Salinas commented: 'at the present day, we have more than enough, so that the doors are now shut and the habit is denied to great wits and talents, because there is no room in all the province'.[12] In effect, if the 'noble spirits' of young creoles prevented them from entering trade or practising a craft, where else could they sustain their pretensions other than by entering the priesthood?

Of central importance to the sudden flowering of ecclesiastical culture were the two Jesuit colleges of San Pablo and San Martín and the university of San Marcos, which, if founded as early as 1549, was effectively established by Toledo in 1576. Salinas hailed San Marcos as 'the workshop of letters, the most fertile mother of numerous and outstanding sons'. The university had sixteen endowed chairs, covering the traditional faculties of theology, philosophy, law and medicine. By 1630 all these posts were occupied by creoles and appointments were so prized that in the oral contests or 'oppositions' for the chairs hundreds attended the sessions. Most successful candidates, like Salinas himself, were pupils of the Jesuit college of San Martín which had over 180 pupils. Academic learning in Lima was dominated by the scholastic tradition still in full vogue in Spain, with memory and dialectical talent much esteemed. Of one holy Jesuit, Salinas recorded that 'he knew by memory all the works of the Angelic Doctor St Thomas'. More to the point, however, the university provided a professional training in law, both civil and canon, in medicine and in theology, which enabled its pupils to compete for high office in Church and State. To advertise the talents of his 'nation' and to encourage young men, Salinas compiled a list of distinguished creoles, all educated at San Marcos, who had won appointment as judges in colonial audiencias, as bishops and canons in the secular clergy, and as provincials and priors in the religious orders. At its head there appeared Fernando Arias de Ugarte, a native of Bogotá, who, after serving as judge in the high courts of Quito and Panama, entered the priesthood and became archbishop of Charcas and Bogotá before his final appointment to the archdiocese of Lima. Apart from the position of viceroy, reserved for scions of the Spanish nobility, the leading offices in Church and State were thus open to creole candidates; it was only Crown neglect and distance from court that prevented them exercising their rightful monopoly on all such places.[13]

No description of early seventeenth-century Lima could omit the presence of six great convents. For these institutions housed no less than 1,366 nuns, 899 slaves and an uncertain number of female lodgers and children, all supported by lavish endowments of property both in the city and the country which yielded a collective annual income of 96,000 pesos. These institutions were still set on a course of growth since, whereas the newly established Dominican convent of Santa Catalina had but 46 nuns and 26 slaves, the Augustinian Encarnación comprised no less than 450 nuns, over 50 novices and 266 slaves, thus forming a community of some 800 women, which by reason of the individual houses occupied by most nuns constituted a veritable city within a city, comprising an entire block of Lima. Since each nun had to offer a dowry of at least 2,000 pesos before entering the convent, recruitment derived from Spanish families of some standing.[14] The existence of such great numbers of women in the religious life required the services of many priests to act as father confessors and spiritual directors.

The significance of Salinas' *Memorial* was that it expressed with exceptional boldness and eloquence the grievances, ambitions and contradictions of the American Spaniards. The ideology of a class rather than of a nation, creole patriotism inherited the frontier aspirations and medieval vision of both conquerors and mendicants. The historical vistas opened by Garcilaso de la Vega and Torquemada provoked a growing acceptance of Indian civilisation as the foundation of their patria's glory, without, however, dimming the insistence on ancestral rights derived from the conquest. So also, Salinas engaged in both a passionate denunciation of the Indians' oppression and a fervid celebration of the creole Church in Lima, without offering a hint of a regret that the ecclesiastical splendours of the capital were sustained and made possible by the daily exertions of the natives. Instead, he chose to excoriate immigrant Spaniards and the export economy they promoted. Yet creole aspirations centred on high office in Church and State, since both their education and status apparently rendered them unfit for entrepreneurial activity. But without the presence of a monarch and his court in Lima how could the natives of the capital obtain the appointments they sought? For the rest, the *Memorial* offered a striking portrait of Lima as physically separated from its hinterland by mountain passes and coastal deserts, an oasis city, its population as much African as Spanish, sustained by the flow of Indian tribute, highland silver and European merchandise – in short, another Byzantium, dwelling self-enraptured, caught up in an endless cycle of liturgical celebration.

III

The chronicler who best expressed the mentality of the generation of creoles who swarmed into the cloisters and colleges of Peru in the first decades of the seventeenth century was Antonio de la Calancha (1584–1654), who wrote his *Crónica moralizada del orden de San Agustín en el Perú* (1638) to commend the spiritual achievements of his province. In particular, he commemorated its apostolic founders, its impressive number of priories, and its holy images. But he also defended the Peruvian Indians from the slander of ill-intentioned critics,

15 Title page of Antonio de la Calancha's *Crónica moralizada del orden de San Agustín*

lauded the qualities of the creoles and questioned the means by which Peru had been conquered. A contemporary of Salinas and Solórzano, he obviously subscribed to their questioning of the exclusion of creoles from high office and their critique of the exploitation of Indian labour. But his interest was equally captured by the fervid world of hispanic piety, in which there was enacted an apparently daily battle between the forces of darkness and light, where holy friars fought demons by fasting and penitence and holy images wrought their miraculous cures. It was also a world of night battles with dreams frequently invaded by apparitions of the Virgin Mary, Christ and countless devils. Although Calancha was praised by his contemporary, Antonio de León Pinelo, as 'a great positive (theologian), an elegant preacher and accomplished in human letters', qualities reflected in his overcharged, discursive style, he exhibited an almost instinctive credulity, tempered only by his Christian orthodoxy and patriotism. A native of Chuquisaca, a city then known as La Plata and now as Sucre, he was educated at the university of San Marcos, passed some years at Potosí and other provincial towns, and became guardian of the great Augustinian priory in Lima, where he acquired a considerable reputation as both a preacher and as a rigorous spiritual director. An impression of both his style and intellect can be obtained from the exordium on Potosí, which he hailed as 'unique in opulence, first in majesty, the ultimate in avarice; it has the form of a sugar-loaf, or, best to say, it is like sugar, since so many ants search for it, soon to grow into giants'. What could be more appropriate than that the imperial city of Potosí should have for its patron St Augustine, the honoured patriarch of the imperial order of Augustinian friars? Was there not a spiritual significance to be found in the identification of the *cerro rico* as Ophir? There was further food for thought in the consideration that in Peru silver grew in great metal trees rooted deep within the earth, the thin veins or lodes encountered by miners but their upper branches, whose substance was constantly renewed by the upward flow of precious ore. Was not the order of St Augustine in Peru a tree of grace, its spiritual sap yielding a rich harvest of souls? It was a holy mine, a sacred Potosí, from which flowed an endless stream of spiritual riches.[15] As this extended conceit illustrates, Calancha, like Salinas and León Pinelo, was awe-struck by his country's material wealth, so dramatically disinterred from the very bowels of the earth. At the same time, it manifests a strain of rhetorical piety for which the only equivalent in English literature is the poetry of Richard Crashaw.

The patriotic character of Calancha's endeavour was clearly revealed in his defence of the Indians, a task undertaken, so he declared, to pay the debt he owed them for having been born in a country once theirs, although he also insisted: 'I have no part Indian, nor did God wish to make me brown, since all I owe this land is the fact of my birth and to Andalusia my parents and clean lineage' (*limpieza*). As against the imperial school led by Acosta and Solórzano, he argued that the natives of the New World were 'free by nature', their nations encompassing both rulers and servants, their society thus endowed with the same range of qualities and talents as any human community. Similarly, he rejected García's notion that the Indians descended from the Ten Lost Tribes of Israel and derided Fr Pedro Simon's theory that they were the descendants of Issachar, the tribe predestined like the strong ass for toil and servitude. Equally decisively, he broke with Acosta and Torquemada in ascribing their patriarchal ancestry to Japhet rather than Ham, thereby associating them with the Spaniards rather than with Africans. Indeed, he argued that the most probable antecedents of the Indians were the Tartars of East Asia. After all, not merely was there a similarity in colour and features, there were also common modes of life. In particular, the Araucanians in Chile greatly resembled the Tartars, since they subsisted off hunting and warfare, lived in small hordes, and abhorred cities and fixed settlements.[16]

In light of these declarations, it comes as no surprise to observe that Calancha unreservedly praised Manco Capac, founder of the Inca dynasty, who 'made politic laws with rewards and punishments, and these, together with those added by his successors, were among the most advanced in reason and the most in conformity with natural law of all that the most politic nations have ordained, excepting those of the Catholic Church and of our kings'. Such an achievement was all the more remarkable since the first men in Peru had dwelt in savagery, similar to the condition of the contemporary natives of Amazonia. Moreover, they had been governed by democracy, 'a pestilential government where all command'. Only slowly had they attained to a stage of aristocracy where local caciques formed small states prior to the advent of the Incas. As it was, Calancha stressed the grandeur of an empire that encompassed over two thousand leagues of territory stretching from Quito to Chile and which had endured over five hundred years. He noted that the *quipus*, the knotted strings used by the Incas, were mnemonic devices used both for computation and for recall of past events, thus serving the purposes of both tribute registers and historical annals. That the Incas propagated the worship of Pachacamac, creator of the universe, only served to confirm the attractive and advanced character of their polity. Despite this glowing commendation, however, Calancha himself did not actively pursue the study of Inca history or religion. Most of his material and reflections derived from Garcilaso, Blas Valera, whom he saluted as 'an eminent linguist and most curious investigator of their antiquities', and Salinas. Only in his description of the coastal shrine of Pachacamac was there any sign of a personal interest. For the rest, he drew on missionary experience to describe features of native religion and on the prior work of Alonso Ramos Gavilán dealing with the Inca temple and the subsequent Christian sanctuary at Copacabana on Lake Titicaca. Moreover, as befitted an Augustinian friar, Calancha agreed with Acosta and Torquemada in defining native religion as inspired by the Devil and his army of fallen angels, whom he described as actively intervening in human affairs, speaking through false oracles, invading dreams and sponsoring cults that required human sacrifice.[17] Already, Ramos Gavilán had recorded that on the chief feasts at Copacabana the Incas had sacrificed up to 200 children, and that no less than 1,000 persons had been slaughtered at the death of the emperor Huayna Capac. In Peru, as much as in Mexico, there thus emerged a confused image of the native past with wise legislators staining their hands with the demonic ritual of their religion.[18]

The degree to which Calancha differed from Garcilaso or failed to comprehend the ideological import of his work is clearly revealed in his reliance on an apostolic visitation to explain the virtues of native society. Citing the treatise on Copacabana, published in 1622 by his fellow Augustinian, Ramos Gavilán, he asserted that there was clear evidence that St Thomas had preached the gospel in South America, travelling from Brazil to Paraguay, thereafter traversing the Andes, before embarking at Callao to return to India. Native *quipus* testified to the arrival of a great sage, bearded and white, called Tumupa, who had set up a famous stone cross at Carabuco as testimony of his mission. It was thanks to his teaching that the Indians believed in the existence of a creator god, in heaven and hell, and the immortality of souls, and had practised rites reminiscent of Christian baptism, confession and communion. If their apprehension of these doctrines remained cloudy, it was because their form of intellect always required spiritual truths to be expressed by means of material objects. To clinch this line of reasoning, Calancha also adduced the theological consideration that since Christ had commanded his disciples to preach the gospel to all nations, it would have been contrary to Divine mercy and natural justice to have allowed the peoples of America to languish for another 1,500 years in ignorance and darkness. In his evocation of St Thomas and Satan as the primal sources of native religion and morality, Calancha thus rejected the essentially naturalistic version of Garcilaso, who had argued that, by reason of the natural light implanted within them, all men could know and worship the one true God and observe the natural law, all without the assistance of Christian revelation. Whereas in Spain, Juan Eusebio Nieremberg depicted the Incas, along with the Lamas of Tibet, as exponents of natural religion, in Peru itself the influence of the Devil was too palpably visible for Garcilaso's views to be so readily accepted. In any conflict between St Augustine and patriotism, the African doctor still commanded the field.[19]

As much as Salinas, Calancha cited Las Casas' *Brevísima relación* as the authoritative text on the Spanish conquest, claiming indeed that it had been printed at the express command of Charles V. More surprising, he also cited Benzoni and inserted the last testament of the conqueror, Mancio de la Sierra, which attested both to the shining virtue of Inca government and the murderous immorality of the Spaniards. True, Calancha praised Pizarro as 'a valiant heart, born for great resolutions' and cited a number of cases where men of humble birth won great empires, but his inclusion of Tamerlane the Great in the list did not help vindicate the conqueror's reputation. Indeed, he denounced the rebellion of Gonzalo Pizarro as inspired by a pernicious desire for 'liberty', compared it to the movement of the *comuneros* in Spain, and pronounced the resulting government as tyrannical as that of the emperor Tiberius. Governed by 'avarice and vainglory', the conquerors had treated the natives like dogs, exploiting them with the greatest cruelty, without the slightest attempt to impart the elements of Christian doctrine. Echoing Gómara, he noted that Providence had punished the conquerors for their crimes, since not merely had the first leaders all died violently, either murdered or executed, but also few of their followers had survived the civil wars or founded families of any substance.[20] Indeed, he surmised that only five lineages could be reckoned to be now comfortable, with an income sufficient to command respect, the remainder often poverty-stricken, reduced to begging on the streets for alms. On Toledo, Calancha adopted an ambiguous approach, since although he praised him as 'the first legislator of the Indies, whose ordinances are today's laws', he strongly condemned the execution of Tupac Amaru, citing Garcilaso's story of Philip II's reproof to the viceroy. He concluded that Toledo could have resolved the problem with 'a less criminal measure', and exclaimed: 'how many nobles have had their hearts hardened by the pestilential [doctrine of] reason of state, the poison of monarchies ... '. Herrera's veiled endorsement of Machiavelli thus found no echo in Calancha.[21]

Despite his condemnation of the conquerors, Calancha defined the conquest itself as an act of Providence, announced by omens and the prophecy of Huayna Capac, and blessed by the apparitions of Santiago and the Virgin Mary at Cuzco. Indeed, without the assistance of heavenly forces, the Spaniards could never have overthrown such a vast empire, the very success of the Araucanians in preserving their independence a proof of this thesis. However, the crimes of the conquerors, and the harsh immorality of the secular clergy who had entered Peru in that epoch, meant that the Indians never approached the mendicants with the veneration displayed by the natives of New Spain. Certainly, Calancha failed to cite any scenes of religious enthusiasm that could compare to the ritual euphoria so proudly described by Torquemada. Instead, he lamented that the friars had 'to conquer legions of demons made princes and millions of idolaters their tributaries'. The spiritual conquest in Peru proved to be an arduous task, a slow demanding campaign which stretched out for over a century. As late as 1609 the archbishop of Lima launched a campaign to extirpate idolatry, since inquiries had shown that the Indians still continued to worship their ancient gods. Calancha knew the leading figures in this campaign, José de Arriaga and Hernando de Avendaño, and obviously supported their efforts to liberate the natives from the power of the Devil. In Catholic terms, Peru was but an occupied territory, the clergy still engaged in remorseless suppression of native rites and beliefs. In this context, it is surely significant that Calancha should have observed that in dealing with the Indians it was necessary 'to assimilate them in treatment to the Spaniards in all things and cases which do not harm their nature, so that in esteeming honour they might forget their obscene customs and vile actions'.[22] It was not sufficient to be a Christian; one also had to be a man of honour; conversion thus entailed hispanisation.

If Calancha disparaged the record of the secular clergy brought over by the first encomenderos, it was to exalt the role of the Augustinians, whose arrival in 1550 inaugurated 'the spiritual conquest of this Peru'. Led by Andrés de Salazar who had laboured for many years in Mexico, the friars sought to apply missionary methods which had succeeded so well in New Spain. It was the Augustinians, so Calancha declared, who first undertook the task of learning Indian tongues so as to preach the gospel in language that the natives could understand. As befitted the founder of a new province, Salazar was described as man of prayer, fasting and penitence, who sought to introduce a regime of austere rigour, obliging his friars to renounce all worldly goods and walk barefoot. Another founding father with experience of Mexico was Agustín de la Coruña, later bishop of Popayán, who begged Toledo to spare the unfortunate Tupac Amaru. In all this, Calancha admirably fulfilled the terms of his brief as chronicler, which was to provide future generations of friars with a series of edifying lives of the founders and holy men of the province. All the emphasis was on penitence, fasting, self-scourging, and prayer, the time-honoured means of achieving heroic sanctity. His narrative reached a climax with the tortures inflicted on Diego Ortíz, a zealous friar, who had ventured into Vilcabamba, the Inca redoubt, with the aim of converting the Indians, only there to suffer a barbarous martyrdom. Calancha marvelled at the paradox that Ortíz was 'a religious without letters, he studied little and converted many . . . a simpleton by nature and a sage through grace'.[23] As the proto-martyr of Peru, there were strong grounds for acclaiming him as the country's patron.

Part of the duty of the monastic chronicler was to provide an account of the foundation and progress of each priory in the province, a task which enabled Calancha to celebrate the qualities of the cities in which they were located. In contrast to Salinas, however, he chose not to expatiate on Lima other than to commend the manifold glory of its ecclesiastical establishment. Instead, he fixed upon his own priory and its great church which was adorned by no less than fourteen altarpieces and chapels. The community generally comprised 150 friars, among whom were sixteen qualified masters of theology and three professors of the university. So wealthy had the house become that it distributed 5,000 pesos each year in alms. So also, he marvelled at the

Augustinian nunnery of the Incarnation, which in 1631 supported a community of over eight hundred women, with the 288 professed nuns attended by a variety of slaves, servants and relatives. The current abbess was daughter of a judge of the high court. Her faithful subjects peopled no less than nine choirs, all accompanied by harps, violins, basses and guitars, whose harmony, so Calancha averred, was worthy of heaven itself.[24]

It was when he came to describe the priory at Potosí, a house which had received no less than 535,000 pesos in alms in the years 1584 to 1611, that Calancha discussed the city and its sterile surroundings. Noting that a census taken in 1611 had enumerated a population of 150,000, served by no less than fourteen parishes, he pronounced that the *cerro rico* offered a veritable image of hell, its open maws devouring the hapless natives that were forced to descend into its depths, only there so often to meet with accident and abuse. Were not the Catholic King supported by the flow of silver, it might well be thought that the discovery of the mines had been prompted by the Devil. Mammon was the idol that was worshipped at Potosí. It was a town much given to discord, with a violent dispute between Basques and Castilians in 1623–4 waxing so fierce that the Augustinian priory had to shelter several Basques from the fury of their opponents and expend all their efforts to secure a reconciliation between the two factions.[25] The frankness of this condemnation of the city, on whose exertions the entire kingdom relied for its prosperity, is surprising and indicates the great divide which separated friars from entrepreneurs.

In pronouncing Potosí to be governed by avarice, Calancha undertook a careful calculation of its astrological determinants, since the influence of the constellations obviously affected the character of its inhabitants. Careful to insist on the orthodox doctrine that man was a free agent, nevertheless, he praised Emperor Leopold of Austria and other Catholic authors, 'great mathematicians', who had offered 'scientific proof', based on 'continuous experience', as to the influence of the stars on human affairs. In consequence, he did not hesitate to provide astrological characters for all the leading cities of Peru, usually, however, tracing favourable effects on their residents. Indeed, 'the stars are most noble creatures', whose influence was invariably benevolent.[26]

If Calancha was so anxious to affirm the kindly nature of the stars, it was because he sought to safeguard the creoles from the accusations of Juan de la Puente and his disciples. So benign was the climate of the New World that some authors had identified the hemisphere as the site of Paradise. With such kind airs, it was only to be expected that the spirit of its inhabitants would be lively. He quoted the well-known texts of Hippocrates and Galen to the effect that owing to the temperance of its climate the inhabitants of Asia were superior in both intellect and character to the natives of Europe. So equally, had not Aristotle argued that the nations who dwelt in the warm zones of the earth were more lively in intellect than the natives of the far north, whose heads were frozen by cold? All this led to the conclusion that the climate of Peru was especially favourable, so that Calancha marvelled at: 'the lordly spirit which this land engenders. The Creoles of this Peru are of keen understanding and happy memory, with children so rapid in the use of reason that a twelve year old often reaches further than a man of forty in other kingdoms.' Despite such an abundance of talent, there were few rewards to sustain the enthusiasm for learning, since the court was so distant. Yet, whereas in Spain it took eight years just to acquire a knowledge of Latin, in the Indies eight years sufficed to produce excellent theologians and jurists. Few Creoles applied themselves to the mechanical arts and still fewer entered trade or became sailors.[27] Even immigrants from the Peninsula felt the influence of the climate, since 'he who was but a labourer in Spain assumes the airs of a noble'. At the same time, he declared that the Indies had been settled by members of the most noble families of Spain, an affirmation that led to the resounding conclusion: 'This Peru is inhabited by noble lineages, wise lawyers and acknowledged saints.' After such a glowing pronouncement, it comes as a surprise to encounter the familiar creole plaint about the decline of conquerors' families and the rise of new men to wealth, a spectacle which provoked Calancha to declare in lapidary style: 'those born in it are strangers in their own land and the newcomers are the heirs of its honours'.[28] In all this, the influence of Salinas was manifest. What is curious is that at no point did Calancha mention that his own province had adopted the *alternativa* in 1629, a sure sign of tension between European and American Spaniards, or, as his successor as chronicler called them, Castilians and Peruvians.[29]

If stars and climate combined to constitute an environment worthy of Paradise, mankind's ancient enemy continued to haunt creoles and Indians alike, ensnaring them into multiple traps. In a learned disquisition on this theme, Calancha cited any number of Church Fathers who all agreed that the Devil and his minions possessed the power to assume animal form, to assail the faithful in dreams, to provoke strange apparitions and voices, and, at the very worst, act as succubi arousing sexual excitement. There was nothing theoretical in Calancha's interest, since he related many anecdotes dealing with demonic possession and intervention in human affairs. The fact that there was an entire army of witches and folk-healers practising their malign arts amidst an Indian population still prone to idolatry only served to heighten his conviction that Peru was a spiritual battle-ground. He related the story of a noble Spaniard who on failing to make his fortune in Potosí had sold his soul to the Devil, a transaction that became evident when, struck by illness, he publicly blasphemed and cursed the name of Christ. In this case, Calancha proved able to rescue the man from demonic possession, raising alms to relieve his debt and comforting him by prayer and exhortation. So too, he recalled a holy friar, much given to night prayer and ascetic rigour, who was thrown into despair on hearing a voice which informed him that a fellow friar, recently dead, whom he had revered for his saintly austerities, was now roasting in hell-fire. Not until a year's tormented prayer had passed, did the Virgin Mary relieve his anxiety, granting him a vision of herself crowned by God the Father and the Holy Spirit, with Christ engaged on the salvation of his beloved mentor. Then again, Calancha heard in Cuzco the dramatic story of two priests attached to the cathedral, the one learned and devout, the other idle and dissolute. The Virgin appeared to the pious cleric in his dreams to inform him that his companion was doomed to die within three days and would be dragged to hell by four devils. After careful consultation with his confessor, he took heed of these dreams and warned the dissolute priest of his impending fate, only to find his counsel scorned. Sure enough, after the three days had passed, the man died without repentance and was hence damned for all eternity.[30] As is obvious from these tales, the Devil's influence was manifest at all levels of society, as much in the cloister as in the tavern. But on all occasions, the forces of darkness could be countered by the heavenly assistance of the Virgin Mary and her Son. What these numerous anecdotes revealed was a world in which magic and the supernatural still invaded the everyday life of priests and laymen alike. If we recall that in sixteenth- and seventeenth-century Europe, witches were burnt in their thousands, then Calancha's obsession with demonic influence clearly derived from fears and theories current among both the Protestant and Catholic Churches.

If he did not exhibit any obvious signs of paranoia over the Devil's dominion, it was because Calancha drew comfort from the spiritual resources of the Church, whose sacraments, saints and images offered powerful assistance to anyone threatened by Satan. Indeed, he devoted many eloquent pages to the miraculous images which numbered among the most treasured possessions of the Augustinian Order in Peru. To start with, its friars attended Our Lady of Guadalupe at Pacasmayo, a copy of the image in Extremadura, which had been commissioned by a wealthy citizen of Trujillo. Once installed in a hill-chapel, the figure had attracted widespread devotion in an area where the Indians were notorious for their worship of the moon. It was largely thanks to the influence and miracles of the Virgin that idolatry was finally vanquished. In a revealing passage which occurred during a eulogy of Our Lady of Grace, a figure venerated in his priory in Lima, Calancha wrote: 'the beauty of the image won popular devotion, which is most important, since in spiritual matters our nature rests in delightful images, which are accustomed to purchase hearts through the eyes'. The material attractions of such a cult were elucidated when he exclaimed that the Virgin had displayed a fine sense of business in choosing to cure the lunatic son of a wealthy woman, since the grateful mother had donated a fertile tract of land to the priory.[31]

Nowhere was the public importance of holy images more clearly described than in Calancha's description of the arrival in 1593 at the port of Callao of a great, life-size crucifix, a replica of the Christ of Burgos, a powerful, tortured carving which ranked among the greatest images of Spain. Escorted by a procession of Augustinian friars, the figure was carried to Lima, its progress accompanied by salvos of cannon-shot and excited crowds which thronged the streets of the capital. On an appropriate Friday, the Augustinians celebrated a high mass in honour of their new image, inviting the viceroy, the judges of the high court, and other dignitaries to attend. Their church was decked with velvet hangings, the altars ablaze with lights, and the great figure of Christ guarded by 'a theatre' of thirty-four great candles, each weighing five pounds of wax. Fireworks and music marked the occasion, albeit then, so Calancha added, 'another music then gave joy to heaven, there entering many penitents, who that day having seen such a bloody, wounded image, now walked scourging their flesh, in sorrow for having sinned, forcing those who saw them to utter unhappy sighs'. So impressed was the viceroy, the Count of Cañete, that he returned in the evening, accompanied by his wife and the court nobility. On the Saturday, the church was crowded all day, services lasting until midnight. Thereafter, a confraternity of distinguished citizens was formed and monies raised to build a richly adorned chapel, their veneration soon joined by two further confraternities, respectively organised for Indians and free blacks, all three bodies parading with their image on Holy Thursday through the streets. So celebrated was this figure of Christ that it was soon copied and became the prototype of many similar images, both in paintings and sculptures, throughout Peru. Its reputation for miraculous intervention in human affairs was confirmed when in 1594 the viceroy pleaded with the image to protect Spanish settlements from the depredations of an English privateer which had entered the waters of the Pacific. When the ship was captured, he led a procession of officials and confraternities to the Augustinian church to offer thanks, an occasion rendered all the more joyful by news that Sir Francis Drake had died off Porto Bello.[32]

For all his pursuit of the miraculous, Calancha found no story that could rival the contemporary account of the Mexican Guadalupe. In Peru all images were either imported from Spain or carved locally, without any alleged heavenly intervention. In tracing the origin of the celebrated cult of Our Lady of Copacabana, Calancha once more drew on the treatise of Ramos Gavilán. As so often in New Spain, the site, a narrow promontory reaching into Lake Titicaca, had been used for pagan rites, the temple dedicated to the sun numbering among the three principal sanctuaries in the Inca empire. It had been a place of pilgrimage and supported a convent of virgins. Once levelled to the ground by the Spaniards, the site remained deserted until 1583 when a local Indian lord, called Alonso Viracocha Inca, commissioned his nephew, at that time resident in Potosí, to carve an image of the Virgin and Child. Once gilded by a Spanish artisan, the figure was installed in a small chapel at Copacabana, where it soon evoked popular devotion, wrought miraculous cures and attracted pilgrims. The Augustinian friars were brought in to officiate at the shrine and by 1613–14 the cult had so increased that it was necessary to enlarge the chapel. By then Spaniards had begun to pray to the Virgin alongside the Indians and the governor of Chucuito attended the ceremonies that marked the consecration of the enlarged sanctuary. The chaplain, Ramos Gavilán, described the image as 'the mother of this barbarian people of Peru', whom he compared to the children of Israel labouring in Egypt for Pharaoh. It was the Indians who were drafted on *mita* service to work at Potosí who especially prayed to Our Lady of Copacabana for assistance, installing a copy of her image in that city. Once again, the influence of the Virgin was seen as decisive in the destruction of the Devil's power over the natives of Peru.[33]

The concordance of views between Calancha and Salinas is impressive and confirms the ideological importance of the Franciscan. Both these friars were concerned to defend Indian nature and Inca achievements from imperial slander, to exalt the qualities of the creoles, to deplore the exploitation of the natives at Potosí and, above all, to celebrate the spiritual glories of Lima and the colonial Church. But Calancha was equally driven to undermine the authority of Garcilaso. For he explained Inca law and morality by means of an apostolic mission and invoked Las Casas and Benzoni to condemn the conquerors, thus rejecting both sides of Garcilaso's visionary patria. Instead, he adopted the perspective of Torquemada and Grijalva, insisting on the foundation role of the spiritual conquest. But he failed to provide any inspiring primal scenes of native enthusiasm and was reduced to mere eulogy of the first Augustinians. Moreover, the presence of the Devil was still too palpable in contemporary Peru for any celebration of an early victory. In the last resort, he fixed upon the miraculous images guarded by his order as evidence of Heaven's blessing on the creole Church.

Whereas the leading exponents of Baroque culture in the hispanic world delved into hermeticism and alchemical science to comprehend the universe, provincial asociates of the movement invoked astrology, magic, images and the Devil to explain the mysteries and dramas that afflicted their lives. Miracles and spirits were part of everyday experience. What is peculiar in Calancha is the dissonance or incongruity between his rhetorical style, burdened with a heavy cargo of classical and patristic citation, and the naïve credulity which informed his seemingly endless fund of anecdotes about apparitions and miracles. Admittedly, much the same incongruity can be observed in many colonial paintings where an imperfectly rendered Renaissance style is deployed on themes which are medieval or merely naïve in spirit and arrangement. That such an evidently learned theologian as Calancha should have grasped at every sign of spiritual forces at work in the world surely demonstrates that in Habsburg Spanish America the clerical elite and the populace participated in a common religious culture.

IV

In the first years of the seventeenth century the City of the Kings, as Lima was officially styled, was the abode of saints. No less than four individuals, two Europeans and two Americans, were eventually canonised by the Holy See. St Toribio Alfonso de Mogrovejo, archbishop of Lima, 1581–1606, was an exemplary prelate, renowned as much for his pastoral dedication as for his personal austerities, his time spent visiting his mountainous diocese and virtually all his great income devoted to alms for the poor. St Francisco Solano (1549–1610) was a Franciscan missionary who preached the gospel in Paraguay and Tucumán before returning to Lima, where in 1604 his sermons provoked scenes of mass penitence, the churches remaining open to provide confession and the faithful sallying forth onto the streets to scourge themselves, for all the world as if a prophet had entered a modern Nineveh. So uplifted in prayer was Solano that at times his feet were seen to leave the ground. The rigour of his fasting and penitence offered a lesson to all religious embarked on the path to sanctity. When he died, the entire city, led by the viceroy and archbishop, mourned at his bier and within a decade testimonies were collected to forward his cause at Rome.[34] Heroic virtue and endless prayer, however, did not constitute sufficient grounds for elevation to that select body of heroes recognised by the Papal court as Catholic saints. It was necessary to provide evidence that the defunct indeed dwelt in heaven and had the power to assist the faithful. The proof of sanctity was the power to work miracles. In short, the recognition accorded by the Roman Church depended on the devotion of the faithful, who testified to the miracles that answered their prayers for assistance. In this sense, a saint was not just a holy man or woman, but rather a public figure, acclaimed by a particular community, whose cult was thereafter diffused across the Church. Saints and their relics were thus essentially thaumaturgic.[35] As the biographer of Solano observed: 'The intercession of this apostolic man, his merits, his relics, the earth of his sepulchre, the oil of the lamps of his sepulchre, calm the weather when there are tempests at sea, have power to smother fire, give joy to the sad, have success in births, heal frights, flows of blood, and put to flight the gout, malign fever . . . ' It was Salinas who promoted Solano's cause at the Roman court, his pleas attracting papal commendation. In the event, new procedures introduced by the Holy See delayed any pronouncement until 1679, when both Mogrovejo and Solano were beatified, with their canonisation finally announced in 1726. Just why the cause of these two Spaniards was promoted so strenuously by the ecclesiastical establishment in Lima and why their Mexican counterparts failed to promote any similar candidates is not clear.[36]

The two creole chroniclers, chiefly responsible for publishing testimonies of the holy lives and miracles of saints in Lima, were the Franciscan Fr Diego de Córdova Salinas and the Dominican Fr Juan Meléndez. Neither man sought to emulate Calancha's patriotism or his anecdotal divagations. Their interest in the Inca past was at best perfunctory and their defence of native abilities merely formal. Despite their praise of Las Casas – Meléndez accepted Remesal's claim that the Dominican had briefly visited Peru – they equally saluted Pizarro for his conquest of 'the blind Babylon of idolatry' and noted that the first Dominicans were 'inseparable companions of the famous Francisco Pizarro'. Indeed, Meléndez allowed Francisco Antonio Montalvo, a Spanish friar who knew Lima, to insert a prefatory commendation in which he asserted that the *Brevísima relación* was a forgery, perpetrated by an unknown Frenchman to slander the Spanish monarchy, a claim that Meléndez himself implicitly dismissed in his laudatory account of Las Casas' career.[37] If the controversies of the conquest period thus no longer troubled the creole chroniclers, the glories of Lima commanded all their attention, since both Córdoba and Meléndez followed Salinas and Calancha in providing a detailed description of the churches, priories, colleges, cathedral, and convents of the capital, together with some mention of local luminaries, distinguished either for their sanctity or learning. A familiar note of creole exasperation was struck by Meléndez when he recounted that on visiting Spain he had been complimented on the quality of his Spanish and questioned whether there were any books in America. Insisting that there were three separate nations in Peru, Indians, blacks and Spaniards, who never intermarried, he remarked of the creoles or 'Indianos', as Spaniards born in the New World were called, that 'their first application is to study and the Church', or failing this, to enter honourable professions. At the same time, he observed that although the Indians prior to the conquest had been governed by the Devil they had in fact followed natural law and were now active as master painters and sculptors.[38]

Both these mendicant chroniclers were obsessed with the gold and silver flowing from the mines of Peru and inevitably turned the phenomenon to spiritual and patriotic account. Córdoba exclaimed: 'as Potosí gives bars of silver to enrich Spain, so the university of Lima can enrich many kingdoms with individuals illustrious in virtue, pure in blood, and celebrated in letters'. That Meléndez chose to entitle his chronicle of the Dominicans in Peru, *Tesoros verdaderos de las Indias* (1681–2) and opened with an estimate of production figures, speaks for itself. Where both these chroniclers abandoned the dulcet vein of eulogy for polemic, was in their joint critique of Calancha, their ire provoked by his assertion of Augustinian primacy in the Peruvian mission-field. The fact of the matter was that the Dominicans had arrived first, closely

16 Juan Meléndez

followed by the Franciscans. Fr Domingo de Santo Tomás, the disciple of Las Casas, had framed an introduction to the Quechua language well before any Augustinian turned his attention to that task. The civil wars had not prevented the mendicants from preaching to the natives. At the same time, neither chronicler preserved any tradition within their respective communities of much Indian enthusiasm for the Christian gospel.[39]

It was Meléndez who presented extended accounts of the lives and works of the two Dominican saints of Lima, St Rosa and St Martín de Porras. Posterity or, best to say, the official Church was slow to appreciate the true value of Porras, a mulatto *donado*, or voluntary servant, bound by personal vow, since he was only beatified in 1837 and not canonised until 1962, his cult sustained through the centuries by popular devotion. The son of a free, black woman, daughter of Africans, and of a Spanish nobleman, Martín de Porras (1579–1639) was not allowed to enter the Dominican Order as a lay brother, since the rules of the province prohibited the entrance of blacks or mulattos. As a *donado*, he was allowed to wear the religious habit and was placed in charge of the infirmary of the great priory in Lima dedicated to Our Lady of the Rosary. In that capacity, he soon became famous for his boundless charity to the poor and his unceasing ministrations to the sick, so that Indians and blacks flocked to the priory in search of treatment and alms. At the same time, he became noted for the extreme rigour of his regimen, regularly scourging his shoulders twice a day, rubbing salt and vinegar into the wounds. On occasion, he persuaded black slaves to whip him. Such was the intensity of his prayer that he was seen suspended in the air, rapt in spiritual ecstasy. By the time he died, Porras had become well known in Lima, received and consulted by dignitaries of Church and State, so that the viceroy and judges of the high court all came to pay their respects at his funeral bier. Although the Dominicans in Peru were careful to prepare testimonies of his life and the subsequent miracles wrought through his heavenly intercession, their priority in Rome was to promote the cause of a Spanish missionary, Fr Vicente Vernedo, destined, however, never to receive an official accolade. The public attention given to Martín de Porras attests to the all-inclusive genius of post-Tridentine Catholicism.[40]

The chief saint to emerge in seventeenth-century Lima was Isabel Flores de Oliva (1584–1617), better known as Rosa de Santa María, who was beatified in 1668 and swiftly canonised in 1671, when she was recognised as patron not merely of Lima and Peru, but of all America. Of humble but honourable creole stock – both her parents were born in the New World – Rosa refused all thought of marriage and from her youth onwards wore a religious habit, frequenting churches where her devotion to the images of Mary, especially Our Lady of the Rosary, soon aroused the attention of pious priests. At the outset, too poor to afford the dowry necessary for entrance into a nunnery and thereafter disinclined to accept the bustle of the great convents of Lima, Rosa figured as a *beata* and in 1607 was admitted to the Third Order of the Dominicans. In effect, she lived at home or lodged with wealthy benefactors, where she became expert at sewing and adept at turning popular song to religious account. She attracted the devotion of a circle of well-connected, pious ladies, several of whose daughters followed her example and became nuns or *beatas*. Unfortunately, the vapid quality of her hagiography does not allow us to discern with any clarity the nature of her appeal, the more especially since the few recorded sentiments and songs betray a dulcet sentimentality. There was little that was soft or sweet, however, in her mortification of the flesh, since she soon abandoned any regular meals, subsisting off a diet of bread and water, supplemented by herbs and juices. So also, she wore bristle cilices around her limbs and regularly scourged herself, on one occasion seeking to administer five thousand blows within the space of eight days, in imitation of Christ's passion. At times she wore a crown of thorns pressed so deep as to cause blood to flow down her cheeks. Such a regimen led to constant headaches and stomach pains and also provoked the assaults of devils, including a spirit whose visits became so frequent that she called him 'El Sarnoso' – the scabby one! Shortly before her death, a portrait of Christ, before which she was rapt in prayer, started to sweat, a phenomenon that aroused immense public speculation. By this time, she was so venerated in the city that in the public exequies that marked her death, the viceroy, the archbishop and all the religious orders attended the ceremonies. Within two years, her remains were removed to a special sepulchre and miracles occurred with such frequency that the authorities hastened to compile testimonies so as to promote her cause in Rome.[41]

If the canonisation of Martín de Porras depended on popular devotion maintained across centuries, by contrast the rapidity with which Isabel Flores was admitted to the pantheon of saints can only be explained by the intensity of the Marian cult in the seventeenth century. At a time when the Virgin Mary was increasingly depicted in her advocation as the Immaculate Conception, Rosa of Lima was clearly viewed as another, living Mary. The current campaign to replace Santiago as patron of Spain by St Teresa of Avila was another pointer in the same direction. The imagination of the hispanic world in this epoch hovered at the limits of passion, with the pursuit of honour and lust depicted by the dramatists forever countered by the opposing practice of mystic prayer and ferocious castigation of the flesh. St Rosa was the spiritual antidote, so to say, of Don Juan. That such an ideal virgin-saint had to win her crown by such intense mortification testifies to the uncompromising demands of the hispanic ideal of sanctity.

In all this, there was little that was peculiar to Peru; indeed, the sheer normality of her type of sanctity confirmed the degree to which Lima was a Spanish city set down on the coast of the Pacific. Her cult certainly offered

17 Angelino Medoro, *Santa Rosa de Lima*

grounds for patriotic pride, but its message lacked any specifically Peruvian content. Was it for that reason that an elderly *émigré* Spanish poet, the Count of La Granja, one-time corregidor of Potosí, felt called to compose a heroic epic in twelve cantos in honour of St Rosa? Whatever the cause, his pen soon exhausted the exiguous incidents of her life, so that he was obliged to mount an

elaborate poetic machinery of a hidden Inca high priest, Bilcaoma, who in
Satanic conclave plotted the destruction of Catholic Peru and the restoration of
the Incas, a campaign in which he was assisted by Queen Elizabeth of England,
Sir Francis Drake and the Dutch privateers, whose incursions into the South
Seas were defeated by the prayers and presence of St Rosa. In this strange
literary scheme, the saint thus emerged as the heavenly patron of Lima, whose
powers were invoked to maintain a Peru founded by that great Christian
warrior, Francisco Pizarro.[42]

V

In the cathedral at Cuzco, a canon paused in the midst of his sermon to
exclaim: 'Ladies, make way for that poor Indian woman: she is my mother.' In
this anecdote, jealously preserved by local tradition, Juan de Espinosa Medrano (1629–88), commonly known as 'El Lunarejo', publicly testified to his
impoverished, mestizo origin. Celebrated for both erudition and eloquence,
Espinosa's talents had won for him ordination as a priest and promotion to the
rank of canon, his career eventually crowned by appointment as archdeacon.
After his relatively early death, two volumes of his Thomist philosophy were
published in Latin at Rome and a collection of his sermons printed in Peru. His
reputation, however, had been assured since his *Apologético en favor de d. Luis
de Góngora* had appeared in Lima in 1662, a work in which his censor hailed
him as 'this Demosthenes of the Indies . . . this Creole Phoenix'. At issue was
the censure of the Portuguese critic, Manuel de Faria y Sousa, who had
denounced Góngora as 'the Mahomet of poetry', his Latinate style and
addiction to hyperbole creating a host of imitators, whose excesses had
corrupted the Castilian language almost beyond redemption. By way of
contrast, Faria adduced the examples of Dante and Camoens, who wrote as
much as prophets as poets, their diction free from the exaggerations of the
Spaniard. That this barbed censure had been advanced some time before his
own birth, did not deter Espinosa from entering the fray, justifying his tardy
contribution by the observation that 'we creoles live very distant'. In his
opinion, it was only with Góngora that Spanish poetry at last attained the high
level of the Latin classics. Through his bold incorporation of learned neolo-
gisms, Góngora had enlarged the empire of the Spanish language, much in the
same way that Cortés had augmented its political power by seizing Moctezuma
in his palace. In any case, how could Góngora be compared to Camoens, when
the two writers were engaged in the different genres of lyric and epic poetry?
Such was the erudition and dialectical skill displayed by Espinosa in this
polemic that his censor proudly pronounced him to be 'the wonder of his
patria, showing the envy which darkly conspires against its sons (called creoles,
a name of unknown etymology) that where God created the highest quality and

most abundant treasures of the earth, He also deposited the intelligence of heaven'.[43]

Despite his formidable Baroque learning, Espinosa Medrano chose not to engage in any exposition of the Inca foundation of his creole patria. The prevailing concept of Peru as a Catholic Ophir, the laws and beliefs of the Andean population derived from the teachings of St Thomas, failed to engender any sustained scholarly interest in the Inca empire. Although the creole elite took great pride in styling their patria 'the great city of Cuzco, head of the kingdoms of Peru', in practice they were decidedly hesitant about crossing the barrier which separated Christian Peru from Tawantinsuyu. There were, of course, good reasons for their diffidence. In the first place, it was remarkably difficult to reconcile Garcilaso's image of the Incas as Platonic guardians with Acosta's insistence that Satan ruled supreme in all the native realms of America, the more especially since the Jesuit's thesis was given practical application in the campaigns to extirpate idolatry which raged across the Andes until the 1660s. The demonic obsessions of Calancha were widely diffused across all levels of colonial society. Moreover, even if Espinosa Medrano had wished to rival Alva Ixtlilxochitl, he would not have easily encountered the materials with which to construct an account of Inca history and culture superior or noticeably different to the interpretations of Garcilaso and Acosta. For the Andean Indians had never developed any system of pictographs and had proved relatively slow to record in Spanish script their oral traditions. As far as can be ascertained, the knowledge encoded in their *quipus*, the knotted strings which served as mnemonic devices, was soon lost. In effect, the natives of Peru had never marked the passage of time with the religious intensity exhibited by their Mesoamerican counterparts and bequeathed posterity little more than the paintings of the twelve legendary monarchs of the Inca dynasty commissioned by the emperor Pachakuti. Then again, the accounts of Andean institutions and beliefs compiled by the first Dominicans and by such observers as Polo de Ondegardo, Juan de Betanzos and Cristóbal de Molina had disappeared from view, gathering dust in inaccessible archives or libraries. The chronicle of Guaman Poma had sunk from sight, leaving but the faintest trace in Salinas' *Memorial*. So too, the Toledan interpretation of the Inca state as a barbaric despotism, guilty of human sacrifice, cruel laws and harsh exploitation of its subjects, never found any extended, coherent exposition in print. In particular, the failure of Bernabé Cobo to publish his *Historia del Nuevo Mundo* (1653) denied critics of the Incas the prime text for the prosecution, since Cobo, the intellectual heir of Acosta and an admiring friend of Solórzano, had presented a mass of new data on native institutions and religion.[44] In its absence, Garcilaso slowly won the day, his victory finally assured by the publication in 1723 of the second edition of the *Comentarios reales*, which enjoyed wide circulation in Peru.

If the creole elite of Cuzco proved so hesitant in their ideological appropriation of Tawantinsuyu, it was because throughout the colonial period the city
housed a rival elite for whom that history was a living memory. The Inca
ayllus, at whose head were the descendants of the emperors, still possessed
noble status and jealously guarded their genealogies. Unlike New Spain where
the native nobility dwindled in status or became absorbed within the hispanic
community, in Peru there still existed an entire class of kurakas distributed
across the Andes who constituted a native gentry, engaging in agriculture and
transport, still acting as vital intermediaries between the rural masses and the
colonial regime. The prominence of this class in Cuzco was clearly depicted in a
series of paintings of the Corpus Christi procession, dating from the late
seventeenth century, in which representatives of the Inca nobility, dressed in all
the finery and insignia of their ancestors, walked at the head of native
confraternities. Earlier in that century, a witness noted that in the celebrations
of the beatification of St Ignatius Loyola in 1610, the Indians of Cuzco had
carried figures of eleven monarchs of the Inca dynasty, from Manco Capac to
Huáscar.[45] Moreover, there existed in Cuzco the college of San Francisco de
Borja, founded by Toledo and administered by the Jesuits, which educated the
children of the native nobility. By the eighteenth century its walls were adorned
with portraits of the Inca monarchs, so that the memory of their empire and its
greatness was sedulously preserved. It became the fashion among the native
nobility to have their own portraits painted, depicting them in traditional
costume, which is to say, in the same attire they wore on ceremonial occasions.
In the celebrations which marked the coronation of Ferdinand VI in 1747, it
was observed that a masque staged by the city's parishes closed with a parade
of 'a squadron of more than twenty Incas, richly dressed in their beautiful
clothes, with their *mascapyachas* . . . ' In effect, if the creole elite were slow to
lay claim to Inca history, it was because it was not a distant past, shrouded in
myth, but rather a living presence, to be observed proudly parading through the
streets, the cultural property of a subordinate but rival elite.[46]

16

MEXICAN PHOENIX

I

IN 1648 the Mexican elite was startled to learn that the image of the Virgin Mary venerated at the 'hermitage' of Guadalupe, situated on a hill-side outside the city, had a miraculous origin. Over a century ago, so the story ran, on Saturday 9 December 1531, a poor Indian from Cuautitlán named Juan Diego heard sweet music as he was passing the hill of Tepeyac on his way to the Franciscan church at Tlatelolco. He then saw a young lady radiant with brilliant light who told him that she was the Virgin Mary, the Mother of the one true God, and that she desired to have a chapel built in her honour at Tepeyac, so that she could show herself to be a merciful mother to Juan Diego and his people and to all the faithful who might seek her assistance. The Virgin commanded him to speak with the Bishop of Mexico and obtain his permission to build the chapel. But when the Indian went to see Juan de Zumárraga he was rebuffed. The next day he again saw the Virgin at Tepeyac and again he went to the bishop, who refused him permission. A third time the Virgin appeared and a third time the bishop rebuffed him, on this occasion demanding that some sign be offered that it was indeed the Virgin Mary and not some devil who had appeared. On the fourth day, by now discouraged, Juan Diego decided to go to Tlatelolco to find a priest for his uncle, Juan Bernardino, who was dying of the plague. But on his way the Virgin appeared to him and commanded him to climb the hill at Tepeyac so as to pick flowers. Despite the winter month, Juan Diego found the hill covered with roses and other flowers which he gathered into his cape, a simple mantle woven from cactus fibre. The Virgin told him to take the flowers to Zumárraga. Sure enough, when he opened his cape before the bishop, the flowers fell to the ground, only to reveal imprinted on the coarse *ayatl* cloth a likeness of the Virgin Mary. Awed by this miracle, the bishop fell to his knees in adoration and then had the image placed in the cathedral until it could be taken with all due ceremony to the chapel which was to be built at Tepeyac. Meanwhile, the Virgin had also appeared to Juan Bernardino, cured him of the plague, and told him that her image was to be known as Holy Mary,

18 Our Lady of Guadalupe

Virgin of Guadalupe. Once the painting was installed at Tepeyac, it soon attracted the veneration of pilgrims and travellers and miraculous cures were performed, a sure sign of its heavenly origin.[1]

The publication of the *Imagen de la Virgen María, Madre de Dios de Guadalupe, milagrosamente aparecida en la ciudad de México* (1648) opened a new epoch in the religious history of New Spain. Although the image had already aroused considerable devotion – a new chapel was completed in 1622 at the order of Archbishop Juan de la Serna – its cult remained confined to its sanctuary and was not noticeably more fervent than the veneration accorded to other Marian images in the Valley of Mexico. Indeed, when Miguel Sánchez, the author of this treatise, died in 1674, a contemporary diarist wrote:

> he composed a learned book, which seems to have been the means by which devotion to this most holy image has extended throughout Christendom, being forgotten even among the citizens of Mexico until this venerable priest made it known, since in all Mexico there was not more than one image of this sovereign lady, which was in the convent of Santo Domingo, and today there is not a priory or church where it is not venerated and very rare the house or the cell of a religious where there is not a copy . . .[2]

A testimony to the excitement caused by Sánchez can be found in the introduction to his book, where Dr Francisco de Siles, a canon of the cathedral chapter and professor of theology in the university of Mexico, pronounced: 'he speaks and writes for all his patria, which receives this history as the executor of its greatness'. As for Luis Lasso de la Vega, chaplain at the shrine of Guadalupe, he roundly exclaimed that he felt like Adam, waking up to find that the Lord Almighty had given him a helpmate. 'I and my predecessors have been sleeping Adams, possessing this second Eve in the paradise of the Mexican Guadalupe.' So stirred was he by the work of Sánchez, whom he saluted as 'the most fortunate creole of all our nation' that in the following year Lasso de la Vega published a short account in Nahuatl of the apparitions and subsequent miracles effected by the image. In simple but poetic language, he told much the same story, but stripped the narrative of all exegesis. About the only noticeable difference was that he described the flowers gathered by Juan Diego as roses of Castile and added a number of miraculous cures. His text also revealed that after listening to a sermon preached by Fr Toribio de Motolinia, the Franciscan missionary, Juan Diego henceforth lived chastely with his wife, serving in the chapel at Tepeyac until his death in 1548.[3]

In the years which followed, sermons, poems and treatises were composed in honour of Our Lady of Guadalupe, the overlapping elite of the cathedral chapter and the university taking the lead. In 1662 Carlos de Sigüenza y Góngora, the greatest Mexican savant of the seventeenth century, wrote an elaborate poem entitled *Primavera indiana* in which he chanted with a superabundance of Gongoresque conceits the innocent charms of the Mexican Virgin, newly appeared in the land of eternal spring. At much the same time, Dr Luis Becerra Tanco (1603–72), professor of mathematics and astrology, published an account of the apparitions entitled *Felicidad de México* (1666, 1675) in which he collated the Spanish and Nahuatl versions and sought to provide some historical substantiation of the story. In 1666 he accompanied two learned canons of the cathedral, Dr Francisco de Siles and Dr Antonio de Gama, on a visit to Cuautitlán to ascertain from elderly villagers whether there survived any local memories of Juan Diego and the apparitions. The aim here was to discover materials which could be presented at Rome, since Siles subsequently led a mission to obtain permission to transfer the feast of Guadalupe from September, where it fell within the Octave of the Feast of Our Lady's Nativity, to 12 December within the Octave of the Feast of the Immaculate Conception.[4] The sheer rapidity with which the cult gained ground was noted by the Jesuit provincial and historian, Francisco de Florencia (1620–95) who in *La Estrella del norte de México* (1688) exclaimed that every town and house in New Spain had a copy of the image. So great was the demand that at Tepeyac there was a resident artist with no other task than to paint such copies.[5] Then again, in the 1670s Dr Isidro Sariñana, a cathedral canon with a reputation as a preacher, joined with Francisco de Siles to raise funds to construct a pilgrim highway to the sanctuary lined with impressive stations or oratories commemorating the fifteen mysteries of the rosary, a costly work which took over ten years to complete. By then a side chapel in the cathedral of Mexico had been dedicated to Our Lady of Guadalupe.[6]

Evidence of the progress of the cult outside the capital can be obtained from *Glorias de Querétaro* (1680) a pamphlet written by Carlos de Sigüenza y Góngora, who confessed that it was not until 1659 that a copy of the image had been brought to the city, commenting: 'a strange case this, that being the Most Holy Mary of Guadalupe the unique and suave magnet of devoted Americans and for Querétaro then to lack her image'. It was the seemingly ubiquitous Francisco de Siles, 'the glory of our nation and patria', who was summoned to preach a sermon to inaugurate the cult in the city.[7] Thereafter, in 1669 a congregation of secular priests was organised under the patronage of the Mexican Virgin and funds raised to construct a handsome church in her honour, the consecration of which in 1680 was marked by extravagant festivities, all faithfully recorded by Sigüenza y Góngora. Querétaro was by no means unique ints newfound devotion and thereafter chapels dedicated to Our Lady of Guadalupe were erected in San Luis Potosí, Oaxaca, Tlaxcala, Chihuahua and Zacatecas. In the course of the eighteenth century the leading cities and most towns of New Spain all established sanctuaries, usually situated *extra muros*, just beyond the limits of urban settlement, linked by a pilgrim way, thus sited in replication of the distance between Tepeyac and Mexico City.

The next important step came in the years 1695–1709 when a handsome new church was built at Tepeyac at an estimated cost of half a million pesos, monies readily subscribed by wealthy laymen and the diocesan treasury. The image was now housed in a sanctuary which rivalled in scale and splendour all but the greatest cathedrals of New Spain. Nor was this the end to the enlargement of the shrine since in the 1780s the current archbishop, Alonso de Haro, established a convent of Capuchin nuns next to the church and in the years 1777–91 presided over the construction of a stylish, octagonal chapel known as the Pocito. Prior to these edifices, devoted benefactors had created a fund, eventually worth over half a million pesos, to finance the foundation of a college of canons to officiate at the sanctuary. The project was delayed by disputes over jurisdiction, the archbishop insisting on his traditional role as patron, so that it was only in 1751 that the college, comprising an abbot and sixteen canons and prebends, was formally installed, the only example of such an institution, common enough in Europe, to be found in New Spain.[8]

A key influence in the development of the cult was the commitment of Juan Antonio de Vizarrón y Eguiarreta, archbishop of Mexico 1730–47 and viceroy of New Spain 1730–40, to whom fell the privilege of presiding over the bicentennial celebrations of the apparitions. But his patronage would have been to no avail had not popular devotion mounted to new heights during the great plague of 1737 which carried off no less than 40,000 victims in the capital alone. In the *Escudo de armas de México* (1746) Cayetano Javier de Cabrera y Quintero described the terrible scenes enacted in the city as both religious communities and confraternities paraded their images through the streets in an attempt to allay popular fears and beseech heaven's assistance. Both Jesuits and Franciscans vied to care for the sick, distributing food and soup, since 'of the innumerable people struck down by fever, most were beset by hunger and lack of care'. The practice of using churches as burial vaults meant that they were soon filled with bodies, creating 'an intolerable stench' so that the authorities were obliged to open new cemeteries. The climax of all attempts to procure Divine intervention came in March 1737 when the image from Tepeyac was ceremonially paraded through the streets, installed in the cathedral, and there formally acclaimed by the City Council of Mexico as their patron, Vizarrón y Eguiarreta in his dual capacity as archbishop and viceroy presiding over the ceremony. The cathedral chapter equally swore homage and in the months which followed the councils of such leading provincial cities as Puebla, Guadalajara and San Luis Potosí also proclaimed the Mexican Virgin as their patron. This sequence reached a grand conclusion in December 1746 when, led by the ailing Vizarrón y Eguiarreta, delegates of all the dioceses of New Spain met to acclaim Our Lady of Guadalupe as their universal patron, a decision which was ratified by the Holy See in 1754.[9] Within the course of a century, the

creole Virgin had thus risen from obscurity to a rank where she could be said to
rival the most celebrated Marian images in Europe.

By the eighteenth century countless copies of Our Lady of Guadalupe were
painted, with famous artists such as Miguel Cabrera competing to demonstrate
their skill in capturing an exact likeness. Orthodox devotion did not allow any
variation on the central image of a young girl standing on a crescent moon
supported by an angel with wings outstretched, her figure enveloped in an
aureoled niche of a hundred rays, her face 'silvery brown' in colour, surmounted by a crown of twelve rays symbolic of stars. Only in the surrounding
space, left vacant in the original, did artists employ their imagination, often
depicting in each corner of the canvas the apparition scenes, and lining the sides
with cherubic angels. It also became the fashion to inscribe on the painting the
famous words, invoked by Pope Benedict XIV: *non fecit taliter omni nationi* (It
was not done thus to all nations), a phrase which captured the singularly
patriotic character of the cult.[10]

II

In his *Monarquía indiana*, Juan de Torquemada lamented that the earthly
remains of Martín de Valencia, the saintly leader of the Franciscan mission to
Mexico, had been lost and that few public miracles were associated with his
name. He concluded that if the spiritual conquest had not been greatly
furthered by miracles, it was because the Indians, moved inwardly by the Holy
Spirit, had readily accepted the Christian gospel.[11] A different explanation was
advanced by Juan de Grijalva, the Augustinian chronicler, who argued that
whereas the primitive Church had required miracles because the Apostles were
poor, ignorant men confronted with all the pride and learning of the Romans
and Jews, by contrast, in America 'the preacher was in all things superior to the
Indians' and hence stood in no need of supernatural assistance.[12] What
obviously preoccupied both men was that the heroic labours of the first
mendicants were passing into oblivion: no friar had been canonised, no tombs
housed relics which attracted popular devotion, and their writings lay unpublished. In part, the erosion of once-cherished reputations derived from the
emergence of a new Church in Mexico, based on the structures laid down by
the Council of Trent, which implicitly rejected any special role for Mexico
within the spiritual economy of the universal Church. By the early seventeenth
century it was an institution dominated at all levels other than that of bishop by
the creole secular clergy, who increasingly viewed friars from the Peninsula as
interlopers. Even within the religious orders the partisan conflict between
creoles and gachupines led to a certain distancing from the dedicated founders of
each province. In short, the spiritual and intellectual leaders of the creole clergy
had come to regard the triumphalism of the spiritual conquest as an embarrass-

ment, since it depicted the foundation of the Mexican Church as a missionary endeavour which had established an overseas replication of the Church in Spain.

It was to assert and demonstrate the independent, spiritual vitality of their Church that the Mexican clergy thirsted for miracles. Had not St Augustine in the closing pages of the *City of God* proclaimed the cures wrought at the tombs of martyrs in North Africa as a sure sign that the Holy Spirit dwelt among the Christian people and that the miracles described in the New Testament still continued?[13] In late antiquity the relics of saints, holy bishops and martyrs aroused increasing veneration, their tombs often enclosed in great basilicas to which pilgrims flocked from afar. Each city came to possess a spiritual patron whose cult was the source of civic pride and the vehicle of corporate solidarity. Christians crowded to touch and beseech the physical relics of holy men, which were thought to embody the spiritual power of heaven, a permanent earthly guarantee of heaven's intervention in the everyday world.[14] In Spain the presumed tomb of St James the Apostle, housed at Compostella, emerged as the spiritual rallying point for the Christian states which fought to halt the Moorish onslaught. Throughout the long centuries of the reconquest, Santiago served as both patron and battle cry of Christian Spain, his shrine a major centre of pilgrimage and a living proof of the apostolic foundation of the Spanish Church.[15] That Santiago was thought to have intervened in the conquest of America, protecting the Spaniards from Indian attack, only served to confirm his role in the militant Catholicism of Castile.

It was from the power of holy images, however, rather than from the relics of holy men, that Spaniards of the Habsburg era most expected miracles to flow. The source of this cult was the Eastern Church whose theologians employed concepts taken from neo-Platonic philosophy to define orthodox icons as 'a likeness of that of which it is the image, in itself showing by imitation the character of its archetype ... the true in the likeness, the archetype in the image'. St Basil the Great wrote: 'What the word transmits through the ear, the painting silently shows through the image ... by these two means, mutually accompanying one another ... we receive knowledge of one and the same thing.' As much as scripture, the icons of Christ and of Mary, the Mother of God, taught the central truths of the incarnation, 'expressive of the silence of God'. When iconoclasts attacked the cult as idolatrous, orthodox theologians defended sacred images as consonant with the doctrines of the incarnation of the Divine Word and of the real presence of Christ in the eucharist.[16] Moreover, the conventional and hieratic portrayals of Christ and his mother were assumed to derive from the Apostolic foundations of the Church and certain images came to be invested with miraculous powers.

In all this there was nothing to shock a Spanish theologian. For although the Latin Church appears to have indulged in little theological speculation over religious paintings and sculptures, content to define them simply as representations whose purpose was to remind worshippers of their heavenly originals, during the late Middle Ages an entire world of miraculous images was created and venerated. In Spain any number of images of the Virgin Mary came to be housed in splendid sanctuaries, the object of pilgrimage and fervent prayer. By far the most venerable of such figures was Our Lady of Pilar at Zaragoza, an image, so it was alleged, brought by the Virgin Mary herself when she accompanied Santiago on his journey to Spain. Other images, such as the famous Virgins of Monserrat in Cataluña, and Guadalupe and Peña de Francia in Extremadura, were found in hill-side caves by herdsmen or shepherds to whom the Virgin Mary had appeared. In the case of Our Lady of Guadalupe, the figure was thought to have been carved by St Luke, then brought to Rome, only later to be despatched by Pope Gregory the Great to St Leandro, archbishop of Seville. Hidden in a cave to escape Muslim desecration, it was discovered in the fourteenth century by a shepherd following the instructions of the Virgin. Virtually all these famous images in Spain were wooden figures of Mary as Mother of God, seated enthroned with the Divine Child in her arms, the texture of the wood blackened by age and candle-smoke.[17] Far from mere representations, such images existed in their own right, so to say, as material conduits of numinous power, which could decisively affect the minds and bodies of pilgrims who came to pray for assistance. Such was the prestige of their sanctuaries that kings and nobles vied to endow them with estates and adorn their churches with rich offerings, a reminder that there was nothing merely popular about cults which joined priests and people, lords and commoners in common devotion.

As was to be expected, the conquerors of the New World brought images with them, often carrying small figures of the Virgin Mary attached to their saddles. Such indeed was the faith of Cortés in the silent witness and inherent power of Christian images that he installed statues of the Virgin in Indian temples both at Tlaxcala and Tenochtitlan, commanding the pagan priesthood to offer them all due honour. Once the conquest was completed, the Spaniards imported a great mass of paintings and sculptures, often ordering copies of the most famous images in the Peninsula. Thus, the powerful, tortured Christ of Burgos was frequently copied and, once brought over, the model for further copies. In contrast to Cortés, however, the first Franciscans in New Spain actively discouraged the veneration of images among their native flock, fearing the evident danger of confusion between pagan idols and Christian statues. Their attitude was also influenced by the Erasmian critique of the late medieval cult of saints' images as mere superstition and as a corruption of the primitive Church's simple worship. Indeed, in his *Regla cristiana breve* Juan de Zumárraga declared that the true Christian had no need to enliven his faith by recourse to such material objects.[18] However, by the first years of the seventeenth century it was clear that Indian religion had come to centre on Christian images as spiritual patrons, devotion to whom became an expression of corporate solidarity. By 1624 Juan de Grijalva observed that the natives were 'extreme in the cult and reverence of images', since each house and family possessed their own altar with a crucifix and various figures of the Virgin Mary and saints. Similarly, each village and its wards had their own patrons which were duly paraded through the streets on their feast-days, during Holy Week and on Corpus Christi.[19] In every region certain images became renowned for their powers to effect cures, often of a miraculous character, and so attracted pilgrims. There was nothing particularly Indian in all this, since the Spanish community and its mestizo and mulatto offspring exhibited an equally strong devotion, so that once an image acquired a reputation for effecting cures, it attracted pilgrims and devotees from all sectors and classes of the colonial population.

The most celebrated image in Mexico at the beginning of the seventeenth century was Our Lady of Los Remedios, a small figure of the Virgin and child, obviously brought over by the conquerors as a 'saddle-image'. Indeed, a similar figure, venerated in Puebla, was known as *la Conquistadora*. In 1621 Luis Cisneros, a Mercedarian friar and university professor, published an account in which he asserted that in all probability the Los Remedios image had been installed by Cortés in the great temple of Huitzilopochtli, only then to be lost or hidden when the Spaniards fled from Tenochtitlan during the *noche triste*. Some time after the conquest, the Virgin Mary appeared to an Indian noble named Juan Tovar, who on her instruction discovered the image hidden on a hill which had once served as the site of a pagan temple. In 1552 or thereabouts, Tovar fell ill, visited the shrine of Our Lady of Guadalupe at Tepeyac, and at her command built a small chapel at Naucalpan, just outside the capital, to house the Spanish image he had found, entrusting its care to the Franciscans at Tlacupa. But the building soon fell into disrepair, and in 1574 a new chapter in the history of the cult began when a wealthy city councillor of Mexico erected a handsome new chapel, formed a confraternity to maintain it, and persuaded the City Council to adopt Our Lady of Los Remedios as its Marian patron. By this time the image had become renowned not merely for miraculous cures but also for its power to bring rain when needed. In the drought years of 1577, 1597 and 1616, the image was taken from her sanctuary in formal procession to the cathedral to beseech heaven's assistance for this purpose. Indeed, it was to commemorate the notable success of its last sally that Cisneros wrote his book, at pains to describe the great parade through the streets, the image accompanied by the massed confraternities and secular clergy, the climax in the cathedral marked by sermons and prayers led by the archbishop. Sure enough, nine days later, the seasonal rain-clouds burst on the expectant capital with all their customary force.[20]

In a description of Marian images in or about Mexico City, Luis Cisneros observed that 'The oldest is that of Guadalupe, which is some leagues from this City to the North, and which is an image of great devotion and attendance, almost since this land was won, which has made and still makes miracles, and for whom a distinguished church is being built which, at the order and care of the archbishop, is almost completed.'[21] The earliest documentary account of this celebrated Mexican Virgin derives from 1554 when Archbishop Alonso de Montufar, the successor of Zumárraga, caused the chapel or hermitage at Tepeyac to be rebuilt, deprived the Franciscans of its care on grounds of neglect, and installed a secular priest as chaplain. The following year he preached a sermon at the sanctuary in praise of Our Lady of Guadalupe at Tepeyac, justifying her cult by allusion to such Marian shrines in Spain as Monserrat, Guadalupe, and Peña de Francia. In this context, it should be noted that Montufar had assisted the Inquisition in proceedings against a leading Erasmian cleric in Seville; in seeking to promote devotion to an image of the Virgin Mary he exhibited his commitment to the maintenance of medieval modes of worship favoured by the Counter-Reformation.[22] He was soon to become embroiled with the mendicants on their refusal to allow Indians to pay tithes to the bishops and their cathedral chapters. Moreover, on this occasion, his sermon elicited a fierce response from the Franciscan provincial, Francisco de Bustamante, who attacked the Marian cult at Tepeyac as a subterfuge for idolatry, arguing that Indians went to the shrine in order to worship their native goddess. For it was well known that Tepeyac had been the site of a substantial temple dedicated to Teotenantzin, 'Mother of the Gods', much frequented by pilgrims, Furthermore, Bustamante claimed that 'an image painted but yesterday by an Indian' named Marcos had been placed in the chapel and was already the object of miracle-mongering.[23] Nor could he adduce any reason as to why the chapel and its image should be called after Guadalupe rather than Tepeyac. It will be recalled that Sahagún in his monumental study of native culture also criticised the cult of Our Lady of Guadalupe as suspect, offering a cloak to the continuance of pagan worship and pilgrimage.[24] Despite these mendicant attacks, derived in good measure both from their Erasmian sympathies and their practical knowledge of Indian religion, the painting at Tepeyac soon came to attract Spanish as well as native devotion, with miraculous cures a sure sign of its inherent power. It was not until 1629, however, that it was accorded the honour of a formal procession from its sanctuary to the cathedral, when its intercession was invoked to lower the great floods which then threatened the very survival of the capital on its island site.

The distinctive feature of the cult at Guadalupe – the name referred as much to the place as to the image – was the story of the miraculous origin of the painting. After all, the Virgin Mary was thought to have appeared both to many herdsmen in Spain and to Indians in Mexico. Most images, invariably carved statues of the Virgin and child, had been discovered in hill-side caves and soon became renowned for their cures and consolations. The story of Los Remedios retailed to Cisneros followed the Spanish pattern with remarkable fidelity. Elsewhere in Mexico and Peru, Marian images were copies brought over from the Peninsula or were carved locally by Indian sculptors. In Spain the great images were generally thought to be of Apostolic provenance, with St Luke recognised as author of the Guadalupe image in Extremadura. The singularity of the Mexican Guadalupe thus consisted in the miraculous impression of the Virgin's image on a poor Indian's cape, the delicate grace of the portrait a haunting testimony of its unique status.

But whence came the story of Juan Diego and Our Lady of Guadalupe? In the case of Los Remedios, Cisneros admitted that the origin of all miraculous images was obscure, but cited the testimony of Juan Tovar's aged daughter. For Miguel Sánchez, writing some 116 years after the apparitions at Tepeyac, there was no such crutch on which to rest: he failed to encounter any written sources and had to rely on oral tradition preserved at the sanctuary. Only for miracles effected by the image was there the evidence of *ex-voto* tablets placed on the walls of the chapel in thanksgiving. Nor did Luis Lasso de la Vega in his Nahuatl version of the story offer any suggestion of prior sources. In consequence, it fell to the savants of the next cycle of publications, which is to say, to Becerra Tanco, Florencia and Sigüenza y Góngora to trace the story past Sánchez back into the sixteenth century. In the second edition of the *Felicidad de México*, revised by Antonio de Gama, Becerra Tanco fixed upon the College of Santa Cruz Tlatelolco as the source of the account in Nahuatl published by Lasso de la Vega, attributing it to Antonio Valeriano, the leading collaborator of Sahagún, the master of Torquemada, and governor of San Juan Tenochtitlan for over thirty years. Moreover, he claimed to have seen the original manuscripts in the possession of a descendant of the kings of Texcoco, who had served as interpreter in the Indian Court, which is to say, Fernando de Alva Ixtlilxochitl, the mestizo historian and associate of Torquemada. Furthermore, he averred that several elderly priests had testified to the truth of the tradition as presented by Sánchez, including one who had heard Valeriano speak about the apparitions.[25] The next commentator, Francisco de Florencia, ascertained that the manuscript mentioned by Becerra Tanco was identical to the Nahuatl account printed by Lasso de la Vega. But he then confused the issue by ascribing its authorship to Jerónimo de Mendieta, the Franciscan chronicler.[26] It was this error which provoked Sigüenza y Góngora, who had been entrusted with Ixtlilxochitl's papers, to pre-empt all further discussion by resolutely affirming that 'the original in Mexican [Nahuatl] is in the letter of Don Antonio Valeriano, who is its true author ... and at the end some miracles in the letter of Don Fernando de Alva also in Mexican ... '.[27]

As yet, modern scholarship has failed to encounter the documentary evidence to prove that Valeriano wrote the original account in Nahuatl of the apparitions to Juan Diego. However, linguistic analysis of the text suggests that the core narrative is written in a classical, poetic style reminiscent of the moral orations recorded by Sahagun. It is doubtful whether a creole priest of the seventeenth century could have simulated such a style.[28] If this indeed be the case, then grounds exist for tracing the entire story back to native sources. Once more, the central role of the College of Santa Cruz Tlatelolco becomes apparent. For here was a group of native intellectuals, men trained in Spanish, Latin, and the rudiments of theology by the Franciscans, who assisted the mendicants translate into Nahuatl prayers, sermons, dramatic interludes and passages of scripture. As we have seen, Sahagún, Torquemada and Fr Juan Bautista all testified to their invaluable assistance, singling out Valeriano both for his knowledge of Latin and his mastery of classical Nahuatl. It was the same group who were probably responsible for the composition of Sahagún's dramatic portrayal of the Indian view of the Spanish conquest and the insistence that Moctezuma welcomed Cortés as Quetzalcoatl. What more striking affirmation of native worth than that the Virgin Mary should have appeared to a poor Indian only ten years after the conquest, assuring him that she would henceforth watch over Mexico as a mother over her children? That Ixtlilxochitl should have acquired the original text and added the section describing subsequent miracles is not improbable since he had studied under Valeriano and had composed Nahuatl hymns, based on the psalms, which he ascribed to Nezahualcoyotl.

III

If Miguel Sánchez (1594–1674) took the facts of the case – the apparitions to Juan Diego and the miraculous imprinting of the Virgin's image on his cape – as already established by tradition and hence in no need of historical substantiation, it was not because he was concerned to tell a simple pious story, designed to stir the hearts of the devout women and ignorant pilgrims. For he composed a densely argued, learned treatise, brimming with scriptural allusions, framed to persuade and illumine the minds of the learned and the great of this world. A well-known preacher, much respected for his knowledge of theology, his manifest piety and deep-seated patriotism, Sánchez chose not to pursue a career which might have brought him honours and promotion, resigning successively from his chaplaincies at the sanctuary of Our Lady of Los Remedios and at a wealthy convent of Jeronymite nuns. Instead, he devoted himself to the study of the works of St Augustine, solitary prayer and attendance at the shrine of Guadalupe.[29] His book was 'a child of silence', evoked by sustained contemplation of an icon in which he came to perceive the very form and essence of the Virgin Mary. If his mode of argument was to appear to later generations extravagant and forced, it was because he wrote as if possessed by a single, blinding idea. In effect, Sánchez employed his knowledge of patristic theology and contemporary biblical exegesis to compose a work which must rank among the most original and daring ever penned by a Mexican author during the colonial period.

It was from St Augustine that Sánchez took his figural approach to biblical history and the Guadalupe narrative. Both in the *City of God* and in his biblical commentaries, the African doctor had interpreted the events and characters of the Old Testament as prophetic 'figures' of Christ, the Church and the New Testament. In this scheme, Noah's Ark became a figure of the Christian Church; Aaron the high-priest, of the Catholic priesthood; the quarrel between Esau and Jacob of the division between Jews and Christians; and Moses a foreshadowing of Christ. Thus two historical persons or events were invoked to explain each other, standing in mutual relation as prophecy and fulfilment, with interpretation reaching both forwards and backwards across the centuries of sacred history. The figural mode of interpreting Christian doctrines enjoyed considerable vogue during the Middle Ages, where it constituted an intellectual premise of Dante's *Divine Comedy*.[30] But whereas St Augustine had defined Christ's incarnation as the complete fulfilment of biblical prophecy, thus depriving Church history of any theological significance other than as a period of expectant anxiety, overshadowed by the prospect of the Last Day and Second Advent of Christ, by contrast Joachim de Fiore extended the figural scheme to include current or imminent events, asserting that the progress of the Christian Church was charged with as much theological significance as the history of the Jews.[31] It was the millennial ideas generated by the application of biblical prophecies to contemporary events which drove Columbus forth across the Atlantic and inspired Motolinia to interpret the conversion of the Indians as a prelude to the Last Age. In short, the method of exegesis bequeathed by St Augustine to the Latin Church was invoked to sustain an approach to Christian history completely at variance with his own distaste for apocalyptic enthusiasm.

The vital premise of Sánchez' interpretation of the Guadalupe image was St Augustine's argument that the woman who figures in chapter 12 of the Apocalypse should be identified as the Virgin Mary. It will be recalled that St John describes a woman heavy with child 'clothed with the sun and the moon under her feet, and upon her head a crown of twelve stars', engaged in fierce battle with a seven-headed dragon, which is to say, Satan, from whom she fled to a desert supported by 'two wings of a great eagle'. In a startling extension of this commonly accepted figural identity, Sánchez declared that the image perceived in prophetic vision by the evangelist on Patmos was precisely the same image and likeness of the Virgin Mary which had been imprinted on Juan Diego's cape at Tepeyac. In obvious excitement, he invited his readers to contemplate 'the original by prophecy in the image of heaven, and the copy

(*transumpto*) by miracle in the image of earth'.[32] The image which St John had
described in mere words had been imparted by the Virgin in a painting, which
as much as any Greek icon silently taught the same Divine message, the vision
on Patmos thus figure and prophecy of the revelation at Tepeyac.

After this bold affirmation, Sánchez did not hesitate to set out its implications, extending his figural applications to magnify yet further his beloved
icon. The image at Guadalupe was hailed as a new ark of the covenant, as an
expression of Divine power equal to the burning bush seen by Moses in Sinai.
That the image first appeared among the flowers gathered in Juan Diego's cape
suggested a far-fetched comparison with Aaron's rod, which, alone among
those belonging to the twelve Tribes, flowered as a symbol of his priestly
vocation. Surely, Sánchez concluded, since the Guadalupe image was the only
likeness of Mary known to have appeared among flowers, then like Aaron's rod
it was especially chosen and indeed might be said to enjoy 'the supreme dignity
of miracle and the primacy of miracles'. By reason of the circumstances of its
origin, the Mexican Virgin was thus the greatest image of Mary in all
Christendom. In the light of these declarations, it comes as no surprise that
Mexicans should have subsequently gloried in the phrase *Non fecit taliter omni
nationi*: which other Christian people had been so honoured? In effect, Sánchez
presented the Spanish conquest as inaugurating a new epoch in Church history,
when the Mother of God offered to the people of Mexico a perfect image of
herself as testimony of her enduring protection. All this led to the conclusion
that Mexico was to become 'a new city of Jerusalem, a city of peace', the Virgin
celebrated as a second Eve intent on founding 'a new paradise'.[33]

Within this frame of interpretation, the seven-headed Dragon of the
Apocalypse was taken to represent the 'imperial monarchy' of Tenochtitlan,
the realm of idolatry, where seven kings paid tribute to the Mexican emperor.
Providence had chosen the Catholic Kings of Castile to effect the conquest and
conversion of the New World, an asseveration which Sánchez further fortified
by saluting Philip II as another Solomon, and as 'a universal Planet Sun' called
to govern the world. In an unlikely metaphor, Cortés and his band were
depicted as an army of angels engaged in cosmic battle against Satan and his
demonic legion. Not that mere human effort sufficed to extirpate the Devil's
influence, since from the outset Mexico 'received the light of the gospel from
the hands of the Virgin Mary, Mother of God, auxiliary conqueror'.[34] Who
could doubt that the rapid disappearance of idolatry in New Spain sprang from
the direct intervention of Mary? As Lasso de la Vega explained, the Virgin had
appeared so as 'to introduce and strengthen the faith which the venerable sons
of St Francis had started to preach'. For Sánchez, however, the final purpose
and significance of the conquest was that it opened the way for the apparitions,
exclaiming that it was 'in this land of Mexico, conquered for such glorious
ends, gained . . . that such an image of God should appear'.[35]

The role of Juan Diego was also found to possess figural meaning, since his conversations with the Virgin Mary at Tepeyac were magnified by comparison with Moses listening to the word of God on Mount Sinai. Were not the ten commandments inscribed on the stone tablets a figure of the likeness of the Mother of God imprinted on Juan Diego's cape? That a poor, ignorant Indian should have been chosen as prophet of the new dispensation only further served to illumine the Christian, not to say Franciscan, quality of the story. As for Zumárraga, Sánchez hailed him as another King David who had placed the new ark of the covenant in its temple on the Mexican Mount Zion at Tepeyac. More suitably, the bishop was also designated as the heir of St Peter, the guardian of authority in the Church, as contrasted to Juan Diego to whom, like his apostolic namesake, had been entrusted care of the Virgin Mary. Noting that the actual miracle had occurred in the bishop's palace, Sánchez inevitably named Zumárraga as another Aaron, commenting: 'To the dignity of bishop, in that prelate God added the estate and patronage of the hermitage of Guadalupe, which until today his illustrious successors possess.' As chief guardian of the sanctuary and its image, the archbishop of Mexico thus enjoyed undisputed primacy over his fellow bishops in New Spain.[36] Both Sánchez and Lasso de la Vega took care to pay tribute to the patronage of the current archbishop, Juan de Manosca.

As weft to warp, Sánchez' fervid religiosity was interwoven with an insistent patriotism, leading him to salute the Guadalupe as 'this prodigious woman and sacred *criolla*'. That the Virgin's likeness was imprinted on a native cape made from cactus fibre signified that it was 'an image which originated in this land and is its primitive *criolla*'. It comes as no surprise to read his familiar plaint that strangers and newcomers (*advenedizos*) of suspect creeds had arrived in Mexico, men whom the Inquisition should invigilate lest they corrupt the faith of the ignorant. At the same time, he surmised that the creoles could be compared to the children of Israel wandering through the desert for forty years, caught between Egypt and the Promised Land.[37] In this context, the figure of the Guadalupe image as the Mexican ark of the covenant acquires a new relevance, especially if it be observed that Sánchez commended it as 'a perpetual entailed estate', an inherited testimony that the Mother of God had chosen Mexico as her patria, so that all Mexicans, no matter what their race or class, could claim her as their countrywoman and patron, bound in enduring covenant. One consequence of Sánchez fixing on the patriotic significance of the Guadalupe was that he mounted a subtle critique of Our Lady of Los Remedios, complaining that whereas the creole image had only been brought into the capital on one occasion, the gachupín image had been so honoured on various occasions. Once more the Old Testament provided a figure, when he compared the two images to Ruth and Naomi, which is to say, to the Moabitess and the Israelite, the stranger and the native.[38]

The powerful impact of Sánchez' doctrine can be best observed in the comments proffered by the learned priests who acted as the censors and commentators of his treatise. Francisco de Siles not merely celebrated the Mexican Virgin as 'our sovereign *criolla* and most holy Mother', he also delved into the Bible to fetch out the story of Esther and Mordechai, who, it will be remembered, had saved the Jews from the persecution of their enemies in Persia, a figure which led him to hail the Guadalupe image as 'another Esther, our head and queen, to whom all those born in this land will ever look for protection and patronage'. More obscurely, Francisco de Bárcenas, who announced himself as a friend of Sánchez for many years, expressed fears that a Jonah might soon appear to denounce the new-found felicity of Mexico, envious of the prosperity of the new Nineveh.[39] Yet more revealing were the comments of Mateo de la Cruz, a Jesuit who in 1660 published a simplified version of the apparition story, since he bluntly contrasted the two great Marian images of Mexico, defining Los Remedios as endowed with power over rain and Guadalupe with power over floods, 'calling that image the conqueror and *gachupina* because it came with the Spanish conquerors, and this image the *criolla*, since it appeared miraculously in this land, where it had its origin in flowers'. Nor did he hesitate to exalt the Mexican Virgin over her Spanish namesake, since the statue in Extremadura had been carved by St Luke, whereas the painting at Tepeyac had been limned by God, or by the Virgin, or, at the very least, by an angel.[40]

It was Cruz who first commented that viewed within the frame of Marian iconography the Guadalupe image was an Immaculate Conception, or, to use the current Spanish term, a *Purísima*, a class of paintings in which the Virgin Mary was invariably depicted without her child as the woman of the Apocalypse, crowned with stars, astride the moon, supported by angels, and often trampling a serpent or dragon. That the apparitions occurred during the octave of the feast of the Immaculate Conception pointed to the same conclusion. The implications of this observation are all-important for the historical interpretation of the painting. For it was not until the close of the sixteenth century that it became at all common in Spain to portray the Virgin Mary in her advocation of the Immaculate Conception. If an Indian artist called Marcos had painted the image in 1554, on what European model did he base his portrait? Alternatively, if the heavenly origin of the image be accepted, then it follows that as early as 1531 the Mother of God had intervened to intimate that she was henceforth to be venerated as the Immaculate Conception. Finally, it should be noted that it was precisely in the first decades of the seventeenth century that the entire hispanic world was roused to public acclamation of the doctrine of 'Mary without spot'.[41]

Surprisingly little doctrinal development in the interpretation of the

Guadalupe story and image occurred after the primordial exegesis of Sánchez. Indeed, his book was not republished during the colonial period and his figural approach was quietly ignored by both Becerra Tanco and Florencia. In the eighteenth century it became an embarrassment. Not that enthusiasm waned, since Florencia exclaimed that the sanctuary at Tepeyac was 'a holy land' which exuded 'an odour of sanctity' more potent than any he had encountered at Marian shrines in Europe, even including the holy house at Loreto. He offered thanks to Mary for 'your miraculous image of Guadalupe, which bound the Devil and in all this Mexican New World drowned the seven-headed dragon of idolatry'. So also, he saluted the Virgin as 'reborn in her image and through her image in this flourishing Christendom of the Mexican empire, amidst the flowers of Guadalupe, in her new Nazareth and patria of the Indies', a trope which led him to boast of 'the land of promise of Mexico'.[42]

The most pointed elucidation of the political bias of Sánchez' work was provided by Jerónimo de Valladolid, chaplain at Tepeyac, who in his prologue to Florencia's book chose to emphasise that the Guadalupe was 'an image born in the palace . . . ' He further noted that the current archbishop, Francisco de Aguiar Seixas y Ulloa, had taken Our Lady of Guadalupe as his patron and had displayed as his coat of arms 'this miraculous sign which gives most credit to his pastoral office'. Moreover, Valladolid observed that if the archbishop possessed Aaron's rod by virtue of being high priest, then Moses' rod was wielded by the corregidor and city council of Mexico. At this stage, it should come as no surprise to learn that if the Guadalupe image was the figural embodiment of Aaron's rod, Los Remedios exemplified Moses' staff of office. On a more general level, Valladolid referred to the Guadalupe painting as 'this hieroglyphic writing', arguing that since the Mexican Indians had preserved their traditions in pictures rather than in script, it was only appropriate that the Virgin should communicate with them by means of a visual rather than a verbal message. Once more, the point was made that whereas St John had related his vision in written words, in Mexico the Virgin had offered her new patria a copy of the very image witnessed by the Apostle.[43] Here was a line of argument remarkably reminiscent of the terms in which Byzantine theologians defended the veneration accorded to icons.

It was in poetry and sermons that the theological implications of Sánchez' theses found full expression. In a skilful variation on a Franciscan theme, Sigüenza y Góngora boldly contrasted the descent of Northern Europe into the dark winter of heresy with the springtide apparition of Our Lady of Guadalupe in North America, a sure sign that the mystical journey of the Church continued ever westward.[44] Another poet echoed Sánchez in hailing Juan Diego as another Moses and Tepeyac as 'the Mexican Horeb', and concluded:

That in New Spain
From another John we hear
Of a new Apocalypse
Although the Revelations are distinct.

In a further flight, one pious author suggested that the image Moses perceived in the burning bush was none other than the Guadalupe.[45] It was now confidently asserted that if the Virgin Mary had dwelt temporarily in the flesh at Nazareth, she had now come to take up permanent residence in her image of Guadalupe. Indeed, Bartolomé de Ita y Parra, a well-known preacher of the eighteenth century, declaimed: 'The image that came to earth to incarnate the Word appeared as the original of this other image that Mary formed and allowed to be seen in Guadalupe.' In short, the icon at Tepeyac was a faithful representation of how the Virgin Mary appeared in the flesh in Palestine. The more creole preachers dwelt on the relation between material image and spiritual reality, the more they were led to a comparison between the Holy Eucharist and the Guadalupe, a path already explored by Greek theologians in their defence against iconoclasm. If the miracle of transubstantiation daily enacted at the Catholic mass changed the sacramental bread and wine into the flesh and blood of Christ, had not the miracle at Tepeyac changed Juan Diego's cape into the image of the Virgin Mary? In a convoluted passage, one preacher sought to justify such a comparison by arguing that the image was 'in certain fashion sacramental, since at first sight the painting appears as an *ayatl*, but it appears that it is not what it appears, since beneath these accidents of material and colour, there is formed in this miraculous frame one that is singular, wonderful and similar to Christ in his divine sacrament'. From this bold statement it was but a short step to affirm that if the Old Testament was given for the Jews, and the New Testament served as the foundation of the Church, then the Virgin Mary had been revealed in the Guadalupe so as to assure the salvation of the peoples of the New World.[46] The third epoch in the universal progress of the City of God had thus been initiated in Mexico under the auspices of Our Lady of Guadalupe.

IV

In an eloquent contrast between medieval and modern civilisation, the American historian, Henry Adams, defined their different sources of power as the Virgin and the dynamo, and concluded: 'An American Virgin would never dare command; an American Venus would never dare exist.' Alas, like so many of his compatriots, Adams knew next to nothing about the Catholic civilisation that flourished in Mexico at a time when New England had barely time to sink roots in North America.[47] Even so, he might have heard that when in 1810 the Mexican people rose in arms to liberate their country from Spanish rule, they marched under the banner of Our Lady of Guadalupe, whom they acclaimed as their mother and patron. Indeed, during the tormented upheaval of the Mexican Revolution, many peasant bands were still to be seen carrying the flag of the Mexican Virgin. If as yet no Mexican Venus has graced the stage of world history, Our Lady of Guadalupe has been recognised by the Holy See as Queen and Patron of America.

Viewed from an historical perspective, the cult of the Guadalupe image appears as a foundation myth. The Spanish conquest had been celebrated by Torquemada in his *Monarquía indiana* as the necessary prelude to the establishment of the mendicant Church. If the first Franciscans had interpreted the joyful conversion of the Mexican Indians as auguring the advent of the millennium, subsequent chroniclers invoked the missionary enterprise as confirmation of the providential mandate of the Catholic monarchy. At this level of spiritual discourse, myth could only be countered by myth. When the creole clergy greeted the revelations of Sánchez with enthusiasm and propagated the cult of the Guadalupe with such zeal, it was in large measure because it provided them with an autonomous, sacred foundation for their Church and country. In effect, the image preserved and venerated at the holy mount of Tepeyac was the Mexican ark of the covenant, a promise of election, a sign that henceforth the Virgin Mary would act as the especial protector of the Mexican people. The cult both united Indians and creoles, rich and poor, in common devotion and served to strengthen the primacy of Mexico and its archbishop over the scattered dioceses of New Spain. Obviously, to comprehend the initial enthusiasm aroused by the image, it is necessary to delve into the devotional world of post-Tridentine Catholicism where the material embodiments of Christian dogmas – the crucifix, the images of the saints, and the very Eucharist – loomed so large in public liturgy and individual prayer. But the subsequent progress of the Guadalupe cult derived from its inextricable intertwining of religious fervour with patriotic enthusiasm. Sharply divided by race, class, customs and even language, the inhabitants of New Spain had little more to bind them together than their common identity as children and subjects of the Mother of God. The last word is best given to Ignacio Manuel Altamirano, a typical, anti-clerical, liberal ideologue of the nineteenth century, who confessed that only before Our Lady of Guadalupe, 'the national deity', did Mexicans stand united and on equal terms: 'It is equality before the Virgin; it is the national idolatry . . . in the last extreme, in the most desperate cases, the cult of the Mexican Virgin is the only bond which unites them.'[48]

17

WESTERN PARADISE

I

IN 1680 the City Council of Mexico erected a triumphal arch to welcome the new viceroy, the Marquis of La Laguna. A grandiose wooden structure, ninety feet high and fifty feet wide, it complied with the rules of architecture, being divided into three levels supported by Corinthian pillars, with sixteen niched pedestals reserved for emblematic statues. Such edifices were a common enough feature of civic celebrations in the early modern period and illustrations still survive of arches designed by Albrecht Dürer in honour of Emperor Maximilian and by Fischer von Erlach for Emperor Charles VI. Loaded with statues and inscriptions, usually culled from classical mythology and history, the purpose of these monuments was as much to instruct as to celebrate, their message conveyed by literary allusion and visual image. As a contemporary savant explained: 'the symbolic doctrine (in which is comprised emblems, hieroglyphs and devices) is a science in which, with brief and comprehensive words, we express certain rare and varied mysteries, some taken from the sayings of the sages and others from histories'. In the Mexican case, the symbolism was remarkably explicit and overtly patriotic. In effect, the viceroy was enjoined to consider that the city he was about to govern had been founded in 1327 and had possessed a line of Indian monarchs prior to the Spanish conquest. The arch carried statues of all twelve Mexican monarchs and leaders, each taken to embody different political virtues. Whereas Huitzilihuitl was praised as a law-giver, the emperor Motecohzuma Ilhuicaminan was depicted as both a warrior and a protector of religion. The second Moctezuma, described as 'this absolute monarch', was commended for his liberality, and his unfortunate successor Cuitlahuitzin hailed for his efforts 'to defend liberty and the patria'. In this pantheon, Cuauhtémoc figured as a native Cato, ever constant in adversity. The entire symbolic structure expressed the hope that 'on some occasion the Mexican monarchs might be reborn from the ashes to which oblivion has consigned them, so that, like Western phoenixes, they may be immortalised by fame ... The heroic ... imperial virtues' of these rulers offered models of statecraft as inspiring as any ancient Roman or Greek, the Mexican past thus invested with the aura of a classical epoch and culture.[1]

Carlos de Sigüenza y Góngora (1645–1700), the author of the arch's design and the pamphlet which explained its meaning, was a Mexican patriot and the chief exponent in New Spain of the cosmological hermeticism of the Austrian Baroque. Professor of mathematics and astrology in the university of Mexico, as a young man he had been expelled from the Company of Jesus and thereafter supported himself by acting as chaplain of the Amor de Dios hospital. The son of a viceregal secretary, he was a distant relative of the Spanish poet, Luis de Góngora, whose latinate style he imitated in his *Primavera indiana*. Although he was widely acclaimed as a savant, delving into history with the same acuity with which he surveyed the heavens, Sigüenza failed to compose or publish anything other than occasional pamphlets, prompted by public commemorations, polemic or official commission. To compensate for the limited range of his own works, he encouraged and indeed inspired an entire circle of friends to write on patriotic themes. It was in part owing to Sigüenza's assistance that Becerra Tanco and Florencia composed their works on the Guadalupe and Agustín de Betancur his history of Mexico. His pre-eminence was freely confessed and Antonio de Gama praised him as 'the best flower of the paradise of letters of our America . . . ' Nor did he lack international recognition since in his *Giro del mondo* (1697–98), the Italian traveller, Giovanni Francesco Gemelli Careri, paid tribute both to his erudition and counsel.[2] He was favoured by the Count of Galve, viceroy of New Spain (1688–96), who financed the publication of several of his works. As much as Buenaventura de Salinas, Sigüenza sought at all points to exalt his patria but succeeded in infusing the common ideology of creole patriotism with a distinctively Mexican content.

The degree to which Sigüenza subscribed to the doctrines of Baroque hermeticism is manifest in his *Teatro de virtudes políticas* (1680) where he cited the Spanish Jesuit, Juan Eusebio Nieremberg as arguing that princes were the living souls of their realms, only then to advert to the opinion of Enrico Farnese, an Italian humanist, that a king was not so much a 'vicar of God' as his 'living image or an earthly god', lofty sentiments which were immediately qualified by St Augustine's admonitions as to the transience of all human dominion. Such a maze of conflicting opinions more served to magnify Sigüenza's erudition than to expose his own sentiments. Nevertheless, he reached to the same sources to justify his innermost convictions, when he quoted Farnese's dictum that 'the citizen is he who lives not for himself but for his patria'. It was to express his commitment to this cause that Sigüenza chose Pegasus, the winged horse of classical mythology, as his personal emblem, signifying 'a man who displays his soul always uplifted to the sublime, in service of his patria'. It was precisely 'this great love I have for my patria', which drove him to explore the Mexican past and style himself, quite simply, a 'Mexican priest'.[3] The urban patriotism of the Italian Renaissance was here quite divorced from any association with the republican doctrines of civic humanism.

In the same way that Garcilaso de la Vega adapted Leo the Hebrew's *Diálogos de amor* to depict the Incas as guided by 'the natural light' given to all men, so equally Sigüenza y Góngora drew upon Athanasius Kircher's *Oedipus Aegyptiacus* (1652–4) to trace the primordial foundations of Mexican culture and religion. But whereas the Jewish philosopher has been as uncherished and migrant as the Inca himself, by contrast Kircher (1601–80) was a German Jesuit, resident in Rome, acclaimed by both monarchs and popes for his vast learning. In a series of monumental volumes dealing with such diverse themes as astronomy, music, volcanoes and earthquakes, Noah's ark, the Tower of Babel, Atlantis, and Egyptian obelisks, Kircher sought to reconcile neo-Platonic Hermetic speculation with scientific research so as to frame a cosmological synthesis which would define and demonstrate Catholic doctrine as the fulfilment of the entire, variegated philosophic and theological quest of humanity. The spirit of his enterprise was best expressed in the declaration that 'there is no doubt that not only the prophets, apostles and other holy men of God but also the Gentile poets, priests and prophets were inspired by this divine *numen* (the Holy Spirit) and made prophets of the birth of the Eternal Word in flesh'. In his culminating work, *Oedipus Aegyptiacus*, Kircher traced the origin of all natural wisdom and religion to ancient Egypt, where he discerned a bitter conflict between the devilish magic and arts of Noah's son Ham, founder of the kingdom, and the secret, pure wisdom of Shem's grandson, Hermes Trismegistus. That both Moses and Plato derived their doctrines from Egypt was thus no coincidence but sure proof of its common source. Not content with the forged texts of patriarchal migrations provided by Annius, Kircher laboured to decipher Egyptian hieroglyphics which he interpreted as symbols of 'the highest mysteries of the Deity', and compared them with both Chinese characters and Aztec pictographs. That he accepted the reality of Atlantis, described by Plato in his *Timaeus*, illustrated Kircher's propensity to accept rather than to question his sources.[4] Obviously, if the Thomist dictum already employed by Las Casas, that grace fulfils rather than destroys nature, provided a theological foundation for Kircher's intellectual enterprise, it was the neo-Platonic, Hermetic strain within the Renaissance, ultimately derived from the patristic school of Alexandria, which inspired his historical and philosophical speculations. In this context, it should be noted that the immediate descendants of Adam, the first Patriarchs, were thought still to have possessed great wisdom and have practised natural morality: the expulsion from Paradise occasioned by the Fall only slowly dissipated mankind's original innocence, thereby subjecting it to the Devil's dominion.

Of Sigüenza's debt to Kircher, whom he hailed as 'a monster of wisdom and the astonishment of the world', there can be little doubt. In his *Teatro de virtudes políticas*, he boldly pronounced that the Mexican Indians were the descendants of Naphtuhim, the son of Misraim, founder and ruler of Egypt. Moreover, the biblical name of their ancestor was but the original form of Neptune, the classical god, who had founded Atlantis with colonists from Egypt. From that continent to America was obviously but a short step. Here was a line of speculation already expounded by both García and Zárate, which Sigüenza strengthened by signalising 'the affinity of American and Egyptian idolatry', and the remarkable similarity in temples, pyramids, clothes and calendars. The clinching argument was their common preference for 'modes of expressing their concepts in hieroglyphs and symbols'.[5] Further exposition of Sigüenza's views can be found in Gemelli Careri where, after describing a visit to the pyramids at Teotihuacan, the Italian traveller reported that the Mexican savant took them to be the work of the Olmecs, immigrants from Atlantis, noting that 'he considered them very ancient and only a little after the Flood'. Elsewhere, he affirmed the similarity of the Egyptian and Mexican calendars as the result of lineal descent from Neptune, the grandson of Ham, citing the false Berosus for confirmation of patriarchal migrations.[6] In proposing such theories, Sigüenza invoked Kircher to rebut Torquemada's *Monarquía indiana* and to endow the Mexican past with an Egyptian foundation. The cultural sequence was thus depicted as a decline from primordial civilisation rather than as a slow ascent from barbarism. Similarities in culture indicated common ancestry and diffusion from Egypt. Moreover, Sigüenza clearly entertained the hope that Mexican pictographs encoded an ancient wisdom, symbolically expressed.

Not content with an Atlantean migration, Sigüenza also conferred on his patria the privilege of an Apostolic visitation. Such a theory had already been proposed in the sixteenth century and Torquemada had been at pains to deny its plausibility, no doubt also aware that Ixtlilxochitl, the mestizo historian, was so persuaded. In Peru the two Augustinian chroniclers, Alonso Ramos Gavilán and Antonio de la Calancha, had argued that St Thomas had preached the gospel both in that country and elsewhere in America. In Mexico both Becerra Tanco and the Franciscan chronicler, Baltazar de Medina, drew on these authors to suggest that St Thomas had come to Anáhuac. Where Sigüenza innovated on such affirmations was in his identification of the apostle with a native deity. In the prologue to one of his last works, it was announced that he had composed a tract entitled 'Phoenix of the West. St Thomas found with the name of Quetzalcoatl', where he described 'the preaching of St Thomas in this land and its primitive Christianity'. Whether Sigüenza ever wrote this work is not clear, although the evidence suggests that in fact he never succeeded in resolving the chronological problems arising from his hypothesis. For as Torquemada had already insisted, the legendary and historical sources concerning Quetzalcoatl all associated the god-hero with ninth-century Tula rather than with an earlier epoch of Mexican history.[7] In this context, it is possibly significant that Sigüenza subscribed to a similar euhemerist explanation of the tribal god, Huitzilopochtli, whom he defined as 'the chief and leader of the Mexicans', who had led that nation through the north steppelands into Anáhuac. Once more, he drew on Kircher and Kaspar Schott to declare that it had been the general practice among early peoples to deify their sages and warrior heroes. If we recall that Torquemada had depicted that personage as Satan incarnate, then the contrast between the two approaches to the Mexican past stands clearly revealed. Not that Sigüenza was inclined to minimise the subsequent descent into idolatry since in his *Paraíso occidental* (1684), he admitted that 'among all nations the Mexican was the one which most gave itself over to the superstitious cult of demons'. Indeed, there is an unattributed passage in Gemelli Careri that asserts that the shape of the Mexican lakes, taken together, had the form of the Beast described in chapter 13 of the Apocalypse. In any case, Sigüenza elsewhere hailed the victory of Our Lady of Guadalupe over the idolatry inspired by the great Beast.[8]

In view of the ephemeral nature of his publications, it is difficult to measure the originality and value of Sigüenza's contribution to Mexican history. It is possibly significant that his good friend, the Franciscan chronicler, Agustín de Betancur, failed in his *Teatro mexicano* (1697–8) to achieve more than rewrite Torquemada and endorse García's theory of multiple pre-hispanic migrations. However, Sigüenza enjoyed the inestimable advantage of possessing the manuscripts and codices of Ixtlilxochitl, a collection given to him by the mestizo's son, Juan de Alva, the cacique of Teotihuacan. In his *Paraíso occidental*, he referred to Ixtlilxochitl as 'the Cicero of the Mexican language' and reproduced translated hymns of Nezhualcoyotl in which the Texcocan monarch addressed 'the Lord and the invisible great Lord God' as a deity whose omnipotence had to be propitiated by prayer and penitence. Elsewhere, he encouraged contemporary nuns to find inspiration in the ascetic virtues of Aztec temple virgins and encouraged the university to note that even in an epoch of apparent barbarism 'Mexico enjoyed polished schools.'[9] The degree to which Sigüenza succeeded in learning how to interpret native pictographs is not clear. Indeed, he complained bitterly that many scholars in Mexico despised the study of 'hieroglyphs' as 'a contemptible futility', so that to find printed illustrations it was necessary to consult the volumes of Samuel Purchas, the English editor of travels, who had acted as if he were 'the most distinguished lover of our patria'. If Kircher had erred on important points about the ancient Mexicans, it was the fault of 'our creole nation' which had failed to undertake the collection and interpretation of the codices.[10] To judge from Gemelli Careri and other reports, Sigüenza himself attempted to unlock the key to the Mexican calendars so as to calculate a correct chronology of the sequence of monarchs and empires. It was these computations that enabled him to affirm with conviction that Tenochtitlan had been founded in 1327. So too, he probably entrusted Gemelli Careri with a copy of the calendar which the traveller printed in his book. In the last resort, however, Sigüenza's greatest contribution lay in his zealous care of Ixtlilxochitl's collection, possibly augmenting it with other manuscripts and codices, all of which he bequeathed to the Jesuit college of St Peter and St Paul.

Like his German masters, Sigüenza y Góngora was a polymath, as much interested in the movements of the heavens as in the events of the past. Oddly enough, it was his scientific studies that occasioned a polemic in which his patriotism found its most embittered expression. In his *Libra astronómica y filosófica* (1690) he launched a fierce attack on Eusebio Kino, a German Jesuit who had spent some years in New Spain primarily engaged in missionary work on the northern frontiers. The cause of the dispute was the difference in interpretation of the appearance of a comet in 1680. Sigüenza had printed a small pamphlet assuring the Marchioness of La Laguna that it should be seen as a natural event without moral significance. By contrast, Kino subscribed to the traditional view that such apparitions presaged great imminent disasters for the human race. Moreover, he asserted that the world was drawing to its close, with no more than three centuries of further existence, so that nature was in decay, its putrefaction causing noxious airs which prompted the formation of more comets than hitherto had been the case. To make matters worse, Kino not merely ignored all the astronomical observations and assistance already provided to him by Sigüenza, he also violently attacked the Mexican savant's naturalistic account of heavenly phenomena and added insult to injury by dedicating his treatise to the Marquis of La Laguna, thus setting the husband to liberate his wife from false counsel.

Infuriated by such dealings – he had already experienced the greatest difficulty in persuading Kino to return his maps and papers – Sigüenza wrote to defend 'not only myself but also my patria and nation', since the Jesuit clearly despised Mexico and Mexican scientists 'through being Spaniards ... and because of this ignorance of the mathematical sciences'. Indeed, he complained that: 'In some parts of Europe and especially in the North, they consider not only the Indians, the original inhabitants of these lands, but also those of us with Spanish parents who happen to be born here, either to walk on two feet only through divine dispensation, or that even with the use of English microscopes our rational parts can be barely discerned.' Since 'I esteem my fame as much as my life', Sigüenza then paraded his vast erudition in contemporary astronomy and science, citing the works of Kircher, Schott, Caramuel, Kepler, Tycho Brahe, Gassendi, Descartes and Quevedo, to mention only the most obvious names.[11] As in his approach to the Mexican past, his most obvious debt was to Athanasius Kircher, who in his *Itinerarium Mysti-*

cum (1656) had argued that comets derived from sun-spots and were of ominous augury for mankind, only then to change his opinion in a subsequent treatise. Encouraged by this rare scepticism in his respected master, Sigüenza proceeded to amass authorities who had denied any connexion between comets and political and natural upheavals on earth, consulting historical annals to rebut any obvious correlations. Moreover, all these authors equally denied that nature was running down or that the world was drawing to its close. If the heavens appeared more filled with eccentric movement than before, it was merely because modern scientists more closely observed its movements. In all this, Sigüenza made clear his debt to both Kircher and to Bishop Juan Caramuel Lobokowitz, whom he described as 'my great friend and most courteous correspondent'. More importantly, he attacked the entire aim of astrology, as distinct from astronomy, observing 'I also am an astrologer and know what is its Achilles heel and on what a very weak foundation the fabric is raised.' Indeed, he denounced astrology as a temptation from the Devil, satisfying 'that desire and propensity which everyone has to know that which is hidden and in the future'. Once more citing Kircher, he traced the origin of the science to Egypt: 'That first and true Zoroaster was Ham, the son of Noah, inventor of all magic and idolatry . . . and illicit arts and sciences.'[12] The very vehemence with which Sigüenza rounded on judiciary astrology suggests former temptations to exploit his knowledge in this direction. It was only in his lifetime that the boundary between science and magic was clearly drawn.

If Sigüenza preferred to exalt the primordial foundation of Anáhuac rather than dwell on the mixed achievements of the Mexican state, it was in part because he was a creole priest and patriot, concerned to celebrate the current glories of his city. He found no problem in praising the 'heroic piety' of Hernán Cortés, whose great deeds merited eternal fame, derived from 'the conquest of such a powerful empire as New Spain'. So also, he celebrated Our Lady of Guadalupe not merely as perpetual protector of Mexico but also as the spiritual conqueror of Satan and his legion of devils. The same contrast was drawn in his commissioned eulogy of the convent of Jesus María where, after observing that so many churches occupied the site of former temples, he opposed the grim skies of Tenochtitlan, darkened by the daily holocaust of human sacrifice, to the sweet incense and pacific liturgy of Catholic Mexico. Nowhere was the celebratory aspect of Sigüenza's talent more obvious than in *Triunfo parténico* (1683) written to record four days of ceremonies in which the university, recently renovated, swore allegiance to the doctrine of the Immaculate Conception of the Virgin Mary. It was an occasion to which all Mexican poets of the epoch were expected to contribute, their pious efforts all greeted with an accolade of fervid eulogy. In his description of the university, Sigüenza drew attention to the portraits of the distinguished alumni who had risen to become bishops, canons and judges. But although Sigüenza followed Balbuena in saluting his patria as 'a delicious paradise of prayer and virtue', he also expressed the familiar creole lament as to 'the little duration of everything in our America which starts in greatness', wondering whether there was 'some malign star' which sterilised the land. Moreover, his idyllic picture of the innocent devotion of the nuns is marred for the modern reader by his emphasis on ascetic rigour. Observing of only holy nun, providentially born in the same year as the execution of Anne Boleyn, that 'all her study was of the crucified Christ', he described in fascinated detail her daily self-scourging, the heavy chains she wore, the great cross she carried round the cloister, and the frequent assault of demons in her cell.[13]

If the glories of the capital were assured, the frontiers of New Spain were far less well guarded. In his *Mercurio volante* (1693) Sigüenza reported the recovery of New Mexico, a province which had been lost in 1680 when the Pueblo Indians rebelled, killing twenty-one religious and expelling all settlers. In 1689 a column of no more than eighty-nine 'Spaniards' and native auxiliaries invaded the province from their base in El Paso and persuaded the Indians to return to their allegiance, their arrival welcomed by reason of Apache attacks on Zuñi villages. So also, Sigüenza was commissioned to celebrate a further renascence of Spanish arms in his *Trofeo de la justicia española* (1691) where he described the defeat inflicted on French forces in Hispaniola, preserving at least part of that island for Spanish occupation. What is notable in this account is the emphasis on God's providence, the clergy offering prayers and penitence in the cathedral to obtain heaven's intercession against enemies who obeyed the doctrines of Machiavelli, seeking to extend their power by force of arms without concern for rights or justice.[14] At the same time, Sigüenza lamented the threat offered to Texas by the French settlement at New Orleans in 1684, a threat which had led to the despatch of missions to that province so as to protect Spanish possession. It was the same threat which occasioned Sigüenza being despatched by the Count of Galve to survey the coasts of Florida with the aim of ascertaining a site for a fort near Panzacola. That his ship was called *Nuestra Señora de Guadalupe*; that Sigüenza should have read Garcilaso's *Florida* as a guide; and that he dubbed some dunes 'with the glorious name of the Apostle St Thomas', all serve to confirm the patriotic purpose of the venture.[15] At the same time, it should be noted that he wrote all these accounts in a plain, unadorned style, the very reverse of Baroque, aureate diction, which he strenuously criticised claiming that 'when I converse, write and preach, I observe the same' (style). In his *Infortunios que Alonso Ramírez padeció* (1690) Sigüenza composed an imaginary tale of a native of Puerto Rico who on a journey to the Philippines was captured by English pirates, led by Bell and Donkin, and then abandoned on a desert shore in the West Indies. Thanks to his devotion to Our Lady of Guadalupe, whose picture he always carried, he was eventually rescued and made his way to Mexico City where he met the Count of Galve and Sigüenza. Once more, we are reminded of the threatened condition of the Catholic monarchy, its frontiers in America subject to the steady encroachment of France and England, and its subjects liable to piratical assault and capture.[16]

The Western paradise was not merely challenged at its limits by buccaneers and Apaches, it was also threatened by rebellion from below. For in June 1692 the populace of Mexico City rose in riot, looted the market in the Zócalo, the main square, and invaded and set fire to the viceregal palace. In his account of these dramatic events, Sigüenza y Góngora traced the causes back to the floods of the preceding summer which had caused the maize and wheat to rot so that harvests were poor and prices consquently high. Despite bringing Our Lady of Los Remedios into the city in May, supplies remained short and, when the expected consignments of maize from Celaya did not arrive, the capital's corn market, the alhóndiga, was forced to close its doors. The result was open riot, led by Indians but soon joined by all elements of the populace. The efforts of both Jesuits and Mercedarians to quieten the mob by procession with cross and sacrament were repulsed with stones. The market in the Zócalo, composed of some 200 wooden booths for selling European cloth and other imported goods, was plundered and its materials used to set fire to the doors of the palace. The viceregal guard lacked bullets for their guns, so that the mob was able to invade the building and sack it. In the event, the worst excesses were prevented by the Count of Santiago, the senior member of the creole aristocracy, who entered the city centre accompanied by his retainers and other leading citizens, all armed and on horseback, firing at the mob which fled without offering any resistance. Had not the populace been more interested in plundering the market, more people in the palace would have been injured than was the case.[17]

Not merely did Sigüenza provide a racy, vivid account of what was the worst riot that capital suffered during the colonial period, he also offered a fascinating profile of his own reactions to these dramatic events. As a trusted adviser of the Count of Galve, he was summoned to the palace to help frame measures to deal with the city's flooding. When the wheat crop was found rotting in the fields, he sallied forth with his microscope, only to find that the grain was infected with a plague of minute insects, invisible to the naked eye. In the same summer of 1691 there occurred an eclipse of the sun, an event widely foretold and eagerly expected by the international community of astronomers. Noting with amusement that the darkening of the sky caused popular consternation in Mexico, with Indian fruit-sellers fleeing in tears to the cathedral, Sigüenza observed that 'on this occasion, I was joyful in extreme, giving repeated thanks to God for having allowed me to see what was happening . . . I was with my quadrant and telescope watching the sun.' His academic quality was put to the test during the riots of the following summer, when he risked his life to rescue the manuscript books of the City Council, endangered by fire in the palace.[18]

What equally distinguished Sigüenza's account was his thorough contempt for the Mexican populace, describing them as 'a common folk so very common . . . composed of Indians, of blacks both locally born and of different nations in Africa, of chinos, mulattos, moriscos, mestizos, zambaigos, lobos, and even Spaniards who are the worst among such a vile mob'. But it was against the natives that Sigüenza most vented his ire, complaining 'the Indians, the most ungrateful, querulous and inquiet people that God has created'. Indeed, when the drains were cleaned, images of Spaniards were found transfixed with pins, 'to such an extreme the Indians hate us'. When the mob of Indians and castas attacked the palace, they shouted: 'Death to the Spaniards and gachupines', exclaiming 'Is this not our land? Why do the Spaniards want it?' Equally revealing were another set of popular cries, which displayed the traditional character of this riot: 'Long live the Most Holy Sacrament! Long live the Virgin of the Rosary! Long live the king! Long live pulque! Death to the viceroy! Death to the Spaniards! Death to bad government!' It was not hunger, but drunkenness, so Sigüenza averred, that had provoked the unrest, since 'Never before has the drunkenness of the Indians reached such excess and dissipation as in these times . . . there is now more pulque consumed in one day in Mexico than in an entire year under idolatry.'[19]

Although Carlos de Sigüenza y Góngora has been described as a Mexican nationalist, he is best defined as a creole patriot who sought to endow the imperial city of Mexico with both a distinguished past and a glorious present. His attitude to the Indians was decidedly ambiguous, since if he took pride in the grandeur of Tenochtitlan, he despised the contemporary native populace as degraded and drunken. At the time he wrote, the very concept of a Mexican nation which might embrace all the variegated ethnic groups and classes which inhabited New Spain had not been invented. Sigüenza wrote as the spokesman of his creole nation and patria. His historical importance lies not in what he achieved, which was little enough, but in what he hoped to do, and in his propagation of the patriot faith. At all points, he sought to evade the authority of Torquemada, replacing the Franciscan antithesis of Babylon and Jerusalem by a vision of a Mexico founded on an Egyptian migration and an apostolic preaching, and redeemed from its lapse into idolatry by the apparition and protection of the Virgin Mary. At a moment when all memory or reliable oral tradition about the native past had disappeared, he preserved the papers of Ixtlilxochitl and transmitted that collection to posterity. In the next generation both Boturini and Veytia were to profit from these manuscripts. In the last resort, Sigüenza's role was to act as a vital, indispensable link between Ixtlilxochitl and the historians of the eighteenth century. More importantly, his patriotic preoccupations were to be turned to political account during the

Insurgency of 1810, when ideologues such as Fray Servando Teresa de Mier and Carlos María de Bustamante appealed to the grandeur of Mexico's native past to justify the rebellion against Spain.

II

'Since the first light of reason struck me, the inclination to letters was so vehement and powerful that neither the reproofs of others, of which I have had many, nor my own reflections, of which I have made not a few, have been enough to make me leave off following this natural impulse which God gave me.'[20] So powerful and personal a voice was not to be heard again in Spanish America until Simón Bolívar dictated his letters. It belonged to Sor Juana Inés de la Cruz (1648–95) a Jeronymite nun and Mexican poet who is generally reckoned to be the last great figure in the cycle of Spanish literature dominated by Góngora and Calderón de la Barca. A precocious talent, fêted at the palace by the wife of the Marquis of La Laguna who arranged for her to be published in Spain, Sor Juana was as much praised for her learning as for her poetry. Like Sigüenza, she was influenced by Kircher and the school of neo-Platonic hermeticism he led. Indeed, in her most difficult and profound poem, *Primero sueño*, in part inspired by Góngora's *Soledades*, she utilised Kircher's cosmological theories to pursue a metaphysical flight of the mind. So difficult and substantial was this work that one clerical wit opined: 'this virgin knows more asleep than most doctors awake'.[21] But her incisive intelligence and wide reading inspired apprehension in a cultural context where nuns were expected to lacerate their flesh in pursuit of sanctity or drink their chocolate in docile quietude. The current archbishop, Francisco Aguiar y Seixas, was a notorious misogynist and ascetic, who devoted all his energies and resources to almsgiving. Even the more enlightened bishop of Puebla, Manuel Fernández de Santa Cruz, took the opportunity of publicly commending Sor Juana to abandon her literary, secular studies in favour of the Bible and other sacred works. Her confessor, Antonio Núñez de Miranda, a Mexican Jesuit who pursued an effective apostolate in the upper spheres of viceregal society, similarly disapproved of her literary activity. Indeed, he was accustomed to say that had not Sor Juana withdrawn to a convent, she would have been the greatest blow to this kingdom that God could possibly have sent, so dangerous was 'the height of her understanding and the singularity of her erudition, joined to no little beauty'.[22] In the last three years of her life, Sor Juana disposed of much of her library and devoted herself to prayer and penitence, dying of the plague when caring for her afflicted brethren. The reasons for this decision are not clear and still a question for debate. Hailed in her own lifetime as the Tenth Muse and a Mexican Phoenix, Sor Juana thereafter became the source of pride for all patriots, with multiple editions of her works all testifying to the magnitude of her achievement.

In the two *loas* or poetic prologues to her plays, *El Divino Narciso* and *El cetro de José*, Sor Juana drew upon Torquemada and possibly Kircher to define the relation between Indian religion and Christian revelation. In one scene she depicted the natives worshipping a harvest deity, the God of seeds, whom she identified as the unknown god whose altar St Paul found at Athens, interpreting both the rites and the sentiments which inspired them as an anticipation and prefiguration of the transubstantiation of the bread and wine into the body and blood of Christ performed in the Catholic mass. In another scene, she admitted that the Indians, misled by the Devil, disregarded the tenets of natural law when they offered human sacrifice, but then proceeded to argue that their intentions were good, since they sought to give their gods the supreme offering – life itself, an argument first advanced by Las Casas and restated by Torquemada. Once enlightened by Christian revelation, the natives would satisfy this sublime imperative by participation at mass, where Christ's sacrifice on the cross was daily re-enacted.[23] In a few remarkably acute lines, Sor Juana thus portrayed the Catholic Eucharist as the fulfilment of natural religion, satisfying mankind's innate desire both to experience sacred communion and to offer ritual sacrifice to the Supreme Deity.

Although she was well acquainted with Sigüenza – he was to deliver her eulogy after she died – Sor Juana was not attracted by the patriotic themes to which he devoted his intellectual energies. Indeed, in 1680 when the cathedral chapter of the capital commissioned her to design a triumphal arch to welcome the Marquis of La Laguna, she chose Neptune as her allegorical theme, using the opportunity to display her knowledge of classical mythology. In his account of this occasion, Sigüenza praised 'the sublimity of her erudition' and 'her capacity in the encyclopedia and universality of letters', observing that through her Mexico enjoyed all that the Graces ever conferred on learned women throughout the centuries. But he then lamented that she had chosen to depict Neptune as the god of fable rather than as the ancestor of the American Indians.[24] In effect, Sor Juana did not contribute to the growth of creole patriotism other than to figure in her own right as a cultural icon, since both her ambition and talent found expression and fulfilment within the universal tradition of Spanish literature.

III

In his *Teatro mexicano* (1697–8) Agustín de Betancur (1620–1700), observed that Mexico now possessed twelve distinct 'families' of religious, a consideration that impelled him to hail the city as 'a new Jerusalem with twelve gates

19 Miguel Cabrera, *Sor Juana Inés de la Cruz*

through which to enter the Jerusalem of triumph, twelve precious stones . . . twelve tribes of Israel . . . which shine like stars in the crown of the woman of the Apocalypse'. In a direct plagiary of Salinas, he further saluted the capital as a Florence in beauty, a Venice in trade, and a Rome in holiness. Further echoing the Peruvian Franciscan, he praised the Mexican creoles since 'the climate, abundance and riches of the patria raise their spirits and ennoble their thoughts . . . so elevated are their spirits that there are few who are inclined towards the crafts and occupations of their fathers'. At the same time, he lamented that although young creoles were quick to master all branches of knowledge, 'at forty most tire of studies', and thereafter passed their lives in idleness, the result, so he averred, of the absence of reward, recognition, or Crown office.[25] The influence of Salinas in Mexico, where he spent the last eight years of his life as commissary-general of the Franciscan provinces of New Spain, can also be observed in the Chrónica de la santa provincia de San Diego (1682), where Baltazar de Medina (1630?–97) was as much concerned to celebrate the glories of Mexico City as to trace the progress of his own reformed branch of the Franciscans. Once again, lists of creole bishops, canons and provincials were compiled. Medina also propounded the theory, taken from Martin del Castillo, that the name of Mexico had a Hebrew or Syriac origin and meant 'of my Messiah'. After exclaiming that 'this Court enjoys some of the qualities of paradise in its climate, freshness, and beauty of roses, flowers and fruits', he further declared that the city was 'like an empress of this kingdom and lady of all the Indian monarchy of both Americas', destined to be 'the monarch of the sceptre and crown of the true Messiah'.[26]

In these dithyrambic phrases, we encounter the creole vision of their patria as a new Zion. To read the first issues of the Gacetas de México (1722–42) edited by Juan Ignacio María de Castorena Ursúa y Goyeneche (1668–1733), is to enter a world in which the Mexican elite appeared immersed in a cycle of theatrical devotion in which new churches and convents were consecrated, images paraded through the streets, and devotion to Our Lady of Guadalupe grew ever more fervid. From these descriptions, it is clear that the Catholic liturgy was celebrated with pomp and splendour, the heavy gilt of altar-pieces that soared to the vaults catching the flickering light of massed banks of candles while orchestras and choirs strained to attain polyphonic crescendos. At such moments, to enter a church was to enter the House of God, to ascend in spirit into the kingdom of heaven. Religious devotion here fused with aesthetic pleasure. For the Gacetas equally reveal a surprising familiarity with the technical language of architecture, suggesting that every detail of new altar-pieces and church façades was scrutinised with critical eye.[27] Moreover, from the 1720s until the 1780s New Spain experienced a striking transformation in style as Churrigueresque exuberance dissolved the architectonic forms of the Baroque, subordinating both sculptural detail and the traditional orders to the concept of the retablo or façade as a unified composition entirely dominated by soaring, vertical movement. The paradox here is that the more the Renaissance vocabulary of architecture was dissolved, the more Baroque became the informing spirit of churches such as the Santa Prisca at Taxco or the Jesuit college at Tepozotlán. The problem is to encounter a literary equivalent of this style which is not tedious or extravagant. For whereas in architecture the physical limitation of the frame imposed a boundary and was ordered according to the perspective of the spectator, by contrast, in literature the deliquescence of classical vocabulary yielded a prose which was often formless and trivial.[28] Examples of this trend are to be found in abundance in *Americana thebaida* (1729) written by the Augustinian chronicler, Matías de Escobar (1690–1748), who praised the remote, fertile valley of Jacona in Michoacán as 'the Cyprus of America, the Elysian Fields of this New World, and the splendid Paradise of these West Indies'. So too, one devout chronicler was saluted as a Homer and Virgil in poetry, a Thucydides and Livy in history and a Demosthenes in eloquence. When the 'celebrated Rodríguez' was simply described as 'an American Titian', it comes as an anticlimax. In short, as classsical epithet was piled on classical epithet, with metaphors multiplied beyond control, meaning was sacrificed to literary effect, and critical acumen destroyed by the imperatives of eulogy.[29] A similar contrast between the same informing spirit yielding remarkably different results in literature and art was observed by Huizinga in Flemish and Burgundian poetry and painting at the close of the Middle Ages, where the application of minute realism uncontrolled by general principles produced brilliant painting and tedious verse.[30]

The architectural splendour and social preponderance of the ecclesiastical establishment in Mexico astonished Gemelli Careri who was informed that men entered the priesthood for want of other means of subsistence. By then the archbishop and cathedral chapter had an income of about 300,000 pesos. A generation later, the Spanish Capuchin, Francisco de Ajofrín, who visited New Spain in 1763, counted no less than 80 churches in the capital, 20 nunneries, all well endowed, and an equal number of priories and colleges. Some clue as to the number of priests and religious resident in Mexico can be obtained from an account of the public exequies of Philip IV held in 1665, where Dr Isidro Sariñana (1630–96), described a procession through the streets of all assembled clergy. On that occasion he counted no less than 1,325 secular priests and 1,080 religious, the latter divided into 340 Franciscans, 160 Dominicans, 180 Augustinians, 130 Jesuits, 120 Mercedarians, 80 Carmelites, and 70 members of two hospital orders. Equally important, he observed 82 Indian confraternities and *mayordomías* on parade, together with 16 brotherhoods catering for black and mulattos and another 19 for Spaniards.[31] In this epoch religious ceremony was not confined to churches, since in Holy Week, on the feast of Corpus Christi, and on great public occasions, it was common for the religious communities and the confraternities to sally forth into the streets, carrying images, banners and crosses, their serried ranks a public demonstration of the hegemony of the Catholic faith.

Although the creole Church concentrated its resources and clerical manpower in the diocesan and viceregal capitals, it also encouraged missionary activity at the frontiers of New Spain. It was in 1693 that the Jesuits opened their first mission in Lower California, in the ensuing decades slowly bringing that Peninsula under Christian sway. Nor did the Company neglect the urban apostolate, since it ministered to both the elite and the populace in mining camps and the capital. Equally important, the Franciscan order experienced a major revival in spiritual fervour with the establishment of missionary colleges at Querétaro (1683), Zacatecas (1707) and Mexico City (1731). In his chronicle of these colleges, published in 1746, Félix Isidro de Espinosa (1679–1755), a native of Querétaro, described the foundation of the Texas mission in 1716–21, an expedition undertaken both to protect that vast province from French penetration and to convert its hitherto isolated peoples. To read his account is to return to the first years of the spiritual conquest of New Spain since we encounter the same story of heroic, devout friars gathering simple natives into villages, teaching them both the gospel and agriculture, only then to witness the inevitable ravages of epidemic disease. At times it was necessary to employ the soldiers of the small garrisons to oblige the Indians to submit to the ministrations of the friars. Apparently unconcerned by the decline in native population, Espinosa remarked: 'the Fathers remained entirely happy and satisfied with the multitude of young children who died, since after being washed with the sacred water of baptism, their happy souls flew to the sacred mansion of heaven'.[32] It was not so easy for the friars themselves to be persuaded of their own salvation. The Franciscan ideal of poverty and imitation of Christ led to an emphasis on extreme asceticism. A leading missionary, Melchor López de Jesús, was described as a 'living portrait of Christ crucified ... Every Friday he left for the fields, barefoot, with a very heavy cross on his shoulders, a cord at his neck, and a crown of thorns so fastened that at times his face could not be seen owing to the blood drawn by the thorns.' Wherever he preached, he erected crosses and calvaries and encouraged the faithful to practise the devotion of the Stations of the Cross. In his mission to Verapaz, the province once converted by Las Casas, he threatened the recalcitrant natives with irons and imprisonment if they did not abandon idolatry, obliging them to attend penitential sessions in which they scourged themselves and carried heavy crosses.[33] Although the most famous of this new wave of missionary Franciscans came over from Spain, creoles like Espinosa were also attracted to enlist in this mendicant elite, the chronicler himself rising to become guardian of the college in Mexico. It is significant that in his account of the 1737 plague in the capital, Cabrera singled out the Jesuits and the Franciscans of this college, San Fernando, for their zeal in attending to the victims of the epidemic. That a later critic should have referred to Espinosa as 'a Julius Caesar' working by day and writing by night, is testimony to the evangelical revival which animated many creoles at this time.[34]

The new Zion, however, was not entirely caught up in the contemplation of heaven and ascetic penitence. Indeed, the populace were generally reckoned to be as drunken as they were devout. Despite his experience of the *lazzaroni* of Naples, Gemelli Careri was appalled by the popular classes of the capital, characterising the blacks and mulattos as insolent and threatening and the Indians as indolent and downtrodden, the two groups united only by a common addiction to theft and drink. So also, Ajofrín exclaimed that 'of a hundred persons you might meet on the streets, you will hardly find one who is properly dressed and shod'. The number of poor in Mexico and Puebla far exceeded anything known in Spanish cities. He found painful the sharp contrast between the mansions and carriages of the rich and the hovels and rags of the poor. 'In this city can be seen two extremes sharply opposed: much wealth and the greatest poverty; many fine clothes and the greatest nakedness; great cleanliness and much filth.' In his visit to the mining town of Guanajuato, he described the workers' lives as both wild and lavish. With high earnings the rule, at the weekend 'they buy taffeta, fine cambric, delicate lace and other rich fabrics so that they dress like princes. By Monday they find themselves without a penny ... and descend the mine nearly naked.'[35] Both the capital and the mining towns were notorious for their crimes and violence. A local patriot counted twenty-eight persons done to death in brawls in Zacatecas during the first eight months of 1728. In the capital, the very Zócalo, the great central square, was filled with a market which embraced both textile booths and vegetable stalls, the latter the source of much filth, the more especially since their owners often passed the night in the market, converting it into a popular encampment.[36]

It was, no doubt, in reaction to popular degradation that the creole elite became so vocal in their disdain for the native inhabitants of their patria. In the introduction to his *Teatro mexicano*, Betancur lamented that the scenes of religious enthusiasm reported by Torquemada had been long since replaced by hostility to the mendicants and a cold indifference to the gospel. The native nobility now preferred to consume their fortunes in elaborate dinners and other festivities without the least regard for the necessities of the Church. Indeed, all classes of Indian society were dominated by drunkenness arising from the consumption of pulque, the fermented juice of the maguey cactus, an endemic vice which caused constant quarrels, infidelities, murders and even idolatry. It was not the plague but alcoholism which had caused the destruction of the Indian population in Mexico.[37] Nor was Betancur alone in this harsh judgement since Florencia and Sigüenza equally lamented native drunkenness. A generation later in *Escudo de armas de México*, Cayetano Cabrera argued that if so many Indians died during the great plagues that periodically devastated the Mexican population, it was because they resorted to pulque for relief and abandoned the sick to their fate, leaving them to die unattended. Citing the reports of several parish priests, he claimed that many natives, especially in the country, were still prone to idolatry, worshipping 'the God of harvests', whom he curiously described as 'that abominable Anti-pope, whose tyrannical power, propagated in great misdeeds, has undermined the entire kingdom'.[38]

A yet more potent source of discontent in the Creole Zion was the presence of so many gachupines. Gemelli Careri remarked that the great import merchants of the capital were mainly immigrants from the Peninsula, men who often employed their wealth to endow new convents and churches. He further noted that the creole sons of these traders often quarrelled bitterly with their fathers, whereas creole women 'have a great affection for Europeans . . . whom even though poor, they prefer to marry rather than their compatriots . . . even though rich, perceiving them as lovers of mulatto women, from whom, together with their milk, they have sucked bad customs'.[39] That such travellers' reports of animosity were not ill-founded was clearly demonstrated by an amusing incident in 1703 when, much to the indignation of the clerical elite, a professor of theology from Alcalá de Henares was installed as dean of the cathedral chapter in Mexico. Unwise enough to sneer at creole preachers, the unfortunate dean then lost the thread of his discourse in the first sermon he preached in the capital. At once, he was violently assaulted in a pamphlet written by Pedro de Avendaño, a celebrated preacher and former Jesuit, who bitterly attacked the appointment of a gachupín as dean, demanding to know what was the difference in talents between Old and New Spain: 'here we have the same men, the same sun, the same books, the same God, the same faith, the same Scripture, but some greater accomplishments, since whereas bearded men in Spain go to school with their primers, here we have schools filled with graduates and doctors'. It was all the result of 'this accursed distance', separating Mexico from Madrid, that the creoles had to accept the imposition of peninsular Spaniards to high office in the Mexican Church.[40]

The depth of feeling which animated creole patriots is best observed in the *Representación politica-legal a la majestad del Sr. D. Felipe V* (1725), written by Juan Antonio de Ahumada, a Mexican-born lawyer, who bluntly demanded of the king that the 'Spaniards of the Indies' should be given preference in all appointments in Church and State. Echoing Solórzano, he pronounced that it was a fundamental premise of both canon law and natural law that the natives of a diocese or country should enjoy its governance and that their sovereign should reward their loyalty by appointment to office. 'What crimes had the creoles committed', he asked, 'that they should not obtain positions which in all Christendom, says the law, should be theirs?' Did not the very Laws of the

Indies decree that the descendants of the conquerors and first settlers should enjoy preference in appointments to office? After all, 'the Indies were conquered, settled and established as provinces with the sweat and toil of the ancestors of the Americans . . . all offices should be theirs'. By contrast what were the European Spaniards now in the New World but mere 'strangers and newcomers', men who arrived burdened with debt, without knowledge of the laws or character of the countries which they came to rule, whose sole aim was to enrich themselves and return home? He defended the character and talents of the creoles from the slander of those who cast doubt on their 'fitness, considering them hardly worthy of the name of a rational being'. Many families sprang from the nobility of Spain. If at times they sank into aimless sloth, it was precisely because they were denied the opportunity and stimulus of high office, existing, as Calancha had observed, as 'strangers in their own land'. It was as if the king had two wives, so Ahumada declared, with the dowry of the second spouse, the Indies, enjoyed by the sons of the first marriage, leaving the Americans deprived of their rightful inheritance.[41] Yet the difference between a king and a tyrant was that the former ruled with love and respect, without resorting to terror or oppression. In conclusion, he rejected any notion that the American Spaniards hated their European cousins arguing that once given office the creoles would prove themselves loyal subjects of the Crown.

The slanderous stereotypes of creole and gachupín, the one an indolent, well-born wastrel and the other an ignorant, avaricious tradesman, thus came to haunt and poison relations between American and European Spaniards. It was a quarrel which had started in the cloisters but which now infected relations even within the family circle. So often, it was a quarrel between fathers and sons, cousins and brothers-in-law, with creole women both the prize and the peacemakers. So common was denigration of creole character and talents among peninsular Spaniards that Benito Feijoo in the fourth volume of his *Teatro crítico universal*, published in 1730, felt obliged to condemn as 'common error' the opinion that creoles developed fast, only then to enter an early decline, the promise of their youth overshadowed by the premature waning of their powers. To counter this widely diffused view, he offered the examples of a Mexican archbishop of Santiago de Compostela, still vigorous at ninety; of the celebrated Peruvian savant, Pedro de Peralta y Barnuevo, whose learning was esteemed by the French Academy; and of Sor Juana de la Cruz, more gifted than any Spanish woman of her century. If there was any tendency to slip into idleness, it was owing to the lack of reward and office, talents languishing in oblivion. That so influential a publicist as Feijoo, so active in preparing Spain to accept the new philosophy and science of the seventeenth century, should have intervened in this debate reveals how heated it had become.[42] Not that his efforts were to much avail, since in the 1760s Ajofrín commented as accepted fact that although the creoles had minds fit to grasp any branch of knowledge, 'at a certain age, such as thirty years, they enter a decline, as much because of their delicate complexion and lack of health as also through lack of encouragement and appointments, for which reason, lacking stimulus, they easily abandon their books and sink into sloth'. He also observed that the creoles did not inherit the business talents of their immigrant parents, so that they often dissipated the fortunes so laboriously accumulated by their gachupín fathers.[43]

IV

In 1743 the viceroy of New Spain ordered the imprisonment of Lorenzo Boturini Benaduci (1702–55), a Milanese nobleman, who had spent six years in the country identified only by an Austrian passport, imperial letters patent of nobility, and a genealogy tracing his ancestry back to ninth-century Aquitaine. During his time in Mexico, Boturini had become so devoted to Our Lady of Guadalupe that at considerable personal expense he had used his circle of acquaintance in Rome to acquire a papal breve authorising the coronation of the Mexican Virgin as 'the sworn, postulated principal patron of this vast empire'. Despite his enthusiasm for the cult, Archbishop Vizarrón y Eguiarreta refused to accept this papal document since it had not been approved by the Council of the Indies. At this point, the newly arrived viceroy, the Count of Fuenclara, learnt of the affair and upon due enquiry found that Boturini had failed to obtain the necessary Spanish licence to enter Mexico, that he had acted as general lieutenant of justice for the district magistrate of Tlaxcala, and that he had solicited funds for the Virgin's coronation entirely on his own initiative. Moreover, he had toured remote Indian villages in search of old documents. Indeed, on further examination, it was found that Boturini had assembled an extensive collection of maps, manuscripts, codices and printed sources dealing with ancient Mexican history and the apparitions of the Virgin Mary at Tepeyac. In fact, the Jesuits had granted him full access to the papers which Sigüenza y Góngora had bequeathed to the college of St Peter and St Paul, so that he had obtained copies and in many cases the originals of such works as Ixtlilxochitl's chronicles, Sigüenza's maps and letters, and much other valuable material.[44] The ease with which he had obtained these documents testifies to the general lack of interest in native antiquities of which Sigüenza had complained a generation before. The upshot of the case was that the viceroy ordered the collection to be confiscated and Boturini deported to Spain.

Once in Madrid, Boturini encountered powerful patronage both from the great savant of Valencia, Gregorio Mayans, and also from a young Mexican nobleman, Mariano Fernández de Echeverría y Veytia, who possessed excellent connexions at court. The result was that in 1747 Boturini was appointed Chronicler of the Indies in recognition of his talents and knowledge. Already in

1746 he had published his *Idea de una nueva historia general de la América Septentrional*, in which he set out a new mode of interpreting the Mexican past. Deprived of his manuscript collection, he perforce had to rely on the published chronicles of Torquemada, Acosta, Herrera, and the codex data printed by Gemelli Careri and Purchas. The novelty and originality of Boturini's approach to the Mexican past did not thus depend on his research or new sources, but rather derived from the application of new hypotheses about the early history of mankind. As he explained in an address to the Valencian Academy, he sought to interpret native religion and history by application of the doctrines of Giambattista Vico (1668–1744), whose *New Science* (1725) he commended as a Catholic antidote to the irreligious ideas of Grotius, Selden and Hobbes. He hailed Vico as 'an eagle and immortal honour of the delicious Pertenope . . . the only man to open the way to penetrate the dense wood of pagan religion' (*gentilidad*).[45] As much as Sigüenza, therefore, Boturini hoped to cast new light on the misty reaches of Toltec myths and Mexican calendars by invoking the most recent European speculations about the primordial history of mankind.

To comprehend the startling character of the transition from Kircher to Vico, it should be recalled that when the Spanish savant, Andrés González de Barcia, obtained permission to republish several American classics, he not merely sponsored second editions of Torquemada's *Monarquía indiana* (1723) and Garcilaso's *Comentarios reales* (1723), he also printed García's *Origen de los Indios* (1729). Moreover, he inserted a great deal of new material in that work, with the aim of incorporating the theories of 'the most learned Athanasius Kircher, wonder of the learned world', and of his Mexican disciple, Sigüenza y Góngora, as reported by Gemelli Careri. The result was to multiply yet further the occasions on which the virginal quiet of the New World was thought to have been broken by invasions from Europe, with the Vikings, St Brendan of Ireland, Prince Madoc of Wales, and the Laplanders all given due credit. But the most significant addition was an exposition of Kircher's thesis that all human culture derived from Egypt, with the Phoenicians, Carthaginians and Atlanteans defined as their descendants or colonists. In part, Barcia delved into the complicated, controverted question of patriarchal chronology, a subject rendered all the more suspect by his doubts as to the veracity of Annius and his false Berosus. But he also rehearsed the chief traits which identified Mexico as an Egyptian offshoot: the construction of pyramids, the system of calendrical computation, and the preference for hieroglyphs. As much as Kircher and Caramuel, he ascribed a hidden wisdom to these hieroglyphs, which encoded symbolic language.[46]

It was in this context of speculation that Boturini pronounced that the cultural development of the American Indians was essentially autochthonous and obeyed 'the natural law of all peoples', ascending through the three great ages governed respectively by gods, heroes and men. If Boturini was so quick

20 Lorenzo Boturini Benaduci

to appropriate Vico's system, it was because the Neapolitan jurist sought to resolve problems which had haunted all serious debate over the origin and character of Indian culture. At the time when Vico came to maturity there were two opposing theories about human development. There was the classical notion, found in Cicero and Lucan, but now developed by Grotius, Selden, Pufendorf and Hobbes, which depicted the first men as forest savages dwelling in a state of nature, dominated by fear, ignorance and aggression, only slowly learning the benefits of association and submission to laws and political authority. It was this school, which, by reason of its rebirth in the new philosophy and science of the seventeenth century, had come to dominate the historical scene and against which Vico formulated his 'new science'. But it should be remembered that until at least the 1680s Kircher and his Hermetic school dominated Catholic culture, so that Vico equally wrote to combat the still surviving notions of patriarchal, hermetic wisdom. Moreover, Vico implicitly fought on a third front, against St Augustine and his disciples, since he quietly excised the Devil from his naturalistic account of the origin of pagan religion and society.[47]

Leaving aside the resounding philosophic premise of Vico's enterprise, that if God alone can know nature because he made it, then men as authors of civil society can discern its principles of development, we are left with the essential perception that the first men lived in a numinous universe in which they worshipped the forces of nature as deities. No matter how savage or terror-struck, mankind everywhere expressed its knowledge in poetic myths and hieroglyphs and was governed by religion and its hierophants. But the age of the gods made way for the age of heroes, great warriors and sages, who framed codes of law and composed poetic epics. In turn this aristocratic epoch was replaced by the age of men, a time of prose and academic learning, when popular government emerged only then to be superseded by monarchy, the most perdurable of all human political arrangements. In framing this account, Vico thus denied that Greek fables or Egyptian hieroglyphs enshrined any esoteric or lofty wisdom; instead, they expressed in poetic form either mere history or 'the vulgar wisdom' of law-givers. Equally important, Vico rejected any diffusionist theories, and ridiculed all claims for Egyptian antiquity. Every nation had its Jove and its Hercules; and Hermes Trismegistus was but a poetic character or symbol of the first men who sought wisdom. In short, Vico advertised his new science as establishing on sure demonstrable foundations 'an ideal, eternal history traversed in time by the history of every nation in its rise, progress, maturity, decline and fall'.[48]

In his *Idea de una nueva historia general*, Boturini set out the Vichian theory of the three ages of mankind but failed to offer any attribution or even mention Vico's name. Since his book was more of a prospectus than a finished work, it consisted of a set of baffling affirmations followed by some intractable demonstrations of intent. On the ever-absorbing question of the origin of the Indians, he rejected outright García's thesis of European migration across the Atlantic and dismissed any descent from the Jews as improbable. The case against diffusionism rested on the philosophic premise that all peoples pass through the same cultural stages and hence any similarity of beliefs, institutions, laws and artefacts has to be ascribed to the common historical experience and nature of humanity rather than to any shared ancestry or patriarchal intervention. In deference to Sigüenza, he accepted the hypothesis that the Mexicans descended from the biblical Naphtuhim, but eviscerated that theory of any explanatory force by insisting that the Indians only slowly wandered across Asia after the fall of the Tower of Babel. He endeavoured to demonstrate that all the original gods of the Mexican pantheon derived from the forces of nature. But Boturini diverged considerably from his mentor's system when, after defining the Toltec period as the Mexican age of heroes, he observed that they preserved much of the wisdom, virtues and arts of the first age when Providence had guided their steps. Moreover, he fully accepted Sigüenza's thesis that St Thomas the Apostle had preached the gospel in Anáhuac and was thereafter worshipped as the hero-god Quetzalcoatl.[49] So too, he interpreted the third age as a period of moral decline, when cities were established and luxury introduced. 'The historical or third age was the unhappy theatre where virtually all that had been an innocent demonstration of Nature [was] corrupted ... the rights and laws of Nature were broken into pieces with so much sacrifice of men, women and innocent children ...' In particular, he blamed the Mexicans as 'butchers and executioners of their own kind', who had perverted the morality imparted by the Toltecs. Only 'the wise emperor of Texcoco, Nezahualcoyotl' preserved the humane philosophy of his ancestors. In his unpublished manuscripts, Boturini devoted much effort to the interpretation of the Mexican calendar and its pictographs, asserting that the hieroglyphs 'hide the most noble, arcane wisdom and symbolic science and high matters of pagan theology' and that the calendar 'does not belong to a people whom Europeans depict as ignorant and incapable of reason, but who are of a most subtle and perspicacious intelligence'. With such views, it comes as no surprise to encounter praise for 'the incomparable Kircher', since in these latter assertions he adopted a position diametrically opposed to his Neapolitan master.[50]

In the appendix to his *Idea*, Boturini provided an annotated catalogue of his Mexican collection. It is there that he traced the documentary sources for the apparition of Our Lady of Guadalupe, questioning that Lasso de la Vega was the author of the first published account in Nahuatl, which, following Sigüenza, he attributed to Antonio Valeriano, an attribution he hoped to prove by comparing signatures from sixteenth-century documents and the original manuscript version of the apparition. He also claimed to have found documentary evidence of the St Thomas mission, although like other enquirers he failed to discover Sigüenza's account of the matter.[51] In effect, although Boturini invoked Vico's 'new science' to clear the Mexican historical landscape of the unwelcome intrusion of Jews, Carthaginians and Atlanteans, he failed to achieve much more than echo Torquemada from whom he borrowed his image of Toltec wisdom and virtue. More significantly, he appears not to have read Acosta's *De procuranda* and hence did not seek to compare the Jesuit's evolutionary sequence based on settlement patterns, forms of government and use of script, with the Vichian scheme of cultural development. Where he did succeed was in offering a naturalistic account of Indian religion, thus eliminating the Devil from his Augustinian role as prime mover of Mexico history and religion. For the rest, his acceptance of the two great elements of creole patriotism, the apostolic mission and the Guadalupe apparition, served to render his book welcome among Mexican readers, most of whom were presumably baffled by his bold affirmations concerning the early history of mankind.

The degree to which Boturini evoked both respect and puzzlement is best observed in the *Historia antigua de México*, written by Mariano Fernández de Echeverría y Veytia (1718–80), the Mexican scion of an influential, bureaucratic family, who fulsomely praised Boturini 'to whom I confess myself entirely the debtor for the first light and instruction of the principal points of this History ... ' During his years in Madrid, 1737–50, he had the opportunity of conversing with the Italian, especially on the thorny question of Mexican chronology. On his return to New Spain, Veytia acted as municipal magistrate in his native city of Puebla and devoted himself to his studies. None of his works were published in his lifetime. His pamphlet entitled *Baluartes de México* ostensibly dealt with the four principal Marian images guarding the capital, but in reality described the progress of the Guadalupe cult, all done in conventional patriotic vein, together with a critique of Los Remedios, in which he argued that the image in Puebla known as 'the conqueror' was the figure which Cortés had placed in the great temple. In his history of the foundation of Puebla, Veytia offered a dry, scholarly account of the construction and consecration of the cathedral, churches and convents of the city.[52] It was a work bereft of civic enthusiasm and entirely lacked the former creole obsession with compiling lists of distinguished compatriots. Despite a latent enthusiasm for Palafox, his praise was tepid and he avoided any open attack on the Jesuits. In short, if Veytia figures in the line of creole patriots, it is entirely by reason of his work on prehispanic history.

Although Veytia repeatedly expressed his gratitude to Boturini, he failed to comprehend the Vichian doctrines expounded in the *Idea* and dissented from his mentor's attempts to decipher the Mexican calendar and chronology. Yet his own work was almost entirely based on the manuscripts and codices collected by the Italian and impounded by the viceregal authorities, chief among which were the papers of Ixtlilxochitl. His most impressive, if not wholly successful exercise, was an exposition of the Mexican calendar, a work, so he averred, which had cost him years of intellectual toil. Here is no place to enter into the details of such a technical question. Sufficient to say that Veytia demonstrated to his own satisfaction that Boturini had failed to understand the principles of the matter, that Gemelli had not fully understood the theories of Sigüenza and, most important, that Torquemada had completely mistaken the character of these figures, alleging that they were ritual notations rather than true calendars. Once again, we here observe the creole imperative to undermine the authority of the Franciscan, albeit in this case with justice and only achieved by recourse to native codices and the papers of Ixtlilxochitl.[53]

Despite his access to new sources, Veytia entirely failed to produce a text which might have replaced Torquemada's masterpiece. In effect, most of his material was narrative in character, so that he entirely lacked the means to re-work the fertile second volume of the *Monarquía indiana* which had incorpor-ated much of Las Casas' *Apologética* and parts of Sahagún. Indeed, he often chose to follow the Franciscan rather than dwell on the implications of his manuscripts. Thus, whereas Ixtlilxochitl clearly distinguished an early Olmec phase from the subsequent Toltec kingdom, Veytia confused the two peoples. In his account of Indian origins he rejected out of hand the theories of García and Sigüenza, only to install seven Toltec, Nahuatl-speaking families as universal ancestors of all the native inhabitants of Anáhuac. Although he confessed that the great pyramid at Cholula derived from the Olmecs, he fixed on the Toltec foundation of Tula in 713 as the start of recorded history. Their monarchy lasted until 1116 when, owing to the evil machinations of the emperor Topiltsin, it was replaced by the Chichimeca empire headed by Xolotl, a state which was finally dissolved by the Mexicans and their Texcocan allies in 1428. In all this, Veytia followed Ixtlilxochitl in attempting to provide an exact chronology and agreed with Sigüenza in ascribing the foundation of Tenochtit-lan to 1327. However, his calculations were not always persuasive, the more especially since he asserted that the last Chichimeca emperor lived for two hundred years, and offered wildly inflated population numbers, claiming that no less than 5.6 million persons died during the wars which destroyed the Toltec realm.[54]

Intermingled with his confused narrative, Veytia advanced certain proposi-tions of clear ideological intent. For a start, he affirmed that the Toltecs believed in a supreme deity, the creator of the universe, and cited Garcilaso de la Vega's definition of Pachacamac, the universal spirit of the Incas, as a parallel. They did not offer their god any blood sacrifice, either of men or of animals. To reinforce this image of a benevolent, natural religion, Veytia invoked the apostolic mission of St Thomas, accepting Sigüenza's identification of the saint with the Indian hero and god, Quetzalcoatl. In confirmation of this theory, he pointed to the evidence of crosses found by the conquerors, of the native 'sacraments' of baptism and communion, and of their triune deity. He thus denied Boturini's argument that it was during the epoch of heroes that the myths concerning native gods had arisen. In fact, although the Chichimecas were barbarians when compared to the Toltecs, they still preserved the primitive monotheism of their forbears. It was not until the advent of the Mexicans, which is to say, in 1298, that the worship of many gods and the practice of human sacrifice became diffused throughout Anáhuac. Just why 'the new religion of the Mexicans' should have gained such wide and rapid acceptance, Veytia did not explain. Unlike Torquemada, however, he did not attribute idolatry to the intervention of the Devil, a figure who is largely absent from his account of native religion. He followed Boturini in defining Huitzilo-pochtli as a tribal leader, later deified, and described the inaugural Mexican vision of an eagle perching on a cactus as a trick of the priests. In contrast to vicious rites and idolatry practised at Tenochtitlan, the emperor Nezahual-coyotl still worshipped the one supreme God, the more especially since he 'hated these sacrifices, holding them to be iniquitous and contrary to natural law'. Taking the lesson of Solís to heart, Veytia endowed the Texcocan state with councils of justice, war, the exchequer, science and arts, and a council of state to advise the monarch, all with their own scribes and archives.[55] In devising this nomenclature, Veytia clearly fulfilled his patriotic aim of incor-porating the peoples of Anáhuac into the comity of civilised nations. As much as Sigüenza and Boturini, he failed to offer a persuasive alternative to Torquemada and hence fell back on unsustainable myth and confused narra-tive. The opportunity to re-write the ancient history of Mexico in a manner acceptable to the eighteenth-century mind thus remained open until it was seized by the exiled Jesuit, Francisco Javier Clavijero.

V

In 1748 creole patriotism reached a new height when in a famous sermon the Mexican Jesuit, Francisco Javier Carranza, declared that the time would come when the Holy See of St Peter would abandon Rome to seek refuge at Tepeyac in New Spain.[56] As always, pride goes before a fall, and clerical patriots were filled with indignation when they read the *Latin Letters* of the Dean of Alicante, Manuel Martí, a celebrated savant, who advised a young friend not to visit America, since it was a literary desert, without books or libraries, fit only for Indians to inhabit. It was to reply to this slanderous attack and to vindicate the honour of his patria that Juan José de Eguiara y Eguren (1696–1763), professor and rector of the university of Mexico, a canon of the cathedral and bishop-elect of Yucatán, compiled a vast bio-bibliography of all known Mexican authors and their works, both published and in manuscript. Although he only published the first volume, the *Biblioteca mexicana* (1755) expressed both the maturity of the Mexican intellectual tradition and its perennial sense of neglect. Eguiara wrote a polemical prologue in which he first sought to defend the cultural achievements of the Mexican Indians, citing the works of Sahagún, Torquemada, Nieremberg and Kircher. In particular, he emphasised that native pictographs were true hieroglyphs rather than mere picture-writing, in this case deploying Sigüenza against Kircher. By implication he accepted the Egyptian origin of the Indians, pointing to the similarity of their religion and writing, and concluded: 'All that concerned their political and domestic government was so much in conformity with reason that had it been united to the norms of the true religion, then nothing would have been wanting to maintain a lasting and complete happiness in such a vast empire.'[57] Turning from this happy spectacle of native virtue, he then lauded contemporary American universities and colleges for their learned faculty, their numerous students, their abundant libraries and the consequent high level of the creole clergy. At the same time, he confessed that Mexico had not produced any great figure of the stature of Aquinas, Duns Scotus, Suárez, Kircher and Caramuel. Indeed, although individual scholars were acquainted with the works of Descartes and Gassendi, the chief schools of philosophy in the university still consisted of Thomists, Scotists and Jesuits. To advertise creole talent, he described the recent examinations for a doctorate taken by Antonio López Portillo, a young priest who had displayed remarkable feats of memory and argument.[58]

Where Eguiara waxed most strongly was in his defence of the mental faculties of the creoles, observing that the roots of the accusations made on this score could be traced back to the constellationary thesis of Juan de la Puente who wrote at the beginning of the seventeenth century. It was a charge that had already been subject to critical review by Feijoo. Nevertheless, Eguiara produced an entire list of venerable creole priests, prelates and professors who had retained vigorous use of all their faculties until a hale old age. He cited Sor Juana Inés de la Cruz and Sigüenza y Góngora as examples of the brilliance and erudition that could be encountered in Mexico. At the same time, he lamented the obstacles and the lack of stimulus to the maintenance of intellectual activity in New Spain, fixing upon the exorbitant cost of publication and the disappearance of such manuscripts as Sahagún's, the location of whose twelve volumes was as yet unknown.[59]

The *Biblioteca mexicana* marked the culmination of an entire cycle of creole culture, framed at a time when it was still possible to entertain the Baroque vision of a Mexico endowed with an Egyptian antiquity and blessed by Providence with the apparition of Our Lady of Guadalupe. It also celebrated the emergence of a Mexican tradition of inquiry into Indian history and hieroglyphs, a difficult and technical study peculiar to creole scholars. The purpose behind the bibliographic project was the old creole desire to exalt their patria's illustrious sons. But the method and standard of inquiry had advanced far beyond the diminutive lists compiled by Medina or Betancur since Eguiara found evidence of no less than a thousand authors of 'the Mexican nation', defining that term as including all persons born in New Spain, Mexican America, both Indians and Spaniards, the first intimation of the existence of such an entity. What Eguiara could not foresee was that the entire cultural value of the authors he cited so proudly was soon to be sharply questioned by the European Enlightenment.

18

PERUVIAN ECLIPSE

I

IN A commissioned eulogy of the current viceroy, published in 1714, Pedro de Peralta y Barnuevo (1664–1743) openly lamented the eclipse of 'that golden age' of Peru, initiated by Toledo, when the Andean highlands had poured forth their seemingly inexhaustible riches to sustain the hegemonic pretensions of the Catholic monarchy. In a sad echo of Nebrija, he declared that arms and the sciences flourish together, only then to cite as examples the Spain of Isabella and Ferdinand and the France of Louis XIV, thus implicitly attesting to the new-found primacy of the Sun King's realm in Europe. Indeed, he composed a long poem in French enlarging on the glorious achievements of that monarch, and had already celebrated in verse the French victory at Villaviciosa which effectively won the Spanish throne for Philip V, the grandson of Louis 'the Great'. With the accession of the Bourbon dynasty ratified at the Peace of Utrecht (1713), it was now possible for Peralta to hail his foreign sovereign as 'a hero-king and a Catholic hero', and compare that indolent, uxorious prince to El Cid, Themistocles and David. If he was so prodigal in eulogy, it was in part because the reign of Charles II (1666–1700), the last, hapless scion of the Habsburgs, had witnessed a radical decline in Spanish military and political strength. The capture and sack of Guayaquil in 1706 by William Rogers, was but the last in an entire series of raids on coastal towns in the Caribbean and the Pacific, in which English, Dutch and French buccaneers threatened the prosperity of the Spanish empire. So powerless were the colonial authorities to deal with the latest English privateer to invade the Pacific that it was found necessary to commission a French trading vessel to pursue his ship.[1] In effect, Spain now figured as a power of the second rank in the European concert, dependent on dynastic alliance with France to preserve its overseas empire from British assault.

Rector and professor of mathematics at the university of San Marcos, Pedro de Peralta acted as 'chief cosmographer'; served as royal accountant in the Court of Audit, a post inherited from his peninsular father; and drew further

21 Cristóbal de Aguilar, *Pedro de Peralta Barnuevo Rocha y Benavides*

income from his wife's landed estates. His expertise in mathematics rendered him an invaluable counsellor to several viceroys, whom he assisted in framing their final reports and in presenting plans for the fortification of Callao. He was also expected to publish an annual almanac, a task he undertook reluctantly, warning the public that astrological predictions lacked any scientific warrant. Saluted by contemporaries as 'a living encyclopedia and an animated library', Peralta was both poet and historian, who composed a clutch of comedies, much occasional verse, and an heroic epic on the foundation of Lima. That he should also have translated a drama of Corneille demonstrated his cultural bias, since no less than three-quarters of the books in his personal library were in French.[2] But although he quoted the French critic, Boileau, with approbation, Peralta still proffered Góngora as a literary model, since as late as the 1730s he organised a poetic competition based on that author's style. Certainly, in his own prose, he decorated his narrative with any number of 'conceits', aphoristic definitions which were more often striking than instructive. To describe the royal mint as uttering 'the political sacrament of Majesty', was no more enlightening than to pronounce of Christ's passion that 'the geometry of mercy is infinite'. It was this preference which led him to declare that although French drama was sublime, its solemnity was alien to Spanish taste which found expression in the lively world of the comedies, concluding that 'the Spaniards are the princes of the theatre'. In this context, it is significant that he should have praised the architectural style of Bernini, the great exponent of the Roman baroque, whose influence was to be discerned in recent churches built in Lima.[3] The penetration of French classicism into the hispanic world, already under way, thus still met with a great deal of resistance.

Cited by Feijoo along with Sor Juana de la Cruz as an example of creole erudition, recognised in Paris for his learning, Peralta composed an epic poem, divided into ten cantos, in which he celebrated the Spanish conquest and the subsequent glories of Lima. If Garcilaso was duly invoked to praise the Incas and Manco Inca portrayed as offering an eloquent defence of the liberty of his patria from Spanish tyranny, nevertheless, the central figure in *Lima fundada* (1732) was Francisco Pizarro, variously described as a Spanish Hercules and another Alexander, whose valour and audacity had enabled him to conquer an entire world. The discovery of America had effected a second redemption, second in importance only to Christ's incarnation, its providential character powerfully demonstrated by the apparitions of the Virgin Mary and Santiago at Cuzco in 1536. If the initial scenes of battle allowed scope for dramatic verse, the ensuing years of viceregal dominion were enlivened only by the occasional depredations of Dutch and English piracy in the Pacific. For the rest, Peralta observed the canons of creole patriotism and framed lists of prudent governors, holy bishops and friars, wise judges and brave soldiers, the often inane exuberance of his classical comparisons soon proving more wearisome than amusing. It is significant that if the three canonised saints of Lima, St Rosa, St Francisco Solano and St Toribio Mogrovejo were all duly incensed, the still unbeatified figure of Martín de Porras was by no means forgotten, testimony of the strength of Limeño devotion to that mulatto friar. In all, Peralta cited no less than five viceroys, ten archbishops, sixty-one bishops and over a hundred judges of the high courts who were natives of Lima, proof enough of the capital's role within the empire. So too, he was able to list no fewer than seventy-four churches and chapels, and fourteen nunneries, and devote eloquent stanzas to the splendour of their 'refulgent altarpieces', lit by lamps like 'falling stars', the very richness of their decoration proof enough that America was won more to serve as an altar than as an empire. In effect, Peralta sought to emulate Camoens and chant in heroic style the imperial glories of his patria. Had not Salinas complained that the deeds of Pizarro were in danger of falling into oblivion, uncommemorated in appropriate form? If Peralta chose verse as the ideal medium of patriotic discourse, it was because he ranked poetry above law, history and the sciences, pronouncing it 'the allegory of the music of reason'. Unfortunately, his ambition outran his talent and the entire project was vitiated by the incongruity between his elevated style and his often banal subject matter, its catalogues of persons mentioned requiring detailed annotation.[4] Despite his invocation of the *Lusiads* as a model, his poem more obviously resembled the Count of La Granja's life of St Rosa.

No contribution to creole patriotism was complete without formal plaint. Sure enough, Peralta seized the occasion to commend Feijoo for his defence of the talents of the American Spaniards. More important, he concluded by asserting that although Lima and the empire had been sustained by the nobility, composed of the descendants of the conquerors, of branches of the best families of Spain, and of merchant families, this class was now threatened with extinction. Here was a theme close to his heart, since in 1714 he had defined the nobility as 'the strength and splendour of the state'. In terms reminiscent of Palafox, he exclaimed that 'all Nature is but spheres and harmonies', so that it was only right that the nobility should figure as the chief delegates of royal authority, power thus descending in graduated hierarchies.[5] In this emphasis on the necessity of high office for the Limeño elite, Peralta echoed the first plaints of creole patriots, a theme which in Mexico had found contemporary expression in the memorial of Juan Antonio de Ahumada. But whereas most petitions mentioned the creoles in general, by contrast, Peralta referred simply to the nobility, choosing thus to act as the spokesman of a social class rather than of a possible nation. In effect, Peralta failed to amplify or build upon the ideological legacy of Salinas and indeed restricted his patriotic concerns to the defence of the interests of a narrow elite.

The merely formal quality of Peralta's patriotism was further illustrated in his account of the celebrations staged in Lima in 1723 to mark the marriage of the Prince of Asturias. After observing that 'Providence had destined the paradise and mine of the world as a colony of Spain', he then paraphrased Salinas to salute Lima as 'a Peruvian Rome . . . the Salamanca of the Indies . . . the Athens of America'. Preceded by bull-fights and followed by comedies, native guilds of the capital paraded through the streets with the twelve Incas at their head, several of these personages played by native nobles from Cuzco, attired in all their traditional finery. After a mock battle between Spaniards, Frenchmen, Turks and Incas, Philip V was hailed as victor with the cry: 'Long live the Catholic Inca, monarch of two worlds!' In his commentary on this scene, Peralta defined Manco Capac as another Lycurgus or Confucius and depicted the Incas as worshipping 'a supreme Cause' and observing the natural law. For the rest he pronounced their realm, renowned for 'its virtues and good government', as greater than the Roman empire and its monuments unrivalled by any edifices of the Ancient World.[6] Apart from the fashionable reference to Confucius, there was nothing here that would not have occurred to any sympathetic reader of Garcilaso or Cieza de León.

If a few pages in an occasional pamphlet exhausted Peralta's interest in the Incas, by contrast, he devoted considerable energy to composing his *Historia de España vindicada* (1730), the first and only volume covering the development of the Peninsula until the advent of the Moors. Opening with the challenging assertion that Spain was to ancient Rome as America was now to Spain, he divided its history into the four epochs of primitive liberty, Roman conquest and empire, Gothic anarchy, and final restoration and greatness. Although he firmly dismissed the 'fictions of the good Annius' and the Platonic myth of Atlantis, he warmly defended the authenticity of Santiago's mission to Spain and the apparition of Our Lady of Pilar at Zaragoza. At no point, however, did he allow his pen to divagate into the favoured terrain of American mythography and speculate on Atlantic migrations or on the journeys of St Thomas across the New World. The only reflection that bore on his Peruvian situation was the dictum that the greater the extension of empires, the less their capacity for action, the burden of weight impeding the exercise of force.[7] For the rest, there was remarkably little to recommend this venture into metropolitan history.

To measure the true quality and bias of Peralta's intelligence, we have to turn to the final report of the Marquis of Castelfuerte, since this survey of Peru during the years 1724–36 betrayed his style and sentiments in every section. Just why the viceroy should have trusted him with this task is not clear. However, he had already subsidised Peralta's publications and in return the savant had hailed the choleric veteran of European campaigns as endowed with the virtues of Caesar, Alexander and any number of other ancient worthies.[8] That the picture of Peru should have been painted in such dark colours was apparently no cause for alarm. In effect, Peralta here displayed an embattled, narrowly Limeño patriotism which identified the interests of the capital with the maintenance of the imperial system as established in the Habsburg epoch.

To start with, Peralta saluted Potosí as 'the synonym of riches and the hyperbole of opulence', only then to confess that whereas its mines used to produce some 11 million pesos of registered silver, not counting a further 3 million escaping in contraband, in the decade which ran from 1724 output of silver and gold in all Peru only reached 3.8 million pesos a year. So too, the great mercury mine at Huancavelica had experienced great difficulties, its

shafts subject to cave-ins and other hazards. Nor were there any solutions for
the industry's problems other than the application of scientific methods in the
refining process. It was precisely this apparently irreversible decline of the
mines which rendered maintenance of the Indian *mita* so necessary. Writing
with unconscionable frankness, Peralta observed: 'In order to maintain the
kingdom, it is necessary to continue bringing it to an end, since the mines which
produce the riches cause the very persons who toil in them to perish.' So
persuaded were the colonial authorities of the devastating effect of the *mita*
that in the last decades of the seventeenth century and again in the years 1716–
20 there were projects to abolish this Toledan institution or, at the very least,
ensure that the Indians drafted for this purpose were paid better wages. In
response to these well-meaning measures, Peralta argued first that it was
virtually impossible to obtain voluntary Indian labour for Huancavelica, by
reason of 'the character of this nation, in whom to indulge idleness is a natural
vice', only then to contradict himself by noting that free labourers demanded a
wage at least double the monies paid to mitayos. Much the same was true of
Potosí.[9] There, Castelfuerte suspended the royal rescripts which had commanded that mitayos should be remunerated for their long journey to the city
and that they should be given the same wages as free workers, arguing that the
industry was barely profitable and depended on the cheap labour of the *mita*
for its survival. In his account of these viceregal decisions, Peralta evinced scant
sympathy for the Indians, since although he admitted that working in the mines
could be lethal, he also attributed the decline in Peru's native population to the
recent plague, inter-breeding with mestizos and excessive consumption of
brandy. In any case, it was a universal law of history that conquered peoples
always suffered a fall in numbers.[10]

    With silver production nearing its lowest level since the discovery of Potosí,
it comes as no surprise to learn that Peru's overseas commerce was in an
equally parlous condition. The great trading fleets which had once sailed
annually for Porto Bello were reduced to arriving every three years after 1656,
and in the period 1707–22 failed to make any appearance. It was in these years
that French merchant vessels swarmed into the Pacific, freely trading in the
leading ports of Peru and Chile. Only in 1723 was a fleet despatched from
Cadiz, thus allowing Castelfuerte to ban all further French interlopers. It was a
decisive action which Peralta hailed as effecting 'a new conquest of Peru'.[11]
However, he had to admit that the revival of the Habsburg system had proved
remarkably difficult to maintain, since the English ship, which under the
provisions of the Peace of Utrecht could be annually despatched to Spanish
colonial ports, had ambushed the trade fair, undercutting the Spanish traders.
In any case, the merchants of Lima soon quarrelled with the Cadiz shippers on
questions of price. Then again, the granting of licences for individual ships to
sail for Buenos Aires equally undermined the old pre-eminence of Lima as the

universal emporium of the viceroyalty. In all this, Peralta displayed a partisan concern for the prosperity of Lima, exclaiming that: 'Buenos Aires is the ruin of two trades, the door through which flies riches, and the window from which Peru is thrown.'[12] That the Andean highlands might have benefited from the cheaper prices of goods brought from the River Plate was of no consideration. After all, in his plan for the fortification of Callao, Peralta declared: 'Quit Lima from Peru and no empire will remain ... With Lima defended, all is defended; with it lost, all is lost ...'[13]

Peralta attested to the disorders that afflicted the interior of Peru during the administration of Castelfuerte. But whereas other chroniclers attributed the riots to popular response to oppressive acts of government, he admitted the deaths of four corregidores, only to explain them by the barbaric character of the rural masses, who refused to pay the tribute justly demanded. It was necessary for royal authority to be re-established and respected. So also, Peralta offered a detailed account of events in Paraguay, ascribing the uproar in part to the animosity of the citizens of Asunción to the wealth and power of the Jesuits, who, so he claimed, had almost 200,000 Indians subject to their command. As for the riotous scene surrounding the execution of José de Antequera in Lima, he roundly denounced the 'barbaric pride' of the Limeño populace, for the most part composed of poor Spaniards, who had been incited by the Franciscans to dispute viceregal dictates.[14] In this contemptuous appraisal of the capital's impoverished inhabitants, Peralta revealed the nobiliary bias of his patriotism.

An extraordinary feature of the *memoria* was its evident animus against the Church. If the viceroy and the high court in Lima were unchallenged, by contrast in the provinces the authority of royal magistrates was overshadowed by 'episcopal splendour', and disputed by the parochial clergy. Referring to the constant conflicts of jurisdiction, Peralta observed that 'the courts compose a commonwealth, not a monarchy'. Each religious order acted as if it were a petty kingdom, 'conquerors of their spiritual empire'. In this context, it was all-important for the viceroy to insist on his authority as vice-patron since 'this royal *patronato* is the most precious jewel in the crown of this kingdom'. After all, the king had funded the construction of most churches and his viceroy had the right to appoint priests to any parish. Yet the bishops now tended to view the Crown as exercising merely secular authority, 'without taking note that if it is not ecclesiastical in jurisdiction, it has a great share of that quality through its protection and even by delegation'. After indulging in the fine Baroque observation that 'pre-eminences are like an honorific money which has currency in the exchange of respect', Peralta concluded that: 'the preaching of the gospel in these parts is a high end in which the eternity of the object is the symbol of the reason of its dominion, within the circle of religion and empire being the beginning and end of its conquest'.[15] By way of insisting on the religious foundation of royal authority, even under the Bourbons, Castelfuerte staged the first public *auto-de-fe* of the Inquisition to be held in living memory in which individuals found guilty of such offences as witchcraft, bigamy and idolatry were punished by scourging, confiscation of property and exile to Chile. The viceroy's ever faithful publicist recorded these proceedings with evident approbation, defining the Inquisition as the very tabernacle of the Catholic faith, its foundation St Dominic's greatest achievement. All this led to the grand conclusion that Spain was a country which had always been 'more of a Church than a Crown, and her kings more protectors of the faith than sovereigns'.[16]

The section which most distinguished Castelfuerte's report from similar viceregal documents was its unqualified advocacy of the pretensions of the creole nobility, which it described as suffering 'a pitiable decadence'. The abolition of encomiendas, the drought on coastal haciendas, but above all, 'the lack of provision of offices which the viceroys used to make', were all cited as the cause of this decline. What Peralta had in mind here was the all-important change which had occurred in the 1680s when the Council of the Indies stripped the viceroys of their traditional right to appoint corregidores to all but the most wealthy towns and districts. Since that pivotal decade in colonial history, the Crown had auctioned these offices in Madrid for terms of five years, with the result that magistrates came to the Indies already in debt and hence determined to exploit their subjects so as to recoup their initial costs and reap high profit for the merchants who financed their operations. Yet the creoles, so Peralta argued, were better acquainted with local laws, knew the character of the people, and by reason of their own gentle disposition generally treated their subjects better. In effect, the new system, now in practice for four decades, damaged the prospects of the creole nobility and was the ruin of the native population. Peralta extended his critique to include the highest levels of colonial government. Observing that the university of San Marcos was thoroughly decadent, with 'more masters than disciples and more doctors than students', he explained its decline, both financial and intellectual, by the absence of any reward or stimulus for academic achievement, it now being possible for candidates to purchase degrees and even acquire doctorates for an outlay of 6,000 pesos. The problem could be best resolved by appointing both bishops and judges of the high courts from the ranks of university professors. After all, it was prelates from Spain who caused most upsets. With the ruin of the nobility now so evident, Peralta warned that: 'few cults are found on altars which do not bestow favours; an empire rules but little when all is power and nothing benefit'. In conclusion, he insisted that Peru was not a mere colony or even a province of the monarchy, but an empire in its own right and that the Crown should thus view it as 'the principal part of its power and, if not the head of its government, the heart of its riches'.[17] That these irreproachable creole sentiments should have found expression in a viceregal memorial was a tribute to Castelfuerte's tolerance and Peralta's presumption.

In many ways, Pedro de Peralta was the Peruvian counterpart of Carlos de Sigüenza y Góngora, albeit born a quarter of a century later. Both men were professors of mathematics and astrology whose numerical expertise was employed to frame almanacs and to counsel viceroys on practical projects which required surveying expertise. Both were creole patriots who took a jaundiced view of the populace of their respective cities. Their skill in verse was equally turned to patriotic account and each man reached out to Europe to assure their reputation as savants. But if Sigüenza looked to Kircher for inspiration and delved in Hermetic myths to establish his patria on Egyptian foundations, by contrast, Peralta saluted the cultural hegemony of France and merely embellished in verse themes already advanced by Salinas. More particularly, the Peruvian polymath exhibited scant interest in the Incas, celebrated Pizarro as the founder of his patria, and generally identified the interests of Lima with the maintenance of the imperial system. Whereas the Mexican at least spoke of his 'creole nation', the Peruvian always wrote on behalf of the creole nobility of Lima. At a vital stage in the development of creole patriotism, Peralta thus failed to infuse that ideology with a Peruvian content and indeed, compared to Salinas, limited its application to the interests of a particular social class.

II

The only chronicler to capture the intensely introverted, often tumultuous life of provincial society in its colonial heyday was Bartolomé Arzáns de Orsúa y Vela (1676–1736). That he also expressed the variegated ideas and sentiments which animated creole patriotism in the Andean highlands demonstrates the social reach of that ideology. Possibly a schoolteacher by profession, albeit without Latin or a secondary education, Arzáns was born and bred in Potosí, his father brought there as a boy from Spain. If his reiterated criticism of pride in lineage be any guide, he was certainly a commoner and possibly, on the side of his mother, a mestizo by descent, although not in status. Whatever his background, Arzáns had access to books, since he had read some history, could quote from a smattering of the classics in translation, and was obviously influenced by chivalrous romances and the comedies which were enacted in the city. Unlike clerical chroniclers, he took a lively interest in the secular life of the city and displayed an obsessive concern with crimes of passion. As much as Fernández de Oviedo or Guaman Poma, he appears to have conceived of his chronicle as a means of rescuing both his city and his name from oblivion. That he wrote more to lament than to laud the events he witnessed only serves to confirm the similarity in form and purpose to the works of his illustrious predecessors. The *Historia de la villa imperial de Potosí* (1705–36) is a vast, sprawling chronicle, organised as annals, which in its modern and only edition comprises three folio volumes and over a million words. If Arzáns completed the historical part of the work in the years 1705–8, thereafter, until his death in 1736, he maintained an open file, recording contemporary events as they occurred. Apparently, sections were read to a circle of friends, since on one occasion a corrupt corregidor sought to have the manuscript impounded, fearful of his deeds being recorded for posterity.[18] Judged in terms of ideology, Arzáns emerges as a faithful disciple of Calancha, whose influence equally extended into the anecdotal form of his chronicle. But in his ability to tell a story and in his fascination with tales of love and honour, he most resembled Juan Rodríguez Freyle, although there is no evidence to suggest that he had ever read *El Carnero*. That his manuscript was later plundered by Ricardo Palma, the nineteenth-century Peruvian *cuentista*, demonstrates the literary genre to which his work can be ascribed.

The sheer exuberance with which Arzáns opened his chronicle can be gauged by the fashion in which he saluted 'the famous, ever great, most rich and inexhaustible Peak of Potosí' as a 'singular work of the power of God, unique miracle of nature . . . emperor of mountains, prince of all mines, lord of 5,000 Indians (who disembowel it), trumpet that sounds across the globe, a paid army against the enemies of the faith . . . '. Drawing on the local treasury accounts, Arzáns stated that between 1556–1719 the mines had produced 330 million pesos in taxes for the Crown, which calculated as just over a fifth, yielded a total registered production of 1,650 million pesos, or an average 10 million pesos a year, figures which had to be augmented by at least a third to take into account contraband shipments shipped through Buenos Aires. Not content with these relatively accurate figures, he also provided estimates of over double that total reaching the approved 3,200 millions cited by other chroniclers. At the height of its prosperity the city had a population of over 150,000, an estimate that made it the largest urban concentration in America. It was to feed these vast numbers, swollen by Indians summoned for *mita* service or engaged in transport, that an entire circle of provinces, from Tucumán and Paraguay to Cuzco and Moquegua produced foodstuffs and other supplies. The city consumed great quantities of coca, flour, maize for chicha beer, wine, brandy, goats, sheep, llamas, sugar, fat, soap, and barley for mules, all of which often had to be brought from considerable distances. To cater for the spiritual needs of this population, fifteen parishes were set up, accompanied by a Jesuit college, six priories of mendicants, two nunneries, and two hospitals. As regards the mining industry, Arzáns stressed the importance of the Toledan reforms which both introduced the amalgamation process of refining silver and established the *mita* of native levies. In particular, he marvelled at the series of great lakes in the hills behind the town that were constructed with dams so as to assure a controlled flow of water for the refining mills. In all this, he drew upon documents and paraded any number of statistics.[19]

However, Arzáns wrote to mourn rather than to praise the new Ophir. In the years when he composed his chronicle, Potosí had entered an apparently irreversible sequence of decline. With only 16,000 houses inhabited, the population was no more than 70,000. So also, the production of silver had fallen dramatically, since in 1703 the fleet only carried 1 million pesos compared to the 5 million common in recent years. The number of Indians arriving on *mita* had also declined radically. The owners of the refining mills, the *azogueros*, owed the treasury close to 1 million pesos for unpaid consignments of mercury. Nor was the city exempt from the effects of this decay, since the secular clergy which depended for subsistence on endowment funds found it increasingly difficult to collect the annual interest and were often reduced to poverty. The sensation of an entire cycle of economic activity drawing to its close was further deepened by the arrival of Frenchmen at Potosí, shipping in merchandise from Buenos Aires, their presence a sure sign of imperial decline.[20]

At the opening of the second part of his chronicle, Arzáns exclaimed that whereas he had started with a story of conquest, vast riches and grandeur, he was now reduced to describing calamities, poverty and decay. If Potosí had once attracted the envy of the world, so now like the seven wonders of the ancient world, its very foundations had crumbled. 'Surely this was one of the most notable declines in the peoples of the world: to see so much vanity, such incomparable riches turned to dust and nothingness.' In a gloomy reflection, Arzáns added: 'there is no prosperity which may not be the start and even the means of adversity and ruin'. The higher the rise, the greater the fall. Moreover, he was moved to question the moral basis of its prosperity, since: 'the greatness of its riches was always motive for offences against God and because of that the cause of its calamities'. For the Christian observer, the pomp and display of a city dedicated to the gratification of greed could only be questionable. Indeed, Arzáns echoed Calancha's description of the mines in the peak as offering the very image of a living hell, devouring the natives who were forced to descend into its depths, since so often they acted as porters clambering up wooden ladders with heavy burdens, always exposed to sudden accident and hurt, abused and exploited by the overseers.[21]

The all-pervasive sense that God had pronounced sentence on Potosí was further strengthened by the experience of the 1719 plague, an infliction which Arzáns interpreted as divine punishment for the city's sins, past and present. In a powerful description, he noted that the churches could not accommodate the corpses in their burial vaults, so that a great pit had to be opened, into which bodies were flung and covered by lime and earth so as to prevent further infection. During the months in which the city was afflicted, the confraternities and religious communities paraded their images through the streets and celebrated penitential sessions to intercede with heaven. As always, the worst affected section of the population were the Indians, with entire settlements destroyed and many of the newly arrived contingent of *mitayos* equally smitten. Among the clergy the Jesuits distinguished themselves for their unremitting care of the sick, assisting the two hospital orders. So great was the mortality that Arzáns calculated that in 10 months some 20,000 persons died, about a third of the current population, with over 800 babies left without mothers. To find an historical parallel for such a disaster, Arzáns cited a description of the Black Death of the fourteenth century presented by Gonzalo de Illescas in his *Historia pontifical*, a work first published in 1569. The 1719 epidemic was the last great onslaught of the bubonic plague and its effects in Peru were comparable to the 1737 epidemic in Mexico which Cabrera was to describe so eloquently.[22]

If Arzáns thus pronounced a strident jeremiad on contemporary Potosí and its inhabitants, he soon slipped from prophetic gravity into recounting moral anecdotes in which he displayed all the art of a born story-teller. What could be better than his cameo sketch, lasting no more than two paragraphs, of a small group of revellers who chose to disregard the plague of 1719, gathering in festive mood to dance, sing and engage in other 'dishonesties', only to hear when they chanted the popular ditty 'This is the life', a deep, frightful voice suddenly answering: 'Now this is but death.' Sure enough, within a few days, all were dead save a woman who immediately rushed to protest her innocence before an image of the Virgin Mary.[23] The everyday world depicted by Arzáns was constantly interrupted by sudden voices, apparitions and omens. As much as Calancha, he attributed spiritual power to the holy images which were venerated in the many churches of the city. A group of Indian miners trapped underground by a sudden fall of earth were thus guided to safety, thanks to their prayers to Our Lady of Copacabana, who was seen by a young boy in the group. The popular devotion accorded to such figures was best exemplified in his account of the arrival in Potosí of an image of Our Lady of Mercedes which had been brought all the way from Quito, touring Peru in quest of alms. In this case, the image was greeted with triumphal arches, and 1,000 Indians danced in its honour, although the clergy's initial welcome soon turned into disapproval, when they encountered the promiscuous escort which accompanied the Virgin. Nevertheless, some 25,000 pesos in alms were collected. Other, more direct apparitions were recorded by Arzáns, as, when describing the virtuous life of a holy priest, he related that the cleric gave his cloak to a poor Indian, only then to have it returned by Christ himself who had assumed that form to test his charity.[24]

As much as Rodríguez Freyle, Arzáns was fascinated by 'the empire that beauty has over men'. Women, he declared, were like fire and had to be at all times treated with the greatest care, since at any moment they were liable to burst into flames, ignited by a sudden gust of passion. To judge from his often rapturous prose, Arzáns himself was by no means exempt from the attractions of young women since in telling the tragic tale of one young maiden, he devoted considerable attention to her marble brow, her snowy cheeks adorned by the faintest blushes, her perfect nose, her well-formed teeth, and so on for an entire paragraph. Despite his moralising, his enthusiasm at times provoked some decidedly un-Christian sentiments as when he exclaimed: 'beauty is the rich and precious dress of souls in which their nobility is revealed ... a crystalline glass through which shines the interior treasure ... ' Moreover, he preferred to see natural beauty adorned, if not expressed, by rich and appropriate attire, since he observed that 'a poorly dressed woman is like false money which does not circulate save at night, or is like a sword that can only kill when unsheathed'. Small wonder that with such susceptibility, Arzáns should have condemned the amorous proclivities of his compatriots with such vehemence, exclaiming 'the most fateful plague that there is among the passions is love', which he declared to be 'composed of all the evils of the world'. He complained about the recent fashion in women's clothes introduced from abroad, in which they uncovered their breasts and hence caused ceaseless provocation. Had not the prophet Hosea condemned women who had bared even their necks to public view? Whatever the case, Arzáns filled his chronicle with stories of passion, seduction and revenge, in which the impulses of lust and honour drove men and women to destruction. In this context, it is surely significant that he should have condemned the comedies enacted in the city as being responsible for filling the minds and hearts of their audiences with examples and principles which ran counter to Christian virtue, encouraging them to sacrifice their lives in pursuit of love.[25] Yet it is probable that many of the tales he related owed more to the theatre than to life, since their plots so often resemble those of the comedies. Whatever the truth of the matter, it is clear that the world of Don Juan, so skilfully depicted by Tirso de Molina, was alive and very much kicking in colonial Potosí.

If Arzáns had cited the Black Death as a parallel for the plague of 1719, in his detailed description of the coronation celebrations of Louis Ferdinand I, held in 1725, he evoked the lavish display of a Burgundian *entrée joyeuse*. For there was staged an elaborate masque in the main square, with young nobles representing the king and his court. There then appeared a triumphal carriage, with statues on its four corners, representing the four continents, two figures of Justice and Mercy, and side images of the Inca kings of Peru from Manco Capac to Atahualpa bearing lamps. Then entered the ambassadors of the kings of France, Great Britain, Portugal, China, Turkey, Ethiopia, and, in person, the Inca king of Peru. Behind the figure of Fame, there appeared nine heroes: three Jews, Joshua, David and Judas Maccabaeus; three gentiles, Alexander, Hector and Julius Caesar; and three Christians, Charlemagne, King Arthur and

Godfrey de Bouillon. Finally, there came the seven planets each with their insignia, the sibyls, and the figures of Fame, Fortune, Deceit and Disillusion. The whole event was preceded by bull-fighting and parades, and followed by three comedies of which Arzáns exclaimed: 'these works of poetry are an animated history ... visible dreams in which reason is transported by the harmony of the senses'.[26] Here was a living public culture, in which spectacle and pageant satisfied both elite and masses, drawing on a tradition that had its roots as much in the Middle Ages as in the Renaissance, and still invoked at the beginning of the eighteenth century without any sense of incongruity or anachronism.

The vein of literary fantasy that enlivened Arzáns' description of contemporary events was even more apparent in the treatment of his patria's history. Indeed, without such gifts he could not have composed such a detailed and entertaining account. For how to write a chronicle about a town without any history? Where were the great deeds on which a narrative could be based? Where were the sources for such a chronicle? These were problems which all would-be creole historians encountered in these middle years of the colonial epoch. Some boldly resolved the difficulty by rewriting the works of their predecessors, a course already adopted by Solís. Others simply turned to annals utilising the records of religious chapters, town councils and other institutions. But Arzáns apparently had neither the inclination nor the opportunity to consult the city archives. With heroic audacity, however, he made a virtue of necessity and proceeded to invent no less than four historians purportedly dating from the period of Potosí's greatness, from whose manuscripts he devised an appropriate sequence of magistrates and events. The result was an action-packed chronicle in which the city was endowed with all the glamour of late medieval Spain, its streets haunted by perpetual affrays, its citizens engaged in violence and seduction, and its public life dignified by tournaments and masques. Nowhere was the element of fantasy more evident than in his account of a pageant allegedly held in 1608, where the 'creole youth and nobility' sallied forth in their richest apparel, all described in great detail, to a joust between two bands of forty knights. That the leader of one party was called Fernando Arzáns Dapifer y Toledo, cousin of the Duke of Alba and married to Elvira Espindola and that he was joined by Ceferino Colón, great-grandson of the Discoverer, only serves to demonstrate the delight with which Arzáns must have read chivalrous romances. At the same time, he asseverated that from 1579 onwards the city was haunted by internecine strife between the different nations of Spaniards and then between Spaniards and creoles. In this case there was a substratum of historical fact since, as Calancha had attested, in 1623–4 there had occurred a violent dispute between Basques and Castilians, in part caused by the arrogance and economic preponderance of the former party. But Arzáns devised entire battles with many deaths and then extended the conflict to encompass the entire seventeenth century.[27] Both the individual combats and the collective assaults which Arzáns described with such monotonous regularity conferred a strangely medieval air on a city whose citizens were primarily devoted to the purpose of self-enrichment.

If so much of Arzáns' chronicle expresses the triumph of literature over history, the source of his imaginings was by no means uncoloured by political prejudice. As his annals approached the period in which he lived, the strife between Basques and creoles, so often ignited by Europeans deriding creoles as mestizos, was transmuted into a constant plaint against the *chapetones*, young Spaniards, fresh from the Peninsula, who came to Potosí in search of wealth and women. Admittedly, Arzáns was obliged to recognise that most of the great fortunes in the city had been put together by immigrant entrepreneurs, either in mining or in trade, and that many of these men had endowed churches and convents and led respectable, pious lives. But he complained bitterly of 'the youth of Spain which always struts with insolence', and deplored their headstrong pursuit of women and addiction to gambling, the twin origins of so much bloodshed and uproar. Moreover, there was constant assertion of superiority, coupled with the insinuation that creoles were mestizos, degraded by impure blood and dishonourable ancestry. It was, no doubt, in response to such charges that Arzáns sung a familiar laud, declaring that the stars and climate of Potosí impelled men to great deeds, so that: 'Great is the intellect, discretion and courage of its creoles, great is their liberality and piety.' He further congratulated his compatriots on their 'acute understanding and happy memory', qualities which allowed them to master all the sciences. Such were their high spirits that few creoles wished to practise artisan crafts or become shopkeepers. Perhaps the only difference that Arzáns rang on this traditional theme was his growing use of the term 'Peruvians' to describe the American Spaniards, a term he applied indiscriminately to all creoles born within the limits of the former Inca empire.[28]

The degree to which Arzáns subscribed to the main tenets of creole patriotism, as enunciated by Calancha and Salinas, is manifest in the opening chapters of his work where he attempted to sketch an historical background. For although he refused to pronounce on the origins of the American Indians, he dwelt in some detail on the extensive travels of St Thomas in the New World. Yet he undercut the theological significance of that event by asserting that the Inca empire had endured for no less than 1,640 years, which is to say, over two centuries before the Incarnation of Christ. Content more to list the names of the Inca monarchs than discuss their achievements, Arzáns defended the Indians in unqualified terms, observing 'in general those of this Peruvian kingdom are of a most fine intelligence, clear understanding and general application'. If they had not developed any script, they had certainly recorded past events on their *quipus*. Since the conquest, the Indians had acted as painters and sculptors and indeed were responsible for building the churches. It was in recognition of their ability that in the 1690s Charles II had issued a rescript authorising the ordination of suitable candidates from the Indian nobility to the priesthood. Citing Solís on Mexico, he noted that 'some writers little friendly to the Spanish nation treat of the Indians as brutes incapable of reason so as to grant less esteem to their conquest'. But as the example of the Araucanians demonstrated, the natives of the New World were courageous and warlike and had it not been for the intervention of Divine Providence the Incas might well have defeated the Spaniards.[29]

If Arzáns displayed only tepid interest in the native past, by contrast he violently denounced the 'unspeakable cruelty of those who are called conquerors', men whose devastation had effected 'the ruin of the New World'. Drawing upon Las Casas' *Brevísima relación*, he lamented the wanton slaughter of millions of natives. At the same time, he was careful to invoke Herrera's description of the debate at Valladolid between Sepúlveda and the Dominican, admitting that the Crown had always sought to restrain the excesses of the conquerors. But it was for Pizarro and his band that Arzáns reserved his strongest condemnation, accusing them of being animated by 'greed, tyranny and ambition'. They had massacred thousands of defenceless natives and had then consumed their ill-gotten fortunes in fratricidal strife. Pizarro was a tyrant who had murdered Atahualpa and whose assassination was but just retribution for his crimes. Like Calancha, Arzáns commented on how few conquerors had survived the civil wars and on their failure to establish families on any lasting basis. Equally predictably, he praised Toledo as another Lycurgus whose laws still governed Peru, only then to lament his execution of Tupac Amaru, once more emphasising Philip II's rebuke to that viceroy, proof enough of the attraction of that story to creole patriots. On considering the entire process of conquest and rebellion, Arzáns marvelled at the contrast that existed between Peru and Mexico, between the just and prudent government established by Cortés and the gross tyranny which Pizarro had inaugurated. Indeed, when he further considered that few fortunes ever seemed to last more than two generations in Peru, he declared that 'without doubt the cause will be [found] in this kingdom being badly acquired by the Spaniards, since apart from the harm done in cold blood to the natives during their first raids, they now treat them worse than if they were slaves, as much in the mines as in the fields'.[30]

In effect, Arzáns defined the colonial regime as founded on violence and sustained by tyranny. On several occasions he questioned the justice of the *mita*, noting that Indians were usually desperate to avoid being drafted to the mines since they feared ill-treatment and accident. With what right did the authorities compel natives to work at Potosí when they had been defined by the Crown as free vassals? Did not the virtual enslavement of the Indians, embodied in the *mita*, confirm the tyrannical nature of the regime established by Pizarro and perpetuated by Toledo? Of their sufferings, 'of all which I am a witness', there could be no doubt. Perhaps the only remedy, so he mused, might be to abolish the *mita* and accept the consequent reduction in silver production as essentially beneficent. After all, the silver was exported so to allow Peru to import European cloth: would it not be better if the population at large wore cloth manufactured in Peru?[31]

The other great abuse of government attributed by Arzáns to Peru's unjust foundation, was 'the insatiable greed of its magistrates, especially of the corregidores of Indian districts'. In this context, he did not distinguish between Peruvian and Spanish magistrates, since both were guilty of the same exploitation of their native subjects. However, the theme that most provoked Arzáns was 'the infernal avarice' of the corregidores who governed Potosí during his lifetime, noting that even the Count of La Granja, whom he praised for his admirable qualities, had carried off a small fortune. He noted that one magistrate was accused of allowing his black slaves to rob and abuse the Indians. Yet when a parish priest publicly denounced one of these men for his murder of a native woman, the corregidor had him imprisoned. This arbitrary act, contrary to canon law, led to the magistrate's excommunication. In conclusion, Arzáns declared that although the Spanish monarchs had striven to protect and assist their subjects, their ministers and judges 'have shown themselves to be impious, lacking in charity, reason and justice, all their efforts going to grab silver and gold, without their greed ever able to satisfy their hydropic thirst for wealth'.[32] In this judgement, he adopted a perspective on the colonial regime which was remarkably similar to the tirades of Guaman Poma a century before.

As his life drew towards its close, Arzáns found more rather than less to bewail. In particular, he denounced the Marquis of Castelfuerte, viceroy of Peru 1724–36, as a 'most cruel tyrant' under whose harsh regime no less than ten corregidores were killed by popular protest. If this number may be too high, it was certainly the case that this viceroy launched what one admiring contemporary called 'the second conquest' of Peru, in an attempt to strengthen royal authority and increase the flow of revenue into the treasury. By far the most unpopular act of his term of government was the execution in Lima of José de Antequera, a creole attorney who had fallen foul of the Jesuits in Paraguay. Here is no place to discuss the complicated tangle of events in that turbulent province where for a period of ten years the citizens of Asunción made and broke governors, sought to expel the Jesuits, and generally testified to the fragility of royal authority. Antequera had been sent to quell the riots but instead had allowed himself to be installed as a popularly acclaimed governor. In the upshot he was tried for treason in Lima and sentenced to death. But his execution provoked popular protests in which the Franciscans joined. To restrain the populace, Castelfuerte ordered his guard to fire on the crowd, thereby killing many people, including two friars. In his detailed report on these proceedings, Arzáns noted that the entire kingdom was indignant at 'the violences and rigour of his Excellency'.[33]

Equally disturbing for the Crown and of great interest to Arzáns was the revolt which broke out in Cochabamba in 1730. In that town, which was inhabited by a numerous body of mestizos, Castelfuerte's agents sought to increase the tribute register by inscribing many mestizos as Indians, the measure rendered all the more hateful by personal insults and menaces. The result was a popular riot led by Alejo Calatayud, a mestizo silversmith, whom Arzáns described as a 'man of high spirit, well-read in histories and of great understanding'. Shouting 'Long live the king! Death to the greedy tyrants of Spain!' the mob looted stores and houses and eventually massacred thirty-nine European Spaniards. Once the religious and parish priests sallied forth with the sacrament, however, the mestizos ceased their depredations and order was restored. As token of their loyalty and deference to the established hierarchy, they allowed the election of two members of the creole elite as municipal magistrates. In the event, these magistrates summoned the creole nobility of the entire valley to assist them, seized Calatayud and his chief associates, and then had the rebel leaders executed. In this case, if Arzáns deplored the arbitrary procedures of the viceroy's officers, he chose not to commend the ensuing rebellion, only expressing the hope that the king would choose ministers willing to rule with justice. The case of Cochabamba was significant in that it formed a prelude to an entire series of revolts in the Andean highlands during the ensuing half century.[34]

Despite his biting attack on the current regime, Arzáns was no closet rebel, since he was persuaded that Providence had intervened to assure Spanish dominion of the New World. Moreover, he fully accepted the contemporary view that political authority derived from heaven, observing that 'kings are the viceroys of God. If the dignity of God is great, then great is that of the king who represents Him ... ' Such reverence, however, did not extend to the king's ministers, since he denounced the so-called statesmen and politicians who framed their counsel in a mode of 'Machiavellian madness', in which ambition and avarice were masked by an appeal to 'reason of state' and 'the common good'. Indeed, Arzáns sharply questioned the entire hierarchy of ethnic and social distinctions which underpinned the colonial regime. In complaining of the arrogance of both peninsular magistrates and immigrant youngsters, he exclaimed: 'Noble and plebeian, poor and rich, black and white – all of us descend from the same father and mother, which was Adam and Eve.' True nobility derived from good deeds rather than from birth or ancestry, and in any case the priesthood was superior in honour to any secular title or state.[35] In another passage, he pronounced that there was far too much emphasis on lineage and honour, so that men 'more prize being nobles than being

Christians', a reflection which led him to the yet more radical conclusion that 'the sovereigns of this world (generally speaking) are arrogant, presumptuous and always filled with ambition'. If we note that Arzáns cited Bodin as arguing that all states began in violence and tyranny, then it can be concluded that he viewed political authority in Peru from an Augustinian perspective, defining the magistrates and ministers of the Crown as inherently corrupt, their regime radically warped by its origin in the violence and injustice of the conquest. In all this, the legacy of Las Casas is manifest.[36]

To close the discussion of Arzáns' chronicle on a note of high political doctrine would be to misread his purpose and the very real achievement of his literary endeavour. The sententious reflections that he inserted into his narrative were generally conventional, at times contradictory, and often borrowed from his reading without acknowledgement. The plaints against the greed of magistrates, no matter how justified, echoed the denunciations of the conquerors' greed launched by Las Casas two centuries before. But whereas the polemic of the Dominican and indeed of Guaman Poma attained a prophetic gravity, by contrast, Arzáns remained a mere witness, a recording angel, so to say, rather than a spokesman for the exploited. In any case, his attention soon turned from civic corruption to yet one more disedifying but fascinating tale of seduction and passion. His literary vocation triumphed over his historical intent.

One last comment appears appropriate. Although Arzáns was happy to condemn 'the viceroy of Lima' for his despotism, he offered few reflections on the state of Peru at large. His patriotism and indeed his experience appear to have been limited to Potosí. In this context, it is possibly significant that he exhibited little enthusiasm for the canonisation of St Rosa, despite her proclamation as patron of Peru. Indeed, since he applied the term *Peruanos* to all creoles born in the vast area that stretched from Quito to Charcas, it is clear that he possessed little if any provincial loyalties.[37] The city of Chuquisaca did not figure as a true capital of the territory subject to its high court. Yet Lima was distant and rarely visited. If creole patriots in the Andean zone failed to encounter any unifying theme which might have served to articulate a more specifically Peruvian ideology, it was because the viceroyalty lacked a true capital and an intellectual elite able to fulfil this role. In its absence, patriotic sentiment remained caught between a generalised creole identity and a particular loyalty to each major city within this vast empire.

III

The absence of any historical sources equivalent to the Mexican codices meant that the Cuzqueño elite's approach to the Inca past continued to be circumscribed by Garcilaso's *Comentarios reales*. Nor did the humdrum life of a

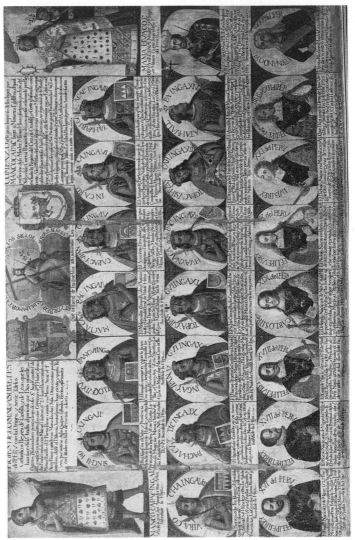

22 Portraits of the monarchs of Peru

provincial capital inspire any chronicle of the kind written by Arzáns y Orsua. Instead, the city was blessed with a careful compilation of its annals, the life-work of Diego de Esquivel y Navia (1700?–1779), an illegitimate son of the creole Marquis of Valleumbroso and eventual dean of the cathedral chapter. Although he warmly embraced Calancha's thesis of an apostolic mission in Peru and dated the foundation of Cuzco as early as 1043, he penned but a stolid account of the Inca regime, bereft of patriotic sentiment, other than in the formal commendation that 'their great deeds . . . in both government and laws, were regulated according to natural law, with the exception of their idolatry and the sensual license of their princes'. If he echoed Garcilaso's condemnation of the executions of Atahualpa and Tupac Amaru, he chose not to question the value of the conquest or dwell on the cruelty of the conquerors. Thereafter, he drew on city and diocesan archives to provide a remarkably precise history of colonial Cuzco, in which he listed the appointment of its magistrates and bishops and the establishment of its chief institutions. He also set out in some detail the elaborate rites that marked the coronation and exequies of reigning monarchs, the consecration of churches, and the incidence of natural disasters. The great earthquake of 1650, which levelled most of the city's churches, was followed by a penitential procession of the religious communities, in which the Franciscans walked naked to the waist, carrying crosses and chains, with crowns of thorns on their heads, and their shoulders bloody from scourging.[38] So too, the plague of 1720, which carried off 20,000 souls in Cuzco alone, was greeted by collective prayer and procession. But it was only as he approached events in his own lifetime – he closed his account in 1749 – that Esquivel allowed his pen to stray into the sort of lively anecdote that Arzáns delighted to recount. Among the most striking passages was his description of the arrival in 1739 of Franciscan preachers, belonging to the newly established college of Propaganda Fide at Ocapa, who terrified their congregations by dire predictions of hellfire for all sinners. So compelling were their sermons – one friar applied a burning taper to his flesh to simulate the pains of the damned – that the city undertook mass penitence, many sinners sallying forth to scourge themselves in public. All this stood in marked contrast to the decline in fervour among the resident religious, since he reported that one Augustinian prior demanded that all his friars should find their own board and lodging, allowing them into the priory only for the celebration of mass and the office.[39]

Although Esquivel rarely interjected comments on the events he described, his perspective, when expressed, was remarkably similar to the views of Arzáns. He did not hesitate to blame a group of young Basques for provoking conflict between American and European Spaniards in which several indivi-duals lost their lives, noting that the immigrants had mocked creoles as mestizos. But he refrained from all but the most discreet reference to his own father, the Marquis of Valleumbroso, who was renowned for his hatred of peninsulars, and whose various acts of arbitrary power, when corregidor of Cuzco, led to his eventual imprisonment. On two separate occasions, however, Esquivel condemned *repartimientos de comercio*, the enforced distribution of merchandise by corregidors as 'contrary to all law and lacking in religion'. Noting the deaths of several of these magistrates during the administration of the Marquis of Castelfuerte, he attributed popular violence to the abuse and oppression of the corregidors. In an echo of Garcilaso, he reported that, on Castelfuerte's return to Spain, the king reproved him so harshly for his arbitrary rule, especially as regards the execution of José de Antequera, that he soon died thereafter, shattered by grief. Equally important, Esquivel recorded that when news reached Cuzco in 1742 of the rebellion in Jauja led by a kuraka who called himself Juan Santos Atahualpa, the authorities at once rounded up a group of Inca nobility resident in the city, fearful of their complicity. Later, he noted that the Franciscans in Jauja had been assured by the rebel leader that he had no quarrel with the Catholic faith, his purpose being 'to restore the kingdom and banish bad government'. Despite the cautious quality of his annals, Esquivel thus testified to the growing unrest among the Andean population in the eighteenth century, disturbances which he blamed on the despotic character of the colonial regime.[40]

No such reflections were allowed to impede the publication of the *Relación de la fundación de la real audiencia del Cuzco*, a brief work published in Madrid in 1795, which both commemorated the establishment of a high court and lauded the glories of Cuzco, in what was the first extended application of the rhetoric of creole patriotism to the former Inca capital. As was customary on such exercises, Ignacio de Castro (1732–92), the rector of the university college of San Bernardo Abad, seized the opportunity to parade his erudition, albeit adorning his account with multiple references to such modern authorities as Montesquieu, Voltaire, Molière, Jaucourt and Bossuet, to mention but the most obvious of his citations. His implicit homage to France was accompanied by a nervous insistence on correct style and good taste, the necessary expression of 'such an enlightened and refined century'. So persuasive were the imperatives of the new refinement that Castro sought to jettison the syllogisms of scholastic philosophy, the heavy cargo of quotations that had accompanied Baroque erudition, and the conceits of a Peralta, replacing these traditional features of learned discourse by simplicity and concision. By way of a practical demonstration of the new felicity in style, he organised a university discussion, in which his students calmly analysed the relative merits of different forms of government. Drawing heavily on Bossuet and Montesquieu, they condemned the anarchy that afflicted the republican constitutions of Poland and Great Britain, scorned the barbaric despotism of the Great Turk, and concluded that absolute monarchy of the sort favoured by the Bourbons offered the most paternal and beneficent mode of exercising political authority. Here was a conclusion that accorded with the speech of the president of the new court at Cuzco, who acclaimed the king as the source of all law and institutions, asserting that 'Majesty is an image of the grandeur of God which is reflected in the Sovereign.'[41]

Despite its insistent modernity, the *Relación del Cuzco* served the thoroughly traditional purpose of civic eulogy. Castro described in some detail the *entrée joyeuse* of the royal seal, the court's legal warrant, which was brought into the city protected from the elements by a canopy of the sort usually reserved for the Eucharist, escorted by a procession of royal officials, Indian caciques and local dignitaries, all parading through carpeted streets lined with curious crowds. High mass in the cathedral was followed by a lavish reception, fireworks, comedies, dances, a pantomime, and three days of bull-fights. So too, Castro listed all the city's many institutions – its cathedral and chapter, two colleges, five priories, six parishes, four hospitals and four nunneries. However, he was obliged to admit that the city was in the midst of an economic decline and that several of its religious institutions were thoroughly decadent. The cathedral could not afford to maintain a full complement of canons and both the Dominican and Augustinian priories housed substantially fewer friars than in earlier years. Only the convent of Santa Clara still thrived, with a population of over five hundred women and girls, of whom only a fifth were professed nuns. If the Church was impoverished, it was because the chief products of the region, sugar and woollens, had suffered from competition, although the crisis in textiles was in part caused by a shift from Spanish-owned establishments to small artisan workshops run by Indians.[42]

Although he noted the European view that Spain had declined precisely because of its dependence on the American empire, Castro argued that Peru and Mexico constituted the foundation of the monarchy's strength, and hailed Philip V as the restorer of its power. His patriotism only became overt in an extended comparison of the two Indian empires, where he asserted that 'Peru exceeded Mexico in policy.' Whereas the Aztec realm had been stained by human sacrifice and despotic demands for tribute, by contrast the Incas were renowned for their public works, moral virtues, riches and the very extent of their empire. Manco Capac was another Confucius and the only equal of Inca roads was the Great Wall of China. Indeed, in terms worthy of his century, he referred to the Incas as endowed with 'minds filled with natural lights, capable of doing honour to humanity'. Castro's animus against Mexico extended into the colonial period, since he declared that the apparitions of the Virgin Mary and Santiago at Cuzco were far more significant than the apparitions of Our Lady of Guadalupe. He lamented the contrasting fates of the two imperial capitals, concluding that 'the exaltation of Lima was the depression of Cuzco', especially since the Andean city had figured for several centuries as a capital: 'it always gave laws, it never received them'. All the more reason, then, to celebrate the inauguration of a high court which at last raised Cuzco to the level of Quito and Chuquisaca.[43] What passed with but fleeting mention in all this was the great Indian rebellion of 1780 in which a local kuraka, José Gabriel Tupac Amaru, had sought to revive the Inca monarchy, only to encounter the determined resistance of the bishop and clergy of Cuzco.

IV

The all pervasive sense of economic decline which haunted the Andean zone in the eighteenth century was matched by a vigorous affirmation of provincial identity. In his *Historia del reino de Quito* (1789), Juan de Velasco (1727–92), an exiled Jesuit and a native of Riobamba, launched a fierce attack on those contemporary European historians who sought to denigrate the character of the American Indians and boldly endowed his patria with an impressive pre-hispanic history. Unlike such fellow Jesuits as Francisco Javier Clavijero and Ignacio Molina, Velasco displayed little comprehension of the issues at stake in the grand controversy over the quality of nature in the New World and its determining effect on all forms of life in the hemisphere. Instead, he compiled lists of rivers, mountains, birds, animals and plants, content simply to transcribe their names in Quechua. For the rest, he lauded the most obvious achievements of the Incas and saluted the talents of contemporary Indians as painters, sculptors and musicians. In effect, Velasco relied on a few primary printed sources supplemented by the notes and manuscripts he had collected prior to his exile in 1767. Persuaded that there were birds generated by flowers on trees and that human hair, once cut and earthed, could turn into snakes, the Ecuadorean Jesuit subscribed to a Baroque world-view, in which miracle, marvel and myth still regularly appeared on the historical horizon. An ardent patriot and a pious Jesuit, he composed the last great colonial chronicle, dedicating it to the current minister of the Indies, Antonio Porlier, so as to obtain its publication, a vain gesture since it was destined to see print only after independence.[44]

On the origin of the American Indians, Velasco was nothing if not eclectic, since he postulated land-bridges both between Brazil and Africa and across the Bering Straits, but supposed that the Peruvians had arrived by sea, slowly traversing the Pacific islands. But, no matter what their first home, all Indians were defined as the descendants of Ham. As for Ecuador, the ancient nation of the Quitas had been 'barbaric, rustic and uncultivated'. Like their Peruvian neighbours, however, they had benefited from the preaching of St Thomas, whose legacy could be discerned in their belief in Pachacamac, the Supreme Being, and in those religious rites which resembled the Christian sacraments. In any case, had not Christ instructed his apostles to preach the gospel to all nations? There was no good reason to suppose that the inhabitants of America had been denied this privilege; indeed, the carvings at Tiahuanuco probably dated from the era of the Christian mission.[45] If there was nothing in these speculations to startle any creole patriot, Velasco innovated decisively in providing Quito with a powerful monarchy that was the exact contemporary of the Inca state. Drawing either on his own fertile imagination or on a manuscript dealing with the civil wars of Atahualpa and Huascar that had been written by Jacinto Collahuazo, the cacique of Ibarra, he asserted that the country had been invaded from the sea by the Caran Scyri, a people of advanced culture. By 1000 AD these newcomers had conquered the uplands and created a realm that was to be governed by fifteen kings of whom, however, Velasco could only name the last four. That they spoke the same language as the Incas demonstrated that they had come from the same overseas country. Somewhat less ingenious than their Peruvian counterparts, they kept records with the help of coloured stones rather than by elaborately knotted strings, but displayed much the same skill in textiles and other applied arts. They worshipped the sun and the moon and built temples which housed observatories.[46] In all this, Velasco freely admitted that, by reason of the absence of reliable evidence, all American history was based on tradition which mingled fable with fact.

The patriotic purpose that inspired Velasco's chronicle was much in evidence when he dealt with the Inca conquest of Quito in 1487, on which material could be gleaned from Garcilaso and Cieza de León. Although he carefully noted that Huayna Capac had defeated the last Scyri king in open battle and thereafter slaughtered some 40,000 men who rebelled against his conquest, Velasco praised 'the wise laws and prudent government' of the great Inca who had punished a coastal people for their practice of sodomy and who maintained the prohibition against all forms of human sacrifice. He lauded the palaces, temples, fortresses and roads of the Incas as proof of their advanced culture and defended their rope bridges as far more practical than any stone structures which were always liable to destruction during earthquake tremors. He emphasised that the Incas believed in a Supreme Being, the immortality of the soul, heaven and hell, and possessed vestiges of the seven Christian sacraments. Their empire resembled a great family, since 'The Incas raised their empire on the powers of the souls and not on the blood of their subjects.' At the same time, he judged their military system to be more remarkable than their religion, based as it was on transplanted communities and the regular guard of *orejones*, and insisted that their conquests derived from 'pure ambition and desire to rule'. Garcilaso's thesis of a benevolent, civilising mission was not borne out by the facts. Indeed, if Velasco proved so willing to praise Inca rule, it was in part because Huayna Capac married the daughter of the last Scyri king and thus legitimised his conquest by marriage to the heir to the throne. It followed that Atahualpa, the fruit of this union, was not the cruel usurper described by Garcilaso, who merely echoed Cuzqueño calumny, but was rather the legitimate king of Quito and a just and prudent king to boot.[47]

In his account of the Spanish conquest and the ensuing civil wars, Velasco quarried from such standard printed sources as Gómara, Jerez, Zárate and Garcilaso a narrative of events in Quito and Popayán, adding material drawn from a manuscript he possessed written by Marcos de Niza, a Franciscan associate of Las Casas, resident in Peru at that time. Although Velasco savagely condemned Pizarro's native interpreter, Filipillo, as 'the most iniquitous man who ever walked on earth', he also sharply criticised the Spanish leader for his treacherous assault on Atahualpa at Cajamarca and still more for the subsequent judicial murder. Pizarro's infamy was further demonstrated by his decision to execute Almagro, the most honest and just of the conquerors. Turning to Quito, Velasco commented that, after the seizure of Atahualpa, the Inca general Rumiñahui, himself a native of the region, massacred the monarch's children and family, sacked temples, and generally acted as a murderous tyrant. In reaction, many native lords welcomed Sebastían de Benalcázar and indeed Atahualpa's uncle, Cuchulima, assisted the Spaniards, accepted baptism and, in return, was recognised as governor of Riobamba, where his descendants continued to thrive for another 150 years. But although Velasco described Benalcázar as a wise, humane governor, he denounced his chief lieutenants as a breed of Neros, guilty of 'bloody cruelties and tyrannies against the Indians of Quito, devastating their villages with fire and blood'. Many caciques were tortured to extract information about Inca treasure and some were thrown to the dogs. Such was the general disruption that fields were left untended and many people later died of famine. Moreover, barely had the conquest finished than there came the infliction of 'the miserable slavery' of encomiendas and the desolation wrought by the civil wars. On Gonzalo Pizarro, Velasco pronounced that all his crimes had derived from 'that bloody monster', Francisco de Carbajal, and denied that he had ever sought to become king of Peru. In a subsequent passage he noted that many Indians had taken refuge in the Amazonian jungles after the fall of Vilcabamba, adding that virtually everyone lamented the execution of Tupac Amaru who 'died with great fortitude and noble spirit and, made an apostle, from the scaffold exhorted his people to receive the faith of Jesus Christ as the only true one'.[48]

In his approach to the conquest, Velasco thus rejected Garcilaso's calm acceptance of its turmoil and came close to echoing the condemnation of Las Casas. In his view the only justification for the Spanish invasion was the opportunity it allowed for the preaching of the gospel. Yet conquerors like Pedro de Alvarado were simply inspired by 'the ambition for more honour, united to the desire to accumulate more riches'. That he exempted Benalcázar from the charges of oppression, however, suggests that he sought to provide an honourable and just foundation for his patria. Indeed, he commented that, because Spanish authors had offered an honest account of the conquest without glossing over cruelties and misdeeds, foreign historians now blamed the entire Spanish nation for these crimes. Yet both Spanish monarchs and their ministers and magistrates had acted to halt these excesses and to punish malefactors. Were there not men like Oliver Cromwell, capable of overturning all laws, to be found in all nations? In any case, in conquering a great empire with so few men, Pizarro had displayed an heroic courage that had won glory for the Spanish name throughout the world. If the Indians had suffered violence and injustice, the conquest ensured that 'they were introduced to a rational, political and civil life, the light of the Gospel greatly compensating for all the evils they suffered'.[49]

On beginning the third part of his chronicle, which he entitled 'modern history', Velasco confessed that it was difficult to cover a period of over 200 years without delving into archives, or indeed, to describe events without causing tedium. He complained that foreigners still applied the term 'kingdoms of Peru' to all Spanish possessions in South America despite the creation of the viceroyalty of New Granada in 1739, which covered the provinces of Venezuela, Panama, New Granada and Quito. Just what lands fell within the kingdom of Quito was not at all clear, since the high court which had been established in 1563 exercised jurisdiction over Popayán as well as 'Quito proper'. The situation was further complicated by ecclesiastical boundaries since, whereas the bishops of Trujillo and Cuenca acknowledged the archbishop of Lima as their metropolitan, the diocese of Quito and Popayán came under Bogotá. Rather than imitate Esquivel and compile annals, a genre more appropriate for a single city, Velasco chose to emulate Fuentes y Guzmán, which is to say, he offered a summary description of each jurisdiction in the kingdom. Not that his data was copious, since on Cuenca, for example, he had little more to say than commend its benign climate. Guayaquil merited mention largely by reason of the several pirate assaults it had suffered. Nor indeed did Velasco write much about Popayán other than to comment on the richness of its gold fields, which were sustained by the labour of imported black slaves, a prosperity which allowed the settlers to repel the attacks of the unsubjugated Indian tribes still lurking on the jungle frontiers.[50]

It was the city of Quito which most attracted Velasco's laud and lament. For here was a capital second only to Lima in size and magnificence, with a population reckoned at over 50,000 souls, served by a cathedral, seven parishes, thirteen priories and colleges of the religious orders, and six nunneries. It possessed two university colleges, founded respectively by the Jesuits and the Dominicans, in which an impressive number of bishops, judges and other notabilities had been educated. The architecture of the city, especially of the Jesuit church, had attracted the commendation of European travellers. Despite these impressive features, Velasco lamented that the city and its immediate

provinces had suffered a profound decline; the golden age of the Habsburg era
was long since past. Quito had once housed forty men who were knights of the
chivalrous orders; now there were but seven titles of nobility in the city. More
important, the wealth which had once flowed into the province, based first on
silver and gold mining, but then more importantly on the production and
export of woollen cloth to Lima, was no longer forthcoming. The opening of
direct trade routes around Cape Horn meant that the merchants of Peru could
purchase European cloth of finer quality and lower price than anything
produced in Quito. The result was that, in Riobamba where twenty *obrajes*
had thrived, only five remained in production and these were threatened with
closure. Since the province still imported goods from Europe but now lacked
exports, its economy lacked sufficient currency to maintain its activities.[51]

For the rest, Velasco listed the eruptions of Pichincha, the volcanic mountain
which periodically splattered Quito with ash and stones, and noted the impact
of epidemics on the population. That a riot in 1592 against the imposition of
the sales tax had been quelled largely thanks to the intervention of the Jesuits
merited its inclusion in his text. But it was the popular tumult of 1765 which
elicited his closest attention. Caused by the establishment of a royal monopoly
in brandy administered by excise officials whose extortions aroused popular
resentment, the riot was precipitated by the European Spaniards, some three
hundred in number, whom the authorities summoned to patrol the streets at
night, an exercise which soon led to dispute and the death of several mestizos.
The result was a mass uprising fired by cries of 'Long Live the King', 'Death to
the *chapetón* rogues.' At this point the judges of the high court chose to defend
the government palace with artillery, a manoeuvre which caused more deaths
and infuriated the mob still more. In the upshot the judges and all European
Spaniards had to go into hiding or flee the city, which was taken over by the
mestizos. It took the creole patricians and the Jesuits some two months to calm
the situation and negotiate a settlement whereby the Europeans were expelled
from the city but saved from murder. By this time, however, the viceroy had
despatched a force of 700 soldiers who were soon able to impose law and order
and allow the Europeans to return. The incident closely resembled the riot in
Cochabamba in 1730 as described by Arzáns y Orsúa, and was but a prelude to
the more serious disturbances which, in 1780, erupted in Arequipa and Socorro.
Although Velasco chose not to comment on the riot other than to note the loyal
intervention of the Jesuits, his sympathies obviously did not lie with the
European Spaniards.[52]

To the east of 'Quito proper', there lay the vast territories covered by the
Amazonian jungles, inhabited by bands of Indians who often strongly resisted
Spanish encroachments. In the province of Macas, for example, extensive gold
deposits were discovered in the sixteenth century, sufficient to maintain several
camps and at least two towns. But in 1599, so Velasco related, the Jívaro

nation, at that time reckoned to number 30,000 souls, joined with their neighbours in a surprise attack on Logroño and succeeded in slaughtering all its male inhabitants and carrying off the women. So fierce and persistent were their attacks that elsewhere camps were deserted and the remaining urban settlements abandoned. What most interested Velasco was the similarity in character of the Jívaros and the Araucanians 'in the multitude of numerous tribes, in the courage and military skill, in the spirit of independence. In their great aversion to the European yoke, they seem to be so similar that it is not easy to discern which enjoys the preference.' As in Chile, controversy raged as to the best way to conquer and convert such Indians, fired in this case by the hope of rediscovering the gold fields. But in 1690–1, when the local governor led an expedition of 1,750 men into the area, he met only with deserted villages and constant ambush, gold conspicuous only by its absence.[53] By the eighteenth century the province had a mere five hundred inhabitants who scratched a bare living growing tobacco.

As a loyal Jesuit, Velasco concluded his 'modern history' with an extended narrative of the Company's missions in the province of Marañon, or Maynas, drawing on earlier printed accounts and manuscript sources. It was a dramatic but unhappy story he had to relate, the constancy of missionary endeavour buffeted by the ebb and flow of native rebellion, epidemic disease and Portuguese invasion, its initial success dissolving into eventual failure. Although the Jesuits here pursued much the same policy and methods as they applied in Paraguay, they failed to establish their missions on a permanent footing, defeated by the jungle environment and the character of the Indians who exhibited, so Velasco averred, a 'natural inclination to sloth and an independent life'. Although the province was explored soon after the foundation of the Jesuit college at Quito in 1585, it was not until 1638 that mission stations were established, their activities not funded by the Crown until 1725. At their height, the Jesuits brought 160,000 Indians under their charge, settled in 74 villages. But the ravages of epidemic disease carried off some 44,000 natives in 1660, and an estimated 66,000 in 1680. Several Indian communities rebelled against the mission regime and many more simply fled further into the jungle, the more especially as they came to associate the Jesuits with the infliction of the plague and smallpox. The culminating blow occurred in 1710 when a force of 1,500 Portuguese, assisted by 4,000 Indians, ascended the Marañon in an armada of canoes, attacked the missions and captured thousands of unfortunate natives for enslavement. By 1767, when the Jesuits were expelled, the surviving missions housed but 18,000 Indians. Small wonder that Velasco should have lamented that 'all the toil, sweat and blood of so many illustrious labourers' in the vineyard should have yielded so little fruit. What is striking here was the degree to which the Jesuits relied on almost equal numbers of American and European Spaniards to staff the missions in the first forty years, only then to recruit Germans and Italians to assist them, so that in the years 1727–67 Velasco counted twenty-six Americans, twenty Spaniards, nineteen Germans and twelve Italians active in the field, clear evidence of the international character of the Company of Jesus. Of all the superiors, however, Velasco singled out Juan Lorenzo Lucero, a native of Pasto, whom he saluted as 'worthy by reason of his wisdom and talent to govern an entire monarchy', the greatest man that the kingdom of Quito produced in the seventeenth century.[54]

One last comment is necessary. At all points in his modern history Velasco inserted miraculous incidents in the most matter-of-fact fashion. After having been pushed into a river, the first Jesuit martyr in Marañón remained stationary and immobile above the waters, calmly preaching penitence to his attackers, before finally sinking beneath the waves. Sufferers from one epidemic were healed simply through being touched by a holy Jesuit, and in another case an epidemic was halted by the prayers of the celebrated Quiteño *beata*, Mariana de Paredes. In Lacatunga, a Jesuit endowed with prophetic powers denounced the disorders associated with the celebration of religious feast-days and foretold an eruption of Mount Cotopaxi if they did not cease. Sure enough, an earthquake soon occurred with considerable loss of life. In Riobamba, when a Lutheran stabbed the host at mass, the angry congregation killed him with their swords, only to find that they drew no blood, the altar thus saved from further desecration. What united all these incidents is that they dealt with natural phenomena: there are no apparitions, inspired dreams or miraculous images described in Velasco's chronicle. Nor did he develop any themes of religious significance which were peculiar to Quito.[55]

In many respects, the *Historia de Quito* was the last great colonial chronicle to be composed within the Baroque convention of creole patriotism. It confirmed what Peralta, Arzáns and Esquivel had implicitly attested, that patriotic identity in the vast territory once ruled by the Incas was confined to the city and its immediate province. The creole elite of Lima had failed to generate myths or images which might have articulated the identity of Peru as the successor of Tawantinsuyu. For, although the wealth of Potosí and the glamour of Lima as an American Ophir dazzled the chroniclers of the Habsburg era, by the eighteenth century the entire region was haunted by a sense of economic decline. The golden age had passed. In this context, Velasco's invention of the Caran Scyri dynasty, when combined with his assertion of Atahualpa's legitimacy, provided Quito with an alternative pre-Inca past, and constituted a legitimate rationale for its future autonomy. Apart from this distinctive past, however, Velasco failed to identify any character, property or myth which distinguished his patria from any other city or province within the Andean zone other than the heroic but disastrous story of its Jesuit missions, an enterprise in which local creoles had acted with great distinction.

In effect, it was only through appeal to their separate histories that the creole elites of the provincial capitals of the Andean zone could lay claim to self-government and local identity. All the more reason, therefore, to resurrect the past, even if the sources had to be invented.

19

HISTORY AND PHILOSOPHY

I

IN 1737 a French scientific expedition led by Charles-Marie de la Condamine (1701–74) arrived in Quito, there to conduct astronomical and physical observations designed to measure the precise limits of the degrees of latitude at the arc of the earth's meridian. The purpose here was to resolve the controversy between Isaac Newton and his opponents as to whether the globe slightly bulged at the equator or at the two poles. In the event it took four distinguished members of the French Academy of Sciences some six years of physical hardship and social deprivation in the high puna of Quito to demonstrate the accuracy of Newton's calculations. A Spanish companion later marvelled that men of rank and learning should have endured the freezing cold and rural isolation for so long. The local population, accustomed to scourge their shoulders in expiation of sins or suffer from cold in search of silver, viewed the expedition's mathematical ardour with incredulity and suspicion. Had it not been for the express orders of Spain's French king, Philip V, the academicians could not have entered South America, still less commanded the assistance of the colonial authorities. As it was, the expedition's high-spirited young physician, Jean Seniergues, angered the dignitaries of Cuenca by arousing the affections of a local beauty and was murdered by the crowd at a bull-fight.[1] The worlds of Newton and Arzáns y Orsúa briefly touched and parted in mutual incomprehension.

In his travel account, published in Paris in 1745–6, La Condamine paid tribute to the enlightened patronage of the Spanish king, thanked the Jesuits of Quito for their hospitality, and deplored the unhappy fate of Seniergues. For the rest, he described his ascent of Mount Cotopaxi and his adventurous voyage down the Amazon. It was his comments on the native inhabitants of the New World that attracted most attention. In phrases worthy of Sepúlveda, the French scientist described the American Indians as 'the enemies of work, indifferent to all motives of glory, honour or knowledge', their lives dominated by current necessities, without thought or feeling for the future. He pronounced: 'they grow old without ever leaving infancy, all of whose faults they preserve'. This stark judgement applied not merely to the savage attached to the Amazonian missions, but also to the unfortunate natives of Peru whose serfdom recalled the condition of contemporary Greeks subject to the Ottoman Turks. La Condamine concluded by expressing his inability to reconcile the elevated image of the Incas provided by Garcilaso de la Vega with the degradation of their descendants, a puzzle rendered all the more intractable by his assertion that Indian languages lacked the terms to express general or abstract ideas.[2] In these observations, the French scientist displayed much the same perspective as the Spanish humanists of the sixteenth century, and thus demonstrated the continuity between the Enlightenment and the Renaissance.

If Philip V took the unprecedented step of allowing foreign academicians to enter his overseas domain, it was in part because, by the early eighteenth century, Spain had acquired a reputation abroad for intellectual retardation. Once feared for its intransigent Catholicism, the Peninsula was now scorned for its cultural inertia. The revolution in science associated with the names of Copernicus, Galileo, Kepler, Boyle, Leibniz and Newton was a European movement in which Spaniards were conspicuous only by their absence. As the Benedictine abbot, Benito Jerónimo Feijoo (1676–1764), admitted in his *Teatro crítico universal* (1726–39), 'physics and mathematics are almost foreigners in Spain'. Indeed, he confessed that in the study of nature Spanish universities still relied on Aristotle, pinned like faded butterflies to the level of 1600. A devoted reader of the memoirs of the French Academy of Science and of other learned societies, Feijoo sought to transmit to a broad public some notion of the recent advances in knowledge, at all points emphasising the primacy of observation and experiment over argument and authority. As cautious as he was orthodox, he remained sceptical about the philosophic systems derived from the new discoveries by Descartes and Gassendi, but openly admitted that in the natural sciences the teachings of Aristotle had been superseded. The patriotic and didactic purpose animating his enterprise can be most clearly observed in his essay on 'The Glories of Spain', in which he repudiated foreign slander, defended the past achievements of his nation, and drew attention to the works of José de Acosta, 'the Pliny of the New World'.[3] For all that, his reliance on French and English sources – he greatly admired Francis Bacon – testified to the all-pervasive sense that Spain had been overtaken by the nations of northern Europe in the pursuit of knowledge.

That Philip V chose two young naval lieutenants to accompany La Condamine's expedition rather than despatch any Spanish savant, testified to the accuracy of Feijoo's comments. For both men had been educated at the recently established Naval Academy at Cadiz, where they had acquired the rudiments of mathematics and astronomy necessary for their profession. It was to counter the unfavourable impression created by La Condamine's travel account that the

Crown encouraged Jorge Juan y Santacilla and Antonio de Ulloa to write their own narrative of the expedition, a work which duly emerged in five volumes entitled *Relación histórica del viaje a la América meridional* (1748) and which was translated into the leading European languages. In this context, it should be noted that the English versions omitted the volume, which consisted of astronomical and physical observations undertaken by Jorge Juan (1713–73) in which the Spaniard amply demonstrated his mathematical expertise. In the second edition of his work, published separately in 1773, Juan inserted a preface in which he provided a brief history of astronomy and praised Newton as 'the greatest of philosophers', who had demonstrated that the heavens and earth were governed by laws that could be expressed in mathematical equations. Although the Papal authorities had once condemned Copernicus, all Europe including Italy now accepted the Newtonian system; for Spain to reject his findings would make the country the laughing-stock of Europe. Jorge Juan also employed his expertise to practical, official advantage when he served as director of the mercury mine at Almadén, acted as commandant of the royal naval arsenal at Ferrol, composed a 'compendium of navigation' and purchased astronomical instruments for the royal observatory at Cadiz.[4] That a naval officer should thus have taken the lead in promoting both the diffusion of scientific knowledge and its practical application in mining, ship construction, cannon-casting and navigation, demonstrates the degree to which the Spanish Enlightenment derived from the encouragement and necessities of the Crown.

The most influential figure of the Spanish Enlightenment to visit and report on the New World was Antonio de Ulloa (1716–95), Jorge Juan's companion in the La Condamine expedition. The son of the Cadiz writer on economic affairs, Bernardo de Ulloa, he first sailed across the Atlantic as a cadet and gained his education at the Naval Academy and on active service. In subsequent years, he served first as governor of Huancavelica, where Peru's mercury mine was situated, and then as governor of Louisiana following the cession of that province to Spain after 1763. Promoted to the rank of admiral, in 1776 he commanded the last great trading fleet to sail from Cadiz to Veracruz. Generally recognised as the principal author of the *Relación histórica*, Ulloa consolidated his reputation as a savant by the publication of *Noticias americanas* (1772) in which he set out his views on the natural history of the New World. A corresponding member of the Royal Society of London, he was described by Voltaire as a 'military philosopher'. What was not known until the following century was that he and Jorge Juan had been commissioned by the chief minister of Spain, the Marquis of Ensenada, to compile a confidential report on colonial government and society, in which Ulloa took the lead in presenting a devastating picture of misrule and corruption.[5] The occasional similarities and the striking differences between the published *Viaje* and the manuscript *Noticias secretas* demonstrate that Ulloa was a zealous servant of the Crown, as ready to suppress topics of colonial embarrassment as to criticise the inhabitants of the New World. In Ulloa's writings we encounter the recrudescence of the imperial tradition of commentary on Spain's overseas empire.

The degree to which the *Relación histórica* served as a work of propaganda can be most clearly observed if Ulloa's description of Lima be compared to the acerbic account presented by Amédée François Frezier, a French naval captain who visited the city in the years 1712–14. Whereas the Frenchman derided the processions of religious flagellants, described the creoles as profligate, idle and superstitious, and commented on the bitter rivalry between American and European Spaniards, by contrast Ulloa chose to emphasise the magnificence of the churches, the wealth of the nobility, the beauty and exotic attire of the women, and the splendour of the ceremonies organised to welcome the viceroy.[6] More generally, he painted an attractive picture of an empire in which each province had its own particular line of agriculture and artisan manufacture. Although he insisted that the flow of European merchandise through the trade fair of Porto Bello was of vital importance for Lima, he also drew attention to the internal trade of South America, in which the woollens of Quito and the cacao of Guayaquil were exchanged for the wheat of Chile and the wines and brandies of Moquegua, the silver of the highlands enlivening this coastal commerce. So too, he described the chain of ports and cities in which he stayed, each town inhabited by a diverse mixture of Spaniards, Indians, blacks mestizos and mulattos. What he omitted were any precise statistics about the volume or value of all this variegated economic activity.

Despite his caution, Ulloa displayed his imperial colours when, in describing Cartagena, he repeated the old canard that after the age of thirty creoles tended to deteriorate, their minds addled by sloth, a condition derived from the absence of 'the incentive of honour' in the form of careers in the judiciary or armed forces. For sure, he admitted that Feijoo had dismissed this generalisation as 'a vulgar error', an admission, however, which did not prevent him from re-opening the subject.[7] Equally important, Ulloa echoed La Condamine's contemptuous account of the natives of Peru. How was it possible to reconcile the glowing image of the Inca empire provided by Garcilaso de la Vega with the all-pervasive degradation of the Indian peasantry encountered by travellers? In an appendix he inserted an historical account of the Incas, effectively summarising the *Comentarios reales*, in which he faithfully repeated its affirmation of observance of natural law. Moreover, he mentioned several Inca ruins he had seen in Quito as offering corroboration for the thesis of an advanced civilisation. Yet contemporary Indians were tranquil to the point of insensibility, bereft of all ideas of honour, religion or wealth, moved neither by fear of punishment nor by hope of reward. In effect, they dwelt in 'an unpolished barbarism ... living almost in imitation of irrational beings, scattered across the countryside'.[8]

As much as Peralta or Sigüenza y Góngora, Ulloa was haunted by the threat of English aggression. Many of the ports he first visited had been sacked by pirates, the capture of Guayaquil by William Rogers in 1709 numbering among the most daring of these exploits. It was towards the completion of La Condamine's labours, in 1739, that war broke out between Spain and Great Britain over smuggling by English traders. In 1742 the naval expedition commanded by Admiral Vernon captured Porto Bello, only then to fail in a disastrous assault on Cartagena. On the opposite side of the continent, Admiral Anson captured the Peruvian port of Paita, sailed northwards to intercept the rich Manila galleon outside Acapulco, and then emulated Sir Francis Drake by circumnavigating the globe. At all points the Spanish empire was thus exposed to British attack. Indeed, Ulloa's return home was interrupted by the capture of his ship, an incident that allowed him to visit Boston and London, where he was more fêted as a member of the La Condamine expedition than treated as an enemy. His *Relación* concluded with a glowing account of New England which he praised for its religious tolerance, its growing, laborious population, the general availability of land for all colonists, the low incidence of taxes and the absence of soldiers. Commenting that 'these provinces have come to be a kind of republic', he cited a French observer who claimed that within a century the colonies would outstrip England and dominate the hemisphere.[9] Framed between the ideal commonwealths of the Incas and the Puritans, the Spanish overseas empire appeared as an anachronism, ripe for reform.

In 1772 Ulloa published his *Noticias americanas*, a relatively brief treatise, in which he drew on the information he had acquired as governor of Huancavelica (1758) and Louisiana (1766). It was not a particularly distinguished performance, since, although he provided a careful description of the Peruvian highlands and its flora and fauna, he abstained from any general reflections. The universe was clearly governed by general laws of nature, but these laws offered no explanation of the diversity of natural phenomena in different zones of the world. Just why certain animals were to be found only in America remained a mystery. All that the naturalist could do was to register the immense complexity of Nature. About the only speculation Ulloa offered was that the 'petrified sea-shells' that were found embedded in highland rocks demonstrated that the Andes were probably the first mountain range to be raised above the waters after the Great Flood. For the rest, he fixed upon the decisive function of altitude in determining both temperature and climate in Peru. In short, all the emphasis was on observation rather than on explanation. The relatively modest advance that Ulloa's work marks when compared to Acosta's *Historia natural*, other than in a greater abundance of precise information, reminds us that in the eighteenth century geology and zoology still trailed far behind physics and mathematics in their capacity to explain phenomena.[10]

Where Ulloa scored was in his discussion of the Peruvian mining industry, since he provided a wide range of statistical information not available elsewhere. By the eighteenth century, the once rich lodes of Potosí were virtually exhausted so that in 1763 the *cerro rico* only received 1,792 hundredweights of mercury to refine its ores out of a total of 5,245 hundredweights then produced at Huancavelica. The remainder went to a wide range of mines, clear proof that the industry no longer depended on a single great source for its ore. For the rest, Ulloa described the amalgamation method of refining silver, drew on his years at Huancavelica to give a precise account of mercury mining, and offered historical estimates of silver production at Potosí. The traditional character of his approach can be best gauged by the reflection that 'the Supreme Author' of the universe had deposited the precious metals at the highest points of the world's surface, thus offering a certain analogy in the moral and physical spheres. He concluded that gold and silver 'give law to the world ... in a certain way their power exceeds the ideas of men'.[11]

The most revealing part of *Noticias americanas* dealt with the origin, character and government of the Indians, a theme which had obsessed Ulloa since his first excursion into the New World. For some reason unsubstantiated in the text, he was now persuaded that since the Indians were so different from any known people of the Old World, they had probably arrived in the Americas in the very first epoch after the Flood, travelling in boats across the Atlantic, first to settle in the Caribbean islands, and then to spread across the mainland. It was possible that some Jews had accompanied them on their travels, since Quechua bore some similarity to Hebrew, and in any case both nations shared an equal fondness for lies and deceit. Whatever their origin, the Indians of Peru had been mere barbarians at the epoch of conquest and thereafter remained submerged in 'rusticity and barbarism'. Such religion as they possessed was a matter of ceremony without 'interior cult'. Like ants or spiders, they lived an entirely material existence, unmoved by either religion or reason. All this led to the conclusion that 'if there are peoples that preserve part of the primitive state of mankind, it has to be the Indians ... ' Not that Ulloa entertained any idyllic view of either childhood or early humanity, since he successively affirmed that 'the life of these peoples should be seen as similar to that of the beasts' and that 'a savant of the first order in Europe' had defined the Indians as grown children, perpetually arrested at the mental age of seven to nine years. Perhaps the most extraordinary proposition that Ulloa advanced, avowedly based on his experience in Peru and Louisiana, was that the American Indians, be they settled or nomad, free or conquered, dwelling in either north or the south, all and everywhere exhibited the same character, invariably governed by 'their propensity to idleness', and such formidable vices as cruelty, drunkenness, insensibility, faithlessness and cowardice. From this obloquy Ulloa exempted only the Incas whose evident achievements, however, suggested that they sprang from 'a more cultivated and civilised race than that of the common Indians'.[12]

This damning image of ineradicable barbarism led Ulloa to justify measures he had previously condemned. For sure, he advocated the abolition of *obrajes*, since these establishments were little better than prisons. But he now argued that the diverse nature of human races required different laws. Such was the innate propensity of all Indians to idleness, that it was necessary to invoke state sanctions to compel them to work. Defending the draft levy of native peasantry for the mines, he pronounced that 'certain punishments are necessary for the Indians'. Moreover, it was 'a blind vulgarity' to imagine that working in the mines was so arduous that it caused depopulation. After all, many mestizos and Indians entered the mines voluntarily, attracted by the high wages. Nor was the *mita*, the forced levy, unjust since, so Ulloa falsely claimed, *mitayos* and free workers were paid the same wage. As it was, more Indians died from the effects of drunkenness than from labouring in the mines. In general, if the native population of Peru had declined, it was owing to the impact of smallpox, drunkenness, and inter-marriage. Such were the hard lessons that Ulloa derived from his experience as a colonial governor.[13]

In his all-pervasive contempt for the inhabitants of the New World, be they creole or Indian, Antonio de Ulloa was the worthy heir of Gonzalo Fernández de Oviedo and Juan Ginés de Sepúlveda. There was an underlying continuity in attitude between the Spanish humanists of the sixteenth century and the philosophers of the eighteenth. At no point was it allowed that the Indian might have the ability to create a civilised society. Whereas Sepúlveda had fixed upon literacy as the essential prerequisite of civilisation, Ulloa declared that it was knowledge of nature and its laws which separated the advanced nations from the inferior races. In both epochs ideology served the interests of political dominion, the barbaric character of the Indians invoked to justify forced labour. In the last resort, Antonio de Ulloa can be best interpreted as the most talented exponent of the recrudescence of the Spanish imperial tradition of commentary on the New World.

II

In 1768 there appeared in Berlin an explosive little book written in French entitled *Recherches philosophiques sur les Américains*, which opened with the forthright declaration that the difference between Europe and America was best defined as the contrast between strength and weakness, between civilisation and savagery. It boasted of the scientific and philosophical achievements of Newton, Leibniz, Descartes, Bayle, Locke, and Montesquieu, and boldly pronounced that not a single book worth reading had ever come out of America. The reader was adjured to regard the American Indians 'as a race of men who have all the faults of a child, as a degenerate species of humanity, cowardly, impotent, without physical force or vigour, and without elevation of spirit'.[14] In a subsequent work on the Chinese and Egyptians, Corneille de Pauw (1739–99), a renegade Dutch cleric, defined the celestial empire as an oriental despotism which more relied on 'the whip and cudgel' than on law to govern a people whose language was incapable of capturing the subtleties of European philosophy, and whose past had been distorted by 'an addiction to historical falsehood'. Noble savages dwelling in their American Eden and mandarin exponents of rational virtue were thus derisively expelled from the Enlightenment Valhalla, all the more to be damned because in part they were both figments of Jesuit fantasy.[15] These slashing attacks on cherished icons found a ready welcome in Europe and Pauw's works were republished in several editions. Such was his reputation that he was commissioned to write the article on America in the supplement to L'Encyclopédie (1776–7), and after his death Napoleon commanded a small monument to be erected. That traces of his influence can be encountered in the works of the two leading historians of America, Guillaume-Thomas Raynal and William Robertson, and that he was bitterly attacked by the creole patriot, Francisco Javier Clavijero, suggests that Pauw was the Sepúlveda of the Enlightenment.

The two premises of Pauw's 'system' were climatic determinism and American exceptionality. He took from Montesquieu, Sir John Chardin, and the Abbé Du Bos the thesis that climate exercised a decisive influence over the character, customs, laws, and politics of nations. Generally speaking it was assumed that the easy climes of Asia and the tropics bred peoples who were prone to indolence of mind and spirit, and hence best suited for despotic forms of government. By contrast, the inhabitants of temperate zones tended to be hardy, enterprising, and persevering in their pursuit of knowledge and freedom. To this general theory Pauw united the hypothesis advanced by George-Louis Leclerc Buffon (1707–88) in his Histoire natural (1747) that, geologically speaking, America was a young continent characterised by a superabundance of great rivers, extensive lakes, and much stagnant swampland. At any given latitude the hemisphere was more cold and moist than the Old World. It was significant that its animal species were less numerous and smaller in physical size than their counterparts across the Atlantic. That European livestock suffered degeneration in America only heightened the contrast. Yet insects, lizards and snakes multiplied and thrived to a degree unknown elsewhere. In effect, so Buffon concluded, 'animated nature, therefore, is less active, less varied and even less vigorous' in the New World. Nor could mankind be exempted from the general rule, since the natives of North America were 'all equally stupid, ignorant, unacquainted with the arts and destitute of industry'. By and large, the inhabitants of the New World were recent arrivals, few in number, scattered in small bands across a vast continent, and sunk in savagery. From his Parisian vantage point, Buffon pronounced: 'In the savage the organs of generation are small and feeble, he has no hair, no beard, no ardour for the females . . . he lacks vivacity or activity of soul . . . ' The only exceptions to this climatic rule were Peru and Mexico where 'are found a polished people, subjected by laws, governed by kings, acquainted with the arts and not destitute of religion'.[16]

All Pauw did was to develop Buffon's arguments in scabrous fashion, citing travellers' accounts by way of corroboration. To add force to his case he attacked Montesquieu for describing America as a fertile land with an equable climate, insisting that it was a poor, sterile country, covered with stagnant waters and rotting vegetation. But, whereas Buffon had argued that America was a young continent, Pauw declared that the hemisphere was ancient and degenerate. At some undetermined point it had suffered such 'convulsions of nature' that its climatic balance had been radically disturbed. The all-pervasive humidity and fetid exhalations of putrid vegetation infected the air with vapours that invaded the breath, blood, and milk of the savages that wandered through its great forests and swamps. Such was the effect of this poisonous climate that their blood was viscous, and hence more resistant to venereal disease (from which they invariably suffered) than was the case with Europeans. The same causes produced a superabundance of lactic fluid in their bodies, so that even the men had milk in their breasts and children were often suckled for many years. The torpidity of these savages was so great that puberty failed to enliven either their instincts or their spirits, the absence of body hair at this stage sure sign of their resemblance to eunuchs. Indeed, the women were often sterile and the men deficient in ardour, often impotent, and much given to sodomy.[17]

Climate and the human physique it produced determined the character, society, and culture of the nations. All peoples, so Pauw declared, started out as mere brutes, more governed by climate than by reason, with no more models for behaviour than their whim and necessity, but all endowed with 'the germ of perfectibility'. Only through agriculture could any group abandon nomad hunting and form settlements and thus advance from 'a wild constitution to a political constitution'. With a sedentary life the arts and sciences emerged and property rights were established. None of this development, however, had proved possible for such peoples as the Eskimos or the blacks in Africa where the extremes of climate prevented any transition from savagery. So too, in America the sterility of nature had created a people so primitive that their languages lacked the means to express abstract or general ideas. They could not even count beyond three or four. Had not travellers like La Condamine and Ulloa united to describe them as insensible creatures, unmoved by fear, honour, avarice, or love? In effect, they were a race of grown children, albeit more degenerate than innocent in their customs and proclivities.[18]

But what of the Incas and Aztecs? How could their evident achievements be reconciled with this image of climatically induced savagery? The contrast between the Incas and contemporary natives had already perplexed both La Condamine and Ulloa. It was a conundrum that Pauw resolved by forthright denial of the veracity of virtually all historical sources dealing with the Indians in the epoch of conquest. For he described the Spanish conquerors as illiterate, cruel adventurers who had perpetrated massacres beyond number, destroying all that they encountered. As for the missionaries, they were ignorant priests, blinded by self-interest, whose accounts of native culture and conversion were not to be trusted. In particular, Pauw rounded on Las Casas, denouncing him as an arch-intriguer, whose defence of the Indians was inspired by the design of becoming their sovereign. A born hypocrite, he was the prime author of the slave trade which had condemned so many Africans to bondage. About the only clerical source that Pauw commended was Acosta's *Historia natural* and whose *De procuranda* he cited. For the rest, he attacked the record of the Jesuits in Paraguay, accusing them of despotism and avarice, citing Palafox's letter to confirm these allegations.[19]

It was 'the story-teller Garcilaso' who 'really revolted' Pauw with his account of Inca *amautas* and their philosophic academy. His *Comentarios reales* was a 'work so indigestible, so pitiful, so radically ill-reasoned' that the French translators of the 1744 edition had been obliged to rewrite the whole thing. In fact, the Inca empire had emerged in 'a savage region, inhabited by barbarians', in which the use of iron or money was unknown. Its only urban settlement was Cuzco, whose buildings more resembled an encampment of Hottentots than a European city. Since La Condamine had found that the Peruvian tongue lacked all means of expressing general ideas, how was it possible to believe Garcilaso's fables about Inca philosophers? Much the same line of reasoning led Pauw to dismiss Gemelli Careri's description of the Aztec calendar as a crude fabrication of his Mexican informant 'Congara', which is to say, Sigüenza y Góngora. Their crude pictures lacked all symbolic meaning. For the rest, the absence of iron and the fine arts, when combined with their addiction to human sacrifice, clearly defined the Aztecs as savages. The 'palace' of Moctezuma was nothing more than a native hut. To add insult to injury, Pauw concluded with a dismissive attack on creole ability, citing travellers such as Frezier and Ulloa to assert that after adolescence the Spaniards born in America declined into indolence and vice, influenced as much as the Indians by the pernicious effects of local climate. A French professor in Lima had failed to encounter a single student able to understand astronomy and mathematics. Not a single native of the New World, Indian or creole, had ever written a book worth reading.[20]

Although Pauw condemned 'those dreadful theologians of the sixteenth century', the facile, mechanical way in which he invoked 'philosophic' theory to damn the American Indians was highly reminiscent of Sepúlveda. If the Spanish humanist relied on Oviedo as a first-hand witness to provide incontrovertible facts, so also Pauw relied on La Condamine and Ulloa for his information. The resemblance is strengthened not merely by their common aversion to Las Casas, but also by their application of classical doctrines. For if we turn to the primordial fount of environmental determinism, which is to say, to Hippocrates' *Airs, Waters, Places*, we find that the Scythians are described as nomads dwelling in a cold, damp, foggy plain, as a people whose physique was gross, flabby and moist, characteristics which prompted infertility in the women, impotence in the men, and in both sexes a torpid indolence. Elsewhere, Hippocrates suggested that lands which are rich, soft and well-watered will tend to have inhabitants who are fleshy, lazy, and cowardly. So too, he set out the grounds for the famous contrast between Greek freedom and Asian despotism. That Pauw should have explicitly compared the American Indians to the ancient Scythians suggests the Hippocratean source of his theories. For his part, he chose to praise Sir John Chardin, who in his *Travels in Persia* (1711) set out the climatic basis of Asian character and despotism, a theory, so Pauw claimed, which Montesquieu was but to develop.[21]

III

The degree to which eighteenth-century history can be interpreted as a sceptical commentary and rewriting of earlier narratives is clearly exemplified in *The History of America* (1777) written by William Robertson (1721-91), a Scots presbyterian minister and for many years principal of Edinburgh university. It was the first sustained attempt to describe the discovery, conquest and settlement of Spanish America since Herrera's *Décadas*. That Robertson also inserted a general discussion of the quality of the American Indians, judiciously measured the degree of civilisation attained by the Aztecs and Incas, and traced the development of colonial society until his own day, indicates the ambitious scope of his work. At all points the text was supported by footnotes, a review of historical sources, and an extensive bibliography. Thanks to the British ambassador in Madrid, Robertson had been able to purchase books and to procure a number of manuscripts dealing with his theme. He also corresponded with the Count of Campomanes. Erudition and industry, however, would not have attracted the praise of such diverse figures as Voltaire and Burke, had they not been joined to 'philosophical investigation'. Already, in his *Charles V,*

Robertson had provided a masterly survey of the progress of European society, in which he traced the erosion of the 'feudal system' caused by the rise of free towns, the revival of learning and Roman law, and by the emergence of royal authority and the balance of power between states. It was the development of commerce, assisted by law and private property, which was held to be chiefly responsible for the advance in civilisation. So too, in his history of America, he deployed concepts elaborated by Adam Smith, Adam Ferguson and John Millar in what they styled 'theoretical or conjectural history'. Nor did he neglect the ideas of Buffon and Montesquieu. In his own day, Robertson was numbered among the luminaries of an intellectual movement which is now saluted as the Scottish Enlightenment. That Edward Gibbon should have informed him that he was honoured to figure in the triumvirate of leading historians, composed of David Hume, Robertson and himself, is proof enough of his standing. In Spain the Royal Academy of History elected him as a member and recommended that his work should be translated and published, subject only to minor emendation.[22]

After such a profusion of contemporary encomium, it comes as something of a shock to find that Robertson's narrative of the discovery of America and conquest of Mexico and Peru is little more than a paraphrase of Antonio de Herrera's *Décadas*. It was no doubt inevitable that the Scotsman should have started with an account of European exploration rather than with a description of the New World and its inhabitants. But why did he have to follow Herrera in interrupting the final siege of Mexico by a description of Magellan's voyage around the world? Anxious to rescue Columbus from Gómara's slander that he had robbed the unknown pilot of the credit of discovering America, he shrank from any full appreciation of the great admiral, merely presenting him as 'a man in whose character the modesty and diffidence of true genius were united with the ardent enthusiasm of a projector'. As regards Cortés, he exculpated him from any responsibility for the massacre at Cholula; followed Herrera in suppressing all mention of Alvarado's massacre at Tenochtitlan; offered the Spanish version of Moctezuma's death; but strongly condemned the conqueror for the murder of Cuauhtémoc. He had few words of praise for Pizarro and censured the execution of Atahualpa as an action that figured among 'the most criminal and atrocious that stains the Spanish name'. In general, he deplored 'the levity, the rapaciousness, the perfidy and corruption prevalent among the Spaniards in Peru'. Owing to Herrera's incorporation of material taken from Las Casas' narrative history, Robertson conceded a prominent place to the Dominican's campaign to defend the Indians, offered a full account of the Cumaná incident, and ascribed the New Laws to his intervention. At the same time, he censured the *Brevísima relación* for its 'evident marks of exaggerated descriptions' and observed of Las Casas' denunciations of population loss that 'with the decisive tone of one strongly prepossessed with the truth of his own

23 William Robertson

system, he imputed all this to a single cause, the exactions and cruelty of his countrymen'. In commending Charles V for his statesman-like vision in promulgating the New Laws, Robertson endorsed Herrera's thesis that the Crown's encouragement of Las Casas signified that the monarchy bore no guilt for the destruction of the Indians.[23]

It was in his analysis of Indian society that Robertson strove to exhibit his quality as a philosophic historian, presenting materials for 'a history of the human mind'. In this grand enterprise, he drew inspiration from Ferguson's remark about the Indians that: 'It is in their present condition that we behold, as in a mirror, the features of our progenitors.' He was also influenced by Adam Smith's emphasis on 'the mode of subsistence' as the criterion by which to measure the special and cultural development of any human group. According to this evolutionary theory, mankind passed through four successive stages, respectively dominated by hunting, herding, agriculture, and commerce. The transition to agriculture was reckoned as all-important, since it was generally accompanied by the emergence of property rights, law, and social ranks. Only with the dominance of commerce, however, was the achievement of civilisation completed. Superimposed on this scheme was the more familiar triad of savagery, barbarism, and civilisation, where barbarism was distinguished from the first phase of human history by the consolidation of political authority and property, characteristics which could co-exist with either the pastoral or agricultural stage.[24] The degree to which Robertson subscribed to these ideas is clearly manifest in his affirmation that

> In every part of the earth the progress of man has always been the same in his career from the rude simplicity of savage life until he attains the industry, the arts and the elegance of polished society ... In every inquiry concerning the operations of men when united together in society the first object of attention should be their mode of subsistence.

It was these general propositions that led Robertson to reject Gregorio García's theory of successive migrations from the Old World in favour of Acosta's hypothesis that America had been settled by small bands of savages from East Asia who lacked livestock, iron and any but the most primitive implements for hunting. The evolution of Indian society was autochthonous: any similarity or reminiscence of Old World customs and concepts in their practices simply indicated a common humanity rather than any immediate ancestry. What rendered the exercise so appealing was that 'in America man appears under the rudest forms in which we can conceive him to subsist ... That state of primaeval simplicity, which was known in our continent only by the fanciful descriptions of the poets really existed in the other.' In short, for Robertson as for John Locke and Claude Lévi-Strauss: 'In the beginning all the world was America.'[25]

Any excitement raised by the alluring promise of an encounter with our first ancestors, miraculously preserved in the New World, was soon dissipated by Robertson's admission that: 'in every part of the earth where man exists, the power of climate operates with decisive influence, upon his condition and character'. Moreover, Robertson also accepted Buffon's thesis of American exceptionality, blithely unconscious that environmental determinism of such pronounced force undermined his previous insistence on the economic determinants of social evolution. As a result, he affirmed that the New World was a cold and moist continent, a vast wilderness rendered unhealthy by stagnant waters and a great mass of putrid vegetation. 'Nature was not only less prolific in the New World, but she appears likewise to have been less vigorous in her productions.' Once again, the smaller number of animal species and their diminutive size was cited, together with the degeneration of European livestock. However, Robertson qualified these propositions by allowing that once the wilderness was cleared, drained and put under cultivation, then the land would become healthier. So too, the dwindling size of European livestock was often the result of poor breeding and insufficient care and pasturage. Until such a transformation, the determinants of climate left the American Indians very close 'to the brute creation', so that 'a feebleness of constitution was universal'. In effect, Robertson followed Buffon and Pauw in fixing upon the absence of beards and body hair as signs of 'a feeble frame and languid desire'. The Indians were indolent, insensible, unmoved by physical desire or love, insensible to the promptings of avarice, honour and fear, childlike and incapable of speculative reasoning. To substantiate this character, Robertson cited in some detail the travel accounts of La Condamine, Bouguer and Ulloa, thus confirming the all-pervasive influence of that expedition on subsequent discussion of the American Indian. Indeed, he explicitly cited Ulloa's extraordinary affirmation that all the native inhabitants of the New World, north and south, free or enserfed, possessed the same character to justify his generalisations. It was only after this venture into climatic determinism and 'characterology' that Robertson invoked the social criteria of the Scottish Enlightenment, noting that the Indians dwelt in the very first stage of savagery, their subsistence dependent on hunting supplemented by desultory agriculture. The lack of livestock, iron, individual property, social ranks, and political authority other than the despotic power of their chieftains, only served to confirm this dismal image. Even at this point, however, he returned to the climatic theme when he contrasted the indolent, easily conquered, despotically governed peoples of the equatorial zone to the hardy, freedom-loving tribes of Chile and North America who had resisted the European advance.[26]

In effect, Robertson emerged from his philosophical investigation with an image of early man remarkably reminiscent of that sketched out by Thomas Hobbes a century earlier. It also echoed, albeit in moderate language, the affirmations of Pauw and Buffon. Clearly, Robertson was well aware that there was a tradition stretching back to Vespucci and Peter Martyr, of depicting the natives of the New World as dwelling in a state of natural innocence, untrammelled by the conventions of European society. It was a tradition which had been most forcefully restated by Jean-Jacques Rousseau who, in his *Discourse on the Arts and Sciences* (1750), had praised the Americas as happy nations, whose customs Montaigne had preferred to the Laws of Plato.

Elsewhere, he described the first state of man as a golden age when each man lived as master of himself, hunting or herding his stock without confinement. It was agriculture which had ushered in the evils of property, government, laws and war.[27] This alternate view of human development had been introduced into the polemic over America by Dom Antoine-Joseph Pernety who sharply criticised Pauw's climatic determinism. The Indians' indifference to money was a sign that they were guided by 'a truly natural philosophy' and were hence free from the prejudices inculcated by education. In short, here was a line of thought which contrasted nature and society and proffered the 'noble savage' as the model by which to judge the artifice and evils of contemporary Europe.[28]

Nowhere did Robertson more clearly nail his liberal colours to the mast than in his discussion of native religion. He boldly pronounced that if religion was not derived 'from rational inquiry or from revelation', then it would consist of a 'wild and extravagant' superstition, a response to childish fears which found expression in oracles, divination and magic, and which invariably served as the handmaiden to political despotism.[29] Here was an image of primitive man that Vico had laboured to eradicate. As yet, the *New Science* was unknown or unread in Scotland. But there existed among the very sources on which Robertson relied a comprehensive statement of an alternative view of Indian religion. In his *Moeurs des sauvages amériquains* (1724) Joseph François Lafiteau, a French Jesuit who had laboured for many years as a missionary in Canada, argued that the religious beliefs and practices of the Iroquois and Huron resembled the ancient cult of the early Greeks and Pelasgians, a resemblance that he attributed to the common inheritance of humanity, the pure, innocent religion of man's first parents. Obviously, a process of corruption had set in, caused by fear, ignorance and the Devil, but significant vestiges of early beliefs and practices had been retained, albeit at times in symbolic form. In effect, Lafiteau here followed Kircher both in tracing the origin of religion and philosophy to early man and in perceiving a twin process of corruption and symbolic transformation. But whereas the German divine had fixed upon Egypt as the fount of wisdom and had sought to interpret hieroglyphics as the original language of mankind, the French Jesuit undertook a detailed investigation of Iroquois religion and society, an ethnographic exercise which still retains its value and has been acclaimed as a pioneering classic. Moreover, Lafiteau rejected current denigration of the Indians, observing: 'They have a good spirit, a lively imagination, an easy conception, an admirable memory. All have at least traces of an ancient, hereditary religion and a form of government.'[30] That Robertson should have quietly ignored a work already much cited by Ferguson demonstrates the degree to which he framed his description of the American Indians according to the preconceptions of the Enlightenment. It is noticeable that Pauw derisively rejected the Jesuit's arguments, observing that 'Lafiteau explained customs as Kircher deciphered hieroglyphs', a striking testimony to the hostility of the Enlightenment to the Jesuit Baroque enterprise.[31]

More confident than Pauw in the veracity of Spanish historians, Robertson offered a judicious assessment of the Inca and Aztec kingdoms, observing that although when compared to the Iroquois they possessed the characteristics of 'polished states', by contrast, when viewed from the perspective of the Old World, 'neither the Mexicans nor the Peruvians will be entitled to rank with these nations which merit the name of civilised'. After all, even the barbarians in Europe had possessed iron tools and weapons and livestock in abundance, a consideration which suggested that the two Indian states had 'hardly advanced beyond the infancy of civil life'. Since Robertson chose not to admit into his discussion evidence of empires earlier than the Aztecs and Incas, he deliberately cut short the duration of settled society. For all that, his ambition was remarkable, since he sought 'to ascertain their place in the political scale, to allot them their proper station between the rude tribes of the New World and the polished states of the ancient . . . ' Whereas Las Casas had once argued for the equivalence of the Aztecs and Incas to the ancient Greeks and Romans, Robertson thus approached his task confident that they occupied a lowly rank in the cultural scale.[32]

As regards the Mexicans, Robertson first fixed upon the institution of property rights, private and communal, as clear proof of their advance towards civilisation. Here was a country with numerous cities, including Mexico itself with a population of 60,000, the existence of which attested to a division of labour between artisans and farmers. A system of irrigation in the central valley and the regular collection of tribute indicated the existence of a fully constituted political authority which was based on a system of social ranks ranging from serfs and free peasants to warriors and a nobility. Robertson concluded that the Mexican state offered 'the image of feudal policy . . . a nobility possessing almost independent authority, a people depressed into the lowest state of subjection, and a king entrusted with the executive power of the state'. However, all this indicated but the first steps towards true civilisation. After all, agriculture was not very advanced, the population was not dense, there was no regular currency and little, if any, commerce. The architecture was of the most primitive kind, with temples built on mounds of pressed earth or, as in the case of Cholula, on natural mounds. That no monuments of any dimension had survived the Spanish conquest demonstrated the insubstantiality of native construction. As for the fabled Mexican hieroglyphs and calendars, what were they but rather simple pictographs which, if certainly signifying an approach to civilisation, nevertheless remained at the very first stage of abstract or symbolic expression? Moreover, in their form they demonstrated all the imperfections of primitive art, since they consisted of 'uncouth representations . . . destitute of grace and propriety . . . the scrawls of children delineate objects almost as accurately'. The neo-classicism of the Enlightenment was thus invoked to damn the crowning proof of Mexican civility.[33] In any case, how was it possible to call a society civilised which conducted unremitting, barbaric warfare, observed a 'gloomy and atrocious religion', and which was corrupted by the vicious practice of human sacrifice?

On the Incas Robertson had less to say. Since Manco Capac was portrayed as the child of the Sun, it followed that religion and the state were identified, with the Inca exercising 'unlimited and absolute authority', applying capital punishment to all offences. But Peruvian religion was a relatively innocent affair, unstained by Mexican cruelty. So too, Inca warfare was undertaken to pacify and civilise other peoples, and the Inca state promoted an advanced agriculture. The stone monuments at Cuzco and elsewhere still survived, sure sign of their impressive quality, and their bridges and roads recalled the achievements of the Romans. Against all this, it had to be emphasised that Cuzco was the only city in the entire empire. There was little evidence of any division of labour and still less of commerce. The population was not warlike and, to judge from recent report, lacked spirit. Robertson concluded that the condition of Peru 'suggests the idea of a society still in the first stages of its transition from barbarism to civilisation'.[34]

In framing his assessment of the Aztecs and Incas, Robertson cited a wide range of historical sources, including certain manuscript material obtained from Spanish archives. First and foremost, however, he drew on the Spanish historians of the sixteenth century, extracting from their profuse materials his own succinct analysis. In other words, he followed the same procedure of paraphrase that he had applied in his narrative account, albeit in this case subjecting his material to the analytical categories developed by the Scottish Enlightenment. But on whom did he most rely to supply him the information he needed? It is his appended notes which offer the answer. In first place, Robertson praised Antonio de Herrera for his 'impartiality and candour' and ranked his *Décadas* 'among the most judicious and useful historical collections'. So too, he praised José de Acosta as 'one of the most accurate and best informed writers on the West Indies'. On the conquest, he found that 'Gómara's historical merit is considerable', albeit he confessed that he was frequently 'inaccurate and credulous'. Bernal Díaz he commended for his first-hand vivacity and authenticity. By contrast to these commendations, he criticised Torquemada for 'his usual propensity for the marvellous' and dismissed Boturini as 'a whimsical, credulous man'. When the Mexican historian, Francisco Javier Clavijero, ventured to question his own accuracy, Robertson took advantage of a second edition of his history to attack the Jesuit for basing his description of ancient Mexico 'on the improbable narratives and fanciful conjectures of Torquemada and Boturini, copying their splendid descriptions of the high state of civilisation in the Mexican empire'. In the same context, he reproached Solís for applying European nomenclature to Indian institutions, observing that such a procedure imposed similarities which did not exist in reality. With such a perspective, it comes as no surprise that he equally dismissed Garcilaso de la Vega as a mere commentary on Spanish sources, adding 'as for composition, arrangement or a capacity for distinguishing between what is fabulous, what is probable, and what is true, one searches for them in vain in the commentaries of the Inca'.[35] In effect, Robertson dismissed out of hand the canonical texts of creole patriotism and at every point preferred the canonical texts of the imperial tradition.

In some ways the most original section of *The History of America* was the concluding chapter which dealt with the progress of colonial society from the conquest until the 1770s. The first and most dramatic consequence of the conquest was the radical decline in Indian population, caused by forced labour, smallpox and the plague, and by the general oppression of 'the indigent and often unprincipled conquerors'. The crown always sought to protect its native subjects as did the Church, since 'the first missionaries who visited America, though weak and illiterate, were pious men ... ' Although the king enjoyed absolute power, in practice the viceroys shared authority with the high courts of justice. What chiefly hampered economic development was the policy of commercial monopoly, restricting intercourse to periodic fleets. The growth of great landed estates and the dominance of mining of precious metals all contributed to economic backwardness, since they impeded the growth of agriculture and the improvement of industry. Citing Ulloa and Frezier, Robertson commented on the engrossment of trade by immigrant Spaniards and the exclusion of creoles from high office, and framed a devastating, if traditional, image of creole character, asserting that 'by the enervating influence of a sultry climate, by the rigour of a jealous government and by the despair of attaining that distinction to which mankind naturally aspires, the vigour of their mind is so entirely broke down, that a great part of them waste their life in luxurious indulgencies, mingled with an illiberal superstition still more debasing'.[35] Indeed, Robertson fixed upon the wealth of the Church, the excessive number of clergy, and the multiplication of religious houses in the cities as sign of the inordinate predominance of an institution which he damned for 'the spirit of low illiberal superstition' that it encouraged, a spirit all too deplorably exemplified in the *Gacetas de Mexico* (1724–9) which he had perused with mounting disgust. Nor had the Church succeeded in inculcating the principles of Christian truth into the dull minds of the Indians, who were barred from priesthood and not infrequently denied admission to the Eucharist.

Anxious not to conclude on too damning a note, Robertson commended the remarkable and far-reaching changes which Charles III and his ministers had introduced. 'The spirit of philosophical inquiry, which it is the glory of the present age to have turned from frivolous and abstruse speculations to the business and affairs of men, has extended its influence beyond the Pyrenees.' In particular, he praised the treatises of Pedro Rodríguez Campomanes on popular industry and wholly commended recent measures to liberate the flow of trade across the Atlantic from former restrictions. His work ended with praise of José de Gálvez, the recently appointed minister of the Indies, who had proceeded with incomparable vigour to reorganise the government of Spain's vast empire, creating new viceroyalties, augmenting the number of judges, and extending free trade.[37]

A Scottish contemporary of Robertson complained that he was a plagiarist, who in conversation 'always paraphrases other people's thoughts'. Much the same can be said about his *History of America*.[38] There was little in his narrative of events that could not be found in Herrera. His analysis of the Aztec and Inca states owed much to Acosta. Indeed, in both perspective and achievement there was a remarkable similarity between the Jesuit humanist and the Presbyterian philosopher. His most original contribution lay in his application of Smith's scheme of modes of subsistence. But the most startling feature of his work was the extent to which he revived and re-stated the Spanish imperial tradition of commentary on America. At every point, from his denigration of Torquemada and Garcilaso to his praise for Gálvez and Charles III, Robertson offended the sensibilities of creole patriots. For its part, the Royal Academy of History in Madrid gladly incorporated him in their ranks and sought to publish a translation of his works in Madrid.

IV

Whereas ancient history offered the magnificent scene of 'great revolutions, heroic manners and extraordinary events', by contrast, nowadays 'the history of the world is become insipid and trifling ... the period of founding and of subverting empires is past'. Such was the balance of power in Europe that warfare was often undertaken for commercial reasons or for the capture of a few frontier towns. Neither 'religious fanaticism' nor 'the spirit of conquest' had any appreciable effect on the course of affairs. In short, 'the annals of nations must hereafter be written by commercial philosophers, as they were formerly by historical orators'. It was in part to substantiate this dictum that Guillaume-Thomas Raynal (1713–96) opened his *Histoire philosophique des ... deux Indes* (1770, 1774, 1781) by affirming that the discovery of the New World and the passage to India 'gave rise to a revolution in commerce and in the power of nations, as well as in the manners, industry and government of the whole world'. From the days of the Phoenicians and the Greeks until the Venetians and Dutch, it had been the commerce of the city states which had created the conditions of peace and liberty in which the arts and sciences flourished most readily.[39]

W. T. RAYNAL F.R.S
Member of the Academy of Sciences
& Belles Lettres of Prussia.

24 Guillaume-Thomas Raynal

Despite these ringing pronouncements, Raynal confessed that when he contemplated the course of European trade and settlement across the world he was more often obliged to weep at the cruelties he was about to narrate than to triumph in its glories. To account for these crimes he fixed upon 'the great assassins who are called conquerors', men animated by an infernal mixture of ambition, avarice and superstition. Moreover, as befitted an erstwhile Jesuit, he blamed organised religion for much of the evils he perceived. In particular, he castigated the Church of Rome and its priesthood as the declared enemies of free inquiry, whose wealth and power have proved formidable obstacles to economic progress and political unity. The existence of a corporation in society dedicated to other-worldy ends must always be detrimental to society. It should be made clear to everyone that 'the state is not made for religion, but religion for the state ... the state has supremacy in everything'. A typical philosophe who belonged to the generation of *L'Encyclopédie*, the Abbé Raynal attacked both the nobility and the Church as remnants of the feudal past, but praised Frederick the Great of Prussia as 'a patriot-king', for his patronage of the arts and sciences.[40]

That the *Histoire des deux Indes* narrated the entire sweep of European overseas expansion testified more to Raynal's literary ambition than to his intellectual grasp. As much an editor as an author, he drew upon the collaboration of several assistants, including Diderot, and steadily augmented his text through three successive editions, published at Amsterdam and Geneva, in which he changed both opinions and facts without compunction. Since he rarely if ever cited any references, readers had little means of tracing the sources of his assertions. In effect, Raynal presented his public with a hodge-podge, a patchwork quilt, in which abstracts of trade statistics jostled for space alongside sentimental anecdotes, learned disquisitions on such technical themes as indigo cultivation, and a great deal of rhetoric. It was a gallimaufry masquerading as a universal history. Moreover, the decision to follow the activities of each European nation in turn prevented any unity of perspective. But it was a device which allowed Raynal to conclude with a survey of the contemporary situation, not omitting the American Revolution, an approach which at times invested his text with the racy immediacy of journalism, the more especially since he favoured reigning monarchs with much high-flown counsel. In effect, Raynal wrote as a leading member of the fourth estate, a philosophe all too well aware of the cultural hegemony of the Enlightenment, who in a brief comparison of European literary achievements, pronounced: 'The French language holds the superiority in prose; if it be not the language of the gods, it is, at least, that of reason and of truth.'[41]

For the inhabitants of Spanish America, however, French truth proved to be rather daunting. Once more, Buffon's thesis was cited as proving that America was 'a world that is still in its infancy'. But whether its manifest immaturity should be interpreted as 'the decay or the infancy of nature', Raynal chose not to say. But he rehearsed the usual proofs, which is to say, the lesser number of animal species, their smaller size, and the degeneration of European livestock. As regards mankind, he commented on the feebleness of the Indians and their subjection to the influence on climate. However, these assertions were offset, if not contradicted, by a lengthy discussion of the Indian tribes of Canada, whom he depicted as a people renowned for their intrepid courage, hardy endurance, and love of liberty. If he referred to 'the infant mind of the savages', he also emphasised that their language was rich in metaphorical terms, a feature demonstrated both in their songs and their oratory. Here, then, was the classic image of the warlike barbarian rather than the witless savage of Pauw's imagining. Moreover, Raynal paid homage to Rousseau when he queried whether his readers might not well envy the free Indians of North America who dwelt so much closer to nature and its laws than the city-dwellers of Europe.[42]

As regards the Aztecs and Incas, Raynal scornfully queried the veracity of the Spanish chroniclers, arguing that, since neither people possessed iron implements, they could not have constructed the cities, fortresses and palaces that figured so largely in these early accounts. What was Mexico but 'a little town, composed of a multitude of rustic huts, irregularly dispersed over a large space of ground', its public edifices 'nothing more than irregular masses of stones heaped one upon the other?' Indeed, cities were mostly conspicuous by their absence, and the much cited roads and bridges of the Incas were of the most rudimentary kind. Both empires were governed by despots who relied on superstition to instil the most abject obedience in their enserfed subjects, a system which offered potent obstacles to the emergence of the arts and sciences. In deference to Garcilaso, however, Raynal admitted the benevolence of Inca rule, admitting that its wise laws ensured the welfare of the conquered peoples. but he speculated as to whether Manco Capac might not have been a shipwrecked European and elsewhere condemned Moctezuma as 'sunk in a state of effeminacy and indolence', the customary marks of oriental despotism. As for the duration of these empires, he pronounced that virtually nothing was known about their history and surmised that until 'philosophers' were allowed to enter America, nothing would be known. With characteristic arrogance he stipulated that 'these learned men shall neither be monks nor Spaniards, but either English or French . . . '.[43]

On turning to narrate the events of the conquest, Raynal found his eyes welling with tears at 'the atrocious acts which the Spaniards were to commit in the New World'. Who was Cortés but 'an assassin covered in innocent blood', a warrior animated by avarice and thirst for fame, who had been 'despotic and cruel' in his treatment of the Indians? As for the conquerors of Peru, what were their civil wars but the inevitable product of 'tyranny and anarchy'? Indeed, he depicted Valverde as urging the Spaniards at Cajamarca to slaughter Atahualpa's entire army. Created 'in an age of barbarism and ignorance', the Spanish empire in America exploited the Indians mercilessly to produce vast quantities of silver which only served to ruin Spain before being shipped to India. Thanks to endless wars, the power of the Church and the restrictions placed on trade, Spain and its empire sank into decline precisely at the time when the nations of northern Europe advanced in both knowledge and prosperity. Raynal drew on Frezier to depict Lima as a kind of colonial Constantinople, filled with overly rich churches and adorned by beautiful, sultry maidens who received their visitors reclining on couches. Indeed, he damned the creoles as immersed in vice, the consequence of idleness and the climate, adding that 'barbarous luxury, pleasures of a shameful kind, a stupid superstition, and romantic intrigues, completes the degradation of their character'. How could America hope to progress when it was governed by 'oriental despotism and Spanish indolence'.[44] In effect, Raynal here implicitly defined Spain as an extension of North Africa, dominated by an ignorant, indolent fanaticism that the Enlightenment associated with Islam and the Orient.

In framing this damning image of the Spanish conquest and empire, Raynal was careful to except Las Casas, observing of his defence of the Indians that 'being more of a *man* than a *priest*, he felt more the cruelties inflicted on them than their ridiculous superstitions'. Were the Americans ever to gain their liberty, they should erect among their first statues a monument to the great man, inscribing on it these words: 'In an age of barbarity, Las Casas, whom thou seest, was a benevolent man.' More surprising, Raynal strongly commended the labours of the Jesuits in Paraguay and Amazonia, stating that they had imitated the Incas in establishing a 'theocratic government' which had protected the Indians from the rapacity of the settlers. Although the Indians lacked liberty, they were ruled in a benevolent fashion, their welfare safeguarded. Finally, Raynal joined with Robertson in commending the reforms of Charles III, fixing upon the increase in naval power and the 1778 declaration of free trade between Spain and its colonies as constituting promise of future progress.[45]

No feature of Raynal's work attracted more attention than his eloquent and repeated denunciations of slavery and the slave trade. It was not that he had any great liking for Africans whom in traditional strain he described as a race dominated by their physical passions. But he condemned the cruelties of their transport across the Atlantic and deplored their servitude in America as destroying the very springs of their humanity. At the beginning of history, 'men were all equals'; nor had ancient slavery proved so degrading as the contemporary institution. Above all else, he attacked enslavement as an affront to the universal principle of human liberty, which at its very minimum could be defined as possession of 'the property of oneself'. One day, so he prophesied, the blacks would rise up in revolution and find a leader able to free them from bondage.[46]

If Raynal dismissed contemporary Spaniards as 'a degenerate race', he displayed the customary French attitude of mingled respect and dislike for the English. After all, Great Britain presented a living example of how freedom, trade and science could promote prosperity and power. It possessed 'the only constitution, perhaps, since man has lived in a social state, where the laws have secured him his dignity, his personal liberty and his freedom of thought; where, in a word, they have made him a citizen . . . ' But British freedom was not exported, since the English had acted as tyrants in Bengal, plundering their recent conquests without mercy. Moreover, 'the English . . . are not only desirous of becoming rich, but of being exclusively so. Their ambition is gain, as that of the Romans was empire.' All their wars were conducted for commercial profit and following their successes in the Seven Years War (1756–63), often obtained by unscrupulous tactics, they aspired to win 'the universal monarchy of the seas'. Writing as a French patriot, Raynal urged the rulers of his country to rebuild the monarchy's naval power and organise a continental coalition against Great Britain.[47]

In the third edition of the *Histoire des deux Indes* (1781), Raynal ended his description of the Thirteen Colonies with a narrative of the American Revolution. Already he had signalised the Quaker establishment of Pennsylvania for its lessons in religious tolerance and had commended the welcome they extended to immigrants of different nations and beliefs. By contrast, he deplored the Puritan fanaticism and their notorious witchhunt at Salem. But it was the struggle of the colonists for liberty against the abuses of the British Crown which evoked his most dithyrambic prose. The figures of Washington and Franklin gave promise of a glorious future, even if the poor soil and limited terrain of the existing provinces meant that they would never support a very large population. For Spanish Americans who read his account the most striking passage here was his paraphrase of Tom Paine's pamphlet, *Common Sense* (1776), where the natural right of any people to establish its own government and to liberate itself from alien despotism was set forth most clearly. Moreover, the inevitability of a separation between America and England was assumed without question. Indeed, Raynal improved on Paine's prose and declaimed: 'Nature has not created a world in order to subject it to the inhabitants of an island in another hemisphere. Nature has established laws of equilibrium, which she follows in all parts, in the heavens as on the earth. By the rule of quantity and of distance, America can belong only to itself.'[48]

In their effect, the contrast between Robertson and Raynal could not have been greater. Although both men were unduly influenced by Buffon's thesis and offered a dispiriting portrait of both Indian savagery and Indian civilisation, nevertheless, their approach to other issues was remarkably different. Whereas the Scot subjected the conquest chronicles to patient and often appreciative review, the Frenchman brushed them aside as completely unreliable. If Robertson was inclined to condone Spanish excesses, Raynal excoriated the conquerors like some latter-day Benzoni. Their disagreement over Las Casas was significant and helps to explain why Raynal could attract creole patriots despite his denigration of the Aztecs and Incas. In the last resort, the political significance of the *Histoire des deux Indes* resided in its implicit comparison between Spain and Great Britain, and, more importantly, between the freedom achieved so recently by the Thirteen Colonies and the oriental despotism to which Spanish America was still subject. What creole patriot could fail to be stirred by the emergence of the new confederated republic, whose inhabitants had been prepared to sacrifice their lives to obtain independence and liberty for their country?

20

JESUIT PATRIOTS

I

THE AMERICAN response to the philosophic assault on the New World expressed both indignation and incredulity that such 'Buffoneries' should win public hearing in a Europe which prided itself on recent advances in the arts and sciences. At a dinner in Paris, Thomas Jefferson and Benjamin Franklin scoffed at the Abbé Raynal, 'a mere shrimp' of a man, for asserting that Europeans degenerated in America, pointing out that all Americans present were taller than their French hosts. Nevertheless, in his *Notes on Virginia* (1784), Jefferson took pains to compile lists of American species, with the aim of showing that the quadrupeds were as large and numerous as their European counterparts. Moreover, he was able to cite the recently discovered bones of a mammoth as clinching proof of the vitality of American fauna. So also, he sharply dissented from Ulloa's view that the Indians were cowardly, describing them as brave, hardy, freedom-loving, affectionate and eloquent. As befitted the citizen of a new republic, he paraded the figures of Washington and Franklin as sign that the Americans would soon equal their British forbears; declared that the increase in population gave promise of a great future; and concluded that the sun had already begun to set on the glory of England.[1]

For the Spanish Americans, still subject to the Bourbon dynasty, the Enlightenment's attack proved all the more hurtful, since its combination of climatic determinism and historical scepticism wounded their patriotic tradition at every point. In his *Historia del reino de Quito* (1789), the exiled Ecuadorean Jesuit, Juan de Velasco, launched a fierce attack on 'the modern sect of anti-American philosophers' and their 'chimerical systems'. Adverting to the great difference in climate between the high plains of the Andes and the low-lying tropical jungles of Amazonia, he compiled long lists of animal species, observing that there were at least thirty different kinds of monkey in his country. The size and strength of species, both American and European, varied according to the province, so that it was impossible to generalise about the entire kingdom, let alone on all America. As for the Indians, he denied the effect of climate on their moral character, observing that good and evil could be found in every clime. The natives of the highlands were healthy and hard-working. If they were often ignorant and without ideas, it was because they lacked all access to education. Since there were no schools for them, how could they hope to become priests or improve themselves? As it was, they were expert musicians, painters, sculptors and architects. Indeed, he was able to cite cases of Indians who were more than qualified to attend university, had the authorities permitted their entrance. Their language had more than sufficient words to express all the abstract notions of Christian theology. If travellers thought the Indians were insensible brutes, it was often because the natives suspected the strangers of seeking to learn their secrets. It was well known in Quito that an Indian questioned by a French academician had returned home in triumph, assuring his friends that he told his interrogator nothing worth knowing.[2]

In his defence of the Incas, Velasco noted that, although Raynal certainly praised their benevolent laws and concern for the welfare of their subjects, he had dismissed as fables their bridges, roads and fortresses. Such was the anti-religious bias of the French philosophe that he had quite failed to mention that the Incas worshipped Pachacamac as Creator of the world and believed in the immortality of the soul. Their rational form of government was enforced by harsh punishments. As for Robertson's judicious summary, where the Scot praised both the laws and monuments of the Incas but cited their lack of writing, commerce and private property as signs of a shortfall in true civility, Velasco insisted on the existence of schools for poets, historians and philoso-phers. What need was there for commerce or property if the empire was organised as if it were a great family, everyone subject to the paternal authority of the Inca? Moreover, the empire possessed over twenty cities and the remains of their fortresses and palaces were to be found in every province of the Andes. Who could doubt, no matter what Pauw, Raynal and Robertson cared to write, that the Peruvians had been 'cultivated and civilised for many centuries'. In suppport of this critique, Velasco simply invoked the authority of Garcilaso de la Vega, Pedro Cieza de León and José de Acosta, corroborated only by the evidence of his own eyes.[3]

A more judicial approach was adopted by Juan Ignacio Molina (1740–1829), an exiled Jesuit from Chile, who in his *Historia geográfica, natural y civil del reino de Chile* (1782–7), simply dismissed Pauw's work as 'more of a romance than a philosophical disquisition', which had as much to do with America as with the moon. Had not all travellers agreed that Chile possessed a temperate climate and a fertile soil, conditions which had offered a propitious environment for European stock? He indicated the problems of nomenclature when dealing with American species and appended a detailed list, arranged according to the Linnaean system of classification and dubbed in Latin. For the rest he argued that if it was only recently that the hispanic population had increased in Chile, this was owing to the continual frontier wars and the commercial monopoly exercised by the merchants of Lima. The main emphasis of his work, however, was on the Araucanians, who once more figure in familiar Tacitean fashion as an intrepid, hardy, freedom-loving nation of warriors. Perhaps the only advance on Ercilla was the invocation of Robertson's four stages of subsistence, which allowed Molina to rank the Araucanians as barbarians, which is to say, well above savagery but below 'civil society', a judgement based on their reliance on agriculture, their clearly defined property rights, and their system of chiefs. They worshipped a Supreme Being but also honoured a pantheon of lesser deities, communicating with the spirits through their shamans and by dreams. A contemporary note was struck when Molina compared their poets to the Celtic bards described by Ossian. For the rest, the perpetual wars between Spaniards and Araucanians loomed large, with Lautaro and Caupolican once more celebrated for their valour, their struggle for independence initiating a conflict that still raged well into the eighteenth century. In effect, Molina seized the opportunity afforded by European curiosity about America, in part aroused by the Pauw polemic, to offer a geographical description of his country and once more recount its epic history.[4] Few countries in Spanish America were so dominated by one primordial text as was Chile by *La Araucana*.

A striking feature of the creole response was the failure of any Peruvian Jesuit or Limeño intellectual to enter the debate over America. Indeed, in the *Mercurio Peruano*, a review published in Lima during the 1790s, a discussion of Indian population cited 'this radical defect of climate ... which in the New World prevents the multiplication of the human species ... '[5] It was not until 1806 that Hipólito Unanue (1755–1833), a distinguished doctor and counsellor of viceroys, published his *Observaciones sobre el clima de Lima* (1806) in which he dismissed the 'frightful picture' of America presented by 'overseas philosophers' and insisted on the necessity of accurate observations. It was to this end that he offered daily meteorological readings of temperature in the capital for two specimen years. So too, he presented the exact measurements of a typical llama. As was to be expected, he provided a valuable survey of diseases and infirmities incurred by the inhabitants of Lima. More generally, he stated that 'the Europeans, who today have triumphed in other parts of the globe as much through the energy of their pens as by their victorious arms, have erected themselves into a court and have pronounced in their favour'. Which was to say, the Europeans thought themselves to be the most intelligent and beautiful of races and had relegated the rest of humanity to an inferior position. Yet, as Unanue adverted, any consideration of history would remind us that civilisation began in the Middle East and that the Arabs had thriving cities when Europe still languished in barbarism. But, although Unanue indicated the benign character of the climate and soil of Lima, he also admitted that 'idleness is an inherent vice of the dwellers in these climes'. Moreover, the melancholy which infected both Indians and creoles in Peru also derived from its climate. Although Unanue qualified these damaging admissions by insisting that with education and discipline man 'is capable of everything' no matter what the weather, he persisted in suggesting that the climate of the torrid zone encouraged the imagination more than other faculties of the mind, an influence clearly demonstrated in the Indian talent for music and painting. It followed from this that children in Lima should be more encouraged to develop their natural interest in the arts and literature than be strained to pursue the aridity of mathematical calculation.[6]

In Europe, the defence of the Incas was left to an Italian Count, Gian Rinaldi Carli, who in his *Cartas americanas* (1780), drew upon Garcilaso to depict the Peruvian monarchs as exponents of a social utopia from which contemporary Europe could learn many a lesson. In more original vein, Carli boldly compared the Spanish conquerors to the North European philosophes, since both groups were united in their contempt of the Indians. Indeed, he ironically pondered whether 'through some extravagant metempsychosis', the soul of Valverde had been resurrected in Pauw.[7] If the Peruvian Jesuits failed to enter the debate over America, by contrast their Mexican brethren were more active. For the Jesuits expelled from New Spain constituted a Pleiad of talent and from their pens soon flowed an entire corpus of historical, literary, and theological work, much of it inspired by patriotic purpose. For the most part, however, their writings were not published and only slowly entered the public domain after independence. In 1804 Pedro Márquez succeeded in setting out in Italian a description of the pyramid at Tajín and an account of an expedition to the ruins at Xochicalco; the plates and texts offered material proof of native skill in astronomy, sculpture and architecture, arts which manifestly disproved the slanders of Pauw and Robertson and demonstrated that the Mexican Indians were 'a civilised nation'.[8] However, the value of these articles was but to confirm the image of Anáhuac presented in magisterial fashion in the most recent history of Mexico.

II

'To serve my country in the best possible way and to restore splendour to a truth which has been obscured by an incredible mob of modern writers on America': such was the stated purpose which drove Francisco Javier Clavijero (1731–87), a Mexican Jesuit exiled in Italy, to compose his *Historia antigua de México* (1780–1), patiently translating his work into Italian so as to secure publication. It was, so he averred, 'a history of Mexico written by a Mexican', expressly designed to answer the slanders of Pauw, Buffon, Raynal and

25 F. C. Giovanni, *Francisco Javier Clavijero*

Robertson, whose works he dismissed as typical of 'an age in which more errors have been published than in all previous centuries, in which authors write with license, lie shamelessly, and when no-one is reputed to be a philosopher who does not mock religion and adopt the language of impiety'. His indignant reaction did not spring from mere obscurantism, however, since as a young man he had greatly admired the writings of Feijoo and Fontenelle. Indeed, his generation of Jesuit college lecturers had aspired to renovate the teaching of philosophy in the Mexican province by incorporating the discoveries of modern science into their courses. Although they were bound by their Order's decree to respect Aristotle's authority, they sought to discard 'the futile bagatelles' of scholastic disputation.[9] As much as their Jansenist opponents, these mid-eighteenth-century Jesuits were thus deeply influenced by the revolution in science, history and philosophy from which the Enlightenment drew its inspiration. In effect, Clavijero rejected the culture of the Baroque and re-stated the creole version of the Mexican past in a style and from an intellectual perspective which he hoped would prove acceptable to contemporary Europe.

In deference to prevailing taste, Clavijero prefaced his narrative with a geographical description of Mexico, clearly distinguishing between the tropical coastlands and the more temperate climate of the central plateau. Despite a tribute to Buffon's standing as a naturalist, he appended two dissertations in which he roundly attacked the entire Buffonian thesis of the exceptionality of American nature. Alert to its historical antecedents, he noted that it had been Acosta who had first commented on the superabundance of waters in the New World and Herrera who had fixed on the paucity of animal species. In fact, there was little evidence to support their case other than the incidence of heavy, seasonal rains. What American lake was larger than the Caspian sea? So too, American bison, bears and wolves were as large as their cousins in the Old World. Why was the mere size of animals reckoned so significant? The elephant, so much admired by Buffon, was surely an ugly beast, with disproportionate members. Indeed, if size was to be the criterion of maturity, then Africa scored high above Europe which should thus be defined as infantile or degenerate. Nor was it true that European livestock declined in America, since in Mexico there were vast numbers of healthy, large oxen, horses and sheep. Even Acosta, who 'was not partial to America' recognised that the Mexican climate was remarkably benign and the soil fertile. Not content with these observations, by turns satirical and commonsensical, Clavijero also cited the *Historia natural* of 'the Pliny of New Spain', Francisco Hernández (1517–87), a Spanish physician and botanist, who had passed several years in Mexico gathering material for his great work, which was published in Latin in the seventeenth century. Drawing on his labours, Clavijero presented numerous additions to the list of Mexican flora and fauna compiled by Buffon, offering thus a potent reminder of the sheer richness of the Spanish cultural tradition, at that time so much condemned in northern Europe.[10]

Among the problems which most perplexed orthodox Catholics was how to connect the biblical account of Noah and the Great Flood with the appearance of mankind and animals in the New World, a problem accentuated by the common acceptance of a mere span of six thousand years for world history. For Clavijero the fact that many Indian peoples of Mexico and Guatemala cherished myths of a flood and of their migration from the north suggested that Acosta had been right in assuming that the Indians had crossed from Asia in the vicinity of the Bering Straits. But he was equally impressed by the hypothesis, found in both Feijoo and Buffon, that the earth's landmass may well have undergone severe dislocations caused by natural 'revolutions'. It was likely that North America had been once united to Asia and Eruope. So too, their very contours suggested that Brazil and Africa may well have been joined.[11] If such was the case, then there was no real difficulty in imagining the slow migration of men and beasts from Noah's ark and the tower of Babel across to the Americas.

If the Buffonian thesis was thus shown to have a weak foundation in natural science, how could the American Indian be redeemed from the charge that he was a feeble, insensible brute? It was easy enough to dismiss the indecent absurdities of Pauw, whose work Clavijero denounced as 'a cesspit or sewer of filth'. But how could the testimony of La Condamine and Ulloa be refuted, especially when many of their slanders were also to be found in Gómara and Herrera? To start with, Clavijero followed Garcilaso de la Vega in sharply distinguishing between the natives of Mexico and Peru and the many American peoples who were 'uncivilised, barbaric and bestial'. After all, he himself described the natives of Lower California as mere savages, 'indolent through lack of stimulus, inconstant ... and much given to puerile games and diversions'. Tribes such as the Iroquois and Caribs were animated by mere caprice, lacked government, law, the arts, and had no idea of the Supreme Being. How could the advanced societies of the Mexicans and Peruvians be understood by comparison with such savages? The origin of such slanders could be traced back to the conquerors whose self-interest had driven them to denigrate native talents, a campaign which had attracted the forthright condemnation of Las Casas and other missionaries.[12]

To answer contemporary disparagement, Clavijero informed his readers that, although he was a creole, born in Veracruz of Spanish parents, he had dealt with Indians since boyhood and as a Jesuit had taught Indian pupils in the college of San Gregorio in Mexico City. He solemnly declared that he had known many Indians, his own pupils among them, who had graduated with honours from college and university, and that several now served as parish priests. They had shown themselves capable of learning all the sciences. These affirmations acquired added force from the moderate, carefully distanced manner in which Clavijero described the character of the Mexican Indians, since although he praised their generosity, fidelity and piety, he also admitted their drunkenness and their distrustfulness. In the last resort, however, their souls were much the same as those of other men, dominated by the same balance of good and evil. As for their physical constitution, how could they be described as feeble, when the entire country depended on their labour? Even Ulloa, who was 'little favourable to the Indians', had testified to their general health and strength. At the same time, Clavijero admitted that the bulk of the native population of Mexico were sunk in misery and deprivation. With education they would certainly improve; but how could they overcome the obstacles created by poverty and exploitation? It was evident that contemporary Indians no longer possessed the fire, the sense of honour, the intrepid courage of their ancestors prior to the conquest. But then, Clavijero queried, who would recognise in the contemporary Greeks, groaning under the rule of the Ottoman Turks, the descendants of Plato and Pericles? It was this strong implicit comparison between Spaniards and Turks that prevented the publication of his work in Spanish until after Independence had been attained.[13]

Ever since La Condamine's travel account, it had been a commonplace among European historians of America that Indian languages lacked the words to express general ideas and mathematical quantities. Here was an assertion which Clavijero answered by drawing on his mastery of Nahuatl, a language for which he had compiled a brief grammar and vocabulary, to offer an entire list of terms used to express such metaphysical and moral concepts as eternity, soul, prudence and justice. As the example of the first missionaries demonstrated, there was no difficulty in translating any passage of the Bible into the Mexican tongue. Indeed, he appended a catalogue of authors who had published vocabularies, grammars and devotional books in native languages. As for terms to denote mathematical quantities, it was possible in Nahuatl to undertaken calculations reaching into the millions. Only in one respect did Clavijero admit a deficiency; classical Nahuatl did not have any equivalent for Greek philosophical concepts such as matter, substance and accidents. But it was a deficiency which Cicero had found also in Latin, and modern European languages had simply borrowed such terms from Greek or Latin. For the rest, Clavijero insisted that 'Mexican' was certainly as euphonious a language as German or Polish.[14]

To dismiss the slanders of ill-informed travellers or malevolent philosophes was a relatively easy task when compared to the challenge of responding to the historical scepticism of Robertson. For the Scotsman had insisted that the destruction of native codices wrought by the first missionaries, when combined with the ambiguous, often undecipherable character of the few codices that did survive, meant that the prime source for any history of ancient Mexico was the materials found scattered in Spanish chronicles. Moreover, whereas Robertson cited Herrera, Gómara, and Acosta with approval, he expressly dismissed Torquemada's subsequent contribution as a fabrication. It was in consequence of this preference that he began his account with the arrival of the Mexica, relegating the Toltecs to the impenetrable shadows of the past. Here, then, was Clavijero's task: he had to vindicate the Mexican tradition of enquiry into the native past in face of a seemingly authoritative, often critical restatement of the imperial school's perspective. But whereas Torquemada had drawn on Franciscan manuscripts, on Las Casas' *Apologética*, and on the codices he had studied with Ixtlilxochitl, what sources hitherto denied to European historians could an eighteenth century Jesuit cite to shatter Robertson's studied disdain?

To start with, Clavijero took a leaf out of Robertson's own book and prefaced his narrative with an annotated bibliography, in which he dismissed Herrera as a mere compendium of Gómara and Acosta; remarked on Gómara's frequent errors; adverted to Acosta's dependence on his Jesuit source, Juan de Tovar; and described Solís as more panegyric than history. By contrast, he listed the early Franciscan authors; praised Sahagún's history as 'a work of immense erudition and fatigue'; cited the contributions of Sigüenza y Góngora; and drew on the work of Gemelli Careri and Boturini, albeit rejecting the latter's 'system of history' as 'too magnificent and as such fantastic'. More important, Clavijero mentioned several Indian and mestizo historians of the sixteenth century, including Ixtlilxochitl, whose manuscripts he had studied in Jesuit libraries. In particular, he drew attention to the two collections of native codices and manuscripts formed respectively by Sigüenza and Boturini, which were preserved at the Jesuit college of St Peter and Paul and in the viceregal archive, where he had consulted them. Fragments from these collections had been published by Gemelli Careri and by Archbishop Lorenzana in his edition of Cortés' letters. In Europe native codices were also to be found in Oxford, Vienna and the Vatican.[15]

The purpose of this bibliographic exercise was eminently patriotic: it was designed to demonstrate the existence of native sources for Mexican history. In both his history and in his appended dissertations, Clavijero was at pains to affirm the veracity, sophistication and variety of Indian 'paintings'. Here were no mere pictures of things and events. Instead, the codices covered a large variety of subjects, ranging from topographical schemes of political boundaries to complicated historical annals. They could only be defined as a form of symbolic writing, the interpretation of which was carefully imparted to young priests and record-keepers by means of songs and other mnemonic devices. For the historian the most revealing documents were the elaborate calendar wheels, since they often indicated the monthly rites and the passage of the years. Such works could only have been produced by 'a most cultured nation' and demonstrated an extensive knowledge of astronomy and mathematics. It was precisely from such materials that native history could be reconstructed. Moreover, after the initial destruction, missionaries such as Olmos, Motolinia and Sahagún had collaborated with the Indian elite to replace what had been lost, especially in the area of calendrical computation and historical annals.[16] Here, then, was an impressive and persuasive statement of the Franciscan creole thesis as to the reliability of native records, sources which underpinned the first volume of Torquemada's *Monarquía indiana*.

The problem for Clavijero was that, although he may well have studied codices and native manuscripts in Mexico, in Italy he entirely lacked such privileged access. In any case, it is by no means clear that he possessed any but the most rudimentary knowledge of how to interpret these often intractable documents. In his dedicatory letter to the University of Mexico, he openly lamented the absence of any professor of antiquities among its faculty and admitted that 'there is no one who currently understands Mexican paintings'. Nor could he draw on the calendrical computations of Sigüenza, Boturini and Veytia, since these still languished in manuscript. The very list of Indian and creole authors he compiled was taken from catalogues of Boturini and Eguiara y Eguren. In effect, when Clavijero sat down in Italy to write his *Historia antigua*, he was obliged to rely on one great source – Torquemada's *Monarquía indiana* – readily available in its eighteenth-century edition. Yet in the bibliography he sharply criticised his great predecessor, observing that despite his diligence, his knowledge of Nahuatl, and his study of the codices, the Franciscan lacked taste and critical acumen, incurred gross contradictions, especially as regards chronology, and fatigued the reader with his superfluous erudition. He confessed that, since the chronicle had 'many valuable things for which one would search in vain in other authors, I found myself obliged to do with this history what Virgil did with Ennius: to search for precious stones among the dung'.[17] It does not require a Freudian analysis to perceive in these harsh words the repugnance of an author who has embarked on the anxious task of rewriting the canonical text of his intellectual tradition.

Although Herrera's contemporary successor as Historiographer and Chief Chronicler of the Indies, Juan Bautista Muñoz, confidently described the *Historia antigua de México* as little more than 'an orderly compendium of Torquemada', it was a much more subtle and daring exercise than that. To start with, Clavijero sought to liberate Anáhuac from the kingdom of darkness. Both Acosta and Torquemada had depicted the Mexica on their journey across the northern wilderness as led by the Devil himself, who deceived them through false oracles and thereafter established his cult in the manifold deities and rites of their empire. In forthright fashion, Clavijero criticised these historians for their naivety in making Satan into an historical personage, arguing that the Almighty had too much respect for his creation to allow the Devil such freedom of action. The practice of idolatry derived from human fears and ignorance and from the trickery and superstition of the pagan priesthood. The advantage of such a view was that it allowed him to offer a naturalistic account of Indian religion, describing in some detail their indistinct notion of a Supreme Being, their pantheon of gods, the colleges of priests, the grandeur of the great temple at Tenochtitlan and its gruesome rites, and the austerity of native morality. Not that he palliated the reality of human sacrifice, since he estimated that some 20,000 individuals were offered to the gods each year in ceremonies which rendered the priests objects 'of disgust and horror'. In effect, Clavijero freed Anáhuac from an Augustinian interpretation of native religion, even if he chose to cite the *City of God* on the obscenity and childish myths of Greek and Roman religion, and boldly concluded that if Mexican religion was more cruel, it was 'less superstitious, less indecent, less puerile and less irrational . . .' than its classical counterpart.[18]

In his historical narrative, Clavijero cleared the text of the mass of classical and biblical allusion which Torquemada had favoured, and proffered a clear chronology. In effect, he began Mexican history with the appearance of the Tolteca in 544, their monarchy enduring until 1051. Newcomers to Anáhuac, they founded cities, cultivated maize, and were subsequently celebrated for the perfection of their arts and calendar, which they bequeathed to their successors. They did not practise human sacrifice and constructed the great pyramids at Cholula and Teotihuacan. Thereafter, Clavijero traced the arrival of the Chichimecas and the rise of the Mexica to empire, providing exact dates for each king from the foundation of the monarchy until 1519. In his description of the Mexican 'constitution', he fixed upon such elements as the election and coronation of kings, the ranks of nobility, the forms of warfare, the activity of courts and magistrates, the practice of agriculture and commerce, the institution of property, both private and communal, and the development of poetry, oratory and drama. In his dissertations, he expanded on the use of cacao as both currency and standard of value; adverted to the laws which governed the relations between states; and admitted that the second Moctezuma had exercised despotic authority, albeit of a quality quite distinct from oriental monarchs who deprived their enserfed subjects of their lands. On the fundamental question of population, he cited Cortés and Bernal Díaz on the size and number of cities in the central valley, asserting that Tenochtitlan possessed at least 60,000 houses. At key points in his text, Clavijero quietly introduced classical comparisons, observing of one brave warrior's exploit that it was 'a memorable action of fidelity to his sovereign, which would be justly celebrated by historians and poets, if the hero had been a Roman or a Greek instead of being an American'. So too, in citing Acosta's description of a drama enacted at Cholula, he exclaimed that it offered 'a living image of the first scenes of the Greeks'. These neo-classical allusions were at times offset by the introduction of contemporary Spanish nomenclature, a device already used to excess by

Solís. Thus, the king's servant responsible for procuring palace supplies was named as 'the general intendant of the royal treasury'. The most persuasive evidence that 'the empire of reason' was not limited to Europe, however, consisted of the colloquies in which parents exhorted their children to adhere to the dictates of morality.[19] The mode of education of the young was the surest sign of the culture of a people and these colloquies revealed a high standard indeed.

The crowning proof of Anáhuac's claim to civilisation was the career and philosophy of Nezahualcoyotl, a monarch whom Torquemada and Ixtlilxochitl had once compared to king David. Clavijero commented that the king not merely instituted councils of war, justice and the treasury, but that he also formed 'a kind of academy for poetry, astronomy, music, painting, history and judicial astrology to which he summoned the most clever professors in the kingdom'. That the king secretly worshipped the Creator of heaven and sought in vain to suppress human sacrifice was agreed by all patriotic historians. But Clavijero also described Nezahualcoyotl as a dedicated naturalist, who procured paintings of distant animals and plants, his collection later proving of assistance to Dr Hernández in forming his catalogue of flora and fauna. In effect, 'he studied with curiosity the causes of the effects he admired in nature and this continued reflection made him realise the insubstantiality and falsity of idolatry'. Commenting on the concurrence of poets, orators and historians at the king's court and the monarch's wisdom in framing his celebrated laws, Clavijero concluded that: 'Texcoco was, so to say, the Athens of Anáhuac and Nezahualcoyotl the Solon of these peoples.'[20] The portrayal of Indian civilisation from the perspective of the neo-classical cult of great heroes and legislators here found appropriate expression.

Although Clavijero declared that 'religion, polity and economy are the three things which principally characterise a nation', and on occasion cited Montesquieu's *Spirit of the Laws*, he failed to develop any logical connection between the various elements that he advanced as proof of the civilised status of the Mexican kingdom. In effect, he substantiated his case by drawing on materials which had been first assembled by Olmos and Motolinia, subsequently enlarged and compressed into logical categories by Las Casas, and thereafter augmented and finally published by Torquemada. Instead of invoking the explicit standards of the Enlightenment, Clavijero unconsciously applied the Aristotelian criteria for a true city, criteria which had been first deployed and developed by Las Casas in his *Apologética*. To insist on his intellectual debt, is not to ignore the profound difference in perspective. For Las Casas had applied to the Indians the Ciceronian scheme of man's upward ascent from hunting and cave-dwelling to agriculture and cities, a scheme which presupposed that the Mexica had barbaric antecedents in the Chichimeca nomads of the North. It was an evolutionary scheme that Torquemada presented in a single chapter. By contrast, Clavijero chose to begin Mexican history with the appearance of the Toltecs and deprecated any attempt to compare the Mexicans with the northern tribes, complaining that 'those who blindly pretend to know the Mexicans in their descendants or in the nations of Canada and Louisiana will take their political system as imaginary and qualify as lies invented by the Spaniards all that we shall say of their lights, their laws and their arts'. At the same time, he drew on the Enlightenment's belief in the uniformity of human civilisation to assert that 'the polity which the Spaniards saw in Mexico (was) greatly superior to that which the Phoenicians and Carthaginians found in our Spain, and the Romans in Gaul and Great Britain'. Clavijero concluded by affirming of the Mexican Indians that 'in essence their souls are the same as those of other men . . . as experience has shown, their intellects are capable of all the sciences'.[21]

With all connection between Anáhuac and savagery boldly severed, it was also imperative to free Indian civilisation from any extraneous influence. In consequence, Clavijero dismissed out of hand the variegated myths which had haunted the creole mind from Ixtlilxochitl onwards. The theories of Gregorio García about the transoceanic migration of historic peoples were scornfully rejected as mere fantasy supported only by some presumed similarity of customs. The same objection applied to the widely held identification of the Toltecs or their predecessors with the ancient Egyptians, a theory entertained by Kircher, Sigüenza and Eguiara. It was a theory which continued to attract Lorenzo Hervás, a Spanish Jesuit savant, who in a letter to Clavijero urged by way of proof the similarity of pyramids, hieroglyphs and calendars. But the Mexican sharply denied all such claims, arguing that the two kinds of pyramids served different purposes and that their calendrical systems were based on a different distribution of months and days. He concluded: 'I am unable to persuade myself that the Mexicans or the Toltecs have been the debtors of any nation in the ancient continent as regards their calendar and method of computing time.' Equally important, he bluntly rejected the identification of Quetzalcoatl as St Thomas the Apostle, which had been proposed by Sigüenza y Góngora and endorsed by Boturini.[22] What need was there for an apostle in a country which he had liberated from Satan's bondage? In effect, Clavijero insisted on the autochthonous quality of a civilisation which he had established on secular foundations.

It is testimony to the perennial ambiguity of creole patriotism that Clavijero should have adopted a decidedly cool attitude to Las Casas, commenting about his writings that 'the excessive fire of his zeal spreads smoke with light, which is to say, truth mixed with error . . .'. Although he praised the great Dominican's defence of the rationality of the Indians, he criticised his denunciation of the conquerors' cruelties as too passionate and exaggerated. In particular, he explicitly denied Cortés' responsibility for the massacre at Cholula, which Las

Casas had urged so strongly, and equally blamed Alvarado's massacre at Tenochtitlan on Tlaxcalan conspiracy, in both cases citing Bernal Díaz as his authority. So too, he accepted the conqueror's account of Moctezuma's death, rejecting the accusation of Sahagún and 'the Mexican historians' that the Spaniards had killed the king. In this context, it is fascinating to observe that Clavijero followed Solís in having Moctezuma attribute the origin of his empire to Quetzalcoatl, so that his peaceful recognition of the authority of Charles V as the heir of this hero-deity could thus be interpreted as an authentic *translatio imperii*. If only the Spaniards had behaved better, the transition might well have occurred without bloodshed. Just why Clavijero should have adopted this imperial stance is made clear in his reflection on the sudden imprisonment of Moctezuma: 'in regard to this and other events of our history it is necessary to adore the highest counsels of Divine Providence, which used the Spaniards as instruments of its justice and mercy to these nations, punishing some for their superstition and cruelty and illumining the remainder with the light of the gospel'.[23] The *Historia antigua* ended abruptly after the torture and death of Cuauhtémoc with the melancholy reflection that 'In spite of the Christian and prudent laws of the Catholic kings, the Mexicans and all the nations that assisted in their ruin were abandoned to misery, oppression and scorn, not merely of the Spaniards, but even of the vilest African slave, God thus avenging on the miserable posterity of these nations, the cruelty, injustice and super-stition of their forbears.' Although in a dissertation Clavijero praised the early Franciscan missionaries as 'those immortal men', whose apostolic zeal, love of poverty and care of the Indians demanded remembrance, in his history he made no attempt to describe the glories of the spiritual conquest, still less record the progress of colonial society.[24] Whereas Torquemada had interpreted the conquest as a providential act which signalised the triumph of Jerusalem over Babylon, by contrast, Clavijero severed the spiritual link between Anáhuac and New Spain, offering little more than a stoic acceptance of a vengeful Providence.

The intellectual achievement of Clavijero was complex, subtle and ambi-guous. At one level, his work successfully defended the contemporary character and historical status of the Mexican people; his patria was thus endowed with a distinguished, not to say, glorious past. So too, he advanced a powerful defence of New Spain's historiographical tradition, its privileged access to native manuscripts and codices. By eliminating all supernatural interference, he presented a persuasive image of Tolteca–Mexica society as a civilisation. So much is obvious. But Clavijero also sought to re-state the creole tradition, and in so doing he effectively ousted Sigüenza y Góngora and his disciples from the seat of honour. Reaching further back, he openly challenged the authority of Torquemada and finally liberated creole patriotism from the intolerable burden of Augustinian damnation and Joachite triumphalism. In effect, he rejected the ideology of both the Baroque savant and the Franciscan chronicler. But his omissions were as important as his affirmations. Within his immediate range there were available two alternate schemes of human development which had been already applied to the Mexican case. Las Casas, Acosta and Robertson had all sketched out an evolutionary scheme whereby mankind slowly ascended from the primitive stage of hunting and wandering, to advanced societies with cities, governments and formed religion. By contrast, Boturini had presented a version of Vico's scheme, where early man figured as a strong poet, his fears transmuted into powerful myths, a stage that gave way to the age of warrior heroes and finally to the prosy condition of urban man. Clavijero made nothing of either scheme. He severed all links between mere savages and the Tolteca–Mexica, who thus appeared on the historical stage already civilised, exponents of natural virtue. It was to explain their origin that he cited Moses' last speech to the children of Israel, a discourse in which the prophet proclaimed that the Almighty had apportioned the lands of the world among the nations and that, despite their manifold transgressions and idolatry, the tribes of Israel were still to receive their inheritance in the Promised Land. So also, the peoples of Anáhuac had set forth from Babel in search of the lands that Noah had assigned them, wandering slowly across Asia, a journey during which they still preserved an indistinct knowledge of the Supreme Being and much of the natural wisdom of the first men [25] Here, then, was a providential design that inspired Clavijero to reject all evolutionary schemes of human development in ancient Mexico.

In the last resort one is impressed by the similarity between Clavijero and Garcilaso de la Vega. Both men wrote in the bitter quietude of European exile, bereft of all historical material other than the printed page, effectively privileged only in their knowledge of native language. Their restrained, judicious style, in itself a testimony to the respective influence of the Renaissance and Enlightenment, masked the intensity of their patriotic commitment. Their common enemy was the imperial tradition of historiography which started with Oviedo, Sepúlveda and Gómara, reached an early climax with Acosta and Herrera, only to be revived and restated by Pauw, Buffon and Robertson. To establish the image of the Incas and Aztecs as civilised nations, they followed Las Casas in framing a comparison no matter how moderate, with the Romans and Greeks. Indian society and religion was purged of all demonic associations and its natural virtue brought into high relief. Neither historian cared much for Las Casas' denunciation of the conquerors, choosing to interpret the conquest as an inexorable act of Providence. Although Clavijero was a creole, he endorsed Garcilaso's vision of a Catholic mestizo patria, when he expressed his regret that the conquerors had not married the daughters of 'the American houses' of nobility, thus opening the way for the emergence of 'a single and individual nation'.[26] That it took a Mexican intellectual more than a century and a half to reach the stage attained by the Peruvian mestizo demonstrates both the decisive originality of Garcilaso and the devastating authority of Torquemada in Mexico. It was only thanks to the historical scepticism promoted by the Enlightenment that the Mexican past could be liberated from its Augustinian devils and Baroque apostles and Egyptians. Whether Clavijero ever read Garcilaso with any care is not known, but the similarity in purpose and situation is startling.

III

In 1790, when the main square in Mexico City was levelled and paved, two pre-hispanic monoliths were discovered lying close to the surface, cast there by the conquerors when they had cleared the ruined enclosure of the great temple. One stone was a monstrous figure of the goddess Coatlicue, carved with bulging skulls and serpents, whose aspect filled spectators with disgust and horror. The other stone, a great disc carved with the glyphs of a calendar wheel, aroused excitement and speculation. In deference to this ambiguous reaction, the authorities had the two relics removed to the university where they were subsequently buried in the courtyard. By then, however, accurate drawings and measurements had been made, and in 1792 were duly published by Antonio de León y Gama (1735–1802) in the *Descripción histórica y cronológica de las dos piedras*. In his approbation, the creole censor, a professor of scholastic theology, exclaimed that although Raynal, Robertson, Buffon, Pauw and 'other enlightened philosophers' had sought to place 'the Indian nation at the level closest to that of the beasts and the most stupid brutes ... this single feature of Indian culture will dispel all such gross errors ... ' Within less than a century the *piedra de sol* was destined to become an emblem of Mexico.[27]

A savant in the tradition of Sigüenza and Peralta, León y Gama was as much an expert in mathematics and astronomy as in Nahuatl and antiquities and like his predecessors had been employed by the viceregal government to conduct astronomical and topographical observations, in this case along the coasts of California. Employed for most of his life as an official in the high court of justice, he confessed that 'I have always had a natural inclination to know with certainty the antiquities of my country.'[28] It was thanks to this prior interest that he was able to seize the opportunity offered by the discovery of the stones to publish the first systematic interpretation of the Mexican calendar. It was a formidable, complicated task, since the Aztecs had employed two parallel systems, a solar year divided into eighteen months of twenty days each, and a ritual year of twenty weeks of thirteen days each. The solar year was completed by a 'dead space' of five days. The glyphs denoting these divisions were inscribed on calendar wheels which also marked the passage of time, divided into indictions of thirteen years and cycles of fifty-two years. Such was the accuracy of this sytem that it was slightly superior to the Gregorian calendar still in use and decidedly superior to the Julian calendar observed by Europe at the time of the conquest. For León y Gama, the deciphering of the calendar was all-important, since it opened the way for a precise reconstruction of Aztec chronology, reaching back from the conquest until 1054 when the Mexica set out from their homeland in Aztlan. In his exposition, he dismissed 'the pretended systems of Gemelli, Boturini, Veytia and Clavijero', with a confidence that was not misplaced, since in the following century, José Fernando Ramírez, an expert interpreter of the codices, signalised his work as 'the first and only strictly rigorous archeological investigation to which Mexico can lay claim'.[29]

The most striking feature of León y Gama's research was the degree to which he relied on the writings of sixteenth-century native annalists, authors such as Cristóbal de Castilla, Hernando Alvarado Tezozomoc and Francisco San Antón Muñón Chimalpahin, who all wrote in Nahuatl. Such works were not easy to understand and it had cost him, so he averred, some twelve years of study, first to learn classical Nahuatl and then to interpret the codices annotated in Nahuatl, which could then be read in the light of information found only in the Indian annalists. Once this was done he could then return to Torquemada and Acosta and revise their statements by comparison with the sources on which they had drawn. In all this bold enterprise which, in scholarly technique far exceeded anything ever done by Robertson, León y Gama worked alone, sustained only by the interest of one or two friends. In effect, he substantiated Clavijero's claim that Mexico possessed native sources which contained the materials for a reconstruction of its ancient history, at least as regards chronology. But none of all this would have been remotely possible had there not existed in Mexico collections of manuscripts and codices on which León y Gama could work. If Fernando de Alva Ixtlilxochitl had not sought out such sources they might well have been lost to posterity. As it was, Sigüenza y Góngora inherited this collection and added to it, bequeathing the materials to the Jesuits, who in turn allowed Boturini to take copies of the originals. It was Boturini's confiscated 'museum' that León y Gama consulted, together with the papers of Veytia and documents held by other individuals.[30] In short, the *Descripción histórica y cronológica* constituted a triumphant vindication of a tradition of inquiry into the native past of Mexico which had been initiated by the Franciscans, assisted by their Indian collaborators at the College of Santa Cruz Tlatelolco, continued by native and mestizo annalists of the late sixteenth century, and thereafter transmitted by the line of creole patriots that started with Ixtlilxochitl and Sigüenza y Góngora. Without that tradition the discovery of the stones might well have passed unnoticed or have been simply treated as a matter of antiquarian curiosity. As it was, the *piedra de sol* was rightly acclaimed as a public monument, an enduring emblem of Mexico, and the most persuasive proof that the peoples of Anáhuac had indeed created a civilisation.

PART 3

RECONQUEST AND REVOLUTION

The great soul of the Legislator is the only miracle that can prove his mission

JEAN-JACQUES ROUSSEAU

21

THE NEW STATE

I

IN 1766 the City Council of Mexico directed an indignant memorial to the Crown complaining of the 'absolute, despotic proceedings' of the newly arrived inspector general of troops, Juan de Villalba, who had sought to levy militia forces without distinction of rank or caste. The creole councillors did not object to the raising of such forces since they admitted that the century had been characterised by almost continuous conflict in Europe between the Great Powers. Although the Crown had despatched two regular regiments of Spanish soldiers to Mexico, there was an obvious need for militia forces to defend the country and maintain internal peace. What the Council condemned was Villalba's summoning of all likely candidates by lot, without separation of nobility and commoners, keeping them kicking their heels in the blazing sun for two days. He had dismissed the City's protests in most brusque fashion and, in treating nobles as if they were blacks, had acted 'against the ordinances, against the constitution of the country'. It appeared that 'the newly arrived officers' believed that 'in this land there is no nobility, nor lineage, nor worth ...'. There had been no attempt to offer the nobility officer rank in the militia, yet the nobility of Mexico descended from the first families of Spain, from the conquerors and from the 'emperors, kings and lords it had in pagan times'.[1] Throughout the period of 242 years that stretched from the foundation of the City under the emperor Charles V until the reign of Charles III the Council had always been accorded the respect and pre-eminence its rank commanded: why now was it subjected to such abuse and disregard?

The worst apprehensions of the creole elite about the new style of government favoured by Charles III were more than fulfilled when in 1767 there arrived a peremptory decree to expel all Jesuits from the territory of the Spanish monarchy. The Walloon viceroy, Francisco de Croix, and the newly arrived visitor-general, José de Gálvez, moved swiftly to implement the order, only to be confronted by a series of riots and uprisings in Guanajuato, San Luis Potosí, Pátzquaro and Uruapan, towns which had already witnessed popular protests against militia enlistment and new excise duties. Drawing upon the troops brought in by Villalba and the militia forces led by creole landowners and miners, Gálvez suppressed this challenge with unprecedented harshness. He hanged 85 persons, flogged 73, banished 117, and sentenced 674 others to various terms of imprisonment. These events marked a watershed in Mexico's colonial history.[2] Peninsular soldiers arrived and Mexican-born Jesuits were expelled; the populace, which did not appreciate the change, were subjected to a brutal exercise in military force. At the same time, a group of creole dignitaries, judges and priests were expelled from Mexico for daring to question the wisdom of these harsh measures.

The ministers of Charles III (1759–88) might have been more prepared to pay heed to these protests had not the plight of the monarchy appeared so grave. For Spain had entered the Seven Years War (1756–63) only to suffer defeat from British naval expeditions which captured Manila and Havana. At the subsequent Treaty of Paris France lost her mainland empire in the New World with the result that, as Gálvez averred: 'Spanish America each day is more exposed to the insatiable ambition of certain European Powers . . . England especially aspires to dominate the entire commerce of both hemispheres.' The case for intervention was rendered all the more pressing since contemporary observers were agreed that Spain's standing as a European power of the second rank, equal to Austria and Prussia, depended on her overseas empire. As Montesquieu wrote in *The Spirit of the Laws* (1748) 'The Indies and Spain are two powers under the same master; but the Indies are the principal, while Spain is only the accessory.' Although the French *philosophe* warned that it was impossible to redress the economic balance since the commerce between Spanish America and Europe was dominated by foreign traders and foreign merchandise, the ministers of Charles III resolutely sought to rebuild the monarchy's power through a radical overhaul of colonial government and a renewal of the colonial economy.[3] In all this, there was a remarkable similarity between the grand designs of the 1560s and the 1760s. On both occasions the Crown despatched visitors and viceroys to strengthen the power of the colonial state so as to extract greater profit from its overseas possessions. If Philip II's ability to wage war in Europe depended on the remission of Peruvian silver procured by the measures of Francisco de Toledo, so equally, Charles III's newfound power in the European concert derived from the upsurge in Mexican silver production engineered by José de Gálvez. In both epochs the interests of the colonists were sacrificed to the necessities of the metropolis. Where the Bourbon ministers scored over their Habsburg predecessors was in their better understanding of the nature of economic activity, an intelligence that largely derived from their reading of mercantilist texts. Here, as in so many aspects of eighteenth-century Spain, innovation consisted in the application of principles and practices first developed in northern Europe.

In his *Theórica y práctica de comercio y de marina*, a lengthy treatise first circulated in 1724 and then published with official sanction in 1742 and again in 1757, Jerónimo de Ustariz, a high-placed official, lamented 'the decadence and annihilation of this monarchy', but interpreted the decline as 'a punishment for our negligence and blindness in the organisation of trade'. It was ill-considered tariffs and excise duties which had destroyed domestic industry and rendered the Peninsula dependent on manufactures imported from abroad. Remedy could only come from a close study and application of 'the new maxim of State', or, as he elsewhere put it, *la nueva política* of France, England and Holland, countries whose trade had thrived at the expense of Spain. Indeed, in 1689 it was estimated that of 27,000 toneladas of merchandise legally shipped from Cadiz to America, only 1,500 originated in the Peninsula. Although obviously conversant with the *arbitristas*, the advocates of reform in the preceding century, Ustariz sought practical guidance in Huet's *Commerce d'Hollande* (of which he promoted a Spanish translation) the French tariffs of 1664–7, and the English Navigation Laws. In particular, he praised Louis XIV's great minister, Jean-Baptiste Colbert, as 'the most zealous and skilful minister concerned with the advance of trade and shipping that Europe has ever known'. His actual recommendations were simple: he insisted that tariff rates must always distinguish between primary produce and elaborated goods; that imported merchandise should always pay higher duties than exports of native manufactures; and that where possible internal excise should be eliminated. More positively, he advocated an active procurement policy in respect of equipment, munitions and uniforms of the armed forces so that all these supplies should come from Spanish workshops and foundries. The main goal here was the creation of a strong navy, its ships built, armed and outfitted in royal arsenals, which would be able to defend the American empire from foreign attack. If 'the establishment of manufactures in Spain [is] the chief measure on which the restoration of the monarchy is to be based', an essential prerequisite was an expansion in the armed might of the Crown.[4]

The application of mercantilist doctrines of the seventeenth century to revive the strength of the monarchy can also be observed in José del Campillo y Cosío's *Nuevo sistema de gobierno económico para la América*, a work written in 1743 and published in 1762 as the second part of Bernardo Ward's *Proyecto económico*. For the starting point of his analysis was a direct comparison between the high profits which accrued to Great Britain and France from their Caribbean sugar islands and the derisory returns of Spain's vast mainland empire. To remedy this sorry state of affairs, he advocated the revival of the Habsburg practice of a general visitation, to be followed by the establishment of permanent intendants, officials especially charged with the development of the economy. He warned against the excessive power and wealth of the Church. In particular, he called for the introduction of what he called *gobierno económico*, by which he clearly meant the doctrines and policies of Colbertian mercantilism. He advocated the termination of the antiquated system of periodic trade convoys sailing from the staple port of Cadiz and sought to open up the chief ports of America and Spain to the free flow of individual shipping. Above all else, Campillo viewed the colonies as a great untapped market for Spanish industry: its population, especially the Indians, were the monarchy's chief treasure. But before the Indians could be incorporated into society, it was necessary to remove malign monopolies, diminish the influence of the Church, distribute unused land, and reform the prevailing system of government. It was also necessary to curb, if not destroy, colonial industry. Throughout his text, Campillo was at pains to assert the supremacy of public interest over private profit, a distinction expressed in the contrast he drew between 'political' trade and 'mercantile' trade.[5]

The impulse to reform also derived from reports from America which attested to the corruption and inefficacy of colonial government. In their *Noticias secretas*, a confidential report commissioned by the Marquis of Ensenada, Antonio de Ulloa and Jorge Juan framed a devastating indictment of the imperial regime in South America. In their prologue they frankly admitted that were their findings to be made public they would cause the same stir as Las Casas' denunciations of the conquerors. As in the *Relación histórica*, Ulloa figured as the chief author, since Juan confined his contribution to a review of the naval defences of the Pacific coast, whose creole and mestizo personnel he castigated for their indiscipline and incompetence, defects all too reminiscent of 'the old Spain'. The remedy, however, lay not in importing European troops, since these were invariably corrupted by the colonial environment and tended to desert, but in recruiting mestizos by state levy and having them trained in Spain, thereafter stationing them across the empire. These impracticable suggestions were matched by a proposal to abolish the trading fleets to Cartagena in favour of licenced shipping round Cape Horn. The imperial concern which animated the report was reinforced by the opening statement in which the Indies were characterised as rich and thriving countries whose inhabitants enjoyed an excessive liberty which rendered them indifferent to their obligation to serve the Crown. Moreover, the distance from Europe allowed governors and other officials to enrich themselves at the expense of both the Crown and their subjects.[6]

If Las Casas had attributed the sufferings of the Indians to the oppression of the encomenderos, so now Ulloa blamed the 'tyrannical government' of the corregidors for the current degradation of the native population of Peru. In particular, he condemned the *repartimientos de comercio*, the enforced distribution of mules, cloth and merchandise, exclaiming that it was 'a system so perverse that it appears to have been imposed as a punishment for these peoples, since one cannot imagine a more tyrannical infliction'. For the district magistrates issued over-priced goods on credit and often exacted payment in labour or in kind, forcing the Indians to work in *obrajes* to weave cloth, or on plantations to grow coca, or employed them as muleteers, carrying goods to distant markets. Alternatively, the Indians entered the hispanic economy on their own account, working in mines and selling their agricultural produce in the highland cities. Generally speaking, the magistrates were retired military men, peninsular Spaniards, whose transactions were financed by the great merchant houses of Lima, where the high court of justice could be readily persuaded to turn a deaf ear to any Indian protests against exploitation. Profits were high and a return of 200,000 pesos on a five-year term of office not uncommon. If the province of Quito was exempt from this system, it was because its Indian communities had lost their land and lived on haciendas where the landlords treated them as if they were serfs. Moreover, many of these estates operated *obrajes* where the natives were often imprisoned and kept in worse conditions than slaves brought over from Africa. In short, if the Indians of Peru so often appeared to European travellers as degraded, insensible and recalcitrant to all incentive, it was precisely because the Crown's magistrates united with the colonial elite to exploit the labour power of the native peasantry in the most tyrannical fashion possible. The only remedy was outright abolition of all *repartimientos de comercio* and restitution of land to the Indian communities. To ensure further protection, Ulloa suggested that the sons of the Indian gentry, the kurakas, should be sent to Spain for their education so that they would acquire sentiments of loyalty to the Crown and on their return serve as protector attorneys for the Indians.[7]

As much as Gemelli Careri or Frezier, Ulloa was shocked by the bitter enmity that characterised the relations of American and European Spaniards, observing that in the Peruvian highlands all the cities were 'a theatre of discord and continual opposition between Spaniards and creoles . . . it suffices to have been born in the Indies to hate the Europeans'. The twin causes of this fierce rivalry were the boundless vanity of the creoles and the poverty of immigrant Spaniards. Although many creoles were in reality mestizos, they all boasted of their noble lineage, demonstrated their status by idleness, and often consumed their inheritance through indulgence in vice. 'They distance themselves from all work or from occupying themselves in trade, the only occupation in the Indies through which fortunes can be maintained without decay.' Not that the creoles were fit for high office, since they were subject to the demands of kinship, so that even the most talented always required European judges or officials at their side to ensure disinterested government. If Ulloa thus adopted an unsympathetic view of the American Spaniards, he was equally disdainful of their peninsular rivals, who were generally men 'of low birth or of little-known lineage in Spain, without education or any other merit'. If immigrants did so well, it was the fault of the creoles who allowed them to dominate trade and often invited them into their houses, accepting all Europeans as nobles, with the result that many of these traders won the hand of creole heiresses. Moreover, the Europeans usually enjoyed the favour of the royal governors and, once established, frequently became town councillors and magistrates. In effect, Ulloa presented the ministry in Madrid with a social analysis that concurred with any number of published travellers' accounts. Not surprisingly, he had little remedy to offer other than the banning of men of low birth from municipal office.[8]

Nowhere did Ulloa display more clearly his character as a philosophe than in his strident condemnation of the colonial clergy, which by reason of its utter failure to observe the rule of celibacy presented a living scandal to all sincere Catholics. The secular priests all had common-law wives and frequently exploited their Indian parishioners, even using their churches as halls for the weaving of cloth. Even worse were the mendicants who led licentious lives, their priories often filled with their concubines. Moreover, the orders were so wealthy that elections to office were often the scene of bitter disputes. Ulloa recalled that he himself had observed friars coming into Quito for the provincial chapter, accompanied by their concubines. By way of remedy, he advocated the abolition of the *alternativa*, since the rotating election of European and creole provincials and priors was the source of perpetual discord and served no useful purpose. For the rest, he recommended that the mendicants should be stripped of their country parishes and restricted to their city priories and frontier missions. Here were measures which were echoed by the current viceroy in Peru, the Marquis of Superunda, and which were to find a ready audience in Madrid.[9]

There was a striking exception to Ulloa's critique of the colonial Church. Both in his published *Relación histórica* and in the *Noticias secretas* he praised the Jesuits for their discipline, dedication and public service. Their great wealth was expended in maintaining excellent colleges and numerous mission stations. They were active as confessors; they did not suffer from any partisan rivalry between Europeans and Americans; and they displayed no compunction in expelling from their society any recalcitrant or corrupted member. Their 'state' in Paraguay offered an exemplary demonstration of how to convert and govern Indians. Indeed, so enamoured was Ulloa with the Jesuits that he recommended that they should be entrusted with the government of all the frontier region in Amazonia, acting as the spearhead of a new 'spiritual conquest'. After all, he argued, had not Garcilaso shown that the Incas had attracted the voluntary allegiance of unsubdued tribes by the very benevolence of their rule? So too, the Jesuits could persuade Indians to accept the authority of the Spanish Crown. Their intervention was all the more desirable since the Portuguese were encroaching upon Spanish territory and the existing Franciscan missions had proved inadequate.[10]

By way of conclusion, Ulloa commented on the sheer weakness of royal authority in the Indies and the failure of Spain to obtain any real profit from its vast overseas empire. It was not simply the case that the corregidors were corrupt, they were also powerless in their dealings with the local elite. Most magistrates rarely employed more than three or four mestizos to assist them, so that they could only quell popular riots by calling upon local landowners to help them. Without the sanction of armed force, so Ulloa averred, it was impossible to uphold the rule of law, the purpose of which was to restrain the vices inherent in human nature. As a result, all royal officials from the viceroy downwards went to the Indies with the sole purpose of enriching themselves. With taxes so light and military service almost unknown, royal authority was at a discount. 'Every individual so much values what he possesses that he considers himself a petty sovereign in his own lands, the absolute owner of them.' In this context, Ulloa praised the Marquis of Castelfuerte, Peralta's patron, for despatching the viceregal guard to imprison a nobleman who had ignored the edicts of the city magistrates.[11]

II

The executive agent of the Bourbon Crown's pursuit of 'profit and power' was José de Gálvez, a lawyer from Málaga, who first as visitor-general of New Spain 1765–71 and then as minister of the Indies 1776–87, drove forward a programme of reform designed to revitalise both the government and the economy of the American empire. The most striking measure was the establishment in 1776 of a new viceroyalty with its capital at Buenos Aires covering the vast area now occupied by Argentina, Uruguay, Paraguay and Bolivia. The result was a dramatic shift in the geo-political balance of the continent, since the subjection of Upper Peru to Buenos Aires meant that Lima suffered a severe loss in status, a blow compounded by the opening of trade routes round Cape Horn which deprived Callao of its entrepôt function. Elsewhere a viceroyalty had been created in New Granada in 1739 to ensure the defence of Cartagena and in 1776 a captain-general was appointed to govern Venezuela with the capital at Caracas. These shifts in jurisdiction were accompanied by the introduction of a new fiscal bureaucracy and the establishment of small standing armies and extensive militia forces in virtually all the leading provinces of the empire. To take the most prominent example, in Mexico regular troops, all recruited locally, eventually numbered some ten thousand men, supported by militia regiments more than double that number. On the fiscal side, the manufacture and sale of tobacco became a highly profitable royal monopoly which required a numerous body of guards and directors to enforce and manage. So too, the collection of the excise duties, the *alcabalas*, was handed over to salaried officials. This expansion in state

EL Exmô. SEÑOR DON JOSE
DE GALVEZ MARQUES
DE SONORA.

26 José de Gálvez

personnel was completed in 1786 with the creation of twelve intendancies in New Spain, each provincial capital then housing a semi-permanent governor, his legal advisor, treasury officials, excise men, tobacco monopoly salesmen, and militia officers. So great was the scale of innovation that when the second Count of Revillagigedo became viceroy in 1789 his predecessor warned him that the final report compiled by his father, who had served as viceroy in the years 1746–55, was inapplicable to the present era since 'the system has varied to such a degree that that wise report ... can assist Your Excellency solely to compare the changes brought about during the course of thirty-five years'.[12]

In the economic sphere the promulgation of the decree of *comercio libre* in 1778 finally terminated the Cadiz monopoly and the periodic despatch of trading convoys. Henceforth, the chief ports of the Peninsula and Spanish America could trade freely with each other by means of individual merchant shipping. In the succeeding decade registered exports tripled and customs revenues more than doubled. Virtually every province of the empire experienced a quickening in the pace of production for export, with New Spain taking the lead, its ouput of silver doubling in the years immediately following the 1760s. As Gálvez declared: 'Since mining is the origin and source of the metals which give spirit and movement to all human occupations and to the universal commerce of the globe, in justice it demands the principal attention of the government.' To encourage production, he halved the price of mercury, the indispensable catalyst in the amalgamation refining process, ensured a more abundant supply from Almadén, offered tax exemptions for enterprises of great risks or high cost, organised the miners into a guild endowed with courts to handle mining litigation, promulgated a new code of law, established both a mining finance bank and a mining college, and conferred titles of nobility on wealthy entrepreneurs. The result of all these measures was to make mining more profitable and to endow the industry with a new aura of respectability. Moreover, the expansion in silver production in Mexico derived from the union of mercantile investment, entrepreneurial skill and state incentive, assisted by an abundant supply of free workers and readily accessible deposits of ore.[13] In the eighteenth century New Spain emerged as the senior province within the empire, second only to the metropolis in its wealth and tax yield.

To draw attention to the scale and success of Gálvez' achievements is not to deny the controversy that his measures aroused. To begin with, in 1768 he joined with Viceroy Croix to call for the abolition of the alcaldes mayores, the district magistrates of New Spain, whom he described as 'a ruinous plague of more than 150 men' whose livelihood derived from their *repartimientos de comercio*, a practice which not merely exploited their Indian subjects through the enforced distribution of over-priced livestock and merchandise, but effectively defrauded the Crown of at least half a million pesos of tribute. Once appointed minister of the Indies, Gálvez obtained from the bishop of Oaxaca a striking denunciation of the system as it then applied in his diocese. Widening the discussion to include some consideration of the thorny question of the Indian's character, the bishop admitted the natives were often guilty of drunkenness, lust and sloth, and generally displayed an 'implacable hatred of Spaniards'. Some observers, especially those with vested interests, 'wish to attribute the cause and origin of his vices to the very nature of the Indian'. But anyone who dealt with the natives 'clearly sees that they were of the same character and inclination as other men, as open to all the virtues and vices in the political, moral Christian spheres of life as those born in Castile. Consequently, the origin of their disorder and lack of application is to be found in the humiliation and abjection in which they were reared and live.' If the repartimientos were abolished, other merchants would be free to trade with the Indians and hence would 'restore to the Indian his natural freedom to treat and deal with whomsoever brings him more return', thus encouraging him to become a hard-working, profit-oriented individual.[14] It was by recourse to such arguments that Gálvez succeeded in justifying the abolition of the alcaldes mayores, the prohibition of repartimientos, and the establishment of the intendants and their subdelegates.

Controversy did not end with the appointment of the intendants, however, since the new system failed to make adequate provision for the maintenance of the subdelegates, the new district magistrates. Moreover, in certain areas, especially in the South, Indians found it difficult to obtain credit for any production aimed at the market, since merchants were reluctant to risk their monies without the sanction of a magistrate's authority. In 1794, when the continued existence of the intendancy system was brought into question, the creole regent of the high court of justice, Baltazar Ladrón de Guevara, recommended that subdelegates should be allowed to trade and distribute goods on credit, albeit without any local monopoly or use of force. He justified this permission by observing:

> It is necessary to suppose that the chief features of Indian character are indolence and abandonment ... if the repartimientos are absolutely necessary for the subsistence of the subdelegates, they are no less necessary for the Indians and the poor, because otherwise ... their misery will increase, since they will lack the most necessary things to exist such as their poor clothing, oxen for the cultivation of their fields, and mules for the transport of their goods.

In 1801 the matter went to the Council of the Indies for a general review, with Peru as much as Mexico the object of discussion. For Jorge de Escobedo, former visitor-general to Peru, the problem 'reduces itself to seek and propose means by which to simulate the Indians to work and supply them with goods, without violence and by hands other than those of their own judges'. It was a former crown attorney in New Spain, Ramón de Posada, who best expressed the distress that the issue provoked in any enlightened mind. He frankly admitted that despite the protection and the laws of the Spanish Kings, the Indians had been oppressed for nearly three centuries. And now they were subjected to a further indignity: 'Such has been the misfortune of the Indians, that in these times, in which even the monuments of their civilisation, greater than those of the Egyptians, Greeks and Romans in some of their periods, have not disappeared, already it is argued that their incapacity makes them slaves by nature.' In effect, the discussion in official circles over the justice of repartimientos was inextricably linked to the perennial debate about the nature of the American Indian, a debate which attracted as much polemic in the eighteenth as in the sixteenth century.[15]

If the Bourbon administrative elite often displayed a creditable compassion for the Indians, seeking to liberate the natives from past abuses and incorporate them into a market economy, by contrast the same men frequently expressed open disdain for the creoles. In a memorandum written before his journey to Mexico, Gálvez voiced disquiet at the number of government places occupied by American Spaniards, asserting that the creoles were too constrained by 'the ties of family and faction to provide a disinterested and impartial government in the New World'. His apprehension was heightened when he found that in the Mexican high court of justice 'the majority of its members were natives of the country'. His fears were echoed in an extraordinary council of state held in Madrid in 1768 to discuss the condition of the American empire. For the two royal attorneys of the Council of Castile, Pedro Rodríguez Campomanes and José Moñino (later the Count of Floridablanca) stated that it was advisable to attract creoles to the Peninsula, both as children for education, and as adults in administrative and military posts. It was necessary, they insisted, 'to maintain the policy of always sending Spaniards to the Indies for the principal offices, bishoprics, and prebendaries, offering the creoles equivalent places in Spain'. When news of this decision reached Mexico, the city council presented a long representation, arguing the case for creole appointments to high office. Nevertheless, once Gálvez became minister in 1776, he issued a decree inviting creoles to present themselves for clerical and judicial appointments in the Peninsula. Henceforth, only a third of all posts in the American courts and cathedral chapters were to be reserved for native-born candidates; the remainder were to be made available to qualified peninsulars.[16]

Heedless of repeated protests from Peru and Mexico, Gálvez relied on lawyers, accountants and soldiers brought in from Spain to drive through his revolution in government. The newly-created fiscal bureaucracy, the intendancies, the standing army, and the high courts of justice were all headed by peninsulars. By the close of his term of office, only a third of the audiencia judges were creoles as compared to a majority when he first arived in Mexico. Even in the Church, for so long a creole preserve at all levels beneath the episcopacy, European priests were appointed to cathedral chapers. Some measure of the disdain with which Gálvez viewed the American Spaniards can be obtained from a letter he wrote to his faithful subordinate, Juan Antonio de Areche, then engaged in a general visitation of Peru, in which he dismissed the inhabitants of Lima as being 'of a quick humour and understanding, but superficial and unreliable in judgement, even though remarkably presumptuous ... they are of little spirit, being timid and submissive'. The vulgar errors which Feijoo had denounced so eloquently were thus now firmly enshrined in the official mind since they afforded a convenient rationale for imperial policy.[17]

What at first sight appears to be a decisive episode in the political education of the creole elite was complicated by issues of class, family and region. For Charles III recruited several of his chief ministers from *manteistas*, which is to say, from lawyers who had not attended the six *colegios mayores*, situated at Salamanca, Valladolid and Alcalá, whose alumni had hitherto dominated the councils of the monarchy. There were families of *colegiales* who served the Crown on both sides of the Atlantic and who constituted an hereditary *noblesse de robe*. Both Floridablanca, Charles III's chief minister after 1776, and his protégé, Gálvez, belonged to the ranks of the *manteistas*, men of relatively humble extraction, raised in the provinces, who were eventually awarded titles of nobility as reward for their service to the Crown. Moreover, Gálvez soon became renowned for his implacable nepotism, appointing first his brother and then his nephew as viceroy of New Spain; other high offices went to more distant relatives and to compatriots from Malaga.

The bias of ministerial policy did not pass unnoticed, since there exists in the archive of the Indies an anonymous document, evidently composed by a high-placed official resident in Madrid during the years 1775–6, who bluntly described Gálvez as a man 'without experience, without prudence and without wisdom'. He described him as 'a minister who completely despises the habits and people' of the New World. Many new government places had been created in these years but nearly all the appointments went to candidates from Spain, thus ignoring the 'due order of promotion' for Americans. Yet on what grounds were the creoles denied access to such offices, the more especially since 'lacking these rewards of study, will not the Americans experience the same fate as the Greeks now subject to the Ottoman empire?' As it was, resentment against the measures grew apace. Even peninsular officials serving in the country had become concerned about the career prospects of their children. He concluded that New Spain 'shall never cease to abominate the rule of the Marquis of Croix during the period of the last visitation'. The country was dismayed to learn that 'the same destructive agent ... should now be placed with greater power to whet his ambition to cause uproar in both hemispheres'. These notes, cast in chronological form, ended on a prophetic note: 'Gálvez has destroyed more than he has built . . . his destructive hand is going to prepare the greatest revolution in the American empire.'[18]

III

The most eloquent of the protests to the Crown against Gálvez' prejudice against the creoles was penned by Antonio Joaquín de Rivadeneira y Barrientos (1710–77?), a native of Mexico City, scion of a noble family of Puebla, who had been educated at the *colegio mayor* of All Saints. At the time a judge on the Mexican high court, he won his appointment after many years practising law in Madrid where he had attracted the patronage of José de Carbajal y Lancaster, the influential minister of Ferdinand VI. He had also demonstrated his talents by the publication of two substantial books in which he paraded his loyalty to the Crown and, more subtly, to his creole patria. That he should have accepted the invitation of the City Council to frame their protest of 1771, written at a time when he was busy defending royal interests in the Fourth Mexican Church Council, indicates the degree to which Gálvez' high-handed measures affronted the creole establishment of Mexico. It further illustrates the contrast of generations, between the *colegiales* favoured by Ferdinand VI and the provincial lawyers promoted by Charles III.[19]

Some measure of Rivadeneira's talents and ideas can be obtained from *El pasatiempo* (1752–3,), three volumes of heavily annotated historical verse, which expeditiously cover the entire span of world history from Creation to the peace treaty signed in 1750 between Spain and Great Britain. Although the Jesuit censor pronounced that 'this book is of the good taste of this century', Rivadeneira still defended the authenticity of St James' apostolic mission to Spain and attributed the conquest of the New World to that saint's intervention. Indeed, he followed the chroniclers of the sixteenth century in ascribing the first discovery of America to an unknown Basque pilot and firmly depicted the ancient Mexicans as subject to Satan's commands in their northern wanderings. Despite his approving citation of Bacon, he affirmed that, since Pope Urban VIII had condemned the Copernican system as contrary to scripture, it was forbidden for Catholics to accept the findings of Newton. That Rivadeneira both prefaced and concluded his work with a eulogy of José de Carbajal y Lancaster, who had been largely responsible for ending Spain's involvement in the War of the Austrian Succession, pointed to his attachment to the house of the Dukes of Linares which had provided a viceroy for Mexico earlier in the century. He also took care to praise the Marquis of Ensenada as 'the declared, passionate director and protector of the Spanish navy'.[20]

At the same time, Rivadeneira displayed no hesitation in pursuing the familiar themes of creole patriotism. He complained about the poor image of the American Indians that prevailed in Spain and stated that there was much to admire in their legislation, arts and government, citing in particular the laws of the Incas and the philosophy and justice of Nezahualcoyotl. Indeed, as a boy he had listened to poetry in Nahuatl and attested to its fine lyrical quality. As for the question of human sacrifice, he exclaimed that all nations had practised idolatry and that in contemporary Europe more men were sacrificed to 'the idol of the Balance of Power' than had ever been offered to native gods. Not that he lamented the fall of Tenochtitlan, since he defined the conquest as the liberation of Mexico from Satan's dominion. As for the contemporary Indians, he admitted that the majority of them were condemned to toiling in the fields, often working twelve hours a day on haciendas to feed and support the rest of society. But he cited the famous memorial on the Mexican Indians written by Juan de Palafox, the bishop of Puebla, as the best guide to their virtues and character. He insisted that 'in general, the Indians have great capacity, as much for the sciences and liberal arts as for the mechanical arts. Among them are to be found very good Latinists, philosophers and great moral theologians . . . the Indians are very fine painters and sculptors.' Indeed, their quality as a people had attracted heavenly approbation since Our Lady of Guadalupe had appeared 'brown in colour like the Indian women and dressed in the same clothes that they wore'. In true creole style, the theme of the Guadalupe led him to cite such well-known authors as Sigüenza y Góngora, Becerra Tanco, and, the most recent in this line of patriots, Juan José de Eguiara y Eguren.[21]

If Rivadeneira employed his literary talent to attract court patronage, he also demonstrated his legal qualifications by publishing a 'manual compendium' on the Crown's rights as patron of the American Church, a work in which he emerged as a strong advocate of royal authority in virtually all ecclesiastical matters other than the purely dogmatic. It is significant that he hailed Juan de Solórzano as 'a genius . . . our common master', since of course the seventeenth-century jurist had defended the rights of creoles to high office. Moreover, in discussing appointments to cathedral chapters, Rivadeneira observed that candidates should be qualified as doctors, masters or licentiates in theology and canon law, preferably with degrees from the universities of Lima and Mexico. He praised his own college of All Saints and deplored the practice of some Mexicans in graduating from Spanish universities. So too, in commenting on the parish clergy, he cautiously urged that preference should be given to priests born in the locality and that in Indian parishes appointments should go to 'the native Indians', preferably to men of noble status who could speak the language of their community.[22]

It was in 1771 that Rivadeneira wrote the Mexican City Council's representation to the Crown defending creole talents and creole rights to high office. The memorial was designed to counter a secret report written by an un-named minister or prelate which had asserted that the spirit of the Americans is submissive and compliant, because it relates well to their humbleness. But if they are raised to power or office, they are exposed to the greatest errors, so that it is best to keep them subject, albeit with places of middle rank. Neither humanity nor my heart proposes that they should be seen as deprived of favour, but experience teaches me that it is best that our Europeans should be placed at the head ...

This recommendation would not have aroused such agitation in creole circles had it not become evident that the Crown now favoured peninsular candidates over their American rivals.[23]

Whereas previous patriots, such as Ahumada and Salinas, had based their argument on the rights of creoles as the descendants of the conquerors, or, in the case of Peralta, on their nobiliary prerogative, Rivadeneira invoked the general principles of natural justice and the legislation of the Spanish Crown and the Church. At the outset he warned that any attempt to deprive American Spaniards of high office in their own countries 'is to seek to transform the law of peoples; it will lead not only to the loss of America, but to the ruin of the State'. Both the laws of Castile promulgated by Henry III in 1396 and the legislation of the Council of Trent provided that appointments in Church and State should go to the natives of each kingdom. He pronounced: 'the appointment of natives to the exclusion of foreigners is a maxim derived from the natural reason which governs hearts. If we cannot class it as a natural right, it is beyond doubt common to all nations and because of this warrants the most sacred observance.' The implications of this forceful pronouncement, based primarily on canon law, was that the Spanish Crown was guilty of contravening the most solemn injunctions of the Catholic Church.[24]

As Rivadeneira was well aware, this line of reasoning could be easily answered by the rejoinder that the kingdom of the Indies formed part of the Crown of Castile so that, constitutionally speaking, the European Spaniards who occupied office in the New World could not be classified as foreigners. It was to meet this objection that Rivadeneira argued that most Spaniards went to the Indies simply to enrich themselves and never identified Peru or Mexico as their *patria*. Indeed, Church prelates incurred great expenses in travelling to their American dioceses and frequently brought with them an entourage of priests for whom they sought prebendaries or parishes, despite their lack of qualification. Much the same was true of royal magistrates. In terms as bold as any employed by Salinas, Rivadeneira declaimed: 'they come to govern a people they do not know, to administer laws they have not studied, to encounter customs with which they are not familiar, and to deal with people they have never seen before'. It was owing to 'the direct government of the Europeans' that the conditon of the Indians continued to deteriorate, since 'the more years that elapse since the conquest, the less is their culture and the greater their misery and rusticity, their very number suffering a decline'. In effect, New Spain was a kingdom in its own right, a creole patria, in which the peninsulars would always be foreigners, no matter what their legal claim or political influence.

The failure to observe the principles of natural justice meant that the American Spaniards were reduced to the condition of serfs, deprived of the honour and fortune afforded by appointment to high office. What crime had the creoles committed that they were denied promotion to the rank of bishop or of judge on the high court? Why were they thus despoiled and degraded in their own country? Yet in regard to the government of the Indies 'the world knows that we *Indianos* are apt for judgement, useful in war, skilful in the management of revenue'. For sure, their enemies justified their exclusion from office by ethnic slander, asserting that they were of humble spirit and condition, in part descended from the Indians. In fact the conquerors and first encomenderos had been hidalgos and thereafter members of the leading families of Spain had settled in Mexico. Creoles were generally raised in comfort and opulence, with all appropriate luxury; they prepared themselves for careers in the Church or in law and never exercised themselves in manual labour. As for commerce, it was dominated by European Spaniards and 'the mechanical arts neither agree well with the lustre of their birth nor in the Indies offer a decent subsistence'. There thus existed in Mexico a numerous class of families of Spanish lineage, whose character was rendered more equable than that of their European ancestors by the 'eternal spring' of the Mexican climate. In a striking metaphor, Rivadeneira defined the creoles as the children of the king's second marriage, denied any share in their mother's dowry, which had been usurped by the children of the first marriage, which is to say, by the sons of Castile.[25]

In his anxiety to distinguish the creoles from the Indians, Rivadeneira admitted that the natives were often low-spirited and downtrodden, adding that 'they are far from being beautiful and indeed are positively of a disagreeable appearance, with very bad colour, rough features, notorious slovenliness when they are not naked, no cleanliness, and even less culture and rationality'. The point of this denigratory description was to deny the possibility of inter-marriage between the races, since 'the Spaniard who would wish to mix with Indian women, would see his children denied the honours of a Spaniard and even excluded from enjoying the privileges conceded to the Indians'.[26] If a poor Spaniard chose a spouse outside his own ethnic stratum, she was invariably drawn from the ranks of the mestizas or mulattas. To provide more substance to his case, Rivadeneira cited Palafox's general report in which the interim viceroy had praised the loyalty of the creoles to the Crown, qualities which at that time were not so evident in several provinces of the Peninsula. Moreover, in 1692 it had been the creole nobility which had sallied forth to quell the popular riot that threatened the safety of the capital. More recently, creole landowners and miners of Guanajuato and San Luis Potosí had taken the lead in repressing the disturbances which had followed the expulsion of the Jesuits in 1767. The two viceroys and the two archbishops of Mexico who had been born in the Indies had all distinguished themselves. In conclusion, Rivadeneira did not insist on the total exclusion of all Europeans from office in America, since he admitted that 'in seeking to maintain two separate and independent bodies under one head, it is necessary to confess a certain political monstrosity'. Yet if the king was to be saluted as the image of God on earth, then he must be seen by the world to be governing with justice, and rewarding the creoles for their loyalty and services.[27]

The 1771 representation was the last grand statement of the traditional themes of creole patriotism in New Spain before the debates of 1808. It exhibited almost exactly the same anguish and embitterment as the memorials of Dorantes de Carranza, Grijalva and Salinas and echoed many of the arguments of Solórzano, Palafox and Ahumada. As much as the pleas of Peralta, it spoke on behalf of the creole elite, and shared the same insistence on nobility. Its condescending description of the Indians clearly betrayed its bias and source. If we recall that by the middle decades of the eighteenth century the community of American Spaniards born and bred in New Spain numbered several hundred thousand, then Rivadeneira's concentration on the issue of creole appointment to high office can be placed in its social context. In the last resort, the representation of 1771 was the manifesto of a colonial elite denied its natural prerogative, the governance of its own country and nation.

IV

The most violent response to Gálvez' grand design to raise more taxes from the American empire occurred in Peru. In 1780 the cacique of Tungasuca, José Gabriel Condorcanki Tupac Amaru (1738–81) called out the Andean peasantry in a rebellion that eventually engulfed the entire territory from Cuzco to Chuquisaca. A contemporary observer estimated that no less than twenty-two corregimientos had been devastated by 'a general revolution'. Dismayed by the sheer scale of the movement, the colonial authorites censored all but the most cursory reference, so that the full story was not made public until after independence. Unknown to Madrid, however, Melchor de Paz, the creole secretary to viceroys Manuel de Guirior (1777–81) and Agustín de Jaúregui (1781–84), took advantage of his position to preserve a record of events, copying eye-witness accounts, rebel letters and proclamations, popular lampoons and official reports and memoranda. His chronicle, entitled *Diálogo sobre los sucesos varios acaecidos en este reino del Perú* (1786), essentially consists of these documents, clumsily woven together in rough chronological sequence, accompanied by a commentary in dialogue form. The result is a shapeless work, bereft of style or any sustained line of narrative, the reliance on dialogue a further source of confusion. In effect, Paz was more of an editor than an author, reluctant to set out his own opinions with any clarity. Yet these defects were also a great strength: his chronicle possesses all the breathless immediacy and pace of a newspaper, the eyewitness reports offering the reader the sensation of participating as a contemporary observer of the often horrific actions described. Not that Paz aspired to impartiality, since he carefully selected documents so as to frame an indictment of the measures favoured by the ministers of Charles III. His *Diálogo* thus figures within the tradition of creole patriotism and is a formidable expression of the Limeño elite's detestation of the Bourbon regime. That it also expressed fear and disdain of the Indian testifies to the perennial contradiction of the American Spaniard's position, forever caught between the intrusive authority of the European metropolis and the explosive discontent of the native masses. Little is known about the life of Melchor de Paz (1730?–96?): his father was from the Peninsula and served briefly as viceregal secretary; he himself was born in Lima, graduated from the San Marcos University, and ended his days as a priest of the Oratory.[28]

To start with, Paz launched a vitriolic attack on Juan Antonio de Areche, visitor-general of Peru 1777–82, whom he described as the 'client and intimate' of José de Gálvez. Part of his animus derived from Areche's quarrel with Guirior, whose sympathy for creole plaints prompted the visitor to persuade Madrid to dismiss him. But Paz also depicted Areche as inflexible and incompetent, a tyrant who was prepared to sacrifice the interests and well-being of the Peruvian population to the single-minded pursuit of raising more revenue for the Crown. Any attempt to question his policies was interpreted as disloyalty and was met by threats of dismissal or posting out of the country. Judged by immediate results, Areche proved successful, since he procured an increase in tax-yield of over a million pesos a year. Yet even in his chosen area of administrative efficiency, he proved incompetent since against all advice he insisted on leasing the management of the Huancavelica mercury mine, a measure which soon led to the ruin of its installations and plummeting production. To drive home his message, Paz inserted several letters to the bishop of Quito, written by an unknown correspondent, in which Gálvez and Areche were accused of being tyrants comparable in depravity to the Pizarros. In particular, the minister of the Indies was denounced for attempting to reconquer the Indies through policies which would soon drive erstwhile loyal subjects into rebellion. To make matters worse, he had created a host of new places in the judiciary and fiscal bureaucracy, only then to fill them with European Spaniards, men often of low social status who despised the Americans. Nor was the minister exempt from the charge of nepotism, since the anonymous author asserted: 'Thus we see regents and the increased number of ministers of these high courts of justice, all relatives, favourites and dependants of Gálvez.'[29]

This biting condemnation of the new regime led directly into Paz' central argument, that, no matter how oppressive *repartimientos de comercio* had been, the chief cause of the Tupac Amaru rebellion was the fiscal measures introduced by Areche. To prove this thesis, he raked across the century and the continent, turning first to the 1730 revolt at Cochabamba, already described by Arzáns and Peralta, which he blamed on the corregidor's attempt to include mestizos in the register of Indian tributaries. But it was the riots at Arequipa in early 1780 which offered him his most persuasive evidence. For in that district the corregidor had not merely issued three repartimientos of merchandise in two years, distributing goods to mestizos living on haciendas as well as to Indian communities, he had also sought to enroll mestizos, mulattos and *cholos* as Indian tributaries, requesting the parish clergy to review the baptismal register with the aim of ascertaining the correct ethnic status of suspect individuals. The gaols were soon filled with unfortunates who could not cover the cost of all these exactions. But popular distress turned to explosive anger when the newly appointed director of *alcabalas* toured the district to ensure that all marketable produce, no matter what its source, paid the excise duty at 6 per cent. The wines and brandy of the coast, which passed through the town en route for the highlands, were charged at even higher rates. The upshot of all this fiscal pressure was popular riot, a movement in part inspired by the local elite, assisted by the Franciscans, in which the customs house was burnt to the ground and its director forced to flee the city to save his life.[30]

For further corroboration, Paz turned first to Quito and then to Bogotá. He cited documents which demonstrated that, whereas previously the alcabala had been collected by the merchant guild on luxury goods imported from Europe, under the present system virtually all produce was now subject to the levy. Indians as much as Spaniards were now liable for payment. The result of all this was to force up prices for the consumer and reduce the profits of the producers. In New Granada the introduction of salaried excise directors and guards, when coupled with the establishment of the royal tobacco monopoly, provoked riots in the town of Socorro. The immediate grievances were the restriction of tobacco cultivation to the district of Tunja, the raising of excise duties from 2 to 6 per cent, the levying of excise on foodstuffs, and the new high prices for *aguardiente*, also a royal monopoly. As in Arequipa the local elite supported the populace. But in this case the riots issued into a widespread movement of *comuneros*, who decided to march on the viceregal capital at Bogotá, incited by cries of 'Long Live Socorro! Long Live the king! Death to bad government!' What was primarily a creole and mestizo rebellion was also joined by Indians, some of whom proclaimed Tupac Amaru as their leader.

Since the viceroyalty had few, if any, regular troops to combat some 20,000 rebels, the archbishop of Bogotá, Antonio Caballero y Góngora, took the lead in negotiating an agreement with the *comuneros*, signing the Capitulations of Zipaquirá, under which all the new fiscal exactions were cancelled. The animus inspiring the rebels can be also observed in their demand for the appointment of 'nationals of America' to government posts, since, so they averred, the Europeans despised the Americans, believing them to be 'inferior servants'. The Archbishop's signing of the capitulations, coupled with promise of amnesty for all rebels who returned home, brought the insurrection to a close. The creole elite who had guided its course thus obtained their goal. In his description of these events, Paz praised Caballero's prudence and skill in handling what might have turned into a disastrous civil war, qualities all too absent in Areche's reaction to a similar challenge in Peru.[31]

Although Paz sought to place the Tupac Amaru rebellion within the context of a general reaction throughout the empire, he also inserted memoranda dealing with the *repartimientos de comercio*, noting that criticism of the system dated back to the seventeenth century. In particular, he drew on a long memorial written in 1778 by Miguel Feijoo de Sosa, a creole accountant in the court of audit, who bluntly condemned the corregidores as thieves and tyrants, who preyed on the native population and perverted their power as magistrates. Moreover, since 1751 when the system had acquired legal sanction, repartimientos had been extended to cover mestizos and landowners, with the result that creole families were threatened with ruin. It was this memorial, when coupled with the outbreak of rebellion, that led Areche to issue a decree in December 1780 finally abolishing *repartimientos de comercio*. Not that Paz was entirely persuaded by the wisdom of this measure, since in the last, unfinished sections of his work, he composed a dialogue, the drift of which was to favour the restitution of some form of repartimientos, preferably without monopoly or force, so as to supply the Indians with mules and domestic cloth, since without such distribution they were likely to sink back into mere subsistence, or, as he would have it, idleness.[32]

It is testimony to Paz' understanding of the official mind, that he correctly traced the origin of the new regime to Campillo's *Nuevo sistema*. To this end, he copied out relevant chapters in which that minister advocated a general visitation, intendancies, and royal monopolies in tobacco and brandy. So too, he noted the comparison between the returns of the Caribbean sugar islands and Peru and Mexico. In the context of the recent rebellion, Campillo's insistence that the true treasure of the Indies was its native population, which had to be liberated from the tyranny of the corregidores, acquired an ironic resonance. The chief aim of the Bourbon revolution of government was to strengthen the monarchy through promoting exports from America and raising more revenue.[33]

If Paz thus framed a general indictment of the new Leviathan, he spared few words of sympathy for its victims. In three separate passages, he presented dialogues in which his invented characters joined in denigrating the Indians. Recalling the projected native uprising in 1750, he cited a contemporary denunciation of the Indian as 'the encyclopaedia of all evils', guilty of idleness, lying, drunkenness, deceit, idolatry, and, above all, consumed by an undying hatred of all Spaniards. He opened a subsequent dialogue with the query 'What sort of thing is an Indian?' only to answer 'the lowest class of rational animal', the prelude to an entire page of inane insult. Moreover, he cited letters from his friend, Juan Bautista Zavala, a landowner in the district of La Paz, who wished to punish the Indians for their cruel attack on creoles by quitting them of their lands, reducing them to serfdom on Spanish-owned estates, measures to be enforced by stationing a small garrison of regular soldiers in each province and burning the Laws of the Indies.[34]

Such diatribes can be more readily understood, if not exonerated, once we recall the sheer savagery of the great Andean insurrection. At the outset there was certainly an attempt to attract the support of creoles and mestizos, but as the movement gathered momentum the Indian peasantry began to attack all Spaniards and their property, whether European or American. Haciendas were looted, *obrajes* destroyed, and towns invaded and sacked. In particular, the southern wing of the rebellion, led by Tupac Catari, alias Julián Apasa, became notorious for its savage massacre of Spaniards, even killing women and children. So too, in Chucuito the rebels took the local towns and murdered their inhabitants, with a column of refugee families from Puno losing a thousand lives before reaching safety in Arequipa. As is always the case at such moments, hysteria infected the creole community and not every report of native savagery should be believed. It appears that the Augustinian friars at the great sanctuary of Our Lady of Copacabana continued to officiate throughout the course of the disturbances, their services once graced with a visit from Tupac Catari. Although some priests were murdered by insurgents, others continued without hurt.[35] The incidence and strength of the rebellion varied from district to district.

In the last resort, the rebellion was defeated, so Paz averred, by the concerted response of the creole elite, the Church and loyal caciques. Had not the cities of Cuzco and La Paz offered such a determined resistance to the assaults of the peasantry, the Crown's authority might have been seriously impaired. As it was, the creole bishop of Cuzco, Juan Manuel de Moscoso y Peralta, mobilised and armed the clergy to defend the city, an action which led Paz to compare him to Juan Caramuel Lobokwitz who in 1648 defended Prague from the Swedes in similar fashion. Moreover, some country clergy were able to rally their parishioners against the rebels. So too, many caciques remained loyal to the Crown and summoned their subjects to join them in the defence of Cuzco

27 Tupac Amaru II

and the pursuit of the rebels, a task in which Mateo Pumacahua, cacique of Chinchoro, especially gained distinction. Equally important, the relief columns despatched from Lima and Buenos Aires were both commanded by creoles, military officers whom Paz promptly dubbed the 're-conquerors of Peru'. Not that the royal forces had an easy task, since the Inspector General, José del Valle, complained that out of 20,000 men he commanded in Cuzco, only 500 were trained soldiers. When he attempted to relieve Chucuito, the Indians in his army acted like bands of Bedouin, robbing villages as they passed, and then returning home once provisions ran down and the weather grew worse. On the other side of the Andes a relief expedition from Cochabamba broke through the cordon surrounding La Paz, only then to disgrace themselves by looting houses in the city. Not until a column of regular troops from Buenos Aires arrived did the president of La Plata launch a concerted campaign of reconquest. Despite their active role in suppressing the rebellion, the creole commanders, so Paz commented, failed to receive from the Crown the recognition and reward their services merited.[36]

What is striking about Paz' approach to the rebellion is his lack of curiosity about Tupac Amaru himself. Apparently, he was unaware that the cacique of Tungasuca had litigated in the high court of Lima to prove his lineal descent from the Tupac Amaru whom Viceroy Toledo had executed in 1572. Educated at the college of San Francisco de Borja in Cuzco, the eighteenth-century Tupac Amaru was a landowner of some substance, the owner of 350 freight mules that plied the routes between Cuzco, Arequipa and Potosí, a mestizo by descent, and hispanicised in culture and costume.[37] Where Paz did score, however, was in his collection of the rebel leader's letters and proclamations. For these documents attest that from the outset Tupac Amaru demanded the abolition of the new excise duties, the *repartimientos de comercio*, and the annual *mita* for Potosí. At one stroke he sought to dismantle the entire structure of exploitation which had brought so much suffering to the Andean peasantry since the days of Toledo. Furthermore, he called for the expulsion of Europeans from Peru and the removal of the corregidors. In short, Tupac Amaru condemned Spanish rule as a manifest tyranny and sought to liberate Peru from its colonial bondage. At the same time, he was at pains to reassure the creoles and mestizos that his movement did not threaten their lives or property, expressing the hope that all races in Peru 'should live as brothers, congregated in one body'. Nor was there any insincerity in this aspiration since he had creoles in his own circle of relatives and advisers. So also, he reminded Bishop Moscoso of his respect for the Church and the Catholic faith in which he had been reared. Indeed, he clearly envisaged that the Crown would continue to levy tribute and the silver tithe and the Church receive its tithe on agricultural produce. Where Tupac Amaru differed from the *comuneros* of New Granada, a distinction which prevented any accommodation with either the Church or the creole elite, was his assumption of the title of Inca and proclamation of descent from the royal house. His right to summon the peasantry into rebellion against the Spanish Crown thus derived from his own hereditary authority as Inca. It was an assertion that awoke messianic expectations among the native masses, fired into action by prophecies of the end of colonial rule. Among Tupac Amaru's papers was found a proclamation in which he styled himself: 'José I, by the grace of God, Inca-King of Peru.' Here was a claim that few creoles could accept without accepting the destruction of the social order from which they derived their status.[38]

If Paz displayed little sympathy for Indian grievances, nevertheless, he provided a description of the execution of Tupac Amaru and his family which was so harrowing as to constitute a virtual condemnation of the entire proceedings. For Areche first ordered the rebel leader to be tortured, dislocating his limbs, and then had him taken out to the great square of Cuzco to witness his wife and eldest son killed, not, however, before he also saw their tongues cut off. Tupac Amaru himself was subjected to a clumsy attempt at execution by means of four horses pulling at each limb, failing which, he was summarily beheaded. Before his death, so Paz reports, the Inca admonished Areche with these words: 'Your Lordship and I are the only men responsible for all the blood which has been shed: Your Lordship for having harassed the kingdom with excessive contributions and new taxes, and I for having wished to liberate it from such tyrannies and oppression.' In this exchange, allegedly taken from first-hand accounts, Paz clearly blamed Areche for causing the rebellion and implicitly exonerated Tupac Amaru, the heroic dignity with which the Inca bore his sufferings further evidence of his patriot character.[39]

What is entirely absent from Paz' *Diálogo* is any consideration of the relation between the Inca empire and the Tupac Amaru rebellion, or best to say, any discussion of the influence of Garcilaso de la Vega in eighteenth-century Peru. Already, both Ulloa and La Condamine had marvelled at the difference between the degraded character of contemporary natives and the elevated image of the Incas as portrayed by the great mestizo historian. But Indian readers of Garcilaso found an equally potent paradox: how was it possible to reconcile the benevolent government of the Incas with the tyranny operated by the Spaniards? In effect, the publication of the second edition of *Comentarios reales* in 1722 proved to be an incendiary event. For in its pages the Indian gentry could learn of the grandeur and justice of the Incas and the cruelty of the Spaniards. Moreover, it assumed contemporary relevance when the kurakas who experienced the full weight of corregidor misrule came to adopt the Inca realm as the political model or criterion by which to judge the abuses of the present era. Nor was this invocation of an ideal past restricted to the native nobility, since in a report to the bishop of Cuzco, written in 1767, Ignacio de Castro, at that time a parish priest in a country district, denounced the depredations of the corregidores, whom he described as 'sanguinary lions and rampant wolves', their 'absolute despotism' a remorseless application of the most cynical maxims of Machiavelli. It was for the bishop to urge the king to protect his subjects from abuse. After all, he added, the Indians had always looked to Cuzco for law and love, 'being kindly seen by the first six monarchs in whom the sole light of natural reason, even without the enlightenment of faith, ruled a government so admirable that its history serves any reader as a model for refined policy'. Here, in a confidential letter, written by a creole priest, we encounter an almost instinctive invocation of Inca benevolence and justice as a yardstick by which to measure contemporary tyranny.[40]

The degree to which *Comentarios reales* fortified the Indian gentry's insistence on their Inca descent was explained by Bishop Moscoso, who in a letter to Areche, written after the siege of Cuzco in 1781, roundly denounced his native flock for their stubborn adhesion to pagan beliefs, ceremonies and 'antiquities'. After more than two centuries of Spanish rule, they still remained entirely bound by their 'gentile' tradition, wearing their own style of clothes and speaking their own language. It had been a capital error to allow the native elite of Cuzco to parade in public dressed in Inca costume and to permit them to have their portraits painted in this fashion. Still more pernicious was the collection of dynastic portraits preserved in the college of San Francisco de Borja, including a likeness of Tupac Amaru, which had been in the refectory. For 'the Indians are a species of rational being who are more impressed by what they see than by what they are told'. The constant sight of Inca portraits and costumes kept alive the memory of the past and indeed converted the Inca empire into an imagined 'golden age'. In effect, Spanish tolerance had sown the seeds of disloyalty. It was now time, so Moscoso urged, to extirpate all vestige of the Inca past, forbidding the caciques to wear any ceremonial garb other than Spanish uniforms and to confiscate all portraits, insignia, books and papers dealing with the Incas. Any criticism of the Spanish conquest should be equally suppressed. Indeed, efforts should be made to extirpate the very use of native languages.[41]

Turning to the rebel leader, whom he had known personally, Moscoso declared:

> if the *Comentarios* of Garcilaso had not been the reading and instruction of the insurgent José Gabriel Tupac Amaru, if his continuous invectives and declamations against the Spaniards had not taken such root in his mind . . . if these and other readings of certain authors of this kingdom had not been accepted by the traitor in all that they uttered about the conquest, Tupac Amaru would not have embarked on the detestable audacity of his rebellion.

Invoking an implicit comparison with Don Quijote, Moscoso declared that if the Andean squireen had not been deceived and bedazzled by the spurious glamour of the books he had read, he would have remained content on his farm, caring for his mule-teams, unknown to the world. To lay the ghost of the past, in 1782 the colonial authorities commanded that all copies of the *Comentarios reales* should be quietly impounded and further circulation in Peru prohibited. Where once Toledo had seized the tracts of Las Casas and banned all further study of the native past, so now Gálvez and his agents sought, albeit in vain, to extirpate the influence of Garcilaso de la Vega.[42]

22

ERASTIAN CHURCH

I

IN 1749 the Crown issued a rescript demanding that all parishes administered by the mendicants in the dioceses of Mexico and Lima should be handed over to the secular clergy. Since the measure provoked little popular unrest, in 1753 it was extended to the entire Spanish American Church. But the high-handed fashion in which the authorities seized both parishes and country convents soon elicited bitter protest. The Franciscans, Dominicans and Augustinians united to complain that friars had been expelled from their cells, allowed to take only their personal belongings, and at times forced to find their own way on foot to the nearest urban priory. 'They were handled as if they were law-breakers, their honour insulted, and treated here in America with a hostility and rigour that was not shown to the Moors and Jews when they were expelled from the Peninsula.' The secularisation of parishes was accompanied by the sequestration of priories. Moreover, since the incoming priest often had no use for such extensive premises, convent buildings were at times leased to serve as stables, as textile workships, or even as popular tenements, with the result that houses such as Santiago Tlatelolco, Acolman and Tzintzuntzan, which en-shrined the historic glory of the spiritual conquest, were now left to ruin. Nor were the Indians served by the change, since the secular clergy had not studied native tongues and hence were unable to minister effectively to their flock who were threatened by a relapse into idolatry. These arguments were confirmed by the Council of Mexico City which observed that to replace groups of eight to ten religious by three secular clergy, all of whom had 'to dress in silk and comport themselves with pomp and authority', was no gain for the Indians, the more especially since the newcomers rarely spoke any language other than Castilian. It was already noticeable that, whereas mendicant churches had been richly adorned, the edifices managed by their rivals were usually bare and ill-kept. One further consequence of the shift was that great numbers of friars would now be crowded into the great priories in Mexico City and Puebla, all in need of alms and occupation.[1]

If the Crown chose to intervene, it was because ministers had received despatches from the viceroys of Peru and New Spain complaining of the excessive numbers, wealth and corruption of the mendicant orders, disorders rendered all the more glaring by their possession of Indian parishes. Although the Mexican hierarchy had attempted to assert their control over the parochial ministry as early as the 1570s, a campaign which reached a stormy climax when the bishop of Puebla, Juan de Palafox, abruptly ejected the friars from all *doctrinas* in his diocese, as late as the 1740s the mendicants still administered two-fifths of the parishes in the dioceses of Mexico and Michoacán. Indeed, small provinces of religious such as the Dominicans of Oaxaca and Puebla only possessed one large central priory and located the majority of their friars in small houses scattered across the countryside where full observances of their rule was virtually impossible. To resolve the matter, Ferdinand VI accepted the advice of his Jesuit father confessor, Manuel de Rábago, and convoked a select committee of 'theologians and jurists' to bring forward proposals for secularisation. But as protests mounted, the minister of the Indies, Julián de Arriaga, modified the severity of the measure by allowing all canonically appointed religious to remain as parish priests until their death, a concession which effectively delayed the transfer for any number of years. So too, the mendicants were allowed to retain all priories which housed at least eight religious, and dioceses such as Oaxaca and Yucatán where qualified secular clergy were scarce continued to rely on the mendicants to minister to the Indians. Despite these concessions the reflux of friars into the city priories was so great that in 1757 the Crown commanded their provincials to reduce the annual intake of novices, with the result that in the next two decades the overall number of friars declined.[2]

If both viceroys and prelates proved so critical of the mendicants, in part it was because they blamed the religious for not teaching the Indians Spanish, a failure which had greatly contributed to the natives' isolation and backwardness. In New Spain Archbishop Manuel Rubio y Salinas seized upon the opportunity afforded by secularisation to command the establishment of parochial schools throughout his diocese. He openly lamented the failure of first missionaries to teach the Indians Spanish since, so he averred, it was impossible to explain the sublime mysteries of the Christian faith in Indian tongues, 'without committing great disonance and imperfection'. Without a knowledge of Spanish the natives would never emerge from the misery and vices which engulfed them, so that 'it is generally necessary to abolish the use of their languages, with the help of royal directives, so that in everything that concerns religion, only Spanish is spoken'. Since such an ideal solution was not at once forthcoming, he scoured his diocese for clergy with some acquaintance with native tongues and created a chair in Mexican (Nahuatl) in his seminary. As it was, disgruntled friars noted that several recently appointed priests were

unable to communicate with their flocks. It was in recognition of this problem
that in 1769 the Crown commanded that henceforth the diocesan seminaries
should allocate a quarter or a third of their places to Indians or mestizos, men
conversant with native languages, who could later administer hill parishes or
act as curates for creole vicars. The extraordinary arrogance which animated
these Spanish prelates appointed by the Bourbon dynasty can be best observed
in a pastoral issued in 1803 by Antonio Bergosa y Jordán, the new bishop of
Oaxaca, who boldly reproached his flock for 'maintaining your rough,
unknown tongues', asserting that, with eighteen different languages, Oaxaca
resembled a Tower of Babel. He observed that 'one of the chief tricks of the
Devil has always been to prevent the use of our Castilian language' and
admonished his Indian subjects to abandon their 'barbarian' tongues, which
had prevented their advance in Christian knowledge and civility.[3]

The religious practices of the Indians, and in particular their veneration of
images and fondness for public procession, also now came under attack. In
1772 the incoming parish priest of Santiago Tlatelolco proposed 'a great reform
as regards images, since they are innumerable and most indecent, ugly and
ridiculous, which far from exciting devotion serve only to provoke mockery
and derision'.[4] In similar vein, the parish priest of San Pedro Paracho, who
confessed that he did not understand Tarascan, nevertheless, denounced the
Holy Week custom whereby an Indian was chosen to represent Christ, his body
painted with the signs of the Passion, 'the face, shoulders and body bathed in
blood'. He commented that although ceremonies were all conducted in
accordance with the Passion story, it all sounded ill to him, 'since I did not see
anything which moved them, even in the outward sense, to devotion'. His
predecessor had wished to extinguish the practice but feared, if he did, to
provoke a riot, since 'they are so tenacious and bound to their customs'. In 1807
the bishop of Michoacán, Antonio de San Miguel, prohibited the procession
and floats which were staged in the town of Celaya on Christmas Eve.
Apparently, the event was a popular fiesta with crowds coming in from miles
around. But the dressing of children of five or six as shepherds and other
figures, when combined with the strange clothes of the Magi and the scene of
the beheading of the Holy Innocents, aroused great levity and was thought by
the local clergy to bring religion into disrepute.[5]

The degree to which the folk Catholicism of the Baroque era was now
ridiculed and repressed by the prelates of the late eighteenth century was
nowhere better illustrated than in Silao, where in 1793 Bishop San Miguel
summarily banned the parade of images during Holy Week. His grounds for
this decision were that the processions caused excessive expense to the Indians
and led to drunkenness and disorders. The images themselves were 'for the
most part indecent in their construction and much more indecent in their
adornment' and hence brought religion into disrepute. The populace did not

care for silent, pious processions, but rather sought occasions which satisfied their inclination for 'uproar, puerile ostentation and pernicious meetings'. What makes this case unusual, however, was the defence offered by the *mayordomos* of the confraternities, who described themselves as Indian tributaries, *'ladinos'* in the Castilian tongue. For they insisted that the faith of the common people, especially the countryfolk, needed to be aroused by 'those living representations or images which so create an impression on them that they form some idea or concept of the sublime mysteries of faith'. Without the stimulus of sight, their faith soon waned, 'since the doors to their intellect are sealed against any discourse', their knowledge of Christian doctrine derived from their senses rather than by even the simplest words or clearest catechism.[6]

The fissure that divided 'enlightened' peninsular prelates from their flock, both creole and Indian, can be clearly observed in the pastorals and edicts of Francisco Antonio de Lorenzana, archbishop of Mexico (1766–72), and of his friend, Francisco Fabián y Fuero, bishop of Puebla (1765–73). In his pastorals, Lorenzana first cited Palafox to admit that 'the Indians have a soul as noble as that of the Europeans', but then repeated the admonitions of his predecessor that Indians should 'know Christian doctrine, not only in their own language, but principally in Spanish'. After all, how could 'Mexican, so thin and barbaric', be compared to Hebrew and Latin? 'Who without caprice could not but admit that as their nation was barbaric, so also was and is their language?' Happy to learn from the Romans and Greeks, this erudite prelate pronounced that it was the right of all conquerors to impose their language on their new subjects. Gravely concerned at the excesses of popular religion, he summarily banned, on pain of twenty-five strokes of the lash, 'all live representations of the Passion of Christ our Redeemer, the Volador pole, the dances of Santiago ... representations of Shepherds and Kings'.[7]

As a tribute to his adopted country, Lorenzana funded the publication of the letters of Hernán Cortés, inserting notes and illustrations. In his preface, he paid tribute to Torquemada, Boturini and Solís and included a figure of Moctezuma's tribute list, copied from Boturini's papers, which he proffered as evidence of 'the opulence, grandeur and majesty of this Mexican empire'. However, he stated that no great monument had survived the conquest and that the Indians were best regarded as minors. He chose not to provide any illustration of pre-hispanic gods, since 'the figures of idols are horrible and ridiculous' and hence unworthy of recollection. In any case, the real history of New Spain began with the conquest and the point of his enterprise was to celebrate the actions of a Spanish hero. Lest it might be thought strange for a bishop to have printed scenes of battle, he asserted that a priest is both a sacred person and 'a faithful vassal' of his king.[8]

It fell to Lorenzana to convoke the Fourth Mexican Church Council of 1771. Its chief purpose, as the royal instruction made clear, was to obtain 'a correction of monastic discipline' and subject the religious to episcopal authority. However, the proceedings were marred by controversy over the intervention of the 'royal representative', the creole judge of the high court, Antonio Joaquín de Rivadeneira y Barrientos (1710–177?), with the result that the Crown never approved the publication of its canons. Indeed, Lorenzana himself admitted that the Papacy would never condone the resolutions of a council in which a layman occupied so prominent a role. Nor was the king's father confessor happy with the measures which were applied to the religious communities. The chief problem here was the bishop of Puebla, Fabián y Fuero, who had stirred up a hornet's nest when he attempted to force the nuns of that city to abandon their comfortable houses within the convent and adopt 'the common life', eating in the refectory rather than preparing meals in their own kitchens. Although Lorenzana issued pastorals supporting his brother bishop, he adopted a more cautious line in implementing a measure which affronted the creole elite, whose daughters had been coerced and insulted. At the Council the royal delegate, whose sister was a nun in Puebla, openly criticised Fabián for his lack of prudence in handling the affair. So too, on the decisive question of limiting the number of religious in each province and priory, the Council failed to reach an agreement, deciding to leave the question to each bishop.[9] In any case, the Crown had already despatched visitors, appointed to inspect each religious order and decide the matter.

That Lorenzana's chief critic at the Council should have been a creole judge points to the complexity of colonial politics. Rivadeneira had published a *Manual compendio* (1756) on canon law, in which he had adopted an extreme regalist position, insisting on the rights and prerogative of the Crown as patron of the American Church. On the controversial question of tithes, he argued that the king had full cognizance of such cases, since the tithes were entirely secular and not, as Palafox had once argued, 'spiritual'. A strong advocate of secularisation, he asserted that in all questions of disputed jurisdiction the *audiencias* possessed the ultimate authority since these high courts exercised the right of the Crown as patron and delegate of the Holy See. In effect, any resolution of an ecclesiastical judge could be overturned by an appeal to the high court, by a procedure known as *recurso de fuerza*. It was in the context of these pronouncements that Rivadeneira saluted royal judges as 'images of the king; organs of his voice; in themselves talking laws ... ministers of God and the King'. Small wonder that he defended Charles III's authority to convoke the Church Council in Mexico by comparing him to Constantine the Great, and as lord of two great empires in the New World.[10]

Despite his ardent regalism, Rivadeneira was a creole aristocrat who denounced the growing burden on rural estates of ecclesiastical annuities, chantries and loans, commenting on the 'hundreds of haciendas and urban properties embargoed because of the capital they bear and the interest they cannot pay'. In effect, these funds often remained charged on the estates in virtual perpetuity, passed on from one generation to another and at times comprised a third or even a half of the estimated value of an hacienda. Whereas agriculture, so Rivadeneira averred, rarely yielded more than a 2 per cent return on capital, all Church loans and funds commanded 5 per cent interest. The result was ruin since at times the greater part of a landowner's income went to satisfy the demands of his clerical creditors. Although Rivadeneira denounced the current practice as a form of usury, he offered few practical solutions to a problem which was to preoccupy Mexican politicians in the next century. Nor did he persuade the Council to address the matter.[11]

It was in his attack on the Council's insistence on Spanish as the preferred instrument of pastoral instruction that Rivadeneira revealed himself as a creole patriot. He openly ridiculed Fabián y Fuero's edict which forbade the parochial clergy to employ any language other than Castilian in their dealings with the Indians. In a risible schedule the bishop of Puebla had demanded that within a year all native children should be taught Spanish and that within a space of four years all Indians within his diocese should be able to recite the elements of Christian doctrine in that language. In sharp reply Rivadeneira commented that it was the Indians themselves and not the clergy who had insisted on speaking their own language, which, as much as any other nation, they loved as their own. In any case, the Mexican tongue possessed all the words and terms necessary for expounding Christian doctrine. If the Indians had failed to learn Spanish over the course of two-and-a-half centuries, they were not about to change their habits within a mere four years. If the edict was enforced the effects would be lamentable: 'to extinguish the Indian tongue is to extinguish the parochial and sacramental language to the detriment of their souls'.[12] In effect, the 'enlightened' prelates who arrived in New Spain in these years despised the inhabitants of America, both creole and Indian, and sought to implement a programme of reform without first acquiring any knowledge of the social realities of the country and people whom they came to govern.

II

In 1767 Charles III summarily expelled all Jesuits from his dominions in Europe and America. A Mexican priest later recalled how one evening a detachment of soldiers abruptly entered his college, ordered the brethren to pack their belongings, and within two days escorted them to Veracruz, their journey broken only by a last, merciful visit for prayer to Our Lady of Guadalupe at Tepeyac. Thereafter, the Jesuits faced a long voyage to Cadiz, followed by an equally arduous journey, first to Corsica, and then to the Papal States. Several elderly or infirm priests died on the way; a few sought release from their vows; and the faithful survivors found lodgings in Italian cities, there to eke out a penurious, obscure existence until their death. In all, about 2,600 priests and brothers were exiled from Spanish America and a similar number from Spain itself. Of the 678 members of the Mexican province, over 500 were creoles, of whom only two were destined to see their country again. The 'urgent, just and compelling causes' which had driven the king to sanction such an apparently arbitrary exercise of power were never divulged to his subjects but remained locked away 'in the royal breast'.[13] In New Spain the popular riots which the expulsion provoked were repressed with unprecedented severity. The unquestioning loyalty demanded by the Bourbon monarchy was expressed by Archbishop Lorenzana who in a pastoral letter warned his flock against even discussing the matter: 'What has to be done is to obey and be silent.' It was the same prelate who persuaded the Fourth Church Council to call for the dissolution of the Company of Jesus, a resolution duly cited by the Spanish ambassador to the Holy See when, in 1774, he successfully obtained from Pope Clement XIV the extinction of the Jesuits as a recognised institute of the Catholic Church.[14]

Although Viceroy Croix warned the Spanish Crown that 'all the clergy and lawyers, since they belong entirely to them (the Jesuits) are also the most resentful', there was little that the creoles could do to express their indignation. Merely for questioning the justice of the decree, Dr Antonio López Portillo, a creole canon celebrated for his erudition in Eguiara's *Biblioteca mexicana*, was despatched to Spain. At one stroke the Jesuit colleges which had provided education in all the chief cities of the empire were closed. In Mexico, the San Ildefonso College had been rebuilt on a majestic scale during the 1740s and was renowned for the distinction of its students who became 'bishops, judges, canons and professors in all the faculties'. In Puebla the Jesuits had just completed the rebuilding of their church and in Guanajuato a new college and a church had been formally opened in 1765 amidst great local rejoicing. All these buildings were constructed in the most elegant Churrigueresque style. Moreover, the Mexican province was in the midst of a movement of intellectual regeneration when the expulsion order arrived. In short, here was no moribund institution ripe for destruction, but a thriving, powerful corporation, whose priests were widely admired for their exemplary zeal and discipline.[15] Among the exiles in Italy were creoles of the first order in learning and intellect.

To account for the expulsion many Jesuits later blamed the Enlightenment, interpreting the destruction of their Company as the first step in a campaign waged by the philosophes to destroy the authority of the Catholic Church, a campaign which was to culminate in the French Revolution. As regards Spain the problem with such an interpretation was that there were but a few freethinkers or philosophes in positions of influence during the reign of Charles III.[16] Sources close to court fixed upon more specific and immediate causes. In part, the king's animosity stemmed from the Jesuits' imprudent identification with Ferdinand VI at a time when that monarch had quarrelled with his brother. Then again, Charles III's father confessor was a Franciscan, Joaquín de Eleta, who came from Osma, Palafox's last see, and who hated the Jesuits. Encouraged by Eleta, the king promoted in Rome the bishop of Puebla's canonisation cause and authorised the publication of a magnificent second edition of the prelate's works, which included his most outspoken criticism of the Company of Jesus. When Eleta counselled the king on the expulsion, he drew attention to the Jesuits' refusal to pay tithe to their bishops, commenting on their notorious wealth that they went to the Indies 'more to win haciendas than souls'. Franciscan jealousy of the worldly success of the sons of St Ignatius, expressed so forcefully when José de Acosta first visited Santo Domingo, here surfaced two centuries later.[17] That in 1758 a Spanish Jesuit, José de Islas, had published a mordant satire on mendicant preaching and education, entitled *Fray Gerundio*, only served to exacerbate the friars' resentment. Nor had Rábago's role in encouraging the secularisation of mendicant parishes in the New World passed unnoticed.

Contemporaries fixed upon the famous *Motín de Esquilache* to explain the Crown's move against the Jesuits. In 1766 the populace of Madrid rioted and invaded the royal palace, shouting: 'Long Live Spain! Death to Squilace!' That an Italian minister should have issued a decree forbidding Spaniards to wear their customary voluminous capes and broad-brimmed hats was too great an insult to Castilian pride. In the event, the distraught king ordered the law to be withdrawn and sent the unfortunate Esquilace back to Italy. But Charles III and his councillors were convinced that such a dramatic challenge to royal authority had been set in motion by a broad coalition of vested interests intent on opposing their programme of reform. It was alleged that the Marquis of Ensenada, Ferdinand VI's chief minister, had conspired to stir the populace into action. So too, sections of the aristocracy and the *colegiales*, the alumni of the *colegios mayores*, were suspected of complicity. But within ministerial circles it soon became an article of faith that it was the Jesuits who were primarily responsible for inciting the mob, and persuading priests to accuse the king in public of being a heretic. This was certainly the view which was expounded by Pedro Rodríguez Campomanes, at that time an influential attorney of the Council of Castile, in a state paper on the riots which was read by the king.[18]

But Charles III would never have dared to expel the Jesuits had he not been assured of the support of an influential party within the Spanish Church. His Minister of Justice, Manuel de Roda, a talented lawyer of humble extraction, was a Jansenist, who soon became notorious for his prejudices, since he was lampooned as having 'a pair of spectacles through which he saw nothing but Jesuits and *colegios mayores*'. According to a later source, it was Roda who was responsible for engineering an alliance of 'free-thinkers and Jansenists' to destroy the Jesuits.[19] The problem here is to define what was meant by Jansenism in this context, the more especially since the Jesuits were accustomed to accuse all their opponents of being Jansenists. What is clear is that churchmen in Bourbon Spain had little interest in the grand Augustinian questions of free will and divine grace that had divided Jesuits and Jansenists so bitterly in seventeenth-century France. There was indeed a great deal of French influence. But it was the Gallican works of Bossuet and the ecclesiastical history of the Abbé Fleury that were most frequently read and cited. Moreover, the Spanish regalist tradition in canon law found reinforcement from the works of Van Espen and 'Febronius', which sharply criticised the papal monarchy and its canon law, defining its absolutist pretensions as a medieval abuse which had undermined the rightful authority of national hierarchies and Church councils.[20] That the Jesuits formed an international body, whose senior members swore a fourth vow of obedience to the Pope, rendered them especially suspect to all regalists intent on elevating the Crown's authority over the Spanish Church.

But eighteenth-century Jansenism would not have proved so influential had it merely been concerned with problems of Church government. Its adherents also questioned the value of the religious orders, choosing more to emphasise the pastoral primacy of the bishops and the parochial clergy. The magnification of asceticism and mystical prayer so prevalent in Habsburg Spain was to be replaced by the teaching of a simple, interior piety and good works. The preaching of the gospel based on scriptural texts was now more esteemed than the pomp and expense of liturgical celebration. As a result, the clergy came to adopt a critical view of popular religion. Indeed, so cautious and orthodox a figure as Feijoo questioned the value of pilgrimages to sanctuaries housing holy images, scorned astrology and oracles, and warned against popular belief in 'miraculous cures'. It was not long before the reforming clergy also fixed upon the extravagant, gilded churches in Baroque and Churrigueresque style as offensive both to Christian piety and good taste. The simple, unadorned lines of the neo-classic style satisfied both Jansenists and philosophes. In the sphere of theology, scholasticism came under attack both for its reliance on Aristotle and for its disputatious method of study. If Feijoo had freely admitted that in natural science Aristotle had been superseded, how could his authority be still invoked in philosophy? Instead, students were now advised to read the early Fathers of the Church and become acquainted with Church history and the proceedings of the Councils. In effect, Spanish Jansenism formed a broad movement of reform and renewal, a current of opinion rather than a party, in which there figured zealots, moderates and place-men, united only by a repudiation of the spiritual and intellectual culture of Baroque, post-Tridentine Catholicism. That Feijoo should have cited Thomas à Kempis and Sir Thomas More in his condemnation of popular devotions attests to the continuity between the Erasmian critique of late medieval religion and the 'Jansenist' attack on the religious orders and popular religion. If the Jesuits were attacked so strongly, it was because, until their expulsion, they had employed their formidable talents to defend scholastic doctrine, encourage popular devotions such as the Sacred Heart of Jesus, and build richly adorned churches.[21]

To observe the way in which these doctrines were applied in New Spain, we need only turn to the second canon of the Fourth Church Council which boldly declared: 'God instituted two great and high dignitaries, which are the priestly or pontifical authority and royal authority: the one as much as the other have the same origin since both issue from God.' As regards the religious orders, a royal rescript commanded that they be warned against any discussion of Jesuit authors and be encouraged to instil 'the reading of Holy Scripture, the Holy Fathers and Councils as the pure sources of the truth and of the constant tradition of the faith, putting to one side all the hatred and party spirit of the schools'.[22] When Archbishop Alonso Nuñez de Haro y Peralta (1772–1800) converted the Jesuit novitiate at Tepozotlan into a seminary he established chairs in Mexican, Otomí and Church history, on which he recommended Fleury as a suitable authority. He defined the bishops as the heirs of the twelve apostles and priests as the successors of the seventy-two disciples sent out by Christ to preach the gospel. In particular, he strongly commended 'the last general Council, which was the Tridentine, in which the discipline was established which in our times ought to serve as an inviolable rule in the direction of souls'.[23]

In an eloquent pastoral, published in 1777, Haro exhorted his diocesan clergy to preserve the purity of Catholic doctrine, warning them that even distinguished divines such as Tertullian and Origen had strayed from orthodoxy. He commended the works of St Augustine, St Charles Borromeo, and the Gallican clergy's declarations. All this was but a prelude to a condemnation of the Jesuit doctrine of probabilism which had promoted, so he averred, moral laxity and a disregard for authority. The social body or community was superior to the individual and hence it was necessary for subjects to obey their monarch, accepting his edicts in a spirit of 'reverential fear'. The king was the minister of God on earth and to resist his authority was to resist God himself, a sin worthy of damnation. Subjects should neither 'inquire into the secrets of the cabinet nor the motives for royal laws', since they could no more understand such arcane policy than they could measure the height of the heavens or the depths of the earth. After such resounding declamations, Nuñez de Haro then broached the substance and occasion of his pastoral, which was a letter from the new Minister of the Indies, José de Gálvez, requesting that he invoke his authority as archbishop to exhort his flock not to defraud the Crown of its legitimate revenue by engaging in contraband. To think or say that it was not a sin to avoid paying taxes was to be guilty of probabilism. Here, in this pronouncement, we observe the doctrinal servility demanded by the Bourbon State: it was a far cry from the independent spirit of Palafox.[24]

III

The minister who expressed with brutal clarity the principles and prejudices which fired the Bourbon assault on the post-Tridentine Church was Pedro Rodríguez Campomanes (1723–1803), an Asturian lawyer of obscure origin and education, who in the years 1762–91 served first as attorney and then as president of the Council of Castile. He had attracted early recognition by publishing an essay on the extinction of the Knights Templar which won him entry into the Royal Academy of History, a body of which he was to become president. Both the bias of his ideas and the extent of his historical learning were readily apparent in his *Tratato de la regalía de amortización* (1765), in which through abundant citation of original sources he demonstrated that in the twelfth century the Christian kings of Europe, with Philip Augustus of France at their head, had issued laws to limit any further acquisition of land by the Church, measures primarily directed against the encroachments of the religious orders. Moreover, he traced 'our fundamental laws' back to the Visigothic era, when the first measures restricting clerical property had been promulgated. Despite this mass of legislation, the religious orders later became notorious for their wealth as landlords and their moral corruption, abuses which in large measure caused the Protestant Reformation. In Spain, however, the number and riches of the clergy continued to grow unabated with the result that by the seventeenth century the very bishops cried halt. By then the Church had become such a burden on society that it was responsible for the depopulation of cities and the impoverishment of the kingdom. The moral that Campomanes drew from this bleak history was uncompromising: the monarchy had ample precedent for prohibiting the Church from acquiring any further property and, indeed, possessed the authority to place restrictions on the number and wealth of the clergy, both religious and secular, measures he considered eminently desirable.[25]

In his all-important state paper on the Motín de Esquilache and the Jesuits, Campomanes detected a grand conspiracy of privileged corporate interests against the monarchy. It was a movement which resembled the *comuneros* of 1519 and the French Fronde of the 1640s. Nor was it the first time that the Jesuits had plotted against the Spanish monarchy, since in 1640 the Portuguese province of the Company had ardently supported the rebellion led by the Duke of Braganza. In any case, the very constitution of the Company of Jesus brought into question the loyalty of its members. For the Jesuits were governed by their father-general who acted as an 'absolute monarch', appointing all provincials and rectors and who demanded blind, unconditional obedience from his subjects, converting them into 'mere machines' without voice or will of their own. For Campomanes, 'the prime vice' of the Company was that it was an international institution, enforcing a loyalty which superseded the obligations of its members as citizens, so that every Jesuit 'is the enemy of the Sovereign Power, depending on a despotic government resident in a foreign country'. It was to strengthen their own freedom of action that Jesuit theologians had insisted on the absolute authority of the Papacy, raising it above the monarchies of Europe. This doctrine was rendered all the more dangerous by their defence of the power of the Pope to depose temporal sovereigns, and still more by their doctrine of tyrannicide.[26]

The most striking feature of Campomanes' report was the prominence given to American issues. The humiliation of so loyal a servant of the Crown as Palafox should never be forgotten, since it offered an object warning to all royal officials. That the Jesuits had sought to place his works on the Index and continued to oppose his canonisation process in Rome was evidence enough of their implacable temper. Moreover, the controversy which caused Palafox's downfall, his attempt to oblige the Jesuits to pay tithe on the produce of their estates, was for Campomanes still a live issue. Drawing upon a report which had traced the history of the whole sorry business, he commented that, although the Crown had decreed in 1657 that the religious orders should pay tithes to the bishops and cathedral chapters, the Jesuits had prolonged their litigation, taking advantage of the debility of the Spanish State and the apprehensions of the hierarchy. Indeed, it was not until 1749 that a settlement was finally reached, a settlement that was remarkably favourable to the Jesuits, since their obligation was reduced to a mere 3 per cent of produce rather than the full tithe. That they obtained such a concession was owing to the intervention of the Marquis of Ensenada and Ferdinand VI's Jesuit confessor, Manuel de Rábago. Here, indeed, was issue tailor-made to infuriate the revenue-conscious ministers of Charles III.[27]

As for Paraguay, what was it, Campomanes queried, other than a kingdom wholly owned by the father-general of the Jesuits? The king of Spain enjoyed but nominal authority over the province if compared to the despotic power exercised by the mission fathers who forced the natives to work on their plantations, selling their produce and employing the profits for unknown purposes. As the case of José de Antequera had clearly shown, any attempt to curb their authority was met by a remorseless campaign of defamation. All this led to the resounding conclusion that, since the kings of Portugal and France had already banished the Jesuits for 'reasons of state', it was now time for the Spanish Crown to exercise its 'economic power' so as to expel the Jesuits, seize their property and ban their doctrines, measures necessary to 'save the country and true religion'.

For the same reason that Campomanes feared the Jesuits, he also denounced the Papacy. In *Juicio imparcial* (1769) he condemned the Pope's attempt to abrogate the Duke of Parma's recent edicts banning all further transfer of lay property to the Church. Drawing upon the 1681 declaration of the Gallican clergy, inspired by 'that great French prelate ... the incomparable Bossuet', he argued that the authority of the Papacy was entirely spiritual and that the Church did not possess any inherent right to coercive or legal jurisdiction. Indeed, he cited the work of Febronius, only published in 1763, in which the entire edifice of canon law on which papal authority rested was subjected to severe criticism. The study of Church history, a discipline especially advanced in France, had demonstrated that the papal claim to exercise a universal monarchy in Christendom stemmed from the twelfth-century campaign of Gregory VII against the Holy Roman Empire, a conflict in which the Pope had encouraged imperial vassals to join him in deposing the emperor. Nor were such pretensions ever forgone, since as late as 1605 Jesuit theologians had supported the papal interdict of Venice, maintaining that the Pope possessed the right to depose princes and kings. Yet there was no good reason to accept that the Papacy had any authority to promote 'the slightest novelty or alteration in States'. Indeed, Campomanes found it incongruous that the Pope should act as a temporal prince in the Papal States, exercising powers of life and death. All this led to the conclusion that 'The Church is the congregation of the faithful who fight at their own expense to acquire the celestial inheritance, without any temporal matter the object of so holy a mother ...'[28]

Not content to question the worldly ambitions of the Papacy, Campomanes also challenged the Pope's right to appoint bishops in the Western Church. Until the twelfth century, Spanish bishops had been elected by diocesan chapters and confirmed by archbishops without any intervention from the Pope. Yet by the fourteenth century the Papacy had sought to invest foreigners with Spanish sees, a manoeuvre which had provoked strong protests from the kings of Castile. Although papal pretensions had been curtailed, it was only through the Concordat of 1749 that the king finally obtained full patronage over all Church appointments, which is to say, a power similar to that he already exercised in the Indies. Yet Rome still admitted appeals on ecclesiastical affairs and despatched rescripts and bulls without consultation with the monarchy. Campomanes concluded that no papal communication with the clergy should be allowed to circulate without prior examination and authorisation by the king's councils. To do otherwise would derogate from the absolute power of the Crown, the more especially since 'kings do not owe their *imperium* to the will of the Roman Court'.[29]

If Campomanes objected so strongly to papal pretensions, it was because he sought to enlarge the absolute authority of the Spanish monarchy. Citing the medieval laws of Partida, which declared that kings are 'vicars of God, each one in his own kingdom', he asserted that their sovereign power derived directly from the Almighty. Furthermore, as 'the anointed of God', kings had the right and obligation to act as protectors of the Church, crushing heresy and invigilating the discipline of the clergy. Had not Constantine the Great presided over General Councils of the Church? In Spain the Visigothic kings had convoked councils to discuss Church affairs and the medieval Cortes had equally intervened in that sphere. Indeed, the privileges, immunities, jurisdiction and property which the Church possessed all derived from the sovereign power of monarchs, who retained the right as much to abrogate as to confirm such temporal rights. After all, 'the Church exists within the State', and the clergy were not exempt from their obligations as 'citizens and subjects'. If the king had no right to intervene in questions of doctrine, nevertheless, as protector, he was bound to maintain orthodoxy through the suppression of heresy. Campomanes concluded by asseverating that the Papacy lacked all authority to question the dispositions of sovereign princes who were not subject to any earthly superior.[30]

Although Campomanes' treatise aroused great disquiet within the Spanish Church, even among Jansenist prelates, his role as spokesman of the Crown was confirmed in 1773 when the ministers ordered 30,000 copies of his *Discurso sobre el fomento de la industria popular* to be circulated across the country, a work which was followed the next year by a tract on artisan education. To start with, he contrasted the current lamentable state of Spanish industry with its thriving condition in the sixteenth century, and drew attention to Holland and England where the rewards and honours given to inventors and improvers of industry had encouraged an expansion of production. Rejecting the physiocratic emphasis on agriculture as the sole source of national wealth, he argued that it was necessary to revive handicraft industry among the peasantry, a proposal which led him more to praise the cottage craftsmen of Galicia than the incipient factories of Barcelona. His aim here was to provide occupation so that the population might grow in number and prosperity. In starkly secular terms he pronounced: 'the most secure barometer by which one ought to measure the progress or decadence of the State' was the progress of industry.[31]

For Spain to emulate its northern neighbours, it was first necessary to eliminate various obstacles to economic growth, chief among which was the existence and power of artisan guilds. Campomanes advocated the abolition of all privileges and limitations on the exercise of their craft by qualified artisans, reducing the guilds' role to issuing certificates of skill, their activities in this regard carefully regulated by local magistrates. He sharply criticised guild confraternities, whose function was to raise monies for religious cults, and demanded their summary abolition. At the same time he sought to encourage foreign artisans to settle in Spain and opined that women should be similarly encouraged to work. In this context he condemned the existence of merchant guilds, the *consulados*, as contrary to public utility. Indeed, he displayed a marked hostility to the mercantile function, declaring that it was quite wrong for peasant craftsmen to depend on merchants and commercial credit to sustain their operations. Rather than relying on self-interest and the pursuit of profit, he aspired to motivate industrial growth by the stimulus of public honour and the achievement of the common good. His chosen instruments were the Economic Societies of the Friends of the Country which, so he hoped, would form the springboard for industrial development. The plan here was to recruit 'the nobility of the provinces who generally live in idle fashion', obtaining their assistance for the collection of economic data, the organisation of schools for design and artisan education, and the promotion of local industry.[32]

Nowhere did Campomanes better attest to his status as a philosophe than when he observed that the activity of men of letters within the commonwealth could be compared to the role of officers in the army. It was for them to write on practical matters, imparting knowledge of mathematics and new techniques, so as to teach the mass of artisans and agriculturists. He denounced the old distinction between the liberal arts and the mechanical or servile arts, and commended those authors who had written on the craft of the tailor or about hemp production. Indeed, the invention of the sewing needle had served humanity far more than all the logic of Aristotle and his countless commentators. In the human sciences the old abstractions and sophistries had been replaced by 'a good reasoning and the geometric order of comparing ideas'. Only the universities lagged behind, still clinging to their antiquated curriculum.[33]

Anxious to defend the record of the Bourbon dynasty, Campomanes took issue with Montesquieu's much cited observations about the decline of Spain. For sure, he agreed that the sudden influx of precious metals into sixteenth-century Spain, when combined with the incessant wars of the epoch, had destroyed national industry and left the country depopulated and exhausted. He rehearsed the various solutions advanced by the *arbitristas* of the following century. But he then argued that with the advent of the Bourbons things had changed for the better, the very War of Succession bringing money into the Peninsula. Thereafter, the procurement policies of the Crown had encouraged ship-building, munitions and textiles. The recent opening of free trade between the Caribbean ports and Spain had already proved so successful that he anticipated complete freedom of trade between the Peninsula and all its American colonies, measures all the more desirable since monopolies and restrictions on the flow of trade were always ruinous for industry.[34]

At every turn, Campomanes thus testified to the immense shift in cultural values that separated the Spanish Enlightenment from the era of the Baroque. So obvious was his disdain for religion that José Climent, Jansenist bishop of Barcelona, condemned him as a free-thinker. Although he purveyed the traditional regalist doctrine of the king as vicar of God, he carefully refrained from suggesting that the monarch might figure as the earthly image of the Almighty, a neo-Platonic conceit still propounded by Bossuet. Instead, he saluted Charles III as a 'patriot-king' and as 'the supreme director of the republic'. He was also much given to invoking 'the State' and 'the Sovereign Power' as the source of earthly dominion. In the preface to one treatise, he wrote that 'the obligation of a citizen moves me to desire the prosperity of the nation'. It was a concern which led him to declare that 'the true foreigner in his country is the idle man', a dictum obviously advanced with the nobility and clergy in mind.[35] Preoccupied as he was with devising remedies for Spain's long decline, Campomanes lacked all sense of the Catholic monarchy's providential mission, failing to perceive that without such an ideology little remained of Spain's claim to dominion in the New World other than the material facts of conquest and possession.

The degree to which the Enlightenment entailed the repudiation of the cultural achievements of the past two centuries of Spanish history can be most clearly observed in the multifarious writings of Gaspar Melchor de Jovellanos (1743–1811), an Asturian lawyer and royal servant, whose works encompassed poetry, drama, political economy, art criticism and legal history.[36] Although he differed from Campomanes in being a noble *colegial* and a Jansenist rather than an obscure *manteista* and free-thinker, Jovellanos was animated by much the same prejudices and principles as regards Spain's economic and cultural decline. Employed by the Crown first as a magistrate in Seville, and thereafter active in various royal academies in Madrid, it was not until 1797–8 that he became minister of Justice where, however, he soon incurred the displeasure of Charles IV's venal favourite, Manuel de Godoy. An assiduous student of political and intellectual developments in France and Britain, Jovellanos sought to introduce and apply the latest doctrines so as to reform and renew Spanish agriculture, architecture, literature, education and religion. To naturalise these policies, however, he constantly scoured the historical record, at all points seeking precedents to justify change.

In a speech delivered to the Royal Academy of History in 1780, Jovellanos lamented that as yet Spain lacked a 'civil history' which would explain 'the origin, progress and alterations of our constitution'. All 'patriots' should study legal history since so many existing institutions, distinctions and laws derived from the distant past. In particular, he commended the Visigothic era, when kings had convoked assemblies of the nobility and bishops, which acted as 'Councils and Cortes', and 'dictated laws which were the expression of the general will, framed by its principal members, who represented the Church and State'. Obviously impressed by Montesquieu's attribution of political freedom to the Germanic tribes, Jovellanos deplored Spain's failure 'to conserve the constitution in its primitive purity'. As it was, the reconquest from the Moors had created a feudal settlement, where the nobility and Church appropriated

28 Francisco-José de Goya, *Gaspar Melchor de Jovellanos*

the land, leaving the masses reduced to servitude. Even so, the Cortes of each kingdom met to sanction laws and remedy abuses: 'In them the general will was united by means of representatives of each estate'. Within the historic constitution there thus existed the elements of renewal.[37]

Despite his retrospective gaze, Jovellanos shared Campomanes' belief in the value of work arguing that an industrious artisan was worth more to society than an idle noble, since he produced things that others wanted. Observing that in the Middle Ages society had been divided into the three classes of priests, warriors and labourers, he reminded his readers that the State now defended the realm from attack, a role which thus deprived the nobility – the descendants of medieval warriors – of their function. Of course the aristocracy were still distinguished by the possession of great wealth; but for the remainder of this class nobility was an accident of birth and sterile in its effect, often preventing men from entering productive activity. But Jovellanos reserved his warmest praise for the strata from which he himself came, which is to say, for families of noble descent but modest means who opted for public service, enlisting in the armed forces or the judiciary. He exclaimed: 'the children of these good patriots are the children of the State'. Elsewhere, he contrasted the spirit of honour which impelled these men to seek fame and reputation in such service with the motive of self-interest which animated merchants and farmers.[38] Whether this preference derived from his nobiliary pretension or expressed an incipient classical republicanism is not clear, although his frequent invocation of the term 'citizen' suggests the latter, albeit in the aristocratic model favoured by Montesquieu.

In Church affairs Jovellanos figured as a leader of the Jansenist party, a sincere Catholic, but averse to the 'ultramontane maxims' which had entered Spain in the thirteenth century. As minister of Justice, he appointed his friend, Antonio de Tavira, as bishop of Salamanca, hoping that he would preside over the regeneration of the university, at that time bitterly divided between Aristotelians and 'philosophers'. He sharply criticised the reactionaries for their defence of scholasticism and for their 'adhesion to the usurpations of the Roman Curia, their aversion to the sovereign authority and its regalias, their ambition to dominate the schools and preserve the influence of the religious orders and, in a word, to perpetuate ignorance.' He observed: 'Tavira is our Bossuet and ought to be the reformer of our Sorbonne.' Like most of his party, Jovellanos was appalled by the excesses of popular religion in Spain. After a visit to the Augustinian church which housed the hallowed image of Christ of Burgos, one of the most frequented sanctuaries in Spain, he confided in his diary that it was 'an effigy of the worst and most horrible form', surrounded by fifty lamps, the shrine and cloister filled with plaques, miniature limbs, and other 'testimonies of the most stupid superstition'. In much the same spirit, Jovellanos derided scholasticism and canon law for their false principles and their disputatious method of argument, recommending that colleges should adopt the study of the Bible, the classics, positive theology, Van Espen on 'the pure and primitive discipline of the Church', and the historical catechism of Fleury.[39]

It was in the sphere of art and architecture that Jovellanos demonstrated greatest reforming zeal, urging the necessity of waging 'bloody war' against the 'works of barbaric and depraved taste'. Not until the reign of Charles III, the patron of the excavations at Pompeii and Herculaneum, had Spain rediscovered 'the recondite and sublime principles of good taste and beauty', which is to say, the art of ancient Greece and Italy, the fount and enduring standard of natural beauty. Although Jovellanos admitted that Gothic cathedrals induced reverence and encouraged prayer, he condemned their lack of proportion and extravagant decoration. These were precisely the same faults that he denounced in the Spanish Baroque, where the influence of Bernini and Borromini had led to the construction of 'braggart buildings, where the richness of the decoration hid the lack of order and system . . . they altered the modules, inverted the orders, disfigured all types of architectural ornament and invented a mass of new forms . . .' In the works of Churriguera, Ribera and Tomé, architects of the early eighteenth century, the extravagance of the retablos had infected the design of façades and porticos.[40] The trend was all the more distasteful since during the sixteenth century Spain had welcomed the Renaissance revival of ancient art, a reception encouraged by Crown patronage, which had reached an early climax in the building of the Escorial, of which Jovellanos wrote: 'the immortal work of San Lorenzo was without doubt the greatest theatre of glory open to the talent of that epoch'. Equally important, Jovellanos discerned the same cycle of efflorescence and corruption in both painting and poetry. Following the death of Velásquez and 'the great Murillo', artists who had assimilated the lessons of the Renaissance, Spanish painting was dominated by the 'over-loaded compositions' of Lucas Jordan. In literature the classic harmony of Garcilaso de la Vega and Luis de León gave way to the conceits of Góngora and 'the irregular and monstruous dramas' of Lope de Vega. In effect, the momentous age when Spain had possessed great soldiers, poets and artists had lasted for little more than a century. It was to cleanse the Augean stable of Baroque decoration that Charles III had imported the German neo-classic artist, Anton Raphael Mengs, whom Jovellanos servilely praised as 'the son of Apollo and Minerva . . . a philosopher-painter', who had exercised 'an impartial and rigid censure against the abortions of extravagance'.[41] It was not until 1777, however, that the Crown finally insisted that all new churches and other public buildings should be constructed in the neo-classic style, their design first approved by the Academy of San Fernando.

By far the most influential of Jovellanos' works was his *Informe en el expediente de ley agraria* (1795) in which he argued that, although a city–state such as Venice might well thrive on the basis of industry and trade, a country like Spain required a thriving agriculture if its population was to grow and prosper. Citing the classic author, Columella, he described agriculture as 'the mother of innocence and of honest work . . . it will be the prime support of the strength and splendour of nations'. Not that he was a mere physiocrat, since he also took from Adam Smith's *The Wealth of Nations* (1776) the thesis of self-interest as the motivating force of economic activity.[42] In line with this liberal approach, he attributed the lamentable state of Spanish agriculture to the concentration in landownership and to the legal, institutional barriers which impeded the free play of self-interest in an open market. To remedy the patient's condition, Jovellanos proposed radical surgery. For a start, he advocated the partition, sale and enclosure of all public lands, be they owned by local councils, village commons or by the Mesta, the powerful guild of sheep-herders which had preserved open grazing rights across the heart of Spain. Yet more radical, he called for the abolition of all *mayorazgos*, the entails by which landowners bequeathed all their estates to a single heir, thus preserving their possessions from testamentary partition between all their children. It was a proposal which protected the current rights of the nobility but which envisaged the eventual dissolution of the economic basis of the Spanish nobility. As regards the clergy, Jovellanos followed Campomanes and urged the sale of all Church lands, the receipts to be invested in state funds so as to yield an equivalent income. At one blow, the centuries-old problem of mortmain was to be resolved and the clergy reduced to the level of state pensioners.[43] To accompany this radical restructuring of landownership, Jovellanos further proposed the elimination of all legal controls on corn prices and land rents, the suspension of internal excise on agricultural goods, and free licence for exports of all produce other than grain. The intervention of the State was henceforth to be limited to the promotion of practical education and such public works as irrigation and road-building. Above all, the aim of these far-reaching reforms was to lift all constraints on individual interest and create a nation of peasant proprietors, entrepreneurial citizen-farmers, from whose labours and production would stem the wealth, freedom and increase of Spain. It was a vision which was to be soon tested by practical implementation and was to have a lasting effect on both sides of the Atlantic.

Despite their avowed interest in history, Campomanes and Jovellanos displayed an intolerant disdain for the immediate past of their country and lacked all sense of its enduring influence on the present. Although they sought to re-shape the culture and economy of Spain according to canons of taste and performance derived from northern Europe, their assimilation of the Enlightenment remained cautious and tentative, more obvious in the aesthetic sphere where Renaissance precedent existed than in religion or politics. Indeed, as their reliance on Bossuet indicates, much of their thinking stemmed directly from seventeenth-century France. Both men were servants of an absolute monarchy who sought to deploy its power to introduce the 'enlightened' reforms they deemed necessary for Spain's salvation. What they failed to comprehend was that their attack on Church privilege, wealth and education signified the demise of the Spanish monarchy. The concept that Spain had been especially chosen by Providence to defend and promote the Catholic cause was anathema to them, the source of the current ills of their country. But how was it possible to remove the Church and its ministers from the centre of society without undermining the stability of the State? For the clergy had preached loyalty and obedience to the Catholic Kings since time immemorial. In effect, the destruction of the religious culture of Habsburg, post-Tridentine Spain eroded the traditional deference of the Spanish people to their kings and laws. In 1808, when French forces invaded the Peninsula and imposed an alien monarch, the hispanic world broke asunder, never to be fully united again.

IV

In 1804 the Spanish Crown commanded that all Church property in New Spain should be sold and the proceeds deposited in the royal treasury which henceforth should be responsible for the payment of the interest on the confiscated capital. Already in Spain itself a similar measure had been introduced in 1798. But whereas the measure was accepted in the Peninsula without great opposition, by contrast, in Mexico, its introduction aroused a storm of protest from all leading institutions. By the time it was cancelled in 1808 over 12 million pesos had been collected, an exaction which infuriated both the colonial elite and the Church. Moreover, the priesthood already had been alienated by a decree of 1795 which breached the clergy's immunity from the jurisdiction of royal courts by investing the criminal bench of the high court with the right to prosecute clerics who were accused of grievous offences.[44] As with amortisation, the policy was enforced despite agitated representations from the hierarchy and cathedral chapters. In effect, if the religious orders had figured as the prime target for reform during the early years of Charles III's reign, by the 1780s the privileges and wealth of the secular clergy became the chief object of attack. Whereas Solórzano had envisaged colonial society as governed by two parallel systems of law, each with their own courts and jurisdiction, each subject to the Catholic king as vicar of God and delegate of the Holy See, by contrast, Campomanes and other ministers now defined the Church as a privileged corporation within the State, whose rights and property derived from the Crown's concession. And what the State or sovereign conferred, it could equally retract.

In 1804 the Archbishop of Mexico, Francisco Javier de Lizana y Beaumont (1802–11) complained bitterly to the Crown of 'the intolerable excess which the abuse of bringing *recursos de fuerza* has reached in this country'. When a bishop issued a judgement against any individual, the lawyers immediately presented an appeal in the high court of justice which now increasingly inclined to find against the hierarchy's rulings. Even in the case of ordination, where a candidate had been refused for confidential reasons, the royal magistrates had intervened. Lizana also lamented the mounting tide of individual secularisations, whereby friars obtained licence from Rome to abjure their vows as religious yet continued to officiate as priests, much to the scandal of the laity. Any attempt to prevent them celebrating mass at once elicited an appeal to the high court. Whether it was 'the corruption of customs, the influence of the country or the blood of infidels' which accounted for this abandonment of the cloister he was not sure, but obviously 'the desire for liberty reigns here far more than in Spain'. He concluded by warning ministers that the 'libertines' sought to destroy all 'hierarchies' and were the Church to be further weakened the authority of the Crown would be threatened. It was in 1809 that Lizana returned to the same theme to complain that the Crown 'has placed many new and successive restrictions on the exercise of ecclesiastical jurisdiction since the middle years of the eighteenth century'. He reminded Madrid that 'it was principally through the secular and regular clergy that the Americans have been and are loyal to God and the king . . . he who has the priests has the Indies' But the ministry, headed by Manuel de Godoy, ignored these warnings and strove to devise new means of exploiting the wealth of the American Church.[45] In 1810 Miguel Hidalgo y Costilla, parish priest of Dolores, called out his native flock into rebellion and thereby sparked off an insurgency in which the creole clergy were to play the leading role.

23

SCIENTIFIC TRAVELLER

I

IN 1802 Alexander von Humboldt (1769–1859) climbed Mount Chimborazo, reaching an altitude of 19,286 feet, only 1,000 feet beneath its majestic snow-capped dome. It was an exploit he always recalled with pride, later exclaiming: 'All my life I have imagined that of all mortals I was the one who had risen highest in the world – I mean on the slopes of Chimborazo.' Although he and his companions suffered from the freezing cold and the thin air, they made barometric observations, collected rock samples, ascertained the limits of vegetation and insect life, and demonstrated that La Condamine's previous measurements were inaccurate. Only two weeks before, Humboldt had climbed Pichincha, a still active volcano close to the city of Quito, boldly peering into its circular gorge where flames dimly flickered and earth tremors shook his instruments. Where once Spanish conquerors and mendicants had sacrificed their lives in quest of silver and souls, so now a German natural scientist expended his energy in pursuit of knowledge, albeit conscious that his intellectual conquest of the New World would win him fame in Europe.[1]

It was in 1799 that Humboldt arrived in Cumaná, there to begin a five-year sojourn in Spanish America, a journey which took him from Venezuela to Lima, included visits to Cuba, and finished with an eleven-month stay in New Spain. In his *Personal Narrative of Travels* (1814–19), he described his voyage into the interior, a 1,500 mile journey up the Orinoco, in which he traversed the burning grasslands of the Llanos, only then to enter the tropical forests of Guiana, eventually reaching the dank, mosquito-ridden jungle where the waters of the Rio Negro, the greatest of the Amazon's tributaries, flowed into the Orinoco through the Casiquiare canal. It was a fabled, desolate zone, once reckoned to be the site of Raleigh's El Dorado and still the object of frontier contention between Spain and Portugal. In carefully modulated prose, Humboldt strove to evoke 'the picturesque beauties which lay open to those who are alive to the majesty of nature'. To this day there are few scenes in travel literature which match the excitement of his landing in the tropics or of his first

29 Alexander von Humboldt

sight of the tropical forest, the lofty trees, heavy with giant creepers, appearing at a distance like some great carpet covering the land. What could be better than the account of entering the vast cavern at Caripe, its darkness filled with the beating wings of innumerable birds and bats that had never seen the light of day? The impact of his book can be judged by the admission of Charles Darwin that 'My whole course of life is due to having read and re-read as a youth his *Personal Narrative*.'[2]

Once back in Europe, Humboldt settled in Paris, there to dedicate the next two decades to the formidable task of publishing the mass of material he had collected during his travels. The thirty volumes, twenty in folio editions, which flowed from his pen, exhibited an unparalleled range of interests, since lavishly illustrated studies of American flora, fauna and geology were matched by comprehensive essays on Aztec history and the political economy of Cuba and New Spain. Where speculation about the New World had once reigned supreme, he now provided a copious mass of precise data. At one stroke the fissure which had opened between the European Enlightenment and American reality was effectively bridged by the intervention of a qualified, critical observer. None of this achievement would have been possible, however, without great wealth, privilege, and remarkable talent. Humboldt belonged to the titled nobility of Prussia and had trained for public service, first by attending a commercial academy at Hamburg, where he learnt how to handle official statistics, and then by enrolling in the school of mines at Freiburg, where he studied under the celebrated geologist, Abraham Werner, a formation which subsequently won him appointment as Director of Mines in Franconia. But Humboldt also came to maturity during the apogee of the *Aufklärung*, a multi-faceted efflorescence of German philosophy and literature, which out-stripped the Enlightenment in France and Scotland and assured Germany the academic leadership of nineteenth-century Europe. After resigning from state service to dedicate himself to scientific research, he came to know Goethe and attended Schiller's lectures at Jena. His brother, Wilhelm von Humboldt, also figured as a young star in the intellectual firmament and was later to win fame as both a reforming statesman and a profound philologist.[3] For his part, Alexander travelled extensively, examining geological strata, and visited revolutionary Paris in company with his close friend, George Forster, whose narrative of travels with Captain Cook in the Pacific fired his ambition to voyage beyond the confines of Europe.[4]

To signalise the individual character of Humboldt's achievement is a commonplace; eminently just; and yet profoundly misleading. It is true that, whereas the great scientific expeditions of this epoch were generally financed by governments, the Prussian baron expended a large part of his own patrimony on a journey in which he was accompanied only by Aimé Bonpland, a French botanist. The published results of his travels compared favourably with the records of both British naval explorations of the Pacific and of the French description of Egypt. But Humboldt traversed a long established empire; he went to America at the recommendation of the Spanish Crown; and encountered an enthusiastic welcome from royal officials and the creole elite. Moreover, he visited the New World at a propitious moment in its history: fifty years before or after, he would not have succeeded in collecting so much raw data on all aspects of life in America. As it was, the confluent effect of the Bourbon revolution in government and the Spanish Enlightenment had created ideal conditions for his venture. Already, in the 1790s, the Crown had despatched German mining experts to Mexico and Peru, and many of these men still remained in the New World, eager to assist their brilliant compatriot. So too, Humboldt placed his talents at the service of the Bourbon State, the very ease with which he collaborated with local officials a tribute to his experience as the servant of an absolute monarchy. When he explored the upper reaches of the Orinoco, he received every possible assistance from local missionaries and officials and in return he communicated the results of his observations of longitude and latitude (which showed that Portugal had advanced well beyond the agreed frontiers) to the governor in Caracas for despatch to Madrid. In New Spain, the viceroy, José de Iturrigaray, commissioned Humboldt to draw an accurate map of the kingdom and to compile statistical tables of population and economic activity, projects which he was later to publish in amplified form in Paris.[5] In all but his strictly scientific works, Humboldt acted as the spokesman of the Bourbon Enlightenment, the approved medium, so to say, through which the collective inquiries of an entire generation of royal officials and creole savants were transmitted to the European public, their reception assured by the prestige of the editor.

II

In his *Personal Narrative*, Humboldt attested that Spanish America no longer consisted of the two great kingdoms of Peru and New Spain: by 1810 an entire circle of provinces, once mere frontier settlements, had emerged as significant zones of population and production for export. As regards Venezuela, François de Pons, in his account published in 1806, had already described in considerable detail the establishment of the captaincy-general at Caracas in 1777 and the consequent introduction of a high court of justice, a merchant guild, an intendant and militia regiments.[6] Rather than repeating this range of information, Humboldt chose not to insert any description of Caracas but instead started with his impressions of the surrounding valley of Aragua, a fertile district where sugar, coffee, cacao and cotton were grown. By then exports from Venezuela were valued at 5 million pesos a year and the population comprised some 750,000 inhabitants, a somewhat low estimate, since other observers reckoned it close to 900,000. He was surprised to find that many of the great plantations leased extensive tracts of land to a numerous class of free mulattos and poor whites, many of whom worked on a seasonal basis for their landlords. These poor farmers generally grew cotton and indigo, leaving the more profitable crops, cacao and sugar, to the plantations whose owners had imported large numbers of slaves from Africa. By the 1800s these slaves numbered at least 60,000 and, depending on estimates, formed anywhere between 6 to 15 per cent of the population, their subsistence dependent on their growing foodstuffs on plots given them for that purpose. By far the most profitable crop was cacao, with two-thirds of the quantity consumed in Europe coming from Venezuela, a trade which formed the basis of the local aristocracy's prosperity.[7]

Both in his travel account and in his *Aspects of Nature* (1807), Humboldt advanced the concept of clearly defined geographical regions, contrasting the fertile upland valleys of Aragua to the Llanos, the vast inland plains of Venezuela, which he compared to the prairies of North America, the pampas of Argentina and the steppelands of Central Asia, commenting on the strange similarity that existed between these grasslands and the great deserts of the world. The Llanos served as a refuge zone for bandits, usually mulattos and blacks, 'who assassinated the whites who fell into their hands'. Here were to be found great herds of cattle, whose owners rarely knew their numbers with any precision, the more especially since many of them were illiterate and lived in the most primitive conditions, relying on a few slaves or mulatto freedmen to handle their stock. Indeed, Humboldt met one estanciero worth an estimated 100,000 pesos who still mounted his horse bare-foot. What clearly emerged from his description was the degree to which the plains had been recently brought under exploitation for the purpose of supplying the coastal valleys and the Caribbean islands with meat, oxen and mules.[8] Despite their lawless, pastoral image, the Llanos were thus increasingly integrated into the Venezuelan economy, the impetus to change derived from population growth and the demands of the coastal settlements.

By contrast, the tropical jungles of Guiana, which together with Amazonia formed a vast plain covered with dense vegetation fed by the superabundant flow of waters from the Andes, appeared to Humboldt as an economically lifeless zone. The problem here was the authority exercised by the mendicant missions. Although he was careful to acknowledge the assistance he had received from these Spanish friars, he deplored their harsh treatment of the Indians, noting that they often beat the natives for trivial offences. The effect of the missions was to quit all spirit or independence from the Indians, who, once converted, soon sank in a listless inertia. Moreover, so Humboldt asserted, the friars excluded other settlers and traders from the considerable territories they controlled, yet failed to encourage their neophytes to engage in agriculture.

Their monopoly and despotism thus obstructed any economic progress, leading Humboldt to conclude that 'the feeble civilisation introduced in our days by the Spanish monks pursues a retrograde course'.[9]

Writing in retrospect, at a time when Venezuela was divided by civil war, Humboldt freely admitted that he had failed to recognise how deep and widespread was the desire for independence, the more especially since during his visit the wealthy classes had expressed their apprehension that any rebellion might well provoke a slave uprising or ethnic conflict between the whites and the coloured sectors of the population. The cruel massacre of French planters in Saint Domingue, which had followed the liberation of its slaves, was much in their minds. What most impressed Humboldt was the spirit of equality that reigned among the creoles, noting that poor whites regarded themselves as the social equals of the wealthy and educated, since 'in the colonies the true badge of nobility is the colour of the skin'. At the same time, he observed how difficult it was for Spaniards living in the tropics to retain any real idea of Europe, so that although Caracas and Havana appeared more aware of events in Europe than was the case in Mexico or Lima, the incongruities were often startling, as when on one occasion he perceived a plantation owner, Raynal in hand, ordering a slave to be beaten for some trifling offence. For the Spanish Americans there were only two events in their history: the conquest, which they condemned for its cruelties, and the struggle for independence. But by rejecting their Spanish heritage, the creoles stood in danger of losing their cultural identity, since 'the colonies have neither history nor national literature', and indeed 'have lost their national individuality'.[10]

If Humboldt offered a lively portrait of Venezuela, he wrote only a few letters about his experience in New Granada, Quito and Peru. His greatest surprise was at the diffusion of scientific knowledge, then invariably called 'the new philosophy'. Such was his own reputation that on his reaching Bogotá, the viceroy, Archbishop Caballero y Góngora, sent out his coach, so that he and Bonpland could be escorted into the city in appropriate style. There, he was received by José Celestino Mutis, a distinguished Spanish botanist, who despite his advanced age was still engaged in preparing an illustrated edition of his extensive collection of plant specimens, which he freely allowed Humboldt to consult. If the Prussian traveller found the society of Bogotá and Quito much to his taste, spending several months in the latter city, by contrast he strongly disliked Lima, commenting that it possessed little cultural life worthy of mention. Whereas in Caracas wealthy landowners often enjoyed an income of 30,000 pesos, in the Peruvian capital it was rare to find anyone with more than 12,000 pesos a year and indeed many families were quite ruined. Moreover, the desert which surrounded the city isolated it from the country of which it was the ostensible capital to such an extent that Humboldt exclaimed: 'Lima is more distant from Peru than London . . . I cannot study Peru in Lima.' In effect, the City of the Kings had lost its former pre-eminence in South America and capitals such as Caracas and Buenos Aires displayed a greater vitality.[11]

In his last volume of travels, published in 1825, Humboldt presented a 'political essay' on Cuba, in which he set out a great mass of data on the sugar industry and slavery. It was largely thanks to its thriving exports that the island's population had risen from 170,000 persons in 1775 to over 600,000 in 1811. By then Havana had 96,000 inhabitants, nearly double the size of Lima's population and in Spanish America second only to Mexico City. The cause of this sudden growth was the slave revolt in Saint Domingue which halted sugar production on that island and caused planters to flee abroad, many seeking refuge in Cuba. It was the Spanish island rather than the British possessions in the West Indies which seized the market opportunity: its planters imported unprecedented numbers of slaves from Africa, introduced new strains of sugar from Tahiti, and invested heavily in refining machinery, including steam engines. The result was a rapid expansion in production. As Humboldt was at pains to observe, none of this increase would have been possible without a sudden surge in the importation of slaves who, by 1810, comprised a third of the Cuban population. Conditions varied from estate to estate, but in general male slaves outnumbered females by four to one and 'there are plantations on which 15 to 18 per cent perish annually', testimony enough of their harsh exploitation. Humboldt commented that it was a sophistry to compare a slave's condition with that of a serf or peasant, affirming that 'slavery is without doubt the greatest of all the evils that afflict humanity'. At the same time, he found that Cuba differed profoundly from the British West Indies in that two-thirds of its population consisted of creoles, mulattos and free blacks, whereas in Jamaica freedmen only numbered a fifth of its inhabitants. As in Venezuela, it was the free small farmers who grew tobacco and produced foodstuffs for the cities, even if the island depended on the United States for its cheap flour. Although Humboldt observed that 'in Havana the people were the best informed of the politics of Europe . . .', it was clear to him that the creole planters' dependence on slavery effectively prevented them from entertaining any projects for independence.[12]

III

To dissipate the fog of Buffonian speculation that still clouded the study of America, Humboldt purchased and travelled with no less than thirty-six of the latest instruments made in Paris, so as to enable him to take observations of latitude, longitude, altitude, temperature, air pressure, and magnetic varia-tions. Both his graphs depicting isothermic lines and his records of magnetic fluctuations marked new departures in these nascent branches of science.[13] So too, he collected rock samples of the diverse terrain he visited, carefully noting their stratigraphic location. For his part, Bonpland surveyed botanical resources and eventually despatched forty-five cases to Paris, containing 6,000 species of plants. It was through the combination of precise measurement and accurate illustration, all based on first-hand observation, that Humboldt won his reputation as a natural scientist.[14] The great harvest of verified facts rather than any advance in theory constituted his prime contribution to knowledge, an achievement that derived directly from his concept of scientific method as 'the art of gathering a great profusion of facts, of ordering them, and of raising them by means of induction to general ideas'. Indeed, at a time when controversy still raged between Neptunists and Vulcanists as to whether the earth's irregular landscape had been caused either by slow subsidence of primordial waters or by volcanic eruption, he chose to eschew all discussion of 'the origin of things', arguing that the scientist's task was to discover 'the laws of nature' which governed the uniform operation of phenomena. In homage to this Newtonian principle, he declared that 'natural philosophy ... is not occupied with the investigation of the origin of beings, but of the laws according to which they are distributed on the globe'. At the same time, he accepted the contemporary thesis that it was climate and physical environment that determined which forms of life thrived or wilted in any given region, including under this rubric the rise and fall of human society.[15]

In his *Essai sur la géographie des plantes* (1805), Humboldt presented a magnificent plate of Mount Chimborazo in which its slopes were divided into five ascending strata. At each level he provided observations of altitude, temperature, humidity and air pressure and carefully listed the varying types of vegetation and animal life found at these heights. In this environment the altitude and the quality of the soil emerged as the key determinants of the distribution of life forms. Here, then, was a bold attempt to offer a total description of a particular landscape, a pioneering essay in ecological analysis, the significance of which was not fully appreciated by geographers until recently. But essentially it was an exercise in descriptive correlation which failed to provide any causal explanation of the phenomena it described.[16] The problem here derived from the very first principles of natural science. For Humboldt certainly succeeded in demonstrating that the geological record in the New World exhibited much the same rock formations and stratigraphy as were to be found in the Old World. Moreover, once the climatic character of particular regions was taken into account, then remarkable similarities could be observed as regards the distribution of flora and fauna in both hemispheres. Highland pines and tropical palms were found across the globe. However, despite his insistence that 'the form of organised life varies according to climate', Humboldt had to admit the 'analogy of climates is often found in the two continents without identity of production', which is to say, that the plants and animals of the New World often differed sharply from those encountered in similar regions of the Old World. It was his failure to discover any explanation for these differences which led him to conclude that 'the causes of the distribution of the species . . . are among the number of mysteries which natural philosophy cannot reach'.[17] In effect, Humboldt's acceptance of the Newtonian paradigm, that the purpose of science was to discover the uniform operation of natural laws, precluded any application of historical method to the problem of distribution. Only with the publication of Charles Darwin's *Origin of Species* (1859) was it finally realised that variations of species sprang from descent and natural selection. If the plants and animals of the new World often differed from their counterparts elsewhere on the globe, it was owing to the grand 'historical fact' of continental drift and the operation of natural selection across the ensuing millennia. Because Humboldt dealt in facts rather than theories and relied on a paradigm of scientific explanation that was soon to become obsolete in geology, zoology and botany, he figures but rarely in any general history of science.[18]

The degree to which Humboldt's acceptance of climatic determinism influenced his interpretation of phenomena can be most clearly observed in his discussion of the nature and achievements of the native inhabitants of the New World. Starting with the premise that 'the civilisation of peoples is almost constantly in inverse ratio to the fertility of the soils they inhabit', he argued that the very harshness of the highland terrain of America had impelled the development of the moral faculties of the Andean and Mesoamerican Indians, who came to form 'a culture similar to that of China and Japan'. By contrast, 'the force of vegetation and the nature of the soil and climate within the torrid zone . . . perpetuated the misery and barbarism of solitary hordes'. In effect, the emergence of both jungle savagery and highland civilisation, the one based on hunting and the other on agriculture, was determined by the Indians' response to their natural environment. The problem here was to locate the mechanism of cultural change, since as Robertson had long since noted, the intermediate stage between hunting and farming – the herding of livestock – was conspicuously absent. This deficiency led Humboldt to conclude that 'In the New World, we seek in vain these progressive developments of civilisation . . . these stages in the life of nations.' Instead, all he discerned was a sharp contrast between civilisation and savagery.[19]

Despite his fondness for Pierre de St Bernardin's *Paul et Virginie*, a romance which celebrated the benign influence of the tropics on humanity's moral character, Humboldt found little to admire among the Indians he encountered in his journey through Guiana, at one point exclaiming: 'How difficult to recognise in this infancy of society, in this assemblage of dull, silent, inanimate Indians the primitive character of our species.' Indeed, he confessed that he found them physically hideous and had no compunction in characterising them as 'dirty and digusting nations', proud of their 'savage independence', a condition which was not to be confused with true freedom, since they often beat their wives and offspring and raided their neighbours in search of women and human flesh. 'Such is the candour and simplicity of manners. Such is the boasted happiness of man in the state of nature.' Rousseau's image of the noble savage was but a fable. Evidently unhappy with the supposition that these natives might resemble early man, Humboldt boldly speculated that contemporary Indians 'far from being the primitive type of our species, are a degenerate race, the feeble remains of nations, who having been long dispersed in the forests are replunged into barbarism ... scattered like the remains of a vast shipwreck'. In the same way that J. R. Forster had suggested that the southern-most inhabitants of the Pacific might well have sunk into savagery through the effects of isolation and their harsh environment, so also Humboldt postulated that the Amazonian Indians may well have originated in the Andean highlands, abandoning the practice of agriculture owing to the pressure of the tropical rain forests.[20] In pursuing this line of speculation, Humboldt was more close to Robertson and Raynal than to Rousseau, whose vision of the noble savage he openly derided.

The most striking affirmation of the environmental determinants of culture came in his *Vues des cordillères et monuments des peuples indigènes de l'Amerique* (1810), in which Humboldt presented a set of plates, accompanied by commentary, depicting volcanic mountains, Mexican and Inca ruins, and Mesoamerican codices, a combination justified by the thesis that the barbaric grandeur of the Andes and the Sierra Madre had exercised a strong influence over the forms of native civilisation. The purpose of the book was to dispel 'the absolute scepticism' of previous historians of America by providing readers with tangible evidence of both the geological record and of human artefacts.[21] One glance at the illustrations of Inca stone-work or of Mexican sculpture at Xochicalco and Mitla sufficed to disprove the contemptuous assertions of Raynal and Robertson. Equally important was Humboldt's decision to present a comprehensive sample of Mexican codices, taken from collections in Vienna, Rome and Madrid, to which he added a careful drawing of the Calendar Stone, which he had personally inspected when in Mexico. The effect was to demonstrate the existence of native sources which could be employed to reconstruct pre-hispanic history, a possibility which Robertson had openly doubted.

It was in his commentary on the codices that Humboldt best revealed his calibre as a scholar. Paying tribute to Antonio de León y Gama's literary executor, Antonio Pichardo, an Oratorian priest who had instructed him on the interpretation of these documents, he accepted without reservation the creole savant's thesis that Mexican chronology could be traced back to the establishment of the Toltec empire in the ninth century. Although he praised Clavijero's history, he relied on León y Gama's work when he came to expound the complexities of the Mexican calendar. What caught his attention, however, was the 'astonishing analogies' that existed between the Mexican system and the calendars employed in China, Tibet and Japan. Whereas Clavijero had simply reinforced the Lascasian comparison with ancient Greece and Rome, Humboldt drew on recent European research on oriental history and religion to demonstrate the remarkable similarities in the nomenclature of the cycle of months and years and in the concept of epochs. So close were these systems that a strong case could be made either for direct contact between Asia and Mexico, or for the existence of 'a common source'. In advancing this hypothesis, Humboldt did not subscribe to any traditional theory of historical migration or genetic descent. He accepted Clavijero's argument that the natives of the New World had arrived from Asia a long time ago, since their unfamiliarity with certain implements, grains and livestock all indicated an early migration by groups still caught in a primitive level of material culture. Such was the force of these considerations that he concluded that the American Indians had followed 'a special route in the development of their intellectual faculties and in their path to civilisation'.[22] But these dutiful remarks were in part superseded by his fascination with the great legislators of Indian society, with Quetzalcoatl and Manco Capac, who had inaugurated the cycle of civilisation in America. If Japan had been converted to Buddhism by a small mission of Chinese monks, might not a similar band have made their way to the New World? In effect, Humboldt here returned to the time-honoured myths surrounding the Mexican mage, but now suggested Buddhist rather than Christian apostles. An isolated mission could well explain the advanced character of calendrical computation and the relatively low level of material civilisation. In first advancing this diffusionist scheme, Humboldt described it as an hypothesis, but later in his life he bluntly asserted that 'the analogies' between American and Asian civilisation 'announce ancient communications and are not simply the result of an identity of position in which these peoples were found at the dawn of civilisation'. In effect, if human society in the New World had no observable, ascending stages, then civilisation had to be introduced by missionary agents from abroad.[23]

If Humboldt proved so anxious to convert the New World into the cultural offshoot of Asia, it was in part because he entirely subscribed to J. J. Winckelmann's thesis that the ancient Greeks had discovered the eternal canons of beauty and the universal principles of political liberty, coeval achievements that owed a great deal to the ideal light of the Mediterranean sky. In this neo-classical creed, freedom and beauty were the prerogative of European civilisation, especially thanks to the efflorescence of the Renaissance and the Enlightenment, and sharply distinguished its society from the oriental despotism of Asian monarchies. In applying these criteria to Mexican artefacts, Humboldt dismissed the figure of Coatlicue, the statue found alongside the

Calendar Stone, as a monstrous but typical example of a people still caught in the 'infancy of the arts'. In effect, he characterised both the Inca and Aztec realms as despotic, their institutions and art forms doomed to re-enact repetitive cycles without any hope of release or true development.

> Enchained by the despotism and barbarity of their social institutions . . . the entire nation was submerged in an unhappy uniformity of habits and supersititions . . . the same causes produced the same effects in ancient Egypt, India, Mexico, and Peru: that is to say, where men do not present but masses animated by the same will, where laws, religion and customs have prevented the perfecting and happiness of the individual.

Despite his endorsement of creole patriots' proud claims as to the advanced character of the Mexican calendar, Humboldt thus firmly relegated both the Incas and Aztecs to an Asiatic status at a time when Asian civilisation was no longer highly esteemed in Europe. The non-classical quality of their art was sufficient to damn them. By way of conclusion, Humboldt assessed the ancient Mexicans as 'a warlike mountain people, strong but of an exaggerated ugliness according to the principles of European beauty, degraded by despotism, accustomed to the ceremonies of a bloody cult, which was little disposed to elevate itself through the cultivation of the fine arts'.[24] In sum, if tropical savagery derived from degeneration caused by the environmental pressure, highland civilisation sprang from Asian missionaries blessed with a culture that precluded any genuine flowering of the human spirit. Social progress and individual development were reserved for Europe.

IV

Unable to return to Europe by way of the Pacific – he had hoped to join a French naval expedition in Lima – in 1800 Humboldt sailed to New Spain and there passed a month in Guanajuato, descending almost daily into the depths of the Valenciana, at that time the greatest silver mine in the New World. Although his interests were primarily geological, he seized the opportunity to ascertain the precise dimension, output and organisation of the enterprise. It formed a vast underground city, serviced by four shafts, from which radiated a multitude of tunnels, rarely more than five yards across, which corkscrewed around the mother lode at all levels and directions. So deep and distant had these tunnels been driven that the owners were obliged to open a new general shaft through the living rock at a projected depth of 600 yards so as to reach the area where most silver was then found. Cut in octagonal form, eleven yards in diameter, with eight mule-drawn whims for hauling the ore to the surface, this shaft was expected to cost 1 million pesos to complete. The investment was all the more necessary since only a quarter of the mine's 3,332 workers actually laboured at the lode face as pick and blast men, with another quarter employed as porters, carrying bags of ore on their shoulders to the foot of the nearest shaft. Humboldt was impressed by the physical strength of these men, whose wages equalled any paid to miners in Germany. Indeed, since the annual earnings of the workforce amounted to some 750,000 pesos, the owners only refined a part of the ore in their own mills, selling the remainder at the pit-head to independent refiners, with the aim of obtaining a weekly cash flow to cover operating costs. In good years the mine produced over 3 million pesos of silver and yielded its owners 1 million pesos in profit.[25] The Valenciana thus figured among the greatest industrial enterprises in the Western world.

In the *Essai politique sur le royaume de la Nouvelle-Espagne* (1807–11), a monumental work printed in two substantial volumes, Humboldt presented an imposing portrait of Mexico as a great empire that stretched from Guatemala to California, inhabited by a variegated population of over 5 million souls. It was a realm that encompassed some 118,000 square leagues of territory, an estimate close to the 136,000 leagues occupied by the Ottoman Turks, albeit much less than the 260,000 leagues claimed by the United States after the Louisiana purchase. In 1803 Mexico City still figured as the most populous city in the hemisphere, its 130,000 inhabitants almost double the number found in Rio de Janeiro or Havana. Nor could cities such as Philadelphia, New York and Boston compare to Mexico as regards the monumental grandeur of its churches, convents and palaces. Given the flourishing state of its mines and overseas trade, who could doubt that New Spain was destined to occupy a leading role in the commerce of the globe, especially as it straddled the routes that linked the Pacific and Atlantic oceans? It already possessed many of the characteristics of an independent state, since in addition to the viceroy, high court, intendants and treasuries, it possessed an army of 10,000 regular soldiers, supported by an extensive network of militia regiments numbering 20,000, the entire force well-armed, recruited in Mexico and financed out of local taxes. In drawing attention to the wealth and sheer extension of New Spain, Humboldt explicitly compared its prospects with the extraordinary progress recently achieved by the United States.[26]

Perhaps the most notable feature of Humboldt's description of Mexico City was his insistence on its modernity. For sure, he cited Clavijero on its foundation in 1325 and inserted material on its Aztec history. But what attracted his attention were institutions such as the Academy of San Carlos, founded in 1782 to promote the principles of neo-classic art and design, which by the time of his visit had formed an entire generation of young artists, importing casts of classic statuary from Europe. He found the Herreran lines of the cathedral impressive and praised Manuel de Tolsa's magnificent equestrian statue of Charles IV which adorned the main square of the capital. Above all else, he lauded the magnificent neo-classical palace which Tolsa had designed to house the newly established mining court and college, a building fit to grace the streets of Naples or Rome. So also, he cited the careers of creole savants, men such as José de Alzate, Miguel Velásquez de León, and Antonio de León y Gama, in particular fixing upon the distinguished astronomical and mineralogical contributions of Velásquez de León, the promoter of the mining court. The existence of these institutions and savants demonstrated beyond doubt that Mexico participated in the universal culture of the Enlightenment.[27]

If Humboldt was so impressed by the effects of the Bourbon revolution in government, it was in part because these institutions and their officials generated much of the data from which he constructed the *Essai politique*. Commissioned by the current viceroy to frame an accurate map of the kingdom and to compile statistical tables of population and production, he drew freely on the reports compiled by intendants, military surveyors, the merchant guilds, the mining court, treasury officials, and the viceregal secretariat. Much of this material had been assembled at the behest of viceroy the Count of Revillagigedo (1789–94), who had conducted a general census of the population and investigated the impact of the 'free trade' edict of 1778. In addition to this statistical data, Humboldt supplied his own impressions, some historical considerations taken from Clavijero and Robertson, materials dealing with Peru and, above all, the memorials of Manuel Abad y Queipo (1751–1825), a liberal canon of the Michoacán diocese, whose critique of New Spain's society accorded with his own observations. The result of all this was a work which dealt successively with the physical geography of New Spain, its population, cities, and provinces, agriculture, mining, trade, industry, state revenue and defence. At one stroke, the vague and sparse information provided by Robertson and Raynal was replaced by a vast mass of precise data, which by reason of its official origin expressed the undoubted achievements of the Bourbon regime.[28]

By far the best informed part of the book dealt with the silver mines. Besides his own expertise, Humboldt also drew on Fausto de Elhuyar, the Director General of the Mining Court, who had been educated at Freiburg; on Andrés del Rio, a distinguished geologist then serving as professor at the Mining College; and on several German mining experts who had come over to Mexico in the 1790s. All their records and inquiries were made available to him and through them he gained access to the private accounts of the Valenciana at Guanajuato. The facts he gathered could not have been more impressive. The mint records revealed that since the 1690s silver production in New Spain had climbed from an annual average of just over 5 million pesos to about 24 million a hundred years later, the rate of increase suddenly accelerating in the 1770s when production almost doubled. To place these figures in historical context, Humboldt printed the tax returns for Potosí, which demonstrated that registered output from the *cerro rico* had not exceeded 10 million pesos in the

1590s and that, despite the Bourbon reforms, production in the Andean area, by then divided between the viceroyalties of La Plata and Peru, had never surpassed the sixteenth-century maximum. By contrast, in the 1790s Mexico was coining five times as many pesos as it had two hundred years earlier and indeed registered about sixty per cent of all the precious metals produced in the New World. In masterly fashion, Humboldt presented estimates of the entire output of bullion since the discovery of America and traced its eventual destination to Asia.[29]

Whereas the first cycle of silver mining had been dominated by the *cerro rico* of Potosí and had depended on the enforced mobilisation of the Andean peasantry, the eighteenth-century boom in New Spain was based on a variegated range of camps, stretching from Real del Monte to Los Alamos, which employed a free, well-paid, often mobile work-force, composed of *castas*, poor Spaniards and Indians. If earlier critics in Peru had always assumed that working in the mines was a lethal experience, Humboldt found the workers in Guanajuato to be remarkably sturdy and attracted to the industry by the prospect of high earnings. Admittedly, he was not impressed by the often primitive techniques still used in Mexican mines – the failure to cut cross galleries to connect the work tunnels, the consequent reliance on human porters, and the use of heavy iron picks similar to those used in sixteenth-century Germany – all this attracted his censure. But he marvelled at the scale of capital investment, often maintained over a period of years, through which the great entrepreneurs of New Spain built their fortunes. Men such as Antonio de Obregón, the first owner of the Valenciana, and the Count of Regla who restored Real del Monte, were millionaires, whose success in mining brought them titles of nobility and enabled them to purchase vast landed estates. Humboldt thus presented a dazzling image of a great colonial industry, then at the height of its prosperity, encouraged by an enlightened government, and driven forward by entrepreneurial skill, extensive capital investment, and a plentiful, well-paid work-force.[30]

It was the success of the mining industry which largely accounted for the sudden surge in trade between Spain and the New World which occurred after the promulgation of the edict of *comercio libre* in 1778. For Mexico, Humboldt drew upon the balances of trade published by the merchant guild of Veracruz, which demonstrated that New Spain exported silver and some cochineal in return for European textiles, paper, iron, and wines, a pattern of commercial exchange which had not changed greatly since the sixteenth century. Extending his purview to encompass the entire American empire, Humboldt noted that Cuba and Venezuela had grown through the export of tropical produce and the importation of African slaves, whereas Peru, Chile and New Granada still relied on the shipment of precious metals to cover the cost of their imports.

Although Buenos Aires exported increasing quantities of hides, its merchants still relied on silver despatched from Potosí and other camps in Upper Peru to pay for the European textiles they distributed across the viceroyalty of La Plata.

A politically sensitive consequence of the silver boom was the increase in Crown revenue, which in New Spain grew from a mere 3.5 million pesos a year in the 1700s to over 20 million pesos by 1800. In this area the Gálvez visitation had constituted a watershed, thanks to the establishment of the royal tobacco monopoly and the appointment of salaried customs and excise men. By 1803 the audited returns showed that tobacco sales yielded the Crown over 3 million pesos net profit, a figure that equalled the combined taxes levied on silver production and the flow of trade, and was more than triple the 1 million pesos collected in tribute from Indians and mulattos. Once the expenses of monopoly materials and production were deducted, the Crown was left with 14.5 million pesos, of which only 4.5 million were expended within the country to cover the costs of administration, justice and defence. By 1803 New Spain 'exported' some 10 million pesos a year in fiscal tribute, monies employed to maintain the royal fleet stationed at Havana, to subsidise imperial administration in the Philippines and the Caribbean, and to assist state expenditure in the Peninsula.[31] Humboldt cited documents which revealed that the Crown's share of bullion shipped abroad from New Spain had grown steadily since the Gálvez visitation and that Mexico was easily Spain's most profitable colony. What these statistics also demonstrated was the traditional character of the Bourbon revival: in effect, Gálvez had emulated the role of Viceroy Toledo in Habsburg Peru and had financed the resurgence of Spanish power in Europe by a more efficient exploitation of Mexican resources, relying as before on the shipment of silver coin to Europe.

Little of this renewal of economic activity would have been possible had not the population of Spanish America grown in equal measure. Drawing on the imperial census conducted in the 1790s, Humboldt calculated that the American empire housed some 14.5 million inhabitants. Once again, the surprising feature here was the emergence of the Southern cone, the Caribbean and the viceroyalty of New Granada. By contrast, the combined population of Lower and Upper Peru did not exceed 2 million. For New Spain the census of 1793 could be supplemented by parish records of baptisms and burials, and by the tribute register. What these records showed was that only 60 per cent of the population still counted as Indians, since the remainder were now listed as Spaniards, mestizos and mulattos, distinctions which by then as much expressed civic and fiscal obligations as genetic reality. By 1803 New Spain supported an estimated 5.3 million inhabitants, and the registered excess of baptisms over burials gave promise of a rapid increase in population.[32] But the census also revealed a heavy concentration of settlement in central Mexico, leaving the provinces that stretched from Zacatecas and San Luis Potosí to Texas and California but thinly inhabited at a time when both Russians and Anglo-Americans had come to menace the security of the northern frontiers.

Not content simply to echo the celebration of economic expansion implicit within official statistics, Humboldt cited the memorials of Abad y Queipo in his comments on the Mexican Indian and the state of agriculture. He thus roundly declared that 'Mexico is the country of inequality . . . a monstrous inequality in rights and fortunes.' Despite recent improvements, it still suffered all the deleterious effects of feudalism, religious intolerance and the cultural retardation of the Indian peasantry. It would take more than a few decades of reform to eradicate the legacy of the past. For although Humboldt generously invoked Clavijero's 'wise researches' into the Indian past, he accepted Robertson's characterisation of the Aztec polity as a 'religious and civil' despotism, and referred to Moctezuma as 'the sultan of Tenochtitlan'.[33] He also followed the Scottish historian in depicting the encomienda as a feudal institution, which in the form of the great estate still dominated the countryside. Moreover, the conquest had exposed the country to the fanaticism of the mendicants who had taught the Indians an external religion in which former idols had been replaced by Catholic images without any real change of belief, so that contemporary Indians devoted all their exiguous resources to religious feasts and processions. To all this there should be added the harmful effects of the commercial monopoly exercised by Spain and the systematic discrimination against the creoles. Like most other travellers, Humboldt noted the ill-feeling which divided European and American Spaniards, commenting that since 1789 there was a distinct tendency for creoles simply to call themselves 'Americans'. Their exclusion from high office was a constant irritant and engendered deep resentment.[34]

It was the degraded condition of the Mexican Indians which prompted Humboldt to express his strongest reservations about the country's capacity for progress. Faithfully reproducing the substance of Abad y Queipo's 1799 memorial, written for Bishop Antonio de San Miguel, he described them as a race of pariahs, trapped within their own communities, by reason of their diverse languages, costume and collective land tenure, who were unable to borrow money, own land or indeed advance themselves in any way. The Laws of the Indies which had been designed to protect them had become their fetters. The remedy, already advanced by Jovellanos for Spain, was to abolish all restrictions on native economic activity, dividing their holdings on an individual basis, and commuting their tribute to other forms of taxation. Liberal measures might well succeed in releasing the energies of the native peasantry. It was in line with these hopes that Humboldt rejected the ethnic prejudice of Ulloa, asserting that the Indians were a vigorous, well-made race, in no way as drunken as the Spanish traveller had claimed, and in Mexico not subject to forced labour. Indeed, with the abolition of *repartimientos de comercio*, effected by the establishment of the intendancies, the Mexican Indian was far superior to the slaves of Cuba and Venezuela as regards conditions of work, and not greatly removed from the serfs of Russia. For all that, the fact that over half the population of New Spain still continued at such a retrograde level of existence, sunk in superstition and ignorance, unmoved by the incentives of profit or freedom, cast grave doubts over the country's future, the more especially if Mexico were compared to the United States where slaves only comprised a sixth of its inhabitants.[35]

The weakest section of the *Essai politique* dealt with agriculture and domestic industry, areas of activity on which the Bourbon bureaucracy had collected few statistics. Once more basing himself on Abad y Queipo, Humboldt condemned the inequalities in landholding which had been created by the emergence of latifundia, estates which were kept intact, generation to generation, by means of entail and the burden of church mortgages. But apart from dismissing these haciendas as the visible legacy of feudalism, he had remarkably little to say about their mode of operation, their work-force or their entrance into the market economy. Instead, he expatiated on the richness of the soil, the distribution of crops and the high yields obtained from both wheat and maize, which were well above anything known in Europe. In particular, he was impressed by the fertility of the Bajío, comparing its landscape, filled with cultivated fields and small towns, to the plains of Lombardy. In this respect, he noted that the increase in mining had benefited agriculture in the surrounding regions, prompting demand for foodstuffs. For the rest, he criticised the royal monopoly in tobacco and noted that, contrary to usual report, Mexico possessed a manufacturing industry which produced cotton textiles at Puebla and woollens at Querétaro. But a brief visit to the obrajes at Querétaro left him appalled at both their primitive technique and the prison conditions in which the labourers were kept.[36] In short, Humboldt depended heavily on the availability of systematic documentation and, where such sources were not forthcoming, he was reduced to the general observations and personal impressions of any traveller.

The *Essai politique* is an essential text for all students of Mexican history and Spanish imperialism. By reason of viceregal patronage Humboldt succeeded in publishing a vast quantity of systematic information that might otherwise have remained locked away in official archives for several generations. It had far-reaching political effects. For the creole elite interpreted its revelations as confirming that Mexico was both notably wealthy and more than ready for independence. In the decades after independence, Liberals cited his critique of the prevailing system of land tenure as further strengthening their case for reform. That he had fixed on the condition of the Indians as a major obstacle to the country's progress helped to place that question on the political agenda. So to signalise the evident merits of *Essai politique* is not to ignore its defects. Its numerical plethora masks vast omissions. Where, for example, is the Mexico City visited by Gemelli Careri and Ajofrín, a great capital dominated by over fifty churches, convents and colleges, their altars decked in churrigueresque splendour? About the only reference Humboldt made to the entire cycle of Baroque architecture and the culture that inspired these buildings, was a puzzled, disdainful mention of the cathedral sacristy chapel as built in 'Moorish or Gothic' style. More important, he provided remarkably little in the way of social analysis: judged by the standard of Alexis de Tocqueville's *Democracy in America* (1835), the *Essai politique* was a lost opportunity. Even in the sphere of economic activity, Humboldt presented an essentially cameralist description, unconversant, it would seem, with the mode of reasoning introduced by Adam Smith other than as a prejudice in favour of free trade. In effect, the *Essai politique* should not be judged as if it were some great work of synthesis: instead, it is best regarded as a source-book. In this light, Humboldt can be seen as an inspired editor and commentator, himself figuring as a contributor in the sections on geology and mining, but otherwise engaged essentially in compiling and presenting the collective research and inquiries of an entire generation of Spanish officials and creole savants. It is precisely this 'representative' character which keeps the book in print and constitutes its enduring value.

V

In the years 1836–9, which is to say, when he was in his late sixties, Humboldt published an extensive, erudite work on Columbus and Vespucci, in which he sought to interpret their discoveries within the context of the growth of geographic knowledge. By then, the Spanish historian, Martín Fernández de Navarrete, had published the extant letters and journals of Columbus, documents which formed the basis of Washington Irving's romantic biography of the great admiral. Not content simply to paraphrase such materials, Humboldt succeeded in locating the early map of Juan de la Cosa and clearly demonstrated that Vespucci was little more than a pilot serving with the Portuguese. Despite the title of his famous work, it was by no means clear that the Florentine fully appreciated the significance of the term 'new world' and probably thought of the lands he explored as the furthest coast of Asia. After proving that it had been the German cartographer, Martin Waldseemuller, who had baptised the new discoveries as America, Humboldt commented that the name was 'a monument to the injustice of man'. Throughout the discussion, he revealed a close familiarity with the principal Spanish chroniclers of the sixteenth century and paid tribute to José de Acosta, expressing his surprise at 'often finding the germ of the most important physical truths in Spanish writers'.[37]

Reacting against the romantic cult of the great man, Humboldt insisted that all the great advances in human knowledge derived from the collective endeavours of several generations of scholars and scientists. The role of the great man was simply to accelerate or animate pre-existent or latent movements of the human spirit. Although the Vikings had undoubtedly reached the New World, they failed either to comprehend or to exploit their achievements. Without the perfecting of nautical instruments and the developments in astronomy, cartography and navigation, the voyages of Columbus would have been unimaginable. In turn, this progress derived from medieval concern with science, an interest already manifest in the works of Roger Bacon and Albert the Great. To these 'double conquests in the physical world and in the intellectual world', had to be added the stimulus of commercial profit which, in turn, depended on the advanced character of the European economy in the fifteenth century.[38]

As for Columbus himself, Humboldt confessed his fascination with the enigmatic complexity of the man, who exhibited 'this triple character of instruction, audacity and patience'. He insisted on the intellectual formation of the great discoverer, his remarkable skill as a navigator, his persistent study of winds and currents, and his oft-expressed wonder at the majesty of nature. At the same time, he fixed on the paradox that Columbus was impelled by millenarian convictions, persuaded that Providence had chosen him to effect the liberation of Jerusalem. Yet the admiral had also initiated the slave trade, seizing the unfortunate natives without scruple. There was thus a positive contradiction between the individual motivation of Columbus and the practical results that flowed from his discoveries. The significance of this paradox deepened, if it be considered that although creative thought had provided great impetus to the march of civilisation, 'the greatest movements have sprung from the action that man is able to exercise over the physical world, the effect of his material discoveries . . . the enlargement of the empire of man over the physical world or the forces of nature, the glory of Christopher Columbus and James Watt . . . presents a more complex problem than the purely intellectual conquests'.[39]

In the last decades of his life, Humboldt resided at the Prussian court and from that vantage point delivered a set of lectures on recent developments of scientific knowledge that was published under the grand title of *Cosmos* (1844). It was an account of the physical universe, starting with the stars and planets and ending with the emergence of man, to which was then added a survey of the history of science from the Greeks to recent discoveries. His purpose was not simply to expound the laws which governed Nature but also to express in fitting terms the sublime grandeur of its primordial harmony. Paying tribute to Goethe's vitalistic theories of metamorphosis, he declared: 'I have ever desired to discern physical phenomena in their widest connection, and to comprehend Nature as a whole, animated and moved by inward forces.' In his discussion of mankind he reiterated the conventional view that all advances to civilisation had occurred in the temperate zone, but carefully rejected 'the cheerless assumption of superior and inferior races of men', citing by way of refutation his brother Wilhelm's noble affirmation of 'the community of the whole human race'.[40]

Celebrated during his life-time as a leading scientist, a great traveller, and a romantic hero, the subject of countless portraits, Alexander von Humboldt was saluted by the contemporary German geographer, Carl Ritter, as 'the scientific re-discoverer of America'. Arriving in the New World at a singularly propitious moment, Humboldt displayed all the voracious energy of an intellectual conqueror, restlessly searching for new ranges of knowledge to survey and master. Yet, at the level of theory, he adopted a remarkably passive, almost unquestioning approach to the mass of data that he collected. He made little attempt to explain or to interpret; he eschewed all inquiry into the causes of things; all his energy went into observing, measuring, describing and compiling. The *Essai politique* still attracts readers because it provides a remarkably comprehensive portrait of New Spain on the eve of independence. By contrast, *Cosmos* is little more than an academic curiosity. But it is thanks to *The Personal Narrative* that Humboldt figures in the roll-call of those great travellers whose exploits and writings still delight and inspire. Perhaps the last word is best given to Charles Darwin who had no hesitation in affirming that Humboldt was 'the greatest scientific traveller who ever lived'.[41]

24

THE GREAT REBELLION

I

IN 1799 there appeared in London a brief but incendiary pamphlet entitled *Carta dirigida a los Españoles Americanos* in which, for the first time, a creole exhorted his compatriots to rebel against the Spanish Crown and secure their liberty. Although Spanish ministers had constantly proclaimed the union and equality of America and Spain, all the benefits of empire accrued to the Peninsula and its inhabitants. Yet had not Montesquieu, 'that sublime genius', observed that of the two powers, 'the Indies are the principal and Spain is the accessory'? Just as a son, separated from his father by a great distance, had the natural right to emancipate himself from parental authority, so equally the American Spaniards had the right to independence. 'Nature has separated us from Spain by immense seas' and this alone 'proclaims our natural independence'. In any case, the Spanish Crown had governed in arbitrary, despotic fashion, ignoring 'the unalienable rights of man and the indispensable duties of all governments'. In past centuries both Holland and Portugal had broken free from Spain, and only recently the English colonies had fought courageously to gain their independence. It was a blasphemy to imagine that the New World had been created for the enrichment of 'a few imbecile rogues' from Spain. The historic moment had arrived when American Spaniards should unite to free the New World of Spanish tyranny and create 'a grand family of brothers', joined in common pursuit of liberty and prosperity.[1]

The author of this inflammatory manifesto was Juan Pablo Viscardo y Guzmán (1748–98), an exiled Peruvian Jesuit, who as early as 1781 had informed the British consul at Leghorn that the creoles were ready to break with Spain. In the years 1789–98 he resided in London, supported by a pension from the British government, seeking to persuade Pitt's cabinet to despatch an expedition to the Pacific, there to seize the Peruvian port of Coquimbo and thus win control of the entire coast from New Granada to Chile. He proposed that a force of up to 6,000 soldiers should be sent, headed by a prince of the royal house, for the purpose of marching to Arequipa, where independence for all

Spanish America should be proclaimed. Provided care was taken to reassure the creoles that liberation rather than conquest was the aim, there was no doubt that the expedition would meet with a warm welcome. For Britain itself there were handsome commercial opportunities in colonial markets and, if territory was required, then Puerto Rico could easily be annexed.[2]

To inform ministers about the current state of Spanish America, Viscardo prepared two extensive memoranda, written in French, in which he was at pains to correct the misleading impression created by the works of Raynal, Robertson and Ulloa. For here was a populous, relatively prosperous empire, most of whose 14 million inhabitants were clothed by the domestic textile industry. Indeed, as even Ulloa's *Viaje* indicated, virtually every province possessed its own line of artisan industry. Contrary to report, the Indians were a laborious race, occupied in agriculture and weaving. In Peru the Laws of the Indies, based on excellent Inca precedent, had ensured that each village owned sufficient land. As a result of the recent expansion in trade, prosperity was on the increase and indeed the Indians might well come to rival the peasantry of Russia or Germany. As for the creoles, the slanders of Robertson and Raynal concerning their character derived from the prejudices of travellers such as Ulloa and Frezier. Yet Italian Jesuits, resident for many years in South America, had praised the American Spaniards for their generosity, high spirits and vigour. There was no evidence that the tropics undermined moral character and in any case the highland airs of South America were far from enervating. Both the creoles and the clergy were respected by the Indians, since they strove to defend the natives from the exploitation of the hated *chapetones*, which is to say, the peninsular Spaniards. In all this, Viscardo criticised Ulloa for his defamation of both Indians and creoles, observing that his prejudices were all the more dangerous owing to his reputation abroad. Yet it was all too clear that 'philosophy never made him forget that he was a *chapetón*'.[3]

Turning to review the disturbances of 1780, Viscardo observed that they had been preceded by uprisings at Cochabamba in 1730 and at Quito in 1764, when the mestizos had rioted against the European Spaniards, movements eventually quelled thanks to the intervention of creole clergy and landowners. By 1780, however, many creoles were so enraged by the new excise duties and tobacco monopoly instituted by the visitors-general in Peru and New Granada that they gave implicit backing to riots at Arequipa, Socorro and around Cuzco. If Tupac Amaru gained native support by his attack on the corregidors and their infamous *repartimientos de comercio*, the initial spark which fired this movement derived from resentment against the new taxes. Although Viscardo noted that several creole aristocrats supported Tupac Amaru, he himself displayed little enthusiasm for the Inca leader and estimated that his rebellion had been ultimately responsible for 60,000 deaths. Indeed, he was more concerned to list the concessions gained by the rebels in New Granada by the capitulations of Zipaquirá. Perhaps the most remarkable feature of his report was the degree to which it coincided with the record of events compiled by Melchor Paz. There was the same insistence that it had been creole generals who had been responsible for the suppression of the rebellion. Moreover, he cited the final dialogue between Areche and the Inca, in which Tupac Amaru accused the visitor-general of being responsible for all the bloodshed and lives lost in Peru. Here, obviously, was a story which enjoyed wide circulation in patriot circles.[4]

In effect, Viscardo testified that the reign of Charles III constituted a watershed in the relations between the Spanish Crown and the creoles. In the first half of the eighteenth century, so he averred, many creoles had been appointed as bishops and judges of the high courts and had prided themselves on their loyalty to Spain. But the arbitrary expulsion of the Jesuits and the equally arbitrary imposition of new taxes had aroused great discontent. Above all, Viscardo castigated José de Gálvez as an inhumane monster, as a minister who had sought to plunder the New World of its wealth, no matter what the price in human lives. Moreover, his 'open and general hatred of all creoles' had led to their systematic exclusion from high office. On all issues, he favoured brutal repression and only his death had saved America from further rebellion. As it was, his successor as minister, Antonio Porlier, had adopted a more conciliatory policy, rewarding Bishop Moscoso's loyalty with appointment as archbishop of Granada. Here, then, is invaluable testimony that the Bourbon reconquest of America launched by Charles III and his ministers, alienated the creole elite and eventually provoked their participation in the movement for independence.[5]

Despite his projects and memoranda, Viscardo failed to attract British support for an expedition to liberate South America, in part, no doubt, because a similar venture to Santo Domingo had suffered grievous losses. All he could do was to continue to emphasise the immense commercial opportunities that would emerge once independence was achieved, and to warn against the danger of French intervention. Condemned to an obscure life in an alien metropolis, Viscardo broadened his reading and revised his opinions. In his last memorandum, written in 1797 and addressed to 'all free peoples', he now invoked Montesquieu and Adam Smith to argue that without freedom prosperity and progress were impossible. It was the remorseless despotism established by Philip II that had destroyed Spain and devastated America. The influx of silver and the commercial monopoly had but completed the process initiated by the tyrannical rule of the first Habsburgs. Moreover, neither the measures of Bourbon ministers nor the projects of such ministerial economists as Ustariz and Ward had succeeded in reviving Spanish industry, so that Cadiz still served as a mere entrepôt where American silver was exchanged for foreign manufactures. Indeed, the French colony of Saint Domingue came close to rivalling the entire Spanish empire in the value of its exports. Yet all travellers commented on the natural fertility and wealth of Spanish America. To explain its retardation, one had only to read Las Casas' *Brevísima relación* where the tragic depopulation of the Indies was set out in all its true horror. Then again, both Raynal and Robertson had demonstrated how the colonies had been subjected to a despotic government based on commercial monopoly and exploitation of the Indians. In recent years, the creoles had been denied all participation in government, their countries thus converted into a vast prison, by a metropolis whose only interest was in the profit of empire. Viscardo concluded with a pointed comparison between the liberty and prosperity of the United States and the degradation and poverty of Spanish America.[6] What, indeed, was the Spanish monarchy in America but an oriental despotism, more similar in government and spirit to the realm of the Great Turk than to any free society?

Whereas the memorandum of 1797 was a confused mixture of commercial statistics, citations from contemporary philosophes, and fiery sentiment, by contrast *Carta dirigida a los Españoles Americanos* was written with a concentrated force not present in his earlier works. Was its lucid passion inspired by intimations of mortality? Whatever the case, its rhetoric produced an immediate impression on creole contemporaries, since one patriot declared that he had read the manifesto with 'holy enthusiasm'. At the time of its composition, Viscardo had clearly despaired of the British cabinet, and shortly before his death entrusted his papers to Rufus King, the American minister in London, who in turn gave them to Francisco de Miranda, the Venezuelan patriot. It was Miranda who arranged for the publication of the *Carta*, first in French and then, two years later, in Spanish. Such was its impact and distribution that in 1807 an Argentine lawyer studying at Chuquisaca, Mariano Moreno, read it and wrote out his own copy. By then, in 1806, Miranda had taken numerous copies on his first expedition to Venezuela, distributing them as propaganda for the independence cause. In this way, the work of an unknown exile suddenly acquired a remarkable influence over the opening ideology of the Spanish American Revolution.

The most striking feature of the *Carta* was the degree to which Viscardo drew on the traditional themes of creole patriotism to substantiate his plea for independence. Although he certainly cited Montesquieu on Spain and America, made mention of natural rights, and echoed Tom Paine on the natural independence conferred by geographical distance, nevertheless, his condemnation of Spanish tyranny derived emotional force from its reiteration of creole plaints that had first emerged in the early seventeenth century. Apart from his wholly contemporary invocation of the redemptive powers of political liberty, there was little in his discourse that would have been unfamiliar or distasteful to Salinas, Arzáns y Orsúa and Calancha. For he chose to address his letter, not to all the inhabitants of America, but solely to the creoles, which is to say, to the nobility, the lawyers, the clergy and their immediate clientele. As much as Rivadeneira and Ahumada, Viscardo spoke on behalf of a ruling class denied its natural and ancestral right – the governance of their own country. 'The New World is our patria and its history is our history', he wrote, since 'our fathers' conquered it at their own expense, initiative and bloodshed, and thus acquired rights superior to those enjoyed by the Goths in Spain. But their loyalty to the Spanish Crown had betrayed them into neglecting the interests and rights of their children and descendants. In this account, the creole once more figured as the dispossessed heir, suffering from the discrimination of kings who appointed foreigners, which is to say, European Spaniards, to high offices, 'which properly speaking belong exclusively to us in our own country'. As much as Salinas, Viscardo combined this insistence on ancestral right with an invocation of Las Casas on the horrors of the conquest, cruelties inflicted on 'peoples whose only offence was their weakness', with the result that 'the splendour of the greatest known conquest was converted into an ignominious stain on the Spanish name'. Moreover, he then cited Garcilaso on Toledo's murder of the first Tupac Amaru and inserted the entire passage where the Inca historian lamented the viceroy's persecution of the mestizos of Cuzco, who were driven forth into exile or beggary, despite the merits of their fathers, the conquerors, and the inherited rights of their Inca mothers. In effect, both the *Brevísima relación* and the *Comentarios reales* were thus installed as significant, antecedent texts in the first creole manifesto for independence.

Where Viscardo scored over his predecessors was in his outright opposition to the absolute monarchy established by the Habsburgs. Whereas in the Middle Ages Spaniards had possessed a wide measure of freedom and indeed under the constitution of Aragon had enjoyed the right to rebel against unjust government, with the advent of Charles V they had lost their liberty. The advantage of this interpretation of Spanish history was that it enabled Viscardo to attribute the exploitation of America to the monarchy itself rather than to its corrupt agents. It had been the court which had enforced the 'mercantile tyranny' of the Cadiz monopoly, which obliged creoles to purchase European goods at grossly inflated prices. For the rest, Viscardo repeated the customary complaint against the corregidores, whose oppressive regime had sacrificed the welfare of the Indians to the profit of 'a mob of adventurers' from Spain. In this catalogue of abuse, which culminated in Charles III's scheme to fund the monarchy's naval power from American revenue, Viscardo refrained from any explicit mention of Tupac Amaru, preferring to laud the 'Americans' of New Granada for their success in forcing the Crown to accept the capitulations of Zipaquirá. Indeed, he proffered the expulsion of the Jesuits as the most compelling proof of contemporary royal tyranny, since it constituted an arbitrary act of power which had violated their natural rights to liberty, property and security.[8]

When Viscardo defined the three centuries of colonial rule as a story of 'ingratitude, injustice, serfdom and devastation', he announced to the world that the American Spaniards now aspired to liberate themselves from the bondage of the past. There was apparently little that was positive in their history. Yet Viscardo unconsciously attested to the determining influence of that history when he reiterated the traditional plaints of creole patriots. That he defined the New World rather than Peru as his patria; that he addressed the creoles rather than all the inhabitants of Spanish America; that he reached back to Las Casas and Garcilaso for antecedent texts; and that he was silent about Tupac Amaru – all this indicated the peculiarly ambiguous character of his ideological enterprise. Unlike their Mexican counterparts, patriots in Peru had failed to create and propagate images and myths through which their patria could be celebrated. For Viscardo the history of his country obviously began with the conquest and not with the Incas. Was it because he was so rooted in the tradition of creole patriotism that he proved unable to assimilate the Enlightenment other than in the most superficial fashion? It was the American rather than the French Revolution which attracted his praise. Montesquieu rather than Rousseau was his mentor. Even so, it was not easy for him to reconcile the interests of a social elite with the universal rights of humanity. Indeed, the real impetus to his engagement in conspiracy and propaganda came from his indignation at the harsh measures of the enlightened despotism that characterised the regime of Charles III. At the same time, his readiness to oppose the Crown obviously stemmed from the collapse of the providential doctrine that had once defined the Catholic monarchy as the chief bulwark of the Church. If the Spanish king no longer enjoyed the mandate of heaven, then on what foundation did his authority in the New World rest? In effect, Viscardo's rejection of the Crown stemmed as much from the silent erosion of the political and cultural values once imparted by post-Tridentine Catholicism as from the direct influence of the Enlightenment.

II

In 1808 Napoleon Bonaparte compelled Charles IV and his recently proclaimed heir, Ferdinand VII, to relinquish their dynastic claim to the throne, and installed his own brother, Joseph, as king of Spain. Under the pretext of a joint invasion of Portugal, French troops had already entered the Peninsula and stood poised to enforce the coup by armed force. Several ministers and high officials welcomed the new king as affording an opportunity of implementing long cherished reforms. But any hopes of a peaceful change of dynasty were abruptly dispelled when peasants and townsmen joined in popular riot to attack the French and hunt down collaborators. Local officials and gentry, who might otherwise have favoured accommodation with the invaders, hastily enlisted in the insurrection and soon established juntas in all leading cities and provinces. In some districts the clergy preached a holy war of resistance. Soon after the coup a Central Junta was established at Aranjuez under the presidency of the aged Count of Floridablanca, the former chief minister of Charles III. But neither the regular army nor the militia raised by the local juntas proved any match for the French troops, who by 1810 occupied most cities in the Peninsula. The Central Junta fled to Seville, there to be abruptly dissolved and replaced by a Regency which then moved to Cadiz, a city impregnable by land and protected at sea by the British fleet.

The abdication of the Bourbon dynasty provoked a constitutional crisis which split the Spanish monarchy asunder. When news of the French invasion reached America, the creole elite re-affirmed its loyalty to Ferdinand VII. But when it became evident that Spain had fallen into anarchy, demands were soon raised for juntas to be established in each major province of the American empire. In 1810 creole juntas ousted the colonial authorities in Buenos Aires, Caracas, Bogotá and Santiago de Chile. Only Lima and Mexico City remained faithful to Spain, albeit more from fear of popular insurrection than from any love of the Spanish people. In effect, a refugee government, which depended on the British alliance for its safety, still sought to exercise authority over the American empire. It was to restore some semblance of legitimacy to government that in 1810 the Regency agreed to summon a general Cortes, to be attended by deputies from both Spain and America.

In the deliberations of the Central Junta, it had been Gaspar Melchor de Jovellanos, the former minister of justice, who had argued most forcefully that the only solution to the constitutional crisis was the convocation of a general Cortes. Confined for eight years in Mallorca at the order of Manuel de Godoy, the infamous chief minister of Charles IV, Jovellanos had rejected King Joseph's offer of a cabinet post, opting instead to serve on the Central Junta. To guide his country through the political shoals, he turned to historical precedent and British example. His own preliminary survey of medieval legislation had been deepened and amplified by his fellow Asturian and protégé, Francisco Martínez Marina (1754–1833), who in 1806 completed a celebrated 'critical-historical essay' designed to introduce a new edition of the Laws of Partida. Once more, the Visigoths were lauded for their 'temperate, monarchical government, mixed with aristocracy and democracy', in which the Crown's measures required the assent of the assembly of nobles and prelates. Above all, it was Alfonso the Wise, the thirteenth-century king of Castile, who had created the medieval constitution, summoning to the Cortes not merely the nobility and prelates but also the representatives of the cities.[9] Here, then, were the elements of an ancient constitution which Jovellanos hoped to restore. At the same time, in 1809–10, he corresponded with Lord Holland, a member of the Whig party and nephew of the former leader, Charles Henry Fox, who recommended him to read Blackstone's *Commentaries on the Laws of England* (1765–9), since there he would encounter 'a very wise way and not a French way of dealing with the questions of liberty and constitution'. In Holland's opinion what Spain required was 'the establishment of liberty without breaking the foundations of hierarchy', a proposition to which the Spanish statesman warmly assented. To judge from his arguments, Jovellanos had already read Edmund Burke's *Reflections on the French Revolution* where the Irishman had condemned the abstract principles and paper constitutions of the republican theorists, invoking by contrast historical prescription and practical experience of politics.[10] Certainly the influence of Montesquieu and Burke appear in Jovellanos' affirmation that: 'I greatly distrust political theories and especially the more abstract. I believe that each nation has its character; and that this is the result of its ancient institutions.' Rather than a new constitution, Jovellanos favoured cautious reform, fixing instead on the necessity of improving public education and ensuring 'the right to associate and to speak', which would dispel errors and promote improvements.[11] The appeal here was both to the prescriptive, determining influence of existing institutions and to the equally potent forces of education and freedom of speech. It was necessary first to change people and only then to change their laws and government: to do otherwise would be to impose a new form of government on a people whose character had been shaped by previous laws and which hence still required those laws. In effect, Jovellanos reiterated Montesquieu's principle that laws should reflect the character, climate and history of a people and hence should vary from country to country, the very opposite of Rousseau's conviction that governments through wise laws should strive to change and improve the character and morals of the people. Implicit here was the contrast beween the parliamentary, aristocratic constitution of Great Britain and the radical democracy of the French Revolution.

In 1810 the Central Junta was abruptly dissolved and replaced by a Regency, a confused, arbitrary seizure of power, which left Jovellanos exposed to persecution. Escaping to Asturias, elderly and infirm, he penned his last work, a long defence of his political beliefs. After noting that he had rejected impressive offers of high office from his several friends who had joined King Joseph, he affirmed that he had re-entered public life, animated solely by 'the burning love I profess for my country'. If he had campaigned for the convocation of a Cortes, it was because he wished 'to re-establish and improve our constitution, violated and destroyed by despotism and time'. For three hundred years Spain had been governed by 'foreign kings', who, starting with Charles V, had neglected to summon the full Cortes of three estates and had imposed 'a despotism over the nation'. To remedy such long-standing ills was not an easy task and precipitate measures were to be avoided. Indeed, Jovellanos denied that any newly assembled Cortes had the power to alter 'the essence of our ancient constitution': all that it could do was to moderate royal prerogative and assure 'the civil and political liberty of the citizen'. To attempt any more sweeping change would expose the country to the opposing but sequential dangers of democracy and despotism.[12] Not content with such negative proposals, Jovellanos then affirmed that it was essential to establish 'a mixed government', in which the respective independence of the executive, the judiciary and the legislature would be assured and the legislative assembly be divided into two chambers. In this respect, Great Britain and the United States were the grand exponents of 'political balance', a principle unknown in the ancient world, which allowed modern governments to incorporate the varying interests of monarchy, aristocracy and democracy within the same constitutional frame. Himself a nobleman, Jovellanos advocated that Spain should revive medieval practice and divide the Cortes into two houses, the first composed of the elected representatives of the people, and the second recruited exclusively from the nobility and upper clergy. Voting rights were to be based on 'qualities of property, rank, and education', thus preventing open democracy.[13]

To the young liberals who dominated the Cortes at Cadiz, Jovellanos' proposals smacked of antiquarian fantasy, one deputy observing that: 'Reason and not the examples taken from old folios should be the master of the Spaniards.' There was no desire to allow the clergy or the nobility any preferential voice in the national assembly. Still less was there any great admiration for Great Britain.[14] Why rummage through old law books or study English practice, when there existed a perfectly applicable model across the border? If Spanish dramatists and poets slavishly observed the neo-classical rules propounded by their French masters, why should not Spanish politicians appropriate the constitutional lessons of the Convention? Not that they were inclined to adopt Jacobin measures, since they were all too conscious of the conservative bias of Spanish society. But the result of their deliberations was none too impressive. The imposing declaration that 'sovereignty resides essentially in the nation' was accompanied by the affirmation that 'the power to execute laws resides exclusively in the king'. But the monarch was stripped of any right to veto or oppose the measures approved by a Cortes that consisted of a single popularly elected chamber. Equally problematic was the forthright assertion that 'the Spanish nation is the reunion of all the Spaniards of both hemispheres', a definition that expressly excluded anyone of African descent. For the rest, the text omitted any declaraion of the rights of man and pronounced that 'the religion of the Spanish nation is and shall be in perpetuity the Catholic, Apostolic and Roman, the only true religion'.[15]

In his letters to Lord Holland, Jovellanos lamented that the young deputies had been so influenced by their reading of Rousseau, Mably and Locke that they had fatally undermined the power of the Crown. He openly admitted that 'my desire was to prepare by means of our plan a constitution modelled on the

English and bettered in so far as it could be'. As it was, 'the ancient constitution' had been destroyed by the inopportune and unnecessary declaration of the sovereignty of the people. By this time, Jovellanos was ill and close to death.[16] But his forebodings were more than justified, since the constitution of 1812 proved unacceptable to a strong faction within the Spanish hierarchy who were soon to call upon Ferdinand VII to restore absolute monarchy. The realities of Spanish society were still averse to liberal projects. On the other hand, Jovellanos' advocacy of nobiliary rights aroused derision even among his disciples. Martínez Marina defined the hereditary nobility as 'a plague of the social order . . . an enemy of the people'. Nor did he imagine that old forms of government could be restored after an interregnum of three centuries; in undertaking historical research, he aspired merely to show that 'In these ruins and vestiges of the ancient political edifice, the nation can learn what it once was and what it ought to be.'[17] Another protégé later wrote that the Asturian statesman 'indulged a deep-seated jealousy to everything popular . . . to a most passionate attachment to the privileges of blood he joins a superstitious veneration for all kinds of external forms . . . He wished to restore the Cortes; but more like a piece of antiquity, in the full costume of the fifteenth century than as an effectual repository of power.'[18]

III

In the years 1810–14 there appeared in London a monthly review entitled *El Español*, edited by José María Blanco y Crespo, better known by his English name of Joseph Blanco White (1775–1841), a native of Seville, who had worked with Jovellanos in 1809, undertaking research into medieval precedents for the Cortes and helping Manuel Quintana edit the *Semanario Patriótico*. The professed aims of *El Español* were to assist the Cortes frame a moderate constitution and, more important, to effect a reconciliation between the insurgent juntas in America and Spain. The editor's motives were impeccable: 'I knew that the Spanish colonies had been cruelly wronged by the mother country, and ardently wished to see them legislating for themselves.' On both heads he advocated moderate liberal solutions, what in contemporary English parlance would have been defined as Whig measures. As he later asserted: 'I am neither what you call a Tory nor a bigot . . . A levelling spirit I detest . . . ' To this end he printed Jovellanos' last work on constitutional reform; delved into the medieval institutions of Aragon; recommended Jeremy Bentham on parliamentary practice; on the American question presented Moreno's memorial and the American deputies' representation at the Cortes; and accepted two long letters from the Mexican exile, Fray Servando Teresa de Mier.[19] Moreover, he offered a critical commentary on the course of the American rebellion baed on data procured from both insurgents and British sources. The only journal of its kind, the influence of *El Español* was immense since its articles were reprinted in the insurgent press, and echoes of its doctrines can be observed in the arguments of both Simón Bolívar and Fray Servando. If the review achieved such prominence it was, in part, because it was strongly backed by the Foreign Office which purchased 100 copies and encouraged British firms trading with Spanish America to take another 500 for distribution. Both the sympathy professed for the patriot cause and the reliance on English sponsorship provoked bitter resentment in Spain where the journal was soon banned, a deputy rising in the Cortes to declaim: 'I recognise in *El Español* an enemy of his country worse than Napoleon.'[20]

Closely advised by Lord Holland and his friend, John Allen, Blanco White openly boasted: 'In the midst of a nation so celebrated for its knowledge of politics, I have the fortune to listen to men who are among the most wise and experienced in this difficult science, which cannot be well learnt save by experience . . . The workship of liberty is open in England before the eyes of all the world.' Once an advocate of the sovereignty of the people, he now cited Bentham on parliamentary procedures and echoed Burke's emphasis on the primacy of practical experience over abstract theory. He roundly criticised the Jacobins for their metaphysical principles of liberty and equality, which had proved the means by which unscrupulous demagogues had gained power, only then to precipitate a descent into anarchy which could only be remedied by military despotism. The abstract universal liberty advocated by Rousseau was not to be confused with the freedom which derived from the laws of individual countries and the configuration of their respective societies. 'Political liberty is one thing in one country and another thing in another. That of Athens was a caprice, in Sparta slavery, and in Rome an open war.' Since the distribution and balance of property and morality differed from country to country, so equally should constitutions vary, their laws and government a reflection of the state of society. Absolute equality was a chimera: 'Civil society is like an association in which individuals have more or less shares or lots according to the wealth with which they enter.' Above all else, the rights and freedom of the individual depended on the prior existence of society and on the laws which its government enforced. With such principles to hand, Blanco White condemned the Cortes for its failure to consider a two-chamber legislature and its enunciation of the doctrine of popular sovereignty. In effect, the Cortes had produced a book, a document that demonstrated their command over political theory but which bore no relation to the political realities of Spanish society.[21] When Ferdinand VII brought the entire experiment to a close in 1814 by announcing a return to absolute monarchy, Blanco White found melancholy confirmation of his worst fears.

As regards America, Blanco White argued that the Cortes should recognise the authority of the insurgent juntas that had appeared in 1810. These bodies

30 Joseph Blanco White

had assumed power in the name of Ferdinand VII and had not broken relations with Spain. To avoid their opting for outright independence, a decision which would entail civil war and bloodshed, it was necessary for Spain to make concessions. All viceroys and governors should be removed, allowing the provinces to elect their own juntas. At the same time, it was necessary to invite delegates from these juntas to attend the Cortes so that the Americans would possess equal representation, a marked contrast to the current situation, where the 53 deputies from the New World faced 158 peninsular Spaniards. To complete these initial proposals, Blanco White further recommended that all commercial restrictions should be lifted, so that foreign shipping would henceforth enjoy free access to the ports of Spanish America.[22] Opposing all initiatives that favoured reconciliation Blanco White discerned two great parties. The first was 'the merchant party of Cadiz', whose livelihood depended on the preservation of Spain's monopoly of trade with the American empire. With the Cortes assembled in their city, these men succeeded in influencing many deputies, the more especially since they were assisted by their fellow merchants in Mexico, who still commanded ample funds to finance their campaign. Equally important, the dominant liberal faction were notably reluctant to apply their principles to America, fearful that any concession might diminish their country's power. Blanco White later described these deputies as 'the Spanish patriotic party, French in their notions, Castilians of the old stamp in their politics, they both cherished a violent jealousy of England, and regarded the American colonies as their property'.[23] Whereas the disciple of Burke advocated reconciliation, the followers of Rousseau aspired to preserve the imperial unity of their monarchy.

If the debate over free trade followed predictable lines of economic interest, the controversy over voting rights opened old wounds anew. At first the peninsular deputies proposed to restrict the franchise in the New World to the American Spaniards, thus depriving the overwhelming majority of the population of any participation in politics. After vehement debate it was agreed that Indians should have the vote, since they had always counted as free subjects of the Crown. But the Cortes then limited the number of seats available for the New World, so that the American constituencies should have a greater number of inhabitants than their equivalents, thus ensuring that deputies from the Peninsula would control the assembly. The measure which most aroused the creole indignation, however, was the exclusion of all persons of African or part African descent from the electoral list, the stigma of slavery thus reckoned irrevocable. It was to assist the American delegates in their protests against this invidious law that Blanco White printed a long dissertation on the intellectual faculties of the blacks, written by William Wilberforce, the prime author of the abolition of the slave trade in the British empire.[24] In effect, the disenfranchisement of all blacks and mulattos entailed the perpetuation of the colonial hierarchy of castes, since registers would have to be maintained for voting purposes.

Initially, Blanco White praised the Caracas junta for their moderation, observing: 'if we had seen that revolution beginning by the proclamation of exaggerated principles of liberty, and impracticable theories of equality like the French Revolution, we would have distrusted the upright intentions of its promoters and would have believed the movement to be the effect of a party'. Subsequently, he sharply criticised the declaration of Venezuelan independence issued in 1811. When the junta then proceeded to frame a federalist constitution, based on the precedent of the United States, adding the French declaration of the rights of man, he condemned their measures as precipitate and ill-advised, exposing their country to 'the stormy gulf of democracy'. The contrast beween high-flown sentiment and social reality was striking, since the Indians and castas lacked both property and education, the essential prerequisites of the true citizen.[25] When this so-called 'fools' republic' was overturned by popular royalist reaction, he commented on the absurdity of adopting a federal system which weakened the central government and noted that, despite their liberal principles, the insurgents had persecuted their opponents. Blanco White's worst fears were realised in New Spain where, after presenting a long account of the insurgency led by Miguel Hidalgo, he declared that this was 'an internecine revolution in which sons struggle against their fathers, people of colour against the whites, and the poor and deprived against the powerful'. It was the threat of anarchy and destruction of property that now bound the creoles to the Crown: the only lasting solution was to establish a representative junta and thus encourage those elements within colonial society who genuinely wished to preserve the union with Spain.[26] But, as the years passed, Blanco White's enthusiasm for the American cause waned, since he came to conclude that: 'All clamour for liberty: but the echo of this voice in their hearts is power, riches and command.' His acquaintance with the American Spaniards in London and elsewhere led him to judge that they were 'naturally quick and intelligent; but they generally want moral principles and steadiness of character ... the characteristic fault among all classes is an habitual disregard of moral obligation'.[27]

At first sight, Blanco White's intervention in the world of independence politics appears like an aberration, the accidental result of his exile in London. For the main course of his life was dominated by a quest for religious certitude which drove him to exchange a comfortable canonry in the cathedral at Seville for a bare subsistence in England. Born a Spaniard, albeit of part Irish ancestry, ordained a Catholic priest, he progressively renounced his vocation, his faith and his nationality. In later years he wrote bitterly: 'I never felt proud of being a Spaniard, for it is as a Spaniard that I found myself mentally degraded, doomed to bow before the nearest priest and layman, who might consign me any day to the prisons of the Inquisition.' Once a Jansenist and then a Jacobin, in England he became a Whig and an Anglican, graduating from the worldly glitter of Holland House to the clerical seclusion of Oriel College at Oxford. Befriended by the Anglican archbishop of Dublin, who made him his chaplain, he once more renounced his Christian faith, ending his days as a Unitarian in Liverpool. Despite his long sojourn in England, he never felt at home, since the climate gave him colds, the stiff formality of English manners dampened his spirits, and the general aversion to argument irritated his restless intellect. Yet he found it painful to write in Spanish, since 'I feel on similar occasions puzzled as to my own identity and have to awake as it were from a melancholy dream and assure myself that I am not again in the country of my love and aversion . . . '[28]

Viewed from the vantage point of the late nineteenth century, it can be seen that Blanco White's tormented quest expressed in extreme form the religious doubts of many hispanic intellectuals of his epoch. Behind the problems of government and constitution there lurked a crisis of religious faith and national identity. In his *Letters from Spain* (1820), Blanco White freely confessed that he had been tempted to welcome Joseph Bonaparte, to whom 'many of the most enlightened and honest Spaniards had attached themselves'. For the French king abolished the Inquisition, banned the excesses of popular religion, and suppressed the religious orders, sequestrating their property. By contrast, the patriot cause drew strength from the clergy's preaching, since an English visitor noted that 'the priests headed by a bishop and several dignitaries of the Church have established a sort of crusade in Extremadura against the French. The initiated wear a cross upon their breasts, like those worn in the Holy Wars and against the infidels.' Blanco White confessed that 'he can see no prospect of liberty behind the cloud of priests who everywhere stand foremost to take the lead of our patriots'.[29] The fissure which opened between the guerilla bands who fought for Spain's independence and the young liberals who debated constitutional issues at Cadiz was not easily bridged.

Above all else, Blanco White detested the religious culture of post-Tridentine Catholicism which, despite the inroads of Enlightenment and Jansenism, still dominated Spanish society. It was the practice of confession, public flagellation in religious processions, popular veneration of images, the overly enthusiastic preaching of the mendicants, the futile disputations of scholasticism, the tedium of systematic meditation, the barbarous confinement of nuns and the celibacy of the clergy – in short, almost the entire configuration of religious practice in Spain – which attracted his condemnation. Spain was a decadent society, still feebly living off the exhausted capital of former ages, which, until it liberated itself from the Church's influence, would never produce any great men again. At one time tempted into atheism, Blanco White ended his days a deist. In his last desolate years in Liverpool, he became persuaded that organised religion in all its multitude of forms and creeds constituted the chief obstacle to mankind's search for truth, effectively blocking all true access to the Deity. For religion relied on authority and imagination, whereas man had to be guided by his reason. 'I consider the Imaginative Faculty – that faculty which clothes every idea in matter – the arch-enemy of those truly spiritual enjoyments. Cleanse the internal sanctuary from idols, if the Deity is to take up his seat within it.' Towards the close of his life, he learnt German and read Fichte and other philosophers, echoing their vocabulary when he declared that 'Reason alone, as Ideality, penetrates the region of Infinitude and leads to what is Necessary and Universal.'[30]

In the light of such principles, it should come as no surprise to find that, although Blanco White actively promoted the diffusion of romanticism in the hispanic world, he failed to comprehend its true significance. In *Variedades o Mensajero de Londres* (1823–5), an illustrated journal he edited for Rudolph Ackerman, he offered translations of Shakespeare and Sir Walter Scott, reviewed books on Islamic Spain, and commended Cervantes and El Cid. But despite this enlargement of perspective, he insisted that the ancient Greeks and Romans had discovered the universal and invariable canons of natural beauty and literary style. Not that he was impressed by contemporary neo-classic verse in Spanish, since it imitated the French school and entirely lacked the depth of English poetry. Elsewhere, he marvelled that the leading Spanish dramatist and poet, Francisco Martínez de la Rosa, still defended the Aristotelian unities of theatrical composition, citing the works of Corneille as a model for the nineteenth century. But, although Blanco White expressed his admiration for Sir Walter Scott's romances, he condemned the poor taste of Elizabethan dramatists, objecting to their redundant verbiage and their commonplace, vulgar opinions. He did not question the excellence of Shakespeare, but suggested that it was better to read his works in private rather than attend the theatre, an institution best left to the populace.[32] In short, he failed to comprehend the romantics' exaltation of Imagination as mankind's most creative faculty and faithfully echoed the neo-classic principles which in his youth had served to liberate Spain of the fading shreds of Churrigueresque extravagance.

Towards the close of his life, Blanco White wrote a parable, obviously personal in application, of a young priest who was granted a vision of Truth, in which he was warned that, whereas most men neglect or cover their mirror of truth, he was destined so to polish his own mirror that it would appear to be black, causing other men to drive him forth as an outcast. 'To be a liberal in Spain', wrote the essayist, Mariano José de Larra, 'is to be a potential emigrant.'[33] In effect, Blanco White was but the forerunner of an intellectual diaspora, suffering in radical mode the common fate, be it of internal alienation or public exile. Was it for this reason that Marcelino Menéndez Pelayo employed all the rhetorical resources of his minatory prose to paint such a searing portrait of the man? For the great critic concluded his history of Spanish heterodoxy with a passionate defence of his country's Catholic foundation: 'Spain, evangelist of half the world; Spain, hammer of heretics, light of Trent, sword of Rome, cradle of St Ignatius: – that is our greatness and unity; we do not have any other.' But that was precisely the Spain that Blanco White had rejected.[34] As much as James Joyce in Dublin, he chose to declare that: 'I will not serve', repudiating the allegiance of both Church and country. Unlike the Irish artist, however, the long, often silent years of his exile brought forth no great work to justify his sacrifice. Instead, he stripped himself of all the consolations provided by organised religion, reaching the point where even verbal prayer appeared as a barrier to his pursuit of truth. Yet, to the end of his days he remained persuaded that God dwelt in his soul, communicating to him through the oracle of conscience. He died convinced that 'my whole existence, with its helplessness, its misery, its anguish, its aspiration, is a Prayer'. When his former friend, John Henry Newman, read his posthumously published journals and autobiography, he was appalled by the spiritual desolation of the last years and concluded that it was the price paid for excessive reliance on the powers of individual reason.[35] But, when he himself came to abandon the Anglican Church, albeit in favour of Catholicism, thereby exiling himself from the exuberant mainstream of Victorian England, was he not also influenced by Blanco White's renunciation of all worldly attachments?

IV

In the bustling port of Buenos Aires, since 1776 the capital of the viceroyalty of La Plata, a vast area which embraced the territories of modern Argentina, Uruguay, Paraguay and Bolivia, it was economic interest rather than metaphysical anguish that drove men to seek independence. For Spain's alliance with France, enforced after its defeat in the war of 1793–5, had provoked a British naval blockade which succeeded in destroying the commercial links between America and the Spanish ports. The export of hides from the River Plate suffered accordingly. Moreover, in 1806 two successive British expeditions arrived, commissioned to occupy the ports of Buenos Aires and Montevideo, thereby establishing bases for colonial rule. At this juncture the viceroy fled to the interior, so that the task of surrounding and defeating the invaders was assumed by the local militia led by creole landowners. Although Ferdinand VII was subsequently acclaimed king, doubts about sovereignty and the rights of colonial officials to continue to exercise power soon appeared. Even the most conservative constitutional texts had allowed that if a dynasty abdicated, then sovereignty returned to the people, its original source. It was to quell creole demands for the establishment of a local junta that the wealthy Peninsula traders who dominated the city council and the merchant guild projected a coup, only to suffer discovery and imprisonment. In May 1810 an open city council meeting, attended by 251 individuals, rehearsed and accepted the arguments concerning the reversion of sovereignty to the people, once legitimate government had lapsed. The current viceroy was deposed and replaced by a patriotic junta, the militia's armed force constituting the chief intrument of the creole seizure of power. Independence, however, was not proclaimed, since the junta ostensibly governed the River Plate in the name of Ferdinand VII.[36] Perhaps the most remarkable feature of these proceedings was the junta's assumption of authority over all the vast territories of the viceroyalty. Expeditionary forces were despatched to the interior to demand obedience, any opposition at once condemned as treason.

The economic interests which fired creole grievances were given eloquent expression by Mariano Moreno (1779–1811), secretary of the first junta. In a memorial addressed to the Central Junta in 1809, he called for the River Plate to be opened to foreign shipping, thereby destroying Spain's commercial monopoly. He roundly denounced the peninsular merchants of Cadiz and Buenos Aires for seeking to maintain their monopoly, ready to sacrifice local interests in pursuit of personal gain. Moreover, the British naval blockades of 1796–1802 and 1804–8 had already destroyed a great part of Spanish shipping, so that in fact the country relied on smuggled imports, usually of British manufacture. Even so, the landowners, 'the most useful, the most noble and the most distinguished part of society' had greatly suffered from the interruption of trade, their hides mouldering in massive lots at the port, with contraband offering only a measure of relief. The true wealth of the province was to be found in the countryside, but how was its progress and prosperity to be assured if Spain retained its monopoly? The Central Junta had recently declared that the American provinces were not colonies but constituted an integral part of the monarchy.[37] If this was the case, then why were American ports denied the access to foreign shipping which all the leading ports in the Peninsula possessed?

Sufficiently impressed, when a student at Chuquisaca, by Viscardo's *Carta* as to take a personal copy, Moreno later graduated to more radical texts. Once in power at Buenos Aires, he arranged for the publication of Rousseau's *Social Contract*, inserting a laudatory preface in which he saluted the Genevan philosopher for dispelling the clouds of despotism through his lucid exposition of the 'rights of peoples' and his tracing the origin of political obligation to 'the social pact'. The text was printed in order to educate the Porteño public of their rights and duties as citizens. Despite his enthusiasm, however, Moreno suppressed those passages where Rousseau had 'the misfortune to wax delirious in religious matters', proof enough, this decision, that the hispanic world was not yet ready for any frontal assault on the truths of revealed religion. The appearance of this celebrated work, the fountainhead of political radicalism, exposed Moreno to the charge of being a Jacobin, intent on challenging the acknowledged hierarchy of society. After his death, his brother defended his reputation, affirming that 'Dr Moreno was far from accepting the principles of a democratic liberty that abhors distinctions, rank, and all that is not perfect equality between citizens.' There is little reason to dispute this statement.[38] Although the creole elite often borrowed the language of the

French Revolution, they had no intention of allowing their social position to be destroyed by mob rule. Had not the application of revolutionary principles in Saint Domingue precipitated slave rebellion, race warfare, and the massacre of the planters?

V

In Peru creole reactions to the Spanish monarchy's political crisis were ambiguous, indecisive and often contradictory, the customary resentment against Europeans in government tempered by fears of insurrection and social dissolution. If Viceroy José Fernando de Abascal (1806–16) moved swiftly to convert Lima into the chief bastion of royal power in South America, eventually despatching military expeditions to suppress the patriotic juntas that had seized power in La Paz, Quito and Santiago de Chile, it was in large measure because he relied on the tacit support of the creole elite. In 1809 the Limeño jurist, Manuel Lorenzo Vidaurre (1773–1841) compared the Spanish resistance to the French invasion with Israel's struggle against the Philistines and organised a public subscription to assist this holy cause, services which won him appointment as judge in the high court at Cuzco. Although he was soon to condemn the current oppression of the Indian peasantry, claiming that the new breed of district magistrates, the subdelegates, were if anything more oppressive than the former corregidores, he welcomed the 1812 Constitution as offering the best opportunity for satisfying the creoles' hunger for self-government. Any overt movement for independence, so he feared, would lead to civil war and destruction of lives and property. In any case, did not the history of ancient Rome and the experience of contemporary France demonstrate that monarchy was the best form of government, animated, as Montesquieu had adverted, by the spirit of honour? By contrast, most republics had fallen prey to faction and disorder, the results of untrammelled self-interest and avarice, each man esteeming himself equally apt for high office. How could a country like Peru, with such a diversity of peoples, thrive under republican rule? Why should Cuzco and Arequipa accept Lima as their capital? To such doubts Vidaurre united a typically Limeño affirmation of his hispanic identity, bluntly stating: 'In the European Spaniard, I see myself ... We American Spaniards are not the conquered, we are the conquerors, equal in everything to the persons who gave us our being.' What was required was an equality in appointments for European and American Spaniards.[39]

In moments of crisis, however, loyalist creoles were apt to arouse the suspicions of the peninsular Spaniards who dominated colonial government. Indeed, any prominence gained in the defence of royal authority was likely to expose them to subsequent persecution. The creole commanders who had led the forces which suppressed the Tupac Amaru rebellion did not obtain the promotion and reward they expected. More extraordinary was the fate of Bishop Juan Manuel Moscoso y Peralta, whose successful defence of Cuzco failed to quell rumours that he had been an accomplice of Tupac Amaru. The new intendant, come fresh from Spain, accused him of being the head of a creole 'party' and warned Gálvez that since Peru was still 'an ecclesiastical monarchy' the continued presence of Moscoso in Cuzco posed a threat to Spanish rule. Exiled to Madrid, the indignant prelate complained that whereas the archbishop of Bogotá, Antonio Caballero y Góngora, had bee made viceroy of New Granada for having negotiated a peace treaty with the rebels of Socorro, his own strenuous efforts to combat the Tupac Amaru revolt had been rewarded by persecution and removal from his country. In the event, Moscoso was exonerated from all charges and honoured by his appointment as archbishop of Granada.[40]

At no point was creole loyalism more decisive than in 1811 when Upper Peru was occupied by forces from Buenos Aires. It was Brigadier Juan Manuel de Goyeneche y Barreda (1776–1846), a native of Arequipa then acting as interim governor of Cuzco, who rallied the creole elite of the two cities to officer the army he had raised to repel the invaders. Thanks to his military formation in Spain, Goyeneche succeeded both in training his forces and in defeating the Argentines, thus restoring Upper Peru to royalist dominion. His achievements soon aroused the suspicions of viceroy Abascal who complained that his army was led by creoles and that his status as 'a native son' had placed him beyond the reach of viceregal authority. When Goyeneche resigned his command in 1813 he complained bitterly of Abascal's slander, noting that it had been largely thanks to his personal and family influence that so many wealthy young creoles had enlisted in the army, enduring considerable hardships to lead forces whose loyalty was often in doubt. For the rest, he observed that unless Buenos Aires could be re-conquered there was little hope of retaining Peru for the Crown, since the peoples of America had lost their traditional acceptance of 'the sanctity of our laws and the beneficence of Spanish government', so that 'fear was the only brake' on what was well-nigh a universal desire for independence.[41]

That some creoles in Cuzco still toyed with the idea of an Inca restoration was demonstrated by the 'spiritual conspiracy' organised in 1805 by José Manuel Ubalde, an impoverished lawyer then acting as legal advisor to the intendant, and Gabriel Aguilar, an intriguing miner. Denizens of the lower strata of creole society, they inhabited a world in which Catholic piety, patriotic fervour and personal ambition were fuelled by visions and dreams. For Aguilar obtained Ubalde's support for proclaiming him Inca emperor of Peru by informing him of a childhood vision in which he had been assured of a great role in his country's history. Both men agreed that Spanish rule was oppressive and that St Thomas Aquinas had recognised the right to rebel against tyranny. When they conferred with like-minded priests, one cleric cited the prediction of Raynal, the 1771 representation of the Mexico City Council, and the example of the 'Americans of Boston'. But the current of religious emotion that underlay these arguments surfaced when another cleric fell into an ecstasy in Aguilar's presence, and claimed later to have seen the pretender crowned in the cathedral of Cuzco. After their arrest, Ubalde was reminded of the traditional doctrine that, since the Catholic king was God's image on earth, any challenge to his authority was an attack on God. By way of reply, he insisted on the right of rebellion against tyranny and argued that natural law did not prescribe loyalty to any particular dynasty. After all, the Papacy had just recognised Napoleon as emperor of the French, despite the claims of the Bourbon dynasty to that throne. He went to his execution convinced that Aguilar had been chosen by providence as a creole Maccabee, called to liberate Peru from Spanish rule.[42]

It was the promulgation of the 1812 Constitution that provided the Cuzqueño elite with the opportunity to assert their right to participate in government. A group of lawyers at once hailed its text as 'the living voice of the people in their re-assumed sovereignty'. Indeed, the newly elected city council called for copies to be widely distributed so as to halt 'the arbitrary despotism which has suffocated and suppressed the unalienable rights of man and the citizen'. After a series of quarrels between Spanish bureaucrats and creole councillors, in 1814 the provincial deputation, the city council and the cathedral chapter, all three bodies dominated by creoles, united to elect a three-man ruling junta and appointed José Angulo, a mestizo landowner, as 'captain-general of the national armies and political governor of this city'. Mateo Pumacahua, the cacique of Chinchoro, whose resistance to Tupac Amaru had won him the rank of brigadier, agreed to serve on the junta and mobilised his Indian followers in support of the rebellion. Expeditions were despatched to La Paz, Arequipa and Huamanga, their capture testimony to the strength and popularity of a movement that for a few months dominated the central highlands. However, neither Angulo nor Pumacahua possessed the qualities necessary to lead an insurrection and their forces disintegrated before the advance of a column of 1,200 trained soldiers loyal to the Crown. By 1815 the rebellion had been crushed and its leaders executed.[43]

Although the authorities in Cuzco proclaimed their loyalty to Ferdinand VII and insisted they wished merely to implement the 1812 Constitution, they also strongly condemned the 'atrocious despotism' of the governors sent from Spain during the last 300 years. In a letter to Abascal, the city council defined Spain as an 'oppressive stepmother patria' and asserted that crimes such as the murder of Ubalde and Aguilar had been unknown 'in the natural state of the Incas'. They complained that the Jesuit college and church 'once a house of prayer, and virtue, and a centre of wisdom', had been converted into a barracks for

Spanish soldiers, one of whom had sacrilegiously stabbed an image of the crucified Christ. Oddly enough, it was a European prebend of the cathedral, Francisco Carrescon, who most clearly advocated separation from Spain, when in a sermon he insisted that the Americas were not 'conquered colonies' but rather countries which possessed as much right as Spain to rebel and fight for their freedom. In an echo of Raynal, he surmised that Nature herself had divided the world into provinces and kingdoms, separated by the oceans. Looking to the future, he hailed Cuzco as 'the centre of all this vast Peruvian empire' and advocated the creation of a state that would span the continent, with Cuzco as its capital and Buenos Aires and Lima in a satellite role. On blessing the national flags, he saluted Angulo as 'our Peruvian Maccabee'. That such hyperbole did not pass unheeded was demonstrated by a letter that Angulo wrote to the aged bishop of Cuzco in which he claimed that Providence had called him to effect the liberation of Peru from Spanish tyranny, adding 'for this great work the King of Peoples chose me as his instrument'.[44]

No aspect of the 1814 rebellion more alarmed royal officials than the involvement of the clergy. In a subsequent report, Manuel Pardo, regent of the high court at Cuzco, asserted that Angulo had been 'surrounded by friars and priests who were his chief counsellors'. He urged that the creole bishop of Cuzco, once the faithful disciple of Moscoso and now aged 87, should be removed from his see on charges of complicity. After noting that, whereas in Spain the clergy supported the Crown by leading the resistance to the French, in America they sought to stir the populace against Spanish rule, he declared that on both sides of the Atlantic their aim was 'to leave religion with the clothing of the exterior cult, sufficient to enable their ministry to obtain from an ignorant people all the profit that their avarice suggests'. But if the monarchy could no longer rely on the clergy to preach loyalty to the Catholic king, on what basis could Spanish rule be maintained in the New World? The problem was all the more pressing since Pardo conceded that anyone who lived in Peru soon became aware of 'the hatred that most creole Spaniards nurse in their hearts against the Europeans and their government'. About the only course of action that this senior colonial judge could recommend was that no creole should be promoted to high office in Church or State whose loyalty was not clearly manifest. For the rest, all militia forces should be disbanded and a strong garrison of European soldiers be stationed permanently in Peru.[45] If the monarchy could no longer depend on the loyalty of its subjects, it had to be ready to quell opposition by armed might.

It was Vidaurre who emphasised the contradictions in royal policy in these last years of imperial rule. Removed from his post as judge in Cuzco under suspicion of complicity in the 1814 revolt, he did not hesitate to present the Crown with memorials, both in Lima and Madrid, in which he openly questioned the reliance on military force. America had been held and could only be held by the exertions of the American Spaniards: Spain lacked the means to garrison a hemisphere. When the bishop-elect of Michoacán, Manuel Abad y Queipo, publicly advocated the despatch of an army of 20,000 men to America and the exclusion of creoles from high office, Vidaurre protested that such measures entailed outright tyranny, and insisted that 'the monarchy depends on a tacit or manifest pact with the individuals that compose it'. Rather than ordering troops to the New World, it would be wiser to send a prince of the royal family, invested with the authority to negotiate a peace treaty with the 'rebels' in Buenos Aires. As a magistrate who had served the Crown over a number of years, Vidaurre assumed the right to remind his European compatriots that 'the glory of a monarch is to rule free souls . . . Spain is not Constantinople'.[46]

The failure of the 1814 rebellion, when taken with the arrival of a strong expeditionary force from Spain, meant that Peru was destined to have its independence imposed by foreign invasion, with José de San Martín and Simón Bolívar competing to liberate the last stronghold of Spanish rule in South America. It was at this juncture that Vidaurre finally quit royal service and in 1823 returned to Peru, there to abjure in his *Plan de Perú* (1823) his former enthusiasm for monarchy. All his hopes for effecting a reconciliation between Spain and America had foundered, so he averred, on the very character of the Spaniards, the essence of which was 'pride, cruelty and avarice'. He presented himself to the Peruvian public as another Las Casas, a witness to the tyranny of Spanish rule, his own career testimony of the persecution endured by creole patriots. However, his quarrel with the monarchial projects of San Martín and his open advocacy of Simón Bolívar's republican dictatorship, soon exposed him to the acrimony of party politics. That he should have urged the necessity of an agrarian law, designed to quit the religious orders of their lands and to break up the great estates, only served yet further to alarm the Limeño élite. Not that Vidaurre was a radical, since he commended the constitution of the United States as the best model for Peru, arguing that it was 'the quintessence or perfection of the British government' and hence the very opposite of the French republic which had fallen prey to a band of savages.[47]

By far the most extraordinary feature of the *Plan de Perú* was its strident attack on Christianity. Careful to mask his own opinions by citing them as the views of a French friend, Vidaurre presented the standard Enlightenment critique of the Catholic Church, openly comparing it to Islam. The Old Testament was but an instrument of moral corruption, the Pope a despot, the Council of Trent's resolutions contrary to human nature, and the reliance on miracles and martyrs the common property of all false religions. More close to home, the great priories of Lima were described as 'asylums of sloth and schools of superstition' which merited immediate suppression. In the university, Aristotle should be replaced by Newton and the chairs of Theology,

Scripture, Canon and Roman Law suppressed. Anxious to claim that he was still a Roman Catholic, Vidaurre argued that what was required in Christian teaching was 'much humanity and few mysteries'.[48] In effect, Vidaurre here attested that Blanco White was by no means the only Spaniard of this epoch to reject the religious culture of Tridentine Catholicism. The crisis of political legitimacy in America was intimately bound to the erosion of faith in the traditional authority of the Catholic Church. Independence was but a prelude to the destruction of the entire Baroque culture on which the Catholic monarchy had based its power and prestige.

VI

As far as can be ascertained, the first European to call for the outright independence of Spanish America was Dominique de Pradt (1759–1837), a French cleric, whose opposition to the Revolution had not prevented him from subsequently serving Napoleon from whom he obtained appointment as archbishop of Malines. In *Les Trois âges des colonies* (1801–2), a work published in Paris, he boldly affirmed that the emancipation of all America was inevitable and would constitute an epoch as memorable in world history as the era of discovery. The man who could resolve the colonial problem would win a fame greater than that enjoyed by Columbus. A disciple of Raynal and Montesquieu, Pradt exhibited all the customary Enlightenment disdain for Spain, whose empire in America he compared to the dominions of the Ottoman Turks, since it more stifled than encouraged economic growth. 'Spain, it is true, like an immense tree, covers a vast extent of ground with her branches, but their shade smothers the fruits which they ought to protect or defend.' Indeed, despite its physical magnitude, the Spanish monarchy did not figure significantly in the political concert of Europe and in the economic sphere acted as a mere entrepôt, through which flowed the commerce of other nations, its agents simply exacting a commission on all transactions.[49] The independence of the United States, the revolutionary convulsions in Europe, and the general ferment of ideas, all presaged the imminent dissolution of its empire in the New World.

A student of Adam Smith, whom he implausibly defined as 'the Rousseau of political economy', Pradt attributed the growth of European prosperity since the sixteenth century to the profits of colonial trade. Marvelling at the rapid increase in the production of tropical crops on Saint Domingue, which 'in fifty years climbed to the first rank in all the European establishments in both worlds', he concluded that: 'The colonies exist but to produce and produce but to afford the means of consumption: this is their nature and purpose.' The entire rationale of the overseas possessions of the European powers was thus to export primary produce and take in the manufactured good of the metropolis. Pursuing his argument to its logical conclusion, Pradt asserted that: 'Riches are, at present, the basis of power, and since colonies are without doubt the most abundant source of riches they are consequently also the source of power.' To these essentially mercantilist considerations, which were supported by an array of commercial statistics, Pradt added a biological metaphor. Colonies were also the children of 'the mother country' and were impelled by a process of growth which would inevitably culminate in maturity and hence result in independence. 'In colonial language, age is not simply the measure of time and duration, but also of force and virility ... Independence is innate in the colonies, as the separation of families is in human nature, the first principle of their independence.'[50] The attraction of this homely metaphor was that it offered no ideological hostages to fortune: what need was there to discuss abstruse questions of sovereignty when the simple facts of family relations could be invoked to justify separation from the parent country?

Despite his admiration for Raynal, Pradt argued that it was essential for colonies to preserve slavery, since he attributed the fall of Saint Domingue to the sudden freeing of the enslaved work-force of its plantations. It followed that any general declaration of human equality would inevitably provoke emancipation and expose the colonies and Europe itself to ruin. In effect, Pradt here warned the Spanish Americans that independence should not be confused with revolution, since any public proclamation of the doctrines of liberty and equality would open the door to the destruction of property and anarchy. Peering into his crystal ball, Pradt predicted the probable emergence of at least fourteen new states in the Americas. He prophesied that Mexico would become a great empire in its own right, by reason of its mineral wealth and its geographical position straddling the commerce of Asia and Europe. As for South America, he saw any number of states about to be born, destined to grow in prosperity, once all barriers to free trade with Europe were removed. Their best hope for political stability, so Pradt argued, was for them to accept European princes as their monarchs.[51]

In the second, revised edition of his work entitled *Des colonies, et de la révolution actuelle de l'Amerique* (1817), published in French, Spanish and English, Pradt advocated the creation of three large empires in Spanish America and called upon the reactionary Holy Alliance powers in Europe to intervene to protect the twin causes of Catholicism and monarchy. Equally important, he enlarged his discussion of the imperial role of Great Britain. Already, he had contrasted the territorial ambitions of France in Europe to the British concentration on shipping and overseas expansion, a contrast which had brought prosperity to the island power. He now argued that by reason of her overwhelming strength in manufactures and shipping, Britain had no cause to seek military or political dominion in Spanish America since its hegemony was assured by its economic preponderence. 'England is the sole colonial power ... The nation which enjoys a superiority in navigation, industry and capital, is the owner of all colonies. That nation has no need to take them into possession, but only to trade with them.' At the same time, Pradt drew attention to the territorial encroachments of Great Britain, alluding to 'the immense chain of trading posts which she has drawn round the globe, to subject it to her dominion and commerce, two things she never separates'.[52]

In the later phases of the Spanish American revolution, the influence of Pradt was unmistakable. Already, in his Jamaica letter of 1815, Simón Bolívar accepted Pradt's definition of the function of colonies and welcomed his prediction that fourteen or more states would emerge from the destruction of Spain's empire. Indeed, after Colombia was finally liberated, he offered the French abbé a pension and invited him to come to the New World so as to 'become our legislator and wise man'. In return, Pradt lauded Bolívar as the Washington, if not the Napoleon, of South America, and warmly defended him from charges of tyranny. So too, in Mexico Servando de Mier paid great heed to his work, echoing his thesis about the inevitability of independence, but warmly attacking both his description of Mexico as a mere colony and his advocacy of monarchy.[53] Throughout Spanish America Pradt's magnification of Britain's global hegemony awoke fears about the possible expansion of that power in the New World.

25

LIBERALS AND PATRIOTS

I

IN NEW SPAIN the first reaction of both officials and the creole nobility to news of the French invasion of the Peninsula was to denounce the imposition of Joseph Bonaparte and warmly acclaim Ferdinand VII as king. But, when agents arrived from the juntas of Seville and Asturias, each demanding recognition of their authority over New Spain, the viceroy, José de Iturrigaray (1803–8), responded that 'Spain is in anarchy, all are supreme juntas and thus there is not one that should be obeyed.' But if the metropolis lacked a government, then on whose behalf did the viceroy govern New Spain? Questions of sovereignty and legitimacy, hitherto confined to legal textbooks, suddenly acquired immediate practical application. It was to resolve the constitutional crisis that Iturrigaray convoked a series of meetings attended by most high officials and some members of the nobility. The Mexico City Council, a creole bastion, invoked the standard natural law doctrines of Pufendorf and Heineccius, as propounded by their Spanish disciple, Joaquín Marín Mendoza, to affirm that the Crown's authority was based on a primordial pact in which the people irrevocably ceded the exercise of sovereignty to the king and his heirs. But with the abdication of the Bourbon monarchs, sovereignty now returned to the people, which was to say, to the city councils which represented the people. In any case, the *Siete Partidas*, the thirteenth-century law code which still governed constitutional matters, provided that, during the minority or absence of a king, a regent should be appointed and a Cortes summoned to advise him. In effect, the viceroy, the high court of justice, the intendants, and the treasury officials no longer possessed legitimate power: hence, 'to fill the immense gap which now exists between the authorities which govern and the sovereign power', it was imperative to convoke a general junta, representative of the city councils, so as to re-validate the legal bases of power.[1] The premiss on which these arguments rested, was that New Spain constituted a true kingdom, endowed with the right to determine its political destiny.

Confronted with such an unprecedented challenge to the colonial system, the

Spanish judges who dominated the high court simply reiterated the traditional thesis that New Spain was an overseas province of the Crown of Castile and hence demanded that Mexico should submit to the dictates of the junta at Seville. When it became clear that the viceroy inclined to the creole side of the argument, these judges conspired with the archbishop and the merchant guild, the bulwark of peninsular dominion, to stage a *coup d'état*. The apprentice traders of the capital, immigrants from Spain, were mobilised to invade the palace and seize Iturrigaray, replacing him as viceroy by an aged, impecunious military man. The lawyers who had prepared the city council's brief were imprisoned. To justify their actions, the conspirators issued a proclamation in which they stated that 'Necessity is not subject to ordinary law. The people have taken power of the person of his Excellency the Viceroy and imperiously demand his resignation for reasons of utility and general convenience.' But which people, and whose necessity or convenience? Such questions found no answer in this resort to arbitrary violence.[2]

In the two years which followed, New Spain experienced an uneasy peace, the European Spaniards jubilant but apprehensive, the American Spaniards embittered but expectant. For creoles they were years filled with rumour, conspiracy, and mounting confidence. The Marquis of Rayas, a friend of Iturrigaray, wrote that in recent events he perceived: 'the finger of God, whose providence and mercy works in favour of a nation He loves, for the very fact that it is the most Catholic and religious'.[3] For his part, the archbishop of Mexico, Francisco de Lizana y Beaumont (1802–11), who briefly figured as viceroy, warned that 'the present government of this colony' depended on the appointment of Europeans to high office in Church and State, 'excluding or postponing the creoles', since it was clear that virtually all the Americans now longed for independence. Only recently, he had imprisoned a priest who had dared to suggest, in a sermon preached in the cathedral before the judges of the high court, that the French invasion was God's punishment on Spain for its corruption and infidelity.[4]

In September 1810, Miguel Hidalgo y Costilla (1753–1811), parish priest of Dolores, called out the masses in rebellion against European dominion. He was joined by Indians and castas, by the farm labourers, artisans and miners of the Bajío. For a banner and symbol of their movement he offered his followers the image of Our Lady of Guadalupe. Acclaimed 'generalísimo of America', Hidalgo led his swollen undisciplined horde to Guanajuato, marching to the cries of 'Long Live Our Lady of Guadalupe! Long Live Ferdinand VII! Death to the gachupines!' On demanding the city's surrender, he explained that the purpose of his insurrection was to expel the Europeans and recover the rights of 'the Mexican nation', and thus end the cruel tyranny of 300 years. 'The present movement is great and it will be yet more great when it attempts to recover the holy rights conceded by God to the Mexicans and usurped by a few cruel conquerors . . . ' Unpersuaded by this rhetoric, the intendant, Juan Antonio de Riaño, concentrated his forces in the Alhóndiga de Granaditas, an impressive neo-classic edifice constructed to serve as a corn market and municipal granary. In the ensuing siege and the massacre that followed its capture, over three hundred Spaniards lost their lives. The populace rampaged through the city sacking the properties owned by the gachupines.[5] These events marked the final rupture between European and American Spaniards; no longer quarrelling cousins, they became suspicious foes, no matter how pressing the need for an alliance against the insurgent masses.

Thereafter, Hidalgo led his forces first to Valladolid and then to Guadalajara, where he had high mass and *Te Deums* celebrated in the cathedrals while in the suburbs peninsular Spaniards were murdered. He abolished slavery and, more important, decreed the abolition of tribute for Indians and mulattos, a measure which thus removed any necessity of preserving records of these invidious distinctions. He also forbade any further leasing of Indian community lands, seeking to protect the integrity of their boundaries. Finally, he called for the expulsion of all gachupines, denouncing them as 'unnatural men, who have broken the closest bonds of blood, abandoning their fathers, brothers, wives, and their own children . . . to cross immense oceans. The force behind all their toil is avarice . . . They are Catholics through policy, their true god is Mammon.'[6] Here, in these passionate words uttered by a rebel leader, we encounter the culminating expression of creole, clerical disdain for the *advenedizos*, the hard-handed peninsular traders who grubbed for fortune in the New World.

Some measure of the sentiments that inspired the priests who served Hidalgo can be obtained from an insurgent periodical, *El Despertador Americano* (1810–11), edited by Francisco Severo Maldonado, a doctor of theology, who warned the Americans against the inroads of atheism that the French forces had propagated in Spain. It was for the Americans to take the lead in defending 'the sacred rights of the altar and the patria'. Religion which had been exterminated in Europe could be preserved in America: if King Joseph had proscribed the religious orders, the creoles should strive to maintain them. Above all, the insurgents served 'Our Holy Mother of Guadalupe, Tutelary Numen of this empire, sworn captain of our legions.' Hidalgo was another Washington, a 'hero liberator', who, after 300 years of tyranny, now sought 'the independence of a nation that has only taken up arms to recover its sacred rights and maintain the religion of its fathers intact'. Why should the gachupines be allowed to own the richest mines, the most thriving haciendas, to marry the wealthiest heiresses, to monopolise trade, to drain the country of its bullion and currency, to occupy the leading positions in Church and State, and, to add insult to injury, then accuse the creoles of idleness? There was a danger that the Europeans might hand over the country to King Joseph.[7] As for the royalist recapture of Guanajuato, Maldonado evoked the shade of Las Casas to witness the horrors of the massacre that followed this event, scenes worthy of Cortés' capture of Tenochtitlan.

In its clerical leadership and invocation of religious symbols, the Mexican insurgency more resembled the Spanish resistance to the French invasion than the independence movements of South America. At the outset the gentry of San Miguel had plotted to use their authority as militia officers to mobilise their troops in what they hoped would prove to be an orderly seizure of power. The intendant of Guanajuato was known to be sympathetic to creole grievances. They had been encouraged by the support of several magnates. Nor were their calculations entirely erroneous, since the militia regiments of Celaya, Valladolid and Guadalajara all joined their movement. But, when their plans were discovered, Miguel Hidalgo seized the leadership of the rebellion, calling upon the masses to follow him in a disorderly rout which soon threatened to degenerate into a general attack on the propertied classes. It was largely thanks to his high standing among the clergy of the Michoacán diocese that so many priests joined the insurgency, often inciting their parishioners to rebel. But the popular character of the movement, which found expression in indiscriminate plundering of property, alarmed many creole landowners and drove them to rally to the royalist cause. The magnates of the northern provinces mobilised their horsemen to form new regiments of militia. The result was that the insurgents' undisciplined horde was easily defeated by New Spain's small regular army, commanded by Félix Calleja. Hidalgo was captured and duly executed. But the rebellion flared anew in the South, where José María Morelos, a parish priest from the *tierra caliente*, succeeded in forming a more disciplined force. It was in this phase of the insurgency that a Congress was summoned and independence at last clearly stated as a national objective. In the event, the royalist reaction proved too strong, especially since Morelos failed to establish his authority over all rebel leaders and, once he was captured, the movement declined into mere banditry.

That Miguel Hidalgo should have headed the Mexican Insurgency was a measure of the crisis in authority and belief that characterised this period. For he numbered among the most learned priests in his diocese and indeed had been accused of Jansenism owing to his admiration for the Church history of the abbé Fleury. His knowledge of French literature and his zeal in promoting artisan industry at Dolores had won him the respect of Intendant Riaño, an official well known for his enlightened ideas. When rector of the San Nicolás college at Valladolid, he had become the good friend of Manuel Abad y Queipo, whose memorials to the Crown had been used to such effect by Alexander von Humboldt.[8] There can be little doubt that the two men shared much the same views about the necessity of economic and social reform in New Spain. But Abad y Queipo was an Asturian, whose liberalism stopped short of any recognition of the right of Mexicans to govern their own country. For his part, when Hidalgo moved into revolt, he suspended his liberal beliefs in favour of the time-honoured themes of creole patriotism. There thus opened a fissure between liberalism and patriotism that was to haunt Mexican politics for many years to come.

II

To explain why the creole clergy should have been so ready to embrace the insurgency cause and to account for the social and economic tensions that converted the movement into a bitter civil war, it is necessary to examine the writings of Manuel Abad y Queipo (1751–1825). The illegitimate son of an Asturian nobleman, he had arrived in New Spain in 1786 as part of the 'official family' of Fray Antonio de San Miguel, the new bishop of Michoacán, who at once appointed him as judge of chantries and pious works, a post which offered him an unrivalled knowledge of ecclesiastical capital and credit. It was in recognition of his talents that the bishop and cathedral chapter commissioned him to write their official protests against the controversial Crown measures to end clerical immunity from royal courts and to sell off all ecclesiastical property. After acquiring degrees in canon and civil law, in 1805, Abad y Queipo became a canon and in 1810, was nominated bishop-elect of Michoacán. By this time he was well known in both Mexico and Spain for his outspoken and often radical proposals for economic and fiscal reform. A student of the 'profound Smith' and his *Wealth of Nations*, Abad y Queipo did not hesitate to cite Montesquieu in his memorials to the Crown and in his reform projects obviously drew on Jovellanos' *Informe de ley agraria*. When he visited Paris in 1805, he presented Alexander von Humboldt with a copy of his extant memorials, a source which the Prussian savant cited frequently in his *Essai politique*, albeit attributing them to Bishop San Miguel. A liberal in both politics and economics, this would-be bishop was subsequently accused of being a Jansenist, no doubt in part because he greatly admired the ecclesiastical history of the abbé Fleury.[9] The most striking feature of the collection of memorials which be published in 1813 was the complete absence of any material dealing with religion. Secularisation could thus affect individual conscience as much as public status.

In his first representation to the Crown, framed on behalf of the Bishop San Miguel and the chapter of Michoacán in 1799, Abad y Queipo strongly protested against the abrogation of the personal immunity of the clergy from royal courts. Already the country had been scandalised to witness the imprisonment and trial of a priest in Puebla. In particular, the criminal bench of the high court was intent on 'the degradation of the American clergy', taking cognizance of cases without paying heed to the bishops' counsel or judgement.

Without immunity, any clergyman could be accused of criminal offences by local magistrates on trumped-up charges and exposed to the humiliation of trial by royal judges. In the villages of Michoacán 'everyone is an Indian or a mulatto; the only white faces are those of the parish priest and the magistrate, if the latter himself is not also a mulatto'. Moreover, the criminal bench of the high court had displayed an alarming tendency to accept any denunciation of the clergy presented by country magistrates, no matter how ill-grounded.[10]

Not content to warn the Crown of the practical consequences of the measure, Abad y Queipo invoked political principles, observing 'the immunities of the Spanish clergy are part of our monarchial constitution and cannot be excessively reduced without altering it ... The right to be tried by judges of his own class is like the most precious property in the mind of each individual, and for this reason all the distinguished classes have obtained their respective *fueros*.' To strengthen his case, Abad y Queipo cited the example of France where the *parlements* had so discredited the clergy in popular esteem by destroying their privileges, that the people eventually turned on the Crown itself. Nor did he hesitate to quote directly from *The Spirit of the Laws* the dictum that 'if in a monarchy you quit the lords, nobility and clergy of their prerogatives, then very soon you will have a popular state'. Moreover, in New Spain four-fifths of the clergy 'do not have a benefice and simply subsist on the low stipends of their office; they do not receive anything from the government that might distinguish them from other classes other than the privilege of their *fuero*'. Since the country clergy were often the only protectors of the masses from the abuses of magistrates and landowners, they still enjoyed great influence, which hitherto they had always employed to preach loyalty and obedience to the Crown. In effect, 'the clerical *fuero* is the only special bond which ties them to the government'.[11]

The secular, not to say utilitarian character, of Abad y Queipo's thinking can be best observed in a confidential report which he prepared in 1805 for Bishop San Miguel on the proposals to create three new dioceses in New Spain, respectively based in Acapulco, Veracruz and San Luis Potosí. He sharply criticised the project on the grounds that it would rob the bishops and canons of Puebla and Michoacán of their tithe income and thus lower their status. At present, so he averred, cathedral chapters were filled with candidates drawn equally from Spain and Mexico: to reduce their salaries would injure the aspirations of the local priesthood. In any case, 'the clergy are a charge on the State' and a burden on the people, who had to pay the contributions which maintained them. To trace the full consequence of erecting a new bishopric, 'it would be necessary to write a treatise of political economy'. In particular, the effects would be ruinous for San Luis Potosí, a city situated on the northern limits of the Michoacán diocese, since it already possessed five mendicant priories, three parishes, a sanctuary dedicated to Our Lady of Guadalupe, twenty-six confraternities, and some thirty clergy living off their chantries. To add a cathedral and canons would be too great a burden for a town with no more than 14,000 inhabitants, surrounded by a province dominated by vast latifundia. In liberal strain, Abad y Queipo confessed: 'The lack of property and the excess of clergy are the true causes of the decay of San Luis Potosí.' In any case, he was less than persuaded of the moral efficacy of episcopal visitations, arguing that their effects were momentary unless they were accompanied by 'other motives capable of redressing human passions such as honour, interest and respect for other men . . . whose force is also proportional to the kind of society in which they exist'.[12]

In both these memorials, Abad y Queipo offered a striking analysis of rural society in New Spain and proffered radical proposals for reform. His starting point was that 'in America there is no graduation or middle ground: everyone is either rich or poverty-stricken, noble or infamous'. Of the estimated $4\frac{1}{2}$ million inhabitants of New Spain, 'the Spaniards compose a tenth of the total population and they alone have almost all the property and riches of the kingdom'. The remainder, which is to say, the Indians and castas, were 'the retainers, servants or workers of the first class'. The result of this deplorable inequality was open hatred and conflict of interest, leading to 'envy, theft and poor service on the part of some; and scorn, usury and harshness on the part of others'. True, in a subsequent passage, Abad y Queipo admitted that beneath the level of the Spaniards, there was a strata comprising a fifth or a third of the population which had sufficient means to feed and clothe itself relatively well, and that of the lower two-thirds the maintained peons of the haciendas were the best off; but such qualifications did not alter his broad conclusion that the majority of the population 'groan under the weight of indigence, ignorance and abjection'. Nor had the recent establishment of intendancies and the abolition of *repartimientos de comercio* bettered the condition of the masses, since the successors of the alcaldes mayores were now paid a mere pittance and hence were even more corrupt than their predecessors. Indeed, the intendants found it difficult to encounter qualified candidates for the post of subdelegate. Although the repartimientos at times had caused hardships, nevertheless, the former district magistrates had brought two great benefits: 'the one was that they administered justice with disinterest and rectitude in the cases to which they were not party, and the other was that they promoted industry and agriculture in lines which were important to them'.[13]

In his description of the rural masses, Abad y Queipo noted that 'the castas find themselves defamed by law as the descendants of black slaves'. It was for this reason that they hated paying tribute and sought to change their status by quietly ascending into the Spanish stratum, albeit always hindered by their poverty and lack of education. But it was on the Indians that Abad y Queipo concentrated his attention, since they still constituted the majority of the

Mexican population. Of their social degradation there could be no doubt: 'the colour, ignorance and poverty of the Indians place them at an infinite distance from a Spaniard'. Unlike Ulloa and other European commentators, however, Abad y Queipo did not blame the condition of the Mexican Indian on his sloth or his drunkenness or indeed, on any innate inherited characteristics. Instead, he blamed the Laws of the Indies. It was the well-meaning but disastrous legislation of the Spanish Crown which had led to the Indians being treated as minors, prevented from borrowing more than five pesos, recently deprived of all credit from district magistrates, and above all, permanently trapped within the system of communal tenure of land. The result was that the Indians dwelt in separation from the remainder of society, could not undertake binding transactions, and, at every point, were denied the means to better their condition. 'Isolated by their language and by the most useless and tyrannical government, they preserve the customs, usages, and gross superstitions, which in each village eight or ten old Indians mysteriously seek to maintain, living idly at the expense of the toil of the others, ruling them with the most harsh despotism.'[14]

To remedy the manifold and obvious ills of New Spain, Abad y Queipo drew heavily, albeit without acknowledgement, on Jovellanos' *Informe de ley agraria*. In the first place he called for 'a law which would establish the absolute civil equality of the class of Indians with the class of Spaniards'. The only way to do this was to abolish the tribute or capitation tax, allow them to incur such debt as they could obtain, and free them from all restrictions on the sale of their produce, concessions, however, to be matched by an obligation to pay sales tax (*alcabalas*) and tithes at the same rate as Spaniards. Much the same concessions should also be extended to the castas, who should be freed of tribute, allowed to take all appointments for which nobility was not required, and enjoy the same status as other subjects of the Crown. Not content with legal and fiscal equality, Abad y Queipo then proposed radical land reform. As regards the Indians, he advocated measures 'to divide the lands of the Indian communities in dominion and property among individuals, leaving only the pasture and rough lands in common'. Furthermore, since 'the bad division of lands' was the chief cause of poverty and dispersion of population, he proposed that all vacant public lands should be distributed among Indians, castas and poor Spaniards. Yet more radical, he suggested that land on haciendas which had been left uncultivated for twenty or thirty years should be thrown open to popular cultivation, presumably by means of tenancy arrangements. Other reforms included the abolition of the sales tax on all property transactions, free licence for the establishment of textile workshops and permission for anyone to live in Indian villages. In short, Abad y Queipo fixed upon the inequitable distribution of property as the chief cause of New Spain's social squalor and advocated individual ownership of land as the chief remedy. In all this the influence of Jovellanos can be clearly discerned, especially in the premiss that every individual, no matter what his race or history, would respond to economic incentives, once government had created a framework of legal equality and availability of land.[15]

In 1805 Abad y Queipo once more addressed a representation to the Crown, this time acting on behalf of the farmers and merchants of Valladolid, to plead for the suspension of the ecclesiastical amortization decree of the previous year, which threatened the destruction of 'the agriculture, industry and commerce of the kingdom and the ruin of the royal exchequer'. What ministers in Madrid had failed to understand or had chosen to ignore, was that in New Spain the Church owned relatively little land, especially after the confiscation and sale of the Jesuit haciendas. Instead, over the three centuries of colonial rule the complex gamut of ecclesiastical institutions, from wealthy nunneries and prestigious confraternities to humble brotherhoods and parochial altar endowments, had accumulated vast sums in the form of annuities, loans, unredeemed mortgages and chantry funds, all secured on haciendas and urban property. Based on his experience as judge of chantries and pious works, responsible for the investments of these monies once they were redeemed or established, Abad y Queipo estimated that this accumulated capital amounted to 44.5 million pesos as against landed property worth 2.5 to 3 million. Yet the Crown now demanded that this vast sum should be redeemed and paid into the royal treasury. The result would be nothing short of disastrous for the propertied and entrepreneurial classes of New Spain. For merchants and miners as much as landowners had raised monies from the Church in order to finance their operations, offering haciendas as security. Moreover, a great part of clerical capital had been charged on estates by their owners as annuity funds for sons who entered the priesthood and as such had never involved any transfer of cash.[16] In effect, the Crown had imposed a savage capital levy on New Spain's landed elite and its effect would be to destroy the country's credit system and drain the economy of its currency. Some 20,000 citizens would have to travel to the diocesan capitals, there to negotiate the rate of redemption over a period of ten years, advertising to all the world the precarious state of their finances. Yet it was precisely the upper fifth of the population who paid virtually all the taxes, supported the weight of foreign trade, and had always been distinguished for their loyalty to the king.

Anxious to seize the opportunity to develop further his analysis of New Spain's economy, Abad y Queipo included in his memorial a discussion of Mexican agriculture. Why was it that Mexican farmers were unable to compete against their Anglo-American counterparts in supplying flour to Cuba? As in the allied question of Indian retardation, the answer was simple: the Mexican countryside was dominated by some 10,000 haciendas, estates which had grown almost continuously since the sixteenth century and which in some cases covered entire districts. The availability of Church funds had enabled the haciendas to grow in size, but had equally prevented their partition. Yet many estates bore so heavy a range of Church funds that the combined sum at times amounted to half the value of the estate, with the result that annual income barely covered interest payments, leaving the owner to rely on years of high sales to extract his profit. Despite this precarious situation, many owners, so Abad y Queipo averred, chose not to lease their land, but left great tracts uncultivated or devoted it to rough pasture, fearful that Indian tenants might appeal to the authorities for recognition as a constituted village and therefore legally entitled to a land endowment. Other factors impeding the development of Mexican agriculture were the Church tithe, the Crown's 6 per cent excise duty, municipal laws governing grain sales, poor roads, the mountainous terrain and irregular rainfall. In the last few years, which was to say, since 1800, New Spain had suffered from a marked scarcity of currency which caused 'a very considerable delay in all payments, a great slowness in the course of business, and much difficulty for new enterprises'. The promissory notes issued by northern miners on merchants houses in Mexico City often circulated for two to three months, endorsed for as many as ten separate transactions. However, no matter how long the list of contributory causes, Abad y Queipo fixed upon the concentration in landownership as the chief cause for the backwardness of Mexican agriculture and the stark contrasts between rich and poor in the Mexican population. He concluded: 'The indivisibility of haciendas, the difficulty in managing them, the lack of property among the people, has produced and continues to produce deplorable effects for agriculture, for the population, and for the State in general.'[17]

That it was Manuel Abad y Queipo, in 1810 bishop-elect of Michoacán, who took the lead in denouncing the insurgency, demonstrated the extent to which Spanish liberalism and Mexican patriotism had parted company. A few months before the outbreak of the rebellion he had urgently warned the Regency that 'our possessions in America and especially this New Spain are very disposed to a general insurrection . . . the electric fire of the French Revolution has put into movement . . . an ardent desire for independence'. Napoleon was more admired than feared in New Spain. The seizure of Iturrigaray had inflamed the traditional enmity of gachupines and creoles to the point where 'the Americans would wish to govern alone and be the exclusive proprietors' of the kingdom. As for the Indians and castas, they hated the Spaniards and would follow the creoles in rebellion, even though their interests were quite different. Indeed, mass rebellion might well degenerate into race warfare and create scenes reminiscent of the revolution in Saint Domingue. It was to forestall these dire events that Abad y Queipo advocated the abolition of the tribute, since it would then be no longer necessary to maintain records of ethnic status. At present, anyone of African descent, no matter how remote or tenuous their ancestry, had to pay this poll tax, which thus served as 'a badge of slavery'. To quell creole discontent, he proposed the abolition of Spain's commercial monopoly, arguing that Mexico could no longer be governed by rules established by Philip II: it required 'a new system, more liberal and just'. These fiscal concessions could be covered by raising the price of tobacco, still a royal monopoly, and by raising excise duties from 6 to 8 per cent. Above all else, however, Abad y Queipo urged the immediate recruitment of a regular army numbering at least 30,000 men: if creole loyalty could no longer be assured, then armed might should prevail.[18]

Confronted with the insurgency, Abad y Queipo invoked his authority as bishop-elect to excommunicate its leader, denouncing him as 'the new Maho-met Hidalgo', who preached a gospel of social hatred, cynically proclaiming the patronage of Our Lady of Guadalupe while encouraging the Indians and castas to plunder property in an insurrection that was 'essentially anarchic'. Admitting his own error in allowing many men of imperfect education and poor morality to become priests, he lamented that the rebellion 'is almost entirely the work of ecclesiastics, since they are its chief authors and those who started and sustain it'. What greater heresy could there be than to challenge the heaven-sent authority of the Spanish monarchy and incite the populace to plunder and murder? Was not Spain this 'chosen portion, a holy nation', a new Israel chosen by 'the special providence' of God to preach the Christian gospel and thus convert and civilise 'so many idolatrous and barbarous nations'. All authority, and indeed the institution of human society, derived from God and to challenge his divine providence was to be guilty of heresy.[19]

Mingled with these traditional affirmations were some remarkably liberal declarations. For Abad y Queipo observed that 'although Spain has been in decadence without intermission for three centuries until this moment, owing to the ambition, ineptitude and apathy of its kings and the despotism of its ministers', nevertheless, it had assured the peace and prosperity of America. Only recently it had 'suffered with resignation the disorders of the disorganised government of Godoy'. But the nation had been reborn in the struggle against the French and at the Cortes of Cadiz had promulgated 'the most liberal, the most just, and the most prudent constitution of all that have been seen until now in human society'. Had it not conceded equal rights to European and American Spaniards? It had avoided the pernicious errors of Rousseau and created a framework of orderly liberty. The patria, so he argued, was not a mere city or a province, as was so often assumed in America: 'Our patria, then, is all the Spanish nation . . . the general association of all the inhabitants of its extended dominions . . . ' As for Mexico, it was neither a colony nor a kingdom in its own right, but rather a province of a united Spanish monarchy, the common patria.[20]

In his anxiety to assist the Spanish cause and suppress the insurgency, Abad y

Queipo did not hesitate to recommend the confiscation of church silver and the taxation of clerical incomes, applying the proceeds to finance the war effort. More important, he advocated the suspension of 'all civil and ecclesiastical privileges and immunities . . . *Salus populi suprema lex*.' Indeed, when in 1812 the viceregal authorities abolished clerical immunity from the jurisdiction of royal courts, he defended the measure as entirely necessary, observing that all privileges derive from the king, who could thus withdraw what he had once conceded. Existing immunities had been based on the canon law issued by the Papacy in the twelfth and thirteenth centuries, legislation based on false documents and history. Not content to nail his colours to the Jansenist mast, Abad y Queipo also displayed his command of liberal economic theory when he defended gachupín avarice against Hidalgo's condemnation. 'The avarice of the gachupines . . . only signifies that innate desire in the heart of man to better his condition, which is the first motive of all human activity and the stimulus of social virtues and of the talent, application, economy, frugality, courage and constancy in enterprises and adversities.' It was the same force which had created the wealth of New Spain and founded many noble families.[21] In proposing these arguments, Abad y Queipo unwittingly testified to the intellectual abyss that separated the clerics of the late eighteenth century from the Franciscans who had founded their church.

But Abad y Queipo did not greatly profit from the vehemence with which he had attacked his former friend, since he was in part held responsible for the widespread participation of the Michoacán diocesan clergy in the insurrection. His public eulogy of the 1812 Constitution and his Jansenist sympathies counted against him when Ferdinand VII restored absolute monarchy. In 1815 he was ordered to resign his see and return to Spain, where he was subjected to confinement by the revived Inquisition. When the Liberal revolution occurred in 1820, he foolishly allowed himself to be nominated as a member of the ruling junta, a testimony of where his sympathies lay, but the cause of his imprisonment once Ferdinand VII regained power. In 1824 he died in captivity, the victim of age and the ill-health caused by the deplorable conditions in which he was kept.[22]

In effect, both Miguel Hidalgo and Manuel Abad y Queipo paid a heavy price for their acceptance of the primacy of secular over spiritual concerns since, although theological doctrine and religious symbols entered their discourse, their application was determined by political ends. Nothing was more ironic than their subsequent reputation. In the years which followed independence, liberals such as Lorenzo de Zavala and José María Luis Mora were to condemn Hidalgo for the popular, religious character of his rebellion and his failure to propound any proposals for reform. By contrast, Mora reprinted Abad y Queipo's memorials of 1799 and 1805, thereby ensuring their influence over the development of Mexican radicalism. In particular, his signalising the all-engrossing magnitude of haciendas and the isolating effect of Indian communal tenure as the twin causes of the Mexican agrarian problem was to frame an agenda for reform which was to affect Mexican politics until the twentieth century. If Hidalgo is acclaimed as the Founding Father of the Mexican republic, Abad y Queipo is best regarded as the intellectual progenitor of Mexican Liberalism.

III

No feature of the debate over the Mexican insurgency was more striking than the violent rhetoric deployed by the Spanish publicists who defended the colonial system. Stereotypes of creole and gachupin character, once the subject of family dispute and travellers' comments, were now invoked as constituting political reasons for dismissing claims to self-government. At the same time an attempt was made to undermine creole pretensions by appealing to popular grievances over land and employment. Much of this debate was staged at Cadiz, both in the Cortes and in short-lived reviews. In this respect Blanco White's *El Español* played a decisive role in the diffusion of information throughout Spanish America about the constitutional issues discussed at Cadiz. What has rarely been noted is that the insurgent press in New Spain often printed articles that had first appeared in *El Español*, and thus brought home to their readers the brutal character of the polemic waged by Spanish propagandists, thereby exacerbating creole anger.

The most vociferous critic of creole pretensions was Juan López de Cancelada (17?–1825), who was hired by the merchant guilds of Mexico and Cadiz to defend their cause in the press. At one time a store-keeper, whose Mexican wife had deserted him, Cancelada acted as editor of the *Gazeta Mexicana*, before his twenty-two years stay in New Spain was abruptly cut short in 1810 when he was deported for secretly accusing a distinguished creole judge of treason, an offence compounded by his contemptuous labelling the archbishop as a creature of Godoy. Once in Cadiz, he edited two short-lived reviews and published pamphlets defending the gachupín seizure of Viceroy Iturrigaray in 1808. His most significant work was *Ruina de la Nueva España* (1811), in which he argued forcefully against opening Mexican ports to foreign shipping and commerce. At present, so he averred, Mexican industry, and especially the textile industries of Puebla and Querétaro, was in a flourishing condition, and supplied at least two-thirds of the population with their necessities. To concede creole petitions for free trade would entail the ruin of industry, since the cheap cottons and woollens of Lancashire and Yorkshire would sell at far lower prices than locally produced cloth. Free trade would bring mass unemployment. Clearly, in presenting this case, Cancelada was more concerned to defend the monopoly profits of Spanish merchants than to protect the wages of Mexican artisans; but that did not detract from the cogency of his argument.[23] Then, in an endeavour to carry the attack into the enemy camp, Cancelada denounced the concentration of land ownership in New Spain, complaining that creole magnates monopolised entire districts, effectively depriving the Indians and castas of any access to land other than as labourers or as seasonal tenants. Citing cases where villages were entirely surrounded by haciendas, he asserted that the majority of the Mexican population survived on a bare subsistence, often wandering from estate to estate in search of employment or land to rent. Since it was their landless condition which had driven so many peasants to enlist in Hidalgo's insurrection, the only remedy for New Spain's social problems was to implement a general distribution of land. When the American deputies vehemently attacked his proposals as an assault on private property, he mocked them, observing that 'in place of asking the Cortes for the distribution of land to all families, the creoles asked for free trade with the English, so as to ruin poor weavers in the country'.[24]

On the subject of appointment to high office, Cancelada produced statistics which purported to demonstrate that creoles occupied far more posts in the colonial bureaucracy than was generally supposed, an assertion which infuriated his opponents. Moreover, he raked over the cinders of colonial stereotypes to spark further controversy when he declared that creoles were born with 'white hands', which was to say, that they were reared to think of themselves as gentlemen and were generally unfit for any trade or form of productive work. Much of the problem, he admitted, stemmed from gachupín fathers who proudly encouraged their creole offspring to attend college or university, hoping 'to give a career to my sons', an education which prepared them for the Church, the law and the bureaucracy. But not all creoles found a profession and many simply dissipated the inheritance bequeathed by their merchant fathers. By contrast, the gachupines came to New Spain as young men, worked diligently for their compatriots or relatives as apprentice merchants; and then graduated to become partners with a third of the profits. Often they married the daughter of their former employer and thus stood to manage the accumulated capital of two immigrant generations.[25] Here, in a controversy arising out of the wars of independence, we encounter stereotypes and sentiments that were already a commonplace in the first decades of the seventeenth century, when Dorantes de Carranza, Gómez de Cervantes and Salinas wrote their memorials to the Crown.

In Cadiz it fell to canon José Miguel Guridi Alcocer (1763–1828), deputy for Tlaxcala, to issue a public rebuttal of Cancelada's assertions. Not deigning to trade insults about the respective characters of American and European Spaniards, he reiterated the current demands for free trade, called for the lifting of all restrictions on the planting of vineyards in America, and accused

Cancelada of advocating an equality of rights reminiscent of the French Revolution, since 'the distribution of land that he promotes is contrary to the sacred right of property which every government ought to protect'. Moving onto the offensive, he demanded that at least half of all appointments in the New World should go to creoles; at present his compatriots were treated with such contempt that doubts had been raised as to whether 'they were men'. If the monarchy was to continue in America, it must observe absolute equality of opportunity for all posts. In more direct response, Guridi Alcocer presented statistics in which he demonstrated that only 4 out of 170 viceroys had been born in America, and a mere 14 out of 602 captains general, presidents and governors. At present there were only 4 creoles among the 28 intendants serving in the New World. The record for judges and bishops was better, since 278 creoles had been appointed as bishops compared with 702 Europeans. Exact figures for the judges of the high courts were not available, but the evidence suggested that about a third had been creoles. But it was noticeable that the proportion of creole prelates and judges had fallen in recent decades. In effect, Cancelada had distorted the figures by counting crown officials of all levels rather than examining the roll call of viceroys, governors, bishops and judges. In the course of his argument, Guridi Alcocer cited Solórzano and Feijoo on the controverted questions of creole talents and rights; but it was his precise calculations on office-holding that were destined to enter the history books.[26]

By far the most notorious intervention in the debates of the Cortes came from the merchant guild of Mexico whose political agents read out a lengthy memorial designed to persuade the assembly not to give voting rights either to Indians or castas. Indeed, these 'European Spaniards of America' proposed that the merchant guilds of Veracruz, Guadalajara and Mexico be vested with the right to elect six deputies for the Cortes, in recognition that 'their condition of conquerors in a conquered land makes them the first inhabitants, the privileged and chosen in all America'. To support their exclusionary demands, they raked across Pauw, Robertson and Raynal to spew forth a farrago of misrepresentation and prejudice. What was the ancient history of the New World, they asked, but 'a chaos of confusion and an abyss of shadows'. When the Europeans first arrived in America, they found 'so few inhabitants, such scarce farming, such an abundance of hunger and nakedness', that all observers concluded that the Indians still dwelt in 'the primitive infancy of the first nations, all too close to the animal state'. The natives of Peru and Mexico were somewhat more advanced, but their polities were marred by 'unbridled despotism, the most bloody and terrible superstition'. It was only thanks to the wise and benevolent laws of the Spaniards that these 'Orang Utang inhabitants of America' were slowly domesticated, albeit still dominated by drunkenness and sloth. Nor were the castas better, since they had much the same character as the Indians, distinguished only by the ardour with which they gratified their vices. As for the creoles, they wasted their inheritance through dissipation, and idly dreamt of public office and independence. It was the Europeans who constituted 'the soul of the prosperity and opulence of the kingdom by reason of their enterprise in mining, agriculture, industry, and commerce, the management of which they enjoy almost exclusively, not so much because of their energy and avarice, but thanks to the neglect and lack of application of the creoles'. The merchant guild concluded with a reiterated demand that voting rights in New Spain be heavily restricted since it was 'a province, the residence of five million automatons, one million disloyal subjects, and a hundred thousand citizens addicted to order ... ' How could there be any equality of rights between Spain the conqueror and such a colony? In these gross insults, worthy of Oviedo or Pauw, the gachupín traders of Mexico, their embattled sensibility still shocked by the massacres at Guanajuato and elsewhere, dismissed the population from whom they drew their livelihood as barely human.[27]

It was Fray Servando Teresa de Mier (1763–1827), an exiled Mexican Dominican, who offered the most forthright response to 'the sovereign army of merchants ... this army of oppression, whose vanguard is Cadiz, its centre in the ports of America, and its rearguard in the capitals of America'. In an open *Carta de un Americano*, which appeared in *El Español*, he contemptuously described the guild's misrepresentation of Indian history as the offscourings of Raynal, Pauw, Ulloa and Muñoz, theories long since refuted by Clavijero, Carli and others. Had not the researches of León y Gama, Boturini and Sigüenza y Góngora conclusively demonstrated that the ancient Mexicans had an advanced civilisation, endowed with libraries and universities, and governed by wise and just laws? If the Indians now appeared degraded, it was entirely the fault of Spanish exploitation. For the rest, Mier questioned Blanco White's condemnation of the Caracas junta's declaration of independence. Far from being Jacobins, the Venezuelans had been more influenced by the example of the United States, since they had promulgated a federal constitution. The Americans had been denied equal representation in the Cortes, and hence possessed the right to opt for independence, since 'the Spanish Americas were never colonies in the modern European sense of that term'.[28] At the same time, Mier denied Cancelada's assertion that only the Indians possessed original rights to America. By reason of their birthplace, their labour and education, both creoles and castas possessed an equal right to the New World. All three groups had suffered from Spanish injustice and all three had 'the right to prove that the climate of America does not degrade or brutalise'. Finally, Mier observed that Spain's title-deed to the New World, the papal donation of 1493, lacked all legitimacy, since the Papacy had no authority to meddle in temporal affairs, still less to divide the world among Iberian predators. In pursuing this Jansenist line of argument, Mier criticised Abad y Queipo's excommunication of Hidalgo, asserting that his presumed authority in this matter derived from medieval canon law which was notoriously based on forged credentials.[29]

The influence of these debates at Cadiz and in *El Español* can be clearly discerned in the insurgent press of New Spain, which consisted of badly printed periodicals of uncertain duration and limited circulation. In his *Semanario patriótico Americano* (1812–13), Andrés Quintana Roo (1787–1851), printed instalments of Mier's letter and thus publicised the contents of the merchant guild's atrocious memorial. He denounced the Regency as the instrument of 'this new mercantile sovereign' and revived the traditional creole plaint against the peninsular immigrants, the *advenedizos*, who monopolised both commerce and high office, frequently married heiresses, and rendered the creoles ashamed to be 'the sons of the country'. The root of all misery in America was the avarice of the Europeans who came determined to exploit its inhabitants, reducing them to virtual slavery.[30] Much the same sentiments were expressed by Carlos María de Bustamante (1774–1848), the former editor of *El Diario de México*, who in his *Correo Americano del Sur* (1813), confessed that, despite the events of 1808–10, he had expected the constitutional order established by the Cortes of Cadiz to bring liberty to Mexico. But he had incurred viceregal censure by his protests at royalist massacres of rebel forces and had fled to join the insurgents. Like Quintana Roo, he printed portions of Mier's letter; excerpted the American deputies' representation to the Cortes; and commented bitterly on both Cancelada's slanders and 'the vile report' of the Mexican merchant guild.[31] The effect of Spanish propaganda was thus to exacerbate creole resentment and strengthen their determination to obtain independence.

IV

The southern phase of the insurgency was, if anything, more dominated by priests than the movement led by Hidalgo. Indeed, Cancelada claimed that José María Morelos, the country vicar who now commanded the rebel forces, had four clear principles: that all Europeans should be expelled from America; that all property should be owned by Americans; that Our Lady of Guadalupe should be obeyed in all things; and that priests should act as God's lieutenants, governing in both the temporal and spiritual spheres. So exasperated was Félix Calleja, the royal commander, at the number of creole clerics joining the rebellion that he suggested bringing in friars from the Peninsula to administer all parishes. The religious character of the movement was best expressed by Carlos María de Bustamante who avowed his devotion to Our Lady of Guadalupe, proclaiming that during the apparition Juan Diego had heard 'the authentic certificate of our liberty. You will call me mother and I will be yours; you will call upon me in your tribulations and I will hear you; you will plead with me for liberty and I will loose your chains . . . '[32]

The decision of the viceregal authorities to suspend clerical immunity from royal jurisdiction, so as to enable military commanders to try and execute rebel priests without reference to their bishops, alarmed the clergy and aroused indignant protest. When the cathedral chapter of Mexico, composed of canons distinguished for their learning, rank and loyalty to the Crown, vigorously condemned the measure, their memorial was printed by Andrés Quintana Roo in his rebel journal. The chapter argued that 'in everything the clergy are distinguished from the secular state: they have a holy, indelible, and eternal character; their persons are sacred and inviolable ...'. Although priests were citizens, endowed with the same rights and obligations as other men, their sacerdotal character conferred rights far superior to any conceded by society or the state. It had been argued that the sovereign power of princes entailed the subjection of the clergy, but this was to forget that the bishops and clergy exercised sovereign power within the Church where the laity only figured as subjects. Since the Church's authority was not of earthly origin, it followed that it was essentially independent of the secular powers of this world. The clergy's immunity from royal jurisdiction was thus 'sacred and inviolable'. It was to signalise his disapprobation that General Mariano Matamoros, one-time vicar of Jantetelco, 'gave his troops for their banner a great black flag with a green cross, similar to that used by the canons on Holy Wednesday, with the arms of the Church and a motto which said: "Die for ecclesiastical immunity."' [33]

It was José María Morelos (1765–1815), who expressed most powerfully the animating ideals of the Insurgency. A casta of artisan stock, albeit a Spaniard in status, educated in the diocesan seminary, Morelos had served in a remote parish in the *tierra caliente*, where he preserved a remarkably archaic, provincial view of society. After assembling his forces, he informed the villagers of Atenango that 'we are only about to change the military and political government that the gachupines have, so that the creoles should have it, removing as many taxes as possible, such as the tribute and other charges which oppress us'. In Oaxaca he pursued the same message, proposing to quit all Europeans from government, adding that 'all taxes should be removed, leaving only the tobacco and excise duties to sustain the military and tithes and parish fees to sustain the clergy'. Here, in these apparently simple proposals, we encounter a medieval image of society, in which the two swords, the warriors and the priests, each possess their own taxes and, by implication, their own courts and jurisdiction. When Morelos convoked a constitutional congress at Chilpancingo, he insisted that all deputies should be qualified theologians or lawyers. But, despite this insistence on corporate privilege, he firmly demanded the destruction of the colonial hierarchy of ethnic castes, that invidious system whereby the civic rights and obligations of an individual were defined at birth by inscription in the respective baptismal registers kept for each group. Henceforward, so he declared, 'with the exception of the Europeans, all other

31 José María Morelos y Pavón

inhabitants will not be named according to their quality as Indians, mulattos and other castes, but all generally as Americans. No one will pay tribute, and there shall be no slaves ... ' Indian lands were no longer to be leased but returned to their respective communities. In effect, Morelos here proclaimed the radical principle of ethnic equality but justified this ideal, not by invoking the universal rights of man, but through the affirmation of common identity as Mexicans.[34] At the same time, he condemned all demands for 'caste-war' or a general confiscation of property, on the grounds that it was not his 'system' to attack 'the rich for being so, and still less the rich creoles ... Since the whites are the first representatives of the kingdom and were the first to take up arms in defence of the natives of the villages and other castes, becoming united with them, for this reason they ought to be the objects of our gratitude, and not of the hatred that some wish to raise against them.' He concluded that all Americans were brothers in Christ, a new Israel struggling for liberation from its oppressors, and once more insisted that 'this equality in *calidad* and liberty is the natural and divine problem. It is only virtue which distinguishes a man and makes him useful to the Church and State.'[35] When his followers acclaimed him 'Generalísimo of North America', Morelos chose to call himself 'the servant of the nation'.

At the Congress of Chilpancingo, summoned in 1813 to frame a Declaration of Independence, Morelos prepared a document called 'Sentiments of the Nation', in which, after once more insisting on the abolition of ethnic distinctions, he urged the assembly to devise laws 'to moderate opulence and poverty', raise the earnings of the poor, and create a nation in which the only distinctions would be of virtue and vice. Sovereignty was vested in the people and now exercised by Congress. All government posts should be reserved for Americans and indeed foreigners were not to be admitted into the country, save as merchants in the ports or as useful artisans. The Catholic religion was to be the only tolerated faith, and the clergy were to be maintained by tithes and parish fees. 'The Most Holy Mary of Guadalupe' was to be acclaimed as 'the patron of our liberty'. Miguel Hidalgo was named as the hero of independence and the nation should henceforth celebrate as national holidays both 15 September and 12 December. It was in his opening speech to the Congress, however, that Morelos widened his perspective, reading a text which had been prepared for him by Carlos María de Bustamante. After a cursory, almost disdainful mention of the doctrine of the sovereignty of the people, brandished by the Spaniards against the French yet denied to the Americans, he compared the Mexicans to the people of Israel in Egypt suffering under Pharaoh. But God himself had now heard their pleas and had decreed their liberation, sending his Spirit to move their hearts and lead them into battle. In an audacious metaphor, the Almighty was compared to the Mexican eagle protecting his people with both wings and talons. At the same time, independence was presented as an act of restoration: 'We are about to re-establish the Mexican empire, improving its government.' The continuity between Aztec past and Mexican present was emphasised in the following invocation:

> Spirits of Moctehuzoma, Cacamatzin, Cuauhtimotzin, Xicotencalt and of Cat-zonzi, as once you celebrated the feast in which you were slaughtered by the treacherous sword of Alvarado, now celebrate this happy moment in which your sons have united to avenge the crimes and outrages committed against you, and to

free themselves from the claws of tyranny and fanaticism that were going to grasp them for ever. To the 12th of August of 1521 there succeeds the 14th of September 1813. In that day the chains of our serfdom were fastened in Mexico-Tenochtitlan, in this day in the happy village of Chilpancingo they are broken for ever.

In this speech we encounter a clear affirmation of a Mexican nation, already in existence before the conquest, now about to recover its independence. That its author – Bustamante – was himself the son of a Spaniard only serves to highlight the drama of the occasion.[36] Creole patriotism, which began as the articulation of the social identity of American Spaniards, was here transmuted into the insurgent ideology of Mexican nationalism. Hidalgo and Cuauhtémoc were thus united in common struggle against the Spanish foe. At the same time, this type of argument allowed the clerical leadership of the insurgency to avoid any emphasis on such doctrines as popular sovereignty and universal human rights.

The actual Act of Independence issued by the Congress was a singularly brief statement, obscurely phrased, and remarkable more for its omissions than for any positive declaration of principle. Apparently, it was the Congress of Chilpancingo rather than the Mexican people which had recovered 'its usurped sovereignty'. Moreover, this happy event derived not from the struggle of the insurgents, but rather from 'the present circumstances in Europe' and 'the inscrutable designs' of Providence. The Act solemnly promised to maintain the Catholic religion in all its purity, banning the practice of other faiths, even in secret. The religious orders were to be conserved and protected. Indeed, the Congress subsequently passed a resolution, proposed by Bustamante, calling for the re-establishment of the Jesuits. The same insistence on a confessional republic can be observed in the Constitutional Decree of Apatzingán, promulgated in 1814, which not merely stated that 'the Catholic, Roman and Apostolic religion is the only one to be professed in the state', but also declared that 'the status of citizen is lost through the crimes of heresy, apostasy, or treason to the nation'.[37]

V

Once Morelos was captured and executed in 1815, the insurgency crumbled into a series of guerilla bands haunting the mountainous periphery of the central plateau, whose operations increasingly partook more of banditry than of warfare. But the young creoles who had enrolled in the royalist army as professional officers still found their path to high command blocked by generals and colonels brought in from the Peninsula. Moreover, in 1820, a liberal revolution occurred in Spain following the mutiny of a military expedition destined for service in South America. The new Cortes once more expelled the Jesuits, abolished the Inquisition, terminated ecclesiastical immunity, and allowed considerable freedom of the press, measures which alienated the hierarchy of the Mexican Church. It was at this point that Agustín de Iturbide, a creole who had hitherto distinguished himself by the brutal energy of his campaigns against the insurgents, now conspired with his brother officers to separate Mexico from Spain. According to Carlos María de Bustamante, he had been disagreeably impressed by Servando de Mier's history of the Mexican revolution, where he received unfavourable mention. But the most important influence on his Plan de Iguala (1821), in which he set out the bases of independence, appears to have been the 1817 edition of the abbé Pradt's work, where Catholicism and monarchy were identified as the twin instruments of political stability for Spanish America.[38]

In his plan, Iturbide began by identifying as Americans all the diverse peoples who resided in Mexico, regardless of their birth-place. He then presented Pradt's biological metaphor, in which the dissolution of empires was interpreted as a natural process, similar to the emancipation of children from their parents, a process which did not injure the affection that characterised their filial relation. It was thanks to Spain, 'the most Catholic, pious, heroic and magnanimous nation' that Mexico had grown in wealth and population to the point where the branch was now equal to the trunk and separation had thus become a necessity. To achieve this end Iturbide offered three guarantees: he promised to maintain the Catholic religion, to achieve independence with a constitutional monarchy, and to preserve the peace and union of Americans and Europeans. Subordinate articles called for the return to the clergy of all their traditional privileges and property; and offered all office-holders the right to continue provided they accepted the Plan. So seductive was this proclamation that Iturbide proved able to effect a virtually peaceful seizure of power, the success of his revolt signalised when the incoming liberal viceroy, Juan O'Donojú, signed the Treaty of Córdoba in which Mexico was recognised as a fully independent empire which was to be governed by a constitutional monarch chosen from the Bourbon dynasty. Despite the conservative character of this settlement, the Act of Independence of 1821, signed by Iturbide and a number of dignitaries, invoked insurgent ideology when it grandly announced that: 'The Mexican nation, which for 300 years has neither had its own will nor free use of its voice, today leaves the oppression in which it has lived'. Within a few months, however, once it had become clear that the Bourbons had no intention of despatching a prince to occupy the Mexican throne, Iturbide proclaimed himself emperor, a manoeuvre which, if acclaimed by the mob, soon provoked armed rebellion.[39] Whereas in South America, the patriot forces won independence on the battle-field, in New Spain it was the royalist army which freed the country from Spanish rule and which was to govern Mexico until the Liberal Reform.

26

INSURGENT CREOLE

I

ON THE feast day of Our Lady of Guadalupe in 1794, Fray Servando Teresa de Mier (1763–1827), a Dominican theologian, preached before the dignitaries of Mexico, including the viceroy and archbishop, who had assembled at Tepeyac to pay homage to the patron of New Spain. What he had to say could not have been more startling. Opening with a customary trope, he compared the congregation to the priests, nobility and magistrates of Israel who had worshipped at the temple in Jerusalem and saluted the image of Mary as 'a new and better ark of the covenant of the Lord and his Mother' with this truly chosen, beloved generation, with their especial people, the Americans'. But he then declared that the recent excavations in the main square, 'more precious than those of Herculaneum and Pompeii', had thrown new light on the ancient history of Mexico and hailed the Calendar Stone as a jewel worth more than all the gold of the Indies. Such was their significance that he now advanced four propositions: that the image of Our Lady of Guadalupe had been imprinted on the cape of St Thomas, 'apostle of this kingdom' and not on that of Juan Diego; that the image had been worshipped by Indians some 1,750 years ago in the sierra of Tenayuca, where St Thomas had built a temple; that when the Indians apostatized, St Thomas hid the image, which remained lost until the Virgin Mary appeared to Juan Diego to reveal its whereabouts; and that the image was a painting of the first century, miraculously imprinted by the Virgin Mary before her death. Known to the Indians as Quetzalcoatl, St Thomas had taught his flock the chief doctrines of the Christian faith and Mary was thereafter venerated as the Mother of God. The sermon concluded with a petition to Our Lady of Guadalupe, 'teotenanzin entirely virgin, trustworthy tonacayona', to protect Mexico: 'Ark especially precious now that the Philistines of France have attacked Israel, do not permit that they should triumph here as they did there owing to the sins of the sons of Heli.'[1]

At one stroke, the abstruse speculations of creole savants were here transformed into a public declaration of the spiritual autonomy of Mexico. If

Spain had St James and Our Lady of Pilar, so equally Mexico had St Thomas and Our Lady of Guadalupe. Each country had been visited by an apostle who had endowed it with a miraculous image of the Virgin Mary. The apparition at Tepeyac simply rescued the Indians from their apostasy and restored their ancient faith. That Fray Servando should have appealed to the authority of the Calendar Stone to justify his assertions suggests that he had not read León y Gama's magisterial interpretation of that monument. Instead, he had accepted the theories of José Ignacio Borunda, an elderly creole lawyer, whose study of Athanasius Kircher, had encouraged him to read the hieroglyphs inscribed on the Stone as embodying an 'arcane philosophy' in which the foundation of Mexico–Tenochtitlan by St Thomas was indisputably revealed. That Mier did not bother to consult Borunda's manuscript suggests that he was already inclined to accept Sigüenza y Góngora's identification of St Thomas as Quetzalcoatl. Just when, however, he decided to incorporate the Guadalupe image into the framework of the apostolic mission, is not clear.[2] In effect, he denied the singularity of the image's apparition and located it within that group of images for which apostolic origin was claimed.

Ecclesiastical retribution for Mier's audacity was swift and punitive. The archbishop of Mexico, Alonso Núñez de Haro, already renowned for his hostility to creole pretensions, ordered him to be confined to his cell and mounted a judicial inquiry. The two creole canons charged with examining the papers ridiculed Borunda as 'a Mexican historical Don Quijote', whose allegorical interpretations were both arbitrary and whimsical. More important, they indicated the basic difficulty in chronology presented by the identification of St Thomas and Quetzalcoatl: the Indian high priest of Tula, described by Torquemada and Clavijero, had lived at least 700 after the apostle. Against Mier, the two canons adopted a more severe line: 'he has deceived the people with false documents and fictions'; his sermon was 'a tapestry of dreams, delirium and absurdities'; and his theories 'are capable of forming a thousand romantic, novelistic historians'. With this sharp condemnation in hand, the archbishop sentenced Mier to ten years exile and confinement at Caldas, a Dominican priory situated in the hills of Santander, a punishment designed 'to contain his spirit, so proud and so inclined to inflated ideas and pernicious novelties'.[3]

Although Mier later declared that 'as a man of honour and birth I received a stab of death from the edict', he soon escaped from Caldas to Madrid where he strove to vindicate his reputation. By then Juan Bautista Muñoz, the current general chronicler of the Indies, had located Sahagún's great history of Mexican things, and had there encountered the Franciscan's dismissal of the cult at Tepeyac as idolatrous. Acting on his advice, the Academy of History exonerated Mier from any error or crime other than of imprudence in questioning 'the fable' of the Guadalupe in so public a fashion. But the matter was not to be so easily resolved. Unknown to Mier, the viceroy had warned the authorities in Madrid that Fray Servando had welcomed the news of the French Revolution and that it was advisable to keep him in Spain. When it appeared likely that Mier would obtain remission of his sentence, the archbishop intervened to complain that the exiled Dominican was 'loose in speaking; and in sentiment and opinion is opposed to the rights of the king and to Spanish dominion'.[4] It was these political considerations as much as his sermon, which led to the Mexican patriot being subjected to further confinement.

In the years which followed, Fray Servando embarked on that picaresque career that he was to describe with so much gusto in his memoirs. In 1801 he fled to France, where he was welcomed by Henri Gregoire, the leader of the constitutionalist clergy; visited Rome to obtain his secularisation from the Dominican order; returned to Spain where he was again imprisoned; escaped to Portugal; returned in 1809 to serve as volunteer chaplain against the French; witnessed the opening of the Cortes of Cadiz; took up residence in London where he contributed to *El Español* and published the first history of the Mexican insurgency; sailed for Mexico in company of Javier Mina, where he was imprisoned and wrote his memoirs; escaped to the United States where he printed a memorial warning his compatriots against accepting a king; returned once more to Mexico and served as a deputy in Congress, campaigning against the radical proposals for a federal constitution; and in 1827 died in the national palace after receiving the last sacraments.[5]

During the long years of European exile, Mier read widely in theology, political theory and Mexican history. He conversed with Joseph Blanco White, Simón Rodríguez, the tutor of Simón Bolívar, and Henri Grégoire. He himself emerged as the chief theorist of the Mexican insurgency. By party affiliation, he can be defined as a Jansenist and a Whig, which is to say, he was an aristocratic republican and a liberal Catholic, who rejected the free-thinking, radical democracy of Rousseau and his disciples. In the hispanic world, he figured as an adherent of Jovellanos and Blanco White and applied their ideas to Mexico. Despite these influences, he never renegued on his belief in the apostolic evangelisation of the New World and towards the close of his life, in July 1822, rose in the newly assembled Mexican Congress to argue that since Jesus Christ had commanded his apostles to preach to all nations under the sun, at least one apostle had come to America. If St Thomas was thus publicly installed as the apostle of the New World, it was, so Mier claimed, because 'the most holy Virgin did not await the passage of 1,600 years in order to be Our Lady and Mother ... '[6] Theological necessity was thus invoked to support patriotic belief.

The degree to which Fray Servando remained obsessed with this question of an apostolic mission is best observed in his *Historia de la revolución de Nueva España antiguamente Anáhuac* (1813), where, much to the confusion of his

English readers, he inserted a long appendix on the subject. Mier here drew as much on García's *Origen de los indios* and Calancha's *Crónica moralizada* as on Sigüenza y Góngora, Becerra Tanco, Veytia (whose manuscripts he had consulted in Madrid), and Boturini. Further corroboration was taken from Kircher's account of St Thomas' mission to India and China. By contrast, he sharply attacked both Acosta and Torquemada for their invocation of the Devil as the author of native religion. However, he now postulated at least two separate missions, the first by St Thomas, and the second in the sixth century led by a Syrian bishop or by the Irish missionary, St Brendan. So also, he accepted García's thesis that the New World had been invaded by any number of distinct peoples prior to the arrival of the Spaniards. Above all else, the similarity in doctrines and rites between Aztec religion and Catholicism pointed to a common origin. 'What was the religion of the Mexicans but a Christianity confused by time and the equivocal nature of the hieroglyphs?' Even the sacrificial consumption of human flesh was but a misunderstanding of the doctrine of The Eucharist.[7] Why should Nezahualcoyotl be called an idolater when it was clear that he worshipped the one true God? Nor was the corruption of Indian Christianity any cause for surprise: had not the French but recently descended into atheism?

The emotional force which animated Mier's convictions was clearly revealed in his *Carta de despedida* (1820), a manuscript which he wrote on the point of sailing for Spain, destined, so it seemed, for permanent exile. He started with a passionate plea that Mexico should reject the Spanish Academy's recent decision to substitute 'j' for 'x' in all Mexican names. For Mexico, as distinct from Mejico, derived from the Indian pronunciation 'Mescico', which meant: 'where Christ is or where he is adored, so that Mexicans are the same as Christians'. To arrive at this etymology, he cited the thesis of Martín del Castillo, sustained by Baltazar de Medina, that Mexi was the Indian pronunciation of the Hebrew Mesias. In effect, Mexico–Tenochtitlan had been founded by St Thomas–Quetzalcoatl and still bore the name which signified its Christian vocation.[8]

If Mier's faith in the apostolic foundation of his country proved unshakeable, by contrast his belief in the story of Guadalupe was soon lost. Prior to the sermon, his doubts had been aroused by José Ignacio Bartolache's observation that the image's canvas was of a different substance from the material used for Indian capes. In any case, the Jansenist clergy with whom he was associated, generally adopted a sceptical view of apparitions, miracles and miraculous images. The story of St James' mission to Spain had become the object of controversy and the authenticity of his tomb at Compostella strongly questioned. When Muñoz's memoir on the Mexican Guadalupe was published in 1817, any vestige of faith Mier still entertained was destroyed, the more especially since Sahagún had identified the cult at Tepeyac as a disguised worship of Tonantzin. In a series of letters to Muñoz, dated 1797 but probably written in 1817–20, Mier now drew attention to the similarity of the apparition story to the biblical account of Moses on Mount Sinai. Citing Sigüenza y Góngora's affirmation that the original manuscript was written by Antonio Valeriano, the Indian governor of Tenochtitlan and a collaborator of Sahagún, he declared: 'The story of Guadalupe is a comedy of the Indian Valeriano, based on Aztec mythology, so that the young students at Santiago Tlatelolco, where he was a professor, could perform it, since at that time they were accustomed to perform in their language the farces that were called *autos sacramentales*.' But Mier did not discuss the origin of the image other than to assert that it was obviously indigenous in both its style and concept.[9] Since he was persuaded that the Mexican Indians had worshipped the Virgin Mary under the guise of Tonantzin for centuries prior to the arrival of the Spaniards, the precise provenance of the image apparently did not concern him.

In effect, Mier's bold attempt to combine the two great creole myths into a single historical event failed to survive his own latent scepticism. He had to admit that Borunda's theories were nonsensical. But although he differed from most creole patriots in doubting that the Virgin Mary had imprinted her image on Juan Diego's cape, his demonstration of an apostolic mission to Mexico met with an enthusiastic reception, the more especially since it was based on a small library of Creole authors. The nineteenth-century scholar, José Fernando Ramírez, assembled a mass of manuscripts and texts dealing with the subject and did not hesitate to insert Mier's dissertation in the Spanish translation of William Prescott's history of the Spanish conquest. As late as the 1880s Manuel Orozco y Berra toyed with the idea that Quetzalcoatl was an Irish missionary.[10] The impetus here derived from the widespread desire to provide Mexico with a Christian foundation and thus liberate the country from the historical necessity of Spanish conquest and evangelisation.

II

If Fray Servando was able to move so easily from country to country in Europe, it was in part because he had become a Jansenist, which is to say, on questions of Church discipline, an extreme Gallican. Granted that he was the victim of episcopal persecution and ardently desired to be freed of his Dominican vows, there was nothing very surprising in this. Whatever the reasons, his memoirs reveal that virtually all the men who protected and assisted him in Spain were accused of belonging to that party. Nor was Mier loath to confess his allegiance, since he declared that 'in Europe they call Jansenist all the men who are solidly instructed in religion and who are friends of the old and legitimate discipline of the Church'. It was thanks to this party affiliation that Mier was welcomed by Henri Grégoire when he fled to France in 1801, since the French bishop corresponded with Jovellanos and other Spanish Jansenists. But the two men were also united by a common admiration for Bartolomé de las Casas, whose tracts Grégoire edited for publication in France, acknowledging in his introduction the assistance he had received from 'a learned American doctor of the University of Mexico'. Ever on the side of the oppressed, Gregoire founded an anti-slavery society in Paris, corresponded with William Wilberforce in London, and warmly supported the independence of Haiti.[11]

If Fray Servando later referred to Grégoire as 'my friend' and as 'a great bishop', it was because he came to share many of his opinions. A Jansenist who founded the Society of Christian Philosophy to propagate his views, Henri Grégoire (1750–1831), had been elected to the National Assembly in 1789 where he soon emerged as an ardent republican, declaiming that 'the history of kings is the martyrology of nations'. He found no difficulty in accepting the Civil Constitution of 1791 which prescribed the popular election of both priests and bishops. Nominated bishop of Blois, he became the leader of the constitutional clergy but was obliged to resign his see in 1804 after Napoleon reached a concordat with the Pope, agreeing to restore the former hierarchy. Although the ultramontane clergy denounced Grégoire as a heretic, he always insisted on his dogmatic orthodoxy in all matters other than the grand question of Church government, on which he adopted a republican, federal position, rejecting the papal monarchy in favour of Gallican autonomy. No friend of either the Jacobins or the philosophes, he sharply condemned 'the corrupting cynicism of the confessions of J. J. Rousseau', and declared that 'Voltaire never had other guides than his own vanity and cupidity'. He had attended the sessions of the Convention dressed as a bishop and strongly opposed the state deism proposed and introduced by Robespierre. Whereas many clergymen reacted against the excesses of the Revolution by favouring an alliance between the Church and absolute monarchy, Grégoire strove to maintain 'the holy alliance of Christianity and democracy', adding that whereas 'J. J. Rousseau claims that Catholicism and liberty are irreconcilable, I believe that Catholicism is irreconcilable with despotism'.[12]

As a patriot from a country where the hierarchy had excommunicated insurgent leaders as heretics, Mier had good reason to echo Grégoire's views. In his contributions to El Español and in his subsequent writings, he openly questioned the legitimacy of the Alexandrine donation of 1493, arguing that the papal monarchy established during the Middle Ages was based on forged documents – the Decretals of St Isidore and the Donation of Constantine – which were expressed in the canon law of Gratian. In good Jansenist fashion, he called for a return to the primitive constitution of the Church where all priests and not merely bishops figured as the heirs of the apostles. Each diocese should possess its own council, vested with an authority superior to the bishop's.

32 Servando Teresa de Mier

The Christian people that compose the defined Church . . . will choose its bishops in company with the clergy and will not accept any bishop against its will . . . Of divine right the parish priests with the bishop compose the court or judgement seat of the Church, so that according to the ancient and true canons a bishop could do nothing without the consultation and consent of his *presbyterium*, composed of the parish priests of his city.[13]

After Mexico achieved independence, Mier intervened in the congressional debates of 1823 to advocate immediate action on the appointment of bishops to replace the Spaniards who had fled the country. On the subject of opening relations with the Papacy, he confessed: 'my ideas in this matter are very liberal since I have been a member of the constitutional clergy of France . . . Whether the Church is a monarchy as the ultramontanes claim, or whether it is a federal republic as the university of Paris teaches, which is my opinion, is a matter for question in the Church.' The Pope was certainly to be acknowledged as the visible head, the centre of the Church's unity, but his right to appoint bishops was a medieval usurpation of powers that resided within each metropolitan see. Concordats with Rome invariably impaired the nation's right to choose the bishops it wanted. Mier concluded: 'Each church has its divine foundation, with all the powers necessary to conserve and propagate itself without any necessity of going to Rome.'[14] His worst apprehensions concerning the Papacy were confirmed in 1824 when Leo XII issued an encyclical in which he exhorted the Spanish Americans to renew their allegiance to the Spanish Crown. This untimely missive aroused great resentment throughout Mexico and Mier published an acerbic pamphlet, reproduced in a leading newspaper, in which he firmly condemned the Holy See's meddling in the temporal affairs of this world. He reminded his readers of the Alexandrine Donation which had unleashed 'bloodstained demons' on the New World and commended the Gallican declarations of 1682 proposed by 'the most learned Bossuet'. Moving on to the offensive, he cited the famous homily of Pius VII, issued when bishop of Imola, which had advocated an alliance of Christianity and democracy, a text which had been printed in Paris by 'my celebrated friend, the wise and virtuous Grégoire', and which in Spanish translation now circulated in Mexico. One of Mier's last letters, written in 1825, strongly criticised Canon Vasquez' mission to Rome, which aimed to arrange the appointment of a new hierarchy for Mexico.[15]

Like his French mentor, Fray Servando continued to regard himself as a Catholic and a priest. In Congress he opposed the implementation of the decrees of the 1820 Cortes which threatened clerical privileges and property, arguing that they would only serve to antagonise the people: 'all the clergy together do not exceed four thousand and among them are the nobility and the enlightened. It is for this reason that the clergy has always been at the head of the insurrection since it knows best the rights of the people, to whom it has always been a father and a protector.' As much as Grégoire, he took a critical view of both philosophes and Jacobins, attributing the crimes of the French Revolution to 'the demoralisation of the people, the work of its philosophers . . . they attacked dogma and with it there fell morality and so there was lacking religion, without which, as Tacitus rightly said, it is as impossible to found a republic as to build a city in the air'. It was for this reason that he advocated the prohibition in Mexico of all impious or blasphemous books, speaking at least three times on the subject in Congress, with Rousseau and Voltaire his especial object of attack. In all this, Mier showed himself a firm exponent of the confessional republicanism favoured by Morelos and Bustamante.[16]

III

It was the French invasion of the Peninsula which provided Fray Servando with an opportunity to intervene in the politics of independence. Unwise enough to return to Spain in 1803, after a visit to Rome in which he claimed to have obtained his secularisation, he was promptly condemned to further confinement, first in Madrid and then in a prison for erring clerics in Seville. The administrator of the prison complained bitterly of his charge, exclaiming that Mier's behaviour and utterances were so extravagant as to 'make me believe that he has suffered a stroke in the brain, since how else to explain his believing such nonsense as to persuade himself that in the midst of all his abjection he is about to leave here to become a dean or a bishop'. When in 1805 he reported Mier's second and successful escape to Portugal, he begged to be allowed to resign, adding 'everything is useless with this class of monster . . . I no longer have the force to struggle with such creatures.'[17] Utterly unabashed, Fray Servando re-entered Spain in 1808, there to serve as chaplain to a volunteer battalion, witnessing the defeat of General Blake at Belchite, despatching an exuberant account of his role in that battle for publication in Mexico. He then boldly made his way to Cadiz and petitioned the Regency to reward his services by appointment as canon in the cathedral of Mexico. Present at the opening of the Cortes, he established close contact with the American deputies and was commissioned by Iturrigaray's widow to refute Cancelada's allegations about the viceroy's actions in 1808. Thereafter, Mier sailed for London where he contributed to *El Español* and published his *Historia de la revolución*, maintained during the years 1811–16 by a small subvention from the British government procured by Blanco White.[18]

The purpose of his *Historia* was to rehearse the constitutional arguments of 1808, comment on the debates at the Cortes of Cadiz, describe the course of the Mexican insurgency, and provide a reasoned case for Mexican independence. It is the capital text for any interpretation of the ideology of the Spanish American revolution. Written in vigorous, polemical style, it marks the axial moment when the traditional themes of creole patriotism were converted into strong arguments against Spanish rule. To assist him, Mier drew also on the Whig emphasis on the ancient constitution propounded by Jovellanos and Blanco White; nor did he hesitate to cite Thomas Paine. At all points, however, he rejected the influence of Rousseau and Jacobin principles of democracy: his appeal was to Mexican history rather than to universal reason, his aim the liberation of the Mexican nation rather than the redemption of humanity.

Here is no place to trace anew the constitutional debates of 1808–12 in Mexico and at Cadiz. Suffice to say that Fray Servando assembled abundant materials, culled from both *El Español* and the American deputies at the Cortes, all designed to demonstrate that the rupture between Spain and America derived from the unprovoked aggression of the Europeans resident in the New World. The seizure of Iturrigaray, the insults of that 'bankrupt pedlar' Cancelada, the denial of free trade, the exclusion of castas of African descent from the electoral register, the refusal to appoint creoles to high office, the atrocious memorial of the Mexican merchant guild, the inequality of representation at the Cortes, and the refusal to recognise the insurgent juntas: here was the substance of a case which had already led Mier to exclaim – 'What have the Americas now to expect of the Spanish nation? What remains for us to propose to such an obstinately tyrannical nation? What terms can we adopt with such a proud nation, that is agonising, drowning, hanging, without an army, without leaders, without fortifications, without a navy, without resources, almost entirely subjugated, yet which still denies us all, despises, insults, threatens, intrigues and boasts when it ought simply to beg pardon for its crimes in America and humbly implore asylum?'[19]

In effect, the customary enmity between creoles and gachupines, already so noticeable a feature of Mexican society since the early seventeenth century here finally exploded into the most bitter recrimination. The plaint against the *advenedizos* now crystallised into a denunciation of the mercantile tyranny exercised by the peninsular Spaniards in America and still sustained by the Regency and Cortes. Equally important, Mier roundly denounced the *alternativa*, that peculiarly colonial system, whereby friars were brought over from Spain for the express purpose of governing the mendicant communities in alternate terms, despite the overwhelming creole majority. As a Dominican, Mier had experienced the persecution of his European confreres, whose predominantly peasant origin constituted a further source of irritation for the aristocratic creoles who entered the order. Furthermore, he attacked Archbishop Nuñez de Haro who had sought to pack cathedral chapters with canons from the Peninsula, thereby denying creoles their due promotion. It was this manifest discrimination which had driven so many Mexican clergy to embrace the insurgent cause.[20]

The reiteration of old grievances acquired a deeper historical resonance when Mier evoked the crimes of the conquerors, only then to fix upon the cruelties perpetrated by contemporary royalist commanders as affording proof that the Spaniards had never changed: they remained the same ferocious nation, ever intent on the destruction of the New World and its inhabitants, be they Indians or creoles. Just as Alvarado had slaughtered the Aztec nobility at Tenochtitlan, so also General Calleja had massacred the population of Guanajuato once that city was recaptured. In Michoacán and Jalisco, where once Nuño de Guzmán had tortured and ravaged, so now General Cruz burnt and killed. Once appointed viceroy, Calleja re-enacted the measures introduced by the Duke of Alba in the Low Countries. The executions of insurgent leaders recalled the official murder of Tupac Amaru ordered by Viceroy Toledo. Not content with rhetoric, Mier extracted from official gazettes a summary of military actions and the numbers of insurgents fallen in battle or executed, which demonstrated, so he argued, that the royalists had far outstripped Cortés in the number of Mexicans they had killed. As much as the conquerors, contemporary Spaniards had acted like wolves let loose in the sheepfold, striving to preserve their dominion by terror and devastation.[21]

In framing this indictment, Mier cited Las Casas' *Brevísima relación de la destrucción de las Indias* as proof of the implacable cruelty of the Spaniards. So persuaded was he of its ideological relevance to the insurgent cause, that he promoted no less than three editions of the tract, in London,

Philadelphia, and Mexico, warning the Spaniards in his preface that: 'neither will there be lacking a new Las Casas to reveal your crimes and expose you once more to the execration of the universe'. Already, in the French edition, he had defended the great Dominican from the slander of 'the story-teller Pauw and his acolyte Robertson', who had accused him of starting the slave trade. So now he saluted Las Casas as 'the tutelary genius of the Americas, father of the Indians', and warmly adopted Raynal's suggestion that after independence Mexico should erect a statue in his honour. As a Dominican, Mier had read the histories of his Order in Mexico written by Dávila Padilla and Remesal, in which Las Casas figured as a virtual saint: so now he applied the virulent denunciation of the conquerors to the contemporary scene and installed Las Casas as prophet for all the inhabitants of America, be they Indian, casta or creole.[22]

At apparent odds with this passionate rejection of the conquest, Mier also asserted that the creoles had been deprived of their ancestral rights as heirs of the conquerors. Here was a traditional line of argument, a commonplace of seventeenth-century petitions for office, already advanced by Juan Antonio Ahumada in the 1720s and sustained by Viscardo y Guzmán in his famous *Carta*. There had existed, so Mier declared, a 'social pact' between the conquerors and the kings of Spain, inherited by their creole heirs, which had been destroyed by the gachupín coup of 1808. It was a binding instrument which should not be confused with the 'anti-social contract' of Rousseau, which he denounced as 'that tapestry of sophistries, decorated with the brilliance of the enchanting eloquence of the Genevan philosopher'. The doctrine of the general will and popular sovereignty had caused the French Revolution and all its excesses; it had prompted the downfall of the Caracas junta; and it had inspired the Constitution of Cadiz, where the creation of a unitary state based on a fictitious Spanish nation had reduced the Americans to perpetual tutelage. Rather than invoking universal rights or general theory, Mier appealed 'to the solemn and explicit pact celebrated between the Americans and the kings of Spain . . . authenticated in the very code of their laws. This is our Magna Carta.' Had not the Indies been conquered by privately financed expeditions, whose leaders subsequently acted as governors, establishing cities and distributing encomiendas? Only later were the conquered territories incorporated into the kingdom of Castile, binding the Americans, however, to the Spanish king and not to the Spanish people.[23]

But Mier did not rest his case on any title-deed conferred by conquest, since he defined the creoles as the spiritual heirs of the early mendicants who had defended the Indians from the exploitation of the conquerors. It was thanks to the campaign launched by Las Casas and his fellow Dominicans that the natives of the New World were declared to be true human beings and free subjects of the Crown. The fruit of their efforts was the New Laws of 1542, which ended the worst abuses of the encomiendas. It was at this period that the Crown promulgated for America 'their fundamental laws or their true constitution. They then laid the foundations of the code of the Indies, whose better laws are little more than conclusions drawn from the writings of Las Casas, as Remesal has well said.' Moreover, to compensate the conquerors for the loss of their encomiendas, the Crown promised that their descendants should enjoy preference for all appointments in Church and State, preferential rights that Mier described as 'compensatory laws annexed to the social pact of the American creoles with their kings'.[24] At much the same time, the Crown celebrated similar pacts with the Indians, recognising the authority of their lords and affirming their status as free subjects.

In effect, Mier applied to America the same kind of historical arguments that Jovellanos and Blanco White had advanced for Spain. If the conquest was execrated, the Laws of the Indies, which enshrined the rights of the conquerors and their descendants, were installed as the ancient constitution of the New World. In accord with Solórzano, Mier then argued that the American territories constituted true kingdoms, endowed with viceroys, governors, high courts, colleges, universities, bishops and convents. Although in legal theory part of the Crown of Castile, the Indies possessed their own Council, comparable in status to the Councils that administered Italy, Flanders and Aragon, and thus possessing 'equal sovereign principality, preserving their laws, rights and pacts'. Like its Spanish exemplar, however, the American constitution had been undermined and ignored by the growing despotism of the Crown, which denied creoles any advancement, reduced the Indians to serfs, and imposed a commercial monopoly. But no matter how eroded and corrupted, the constitution still endured as the political foundation of Mexico, offering clear proof that once the Bourbon dynasty abdicated, sovereignty had to return to the Americans, with whom the Crown had celebrated the original pact. It followed that the Cortes lacked all authority to promulgate a new constitution, uniting Spain and America in a unitary state. Praising Blanco White for 'the clarity of his judgment, for the rectitude and impartiality of his heart, and for his complete union of enlightenment and political knowledge', Mier signalised the manifold deficiencies of the Cadiz constitution, fixing on its weak executive, its lack of a second legislative assembly, and the absence of an independent judiciary. Essentially the work of doctrinaires, it replaced the positive if imperfect legislation of over two centuries by administrative chaos.[25]

Although Fray Servando appealed to history to justify the insurgent cause, he also advanced several arguments based on the natural rights created by geography, birth and race. For he clinched his case by citing Tom Paine's *Common Sense*, paraphrasing a passage that had already appeared in both Raynal and Viscardo: 'Nature has not created a world in order to submit it to the inhabitants of a peninsula in another universe . . . By the law of masses and of distances America can belong only to itself . . . so rich a world cannot be the slave of a miserable corner.' In addition, he defended the rights conferred by birth and upbringing, exclaiming: 'Americans, we have the same rights over America as the Indians, who came from Asia . . . that of being born here, cultivating the land, building and defending its towns.'[26] Not content simply to assert the parity of creoles and Indians, he also emphasised the relevance of *mestizaje*. After all, Tom Paine had argued that Great Britain could not be regarded as the mother country of the United States since the continent had attracted immigrants from all Europe. So now, Mier asserted that, since Spanish migration had been primarily masculine, many conquerors and settlers had married or bred with Indian women, so that Spain could not be described as the mother country of Mexico. 'All we creoles are mestizos . . . in our veins flow the pure blood of the native lords of the country.' It was some years later, in a memorial published in 1821, that Mier brought all these arguments together in a passage which drew in equal measure on Viscardo, Garcilaso de la Vega and Tom Paine. Alluding to recent Spanish territorial treaties with the United States he wrote:

> All these concessions are insults we suffer, not only on account of the rights of our mothers who were Indians, but also by reason of the pacts of our fathers, the conquerors, who gained everything at their own cost and risk, with the kings of Spain . . . America is ours because our fathers gained it, thus creating a right; because it was of our mothers, and because we are born in it. This is the natural right of all peoples in their respective regions. God has separated us from Europe by an immense sea and our interests are distinct. Spain never had any right here.

By then Mier had come to present himself as the symbolic Mexican patriot, declaring: 'I myself descend from the last emperor, Cuauhtémoc . . . This is the true reason why I was exiled to Spain twenty-five years ago and why I was not allowed to return . . .'[27]

IV

In 1816 Fray Servando finally left England, sailing for Mexico in the company of Javier Mina, a foolhardy Spanish soldier who planned to overthrow Ferdinand VII by initiating a revolt in Mexico. The expedition soon met with defeat and Mina, together with most of his companions, lost his life. As always Mier survived, this time by reason of his non-combatant status and his family connections with the northern nobility. But he spent the next five years in gaol, first under the Inquisition and then in the grim fortress of San Juan de Ulúa. It was in this period of confinement that he wrote his memoirs and drafted several essays in which he defended his ideas and career. In 1821 he escaped from the ship that was taking him back to Spain and fled to Philadelphia, where he published his *Memoria político-instructiva*. By then Mier was a national figure, a legend in his own life-time, wherein the borderline between fact and fantasy was not always clear, even to himself. 'Being from a country as distant as Mexico made me a sort of mythological creature ... no-one could persuade themselves that a man of my knowledge and education could be an ordinary man.' To a Spanish official, 'my history appeared like a story and surely invented'. And indeed, so it was, since in these years Mier not merely described himself as a 'celebrated writer and descendant of the last emperor of Mexico'; he also claimed to have been appointed archbishop of Baltimore. Less dramatically, he asserted that during his visit to Rome he had obtained secularisation from the Dominican Order and had been named apostolic pronotary, a rank which allowed him to wear episcopal scarlet.[28] None of these whims detracted from his political influence since the Inquisition appraised him in these sober terms: 'Fray Servando is among the most prejudicial and feared men among the many that have been known. In character he is arrogant, proud and presumptuous. He possesses a vast knowledge of bad literature. In person he is tough, lively and daring ... he still preserves an inflexible mind and a tranquil spirit, superior to all his misfortunes.'[29]

In his memoirs, Fray Servando painted a bitter, scornful picture of the Spain of Godoy. The country was poor, its land infertile, its climate wretched, and the people ridden with disease. 'In Castile there is bread and wine and nothing else.' Provincial differences were great: 'they only agree in all being fierce and proud, more or less, and in being ignorant and superstitious'. He depicted the government as corrupt, despotic and dominated by a nobility which was both ignorant and vicious: 'almost all public officials are the servants and lackeys of the grandees or relatives of their mistresses'. After his sojourn in Paris, he found Spain provincial: 'the Spaniards are the perpetual apes of the clothes and customs of the other Europeans, and especially of the French'. Not that he himself cared much for Napoleonic France, since he wrote contemptuously of 'the light and comic genius of the French which has ended in their being the slaves of a despot ... never did I see a people more superficial, changeable and futile as the French'. Indeed, what impressed Mier in France was neither its politics nor its military glory, but rather the French Church with its Gallican rites and Jansenist clergy, his residence in that country serving only to confirm his detestation of the philosophes. It was in his published *Memoria*, written in Philadelphia, that Mier transmuted these commonplace remarks into a political, not to say, philosophic, antithesis between Europe and America. 'When one leaves our abundant, temperate and delicious climate to go to Europe, he feels the same disadvantage that Adam felt on leaving Paradise to enter a land full of nettles and thorns, which to obtain bread he had to till with the sweat of his brow. On the other side of the ocean, one naturally feels the idea of an original sin.' Were not the Europeans 'decrepit peoples, corrupted by luxury, ambition, immorality and license?' For a man so impressed by the burden of history, however, this optimistic view of the New World as another Eden proved to be but a passing phase, the result, no doubt, of Philadelphian air and hospitality.[30]

Chief among the influences on Mier's thinking in these years was the recently published work of the abbé Pradt whose biological metaphor of independence as a natural process of growth and maturity he welcomed, echoing the argument almost word for word when he wrote of Spanish America: 'independence is nothing more than the declaration of the coming of age. Now that we have a larger population than the mother country, equal culture, and greater wealth, we believe that we are now ready to emancipate ourselves. To call us rebels because of this is to call Nature a rebel because it emancipates children when they no longer need their parents.' But Mier indignantly rejected Pradt's definition of Spanish America as a mere colony, which is to say, the simple property of the metropolis, whose purpose was but to produce and consume. Such a description might well be true of the Antilles, but it certainly could not be applied to Mexico which possessed all the institutions of a true country. Despite his earlier praise of English freedom, he now endorsed Pradt's warning about the threat of British expansion, observing 'I have heard their ministers say that no-one exceeded Machiavelli in practical wisdom. That is their bible . . . the policy of Albion, as obscure as its climate, is in opposition to the liberty and prosperity of the world.'[31]

But it was Pradt's advocacy of monarchy for Spanish America which most alarmed Mier and drove him to write his *Memoria político-instructiva*. In his earlier works, he had eschewed any discussion of the forms of government other than to condemn federalism as a recipe for anarchy. After all, Regency England was no place in which to publish an open attack on the principle of monarchy. Yet Mier already had been greatly influenced by Grégoire and Tom Paine, both of whom were staunch republicans, and when he now asserted the necessity of a republic for Mexico, he turned to these men again. 'In the long term, liberty and a king are incompatible . . . What is the history of kings, as a great bishop has said, but the martyrology of nations? . . . Kings are so many idols manufactured by pride and adulation'. Had not the prophet Samuel warned the Israelites against choosing a king? As Tom Paine had observed, 'God Himself gave his chosen people a republican government.' Apart from its inherent tyranny, monarchy was also inextricably European, so that a king would involve Mexico in the wars of the Old World and prevent the achievement of true independence. 'The dynasties of Europe do not have any more rights over America than those of thieves and brigands . . . Through the ties of family, throne and the interests of Europe, a king would trap us in the interminable wars of that old, rotten, needy and intriguing whore, as Napoleon called Europe.'[32]

On a more positive note, Mier declared that 'republican government is the only one, in which particular interests, always active, are the same as the general interest of the government and state'. He offered the United States, 'our compatriots', as the model of progress for Mexico. The excesses of the French Revolution did not derive from its republicanism; they were to be attributed to the prevalent irreligion caused by the writings of the philosophes; to the intrigues of foreign powers; and to the national character of the French who always crave a master. Following the same line of argument, Mier favoured a republic in Mexico because it was the form of government best suited to 'our genius and character, which is as docile, light, vivacious, sweet and benign as our climate'. He feared that a king would soon attract 'an army of flatterers, officials, servile missionaries, monarchical theologians and inquisitors . . . I am convinced that kings are not suitable for our sweetness. The king of the sheep, which is what we Mexicans are, can only be the wolf. The general spirit is republican.'[33] This reliance on national character as a mode of explanation once more reveals Mier's preference for historical and geographical arguments over any abstract reasoning in politics, a preference supported by his reading of Montesquieu, Blanco White and Jovellanos.

On his return to Mexico from the United States, Mier was captured by the Spanish garrison that still occupied San Juan de Ulúa, so that by the time he obtained his release in 1822, Agustín de Iturbide had proclaimed himself emperor of Mexico. Entering Congress as deputy for New Leon, Mier vigorously opposed the new monarch and denounced the proposal to establish military courts: 'this measure at once recalls the disastrous times of Robespierre, of Venegas and Calleja'. In the debates he drew on his European experience to inform the assembly that 'in most free countries like England, there has always been a party for opposition', only then to express his doubts as to whether the Mexicans could maintain such a system: 'more likely, we shall embrace the extremes, like the French, being either very servile or very radical'. He soon moved into open conspiracy against the regime, suffered his last term of prison, and then escaped to join the former insurgent generals, Vicente Guerrero and Nicolás Bravo, in their revolt against the emperor. A government pamphlet affirmed that 'as for Padre Mier, all the evidence combines to condemn him as the chief director of the enterprise'.[34]

When Congress re-assembled after the overthrow of Iturbide, Mier played an important, but largely unsuccessful role in the political manoeuvres and debates that followed. Although he helped to outwit the conservative 'Bourbon' party, he himself was in turn defeated by the radicals. Rather like Jovellanos in 1810, he lamented that for many deputies 'there is nothing more to know than Montesquieu, Rousseau and Raynal'. Although the great majority wanted a republic, there were considerable divisions as to the precise form of its government: 'we differ in that some want a confederation and I . . .

want a centralised republic for at least ten or twelve years'. But although both Padre Mier and Carlos María de Bustamante joined forces to advocate a centralised republic endowed with a strong executive, the radical majority in Congress opted for a federal constitution, prompted in large measure by the instructions of their state capitals, where local politicians were anxious to liberate their territories from the dominion of Mexico City.[35] The 1824 Constitution was later described as 'a monstrous graft of that of the United States on that of Cadiz of 1812', which was to say, that it created a federation of sovereign states but rendered the executive subordinate to congress. Its promulgation was preceded by the Constitutive Act of the Mexican Federation, which declared that: 'The Mexican nation is composed of the provinces comprised in the territory of the viceroyalty formerly called New Spain.' The actual constitution came with a proclamation in which 'the flourishing republic of our neighbours in the North' was lauded as offering a prime example of political practice. The federation was defended on the grounds that the sheer size and physical diversity of the new republic required delegation of authority, since different states would require different laws. Respectful reference was made to the writings of Rousseau, Montesquieu and Franklin; and Washington was saluted as 'an immortal man'. Like its exemplar of Cadiz, the document omitted all reference to the rights of man and largely dealt with the organisation of government.[36] The Roman Catholic religion was installed as the official religion of the republic. In effect, here was no Jacobin manifesto, but rather a text which faithfully expressed the interests of the provinces and the illusions of the radicals; it further implicitly attested to the dominance of the United States in the sphere of political culture.

In December 1823, Mier rose in Congress to deliver his Political Prophecy. In essence, he argued that a constitution should not be introduced as an instrument of reform but rather should take into account national character and social reality. Although federation was the best form of republican government, Mexico required a federation that was 'very compact, being thus more analogous to our education and customs'. As much as the radicals, he accepted that the United States had attained 'the height of social perfection'. But before their type of government and political practice could be adopted in Mexico, society had to change, since any mere copying of foreign models would bring disaster. To drive home this argument, he contrasted both the history and the character of the Mexicans and their northern neighbours, insisting on the immense differences which separated the two nations. For the Anglo-Americans were 'a new people, homogeneous, industrious, diligent, enlightened and full of social virtues, educated as a free nation'. For years they had lived under a constitution which was essentially republican and had formed their confederation to unite against the oppression of England. Each state had ports and access to the sea and thus enjoyed a considerable measure of independence. By contrast, the Mexicans were 'an old people, hetero-geneous, without industry, hostile to work, who wish to live off public office like the Spaniards, as ignorant in the general mass as our fathers, and rotten with the vices that derive from the slavery of three centuries'. In this context, it was absurd to imitate the Americans and divide the country into separate states, especially since only some provinces possessed ports and 'nature itself, so to say, has centralised us'.[37]

After this stark assessment, Mier moved to attack the radicals on their chief principle, their belief in the sovereignty of the general will, arguing that majority rule simply meant the dominance of 'the will of gross and ignorant men, who compose the general mass of people'. He warned that reliance on this 'sophistry' could lead to demagoguery and the tyranny of the mob: 'The people can be as tyrannical as a monarch ... The people have always been the victims of the seduction of turbulent demagogues.' It was the self-same principle, taken from Rousseau, that had led to the Jacobin terror of the French Revolution: 'Principles, if you wish, metaphysically true; but inapplicable in practice, because they consider man in the abstract and such a man does not exist in society.' In Europe only England had escaped the contagion of anarchy. It was during his residence in London that he himself had finally renounced Jacobi-nism. Persuaded by 'my celebrated friend *El Español* Blanco White ... I studied in that old school of practical politics; I read its Burkes, its Paleys and its Benthams'. The English relied on a few fundamental laws which protected individual liberties; they preferred not to write a constitution. Mexico, he thought, was not yet ready to frame a permanent constitution; he warned of the French example. 'It is characteristic of the comic genius of the French to fabricate constitutions arranged by scenes like comedies.' As it was, Mier reiterated his support for a moderate federation endowed with a strong central executive. Sovereignty resided in 'the legal will' of the constituted bodies of government and their elected representatives rather than in the people itself. Applying the classic Burkean analysis, he predicted that Mexico would suffer a period of anarchic demoguery followed by military despotism. He con-cluded: 'I protest that I have not played any part in the evils that are about to descend on the peoples of Anáhuac. They have been seduced to demand what they neither know nor understand. I foresee divisions, emulation, disorders, ruin and the upheaval of our land to its very foundation.'[38]

Few prophets have been more accurate in their predictions than Padre Mier. Awarded a pension and lodgings in the National Palace by President Guada-lupe Victoria, a former insurgent leader, the ageing patriot watched with growing dismay the onset of political divisions that threatened to destroy the country. The rich province of Jalisco openly challenged the authority of the central government and had to be reduced to submission by military force. Worse still, politicians organised masonic lodges which reflected their diverse ideological aspirations. In his correspondence, Mier denounced the radical lodges as composed of a union of former Iturbidistas and 'anarchists, recruited from all the scum and the most immoral adventurers'. It was these Yorkinos who were to bring in legislation expelling all Spaniards from Mexico and thus effectively challenge the post-colonial settlement on which Iturbide had based his proposals for independence. These measures formed but a prelude to the radical legislation of the Reform (1856–9) which confiscated all Church property, banned the religious orders, and separated Church and State. But long before that tumultuous epoch, in 1827, Mier died in the National Palace. On receiving the last sacraments, he solemnly warned his friends and associates against the dangers of freemasonry and federalism, and affirmed that he died a loyal Catholic.[39] Denied peace even in his grave, Mier's mummified carcass was exhumed by the radicals in 1861 and, along with his fellow Dominicans, sold to a circus owner for public exhibition.

V

In his *Common Sense* (1776), Tom Paine wrote: 'The cause of America is, in great measure, the cause of all mankind . . . We have it in our power to begin the world again.' Despite the cosmic exuberance of this pronouncement, the Anglo-Americans proved remarkably cautious in their constitutional delibe-rations. Before independence they had possessed local assemblies, enjoyed considerable freedom of the press, and avidly read the pamphlets of the radical Whig opposition in England. They had studied the classical texts of Locke and Montesquieu. Although they justified their rebellion by appeal to the universal rights of mankind, they framed a constitution that in many respects was an improved version of its British exemplar, albeit inspired by rational principles and carefully designed to accommodate the local automony of the component states.[40] In effect, the Anglo-Americans had been raised in a tradition of politics that stretched back to the seventeenth century; they were the heirs of Parliament's victory over the Crown.

How different was the case of Mexico! As much as their northern neigh-bours, Servando de Mier and Carlos María de Bustamante were the heirs of a tradition of creole patriotism that could be traced back to the early seventeenth century. But its predominant forms of expression were historical and religious, all cast in a particular rather than a universal mode. It offered few lessons in political theory other than an incessant plaint over access to high office. Instead the creole mind dwelt endlessly on the dramatic scenes of the conquest and the grandeur of Tenochtitlan, fixing on the figures of Cortés, Las Casas, Mocte-zuma and Cuauhtémoc. As much as the Poles and the Irish, the Mexicans could never forget the past. Deficient in formal ideology, the movement for indepen-dence at times degenerated into a family quarrel between peninsulars and creoles which fed off ethnic slander and social prejudice. To rally the mass of the population against Spain, Mier and Bustamante propagated the myth of a Mexican nation, already in existence prior to the conquest and now, after 300 years of enslavement, about to recover its freedom. In practice, however, it was the image of Our Lady of Guadalupe, the patron and mother of all inhabitants of New Spain which was invoked to rally the masses and the elite in common insurgency against Spain. The rebels' passionate rejection of all ethnic distinctions was justified by the affirmation of a common identity as Mexicans. In effect, the themes and symbols of creole patriotism – that idiosyncratic amalgam of Marian devotion, hatred of Spanish immigrants, and identification with the Aztec past – were here transmuted into the precocious rhetoric of a Mexican nationalism which was designed to unite creoles, mulattos, mestizos and Indians in the struggle for independence. With such an original and potent ideological vehicle, what need was there to invoke the universal principles of Western liberalism other than in the most perfunctory fashion?

Unfortunately, the insurgent rhetoric had little to say about which forms of government would best suit an independent Mexico. The result was that the influence of European radicalism soon threatened to overwhelm the creole political tradition. Indeed, the first generation of Mexican liberals, Lorenzo de Zavala and José María Luis Mora, scornfully criticised the insurgency for its clerical leadership, its lack of principles, and its populist leanings. In these early years it fell to Servando de Mier to demonstrate that a middle ground existed between the *exaltados* and the *serviles*, which is to say, between the radicals and conservatives. In essence, a disciple of Jovellanos, Blanco White and, at second remove, of Edmund Burke, he came close to being what at that time the English would have called a Whig. He was an aristocratic republican, a liberal Catholic and a Mexican nationalist, viewing Jacobins, monarchists and military adventurers with equal disdain. Bereft of the assistance of German idealism, Mier remained a proto-nationalist, attracted by the same emphases on national character and the national past, but unable to articulate his ideas beyond the stage of a few historical examples and arguments. Moreover, Mier never freed himself from the perennial ambiguity of creole patriotism with its contradictory appeal to ancestral rights and Aztec grandeur. But he succeeded brilliantly in endowing the Mexican nation with a patriotic pedigree in which Moctezuma and Cuauhtémoc figured as the predecessors of Hidalgo and Morelos, united in their stand against the cruel tyranny of Spain. It was largely thanks to the intervention of Mier and Bustamante that creole patriotism not merely served as the animating ideology of the insurgency but, equally important, bequeathed a legacy which was renewed during the Mexican Revolution when many of its most cherished themes were integrated into the liberal nationalism of that movement by thinkers as diverse as Manuel Gamio, José Vasconcelos and Andrés Molina Enríquez.

27

REPUBLICAN HERO

I

IN SOUTH AMERICA independence was won by patriot armies on the field of battle. The contrast with Mexico could not have been greater. The achievement was all the more remarkable if we recall that by 1815 the Spanish monarchy had re-established its dominion over virtually all the vast territories that lay between the Rio Grande and Tierra del Fuego. Only the provinces of the River Plate had succeeded in preserving their autonomy. Elsewhere, the insurgent juntas that had seized power in 1810 had all fallen prey to internal dissension, popular uprising and the royalist reaction. From the start, Lima had remained loyal to the Crown and it was from Peru that armies sallied forth to reconquer Quito, Chile and Upper Peru. As in Mexico, young creoles eagerly enrolled in the royal army and there acquired the ethos of the professional soldier, their loyalty to Ferdinand VII only strengthened by the challenge of popular rebellion. Moreover, the defeat of Napoleon allowed Spain to despatch veteran regiments to reinforce the colonial army. In Venezuela, it was troops from the Peninsula who pacified the coastal valleys and restored royal control over New Granada.[1]

The first real challenge to the resurgent monarchy came in 1817 when José de San Martín, an Argentine general who had served for many years in the Spanish army in Europe, led the soldiers he had recruited and trained in Cuyo across the Andes into Chile. Acting in alliance with patriot forces, he succeeded in defeating the royalists at the hard-fought battle of Maipú. Thereafter, in 1820, he organised an expeditionary force of Argentinian and Chilean troops, which succeeded in capturing Lima and liberating the coastal districts of Peru. But, although many creole officers and bureaucrats now changed sides and set about organising a Peruvian state, the viceroy and his army still commanded the entire mountainous region that stretched from Potosí to Quito. By then Buenos Aires and its provinces were racked by civil war so that San Martín could not expect any further assistance from that quarter. The result was a stalemate which could be broken only by a peaceful settlement effected between patriot and royalist creoles or by armed intervention from the outside. In the event, it was Simón Bolívar who took upon himself the task of destroying the last vestiges of Spanish dominion in South America, employing for that purpose the army he had formed to win the liberation of Venezuela and New Granada.

If Venezuela acted as the mainspring of insurgency in South America, it was in part because its location and terrain allowed easy access to ideas, volunteers and supplies from abroad and afforded ideal conditions for guerilla warfare. Its tardy emergence as a unified and wealthy province during the last decades of the eighteenth century meant that the institutions of Church and State commanded far less influence than in Peru or New Spain. As early as 1780 the American proclamation of Philadelphia had circulated in manuscript, translated by a creole dean of the cathedral in Caracas. In 1797 a conspiracy of mulattos and black slaves in Coro revealed the infiltration from Haiti of doctrines of social equality and popular sovereignty. A French traveller noted that the priories of the mendicant orders were half empty and that young creoles 'at present seek an epaulette with as much avidity as they did formerly the tonsure'. Moreover, the wealthy landowners whose income depended on the export of cacao were aggrieved to find their petitions for access to foreign shipping during the British naval blockades of 1797–1802 and 1804–8 rejected by the ministry in Madrid.[2] The most remarkable of the precursors of the independence movement, Francisco de Miranda, was a Venezuelan who, in 1806, led an ill-fated expedition to the coasts of his native land, distributing copies of Viscardo's *Carta* as propaganda.

It was the Caraqueño elite, the wealthy landowners and their legal associates, who ousted the colonial authorities in 1810, proclaimed independence and, in 1812, issued a remarkably liberal constitution in which both the rights of man and popular sovereignty were clearly enunciated. A federal republic was established, based on the example of the United States, which was governed by a two-chamber legislative assembly and a triumvirate board as the executive. Although ethnic distinctions were expressly abolished and the legal equality of all citizens prescribed, the right to vote was limited by property qualifications and candidacy to the Senate restricted to men who possessed property worth at least 6,000 pesos. Despite its proclamations, however, the regime acted as if the invidious distinctions between creoles and *pardos*, as the inhabitants of African extraction were called, still remained in force, so that the pardo regiments of militia still survived. Moreover, the two provinces of Coro and Maracaibo refused to join the federation, fearful that rejection of royal authority might prompt a slave rebellion. Irresolute in action, divided in counsel, the leaders of this 'Fools' Republic' failed to recruit a regular army, choosing rather to rely on a citizen militia to defend their state.[3] In these circumstances, it required little more than an earthquake which devastated the capital to drive the populace into rebellion and thus allow the Church and the resident peninsular Spaniards to proclaim the restoration of royal authority. That a pardo uprising should have so rudely destroyed creole dreams of governing their own country indicated the divided nature of Venezuelan society.

It was during the fighting against this popular rebellion that Simón Bolívar (1783–1830) first came to the fore, acting as chief lieutenant to Francisco de Miranda. On escaping to New Granada, at that time a bitterly divided federal republic, he drew the appropriate lessons from the recent catastrophe: that federalism was a recipe for political disaster; that a citizen militia was no substitute for a trained army; and that undue clemency to the enemy was a sign of weakness. In lapidary fashion, he concluded: 'We had philosophers for leaders; philanthropy for laws; dialectic for tactics; and sophists for soldiers.' It was in 1813 that he first won his title of Liberator when, after assembling a small force in New Granada, he swept into Venezuela and in 'the wonderful campaign' freed Caracas from royalist rule.[4] However, despite his ruthless measures against the Spaniards, executing prisoners without mercy, his regime was toppled by a sudden onslaught of *llaneros*, the savage horsemen of the inland plains, who drove him once more to seek refuge in New Granada. On a second occasion a popular uprising had overturned the creole republic. In 1815 an expeditionary force of 10,000 Spaniards arrived, many of them veterans of the Peninsula war, who moved rapidly to quell the power of the *llaneros* and restore the forms of colonial society. By then many creoles welcomed the return of Spanish rule, their fears of popular disturbance amply confirmed by the events of previous years.

After several months' residence in Jamaica and Haiti, in 1817 Bolívar succeeded in establishing a base at Angostura, deep within the jungles of Guiana, but connected by river to the sea. It was an ideal location for guerilla warfare and was chosen because Bolívar lacked the military resources to dislodge the Spanish infantry in Caracas. His first step was to attract the support of the bands of *llanero* rebels led by José Antonio Paéz, an untutored chieftain whose physical prowess allowed him to quell all challenge to his authority by personal combat. In his memoirs, Paéz later explained that he accepted the creole aristocrat as his leader in deference to Bolívar's military gifts and his international prestige, and, above all, because of the many advantages accruing from having 'a supreme authority and a centre that could direct the various leaders'. He added that the patriots then possessed the indispensable elements with which to conduct a war: 'the intellectual force to direct and form plans and the material force to bring them to the determined result'.[5] Paéz praised the Liberator's knowledge of military strategy, derived both from his reading and his experience of previous campaigns. He also recalled that Bolívar possessed an unexpectedly strong physical constitution which enabled him to endure the rigours of guerilla warfare as well as any *llanero*. Had he not been able to ride and shoot as well as any of his half-savage

33 José Gil de Castro, *Simón Bolívar en Lima*

followers, the Liberator might well have failed to command the allegiance of the insurgent caudillos. Even so, the common struggle against the Spaniards barely masked the conflicts of class and race that divided the rebels. Indeed, Bolívar was driven to order the execution of Manuel Piar, a popular and effective leader, for advocating a war of extermination against all whites. In condemning this menace to his class, Bolívar proclaimed: 'Who are the agents of this revolution? Are they not the whites, the rich, the titles of Castile . . . ?' In practice, the Liberator was usually accompanied by a small circle of aides and associates, among whom were to be found aristocratic relatives and foreign volunteers.[6]

Where Bolívar's prestige and experience most assisted the rebel cause was in his ability to recruit volunteers from Europe. Acting through their agents in London, the Venezuelan insurgents enlisted no less than 3,000 soldiers in Great Britain, Ireland and Germany, men who generally had fought in the Napoleonic Wars and who sailed for the New World in search of reward and adventure. The patriot command of the Guayana river, combined with the benevolent neutrality of the British squadron in the Caribbean meant that most of these soldiers came fully equipped, ready for battle. It was the fate of many volunteers to die of fever and other tropical diseases; some laid down their lives in battle; and the remainder were eventually paid off and sent home. The steady flow of recruits from Europe during the years 1818–21 allowed Bolívar to form effective infantry units, at times mingling foreign and native troops, able to withstand Spanish canon barrage. Their presence in Venezuela augmented his authority when dealing with the guerilla chieftains and afforded him the basis of a regular army.[7] Moreover, his immediate entourage benefited from the faithful services of Daniel O'Leary, his future biographer, William Ferguson, and Belford Hinton Wilson.

The third element in Bolívar's coalition of forces derived from his masterly surprise conquest of New Granada in 1819, the reward for an arduous month's treck from the tropical plains of Venezuela, up through the mountain passes of the Andes, and into the valleys of Cundinamarca where, in 1819, he defeated Spanish troops at the battle of Boyacá. With New Granada liberated, Bolívar freely drew on its resources, both for provisions and manpower, to prepare for the eventual assault on Caracas. That he delayed his attack for two years, a period when many of his Colombian and British recruits succumbed to tropical disease, indicated the strength of the royalist position. In 1822 victory was finally won at the battle of Carabobo and Venezuela liberated. It is noticeable in the accounts of these military engagements that, although the impetuous charge of the *llanero* cavalry decided the outcome, the sturdy defence presented by the British legion proved indispensable in enabling the patriot lines to withstand Spanish attack.

To provide his campaign with political legitimacy, in 1819 Bolívar convoked a national congress at Angostura which elected him president and then proclaimed the republic of Colombia, an entity which was established to inherit the territorial rights of the former viceroyalty of New Granada, which is to say, to encompass the area of the modern states of Venezuela, Colombia, Panama and Ecuador. In later years, Bolívar admitted that this congress consisted of little more than a handful of selected individuals meeting at his command, so as to provide a cloak of political legality for his imminent conquest of New Granada. It was a farce designed to impress international opinion. Indeed, the text of his address to the congress was despatched immediately to Europe where it was published in an English translation in London the very same year.[8] As much as Hernán Cortés, Bolívar thus employed his command of the written word to legitimise his audacious enterprise.

After enforcing his authority in Quito, in 1823 Bolívar embarked on the conquest of Peru. Prior to entering on that campaign, however, he had a celebrated interview with San Martín at Guayaquil, an experience that left neither man particularly impressed with the other, the taciturn professional soldier dismayed by the vainglorious rhetoric of the Venezuelan, and the aristocratic patriot disdainful of the Argentinian's lack of imagination, subsequently commenting that San Martín 'does not appear to me sufficiently sensible to the kinds of sublimity there are in ideas and enterprises'. In the event, San Martín withdrew from Peru, leaving the way open to Bolívar to challenge the royalist army which still numbered some 20,000 men, almost entirely recruited from the Andean peasantry, with no more than 500 Spaniards to serve as officers and sergeants. But the Liberator's intervention met with but a tepid welcome from the Peruvian president, the Marquis of Torre Tagle, a former intendant, who still hoped to achieve a peaceful settlement with the royalist army, the more especially since it still possessed many creole officers. But Bolívar pressed forward, relying on his military machine to recruit soldiers in Ecuador to supplement the troops brought down from New Granada and Venezuela. Torre Tagle was soon accused of treachery to the patriot cause and a congress installed in Lima which duly acclaimed Bolívar as dictator of Peru, an office he occupied in addition to being president of Colombia. In 1824 at the two great battles of Ayacucho and Junín, Bolívar and his faithful lieutenant, José Antonio de Sucre, defeated the royalist forces and brought Spanish rule to an end in South America.[9] The following year Bolívar recognised the establishment of a republic in Upper Peru and graciously allowed the new state to assume his name, thereafter endowing it with a freshly devised constitution.

II

To understand the springs of Bolívar's heroic achievements, it has to be emphasised that, although he was a creole aristocrat, heir to a great fortune in plantations and slaves, blessed with an ancestral line that stretched back to the foundation of Caracas, he was educated and came to intellectual maturity in Europe. Apart from the few months of his tragically short marriage to the daughter of the Marquis of Toro, he spent the entire period, 1799–1806, which is to say, between the ages of sixteen and twenty-three, on Grand Tour, attending the Spanish court, entering society in Paris, and travelling to Italy. During these years, so he later averred, he read widely in European literature and, in particular, studied the chief texts of the French Enlightenment. Both the events he witnessed and the books he read impelled him to adopt the creed of classical republicanism. The ground had been prepared by Simón Rodríguez, his boyhood tutor, whom Bolívar later warmly saluted as his master and mentor, who had shown him the path he was to follow in life. Although the charming story that Rodríguez educated his young charge according to the principles of Rousseau's *Emile* apparently lacks foundation, there is no doubt that this eccentric, unsociable man was a radical who was involved in the *pardo* conspiracy of 1797. The two men met again in Paris (where Rodríguez also associated with Fray Servando de Mier), and in 1805 travelled together to Italy, pausing on their way at Chambéry to pay their respects to the memory of Rousseau. At Milan they witnessed the coronation of Napoleon as king of Italy; in Venice meditated on the rise and fall of republics; and at Florence studied the works of Machiavelli. It was at Rome on Monte Sacro (the Aventine) that Bolívar solemnly swore never to rest until his country was freed from the chains of Spanish power. According to Rodríguez, the young Venezuelan first reflected on the political vicissitudes of the Roman republic and early empire, no doubt drawing on his reading of Plutarch, and then expressed the hope that the cause of liberty, so often defeated in Europe, would prove victorious in the New World, following the trajectory of civilisation which moved ever westward.[10] It was a heady moment. the reading of Rousseau and Machiavelli, the spectacle of Napoleon, the fate of Rome – all these influences joined to produce a scene worthy of a canvas by David, the neo-classic French painter, in which the young hero renounced domestic comfort and eternal salvation in favour of public glory achieved in the service of his patria.

In this context it should be noted that classical republicanism did not merely entail the repudiation of monarchy as a form of government, it comprised a secular philosophy of life which taught that man could only pursue or achieve true virtue in his capacity as an active citizen of a republic. The origin of this doctrine can be traced back to fifteenth-century Florence, to the civic human-ism of Bruni and Guicciardini and, more particularly, to Machiavelli, who so emphatically asserted the primacy of political action over other human or Christian values. From the start, humanists were prone to celebrate the glories of great warriors. In eighteenth-century France, Montesquieu provided a

comparative, historical perspective on the doctrine when he divided governments into three great types – monarchy, despotism and republics – animated
respectively by the principles of honour, fear and virtue. He divided republics
into aristocracies and democracies, but praised the balance and moderation of
the former, qualities that he discerned in the British constitution. These
distinctions were radicalised by Rousseau, who argued that it was only as a
citizen of a free republic that a man could enjoy freedom and equality, or
indeed fulfil himself as a social being. Both Machiavelli and Rousseau sharply
criticised Christianity for its other-wordly concerns, which distracted men
from the pursuit of civic action, political virtue and military glory. For all these
authors, the republics of the classical world offered an arsenal of examples,
usually culled from Plutarch, which served as a standard for the present, with
Sparta rather than Athens the preferred model.[11]

For Simón Bolívar the central texts of this tradition, *The Prince* and *The
Social Contract*, offered important lessons. No doubt he took heed of Machiavelli's acceptance of the necessity of pre-emptive violence and dissimulation,
the political value of which had been demonstrated by the Jacobins in their
revolutionary Terror. But it was the emphasis given to the role of the legislator,
the ruler and founder of a new state, which most attracted his attention. Why
had Lycurgus succeeded in Sparta and Solon failed in Athens? How to account
for the enduring influence of Moses? The problem here was to find the means of
endowing a new republic with the time-hallowed legitimacy of ancient
monarchies. It was for this reason that Machiavelli commended the armed
prophet and Rousseau insisted that the legislator should emulate Moses and
invest his laws with a numinous aura.[12] Nor was all this a question of theory,
since the career of Napoleon Bonaparte offered a practical application of these
principles. Only a year before swearing the oath to liberate his patria, Bolívar
had witnessed the grand spectacle of the French emperor's coronation in Paris,
an event which inflamed his imagination, since he later declared that the
prospect of having one's glorious deeds admired by a million persons constituted 'the ultimate grade of human aspirations, the supreme desire and
ambition of man'. Although he disapproved of Napoleon's title as a 'gothic'
charade, Bolívar later confessed that he admired him as 'the first captain of the
world, both as a statesman and as a philosopher'.[13]

Of Bolívar's commitment to classical republicanism there can be no doubt.
By all accounts he was a free-thinker who admired Voltaire and spurned
Christianity. In a letter to the bishop of Popayán, he explicitly contrasted the
careers of the warrior and the priest, distinguished the republican virtues of
Cato and Socrates from the qualities of a saint, and concluded: 'the world is
one thing, religion is another'. He displayed no compunction in massacring
prisoners of war and later mused that he had probably ordered more men to be
executed than had Napoleon. Moreover, his letters were peppered with

allusions to Brutus and Sulla, to Lycurgus and Solon, to Camillus and Caesar. Where Mexican patriots turned to the figures of Cuauhtémoc, Quetzalcoatl and Las Casas for inspiration, Bolívar's imagination constantly dwelt on the austere examples presented by Plutarch, Montesquieu and Livy. This neo-classical perspective also governed his appreciation of literature, since he advised the creole poet, Juan José de Olmedo, to observe the rules of Boileau in his odes celebrating insurgent victories. Above all else, here was a creed which presented him with the image of the republican hero whose pursuit of glory was justified by the liberation of his patria and defence of liberty.[14]

It was in his *Carta de Jamaica* (1815) that Bolívar first set out his political beliefs in some detail. Written to an Englishman sympathetic to the rebel cause but manifestly bewildered by Servando de Mier's history of the Mexican revolution, this text marked the moment when the customary themes of creole patriotism were transmuted into an affirmation of classical republicanism. To be sure, Bolívar paid tribute to 'the philanthropic bishop of Chiapas, the apostle of the Indies, Las Casas', who had denounced the cruelties of the conquerors with such valour. His message was still relevant since Spain, that 'denaturalised stepmother', was now guilty of committing similar barbarities against 'the heroic and unhappy Venezuela'. Where native monarchs had once been seized and murdered, so now countless patriots were slaughtered. Although Spain was bereft of power, wealth and credit, it still sought to dominate half the world. Yet the editor of *El Español* had demonstrated beyond all doubt that, with the abdication of the Bourbon kings, sovereignty had returned to the people, so that the Regency had no legitimate cause to withhold recognition from the insurgent juntas in America. Certainly it was the case, as Mier had argued, that the conquerors had formed a 'social pact' with Charles V, but its provisions had never been observed, with the consequence that 'we were never viceroys nor governors, save for the most extraordinary reasons; seldom archbishops and bishops; never diplomats; soldiers only in subordinate rank; nobles without privileges; in effect, we were never magistrates, nor financiers and rarely even merchants'. In this famous statement, Bolívar gave eloquent expression to creole plaints which had echoed across the generations since the early seventeenth century.[15] But he then invoked Montesquieu's concept of despotism, a category largely based on the realm of the Ottoman Turks, to define the Spanish empire in the New World as an oriental despotism, more oppressive than the regimes that governed Turkey and Persia, since in those countries the monarchs at least employed native ministers. The 'active tyranny' of Spain had reduced the creoles to perpetual infancy, their action confined to the economic sphere, acting as simple producers and consumers of commodities, their countries mere colonies of the metropolis. In effect, Bolívar accepted Pradt's definition of the function and character of a colony, largely derived from his knowledge of the Antilles, and applied that concept to Spanish America. At the same time he implicitly assumed that social manhood depended on the exercise and pursuit of political power and office: without access to political action men remained mere subjects, no matter how free they were to enrich themselves. This republican perspective differed intensely from Mier's reformulation of creole patriotism.

Turning to the contemporary scene, Bolívar complained that Europe and the United States had remained mere spectators of a struggle that was about to determine the fate of an entire world, an event for which the only historical parallel was the dissolution of the Roman empire. He did not dare to predict the precise outcome. What had already become clear, however, was that 'the democratic and federal form' of government had precipitated a crisis in Venezuela, leaving the country exposed to a royalist *revanche*. Had not Montesquieu insisted on the difficulty of giving freedom to peoples accustomed to serfdom? How could the equilibrium between liberty and effective government be maintained? It was all too easy to descend into anarchy or revert to despotism. As for the future, Bolívar ruled out the possibility of any consolidated state, be it a republic or a monarchy, emerging to unite Spanish America: the magnates of the provincial capitals who had inspired the rebellion would not countenance any over-arching authority which would deny them full independence. Instead, he accepted Pradt's view that some fourteen or more states would come into existence, albeit republics rather than monarchies.[16] At the same time he adverted to the immense differences in climate, character and customs that distinguished each province, arguing that in consequence similarly different forms of government would prevail. In line with this proposition he suggested that Mexico would eventually be ruled by a powerful, elected president; that Chile would enjoy an exceptional degree of freedom; and that Peru would dwell in perpetual serfdom. As for Colombia, he hoped that it would imitate Great Britain and install a powerful executive balanced by an hereditary senate.

In the last section of his letter, Bolívar sought to resolve his correspondent's perplexity concerning the possible role of Quetzalcoatl in the Mexican insurgency. Here was certainly a theme which had fascinated most authors in New Spain, even if they were divided on the question as to whether the Indian hero was St Thomas the Apostle, but it was a theme about which the masses knew nothing. Instead, 'the leaders of the independence movement in Mexico have happily profited from fanaticism with the greatest skill, proclaiming the famous Virgin of Guadalupe as queen of the patriots'. The result was that 'political enthusiasm has formed a mixture with religion, which has produced a vehement fervour for the sacred cause of liberty'.[17] In effect, Bolívar here signalised the profound difference that separated the insurgency in New Spain from the movement he led in Venezuela.

The most systematic exposition of Bolívar's views on government came in his *Discurso de Angostura* (1819) delivered to the Venezuelan constituent congress he had convoked. Formally renouncing his power as dictator and supreme chief of the Republic, he affirmed that he was but the simple instrument of the 'revolutionary hurricane' which had first convulsed and now threatened to destroy Venezuela. Once more he reverted to the despotic character of the colonial regime which submitted the American people to 'the triple yoke of ignorance, tyranny and vice', so that they had acquired 'neither knowledge, power nor virtue'. If liberty, as Rousseau had observed, was a dangerous food, how much more so was it for such a population: nothing was more easy than to lose political balance and revert to despotism. After all, history amply demonstrated that monarchy and aristocracy offered far more effective bases for stable and enduring government than did democracy which so often had descended into demagoguery and anarchy. The Venezuelan Constitution of 1812 was an admirable document, blessed with the most enlightened precepts of liberty, equality and national sovereignty. In large measure it had been fashioned according to the model of the United States. But had not Montesquieu declared that laws should fit and reflect the climate, character and customs of the people for whom they were framed and that different peoples required different laws? How could one compare the Anglo-Americans and the Spanish Americans? Their climate, religion, character, history, wealth and customs differed in almost every respect. In particular, it was manifest that 'our moral constitution' did not admit a federalism that was more appropriate for 'a republic of saints'.[18]

Following the same line of reasoning, Bolívar defended the principle of political and legal equality of all citizens, only then to insist on the immense moral and physical inequalities that divided the existing population. The Venezuelans formed a mixture of races in which Africa and America weighed more heavily than Europe. At the same time he demanded the emancipation of all slaves, arguing that the survival of slavery was incompatible with republican freedom. For the rest he suggested that the most perfect form of government was the regime which provided the greatest degree of special security and political stability. Obviously, the country wanted a republic based on the principle of popular sovereignty. But absolute democracy was notoriously unstable, as the collapse of Athens before Sparta had demonstrated. In the contemporary world, it was Great Britain which had achieved the best balance of liberty and stability. In all this it was necessary to avoid 'abstract theories' and devise a system that would strengthen national unity.[19]

Although Bolívar averred that 'perfectly representative institutions are not suited to our character', he accepted that the lower house of the legislative assembly should be elected by popular vote. But he then advocated the establishment of an hereditary senate which would form, so he hoped, 'the base, the bond and the soul of the Republic'. In the first instance it was to be composed of the insurgent leaders who had distinguished themselves in the struggle for independence, joined later by wealthy landowners and public officials, all in possession of property worth at least 6,000 pesos. He expected that a special school would be set up to educate the children of 'the liberators'. When a critic later fixed upon the hereditary senate as unrepublican, he responded that it would serve 'to temper democracy, since it is by now well established that an absolutely democratic government can be as tyrannical as any despot'. That he inisisted on a strong executive, whose authority was to be protected by a clear division of powers between the three branches of government, goes without saying. Finally, Bolívar advocated the establishment of an Areopagus, a Board of Censors, divided into two councils, the one to superintend education, the other to safeguard the republic from corruption by invigilation of public morality. In defence of this 'truly holy court', he cited Lycurgus who had constrained the Spartans to virtue through the imposition of wise laws. All these proposals rested on the premiss that 'only a balanced or tempered government can be free', an assumption derived from Bolívar's reading of Montesquieu and El Español, where Jovellanos's constitutional defence of the Central Junta had been published.[20]

Notwithstanding his eloquence, Bolívar signally failed to impress the lawyers who met at Cúcuita in 1821 to frame a constitution for the republic of Colombia. They ignored most of his proposals and proceeded to divide the vast territories of the former viceroyalty of New Granada into a series of provinces, each governed by an intendant. Much to the anger of the Venezuelan caudillos, the capital was located at Bogotá. In letters he dictated after the event, Bolívar sarcastically cited Plato on the desirability of banning lawyers from the republic, observing that 'these gentlemen think that the will of the people consists in their opinion, not realising that in Colombia the people is in the army'. It had been the people in arms who had conquered liberty and who therefore possessed the right to determine the political destiny of their country, the more especially since the rest of the population had acted as passive spectators. As it was, the legislators had ignored the character of the people and their country, prescribing a complicated paper constitution which called to mind 'a Greek temple built on a Gothic base near a volcano'.[21]

III

In 1823, when he was already president of Colombia and about to embark on the liberation of Peru, Bolívar wrote a brief account entitled 'My rapture on Mount Chimborazo', where he described how, following in the footsteps of La Condamine and Humboldt, he had climbed this highest peak of the Andes. In fervid prose, he stated that, as he made the ascent, he felt possessed by a divine spirit, which he identified as the God of Colombia. At the summit he encountered Time itself, decked in the conventional form of an elderly sage, scythe in hand, who reminded him of the cosmic insignificance of all human action. Overcome with terror, Bolívar questioned the sage as to why he had surpassed all other men in fortune, only then to perceive, as in a vision, profound truths about human history and the universe. Since Bolívar never deigned to reveal the contents of this revelation, the significance of this rather contrived piece of literature lies in the testimony it affords about the Liberator's perception of his own mission and status. He obviously conceived himself to be an armed prophet, chosen by destiny to destroy an empire and create a new political order. Indeed, in a subsequent letter written to an English correspondent he exclaimed: 'It is not known in Europe what it costs me to maintain the equilibrium in some of these regions. Can one man alone succeed in constituting half the world?' Nor was Bolívar alone in this assessment of his task since Simón Rodríguez later argued that, in the future, the world would be dominated by political prophets, which is to say, by philosophers 'who calculate so as to predict events which are in the order of things'.[22]

The utopian quality of Bolívar's thinking in these years of triumph, when victory followed victory, was all too clearly revealed in the constitution he framed for the republic of Bolivia, formerly Upper Peru. Acting as sole legislator, he drafted a document which was both fanciful and complex. The new republic was endowed with a life-long president, an hereditary vice-presidency, and a tri-cameral legislative assembly. In a warning against the twin dangers of tyranny and anarchy, he declared: 'The President of the republic figures in the constitution as the Sun which, from its centre, gives life to the universe. This supreme authority ought to be perpetual.' True to his early convictions, he outlawed slavery as offensive to the sacred principle of equality, and defined the sovereignty of the people as 'the only legitimate authority of nations'. The true meaning of Bolivia, he added, should be 'an unbridled love of liberty'. Despite this striking affirmation, however, he restricted the exercise of political rights to those citizens who were both literate and solvent, a measure which effectively disenfranchised the overwhelming majority of the inhabitants of a country that was still predominantly Indian. Moreover, since most government positions were to be filled by nomination, popular elections were restricted to the minimum. In effect, the constitution was more a work of imagination than a form of government, and was never put into practice. Not that Bolívar neglected his own interests in the matter, since he procured the appointment of his faithful lieutenant, José Antonio de Sucre, as the first president, observing that 'General Sucre is necessary for this constitution and without him there is nothing.'[23]

The magnitude of Bolívar's achievements in these years of triumph was matched by the scale of his projects. In 1826 he convoked a congress in the Isthmus of Panama to discuss the possibility of a grand federation of Spanish

American republics. He discussed with agents from Buenos Aires the possibility of a union between Argentina and Bolivia, and talked of entering the River Plate provinces at the head of an army so as to help free Uruguay from Brazilian occupation. Exclaiming that 'the demon of glory ought to take us as far as Tierra del Fuego', he noted that he had been summoned 'to exercise the Protectorate of America'. In his dual capacity as president of Colombia and dictator of Peru, he toyed with the idea of forming an Andean confederate republic, composed of five or six states, which was to say, Bolivia, South Peru, North Peru, Ecuador, New Granada and Venezuela. To support this proposal he invoked Montesquieu's endorsement of the confederate republic as the state most fit to dominate and survive the conflicts that were bound to haunt single provinces, an argument that James Madison had already deployed to great advantage in *The Federalist* (1787). Certainly, if account was taken of the disintegration of Argentina into a series of petty, warring fiefdoms, the advantages of a strong, over-arching federation were obvious. But Bolívar never seems to have advanced the project beyond the stage of conversation and letters. Moreover, although the federation was to have 'one flag, one army, and one nation', the chief instrument of union was to be 'that clever modern invention, the army of occupation', a force that was to be recruited from 'the ten thousand immortals', the Colombian soldiers who had defeated the Spaniards at Ayacucho and Junín, men who were now to serve as 'the guardians of our tranquillity'. As for his own role, Bolívar suggested that 'the Liberator, as supreme chief, will march each year to visit the departments of each state', a task which clearly indicated his dislike of the practical duties of civil administration.[24]

The failure of all these grand projects demonstrated how frail were the foundations on which Bolívar sought to erect his grandiose structure. In many respects the liberation of Peru was a conquest and, like most conquests, provoked bitter resentment among injured and displaced parties. After all, the battles of Ayacucho and Junín had been fought between predominantly Peruvian armies and patriot forces recruited in Colombia. Moreover, once Bolívar left Peru in 1826, the former royalist officers who had welcomed San Martín seized power, expelled the last remaining Colombian troops and, the following year, invaded Ecuador in an unsuccessful bid to aggregate that province to their country. In Bolivia Sucre was soon ousted from office and replaced by Andrés de Santa Cruz, a general who had served the Crown for several years before embracing the rebel cause. Nor did the division of the central Andean region into two distinct countries meet with universal approval, since during the 1830s Santa Cruz introduced a short-lived federation of Bolivia and Peru.

In all the flurry of geo-politics, at a time when Bolívar depicted himself as a Sisyphus attempting to maintain the political balance of half a world, there was thus a striking contrast between the shrewd realism that underlay his mastery of men and the abstract, fanciful quality of his projects. The explanation surely lies in his self-conceived role as a secular prophet, charged with the founding of new republics. Orphaned at an early age, a widower at nineteen, without an heir, his formative years spent in Europe, Bolívar took little interest in managing the estates he inherited. Once in public life, he freed his slaves, abandoned the plantations and squandered any gifts or monies that came his way during his career, so that by his death he was solely dependent on his presidential pension. This spend-thrift quality demands emphasis because it sharply distinguished Bolívar from the caudillos of his epoch, most of whom strove to lay the foundations of great family fortunes. He displayed little attachment to Venezuela or even to Caracas, rarely visiting the country after its liberation other than to reprove its turbulent caudillos. Indeed, he wrote to his old friend, the Marquis of Toro, that henceforth he must be regarded not as a son of Caracas, but rather as the leader of Colombia. For here was the focus of his allegiance, the patria for which he fought and which he died commending – Colombia – that union of New Granada, Venezuela and Ecuador, which he had both created and named. It was a state which he had established to sustain his campaigns of liberation and which, in turn, was sustained solely by the prestige and authority of the Liberator. It was also a state which was detested in equal measure by the lawyers of New Granada and the caudillos of Venezuela. The personal function of the state was explicitly recognised when, in 1830, the Venezuelan congress declared that it wished to dissolve the union so as 'to separate us from the government of Bogotá and no longer depend on the authority of his Excellency the Liberator, General Simón Bolívar'. In a letter Bolívar referred to his tutor Rodríguez as 'a cosmopolitan philosopher, without a patria, family or home'. At the end of his days, with Colombia dissolved, much the same could have been said of the Liberator.[25]

If his utopian projects and obsession with glory prevented Bolívar from consolidating the state he had founded, his premonitions of impending disaster grew ever more prophetic. As early as 1822 he had cast scorn on Colombia's high-principled constitution, describing the inhabitants of the republic in dire terms: 'one part is savage, the other slave; most hate each other; and all are corrupted by superstition and despotism'. If he had little sense of belonging to a class of landowners, Bolívar was acutely aware of his position as a creole, which was to say, as a white man attempting to dominate a population which was largely coloured. Although he insisted on legal equality and was a passionate advocate of the abolition of slavery, he came to fear the masses, commenting in 1825 that 'legal equality does not satisfy the spirit of the people who want absolute equality ... and after that a *pardocracy* ... and the extermination of the privileged classes'. He later lamented: 'Where is the army of occupation that will keep us in order? We shall have Guinea and more

Guinea . . . he who escapes with his white face will be fortunate indeed.' It was precisely this fear of race warfare that had driven him to execute General Piar.[26]

His predictions for the future of his country were grounded on the observation that the colonial regime had been sustained by despotic fear and that neither independence nor the constitution had changed the character of the people and the nature of its government. In a famous letter, written in 1826, Bolívar declared: 'I am convinced to the very marrow of my bones that only a clever despotism can govern in America.' On two occasions, widely separated in time, he quoted from Montesquieu a dictum, to which Rousseau had already adverted, that 'a free nation may have a liberator; an enslaved nation can only have another oppressor'. But the dictum had a corollary, which Bolívar did not cite but which he had obviously read: 'Any man who had sufficient power to expel the absolute master of a state, has power enough to become absolute himself.' In fact, both at the outset and at the conclusion of his career, Bolívar exercised supreme power as dictator, himself admitting that 'dictatorship has been my constant authority; this magistracy is republican; it has saved Rome, Colombia and Peru'. But when in 1826 Paéz, the Venezuelan caudillo, urged him to crown himself emperor, he vehemently rejected the suggestion, asserting that America had nothing in common with France and that the coloured population would interpret monarchy as a denial of all their hopes for equality. As for himself, 'I am not Napoleon and do not wish to be him; nor do I wish to imitate Caesar, and still less Iturbide. Such examples appear to me unworthy of my glory. The title of Liberator is superior to all those that human pride has received.' The very vehemence of his denial suggests that Bolívar had indeed experienced the temptation of establishing a permanent form of absolute rule so as to avert the anarchy that threatened to destroy the countries he had freed.[27]

In 1829 Bolívar wrote a survey of Spanish America, in which he described, country by country, the civil wars and struggles for power that currently afflicted almost every region and province of the continent. Just as the fall of the Roman expire had ushered in the Dark Ages, so equally the destruction of the Spanish empire in America had brought political anarchy and social dissolution. Every republic was threatened with disintegration as local chieftains carved out fiefdoms and cities were racked by riot and faction. He concluded: 'There is no good faith in America, nor between nations. Treaties are pieces of paper; constitutions mere books; elections open combat; liberty is anarchy and life itself a torment.' Only a month before he died in 1830 he received news of the assassination of General Sucre, the most distinguished and loyal of his lieutenants. In a sombre letter commenting on the event, he stated that twenty years of command had yielded him the following reflections: 'America is ungovernable to us. He who serves the revolution ploughs the sea . . . This country will infallibly fall into the hands of uncontrollable multitudes, thereafter to pass under almost imperceptible tyrants of all colours and races.'[28]

In these last, despairing years, Bolívar lamented that 'our peoples do not offer the basis for any heroic enterprise ... instinct alone will make us live, albeit almost without object. For what object can there be in a people where neither glory nor happiness stimulate the citizens?' In effect, Bolívar found it remarkably difficult to accommodate himself to the public penury and endless conspiracies that characterised the new republics, a situation which allowed the maintenance of only the most rudimentary regular army. When Paéz first rebelled against the authority of Bogotá, the Liberator shrank from the prospect of yet another civil war, not simply on account of its inevitable cost in bloodshed, but also because such an action would injure his reputation. By this time he was weary of politics, and no doubt apprehensive as to whether his troops could defeat Paéz' *llaneros*. But the more he approached the close of his career, the more he dwelt on the verdict of posterity. By 1829 he reflected: 'My name already belongs to History ... my patriotism is equal to that of Camillus. I love freedom no less than Washington and no-one can deny that I have the honour of having humiliated the Spanish Lion from the Orinoco to Potosí.' If he refrained from the harsh repression necessary to perpetuate his command over Colombia, it was, so he averred, because he had no desire to end his career as a tyrant. Ever faithful to his republican creed and its repertoire of classical heroes, he wrote to Paéz that he did not want to abandon 'the noble character of a free man and the sublime title of Liberator. To save the *patria* I ought to have been a Brutus, and to preserve it in a civil war I ought to be a Sulla.' The imperatives of his personal vision which had inspired the heroic venture of emancipation equally prevented him from engaging in the despotic measures necessary to preserve Colombia.[29] It would thus be an error to interpret his political rhetoric and projects as a splendid mask for his personal ambition, to discern the cruel lineaments of the Prince behind the benevolent guise of the Liberator. Bolívar was essentially a man of action, a soldier more than a statesman, who was driven into action by a few strong ideas that he had adopted during his stay in Europe. He was indeed a prince who created his own state, but he was also a republican hero whose fame rested on public esteem. To the end, the doctrines of Rousseau and Machiavelli, the competing claims of personal virtue and public liberty, jostled for primacy in his soul.

IV

In his lectures on heroes and hero-worship, Thomas Carlyle declared that 'Universal History ... is at bottom the History of the Great Men who have worked here.' In politics the prime task of the hero was to act as 'the missionary of Order', striving to master and direct the tumult and licence of revolution. It was Cromwell, 'the inarticulate prophet', a man without ambition, rooted deep in 'the great Empire of Silence', who best exemplified the qualities of the 'Commander over Men'. By contrast, Napoleon had betrayed his mission and declined into a mere charlatan, his empire a masquerade of rhetoric and costume. Whereas Cromwell expressed the true essence of the Puritan Revolution, Napoleon converted the apocalypse of the French Revolution into a charade.[30] Here was a contrast which was implicitly invoked by Bartolomé Mitre, the Argentine historian and statesman, in his *Historia de San Martín* (1885), where he portrayed the taciturn soldier as another Cromwell, 'a living statue of balanced force', a shrewd political realist who despised the rhetoric and vanity of other insurgent chieftains. In his celebrated description of the interview at Guayaquil, he depicted Bolívar as a rootless visionary, obsessed with his own glory, whose grandiose projects all came to naught. As if to anticipate such comparisons, Bolívar himself had already insisted on the chasm which separated the splendour of the French emperor's court from the republican simplicity of his own entourage. Ever anxious to defend his former pupil, in 1828 Simón Rodríguez commented that in Europe generals travelled to the battle-field in carriages, whereas in America rebel leaders like Bolívar had had to suffer much the same hardships as their followers. If Napoleon had ridden the tide of revolutionary conquest and was thus 'the creature' of France, Bolívar had given Colombia its very being and still sustained its republican government.[31]

The last word is best left to Enrique Rodó (1871–1917), the Uruguayan essayist who, in *El mirador de Próspero* (1913), declared that Bolívar had 'embodied in its total complexity of means and forms the energy of the Revolution' in Spanish America. For all his manifold virtues, San Martín was simply a good soldier, a general whose talents would have brought him distinction in any European army, whereas Bolívar was an American Alcibiades, an aristocrat endowed with the prophetic powers of true genius. In both Argentina and Venezuela there was a radical difference between the chieftains who succeeded in mastering the wild bands of gauchos and *llaneros* who dominated the great plains and the generals who led the regular armies which defeated the Spaniards on the field of battle. But whereas San Martín never had to confront these gaucho caudillos, men such as José de Artigas, the founder of Uruguay, by contrast, Bolívar first had to master the Venezuelan llaneros, bending Paéz to his will, before he was able to recruit and command the patriot armies at Carabobo and Junín. Bolívar also defended the insurgent cause by speeches and letters and, once liberation was achieved, acted as legislator and statesman. In effect, he combined the roles of Artígas, San Martín and Moreno. In terms reminiscent of Carlyle, Rodó concluded that Bolívar 'personified all that is characteristic and essential in our history. He is the clay of America moved by the breath of genius.'[32]

28

CIVILISATION AND BARBARISM

I

WHEN CHARLES DARWIN (1809–82) traversed the coasts of South America in 1833, acting as naturalist for HMS *Beagle*, he had occasion to meet General Juan Manuel Rosas, then engaged in a campaign against the pampa Indians. In his diary he noted that the general, a great estanciero who owned 74 square leagues of country and over 300,000 head of cattle, had attracted public attention by his success in disciplining the several hundred peons who were employed on his estates, forming them into a frontier militia. He added that Rosas was 'a perfect gaucho: his feats of horsemanship are very notorious', and that he had won great popularity by visiting the British minister, Lord Ponsonby, dressed as a gaucho, observing that the costume of the country was 'the proper and therefore most respectful dress'. It was thanks to such means that Rosas had gained an extraordinary ascendancy over the masses and 'in consequence despotic power'. If Buenos Aires enjoyed a prosperous, if sombre peace, by contrast Peru presented the spectacle of anarchy, with no less than four candidates for the presidency engaged in armed contention. Attending high mass at the cathedral in Lima to mark the anniversary of Independence, Darwin was shocked to observe that at the *Te Deum*, 'instead of each regiment displaying the Peruvian flag, a black one with a death's head was unfurled', as a sign of their determination to die for their cause.[1] When Darwin fixed upon 'the struggle for life' as nature's means of ensuring the preservation of favoured races, did he ever give any thought to the competition for political power that he had witnessed in South America?

It was to explain how Rosas and men like Rosas had come to dominate Argentine politics that Domingo Faustino Sarmiento (1811–88) wrote *Civiliza-ción y barbarie. Vida de Juan Facundo Quiroga* (1845). First published as instalments in a Chilean newspaper, written in haste, *Facundo* was a work of startling originality and high ambition. Its author, a provincial autodidact, a native of San Juan, a town of no more than 10,000 inhabitants situated on the eastern flanks of the Andes, had devoured the French periodical literature of the epoch and had familiarised himself with historians such as Guizot, Thierry and Michelet. The measure of his ambition can be gauged by his observation in the prologue that South America as yet lacked any work comparable to Alexis de Tocqueville's *Democracy in America* (1839), which was to say, any examination of the principles which animated its society. The regime of Rosas, he declared, was no aberration, it personified the political character of the Argentine people. To assist him explore that character, Sarmiento drew inspiration from the Spanish *costumbrista* essayist, José Mariano de Larra, whose satirical sketches of popular manners and scenes enjoyed great popularity in South America. More surprising, he cited the novels of Fenimore Cooper, especially *The Prairie*, which included a description of 'the great North American desert', as the mid-Western grasslands were then called.[2] Further in the background was the influence of Montesquieu and his emphasis on the environmental determinants of human polities.

To start with, Sarmiento provided a memorable description of the Argentine pampas, which he freely compared to the steppelands of central Asia and the deserts of the Middle East, a comparison that Humboldt had initiated. In all these areas, which were inhabited by bands of nomads and crossed only by occasional caravans, nature imposed much the same kind of human society. For the gauchos passed their life on horse-back, herding cattle or hunting, incapable of fixed settlement or agriculture, gathering to drink and fight in crude *pulperías*, their fondness for music and poetry matched only by a swift resort to the knife when tempers were aroused. Among these horsemen were to be found skilled trackers, masters of the countryside, bards and outlaws. But, although Sarmiento multiplied his comparisons with the Bedouin and the Tartars, he also conceded that the gauchos were often employed by the owners of the great estates as cow-hands. In such cases the landlords acted like feudal barons, wielding patriarchal authority in the rural isolation of their estancias. Whatever the character of their association, the gauchos all required an iron discipline, their captains or caudillos quick to quell any challenge to their commands by appeal to the knife. As much as the Arabs, they needed a stern judge, a veritable Mahomet, to master and direct them.[3] In effect, the natural environment of the great plains created a society which had to be restrained by despotic forms of authority if it were not to lapse into anarchy or banditry.

It was the revolution of 1810 which had offered the gaucho chieftains their opportunity to seize power. For the political elite of Buenos Aires were so intent on raising armies to defeat the Spaniards that they neglected to create a regime sufficiently stable to master the countryside. 'The patriotic revolutionary army' which followed José de San Martín into Chile consisted of forces largely raised in Cuyo (the province which comprised Mendoza, La Rioja and San Juan), officered in part by creoles who had embraced the military career as professional soldiers. But San Martín refused to raise his sword in civil war, choosing rather to liberate Peru. Nevertheless, in the 1820s Bernardino Rivadavia succeeded in becoming governor of Buenos Aires and then president of the federation. A moderate but committed liberal, he introduced a reform programme designed to transform the country and provide it with a strong central government. For Sarmiento, 'Rivadavia was the living embodiment of that grandiose, poetic spirit which then dominated society', a spirit expressed in the ambition to create 'a great American state, a republic'. But Sarmiento equally confessed that the president and his Unitarian party were blinded by their abstract political principles and entirely failed to perceive the harsh realities of Argentine society. When an attempt was made to employ the remnants of the regular army against the opposing faction, the gaucho chieftains of the pampas and the provinces mobilised their hordes to oust the liberals from power. At this juncture, only José María Paz, a career officer leading a force of veteran infantrymen, proved any match for the irregular cavalry of the caudillos.[4] But the influence of Rosas in the province of Buenos Aires was too pervasive for any single victory in battle to count for much and he was obliged to seek safety in exile.

The Argentine Revolution, so Sarmiento argued, consisted of two distinct movements: in the first phase the cities fought to liberate the country from the Spaniards; in the second, the country chieftains fought to conquer the cities. The first of these caudillos to emerge on the political stage was José de Artigas, who attracted the outlaw gauchos of the frontier districts of Uruguay to enlist under his command. Thereafter, similar figures, virtually all of them commanders of frontier militias, mobilised their forces to support the federalist cause and seize power throughout the states of the republic. By far the most sinister of these rural chieftains was Juan Facundo Quiroga, 'the tiger of La Rioja', a man of known family, who embodied all the vices of the bad gaucho. Irascible, cruel, governed by his passions, Facundo came to dominate the provinces of the interior, terrorising and plundering towns like San Juan, La Rioja and Mendoza, executing opponents without compunction. From his personal knowledge of the district and the man Sarmiento drew a searing portrait of this caudillo, providing the reader with a vivid catalogue of horror and atrocity.[5]

Determined as much to explain events as to describe them, Sarmiento defined the conflict in Argentina as a struggle between civilisation and barbarism, between liberty and despotism, progress and stagnation, and above all, between the cities and the desert. That he also described it as a conflict between Europe and America only served to sharpen the polemical intent of these grand antitheses. Buenos Aires was the hope of the future, a city destined to rank as the great metropolis, the very fount of nineteenth-century liberal values in Argentina. But it was José María Paz rather than Rivadavia or Moreno, whom Sarmiento pitched upon as the personification of those

European values, decribing him as 'an artillery man and hence a mathematician, a scientist . . . the first citizen general who has triumphed over the pastoral element'. By contrast, Facundo was 'the most American figure that the Revolution presents', the embodiment of gaucho passion, who 'used terror as a system of government'. Indeed, thanks to this instrument of power he had survived military defeat and rebuilt his authority, a spectacle that caused Sarmiento to reflect: 'One should not deceive oneself: terror is a means of government that produces better results than patriotism and spontaneity.' It was this famous admission that caused later critics to accuse him of having written a manual for caudillos.[6]

The polemical intent of Sarmiento's work becomes immediately obvious when, shifting his focus to Rosas, he argued that the *Restaurador's* government was impelled by the same principle of terror as Facundo's, albeit now applied in a systematic and rational fashion. Rosas brought to the city all the values of the wilderness and governed the capital as if it were a great estancia. But Sarmiento had to admit that Rosas, whom he dubbed 'the legislator of this Tartar civilisation', came from a family of Goths, which is to say, of creole conservatives, and that he enforced severe discipline on his estancias, forbidding his gauchos to carry knives. Moreover, he had procured the assassination of Facundo, when that chieftain threatened his position, and thereafter established his hegemony over the governors of the interior, thus preventing any further outbreak of civil war. The result was a substantial measure of internal peace and economic prosperity. Indeed, with European immigrants beginning to enter the country in increasing numbers, change was assured, no matter for how long Rosas clung to power. In all this, the general served as 'a great and powerful instrument of Providence', through whom the country was slowly entering the path of Progress.[7]

Contemporaries of Sarmiento were not impressed by his grand antitheses. In a biting critique, Juan Bautista Alberdi (1810–84) insisted that the Buenos Aires revolution of 1810 was not caused by ideas, but by the economic interests of the estancieros. It was to defend the principle of free trade that Moreno had written his famous representation of 1809. So too, the prime cause of the civil wars had been the Buenos Aires junta's unilateral assumption of authority over the territories of the viceroyalty, appointing governors without obtaining the assent of the provincial elites. 'The revolution was made by Buenos Aires, and hence for Buenos Aires; without the provinces, and hence against the provinces.' The ensuing civil war had been waged between two countries, the coast and interior, a division obscured by the sobriquets of the Unitarian and Federalist parties. Above all, Alberdi attacked Sarmiento's antithesis of city and wilderness. In fact, the pampas were the chief source of wealth and civilisation in Argentina, exporting hides and salted beef in ever increasing quantities.

Moreover, the greatest estancieros resided in Buenos Aires and from that urban base governed the country. Alberdi concluded: 'Terror is not the means of government, as Sarmiento states, it is money, riches.' In effect, Rosas had used the rural chieftains of the interior to oust the Unitarian clique from power; but his regime consolidated the capital's political hegemony. Such conflict as occurred in Argentina was between the sixteenth and nineteenth centuries, between the coastal provinces and the interior. Where Alberdi agreed with Sarmiento was in his disdain for Argentina's colonial inheritance, later confessing that in his youth he had detested 'everything that was Spanish'. Similar also was his depreciation of the New World, as when he asserted that 'all the civilisation of our land is European . . . In America everything that is not European is barbarous.'[8]

The contrast that Alberdi drew between the sixteenth and nineteenth centuries expressed the familiar contemporary antithesis between liberal progress and Catholic reaction, with France, Great Britain and the United States hailed as the exemplars of contemporary civilisation, and Spain relegated to the status of a semi-African excrescence. In *Facundo* Sarmiento inserted a satirical account of Córdoba, an episcopal city which, since the foundation of its university in 1613, had acted as the centre of academic culture in Argentina. Even after independence, its spirit remained 'monastic and scholastic', its schools still dominated by the study of theology and canon law, with the clergy so dominant that the city resembled 'a vast cloister'.[9] In his *Recuerdos de provincia* (1850), Sarmiento provided substance to these charges by recounting the career of Dean Gregorio Funes, an enlightened but orthodox patriot, who had sought to reform the curriculum of Córdoba's university by introducing the study of mathematics, physics and music. His participation in national politics won him many enemies and he ended his days selling his books, one by one, to cover his subsistence. What Sarmiento here revealed was the great influence the clergy still enjoyed in the interior provinces, an influence at times employed in the federalist cause, since many priests saw Rivadavia's reforms as undermining the privileges and power of the Church. Despite his admiration for the local clergy, several of whom were close relatives and mentors, Sarmiento was appalled by the public manifestations of popular religion and denounced the processions of images and the self-scourging of penitents as 'horrible practices that presented the ultimate degree of degradation to which a man can arrive'.[10] Towards the end of his life, he asserted that Islam had left an indelible imprint on Spanish character and culture and derisively characterised Philip II as the commander of the faithful, an Iberian Caliph. In effect, he identified Spain with the medieval stagnation and feudalism that he had encountered in the Argentine countryside, an identification assisted by the suggestion that both had been influenced or were analogous in their development to Islam, a thesis that led to the assertion: 'Americanism is the reproduction of the old Castilian tradition, the immorality and pride of the Arab.'[11]

If Sarmiento thus shared the conventional liberal critique of Spain and post-Tridentine Catholicism, why did he choose instead to emphasise the contrast between the city and the wilderness? The case is all the more puzzling if we consider that there was little in his reading to suggest such a sharp dualism. Although the historians he cited, Guizot, Thierry and even Robertson, had traced the rise of European civilisation from the barbarism of the Dark Ages and had depicted the cities as the cradles of trade, freedom and learning, there was little attempt in any of these authors to force their concepts into any schematic antithesis. As for Fenimore Cooper, he had portrayed the solitary hunters of the great forests and prairies as the favoured children of nature, their simple virtue exempt from the artificial vices of urban civilisation and the predatory advance of frontier settlement. Only Charles François de Volney, in his *Les Ruines* (1791), a work Sarmiento cited, attributed the destruction of cities to the barbarian incursions which emerged from the deserts and mountains. But if empires fell, it was because they suffered from moral decay and the devastating rule of tyrants.[12] In the Fertile Crescent the desert dwellers thus formed human reservoirs of barbaric virtue, unaffected by the corruption of urban civilisation. Much the same contrast was drawn in many a nineteenth-century work between the fierce, hardy, freedom-loving barbarians of the German forests and the effete inhabitants of the later Roman empire, a contrast that can be traced back to Tacitus. But of all this, there is remarkably little in Sarmiento. *His* barbarians were a drunken, savage crew of wastrels and robbers of whom the world was best rid. In an iniquitous letter, written in 1863 when he was governor of San Juan, he proudly celebrated the execution of the last gaucho caudillo, El Chacho, adding 'I do not try to economise with gaucho blood ... blood is the only thing they have which is human.' Later in life, he was to define the American Indians as the remnants of 'a prehistoric, servile race', and mock Ercilla's *Araucana* for its eulogy of a horde of 'filthy Indians'.[13]

In effect, the celebrated antithesis between urban civilisation and rural barbarism sprang from Sarmiento's personal experience of Argentine politics. In 1829 he had fought with General Paz against the federalist caudillos and, after capture, only narrowly escaped with his life. It was thanks to his outspoken opposition to the local governor's despotism that he was forced to take refuge in Chile, there to eke out an impecunious existence as a school-teacher and journalist. But his detestation of the gaucho had come even earlier when, one day, as a mere stripling sixteen years old, working as a petty shopkeeper in San Juan, he had witnessed the arrival of Facundo's *montonera*, a band of some 600 gauchos riding through the hitherto peaceful streets of the small town, cursing and shouting, their grimy faces peering above the great leather shields that protected their legs from thorns, as if they were so many devils riding with wings through the dust-storm thrown up by their terrified horses. In describing this scene, Sarmiento exclaimed: 'here was the vision of the Road to Damascus, of liberty and civilisation. All that was wrong with my country was revealed in that one, unexpected moment: barbarism!' Hitherto, he had accepted his family allegiance to the Federalists; henceforth, he was their unremitting enemy.[14]

To understand the intensity of Sarmiento's reaction to the sudden irruption of the gauchos we must turn to his *Recuerdos* where he portrayed the distinguished members of his family and described his upbringing and education. He came from a creole lineage that could trace its ancestors back to the sixteenth-century settlers of the region and which, generation by generation, had destined its ablest children for careers in the Church. Within his extended circle of relatives he could count bishops, Congress deputies, historians, zealous friars, and learned parish priests. But for all their illustrious ancestry, his parents were poverty-stricken, his mother supporting the family by weaving and spinning cloth, his father acting as a muleteer when not embroiled in the wars of independence. Indeed, 'of the other eleven brothers and sisters of my mother, several of their children now go dressed in a poncho, earning 1½ *reales* a day as peons'. Such was not Sarmiento's destiny: his natural intelligence and aptitude for learning soon attracted attention and he boarded with an uncle, the parish priest of San Luis, who taught him Latin and theology and encouraged his interest in literature. In a striking affirmation of his status, Sarmiento recalled: 'in the bosom of poverty, I was raised as a gentleman and my hands were never employed in more than what was required for my games and past-times'. If his father proffered the dubious example of a soldier's career, his mother and family tradition urged the priesthood as the only fitting profession for a man of his education and talents. Small wonder that he felt ashamed on becoming a shopkeeper and soon abandoned that employment, first to serve as a soldier and then, more sensibly, to open a school.[15] In effect, Sarmiento came from a typical creole family, which had maintained its leadership of colonial society as much by reason of its reiterated ecclesiastical distinction as from its economic standing. With independence and the widespread disenchantment with the Church the sons of such families entered politics, only to find their expectations of high office destroyed by the sudden emergence of rural caudillos who moved swiftly to dominate the states of the interior. Sarmiento had saluted 'the democratic nobility ... of patriotism and talent', which should have led the new republic on its predestined path towards civilisation. Once more, however, the creole Jacob found himself deprived of his birthright, albeit now, not by Spanish magistrates and merchants, but by ignorant popular leaders who had ridden the tide of revolution. It was this context of disappointed expectation that accounted for the intensity of Sarmiento's adolescent vision.

In the last resort, *Civilización y barbarie* is best compared with Las Casas' *Brevísima relación*. Both are works of prophetic force and personal vision. If Las Casas had mourned the failure of the Catholic Kings to ensure social justice and peaceful conversion for the native inhabitants of the New World, so now Sarmiento lamented the failure of the Independence movement to provide the Argentinian people with liberty and progress. In both cases, largely defenceless nations, accustomed to the rule of law and custom, had fallen prey to the onslaught of ruthless tyrants, intent only on self-enrichment and power, who established their dominion through the remorseless application of terror. Henceforward, the rural caudillo was to rank with the Spanish conqueror as the very symbol of Spanish America's failure to encounter legitimate forms of government. Even if such men often acted as the agents of economic interests, as Alberdi argued, their reliance on terror as an instrument of power proved the accuracy of Sarmiento's indictment. It was for this reason that *Facundo* proved to be such a seminal work, initiating what was to grow into a small library of books, all devoted to the unhappy task of describing the caudillos, caciques and generals who were to govern so much of the hemisphere during the ensuing two centuries. For the rest, if Sarmiento proved sufficiently adept as to learn the practical lessons of politics taught by Rosas and rise to become governor of San Juan and president of the Argentine Republic, publishing any number of pamphlets and books, it is only thanks to *Facundo* that he still figures so largely in any account of the thought and literature of Spanish America.

II

In 1839 John Lloyd Stephens entered Guatemala, charged by President Van Buren with a diplomatic mission to the Confederation of Central American States. He found the republic racked by civil war and about to dissolve into its component parts. As in Argentina, provincial antagonism combined with ideological difference to produce a political crisis which broke the central government. The anti-clerical, liberal policies favoured by Francisco Morazán, a native of Honduras, were bitterly opposed by the creole aristocracy and Church hierarchy in Guatemala. But to oust Morazán from office the conservatives called upon Rafael Carrera, a young mestizo leader, who enjoyed a remarkable ascendancy over the Indian peasantry. Stephens found politics in Central America to consist of little more than 'a bloody scramble for power and place'. Although Carrera conversed amiably with him, he feared that the creole élite had unleased 'a wild animal that might at any moment turn and rend them'. The caudillo had already conducted several massacres of opponents and openly appealed to the ethnic resentments of his native followers, not allowing any white men to serve as officers. If the Federation was doomed, it was because there was 'no such thing as national feeling' to bind Central America together.[16]

The reason why Stephens went to Central America, however, was not to conduct diplomacy but to gather material for a book. An experienced author, he had already published accounts of his travels in Egypt, Arabia and Eastern Europe, which had sold well. His interest in Guatemala and Mexico had been awakened by reading a description of the Maya ruins at Palenque and it was with the aim of surpassing previous accounts that he persuaded Frederick Catherwood, a skilled English draughtsman, to accompany him, covering his costs. The result was *Incidents of Travel in Central America, Chiapas and Yucatan* (1841), in which Stephens described both his adventurous encounters with local politicians and his exploration of the Maya sites at Copán, Palenque, Uxmal and elsewhere. Such was the calibre of Catherwood's illustrations that any reader could at once judge the quality of native art, the engravings offering a better guide than modern photographs. Moreover, Stephens himself boldly invoked his knowledge of Middle Eastern antiquities to pronounce that the sculptures, stelae and friezes at Copán were 'in workmanship equal to the remains of Egyptian art', and thus demonstrated that 'the people who once occupied the Continent of America were no savages'. Influenced by Volney's reflections on the rise and fall of empires, he surmised that the buildings at Palenque were 'the remains of a cultivated, polished and peculiar people', constructed in the midst of their golden age, who had perished without leaving any memory among the modern inhabitants of the district. The spectacle afforded by Copán, of an entire city covered by jungle foliage, suggested 'the idea of a holy city – the Mecca or Jerusalem of an unknown people'. Despite these romantic effusions, Stephens rejected the theories of recent explorers who had ascribed Palenque to the work of Romans, Egyptians, and even of settlers from Atlantis. Had not Bernal Díaz described temples and pyramids in Yucatán that were remarkably similar to those found at Uxmal and Palenque? It was the American Indians who had constructed these buildings and whose civilisation had been destroyed by the Spanish conquest.[17] That modern peasants lacked all notion of their ancestors' achievements held no surprise for any traveller to Egypt or Iraq.

The impact of Stephens' book was impressive – it rapidly ran through several editions – but, if judged from the Spanish American perspective, not entirely fortunate. For it presented a contrast between ancient, forgotten civilisation and contemporary political barbarism, the high aesthetic appeal of Maya sculpture undercut by the appalling civil wars of the present era. Moreover, the entire colonial cycle was ignored, other than in the descriptions of popular religion and the churches in which its ritual was enacted. For the rest, a decidedly American note was struck when Stephens bought the site at Copán for 50 dollars, and was only deterred from purchasing Palenque for 1,500 dollars by the obligation to acquire Mexican citizenship. On viewing the volcano at Mosaya, he reflected grandly on the 'power of the great Architect' to scatter such marvels across the world, only then to move swiftly from the sublime to the commercial, when he reflected that 'at home this volcano would be worth a fortune . . . with a good hotel on top, a railing round to keep the children from falling in, a zigzag staircase down the sides, and a glass of lemonade at the bottom . . .' Here, indeed, was the voice of a new civilisation.[18]

Nothing is more striking than the sheer confidence with which Anglo-American authors of the early nineteenth century invaded Hispanic American history, re-writing the chronicles of an earlier epoch to suit their own preconceptions and purposes. The forerunner of the new school was Washington Irving's *Life and Voyages of Christopher Colombus* (1828), which was based on the documents, including the discoverer's letters, recently printed by the Spanish naval historian, Martín Fernández de Navarrete. For Irving cast Columbus in a Protestant mould, hailing his 'visionary spirit, his penetrating genius . . . his heroic courage', and identified him as the true representative of an epoch in which 'the revival of science accompanied the revival of letters'. Before embarking on his voyage, the great admiral had to vanquish scholastic 'errors and prejudices' that derived from 'the long night of monkish bigotry and false learning'. But he would not have succeeded had he not been inspired by 'the solemn belief that he was a peculiar instrument in the hands of providence', chosen to undertake 'a sublime and awful mission'. Although Irving admitted that his hero had erred in enslaving Indians, he simply stated that 'he sinned against the natural goodness of his character'.[19] For the rest, Irving praised Las Casas, who 'exhibited a zeal and constancy and intrepidity worthy of an apostle', and whose *Historia de las Indias*, which he had consulted in Madrid, bore 'the stamp of sincerity and truth'. Indeed, much of Herrera's history was little more than a transcript of Las Casas' narrative, albeit purged of its critique of the conquerors. By far the most revealing feature of Irving's narrative was his description of the Indians of Hispaniola as 'a singularly idle and improvident race', content with a bare subsistence in an easy climate, who soon fell prey to the Spaniards who presented 'an epitome of the gross vices which degrade civilisation'. In effect, Washington established a decidedly American antithesis between a native paradise, where the Indians exhibited 'a natural liberty of ignorant content and loitering idleness', and the white man's civilised purgatory, which was governed by 'avarice, and pride and ambition, and pining care, and sordid labour'.[20]

By far the most accomplished of these American historians was William Hickling Prescott (1796–1859) whose *History of the Conquest of Mexico* (1843), brought him universal acclaim. A man of independent means, he had

Spain scoured for all available texts both printed and manuscript that dealt with his theme, drawing in equal measure on established classics like Torquemada and Clavijero and on newly available works by Ixtlilxochitl and Sahagún. On the conquest he relied on Bernal Díaz to enliven the narrative of Gómara and Cortés, confessing in a letter that 'such letters as Peter Martyr's, such notices as the Quincuagenas of Oviedo, and such gossiping chronicles as Bernal Díaz's, are worth an ocean of state papers for the historian of life and manners who would paint the civilisation of a period'. Although his aim was to describe the conquest, he prefaced the narrative with an extended discussion of Aztec history and culture. At all points his text was supported by numerous references, accompanied by incisive notes on earlier chroniclers. It was this combination of erudition and literary style that won Prescott such a wide audience.

To understand the spirit in which Prescott approached Mexican history it should be noted that he belonged to the New England school of romantic, liberal historians, among whom also figured George Bancroft, Francis Parkman and John Lothrop Motley. Theirs was the romanticism of Sir Walter Scott, whose novels had taught them that the great figures of the past could be portrayed as living persons, their thoughts and character vivified by the historian's imagination. In effect, these New Englanders regarded history as a branch of literature and sought to capture public interest by striking portraits of great men and carefully painted scenes of dramatic events. Despite their romantic method, however, they were all firmly committed to the liberal, Protestant version of the past in which political freedom and commercial expansion proceeded together, flowering first in Holland and England, only then to find a lasting home in the United States. By contrast, they dismissed the absolute monarchies of Spain and France, and still more the Catholic Church, as obstacles to progress, mere dwindling remnants of feudalism and superstition which were doomed to defeat when confronted with the rational, hardy virtue of northern Protestants. As for the Indians of North America, they were depicted as savages who were destined to disappear before the remorseless march of progress. So also, they echoed Montesquieu and condemned the states of the Orient as marred by despotism and superstition, their rulers sunk in a luxury that rendered them effeminate. Within this scale the Spaniards figured ambiguously since, when judged by the standard of the Moors, they appeared as sturdy Christian warriors but, when viewed in company of the Dutch and English, were soon dismissed as superstitious and despotic.[21] Governing the attitude of these New England historians to other cultures was a deep-seated Puritanism which found immediate expression in their aversion to the liturgy, monastic ideals and hierarchical principles of the Catholic Church.

In his discussion of Aztec culture, Prescott skilfully steered a middle course between the opposing interpretations of Robertson and Clavijero. Eschewing any general survey of the gradations of Indian society in the New World, he started his book with the Toltecs, asserting that 'the Aztec and Texcocan races were advanced in civilisation far beyond the wandering tribes of North America ... in degree not short of our Saxon ancestors under Alfred ...' Not only did he thus accept Clavijero's sharp dissociation of Anáhuac from the northern barbarians, he also rejected Humboldt's suggestion of direct cultural influence from Asia, arguing that ancient Mexico formed 'in its essential features a peculiar and indigenous civilisation'. In arriving at this conclusion he also cited Stephens' descriptions of Maya ruins. But Prescott also defined this American civilisation as unmistakably oriental in its mode of government. If he echoed Ixtlilxochitl's portrayal of Nezahualcoyotl as a philosopher king who abhorred human sacrifice and worshipped the supreme deity, nevertheless, he affirmed that the pomp and luxury of the Texcocan court were reminiscent of 'Asiatic and Egyptian despotism'. Nor did he exculpate the Mexicans' addiction to human sacrifice, since he concluded that 'the debasing institutions of the Aztecs furnish the best apology for their conquest'. The only exception to this all-pervasive image of oriental despotism was afforded by Tlaxcala which Prescott defined, somewhat oddly, as a feudal, mountainous republic, whose hardy peasantry were more free than the other peoples of Anáhuac.[22]

Once embarked on his narrative of the conquest, Prescott changed his perspective and depicted the struggle as a conflict between progress and savagery, declaring that 'the time had now come when these imperfect tactics and rude weapons of the barbarian were to be brought into collision with the science and engineering of the most civilised nations of the globe'. Once more 'the white man, the destroyer' was to conquer and break asunder native societies whose barbarism doomed them to subjection and decay. In this schematic conflict, the characters of Cortés and Moctezuma exemplified the contrasting qualities of the Christian warrior and an oriental despot. Despite his copious citation of Bernal Díaz, Prescott presented Cortés as the hero of the story, a fit representative of a country which, although still feudal and Catholic, possessed abundant vigour and invention. 'It was the expiring age of chivalry and Spain, romantic Spain, was the land where its light lingered longest above the horizon.' By contrast, Prescott scornfully portrayed Moctezuma as the embodiment of the debilitating effects of despotism, asserting that 'his pusilla-nimity sprang from his superstition', the advent of the Spaniards tormenting his 'effeminate' character. In his concluding reflections Prescott endorsed the conquest as beneficial, since it rescued the natives from the Aztec reign of terror. But he made no attempt to excuse the Spanish massacres at Cholula and Tenochtitlan, and opined that the torments of the Inquisition were but a poor improvement over the sacrifices of the Mexica. However, he confessed that Catholicism was better suited to Indian needs than any form of Protestantism that relied on 'cold abstractions' and the 'pale light of reason' since the liturgical pomp of the Roman Church resembled pagan ritual and evoked 'a tempest of passion' within its barbaric participants.[23]

If Prescott had found an ideal subject for his pen in the conquest of Mexico, by contrast he found little to excite his interest in either the native history or the civil wars in Peru. Although he confessed to the charm of Garcilaso's prose, he complained of 'the exaggerated tone of panegyric ... worthy of a Utopian philosopher'. Indeed, the very concern for the welfare of their subjects exhibited by the Incas was interpreted by Prescott as a denial of 'the taste, the prejudices and the principles of our nature', since the peasantry were deprived of private property rights and freedom of movement. No matter how benevolent its intentions, no matter how admirable its architecture and agriculture, the Inca empire was 'a despotism, mild in character, but in its form a pure and unmitigated despotism', comparable to the regimes that dominated east Asia. If no one starved in ancient Peru, there was no possibility of progress since 'ambition, avarice, the love of change, the morbid spirit of discontent ... found no place in the bosom of the Peruvian'. So distasteful did Prescott find this alien spectacle, enacted in the hemisphere where freedom and progress were destined to triumph, that he evoked the contrary image of 'our own free republic where any man can aspire to high honour, carve out a fortune ...' Yet avarice and ambition were precisely the qualities that distinguished Pizarro and his quarrelling band of followers, since in their conquests 'gold was the incentive and gold the recompense'. Weary of the interminable round of civil wars he had to describe, Prescott found relief in the figures of Las Casas, 'the uncompromising friend of freedom', and of La Gasca, with whose equitable settlement he closed his narrative, concluding that 'with some honourable exceptions it was the scum of her chivalry that resorted to Peru'.[24]

Embedded within his Peruvian narrative, Prescott offered a revealing comparison of Spanish America and New England. The conquerors were the last crusaders, albeit more animated by avarice than religion, whose cruelties towards the Indian, worthy of any Muslim prince, were cloaked by their Catholic banner. Their rapid conquests could be best compared to 'the sudden splendours of a tropical vegetation', which exhibited 'even in their prime, the sure symptoms of decay'. By contrast, the Anglo-Saxons in the New World were animated by the desire for 'independence – independence, religious and political'. Suffering the privations of the wilderness they were content with nothing but a bare subsistence, 'watering the tree of liberty with their tears and the sweat of their brow, till it took deep root in the land and sent up its branches high towards the heavens'. In effect, if Prescott defined the Indian states of Mexico and Peru and sixteenth-century Spain as civilisations, he found them decidedly inferior when compared to the enlightenment and progress achieved by the United States.[25] In the last resort his masterly romantic evocation of the conquest epoch, no matter how sympathetically drawn, was framed within a perspective that was irredeemably liberal and Protestant.

In Mexico Prescott's work was widely welcomed and soon translated. But, in his notes to the 1844 edition, the conservative statesman, Lucas Alamán, cautioned readers about the anti-Catholic bias that underlay many of the New Englander's passing remarks. Rather than engage in any general critique, Alamán simply defended the possibility of a Christian mission to Mexico long before the arrival of the Spaniards and inserted Servando de Mier's celebrated dissertation on St Thomas and Quetzalcoatl as an appendix.[26] It fell to José Fernando Ramírez (1804–71), an erudite patriot, to offer the most balanced commentary. After praising Prescott's literary power and his wide knowledge of historical sources, he criticised the 'racial disdain' which pervaded the text and determined the very vocabulary used to describe the behaviour of the Mexica. In virtually all the accounts of battles between the Spaniards and Indians, the Aztecs were referred to as barbarians and savages, much given to shrieking or shouting their war-cries. Noting that Prescott described Nahuatl as an unmusical language, Ramírez queried how a man accustomed to the tunes of *Yankee Doodle* could judge the tonality of a language he had never heard. Nor was he entirely happy with the New Englander's assessment of native civilisation, observing that the distinction drawn between Texcoco and Tenochtitlan was far too stark, since in both cities much the same religious ceremonies were performed. On the central issue of human sacrifice, Ramírez drew on the works of Joseph de Maistre to argue that all religion sprang from the fear of death and the necessity of propitiating Heaven by means of offerings. Human sacrifice had occurred in many countries and everywhere marked a stage in social development when religious ideas had attained a certain level of complexity. It thus measured civilisation rather than barbarism. As for the consumption of human flesh among the Aztecs, this always entailed a religious rite and was never used as a source of nutrition. For the rest, Ramírez complained of Prescott's distrust of native historical sources, which is to say, the codices and annals of the post-conquest period, from which, so he argued, Indian history could be reconstructed for several centuries. It was his neglect of these sources that had led Prescott to ignore Moctezuma's belief that Cortés was the herald of Quetzalcoatl's return to Anáhuac.[27]

III

Saluting José María Morelos as he embarked on campagin to liberate his country from Spanish rule, Carlos María de Bustamante (1774–1848) exclaimed: 'Go with God, favoured son of victory. The guardian angel of America guides you; and in the silence of the night Moctezuma's shade

34 Miguel Mata, *Carlos María de Bustamante*

ceaselessly demands that you exact vengeance for his gods and for those innocent victims whom Alvarado sacrificed in the temple of Huitzilopochtli.' No feature of the *Cuadro histórico de la revolución de la América mexicana* (1821–7) was more startling than the rhetorical confidence with which its author conjured spirits and shades from the conquest epoch, their brooding presence conferring historical resonance on the most dramatic moments of his narrative. Reflecting on the slaughter of Spaniards wrought by the insurgents at the Alhóndiga de Granaditas in Guanajuato, Bustamante invoked the shades of Cortés, Alvarado and Pizarro, whom he depicted weeping over the corpses of their compatriots, only to be sternly reproached by the Spirit of America who reminded them of the conquerors' massacres at Cholula and Tenochtitlan, and of the murders of Moctezuma and Cuauhtémoc, vengeance for which had at last been taken. At the conclusion of his long work, when Bustamante described Iturbide's triumphant march through the streets of Mexico City, he seemed to see, as in his mind's eye, the shades of the ancient Mexican emperors rising from their tombs in Chapultepec to lead the parade.[28] The purpose of these images was to affirm the existence of a Mexican nation at the time of the Spanish conquest and to assert that the self-same nation was now about to recover its liberty after 300 years of colonial rule, the Insurgency thus portrayed as reparation for the historical injustice of conquest. The often antiquarian bias of creole patriotism was here transmuted into the ideology of a national liberation movement. Had not Morelos himself in his inaugural speech to the Congress of Chilpancingo, a text written by Bustamante, declared that the insurgents were about to free the Mexican people from the chains of serfdom imposed on them in 1521?

Published in irregular weekly instalments, only twelve pages in length, reprinted in five volumes in 1843–6, the *Cuadro histórico* exercised a pervasive and enduring influence over all subsequent interpretation of the struggle for independence in Mexico.[29] That Bustamante had met or known most of the men whose actions he related, and that he himself had participated at the congress in Chilpancingo, meant that he wrote with all the authority of an eyewitness. Nor did he hesitate to swell his pages by inclusion of contemporary memoirs, letters and official documents. The result was a passionate, intimate evocation of a nation in arms, its leaders and their followers sacrificing their lives to free their country from Spanish rule. Written to magnify 'the glory of the Mexican nation', the *Cuadro histórico* succeeded brilliantly, installing the insurgency led by Hidalgo and Morelos as the historical foundation of the Mexican Republic, and thus relegated Iturbide's revolt to the level of a mere consequence or historical accident. At a time when former royalists commanded the army and were to govern Mexico as presidents for years to come, Bustamante snatched ideological victory from the jaws of military defeat and advanced an interpretation of the independence movement that was to serve as a decisive link in the formation of the Mexican political tradition.

In fluent, often colloquial prose, Bustamante provided his readers with an attractive portrait of Hidalgo as a dedicated parish priest, who strove to develop the agriculture and industry of Dolores. An acknowledged authority on Church history, he was a widely respected figure among the clergy of the Michoacán diocese, whose decision to call out the masses against the colonial authorities caused many other priests to join the rebellion. Elsewhere, Bustamante was to recall that he had met Hidalgo before 1810 and had been impressed by his 'gentle character, his amenable and learned conversation, his popularity and gentlemanly manners'. But he freely admitted that his character was flawed by a vein of hatred against the Spaniards, which drove him to condone the slaughter of captured Europeans at Valladolid and Guadalajara. Indeed, Bustamante later speculated that, had Hidalgo sought to prevent such massacres, he might well have succeeded in liberating the country in six months.[30] By contrast, Bustamante had little but praise for Morelos, the son of a carpenter, who had worked on an hacienda before acquiring the rudiments of Latin necessary to qualify for the priesthood. Appointed to a parish in the *tierra caliente*, he had laboured devotedly, oblivious to national events, until a visit to Valladolid awakened him to his country's servitude. Brave, honest, reserved, fearless, Morelos had few faults other than a certain fondness for women and, through his skilful campaigning, came close to victory. But these two leaders were but the most prominent in an entire gallery of patriotic portraits presented by Bustamante. That the insurgent leaders sprang from such a diversity of social backgrounds only served to emphasise the popular character of the movement. Whereas Nicolás Bravo came from a landowning family whose local influence brought many followers into the rebel camp, Vicente Guerrero was a casta, whose rustic language was later to evoke supercilious comment. It was Bustamante who first rescued from obscurity the heroic action of Pipila in setting fire to the door of the Alhóndiga at Guanajuato, and who celebrated the patriotic constancy of Félix Fernández, better known as Guadalupe Victoria.[31] In effect, the *Cuadro histórico* bequeathed to posterity a stirring account of an entire movement, the very complexity and disorder of the narrative a testimony to its author's ambition to portray a nation struggling for liberty rather than simply dwell on the great deeds of its principal leaders.

But if Bustamante opened his chronicle sounding a patriotic paean, in its middle passages he narrated with growing dismay the bitter internal divisions of the rebels, especially once the capture of Morelos had robbed the movement of any coherent focus of command. The 'national congress', on which he served as a deputy, was abruptly dissolved by order of a chieftain nominally subject to its authority. The rebels were now led by petty caudillos, each with his own court of followers, who showered him with adulation and promoted rivalry with other leaders. It was a spectacle that prompted Bustamante to recall the quarrels of the Pizarros and Almagros in Peru, causing him to confess that 'even in this we are the sons of the Spaniards'. But worse was to come. For several insurgent bands turned to banditry, more apt to prey on their fellow Mexicans than to combat the royalist troops. Of one popular leader, notorious for his sadistic delight in beating prisoners, Bustamante declared: 'I knew this monster, a disgrace to the human species.' As for the Villagrán family in Huichapán, they had simply taken advantage of the rebellion to terrorise an

entire district, their depredations worse than any deeds of the Spaniards. In
words reminiscent of Oviedo describing Hernando de Soto, Bustamante stated
that Padre Torres, the infamous rebel chieftain of Guanajuato, had no other
purpose in mind than 'to kill, rob and burn'.[32] Lurking within the pages of the
Cuadro histórico are scenes as violent and savage as any penned by Sarmiento.
In Mexico the social disorders caused by the independence movement thus
unleashed figures comparable with Facundo.

In accordance with his patriotic purpose, Bustamante vilified the Spanish
commanders and officials who defeated the rebellion. Both the judges of the
high court who organised the 1808 coup and Viceroy Venegas were condemned. But it was Félix Calleja, the general who used his family connexions in
San Luis Potosí to rally the northern landlords to the royalist side, who was
subjected to the most bitter criticism, especially since he had executed many
suspected insurgents in Guanajuato. But Bustamante readily conceded that
Juan Antonio Riaño, the intendant of Guanajuato, who had died in the
Alhóndiga in 1810, had been an enlightened governor who had striven to
promote the welfare of his subjects. So too, he admitted that Viceroy Juan Ruiz
de Apodaca sought to effect a reconciliation with creoles and had attracted a
considerable degree of support. In effect, Bustamante recognised that, as the
insurgents quarrelled among themselves and increasingly turned to banditry, so
the propertied classes rallied ever more strongly to the royalist cause. Young
creoles enlisted as soldiers, adopting the ethos of professional soldiers, so that
by the close of the conflict the army comprised no less than 39,000 men,
including both regular and militia units. Distributed across the country, this
force was funded from Mexican revenues, recruited from the Mexican
population, and had successfully defeated the Insurgency. Indeed, Bustamante
cited a letter written by Calleja to Venegas, in which the general complained of
the narrow egotism of the European Spaniards resident in Mexico and openly
admitted that it was only thanks to the 'good Americans' that the royalist
armies had prevailed. It was from their ranks that Agustín de Iturbide emerged
to organise the orderly rebellion that freed the country from Spanish rule. But
for Bustamante the agreement to install a Bourbon prince as emperor of
Mexico, embodied in the Treaty of Córdoba, was a betrayal of the independence cause.[33] In effect, the former insurgent found it remarkably difficult to
recognise that Iturbide succeeded where Hidalgo and Morelos had failed.

In the years immediately following 1821 Bustamante reinforced the argument of the *Cuadro histórico* by publishing any number of colonial chronicles
and documents. Whereas in his first journal he had commended Boturini and
'the precious work' of Clavijero, he now compiled an attractive portrait of
ancient Texcoco by the simple expedient of joining Mariano Veytia's account
of that state to Ixtlilxochitl's laudatory description of Nezahualcoyotl and his
court. So too, he published Ixtlilxochitl's narrative of the conquest, albeit with

the unpromising title of *Horribles crueldades de los conquistadores de México*, and printed both parts of Antonio León y Gama's description of the Calendar Stone and Coatlicue. His most significant coup was to obtain a copy of Bernardino de Sahagún's monumental history of Indian 'things', bringing out a complete edition in 1829–30.[34] Not content with such editorial contributions, in his *Mañanas de la Alameda* (1835–6) he presented dialogues dealing with native history, aiming to instruct young ladies so that 'they can look upon our ancient nations as politic and cultured peoples'.[35] It was at this time that he printed the history of Mexico City, written by the exiled Jesuit, Andrés Cavo, to which he added a supplement dealing with the late eighteenth century and the insurgency. His desire to re-establish the Jesuits in Mexico also induced him to publish the history of the Company of Jesus in Mexico, written by Francisco Javier Alegre.

If Bustamante thus moved swiftly to provide the Mexican public with texts on which all previous patriotic historians had drawn, he himself displayed little inclination to engage in any serious study of these chronicles and did not hesitate to cut, to interpolate comments or, indeed, to amend the texts he published, his essentially political enthusiasm over-riding any academic purpose. As a disciple of Servando de Mier, whom he described as 'my honourable and very dear friend and companion', he fully subscribed to the time-honoured thesis of an apostolic mission to Mexico and inserted Mier's famous dissertation on St Thomas and Quetzalcoatl into his edition of Sahagún's history. In his popular dialogues, he expounded all the usual arguments in favour of the hypothesis, from the presence of crosses in pre-conquest Mexico to the similarity in ritual and belief of Indian religion and Christianity, and elsewhere confidently asserted: 'at present there can be no doubt that the gospel was announced in America to the ancient Indians'.[36]

In this context it should come as no surprise that Bustamante fervently believed in the apparition of the Virgin Mary at Tepeyac and in the miraculous origin of the image of Our Lady of Guadalupe. Assisting in the tricentenary celebrations in 1831, he wrote several pamphlets defending the authenticity of the traditional account. For him the Virgin of Tepeyac appeared as 'a sweet young Indian woman, dark and full of kindness'. To respond to the objections presented by the Spanish historian, Juan Bautista Muñoz, that Sahagún had condemned the cult as a subterfuge for idolatry, Bustamante constructed an ingenious defence. In 1840 he published the 1585 version of Sahagún's Book 12 under the thoroughly misleading title of *La aparición de Nuestra Señora de Guadalupe de México*, in which he seized upon the Franciscan's admission that in his first account of the conquest he had remained silent about certain matters. Here was the explanation of his failure to mention the apparition: fear of Spanish punishment had prevented contemporaries from testifying to the facts of the miracle. After the conquest, 'for many years throughout all parts the air of this America breathed death, hatred, devastation and slavery'. What would have happened, Bustamante queried, had any patriot in the years 1810–21 claimed to have seen the Virgin? The Spaniards would have executed him on the spot. In any case, the manuscript of Sahagún was corrupt, since the enemies of Mexico had altered the text.[37] In this summary fashion he quelled doubts and maintained the truth of the traditional version.

In addition to publishing any number of short-lived journals, pamphlets and texts, Bustamante also kept a political diary in which he recorded contemporary events. Since he served as congressional deputy for Oaxaca, his home state, for most of this period he had an admirable vantage point from which to comment on the turbulent politics of the first republic. Thereafter, he had printed a series of volumes in which he described with mounting dismay the cycle of military *pronunciamientos* and revolutions that destroyed all hope of stable government. In effect, the generals, who had joined Iturbide to liberate the country from Spanish rule, continued to govern Mexico until the Liberal Reform of the 1850s, forming an unhappy band of quarrelling rivals, ever ready to rebel, acting in alliance with diverse political factions. The result was a system of institutionalised disorder, in which the republic lurched from crisis to crisis, the steadily growing burden of foreign and domestic debt the best measure of the republic's debility. About the only advantage the army brought Mexico was its swift suppression of provincial separatism and the protection of the leading cities from rural assault. Although chieftains like Facundo certainly existed in Mexico, they were largely confined to the backlands, the northern frontier, and the mountainous periphery of the central plateau. The price for these decades of internal conflict was paid in 1845–8, when the United States declared war and inflicted an overwhelming defeat on a demoralised and divided Mexican army.

In his self-elected role of national chronicler, Bustamante made little attempt to conceal his partisan bias, punctuating the record of events with often violent effusions of opinion. Like Padre Mier, he detested radicals, monarchists and military dictators. As early as 1823 he had joined with Mier to oppose the federal clauses of the Constitution and thereafter became embroiled in a pamphlet polemic with the radicals, suffering temporary imprisonment for his pains. Whereas he warmly commended the regime of his military namesake, General Anastasio Bustamante, he sharply attacked the liberal government of 1832–4, later writing: 'The memory of the government of Gómez Farías chills the heart of all Mexicans as much as that of Robespierre for the French ... It was not a Congress, it was a club of ferocious Jacobins.' Whereas the preceding assembly, in which he had served as deputy for Oaxaca, had been 'composed in the main of scholars, nobles and men of honour', the radicals were often 'so crude and mean that at first sight one knew what to expect, since both their manners and dress proclaimed their low origin'. The son of a Spaniard, educated as a lawyer, Bustamante openly lamented that 'cobblers, tailors and other base, drunken fellows', should now use the liberal masonic lodges to obtain election as municipal councillors. His experience as an insurgent had not induced any great respect for the populace, since he observed: 'The people is a ferocious and ungrateful beast which is not easy to subdue once it has lost respect for the powers that be.'[38]

What Bustamante most detested about the radicals, however, was their attack on the privileges and wealth of the Church. On noting that the liberals had denounced 'gothic institutions' as contrary to 'the philosophic spirit of the century', he explained to his readers that 'these gothic institutions are the prosperity of the goods owned by the religious communities, intolerance in public worship, ecclesiastical charges to support the Catholic cult, the perpetuity of religious vows, the private jurisdiction of the Church and other pious matters'. When the radicals moved to expropriate clerical property, he argued that the funds administered by the diocesan courts acted as a finance bank for agriculture. In any case, what right had government to sequester monies that were primarily employed for charitable or pious purposes, given for that purpose by private donors? If only he had the pen of a Chateaubriand, he lamented, to describe how the Franciscans and other mendicants had defended the Indians from the exploitation of the conquerors. So committed was Bustamante to the Catholic cause that he opposed freedom of worship as a threat to national unity, arguing that 'tolerance in an entirely Catholic country ... is a much a blunder in the moral sphere as was the introduction of a federal system in politics.' At the same time, he eschewed ultramontanism, insisting that the republic had inherited the Spanish Crown's *patronato* over the Church, which is to say, that the State possessed the right to intervene in the sphere of ecclesiastical appointments. But, when the radicals refused to approve papal nominations for the hierarchy, he claimed that they threatened to plunge Mexico into schism, raising the spectre of a national Church. For his part, Bustamante repeatedly urged Congress to allow the Jesuits to return to Mexico and protested: 'I am no Jansenist but very much an apostolic Roman Catholic.'[39]

The sharp limitations on Bustamante's rhetorical appeal to the native past were now revealed when he stridently attacked former insurgents such as Vicente Guerrero for inciting the Indians to claim lands belonging to great estates. It was not that he was unsympathetic to the condition of the native population, since he supported the abolition of aristocratic entails in the hope that the great estates might be divided. He suggested that tenants should be given some measure of security and admitted that hacienda peons were no better than serfs, observing that 'in truth the Indians are slaves, comparable to the helots of Sparta'.[40] But he was horrified when radical deputies in the State of Mexico openly argued that, since the Spanish conquest was an injustice, all land titles derived from that crime were invalid. Indeed, one rural leader informed the Indians that 'they were the true lords of all America and that the whites should restore all their occupied lands'. So too, he noted with alarm that Vicente Guerrero was passing himself off as 'a descendant of the kings of Texcoco ... it is greatly to be feared that once the Indians were aroused by Guerrero they would form a party that would lead to caste war'. Bustamante's fears about an Indian uprising grew more strident when he learnt that, in 1843, Juan Alvarez, the popular cacique who dominated the mountainous state of Guerrero, had 'formed a revolution in the South by means of the Indians, whom he has made believe that he is going to give them possession of all the lands and haciendas of the whites'. Over a hundred villages were involved in the movement, led by 'a breed of caciques ... petty captains to move the masses'. For Bustamante it was the height of irresponsibility to arm the natives, since there were 'tribes that are truly barbarian, that have always been ready to destroy the Hispano-American race'. That a local dispute over land rights, a conflict between villages and haciendas, should have evoked such sentiments in this elderly journalist reveals how deep-rooted were the fears of social dissolution in Mexico during the tragic decade of the 1840s.[41] If it be recalled that both Guerrero and Alvarez were former insurgents and that their chief local opponent was Nicolás Bravo, whom Bustamante consistently praised as the most patriotic of Mexico's military presidents, then the extent of the fissure that had opened between the radical and conservative wings of the Insurgency is clearly revealed.

Any doubts about Bustamante's conservatism are removed by his assertion that 'in truth Don Lucas Alamán is the great statesman of the republic'. For Alamán was the arch-reactionary of the epoch, chief minister of General Bustamante in 1830–2, who sought to create a strong central government, based on a close alliance of the army, the Church, and landed classes. Moreover, Alamán established a state bank to finance the mechanisation of Mexican industry, introducing a wide measure of protection for national manufactures. Here was a project to which Bustamante gave enthusiastic support, since he roundly denounced 'the false economists', the liberal disciples of Adam Smith and J. B. Say, who had opened the ports to foreign imports, thereby ruining Mexican industry. Whereas prior to 1810 the workshops and artisans of New Spain had thrived, especially when the British naval blockade halted the flood of cheap textiles from Lancashire, after Independence thousands of men had been thrown out of work, often turning to banditry to survive. What did free trade mean other than the dominion of Great Britain? Echoing the warnings of the abbé Pradt, Bustamante asserted that the British 'want us to be a mere colony, consumers of their products and more enslaved than we were to the Spaniards'.[42] It was only through the interventionist policies favoured by Alamán that Mexico could recover its economic independence.

Was it because of his growing conservatism that Bustamante failed to issue any general condemnation of the disastrous role played by the military in Mexican politics? In 1836 he participated in the framing and implementation of the Centralist Constitution of 1836, a project headed by General Anastasio Bustamante, and denounced with ever greater virulence General Antonio López de Santa Anna, whose manoeuvres for the presidency threw the republic into continual conflict. On witnessing Santa Anna's first triumphal parade in 1833, when he was accorded honours more worthy of a monarch than a president, he asked himself: 'If Hidalgo could have imagined this farce would he have uttered the *Grito de Dolores?*' That the general twice came to power, acting in alliance with the radicals, only deepened his detestation of the man whom he described as 'a monster whose deformities my poor pen cannot depict'. When he came to narrate the disastrous years of Santa Anna's presidency of 1841–3, which had been distinguished only by their venality, adulation and irresponsibility, he concluded with a searing indictment: 'You are like Attila, a scourge of God. Your power has been like that of Satan, a power of corruption and extermination.' All this contrasted strongly with Bustamante's reiterated praise of General Nicolás Bravo, whose insurgent experience and current conservatism he found most congenial.[43]

The mounting dismay with which Bustamante chronicled the political chaos that afflicted Mexico turned to prophetic despair when, during the tragic years 1845–8, the United States despatched armies which rapidly succeeded in occupying great tracts of national territory. Within little more than seven months, an American expeditionary force of 14,000 men landed at Veracruz and, after a series of hard-fought battles, entered Mexico City. At the subsequent Treaty of Guadalupe Hidalgo (1848), Mexico ceded to the United States virtually all its territories that lay north of the Rio Grande, even including New Mexico, which had been settled since the seventeenth century. It was while the capital was in foreign hands that Bustamante published his last work, *El nuevo Bernal Díaz del Castillo* (1847), whose very title emphasised the shaming similarity between the Spanish and American conquests of Mexico, a comparison which had already been drawn by the invaders themselves. The patriotic identification with Moctezuma and Cuauhtémoc, which Bustamante had deployed so vehemently against the Spaniards thus acquired a deeper, more bitter resonance. But the former insurgent had relatively little to say about the Americans other than to note that at Puebla 'the people show neither respect nor much hatred for the invaders', more surprised than impressed by their white-haired officers and the filthy, often bizarre uniforms of the volunteers, among whom they noted Irishmen. In any case, he had already described the

United States as 'the strangest and most ridiculous anomaly in history', since it was a nation composed of immigrants, who boasted of their liberty and democracy, yet who condemned the blacks to 'the most cruel slavery', treating them worse than beasts.[44]

What most pre-occupied and haunted Bustamante in *El nuevo Bernal Díaz* was the welter of political intrigue and armed coups that dominated Mexican politics in the very months when American troops pushed ever deeper into national territory. In a nightmare sequence, all the factions and men whom he most feared and detested came to power, their brief terms of office and their violent shifts in policy affording tragic testimony of the desperation that then characterised the political nation. To start with, General Mariano Paredes, acting with the discreet support of Lucas Alamán, openly advocated installing a European prince on the Mexican throne, a scheme that Bustamante roundly denounced as entailing the abandonment of Independence. After citing the prophet Samuel's warning about the tyranny of kings, he declared: 'I have served my country for thirty-five years and I can say that I have gambled my life in various kinds of combat so as not to be governed by a king.' Hardly had Paredes departed for Europe than he was replaced by Valentín Gómez Farías, brought to office by an alliance with Santa Anna, who at once sought to expropriate Church wealth and curtail clerical privileges, measures which provoked an armed rebellion of the capital's national guard. It was this radical attack on Mexico's Catholic institutions that drove Bustamante to publish his last pamphlet. Worse was to come, however, when Santa Anna was offered the title and powers of dictator. When the general failed to defend the capital from American assault and fled ignominiously abroad, Bustamante closed his chronicle with a final acerbic attack, naming Santa Anna as a Judas Iscariot who had betrayed his country.[45] By then Bustamante himself was close to death, already reduced to begging the College of San Gregorio to provide him with meals, 'the most sensitive fibre of my heart' wounded by his country's misfortunes.[46]

In his *Cuadro histórico*, Bustamante explained that he was 'the annalist of Mexican America, since I do not merit the name of historian in the true sense of the word'. As much as Bernal Díaz he aspired to present a 'true history' of events, asserting that 'I wrote what I saw or what I understood to be true', leaving to the 'master's hand' of a future Robertson or Mariana the composition of an impartial, philosophic history.[47] Where Servando de Mier had sought to advance reasons to justify independence, Bustamante was content to provide a simple record of events. But although he cited Bernal Díaz as his model, he more closely resembled Gonzalo Fernández de Oviedo, both as regards his method and the scope of his work. It is only in Bustamante's chronicles that the modern reader can obtain any real impression either of the popular complexity of the Mexican insurgency or of the dizzying pace of

Mexican politics after independence. The comparison with Oviedo is strengthened if we consider that both their chronicles are packed with incident but are entirely bereft of explanation, the disasters and failures they recount with such monotonous lamentation invariably ascribed to individual ambition or avarice. Judged by the standards of contemporary educated taste, the works of Oviedo and Bustamante appeared old-fashioned and popular, closer in style and attitude to the men whose deeds they chronicled than to the humanists and philosophic historians who were later to use their materials. If Oviedo belonged to the late medieval world of the fifteenth-century courts, so equally Bustamante preserved the provincial baroque culture of an earlier epoch, his very fondness for citing Don Quijote testimony of the enduring influence of the Spanish literary tradition. Each man suffered a similar fate. For Oviedo's sprawling work was soon summarised in elegant prose by Gómara, whose exuberant eulogy of the conquerors was destined to relegate the chronicler to relative obscurity. As for Bustamante, his materials were soon to be appropriated by both liberal and conservative historians, whose political discord did not inhibit their common rejection of his patriotic excesses. But, despite their scorn, Bustamante largely succeeded in his self-elected mission: he provided the new republic with a portrait gallery of its founding fathers, the insurgent heroes, who were thereafter to figure in every patriotic text.[48] That in El nuevo Bernal Díaz he also wrote an epitaph on the first republic is less widely remarked.

The attack on Bustamante was first launched by Lorenzo de Zavala (1788–1836), an acerbic radical who, in his aptly named Ensayo crítico (1831–2) on the revolutions in Mexico, openly derided him, stating that 'this man, without critical sense, enlightenment or good faith, has woven a tapestry of tales ... What can one think of a man who in his writings seriously says that devils appeared to Moctezuma?' Moreover, whereas Gómara echoed Oviedo's praise of the conquerors, by contrast, Zavala questioned the value of the insurgency, claiming that 'Hidalgo operated without a plan, a system, or a fixed objective. Viva la Señora de Guadalupe was the only basis of his campaign; the national flag on which her image was painted, his code of laws and institutions.' Similarly, the other liberal historian of this epoch, José María Luis Mora, also condemned Hidalgo for leading an essentially destructive movement and found more inspiration in Abad y Queipo's social analysis than in Bustamante's narrative.[49]

Despite Bustamante's ardent Catholicism, his advocacy of a centralist republic, and his pamphlet war against the radicals, his insurgent anti-Spanish polemic offended the conservatives. It was left to Lucas Alamán (1792–1853) to write his obituary and expose the contradictions of his nationalist rhetoric. After paying tribute to his honest, disinterested patriotism, he dismissed the attempt to constitute the Aztec empire as the historical foundation of contemporary Mexico, arguing that 'the conquest ... has eventually created a new nation in which all trace of the past has been erased: religion, customs, language, people: all come from the conquest'.[50] In any case, the republic encompassed vast territories which lay outside the confines of ancient Anáhuac, lands colonised under Spanish rule. To drive home this argument, Alamán wrote a short laudatory account of Cortés, whom he saluted as the founding father of his country; that he chose not to dwell on the sixteenth century demonstrates how pressing were the demands of contemporary politics. It was in his *Historia de Méjico* (1849–52), a magisterial work written in austere neo-classic prose, that Alamán presented the conservative version of the Insurgency and the first republic. Although he used the wealth of material presented in the *Cuadro histórico* he roundly condemned Hidalgo for exposing the country to social anarchy. He concluded that 'those years of warfare were nothing more than the endeavour of the educated and propertied classes, acting in conjunction with the Spanish government, to subdue a vandalistic revolution that would have destroyed the civilisation of the country ... it was an uprising of the proletariat against all wealth and culture'. In effect, Alamán was possessed by the same fears as Sarmiento, that his country might fall prey to the barbaric caudillos who haunted the backlands, the threat rendered all the more fearful by the demagogic tactics of radical politicians. A devout Catholic, a keen student of Burke and De Maistre, Alamán was a reactionary who saluted Iturbide as the liberator of Mexico and ended his days persuaded that his country needed a European prince to provide stable government and economic progress. In his history he framed an acerbic contrast between the prosperity and enlightened government of New Spain under the last Bourbons, so brilliantly described by Humboldt, and the desperate penury and political disorder of the Mexican republic in 1850, its armies defeated, its public treasury bankrupt, and its people demoralised. Apprehensive of further Anglo-American expropriations, he defined the Church as 'the only common bond which unites all Mexicans when all other ties have been broken and the only one capable of sustaining the Spanish American race and protecting it from the great dangers to which it is exposed'.[51] In Alamán's disenchanted vision there was thus no room for the Catholic insurgent, *indigenista* enthusiasm of Mier and Bustamante: the Church was Spain's chief legacy to Mexico and it was the Church which alone constituted the basis of national unity and survival.

IV

Just prior to the 1808 French invasion of Spain, the abbé Pradt warned the Spanish Americans that the great challenge facing them was to obtain independence without unleashing a revolution. Had not the slave rebellion in Saint Domingue caused the extermination of the French creoles? In the event, it proved impossible to expel the Spaniards without calling upon the masses to fight for independence. Loyalty to the Crown, still a potent force in many provinces of the American empire, was strengthened by fears of social disorder, and in both New Spain and Peru young creoles enlisted in the royal armies which were raised to quell the insurgency. During the ensuing civil wars popular leaders emerged whose guerilla operations were often indistinguishable from mere banditry. The ethnic tensions which divided colonial society soon found expression in outright massacre of Europeans and in widespread suspicion of the creoles. It was easy enough to invite the rural masses into rebellion against the Spanish Crown and its constituted authorities: it was considerably more difficult to master the often savage bands that emerged during the civil wars that ensued. The result was that most republics fell prey to endemic conflict and military coups, with several states disintegrating into their component provinces.

A British naval officer, who visited Colombia during the rebellion, observed that 'revolution not merely ruffles the surface of society, it descends into its deepest and most hidden recesses'. At all levels of the social hierarchy 'the native force of individual character and genius rise above the artificial restraints which law and custom impose', so that the very principle of hierarchy was threatened.[52] Much the same reflections occurred to Lorenzo de Zavala, who commented of Mexico that 'along with the chains that once oppressed it, there has also disappeared the old bonds of subordination, a good part of the old habits of order and, to a certain extent, the very common interest that should sustain it'.[53] In effect, the destruction of the traditional authority of the Crown entailed the erosion of most forms of political deference, so that at times mere violence became the basis of government. It was the decomposition of the central State that allowed rural caudillos such as Facundo to emerge. In Mexico the presence of the army created a paradoxical situation since, if caudillos were confined to the backlands, the leaders of the army, especially Santa Anna, themselves became agents of disintegration. It was only in the middle decades of the nineteenth century that statesmen emerged who succeeded in mastering the diverse forces that had thrust the hemisphere into such disorder, men who preached liberal reform but whose achievement was the re-creation of the State.

29

MEXICAN LEVIATHAN

I

IN 1859, at the height of the Three Years War, the Liberal cabinet headed by Benito Juárez, promulgated the Reform Laws which separated Church and State, suppressed the religious orders and confraternities, expropriated all Church property, and left the clergy henceforth dependent on the offerings of the Catholic laity. In their public statement justifying these measures, the radicals claimed that to defend their privileges and wealth 'the high clergy' and the military had thrown the country into civil war. It was now time to expel from the public life of the republic these last elements of 'the colonial system', which impeded the incorporation of Mexico into contemporary civilisation. With remarkable confidence they declared that the Liberal party embodied in the government was not a faction, but the nation itself, 'the very symbol of reason, order, justice and civilisation'. Whereas the Catholic Kings had demanded that all their subjects enter the Roman Catholic Church, so the Mexican nation now decreed that religion was a matter for private conscience, albeit subject to government in all its public manifestations.[1] When the Liberals returned to power in 1861 they expelled the religious communities from their houses and destroyed the great priories and convents in which creole patriots had once so gloried. At one level, the Reform Laws completed the campaign against the Catholic Church initiated by the enlightened ministers of the Bourbon dynasty. At a deeper level, they marked the destruction of the last remnants of the traditional order. New Spain had been built on the ruin of Anáhuac: it was now time for Mexico to be built on the ruin of New Spain.

To understand why Mexican Liberalism fixed upon the Church as the chief obstacle to progress, it is necessary to examine the writings of José María Luis Mora (1794–1850) who, in his *México y sus revoluciones* (1867) and *Obras sueltas* (1837), set out the case against the Roman Catholic clergy with remarkable clarity. Educated and ordained as a priest, a lecturer in the college of San Ildefonso, Mora came from a wealthy farming family of the Bajío, who were ruined by the 1810 insurgency. After independence he openly paraded his liberal views and served as chief counsellor to Valentín Gómez Farías during the short-lived radical government of 1832–4, his advocacy of radical measures against the Church wealth and institutions arousing such conservative ire that he was thereafter obliged to live in European exile. Despite his fame as a radical, he preferred Montesquieu to Rousseau, admired Washington and the American Revolution, and condemned the excesses of Robespierre and the French Jacobins. Within the hispanic tradition he was indebted to Jovellanos, whose essays he had published in Mexico, and relied heavily on the writings of Manuel Abad y Queipo for his analysis of Mexican society. In effect, Mora incorporated the principles of the Spanish Enlightenment into the ideology of Mexican Liberalism, thereby acting as the essential link between the Bourbon ministers and the Reform. Accustomed to tell his friends that 'I am just a philosopher', Mora was described by Melchor Ocampo as 'sententious as Tacitus, biased as a reformer, presumptuous as a scholastic'.[2]

Nowhere was Mora's philosophic approach more evident than in his disdain for Bustamante and his insurgent nationalism. When he sketched the historical causes of contemporary problems he began his account with conquest, pausing only to insist that Mexico had as many Indian inhabitants in 1810 as in 1519. If he did not seek to palliate the massacres inflicted by the Spaniards, he had no hesitation in acclaiming Cortés as a great man and the effective founder of the country. But there was little in colonial society that attracted his praise or sympathy other than the reforming measures of Charles III and his ministers. Indeed, he provided an attractive portrait of Juan Antonio Riaño, the intendant of Guanajuato, asserting that he might well have embraced an orderly bid for independence. As for the Insurgency, Mora defined it as 'necessary for obtaining Independence but destructive and pernicious for the country'. Like Zavala he criticised Hidalgo for his failure to ennunciate any political principles or objectives, and condemned the massacres of Spaniards that accompanied the capture of Valladolid and Guadalajara. By contrast, he found Morelos' title of 'servant of the nation', an attractive lesson for all citizens.[3] In effect, Mora rejected virtually all the elements of the patriotic creed propounded by Mier and Bustamante.

Connected by friendship with leading figures in the capital's social and intellectual elite, Mora openly denounced the measures favoured by the Yorkino radicals during the 1820s. Neither the expulsion of Spaniards nor the erection of protective tariffs for cheap textiles met with his approval. The alliance between urban ideologues like Lorenzo de Zavala and the populist wing of the insurgents led by Vicente Guerrero aroused his suspicion of a betrayal of liberal principle. By contrast he favoured Francisco García, the progressive governor of Zacatecas and Gómez Farías, whom he urged to impose reform by means of a revolutionary dictatorship. In his subsequent history of this hectic period in Mexican politics, Mora interpreted the party conflict, not in terms of social classes, but rather as a struggle between the nation and the privileged corporations, which is to say, between the states and the army and Church. Here was the underlying cause of the hostilities between Federalists and Centralists, since the two great corporations which sought to dominate the country had their chief base in Mexico City. In immediate terms, it was the existence of the army, divided in some seventeen brigades, each led by a commandant general, which undermined the authority of the state governors and constituted 'a principle of disorder and anarchy'. In effect, the army consumed the bulk of federal revenues and after each revolt obliged the republic to assume an additional burden of debt.[4] No progress could come while Mexico was subject to the rule of this praetorian guard.

But it was in the Church that Mora descried the chief obstacle to social, economic and intellectual change. That the clergy had preserved their legal immunity and privilege ran counter to the basic principle of the legal equality of all citizens, establishing the Church as a powerful corporation with vested interests which were separate from the general interest of the nation. Nowhere was the sinister influence of the clergy more deplorable than in their control of education, since 'instead of inspiring youth with a spirit of inquiry and doubt, which will always lead the human spirit to approach the truth, they instil habits of dogmatism and disputation'. It was to remedy this situation that Mora advised Gómez Farías to suppress the university and existing colleges, replacing them by secular institutes blessed with a curriculum based on science, law, medicine and literature.[5] Equally deleterious was the clergy's influence on the 'moral condition' of the population, since they failed to inculcate the distinction between crime and sin, with the result that most Mexicans generally confused the obligations of a citizen with the duties of a Christian. The clergy sat in judgement on the civil law since, unless they condemned an offence as a sin, their parishioners ignored the prohibitions of the law. Moreover, at times, priests still sought to censor publications as contrary to the Christian faith, thereby challenging the constitutional right of free expression. Finally, Mora criticised the clergy for their encouragement of popular religion, in which the masses worshipped images and incurred needless expense in superstitious rites that had nothing to do with true Christianity.[6] In this summary of clerical offences, Mora simply echoed the eighteenth-century Jansenist critique and carefully eschewed any challenge to Catholic dogma.

Just how radical were Mora's views on Church reform can be judged by inspecting his 'Dissertation on ecclesiastical property and revenue', written in 1831 to guide the governor of Zacatecas. To start with, he proposed that the Church's right to levy a tithe on all agricultural production should be abolished since the tax was an unjust, heavy burden on farmers, and the proceeds used to maintain bishops and cathedral chapters in unnecessary splendour. So too, the mass of chantry funds and endowments which supported the unbeneficed clergy should be confiscated since they enabled a large number of priests to live in idleness. Much the same was true of the religious orders, whose members were frequently corrupt, idle and without the slightest utility to society: they should be disbanded and their estates and urban property expropriated. Equally ripe for suppression were the confraternities, whose considerable wealth was expended in liturgical excess. Indeed, about the only worth-while element that Mora discerned in the contemporary Mexican Church was the parochial clergy, whose arduous ministry was often but poorly rewarded. Even here, however, he criticised the reliance on fees charged for the rites of baptism, marriage and funerals, since these monies were often exacted from the poor. In short, Mora anticipated virtually the entire programme of the Reform, only stopping short of advocating outright separation of Church and State. Although he deprecated the 1824 Constitution's affirmation of Catholicism as the national religion, he proposed the establishment of a capital fund, to be administered by the states, which would yield sufficient interest to pay salaries to the clergy.[7] It was for this reason that he suggested the appointment of a bishop in each state of the federation.

The strangest feature of Mora's discussion of Church wealth was the way in which he over-estimated its value. In a bizarre calculation, he stated that the overall tithe income of 2.3 million pesos represented a capital fund of 46 million pesos, thus defining it as 5 per cent interest on estates or monies actually owned by the Church. So too, he grossly over-estimated the amounts invested in chantry funds, church fabrics and adornments, with the result that he reached a final estimate that total Church wealth came to 179 million pesos. The attraction of these calculations was that they could serve as tempting bait for the politicians: Church wealth could be used to redeem the ever growing burden of the domestic national debt. At the same time, Mora criticised Zavala for proposing that Church property be expropriated and sold on the open market, since this procedure would ruin sitting tenants and break the land market. In yet one further anticipation of Reform legislation, Mora advocated that all tenants be given the first option on purchase and that, following the precedent of the 1804 consolidation measure, their payments be made in instalments spread across the years.[8]

To justify expropriation, Mora had recourse to Campomanes and other Jansenist authors, arguing that the Church had two, quite separate characters. First and foremost, the Church was 'a mystical body ... eternal and enduring, eternally independent of the temporal power'. But it was also 'a political community', whose rights and property derived from the civil authorities. In making this distinction, Mora claimed that the primitive Church had been nothing but a mystical body: its bishops and clergy depended on the faithful's offerings for their maintenance and possessed a merely voluntary authority. It was thanks to the Emperor Constantine and his successors that the situation changed, when bishops came to exercise a jurisdiction with their own courts and laws, administer property and levy taxes such as the tithe. Yet all these new-found rights and privileges were based on concessions from the civil power and, what the State could give, the State could take away. In any case, since ecclesiastical institutions administered their property as trustees, they entirely lacked the virtue and rights of private ownership. In effect, Mora sought to dismantle the entire system of canon law and jurisdiction which had been created during the Middle Ages and which had been transplanted by Spain into the New World. Even if he did not openly advocate separation of Church and State, that outcome was implicit in his dictum: 'the end and object of civil government is to maintain the social order and not to protect this or that religion'.[9] In an ideal world the Church would simply figure as the voluntary association of the faithful, bereft of any public voice or status.

In contrast to this bold approach to Church wealth, Mora accepted that possessive liberalism forbade the state to meddle with private property. In terms which echoed John Locke, he declared that 'the right to acquire [property] which an individual has, is prior to society and corresponds to him as a man, so that society does no more than assure his possession'. Whereas the Church in its character of 'a political community' had been created by society, by contrast, individuals were reckoned to have owned property before agreeing to the social contract which established society and the civil authorities. Even trading and industrial companies were exempt from expropriation since they were 'associations of individuals', whose shares embodied the principle of private ownership. In this Liberal scheme of things, the force which drove society forward was the self-interest of the individual proprietor, operating in a market free from state intervention. It was this principle that inspired Mora to reject Alamán's project to promote the mechanisation of Mexican industry by tariff protection and a state finance bank, affirming that 'private interest and free competition untrammelled by government protection should dictate capital investment and determine the industry of a country . . . the government should not directly help any industry'.[10] In any case, economic logic suggested that Mexico should concentrate on mining and agriculture, activities favoured by its natural environment and the talents of the population, leaving manufacturing to Europe.

The degree to which Mora's philosophic radicalism determined his social analysis was most evident in his discussion of Mexico's agrarian problem. The facts of the case had been spelt out already by Abad y Queipo, and Mora simply echoed his conclusion that the distribution of landed property between the vast territories of the haciendas and the communal holdings of the Indian villages was a recipe for stagnation. Progress could only come from the 'individual interest' of a numerous class of proprietary farmers. But he asserted that the chief reason why the great estates had not been divided between heirs or partitioned for sale was their heavy burden of Church endowments and annuities. For the diocesan courts which administered these funds sought to protect their investment by preventing any division of estates until the debts were redeemed. If these charges were removed, so Mora argued, the operation of individual interest, the testamentary laws, and the free market would inevitably promote the division of the haciendas. But, even if this were not to occur, it was still wrong to allow the State to intervene, since 'the Legislator cannot give laws which directly affect private property'. In this respect, all he could recommend was the example of Francisco García, governor of Zacatecas, who had used state revenues derived from a mining boom to purchase haciendas and effect their partition.[11]

When he praised the proprietary farmer as the ideal agriculturist, by no means did Mora envisage a nation of peasants. In his discussion of the expropriation of haciendas owned by the Church, he proposed that these estates should be divided into properties worth about 12,000 pesos, which is to say, into substantial farms worked by hired labour. That this was not an arbitrary suggestion was shown by the level of property qualification for voters and elected officials that he recommended. For, after condemning the election of deputies and councillors without means as a cause of abuse and corruption, he suggested that all such citizens should possess an annual income of about 1,000 pesos or own property that was assessed for tax purposes at about 6,000 pesos. If such figures be compared to contemporary land prices in the Bajío, then it becomes clear that Mora conceived the ideal citizen and politician as a farmer who had about 1,000 acres to his name.[12]

If the rights of private property prevented the State from intervening to divide the great estate, by contrast there was nothing to prevent politicians from meddling in the affairs of the Indian villages. Once more, Mora echoed Abad y Queipo and pronounced that the communal tenure of land vested in each village was the chief cause of their backwardness. In this regard, the Laws of the Indies, no matter how benevolently conceived, had disastrously isolated the natives, maintaining them in a condition of perpetual tutelage. The first missionaries had operated under erroneous principles, since 'all their concern consisted in that they [the Indians] should be Christians, without first taking care to make men of them'. For the Indians 'civil society' lacked the fundamental basis of private property, which alone would have brought progress. Moreover, the legal right of every Indian *pueblo* to claim a collective endowment of land, a right set out in the Laws of the Indies and still enforced under the republic, had provoked a series of disputes between villages and haciendas, in which the Indians were often the aggressors.[13] Although Mora did not follow Abad y Queipo in recommending the distribution of Indian lands among individual villagers, he clearly would have supported such a measure, since it was inherent in his analysis.

As much as priests and soldiers, Indians were a privileged class according to Mora, since they were protected by laws and institutions which catered solely for their interests, thereby separating them from the general mass of Mexican citizens. Did not virtually all the Laws of the Indies define them as minors? Yet it was 'an unpardonable error' to suppose that one race was either superior or inferior to another race, especially since all nations had changed across the centuries. Who could doubt that the Indians were equal in intellect and aptitude to other Mexicans? But, whereas the effect of independence had been to destroy the differences between the creoles and castas, by contrast, the Indians still remained a people apart, unable or unwilling to take advantage of the legal equality as citizens that had been theirs since the establishment of the republic. The way forward was by assimilation through education, Mora asserted, since 'education can do everything'.[14] It was for this reason that he sharply condemned Juan Rodríguez Puebla, the rector of the College of San Gregorio, for his campaign to preserve specifically Indian institutions and the laws that protected them. Instead, he commended Gómez Farías who, in all government measures, had refused to recognise any distinction between Indians and non-Indians, merely referring to the rich and the poor, thus seeking 'to hasten the fusion of the Aztec race with the general body of citizens', aware that 'the existence of different races in the same society has to be an eternal cause of conflict'.[15] Once again, Mora here anticipated what were to be the aims and perspective of the Liberal Reform.

Perhaps the most perplexing feature of Mora's analysis was his failure to discuss how the Liberals were to carry through a massive transformation of property relations without creating a strong central executive. If both army and Church operated on the national level then, so equally, the political nation had to create the institutional means to defeat them. The nightwatchman view of the central state and the emphasis on the states of the federation could not survive any strong challenge to the role of elected authorities. Moreover, if Mora had little or no theory of state action, so too, he failed to present any image of the Mexican patria or nation. Whereas creole patriotism had laboured across the centuries to glorify the Indian past and to depict Mexico as especially chosen by the Virgin Mary for her protection, all that occurred to Mora was to compare Mexico to Ireland as a country desperately in need of reform.[16] In effect, the Liberal insistence on the primacy of individual self-interest left little room for any positive theory of the nation, the state, and politics. To incorporate Mexico into the civilisation of the nineteenth century was an admirable aim, but how was this to be done without demanding self-sacrifice from many citizens?

The influence Mora exercised on his contemporaries can be best observed in the essays of Mariano Otero (1817–50), a leading figure among the moderate Liberals of the 1840s, who argued that 'the middle class which embodies the

truc character of the population ... shall naturally come to form the true
constitutive principle of the republic'. But this striking affirmation was
immediately qualified when he admitted that the chief merchants and most
skilled artisans were foreigners, since in Mexico 'to be counted respectable, a
man has to be a soldier, a bureaucrat, a priest, a lawyer, or at least a doctor'.
Drawing on Montesquieu, he attributed the constant revolts and civil conflict
that Mexico suffered to a basic indecision or lack of consensus as to where the
country's future lay, arguing that 'in constituted societies there is a dominant
principle which decides political and administrative questions as they arise'.[17]
Although he was confident that Mexico would adopt the forms of contemporary civilisation, his optimism was shaken by the defeats inflicted by the Anglo-
American invasion. Noting that foreign newspapers had depicted the Mexicans
a 'a degenerate race which does not know how to govern or defend itself', he
confessed that most of the population had been but passive spectators during
the war. Moreover, the Church hierarchy, intent on defending its wealth and
privilege, had engineered a revolt against Gómez Farías and conspired with
General Paredes to import a monarch from Europe. For Otero, Mexico's chief
problem was that 'there is no nation', and hence no 'national spirit'.[18] In
circumstances so desperate, what point was there in appealing to the liberal
concept of self-interest of the individual?

If the Liberals clamoured ever more loudly against the Church, for their part
the clergy now abandoned their Jansenist opinions and adopted an intransigent
ultramontanism that rendered the separation of Church and State a practical
necessity for bishops and politicians alike. When Melchor Ocampo (1814–61),
a former governor of Michoacán who was about to resume office, asserted in
1851 that the state authorities had the right to regulate the fees charged by the
clergy for baptism, marriage and funerals, he was roundly condemned by an
anonymous parish priest for attempting 'to usurp the Church's sovereignty, to
secularise religious society, and to impose the civil power over and above the
divine jurisdiction of the bishops'. Ocampo had failed to realise that the
Church was 'a universal society, sovereign and independent', whose 'sovereigns', the bishops, alone possessed the right to determine what charges, if any,
to make for its ministrations and how best to ensure its material maintenance.
For the Council of Trent had defined Christ as a 'legislator', and affirmed that
bishops exercised the powers conferred by Christ on the apostles. Ocampo
must recognise that 'the Church is one, States are many ... the clergy are as
independent of the State as is Mexico of England ... ' To question the canons
of Trent was to incur the danger of excommunication and to infringe the
Mexican constitution which had recognised Catholicism as the national
religion. When Ocampo asserted that every man had a natural right to worship
God in the manner dictated by his conscience, he was at once informed that the
exercise of private judgement in religion was 'a criminal heresy' which, if

applied widely, would lead to anarchy, socialism, and the crimes of the French Revolution.[19] If we pause to consider that this tirade was elicited by an objection raised by municipal authorities to the practice of the parochial clergy in levying fees according to a diocesan schedule published in 1737 that imposed differential rates for Indians, castas and Spaniards, a schedule which thus infringed the republic's abolition of legal ethnic distinctions, then the ideological abyss that separated the clergy from the liberals can be plumbed.

Once the radicals swept to power in 1855 they set about implementing Mora's proposals. The first measure was to quit the clergy of all their legal privileges and immunity. But it was the 1856 Law brought in by Miguel Lerdo de Tejada which dealt the Church the most effective blow by demanding the sale of all Church property, an act which completed the process initiated by the 1804 Consolidation decree. As regards urban property, tenants were given first option on purchase. The terms of payment were decidedly generous since 60 per cent of the sum required, a figure estimated by reckoning current rent as 6 per cent of capital value, could be paid by presenting national debt bonds, instruments which could be readily purchased at about 10 per cent of their nominal value. The 40 per cent to be paid in cash was divided into instalments spread over forty months. As for haciendas, their owners were allowed to free their properties of the inherited, accumulated burden of chantry funds and other endowments by simply paying 15 per cent of the capital value, which is to say, the equivalent of three years' current rent. The effect of these transactions, when combined with the outright sale of the lands and urban property directly owned by Church institutions, was to reduce the domestic national debt, create a new class of house-owners in the leading cities, and write off all the wealth of the Church that had accumulated over three centuries.[20] The Lerdo Law equally applied to civil corporations and to Indian *pueblos*. Any lands that had been leased to private individuals were immediately adjudicated to tenants. But it was the abolition of Indian communal tenure and the distribution of land in small plots among individual villagers that aroused vehement protests and outright rebellion, especially when local elites conspired with officials to defraud their neighbours and fellow-villagers of their rightful shares of land.[21] Few laws in Mexican history have been so dramatic or unfortunate in their effect as the Lerdo Law. The battery of Liberal reform was completed with the promulgation of a new Constitution in 1857, which installed the language of natural rights into the national charter. It also provided for congressional supremacy over the executive branch and, through its omission of any declaration about national religion, effectively de-established the Catholic Church. Moreover, in separate clauses, the Church was prohibited from owning property, the clergy forbidden to act as deputies, and the federal authorities given unspecified powers to regulate religion and 'its external discipline'.[22]

The assault on the Church provoked a furious reaction in which the Mexican bishops, supported by the Papacy, exhorted the faithful not to accept the Liberal constitution. The result was a cruel civil war that effectively broke the political power of both the army and the hierarchy. In consequence, when Napoleon III chose to take advantage of the American Civil War and intervene in Mexico in 1862, the bishops welcomed the French invasion and actively supported the conservatives' invitation to Maximilian of Austria to become emperor of Mexico. Expelled from the country by the Liberals, the archbishop of Mexico, Pelagio Antonio de Labastida, served briefly as president of the Council of State. But Maximilian refused to restore the privileges and wealth of the Church and sought to consolidate his regime by recognising the Lerdo Law, appointing moderate Liberals to his cabinet. However, his regime depended on French bayonets and, when the Americans demanded and obtained the removal of all European troops from Mexican soil, Maximilian was doomed, suffering execution in 1867. Throughout this prolonged period of civil war, from 1858 onwards Benito Juárez (1806–72) a Zapotec lawyer and former governor of Oaxaca, acted as president. But, whereas during the Three Years War he was overshadowed by his powerful ministers, Miguel Lerdo de Tejada and Melchor Ocampo, in the war against the French occupation he emerged as the focus of the national unity, expressing the common resolve to preserve Mexican independence. That the Mexicans succeeded in organising their defence without assistance from abroad was a matter for self-congratulation, a feat that Juárez himself described as 'the greatest glory that I desire for my country'.[23]

Of the several paradoxes that haunted the Reform, the growing contradiction between its liberal principles and its main political achievement was the most striking. From a movement that for over a generation had advocated a powerful Congress and a weak executive, there eventually emerged an authoritarian regime headed by Benito Juárez. As early as 1861 the president had complained bitterly of the limitations on his authority, exclaiming: 'under these conditions it is impossible to govern: no one obeys me and I am not able to oblige anyone to obey'. But, when the French invasion caused the legislature to dissolve, Congress conferred plenary powers on Juárez, with 'no other restrictions than the salvation of independence, the integrity of the nation, the constitutional form of government and the Reform laws'. It was in virtue of these powers that the president prorogued his term of office in 1865, justifying his decision by the necessity of offering the invaders a clear focus of resistance.[24] Thereafter, during the restored republic, Juárez skilfully deployed the prestige and loyal following he had won by his unyielding resistance, to remain in office, obtaining re-election in 1868 and 1872. Throughout this period he was regularly voted 'extraordinary powers' by Congress so as to allow him to deal with the crises and revolts that threatened his government. But, although his retention of power was only made possible by the support given him by state governors, the army and leading politicians, many radicals never forgave Juárez for his betrayal of their liberal principles. That his enemies often looked to Porfirio Díaz, a general who had won a high reputation in the war against the French, to restore the constitution, only serves to illustrate the paradoxical shifts of Mexican politics in this period, since Díaz himself was eventually to be re-elected president eight times, governing the country until 1911.

II

The Reform movement attracted the services of an entire circle of literary intellectuals, who entered government with the aim of transforming their country into a modern, liberal society. Among the most prominent of these men was Ignacio Ramírez (1818–79), a mestizo from the Bajío, where his father had gained notoriety as a Yorkino politician. Educated at the College of San Gregorio in Mexico City, he soon moved into politics and journalism, where he acquired fame under the pseudonym of 'El Nigromante'. In the 1840s he founded the Literary Institute at Toluca and taught there for some time. His political career reached its climax when, in 1861, he served under Juárez as Minister of Justice and Public Instruction. Thereafter, he quarrelled with the president and, under the restored republic, waged fierce journalistic war against his erstwhile leader. He also served as judge in the Supreme Court and finally, in 1879, entered the first cabinet of Porfirio Díaz, once more acting as Minister of Justice.[25] His chief disciple and associate was Ignacio Manuel Altamirano (1834–93), an Indian born in Tixtla, the home town of Vicente Guerrero, who was educated at the Toluca Institute when Ramírez taught there. During the Three Years War he served as secretary to Juan Alvarez, the governor of Guerrero and, after a period in Congress, enlisted in the army to combat the French, rising to the rank of colonel. Thereafter, he acted as attorney and judge of the Supreme Court, lectured at various institutions, and engaged in journalism, both literary and political. He joined Ramírez both in his opposition to Juárez and in his support for Díaz, receiving several official appointments in the 1880s.[26] Despite their common viewpoint in politics, the two men differed greatly in character and style. Whereas Ramírez was a leading politician, a student of political economy and an acerbic journalist, Altamirano was more the man of letters, conciliatory in temper, much given to romantic nostalgia, who had a considerable literary achievement to his credit. Both men epitomised the emergence in Mexico of a new class of intellectuals, who relied on their brains and their fluent pens to rescue them from obscurity, albeit rarely from poverty. That they should have intervened so prominently in the public life of their country demonstrates the central role of liberal culture in Mexican politics during the Reform period.

The tap-root of radicalism in Mexico continued to be detestation of the

Catholic Church, the power and influence of which was conceived as the chief obstacle to social, economic and moral progress. Without the destruction of its public authority it would be impossible to create a modern, secular society committed to the principles of the French Revolution. As Minister of Justice and Public Instruction in the radical cabinet of 1861, Ignacio Ramírez soon became renowned for the zeal with which he applied the Laws of the Reform. Under his direction the religious orders, both male and female, were expelled from their cloisters and their property confiscated. Several of the great convents were destroyed so as to facilitate urban development and others were appropriated for public use, former churches now serving as libraries. Their paintings, images and treasures were dispersed or destroyed. Indeed, so determined was Ramírez to rid Mexico of all evidence of past glories that, when he learnt that workers at the national mint were reluctant to melt down precious monstrances and chalices, he himself hastened to seize a hammer to inflict the first blows. Whereas many Liberals were deists or closet Catholics, Ramírez made no secret of his atheism and aversion to all religion. As early as 1836 he had shocked a literary gathering with the ringing declaration: 'There is no God.' Later, as political head of Tlaxcala, he attempted to ban the annual procession staged in honour of Our Lady of Ocotlán, an image housed in the chief sanctuary of that city, only to be expelled by an indignant populace and clergy.[27] Evidently, Ramírez inculcated anti-clericalism at the Literary Institute at Toluca, since his young disciple, Ignacio Manuel Altamirano, acquired the sobriquet of 'the Marat of the Radicals' on account of his fiery speeches in the 1861 Congress. On one occasion, he passionately denounced proposals for a general amnesty for conservatives, recently defeated in the Three Years War, and openly lamented: 'the government banished the bishops, instead of hanging them, as those apostles of iniquity deserved'. In later years he congratulated the governor of Mexico for banning the Holy Week processions at Tacubaya, observing 'this spectacle has nothing in common with the Christian religion and is an affront to the culture of this century'. By contrast with Ramírez, however, Altamirano favoured a purified form of religion and indeed argued that 'the liberal party is the true observer of the Gospel'. It was the Catholic Church, as it was then constituted, which was the enemy, not the teachings of Christ.[28]

In their approach to the economic problems of their country, the radicals upheld the *laissez-faire* doctrines of classical liberalism, fixing upon individual self-interest as the chief motor of material progress. For his part, Ramírez was keenly aware of the injustices inflicted on the masses by both landlords and industrialists and indeed on one occasion was accused of inciting Indians to rebel against their exploitation. But in general he preached 'the gospel of [Adam] Smith' and insisted on 'the principle of non-intervention by the state in production and consumption'. Indeed, he affirmed that the chief purpose of achieving independence from Spain was to create a free market economy in Mexico. It followed that he condemned all measures of tariff protection, arguing that, if Mexico was to move beyond its current 'industrial barbarism', it should import as many manufactured goods as it could afford. In a clear echo of the earlier liberal attack on Lucas Alamán's project for the mechanisation of Mexican industry by means of state finance and tariffs, Ramírez denounced as injurious to the national interest any attempt to introduce protection, which would only benefit, so he averred, some 5,000 workers and '200 speculators'. At the same time, he took sufficient interest in European affairs to realise that conflict between capital and labour was inevitable, a view which led him to advocate the formation of trade unions to protect the workers' interest. However, he equally warned of the dangers inherent in any advance to socialism or communism, arguing that the restrictions on individual liberty inherent in their proposals would result in collective serfdom. These fears led him to inform his fellow radical Guillermo Prieto, that 'the right to work cannot be realised other than by means of communism'. More positively, his advocacy of an open economy was expressed in the encouragement he offered as minister to the construction of railways and the establishment of agricultural colonies. Undeterred by the history of Texas, he favoured European immigration and called for French settlement in Sonora and Sinaloa. Similarly, he welcomed foreign investment and declared: 'all capital, by the simple fact of its existence in Mexico, should be regarded as Mexican'.[29] It should be remembered, of course, that he died before the country received any major influx of investment from abroad.

In the sphere of political authority, Ramírez retained the customary liberal suspicion of the state, but whereas his predecessors had fixed upon the federal system of sovereign states to offset the power of central government, he identified the *municipio*, the township, as the chief bastion of civic liberty. To justify this preference, he cited the authority of Alexis de Tocqueville and the example of the 1871 Paris commune. Once again, he warned of communism, insisting that each municipality should express the political union of individual property-holders, be they farmers or artisans. Once property was divided among the greatest number of citizens, then society should exercise self-government through local institutions. The example of the United States was here a potent lesson in democracy, much admired by Ramírez. It was in part his opposition to all forms of administrative centralisation that impelled Ramírez to break with Benito Juárez. He resumed his beliefs in this lapidary formula: 'the individual is sovereign, the *muncipio* is the nation'.[30]

Public education was the Liberals' panacea for their country's ills, both social and civic. As minister, Ramírez arranged for the confiscated books of the great convents to be deposited in the former church of the Augustinian friars so as to form a national library in Mexico City. But state funds for education were not

forthcoming until the Porfirian settlement. Altamirano lamented the failure of
Mexican statesmen to make adequate provision for the establishment of
primary schools. Yet without a system of obligatory primary education, how
could the masses be rescued from the superstitions taught by the Church or be
prepared to exercise their democratic rights? Without such measures, the
inhabitants of the republic would remain sharply divided, with any hope of
social equality a delusion. In a passage that tells us much about Mexico at that
time, Altamirano declared: 'We, the agents of progress and regeneration, after
many years of propaganda and struggle, have succeeded in destroying all the
social distinctions that rendered equality at law a joke in the republic.' The men
of wealth and privilege in Mexico had lost their former influence in both society
and politics. But there still remained the all-important distinction between the
classes 'that educate themselves and those who remain in a state of ignorance'.
Until universal education was introduced, the country would continue to be
divided between an aristocracy of patricians and intellectuals and the masses,
with knowledge rather than religion or military power the source of privilege.[31]

To judge from their published works, the radicals did not question the effects
of the Ley Lerdo of 1856 on Indian landholdings. Their silence is all the more
remarkable if we consider that subsequent radicals were to condemn the
abolition of communal tenure and the distribution of land among villagers as a
measure which led to widespread appropriation of *pueblo* territory by mestizos
and neighbouring landlords. In this respect, the task of the Revolution was to
reverse the work of the Reform. It would appear that Ramírez and Altamirano were blinded by their belief in the supreme value of individual, private
property, persuaded that once the Indian peasantry became petty proprietors
the play of self-interest would promote material improvement.[32] In any case,
they viewed the survival of the Indian *pueblo* as an obstacle to the social
integration of the native population, a view they inherited from Mora. For his
part, Ramírez asserted that by reason of their isolation and the multiplicity of
their languages, the Indians could not be defined as Mexicans, since 'these races
still conserve their own nationality, protected by family and language'. As a
rule, their village life pursued its own dull rhythm, quite untouched by any
questions of national concern. The natives more resembled industrious ants
than the citizens of a republic. To what point liberal institutions in Mexico, if
the rural masses remained submerged in political apathy, ignorant of all that
occurred beyond the confines of their immediate locality? In an unconscious
echo of Viceroy Toledo and José de Acosta, Ramírez bluntly questioned the
very humanity of the Indians: 'to count them citizens, first we have to start to
make them into men ... we have republican institutions, but we do not have
citizens, since we do not even have men ...' Needless to say, it was not any
theory of ethnic superiority or inferiority which prompted these remarks but
rather the conviction that the exercise of human virtue and talent required a

foundation on individual property and free expression in the political life of the republic.[33]

Where the radicals of the Reform differed markedly from their liberal predecessors was in their new-found emphasis on the *patria*, and, still more, in their saluting the 1810 Insurgency as the historical foundation of their liberal patria. They ignored the critique of that movement advanced by Zavala and Mora and openly adopted Bustamante's exuberant celebration of the insurgent heroes. Indeed, Ramírez affirmed that the Mexican people could not return to the epoch of the Aztecs, still less consider themselves Spaniards; instead: 'We come from the village of Dolores. We descend from Hidalgo.'[34] Obviously, it was not as a priest that the insurgent leader was hailed, since Ramírez chose to praise Hidalgo as a proponent of progress and science, who actively encouraged local industry in his parish. Similarly, Altamirano not merely saluted the *cura* of Dolores as 'Father of the patria and liberator of Mexico', but also asserted that his decrees which freed all slaves and abolished Indian tribute raised him in stature above both Washington and Bolívar. In a brief account of Mexican history since Independence, he characterised the Insurgency as a popular movement in which the Mexican people rebelled against the exploitation of the privileged classes, composed of 'the colonial nobility, the upper clergy, landowners and rich merchants'. With the failure of the revolt, these same elements of privilege assisted Iturbide to engineer his coup so as to maintain their threatened status and property. Not until the Reform did the liberals, 'the party of the nation', succeed in wresting power from the Church and the army. Unlike Zavala and Mora, Altamirano thus postulated an underlying continuity of purpose between the insurgents and liberals based on a common popular constituency. What we here encounter is the surfacing at the literary level of the political views and action of Guerrero and Juan Alvarez, former insurgents who, unlike Nicolás Bravo and Carlos María de Bustamante, fought in coalition with urban radicals and ideologues. As a native of Tixtla, and one-time secretary of Alvarez, Altamirano expressed the popular commitment to both the Insurgency and the Reform. But it was Ramírez who interpreted the *Grito de Dolores* as conferring on the Mexican people a radical birthright which demanded insurrection against tyranny and foreign rule. If Hidalgo had failed to frame a constitution or elaborate any political doctrine, it was because he was inspired and animated by the image of his patria liberated from colonial exploitation. His decision to call out the masses in revolt against Spain thus constituted an enduring principle of political action. The example set by Hidalgo became all the more significant when Mexico was confronted with the French invasion and Maximilian's empire, since these events obviously meant that the aims of the 1810 movement had yet to be fully attained. The intensity with which Ramírez reacted to the threat to independence can be gauged from a remark he made in 1865 when he fled northwards from the

French advance: 'Death to the gachupines! Is there any Mexican who in his life has not uttered these sacramental words?'[35]

If the liberal patria had its roots in the Insurgency, its animating spirit derived from the ideals and example of the French Revolution. Both Ramírez and Altamirano paid tribute to France as the 'wet-nurse' of all Mexican politicians in the sphere of ideas. The radicals of the Reform advanced beyond the cautious liberalism of Mora to adopt the ideology of classical republicanism which had already so influenced Simón Bolívar. In this context we should note that, whereas liberalism conceived of society as a concourse of individuals, each engaged in the pursuit of self-interest, constituting a confederation of property-holders bound by contractual obligation, by contrast classical republicanism taught that men only find fulfilment in political action undertaken as citizens of a free republic and encouraged such citizens to win glory by sacrifice of their lives in the service of their country.[36] It appears that this ideology was transmitted to the Mexican radicals by Jules Michelet, Victor Hugo and Edgar Quinet, who converted the Plutarchian republicanism of the Revolution into a form of jacobin nationalism. It was Michelet who celebrated la patrie as an immortal god, a living school, a great friendship, animated since the Revolution by 'the gospel of equality'. He asserted that 'the vast legion of proprietary peasant-soldiers' of contemporary France offered a basis for liberty denied to countries already subject to the serfdom imposed by modern industry. Michelet and Quinet frequently applied a religious vocabulary to national heroes and events, seeking to create a civic religion, endowed with its own pantheon of saints, calendar of feasts, and civic edifices adorned with statues. But nationalism in this case was decked in neo-classical rather than in the more customary gothic garb, la patrie defined not by appeal to history but with invocation of the radical ideals of the republic and revolution. The distinction was made clear by Victor Hugo when he observed that the English 'still cherish feudal illusions. They believe in heredity and hierarchy ... they still think of themselves as a nation, not as a people.' By contrast, France had inherited the torch of civilisation from ancient Greece and Italy, its republican ideals thus an expression of a permanent mission civilatrice.[37]

The degree to which the Mexican radicals adopted this rhetoric can be clearly observed in the early speeches of Altamirano in which he declared: 'the apostles of the cult of the patria, contrary to the apostles of religion, should die fighting'. In much the same vein, he presented himself as 'a humble apostle of the cult of the patria' and saluted Juárez as 'the high priest of the republic ... our immortal president ... the second father of Mexican independence'. Indeed, he defended Juárez from the criticism that he had not written any books by observing that Socrates and Christ were venerated for their living example rather than for any book. In subsequent addresses to school children, Altamirano exhorted them 'to love the patria and consecrate themselves to science', singling out the ideals of the French Revolution as a permanent goal and inspiration for Mexico. In a personal aside, he averred that he himself had always pursued glory seeking to serve his country in politics and literature. But he warned the children that without patriotism and self-sacrifice, public action lost its dignity and honour, dwindling into mere egoism and ambition. If Ramírez was less explicit, the bias of his comments points in the same direction. During the French intervention he wrote that it was more important to provide citizens with arms than with clothes, summoning up the image of a nation at war, all citizens potential soldiers. Moreover, his subsequent visit to San Francisco left him more depressed than elated at the spectacle of so much human energy expended on the pursuit of enrichment, his republican ideals offended by its *laissez-faire* individualism.[38]

The classical republicanism espoused by Ramírez and Altamirano could not be easily reconciled with the presidential autocracy progressively introduced by Juárez after 1867. Neither man accepted his retention of the presidency in 1864 and thereafter they campaigned in the press against his successive re-election in 1868 and 1872. Whether the violence of their denunciations sprang simply from their distaste for dictatorship or was influenced by their support for the candidacy of General Porfirio Díaz is difficult to say. Elected a judge of the Supreme Court, Ramírez found that the government was unable or unwilling to pay his salary since public revenue was absorbed by the army or, so he asserted, went 'to win votes in Congress, to purchase votes at the ballot-box, and to impose governors in the states'. At least half the deputies in Congress were place-men, obliged to support the government by reason of their office. The result was that 'in the Mexican republic there does not now exist a legitimate government' since Juárez used his command over Congress to obtain the suspension of the Constitution, ruling as dictator by virtue of his 'extraordinary faculties'. In a scathing attack, Ramírez castigated his erstwhile leader: 'Don Benito, you and all yours reduce politics to electoral intrigue, secret expenses, corruption of deputies and the shedding of blood. Yet the nation desires and needs something very different: roads, bridges, colonies, and municipal liberty.' As it was, more Mexicans had lost their lives in civil war under Juárez than in all the struggle against the French and Maximilian. He noted with disgust that one congressional deputy had described the president as *el hombre-constitución*, as the constitution personified. That these charges did not spring merely from an anguished republicanism was made clear when Ramírez defined the three parties into which the liberal coalition had divided. For if he damned the *juaristas* as office-holders and described the followers of Sebastian Lerdo de Tejada as men of wealth and intelligence, he identified the supporters of Porfirio Díaz as 'the party of the people'. Since the days of the alliance between Valentín Gómez Farías and General Antonio López de Santa Anna, the radicals had always exhibited a fascination with military leaders.[39]

Although Altamirano proved ever willing to recognise the greatness of Juárez in offering indomitable resistance to the French, he never condoned the president's 'ambition for power' that thrust the country into rebellion and civil war. In his brief history of Mexico, written in 1883, he pronounced a damning verdict in which after conceding that Juárez possessed a 'will of granite' which allowed him to overcome all reverses, he condemned his implacable pursuit of personal emnities. 'He pardoned the enemy of his ideas ... and promoted traitors of the country, if they had not attacked his person, and proscribed and tenaciously persecuted or had spotless liberals and distinguished patriots shot, if they had the misfortune not to be his personal supporters or had offended him in some way.' In particular, he criticised Juárez for retaining the same ministers in cabinet for many years and for his 'system of coalition' by which he used the army or state governors to impose official candidates at all levels of government.[40] The essay ended with a measured panegyric of Porfirio Díaz and his successor as president, Manuel González, who had succeeded in effecting a reconciliation between the diverse factions of 'the liberal family'. Moreover, their achievement in governing Mexico without provoking any further armed revolts was accompanied by the construction of railways and foreign investment which promised to open an era of progress and prosperity.

It fell to the Científicos, the conservative liberals who served Porfirio Díaz, to make a virtue of necessity and defend presidential autocracy as the instrument of economic progress. In particular, Justo Sierra (1848–1912), Altamirano's chief disciple, argued that the apathy and ignorance of the masses, the reactionary sympathies of the Church and the social élite, and the threat from the United States, all indicated the necessity of a strong central executive. Dismissing the 1857 Constitution as 'a generous, liberal utopia', he urged that the Liberals should convert themselves into 'a government party, profoundly conservative, but faithful to free institutions', a party which should continue 'the same policy of conservation and order, in a word, authoritarian, initiated by Juárez'. At the conclusion of his history of the Mexican people, published in 1902, Sierra defended the prolonged presidency of Porfirio Díaz, 1877–80, 1884–1911, as a form of 'social dictatorship, a spontaneous caesarism', in which 'the political evolution of Mexico has been sacrificed for other phases of its social evolution'.[41]

As the celebration of the 1906 centennial anniversary of Juárez' birth gathered pace, the Porfirian establishment was disturbed by a withering attack on the great president launched by Francisco Bulnes (1847–1924), a dissident Científico, who in two widely read books, reiterated and extended the critique initiated by Ramírez and Altamirano. The central accusation levelled against Juárez was that he was the passive, residual legatee of the toil and sacrifice of an entire generation of liberal heroes, a virtual spectator during the wars of the Reform and Intervention, who had depended on the initiative and energy of his ministers and generals. But, if Juárez had retained power for so long, it was because 'throughout his presidency, he was seen constantly to spend and nullify men of true merit who might have lent true service to their country, simply through fearing them as rivals in respect to the supreme command'. He concluded that Juárez was best defined as 'a secular Zapotec Buddha', whose apotheosis derived from the residual Catholicism of the Mexican people, 'which always look for an image, a cult, a piety for social emotion'.[42] Careful to protect his liberal credentials, he attacked the clergy as natural traitors, who would always place religion above their country's best interests. Although he admitted that the majority of the population remained Catholic, he argued that the Liberals comprised the active minority, the men of intelligence and enterprise, the political nation, and hence saluted the separation of Church and State as the Reform's lasting achievement. But Bulnes also insisted on the contribution of regional chieftains to the radical victory, asserting that 'the effective force of the Mexican Liberal party has always been the *caciques*'. In a pioneering social analysis, reminiscent of Sarmiento, he argued that, although the Insurgency had been defeated, its local leaders had survived, exercising a personal, despotic power over districts and regions, their national ambitions quelled only by the presence of the regular army, whose generals effectively governed Mexico after Independence. In effect, the conflict between Federalists and Centralists was little more than a struggle for power between two rival sets of tyrants, and if victory went to the caciques, it was because their authority rested on complex local networks of clients, relatives and associates, whereas the generals simply relied on the national treasury to fund their forces.[43] If the Liberal victory in the Reform derived from a loose alliance of regional chieftains, progressive state governors and radical intellectuals, the doubtful achievement of Juárez was to unite all these elements into a permanent coalition of office-holders, united by a common desire to retain power.

It was Justo Sierra who entered the fray with Bulnes to the greatest effect, turning aside from his official labours as Secretary of Education to compose a stirring, romantic biography of Juárez which possessed all the authority of an eye-witness account. Drawing on his youthful memories of the Reform period, he painted attractive portraits of the radical leaders, only then to conclude that all their efforts 'were resumed in the authority of Juárez'. Throughout his work, Sierra emphasised the Indian nature of the president, whose greatest quality was an indomitable, stoic character which allowed him to resist the French and to master the tortuous currents of Mexican politics.[44] Readily admitting that the president lacked eloquence, deferred to the judgement of his ministers, and was often silent, Sierra thereby implied that Juárez possessed an adamantine quality, a rootedness in the Mexican people, and dwelt in that 'empire of silence' which Carlyle had defined as the source of Cromwell's authority. As much as his English counterpart, the Zapotec president was 'an inarticulate prophet', who nevertheless discerned and expressed the inner will of his country and people far better and more deeply than any man of ideas or words. That Sierra halted his narrative at the French invasion meant that he omitted any discussion of the controversial means by which Juárez retained the presidency and re-built the Mexican state on authoritarian lines. Nor did he include any discussion of the part played by caciques in the Liberal victory. In effect, he raised a literary monument to an immaculate liberal patriot. Had not Machiavelli and Rousseau argued that the prince and legislator who sought to create a new state would have a greater chance of success if their authority and laws could be invested with a sacral aura?[45] Here, then, was the inner purpose of Sierra's work: it was to legitimise the Mexican state through the consecration of Juárez as its lawgiver and founding father. That the Mexican Moses should have been a man of law rather than a soldier, a civilian leader presiding over a coalition of popular caudillos and regional caciques, only served to strengthen the image and its political message. The contrast with Bolívar could not have been greater.

Liberal patriotism was the Mexican version of classical republicanism. Unlike their French mentors, however, the radicals and their Científico heirs failed to elaborate any form of nationalism. 'The God of nations' may well have spoken through France, as Michelet declared, but his radical word was not revealed to any Mexican prophet. Asserting the priority of political action over private profit, they incited Mexicans to serve and die for their country. Their rhetoric was destined to become the staple discourse whenever 'the liberal family' gathered in civic ceremony to celebrate its heroes and victories. It was also used to instruct generations of school-children in the glories of their country's history. It found material embodiment in the Paseo de la Reforma, a grand avenue in Mexico City, lined with the busts of liberal heroes, its passage periodically broken by monuments dedicated to Columbus, Cuauhtémoc, and the leaders of the Insurgency. It was Justo Sierra who unwittingly defined the limitations of this rhetoric when, in a ringing description of the Reform and Intervention, he concluded: 'Liberty had triumphed; the great reforming revolution had become confounded with a war of independence, and Patria, Republic and Reform were henceforth the same thing.' Elsewhere he asserted that 'the liberal party was the nation'.[46] But the unspoken corollary of these bold affirmations was, so to say, the ideological expatriation of all conservatives and committed Catholics, who obviously did not figure as members of this liberal patria. Equally absent were the Indian pueblos who, if we are to believe Ramírez, still formed separate nationalities, blissfully unaware of their Mexican identity. Moreover, when Sierra eulogised Juárez, he perpetuated the extraordinary dichotomy, not to say contradiction, between the radical, republican ideals advanced in his texts on national history and the political realities of the authoritarian state installed by Juárez and sustained by Porfirio Díaz.

III

It was in the realm of culture that the character and contradictions of liberal patriotism can be most readily observed. In the first years of the restored republic, Altamirano staked out a role for himself as promoter of national literature, organising literary gatherings attended by writers of diverse political hues. He founded a critical review, and he himself wrote essays and novels to expound his message. The reason for such promotion was obvious: 'Here in Mexico . . . we still have not all dared to utter *el grito de Dolores* in all matters.' In literature the Spanish tradition still imposed its authority, stifling any real address to national themes. The contrast with the situation elsewhere in the New World was striking, since 'the literature of the peoples of South America was conceived from patriotism'. Had not José Joaquín de Olmedo immediately penned a patriotic ode to celebrate the victory of Simón Bolívar at Junín, saluting the Liberator as 'the personification of liberty'? Thereafter, the disciples of Andrés Bello devoted their literary talents to poetic description of the magnificent landscape of America, its mountains, rivers and pampas their chosen themes. Yet in Mexico, apart from the well-meaning but indigestible chronicles of Carlos María de Bustamante, the history of the Insurgency had still to be written. Indeed, the character and deeds of its leaders had been slandered by Lucas Alamán, the arch-reactionary 'of malign memory'. Moreover, popular songs and verse still reflected 'the profoundly religious character' of the Mexican people. If in recent years Guillermo Prieto had sought to reach a popular audience with his poetry, nevertheless, he had restricted himself 'to the mestizos who speak Castilian' and avoided 'the sombre and melancholic world of the native race'.[47]

The radical adoption of the Insurgency as the foundation of their country did not prompt any sympathy for the cherished themes of creole patriotism. Although Ramírez had been educated at the College of San Gregorio, an institution established by the Jesuits for the Indian nobility and in his time administered by Juan Rodríguez Puebla, a fervent *indigenista*, he displayed little concern for the Indian past. It is true that he derided any suggestion of external influence on the autochthonous development of native civilisation, composing a mordant sketch about the alleged mission of St Thomas the Apostle to Anáhuac. Indeed, he advocated the establishment of a national institute for the study of Nahuatl and native culture and history, asserting that 'all national wisdom must be founded on a native basis'. But all this was more than offset by his radical disdain for a society that was dominated by religion

35 Santiago Rebull, *Ignacio Manuel Altamirano*

and fear, the remnants of its literature that survived notable for its incoherence and barbarism. What lessons were to be learnt from texts which allowed that 'the first Mexican emperor ate his wife during their wedding night and before the sun rose the next day changed her into a goddess'? As regards the political order, he observed: 'all these classes only consisted of a hierarchy, the people composed of subjects and slaves . . . terror pervaded the entire social body'. In short, he defined the Aztec confederation as an oriental despotism, a view purveyed as much by Alexander von Humboldt as by William Prescott. It was a view also adopted by Altamirano who referred to 'the sultans of Anáhuac and their beautiful, odalisque princesses'.[48] But, apart from a brief eulogy of the bravery of Cuauhtémoc in the defence of Mexican liberty, Altamirano abstained from any pronouncement on the character and achievements of his pagan ancestors, his silence about native history as notable as his detachment from the problems of contemporary Indians.

Needless to say, Ramírez and Altamirano united to excoriate the three hundred years of colonial rule as a Dark Age when the country resembled a vast convent, terrorised by the Inquisition and exploited for the benefit of Spain. Neither its art nor its literature were thought to have the slightest value and, indeed, were probably best destroyed lest they corrupt contemporary taste. A neo-classic in his approach to the arts, Ramírez called for the destruction of the fine baroque relief depicting St Augustine, which adorned the façade of the new National Library, denouncing its tortured outline as a barbarous example of 'monkish art'. So also, Altamirano condemned an exhibition of colonial art paintings for their 'sad and enervating character of asceticism', denying that they could be considered as Mexican. In similar vein, Ramírez dismissed Sor Juana de la Cruz as love-lorn and pious, her verse comparable to the vapourings of Manuel Carpio, a contemporary poet of religious bent, whom he described as 'tearful, sentimental and pious, like Nezahualcoyotl and Sor Juana'; in one all-encompassing sentence quashing entire cycles of creole exaltation.[49]

Although Altamirano insisted that Mexican history offered both poets and novelists 'a spring of magnificent and poetic legends', he warned a young poetess against chivalrous romance as a possible theme in Mexico, 'where there are no more ruins than those of the Aztec pyramids ... where there have been no other crusades than those against the Indians, nor more chivalrous memories than the greed of the old encomenderos ...' His aversion to New Spain was manifest in his scorn for Sor Juana, 'whom it is necessary to leave quiet and snug at the bottom of her grave and between the parchment of her books', since she had lived in the malign period of 'literary conceits, of the Inquisition and scholastic theology'. So dark was the shadow cast by Spanish rule that it required no less a figure than Alexander von Humboldt to illumine the country with the science and philosophy of the Enlightenment, his effect signalised by Ramírez in these striking terms: 'Progress required its Columbus and it was Humboldt, the conqueror, the missionary of philosophy.'[50]

The critical principles which guided Altamirano in his judgement of the arts can be best observed in his comments on paintings. Not merely did he damn the output of the Colony as un-Mexican, he also criticised the revival of the Academy of San Carlos, inaugurated by the Catalan painter, Pelegrín Clavé, for its insistence on European models and criteria. However, he was happy to report that after 1867 a new generation of Mexican painters had appeared, men anxious to depict scenes of national interest. Such indeed was the ambition of José María Velasco, whose landscapes figure among the most esteemed paintings to have come out of Mexico. But his portrayal of the central plateau met with but tepid appreciation from Altamirano, who perfunctorily commended his work as 'most worthy of praise'. For what the radical patriot wanted to see were canvases that dealt with historic scenes and figures, a preference rendered explicit in his lament at one exhibition where he found not 'a single hero of Independence nor any martyr of the Reform' portrayed. By way of consolation, he fixed on the two compositions of Félix Parra that deal respectively with the massacre wrought by Cortés at Cholula and with Bartolomé de las Casas, the great defender of the Indians. 'This is indeed national painting' he declared, 'without doubt, Félix Parra is today the first painter in Mexico'. As much as any Victorian, Altamirano wanted a picture to have a message, albeit more patriotic than moral.[51]

What Altamirano most awaited, but awaited in vain, was the appearance of an epic novel dealing with the national experience during the Insurgency and Reform. The novel was the chief art-form of the nineteenth century, in its sphere as modern and original as the railway or the telegraph. Where else could one find persuasive and realistic portrayal of history and politics, of the individual and love, of landscape and cities, of manners and society, of heroes and wars, all encompassed within the pages of a single work, as much accessible to the literate populace as to the intellectual elite? As always, Altamirano's purpose was didactic and patriotic. Commenting on the skill with which the Church inculcated dogma through dramatic sermons and hymns, he identified the novel as the ideal medium for the propagation of liberal and patriotic sentiment. So also, its presentation of manners could assist in popular education. The models for this 'national epic' were the works of Sir Walter Scott, Fenimore Cooper, Alexandre Dumas, Victor Hugo and the Spanish author, Manuel Fernández y González. In short, if the drift of his literary prescription suggested a Mexican equivalent of *War and Peace*, what he actually had in mind was *Waverley* and *Les Misérables*. Even at this diminished level, however, his expectations were not crowned with achievement, since although any number of novels, both historical and contemporary, were written in Mexico at this time, few possessed any enduring artistic value.[52] Altamirano himself composed several novels of which *El Zarco* was the most ambitious, but in its deployment of brown-skinned heroes and blue-eyed villains the work was overtly didactic and its eulogy of vigilante justice overdone. Written to order, so to say, *El Zarco* entirely lacked the irony, vitality and breadth of Manuel Payno's *Los bandidos de Río Frío*, the only Mexican novel of the nineteenth century to approach an adequate and persuasive portrayal of the tragi-comedy of national politics and life in the decades before the Reform. For his part, Altamirano was too taken with the notion that the purpose of literature was 'to create national character', to be able to infuse his narrative with the satirical verve which animated Payno's great work.[53]

It is as an essayist rather than as a novelist that Altamirano deserves to be remembered. In the 1880s he took advantage of the newly constructed railways to travel and record his impressions of the country. If he now displayed an interest in sixteenth-century Mexico, it was in part because Joaquín García Icazbalceta, a conservative Catholic historian, had located and printed both the chronicles of Motolinia and Mendieta, together with a copious selection of letters and memorials which amply demonstrated that the first mendicants had striven to defend the Indians from Spanish exploitation. In a description of Texcoco, Altamirano confessed his disappointment at finding a town that was 'hybrid in its buildings, hybrid in its inhabitants and in their customs and physiognomy', and which possessed 'the same ordinary aspect, monotonous and sad, that characterises the mestizo villages of the State of Mexico'. This joyless and impoverished condition was soon to be transformed, so he hoped, by the arrival of the railway, through which prosperity and knowledge would be diffused, rescuing the population from their previous isolation. What is striking about the essay is Altamirano's patent lack of interest in the former glories of Texcoco, when Nezahualcoyotl had held court in the city. There was no more connexion between the Aztec past and the contemporary population than between ancient Babylon and modern Iraqi peasants. Instead, the monument from the past which caught Altamirano's attention was the Franciscan church which promptly evoked a series of reflections about the missionary labours of the mendicants in Mexico. He admitted that he had been reading the chronicles of the friars, published by García Icazbalceta, which revealed how selflessly they had ministered to the Indians. In particular, he had been impressed by the account of Pedro de Gante, who had taught the natives Spanish arts and crafts. Surely, he exclaimed, all Mexicans should be willing 'to pay homage to the holy memory of the first Franciscans'.[54] Nor was this sudden enthusiasm a transient reflection, since in a separate essay on the shrine at Sacramonte in Amecameca, where an image of Christ was venerated in a cave formerly used as a hermitage by Martín de Valencia, the leader of the first Franciscan mission to Mexico, Altamirano praised the chronicle of Jerónimo de Mendieta for its 'easy, sweet and picturesque style' and its 'innocent and infantile grace', and then saluted the mendicants as 'the first friends of the Indians, the messengers of enlightenment, the true heroes of Latin American civilization'. At much the same time, he took the opportunity of a school speech to describe the Franciscan college of Santa Cruz Tlatelolco as 'the first sanctuary of civilisation' in Mexico. All this was a far cry from the anticlericalism of his youth.[55]

The growing fissure between Altamirano's public radicalism and his private nostalgia for the religion of his childhood is nowhere more clearly revealed than in 'Holy Week in my Village', an essay in which he recalled his early memories of Tixtla, when he still spoke Nahuatl. The result is a rare piece of writing, full of charm, imbued with almost painful nostalgia, a portrait of lost innocence. Whereas Indians usually figured in Mexican literature of the period as country clowns, by turns drunken, sullen, idolatrous and impassive, by contrast in Altamirano's account they are depicted as fervent Catholics, their life centring on the liturgy and feasts of the Church. He described the expedition of the children to cut palms for Holy Week and the procession on Holy Thursday when every household sallied forth onto the streets carrying their own crucifix or image of Christ, over a thousand images illumined by the flickering torches at night. He reflected that 'religion is the good fairy of childhood' and confessed that in writing the piece he had relived some of the joys of his early years. Since Altamirano elsewhere publicly applauded the decision of the governor of Mexico to ban Corpus Christi processions in the environs of the capital, it is clear that he could only approach or sympathise with the Church by relegating its virtues to childhood or the past. Oddly enough, it was in his novella, *La navidad en las montañas*, that he came closest to resolving the contradiction. For there he presented an attractive description of a Spanish priest, once a Carmelite, who preached a simple gospel of good works and brotherhood, setting up a school for his parish and encouraging agriculture. He had abolished the collection of all fees for masses and the sacraments and had swept his church clean of images and side-altars. All this led to the conclusion that true Christianity, as distinct from the practices and dogmas of the contemporary Church, was very close to the ideals of liberalism.[56]

The degree to which his recognition of the force of religious sentiment in Mexico inhibited Altamirano and other radicals from any attempt to strengthen liberal patriotism by an appeal to nationalism can be best observed in his essay on the cult of Our Lady of Guadalupe, the only systematic study to issue from his pen. Here he offered a survey of the complex bibliography that surrounded the story of the apparition of the Virgin Mary to the Indian, Juan Diego, at Tepeyac. But, whereas García Icazbalceta was later to deny that the apparition had any documentary evidence, Altamirano discussed the question without polemic, content to let his readers draw their own conclusions. His purpose was not to discuss the miracle, if such it was, but rather to examine its political significance. Already by the eighteenth century 'a spirit of nationalism' surrounded the cult of the Guadalupe, which by then had assumed 'a patriotic character'. Indeed, during the Insurgency the Virgin became 'a symbol of nationality'; and, so devoted was Guerrero to Mexico's patron saint, that in 1828 he deposited the flags captured from the Spaniards in the basilica at Tepeyac. Thereafter, until the accession of Juárez, all rulers of Mexico, including Juan Alvarez and Maximilian, paid their respects to the 'national deity'. So honoured was the Virgin that the liberals exempted the sanctuary from the application of the laws of the Reform. Not content, however, with assessing the historical significance of the cult, Altamirano openly confessed that it was only when joined in worship of Our Lady of Guadalupe that all Mexicans, no matter what their race or class, were equal and united: this was the living reality, all else was a question of theory and law. 'It is equality before the Virgin; it is the national idolatry ... in the last extreme, in the most desperate cases, the cult of the Mexican Virgin is the only bond which unites them.' Altamirano concluded that the day Our Lady of Guadalupe was not venerated, 'the Mexican nationality' would have disappeared.[57] If such indeed was the case, then on what basis could a secular theory of nationalism be founded?

In these surprising affirmations, Altamirano signalised the gulf that separated the popular Catholicism of the insurgents from the bitter anti-clericalism of the radicals. But he also implicitly admitted that the ideals of the Liberal republic were alien to the majority of the Mexican people. The radicals had created a state: they had yet to form a nation. Indeed, their exclusion of committed Catholics from public life and their assault on the communal land-holdings of the Indian villages had left them with but a narrow base of political support. When Altamirano and Sierra confidently declared that 'the Liberal party is the nation', they referred to the constituted authorities of the republic, which is to say, to the political nation which inhabited the city chambers, the state assemblies, and the offices of central government. Anxious to diffuse their creed throughout society, the Liberals promoted public education, providing schools with texts on *historia patria*, which set out the radical interpretation of Mexican history and politics. But whereas creole patriots had celebrated Mexico's special destiny, by contrast the Liberals simply urged their country's incorporation into the civilisation of the nineteenth century. Moreover, if the reiterated force of their civic rhetoric succeeded in enshrining Juárez as the national hero, it also implicitly indicated the glaring contradiction between the democratic aspirations of the Reform and the authoritarian character of contemporary government. The initial goal of the men who instigated the 1910 revolution was to bridge the abyss that separated the Mexican people from the Mexican state by bringing in some form of representative government. By then, diverse theories of nationalism, based on history, race and culture, commanded considerable support and were destined to influence the policies of the revolutionary state. But that is another story and another book.

NOTES

ABBREVIATIONS

AGI   Archivo General de Indias
BAE   Biblioteca de Autores Españoles
BA   Biblioteca Ayacucho
BP   Biblioteca Porrúa
HAHR   *Hispanic American Historical Review*
JLS   *Journal of Latin American Studies*

PROLOGUE

1 Thomas Babbington Macaulay, *Critical and Historical Essays contributed to the Edinburgh Review*, 3 vols. (London, 1843), III, 109.
2 G. M. Young, *Victorian England. Portrait of an Age* (Oxford, 1964), p. vi.
3 George Kubler, *The Shape of Time. Remarks on the History of Things* (New Haven, 1970), p. 112.

1 A NEW WORLD

1 Samuel Eliot Morison, *The European Discovery of America. The Southern Voyages A.D. 1492–1616* (Oxford, New York, 1974), pp. 26–40. There is an excellent bibliography about Columbus on pp. 19–25. The citation from *The Divine Comedy* comes from *The Inferno*, canto 26, lines 76–142; see also Isaiah lx, 19.
2 Hernando Colón, *Vida del Almirante Don Cristóbal Colón*, ed. Ramón Iglesia (Mexico, 1947), pp. 34–56.
3 Cristóbal Colón, *Textos y documentos completos*, ed. Consuelo Varela (Madrid, 1982), p. 84.
4 *Ibid.*, p. 249.
5 Morison, *European Discovery*, pp. 30–42.
6 Francisco López de Gómara, *Historia general de las Indias*, ed. Jorge Gurría Lacroix, BA 64 (Caracas, 1979), pp. 28–9.
7 Colón, *Textos*, p. 255.
8 *Ibid.*, p. 302; Morison, *European Discovery*, p. 34; see also Alain Milhou, *Colón y su mentalidad mesiánica en el ambiente franciscanista español* (Valladolid, 1983), *passim*.

9 Colón, *Textos*, pp. 217–21, 286–7, 302.

10 *Ibid.*, pp. 297–8.

11 Morison, *European Discovery*, pp. 272–312.

12 Americo Vespucci, *El Nuevo Mundo*, ed. Roberto Levillier (Buenos Aires, 1951), pp. 187, 173, 181–3.

13 *Ibid.*, p. 211.

14 Peter Martyr D'Anghera, *De Orbe Novo: The Eight Decades*, trans. F. A. MacNutt, 2 vols. (New York, 1912), I, 80, 104.

15 *Ibid.*, II, 39, 46.

16 *Ibid.*, I, 106, 217; II, 49.

17 *Ibid.*, I, 376; II, 52, 248–50, 271–2.

18 *The Essays of Montaigne*, ed. and trans., E. J. Trechmann, 2 vols. (Oxford, 1927), I, 476–7; II, 202–15, 372–7.

19 Robert B. Tate, *Ensayos sobre la historiografía peninsular del siglo XV* (Madrid, 1970), pp. 75–99, 289–94.

20 Antonio de Nebrija, *Gramática de la lengua castellana*, ed. Ignacio González-Llumbrera (Oxford, 1926), pp. 3, 6–7; Ramón Menéndez Pidal, *España y su historia*, 2 vols. (Madrid, 1957), II, 27.

21 John Lynch, *Spain under the Habsburgs*, 2 vols. (London, 1964), I, 58.

22 Pierre Chaunu, *La España de Carlos V*, 2 vols. (Barcelona, 1976), II, 148–55.

23 *Ibid.*, II, 200–10; Peter Russell, 'Arms versus letters: towards a definition of Spanish fifteenth-century humanism' in Archibald R. Lewis, ed., *Aspects of the Renaissance* (Austin, 1967), pp. 47–58; Tate, *Ensayos*, pp. 281–6.

24 Angus MacKay, *Spain in the Middle Ages. From Frontier to Empire 1000–1500* (London, 1977), pp. 133–8.

25 Hernando de Acuña, *Varias poesías*, ed. E. Catena de Vindel (Madrid, 1954), p. 342.

26 Jacob Burckhardt, *The Civilization of the Renaissance in Italy* (Phaidon Press, London, 1955), pp. 171–3.

27 Alexander von Humboldt, *Examen critique de l'historie de la géographie du Nouveau Continent et des progrès de l'astronomie nautique aux quinzième et seizième siècles*, 5 vols. (Paris, 1836–9), III, 9–12, 234–49.

2 CONQUERORS AND CHRONICLERS

1 Martyr, *De Orbe Novo*, II, 144.

2 Hernán Cortés, *Cartas y documentos*, ed. Mario Hernández Sánchez-Barba, BP 2 (Mexico, 1963), pp. 33, 72–80, 114.

3 J. H. Elliott, 'Cortés, Velásquez and Charles V', introduction to Hernán Cortés, *Letters from Mexico*, trans. Anthony Pagden (New Haven and London, 1971).

4 Cortés, *Cartas*, pp. 43–4.

5 *Ibid.*, pp. 59, 68–9.

6 *Ibid.*, p. 318.

7 Mario Góngora, *Studies in the Colonial History of Spanish America*, trans. Richard Southern (Cambridge, 1975), pp. 1–32.

8 *Ibid.*, pp. 98–114; J. H. Elliott, 'The Spanish Conquest and settlement of America' in Leslie Bethell, ed., *The Cambridge History of Latin America*, 5 vols. (Cambridge, 1984–6), I, 176–80, 188–96.

9 Bernal Díaz del Castillo, *Historia verdadera de la conquista de la Nueva España*, ed. Joaquín Rámirez Cabañas, 2 vols. (Mexico, 1968), II, 71–4.

10 Woodrow Borah, *Early Colonial Trade and Navigation between Mexico and Peru* (Berkeley and Los Angeles, 1954), pp. 8–16.

11 Guillermo Lohman Villena, *Las ideas jurídico-políticas en la rebelión de Gonzalo Pizarro* (Valladolid, 1977), pp. 101–2.

12 Francisco de Jerez, 'Verdadera relación de la conquista del Perú y provincia del Cuzco' in *Crónicas de la conquista del Perú*, ed. Julio Le Reverend (Mexico, n.d.), pp. 30, 83, 114.

13 *Ibid.*, pp. 110–11; James Lockhart, *The Men of Cajamarca* (Austin, 1972), pp. 79–81.

14 The best study of Oviedo is by Juan Pérez de Tudela in his introduction to Gonzalo Fernández de Oviedo, *Historia general y natural de las Indias*, BAE 117–21, 5 vols. (Madrid, 1959); see also Demetrio Ramos, *Ximénez de Quesada y el epítome de la conquista del nuevo reino de Granada* (Seville, 1977), p. 176; Antonello Gerbi, *La naturaleza de las Indias Nuevas* (Mexico, 1978), *passim*.

15 Oviedo, *Historia*, IV, 336; II, 341.

16 Gonzalo Fernández de Oviedo, *Quinquagenas de la nobleza de España*, ed. Juan Bautista Avalle-Arce, 2 vols. (Chapel Hill, N.C., 1974), I, 89; II, 415, 596–7; Oviedo, *Historia*, I, 157.

17 Oviedo, *Historia*, I, 25; II, 29, 86, 238.

18 *Ibid.*, II, 96; V, 14.

19 *Ibid.*, IV, 36, 42, 97.

20 *Ibid.*, I, 39; II, 325.

21 For this interpretation see Gerbi, *La naturaleza*, pp. 163, 299.

22 Juan Bautista Avalle-Arce, 'El novelista Gonzalo Fernández de Oviedo y Valdés', in Andrew Debicki and Enrique Pupo-Walker, eds., *Estudios de literatura hispano-americana en honor a José J. Arrom* (Chapel Hill, N.C., 1974), pp. 23–46.

23 Oviedo, *Quinquagenas*, I, 142–4, 245.

24 Oviedo, *Historia*, I, 16, 33.

25 *Ibid.*, I, 17–18.

26 *Ibid.*, III, 26, 235.

27 *Ibid.*, II, 156, 172–3.

28 *Ibid.*, IV, 259–66.

29 *Ibid.*, V, 30–3, 194, 243–4; Oviedo, *Quinquagenas*, I, 255, 269.

30 Oviedo, *Quinquagenas*, I, 44–5, 163, II, 247–8; Oviedo, *Historia*, V, 230–1.

31 Oviedo, *Historia*, II, 165, 400.

32 *Ibid.*, I, 10, 80.

33 *Ibid.*, III, 199; IV, 391; Oviedo, *Quinquagenas*, I, 149.

34 Oviedo, *Quinquagenas*, II, 409, 625–36; Oviedo, *Historia*, II, 411–12, 432–3; III, 248; IV, 367, 383–4.

35 Oviedo, *Quinquagenas*, I, 85, 125–7; II, 469, 499–504, 679–81; Oviedo, *Historia*, V, 243.

36 Oviedo, *Historia*, I, 67–8, 111, 115; III, 340.

37 *Ibid.*, III, 82, 122; IV, 49, 419; V, 42, 51.

38 *Ibid.*, I, 111–24, 67–9, 96; II, 115–16.

39 Oviedo, *Quinquagenas*, I, 373.

40 Oviedo, *Historia*, II, 194–201.

41 *Ibid.*, IV, 263–4; Oviedo, *Quinquagenas*, II, 595; Francisco López de Gómara, *Annals of the Emperor Charles V*, ed. Roger Bigelow Merriman (Oxford, 1912), p. 258.

42 J. Huizinga, *The Waning of the Middle Ages* (London, 1955), pp. 281–320; Oviedo, *Historia*, II, 16, 96.

43 Oviedo, *Historia*, I, 189; II, 7–9.

44 *Ibid.*, I, 14; II, 56; IV, 108; see also Arnaldo Momigliano, *Studies in Historiography* (London, 1966), p. 137.

45 Ramos, *Ximénez de Quesada*, pp. 113–14, 183–4, 198.

46 Gómara, *Annals of Charles V*, pp. 173–7, 232–3.

47 On Giovio see Eric Cochrane, *Historians and Historiography in the Italian Renaissance* (Chicago, 1981), pp. 3–9, 366–77; on Gómara see Ramón Iglesia, *Cronistas e historiadores de la conquista de México* (2nd edn, Mexico, 1972), pp. 150–328.

48 On Mexía see Ramos, *Ximénez de Quesada*, pp. 91–109.

49 Gómara, *Historia general*, pp. 7–8, 118–19, 319.

50 *Ibid.*, pp. 28, 35–8, 219–21.

51 *Ibid.*, pp. 319–20; Gómara, *Annals of Charles V*, p. 248.

52 Gómara, *Historia general*, pp. 7, 47, 180–1, 280–3.

53 Francisco López de Gómara, *Historia de la conquista de México*, ed. Jorge Gurría Lacroix, BA 65 (Caracas, 1979), pp. 366–7.

54 *Ibid.*, p. 367.

55 *Ibid.*, pp. 38, 361–4.

56 On Díaz see Carmelo Saénz de Santa María, 'Introducción crítica de la "Historia Verdadera" de Bernal Díaz del Castillo', *Revista de Indias*, XXVI (1966), pp. 328–416; also Iglesia, *Cronistas e historiadores*, pp. 210–30.

57 Díaz del Castillo, *Historia verdadera*, I, 199.

58 *Ibid.*, I, 115.

59 *Ibid.*, I, 260.

60 *Ibid.*, II, 39–40.

61 *Ibid.*, II, 357, 366–7, 378.

62 See Victor Frankl, *El 'Anti-jovio' de Gonzalo Jiménez de Quesada* (Madrid, 1963), pp. 93–8, 391–421; Oviedo, *Historia*, III, 101; Cochrane, *Historians and Historiography*, pp. 366–77.

63 Gonzalo Jiménez de Quesada, *El Antijovio* (Bogotá, 1952), pp. 29, 137–44, 177–8, 617–20.

64 *Ibid.*, pp. 123, 296, 349–50, 364–5, 397–8.

65 José Toribio Medina, *Vida de Ercilla* (Mexico, 1948), *passim*.

66 Two useful studies are Juan María Corominas, *Castiglione y la Araucana* (Madrid, 1980), and F. Pierce, *Alonso de Ercilla y Zúñiga* (Amsterdam, 1984).

67 Alonso de Ercilla, *La Araucana*, ed. Ofelia Garza de del Castillo (Mexico, 1975), pp. 180, 187.

68 *Ibid.*, pp. 501–2, 512.

3 THE UNARMED PROPHET

1 Bartolomé de las Casas, *Obras escogidas*, ed. with a critical study by Juan Pérez de Tudela Bueso, BAE 95–6, 105–6, 110, 5 vols. (Madrid, 1957), V, 43–55.

2 *Ibid.*, V, 50.

3 For his conversion see Bartolomé de las Casas, *Historia de las Indias*, ed. Agustín Millares Carlo and Lewis Hanke, 3 vols. (Mexico, 1951), III, 92–100.

4 A general guide to Las Casas is Juan Friede and Benjamin Keen, eds., *Bartolomé de las Casas in History* (De Kalb, Illinois, 1971). The best guide to his works is Henry Raup Wagner and Helen Rand Parish, *The Life and Writings of Bartolomé de las Casas* (Albuquerque, New Mexico, 1967), pp. 251–93; for the revised date of birth see Helen Rand Parish and Harold E. Weidmann, 'The correct birth-date of Bartolomé de las Casas', *HAHR*, 56 (1976), pp. 385-405.

5 Las Casas, *Historia de las Indias*, II, 383–5, 440–1.

6 *Ibid*, II, 264.

7 Las Casas, *Obras*, V, 3–24.

8 *Ibid.*, V, 31–9.

9 Las Casas, *Historia de las Indias*, III, 352–401.

10 Las Casas, *Obras*, V, 56–68.

11 On this mission see André Saint-Lu, *La Vera Paz: esprit évangelique et colonisation* (Paris, 1968), *passim*.

12 Wagner and Parish, *Las Casas*, pp. 83–107.

13 Bartolomé de las Casas, *Del único modo de atraer a todos los pueblos a la verdadera religión*, ed. Lewis Hanke and Agustín Millares Carlo (Mexico, 1942, reprinted 1975), pp. 65–73, 157, 250–79, 311–14.

14 *Ibid.*, pp. 345, 390–402, 415–17.

15 Las Casas, *Obras*, V, 69–133.

16 For a facsimile reprint and transcription of the *Brevísima relación* see Bartolomé de las Casas, *Tratados*, ed. Lewis Hanke *et al.*, 2 vols. (Mexico, 1965), I, 3–173.

17 Bartolomé de las Casas, *Los tesoros del Perú*, ed. and trans. Angel Losada García (Madrid, 1958), pp. 309–10; Las Casas, *Historia de las Indias*, III, 227.

18 Las Casas, *Obras*, V, 120–33.

19 Wagner and Parish, *Las Casas*, pp. 108–19.

20 Las Casas, *Obras*, V, 199–233; see also Helen Rand Parish, *Las Casas as a Bishop* (Washington, 1980), *passim*.

21 The *Confesionario* is printed in Las Casas, *Tratados*, II, 853–914.

22 See introduction to Bartolomé de las Casas, *De regia potestate*, ed. Luciano Pereña *et al.* (Madrid, 1969), pp. 174–226; Las Casas, *Obras*, V, 467–76.

23 Las Casas, *Obras*, V, 453–9.

24 *Ibid.*, V, 469–76.

25 See José Ignacio Tellechea Idígoras, *El arzobispo Carranza y su tiempo*, 2 vols. (Madrid, 1968), II, 32–43; Wagner and Parish, *Las Casas*, pp. 223–4.

26 Las Casas, *Obras*, V, 534–9. This summarised his *Tratado de doce dudas*, printed on pp. 478–532.

27 Las Casas, *Historia de las Indias*, I, 19–24.

28 *Ibid.*, I, 25–7. The Latin *Apologia* is available in English translation as Bartolomé de las Casas, *In Defence of the Indians*, ed. and trans., Stafford Poole (De Kalb, Illinois, 1974), p. 138.

29 Las Casas, *Historia de las Indias*, I, 152–60, 186–9, 208–9, 364; II, 107–11, 330–2.

30 *Ibid.*, II, 487; III, 14, 35–7, 170, 185–8. See also Manuel Giménez Fernández, *Bartolomé de las Casas: capellán de Su Majestad Carlos I* (Seville, 1960), *passim*.

31 Las Casas, *Historia de las Indias*, II, 41–61; II, 347–54, 468–70.
32 *Ibid.*, II, 446–9.
33 *Ibid.*, II, 539; III, 92–107, 170–89, 376, 382.
34 *Ibid.*, I, 129–34, 144; III, 177–9.
35 *Ibid.*, on Oviedo see II, 203, 390–1, 518; III, 313, 333, 383; on Gómara see II, 529; III, 251, 321, 385.
36 *Ibid.*, II, 528–9; III, 222–7; Las Casas, *Los tesoros*, p. 373.
37 Las Casas, *In Defence of the Indians*; Las Casas, *Obras*, V, 539–40.
38 J. H. Hexter, *The Vision of Politics on the Eve of the Reformation* (London, 1973), pp. 179–203; Vicente Beltrán de Heredia, 'Las corrientes de espiritualidad entre los Dominicos de Castilla durante la primera mitad del siglo XVI' in *Miscelánea*, 4 vols. (Salamanca, 1972), III, 520–659.

4 THE GREAT DEBATE

1 Juan López de Palacios Rubios, *De las islas del mar Oceáno*, ed. Silvio Zavala and Agustín Millares Carlo (Mexico, 1954), pp. 8–39.
2 *Ibid.*, pp. 89–108, 128–33, 182–3.
3 Las Casas, *Historia de las Indias*, II, 450–7; III, 26–30.
4 Robert P. Adams, *The Better Part of Valor – More, Erasmus, Colet and Vives on Humanism, War and Peace 1496–1525* (Seattle, 1962), pp. 190–3, 224–5.
5 Saint Augustine, *Of the City of God: with the learned comments of Io. Lodivicus Vives* (2nd edn, London, 1620), bk. IV, cap. 4, p. 150.
6 Juan Luis Vives, *Concordia y discordia*, ed. Laureano Sánchez Gallego (Mexico, 1940), pp. 65–6, 113–16, 136–43.
7 *Ibid.*, pp. 227, 441–9.
8 Francisco de Vitoria, *Relectio de Indis*, ed. L. Pereña and J. M. Pérez Prendes (Madrid, 1967), p. 137; St Thomas Aquinas, *Philosophical Texts*, ed. Thomas Gilby (Oxford, 1951), pp. 323, 368–76, 380–8; see also St Thomas Aquinas, *Selected Political Writings*, ed. A. P. D'Entrèves (Oxford, 1954), pp. 3–23.
9 Vitoria, *De Indis*, pp. 100–123; see also Anthony Pagden, *The Fall of Natural Man: the American Indian and the origins of comparative ethnology* (Cambridge, 1982), pp. 57–108.
10 J. A. Fernández-Santamaría, *The State, War and Peace. Spanish Political Thought in the Renaissance 1516–1559* (Cambridge, 1977), pp. 168–91; Pagden, *Fall of Natural Man*, pp. 109–18.
11 Juan Ginés de Sepúlveda, *Tratado sobre las justas causas de la guerra contra los indios*, ed. Manuel García-Pelayo (Mexico, 1941, reprinted 1971,), pp. 101, 105.
12 *Ibid.*, pp. 105, 109–10, 133; on Cortés, pp. 103–9.
13 Antonio María Fabie, *Vida y escritos de las Casas*, 2 vols. (Madrid, 1879), II, 335–53.
14 Bartolomé de las Casas, *Apologética historia sumaria*, ed. Edmundo O'Gorman, 2 vols. (Mexico, 1967); Pagden, *Fall of Natural Man*, pp. 119–45.
15 Las Casas, *Apologética* I, 102, 108–9, 152, 172–6.
16 M. T. Cicero, *De inventione*, Loeb Classical Library (London, 1949), pp. 3–7.
17 M. T. Cicero, *Treatises*, ed. C. D. Yonge (London, 1853) pp. 408–11; Las Casas, *Apologética*, I, 249–50.

18 Las Casas, *Apologética*, I, 370–91, 451–62.
19 *Ibid.*, II, 251.
20 *Ibid.*, II, 203–42, 260–70.
21 *Ibid.*, II, 242–5; Las Casas, *De regia*, p. 238; Las Casas, *In defence of the Indians*, pp. 226–42.
22 Las Casas, *Historia de las Indias*, II, 387, 436–47, 579–609, 330.
23 *Ibid.*, II 637–54.
24 Antonio de Remesal, *Historia general de las Indias Occidentales*, ed. Carmelo Sáenz de Santa María, BAE 175, 189, 2 vols. (Madrid, 1964–6) II, 369.
25 Las Casas, *Apologética*, II, 242.
26 Las Casas, *In defence of the Indians*, pp. 55–7, 65–6, 106–17, 304–11.
27 *Ibid.*, pp. 35–9, 118–19, 171–82, 270–97, 319.
28 *Ibid.*, pp. 145, 168–70, 259–60, 351–7.
29 Las Casas, 'Tratado comprobatorio del imperio soberano y principado universal que los reyes de Castilla y León tienen sobre las Indias', in *Tratados*, II, 1033, 1117, 1153, 1129.
30 Las Casas, *De regia*, pp. 34–5, 41–4, 76–7, 87–9, 103–4.
31 Las Casas, *Los tesoros del Perú*, pp. 129, 185, 199, 229, 265.
32 *Ibid.*, pp. 265–9, 295, 307, 313–15.
33 *Ibid.*, pp. 81, 131, 191, 311; see also Quentin Skinner, *The Foundations of Modern Political Thought*, 2 vols. (Cambridge, 1978), I, 9–11, 51–65.
34 Las Casas, *In defence of the Indians*, pp. 321–5; Las Casas, *Historia de las Indias*, II, 414–15.
35 Las Casas, *Obras*, V, 50; St Augustine, *City of God* (London, 1967), p. 139.
36 Saint Augustine, *Of the City of God* (London, 1620), p. 150.
37 Las Casas, *Historia de las Indias* II, 466–7, 517; St Augustine, *City of God* (1967) p. 890.
38 Servando Teresa de Mier, *Historia de la revolución de la Nueva España antiguamente Anáhuac*, 2 vols. (Mexico, 1922), II, 285, 320–1.

5 FRANCISCAN MILLENNIUM

1 For this scene see Bernal Díaz, *Historia verdadera*, II, 177.
2 Robert Ricard, *The Spiritual Conquest of Mexico* (Berkeley and Los Angeles, 1966), pp. 272–3.
3 France V. Scholes and Eleanor B. Adams, eds., *Don Diego Quijada Alcalde Mayor de Yucatán 1561–1565: Documentos*, 2 vols. (Mexico, 1938), I, 169–84, 289–331; II, 213–14. See also Inga Clendinnen, *Ambivalent Conquests. Maya and Spaniard in Yucatán, 1517–1570* (Cambridge, 1987), pp. 72–93.
4 Joaquín García Icazbalceta, *Bibliografía mexicana del siglo XVI*, ed. Agustín Millares Carlo (Mexico, 1954), pp. 90–104.
5 Gómara, *Conquista de México*, pp. 361–6, 371–2; Gómara, *Historia general*, p. 283.
6 Georges Baudot, *Utopie et Histoire au Mexique* (Toulouse, 1977), pp. 74–86; Silvio Zavala, *Sir Thomas More in New Spain* (London, 1935); Fintan B. Warren, *Vasco de Quiroga and his Pueblo-Hospitals of Santa Fe* (Washington D.C., 1963), *passim*.
7 George Kubler, *Mexican Architecture in the Sixteenth Century*, 2 vols. (New Haven, Conn., 1948), II, 231–84.

8 Motolinia (Toribio de Benavente), *Historia de los indios de la Nueva España*, ed. Joaquín García Icazbalceta, BP 47 (Mexico, 1858, facsimile 1971) pp. 67–98, 106, 115; Baudot, *Utopie et Histoire*, pp. 241–386.

9 Motolinia, *Historia*, pp. 62, 112; Motolinia (Toribio de Benavente), *Memoriales ó libro de las cosas de la Nueva España y de las naturales de ella*, ed. Edmundo O'Gorman (Mexico, 1971), pp. 85–6, 237–42; Baudot, *Utopie et Histoire*, pp. 122–36, 182–4, 237–8.

10 Motolinia, *Memoriales*, pp. 310–12, 322.

11 Motolinia, *Historia*, p. 7.

12 *Ibid.*, pp. 5, 186; Motolina, *Memoriales*, pp. 212, 353.

13 Motolinia, *Historia*, pp. 15–21, 28, 206–7; Motolinia, *Memoriales*, pp. 138, 294.

14 Marjorie Reeves, *The Influence of Prophecy in the Later Middle Ages. A Study of Joachism* (Oxford, 1969), pp. 180–200, 224–30, 236–7, 271, 365.

15 Motolinia, *Historia*, p. 144; Motolinia, *Memoriales*, pp. 219–20, 387–8; Toribio de Motolinia, 'Carta al emperador Carlos V', in *Colección de documentos para la historia de México*, ed. Joaquín García Icazbalceta, BP 47–8, 2 vols. (Mexico, 1858, facsimile 1971), I, 263.

16 Motolinia, *Historia*, pp. 154–60, 177, 196; Motolinia, *Memoriales*, p. 222.

17 Motolinia, 'Carta al emperador', pp. 264–5, 270–3.

18 *Ibid.*, pp. 257–63, 274.

19 Jerónimo de Mendieta, *Historia eclesiástica indiana*, ed. Joaquín García Icazbalceta BP 46 (Mexico, 1870, facsimile 1971), pp. 556–62, 514–15; on Mendieta see John Leddy Phelan, *The Millennial Kingdom of the Franciscans in the New World* (2nd edn, Berkeley and Los Angeles, 1970), pp. 41–110.

20 Mendieta, *Historia*, pp. 651–3; 222, 250.

21 *Ibid.*, pp. 540, 220–2.

22 *Ibid.*, pp. 500–13, 529.

23 *Códice Mendieta: documentos franciscanos siglo XVI y XVII*, 2 vols. (Mexico, 1892, facsimile 1971), II, 9–11.

24 Mendieta, *Historia*, p. 448.

25 Charles Gibson, *The Aztecs under Spanish Rule 1519–1810* (Stanford, 1964), pp. 200–3, 227–35.

26 Mendieta, *Historia*, pp. 519–29; *Documentos inéditos del siglo XVI para la historia de México*, ed. Mariano Cuevas, BP 62 (Mexico, 1914, facsimile 1975), pp. 354–68, 416–17; *Códice Mendieta*, I, 223–9, 246–7; *Cartas de religiosos de Nueva España*, ed. Joaquín García Icazbalceta (Mexico, 1886, 2nd edn, 1941), pp. 163–6.

27 Jerónimo Valderrama, *Cartas y otras documentos sobre su visita al gobierno de Nueva España*. 1563–67, ed. France V. Scholes and Eleanor B. Adams (Mexico, 1961), pp. 57–8, 66, 75; *Cartas de religiosos*, pp. 5–17; *Instrucciones que los virreyes de Nueva España dejaron a sus sucesores* (Mexico, 1867), p. 245.

28 Mendieta, *Historia*, pp. 556–63; *Cartas de religiosos*, pp. 5–28, 102–6.

29 Mendieta, *Historia*, pp. 15–17, 175–6, 210–12.

30 *Ibid.*, pp. 556–63.

31 Ricard, *Spiritual Conquest*, pp. 48–9; Arthur J. O. Anderson *et al.*, eds., *Beyond the Codices: the Nahua View of Colonial Mexico* (Berkeley and Los Angeles, 1976), *passim*.

32 Paul Kirchhoff, Lina Odena Guemes and Luis Reyes García, ed. *Historia Tolteca Chichimeca* (facsimile Mexico, 1976); Motolinia, *Historia*, p. 3.

33 García Icazbalceta, *Bibliografía*, pp. 474–8.
34 Munro S. Edmonson, ed., *Sixteenth-Century Mexico: the work of Sahagún* (Albuquerque, New Mexico, 1974); Howard F. Cline, 'Bernardino de Sahagún 1499–1590', in Robert Wauchope (general editor), *Handbook of Middle American Indians*, 16 vols. (Austin, Texas, 1964–76), XIII, 188–239.
35 Baudot, *Utopie et Histoire*, pp. 475–508.
36 Andrés Martín Melquiades, 'Pensamiento teólogico y vivencia religiosa en la reforma Española 1400–1600', in Ricardo García-Villoslada, ed., *Historia de la Iglesia en España, siglos XV y XVI*, vol. 3 (Madrid, 1980), pp. 303–5.
37 Bernardino de Sahagún, *Historia general de las cosas de Nueva España*, ed. Angel María Garibay K, BP 8–11, 4 vols. (Mexico, 1956), I, 27, 105, 268.
38 *Ibid.*, III, 158–68.
39 *Ibid.*, III, 352–6, 359–60; IV, 19.
40 *Ibid.*, III, 352–3, 357.
41 *Ibid.*, I, 105–8; García Icazbalceta, *Bibliografía*, pp. 322–88.
42 Sahagún, *Historia*, IV, 27, 45, 86–9.
43 *Ibid.*, IV, 101, 106–8, 113, 123, 136–62; Arthur J. O. Anderson and Charles E. Dibble, *Florentine Codex: The General History of the Things of New Spain of Bernardino de Sahagún*, 13 parts (Santa Fe, New Mexico, 1951–5), Book 12, *The Conquest of Mexico*.
44 Agustín Dávila Padilla, *Historia de la fundación y discurso de la provincia de Santiago de México de la orden de predicadores*, facsimile 2nd edn of 1625 (Mexico, 1955), pp. 93–105, 37–48, 93–103.
45 *Ibid.*, pp. 79–86, 101–3
46 *Ibid.*, pp. 91–2, 303–27; citation on p. 308.
47 *Ibid.*, pp. 328–41.

6 THE PROCONSUL

1 Roberto Levillier, *D. Francisco de Toledo* (Madrid, 1935), pp. 321–52; Antonio de la Calancha, *Corónica moralizada del orden de San Agustín en el Perú*, ed. Ignacio Prado Pastor, 6 vols. (Lima, 1974), III, 1586.
2 George Kubler, 'The Neo-Inca State 1537–1572', *HAHR*, 27 (1947), pp. 189–203; Steve J. Stern, *Peru's Indian Peoples and the Challenge of Spanish Conquest* (Madison, Wisconsin, 1982), pp. 50–79; Levillier, *Toledo*, pp. 366–70, 394.
3 Levillier, *Toledo*, pp. 14–81; Lewis Hanke, ed., *Los virreyes españoles en América durante el gobierno de la Casa de Austria: Perú*, BAE 281–6, 6 vols. (Madrid, 1978–80), I, 127.
4 Ricardo Beltrán y Rózpide, ed., *Colección de las memorias ó relaciones que escribieron los virreyes del Perú*, 2 vols. (Madrid, 1921–30), I, 157.
5 Juan de Matienzo, *Gobierno del Perú 1567*, ed. Guillermo Lohmann Villena (Paris–Lima, 1967), pp. 94–8, 101, 111; 'Anónimo de Yucay: Dominio de las Yngas en el Perú y del que Su Majestad tiene en dichos reinos', ed. Josyane Chinese, *Historia y Cultura*, 4 (1970), pp. 106–47.
6 Levillier, *Toledo* pp. 238, 257–9; Roberto Levillier, ed., *Gobernantes del Perú: cartas y papeles, siglo XVI*, 14 vols. (Madrid, 1921–6), I, 406–29; IV, 60, 121–2.
7 Levillier, *Toledo*, pp. 96, 131–2; Karen Spalding, *Huarochirí: An Andean Society*

under Inca and Spanish Rule (Stanford, 1984), pp. 54–8, 178–83; Hanke, *Los virreyes*, I, 130–9.

8 Spalding, *Huarochirí*, pp. 158–64.

9 Josep M. Barnardas, *Charcas 1535–1565* (La Paz, 1973), pp. 296–9.

10 Levillier, *Toledo*, p. 315; Hanke, *Los virreyes*, II, 130–1, 139.

11 Stern, *Peru's Indian Peoples*, pp. 75, 92–106.

12 Levillier, *Gobernantes*, IV, 9–14; Pierre Duviols, *La destrucción de las religiones andinas* (Mexico, 1970), pp. 132–43.

13 Hanke, *Los virreyes*, I, 129–30; Levillier, *Gobernantes*, IV, pp. 9–14; Levillier, *Toledo*, pp. 122–7.

14 Barnardas, *Charcas*, pp. 311–22, 266, 361–6; Luis Capoche, *Relación general del asiento y villa imperial de Potosí*, ed. Lewis Hanke, BAE 122 (Madrid, 1959), pp. 115–21.

15 Matienzo, *Gobierno*, pp. 29, 33, 63; Capoche, *Relación*, pp. 108–9.

16 Capoche, *Relación*, pp. 135–41; Peter J. Bakewell, *Miners of the Red Mountain. Indian Labor in Potosí 1545–1650* (Albuquerque, New Mexico, 1984), *passim*.

17 Matienzo, *Gobierno*, pp. 208–11, 279; Levillier, *Gobernantes*, IV, 162–8.

18 *Anónimo de Yucay*, pp. 106–7, 115–16, 126.

19 Levillier, *Gobernantes*, IV, 442; V, 310–12.

20 *Ibid.*, III, 304–5; Matienzo, *Gobierno*, pp. 13–14; *Anónimo de Yucay*, pp. 119, 122.

21 Pedro de Cieza de León, *El señorío de los Incas* (Lima, 1967), pp. xxxiii, 28–83.

22 Pedro de Cieza de León, 'La crónica del Perú', in Julio le Reverend Brusone, ed., *Crónicas de la conquista del Perú* (Mexico, n.d.), pp. 177–200, 261, 306–7, 372, 444.

23 Pedro Sarmiento de Gamboa, *History of the Incas*, ed. Clements Markham, Hakluyt Society (Cambridge, 1907), pp. 15–37, 119–20, 139–40.

24 *Ibid.*, pp. 190–5.

25 *Ibid*, pp. 199–201; Levillier, *Toledo*, pp. 285–95; Levillier, *Gobernantes*, IV, 54–60; VI, 41–3; see also Baudot, *Utopie et Histoire*, p. 504.

26 Matienzo, *Gobierno*, pp. 18–22, 57.

27 *Ibid.*, pp. 17–18, 60–1, 135.

28 *Informaciones acerca del señorío de los Incas*, ed. Marcos Jiménez de la Espada (Madrid, 1882), pp. 186–97, 200–4.

29 Hanke, *Los virreyes*, I, 138–40.

30 *Ibid.*, I, 139; Levillier, *Gobernantes*, VII, 50–2, 468–96.

31 Geoffrey Parker, *The Army of Flanders and the Spanish Road 1567–1659* (Cambridge, 1972), p. 239.

7 ANDEAN PILGRIM

1 Felipe Guaman Poma de Ayala (Waman Puma), *El primer nueva corónica y buen gobierno*, ed. John V. Murra, Rolena Adorno and Jorge L. Uriosto, 3 vols., continuous pagination (Mexico, 1980), III, 1008–9.

2 *Ibid.*, III, 1017–22.

3 *Ibid.*, III, 1014–15.

4 *Ibid.*, III, 1025.

5 See Rolena Adorno, *Guaman Poma: writing and resistance in Colonial Peru*

(Austin, Texas, 1986), *passim*; Raúl Porras Barrenechea, *El cronista indio Felipe Huaman Poma de Ayala* (Lima, 1948), p. 29; Juan Ossio, 'Guaman Poma y la historiografía indianista de los siglos XVI y XVII', *Historia y Cultura*, 10 (1978), pp. 181–206.

6 Guaman Poma, *Corónica*, I, 39–53; see also Nathan N. Wachtel, 'Pensée sauvage et acculturation. L'espace et le temps chez Felipe Guaman Poma de Ayala et l'Inca Garcilaso de la Vega', *Annales, Economies, Sociétés, Civilisations*, 26 (1971), pp. 793–840.

7 Guaman Poma, *Corónica*, I, 63, 70–2, 89–97.

8 *Ibid.*, I, 160–95; III, 1172–61; citation on II, 804.

9 *Ibid.*, II, 342–4, 347, 380; III, 997; also Adorno, *Guaman Poma*, pp. 4–35.

10 Guaman Poma, *Corónica*, I, 349, 375–6, 382, 399, 521.

11 *Ibid.*, I, 35, 72, 342; III, 914–15, 1158.

12 *Ibid.*, II, 413–14, 420.

13 *Ibid.*, III, 885, 890.

14 *Ibid.*, II, 419, 424.

15 *Ibid.*, II, 458–78, 642–51.

16 *Ibid.*, II, 461, 467, 535–9, 545, 574, 824; for his accusations against Morrúa see II, 615; III, 848.

17 *Ibid.*, II, 490, 511, 711, 724, 734, 803–9, 890–1, 911.

18 *Ibid.*, II, 655–6, III, 850; I, 75.

19 *Ibid.*, I, 290; II, 508, 567, 599–613; for Franciscans see II, 596.

20 On *Taki onquoy* see Stern, *Peru's Indian Peoples*, pp. 51–70; Guaman Poma, *Corónica*, I, 209, 253; II, 638; on Christ, II, 533; on Guaman Poma himself, III, 845–6.

21 *Ibid.*, II, 421, 620; III, 858; II, 511.

22 *Ibid.*, II, 420–1, 620, 763; Abraham Padilla Bendezu, *Huaman Poma: el indio cronista dibujante* (Mexico, 1979), pp. 30–67.

23 Guaman Poma, *Corónica*, III, 896, 898–911; II, 692–744, 767.

24 Francisco de Avila, *Dioses y hombres de Huarochirí*, ed. José María Arguedas (Lima, 1966), pp. 117–23.

25 *Codex Pérez and the Book of Chilam Balam of Maní*, ed. Eugene R. Craine and Reginold C. Reindrop (Norman, Oklahoma 1979), pp. 88–90, 143, 182–5.

26 *The Book of Chilam Balam of Chumayel*, cd. and trans. Ralph L. Roys (Norman, Oklahoma, 1967) p. 79; Victoria Reifler Bricker, *The Indian Christ, The Indian King. The Historical Substrate of Maya Myth and Ritual* (Austin, Texas, 1981), pp. 22–4.

27 Roys, *Chilam Balam*, pp. 107–9, 157.

28 Guaman Poma, *Corónica*, I, 338; III, 896, 1008.

29 Adorno, *Guaman Poma*, pp. 13–32, 57–62; Guaman Poma, *Corónica*, III, 848, 997–8.

30 Guaman Poma, *Corónica*, II, 661–2.

31 Porras Barrenechea, *Huaman Poma*, p. 69.

8 JESUIT TRIUMPHS

1 José de Acosta, *Obras*, ed. Francisco Mateos, BAE 73 (Madrid, 1954), pp. 255–7.

2 André Ravier, *Ignatius of Loyola and the Founding of the Society of Jesus* (San

Francisco, 1973), *passim*; Jean Delumeau, *Catholicism between Luther and Voltaire: a new view of the Counter-Reformation* (London, 1977), pp. 34, 61–3; and H. Outram Evennett, *The Spirit of the Counter-Reformation*, edited with a postscript by John Bossy (Cambridge, 1968; reprinted, Notre Dame, 1970), pp. 74–83.

3 Alonso de Sandoval, *De instauranda Aethiopum salute. Naturaleza, policía sagrada y profana, costumbres i ritos, disciplina y catechismo evangélico de todos etíopes*, ed. Angel Valtierra (3rd edn, Bogotá, 1956), pp. 105–10.

4 *Ibid.*, pp. 379–438.

5 *Ibid.*, pp. 105–6, 194–208, 346.

6 *Ibid.*, pp. 14, 26–7, 57–64.

7 *Ibid.*, pp. 97–103.

8 Angel Valtierra, *Peter Claver, Saint of the Slaves* (London, 1960), *passim*.

9 Sandoval *De instauranda*, pp. 479–95, 532–63.

10 *Ibid.*, pp. 280–302, 316–21, 502–7, 532–63.

11 *Ibid.*, pp. 498–520 on St Ignatius; pp. 35–7, 152–63 on St Thomas; p. 586 on Jesuits as merchants.

12 Antonio Ruiz de Montoya, *Conquista espiritual hecha por los religiosos de la Compañía de Jesús en las provincias del Paraguay, Paraná, Uruguay y Tape* (2nd edn, Bilbao, 1892), pp. 123–44.

13 *Ibid.*, pp. 142, 193–9, 226, 274.

14 *Ibid.*, pp. 95–109.

15 *Ibid.*, pp. 35–42, 191.

16 *Ibid.*, pp. 144–66, 297–8.

17 Adalberto López, *The Revolt of the Comuneros, 1721–1735* (Cambridge, Mass., 1976), pp. 34–46.

18 Andrés Pérez de Ribas, *Historia de los triumphos de nuestra Santa Fe entre gentes de las más bárbaras y fieras del nuevo orbe: conseguidos por los soldados de la milicia de la Compañía de Jesús en las misiones de Nueva España* (Madrid, 1645), pp. 409–11, 418–19, 751–2.

19 *Ibid.*, pp. 283–5, 411–13, 426–32.

20 *Ibid.*, pp. 58–70; the definition of the spiritual conquest occurs in the unpaginated prologue.

21 *Ibid.*, pp. 731–42.

22 *Ibid.*, pp. 452–65.

23 Herman W. Konrad, *A Jesuit Hacienda in Colonial Mexico: Santa Lucía 1576–1767* (Stanford, 1980), p. 71.

24 Antonio Astraín, *Historia de la Compañía de Jesús en la asistencia de España*, 7 vols. (Madrid, 1902–25), V, 321–5.

25 Konrad, *A Jesuit Hacienda*, pp. 70–4, 82, 98.

26 Alonso de Ovalle, *Histórica relación del reyno de Chile y de las misiones y ministerios que exercita en el la Compañía de Jesús* (Rome, 1646), pp. 3, 83–95, 435.

27 *Ibid.*, pp. 268–90, 313–16.

28 *Ibid.*, pp. 338–45.

29 *Ibid.*, pp. 345–62.

30 *The Spiritual Exercises of Saint Ignatius of Loyola*, trans. W. H. Longridge (London, 1919), pp. 100–8; see also Evennett, *The Counter-Reformation*, pp. 43–66.

31 Longridge, *The Spiritual Exercises*, pp. 198–9.

32 Hughes Didier, *Vida y pensamiento de Juan E. Nieremberg* (Madrid, 1976), pp. 124–5, 164–7.

33 Evennett, *The Counter-Reformation*, pp. 97–102, 135–7.

9 HISTORY AND MYTH

1 William Robertson, *The Works of William Robertson, D.D.*, 8 vols. (Oxford, 1825), VI, 409, 431.

2 Acosta, *Obras*, see introduction by Francisco Mateos and pp. 370–2.

3 *Ibid.*, pp. 353–60.

4 José de Acosta, *Historia natural y moral de las Indias*, ed. Edmundo O'Gorman (Mexico, 1962), pp. 13, 71, 89.

5 *Ibid.*, pp. 42–6, 59–62.

6 *Ibid.*, pp. 46, 63–4.

7 José de Acosta, *De procuranda Indorum salute*, ed. Francisco Mateos (Madrid, 1952) pp. 45–8; Acosta, *Historia*, pp. 293–305; see also Pagden, *Fall of Natural Man*, pp. 146–200; John Howland Rowe, 'Ethnography and ethnology in the sixteenth century', *The Kroeber Anthropological Society Papers*, 30 (1964), pp. 1–20; Margaret T. Hodgen, *Early Anthropology in the Sixteenth and Seventeenth Centuries* (Philadelphia, 1964), pp. 313–17.

8 Acosta, *Historia*, pp. 285–88; Acosta, *Obras*, pp. 331–44.

9 Acosta, *De procuranda*, pp. 47–8, 191–9.

10 *Ibid.*, pp. 155–65, 186–7.

11 *Ibid.*, pp. 155–61, 191–6.

12 *Ibid.*, pp. 160, 187–8, 223–4.

13 *Ibid.*, pp. 218–20, 185–6.

14 *Ibid.*, pp. 58–9, 86–9, 91–2.

15 *Ibid.*, pp. 15, 293–5, 403–5, 410.

16 *Ibid.*, pp. 58, 131, 332–8, 539–64, 582–3; on mestizos see pp. 359–60, 583.

17 *Ibid.*, pp. 237–46, 254, 281–91.

18 Acosta, *Historia*, pp. 216–280. The English translation comes from Joseph de Acosta, *The Natural and Moral History of the Indies*, ed. Clements R. Markham, The Hakluyt Society, 2 vols. (London, 1880).

19 Acosta, *Historia*, pp. 216–20, 235, 325–9.

20 *Ibid.*, pp. 293, 297–300, 281–2, 349.

21 *Ibid.*, pp. 371–7.

22 *Ibid.*, pp. 148–66; 142–3.

23 Acosta, *De procuranda*, pp. 427–39; Marcel Bataillon, *Estudios sobre Bartolomé de las Casas* (Madrid, 1976), pp. 353–67; Duviols, *Destrucción de las religiones andinas*, pp. 41–2, 363–4.

24 Matteo Ricci, *China in the Sixteenth Century. The Journals of Matteo Ricci*, trans. Louis J. Gallagher (New York, 1953), pp. 93–4.

25 Gregorio García, *Origen de los indios del Nuevo Mundo*, ed. Andrés González de Barcia (Madrid, 1729; facsimile Mexico, 1980). On Berosus see Don Cameron Allen, *The Legend of Noah* (Urbana, Illinois, 1949), pp. 114–21; T. D. Kendrick, *British Antiquity* (London, 1950), pp. 71–2.

26 García, *Origen*, pp. 7–15, 34, 68–71.

27 *Ibid.*, pp. 81–2, 85–7, 100–2, 110–12; see p. 121 for Mexico as Mesi.

28 *Ibid.*, pp. 44–9, 130–41.

29 *Ibid.*, pp. 141–60, 165–71, 183–6, 203, 242–3.

30 *Ibid.*, pp. 75, 102–3.

31 Juan de la Puente, *Tomo primero de la conveniencia de las dos monarquías Católicas, la de la Iglesia Romana y la del Imperio Español, y defensa de la precedencia de los Reyes Católicos de España a todos los reyes del mundo* (Madrid, 1612), pp. 9–10, 11, 201–3, 245–8.

32 *Ibid.*, pp. 248, 263.

33 Antonio de León Pinelo, *Epítome de la biblioteca oriental i occidental naútica i geográfica* (Madrid, 1629, facsimile edn, with preliminary study by Agustín Millares Carlo; Washington, 1958); Antonio de León Pinelo, *El paraíso en el Nuevo Mundo*, ed. Raúl Porras Barrenechea, 2 vols. (Lima, 1943), I, 114–24, 139–51; II, 431.

34 León Pinelo, *Paraíso*, I, v–vii; León Pinelo, *Epítome*, p. 4.

35 *Ibid.*, I, 165–86, 195–6.

36 *Ibid.*, II, 3–5, 27–32, 525–7.

37 *Ibid.*, I, 230–59, 277–8, 286, 272.

38 *Ibid.*, II, 143, 162, 317–29, 368–70; I, 328.

39 Antonio de León Pinelo, *El Gran Canciller de Indias*, ed. Guillermo Lohmann Villena (Seville, 1953), pp. 41–3.

40 M. Girolamo Benzoni, *La historia del Mundo Nuevo*, ed. Marisi Vennini (Caracas, 1967), pp. 24–5, 57, 64–9, 72–5, 90–5, 156–64.

41 On the appointment of Velasco see Rómulo D. Carbia, *La crónica oficial de las Indias Occidentales* (Buenos Aires, 1940), pp. 100–4; see also V. Afansiev, 'The literary heritage of Bartolomé de las Casas', in Friede and Keene, *Las Casas in History*, pp. 539–80.

42 Antonio de Herrera, *Historia general de los hechos de los castellanos en las Islas i Tierra Firme de Mar Océano*, 4 vols. (Madrid, 1601–15); on Herrera see Manuel Ballesteros Gaibros, 'Antonio de Herrera 1549–1625' in Wauchope, ed., *Handbook of Middle American Indians*, XIII, 240–55. There is a modern edition of Herrera, with a valuable introduction by Antonio Ballesteros y Beretta, 17 vols. (Madrid, 1934–57).

43 Herrera, *Historia*, I, unpaginated prologue; José Toribio Medina, ed., *El descubrimiento del Océano Pacífico*, 3 vols. (Santiago de Chile, 1913), II, 516–47, 571–4.

44 Herrera, *Historia*, I, 80–8.

45 *Ibid.*, II, 41, 112; III, 58–62; Medina, *Descubrimiento*, II, 518, 532.

46 Herrera, *Historia*, I, 52.

47 Carlos Bosch García, 'La conquista de la Nueva España en las *Décadas* de Antonio de Herrera y Tordesillas', in Hugo Díaz Thomé *et al.*, *Estudios de historiografía de la Nueva España* (Mexico, 1945), pp. 143–202; Antonio Ballesteros y Baretta, ed., Herrera, *Historia* (Madrid, 1934), I, lxxi.

48 Herrera, *Historia*, III, decade V, lib. III, cap. iv.

49 *Ibid.*, I, 10–11, II, 32, 208, 241; IV, 236, 276–7.

50 Giovanni Botero, *The Reason of State*, ed. D. P. Waley (New Haven, Conn. 1956), pp. 63–9.

51 Antonio de Solís y Rivadeneyra, *Historia de la conquista de Méjico* (Paris, 1838), pp.

4–5, 108–9; see also Luis A. Arocena, *Antonio de Solís. Cronista indiano* (Buenos Aires, 1963), *passim.*

52 Solís, *Historia*, pp. 55, 75, 174–8, 294.

53 *Ibid.*, pp. 150–1, 53–5, 196–220, 195, 307.

54 *Ibid.*, pp. 189, 249–51.

55 *Ibid.*, pp. 136, 211.

10 THE CATHOLIC MONARCHY

1 Juan de Solórzano Pereira, *Obras pósthumas* (Zaragoza, 1676), pp. 365, 373, 383, 387.

2 *Recopilación de leyes de los reynos de las Indias*, ed. Juan Manzano Manzano (facsimile edn of 1681, 4 vols.; Madrid, 1973), introduction; see also Antonio de León Pinelo, *Discurso sobre la importancia, forma y disposición de la recopilación de leyes de las Indias Occidentales*, ed. Aniceto Almeyda (Santiago de Chile, 1956), pp. 72–4, 100–2.

3 *Recopilación*, I, f. 1; MacKay, *Spain in the Middle Ages*, pp. 133, 137, 154; Solórzano, *Obras Posthumas*, p. 253.

4 *Recopilación*, II, f. 1.

5 Antonio de León Pinelo, *Tratado de confirmaciones reales de encomiendas, oficios i casos* (Madrid, 1630), pp. 51, 68, 72, 98.

6 *Ibid.*, pp. 95–6, 101–11.

7 Juan de Solórzano y Pereira, *Política indiana*, ed. Miguel Angel Ochoa Brun, BAE 252–6, 5 vols. (Madrid, 1972), I, xxxii–xxxix.

8 *Ibid.*, I, 81–8, 97–105, 113–14.

9 *Ibid.*, I, 92–5, 119–32, 58–81.

10 *Ibid.*, I, 137–60, 156, 176–84, 207, 233–4.

11 *Ibid.*, I, 263–310, citation p. 285; invocation of Daniel, pp. 283–4, 166.

12 *Ibid.*, I, 316–21, 372–6, 384–90, 398, 418–22.

13 *Ibid.*, II, 283–4, 8–22, 317, 307.

14 *Ibid.*, II, 391–407.

15 *Ibid.*, IV, 25–31, 40–7, 67, 71, 138–41; on Viceroys see pp. 199–216, 223.

16 *Ibid.*, III, 6, 359–64; for *Patronato*, pp. 18–23, 33; on bishops pp. 43, 120, 165; IV, 7.

17 *Ibid.*, III, 221–7, 244–9, 255–67.

18 *Ibid.*, III, 318–24.

19 *Ibid.*, III, 295–307, 413–23.

20 *Ibid.*, I, 443–5; IV, 70–1, 248–51.

21 Didier, *Nieremberg*, pp. 398–401.

22 Juan Caramuel Lobkowitz, *Architectura civil recta y obliqua* (Vegeren, 1678), pp. 19–26, 49–52; Eusebius of Caesarea, *The Church History and other writings* (New York, 1890), pp. 586–7.

11 TRIDENTINE PRELATE

1 Juan de Palafox y Mendoza, *Tratados mejicanos*, ed. Francisco Sánchez-Castañer, BAE 117–18, 2 vols. (Madrid, 1968), introduction.

2 J. I. Israel, *Race, Class and Politics in Colonial Mexico 1610–1670* (Oxford, 1975), pp. 199–246; J. H. Elliott, *The Count-Duke of Olivares* (New Haven, Conn, 1986), pp. 489–90, 518, 553–85.

3 Palafox, *Tratados*, II, 14–32.

4 Juan Diez de la Calle, *Memorial informatorio al Rey nuestro Señor* (Madrid, 1645), p. 12.

5 AGI, Mexico 2710, Palafox to Crown, 25 January 1645; Palafox, *Tratados*, I, 146–7; Israel, *Race, Class and Politics*, p. 206.

6 Palafox, *Tratados*, I, 129; Israel, *Race, Class and Politics*, p. 216.

7 Francisco Javier Alegre, *Historia de la provincia de la Compañía de Jesús de Nueva España*, ed. Ernest J. Burrus and Félix Zubillaga, 4 vols. (Rome, 1956–60), III, 423. On Salinas see Baltazar de Medina, *Chrónica de la santa provincia de San Diego de México de religiosos descalzos de N.S.P.S. Francisco en la Nueva España* (Mexico, 1682), pp. 41, 160, 212–13; Palafox, *Tratados*, II, 43.

8 Palafox, *Tratados*, I, 79–81, 94, 102–3; II, 91–117.

9 *Fuentes para la historia del trabajo en Nueva España*, ed. Silvio Zavala and María Castelo, 8 vols. (Mexico, 1939–45), VII, x–xi, 457–60, 487–8; see also AGI, Mexico 2709, where Palafox suggested giving mendicant priories forty to fifty *indios adscripticios* to serve as carpenters, masons and cooks.

10 Palafox, *Tratados*, II, 165–72; see also Juan de Mendoza y Palafox, *Obras*, 13 vols. (Madrid, 1762), XI, 194–202.

11 Palafox, *Tratados*, I, 195–208.

12 Palafox, *Tratados*, I, 21, 33–4; Palafox, *Obras*, X, 26–7; XII, 5–12.

13 Palafox, *Tratados*, I, 19–26; Alegre, *Historia*, III, 416.

14 Palafox, *Tratados*, I, 22–5.

15 D. A. Brading, 'Tridentine Catholicism and Enlightened Despotism in Bourbon Mexico', *JLS* 15 (1983), pp. 1–22.

16 Palafox, *Tratados*, I, 72–7, 98–9, 114.

17 Palafox, *Obras*, XIII, 354, 387; I, 57; *Documentos inéditos o muy raros para la historia de México. VIII. Don Juan de Palafox y Mendoza*, ed. Genaro García and Carlos Pereyra, 2nd edn, BP 58 (Mexico, 1974) pp. 524–7, 593–5; Serge Gruzinski, *Man-gods in the Mexican Highlands* (Stanford, 1989), pp. 97–8.

18 Palafox, *Obras*, I, 15–45, 132; XIII, 157, 624.

19 *Ibid.*, I, 194–6, 205, 220–30.

20 Palafox, *Tratados*, II, 169; *Obras*, I, 132–81, 229.

21 Palafox, *Obras*, II(I), 10–7; II(II), 569–70; III(II), 9–11; IV, 138–40.

22 *Ibid.*, II(II), 23, 227, 282–3, 292–9.

23 *Ibid.*, X, 8; V, 314–15.

24 *Ibid.*, V, 324; IX, 187, 409, 586–95; I, 356, 541–5, 650–5.

25 *Ibid.*, V, 297; X, 7–8; I, 361.

26 *Ibid.*, III(I), 7–8; III(II), 404; X, 23–6. On Borromeo see A. D. Wright, *The Counter-Reformation: Catholic Europe and the Non-Christian World* (London, 1982), pp. 52–4, 189–91.

27 Palafox, *Obras*, XI, 30–2; Astraín, *Historia de la Compañía de Jesús*, V, 321–5.

28 Palafox, *Tratados*, I, 125–58.

29 Alegre, *Historia*, III, 423; Israel, *Race, Class and Politics*, pp. 103–6; Palafox, *Carta al sumo pontífice Innocent X* (3rd edn, Madrid, 1767), p. 159. Note that Palafox

claimed that one Provincial expelled 38 priests and brothers out of some 300 members of the Mexican province.

30 Palafox, *Obras*, XII, 23–47.

31 *Ibid.*, XII, 195–201 for Salinas; XI, 197 for citation; also *Tratados*, II 36–89.

32 Palafox, *Tratados*, I, 45; the *Defensa canónica* is printed in *Obras*, XII, where Rada's resistance is on pp. 390–2; on Palafox's career at Osma, see *Obras*, XIII, 140–51, 283–6.

33 Palafox, *Obras*, XI, 185–97, 212–14, 302–14; *Carta al Innocent X*, pp. 137–9, 144–9, 163–78.

34 Juan de Palafox y Mendoza, *Diario del viaje a Alemania*, ed. Xristina de Arteaga (Madrid, 1935), pp. 90–4; Palafox, *Obras*, X, 56–68; IV, 516–28; V, 333; IX, 187, 382–6.

35 Palafox, *Obras*, X, 76–85; *Viaje al Alemania*, pp. 37, 42, 56–8.

36 *Ibid.*, X, 37–49.

37 *Ibid.*, V, 322; X, 275, 373, 411.

38 *Ibid.*, III(II), 510, 512–13.

39 Pedro Rodríguez de Campomanes, *Dictamen fiscal de expulsión de los jesuitas de España (1766–1767)*, ed. Jorge Cejudo and Teófanes Egido (Madrid, 1977), pp. 74, 107–11, 125, 167.

40 Evennett, *The Counter-Reformation*, pp. 139–41; Henri Bremond, *A Literary History of Religious Thought in France*, 3 vols. (London, 1928–36), III, 14–17, 134–47, 174–5, 440–1.

12 INCA HUMANIST

1 On Garcilaso see José Durand, *El Inca Garcilaso, clásico de América* (Mexico, 1976); Aurelio Miró Quesada, *El Inca Garcilaso y otros estudios garcilasistas* (Madrid, 1971); J. G. Varner, *El Inca. The Life and Times of Garcilaso de la Vega 1539–1616* (Austin, Texas, 1968); Enrique Pupo-Walker, *Historia, creación y profecía en los textos del Inca Garcilaso de la Vega* (Madrid, 1982).

2 For these autobiographical statements see Eugenio Asensio, 'Dos cartas desconocidas del Inca Garcilaso', *Nueva Revista de Filología Hispánica*, VII (1953), pp. 583–93; Inca Garcilaso de la Vega, *Historia general del Perú*, ed. Angel Rosenblat, 3 vols. (Buenos Aires, 1944), II, 216; Inca Garcilaso de la Vega, *Obras completas*, ed. Carmelo Sáenz de Santa María, BAE 122–5, 4 vols (Madrid, 1960), I, 5–8, 231–8; Inca Garcilaso de la Vega, *La Florida del Inca* (Mexico, 1956) pp. 5–10.

3 Garcilaso, *Obras* I, 5–81; *La Florida*, p. 112.

4 Garcilaso, *La Florida*, pp. 368–70, 429; Oviedo, *Historia*, II, 156–79.

5 Miró Quesada, *Garcilaso*, pp. 150–5; Pupo-Walker, *Historia, creación y profecía*, pp. 52–3.

6 Garcilaso, *La Florida*, pp. 18–20, 109, 137–8, 151, 214, 261, 271, 342.

7 *Ibid.*, pp. 84, 94, 112, 442–3; P. Cornelius Tacitus, *On Britain and Germany* (London, 1948) p. 80.

8 Cochrane, *Historians and Historiography*, pp. 18–20, 304.

9 Jean Bodin, *Method for the Easy Comprehension of History* (New York, 1945), pp. 15, 297–8.

10 For *Los diálogos de amor* see Garcilaso, *Obras*, I, 1, 30, 56, 73, 102, 193, 200–4; see

also D. P. Walker, *The Ancient Theology* (London, 1972), pp. 102–3, 200–3; and William D. Ilgen, 'La configuración mítica de la historia en los *Comentarios reales del Inca Garcilaso de la Vega*' in A. P. Debicki and E. Pupo-Walker, ed., *Estudios de literatura hispanoamericana en honor a José J. Arrom* (Chapel Hill, North Carolina, 1974), pp. 37–46.

11 Garcilaso, *Obras*, I, 67–9.

12 Jerónimo Román y Zamora, *Repúblicas de Indias, idolatrías y gobierno en México y Perú antes de la conquista*, 2 vols. (Madrid, 1897). For Las Casas see I, 46, 93, 187; for Incas see I, 160, 270–2; II, 42–3, 72.

13 Garcilaso de la Vega, *Comentarios reales de los Incas*, ed. Angel Rosenblat, 2 vols. (Buenos Aires, 1943), I, 20, 88, 124, 233; *La Florida*, p. 112; Duviols, *Destrucción de las religiones andinas*, pp. 41–2.

14 Garcilaso, *Comentarios*, I, 29–39; II, 126.

15 *Ibid.*, I, 39–67.

16 *Ibid.*, I, 66–7, 78–83, 103, 136.

17 *Ibid.*, I, 266–44; II, 102–10.

18 *Ibid.*, I, 66, 79, 244; II, 27–34.

19 See José de la Riva Agüero, *Obras completas*, 11 vols. (Lima, 1962–75), IV, 51–7.

20 Bernabé Cobo, *Historia del Nuevo Mundo*, ed. Francisco Mateos, BAE 91–2, 2 vols. (Madrid, 1956), II, 133–5, 172–4, 147–8.

21 José Durand, 'Perú y Ophir en Garcilaso Inca, el Jesuita Pineda y Gregorio García', *Histórica*, 3 (1979), pp. 33–54; Garcilaso, *Obras* I, 234–5; *Comentarios*, I, 245.

22 Román y Zamora, *Repúblicas*, II, 221–3; Garcilaso, *Historia del Perú*, I, 7, 20–1, 234, 261–7.

23 Garcilaso, *Historia del Perú*, I, 59–75.

24 *Ibid.*, I, 302–9; II, 14–16, 215–16.

25 *Ibid.*, II, 133–6.

26 *Ibid.*, III, 243–51.

27 *Ibid.*, III, 124–4, 301.

28 Acosta, *Historia*, pp. 360–1, 371–4; Garcilaso, *Historia del Perú*, I, 177–9.

29 Miró Quesada, *Garcilaso*, p. 215; Bodin, *Method for History*, pp. 15, 297–8.

30 Garcilaso, *Historia del Perú*, I, 113; III, 218–32.

31 James Joyce, *A Portrait of the Artist as a Young Man* (London, 1930), p. 281.

32 John Rowe, 'El movimiento nacional inca del siglo XVIII' in Alberto Flores Galindo, ed., *Tupac Amaru II. 1780* (Lima, 1976), pp. 25–32.

13 THE TWO CITIES

1 Fernando de Alva Ixtlilxochitl, *Obras históricas*, ed. Edmundo O'Gorman, 2 vols. (Mexico, 1975), I, 204, 526–6; *Códice Xolotl*, Charles E. Dibble, ed., 2 vols. (Mexico, 1980), *passim*.

2 Ixtlilxochitl, *Obras*, I, 418–25; II, 7–9, 35.

3 *Ibid.*, I, 385, 405, 447, 439; II, 61–137.

4 *Ibid.*, I, 418–28, 492–517.

5 Juan de Torquemada, *Los veinte y un libros rituales y monarquía indiana*, ed. Miguel León-Portilla *et al.*, 7 vols. (Mexico, 1975–83). Vol. 7 consists of analysis and discussion by the editors.

6 Herrera, *Historia*, decade VI, lib. III, cap. xix.

7 Torquemada, *Monarquía*, I, xxvi–xxxi, 361; García Icazbalceta, *Bibliografía*, pp. 477–8; Miguel León-Portilla, 'Biografía de fray Juan de Torquemada' in *Monarquía*, VII, 13–48.

8 Ixtlilxochitl, *Obras*, II, 137; Torquemada, *Monarquía*, VII, 93–267 presents a detailed analysis of sources of each chapter.

9 Torquemada, *Monarquía*, I, 34–45.

10 *Ibid.*, I, 46; IV, 353–5, 361–7; V, 355.

11 *Ibid.*, I, 55–94; for Las Casas extract see I, 69– 74; in religion III, 174.

12 *Ibid.*, I, 69–74.

13 *Ibid.*, I, 350–2; III, 81–7.

14 *Ibid.*, I, 114, 132–5, 236–7, 397; III, 174–5.

15 *Ibid.*, II, 235, 284.

16 *Ibid.*, I, 164–8, 230–40, 291–9.

17 *Ibid.*, III, 23–8, 160–5; IV, 98–109, 261.

18 *Ibid.*, I, 283–4, 314–15, 396–7; III, 216–29.

19 *Ibid.*, I, 120, 298; III, 28, 52–3, 119, 127–8, 174–5; for citation IV, 261.

20 Diego Durán, *Historia de las Indias de Nueva España e Islas de la Tierra Firme*, ed. Angel M. Garibay K., BP 36–7, 2 vols. (Mexico, 1967), I, xxix, 9–15, 186–7; II, 14– 18, 28, 101, 205, 343–68.

21 *Ibid.*, II, 22, 514–15, 548–9, 574–5.

22 Torquemada, *Monarquía* II, 59–63, 137–9, 154, 203–5; VII, 80, 175.

23 *Ibid.*, II, 212–16.

24 *Ibid.*, II, 318–26.

25 *Ibid.*, II, 9–10, 39, 326–30.

26 *Ibid.*, V, 314, 339–40, 344, 355.

27 García Icazbalceta, *Códice Mendieta*, II, 172–5.

28 Torquemada, *Monarquía*, II, 414–16, 519, 467–72.

29 *Ibid.*, V, 10–15, 74–5.

30 *Ibid.*, VI, bk. 20, cap. xlvi.

31 *Ibid.*, VI, bk. 20, cap. lxxiii.

32 García Icazbalceta, *Códice Mendieta*, II, 130–62; Torquemada, *Monarquía*, II, 410–14.

33 Torquemada, *Monarquía*, II, 374, 381–2, 390–402.

34 *Ibid*, II, 403–16; citation on p. 414.

35 Juan Suárez de Peralta, *Tratado del descubrimiento de las Indias*, ed. Federico Gómez de Orozco (Mexico, 1949), pp. 99–100, 169.

36 Torquemada, *Monarquía*, I, 408–15, 418–21; *Instrucciones que dejaron los virreyes de Mexico*, p. 245.

14 CREOLE PATRIOTS

1 Silvio A. Zavala, *La encomienda Indiana*, BP 53 (2nd edn, Mexico, 1973), pp. 610–13.

2 Gonzálo Gómez de Cervantes, *La vida económica y social de Nueva España al finalizar el siglo XVI*, ed. Alberto María Carreño (Mexico 1944), pp. 77–82, 132.

3 *Ibid.*, pp. 91–4, 101, 117–18, 122–6, 132, 184–5.

4 *Ibid.*, pp. 99–110, 124, 137–8.

5 Baltazar Dorantes de Carranza, *Sumaria relación de las cosas de la Nueva España*, ed. José María de Agreda y Sánchez (Mexico, 1902, reprinted 1970), pp. 17–21, 234, 258.

6 *Ibid.*, pp. 113–14.

7 Calancha, *Crónica*, I, 164.

8 Carranza, *Sumaria relación*, pp. 8–10, 47–86; see Ernesto de la Torre Villar, 'Baltazar Dorantes de Carranza y la *Sumaria relación*', in Díaz-Thomé, *Estudios de historiografía*, pp. 203–62.

9 Carranza, *Sumaria relación*, pp. 17–25, 42, 96–9, 113–18.

10 Torquemada, *Monarquía*, VI, bk. 20, cap. lxxiii; García Icazbalceta, *Cartas de religiosos*, p. 28; Cuevas, *Documentos*, p. 299; Sahagún, *Historia*, III, 160.

11 Francisco Morales, *Ethnic and Social Background of the Franciscan Friars in Seventeenth-Century Mexico* (Washington, 1973), pp. 56–9, 66–8.

12 De la Puente, *Conveniencia de las dos monarquías*, p. 363; Diego Cisneros, *Sitio, naturaleza y propiedades de la Ciudad de México* (Mexico, 1618), pp. 113–14; Enrico Martínez, *Reportorio de los tiempos e historia natural de Nueva España*, ed. Francisco de la Maza (Mexico, 1948), pp. 176–8; Juan de Cárdenas, *Problemas y secretos maravillosos de las Indias* (facsimile of 1591 Mexican edition, Madrid, 1945), fs. 176–82.

13 Juan de Grijalva, *Crónica de la orden de N.P.S. Agustín en las provincias de la Nueva España* (Mexico, 1624), pp. 21–2.

14 *Instrucciones que dejaron los virreyes*, pp. 249, 254–5.

15 García, ed., *Documentos inéditos*, p. 312; Bernardo de Balbuena, *La grandeza mexicana*, ed. Luis Adolfo Domínguez (Mexico, 1971), pp. 94–9, 116–19.

16 Gaspar Pérez de Villagra, *Historia de la Nueva México* (Alcalá, 1610), pp. 40–56, 271.

17 Juan Rodríguez Freyle, *El Carnero*, ed. Darío Achury Valenzuela, BA 66 (Caracas, 1979), pp. 17, 23, 36, 314–18; on creoles see pp. 367–70, 411–24.

18 *Ibid.*, pp. 258, 289–91, 328–9; 291, 304, 390.

19 Francisco Núñez de Pineda y Bascuñán, 'Cautiverio feliz y razón de las guerras dilatadas de Chile', in Diego Barrós Arana, ed., *Colección de Historiadores de Chile*, vol. III (Santiago de Chile, 1863), pp. 2, 214, 423; see also Sergio Correa Bello, *El Cautiverio feliz en la vida política chilena del siglo XVII* (Santiago de Chile, 1965), *passim*.

20 Núñez de Pineda, *Cautiverio feliz*, pp. 83, 158–9, 251, 289.

21 *Ibid.*, pp. 67, 98–9, 104, 122–4, 172–80, 195, 362–3.

22 *Ibid.*, pp. 6–7, 162, 171, 252–64, 307.

23 *Ibid.*, pp. 70, 128–30, 264–7.

24 *Ibid.*, pp. 15, 118, 230–6, 410, 421–6.

25 *Ibid.*, pp. 117, 163, 216, 332; 389, 518; on St Augustine, p. 239.

26 Francisco Antonio de Fuentes y Guzmán, *Recordación florida: discurso historial, natural, material, militar y político del reino de Goathemala*, ed. Carmelo Sáenz de Santa María, BAE 230, 251, 259, 3 vols. (Madrid, 1969–72), II, 190–4; II, 197, 249–52; III, 314. See also Severo Martínez Peláez, *La patria del criollo* (Guatemala, 1971), pp. 38–61.

27 Fuentes, *Recordación*, I, lxiv, 117, 133–9, 199, 162.

28 Ibid., I, 230, 255, 357–9; II, 71–5, 150–5, 283 4; III, 92–4.

29 Ibid., I, 321; III, 13, 290–8, 310–11.

30 Ibid., I, 226, 316, 356; III, 11, 28, 28.

31 Ibid., III, 99, 103–4, 138–46, 277–80.

32 Ibid., I, 159, 166–73; II, 8, 179–93.

33 Ibid., I, 197; II, 164–5, 278–9; III, 71–5, 87, 201–4.

34 José de Oviedo y Baños, Historia de la conquista y población de la provincia de Venezuela (Caracas, 1967), pp. 6–7, 24–39; on Aguirre see pp. 277, 328–35.

35 Ibid., pp. 422–48.

36 José Martín Félix de Arrate, Llave del Nuevo Mundo, ed. Julio J. Le Reverend Brusone (Mexico, 1949), pp. 63–4, 90–1, 139–41, 148–51, 168–9, 194–6.

37 Ibid., pp. 18–21, 39–40.

38 Ibid., 93–5, 141–4, 231–51.

15 ANNALS OF OPHIR

1 García, Origen de los Indios, pp. 15–17; Fernando de Montesinos, Memorias antiguas, historiales y políticas del Perú, ed. Horacio Urteaga (Lima, 1930), pp. 3–5.

2 Buenaventura de Salinas y Córdova, Memorial de las historias del Nuevo Mundo, Pirú, ed. Luis E. Valcárcel and Warren L. Cook (Lima, 1957), pp. xlvi–lvi. There are apparently several printed versions of Memorial del P. Fray Buenaventura de Salinas; I consulted the British Library's copy which was printed after January 1651.

3 Ibid., pp. 249–80, 284, 297–303, 321.

4 Ibid., pp. 274–8.

5 Ibid., pp. 86–9, 162, 246, 275–7.

6 Ibid., pp. 89–91, 106–14, 248–55, 330.

7 Ibid., pp. 260–8.

8 Ibid., pp 284 5, 294–310.

9 Ibid., pp. 12, 13–20.

10 Ibid., pp. 38, 48–50, 76–82.

11 Ibid., pp. 191–246, number of masses on p. 244.

12 Ibid., pp. 228, 217.

13 Ibid., pp. 162–82, 230–43, 176 8, 188–9.

14 Ibid., p. 198.

15 Antonio de la Calancha, Crónica moralizada del orden de San Agustín en el Perú, 6 vols, continuous pagination (Lima, 1974–81), I, 26–36; León Pinelo, Paraíso, II, 436.

16 Calancha, Crónica, I, 88–107.

17 Ibid., I, 108, 205–22.

18 Alonso Ramos Gavilán, Historia del célebre santuario de N. Señora de Copacabana y sus milagros e invención de la Cruz de Carabuco (Lima, 1621), pp. 14–16, 27–8, 111.

19 Calancha, Crónica, II, 701–69; Ramos Gavilán, Historia, pp. 30–53, 164, 233, 256; Didier, Nieremberg, p. 216.

20 Calancha, Crónica, I, 238–423, 253–5, 263, 284–98; on Las Casas p. 183.

21 Ibid., III, 976; IV, 1586.

22 Ibid., III, 798–811, 906; I, 253–4; IV, 1428–30.

23 *Ibid.*, I, 22, 292–3, 302; II, 436–45; IV, 1579–86; V, 1771–3.

24 *Ibid.*, II, 564–9; III, 984.

25 *Ibid.*, V, 1675–91.

26 *Ibid.*, II, 546–9.

27 *Ibid.*, I, 153–7.

28 *Ibid.*, I, 157, 164.

29 Antonio de la Calancha and Bernardo de Torres, *Crónicas agustinianas del Perú*, ed. Manuel Merino, 2 vols. (Madrid, 1972), II, 547–59, 773–4.

30 Calancha, *Crónica*, II, 581–3; III, 1138–40; IV, 1428–35; V, 1692–701.

31 *Ibid.*, pp. II, 573–4; IV, 1238–65.

32 *Ibid.*, II, 623–5, 642–4.

33 *Ibid.*, pp. V, 1955; Ramos Gavilán, *Historia*, pp. 101, 184–207, 235–8, 365–74; on comparison with Israel, p. 333; citation p. 382.

34 Diego de Córdova Salinas, *Corónica de la religiosíssima provincia de los doze apóstoles del Perú de la orden de N.S.P. San Francisco*, ed. Lino G. Canedo (Mexico, 1957), pp. 515–61 for Mogrovejo; pp. 542–66 for Solano.

35 Pierre Delooz, 'Towards a sociological study of canonized sainthood in the Catholic Church', in Stephen Wilson, ed., *Saints and their Cults* (Cambridge, 1983), pp. 189–216; see also Peter Brown, *Society and the Holy in Late Antiquity* (London, 1982), pp. 103–66, 222–50.

36 Córdova Salinas, *Corónica*, p. 539.

37 Juan Meléndez, *Tesoros verdaderos de las Indias. Historia de la provincia de San Juan Baptista del Perú de la orden de Predicadores*, 3 vols. (Rome, 1681–2), Montalvo's assertion about Las Casas is in the unpaginated introduction, vol. I and II, 172; but see I, 27–33, 248–9; Córdova, Salinas, *Corónica*, p. 33.

38 Meléndez, *Tesoros*, I, 349–57.

39 Córdova Salinas, *Corónica*, pp. 79, 482, Meléndez, *Tesoros*, I, unpaginated introduction, 199–217.

40 Meléndez, *Tesoros*, III, 201–338; see also Rubén Vargas Ugarte, *Vida de San Martín de Porras* (Buenos Aires, 1963), pp. 149, 162–3, 461, 478–83.

41 Meléndez, *Tesoros*, II, 177–490; Rubén Vargas Ugarte, *Vida de Santa Rosa de Lima* (Buenos Aires, 1961), *passim*.

42 Luis Antonio de Oviedo y Herrera, *Vida de Santa Rosa de Santa María, natural de Lima y patrona de Perú* (Madrid, 1711), pp. 287, 442.

43 Juan de Espinosa Medrano, *Apologético en favor de D. Luis de Góngora* (Lima, 1662), see unpaginated prologue, pp. 3–9, 15, 25. For scene in cathedral see Diego de Esquivel y Navia, *Noticias cronológicas de la gran ciudad del Cuzco*, ed. Félix Denegri Luna, 2 vols. (Lima, 1980), II, 148–9.

44 Cobo, *Obras*, II, 280.

45 José de Mesa and Teresa Gisbert, *Historia de la pintura cuzqueña*, 2 vols. (Lima, 1982), I, 177–80, 283–7; II, 229–42; Cobo, *Obras*, II, 61.

46 Esquivel, *Noticias*, II, 405.

16 MEXICAN PHOENIX

1 Miguel Sánchez, *Imagen de la Virgen María, Madre de Dios de Guadalupe, milagrosamente aparecida en la ciudad de México. Celebrada en su historia, con la*

profecía del capítulo doce del Apocalipsis (Mexico, 1648), pp. 19–45. This and other early accounts are reprinted in Ernesto de la Torre Villar and Ramiro Navarro de Anda, ed., *Testimonios históricos guadalupanos* (Mexico, 1982). The best introduction to the subject remains Francisco de la Maza, *El guadalupanismo mexicano* (2nd edn, Mexico, 1984).

2 Antonio de Robles, *Diario de sucesos notables (1665–1703)*, ed. Antonio Castro Leal, 3 vols. (Mexico, 1946), I, 144–6.

3 Sánchez, *Imagen*, unpaginated introduction; see also Luis Lasso de la Vega, *Huei tlamahuicoltica . . . Santa María Totlaconantzin Guadalupe* (Mexico, 1649). This is translated in Torre Villar, *Testimonios*, pp. 284–308.

4 Luis Becerra Tanco, *Felicidad de México en el principio y milagroso origen que tubo el santuario de la Virgen María N. Señora de Guadalupe* (2nd edn, Mexico, 1675), pp. 14–30.

5 Francisco de Florencia, *La Estrella del Norte de México*, reprinted in *Colección de obras y opúsculos pertenecientes a la aparición de Nuestra Señora de Guadalupe*, 2 vols. (Madrid, 1785), II, 218–29, 281, 289–91, 388–9, 500. Note that Torre Villar, *Testimonios*, does not print the complete text of *Estrella del Norte*.

6 Robles, *Diario*, I, 189; Florencia, *Estrella*, pp. 150–4, 637.

7 Carlos de Sigüenza y Góngora, *Glorias de Querétaro* (Querétaro, 1945), pp. 10–11.

8 For the development of the cult see Mariano Fernández de Echeverría y Veitia, *Baluartes de México* (Mexico, 1820, facsimile edn 1967), pp. 41–62; Jacque Lafaye, *Quetzalcoatl et Guadalupe* (Paris, 1974), pp. 281–399.

9 Cayetano Javier de Cabrera y Quintero, *Escudo de armas de México* (Mexico, 1746), pp. 206–15, 228, 367–91, 471–95.

10 The phrase occurs first in Florencia, *Estrella*, p. 499.

11 Torquemada, *Monarquía*, VI, bk. 20, cap. xiv–xv.

12 Grijalva, *Crónica*, p. 42.

13 Saint Augustine, *City of God* (Penguin edn), bk. XXII, cap. 8–9, pp. 1033–47.

14 Peter Brown, *The Cult of the Saints* (London, 1981), *passim*.

15 T. D. Kendrick, *St James of Spain* (London, 1960), *passim*.

16 Jaroslav Pelikan, *The Christian Tradition. A History of the Development of Doctrine*, 4 vols. (Chicago, 1971–84), II, pp. 118–23, 133–5.

17 William A. Christian Jr, *Apparitions in Late Medieval and Renaissance Spain* (Princeton, 1981), pp. 23, 38, 87–93.

18 Ricard, *Spiritual Conquest*, pp. 102–3.

19 Grijalva, *Crónica*, pp. 72–3.

20 Luis de Cisneros, *Historia de el principio y origen, progressos venidos a México y milagros de la Santa Ymagen de Nuestra Señora de los Remedios, extramuros de México* (Mexico, 1621), *passim*; see also Grijalva, *Crónica*, pp. 82–5.

21 Cisneros, *Ymagen de los Remedios*, p. 20.

22 Edmundo O'Gorman, *Destierro de sombras. Luz en el origen de la imagen y culto de Nuestra Señora de Guadalupe del Tepeyac* (Mexico, 1986), pp. 65–73, 114–34.

23 *Ibid.*, pp. 84–91; the documents of the case are printed in Torre Villar, *Testimonios*, pp. 36–141.

24 Sahagún, *Historia*, III, 352.

25 Becerra Tanco, *Felicidad de México*, pp. 14, 17.

26 Florencia, *Estrella*, pp. 314–19, 373, 383.

27 Carlos de Sigüenza y Góngora, *Piedad heroyca de Don Fernando Cortés*, ed. Jaime Delgado (Madrid, 1960), pp. 64–5.

28 For this argument see Angel María Garibay K., *Historia de la literatura nahuatl*, BP 1, 5, 2 vols. (Mexico, 1954), II, 256–66; O'Gorman, *Destierro de sombras*, pp. 41–61.

29 Robles, *Diario*, I, 144–6; Florencia, *Estrella*, p. 356.

30 Erich Auerbach, *Scenes from the Drama of European Literature* (Manchester, 1984), pp. 11–76.

31 Reeves, *Prophecy in the Later Middle Ages*, pp. 16–28.

32 Sánchez, *Imagen de la Virgen María*, p. 51.

33 *Ibid.*, pp. 17, 45, 66.

34 *Ibid.*, pp. 6, 10, 17.

35 *Ibid.*, p. 5; Torre Villar, *Testimonios*, p. 307.

36 *Ibid.*, p. 34.

37 *Ibid.*, p. 50.

38 *Ibid.*, pp. 83–4.

39 *Ibid.*, unpaginated introduction.

40 *Colección de obras y opúsculos*, I, 407.

41 *Ibid.*, 408–9; see also Manuel Trens, *María. Iconografía de la Virgen en el arte español* (Madrid, 1946), pp. 118, 149, 189.

42 Florencia, *Estrella*, pp. 161, 565, 599, 731.

43 *Ibid.*, pp. 6–12, 17.

44 Torre Villar, *Testimonios*, pp. 346–7.

45 De la Maza, *El guadalupanismo*, pp. 113, 144.

46 *Ibid.*, pp. 150, 136, 160, 168.

47 Henry Adams, *The Education of Henry Adams*, Modern Library Edition (New York, 1931), p. 385.

48 Ignacio Manuel Altamirano, *Obras completas*, 12 vols (Mexico, 1986–88), V, 116–18.

17 WESTERN PARADISE

1 Carlos de Sigüenza y Góngora, *Obras históricas*, ed. José Rojas Garcidueñas (Mexico, 1960), pp. 259–79, 269, 343–52, 230, 241; the savant cited was Athanasius Kircher.

2 On his life see Irving A. Leonard, *Don Carlos de Sigüenza y Góngora* (Berkeley, 1929), *passim*; on works Ramón Iglesia, *El hombre Colón y otros ensayos* (Mexico, 1944), pp. 119–44; on reputation, Giovanni Francesco Gemelli Careri, *Viaje a la Nueva España*, ed. Francisca Perajo (Mexico, 1976), pp. 52–3, 118–19, 130; for Gama's praise see Florencia, *Estrella*, p. 42.

3 Sigüenza, *Obras históricas*, pp. 238–41; Carlos de Sigüenza y Góngora, *Paraíso occidental* (Mexico, 1684), unpaginated prologue.

4 On Kircher see R. J. W. Evans, *The Making of the Habsburg Monarchy 1500—1700* (Oxford, 1979), pp. 433–42; Joscelyn Godwin, *Athanasius Kircher. A Renaissance Man and the Quest for Lost Knowledge* (London, 1979), pp. 18–23; citations on pp. 19, 56; see also Erick Ivesen, *The Myth of Egypt and its Hieroglyphs in European Tradition* (Copenhagen, 1961), pp. 89–98; Walker, *The Ancient Theology*, pp. 102–3.

5 Sigüenza, *Obras históricas*, pp. 247, 255, 257–9.

6 Gemelli Careri, *Viaje*, pp. 50, 55, 129–30.

7 Becerra Tanco, *Felicidad de México*, p. 27; Medina, *Chrónica*, p. 227; Carlos de Sigüenza y Góngora, *Libra astronómica y filosófica*, ed. José Gaos (Mexico, 1954), p. 16; Sigüenza, *Paraíso occidental*, unpaginated prologue.

8 Sigüenza, *Obras históricas*, pp. 284–6; *Paraíso occidental*, p. 3; Gemelli Careri, *Viaje*, pp. 43–5.

9 Carlos de Sigüenza y Góngora, *Triunfo Parténico*, ed. José Rojas Garcidueñas (Mexico, 1945), p. 37; *Paraíso occidental*, pp. 3–5. ·

10 Sigüenza, *Obras históricas*, pp. 255–6; Gemelli Careri, *Viaje*, p. 25.

11 Sigüenza, *Libra astronómica*, pp. 3, 7, 141, 151; see Elías Trabulse, *Ciencia y religión en el siglo XVII* (Mexico, 1974), pp. 20–46.

12 Sigüenza, *Libra astronómica*, pp. 13–14, 33, 43, 147–9, 162.

13 Sigüenza, *Piedad heroyca*, p. 29; *Paraíso occidental*, pp. 5, 18, 48, 107–15; *Triunfo Parténico*, pp. 44, 82, 244–8.

14 Sigüenza, *Obras históricas*, pp. 99–100, 113, 141–3, 176–7.

15 Carlos de Sigüenza y Góngora, *Documentos inéditos*, ed. Irving A. Leonard (Mexico, 1963), pp. 46, 56, 65–8.

16 Sigüenza, *Paraíso occidental*, unpaginated prologue; his *Alonso Ramírez* is printed in *Obras históricas*, pp. 1–76.

17 Carlos de Siguenza y Góngora, *Relaciones históricas*, ed. Manuel Romero de Terreros (Mexico, 1954), pp. 110–19, 151–5, 160–2.

18 *Ibid.*, pp. 123–4.

19 *Ibid.*, pp. 133, 137–9, 152–8, 171–2.

20 Sor Juana Inés de la Cruz, *Obras completas*, ed. Alfonso Méndez Plancarte, 4 vols. (Mexico, 1951–7), IV, 444.

21 Octavio Paz, *Sor Juana: Her Life and Her World* (London, 1988); Marié-Cécile Benassy-Berling, *Humanismo y religión en Sor Juana Inés de la Cruz* (Mexico, 1983).

22 Juan de Oviedo, *Vida exemplar, heroicas virtudes y apostólicos ministerios de el V. P. Antonio Núñez de Miranda* (Mexico, 1702), p. 133. This passage is reprinted in Francisco de la Maza, ed., *Sor Juana Inés de la Cruz ante la Historia* (Mexico, 1980), pp. 278–82.

23 Sor Juana de la Cruz, *Obras*, III, 3–21, 184–200; see Paz, *Sor Juana*, pp. 339–56.

24 Sigüenza, *Obras históricas*, pp. 246–7.

25 Agustín de Betancur, 'Tratado de la Ciudad de México', printed with separate pagination in his *Teatro mexicano*, BP 45, facsimile of 1697–8 edn (Mexico, 1971), pp. 3–4, 40–1.

26 Baltazar de Medina, *Chrónica de la santa provincia de San Diego* (1682), pp. 230–1, 235.

27 Juan Ignacio María de Castorena Ursúa y Goyeneche, *Gacetas de México*, ed. Francisco González de Cossío, 3 vols. (Mexico, 1949), I, 33–5, 135–7, 150–1, 191–4.

28 Eliza Vargas Lugo, *La iglesia de Santa Prisca de Taxco* (Mexico, 1974); Anthony Blunt *et al.*, *Baroque and Rococo, architecture and decoration* (London, 1978), pp. 299–328.

29 Matías de Escobar, *Americana thebaida*, ed. Nicolás B. Navarrete (2nd edn, Morelia, 1970), pp. 194, 244, 296–302, 312, 374, 456.

30 Huizinga, *The Waning of the Middle Ages*, pp. 275–321; D. A. Brading, *Myth and Prophecy in Mexican History* (Cambridge, 1984), pp. 32–5.

31 Isidro Sariñana, *El llanto del Occidente en el ocaso del más claro sol de las Españas; demostraciones fúnebres de México en las exequias del Sr. Felipe IV* (Mexico, 1666), pp. 99–110; Gemelli Careri, *Viaje*, p. 22; Francisco de Ajofrín, *Diario del viaje que hizo a la América* (Mexico, 1964), pp. 61–6.

32 Félix Isidro de Espinosa, *Crónica de los colegios de propaganda fide de la Nueva España*, ed. Lino Gómez Canedo (2nd edn, Washington, 1964), pp. 677–80, 746–7, 776.

33 *Ibid.*, pp. 569–71, 608–9.

34 Cabrera, *Escudo de armas*, pp. 212–13; José Mariano Beristain de Souza, *Biblioteca hispano-Americana septentrional*, 5 vols. in 2 (third edn, Mexico, 1957), II, 240.

35 Gemelli Careri, *Viaje*, pp. 63–4; Ajofrín, *Viaje*, pp. 77, 213–14.

36 José de Rivera Bernárdez, *Descripción muy breve de la muy noble y leal ciudad de Zacatecas* (Mexico, 1732), p. 17; D. A. Brading, 'The city in Bourbon Spanish America: elite and masses', *Comparative Urban Research*, 8 (1980), pp. 71–85.

37 Betancur, *Teatro mexicano*, unpaginated introduction, II, 91–100.

38 Cabrera, *Escudo de armas*, pp. 60–72, 74–7.

39 Gemelli Careri, *Viaje*, p. 22.

40 Vicente P. Andrade, *Ensayo bibliográfico mexicano del siglo XVII*, facsimile of 1889 edn (Mexico, 1971), pp. 654–68.

41 Juan Antonio de Ahumada, *Representación política-legal a la majestad del Sr. D. Felipe V en favor de los españoles americanos* (Madrid, 1725). I have only been able to consult the mss. copy in Biblioteca Nacional (Mexico), mss. 1187; references are to ff. 7–14, 23–5, 32, 36, 54, 61.

42 Benito Jerónimo Feijoo Montenegro, *Teatro crítico universal*, 8 vols. (8th edn, Madrid, 1753–5), III, 110–25.

43 Ajofrín, *Viaje*, 82, 85.

44 AGI, Mexico 1337, Count of Fuenclara to Crown, 28 February 1743; see also Alvaro Matute, *Lorenzo Boturini y el pensamiento de Vico* (Mexico, 1976), *passim*; Benjamin Keen, *The Aztec Image in Western Thought* (New Brunswick, New Jersey, 1971), pp. 225–40.

45 Lorenzo Boturini Benaduci, *Idea de una nueva historia general de la América Septentrional*, ed. Miguel León-Portilla (Mexico, 1974). This edition prints the Valencia *discurso*, and has a valuable introduction; see pp. lxvi–lxvii, lxxi; also Lorenzo Boturini Benaduci, 'Historia general de la América Septentrional' in Manuel Ballesteros Gaibros, ed., *Documentos inéditos para la historia de España: Papeles de Indias*, vols. V and VI (Madrid, 1947–9), I 25–6.

46 García, *Origen de los Indios*, pp. 199, 248–54.

47 Giambattista Vico, *The New Science*, 3rd edn of 1744, ed. T. G. Bergin and M. H. Fisch (Cornell, Ithaca, New York, 1968), pp. 31–6; Leon Pompa, *Vico: a study of the 'New Science'* (Cambridge, 1975), pp. 8–11.

48 Vico, *New Science*, pp. 36, 65–8, 85–6, 93, 106–11.

49 Boturini, *Idea*, pp. 33, 77–91.

50 Boturini, 'Historia', II, 144, 163, 172, 187; *Idea*, pp. 87, 103.

51 Boturini, *Idea*, pp. 131, 147–50.

52 Mariano (Fernández de Echeverría y) Veytia, *Historia antigua de México*, ed. C. F. Ortega, 2 vols. (2nd edn, Mexico, 1944), I, 34; Veytia, *Baluartes de México*, p. 66; Mariano Fernández de Echeverría y Veytia, *Historia de la fundación de la ciudad de la Puebla de los Angeles*, ed. Efraín Castro Morales, 2 vols. (Puebla, 1962), I, xxiii; II, 55–69, 292–3.

53 Veytia, *Historia antigua*, I, 35, 68–71.

54 *Ibid.*, I, 109, 149, 156, 207–9, 230.

55 *Ibid.*, I, 115–39, 175–88, 289, 315–29; II, 40–1, 139, 164, 182.

56 Beristain, *Biblioteca*, II, 52–3.

57 Juan José de Eguiara y Eguren, *Prólogos a la biblioteca mexicana*, ed. Agustín Millares Carlo (Mexico, 1944), pp. 66–7, 72, 77–8, 92–3.

58 *Ibid.*, pp. 101–20, 167, 178, 191.

59 *Ibid.*, pp. 142–6, 199, 219–20.

18 PERUVIAN ECLIPSE

1 Pedro de Peralta Barnuevo y Rocha, *Imagen política del gobierno del Exmo. Señor D. Diego Ladrón de Guevara* (Lima, 1714), pp. 43–4, 64–6, 80, 94; Pedro de Peralta Barnuevo, *Obras dramáticas*, ed. Irving A. Leonard (Santiago de Chile, 1937), pp. 261, 350–1, 358–71.

2 Luis Alberto Sánchez, *El Doctor Océano* (Lima, 1967), pp. 15–50, 77; his library p. 99; citation p. 242; Pedro de Peralta Barnuevo Rocha y Benavides, *Lima fundada o conquista del Perú*, 2 vols. (Lima, 1732), unpaginated prologue.

3 Peralta, *Imagen política*, pp. 46–9; Peralta, *Lima fundada*, II, 259.

4 Peralta, *Lima fundada*, I, 47; II, 259, 347–9, 355, 472; cclxxi–vi.

5 Peralta, *Imagen política*, pp. 82–6; Peralta, *Lima fundada*, II, canto 7, cclxxxi; canto 10, cxvi, note 67 on nobility.

6 Pedro de Peralta Barnuevo y Rocha, *Júbilos de Lima y fiestas reales* (Lima, 1723), unpaginated throughout.

7 Pedro de Peralta Barnuevo y Rocha, *Historia de España vindicada* (Lima, 1730), pp. 2, 150–8, 191, 660–705, 1214–15.

8 *Memorias de los virreyes que han gobernado el Perú*, ed. Manuel A. Fuentes, 6 vols. (Lima, 1859), III, 56–364; for Peralta's praise of Castelfuerte as his Maecenas see his *Lima fundada*, prologue.

9 Fuentes, *Memorias*, III, 56, 169–71, 242; for Huancavelica *mita*, pp. 153–61.

10 *Ibid.*, III, 132–4, 169–82.

11 *Ibid.*, III, 238–46.

12 *Ibid.*, III, 246–63.

13 Pedro de Peralta Barnuevo y Rocha, *Lima inexpugnable*, ed. Luis Antonio Eguiguren Escudero (2nd edn, Lima, 1966), xxv, xxxii.

14 Fuentes, *Memorias*, III, 278–83, 292–324.

15 *Ibid.*, III, 65–80, 99, 104–19.

16 Peralta, *Relación del auto de Fe* (Lima, 1733), unpaginated.

17 Fuentes, *Memorias*, III, pp. 59–61, 126–9, 139–41.

18 Bartolomé Arzáns de Orsúa y Vela, *Historia de la villa imperial de Potosí*, ed. Lewis Hanke and Gunnar Mendoza, 3 vols. (Providence, Rhode Island, 1965), I, xxxiv–xlviii. I am indebted to Gunnar Mendoza's introduction.

19 Arzáns, *Historia*, I, 3, 7–10, 63–5, 158–68.

20 *Ibid.*, I, 10, 64; II, 416, 420, 443; III, 59.

21 *Ibid.*, II, 156, 321–2; III, 119; on mines as hell, I, 65.

22 *Ibid.*, III, 82–99.

23 *Ibid.*, III, 86.

24 *Ibid.*, II, 144–6; III, 339–42.

25 *Ibid.*, II, 147, 202–3, 342; III, 180–1, 261.

26 *Ibid.*, III, 185–8.

27 *Ibid.*, on invented historians and civil war see introduction, I, xlix–lx, lvii–viii; on Masque, I, 268–76; on Basques, I, 337–9.

28 *Ibid.*, on Europeans, I, 201; II, 157; III, 74, 80, 365; on creoles, II, 161, 333–4.

29 *Ibid.*, I, 12–6, 20–1, 31.

30 *Ibid.*, I, 30–52; on Toledo I, 145, 154–5; on Mexico and Peru I, 94; citation II, 139.

31 *Ibid.*, II, 10–16, 189.

32 *Ibid.*, I, 94; II, 190, 407–8, 412, 417, 435; citation, III, 317.

33 *Ibid.*, III, 330, 344; on Antequera, III, 171, 195, 327–30.

34 *Ibid.*, III, 317–24; see also Scarlett O'Phelan Godoy, *Rebellions and Revolts in Eighteenth-Century Peru and Upper Peru* (Cologne, 1985), pp. 58–85.

35 *Ibid.*, III, 73, 368, 393–5.

36 *Ibid.*, II, 363, 386; on Bodin, III, 10.

37 *Ibid.*, III, 166, 343; II, 253.

38 Esquivel, *Noticias*, I, 4–7, 60, 65; on Toledo I, 229–41; II, 90–6.

39 *Ibid.*, II, 220–4, 264–6, 344, 347.

40 *Ibid.*, I, xxi–xxxix for father; for *repartimientos*, I, 216; II, 239, 249; on Castelfuerte, II, 280; on Juan Santos, II, 276, 295, 300, 342.

41 Ignacio Castro, *Relación de la fundación de la Real Audiencia del Cuzco*, ed. Carlos Daniel Valcárcel (Lima, 1978), pp. 13, 17–18, 148–53, 162–76; see also Daniel Valcárcel, *Ignacio de Castro* (Lima, 1953), *passim*.

42 Castro, *Relación*, pp. 49–51, 59–61, 79–90.

43 *Ibid.*, pp. 17–24, 34–5, 41–2, 67.

44 Juan de Velasco, *Historia del reino de Quito*, 3 vols. (Quito, 1946), I, 101–3.

45 *Ibid.*, I, 196–9, 202, 214–15, 267.

46 *Ibid.*, I, 255; Juan de Velasco, *Historia del reino de Quito en la América Meridional*, ed. Alfredo Pareja Diezcanseco, BA 82 (Caracas, 1981). This edition prints only Parts II and III of the *Historia*, see pp. 11–17, 31.

47 Velasco, *Historia*, (1981), pp. 19–36, 54, 59–60, 69.

48 *Ibid.*, pp. 98–9, 107, 112; on Quito, pp. 141–5, 155, 175, 235–6; on Tupac Amaru, pp. 483–6.

49 *Ibid.*, pp. 158, 205, 147, 241, 243–4.

50 *Ibid.*, pp. 244–50, 284–96.

51 *Ibid.*, pp. 301–16.

52 *Ibid.*, pp. 325, 330–3; on riot, pp. 334–7.

53 *Ibid.*, pp. 422–35; citation p. 427; 447.

54 *Ibid.*, pp. 403–12, 459–60, 481–2, 522–5, 537–8; on Jesuit recruitment pp. 501–2, 512–14; on Lucero, pp. 495, 446.

55 *Ibid.*, pp. 328–9, 347, 356, 416.

19 HISTORY AND PHILOSOPHY

1 Charles-Marie de la Condamine, *Journal du voyage fait por ordre du Roi a l'Equateur servant d'introduction a la mesure des trois premiers degrés du Méridien* (Paris, 1751), pp. 85, 127–8; see also Victor W. von Hagen, *South America Called Them* (London, 1949), pp. 3–108.

2 Charles-Marie de la Condamine, *Relation abrégée d'un voyage fait dans l'intérieur de l'Amérique Méridionale* (Maestricht, 1778), pp. 50–5.

3 Feijoo, *Teatro crítico*, IV, 378, 384; V, 248–93; VII, 15, 319–24.

4 Jorge Juan, *Observaciones astronómicas y phísicas hechas de orden de S.M. en los reynos del Perú* (2nd edn, Madrid, 1773), the introduction presents his biography.

5 Arthur P. Whitaker, 'Antonio de Ulloa', *HAHR*, 15 (1935), pp. 155–94; there is an attractive description of Ulloa in Joseph Townsend, *A Journey through Spain in the years 1786 and 1787*, 3 vols. (London, 1792), II, 152.

6 Amédée François Frezier, *A Voyage to the South Seas in the years 1712, 1713 and 1714* (London, 1717), pp. 126, 228–31, 250–3; Jorge Juan and Antonio de Ulloa, *Relación histórica del viaje a la América meridional*, 5 vols. (Madrid, 1748), II, 45–7, 70–81.

7 Juan and Ulloa, *Viaje*, I, 47.

8 *Ibid.*, I, 541, 542–60.

9 *Ibid.*, II, 506–13.

10 Antonio de Ulloa, *Noticias americanas* (Buenos Aires, 1944), pp. 14, 19, 83–4, 112, 229–37.

11 *Ibid.*, pp. 175–6, 187–205.

12 *Ibid.*, pp. 8, 176, 244–56, 159, 260, 290, 306–13, 293 301.

13 *Ibid.*, 176, 211, 263–7.

14 Cornelius de Pauw, *Recherches philosophiques sur les Américains*, 3 vols. (London, 1771), I, iv, xii; on Pauw see Antonello Gerbi, *The Dispute of the New World. The History of a Polemic 1750–1900*, trans. Jeremy Moyle (Pittsburgh, 1973), pp. 52–80.

15 Cornelius de Pauw, *Philosophical Dissertations on the Egyptians and Chinese*, 2 vols. (London, 1795), I, 5–9, 240; II, 166, 179, 292.

16 Georges-Louis Leclerc Buffon, *Natural History*, 10 vols. (London, 1747), I, 211; IV, 312–39; VII, 15, 48.

17 Pauw, *Recherches*, I, 5–12, 24–7, 128–34; I, 40–77, 173.

18 *Ibid.*, I, 115–21, 85, 131–4; II, 147–53.

19 *Ibid.*, on Las Casas, I, 18, 144–5; on Acosta, I, 122, II, 307; on Jesuits, II, 405–10.

20 *Ibid.*, on Garcilaso, I, 78–80, 259, II, 143; on Incas, II, 181–91; on Aztecs, II, 201–7; on creoles, II, 157–60, III, 176.

21 *Ibid.*, I, 140; III, 170, 410, 449; see also Hippocrates, *Airs, Waters, Places*, Loeb Library (London, 1973), pp. 107, 115, 121–37.

22 Robertson, *The Works of William Robertson D.D.*, III, 12–13, 74, 133, 168–9; see Dugald Stewart, *Account of the Life and Writings of William Robertson D.D.* (2nd edn, London, 1802), pp. 108, 117–18, 274.

23 Robertson, *Works*, VI, 61, 200–18, 397–9; VII, 172, 210–15, notes 7.

24 Ronald L. Meek, *Social Science and the Ignoble Savage* (Cambridge, 1976), pp. 113–17, 151–3; Duncan Forbes' introduction to Adam Ferguson, *An Essay on the History of Civil Society*, ed. Duncan Forbes (Edinburgh, 1966), xx–xxiv; Dugald

Stewart, *The Works*, 7 vols. (Cambridge, 1829), VII, 30–2; Robertson, *Works*, VI, 259.

25 Robertson, *Works*, VI, 246, 260, 298; Meek, *Social Science*, p. 22.

26 Robertson, *Works*, VI, 383, 236–42, 284–316, 320, 383–5; for Ulloa and Condamine, VI, 423–8.

27 Jean-Jacques Rousseau, *The Social Contract and Discourses* (Everyman edn, London, n.d.), pp. 135–6, 214–15.

28 Pernety's dissertation is printed in Pauw, *Recherches*, III; see III, 135–7.

29 Robertson, *Works*, VI, 321, 247, 354–62; Meek, *Social Science*, pp. 82–9.

30 Joseph François Lafiteau, *Customs of the American Indians compared with the Customs of Primitive Times*, ed. and trans. by W. N. Fenton and E. L. Moore, 2 vols. (Toronto, 1974), I, 90, 100, 278.

31 Pauw, *Recherches*, II, 73; Pauw, *Dissertations on Egyptians*, I, 320; II, 121, for a sharp critique of Kircher.

32 Robertson, *Works*, VII, 248–9.

33 *Ibid.*, VII, 256, 260–1, 265–6, 270–1.

34 *Ibid.*, VII, 286–9, 300–2.

35 *Ibid.*, VI, xiii–iv, 431; VII, Notes, 3, 16–7, 25, 29–32.

36 *Ibid.*, VII, 340, 350–4; Notes, 48.

37 *Ibid.*, VII, 384, 389–91, 402; Notes, 58.

38 Alexander Carlyle, *Autobiography*, ed. John Hill Burton (London, 1910), pp. 129, 301.

39 Guillaume-Thomas Raynal, *A Philosophical and Political History of the Settlements and Trade of the Europeans in the East and West Indies*, trans. J. O. Justamond, 6 vols. (3rd edn, London, 1798), II, 349–51, I, 1–4.

40 *Ibid.*, I, 24; II, 221–2, 413; III, 1–2; IV, 43; VI, 295–6.

41 *Ibid*, VI, 458; see Hans Wolpe, *Raynal et sa Machine de Guerre: l'histoire des Deux Indes et ses perfectionnements* (Paris, 1956), pp. 10–29, 72, 129–30.

42 *Ibid.*, V, 137, 292–302; Gerbi, *Dispute of the New World*, pp. 45–50.

43 *Ibid.*, II, 381, 398–404; III, 18, 25–32; II, 406.

44 *Ibid.*, II, 376, 409; III, 14, 32, 129–32, 189, 214–23, 232.

45 *Ibid.*, III, 62, 197 on Las Casas; III, 148–87, 233–62.

46 *Ibid.*, III, 193; IV, 33, 97–109, 116–29.

47 *Ibid.*, III, 458–85; IV, 472–3.

48 *Ibid.*, VI, citation from Paine p. 163; see also *The Thomas Paine Reader*, ed. Michael Foot and Isaac Kramnick (London, 1987), p. 86.

20 JESUIT PATRIOTS

1 Thomas Jefferson, *The Writings*, Library of America (New York, 1984), pp. 169–82, 184–9, 190–2, 800–1; Gerbi, *Dispute of New World*, pp. 242–3.

2 Velasco, *Historia* (1946), I, 14–15, 109, 120–8, 247–56.

3 *Ibid.*, I, 271–95.

4 Juan Ignacio Molina, *The Geographical, Natural and Civil History of Chile*, 2 vols. (London, 1809), I, xvi–xvii, 30–1, 273; II, 19–25, 55–8, 81, 104, 168; Gerbi, *Dispute of the New World*, pp. 212–16.

5 *Mercurio Peruano*, 31 (12 April 1791), p. 282.

6 Hipólito Unánue, *Obras científicas y literarias*, 3 vols., facsimile of 1914 edn (Lima, 1975), I, 39, 67–8, 73–5, 79, 174.

7 Gerbi, *Dispute of the New World*, pp. 233–9.

8 Pedro José Márquez, *Sobre lo bello en general y dos monumentos de arquitectura mexicana, Tajín y Xochicalco*, ed. Justino Fernández (Mexico, 1972), pp. 132–3, 152–3.

9 Francisco Javier Clavijero, *Historia antigua de México*, ed. Mariano Cuevas (Mexico, 1964), pp. xviii, xxi, 422; Charles E. Ronan, *Francisco Javier Clavijero S.J. (1731–1787). Figure of the Mexican Enlightenment. His Life and Works* (Rome, 1977), pp. 16–28, 60–76; Luis Villoro, *Los grandes momentos del indigenismo en México* (2nd edn, Mexico, 1979), pp. 93–126.

10 Clavijero, *Historia*, pp. 11, 25, 455–72, 478–93.

11 *Ibid.*, pp. 34–41.

12 *Ibid.*, pp. 201, 423, 525; Francisco Javier Clavijero, *Historia de la antigua o Baja California*, ed. Miguel León-Portilla (Mexico, 1970), pp. 52–3.

13 Clavijero, *Historia*, pp. 45–7, 503–10, 517–19.

14 *Ibid.*, pp. 239–43, 525, 542–7.

15 *Ibid.*, pp. xxv–xxxvii.

16 *Ibid.*, pp. xxxv–xxxvii, 193–4, 248, 531–6.

17 *Ibid.*, pp. xvii, xxx; Ronan, *Clavijero*, pp. 188–9; Julio Le Reverend Brusone, 'La historia antigua de Mexico del Padre Francisco Javier Clavijero', in Díaz-Thomé, *Estudios de historiografía*, pp. 293–323.

18 Clavijero, *Historia*, pp. 86, 159–93, 571–9, 93–126; for Muñoz' critique see Ronan, *Clavijero*, pp. 164–5; also Frank E. Manuel, *The Eighteenth-Century Confronts the Gods* (Harvard, 1959), pp. 42–4, 103–8.

19 Clavijero, *Historia*, pp. 48–66, 203–6, 210–31, 241–3, 444, 553–4.

20 *Ibid.*, pp. 103–4, 113–14.

21 *Ibid.*, pp. 147, 525–6; citation, 45, 201; Ronan, *Clavijero*, p. 214; John Leddy Phelan, 'Neo-Aztecism in the eighteenth century and the genesis of Mexican nationalism' in Stanley Diamond, ed., *Culture in History: Essays in Honour of Paul Radin* (New York, 1960), pp. 764–70.

22 Clavijero, *Historia*, pp. 151–2, 288–92, 428–37.

23 *Ibid.*, pp. xxix, 325–7, 336–7, 344, 356, 362–3.

24 *Ibid.*, pp. 418, 568.

25 *Ibid.*, pp. 431–2.

26 *Ibid.*, p. 213.

27 Antonio de León y Gama, *Descripción histórica y cronológica de las dos piedras*, facsimile of 1792 and 1832 edns (Mexico, 1978), unpaginated introduction.

28 AGI, Mexico 1883, Gama to Crown, 26 September 1790.

29 Gama, *Descripción*, pp. 15–30, 47, 60; José Fernando Ramírez, 'Notas y esclarecimientos' in William H. Prescott, *Historia de la conquista de México*, ed. Juan A. Ortega y Medina (Mexico, 1970), p. 658.

30 Gama, *Descripción*, pp. 33–4, 48, 85–6; Part II, pp. 3–4, 108.

21 THE NEW STATE

1 Biblioteca Nacional (Madrid), mss. 3650–1, City Council of Mexico to Crown, February 1766.

2 D. A. Brading, *Miners and Merchants in Bourbon Mexico 1763–1810* (Cambridge, 1971), pp. 25–8.

3 *Ibid.*, p. 26; Baron de Montesquieu, *The Spirit of the Laws*, trans. Thomas Nugent, 2 vols. in 1 (New York, 1949), I, 372.

4 Jerónimo de Ustariz, *Theórica y práctica de comercio y de marina* (3rd edn, Madrid, 1757), pp. 4, 46, 96, 238.

5 José del Campillo y Cosío, *Nuevo sistema de gobierno económico para la América* (Madrid, 1789), p. 32.

6 Jorge Juan and Antonio de Ulloa, *Noticias secretas de América*, 2 vols., continuous pagination, facsimile of 1826 edn (Madrid, n.d.), I, 93–106, 223; Arthur P. Whitaker, 'Jorge Juan and Antonio de Ulloa's Prologue to their Secret Report of 1749 on Peru', *HAHR*, 18 (1938), pp. 507–13.

7 Juan and Ulloa, *Noticias secretas*, II, 238–88, 317.

8 *Ibid.*, II, 417–28, 434.

9 *Ibid.*, II, 490–518; see Luis Merino, *Estudio crítico sobre las 'Noticias secretas de América' y el clero colonial (1720–1765)* (Madrid, 1946), pp. 135–46.

10 Juan and Ulloa, *Noticias secretas*, II, 330, 364, 385–93, 406–8, 529–34.

11 *Ibid.*, II, 394–7, 432–42.

12 D. A. Brading, 'Bourbon Spain and its American Empire' in *Cambridge History of Latin America*, ed. Leslie Bethell, 5 vols. (Cambridge, 1984–6), I, 389–434.

13 Brading, *Miners and Merchants*, pp. 14–15, 26–30.

14 *Ibid.*, pp. 45–51.

15 *Ibid.*, pp. 86–9.

16 *Ibid.*, pp. 36–40.

17 Mark A. Burkholder and D. S. Chandler, *From Impotence to Authority: The Spanish Crown and the American Audiencias 1687–1808* (Columbia, Missouri, 1977), pp. 97–124.

18 Brading, *Miners and Merchants*, pp. 37–42.

19 On Rivadeneira see Beristain, *Biblioteca*, III, 210–12; also Félix Osores, 'Noticias bio-bibliográficas de alumnos distinguidos del Colegio de San Pedro, San Pablo y San Ildefonso de México' in Genaro García, *Documentos inéditos o muy raros para la historia de México*, BP 60 (2nd edn, Mexico, 1975), pp. 847–8.

20 Antonio Joaquín de Rivadeneira y Barrientos, *El Pasatiempo*, 3 vols. (Madrid, 1752–3), I, 64; II, 13–14, 105, 221, 256–7; III, 72, 233.

21 *Ibid.*, II, 241–51, 258–65, 268, 301, 337.

22 Antonio Joaquín de Rivadeneira y Barrientos, *Manual compendio del regio patronato indiano* (Madrid, 1755), pp. 13, 181–3, 266, 272–3.

23 'Representación humilde que hace la imperial, nobilísima y muy leal ciudad de México en favor de sus naturales (1771)' in *Colección de documentos para la historia de la guerra de independencia de México de 1808 a 1821*, ed. J. E. Hernández y Davalos, 6 vols., facsimile of 1877 edn (Mexico, 1985), I, 427–55; citation on p. 427; for identification of Rivadeneira as author see Mark A. Burkholder and D. S. Chandler, *Biographical Dictionary of Audiencia Ministers in the Americas, 1687–1821* (Westport, Conn., 1982), pp. 285–6, and their *From Impotence to Authority*, p. 98.

24 Hernández, *Colección*, I, 428–30.

25 *Ibid.*, I, 431–5, 437–8.

26 *Ibid.*, I, 441.

27 *Ibid.*, I, 444–6, 450–2.

28 Melchor Paz, 'Diálogo sobre los sucesos varios acaecidos en este reyno del Perú' in *Guerra separatista. Rebeliones de Indios en Sur América, la sublevación de Tupac Amaru*, ed. Luis Antonio Eguiguren, 2 vols. (Lima, 1952), I, 11–14; II, 263. On the Tupac Amaru rebellion see O'Phelan Godoy, *Rebellions and Revolts*, pp. 161–275; Flores Galindo, *Tupac Amaru II*, *passim*.

29 Paz, *Diálogo*, I, 222–3, 285; II, 104–5, 117, 127–36.

30 *Ibid.*, I, 85–7, 107–11, 132–7, 162, 188–92.

31 *Ibid.*, I, 421; II, 77–86; see John Leddy Phelan, *The People and the King. The Comunero Revolution in Columbia, 1781* (Madison, 1978), *passim*.

32 Paz, *Diálogo*, II, 293–357, 419–21; I, 103.

33 *Ibid.*, II, 388–418.

34 *Ibid.*, I, 206–7, 293–4; II, 185, 299, 419–21.

35 *Ibid.*, I, 244, 279, 341–6, 386–97, 433; II, 102.

36 *Ibid.*, II, 91–3, 107, 109–210, 263–5, 292, 297; I, 276, 412–16.

37 Daniel Valcárcel, *La rebelión de Tupac Amaru* (Mexico, 1965), pp. 42–7, 144.

38 Paz, *Diálogo*, I, 285–6, 250, 328–31, 361–2.

39 *Ibid.*, I, 405–6, 411.

40 *Tupac Amaru y la Iglesia: antología* (Lima, 1983), pp. 152–61.

41 *Ibid.*, pp. 270–2.

42 *Ibid.*, pp. 276–7; also Rowe, 'El movimiento nacional inca del siglo XVIII' in Flores Galindo, *Tupac Amaru II*, pp. 25–32.

22 ERASTIAN CHURCH

1 D. A. Brading, 'Tridentine Catholicism and enlightened despotism in Bourbon Mexico', *JLS*, 15 (1983), pp. 1–22.

2 *Ibid.*, pp. 8–10.

3 Serge Gruzinski, 'La "segunda aculturación": el estado ilustrado y la religiosidad indígena en Nueva España (1775–1800)', *Estudios de Historia Novohispana*, 8 (1985), pp. 175–200; AGI, Mexico 2714, Manuel Rubio y Salinas to Julián de Arriaga, 21 April 1756; Bergosa's printed pastoral can be found in AGI, Mexico 2651.

4 Cited in Gruzinski, 'La "segunda aculturación"', pp. 183–4; Brading, *Tridentine Catholicism*, pp. 17–19.

5 Brading, *Tridentine Catholicism*, p. 18.

6 This case can be found in Archivo General de la Nación, Historia 437.

7 Francisco Antonio de Lorenzana y Buitrón, *Cartas pastorales y edictos* (Mexico, 1770), pp. 38, 45, 68–71, 91–9.

8 Francisco Antonio Lorenzana y Buitrón, *Historia de Nueva España escrita por su esclarecida conquistador Hernán Cortés* (Mexico, 1770), pp. 1–3, 175.

9 Manuel Giménez Fernández, *El Concilio IV Provincial Mejicano* (Seville, 1939), pp. 34–8, 43–5; N. M. Farriss, *Crown and Clergy in Colonial Mexico, 1759–1821* (London, 1968), pp. 35–8.

10 Rivadeneira, *Manual compendio*, pp. 52, 74–5, 115–16, 132, 206.

11 Antonio Joaquín de Rivadeneira y Barrientos, *Disertaciones que el asistente real*

escribió sobre los puntos que se le consultaron por el cuarto concilio mejicano en 1774 (Madrid, 1881), pp. 5–18.

12 *Ibid.*, pp. 58–62.

13 *Tesoros documentales de México siglo XVIII: Priego, Zelis, Clavijero*, ed. Mariano Cuevas (Mexico, 1944), pp. 23–59, 234–97; Ludwig von Pastor, *The History of the Popes from the close of the Middle Ages*, trans. E. E. Peele, 40 vols. (London, 1950), XXXVII, 7–9, 99, 180–1, 414.

14 There is a copy of Lorenzana's pastoral in AGI, Mexico 1710, 26 September 1768; see also Giménez Fernández, *El concilio*, pp. 78–9; von Pastor, *History of the Popes*, XXXVIII, 239, 289.

15 Brading, *Miners and Merchants*, 34–5, 39–41, 233–5; Alegre, *Historia* IV, 16.

16 Javier Herrero, *Los orígenes del pensamiento reaccionario español* (Madrid, 1971), pp. 181–7.

17 AGI, Indiferente General 2973, Joaquín de Osma, 28 January 1765; on Palafox canonisation see von Pastor, *History of the Popes*, XXXVII, 409–13; on Franciscan–Jesuit rivalry see Joseph Blanco White (Leucadio Doblado), *Letters from Spain* (London, 1822), pp. 445–60.

18 Teófanes Egido, 'La expulsión de los jesuitas de España' in Ricardo García-Villoslada, *Historia de la Iglesia en España, IV. siglos XVII y XVIII* (Madrid, 1979), pp. 746–95.

19 Blanco White, *Letters from Spain*, pp. 447–9.

20 Owen Chadwick, *The Popes and the European Revolution* (Oxford, 1981), pp. 392–424; Teófanes Egido, 'El regalismo y las relaciones Iglesia–Estado en el siglo XVIII' in Ricardo García-Villoslada, ed., *Historia de la Iglesia*, IV, 125–253.

21 Feijoo, *Teatro crítico*, I, 189–215; II, 6–20; III, 97–9; VII, 319–26; Joel Saugnieux, *Les jansénistes et le renouveau de la prédication dans L'Espagne de la seconde moitié du XVIIIᵉ siècle* (Lyons, 1976), *passim*.

22 Cited in Giménez Fernández, *El concilio*, p. 168; AGI, Indiferente general 3041, 21 August 1769; see also Mario Góngora, 'Estudios sobre el Galicanismo y la "Ilustración católica" en América Española', *Revista Chilena de Historia y Geografía*, 125 (1957), pp. 96–151.

23 Alonso Núñez de Haro y Peralta, *Sermones escogidos, pláticas espirituales privadas y dos pastorales*, 3 vols. (Madrid, 1806), III, 79–80, 121, 150, 160.

24 *Ibid.*, III, 229–32, 240–2, 288–311.

25 Pedro Rodríguez Campomanes, *Tratado de la regalía de amortización* (Madrid, 1765), pp. 9, 23–5, 46, 57, 195–6, 212, 254.

26 Pedro Rodríguez Campomanes, *Dictamen fiscal de expulsión de los jesuitas de España (1766–1767)*, ed. Jorge Cejuda and Teófanes Egido (Madrid, 1977), pp. 51, 60–3, 70–3, 84–6, 147, 155–64.

27 *Ibid.*, pp. 52, 74, 97–115, 125, 129–35, 159–67.

28 Pedro Rodríguez Campomanes, *Juicio imparcial* ... (Madrid, 1769) pp. 12–13, 25, 47, 82–6, 94–100, 147–54, 319–20; see also Chadwick, *The Popes*, pp. 402–8.

29 Campomanes, *Juicio imparcial*, pp. 191–206, 211–20, 235–6.

30 *Ibid.*, prologue, pp. 57–8, 93–5, 154–9, 262–6, 300–8.

31 Pedro Rodríguez Campomanes, *Discurso sobre el fomento de la industria popular (1774); Discurso sobre la educación popular de los artesanos y su fomento (1775)*, ed. John Reeds (Madrid, 1975), pp. 16–18, 33–6, 51–6, 76, 83, 119–23.

32 *Ibid.*, pp. 60, 71–2, 90–5, 104–12, 130, 169–70, 246.

33 *Ibid.*, pp. 48, 112, 153–4, 169–70.

34 *Ibid.*, pp. 306–29.

35 Campomanes, *Tratado de la regalía*, unpaginated prologue; *Juicio imparcial*, p. 159; *Discursos*, pp. 23, 148; Saugnieux, *Les jansénistes*, p. 228.

36 Gaspar Melchor de Jovellanos, *Obras*, ed. Miguel Artola, BAE 46, 50, 85–7, 5 vols. (Madrid, 1951–6). See Artola's critical study in introduction of vol. III; also John H. R. Polt, *Gaspar Melchor de Jovellanos* (New York, 1971), *passim*.

37 *Jovellanos en la Real Academia de la Historia* (Madrid, 1911), pp. 258–83.

38 Jovellanos, *Obras*, II, 12–9; I, 104–5.

39 *Ibid.*, IV, 14–15; III, 256; I, 201–5, 215.

40 *Ibid.*, I, 350–1, 357, 372, 387.

41 *Ibid.*, I, 362–61, 372.

42 *Ibid.*, II, 120–1, 81–2.

43 *Ibid.*, 83–120.

44 Farriss, *Crown and Clergy*, pp. 163–96.

45 AGI, Mexico 1892, Archbishop to Crown, 24 October 1804; AGI, Mexico 2256, Archbishop to Crown, 10 April 1809.

23 SCIENTIFIC TRAVELLER

1 Douglas Botting, *Humboldt and the Cosmos* (London, 1973), pp. 142–61; Helmut de Terra, *The Life and Times of Alexander von Humboldt, 1769–1859*) (New York, 1955), p. 125.

2 Alexander von Humboldt, *Personal Narrative of Travels to the Equinoctial Regions of the New Continent during the years 1799–1804*, trans. Helen Maria Williams, facsimile of 1818–29 edn, 7 vols. in 6 (New York, 1966), III, 36, 126–46; IV, 293, 464–5; V, 290, 484–97; see also Gertrude Himmelfarb, *Darwin and the Darwinian Revolution* (New York, 1968), p. 46.

3 Hanno Beck, *Alexander von Humboldt* (Mexico, 1971), pp. 251, 311; Charles Minguet, *Alexandre de Humboldt: historien et géographe de l'Amérique espagnole 1799–1804* (Paris, 1969), *passim*.

4 George Forster, *A Voyage round the World in his Britannic Majesty's sloop Resolution commanded by Captain James Cook during the years 1772–75*, 2 vols. (London, 1777); Alexander von Humboldt, *Aspects of Nature in Different Lands and Different Climates*, 2 vols. (London, 1850), II, 301.

5 Humboldt, *Narrative*, V, 413; Beck, *Humboldt*, pp. 139, 153, 193–5, 227–8.

6 François de Pons, *Travels in South America*, 2 vols. (London, 1807), *passim*.

7 Humboldt, *Narrative*, III, 423–30; IV, 128, 189–239.

8 *Ibid.*, III, 363; IV, 311–43, 414; VI, 56; *Aspects of Nature*, I, 1–27.

9 Humboldt, *Narrative*, IV, 532–4; V, 74, 161, 234–8.

10 *Ibid.*, I, 292–4; III, 472–8; Alexander von Humboldt, *Cartas americanas*, ed. Charles Minguet, BA 74 (Caracas, 1980), pp. 69, 275.

11 Humboldt, *Cartas americanas*, pp. 85–107; *Narrative*, I, 233–4; Botting, *Humboldt*, pp. 142–64; Beck, *Humboldt*, pp. 193–205, 218–19.

12 Humboldt, *Narrative*, VII, 25–9, 99; 116, 144–58, 193–4, 261–5.

13 For a list of instruments see Humboldt, *Narrative*, I, 34–40; also Julián Adem,

'Humboldt y la geofísica' in Marianne O. de Bopp, *et al.*, *Ensayos sobre Humboldt* (Mexico, 1962), pp. 48–55; Botting, *Humboldt*, pp. 209, 254.

14 Beck, *Humboldt*, pp. 235–7; Humboldt, *Cartas americanas*, pp. 39–41; Barbara Maria Stafford, *Voyage into Substance. Art, Science, Nature and the Illustrated Travel Account 1760–1840* (Cambridge, Mass., 1984), pp. 92–3.

15 Beck, *Humboldt*, p. 398; Humboldt, *Narrative*, III, 146; V, 180; VI, 392.

16 Alexander von Humboldt, 'Essai sur la géographie des plantes', published as *Voyage de Humboldt et Bonpland. Première Partie* (Paris, 1807), *passim*; see also Margarita Bowen, *Empiricism and Geographical Thought from Francis Bacon to Alexander von Humboldt* (Cambridge, 1981), pp. 225–7.

17 Humboldt, 'Essai sur la géographie', p. 19; *Narrative*, III, 493–6; V, 180–3; *Aspects of Nature*, I, 14–15.

18 For the scientific background see Charles Coulston Gillespie, *Genesis and Geology* (Cambridge, Mass., 1951); Stephen Jay Gould, *Time's Arrow, Time's Cycle. Myth and Metaphor in the Discovery of Geological Time* (London, 1988).

19 Humboldt, *Essai sur la geographie*, pp. 139–40; *Narrative*, III, 14–15; V, 161, 271–2.

20 Humboldt, *Narrative*, III, 208–9; IV, 511–12; V, 14, 30, 46–7, 117; VI, 30; Alexander von Humboldt, *Cosmos*, 3 vols. (7th edn, London, 1849), III, 64–73; Forster, *Voyage round the World*, II, 287–318.

21 Alejandro de Humboldt, *Vistas de las cordilleras y monumentos de los pueblos indígenas de América*, ed. Jaime Labastida (Mexico, 1974), pp. 6–9.

22 *Ibid.*, pp. 97, 112, 130, 146–85.

23 *Ibid.*, pp. 101–2, 299, 370; also Alexander de Humboldt, *Examen critique de l'histoire de la géographie du Nouveau Continent et des progrès de l'astronomie nautique aux quinzième et seizième siècles*, 5 vols. (Paris, 1836–9), II, 68.

24 Freidrich Meinecke, *Historism. The Rise of a New Historical Outlook*, trans. J. E. Anderson (London, 1972), pp. 240–9; Humboldt, *Vistas*, pp. 79–83, 87, 95.

25 Alexander de Humboldt, *Ensayo político sobre el reino de la Nueva España*, ed. Juan A. Ortega y Medina (Mexico, 1966), pp. 352–7; Humboldt, *Cartas americanas*, pp. 219–20; Brading, *Miners and Merchants*, pp. 284–91.

26 Humboldt, *Ensayo político*, pp. 43–51, 103, 118–21, 210, 538, 556–7.

27 *Ibid.*, pp. 79–82, 121–2.

28 The intellectual foundations on which the *Political Essay* rests is his 'Tablas geográficas políticas del reino de Nueva España' (1804), for which see Enrique Florescano and Isabel Gil, eds., *Descripciones económicas generales de Nueva España 1784–1817* (Mexico, 1973), pp. 128–70.

29 Humboldt, *Ensayo político*, Bk. IV, pp. 320–441. This is still the starting point for all inquiry into the production of silver in the New World.

30 *Ibid.*, pp. 366–71, 352–71; Brading, *Miners and Merchants*, pp. 129–207, 261–302.

31 Humboldt, *Ensayo político*, pp. 472–97, 500–9.

32 *Ibid.*, pp. 31–51, 204–7.

33 *Ibid.*, pp. 5–6, 56–76, 95, 316–18.

34 *Ibid.*, pp. 76, 450.

35 *Ibid.*, pp. 6, 55–68.

36 *Ibid.*, pp. 316–18, 251–8, 449–58.

37 Humboldt, *Examen critique*, I, 3–5; IV, 99–108, 267–306; V, 170, 217–20.

38 *Ibid.*, I, 3, 55; II, 34; III, 155–9.

39 *Ibid.*, III, 10–12, 15–25, 228–35, 272–3.
40 Humboldt, *Cosmos*, I, 22–4, 355–6.
41 Beck, *Humboldt*, p. 237; Himmelfarb, *Darwin*, p. 47.

24 THE GREAT REBELLION

1 Juan Pablo Viscardo y Guzmán, *Carta dirigida a los Españoles americanos por uno de sus compatriotas*, ed. Rubén Vargas Ugarte (Lima, 1971), pp. 109, 118–19, 243–53.
2 Juan Pablo Viscardo y Guzmán, *Los escritos de Juan Pablo Viscardo y Guzmán, precursor de la independencia Hispanoamericana*, ed., Merle E. Simmonds (Caracas, 1983), pp. 167–9, 174–87, 206–30.
3 Simmons, ed., *Los escritos de Viscardo*, pp. 206–30.
4 *Ibid.*, pp. 188–98.
5 *Ibid.*, pp. 235–9, 190, 200–1.
6 *Ibid.*, pp. 283–9, 300, 317–20, 326–9, 333–45.
7 Viscardo, *Carta*, pp. 82–91, 97–9, 104–7, 122; see Simmons, *Los escritos de Viscardo*, p. 227 for definition of creoles as a nobility.
8 Viscardo, *Carta*, pp. 101–4, 110–16.
9 For the events of these years see Raymond Carr, *Spain 1808–1939* (Oxford, 1966), pp. 79–119; Francisco Martínez Marina, *Obras escogidas*, ed. José Martínez Cardos, BAE 194, 219, 2 vols. (Madrid, 1966–8), II, 14–16, 24–31.
10 Jovellanos, *Obras*, IV, 347, 377–80.
11 *Ibid.*, IV, 377.
12 *Ibid.*, I, 505–15, 533–8.
13 *Ibid.*, I, 549–54.
14 María Esther Martínez Quintero, *Los grupos liberales antes de las Cortes de Cádiz* (Madrid, 1978), pp. 151–8, 168–71; citation from p. 174.
15 Felipe Tena Ramírez, *Leyes fundamentales de México 1808–1967* (Mexico, 1967), pp. 60–1, 80; Martínez Quintero, *Los grupos liberales*, p. 183.
16 Jovellanos, *Obras*, IV, 471–3.
17 Martínez Marina, *Obras*, II, 28, 44.
18 Blanco White, *Letters*, p. 342; *The Life of the Rev. Joseph Blanco White*, ed. John Hamilton Thom, 3 vols. (London, 1845) I, 150.
19 Blanco White, *Life*, I, 184; Blanco White, *Letters from Spain*, p. 34; José María Blanco y Crespo, ed., *El Español*, 8 vols. (London, 1810–14), I, 229–32, 411–35; III, 268–70; IV, 372–88, 279–316.
20 Martin Murphy, *Blanco White. Self-Banished Spaniard* (New Haven, Conn., 1989), pp. 61–92; André Pons, 'Recherches sur Blanco White et l'Independance des Colonies Espagnoles D'Amerique' (thesis, La Sorbonne Nouvelle, Paris III, 1974), pp. 57–9.
21 Blanco y Crespo, *El Español*, II, 84–6, 101–27, 130–48, 166–200; III, 282–90; VIII, 239–52.
22 *Ibid.*, II, 49–54, 336–43.
23 *Ibid.*, II, 337–8; Blanco White, *Life*, I, 188.
24 Blanco y Crespo, *El Español*, IV, 26, 65–79, 109–32; James Ferguson King, 'The coloured castes at the Cortes of Cadiz', *HAHR*, 32 (1953), pp. 33–64.
25 *El Español*, I, 316; IV, 26, 44–6, 81–94.

26 *Ibid.*, V, 410–24; III, 22–35.

27 *Ibid.*, IV, 421; Blanco White, *Life*, I, 200.

28 Blanco White, *Life*, I, 141, 395; Murphy, *Blanco White* traces his spiritual journey with great delicacy.

29 Blanco White, *Letters*, pp. 40–2; Elizabeth, Lady Holland, *The Spanish Journal*, ed. The Earl of Ilchester (London, 1910), pp. 140–1; see also *La guerra de la independencia (1808–1814): su momento histórico*, 2 vols. (Centro de Estudios Montañés, Santander, 1982), II, 208–11, 617–50.

30 Blanco White, *Letters*, pp. 57–63, 118, 218–326; Blanco White, *Life*, I, 29–114; III, 116, 122–3.

31 Joseph Blanco White, *Variedades o mensagero de Londres* (London, 1823–5), I; (1824), 69, 115, 342.

32 *Obra inglesa de D. José María Blanco White*, ed. Juan Goytisolo (Buenos Aires, 1972), pp. 312–14, 316, 321.

33 Blanco White, *Life*, III, 457–66; Vicente Llorens Castillo, *Liberales y románticos. Una emigración española en Inglaterra (1823–1834)* (Mexico, 1954), pp. 327–51.

34 Marcelino Menéndez Pelayo, *Historia de los heterodoxos españoles*, 2 vols. (3rd edn, Madrid, 1978), II, 790–819, 1038.

35 Blanco White, *Life*, II, 278; Murphy, *Blanco White*, 198–201.

36 John Lynch, *The Spanish American Revolutions 1808–1826* (London, 1973), pp. 37–87.

37 Mariano Moreno, *Escritos políticos y económicos* (Buenos Aires, 1915), pp. 129–47, 155–8.

38 Manuel Moreno, *Vida y memorias de Mariano Moreno* (Buenos Aires, 1918), p. 247.

39 Manuel Lorenzo de Vidaurre, 'Plan de Perú y otros escritos', *Colección documental de la independencia I. Los ideólogos*, ed., Alberto Tauro, vol. 5 (Lima, 1971), pp. 217–27, 173–85, 300, 306.

40 Luis Durand Flores, *Criollos en conflicto. Cuzco después de Tupac Amaru* (Lima, 1985), pp. 42–8, 79–82, 150, 219–41.

41 Luis Herreros de Tejada, *El Teniente General D. José Manuel de Goyeneche Primer Conde de Guaqui* (Barcelona, 1923), pp. 466–505; citations on pp. 466–8, 485–9.

42 Gregorio Loza and Josep Barnardas, ed., *El conato revolucionario de 1805* (La Paz, 1976), pp. 46, 54–8, 67, 173–97; see also Alberto Flores Galindo, *Buscando un Inca: identidad y utopía en las Andes* (Lima, 1987), pp. 145–208.

43 Horacio Villanueva Urteaga, ed., 'La revolución del Cuzco de 1814', *Colección documental de la independencia del Perú. III. Conspiraciones y rebeliones en el siglo XIX*, vol. 6 (Lima, 1971), pp. 85, 105, 183–93, 306.

44 *Ibid.*, pp. 211, 216–18; Manuel Jesús Aparicio Vega, ed., *Colección documental de la independencia*, III, vol. 7 (Lima, 1974), pp. 24–5, 547–54, 568.

45 *Ibid.*, pp. 261–70.

46 Vidaurre, 'Escritos', pp. 245–62, 275, 292, 301, 309; Durand Flores, *Criollos en conflicto*, pp. 150–5.

47 Vidaurre, 'Escritos', pp. 9–10, 199–200, 360–5, 394, 425–39.

48 *Ibid.*, pp. 40–68, 96–107.

49 Dominique de Pradt, *Les Trois ages des colonies*, 2 vols. in 3 (Paris, 1801–2), I, xxviii, 182–3; II, 189–90, 203–17; III, 475–77, 509.

50 *Ibid.*, I, 20–3, 158–62; II, 22–7; III, 306, 371; also Dominique de Pradt, *Europe and America in 1821*, 2 vols. (London, 1822), p. 87.

51 Pradt, *Les Trois ages*, I, 57–80, 95–116; III, 382–3, 404–35.

52 Abbé de Pradt, *The Colonies and the Present American Revolution*, 2 vols. (London, 1817), I, viii–x, 402–3, 129, 301–4, 443.

53 Manuel Aguirre Elorriaga, *El Abate de Pradt en la emancipación hispanoamericana 1800–30* (Buenos Aires, 1946), pp. 68–74, 121, 228–9; Pradt, *Europe and America*, II, 156, 327.

25 LIBERALS AND PATRIOTS

1 Juan López de Cancelada, *Conducta de Iturrigaray ...* (Cadiz, 1812), p. 52; Servando Teresa de Mier, *Historia de la revolución de la Nueva España antiguamenta Anáhuac*, 2 vols. (London, 1813), I, xxxvi–xl, 42.

2 Lucas Alamán, *Historia de Méjico*, 5 vols. (4th edn, Mexico, 1968), I, 164.

3 AGI, Mexico 1472, Marquis of Rayas, 13 February 1809.

4 AGI, Mexico 2545, Archbishop Lizana, 20 February 1809.

5 Ernesto de la Torre Villar *et al.*, ed., *Historia documental de México*, 2 vols. (Mexico, 1964), II, 40–9.

6 Alamán, *Historia*, II, 391–3.

7 Francisco Severo Maldonado, 'El Despertador Americano' in *Periodismo insurgente*, 2 vols., facsimiles without continuous pagination (Mexico, 1976), I, pp. 4–5, 17, 27–8, 40 3.

8 Luis Castillo Ledón, *Hidalgo. La vida del Héroe*, 2 vols. (Mexico, 1948), I, 54–5, 69, 88; II, 279.

9 Lillian E. Fisher, *Champion of Reform. Manuel Abad y Queipo* (New York, 1955), *passim*.

10 'Escritos del Obispo electo de Michoacán Don Manuel Abad y Queipo', in vol. I of José María Luis Mora, *Obras sueltas*, 2 vols. (Paris, 1837), pp. 4–5, 25–6, 39–41, 44, 175–273.

11 *Ibid.*, pp. 6, 12, 22, 32–3, 64.

12 AGI, Mexico 2603, posthumous report of Bishop Antonio de San Miguel, 8 February 1805.

13 Abad y Queipo, 'Escritos', pp. 54–7, 61–2.

14 *Ibid.*, pp. 54–6.

15 AGI, Mexico 2603, 8 February 1805; Abad y Queipo, 'Escritos', p. 60.

16 Abad y Queipo, 'Escritos', pp. 80–1, 101–2.

17 *Ibid.*, pp. 86–9, 94–5.

18 *Ibid.*, pp. 146–9, 154–67.

19 Manuel Abad y Queipo, *Colección de los escritos más importantes que en diferentes épocas dirigió al Gobierno* (Mexico, 1813); *Escritos*, pp. 4–5, 25–6, 39–44; also Manuel Abad y Queipo, *Cartas pastorales*, separate pagination (Mexico, 1811–13), 'Edicto Instructivo', 30 September 1810; 'Carta pastoral', (1813), pp. 2, 34, 49.

20 Abad y Queipo, *Carta pastoral*, 15 February 1811, p. 12; *Carta pastoral*, (1813), pp. 6–7, 19, 23–5, 29.

21 *Ibid.*, *Carta* (1813), pp. 73–81, 88–101, 50–2.

22 AGI, Mexico 2571, last petition, 30 June 1825.

23 Juan López de Cancelada, *Ruina de la Nueva España* (Cadiz, 1811), pp. 23–6, 56–8.

24 *Ibid.*, pp. 81–3; Juan López de Cancelada, *El Telégrafo Mexicano* (Cadiz, 1813), pp. 18–20.

25 Juan López de Cancelada, *El Telégrafo Americano* (Cadiz, 1812), no. 20, 19 February 1812, p. 254.

26 José Miguel Guridi Alcocer, *El Censor extraordinario* (Cadiz, 1812), no. 59, pp. 2–27, 37, 133–5. This issue prints his speech to the Cortes of 8 January 1811.

27 Andrés Cavo, *Los tres siglos de México durante el gobierno español hasta la entrada del ejército trigarante*, ed. with supplement by Carlos María de Bustamante, 4 vols. (Mexico, 1836–8), III, 339–77. The last two volumes are written by Bustamante.

28 Servando Teresa de Mier, 'Cartas de un Americano', *El Español*, 11 November 1811, 26 May 1812, reprinted in vol. IV of José Eleuterio González, *Obras completas* (Monterrey, 1888), pp. 25, 47–50, 100–9, 150–61.

29 Mier, 'Cartas de un Americano', pp. 20, 82–5, 139, 40.

30 Andrés Quintana Roo, 'Semanario Patriótico americano', facsimile in *Periodismo insurgente*, pp. 12–165, where Mier's letters were reprinted by instalments, 13 September to 22 November 1812.

31 Carlos María de Bustamante, 'Correo Americano del Sur', facsimile in *Periodismo insurgente*, pp. 152–8, 209–20.

32 Cancelada, *El Telégrafo Mexicano*, p. 254; Bustamante, 'Correo Americano', pp. 194–5.

33 Quintana Roo, 'Semanario patriótico', pp. 12–22; Carlos María de Bustamante, *Cuadro histórico de la revolución mexicana*, 3 vols. (Mexico, 1961), I, 444.

34 Ernesto Lemoine Villacaña, *Morelos* (Mexico, 1965), pp. 13–31, 83–6, 181, 264.

35 *Ibid.*, pp. 184–90, 264.

36 *Ibid.*, pp. 365–79; citation on pp. 368–9. Bustamante wrote the speech, but Morelos corrected it, eliminating all reference to Ferdinand VII.

37 Tena Ramírez, *Leyes fundamentales*, pp. 31–5.

38 Bustamante, *Cuadro histórico*, I, 11; Guadalupe Jiménez Codinach, *México en 1821: Dominique de Pradt y el Plan de Iguala* (Mexico, 1982), pp. 131–43.

39 Tena Ramírez, *Leyes fundamentales*, pp. 113–19, 122–3.

26 INSURGENT CREOLE

1 Servando Teresa de Mier, *Obras completas: El heterodoxo guadalupano*, ed. Edmundo O'Gorman, 3 vols. (Mexico, 1981), I, 227–55.

2 *Ibid.*, II, 63–109; see also Nicolás León, *Bibliografía mexicana del siglo XVIII*, 5 vols. (Mexico, 1902–8), III, 195–351.

3 Mier, *Obras completas*, I, 119–22, 151, 165–71, 178–80.

4 Servando Teresa de Mier, *Memorias*, ed. Antonio Castro Leal, 2 vols. (Mexico, 1946), I, 108, 113, 231–8, 271–3; AGI, Mexico 1894, Alonso Haro to Crown, 24 February 1798; AGI, Mexico 1440, Branciforte to Crown, 1 May 1795.

5 D. A. Brading, *The Origins of Mexican Nationalism* (Cambridge, 1985), pp. 24–65.

6 Carlos María de Bustamante, *Continuación del cuadro histórico de la revolución mexicana*, ed. Jorge Gurría Lacroix, 4 vols. (Mexico, 1953–63), I, 92–3.

7 José Guerra (Servando Teresa de Mier), *Historia de la revolución de Nueva España*

antiguamenta Anáhuac, 2 vols. (Mexico, 1922), II, appendix i–xliii; Servando Teresa de Mier, *Escritos inéditos*, ed. J. M. Miquiel and Hugo Díaz Thomé (Mexico, 1944), p. 141.

8 Servando Teresa de Mier, *Escritos y memorias*, ed. Edmundo O'Gorman (Mexico, 1945), pp. 33–52.

9 For the dating of these letters see Mier, *Obras completas*, III, 59–88; for Valeriano see *Obras completas*, III, 177–82 and Mier, *Memorias*, I, 43.

10 See León, *Biblografía*, III, 253–560; Manuel Orozco y Berra, *Historia antigua y de la conquista de México*, ed. Angel María Garibay K., 4 vols. (Mexico, 1960), II, 430.

11 Mier, *Memorias*, II, 17; *Oeuvres de Don Barthélemi de las Casas*, ed. J. A. Llorente, 2 vols. (Paris, 1822), II, 345, 398–428; Ruth F. Necheles, *The Abbé Gregoire* (Westport, Conn., 1971), pp. 174, 246.

12 Henri Grégoire, *Mémoires*, 2 vols. (Paris, 1837), I, 321; II, 4, 51, 360; see also Henri Grégoire, *Histoire Patriotique des Arbres de la Liberté*, preceded by essay on his life and works by Charles Dugaste (Paris, 1833), p. 38.

13 Mier, *Memorias*, I, 206–7; also 'Cartas de un americano', pp. 137, 343–5.

14 Juan A. Mateos, *Historia parlamentaria de los congresos mexicanos*, 11 vols. (Mexico, 1978–86), II, 270–1; reprinted in *Pensamiento político del padre Mier*, ed. Edmundo O'Gorman (Mexico, 1945), p. 83.

15 *Discurso del doctor don Servando Teresa de Mier sobre la encíclica del Papa León XII* (5th edn, Mexico, 1825), *passim*.

16 Mier, *Escritos inéditos*, p. 376; *Cartas de un Americano*, p. 142; Mateos, *Historia parlamentaria*, I, 760, 774; II, appendix, 85.

17 AGI, Mexico 1894, September 1805; AGI, Mexico 2697, 29 March 1811.

18 Hernández, *Colección de documentos*, VI, 757, 806–26, 877–8; Murphy, *Blanco White*, p. 178.

19 Brading, *Origins of Nationalism*, pp. 67–70; Mier, *Cartas de un Americano*, p. 51.

20 Mier, *Historia de la revolución*, I, 238–40; *Memorias*, I, 106, 187–9.

21 Mier, *Historia de la revolución*, I, 298–9; II, 3–4, 104–5.

22 *Ibid.*, II, 321; Bartolomé de las Casas, *Destrucción de las Indias Occidentales*, with preliminary discourse by Servando Teresa de Mier (Mexico, 1822), p. 29.

23 Mier, *Historia de la revolución*, II, 166–7.

24 Mier, *Escritos inéditos*, p. 269; *Historia de la revolución*, II, 285.

25 Mier, *Historia de la revolución*, II, 197–9.

26 *Ibid.*, II, 273; *Cartas de un americano*, pp. 84, 324.

27 Mier, *Historia de la revolución*, II, 30; Servando Teresa de Mier, *Memoria político-instructiva enviada desde Filadelfia a los gefes independientes del Anáhuac llamado por los españoles Nueva España* (2nd edn, Mexico, 1822), pp. 124, 72.

28 For expedition see William David Robinson, *Memoirs of the Mexican Revolution* (Philadelphia, 1820); also Mier, *Memorias*, II, 61, 203; Alfonso Junco, *El increíble Fray Servando: psicología y epistolario* (Mexico, 1959), pp. 96, 135.

29 Hernández, *Colección de documentos*, VI, 839; see also Alamán, *Historia de Méjico*, V, 408.

30 Mier, *Memorias*, II, 52, 138, 146, 166 on Spain; II, 21, 38, 50 on France; *Memoria político-instructiva*, p. 89.

31 Mier, *Escritos inéditos*, pp. 83, 90–1, 158.

716   NOTES TO PAGES 597–611

32 Mier, *Memoria político-instructiva*, pp. 53–6; *Escritos inéditos*, pp. 382, 405–8.
33 Mier, *Memoria político-instructiva*, pp. 53, 81–3, 90–2; *Escritos inéditos*, pp. 382, 411.
34 Mateos, *Historia parlamentaria*, I, 732, 797; *Idea de la conspiración descubierta en la capital del imperio mexicano*, Anon. (Mexico, 1822), p. 12.
35 Mier, 'Epistolario' in Junco, *El increíble Fray Servando*, pp. 97, 164–6.
36 This speech is printed in Mier, *Pensamiento político*, pp. 127–32.
36 Tena Ramírez, *Leyes fundamentales*, pp. 154, 163, 165–66.
37 Mier, *Pensamiento político*, pp. 127–31.
38 *Ibid.*, p. 140.
39 Mier, *Epistolario*, p. 191.
40 *The Tom Paine Reader*, p. 65; Bernard Bailyn, *The Ideological Origins of the American Revolution* (Cambridge, Mass., 1971), pp. 34–53.

27 REPUBLICAN HERO

1 Lynch, *The Spanish American Revolutions*, pp. 157–84.
2 De Pons, *Travels in South America*, I, 361.
3 Miguel Izard, *El miedo de la revolución: la lucha para la libertad en Venezuela 1777–1830* (Madrid, 1979), *passim*; Lynch, *Spanish American Revolutions*, pp. 198–218.
4 Simón Bolívar, *Obras completas*, ed. Vicente Lecuna, 3 vols. (Caracas, 1964), II, 54; Gerhard Masur, *Simón Bolívar* (Albuquerque, New Mexico, 1968), is still the best life of the Liberator.
5 José Antonio Paéz, *Autobiografía*, 2 vols. (New York, 1870), I, 136, 141. On these caudillos see John Lynch, 'Bolívar and the Caudillos', *HAHR*, 63 (1983), pp. 3–36.
6 Bolívar, *Obras*, III, 647–8.
7 H.L.V. Ducoudray Holstein, *Memoirs of Simón Bolívar*, 2 vols. (London, 1830), II, 121, 167–72; L. Peru de la Croix, *Diario de Bucaramanga* (2nd edn, Lima, 1965), pp. 36, 39.
8 Croix, *Diario*, pp. 76–81.
9 Bolívar, *Obras* I, 662; Lynch, *Spanish American Revolutions*, pp. 266–90.
10 For this scene see Simón Rodríguez, *Obras*, ed. Pedro Grases, 2 vols. (Caracas, 1975), II, 328. Daniel Florencio O'Leary, *Bolívar y la emancipación de Sur-América*, 2 vols. (Madrid, 1915), I, 88; Bolívar, *Obras*, II, 139.
11 J. G. A. Pocock, *The Machiavellian Moment. Florentine Political Thought and the Atlantic Republican Tradition* (Princeton, 1975), pp. 48–82, 156–219; Montesquieu, *The Spirit of the Laws*, I, 8–27; on Rousseau see Judith N. Shklar, *Men and Citizens* (Cambridge, 1969), p. 212.
12 Niccolò Machiavelli, *The Prince* (London, 1961), pp. 52, 128, 135–6; Rousseau, *The Social Contract and other Discourses*, p. 38; Shklar, *Men and Citizens*, pp. 154–65.
13 Croix, *Diario*, pp. 42, 82–3.
14 Bolívar, *Obras*, I, 646; II, 176–8; Croix, *Diario*, pp. 71, 121–2; for the cult of the republican hero see Robert L. Herbert, *David, Voltaire, Brutus and the French Revolution* (London, 1972), pp. 70–1, 109; also Robert Rosenblum, *Transformations of Late Eighteenth-Century Art* (Princeton, 1967), pp. 70–2; Hugh Honour, *Neo-classicism* (London, 1968), pp. 34–6, 171.

15 Bolívar, *Obras*, I, 161–6.
16 *Ibid.*, I, 168–72.
17 *Ibid.*, I, 173–4.
18 *Ibid.*, III, 674–81.
19 *Ibid.*, III, 682–6.
20 *Ibid.*, III, 686–90; I, 442–3.
21 *Ibid.*, I, 551, 165–6; see Jaime Duarte French, *Poder y política en Colombia 1810–1827* (Bogotá, 1980), pp. 13–14, 130–6.
22 Bolívar, *Obras*, III, 729–30; Pedro Grases, 'Estudios Bolivarianos', vol. IV of *Obras completas* (Barcelona, 1981), pp. 367–84; Rodríguez, *Obras*, II, 310.
23 A contemporary English translation of the Bolivian Constitution can be found in John Miller, *Memoirs of General Miller*, 2 vols. (London, 1828), II, 404–39; see also Bolívar, *Obras*, III, 762–70; II, 294.
24 Bolívar, *Obras*, II, 88–91, 229, 364–7, 464; III, 294; see also Alexander Hamilton, J. Jay, and James Madison, *The Federalist* (Everyman Books, London, n.d.), no. 10, pp. 41–8.
25 Bolívar, *Obras*, III, 422–9; I, 683–5; II, 158; Paéz, *Autobiografía*, II, 34; see also, J. H. Hexter, *The Vision of Politics*, pp. 150–78.
26 Bolívar, *Obras*, I, 709; II, 116, 431.
27 *Ibid.*, II, 430; Bolívar cited this dictum in his Jamaica Letter, *Obras* I, 168; and in 1828, *Obras* II, 823. On dictatorship see *Obras*, II, 324, 486.
28 *Ibid.*, III, 501, 844–6.
29 *Ibid.*, III, 20–1; II, 214, 405; III, 255. The source of his horror at Sulla's reputation came from Montesquieu's 'Le dialogue de Sylla et d'Eucrate' published with *Considérations sur les causes de la grandeur des Romains et leur décadence* (Paris, 1954), pp. 139–45.
30 Thomas Carlyle, *Complete Works*, 17 vols (London, 1888), IV, 167, 178–83, 190–97.
31 Bartolomé Mitre, *Historia de San Martín y de la emancipación sudamericana*, 2 vols. (Buenos Aires, 1950), I, 55–6; II, 627, 887–97, 987–98; Croix, *Diario*, pp. 31–2; Rodríguez, *Obras*, II, 198, 242.
32 José Enrique Rodó, *Obras completas*, ed. Emir Rodríguez Monegal (Madrid, 1967), pp. 529–44; citations on pp. 551–3.

28 CIVILISATION AND BARBARISM

1 R. D. Keynes (ed.), *The Beagle Record* (Cambridge, 1979), pp. 148, 282.
2 Domingo Faustino Sarmiento, *Civilización y barbarie. Vida de Juan Facundo Quiroga*, colección Hispánica (New York, 1961), pp. 13–15, 44–5; Paul Verdevoye, *Domingo Faustino Sarmiento. Educateur et publiciste entre 1839 et 1852* (Paris, 1963), pp. 52–9, 89–91.
3 Sarmiento, *Facundo*, pp. 27–42, 58–62.
4 *Ibid.*, pp. 64, 113–18, 136, 145–7.
5 *Ibid.*, pp. 66–71, 88–94.
6 *Ibid.*, pp. 15–18, 36, 116–17, 143–51, 160.
7 *Ibid.*, pp. 88, 177, 221–7, 250.
8 Juan Bautista Alberdi, *Grandes y pequeños hombres del Plata* (Paris, n.d.), pp. 45, 139, 298, 312, 329–30; Alberdi, *Autobiografía* (Buenos Aires, 1927), p. 64; Alberdi,

Bases y puntos de partido para la organización de la República Argentina (Buenos Aires, 1943), pp. 67–8.

9 Sarmiento, *Facundo*, pp. 110–12.

10 Domingo Faustino Sarmiento, *Recuerdos de provincia*, ed. Guillermo Ara (Buenos Aires, 1966), pp. 147–66, 177.

11 Cited in Verdevoye, *Sarmiento*, p. 379.

12 On Cooper see Henry Nash Smith, *Virgin Land. The American West as Symbol and Myth* (Cambridge, Mass., 1970), pp. 59–70; Vernon L. Parrington, *The Romantic Revolution in America, 1800–1860* (New York, 1954), pp. 214–29; Charles François de Volney, *The Ruins: or, A survey of the revolutions of empires* (London, 1807), pp. 54–61.

13 Cited in Enrique Anderson Imbert, *Genio y figura de Sarmiento* (Buenos Aires, 1967), p. 122; Domingo Faustino Sarmiento, *Conflicto y armonías de las razas en América*, ed. José Ingenieros (Buenos Aires, 1915), pp. 409, 449.

14 Cited in Anderson Imbert, *Sarmiento*, pp. 17–18.

15 Sarmiento, *Recuerdos*, pp. 71, 94, 182, 205–6.

16 John Lloyd Stephens, *Incidents of Travel in Central America, Chiapas and Yucatan*, 2 vols. (London, 1841), I, 49, 62, 199–202, 247–50, 305, 360; II, 52, 89–91, 11–15, 207–9.

17 *Ibid.*, I, 102–3, 155–60; II, 291–300, 356, 437–55; see also Victor W. von Hagen, *Search for the Maya. The Story of Stephens and Catherwood* (Farnborough, 1973), pp. 110, 173.

18 Stephens, *Incidents*, I, 128; II, 13, 363.

19 Washington Irving, *A History of the Life and Voyages of Christopher Columbus*, 4 vols. (London, 1828), I, 4, 11, 50, 120–8; III, 286; IV, 51–9.

20 *Ibid.*, IV, 349, 359, 388; II, 52, 125–8.

21 George Ticknor, *Life of William Hickling Prescott* (Boston, 1864), pp. 190, 208; David Levin, *History as Romantic Art* (Stanford, 1959), *passim*.

22 William H. Prescott, *History of the Conquest of Mexico*, The Modern Library (New York, n.d.), pp. 21, 33, 52, 91, 103, 223, 714.

23 *Ibid.*, pp. 159, 171, 195, 415, 438, 531.

24 *Ibid.*, *History of the Conquest of Peru*, pp. 741–4, 762–3, 790, 817, 879–82, 988, 1124, 1232.

25 *Ibid.*, p. 829.

26 William H. Prescott, *Historia de la conquista de México, anotada por Don Lucas Alamán y con notas críticas y esclarecimientos de Don José Fernando Ramírez*, ed. with prologue by Juan A. Ortega y Medina (Mexico, 1970), pp. 34–5.

27 *Ibid.*, pp. 657–99.

28 Carlos María de Bustamante, *Cuadro histórico de la revolución mexicana*, 3 vols. (Mexico, 1961), I, 38–9, 336; III, 332.

29 For an invaluable list of Bustamante's writings see Edmundo O'Gorman, *Guía bibliográfica de Carlos María de Bustamante* (Mexico, 1967), pp. 39–51; Josefina Vásquez de Knauth, *Nacionalismo y educación en México* (Mexico, 1970), pp. 32–9, 78–9.

30 Bustamante, *Cuadro histórico*, I, 200–7; Cavo, *Los tres siglos de México*, III, 329.

31 Bustamante, *Cuadro histórico*, I, 37, 336–43, 367; II, 178–89, 214–22, 467.

32 *Ibid.*, I, 431–2, 596–7; II, 5, 35, 222–3, 724.

33 Ibid., I, 51, 130–2, 395–6; II, 264–5, 426–8, 540–3; III, 35–8, 341–3.

34 See O'Gorman, Guía bibliográfica, pp. 103–11.

35 Carlos María de Bustamante, Mañanas de la Alameda en México, 2 vols. (Mexico, 1835–6), II, 1.

36 Bernardino de Sahagún, Historia general de las cosas de la Nueva España, 3 vols. (Mexico, 1829–30). Mier's dissertation was inserted without pagination between pp. 277–9, vol. I; see also Bustamante, Mañanas de la Alameda, I, 108–20; Carlos Maria de Bustamante, La aparición guadalupana de México (Mexico, 1843), p. 69; on his editorial methods see Ernesto Lemoine's introduction to Carlos María de Bustamante, Texcoco en los ultimos tiempos de sus antiguos reyes, facsimile of 1826–7 edition (Mexico, 1970), pp. 9–51.

37 Bustamante, La aparición guadalupana, pp. 6–7, 61; see also Bustamante, La aparición de Nuestra Señora de Guadalupe de México (Mexico, 1840), pp. v–xvii.

38 Bustamante, Continuación del cuadro histórico, III, 340; IV, 42, 126, 133, 151, 157, 247.

39 Carlos María de Bustamante, Análisis crítico de la Constitución de 1836 (Mexico, 1842), p. 30; Bustamante, Abajo gente baldía gritan los reformadores ó sea defensa de las órdenes religiosas (Mexico, 1833), pp. 2–5, 15–16; Bustamante, Continuación del cuadro histórico, IV, 14, 18, 30, 242.

40 Carlos María de Bustamante, Juguetillo Octavo (Mexico, 1820), pp. 3–4, 8.

41 Bustamante, Continuación del cuadro histórico, III, 225–9; Carlos María de Bustamante, Representación que los vecinos emigrados de la villa de Chilapa han hecho ... (Mexico, 1845), pp. 3–6; Carlos María de Bustamante, El nuevo Bernal Díaz del Castillo ó sea historia de la invasión de los angloamericanos en México, 2 vols. (Mexico, 1847), I, 78.

42 Bustamante, Continuación del cuadro histórico, II, 228; III, 219–20, 443–6.

43 Ibid., IV, 53, 233, 372; Carlos María de Bustamante, Apuntes para la historia del gobierno del general D. Antonio López de Santa-Anna (Mexico, 1845), pp. 384–6.

44 Bustamante, El nuevo Bernal Díaz, II, 172; Cavo, Los tres siglos, III, 217–18.

45 Bustamante, El nuevo Bernal Díaz, I, 116–17, 134–45; II, 218, 223.

46 Ibid., I, 60; O'Gorman, Guia bibliográfica, pp. 22–7, 191.

47 Bustamante, Cuadro histórico, I, 327; II, 663.

48 See Ernesto Lemoine's introduction to Carlos María de Bustamante, Viaje a Toluca en 1834 (Mexico, 1969), pp. 37–8.

49 Lorenzo de Zavala, Ensayo crítico de las revoluciones de México desde 1808 hasta 1830, ed. Manuel González Ramírez, BP 30 (Mexico, 1969), pp. 7, 48; José María Luis Mora, México y sus revoluciones, ed. Agustín Yañez, 3 vols. (Mexico, 1950), III, 9.

50 Lucas Alamán, Disertaciones, 3 vols. (Mexico, 1969), I, 103, 109; Lucas Alamán, Documentos diversos, 4 vols. (Mexico, 1946), III, 315–19, 324–8.

51 Lucas Alamán, Historia de Méjico, 5 vols. (Mexico, 1969), IV, 461; V, 568.

52 Recollections of Service of Three Years during the War of Extermination in the Republics of Venezuela and Columbia by an officer of the Columbian Navy, Anon., 2 vols. (London, 1828), I, 185–6.

53 Zavala, Ensayo crítico, p. 579.

29 MEXICAN LEVIATHAN

1 Tena Ramírez, *Leyes fundamentales*, pp. 634–41, citation on p. 637; see also Edmundo O'Gorman, *La supervivencia política Novo-Hispana* (Mexico, 1969), pp. 60–1.

2 Mora, *Obras sueltas*, pp. 567–74, 587–94, 650–1; Mora, *México y sus revoluciones*, I, xix; Melchor Ocampo, *Obras completas*, ed. Angel Pola, 3 vols. (Mexico, 1978), III, 56; Charles Hale, *Mexican Liberalism in the Age of Mora, 1821–1853* (New Haven, Conn., 1968), pp. 56–77, 122.

3 Mora, *México y sus revoluciones*, II, 8–12, 168–70, 230; III, 8–25, 45–7, 253–5.

4 Mora, *Obras sueltas*, pp. 6–13, 27, 47, 57–61, 110; *México y sus revoluciones*, I, 88–94, 354–76.

5 Mora, *Obras sueltas*, pp. 121–7.

6 Mora, *México y sus revoluciones*, I, 457–68.

7 The dissertation is printed in Mora, *Obras sueltas*, pp. 278–319.

8 *Ibid.*, pp. 29, 84–9, 375–93.

9 *Ibid.*, pp. 280–7.

10 *Ibid.*, pp. 305–6; Mora, *México y sus revoluciones*, I, 46–8, 452–3.

11 Mora, *México y sus revoluciones*, I, 444–56; *Obras sueltas*, pp. 305–12.

12 Mora, *Obras sueltas*, pp. 335, 377; *México y sus revoluciones*, I, 281–5; Hale, *Mexican Liberalism*, pp. 178–9.

13 Mora, *México y sus revoluciones*, I, 66–72, 176–8.

14 *Ibid.*, I, 65–71, 168–74.

15 Mora, *Obras sueltas*, pp. 152–3; Hale, *Mexican Liberalism*, pp. 224–39.

16 Mora, *México y sus revoluciones*, I, 444.

17 Mariano Otero, *Obras*, ed. Jesús Reyes Heroles, BP. 33, 34, 2 vols. (Mexico, 1967), I, 35, 52, 58, 110.

18 *Ibid.*, I, 99, 124–7.

19 Ocampo, *Obras*, I, 32–6, 90–1, 106, 144, 146, 152. The whole volume deals with this dispute.

20 Jan Bazant, *Alienation of Church Wealth in Mexico: Social and Economic Aspects of the Liberal Revolution, 1856–1875* (Cambridge, 1971), pp. 53–94, 168, 182, 209.

21 Richard N. Sinkin, *The Mexican Reform, 1855–1876. A Study in Liberal Nation-Building* (Austin, Texas, 1979), pp. 172–3.

22 Tena Ramírez, *Leyes fundamentales*, pp. 610, 615, 625.

23 Jorge L. Tamayo, ed., *Epistolario de Benito Juárez* (Mexico, 1972), p. 496.

24 Cited in Sinkin, *The Mexican Reform*, pp. 86, 90; see also Justo Sierra, *Obras*, 14 vols. (Mexico, 1948), XIII, 274.

25 David R. Maciel, *Ignacio Ramírez. Ideólogo del liberalismo social en México* (Mexico, 1980), *passim*.

26 Luis González Obregón *et al, Homenaje a Ignacio M. Altamirano* (Mexico, 1935), pp. 3–19.

27 Ignacio M. Altamirano, 'Biografía de Ignacio Ramírez', in his *La literatura nacional*, ed. Antonio Castro Leal, 3 vols. (Mexico, 1949), II, 189–234. For the incident at the mint see Sierra, *Obras*, XIII, 268.

28 Ignacio M. Altamirano, *Discursos* (Paris, 1982), p. 32. Note there are two different collections of Altamirano's essays published with the same title, published respecti-

vely in 1949 and 1974. See Altamirano, *Paisajes y leyendas. Tradiciones y costumbres de México*, 2nd series (Mexico, 1949), p. 228.

29 Ignacio Ramírez, *Obras*, 2 vols. facsimile of 1889 edn (Mexico, 1966), II, 90–101, 111, 126, 159–61.

30 *Ibid.*, II, 226–46, 541–2.

31 Altamirano, *Discursos*, pp. 253–6.

32 See Andrés Molina Enríquez, *La Reforma y Juárez* (Mexico, 1906), pp. 72–6.

33 Ramírez, *Obras*, I, 190–1; II, 183, 192.

34 *Ibid.*, I, 136.

35 Ignacio M. Altamirano, 'Revista histórica y política' in Manuel Caballero, ed., *Primer almanaque histórico, artistico y monumental de la república mexicana* (New York, 1883–4), p. 5; Altamirano, *Biografía de D. Miguel Hidalgo y Costilla* (Mexico, 1960), pp. 10–3; also, Ramírez, *Obras*, I, 180–3, 317.

36 Pocock, *The Machiavellian Moment*, pp. 462–505.

37 Ramírez, *Obras*, I, 156. According to Juan Sánchez Azcona, Altamirano worshipped Victor Hugo as a 'demi-god': see González Obregón, ed., *Homenaje a Altamirano*, p. 79. Raoul Girardet defines this ideology as uniting 'le chauvinisme cocardier et le messianisme humanitaire' in his *Le Nationalisme français 1871–1914* (Paris, 1966), pp. 12–14. See also Jules Michelet, *Le Peuple*, ed. Lucien Refort (Paris, 1946), pp. 45, 71, 239–48, 262–6; Victor Hugo, *Les misérables*, 2 vols. (London, 1980), I, 316; II, 328, 351.

38 Altamirano, *Discursos*, pp. 59, 94, 109, 135, 368–74, 388–90; Ramírez, *Obras*, I, 148, 368–89.

39 Ramírez, *Obras*, I, 372, 411; II, 286–8, 355, 368, 392, 402, 495, 504.

40 Altamirano, *Discursos*, pp. 351–2; Altamirano, *Revista histórica y política*, pp. 60–3, 72–4.

41 Sierra, *Obras*, IV, 143, 230; IX, 165; XII, 395–6.

42 Francisco Bulnes, *El verdadero Juárez y la verdad sobre la intervención y el imperio* (Mexico, 1965), pp. 451, 652–4, 687, 823–6, 843–5, 857.

43 Francisco Bulnes, *Juárez y las revoluciones de Ayutla y de Reforma* (Mexico, 1967), pp. 16, 19–21, 302–10, 477, 258–76, 483.

44 Sierra, *Obras*, XIII, 187, 257–8, 268, 277.

45 Carlyle, *Complete Works*, IV, 167, 178–83, 190–7; Machiavelli, *The Prince*, pp. 52, 128, 135–6; Rousseau, *Social Contract*, 35–8.

46 Sierra, *Obras*, XII, 359; XIII, 565.

47 Altamirano, *La literatura nacional*, I, 234–7, 262–5; II, 15, 144–5. See also Nicole Girón, 'La idea de "cultura nacional" en el siglo XIX: Altamirano y Ramírez' in Hector Aguilar Camín, ed., *En torno a la cultura nacional* (Mexico, 1976), pp. 51–84; Catalina Sierra Casasus, 'Altamirano íntimo', *Historia mexicana*, I (1951), pp. 97–103.

48 Ramírez, *Obras*, I, 221–2; II, 206–9; Altamirano, *La literatura nacional*, I, 11.

49 Ramírez, *Obras*, I, 466–72.

50 Altamirano, *La literatura nacional*, I, 10; II, 60–7, 126, 150; Altamirano, *Discursos*, p. 288; Ramírez, *Obras*, I, 476.

51 Altamirano, 'Revista artística y monumental' in Caballero, ed., *Primer almanaque*, pp. 90–107.

52 Altamirano, *La literatura nacional*, I, 12, 18–81.

53 Manuel Payno, *Los bandidos de Río Frío*, ed. Antonio Castro Leal, 5 vols. (Mexico, 1965), *passim*; D. A. Brading, *Myth and Prophecy in Mexican History* (Cambridge, 1984), pp. 55–8.

54 Altamirano, *Paisajes y leyendas* (1949), pp. 172–84, 192–4, 235.

55 Altamirano, *Paisajes y leyendas* (Mexico, 1974), pp. 4–7; *Discursos*, p. 364.

56 Altamirano, *Paisajes y leyendas* (1974), pp. 9–19; Altamirano, *Clemencia y La navidad en las montañas* (Mexico, 1966), *passim*.

57 Altamirano, *Paisajes y leyendas* (1974), pp. 56–7, 95, 119, 125, 128.

BIBLIOGRAPHY

This bibliography lists the works cited in the text and notes and refers to the editions used by the author. For all printed works the date of the original edition is given in the text when that work is first discussed. Note that authors are here listed under their most commonly used name, *e.g.*, Gómara rather than López de Gómara.

GUIDES AND BIBLIOGRAPHIES

Andrade, Vicente P. *Ensayo bibliográfico mexicano del siglo XVII*, facsimile of 1889 edn (Mexico, 1971)
Beristáin de Souza, José Mariano. *Biblioteca hispano-americana septentrional*, 3rd edn, 5 vols. (Mexico, 1957)
Cline, Howard. 'Guide to ethnohistorical sources', *Handbook of Middle American Indians*, vol. 13, ed. Robert Wauchope (Austin, Texas, 1973)
Esteve Barba, Francisco. *Historiografía indiana* (Madrid, 1964)
García Icazbalceta, Joaquín. *Bibliografía mexicana del siglo XVI*, 2nd edn, ed. A. Millares Carlo (Mexico, 1954)
León, Nicolás. *Bibliografía mexicana del siglo XVIII*, 5 vols. (Mexico, 1902–8)
Mendiburu, Manuel de. *Diccionario histórico biográfico del Perú*, 2nd edn, with notes and appendix by Evaristo San Cristóval, 15 vols. (Lima, 1931–8)
Menéndez Pelayo, Marcelino. *Historia de los heterodoxos españoles*, Biblioteca de autores cristianos, 2 vols. (Madrid, 1956)
Porras Barrenechea, Raúl. *Fuentes históricas peruanas* (Lima, 1954)
  Los cronistas del Perú. 1528–1650, ed. C. Y. Franklin Pease (Lima, 1986)
Riva Agüero, José de la. *La historia en el Perú*, 2nd edn (Lima, 1965)

MANUSCRIPT SOURCES

AGI Archivo General de Indias
  Audiencia de México, legajos 1337, 1440, 1472, 1710, 1883, 1892, 1894, 1895, 2256, 2545, 2571, 2603, 2651, 2697, 2714
  Indiferente General, legajo 2973
AGN Archivo General de la Nación (Mexico), ramo de Historia, vol. 437
Biblioteca Nacional (Madrid), mss. 3650
Biblioteca Nacional (Mexico), mss. 1187

PRIMARY SOURCES

Abad y Queipo, Manuel. *Cartas pastorales* (Mexico, 1811–13)
  'Escritos del obispo electo de Michoacán Don Manuel Abad y Queipo' in José María
  Luis Mora, *Obras sueltas*, 2 vols. (Paris, 1837)
Acosta, José de. *De Procuranda Indorum Salute*, ed. Francisco Mateos (Madrid, 1952)
  Historia natural y moral de las Indias, ed. Edmundo O'Gorman (Mexico, 1962)
  Obras, ed. Francisco Mateos, BAE 73 (Madrid, 1954)
Acuña, Hernando de. *Varias poesías*, ed. E. Catena de Vindel (Madrid, 1954)
Ahumada, Juan Antonio de. *Representación política-legal a la majestad del Sr. D. Felipe
  V en favor de los españoles americanos* (Madrid, 1725)
Ajofrín, Francisco de, *Diario del viaje que hizo a la América* (Mexico, 1964)
Alamán, Lucas. *Disertaciones*, 3 vols. (Mexico, 1969)
  Documentos diversos, 4 vols. (Mexico, 1946)
  Historia de Méjico, 4th edn, 5 vols. (Mexico, 1968–9)
Alberdi, Juan Bautista. *Autobiografía* (Buenos Aires, 1927)
  Bases y puntos de partido para la organización de la República Argentina (Buenos
  Aires, 1943)
  Grandes y pequeños hombres del Plata (Paris, n.d.)
Alegre, Francisco Javier. *Historia de la provincia de la Compañía de Jesús de Nueva
  España*, ed. Ernest J. Burrus and Félix Zubillaga, 4 vols. (Rome, 1956–60)
Altamirano, Ignacio Manuel. *Biografía de D. Miguel Hidalgo y Costilla* (Mexico, 1960)
  Discursos (Paris, 1982)
  Clemencia y La navidad en las montañas (Mexico, 1966)
  La literatura nacional, ed. Antonio Castro Leal, 3 vols. (Mexico, 1949)
  Paisajes y leyendas (Mexico, 1974)
  Paisajes y leyendas. Tradiciones y costumbres de México, 2nd ser. (Mexico, 1949)
Anónimo de Yucay. 'Dominio de las Yngas en el Perú y del que su Majestad tiene en
  dichos reinos', ed. Josyane Chinese, *Historia y Cultura*, 4 (1970), pp. 106–47
Aquinas, St Thomas. *Philosophical Texts*, ed. Thomas Gilby (Oxford, 1951)
  Selected Political Writings, ed. A. P. D'Entreves (Oxford, 1954)
Arrate, José Martín Félix de. *Llave del Nuevo Mundo*, ed. Julio J. Le Reverend Brusone
  (Mexico, 1949)
Arzáns de Orsúa y Vela, Bartolomé. *Historia de la villa imperial de Potosí*, ed. Lewis
  Hanke and Gunnar Mendoza, 3 vols. (Providence, Rhode Island, 1965)
Augustine, Saint. *City of God*, Penguin edn (London, 1967)
  Of the City of God: with the learned comments of Io. Lodivicus Vives, 2nd edn
  (London, 1620)
Avila, Francisco de. *Dioses y hombres de Huarochirí*, ed. José María Arguedas (Lima,
  1966)
Balbuena, Bernardo de. *La grandeza mexicana*, ed. Luis Adolfo Domínguez (Mexico,
  1971)
Becerra Tanco, Luis. *Felicidad de México en el principio y milagroso origen que tubo
  el santuario de la Virgen María N. Señora de Guadalupe*, 2nd edn (Mexico,
  1675)
Benzoni, M. Girolamo. *La historia del Mundo Nuevo*, ed. Marisi Vannini (Caracas,
  1967)

Betancur, Agustín de. *Teatro mexicano*, facsimile of 1697–98 edn, BP 45 (Mexico, 1971)

Blanco White, Joseph, ed., *El Español*, 8 vols. (London, 1810–14)

   Letters from Spain, published under pseudonym of Leucadio Doblado (London, 1822)

   Obra inglesa de D. José María Blanco White, ed. Juan Goytisolo, (Buenos Aires, 1972)

   The Life of the Rev. Joseph Blanco White, ed. John Hamilton Thom, 3 vols. (London, 1845)

   Variedades o mensagero de Londres (London, 1823–5)

Bodin, Jean. *Method for the Easy Comprehension of History* (New York, 1945)

Bolívar, Simón. *Obras completas*, ed. Vicente Lecuna, 3 vols. (Caracas, 1964)

Botero, Giovanni. *The Reason of State*, ed. D. P. Waley (New Haven, Conn., 1956)

Boturini Benaduci, Lorenzo. 'Historia general de la América Septentrional' in *Documentos inéditos para la historia de España: papeles de Indias*, ed. Manuel Ballesteros Gaibros, vols. V–VI (Madrid, 1947–9)

   Idea de una nueva historia general de la América Septentrional, ed. Miguel León-Portilla (Mexico, 1974)

Buffon, Georges-Louis Leclerc. *Natural History*, 10 vols. (London, 1747)

Bulnes, Francisco. *El verdadero Juárez y la verdad sobre la intervención y el imperio* (Mexico, 1965)

   Juárez y las revoluciones de Ayutla y de Reforma (Mexico, 1967)

Bustamante, Carlos María de. *Abajo gente baldía gritan los reformadores ó sea defensa de las órdenes religiosas* (Mexico, 1833)

   Análisis crítico de la constitución de 1836 (Mexico, 1842)

   Apuntes para la historia del gobierno del general D. Antonio López de Santa-Anna (Mexico, 1845)

   Continuación del cuadro histórico de la revolución mexicana, ed Jorge Gurría Lacroix, 4 vols. (Mexico, 1953–63)

   'Correo Americano del Sur', facsimile in *Periodismo insurgente*, 2 vols. (Mexico, 1976)

   Cuadro histórico de la revolución mexicana, 3 vols. (Mexico, 1961)

   El nuevo Bernal Díaz del Castillo ó sea historia de la invasión de los angloamericanos en México, 2 vols. (Mexico, 1847)

   Juguetillo Octavo (Mexico, 1820)

   La aparición de Nuestra Señora de Guadalupe de México (Mexico, 1840)

   La aparición guadalupana de México (Mexico, 1843)

   Mañanas de la Alameda en México, 2 vols. (Mexico, 1835–6)

   Representación que los vecinos emigrados de la villa de Chilapa han hecho ... (Mexico, 1845)

   Texcoco en los últimos tiempos de sus antiguos reyes, facsimile of 1826–27 edn with introduction by Ernesto Lemoine (Mexico, 1970)

   Viaje a Toluca en 1834, ed. Ernesto Lemoine (Mexico, 1969)

Cabrera y Quintero, Cayetano Javier de. *Escudo de armas de México* (Mexico, 1746)

Calancha, Antonio de la. *Crónica moralizada del orden de San Agustín en el Perú*, ed. Ignacio Prado Pastor, 6 vols. (Lima, 1974)

   Crónicas agustinianas del Perú, ed. Manuel Merino, 2 vols. (Madrid, 1972)

Campillo y Cosío, José del. *Nuevo sistema de gobierno económico para la América* (Madrid, 1789)

Campomanes, Pedro Rodríguez. *Dictamen fiscal de expulsión de los jesuitas de España (1766–1767)*, ed. Jorge Cejudo and Teófanes Egido (Madrid, 1977)

Discurso sobre el fomento de la industria popular (1774); Discurso sobre la educación popular de los artesanos y su fomento (1775), ed. John Reeds (Madrid, 1975)

Juicio imparcial sobre las letras de forma de Breve que ha publicado la Curia Romana en que intenta derogar ciertos Edictos del Serenísimo Señor Infante Duque de Parma, y disputarle la soberanía temporal con este pretexto (Madrid, 1769)

Tratado de la regalía de amortización (Madrid, 1765)

Cancelada, Juan López de. *Conducta de Iturrigaray* ... (Cadiz, 1812)

El Telégrafo Americano (Cadiz 1812)

El Telégrafo Mexicano (Cadiz, 1813)

Ruina de la Nueva España (Cadiz, 1811)

Capoche, Luis. *Relación general del asiento y villa imperial de Potosí*, ed. Lewis Hanke, BAE 122 (Madrid, 1959)

Caramuel Lobkowitz, Juan. *Architectura civil recta y obliqua* (Vegeren, 1678)

Cárdenas, Juan de. *Problemas y secretos maravillosos de las Indias*, facsimile of 1591 Mexican edn (Madrid, 1945)

Carlyle, Alexander. *Autobiography*, ed. John Hill Burton (London, 1910)

Cartas de religiosos de Nueva España, ed. Joaquín García Icazbalceta, 2nd edn (Mexico, 1941)

Castorena Ursua y Goyeneche, Juan Ignacio Maria de, *Gacetas de México*, ed. Francisco González de Cossío, 3 vols. (Mexico, 1949)

Castro, Ignacio. *Relación de la fundación de la Real Audiencia del Cuzco*, ed. Carlos Daniel Valcárcel (Lima, 1978)

Cavo, Andrés. *Los tres siglos de México durante el gobierno español hasta la entrada del ejército trigarante*, ed. with supplement by Carlos María de Bustamante, 4 vols. (Mexico, 1836–8)

Chilam Balam, The Book of Chumayel, ed. Ralph L. Roys (Norman, Oklahoma, 1967)

Cicero, M. T. *Treatises*, ed. C. D. Yonge (London, 1853)

Cieza de León, Pedro de. *El señorío de los Incas* (Lima, 1967)

'La crónica del Perú' in *Crónicas de la conquista del Perú*, ed. Julio le Reverend Brusone (Mexico, n.d.)

Cisneros, Diego. *Sitio, naturaleza y propiedades de la ciudad de México* (Mexico, 1618)

Cisneros, Luis de. *Historia de el principio y origen, progressos venidas a México y milagros de la Santa Ymagen de Nuestra Señora de los Remedios, extramuros de México* (Mexico, 1621)

Clavijero, Francisco Javier. *Historia antigua de México*, ed. Mariano Cuevas (Mexico, 1964)

Historia de la antigua o Baja California, ed. Miguel León-Portilla (Mexico, 1970)

Cobo, Bernabé. *Historia del Nuevo Mundo*, ed. Francisco Mateos, BAE 91–2 (Madrid, 1956)

Codex Pérez and the Book of Chilam Balam of Maní, ed. Eugene R. Craine and Reginold C. Reindrop (Norman, Oklahoma, 1979)

Códice Mendieta: documentos franciscanos siglo XVI y XVII, ed. Joaquín García Icazbalceta, 2 vols., facsimile of 1892 edn (Mexico, 1971)

Códice Xolotl, ed. Charles E. Dibble, 2 vols. (Mexico, 1980)

Colección de documentos para la historia de la guerra de independencia de México de

1808 hasta 1821, ed. J. E. Hernández y Dávalos, 6 vols., facsimile of 1877 edn (Mexico, 1985)

Colección de documentos para la historia de México, ed. Joaquín Garcia Icazbalceta, BP 47–8, 2 vols. (Mexico, 1858, facsimile, 1971)

Colección de las memorias ó relaciones que escribieron los virreyes del Perú, ed. Ricardo Beltrán y Rózpide, 2 vols. (Madrid, 1921–30)

Colección de obras y opúsculos pertenecientes a la aparición de Nuestra Señora de Guadalupe, 2 vols. (Madrid, 1785)

Colección documental de la independencia del Perú, vols. V–VII (Lima, 1971–4)

Colón, Cristobal. *Textos y documentos completos*, ed. Consuelo Varela (Madrid, 1982)

Colón, Hernando. *Vida del Almirante Don Cristóbal Colón*, ed. Ramón Iglesia (Mexico, 1947)

Condamine, Charles-Marie de la. *Journal du voyage fait por ordre de Roi a l'Equateur servant d'introduction a la mesure des trois premiers degrés du Méridien* (Paris, 1751)

Relation abregée d'un voyage fait dans l'interieur de l'Amerique Méridionale (Maestricht, 1778)

Córdova Salinas, Diego de. *Corónica de la religiosíssima provincia de los doze apóstoles del Perú de la orden de N.S.P. San Francisco*, ed. Lino G. Canedo (Mexico, 1957)

Cortés, Hernán. *Cartas y documentos*, ed. Mario Hernández Sánchez-Barba, BP 2 (Mexico, 1963)

Croix, L. Peru de la. *Diario de Bucaramanga*, 2nd edn (Lima, 1965)

Cruz, Sor Juana Inés de la. *Obras completas*, ed. Alfonso Méndez Plancarte, 4 vols. (Mexico, 1951–7)

Dávila Padilla, Agustín. *Historia de la fundación y discurso de la provincia de Santiago de México de la orden de predicadores*, facsimile of 1625 edn (Mexico, 1955)

Díaz del Castillo, Bernal. *Historia verdadera de la conquista de la Nueva España*, ed. Joaquín Ramírez Cabañas, BP 6–7 (Mexico, 1968)

Diez de la Calle, Juan. *Memorial informatorio al Rey nuestro Señor* (Madrid, 1645)

Documentos inéditos del siglo XVI para la historia de México, ed. Mariano Cuevas, facsimile of 1914 edn BP 62 (Mexico, 1975)

Documentos inéditos o muy raros para la historia de México, ed. Genaro García and Carlos Pereyra, 2nd edn, BP 58–60 (Mexico, 1974–5).

Dorantes de Carranza, Baltazar. *Sumaria relación de las cosas de la Nueva España*, ed. José María de Agreda y Sánchez, 2nd edn (Mexico, 1970)

Ducoudray Holstein, H. L. V. *Memoirs of Simón Bolívar*, 2 vols. (London, 1830)

Durán, Diego. *Historia de las Indias de Nueva España e Islas de la Tierra Firme*, ed. Angel M. Garibay K., BP 36–7 (Mexico, 1967)

Eguiara y Eguren, Juan José de. *Prólogos a la biblioteca mexicana*, ed. Agustín Millares Carlo (Mexico, 1944)

Ercilla, Alonso de. *La Araucana*, ed. Ofelia Garza de del Castillo (Mexico, 1975)

Escobar, Matías de. *Americana Thebaida*, ed. Nicolás B. Navarrete, 2nd edn (Morelia, 1970)

Espinosa, Félix Isidro de. *Crónica de los colegios de propaganda fide de la Nueva España*, ed. Lino Gómez Canedo, 2nd edn (Washington, 1964)

Espinosa Medrano, Juan de. *Apologético en favor de D. Luis de Góngora* (Lima, 1662)

Esquivel y Navia, Diego de. *Noticias cronológicas de la gran ciudad de Cuzco*, ed. Félix Denegri Luna, 2 vols. (Lima, 1980)

Eusebius of Caesarea. *The Church History and other writings* (New York, 1890)

Feijoo Montenegro, Benito Jerónimo. *Teatro crítico universal*, 8th edn, 8 vols. (Madrid, 1753–5)

Florencia, Francisco de. *La estrella del norte de México*, reprinted in *Colección de obras y opúsculos pertenecientes a la aparición de Nuestra Señora de Guadalupe*, 2 vols. (Madrid, 1785)

Forster, George. *A Voyage round the World in his Britannic Majesty's sloop Resolution commanded by Captain James Cook during the years 1772–75*, 2 vols. (London, 1777)

Freyle, Juan Rodríguez. *El Carnero*, ed. Darío Achury Valenzuela, BA 66 (Caracas, 1979)

Frezier, Amédée François. *A Voyage to the South Seas in the years 1712, 1713 and 1714* (London, 1717)

Fuentes para la historia del trabajo en Nueva España, ed. Silvio Zavala and María Castelo, 8 vols. (Mexico, 1939–45)

Fuentes y Guzmán, Francisco Antonio de. *Recordación florida: discurso historial, natural, material, militar y político del reino de Goathemala*, ed. Carmelo Sáenz de Santa María, BAE 230, 251, 259 (Madrid, 1969–72)

García, Gregorio. *Origen de los indios del Nuevo Mundo*, ed. Andrés González de Barcia, facsimile of 1729 Madrid edn (Mexico, 1980)

Garcilaso de la Vega, El Inca. *Comentarios reales de los Incas*, ed. Angel Rosenblat, 2 vols. (Buenos Aires, 1943)

Historia general del Perú, ed. Angel Rosenblat, 3 vols. (Buenos Aires, 1944)

La Florida del Inca, ed. Emma Susana Speratti Piñero (Mexico, 1956)

Obras completas, ed. Carmelo Sáenz de Santa María, BAE 122–5 (Madrid, 1960)

Gemelli Careri, Giovanni Francesco. *Viaje a la Nueva España*, ed. Francisca Perajo (Mexico, 1976)

Ginés de Sepúlveda, Juan. *Tratado sobre las justas causas de la guerra contra los indios*, ed. Manuel García-Pelayo (Mexico, 1971)

Gobernantes del Perú: cartas y papeles, siglo XVI, ed. Roberto Levillier, 14 vols. (Madrid, 1921–6)

Gómara, Francisco López de. *Annals of the Emperor Charles V*, ed. Roger Bigelow Merriman (Oxford, 1912)

Historia de la conquista de México, ed. Jorge Gurría Lacroix, BA 65 (Caracas, 1979)

Historia general de las Indias, ed. Jorge Gurría Lacroix, BA 64 (Caracas, 1979)

Gómez de Cervantes, Gonzalo. *La vida económica y social de Nueva España al finalizar el siglo XVI*, ed. Alberto María Carreño (Mexico, 1944)

Grégoire, Henri. *Mémoires*, 2 vols. (Paris, 1837)

Grijalva, Juan de. *Crónica de la orden de N.P.S. Augustín en las provincias de la Nueva España* (Mexico, 1624)

Guaman Poma de Ayala, Felipe. *El primer nueva corónica y buen gobierno*, ed. John V. Murra, Rolena Adorno and Jorge L. Urioste, 3 vols. (Mexico, 1980)

Guridi Alcocer, José Miguel. *El Censor extraordinario* (Cadiz, 1812)

Haro y Peralta, Alonso Núñez de. *Sermones escogidos, pláticas espirituales privadas y dos pastorales*, 3 vols. (Madrid, 1806)

Herrera y Tordesillas, Antonio de. *Historia general de los hechos de los castellanos en las Islas i Tierra Firme de Mar Oceáno*, 4 vols. (Madrid, 1601–15)

Hippocrates. *Airs, Waters, Places*, Loeb Library (London, 1973)

Historia documental de México, ed. Ernesto de la Torre Villar *et al.*, 2 vols. (Mexico, 1964)

Historia Tolteca Chichimeca, ed. Paul Kirchhoff, Lina Odena Guemes and Luis Reyes García, facsimile edn (Mexico, 1976)

Holland, Lady Elizabeth, *The Spanish Journal*, ed. The Earl of Ilchester (London, 1910)

Humboldt, Alexander von. *Aspects of Nature in Different Lands and Different Climates*, 2 vols. (London, 1850)

  Cartas americanas, ed. Charles Minguet, BA 74 (Caracas, 1980)

  Cosmos, 3 vols., 7th edn (London, 1849)

  Ensayo político sobre el reino de la Nueva España, ed. Juan A. Ortega y Medina (Mexico, 1966)

  'Essai sur la géographie des plantes', published as *Voyage de Humboldt et Bonpland. Première Partie* (Paris, 1807)

  Examen critique de l'historie de la géographie du Nouveau Continent et des progrès de l'astronomie nautique aux quinzième et seizième siècles, 5 vols. (Paris, 1836–9)

  Personal Narrative of Travels to the Equinoctial Regions of the New Continent during the years 1799–1804, trans. Helen Maria Williams, facsimile of 1818–29 edn, 7 vols. in 6 (New York, 1966)

  'Tablas geográficas políticas del reino de Nueva España' in *Descripciones económicas generales de Nueva España 1784–1817*, ed. Enrique Florescano and Isabel Gil (Mexico, 1973)

  Vistas de las cordilleras y monumentos de los pueblos indígenas de América, ed. Jaime Labastida (Mexico, 1974)

Idea de la conspiración descubierta en la capital del imperio mexicano (Mexico, 1822)

Ignatius of Loyola, Saint. *The Spiritual Exercises*, ed. W. H. Longridge (London, 1919)

Informaciones acerca del señorío de los Incas, ed. Marcos Jiménez de la Espada (Madrid, 1882)

Instrucciones que los virreyes de Nueva España dejaron a sus sucesores (Mexico, 1967)

Irving, Washington. *A History of the Life and Voyages of Christopher Columbus*, 4 vols. (London, 1828)

Ixtlilxochitl, Fernando de Alva. *Obras históricas*, ed. Edmundo O'Gorman, 2 vols. (Mexico, 1975)

Jefferson, Thomas. *The Writings*, Library of America (New York, 1984)

Jerez, Francisco de. 'Verdadera relación de la conquista de Perú y provincia del Cuzco' in *Crónicas de la conquista de Perú*, ed. Julio le Reverend Brusone (Mexico, n.d.)

Jovellanos, Gaspar Melchor de. *Obras*, ed. Miguel Artola, BAE, 46, 50, 85–7 (Madrid, 1951–6)

Juan, Jorge. *Observaciones astronómicas y phísicas hechas de orden de S.M. en los reynos del Perú*, 2nd edn (Madrid, 1773)

Juárez, Benito. *Epistolario*, ed. Jorge L. Tamayo (Mexico, 1972)

Lafiteau, Joseph François. *Customs of the American Indians compared with the Customs of Primitive Times*, ed. and trans. W. N. Fenton and E. L. Moore, 2 vols. (Toronto, 1974)

Las Casas, Bartolomé de. *Apologética historia sumaria*, ed. Edmundo O'Gorman, 2 vols. (Mexico, 1967)

Del único modo de atraer a todos los pueblos a la verdadera religión, ed. Lewis Hanke and Agustín Millares Carlo (Mexico, 1975)

De regia potestate, ed. Luciano Pereña (Madrid, 1969)

Historia de las Indias, ed. Agustín Millares Carlo and Lewis Hanke, 3 vols. (Mexico, 1951)

In Defence of the Indians, ed. and trans. Stafford Poole (De Kalb, Ill., 1974)

Los tesoros del Perú, ed. and trans. Angel Losada García (Madrid, 1958)

Obras escogidas, ed. Juan Pérez de Tudela Bueso, BAE, 95–6, 105–6 (Madrid, 1957)

Tratados, ed. Lewis Hanke *et al.*, 2 vols. (Mexico, 1965)

Lasso de la Vega, Luis. *Huei tlamahuicoltica . . . Santa María Totlaconantzin Guadalupe* (Mexico, 1649)

León Pinelo, Antonio de. *Discurso sobre la importancia, forma y disposición de la recopilación de leyes de las Indias Occidentales*, ed. Aniceto Almeyda (Santiago de Chile, 1956)

    El Gran Canciller de Indias, ed. Guillermo Lohmann Villena (Seville, 1953)

    El Paraíso en el Nuevo Mundo, ed. Raúl Porras Barrenechea, 2 vols. (Lima, 1943)

    Epítome de la Biblioteca Oriental i Occidental, naútica y geográfica, ed. Agustín Millares Carlo, facsimile of 1629 Madrid edn (Washington, 1958)

    Tratado de confirmaciones reales de encomiendas, oficios i casos (Madrid, 1630)

León y Gama, Antonio de. *Descripción histórica y cronológica de las dos piedras*, facsimile of 1792 and 1832 edns (Mexico, 1978)

Lorenzana y Buitron, Francisco Antonio de. *Cartas pastorales y edictos* (Mexico, 1770)

    Historia de Nueva España escrita por su esclarecido conquistador Hernán Cortés (Mexico, 1770)

Los virreyes españoles en América durante el gobierno de la Casa de Austria: Perú, ed. Lewis Hanke, BAE 281–6 (Madrid, 1978–80)

Machiavelli, Niccolò, *The Prince* (London, 1961)

Madison, James. *The Federalist*, Everyman Books (London, n.d.)

Márquez, Pedro José. *Sobre lo bello en general y dos monumentos de arquitectura mexicana, Tajín y Xochicalco*, ed. Justino Fernández (Mexico, 1972)

Martínez, Enrico. *Reportorio de los tiempos e historia natural de Nueva España*, ed. Francisco de la Maza (Mexico, 1948)

Martínez Marina, Francisco. *Obras escogidas*, ed. José Martínez Cardos, BAE 194, 219 (Madrid, 1966–8)

Martyr D'Anghera, Peter. *De orbe novo: the eight decades*, trans. F. A. MacNutt, 2 vols. (New York, 1912)

Matienzo, Juan de. *Gobierno del Perú 1567*, ed. Guillermo Lohmann Villena (Paris–Lima, 1967)

Maza, Francisco de la, ed. *Sor Juana Inés de la Cruz ante la Historia* (Mexico, 1980)

Medina, Baltazar de. *Chrónica de la santa provincia de San Diego de México de religiosos descalzos de N.S.P. San Francisco de la Nueva España* (Mexico, 1682)

Meléndez, Juan. *Tesoros verdaderos de las Indias. Historia de la provincia de San Juan Baptista del Perú de la orden de predicadores*, 3 vols. (Rome, 1681–2)

Memorias de los virreyes que han gobernado el Perú, ed. Manuel A. Fuentes, 6 vols. (Lima, 1859)

Mendieta, Jerónimo de. *Historia eclesiástica Indiana*, ed. Joaquín García Icazbalceta, facsimile of 1870 edn, BP 46 (Mexico 1971)

Mercurio Peruano, 12 vols., facsimile of 1791–5 edn (Lima, 1964–6)

Michelet, Jules. *Le Peuple*, ed. Lucien Refort (Paris, 1946)

Mier, Servando Teresa de. *Discurso del doctor Don Servando Teresa de Mier sobre la encíclica del Papa León XII*, 5th edn (Mexico, 1825)

'Cartas de un Americano', *El Español* (London, 1811–12); reprinted in vol. IV of José Eleuterio González, *Obras completas* (Monterrey, 1888)

Escritos inéditos, ed. J. M. Miquiel and Hugo Díaz Thomé (Mexico, 1944)

Escritos y memorias, ed. Edmundo O'Gorman (Mexico, 1945)

'Epistolario', in Alfonso Junco, *El increíble Fray Servando: psicología y epistolario* (Mexico, 1959)

Historia de la revolución de Nueva España antiguamente Anáhuac, 2 vols. (Mexico, 1922)

Memoria político-instructiva enviada desde Filadelfia a los gefes del Anáhuac llamado por los españoles Nueva España, 2nd edn (Mexico, 1822)

Memorias, ed. Antonio Castro Leal, 2 vols. (Mexico, 1946)

Obras completas: el heterodoxo guadalupano, ed. Edmundo O'Gorman, vols. I–III (Mexico, 1981)

Pensamiento político del padre Mier, ed. Edmundo O'Gorman (Mexico, 1945)

Miller, John. *Memoirs of General Miller*, 2 vols. (London, 1828)

Molina, Juan Ignacio. *The Geographical, Natural and Civil History of Chile*, 2 vols. (London, 1809)

Montaigne, Michel de. *The Essays of Montaigne*, ed. and trans. E. J. Trechmann, 2 vols. (Oxford, 1927)

Montesinos, Fernando de. *Memorias antiguas, historiales y políticas del Perú*, ed. Horacio Urteaga (Lima, 1930)

Montesquieu, Charles de Secondat, Baron de. 'Le dialogue de Sylla et d'Eucrate', published with his *Considérations sur les causes de la grandeur des Romains et leur décadence*, (Paris, 1954)

The Spirit of the Laws, trans Thomas Nugent, 2 vols. (New York, 1949)

Mora, José María Luis. *México y sus revoluciones*, ed. Agustín Yañez, 3 vols. (Mexico, 1950)

Obras sueltas, BP 26 (Mexico, 1963)

Moreno, Manuel. *Vida y memorias de Mariano Moreno* (Buenos Aires, 1918)

Moreno, Mariano. *Escritos políticos y económicos* (Buenos Aires, 1915)

Motolinia, Toribio de Benavente. 'Carta al Emperador Carlos V' in *Colección de documentos para la historia de México*, ed. Joaquín García Icazbalceta, facsimile of 1858 edn, BP 47 (Mexico, 1971)

Historia de los indios de la Nueva España, ed. Joaquín García Icazbalceta, facsimile of 1858 edn BP 47 (Mexico, 1971)

Memoriales ó libro de las cosas de la Nueva España y de los naturales de élla, ed. Edmundo O'Gorman (Mexico, 1971)

Nebrija, Antonio de. *Gramática de la lengua castellana*, ed. Ignacio González-Llumbrera (Oxford, 1926)

Ocampo, Melchor. *Obras completas*, ed. Angel Pola, 3 vols. (Mexico, 1978)

Otero, Mariano. *Obras*, ed. Jesús Reyes Heroles, BP 33–4 (Mexico, 1967)

Ovalle, Alonso de. *Histórica relación del reyno de Chile y de las misiones y ministerios que exercita en él la Compañia de Jesús* (Rome, 1646)

Oviedo, Juan de. *Vida exemplar, heroicas virtudes y apostólicos ministerios de el V.P. Antonio Núñez de Miranda* (Mexico, 1702)

Oviedo y Baños, José de. *Historia de la conquista y población de la provincia de Venezuela* (Caracas, 1967)

Oviedo y Herrera, Luis Antonio de. *Vida de Santa Rosa de Santa María, natural de Lima y patrona de Perú* (Madrid, 1711)

Oviedo y Valdés, Gonzalo Fernández de. *Historia general y natural de las Indias*, ed. Juan Pérez de Tudela, BAE 115–21 (Madrid, 1959)

    Quinquagenas de la nobleza de España. ed. Juan Bautista Avalle-Arce, 2 vols. (Chapel Hill, NC, 1974)

Paéz, José Antonio. *Autobiografía*, 2 vols. (New York, 1870)

Paine, Thomas. *The Thomas Paine Reader*, ed. Michael Foot and Isaac Kramnick, Penguin Books (London, 1987)

Palacios Rubios, Juan López de. *De las Islas del mar Oceáno*, ed. Silvio Zavala and Agustín Millares Carlo (Mexico, 1954)

Palafox y Mendoza, Juan de. *Carta al sumo pontífice Innocent X*, 3rd edn (Madrid, 1767)

    Diario del viaje a Alemania, ed. Xristina de Arteaga (Madrid, 1935)

    Tratados mejicanos, ed. Francisco Sánchez-Castañer, BAE 117–18 (Madrid, 1968)

    Obras, 13 vols. (Madrid, 1762)

Pauw, Cornelius de. *Philosophical Dissertations on the Egyptians and Chinese*. 2 vols. (London, 1795)

    Recherches philosophiques sur les Americains, 3 vols. (London, 1771)

Paz, Melchor. 'Diálogo sobre los sucesos varios acaecidos en este reyno del Perú' in *Guerra separatista. Rebeliones de indios en Sur América, la sublevación de Tupac Amaru*, ed. Luis Antonio Eguiguren, 2 vols. (Lima, 1952)

Peralta Barnuevo y Rocha, Pedro de. *Historia de España vindicada* (Lima, 1730)

    Imagen política del gobierno del Exmo. Señor D. Diego Ladrón de Guevara (Lima, 1714)

    Júbilos de Lima y fiestas reales (Lima, 1723)

    Lima inexpugnable, ed. Luis Antonio Eguiguren Escudero, 2nd edn (Lima, 1966)

    Lima fundada ó conquista del Perú, 2 vols. (Lima, 1732)

    Relación del auto de Fe (Lima, 1733)

    Obras dramáticas, ed. Irving A. Leonard (Santiago de Chile, 1937)

Pérez de Ribas, Andrés. *Historia de los triumphos de nuestra Santa Fe entre gentes de las más bárbaras y fieras del nuevo orbe: conseguidos por los soldados de la milicia de la Compañía de Jesús en las misiones de Nueva España* (Madrid, 1645)

Pérez de Villagra, Gaspar. *Historia de la Nueva México* (Alcalá, 1610)

Pineda y Bascuñán, Francisco Núñez de. 'Cautiverio feliz y razón de las guerras dilatadas de Chile', in *Colección de Historiadores de Chile*, ed. Diego Barrós Arana, vol. III (Santiago de Chile, 1863)

Pons, François de. *Travels in South America*, 2 vols. (London, 1807)

Pradt, Dominique de. *Europe and America in 1821*, 2 vols. (London, 1822)

    Les Trois âges des colonies, 2 vols. in 3 (Paris, 1801–2)

    The Colonies and the Present American Revolution, 2 vols. (London, 1817)

Prescott, William H. *The History of the Conquest of Mexico and The History of the Conquest of Peru*, The Modern Library (New York, n.d.)

Puente, Juan de la. *Tomo primero de la conveniencia de las dos monarquías Católicas, la de la Iglesia Romana y la del Imperio Español, y defensa de la precedencia de los Reyes Católicos de España a todos los reyes del mundo* (Madrid, 1612)

Quesada, Gonzalo Jiménez de. *El Antijovio* (Bogotá, 1952)

Quijada, Diego. *Don Diego Quijada Alcalde Mayor de Yucatán 1561–1565: Documentos*, ed. France V. Scholes and Eleanor B. Adams, 2 vols. (Mexico, 1938)

Quintana Roo, Andrés. 'Semanario Patriótico Americano', facsimile of 1811–12 edn, in *Periodismo insurgente*, 2 vols. (Mexico, 1976)

Ramírez, Ignacio. *Obras*, facsimile of 1889 edn, 2 vols. (Mexico, 1966)

Ramírez, José Fernando. 'Notas y esclarecimientos' in William H. Prescott, *Historia de la conquista de México*, ed. Juan A Ortega y Medina (Mexico, 1970)

Ramos Gavilán, Alonso. *Historia del célebre santuario de Nuestra Señora de Copacabana y sus milagros e invención de la Cruz de Carabuco* (Lima, 1621)

Raynal, Guillaume-Thomas. *A Philosophical and Political History of the Settlements and Trade of the Europeans in the East and West Indies*, trans. J. O. Justamond, 3rd edn, 6 vols. (London, 1798)

Recollections of Service of Three Years during the War of Extermination in the Republics of Venezuela and Colombia by an officer of the Colombian Navy, Anon., 2 vols. (London, 1828)

Recopilación de leyes de los reynos de las Indias, ed. Juan Manzano Manzano, facsimile of 1681 edn, 4 vols. (Madrid, 1973)

Remesal, Antonio de. *Historia general de las Indias Occidentales*, ed. Carmelo Sáenz de Santa María, BAE 175, 189 (Madrid, 1964–6)

Ricci, Matteo. *China in the Sixteenth Century. The Journals of Matteo Ricci*, trans. Louis J. Gallagher (New York, 1953)

Rivadeneira y Barrientos, Antonio Joaquín de. *Disertaciones que el asistente real escribió sobre los puntos que se le consultaron por el cuarto concilio mejicano en 1774* (Madrid, 1881)

Manual compendio del regio patronato indiano (Madrid, 1755)

El pasatiempo, 3 vols. (Madrid, 1752–53)

'Representación humilde que hace la imperial, nobilísima y muy leal ciudad de México en favor de sus naturales' in *Colección de documentos para la historia de la guerra de independencia de México de 1808 de 1821*, ed. J. E. Hernández y Dávalos, vol. I (Mexico, 1877)

Rivera Bernárdez, José de. *Descripción muy breve de la muy noble y leal ciudad de Zacatecas* (Mexico, 1732)

Robertson, William. *The Works of William Robertson D.D.*, 8 vols. (Oxford, 1825)

Robinson, William David. *Memoirs of the Mexican Revolution* (Philadelphia, 1820)

Robles, Antonio de. *Diario de sucesos notables* (1665–1703), ed. Antonio Castro Leal, 3 vols. (Mexico, 1946)

Rodó, José Enrique. *Obras completas*, ed. Emir Rodríguez Monegal (Madrid, 1967)

Rodríguez, Simón. *Obras*, ed. Pedro Grases, 2 vols. (Caracas, 1975)

Román y Zamora, Jerónimo. *Repúblicas de Indias, idolatrías y gobierno en México y Perú antes de la conquista*, 2 vols. (Madrid, 1897)

Rousseau, Jean-Jacques. *The Social Contract and Discourses*, Everyman edn (London, n.d.)

Ruiz de Montoya, Antonio. *Conquista espiritual hecha por los religiosos de la Compañía de Jesús en las provincias del Paraguay, Paraná, Uruguay y Tape*, 2nd edn (Bilbau, 1892)

Sahagún, Bernardino de. *Historia general de las cosas de Nueva España*, ed. Angel María Garibay K., BP 8–11 (Mexico, 1956)

   Florentine Codex: The General History of the Things of New Spain, trans. Arthur J. O. Anderson and Charles E. Dibble, 13 parts (Santa Fe, New Mexico, 1951–5)

Salinas y Córdova, Buenaventura de. *Memorial de las historias del Nuevo Mundo, Pirú*, ed. Luis E. Valcárcel and Warren L. Cook (Lima, 1957)

   Memorial del P. Fray Buenaventura de Salinas (n.p., 1651)

Sánchez, Miguel. *Imagen de la Virgen María, Madre de Dios de Guadalupe, milagrosamente aparecida en la ciudad de México. Celebrada en su historia, con la profecía del capítulo doce del Apocalipsis* (Mexico, 1648)

Sandoval, Alonso de. *De Instaurando Aethiopum Salute. Naturaleza, policía sagrada y profana, costumbres i ritos, disciplina y catechismo evangélico de todos etíopes*, ed. Angel Valtierra, 3rd edn (Bogotá, 1956)

Sariñana, Isidro. *El llanto del Occidente en el ocaso del más claro sol de las Españas; demostraciones fúnebres de México en las exequias del Señor Felipe IV* (Mexico, 1666)

Sarmiento, Domingo Faustino. *Civilización y barbarie. Vida de Juan Facundo Quiroga*, col. Hispánica (New York, 1961)

   Conflicto y armonías de las razas en América, ed. José Ingenieros (Buenos Aires, 1915)

   Recuerdos de provincia, ed. Guillermo Ara (Buenos Aires, 1966)

Sarmiento de Gamboa, Pedro. *History of the Incas*, ed. Clements Markham, Hakluyt Society (Cambridge, 1907)

Severo Maldonado, Francisco. 'El despertador americano', in *Periodismo insurgente*, facsimile of 1810–11 edn, 2 vols. (Mexico, 1976)

Sierra, Justo. *Obras*, 14 vols. (Mexico, 1948)

Sigüenza y Góngora, Carlos de. *Documentos inéditos*, ed. Irving A. Leonard (Mexico, 1963)

   Glorias de Querétaro (Querétaro, 1945)

   Libra astronómica y filosófica, ed. José Gaos (Mexico, 1954)

   Obras históricas, ed. José Rojas Garcidueñas (Mexico, 1960)

   Paraíso Occidental . . . (Mexico, 1684)

   Piedad heroyca de Don Fernando Cortés, ed. Jaime Delgado (Madrid, 1960)

   Relaciones históricas, ed. Manuel Romero de Terreros (Mexico, 1954)

   Triunfo Parténico, ed. José Rojas Garcidueñas (Mexico, 1945)

Solís y Rivadeneyra, Antonio de. *Historia de la conquista de Méjico* (Paris, 1838)

Solórzano Pereira, Juan de. *Obras Pósthumas* (Zaragoza, 1676)

   Política Indiana, ed. Miguel Angel Ochoa Brun, BAE 252–6 (Madrid, 1972)

Sor Juana Inés de la Cruz ante la historia, ed. Francisco de la Maza (Mexico, 1980)

Stephens, John Lloyd. *Incidents of Travel in Central America, Chiapas and Yucatan*, 2 vols. (London, 1841)

Stewart, Dugald. *The Works*, 7 vols. (Cambridge, 1829)

Suárez de Peralta, Juan. *Tratado del descubrimiento de las Indias*, ed. Federico Gómez de Orozco (Mexico, 1949)

Tacitus, P. Cornelius, *On Britain and Germany* (London, 1948)

Tena Ramírez, Felipe. *Leyes fundamentales de México 1808–1967* (Mexico, 1967)

Tesoros documentales de México siglo XVIII: Priego, Zelis, Clavijero, ed. Mariano Cuevas (Mexico, 1944)

Testimonios históricos guadalupanos, ed. Ernesto de la Torre Villar and Ramiro Navarro de Anda (Mexico, 1982)

Torquemada, Juan de. *Los veinte y un libros rituales y Monarquía indiana*, ed. Miguel León-Portilla, 3rd edn, 7 vols. (Mexico, 1975–83)

Torres, Bernardo de. *Crónicas agustinianas del Perú*, ed. Manuel Merino, 2 vols. (Madrid, 1972)

Townsend, Joseph. *A Journey through Spain in the years 1786 and 1787*, 3 vols. (London, 1792)

Tupac Amaru y la Iglesia: antología (Lima, 1983)

Ulloa, Antonio de. *Noticias Americanas* (Buenos Aires, 1944)

(with Jorge Juan). *Noticias secretas de América*, facsimile of 1826 edn, 2 vols. (Madrid, n.d.)

(with Jorge Juan). *Relación histórica del viaje a la América meridionel*, 5 vols. (Madrid, 1748)

Unánue, Hipólito. *Obras científicas y literarias*, facsimile of 1914 edn, 3 vols. (Lima, 1975)

Ustariz, Jerónimo de. *Theórica y práctica de comercio y de marina*, 3rd edn (Madrid, 1757)

Valderrama, Jerónimo. *Cartas y otros documentos sobre su visita al gobierno de Nueva España. 1563–67*, ed. France V. Scholes and Eleanor B. Adams (Mexico, 1961)

Velasco, Juan de. *Historia del reino de Quito*, 3 vols. (Quito, 1946)

Historia del reino de Quito en la América Meridionel, ed. Alfredo Pareja Diezcanseco, BA 82 (Caracas, 1981)

Vespucci, Americo. *El Nuevo Mundo*, ed. Roberto Levillier (Buenos Aires, 1951)

Veytia, Mariano Fernández de Echeverría y. *Baluartes de México*, facsimile of 1820 edn (Mexico, 1967)

Historia antigua de México, ed. C. F. Ortega, 2nd edn, 2 vols. (Mexico, 1944)

Historia de la fundación de la ciudad de la Puebla de los Angeles, ed. Efraín Castro Morales, 2 vols. (Puebla, 1962)

Vico, Giambattista. *The New Science*, 3rd edn of 1744, ed. and trans. T. G. Bergin and M. H. Fisch (Cornell, Ithaca, New York, 1968)

Viscardo y Guzmán, Juan Pablo. *Carta dirigida a los Españoles Americanos por uno de sus compatriotas*, ed. Rubén Vargas Ugarte (Lima, 1971)

Los escritos de Juan Pablo Viscardo y Guzmán, precursor de la independencia hispanoamericana, ed. Merle E. Simmons (Caracas, 1983)

Vitoria, Francisco de. *Relectio de Indis*, ed. L. Pereña and J. M. Pérez Prendes (Madrid, 1967)

Vives, Juan Luis. *Concordia y discordia*, ed. Laureano Sánchez Gallego (Mexico, 1940)

'The learned comments of I. Lodivicus Vives' in Saint Augustine, *Of the City of God* (London, 1620)

Volney, Charles François de. *The Ruins: or, A survey of the revolutions of empires* (London, 1807)

Zavala, Lorenzo de. *Ensayo crítico de las revoluciones de México desde 1808 hasta 1830*, ed. Manuel González Ramírez, BP 30 (Mexico, 1969)

SECONDARY WORKS

Adams, Henry. *The Education of Henry Adams*, Modern Library (New York, 1931)

Adams, Robert P. *The Better Part of Valor – More, Erasmus, Colet and Vives on Humanism, War and Peace 1496–1525* (Seattle, 1962)

Adem, Julián. 'Humboldt y la geofísica' in *Ensayos sobre Humboldt*, ed. Marianne O. de Bopp (Mexico, 1962)

Adorno, Rolena. *Guaman Poma: writing and resistance in Colonial Peru* (Austin, Texas, 1986)

Allen, Don Cameron. *The Legend of Noah* (Urbana, Ill., 1949)

Anderson, Arthur J. O. *Beyond the Codices: the Nahua View of Colonial Mexico* (Berkeley and Los Angeles, 1976)

Anderson Imbert, Enrique. *Genio y figura de Sarmiento* (Buenos Aires, 1967)

Arocena, Luis A. *Antonio de Solís. Cronista Indiano* (Buenos Aires, 1963)

Asensio, Eugenio. 'Dos cartas desconocidas del Inca Garcilaso', *Nueva Revista de Filología Hispánica*, VII (1953), pp. 583–93

Astraín, Antonio, *Historia de la Compañía de Jesús en las asistencia de España*, 7 vols. (Madrid, 1902–25)

Auerbach, Erich. *Scenes from the Drama of European Literature* (Manchester, 1984)

Avalle-Arce, Juan Bautista. 'El novelista Gonzalo Fernández de Oviedo y Valdés' in *Estudios de literatura hispanoamericana en honor a José J. Arrom*. ed. Andrew Debicki and Enrique Pupo-Walker (Chapel Hill, N.C., 1974)

Bailyn, Bernard. *The Ideological Origins of the American Revolution* (Cambridge, Mass., 1971)

Bakewell, Peter J. *Miners of the Red Mountain. Indian Labor in Potosí 1545–1650* (Albuquerque, New Mexico, 1984)

Barnadas, Josep M. *Charcas 1535–1565* (La Paz, 1973)

Bataillon, Marcel. *Estudios sobre Bartolomé de las Casas* (Madrid, 1976)

Baudot, Georges. *Utopie et Histoire au Mexique* (Toulouse, 1977)

Bazant, Jan. *Alienation of Church Wealth in Mexico: Social and Economic Aspects of the Liberal Revolution, 1856–1875* (Cambridge, 1971)

Beck, Hanno. *Alexander von Humboldt* (Mexico, 1971)

Beltrán de Heredia, Vicente. 'Las corrientes de espiritualidad entre los Dominicos de Castilla durante la primera mitad del siglo XVI' in his *Miscelánea*, vol. III (Salamanca, 1972)

Benassy-Berling, Marié–Cécile. *Humanismo y religión en Sor Juana Inés de la Cruz* (Mexico, 1983)

Blunt, Anthony. *Baroque and Rococo: architecture and decoration* (London, 1978)

Borah, Woodrow. *Early Colonial Trade and Navigation between Mexico and Peru* (Berkeley and Los Angeles, 1954)

Bosch García, Carlos. 'La conquista de la Nueva España en las *Décadas* de Antonio de Herrera y Tordesillas', *Estudios de historiografía de la Nueva España*, ed. Hugo Díaz Thomé (Mexico, 1945)

Botting, Douglas. *Humboldt and the Cosmos* (London, 1973)

Bowen, Margarita. *Empiricism and Geographical Thought from Francis Bacon to Alexander von Humboldt* (Cambridge, 1981)

Brading, D. A. 'Bourbon Spain and its American Empire', *Cambridge History of Latin America*, ed. Leslie Bethell, vol. I (Cambridge, 1984)

Miners and Merchants in Bourbon Mexico 1763–1810 (Cambridge, 1971)

Myth and Prophecy in Mexican History (Cambridge, 1984)

'The City in Bourbon Spanish America: Elite and Masses', *Comparative Urban Research*, 8 (1980), pp. 71–85

The Origins of Mexican Nationalism (Cambridge, 1985)

'Tridentine Catholicism and Enlightened Despotism in Bourbon Mexico', *JLS*, 15 (1983), pp. 1–22

Bremond, Henri. *A Literary History of Religious Thought in France*, 3 vols. (London, 1928–36)

Bricker, Victoria Reifler. *The Indian Christ, The Indian King. The Historical Substrate of Maya Myth and Ritual* (Austin, Texas, 1981)

Brown, Peter. *Society and the Holy in Late Antiquity* (London, 1982)

The Cult of the Saints (London, 1981)

Burckhardt, Jacob. *The Civilization of the Renaissance in Italy* (London, 1955)

Burkholder, Mark A. and Chandler, D. S. *Biographical Dictionary of Audiencia Ministers in the Americas, 1687–1821* (Westport, Conn. 1982)

From Impotence to Authority: the Spanish Crown and the American Audiencias 1687–1808 (Columbia, Miss. 1977)

Carbia, Rómulo D. *La crónica oficial de las Indias Occidentales* (Buenos Aires, 1940)

Carlyle, Thomas. *Complete Works*, 17 vols. (London, 1888)

Carr, Raymond. *Spain 1808–1939* (Oxford, 1966)

Castillo Ledón, Luis, *Hidalgo, La vida del Héroe*, 2 vols. (Mexico, 1948)

Chadwick, Owen. *The Popes and the European Revolution* (Oxford, 1981)

Chaunu, Pierre. *La España de Carlos V*, 2 vols. (Barcelona, 1976)

Christian, William A. *Apparitions in Late Medieval and Renaissance Spain* (Princeton, 1981)

Clendinnen, Inga. *Ambivalent Conquests. Maya and Spaniard in Yucatán 1517–1570* (Cambridge, 1987)

Cochrane, Eric. *Historians and Historiography in the Italian Renaissance* (Chicago, 1981)

Corominas, Juan María. *Castiglione y la Araucana* (Madrid, 1980)

Correa Bello, Sergio. *El Cautiverio Feliz en la vida política chilena del siglo XVII* (Santiago de Chile, 1965)

Delooz, Pierre. 'Towards a sociological study of canonized sainthood in the Catholic Church' in *Saints and their Cults*, ed. Stephen Wilson (Cambridge, 1983)

Delumeau, Jean. *Catholicism between Luther and Voltaire: a new view of the Counter-Reformation* (London, 1977)

Didier, Hughes, *Vida y pensamiento de Juan E. Nieremberg* (Madrid, 1976)

Duarte French, Jaime. *Poder y política en Colombia 1810–1827* (Bogotá, 1980)

Durand, José. *El Inca Garcilaso, clásico de América* (Mexico, 1976)

'Perú y Ophir en Garcilaso Inca, el Jesuita Pineda y Gregorio García', *Histórica*, 3 (1979), pp. 33–54

Durand Flores, Luis. *Criollos en conflicto. Cuzco después de Tupac Amaru* (Lima, 1985)

Duviols, Pierre. *La destrucción de les religiones Andinas* (Mexico, 1970)

Edmonson, Munro S. ed, *Sixteenth–Century Mexico: the work of Sahagún* (Albuquerque, New Mexico, 1974)

Egido, Teófanes. 'La expulsión de los jesuitas de España' and 'El regalismo y las relaciones Iglesia-Estado en el siglo XVIII', *Historia de la Iglesia en España siglos XVII y XVII*, ed. Ricardo García-Villoslada, vol. IV (Madrid, 1979)

Elliott, J. H. 'Cortés, Velásquez and Charles V', introduction to Hernán Cortés, *Letters from Mexico*, trans. Anthony Pagden (New Haven, Conn. 1971)

   The Count-Duke of Olivares. The Statesman in an Age of Decline (New Haven and London, 1986)

   'The Spanish Conquest and Settlement of America', *Cambridge History of Latin America*, ed. Leslie Bethell, vol. I (Cambridge, 1984)

Evans, R. J. W. *The Making of the Habsburg Monarchy 1500–1700* (Oxford, 1979)

Evennett, H. Outram. *The Spirit of the Counter-Reformation*, ed. with postscript by John Bossy (Cambridge, 1968)

Fabie, Antonio María. *Vida y escritos de las Casas*, 2 vols. (Madrid, 1879)

Farriss, N. M. *Crown and Clergy in Colonial Mexico, 1759–1821* (London, 1968)

Fernández-Santamaría, J. A. *The State, War and Peace. Spanish Political Thought in the Renaissance 1516–1559* (Cambridge, 1977)

Fisher, Lillian E. *Champion of Reform. Manuel Abad y Queipo* (New York, 1955)

Flores Galindo, Alberto. *Buscando un Inca: identidad y utopía en las Andes* (Lima, 1987)

Frankl, Victor. *El 'Anti-jovio' de Gonzalo Jiménez de Quesada* (Madrid, 1963)

Friede, Juan and Benjamin Keen. *Bartolomé de las Casas in History* (De Kalb, Illinois, 1971)

Garibay, Angel María. *Historia de la literatura nahuatl*, 2 vols. (Mexico, 1954)

Gerbi, Antonello. *La naturaleza de las Indias Nuevas* (Mexico, 1978)

   The Dispute of the New World. The History of a Polemic 1750–1900, trans. Jeremy Moyle (Pittsburgh, 1973)

Gibson, Charles. *The Aztecs under Spanish Rule 1519–1810* (Stanford, 1964)

Gillespie, Charles Coulston. *Genesis and Geology* (Cambridge, Mass. 1951)

Giménez Fernández, Manuel. *Bartolomé de las Casas: capellán de Su Majestad Carlos I* (Seville, 1960)

   El Concilio IV Provincial Mejicano (Seville, 1939)

Girardet, Raoul. *Le Nationalisme français 1871–1914* (Paris, 1966)

Godwin, Joscelyn. *Athanasius Kircher. A Renaissance Man and the Quest for Lost Knowledge* (London, 1979)

Góngora, Mario. 'Estudios sobre el Galicanismo y la "Ilustración católica" (1957), pp. 96–151

   Studies in the Colonial History of Spanish America, trans. R. Southern (Cambridge, 1975)

González Obregón, Luis, *et al. Homenaje a Ignacio M. Altamirano* (Mexico, 1935)

Gould, Stephen Jay. *Time's Arrow, Time's Cycle. Myth and Metaphor in the Discovery of Geological Time* (London, 1988)

Grases, Pedro. 'Estudios Bolivarianos', vol. IV of his *Obras completas* (Barcelona, 1981)

Hagen, Victor W. von. *South America Called Them* (London, 1949)

   Search for the Maya. The Story of Stephens and Catherwood (Farnborough, 1973)

Hale, Charles. *Mexican Liberalism in the Age of Mora, 1821–1853* (New Haven, Conn., 1968)

Herrero, Javier. *Los orígenes del pensamiento reaccionario español* (Madrid, 1971)

Herreros de Tejada, Luis. *El Teniente General D. José Manuel de Goyeneche Primer Conde de Guaqui* (Barcelona, 1923)

Hexter, J. H. *The Vision of Politics on the Eve of the Reformation* (London, 1973)

Himmelfarb, Gertrude. *Darwin and the Darwinian Revolution* (New York, 1968)

Hodgen, Margaret, T. *Early Anthropology in the Sixteenth and Seventeenth Centuries* (Philadelphia, 1964)

Honour, Hugh. *Neo-classicism* (London, 1968)

Huizinga, J. *The Waning of the Middle Ages* (London, 1955)

Iglesia, Ramón. *Cronistas e historiadores de la conquista de México,* 2nd edn (Mexico, 1972)

El hombre Colón y otros ensayos (Mexico, 1944)

Ilgen, William D. 'La configuración mítica de la historia en los *Comentarios Reales* del Inca Garcilaso de la Vega', *Estudios de literatura hispanoamericana en honor a José J. Arrom,* ed. A. P. Debicki and E. Pupo-Walker (Chapel Hill, N.C., 1974)

Israel, J. I. *Race, Class and Politics in Colonial Mexico 1610–1670* (Oxford, 1975)

Iveson, Erick. *The Myth of Egypt and its Hieroglyphs in European Tradition* (Copenhagen, 1961)

Izard, Miguel. *El miedo de la revolución: la lucha para la libertad en Venezuela 1777–1830* (Madrid, 1979)

Jiménez Codinach, Guadalupe. *México en 1821: Dominique de Pradt y el Plan de Iguala* (Mexico, 1982)

Keen, Benjamin. *The Aztec Image in Western Thought* (New Brunswick, New Jersey, 1971)

Kendrick, T. D. *British Antiquity* (London, 1950)

St James of Spain (London, 1960)

Keynes, R. D. *The Beagle Record* (Cambridge, 1979)

Konrad, Herman W. *A Jesuit Hacienda in Colonial Mexico: Santa Lucía 1576–1767* (Stanford, 1980)

Kubler, George. *Mexican Architecture in the Sixteenth Century,* 2 vols. (New Haven, Conn., 1948)

The Shape of Time. Remarks on the History of Things (New Haven, Conn., 1970)

'The Neo-Inca State 1537–1572', *HAHR,* 27 (1947), pp. 189–203

Lafaye, Jacques. *Quetzalcoatl et Guadalupe* (Paris, 1974)

Lemoine Villacaña, Ernesto. *Morelos* (Mexico, 1965)

Leonard, Irving A. *Don Carlos de Sigüenza y Góngora* (Berkeley, 1929)

Le Reverend Brusone, Julio. 'La historia antigua de México del Padre Francisco Javier Clavijero', *Estudios de Historiografía de la Nueva España,* ed. Hugo Díaz-Thomé (Mexico, 1945)

Levillier Roberto. *D. Francisco de Toledo* (Madrid, 1935)

Levin, David. *History as Romantic Art* (Stanford, 1959)

Llorens Castillo, Vicente. *Liberales y románticos. Una emigración española en Inglaterra (1823–1834)* (Mexico, 1954)

Lockhart, James. *The Men of Cajamarca* (Austin, Texas, 1972)

Lohmann Villena, Guillermo. *Las ideas jurídico-políticas en la rebelión de Gonzalo Pizarro* (Valladolid, 1977)

López, Adalberto. *The Revolt of the Comuneros 1721–1735* (Cambridge, Mass. 1976)

Lynch, John. 'Bolívar and the Caudillos', *HAHR*, 63 (1983), pp. 3–36
Spain under the Habsburgs, 2 vols. (London, 1964)
The Spanish American Revolutions 1808–1826 (London, 1973)

Macaulay, Thomas Babington. *Critical and Historical Essays contributed to the Edinburgh Review*, 3 vols. (London, 1843)

Maciel, David R. *Ignacio Ramírez. Ideólogo del liberalismo social en México* (Mexico, 1980)

MacKay, Angus. *Spain in the Middle Ages. From Frontier to Empire 1000–1500* (London, 1977)

Manuel, Frank E. *The Eighteenth Century Confronts the Gods* (Cambridge, Mass., 1959)

Martínez Peláez, Severo. *La Patria del criollo* (Guatemala, 1971)

Martínez Quintero, María Esther. *Los grupos liberales antes de las Cortes de Cádiz* (Madrid, 1978)

Masur, Gerhard. *Simón Bolívar* (Albuquerque, New Mexico, 1968)

Matute, Alvaro. *Lorenzo Boturini y el pensamiento de Vico* (Mexico, 1976)

Maza, Francisco de la. *El guadalupanismo mexicano*, 2nd edn (Mexico, 1984)

Medina, José Toribio. *El descubrimiento del Océano Pacífico*, 3 vols. (Santiago de Chile, 1913)
Vida de Ercilla (Mexico, 1948)

Meek, Ronald L. *Social Science and the Ignoble Savage* (Cambridge, 1976)

Meinecke, Freidrich. *Historism. The Rise of a New Historical Outlook*, trans. J. E. Anderson (London, 1972)

Melquiades, Andrés Martín. 'Pensamiento teólogico y vivencia religiosa en la reforma española 1400–1600', *Historia de la Iglesia en España*, ed. Ricardo García-Villoslada, vol. 3 (Madrid, 1980)

Menéndez Pidal, Ramón. *España y su historia*, 2 vols. (Madrid, 1957)

Merino, Luis. *Estudio crítico sobre las 'Noticias secretas de América' y el clero colonial (1720–1765)* (Madrid, 1946)

Mesa, José de and Gisbert, Teresa. *Historia de la pintura cuzqueña*, 2 vols. (Lima, 1982)

Milhou, Alain. *Colón y su mentalidad mesiánica en el ambiente franciscanista español* (Valladolid, 1983)

Minguet, Charles. *Alexandre de Humboldt: historien et geographe de l'Amerique espagnole 1799–1804* (Paris, 1969)

Miró Quesada, Aurelio. *El Inca Garcilaso y otros estudios garcilasistas* (Madrid, 1971)

Mitre, Bartolomé. *Historia de San Martín y de la emancipación sudamericana*, 2 vols. (Buenos Aires, 1950)

Molina Enríquez, Andrés. *La Reforma y Juárez* (Mexico, 1906)

Momigliano, Arnaldo. *Studies in Historiography* (London, 1966)

Morales, Francisco. *Ethnic and Social Background of the Franciscan Friars in Seventeenth-Century Mexico* (Washington, 1973)

Morison, Samuel Eliot. *The European Discovery of America. The Southern Voyages A.D. 1492–1616* (Oxford, New York, 1974)

Murphy, Martin. *Blanco White. Self-Banished Spaniard* (New Haven, Conn. 1989)

Necheles, Ruth F. *The Abbé Gregoire* (Westport, Conn., 1971)

O'Gorman, Edmundo. *Destierro de sombras. Luz en el origen de la imagen y culto de Nuestra Señora de Guadalupe del Tepeyac* (Mexico, 1986)

Guía bibliográfica de Carlos María de Bustamante (Mexico, 1967)

La supervivencia política Novo-Hispana (Mexico, 1969)

O'Leary, Daniel Florencio. *Bolívar y la emancipación de Sur-América*, 2 vols. (Madrid, 1915)

O'Phelan Godoy, Scarlett. *Rebellions and Revolts in Eighteenth-Century Upper Peru* (Cologne, 1985)

Ossio, Juan. 'Guaman Poma y la historiografía indianista de los siglos XVI y XVII', *Historia y Cultura*, 10 (1978), pp. 181–206

Padilla Bendezu, Abraham. *Huaman Poma, el indio cronista dibujante* (Mexico, 1979)

Pagden, Anthony. *The Fall of Natural Man: the American Indian and the origins of comparative ethnology* (Cambridge, 1982)

Parish, Helen Rand. *Las Casas as a Bishop* (Washington, 1980)

'The correct birth-date of Bartolomé de las Casas', *HAHR*, 56 (1976), pp. 385–405

Parker, Geoffrey. *The Army of Flanders and the Spanish Road 1567–1659* (Cambridge, 1972)

Parrington, Vernon L. *The Romantic Revolution in America, 1800–1860* (New York, 1954)

Pastor, Ludwig Von. *The History of the Popes from the close of the Middle Ages*, trans. E. E. Peele, 40 vols. (London, 1950)

Paz, Octavio. *Sor Juana: Her Life and Her World* (London, 1988)

Pelikan, Jaroslav. *The Christian Tradition. A History of the Development of Doctrine*, 4 vols. (Chicago, 1971–81)

Phelan, John Leddy. 'Neo-Aztecism in the eighteenth century and the genesis of Mexican nationalism', *Culture in History: Essays in Honour of Paul Radin*, ed. Stanley Diamond (New York, 1960)

The Millennial Kingdom of the Franciscans in the New World, 2nd edn (Berkeley and Los Angeles, 1970)

The People and the King, The Comunero Revolution in Colombia 1781 (Madison, 1978)

Pierce, Frank. *Alonso de Ercilla y Zúñiga* (Amsterdam, 1984)

Pocock, J. G. A. *The Machiavellian Moment. Florentine Political Thought and the Atlantic Republican Tradition* (Princeton, 1975)

Polt, John H. R. *Gaspar Melchor de Jovellanos* (New York, 1971)

Pompa, Leon. *Vico: a study of the 'New Science'* (Cambridge, 1975)

Pons, André. *Recherches sur Blanco White et l'independance des colonies espagnoles d'Amerique* (thesis, La Sorbonne Nouvelle, Paris, 1974)

Porras Barrenechea, Raúl. *El cronista indio Felipe Huaman Poma de Ayala* (Lima, 1948)

Pupo-Walker, Enrique. *Historia, creación y profecía en los textos del Inca Garcilaso de la Vega* (Madrid, 1982)

Ramos, Demetrio. *Ximénez de Quesada y el epítome de la conquista del reino de Nuevo Granada* (Seville, 1977)

Ravier, André. *Ignatius Loyola and the Founding of the Society of Jesus* (San Francisco, 1973)

Reeves, Marjorie. *The Influence of Prophecy in the Later Middle Ages. A Study of Joachism* (Oxford, 1969)

Ricard, Robert. *The Spiritual Conquest of Mexico* (Berkeley and Los Angeles, 1966)

Ronan, Charles E. *Francisco Javier Clavijero S. J. (1731–1787). Figure of the Mexican Enlightenment. His Life and Works* (Rome, 1977)

Rosenblum, Robert. *Transformations of Late Eighteenth Century Art* (Princeton, 1967)

Rowe, John Howland. 'El movimiento nacional inca del siglo XVIII', *Tupac Amaru II. 1780*, ed. Alberto Flores Galindo (Lima, 1976)

'Ethnography and ethnology in the sixteenth century', *The Kroeber Anthropological Society Papers*, 30 (1964), pp. 1–20

Russell, Peter. 'Arms versus letters: towards a definition of Spanish fifteenth-century Humanism', *Aspects of the Renaissance*, ed. Archibald R. Lewis (Austin, Texas, 1967)

Sáenz de Santa María, Carmelo. 'Introducción crítica de la "Historia Verdadera" de Bernal Díaz del Castillo', *Revista de Indias*, XXVI (1966), pp. 328–416

Saint-Lu, André. *La Vera Paz: esprit évangelique et colonisation* (Paris, 1968)

Sánchez, Luis Alberto. *El Doctor Oceáno* (Lima, 1967)

Saugnieux, Joel. *Les Jansénistes et le renouveau de la prédication dans l'Espagne de la seconde moitié du XVIIIᵉ siècle* (Lyons, 1976)

Shklar, Judith N. *Men and Citizens* (Cambridge, 1969)

Sierra, Justo. *Obras*, 14 vols. (Mexico, 1948)

Sinkin, Richard N. *The Mexican Reform, 1855–1876. A Study in Liberal Nation-Building* (Austin, Texas, 1979)

Skinner, Quentin. *The Foundations of Modern Political Thought*, 2 vols. (Cambridge, 1978)

Smith, Henry Nash. *Virgin Land. The American West as Symbol and Myth* (Cambridge, Mass., 1970)

Spalding, Karen. *Huarochirí: an Andean Society under Inca and Spanish Rule* (Stanford, 1984)

Stafford, Barbara Maria. *A Voyage into Substance. Art, Science, Nature and the Illustrated Travel Account 1760–1840* (Cambridge, Mass., 1984)

Stern, Steve J. *Peru's Indian Peoples and the Challenge of Spanish Conquest* (Madison, Wis., 1982)

Tate, Robert B. *Ensayos sobre la historiografía peninsular de siglo XV* (Madrid, 1970)

Tellechea Idígoras, José Ignacio. *El arzobispo Carranza y su tiempo*, 2 vols. (Madrid, 1968)

Terra, Helmut de. *The Life and Times of Alexander von Humboldt 1769–1859* (New York, 1955)

Ticknor, George. *Life of William Hickling Prescott* (Boston, 1864)

Torre Villar, Ernesto de la. 'Baltazar Dorantes de Carranza y la *Sumaria Relación*', *Estudios de historiografía de la Nueva España*, ed. Hugo Díaz-Thomé (Mexico, 1945)

Trabulse, Elías. *Ciencia y religión en el siglo XVII* (Mexico, 1974)

Trens, Manuel. *María. Iconografía de la Virgen en el arte español* (Madrid, 1946)

Valcárcel, Daniel. *Ignacio de Castro* (Lima, 1953)

La rebelión de Tupac Amaru (Mexico, 1965)

Valtierra, Angel. *Peter Claver, Saint of the Slaves* (London, 1960)

Vargas Lugo, Elisa. *La iglesia de Santa Prisca de Taxco* (Mexico, 1974)

Vargas Ugarte, Rubén. *Vida de San Martín de Porras* (Buenos Aires, 1963)
  Vida de Santa Rosa de Lima (Buenos Aires, 1961)

Varner, J. G. *El Inca. The Life and Times of Garcilaso de la Vega 1539–1616* (Austin, Texas, 1968)

Vázquez de Knauth, Josefina. *Nacionalismo y educación en México* (Mexico, 1970)

Villoro, Luis. *Los grandes momentos del indigenismo en México*, 2nd edn (Mexico, 1979)

Wachtel, Nathan N. 'Pensée sauvage et Acculturation. L'espace et le temps chez Felipe Guaman Poma de Ayala et l'Inca Garcilaso de la Vega', *Annales, Economies, Sociétés, Civilisations*, 26 (1971), pp. 793–840

Wagner, Henry Raup, and Helen Rand Parish. *The Life and Writings of Bartolomé de las Casas* (Albuquerque, New Mexico, 1967)

Walker, D. P. *The Ancient Theology* (London, 1972)

Warren, Fintan B. *Vasco de Quiroga and his Pueblo-Hospitals of Santa Fe* (Washington, D.C., 1963)

Whitaker, Arthur. 'Antonio de Ulloa', *HAHR*, 15 (1935), pp. 155–94
  'Jorge Juan and Antonio de Ulloa's Prologue to their Secret Report of 1749 on Peru', *HAHR*, 18 (1938), pp. 507–13

Wolpe, Hans. *Raynal et sa Machine de Guerre: l'histoire des Deux Indes et ses perfectionnements* (Paris, 1956)

Wright, A. D. *The Counter-Reformation: Catholic Europe and the Non-Christian World* (London, 1982)

Young, G. M. *Victorian England. Portrait of an Age* (Oxford, 1964)

Zavala, Silvio. *St Thomas More in New Spain* (London, 1955)
  La encomienda indiana, 2nd edn BP. 53 (Mexico, 1973)

INDEX